D0141723

#50685785
WB
60
C761
2003

CONTEMPORARY ISSUES IN BIOETHICS

SIXTH EDITION

Edited by

Tom L. Beauchamp & LeRoy Walters
Kennedy Institute of Ethics and Department of Philosophy
Georgetown University

Australia • Canada • Mexico • Singapore • Spain • United Kingdom • United States

Publisher: Holly J. Allen
Philosophy Editor: Steve Wainwright
Assistant-Editor: Lee McCracken
Editorial Assistant: Anna Lustig
Technology Project Manager: Susan DeVanna
Marketing Manager: Worth Hawes
Marketing Assistant: Justine Ferguson
Advertising Project Manager: Bryan Vann
Print/Media Buyer: Karen Hunt
Composition Buyer: Ben Schroeter
Permissions Editor: Joohee Lee
Production Service: Matrix Productions
Copy Editor: Vicki Nelson
Cover Designer: Ross Carron
Compositor: ATLIS Graphics
Cover & Text Printer: Maple-Vail/Binghamton

COPYRIGHT © 2003 Wadsworth, a division of Thomson Learning, Inc. Thomson Learning™ is a trademark used herein under license.

ALL RIGHTS RESERVED. No part of this work covered by the copyright hereon may be reproduced or used in any form or by any means—graphic, electronic, or mechanical, including but not limited to photocopying, recording, taping, Web distribution, information networks, or information storage and retrieval systems—without the written permission of the publisher.

Printed in the United States of America

1 2 3 4 5 7 06 05 04 03 02

For more information about our products, contact us at:
Thomson Learning Academic Resource Center
1-800-423-0563
For permission to use material from this text, contact us by:
Phone: 1-800-730-2214
Fax: 1-800-730-2215
Web: http://www.thomsonrights.com

Library of Congress Control Number: 2002105603

Wadsworth—Thomson Learning
10 Davis Drive
Belmont, CA 94002-3098
USA

Asia
Thomson Learning
60 Albert Street, #15-01
Albert Complex
Singapore 189969

Australia
Nelson Thomson Learning
102 Dodds Street
South Melbourne, Victoria 3205
Australia

Canada
Nelson Thomson Learning
1120 Birchmont Road
Toronto, Ontario M1K 5G4
Canada

Europe/Middle East/Africa
Thomson Learning
Berkshire House
168-173 High Holborn
London WC1V 7AA
United Kingdom

Latin America
Thomson Learning
Seneca, 53
Colonia Polanco
11560 Mexico D.F.
Mexico

Spain
Paraninfo Thomson Learning
Calle/Magallanes, 25
28015 Madrid, Spain

CONTENTS

PREFACE

This sixth edition of CIB differs significantly from the fifth and earlier editions. It reflects numerous changes in the field and incorporates several new issues. For example, it reprints thought-provoking essays on ethical dilemmas arising in many parts of the world. Sixty-six of the 113 selections in this edition are new, when compared with the selections in the previous edition. This edition includes novel topics—human embryonic stem cell research and bioterrorism—as well as updated discussions of the global AIDS epidemic, reproductive cloning, managed health care, and physician-assisted death. Numerous other topics have also been carried forward from the fifth edition.

In each chapter we have tried to give students and faculty members a sense of the cutting-edge of contemporary ethical discussion and debate. For example, the chapter on end-of-life decisionmaking includes important new materials on palliation and alternatives to physician-assisted death. The research chapter includes several striking historical examples of the abuse of human subjects—in the Tuskegee syphilis study, in the radiation experiments conducted by the U.S. Atomic Energy Commission, and in China under Japanese occupation. In Chapters 6 and 9, third-world perspectives on questions of global justice in health care are included for the first time.

This book has again been a collaborative effort from start to finish. Tom Beauchamp has assumed primary responsibility for Chapters 1 through 5. LeRoy Walters took the lead on Chapters 6 through 9. However, we have shared a common goal—to identify and reprint a spectrum of views on each of our topics—views advanced by some of the most articulate and widely-respected commentators in the field of bioethics. In this effort we have both been ably assisted by Derrick C. Pau, Michael Hammer, Ahmed Humayun, Joe Folio, and Megan Hughes—our research assistants. These able students helped us to identify pertinent literature, gathered candidate documents, tracked down elusive references, and compiled bibliographies. Our lists of suggested readings give but a small indication of the many authors, committees, and commissions whose work we would like to have included in this volume.

We have again been fortunate to be assisted by the finest library and information-retrieval colleagues in the world. In particular, we acknowledge the exceptional work of Doris Goldstein, Director of Library and Information Services, and her dedicated colleagues, Frances Abramson, Laura Bishop, Martina Darragh, Roxie France-Nuriddin, Jeanne Furcron, Harriet Gray, Lucinda Huttlinger, Joy Kahn, Pat McCarrick, Patricia Martin, Mara McGarry, Hannelore Ninomiya, Anita Nolen, Cecily Orr Nuckols, Susan Poland, Kathleen Reynolds, and Mary Ruof. Martina Darragh deserves special thanks for the many database searches that she performed on our behalf.

Our faculty colleagues have been sources of inspiration and support in all of our academic endeavors. We especially thank our Director, Madison Powers, for his forward-looking and efficient leadership of the Kennedy Institute. We have also been supported in our research by the many acts of kindness and generosity of Wayne Davis, Linda Powell, and Sally Schofield.

Ms. Moheba Hanif has accompanied us in the work on this edition from the beginning of the project. She and Derrick Pau have worked tirelessly to secure permission to reprint the selections that we include in this edition.

At Wadsworth Publishing Company, we thank our new editor, Steve Wainwright, for his helpful suggestions and Jerry Holloway for coordinating the publishing process. At

Matrix Productions in Tucson, Merrill Peterson has once again efficiently overseen the copyediting process and the conversion of our text into pages. At ATLIS Graphics in Camp Hill, Pennsylvania, multiple typesetters with whom we have not spoken directly have done a superb job of accurately keying the pages that follow.

We are also grateful to the reviewers who have used previous editions of CIB in their teaching and who suggested numerous ways to improve this sixth edition: Dr. Ronnie Hawkins, University of Central Florida; James J. McCartney, Ph.D., Villanova University; Anthony Preus, Binghamton University; Lawrence P. Ulrich, Ph.D., University of Dayton; and Dr. Victoria S. Wike, Loyola University Chicago.

Finally, we want to acknowledge the patience and support of our spouses, Ruth and Sue, and of our children, Karine and Zack, and David and Robert, throughout the always-arduous process of reading, selecting, editing, introducing, and proofreading.

We hope that this book will stimulate discussion in academic settings and make a modest contribution to the development of more enlightened public policies on these important biomedical topics.

June 2002

Tom L. Beauchamp and LeRoy Walters
Kennedy Institute of Ethics and Department of Philosophy
Georgetown University

Part I

INTRODUCTION TO ETHICS

1. Ethical Theory and Bioethics

The moral problems discussed in this book have emerged from professional practice in the fields of clinical medicine, biomedical research, nursing, public health, and the social and behavioral sciences. The goal of this first chapter is to provide a basis in language, norms, and theory sufficient for reading and criticizing the selections in the later chapters.

Everyone is aware that ethics in the biomedical professions has had a distinguished history. Among the most influential sources of medical and nursing ethics are its traditions: the concepts, practices, and norms that have long guided conduct in these fields. The history and precise character of these traditions may be the logical starting point in reflecting on professional ethics, but great traditions such as Hippocratic ethics often fail to provide a comprehensive, unbiased, and adequately justified ethics. Indeed, the history of medical ethics over the last two thousand years is a particularly disappointing history from the perspective of today's concerns in bioethics about the rights of patients and research subjects.

Prior to the early 1970s, there was no firm ground in which a commitment to principles outside of Hippocratic medical ethics could take root and flourish. Particular ethical codes written for the medical, nursing, and research professions had always been written by their own members to govern their own conduct. To consult persons outside the profession was thought not only unnecessary, but dangerous. This conception has collapsed in the face of the pressures of the modern world. Such a professional morality has been judged not adequately comprehensive, coherent, or sensitive to conflicts of interest. The birth of bioethics occurred as a result of an increasing awareness that this older ethic had become obsolete.

FUNDAMENTAL PROBLEMS

THE STUDY OF MORALITY

Some Basic Concepts and Definitions. The field of ethics includes the study of social morality as well as philosophical reflection on its norms and practices. The terms *ethical theory* and *moral philosophy* refer exclusively to philosophical reflection on morality. The term *morality,* by contrast, refers to traditions of belief about right and wrong human conduct. Morality is a social institution with a history and a code of learnable rules. Moral standards and responsibilities predate us and are transmitted across generations. Like political constitutions and languages, morality exists before we are instructed in its relevant rules, and thus it has a transindividual status as a body of guidelines for action.

Since virtually everyone grows up with a basic understanding of the institution of morality, its norms are readily understood. All persons who are serious about living a moral life already grasp the core dimensions of morality. They know not to lie, not to steal property, to keep promises, to respect the rights of others, not to kill or cause harm to innocent persons, and the like. Individuals do not create these moral norms, and morality therefore cannot be purely a personal policy or code. The core parts of morality exist before their acceptance by individuals, who learn about moral responsibilities and moral ideals as they grow up.

Individuals also eventually learn to distinguish the general morality that holds for all persons—sometimes called the common morality (see later)—from rules that bind only members of special groups, such as physicians. We learn moral rules alongside other important social rules, which is one reason it later becomes difficult to distinguish the two. For example, we are constantly reminded in our early years that we must observe social rules of etiquette, such as saying "Please" when we want something and "Thank you" when we receive it, as well as more specific rules, such as "A judge is addressed as 'Judge.'" We are also taught rules of prudence, including "Don't touch a hot stove," together with rules of housekeeping, dressing, and the like.

Morality enters the picture when certain actions ought or ought not to be performed because of the considerable impact these actions can be expected to have on the interests of other people. We first learn maxims such as "Keep your promises" and "Respect the rights of others." These are elementary instructions in morality; they express what society expects of us and of everyone in terms of taking the interests of other people into account. We thus learn about moral instructions and expectations, and gradually we come to understand morality as a set of normative standards about doing good, avoiding harm, respecting others, keeping promises, and acting fairly. We also absorb standards of character and moral excellence.

The Common Morality. The set of norms that all morally serious persons share is the *common morality*. This morality binds all persons in all places. In recent years, the favored category to represent this universal core of morality in public discourse has been human rights, but moral obligation and moral virtue are no less vital parts of the common morality. The norms in the common morality do not deviate from what every morally serious person already knows. Every such person believes that we should not lie to others, should keep our promises, should take account of the well-being of others, and should treat them fairly. This background in morality is the raw data for theory and is why we can speak of the origins of moral principles as located in the common morality that we all already share.

A distinction is needed, however, between morality in the narrow sense and morality in the broad sense. The universal principles of the common morality comprise only a narrow range or skeleton of a well-developed body of moral standards. *Morality in the narrow sense* is comprised of universal principles, whereas *morality in the broad* (full-bodied) *sense* includes divergent moral norms, obligations, ideals, and attitudes that spring from particular cultures, religions, and institutions. For example, different standards of allocating resources for health care and different standards of giving to charitable causes are parts of morality in the broad sense. A pluralism of judgments and practices is the inevitable outcome of historical developments in cultures, moral disagreement and resolution, and the formulation of complex institutional and public policies.

Sometimes persons who suppose that they speak with an authoritative moral voice operate under the false belief that they have the force of the common morality (that is, universal morality) behind them. The particular moral viewpoints that such persons represent may be acceptable and even praiseworthy, but they also may not bind other persons or communities. For example, persons who believe that scarce medical resources such as transplantable organs should be distributed by lottery rather than by medical need may have very good moral reasons for their views, but they cannot claim the force of the common morality for those views.

A theory of common morality does not hold that all *customary* moralities qualify as part of the *common* morality; and use of the common morality in moral reasoning need not lead to conclusions that are socially received. An important function of the general norms in the common morality is to provide a basis for the evaluation and criticism of groups or communities whose customary moral viewpoints are in some respects deficient. Critical reflection may ultimately vindicate moral judgments that at the outset were not widely shared.

Four Approaches to the Study of Ethics. Morality can be studied and developed in a variety of ways. In particular, four ways of either studying moral beliefs or doing moral philosophy appear prominently in the literature of ethics. Two of these approaches describe and analyze morality without taking moral positions, and these approaches are therefore called *nonnormative*. Two other approaches do involve taking moral positions and are therefore called *normative.* These four approaches can be grouped as follows:

A. *Nonnormative approaches*
    1. Descriptive ethics
    2. Metaethics
B. *Normative approaches*
    3. General normative ethics
    4. Practical normative ethics

It would be a mistake to regard these categories as expressing rigid, sharply differentiated approaches. They are often undertaken at the same time, and they overlap in goal and content. Nonetheless, when understood as broad polar contrasts exemplifying models of inquiry, these distinctions are important.

First among the two nonnormative fields of inquiry into morality is *descriptive ethics,* or the factual description and explanation of moral behavior and beliefs. Anthropologists, sociologists, and historians who study moral behavior employ this approach when they explore how moral attitudes, codes, and beliefs differ from person to person and from society to society. Their works often dwell in detail on matters such as professional codes and practices, codes of honor, and rules governing permissible killing in a society. Although philosophers do not typically engage in descriptive ethics in their work, some have combined descriptive ethics with philosophical ethics—for example, by analyzing the ethical practices of Native American tribes or researching Nazi experimentation during World War II.

The second nonnormative field, *metaethics,* involves analysis of the meanings of central terms in ethics, such as *right, obligation, good, virtue,* and *responsibility*. The proper analysis of the term *morality* and the distinction between the moral and the nonmoral are typical metaethical problems. Crucial terms in bioethics, including *physician-assisted suicide, informed consent,* and *universal access* to health care, can be and should be given careful conceptual attention, and they are so treated in various chapters in this volume. (Descriptive ethics and metaethics may not be the only forms of nonnormative inquiry. In recent years there has been an active discussion of the biological bases of moral behavior and of the ways in which humans do and do not differ from animals.)

General normative ethics attempts to formulate and defend basic principles and virtues governing the moral life. Ideally, any ethical theory will provide a system of moral principles or virtues and reasons for adopting them and will defend claims about the range of their applicability. In the course of this chapter the most prominent of these theories will be examined, as will various principles of respect for autonomy, justice, and beneficence that have played a major role in some of these theories.

General normative theories are sometimes used to justify positions on particular moral problems such as abortion, euthanasia, the distribution of health care, and research involving human subjects. Usually, however, no direct move can be made from theory or principles to particular judgments, and theory and principles therefore typically only *facilitate* the development of policies, action guides, or judgments. In general, the attempts to delineate practical action guides are referred to as *practical ethics* (B.4 in the outline).

Substantially the same general ethical theories and principles apply to problems across different professional fields and in areas beyond professional ethics as well. One might appeal to principles of justice, for example, in order to illuminate and resolve issues of taxation, health care distribution, criminal punishment, and affirmative action in hiring. Similarly, principles of veracity (truthfulness) are invoked to discuss secrecy and deception in international politics, misleading advertisements in business ethics, balanced reporting in journalistic ethics, and the disclosure of the nature and extent of an illness to a patient in medical ethics.

MORAL DILEMMAS AND DISAGREEMENTS

In the teaching of ethics, moral problems are often examined through cases—in particular, law cases, clinical cases, and public policy cases. These cases, which appear in virtually every chapter in this book, vividly display dilemmas and disagreements that require students to identify and grapple with real moral problems.

Moral Dilemmas. In a case presented in Chapter 3, two judges became entangled in apparent moral disagreement when confronted with a murder trial. A woman named Tarasoff had been killed by a man who previously had confided to a therapist his intention to kill her as soon as she returned home from a summer vacation. Owing to obligations of confidentiality between patient and physician, a psychologist and a consulting psychiatrist did not report the threat to the woman or to her family, though they did make one unsuccessful attempt to commit the man to a mental hospital.

One judge held that the therapist could not escape liability: "When a therapist determines, or pursuant to the standards of his profession should determine, that his patient presents a serious danger of violence to another, he incurs an obligation to use reasonable care to protect the intended victim against such danger." Notification of police and direct warnings to the family were mentioned as possible instances of due care. The judge argued that although medical confidentiality must generally be observed by physicians, it was overridden in this case by an obligation to the possible victim and to the "public interest in safety from violent assault."

In the minority opinion, a second judge stated his firm disagreement. He argued that a patient's rights are violated when rules of confidentiality are not observed, that psychiatric treatment would be frustrated by nonobservance, and that patients would subsequently lose confidence in psychiatrists and would fail to provide full disclosures. He also suggested that violent assaults would actually increase because mentally ill persons would be discouraged from seeking psychiatric aid.[1]

The Tarasoff case is an instance of a moral dilemma because strong moral reasons support the rival conclusions of the two judges. The most difficult and recalcitrant moral controversies that we encounter in this volume generally have at least some dilemmatic features. They may even involve what Guido Calabresi has called "tragic choices." Everyone who has been faced with a difficult decision—such as whether to have an abortion, to have a pet "put to sleep," or to commit a family member to a mental institution—knows through deep anguish what is meant by a dilemma.

Dilemmas occur whenever good reasons for mutually exclusive alternatives can be cited; if any one set of reasons is acted upon, events will result that are desirable in some respects but undesirable in others. Here an agent morally ought to do one thing and also morally ought to do another thing, but the agent is precluded by circumstances from doing both. Although the moral reasons behind each alternative are good reasons, neither set of reasons clearly outweighs the other. Parties on both sides of dilemmatic disagreements thus can *correctly* present moral reasons in support of their competing conclusions. The reasons behind each alternative are good and weighty, and neither set of reasons is obviously the best set. Most moral dilemmas therefore present a need to balance rival claims in untidy circumstances.

One possible response to the problem of public moral dilemmas and disputes is that we do not have and are not likely ever to have a single theory or method for resolving public disagreements. In any pluralistic culture there may be many sources of moral value and consequently a pluralism of moral points of view on many issues: bluffing in business deals, providing national health insurance to all citizens, involuntarily committing the mentally disturbed, civil disobedience in pursuit of justice, and so on. If this response is correct, we can understand why there seem to be intractable moral dilemmas and controversies both inside and outside professional philosophy. However, there also are ways to alleviate at least some dilemmas and disagreements, as we shall now see.

The Resolution of Moral Disagreements. No single set of considerations is an entirely reliable method for resolving disagreement and controversy, but several methods for dealing constructively with moral disagreements have been employed in the past. Each deserves recognition as a method of constructively contending with disagreement.

1. *Obtaining Objective Information.* First, many moral disagreements can be at least facilitated by obtaining factual information concerning points of moral controversy. It has often been assumed that moral disputes are produced solely by differences over moral principles or their interpretation and application, rather than by a lack of information. However, disputes over what morally ought or ought not to be done often have nonmoral elements as central ingredients. For example, debates about the justice of government allocation of health dollars to preventive and educational strategies have often bogged down over factual issues of whether these strategies actually function to prevent illness and promote health.

In some cases new information facilitates negotiation and compromise. New information about the alleged dangers involved in certain kinds of scientific research, for instance, have turned public controversies regarding the risks of science and the rights of scientific researchers in unanticipated directions. In several controversies over research with a high level of uncertainty, it has been feared that the research might create an irreversible and dangerous situation (for example, by releasing an organism of pathogenic capability that known antibodies would be unable to combat and that could produce widespread contagion).

Controversies about sweetening agents for drinks, toxic substances in the workplace, pesticides in agriculture, radiation therapies, and vaccine dissemination, among others, have been laced with issues of both values and facts. Current controversies over whether there should be compulsory screening for AIDS sometimes turn chiefly on factual claims about how much can be learned by screening, how many persons are threatened, whether health education campaigns can successfully teach safe sex practices, and the like.

The arguments used by disagreeing parties in these cases sometimes turn on a dispute about liberty or justice and therefore sometimes are primarily normative, but they may also rest on purely factual disagreements. New information may have only a limited bearing on the resolution of some of these controversies, whereas in others it may have a direct and almost overpowering influence. The problem is that rarely, if ever, is all the information obtained that would be sufficient to settle factual disagreements.

2. *Providing Definitional Clarity.* Second, controversies have been calmed by reaching conceptual or definitional agreement over the language used by disputing parties. Controversies over the morality of euthanasia, for example, are often needlessly entangled because disputing parties use different senses of the term and have invested heavily in their particular definitions. For example, it may be that one party equates euthanasia with mercy killing and another party equates it with voluntarily elected natural death. Some even hold that euthanasia is by definition *nonvoluntary* mercy killing. Any resulting moral controversy over the concept *euthanasia* is ensnared in terminological problems, rendering it doubtful that the parties are even discussing the same problem. Fortunately, conceptual analysis does often facilitate discussion of issues, and many essays in this volume dwell at some length on conceptual analysis.

3. *Adopting a Code.* Third, resolution of moral problems can be facilitated if disputing parties can come to agreement on a common set of moral guidelines. If this method requires a complete shift from one starkly different moral point of view to another, disputes will virtually never be eased. Differences that divide persons at the level of their most cherished principles are deep divisions, and conversions are infrequent. Various forms of discussion and negotiation can, however, lead to the adoption of a new or changed moral framework that can serve as a common basis for discussion.

For example, a national commission appointed to study ethical issues in research involving human subjects unanimously adopted a common framework of moral principles. These principles provided a general background for deliberation about particular problems. Commissioners utilized three moral principles: respect for persons, beneficence, and justice. The principles were then used, along with other considerations, to justify a position on a wide range of moral problems that confronted the commission.[2] This common framework of principles facilitated discussion of controversies and opened up avenues of agreement that might otherwise not have been spotted.

Virtually every professional association in medicine and nursing has a code of ethics, and the reason for the existence of these codes is to give guidance in a circumstance of uncertainty or dispute. Their rules apply to all persons in the relevant professional roles in medicine, nursing, and research and often help resolve charges of unprofessional or unethical conduct. These codes are very general and cannot be expected to cover every possible case, but agreed-upon general principles do provide an important starting point.

4. *Using Examples and Counterexamples.* Fourth, resolution of moral controversies can be aided by a constructive method of example and opposed counterexample. Cases or examples favorable to one point of view are brought forward, and counterexamples to these cases are thrown up against the examples and claims of the first. This form of debate occurred when the commission mentioned in the preceding section considered the level of risk that can justifiably be permitted in scientific research involving children as subjects, where no therapeutic benefit is offered to the child. On the basis of principles of acceptable risk used in their own previous deliberations, commissioners were at first inclined to accept the view that only low-risk or *minimal-risk* procedures could be justified in the case of children (where *minimal risk* refers analogically to the level of risk present in standard medical examinations of patients). Examples from the history of medicine were cited that revealed how certain significant diagnostic, therapeutic, and preventive advances in medicine would have been unlikely, or at least slowed, unless procedures

that posed a higher level of risk had been employed. Counterexamples of overzealous researchers who placed children at too much risk were then thrown up against these examples, and the debate continued in this way for several months.

Eventually a majority of commissioners abandoned their original view that nontherapeutic research involving more than minimal risk was unjustified. The majority accepted the position that a higher level of risk can be justified by the benefits provided to other children, as when a group of terminally ill children become subjects of research in the hope that something will be learned about their disease that can be applied to other children. Once a consensus on this issue crystallized, resolution was achieved on the primary moral controversy about the involvement of children as research subjects (although two commissioners never agreed).

5. *Analyzing Arguments*. Fifth and finally, one of the most important methods of philosophical inquiry is the exposing of inadequacies, gaps, fallacies, and unexpected consequences of an argument. If an argument rests on accepting two incoherent points of view, then pointing out the incoherence will require a change in the argument. There are many subtle ways of attacking an argument. For example, in Chapters 4–5 there are discussions of the nature of "persons" dealing with problems of the right to die and euthanasia. Some writers on these topics have not appreciated that their arguments about persons were so broad that they carried important but unnoticed implications for both infants and animals. Their arguments implicitly provided reasons they had not noticed for denying rights to infants (rights that adults have), or for granting (or denying) the same rights to fetuses that infants have, and in some cases for granting (or denying) the same rights to animals that infants have.

It may, of course, be correct to hold that infants have fewer rights than adults, or that fetuses and animals should be granted the same rights as infants. The point is that if a moral argument leads to conclusions that a proponent is not prepared to defend and did not previously anticipate, the argument will have to be changed, and this process may reduce the distance between the parties who were initially in disagreement. This style of argument may be supplemented by one or more of the other four ways of reducing moral disagreement. Much of the work published in journals takes the form of attacking arguments, using counterexamples, and proposing alternative principles.

To accept this ideal of criticism is not to assume that conflicts can always be eliminated. The moral life will always be plagued by forms of conflict and incoherence. Our pragmatic goal should be a method that helps in a circumstance of disagreement, not a method that will always eradicate problems. We need not claim that moral disagreements can always be resolved, or even that every rational person must accept the same method for approaching problems. However, if something is to be done to alleviate disagreement, a resolution is more likely to occur if the methods outlined in this section are used.

THE PROBLEM OF RELATIVISM

The fact of moral disagreement and the idea of a universal common morality raise questions about whether moral judgments can be reached impartially and hold for everyone, or instead lead to an inescapable relativism.

Cultural Relativism. Relativists have often appealed to anthropological data indicating that moral rightness and wrongness vary from place to place and that there are no absolute or universal moral standards that could apply to all persons at all times. They maintain that rightness is contingent on cultural beliefs and that the concepts of rightness and wrongness are meaningless apart from the specific contexts in which they arise. The claim is that patterns of culture can only be understood as unique wholes and that moral beliefs are closely connected in a culture.

Although it is certainly true that many cultural practices and individual beliefs vary, it does not follow that morally serious people disagree about the moral standards that were described earlier in this chapter as norms in the common morality. Two cultures may agree about these norms and yet disagree about how to apply them in particular situations or practices. The two cultures may even agree on all the basic principles of morality yet disagree about how to live by these principles in particular circumstances.

For example, if personal payments for special services are common in one culture and punishable as bribery in another, then it is undeniable that these customs are different, but it does not follow that the moral principles underlying the customs are relative. One culture may exhibit a belief that practices of grease payments produce a social good by eliminating government interference and by lowering the salaries paid to functionaries, while the people of another culture may believe that the overall social good is best promoted by eliminating all special favors. Both justifications rest on an appraisal of the overall social good, but the people of the two cultures apply this principle in disparate and apparently competing ways.

This possibility suggests that a basic or fundamental conflict between cultural values can only occur if apparent cultural disagreements about proper principles or rules occur at the level of ultimate moral principles. Otherwise, the apparent disagreements can be understood in terms of, and perhaps be arbitrated by, appeal to deeper shared values. If a moral conflict were truly fundamental, then the conflict could not be removed even if there were perfect agreement about the facts of a case, about the concepts involved, and about background beliefs.

We need, then, to distinguish *relativism of judgments* from *relativism of standards:* Different judgments may rely upon the same general standards for their justification. Relativism of judgment is so pervasive in human social life that it would be foolish to deny it. When people differ about whether one policy for keeping hospital information confidential is more acceptable than another, they differ in their judgments, but they need not have different moral standards of confidentiality. They may hold the same moral standard on protecting confidentiality but differ over how to implement that standard.

Showing the falsity of a relativism of standards is more than we can hope to achieve here, but we can show how difficult it would be to show that it is true. Suppose, for the sake of argument, that disagreement exists at the deepest level of moral belief; that is, suppose that two cultures disagree on basic or fundamental norms. It does not follow even from a relativity of *standards* that there is no ultimate norm or set of norms in which everyone *ought* to believe. Consider an analogy to religious disagreement: From the fact that people have incompatible religious or atheistic beliefs, it does not follow that there is no single correct set of religious or atheistic propositions. Nothing more than skepticism is justified by the facts about religion that are adduced by anthropology; and, similarly, nothing more than this skepticism would be justified if fundamental conflicts of social belief were discovered in ethics.

Normative Relativism. Consider now a second type of relativism. Some relativists interpret "What is right at one place or time may be wrong at another" to mean that *it is right* in one context to act in a way that *it is wrong* to act in another. This thesis is normative, because it makes a value judgment; it delineates *which standards or norms correctly determine right and wrong behavior*. One form of this normative relativism asserts that one ought to do what one's society determines to be right (a group or social form of normative relativism), and a second form holds that one ought to do what one personally believes is right (an individual form of normative relativism).

This normative position has sometimes crudely been translated as "Anything is right or wrong whenever some individual or some group judges that it is right or wrong." However, less crude formulations of the position can be given, and more or less plausible examples can be adduced. One can hold the view, for example, that in order to be right something must be conscientiously and not merely customarily believed. Alternatively, it might be formulated as the view that whatever is believed to be right is right if it is part of a well-formed traditional moral code of rules in a society—for example, a medical code of ethics developed by a professional society.

The evident inconsistency of this form of relativism with many of our most cherished moral beliefs is one major reason to be doubtful of it. No general theory of normative relativism is likely to convince us that a belief is acceptable merely because others believe it in a certain way, although that is exactly the commitment of this theory. At least some moral views seem relatively more enlightened, no matter how great the variability of beliefs. The idea that practices such as slavery cannot be evaluated across cultures by some common standard seems morally unacceptable, not morally enlightened. It is one thing to suggest that such beliefs might be *excused,* still another to suggest that they are *right.*

We can evaluate this second form of relativism by focusing on (1) the objectivity of morals within cultures, and (2) the stultifying consequences of a serious commitment to moral relativism. (The first focus provides an argument against *individual* relativism and the second provides an argument against a *cultural* source of relativism.)

We noted previously that morality is concerned with practices of right and wrong transmitted within cultures from one generation to another. The terms of social life are set by these practices, whose rules are pervasively acknowledged and shared in that culture. Within the culture, then, a significant measure of moral agreement (objectivity) exists, and morality cannot be modified through a person's individual preferences.

For example, a hospital corporation cannot develop its professional ethics in any way it wishes. No hospital chain can draw up a code that brushes aside the need for confidentiality of patient information or that permits surgeons to proceed without adequate consents from patients, and a physician cannot make up his or her individual "code" of medical ethics. If codes deviate significantly from standard or accepted rules, they will rightly be rejected as subjective and mistaken.

Room for invention or alteration in morality is therefore restricted by the broader understanding of social morality. Beliefs cannot become *moral* standards simply because an individual so labels them. Because individual (normative) relativism claims that moral standards can be invented or labeled, the theory seems *factually* mistaken. This critique of *individual* relativism does not count against *cultural* relativism, however, because a cultural relativist could easily accept this critique. Our discussion needs to shift, then, to a second argument, which is directed at cultural forms of normative relativism.

The problem is this: In circumstances of disagreement, moral reflection is needed to resolve moral issues whether or not people accept different norms. When two parties argue about a serious, divisive, and contested moral issue—for example, conflicts of interest—most of us think that some fair and justified compromise may be reached despite the differences of belief causing the dispute. People seldom infer from the mere fact of a conflict between beliefs that there is no way to judge one view as correct or as better argued or fairer minded than the other. The more implausible the position advanced by one party, the more convinced others become that some views are mistaken or require supplementation.

People seldom conclude, then, that there is not a better and worse ethical perspective or a more reasonable form of negotiation. If cultural normative relativists deny the acceptability of these beliefs, they seem to give up too early on the possibility that moral agreement may be achieved.

THE ACCEPTABILITY OF MORAL DIVERSITY AND MORAL DISAGREEMENT

Even conscientious and reasonable moral agents who work diligently at moral reasoning sometimes disagree with other equally conscientious persons. They may disagree about whether disclosure to a fragile patient is appropriate, whether religious values about brain death have a central place in secular ethics, whether physician-assisted suicide should be legalized, and hundreds of other issues in bioethics. Such disagreement does not indicate moral ignorance or moral defect. We simply lack a single, entirely reliable way to resolve all disagreements.

This fact returns us to the questions about morality in the particular (or broad) sense that opened this chapter. Neither morality nor ethical theory has the resources to provide a single solution to every moral problem. Moral disagreement can emerge because of (1) factual disagreements (for example, about the level of suffering that an action will cause), (2) scope disagreements about who should be protected by a moral norm (for example, whether fetuses or animals are protected), (3) disagreements about which norms are relevant in the circumstances, (4) disagreements about appropriate specifications, (5) disagreements about the weight of the relevant norms in the circumstances, (6) disagreements about appropriate forms of balancing, (7) the presence of a genuine moral dilemma, and (8) insufficient information or evidence.

Different parties may emphasize different principles or assign different weights to principles even when they do not disagree over which principles are relevant. Such disagreement may persist even among morally serious persons who conform to all the demands that morality makes upon them. Moreover, when evidence is incomplete and different sets of evidence are available to different parties, one individual or group may be justified in reaching a conclusion that another individual or group is justified in rejecting. Even when both parties have incorrect beliefs, each party may be justified in holding those beliefs. We cannot hold persons to a higher standard in practice than to make judgments conscientiously in light of the relevant norms and the available and relevant evidence.

These facts about the moral life sometimes discourage those who must deal with practical problems, but the phenomenon of reasoned moral disagreement provides no basis for skepticism about morality or about moral thinking. Indeed, it offers a reason for taking morality seriously and using the best tools that we have to carry our moral projects as far as we can. We should not forget that we frequently obtain near complete agreement in our moral judgments and that we have the universal basis for morality considered earlier in this chapter.

When disagreements arise, a moral agent can—and often should—defend his or her decision without disparaging or reproaching others who reach different decisions. Recognition of legitimate diversity (by contrast to moral violations that call for criticism) is exceedingly important when we evaluate the actions of others. What one person does may not be what other persons should do even when they face the same problem. Similarly, what one institution or government should do may not be what another institution or government should do. From this perspective, individuals and societies legitimately construct different requirements that comprise part of the moral life (consistent with what we have called morality in the broad sense), and we may not be able to judge one as better than another.[3]

MORAL JUSTIFICATION

Typically we have no difficulty in deciding whether and how to act morally. We make moral judgments through a mix of appeals to rules, paradigm cases, role models, and the like. These moral beacons work well as long as we are not asked to deliberate about or justify our judgments. However, when we experience moral doubt or uncertainty, we are led to moral deliberation, and often from there to a need to justify our beliefs. As we deliberate, we usually consider which among the possible courses of action is morally justified—that is, which has the strongest moral reasons behind it. The reasons we finally accept express the conditions under which we believe some course of action is morally justified.

The objective of justification is to establish one's case by presenting a sufficient set of reasons for belief and action. Not all reasons, however, are good reasons, and even good reasons are not always sufficient for justification. There is, then, a need to distinguish a reason's *relevance* to a moral judgment from its final *adequacy* for that judgment; and also to distinguish an *attempted* justification from a *successful* justification. For example, a good reason for involuntarily committing certain mentally ill persons to institutions is that they present a clear and present danger to other persons. By contrast, a reason for commitment that is sometimes offered as a good reason, but that many people consider a bad reason (because it involves a deprivation of liberty), is that some mentally ill persons present a clear and present danger to themselves or that they require treatment for a serious mental disorder.

If someone holds that involuntary commitment on grounds of danger to self is a good reason and is solely sufficient to justify commitment, that person should be able to give some account of why this reason is good and sufficient. That is, the person should be able to give further justifying reasons for the belief that the reason offered is good and sufficient. The person might refer, for example, to the dire consequences for the mentally ill that will occur if no one intervenes. The person might also invoke certain principles about the moral importance of caring for the needs of the mentally ill. In short, the person is expected to give a set of reasons that amounts to an argued defense of his or her perspective. These appeals are usually either to a coherent group of moral principles or to consequences of actions, and they form the substantive basis of justification.

Many philosophers now defend the view that the relationship between general moral norms and particular moral judgments is bilateral (neither a unilateral "application" of general norms nor a unilateral abstraction from particular case judgments). John Rawls's celebrated account of *reflective equilibrium* has been the most influential model in this literature. In developing and refining a system of ethics, he argues, it is appropriate to start with the broadest possible set of *considered judgments* (see later) about a subject and to erect a provisional set of principles that reflects them. Reflective equilibrium views investigation in ethics (and theory construction) as a reflective testing of moral principles, theoretical postulates, and other relevant moral beliefs to render them as coherent as possible. Starting with paradigms of what is morally right or wrong, one searches for principles that are consistent with these paradigms as well as one another. Such principles and considered judgments are taken, as Rawls puts it, "provisionally as fixed points," but also as "liable to revision."

Considered judgments is a technical term referring to judgments in which moral beliefs and capacities are most likely to be presented without a distorting bias. Examples are judgments about the wrongness of racial discrimination, religious intolerance, and predatory sexual behavior. The goal of reflective equilibrium is to match, prune, and adjust considered judgments and principles so that they form a coherent moral outlook. This model demands the best approximation to full coherence under the assumption of a never-ending search for consistency and unanticipated situations. From this perspective, ethical theories and individual moral outlooks are never complete, always stand to be informed by practical contexts, and must be tested for adequacy by their practical implications.

Although the justification of particular moral *judgments* is often the issue, philosophers are as also concerned with the justification of general ethical *theories*. Which theory, we can now ask, is the best theory? Or do all theories fail tests for considered judgments and coherence?

TYPES OF ETHICAL THEORY

Many writers in bioethics believe that we would justifiably have more confidence in our individual and communal moral judgments if only we could justify them on the basis of a comprehensive ethical theory. The ambition of such an ethical theory is to provide an adequate normative framework for processing, and hopefully resolving, moral problems.

To deal with these issues, the reader should be prepared not only to understand ethical theory but also to make some assessment of its value for bioethics. Our objective in this section is not to show how ethical theory actually can resolve problems in health care, but only to present several influential types of ethical theory. These theories should be situated under the category that we earlier called general normative ethics. We will concentrate on utilitarianism, Kantianism, virtue (or character) ethics, the ethics of care, and casuistry. Some knowledge of these theories is indispensable for reflective study in bioethics because a sizable part of the field's literature draws on methods and conclusions found in these theories.

UTILITARIAN THEORIES

Utilitarianism is rooted in the thesis that an action or practice is right (when compared to any alternative action or practice) if it leads to the greatest possible balance of good consequences or to the least possible balance of bad consequences in the world as a whole. Utilitarians hold that there is one and only one basic principle of ethics: the principle of utility. This principle asserts that we ought always to produce the maximal balance of good consequences over bad consequences. The classical origins of this theory are found in the writings of Jeremy Bentham (1748–1832) and John Stuart Mill (1806–1873).

Utilitarians invite us to consider the larger objective or function of morality as a social institution, where *morality* is understood to include our shared rules of justice and other principles of the moral life. The point of the institution of morality, they insist, is to promote human welfare by minimizing harms and maximizing benefits: There would be no point in having moral codes unless they served this purpose. Utilitarians thus see moral rules as the means to the fulfilment of individual needs as well as to the achievement of broad social goals.

Mill's Utilitarianism. In several types of ethical theory, classic works of enduring influence form the basis for development of the theory. The most influential exposition of utilitarianism is John Stuart Mill's book *Utilitarianism* (1863). In this work Mill refers to the principle of utility as the Greatest Happiness Principle: "Actions are right in proportion as they tend to promote happiness, wrong as they tend to produce the reverse of happiness, i.e., pleasure or absence of pain." Mill's view seems to be that the purpose of morality is to tap natural human sympathies so as to benefit others while at the same time controlling unsympathetic attitudes that cause harm to others. The principle of utility is conceived as the best means to these basic human goals.

For Mill and other utilitarians, moral theory is grounded in a theory of the general goals of life, which they conceive as the pursuit of pleasure and the avoidance of pain. The production of pleasure and pain assumes moral and not merely personal significance when the consequences of our actions affect the pleasurable or painful states of others. Moral rules and moral and legal institutions, as they see it, must be grounded in a general theory of value, and morally good actions are alone determined by these final values.

Essential Features of Utilitarianism. Several essential features of utilitarianism may be extracted from the reasoning of Mill and other utilitarians. In particular, four conditions must be satisfied in order to qualify as a utilitarian theory.

1. The Principle of Utility: Maximize the Good. First, actors are obliged to maximize the good: We ought always to produce the greatest possible balance of value over disvalue (or the least possible balance of disvalue, if only bad results can be achieved). But what is the good or the valuable? This question takes us to the second condition.

2. A Theory of Value: The Standard of Goodness. The goodness or badness of consequences is to be measured by items that count as the primary goods or utilities. Various theories of value (or theories of the good) held by utilitarians point to (1) happiness, (2) the satisfaction of desires and aims, and (3) the attainment of such conditions or states of affairs as autonomy, understanding, various kinds of functioning, achievement, and deep personal relationships.

Many utilitarians agree that ultimately we ought to look to the production of *agent-neutral* or intrinsic values, those that do not vary from person to person. That is, what is good in itself, not merely what is good as a means to something else, ought to be produced. Bentham and Mill are hedonists; they believe that only pleasure or happiness (which are synonymous terms in this context) can be intrinsically good. Pluralistic utilitarian philosophers, by contrast, believe that no single goal or state constitutes the good and that many values besides happiness possess intrinsic worth—for example, the values of friendship, knowledge, love, personal achievement, culture, freedom, and liberties can all qualify.

Both the hedonistic and the pluralistic approaches have seemed to some recent philosophers relatively problematic for purposes of objectively aggregating widely different interests in order to determine where maximal value, and therefore right action, lies. Many utilitarians interpret the good as that which is *subjectively* desired or wanted. The satisfaction of desires or wants is seen as the goal of our moral actions. To maximize an individual's utility is to maximize what he or she has chosen or would choose from the available alternatives.

3. Consequentialism. Whatever its value theory, any utilitarian theory decides which actions are right entirely by reference to the *consequences* of the actions, rather than by reference to any intrinsic moral features the actions may have, such as truthfulness or fidelity. Here the utilitarian need not demand that all future consequences or even all avoidable consequences be anticipated. A utilitarian demands only that we take account of what can reasonably be expected to produce the greatest balance of good or least balance of harm. In judging the *agent* of the action, we should assess whether the agent conscientiously attempts to produce the best utilitarian outcome.

4. Impartiality (Universalism). Finally, in the utilitarian approach all parties affected by an action must receive *impartial consideration.* Utilitarianism thus stands in sharp contrast to egoism, which proposes maximizing consequences for oneself rather than for all parties affected by an action. In seeking a blinded impartiality, utilitarianism aligns good and mature moral judgment with moral distance from the choices to be made.

Act and Rule Utilitarianism. Utilitarian moral philosophers are conventionally divided into several types, and it is best to think of "utilitarianism" as a label designating a family of theories that use a consequentialist principle. A significant dispute has arisen among utilitarians over whether the principle of utility is to be applied to *particular acts* in particular circumstances or to *rules of conduct* that determine which acts are right and wrong. For the *rule utilitarian,* actions are justified by appeal to rules such as "Don't deceive" and "Don't break promises." These rules, in turn, are justified by appeal to the principle of utility. An *act utilitarian* simply justifies actions directly by appeal to the principle of utility. Act utilitarianism is thus characterized as a "direct" or "extreme" theory because the act utilitarian directly asks, "What good and evil consequences will result directly from this action in this circumstance?"—not "What good and evil consequences will result generally from this sort of action?"

Consider the following case, which occurred in the state of Kansas and which anticipates some issues about euthanasia encountered in Chapter 4. An elderly woman lay ill and dying. Her suffering came to be too much for her and her faithful husband of fifty-four years to endure, so she requested that he kill her. Stricken with grief and unable to bring himself to perform the act, the husband hired another man to kill his wife. An act utilitarian might reason that *in this case* hiring another to kill the woman was justified, although *in general* we would not permit persons to perform such actions. After all, only this woman and her husband were directly affected, and relief of her pain was the main issue. It would be unfortunate, the act utilitarian might reason, if our "rules" against killing failed to allow for selective killings in extenuating circumstances, because it is extremely difficult to generalize from case to case. The jury, as it turned out, convicted the husband of murder, and he was sentenced to twenty-five years in prison. An act utilitarian might maintain that a *rigid* application of rules inevitably leads to injustices and that rule utilitarianism cannot escape this problem of an undue rigidity of rules.

Many philosophers object vigorously to act utilitarianism, charging its exponents with basing morality on mere expediency. On act-utilitarian grounds, they say, it is desirable for a physician to kill babies with many kinds of birth defects if the death of the child would relieve the family and society of a burden and inconvenience and would lead to the greatest good for the greatest number. Many opponents of act utilitarianism have thus argued that strict rules, which cannot be set aside for the sake of convenience, must be maintained. Many of these apparently desirable rules can be justified by the principle of utility, so utilitarianism need not be abandoned if act utilitarianism is judged unworthy.

Rule utilitarians hold that rules have a central position in morality and cannot be compromised in particular situations. Compromise threatens the rules themselves. The rules' effectiveness is judged by determining whether the observance of a given rule would maximize social utility better than would any substitute rule (or having no rule). Utilitarian rules are, in theory, firm and protective of all classes of individuals, just as human rights firmly protect all individuals regardless of social convenience and momentary need.

Nonetheless, we can ask whether rule-utilitarian theories offer anything more than act utilitarianism. Dilemmas often arise that involve conflicts among moral rules—for example, rules of confidentiality conflict with rules protecting individual welfare, as in the Tarasoff case. If there are no rules to resolve these conflicts, perhaps the rule utilitarian cannot be distinguished from the act utilitarian.

KANTIAN THEORIES

We have seen that utilitarianism conceives the moral life in terms of intrinsic value and the means to produce this value. A second type of theory departs significantly from this approach. Often called *deontological* (i.e., a theory that some features of actions other than or in addition to consequences make actions obligatory), this type is now increasingly called *Kantian,* because of its origins in the theory of Immanuel Kant (1724–1804).

Duty from Rules of Reason. Kant believed that an act is morally praiseworthy only if done neither for self-interested reasons nor as the result of a natural disposition, but rather from *duty*. That is, the person's motive for acting must be a recognition of the act as resting on duty. It is not good enough, in Kant's view, that one merely performs the morally correct action, because one could perform one's duty for self-interested reasons having nothing to do with morality. For example, if an employer discloses a health hazard to an employee only because he or she fears a lawsuit, and not because of a belief in the importance of truth telling, then this employer acts rightly but deserves no moral credit for the action.

Kant tries to establish the ultimate basis for the validity of moral rules in pure reason, not in intuition, conscience, or utility. He thinks all considerations of utility and self-interest secondary, because the moral worth of an agent's action depends exclusively on the moral acceptability of the rule on the basis of which the person is acting. An action has moral worth only when performed by an agent who possesses a good will, and a person has a good will only if moral duty based on a universally valid rule is the sole motive for the action. Morality, then, provides a rational framework of principles and rules that constrain and guide everyone, without regard to their personal goals and interests.

Kant's supreme principle, *the categorial imperative,* also called *the moral law,* is expressed in several ways in his writings. His first formulation may be roughly paraphrased in this way: "Always act in such a way that you can will that everyone act in the same manner in similar situations." Kant's view is that wrongful practices, such as lying, theft, cheating, and failure to help someone in distress when you can easily do so, involve a kind of contradiction. Consider the example of cheating on exams. If everyone behaved as the cheater did, exams would not serve their essential function of testing mastery of relevant material, in which case there would effectively be no such thing as an exam. But cheating presupposes the background institution of taking exams, so the cheater cannot consistently will that everyone act as she does.

The categorical imperative is categorical, Kant says, because it admits of no exceptions and is absolutely binding. It is imperative because it gives instruction about how one must act. Kant clarifies this basic moral law by drawing a distinction between a categorical imperative and a *hypothetical imperative*. A hypothetical imperative takes the form, "If I want to achieve such and such a valued end, then I must do so and so." These prescriptions—so reminiscent of utilitarian thinking—tell us what we must do, provided that we already have certain desires, interests, or goals. An example is, "If you want to regain your health, then you must take this medication," or "If you want to improve infant mortality rates, then you must improve your hospital facilities." These imperatives are not commanded for their own sake. They are commanded as means to an end that has already been willed or accepted. Hypothetical imperatives are not moral imperatives in Kant's philosophy because moral imperatives tell us what must be done independently of our goals or desires.

Kant emphasizes the notion of *rule as universal law*. Rules that determine duty are made correct by their universality, that is, the fact that they apply to everyone. This criterion of universality offers some worthwhile lessons for bioethics. Some of the clearest cases of immoral behavior involve a person's trying to make a unique exception of himself or herself purely for personal reasons. This conduct could not be made universal, or the rules presupposed by the idea of "being an exception" would be destroyed. If carried out consistently by others, this conduct would violate the rules presupposed by the system of morality, thereby rendering the system inconsistent—that is, having inconsistent rules of operation.

Kant's view is that wrongful practices, including invasion of privacy, theft, and manipulative suppression of information, are "contradictory"; that is, they are not consistent with the very duties they presuppose. In cases of lying, for example, the universalization of rules that allow lying would entitle everyone to lie to you, just as you would be entitled to lie to them. Such rules are inconsistent with the practice of truth telling that they presuppose. Similarly, fraud in research is inconsistent with the practice of publishing the truth. All such practices are inconsistent with a rule or practice that they presuppose.

The Requirement to Never Treat Persons as Means. A second formulation of Kant's categorical imperative—one more frequently invoked in medical ethics—may be paraphrased in this way: "Treat every person as an end and never solely as a means."[4] This principle requires us to treat persons as having their own established goals. Deceiving prospective subjects in order to get them to consent to participate in nontherapeutic research is one example of a violation of this principle.

It has commonly been said that Kant is here arguing that we can never treat another as a means to our ends. This interpretation, however, misrepresents his views. He argues only that we must not treat another *exclusively* as a means to our own ends. When adult human research subjects are asked to volunteer, for example, they are treated as a means to a researcher's ends. However, they are not exclusively used for others' purposes, because they do not become mere servants or objects. Their consent justifies using them as means to the end of research.

Kant's imperative demands only that persons in such situations be treated with the respect and moral dignity to which all persons are always entitled, including the times when they are used as means to the ends of others. To treat persons merely as means, strictly speaking, is to disregard their personhood by exploiting or otherwise using them without regard to their own thoughts, interests, and needs. It involves a failure to acknowledge that every person has a worth and dignity equal to that of every other person and that this worth and dignity cannot be compromised for utilitarian or any other reasons.

CONTEMPORARY CHALLENGES TO THE TRADITIONAL THEORIES

Thus far we have treated only two types of theory: utilitarianism and Kantianism. These theories combine a variety of moral considerations into a surprisingly systematized framework, centered around a single major principle. Much is attractive in these theories, and they have been the dominant models in ethical theory throughout much of the twentieth century. During the 1970s and much of the 1980s, utilitarian and deontological approaches exerted enormous influence on the literature and discourse of bioethics.

Although utilitarian and deontological arguments or patterns of reasoning are still common today, the theories themselves now hold a much diminished stature in the field. The reasons for the demotion of utilitarian and single-principle deontological theories concern the disadvantages of any approach that attempts to characterize the entire domain of morality with one supreme principle. Three disadvantages are especially worthy of note. First, there is a problem of authority. Despite myriad attempts by philosophers in recent centuries to justify the claim that some principle is morally authoritative—that is, correctly regarded as the supreme moral principle—no such effort at justification has persuaded a majority of philosophers or other thoughtful people that either the principle or the moral system is as authoritative as the common morality that supplies its roots. Thus to attempt to illuminate problems in bioethics with a single-principle theory has struck many as misguided as well as presumptuous or dogmatic.

Second, even if an individual working in this field is convinced that some such theory is correct (authoritative), he or she needs to deal responsibly with the fact that many other morally serious individuals do not share this theory and give it little or no authority. Thus, problems of how to communicate and negotiate in the midst of disagreement do not favor appeals to rigid theories or inflexible principles, which can generate a gridlock of conflicting principled positions, rendering moral discussion hostile and alienating.

Third, there is the problem that a highly general principle is indeterminate in many contexts in which one might try to apply it. That is, the content of the principle itself does not always identify a unique course of action as right. It has increasingly become apparent that single-principle theories are significantly incomplete, frequently depending on independent moral considerations with the help of which the theories can serve as effective guides to action.

Much recent philosophical writing has focused on weaknesses in utilitarian and Kantian theories and on ways in which the two types of theory actually affirm some broader and less controversial conception of the moral life. Critics of utilitarian and Kantian models believe that the contrast between the two "types of theory" has been overestimated and that they do not merit the attention they have received and the lofty position they have occupied. Three accounts have been popular in bioethics as replacements for, or perhaps supplements to, utilitarian and Kantian theories. They are (1) virtue theory (which is character based), (2) the ethics of care (which is relationship based), and (3) casuistry (which is case based). These are the topics of the next three sections.

VIRTUE ETHICS

In discussing utilitarian and Kantian theories, we have looked chiefly at obligations and rights. Beyond obligations and rights, we often reflect on the agents who perform actions, have motives, and follow principles. Here we commonly make judgments about good and evil character in persons; virtue ethics gives good character a preeminent place.

Virtue ethics descends from the classical Greek tradition represented by Plato and Aristotle. Here the cultivation of virtuous traits of character is viewed as morality's primary function. Moral virtues are understood as morally praiseworthy character traits, such as courage, compassion, sincerity, reliability, and industry. In virtue ethics, the primary concern is with what sort of person is ideal, while action is considered to have secondary importance. People are viewed as acquiring virtues much as they do skills such as carpentry, playing an instrument, or cooking. They become just by performing just actions and become temperate by performing temperate actions. Virtuous character is cultivated and made a part of the individual, much like a language or tradition.

However, an ethics of virtue is more than habitual training. One must also have a correct *motivational structure*. A conscientious person, for example, not only has a disposition to act conscientiously, but a morally appropriate desire to be conscientious. The person characteristically has a moral concern and reservation about acting in a way that would not be conscientious.

Imagine a Kantian who always performs his or her obligation because it is an obligation but intensely dislikes having to allow the interests of others to be of importance. Such a person does not cherish, feel congenial toward, or think fondly of others, and respects them only because obligation requires it. This person can, on a theory of moral obligation such as Kant's (or Mill's), perform a morally right action, have an ingrained disposition to perform that action, and act with obligation as the foremost motive. It is possible (1) to be disposed to do what is right, (2) to intend to do it, and (3) to do it while also (4) yearning to be able to avoid doing it. If the motive is improper, a vital moral ingredient is missing, and if a person *characteristically* lacks this motivational structure, a necessary condition of virtuous character is absent.

Consider a physician who meets his moral obligations because they are his obligations and yet has underlying motives that raise questions of character. This physician detests his job and hates having to spend time with every patient who comes through the door. He cares not about being of service to people or creating a better environment in the office. All he wants to do is make money, avoid malpractice suits, and meet his obligations. Although this man never acts immorally from the perspective of duty, something in his character is deeply defective morally. The admirable compassion and dedication guiding the lives of many health professionals is absent in this person, who merely engages in rule-following behavior.

Virtue ethics may seem only of intellectual interest, but it has practical value in that a morally good person with right desires or motives is more likely to understand what should be done, to perform required acts, and to form moral ideals than is a morally bad or indifferent person. A trusted person has an ingrained motivation and desire to do what is right and to care about whether it is done. Whenever the feelings, concerns, and attitudes of others are the morally relevant matters, rules and principles are not as likely as human warmth and sensitivity to lead a person to notice what should be done. From this perspective, virtue ethics is at least as fundamental in the moral life as principles of basic obligation.

We also often morally evaluate a person's emotional responses—which tend to reflect one's character—even where no particular action is called for. One might admire a social worker's genuine sorrow at the news that another social worker's patient committed suicide; her expression of sorrow reflects her caring and sympathy. Moreover, in practice, well-established virtues may prove at least as important as mastery of principles, rules, and other action guides. For example, it may be the case that being truthful, compassionate, perceptive, diligent, and so forth is a more reliable basis for good medical practice than knowledge of the principles and rules of bioethics.

A proponent of character ethics need not claim that analysis of the virtues subverts or discredits ethical principles, rules, or theories. It is enough to argue that ethical theory is more complete if the virtues are included and that moral motives deserve to be at center stage in a way some leading traditional theories have inadequately appreciated. It is not difficult to see the compatibility of virtue ethics and duty ethics.

Indeed, it is doubtful that virtue can be adequately conceptualized without some background assumptions about right action. For example, seeing truthfulness as a virtue seems inseparable from seeing truth telling as a prima facie obligation. If we ask why one should generally be truthful, it seems evasive to say, "Because virtuous people are that way." A more adequate response would show how truthfulness displays respect for people's autonomy, tends to promote certain benefits, and ordinarily avoids certain kinds of harm.

THE ETHICS OF CARE

Related to virtue ethics in some respects is a relatively new body of moral reflection often called the "ethics of care." This theory develops some of the themes in virtue ethics about the centrality of character, but the ethics of care focuses on a set of character traits that people all deeply value in close personal relationships: sympathy, compassion, fidelity, love, friendship, and the like. Noticeably absent are universal moral rules and impartial utilitarian calculations such as those espoused by Kant and Mill.

To understand this approach, consider the traditional theories' criterion of impartiality in moral judgment. This criterion of distanced fairness and treating similar cases similarly makes eminently good sense for courts, but does it make good sense of intimate moral relationships? The care perspective views this criterion as cutting away too much of morality in order to get to a standpoint of detached fairness. Lost in the traditional *detachment* of impartiality is *attachment*—that which we care about most and which is closest to us. In seeking blindness, we may be made blind and indifferent to the special needs of others. So, although impartiality is a moral virtue in some contexts, it may be a moral vice in others. The care perspective is especially important for roles such as parent, friend, physician, and nurse, where contextual response, attentiveness to subtle clues, and discernment are likely to be more important morally than impartial treatment.

Being cautious about abstract principles of obligation—the instruments of impartiality—is also characteristic of the ethics of care. Defenders of the ethics of care find principles often to be irrelevant, vacuous, or ineffectual in the moral life. A defender of principles could say that principles of care, compassion, and kindness structure our understanding of when it is appropriate to respond in caring, compassionate, and kind ways, but there is something hollow about this claim. It seems to best capture our moral experience to say that we rely on our emotions, our capacity for sympathy, our sense of friendship, and our knowledge of how caring people behave.

Exponents of the ethics of care have also criticized the autonomous, unified, rational beings that typify both the Kantian and the utilitarian conception of the moral self. They argue that moral decisions often require a sensitivity to the situation as well as an awareness of the beliefs, feelings, attitudes, and concerns of each of the individuals involved and of the relationships of those individuals to one another.

Additional reasons exist for thinking that a morality centered on care and concern cannot be squeezed into a morality of rules. For example, it seems very difficult to express the responsibilities of a health care professional adequately through principles and rules. We can generalize about how caring physicians and nurses respond in encounters with patients, but these generalizations do not amount to principles, nor will such generalizations be subtle enough to give sound guidance for the next patient. Each situation calls for a different set of responses, and behavior that in one context is caring seems to intrude on privacy or be offensive in another context.

A morality centered on care and concern can potentially serve health care ethics in a constructive and balanced fashion, because it is close to the processes of reason and feeling exhibited in clinical contexts. Disclosures, discussions, and decision making in health care typically become a family affair, with support from a health care team. The ethics of care maintains that many human relationships in health care and research involve persons who are vulnerable, dependent, ill, and frail and that the desirable moral response is attached attentiveness to needs, not detached respect for rights. Feeling for and being immersed in the other person establish vital aspects of the moral relationship. Accordingly, this approach features responsibilities and forms of empathy that a rights-based account may ignore in the attempt to protect persons from invasion by others.

CASUISTRY

A third alternative to classic theories has been labeled *casuistry.* It focuses on decision making using particular cases, where the judgments reached rely on judgments reached in prior cases. Casuists are skeptical of the power of principles and theory to resolve problems in specific cases. They think that many forms of moral thinking and judgment do not involve appeals to general guidelines, but rather to narratives, paradigm cases, and precedents established by previous cases.[5]

Casuists concentrate our attention on practical decision making in particular cases and on the implications of those cases for other cases. Here we proceed by identifying the specific features of, and problems present in, the case. We may attempt to identify the relevant precedents and prior experiences we have had with related cases, attempting to determine how similar and how different the present case is from other cases. For example, if the case involves a problem of medical confidentiality, analogous cases would be considered in which breaches of confidentiality were justified or unjustified in order to see whether such a breach is justified in the present case.

Consider the way a physician thinks in making a judgment and then a recommendation to a patient. Many individual factors, including the patient's medical history, the physician's successes with other similar patients, paradigms of expected outcomes, and the like will play a role in formulating a judgment and recommendation to this patient, which may be very different from the recommendation made to the next patient with the same malady. The casuist views moral judgments and recommendations similarly. One can make successful moral judgments of agents, actions, and policies, casuists say, only when one has an intimate understanding of particular situations and an appreciation of treating similar cases similarly.

An analogy to case law is helpful in understanding the casuist's point. In case law, the normative judgments made by courts of law become authoritative, and it is reasonable to hold that these judgments are primary for later judges who assess other cases—even though the particular features of each new case will be different. Matters are similar in ethics, say casuists. Normative judgments about certain cases emerge through case comparisons. A case under current consideration is placed in the context of a set of cases that shows a family resemblance, and the similarities and differences are assessed. The relative weight of competing values is presumably determined by the comparisons to analogous cases. Moral guidance is provided by an accumulated mass of influential cases, which represent a consensus in society and in institutions reached by reflection on cases. That consensus then becomes authoritative and is extended to new cases.[6]

Cases like the Tarasoff case have been enormously influential in bioethics. Writers have used it as a form of authority for decisions in new cases. Features of their analyses have then been discussed throughout the literature of bioethics, and they become integral to the way we think and draw conclusions in the field. The leading cases become enduring and authoritative sources for reflection and decisionmaking. Cases such as the Tuskegee syphilis experiment case (in which a group of men were intentionally not given treatment for syphilis in order to follow the course of the disease) are constantly invoked to illustrate *unjustified* biomedical experimentation. Decisions reached about moral wrongs in this case serve as a form of authority for decisions in new cases. These cases profoundly influence our standards of fairness, negligence, paternalism, and the like. Just as case law (legal rules) develops incrementally from legal decisions in cases, so the moral law (moral rules) develops incrementally. From this perspective, principles are less important for moral reasoning than cases.

At first sight, casuistry seems strongly opposed to the frameworks of principles in traditional duty-based theory. However, closer inspection of casuistry shows that its primary concern (like the ethics of care) is with an excessive reliance in recent philosophy on impartial, universal action guides. Two casuists, Albert Jonsen and Stephen Toulmin, write that "*good* casuistry . . . applies general principles to particular cases with discernment." As a history of similar cases and similar judgments mounts, we become more confident in our general judgments. A "locus of moral certitude" arises in the judgments, and the stable elements crystallize into tentative principles. As confidence in these generalizations increases, they are accepted less tentatively and moral knowledge develops.[7]

Today's casuists have resourcefully reminded us of the importance of analogical reasoning, paradigm cases, and practical judgment. Bioethics, like ethical theory, has sometimes unduly minimized this avenue to moral knowledge. Casuists also have rightly pointed out that generalizations are often best learned, accommodated, and implemented by using cases, case discussion, and case methods. These insights can be utilized by connecting them to an appropriate set of concepts, principles, and theories that control the judgments we make about cases.

Nonetheless, this form of reasoning can be misleading. Casuists sometimes write as if cases lead to moral paradigms, analogies, or judgments entirely by their facts alone (or perhaps by appeal only to the salient features of the cases). This premise is suspect. No matter how many facts are stacked up, we will still need some value premises in order to reach a moral conclusion. The properties that we observe to be of moral importance in cases are picked out by the values that we have already accepted as being morally important. In short, the paradigm cases of the casuists are value laden.

The best way to understand this idea of paradigm cases is as a combination of (1) *facts* that can be generalized to other cases—for example, "The patient refused the recommended treatment"—and (2) *settled values*—for example, "Competent patients have a right to refuse treatment." In a principle-based system, these settled values are called principles, rules, rights claims, and the like; and they are analytically distinguished from the facts of particular cases. In casuistical appeals to cases, rather than keeping values distinct from facts, the two are bound together in the paradigm case; the central values are generalizable, however, and must be preserved from one case to the next.

ETHICAL PRINCIPLES

Various basic principles are accepted in classic ethical theories and also seem to be presupposed in traditional codes of ethics. There is an "overlapping consensus" about the validity of these principles. But what is a principle, and which ones overlap the different theories?

A *principle* is a fundamental standard of conduct from which many other moral standards and judgments draw support for their defense and standing. For example, universal moral rights and basic professional duties can be delineated on the basis of moral principles. Ideally, a set of general principles will serve as an analytical framework of basic principles that expresses the general values underlying rules in the common morality and guidelines in professional ethics.

Three general moral principles have proved to be serviceable as a framework of principles for bioethics: respect for autonomy, beneficence, and justice. These three principles should not be construed as jointly forming a complete moral system or theory, but they can provide the beginnings of a framework through which we can reason about problems in bioethics. Each is treated in a separate section here.

One caution is in order about the nature and use of such principles. Moral thinking and judgment must take account of many considerations besides ethical principles and rules, and principles do not contain sufficient content to determine judgments in a great many cases. Often the most prudent course is to search for more information about cases and policies rather than trying to decide prematurely on the basis of either principles or some general theoretical commitments. More information sometimes will resolve problems and in other cases will help fix the principles that are most important in the circumstances.

Principles provide a starting point for moral judgment and policy evaluation, but—as we saw in the previous section and will see in the section on public policy—more content is needed than that supplied by principles alone. They are tested and reliable starting points, but they rarely are sufficient for moral thinking.

RESPECT FOR AUTONOMY

One principle at the center of modern bioethics is *respect for autonomy*. It is rooted in the liberal moral and political tradition of the importance of individual freedom and choice. In moral philosophy *personal autonomy* refers to personal self-governance: personal rule of the self by adequate understanding while remaining free from controlling interferences by others and from personal limitations that prevent choice. *Autonomy* thus means freedom from external constraint and the presence of critical mental capacities such as understanding, intending, and voluntary decision-making capacity.[8]

To respect an autonomous agent is to recognize with due appreciation that person's capacities and perspective, including his or her right to hold certain views, to make certain choices, and to take certain actions based on personal values and beliefs. The moral demand that we respect the autonomy of persons can be expressed as a principle of respect for autonomy: Autonomy of action should not be subjected to control by others. The principle provides the basis for the right to make decisions, which in turn takes the form of specific autonomy-related rights.

For example, in the debate over whether autonomous, informed patients have the right to refuse self-regarding, life-sustaining medical interventions, the principle of respect for autonomy suggests a morally appropriate response. But the principle covers even simple exchanges in the medical world, such as listening carefully to patients' questions, answering the questions in the detail that respectfulness would demand, and not treating patients in a patronizing fashion.

Respect for autonomy has historically been connected to the idea that persons possess an intrinsic value independent of special circumstances that confer value. As expressed in Kantian ethics, autonomous persons are ends in themselves, determining their own destiny, and are not to be treated merely as means to the ends of others. Thus, the burden of moral justification rests on those who would restrict or prevent a person's exercise of autonomy.

To respect the autonomy of self-determining agents is to recognize them as *entitled* to determine their own destiny, with due regard to their considered evaluations and view of the world. They must be accorded the moral right to have their own opinions and to act upon them (as long as those actions produce no moral violation). Thus, in evaluating the self-regarding actions of others, we are obligated to respect those people as persons with the same right to their judgments as we possess to our own, and they in turn are obligated to treat us in the same way.

Medical and nursing codes have begun in recent years to include rules that are explicitly based on this principle. For example, the first principle of the American Nurses' Association Code reads as follows:

> The fundamental principle of nursing practice is respect for the inherent dignity and worth of every client. Nurses are morally obligated to respect human existence and the individuality of all persons who are the recipients of nursing actions. . . . Truth telling and the process of reaching informed choice underlie the exercise of self-determination, which is basic to respect for persons. Clients should be as fully involved as possible in the planning and implementation of their own health care.[9]

The controversial problems with the noble-sounding principle of respect for autonomy, as with all moral principles, arise when we must interpret its significance for particular contexts and determine precise limits on its application and how to handle situations when it conflicts with such other moral principles as beneficence and justice. Among the best known problems of conflict are found in cases of overriding refusals of treatment by patients, as in Jehovah's Witnesses' refusals of blood transfusions.

Many controversies involve questions about the conditions under which a person's right to autonomous expression demands actions by others and also questions about the restrictions society may rightfully place on choices by patients or subjects when these choices conflict with other values. If an individual's choices endanger the public health, potentially harm another party, or involve a scarce resource for which a patient cannot pay, it may be justifiable to restrict exercises of autonomy. If restriction is in order, the justification will rest on some competing moral principle such as beneficence or justice. This issue of both specifying and balancing the demands made by conflicting moral principles can now be seen to apply to each of these principles.

BENEFICENCE

The welfare of patients is the goal of health care. This welfare objective is medicine's context and justification: Clinical therapies are aimed at the promotion of health by cure or prevention of disease. This value has long been treated as a foundational value—and sometimes as *the* foundational value—in medical and nursing ethics. Among the most quoted principles in the history of codes of medical ethics is the maxim *primum non nocere:* "Above all, do no harm." Although the origins of this abstract principle are obscure and its implications often unclear, it has appeared in many medical writings and codes, and it was present in nursing codes as early as Florence Nightingale's Pledge for Nurses. Many current medical and nursing codes assert that the health professional's "primary commitment" is to protect the patient from harm and to promote the patient's welfare.

Other duties in medicine, nursing, public health, and research are expressed in terms of a *more positive* obligation to come to the assistance of those in need of treatment or in danger of injury. In the International Code of Nursing Ethics, for example, it is said that "[T]he nurse shares with other citizens the responsibility for initiating and supporting action to meet the health and social needs of the public."[10] Various sections of the Principles of Medical Ethics of the American Medical Association express a virtually identical point of view.

The range of duties requiring abstention from harm and positive assistance may be conveniently clustered under the single heading of *beneficence*. This term has a broad set of meanings, including the doing of good and the active promotion of good, kindness, and charity. But in the present context the principle of beneficence has a narrower meaning: It requires us to abstain from injuring others and to help others further their important and legitimate interests, largely by preventing or removing possible harms. Presumably such acts are required when they can be performed with minimal risk to the actors; one is not under an obligation of beneficence in all circumstances of risk.

According to William Frankena, the principle of beneficence can be expressed as including the following four elements: (1) One ought not to inflict evil or harm (a principle of nonmaleficence). (2) One ought to prevent evil or harm. (3) One ought to remove evil or harm. (4) One ought to do or promote good.[11] Frankena suggests that the fourth element may not be an obligation at all (being an act of benevolence that is over and above obligation) and contends that these elements appear in a hierarchical arrangement so that the first takes precedence over the second, the second over the third, and the third over the fourth.

There are philosophical reasons for separating passive nonmaleficence (as expressed in element 1) and active beneficence (as expressed in elements 2–4). Ordinary moral thinking often suggests that certain duties not to injure others are more compelling than duties to benefit them. For example, we do not consider it justifiable to kill a dying patient in order to use the patient's organs to save two others. Similarly, the obligation not to injure a patient by abandonment seems to many stronger than the obligation to prevent injury to a patient who has been abandoned by another (under the assumption that both are moral duties).

Despite the attractiveness of this hierarchical ordering rule, it is not firmly sanctioned by either morality or ethical theory. The obligation expressed in element 1 may not *always* outweigh those expressed in elements 2–4. For example, the harm inflicted in element 1 may be negligible or trivial, whereas the harm to be prevented in element 2 may be substantial: Saving a person's life by a blood transfusion clearly justifies the inflicted harm of venipuncture on the blood donor. One of the motivations for separating nonmaleficence from beneficence is that they themselves conflict when one must *either* avoid harm *or* bring aid. In such cases, one needs a decision procedure for choosing one alternative rather than another. But if the weights of the two principles can vary, as they can, there can be no mechanical decision rule asserting that one obligation must always outweigh the other.

One of the most vexing problems in ethical theory is the extent to which the principle of beneficence generates *general moral duties* that are incumbent on everyone—not because of a professional role but because morality itself makes a general demand of beneficence. Any analysis of beneficence, in the broad sense just delineated, would potentially demand severe sacrifice and extreme generosity in the moral life—for example, giving a kidney for transplantation or donating bone marrow. As a result, some philosophers have argued that this form of beneficent action is virtuous and a moral *ideal,* but not an obligation. We are not *required* by the general canons of morality to promote the good of persons, even if we are in a position to do so and the action is morally *justified.*

Several proposals have been offered in moral philosophy to resolve this problem by showing that beneficence *is* a principle of obligation, but these theoretical ventures are extraneous to our concerns here. The scope or range of acts required by the obligation of beneficence is an undecided issue, and perhaps an undecidable one. Fortunately, we do not need a resolution in the present context. That we are morally obligated on *some* occasions to assist others—at least in professional roles such as nursing, medicine, and research—is hardly a matter of moral controversy. Beneficent acts are demanded by the roles involved in fiduciary relationships between health care professionals and patients, lawyers and clients, researchers and subjects (at least in therapeutic research), bankers and customers, and so on.

We can treat the basic roles and concepts that give substance to the principle of beneficence in medicine as follows: The positive benefits that the physician and nurse are obligated to seek all involve the alleviation of disease and injury, if there is a reasonable hope of cure. The harms to be prevented, removed, or minimized are the pain, suffering, and disability of injury and disease. In addition, the physician and nurse are enjoined from *doing* harm if interventions inflict unnecessary pain and suffering on patients.

Those engaged in both medical practice and research know that risks of harm presented by interventions must be weighed against possible benefits for patients, subjects, and the public. The physician who professes to "do no harm" is not pledging never to cause harm, but rather to strive to create a positive balance of goods over inflicted harms. This is recognized in the Nuremberg Code, which enjoins: "The degree of risk to be taken should never exceed that determined by the humanitarian importance of the problem to be solved by the experiment."

JUSTICE

Every civilized society is a cooperative venture structured by moral, legal, and cultural principles that define the terms of social cooperation. Beneficence and respect for autonomy are principles in this fabric of social order, but *justice* has been the subject of more treatises on the terms of social cooperation than any other principle. A person has been treated justly if treated according to what is fair, due, or owed. For example, if equal political rights are due all citizens, then justice is done when those rights are accorded.

The term *distributive justice* refers to fair, equitable, and appropriate distribution in society determined by justified norms of distribution that structure part of the terms of social cooperation. Usually this term refers to the distribution of primary social goods, such as economic goods and fundamental political rights. But burdens are also within its scope. Paying for forms of national health insurance is a distributed burden; medicare checks and grants to do research are distributed benefits.[12]

Recent literature on distributive justice has tended to focus on considerations of fair economic distribution, especially unjust distributions in the form of inequalities of income between different classes of persons and unfair tax burdens on certain classes. But many problems of distributive justice exist besides issues about income and wealth, including the issues raised in prominent contemporary debates over health care distribution, as discussed in Chapter 2.

There is no single principle of justice. Somewhat like principles under the heading of beneficence, there are several *principles* of justice, each requiring specification in particular contexts. But common to almost all theories of justice is a minimal, beginning principle: Like cases should be treated alike, or, to use the language of equality, equals ought to be treated equally and unequals unequally. This elementary principle is referred to as the *formal principle of justice,* or sometimes as the *formal principle of equality*—formal because it states no particular respects in which people ought to be treated. It merely asserts that whatever respects are under consideration, if persons are equal in those respects, they should be treated alike. Thus, the formal principle of justice does not tell us how to determine equality or proportion in these matters, and it therefore lacks substance as a specific guide to conduct. Equality must here be understood as "equality in the relevant respects." Many controversies about justice arise over what should be considered the relevant characteristics for equal treatment. Principles that specify these relevant characteristics are often said to be *material* because they identify relevant properties for distribution.

The following is a sample list of major candidates for the position of valid material principles of distributive justice (though longer lists have been proposed): (1) To each person an equal share. (2) To each person according to individual need. (3) To each person according to acquisition in a free market. (4) To each person according to individual effort. (5) To each person according to societal contribution. (6) To each person according to merit. There is no obvious barrier to acceptance of more than one of these principles, and some theories of justice accept all six as valid. Most societies use several principles in the belief that different rules are appropriate to different situations.

Because the formal and material principles leave space for differences in the interpretation of how justice applies to particular situations, philosophers have developed diverse *theories* of justice that provide material principles, specify the principles, and defend the choice of principles. These theories attempt to be more specific than the formal principle by elaborating how people are to be compared and what it means to give people their due. Egalitarian theories of justice emphasize equal access to primary goods; libertarian theories emphasize rights to social and economic liberty; and utilitarian theories emphasize a mixed use of such criteria so that public and private utility are maximized.

The *utilitarian theory* follows the main lines of the explanation of utilitarianism given earlier, and thus economic justice is viewed as one among a number of problems concerning how to maximize value. The ideal economic distribution, utilitarians argue, is any arrangement that would have this maximizing effect.

Egalitarianism holds that distributions of burdens and benefits in a society are just to the extent they are equal, and deviations from equality in distribution are unjust. Most egalitarian accounts of justice are guardedly formulated, so that only *some* basic equalities among individuals take priority over their differences. In recent years an egalitarian theory discussed earlier in the section on Kantian theories has enjoyed wide currency: John Rawls's *A Theory of Justice*. This book has as its central contention that we should distribute all economic goods and services equally except in those cases in which an unequal distribution would actually work to everyone's advantage, or at least would benefit the worst off in society.

Sharply opposed to egalitarianism is the *libertarian* theory of justice. What makes libertarian theories libertarian is the priority afforded to distinctive processes, procedures, or mechanisms for ensuring that liberty rights are recognized in economic practice—typically the rules and procedures governing social liberty and economic acquisition and exchange in free market systems. Because free choice is the pivotal goal, libertarians place a premium on the principle of respect for autonomy. In some libertarian systems, this principle is the sole basic moral principle, and there thus are no other principles of justice. We will see in Chapter 2 that many philosophers believe that this approach is fundamentally wrong because economic value is generated through an essentially communal process that our health policies must reflect if justice is to be done.

Libertarian theorists, however, explicitly reject the conclusion that egalitarian patterns of distribution represent a normative ideal. People may be equal in a host of morally significant respects (for example, entitled to equal treatment under the law and equally valued as ends in themselves), but the libertarian contends that it would be a basic violation of *justice* to regard people as deserving of equal economic returns. In particular, people are seen as having a fundamental right to own and dispense with the products of their labor as they choose, even if the exercise of this right leads to large inequalities of wealth in society. Equality and utility principles, from this libertarian perspective, sacrifice basic liberty rights to the larger public interest by coercively extracting financial resources through taxation.

These three theories of justice all capture some of our intuitive convictions about justice, and each exhibits strengths as a theory of justice. Perhaps, then, there are several equally valid, or at least equally defensible, theories of justice and just taxation. This problem will be studied further in Chapter 2.

The Prima Facie Nature of Principles. W. D. Ross, a prominent twentieth-century British philosopher, developed a theory intended to assist us in resolving problems of a conflict between principles. Ross's views are based on an account of what he calls prima facie duties, which he contrasts with actual duties. A *prima facie duty* is a duty that is always to be acted upon unless it conflicts on a particular occasion with an equal or stronger duty. A prima facie duty, then, is always right and binding, all other things being equal;

it is conditional on not being overridden or outweighed by competing moral demands. One's *actual duty,* by contrast, is determined by an examination of the respective weights of competing prima facie duties.

Ross argues that several valid principles, all of which can conflict, express moral duties (that is, obligations). These principles do not, Ross argues, derive from either the principle of utility or Kant's categorical imperative. For example, our promises create duties of fidelity, wrongful actions create duties of reparation, and the generous gifts of our friends create duties of gratitude. Ross defends several additional duties, such as duties of self-improvement, nonmaleficence, beneficence, and justice. Unlike Kant's system and the utilitarian system, Ross's list of duties is not based on any overarching principle. He defends it simply as a reflection of our ordinary moral conventions and beliefs.

The idea that moral principles are absolute values that cannot be overridden has had a long, but troubled, history. It seems beyond serious dispute that all moral norms can be justifiably overridden in some circumstances. For example, we might withhold the truth in order to prevent someone from killing another person; and we might disclose confidential information about one person in order to protect the rights of another person. Principles, duties, and rights are not absolute or unconditional merely because they are universal. Both utilitarians and Kantians have defended their basic rule (the principle of utility and the categorical imperative) as absolute, but this claim to absoluteness is dubious. For Ross's reasons, among others, many moral philosophers have with increasing frequency come to regard principles, duties, and rights not as unbending standards but rather as strong prima facie moral demands that may be validly overridden in circumstances of competition with other moral claims.

Although no philosopher or professional code has successfully presented a system of moral rules that is free of conflicts and exceptions, this fact is no cause for either scepticism or alarm. Prima facie duties reflect the complexity of the moral life, in which a hierarchy of rules and principles is impossible. The problem of how to weight different moral principles remains unresolved, as does the best set of moral principles to form the framework of bioethics. Nonetheless, the general categories of prima facie principles discussed here have proven serviceable as a basic starting point and source for reflection on cases and problems. The main difficulty with these principles is that in most difficult contexts they must be specified.

The Specification of Principles. Practical moral problems often cannot, as we noticed earlier, be resolved by appeal to highly general principles. Practical problems typically require that we make our general norms suitably specific.[13] Universal norms are mere starting points that almost always must be transformed into a more specific and relevant form in order to create policies, bring controversial cases to closure, resolve conflicts, and the like. The implementation of the principles must take account of feasibility, efficiency, cultural pluralism, political procedures, uncertainty about risk, noncompliance by patients, moral dilemmas, and the like. In short, the principles must be specified for a context.

Specification is not a process of producing general norms; it assumes that they are already available. It is the process of making these norms concrete so that they can meaningfully guide conduct. This process requires reducing the indeterminateness of the general norms to give them increased action-guiding capacity while retaining the moral commitments in the original norm. Filling out the commitments of the norms with which one starts is accomplished by narrowing the scope of the norms, not merely by explaining what the general norms mean. For example, without further specification the principle *respect the autonomy of competent persons* is too spare to handle complicated problems of what to say or ask for in clinical medicine and research involving human subjects. A mere definition of *respect for autonomy* (as, say, "allowing competent persons to exercise their liberty rights") might clarify one's meaning, but would not narrow the general norm or render it more specific. Specification is a different kind of spelling out than analysis of meaning. It adds content. For example, one possible specification of *respect the autonomy of competent persons* is "respect the autonomy of competent patients after they become incompetent by following their advance directives."

After this specification, when one subsequently encounters difficult cases of vague advance directives and must decide whether to observe them, one could further specify as follows: "Respect the autonomy of competent patients (after they become incompetent) by following their advance directives if and only if the directives are clear and relevant." As other problems and conflicts of norms emerge, the process of specification must continue. That is, already specified rules, guidelines, policies, and codes must be further specified to handle new or more complex circumstances. Such progressive specification is the way we do and should handle problems that arise in devising internal standards of medical morality.

A specification, by definition, must retain the initial norm while adding content to it. In the case of progressive specification, there must remain a transparent connection to the initial norm that gives moral authority to the string of norms that develop over time. Of course, there is always the possibility that more than one line of specification will issue from one or more initial norms. That is, different persons may offer different specifications. In this process of specification, overconfidence in one's specifications can lead to a dogmatic certainty of the sort found in the authoritative pronouncements of professional medical associations. Moral disagreement in the course of formulating specifications is inevitable and may not be eliminated by even the most conscientious specifications. In any given problematic or dilemmatic case, several competing specifications are virtually certain to be offered by reasonable parties. Alternative specifications are no more a matter of regret than are other contexts in which reflective persons offer alternative solutions to practical problems.

LAW AND POLICY

Moral principles are often already embedded in public morality, public policies, and institutional practices, but if these values are already in place, how can moral reflection on philosophical theory assist us in the complicated task of forming and criticizing institutional policies, public policies, and laws?

ETHICS AND PUBLIC AFFAIRS

Institutional and public policies are almost always motivated by and incorporate moral considerations. Policies such as those that fund health care for the indigent and those that protect subjects of biomedical research are examples. Moral analysis is part of good policy formation, not merely a method for evaluating already formed policy. A *policy,* in the relevant sense, is comprised of a set of normative, enforceable guidelines that govern a particular area of conduct and that have been accepted by an official body, such as an institutional board of trustees, an agency of government, or a legislature. The policies of corporations, hospitals, trade groups, and professional societies are private rather than public, but the discussion that follows is directed at all forms of policy.

Many articles in this volume are concerned with the use of ethical theory for the formulation of public affairs. Joel Feinberg has made a suggestive comment about one way in which the problems raised in these essays might be viewed from an ideal vantage point:

> It is convenient to think of these problems as questions for some hypothetical and abstract political body. An answer to the question of when liberty should be limited or how wealth ideally should be distributed, for example, could be used to guide not only moralists, but also legislators and judges toward reasonable decisions in particular cases where interests, rules, or the liberties of different parties appear to conflict. . . . We must think of an ideal legislator as somewhat abstracted from the full legislative context, in that he is free to appeal directly to the public interest unencumbered by the need to please voters, to make "deals" with colleagues, or any other merely "political" considerations. . . . The principles of the ideal legislator. . . . are still of the first practical importance, since they provide a target for our aspirations and a standard for judging our successes and failures.[14]

However, policy formation and criticism usually involve complex interactions between moral values and cultural and political values. A policy will be shaped by empirical data and information in relevant fields such as medicine, economics, law, and the like. By taking into consideration factors such as efficiency and clientele acceptance, we interpret principles so that they provide a practical strategy for real-world problems that incorporate the demands of political procedures, legal constraints, uncertainty about risk, and the like.[15] For example, in this book we will consider policies pertaining to physician-assisted suicide, ethics committees in hospitals, public allocations for health care, regulation of risk in the workplace, protection of animal and human subjects of research, legislative definitions of death, liability for failures of disclosure and confidentiality, policies to control developments in genetics, the control of epidemics, and a host of other moral problems of institutional and public policy.

A specific example of ethics at work in the formulation of policy is found in the work of the previously mentioned National Commission for the Protection of Human Subjects of Biomedical and Behavioral Research, which was established by a federal law. Its mandate was to develop ethical guidelines for the conduct of research involving human subjects and to make recommendations to the Department of Health and Human Services (DHHS). To discharge its duties, the commission studied the nature and extent of various forms of research, its purposes, the ethical issues surrounding the research, present federal regulations, and the views of representatives of professional societies and federal agencies. The commission engaged in extensive deliberations on these subjects in public, a process in which moral reasoning played as central a role as the information and methods supplied from other fields.

Subsequent government regulations regarding research issued by the relevant agency (DHHS) were developed on the basis of work provided by the commission. These public laws show the imprint of the commission in virtually every clause. The regulations cannot be regarded as exclusively ethical in orientation, but much distinctive ethical material is found in the commission documents, and ethical analysis provided the framework for its deliberations and recommendations. The commission also issued one exclusively philosophical volume, which sets forth the moral framework that underlies the various policy recommendations it made. It is among the best examples of the use of moral frameworks for actual (not merely theoretical or programmatic) policy development and of a philosophical publication issued through a government-sponsored body.

Several U.S. federal branches, agencies, and courts regularly use ethical premises in the development of their health policies, rules, or decisions. These include the Centers for Disease Control (CDC), the National Institutes of Health (NIH), the Agency for Health Care Policy and Research (AHCPR), and the U.S. Supreme Court. Ethical analysis also often plays a prominent role in policy formation in bioethics. Examples include the widely examined work of the Oregon legislature on rationing in health care, the New York

Task Force on Life and the Law, the New Jersey Bioethics Commission, and so on. Their reports and legislative actions raise vital questions explored at various points in this book about the proper relation between government and professional groups in formulating standards of practice.

MORALITY AND LAW

The "morality" of many actions that have a public impact is commonly gauged by whether the law prohibits that form of conduct. Law is the public's agent for translating morality into explicit social guidelines and practices and for determining punishments for offenses. Both case law (judge-made law expressed in court decisions) and statutory law (federal and state statutes and their accompanying administrative regulations) set standards for science, medicine, and health care, and these sources have deeply influenced bioethics.

In these forms law has placed many issues before the public. Case law, in particular, has established influential precedents that provide material for reflection on both legal and moral questions. Prominent examples include judicial decisions about informed consent and terminating life-sustaining treatment. The line of court decisions since the Karen Ann Quinlan case in the mid-1970s, for example, constitutes an important body of material for moral reflection. Most of the chapters in this book contain selections from case law, and selections in the chapters frequently mention actual or proposed statutory law.

Moral evaluation is, nonetheless, very different from *legal* evaluation. Issues of legal liability, costs to the system, practicability within the litigation process, and questions of compensation demand that legal requirements be different from moral requirements. The law is not the repository of our moral standards and values, even when the law is directly concerned with moral problems. A law-abiding person is not necessarily morally sensitive or virtuous, and from the fact that an act is legally acceptable it does not follow that this act is morally acceptable.

The judgment that an act is morally acceptable also does not imply that the law should permit it. For example, the moral position that various forms of euthanasia are morally justified is consistent with the thesis that the government should legally prohibit these acts, on grounds that it would not be possible to control potential abuses.

Bioethics in the United States is currently involved in a complex and mutually stimulating relationship with law. The law often appeals to moral duties and rights, places sanctions on violators, and in general strengthens the social importance of moral beliefs. Morality and law share concerns over matters of basic social importance and often acknowledge the same principles, obligations, and criteria of evidence. Nevertheless, the law rightly backs away from attempting to legislate against everything that is morally wrong.

LEGAL AND MORAL RIGHTS

Much of the modern ethical discussion that we encounter throughout this volume turns on ideas about rights, and many public policy issues concern rights or attempts to secure rights. Our political tradition itself has developed from a conception of human rights. However, until the seventeenth and eighteenth centuries problems of social and political philosophy were rarely discussed in terms of rights. New political views were introduced at this point in history, including the notion of universal natural (or human) rights. Rights quickly came to be understood as powerful assertions of claims that demand respect and status.

Substantial differences exist between *moral rights* and *legal rights,* because legal systems do not formally require reference to moral systems for their understanding or grounding, nor do moral systems formally require reference to legal systems. One may have a legal right to do something patently immoral or have a moral right without any corresponding legal guarantee. Legal rights are derived from political constitutions, legislative enactments, case law, and the executive orders of the highest state official. Moral rights, by contrast, exist independently of, and form a basis for, criticizing or justifying legal rights.

Philosophers have often drawn a distinction between positive and negative rights. A right to well-being—generally the right to receive goods and services—is a *positive right,* and a right to liberty—generally a right not to be interfered with—is a *negative right*. The right to liberty is a negative right because no one has to do anything to honor it. Presumably all that must be done to honor negative rights is to leave people alone. The same is not true of positive rights. To honor those rights, someone has to provide something. For example, if a person has a human right to well-being and is starving, then someone has an obligation to provide that person with food. This important distinction between positive and negative rights is analyzed in Chapter 2 under the subject of the right to health care.

Because general negative rights are rights of noninterference, their direct connection to individual self-determination is apparent. Because general positive rights require that all members of the community yield some of their resources to advance the welfare of others by providing social goods and services, there is a natural connection in theories that emphasize positive rights to a sense of *the commons* that limits the scope of individualism. The broader the scope of positive rights in a theory, the more likely that theory is to emphasize a scheme of social justice that confers positive rights to redistributions of resources.

Accordingly, a moral system composed of a powerful set of general negative obligations and rights is antithetical to a moral system composed of a powerful set of general positive obligations and rights, just as a strong individualism is opposed to a strong communitarianism. Many of the conflicts that we encounter throughout this book spring from these basic differences over the existence and scope of negative and positive rights and obligations, especially regarding the number, types, and weight of positive rights and obligations.

LAW, AUTHORITY, AND AUTONOMY

As important as autonomy rights are, no autonomy right is strong enough to entail a right to unrestricted exercises of autonomy. Acceptable liberty must be distinguished from unacceptable, but how are we to do so?

Liberty-Limiting Principles. Various principles have been advanced in the attempt to establish valid grounds for the limitation of autonomy. The following four "liberty-limiting principles" have all been defended.

1. *The Harm Principle:* A person's liberty is justifiably restricted to prevent harm to others caused by that person.
2. *The Principle of Paternalism:* A person's liberty is justifiably restricted to prevent harm to self caused by that person.
3. *The Principle of Legal Moralism:* A person's liberty is justifiably restricted to prevent that person's immoral behavior.
4. *The Offense Principle:* A person's liberty is justifiably restricted to prevent offense to others caused by that person.

Each of these four principles represents an attempt to balance liberty and other values. The harm principle is universally accepted as a valid liberty-limiting principle, but the other three principles are highly controversial. Only one of these controversial principles is pertinent to the controversies that arise in this volume: paternalism. Here the central problem is whether this form of justification for a restriction of liberty may ever validly be invoked, and, if so, how the principle is to be formulated.

Paternalism. The word *paternalism* refers to treating individuals in the way that a parent treats his or her child. Paternalism is the intentional limitation of the autonomy of one person by another, where the person who limits autonomy appeals exclusively to grounds of benefit for the person whose autonomy is limited. The essence of paternalism is an overriding of a person's autonomy on grounds of providing that person with a benefit—in medicine, a medical benefit.

Examples in medicine include involuntary commitment to institutions for treatment, intervention to stop "rational" suicides, resuscitating patients who have asked not to be resuscitated, withholding medical information that patients have requested, compulsory care, denial of an innovative therapy to patients who wish to try it, and some government efforts to promote health. Other health-related examples include laws requiring motorcyclists to wear helmets and motorists to wear seat belts and the regulations of governmental agencies such as the Food and Drug Administration that prevent people from purchasing possibly harmful or inefficacious drugs and chemicals. In all cases the motivation is the beneficent promotion of individuals health and welfare.

Paternalism has been under attack in recent years, especially by defenders of the autonomy rights of patients. The latter hold that physicians and government officials intervene too often and assume too much paternalistic control over patients' choices. Philosophers and lawyers have generally supported the view that the autonomy of patients is the decisive factor in the patient-physician relationship and that interventions can be valid only when patients are in some measure unable to make voluntary choices or to perform autonomous actions. The point is that patients can be so ill that their judgments or voluntary abilities are significantly affected or are incapable of grasping important information about their case, thus being in no position to reach carefully reasoned decisions about their medical treatment or their purchase of drugs. Beyond this form of intervention, many have argued, paternalism is not warranted.

However, paternalism also has defenders, even under some conditions in which autonomous choice is overridden. Any careful proponent of a principle of paternalism will specify precisely which goods and needs deserve paternalistic protection and the conditions under which intervention is warranted. Some writers have argued that one is justified in interfering with a person's autonomy only if the interference protects the person against his or her own actions where those actions are extremely and unreasonably risky (for example, refusing a life-saving therapy in nonterminal situations) or are potentially dangerous and irreversible in effect (as some drugs are). According to this position, paternalism is justified if and only if the harms prevented from occurring to the person are greater than the harms or indignities (if any) caused by interference with his or her liberty and if it can be universally justified, under relevantly similar circumstances, always to treat persons in this way.

This moderate formulation of paternalism still leaves many critics resolutely opposed to all possible uses of this principle. Their arguments against paternalism turn on some defense of the importance of the principle of respect for autonomy. We will many times encounter such appeals in this volume, especially as applied to rightful state intervention in order to benefit patients or subjects without their authorization.

T.L.B.

NOTES

1. *Tarasoff v. Regents of the University of California,* California Supreme Court (17 California Reports, 3d Series, 425. Decided July 1, 1976). Reprinted in Chapter 3 of this volume.

2. These principles and their analysis by the National Commission for the Protection of Human Subjects of Biomedical and Behavioral Research have been published as *The Belmont Report: Ethical Principles and Guidelines for the Protection of Human Subjects of Research* (Washington, DC: U.S. Government Printing Office, DHEW Publication, 1978).

3. Cf. Walter Sinnott-Armstrong, *Moral Dilemmas,* 216–27; and D. D. Raphael, *Moral Philosophy* (Oxford: Oxford University Press, 1981), 64–65.

4. Immanuel Kant, *Foundations of the Metaphysics of Morals,* trans. Lewis White Beck (Indianapolis, IN: Bobbs-Merrill, 1959), 47.

5. Albert R. Jonsen, "Casuistry as Methodology in Clinical Ethics," *Theoretical Medicine* 12 (December 1991); Jonsen and S. Toulmin, *Abuse of Casuistry* (Berkeley: University of California Press, 1988); Jonsen, "Casuistry: An Alternative or Complement to Principles?" *Kennedy Institute of Ethics Journal* 5 (1995), 237–51.

6. John D. Arras, "Principles and Particularity: The Role of Cases in Bioethics," *Indiana Law Journal* 69 (Fall 1994): 983–1014 (with two replies); and "Getting Down to Cases: The Revival of Casuistry in Bioethics," *Journal of Medicine and Philosophy* 16 (1991), 29–51.

7. Jonsen and Toulmin, *Abuse of Casuistry,* 16–19, 66–67; Jonsen, "Casuistry and Clinical Ethics," 67, 71.

8. For autonomy-based theory, see Robert Nozick, *Anarchy, State, and Utopia* (New York: Basic Books, 1974); H. Tristram Engelhardt, Jr., *The Foundations of Bioethics,* 2nd ed. (New York: Oxford University Press, 1996); Joel Feinberg, *The Moral Limits of the Criminal Law* (New York: Oxford University Press, 1984–87); Jay Katz, *The Silent World of Doctor and Patient* (New York: The Free Press: 1984).

9. American Nurses' Association, *Code for Nurses with Interpretive Statements* (Kansas City, MO: ANA, 1985), 2–3.

10. 1953 and 1973 International Codes of Nursing Ethics of the International Council of Nurses.

11. William Frankena, *Ethics,* 2nd ed. (Englewood Cliffs, NJ: Prentice-Hall, 1973), 47.

12. For accounts of justice that have influenced contemporary bioethics, see John Rawls, *A Theory of Justice* (Cambridge: Harvard University Press, 1971); Norman Daniels, *Just Health Care* (New York: Cambridge University Press, 1985); Allen Buchanan, "Health-Care Delivery and Resource Allocation," in *Medical Ethics,* ed. Robert Veatch, 2nd ed. (Boston: Jones and Bartlett Publishers, 1997); Daniel Callahan, *Setting Limits: Medical Goals in an Aging Society* (New York: Simon & Schuster, 1987).

13. Henry S. Richardson, "Specifying Norms as a Way to Resolve Concrete Ethical Problems," *Philosophy and Public Affairs* 19 (Fall 1990), 279–310.

14. Joel Feinberg, *Social Philosophy* (Englewood Cliffs, NJ: Prentice-Hall, 1973), 2–3.

15. Dennis Thompson, "Philosophy and Policy," *Philosophy and Public Affairs* 14 (Spring 1985), 205–18.

SUGGESTED READINGS FOR CHAPTER 1

MORALITY AND MORAL PHILOSOPHY

Beauchamp, Tom L. *Philosophical Ethics.* 3rd ed. New York: McGraw-Hill, 2001.

Copp, David. *Morality, Normativity, and Society.* New York: Oxford University Press, 1995.

Holmes, Robert L. *Basic Moral Philosophy.* Belmont, CA: Wadsworth, 1993.

Mason, Homer E., ed. *Moral Dilemmas and Moral Theory.* New York: Oxford University Press, 1996.

Regan, Tom, ed. *Matters of Life and Death.* 3rd ed. New York: Random House, 1992.

Singer, Peter, ed. *A Companion to Ethics.* Cambridge: Blackwell, 1991.

———. *Practical Ethics.* 2nd ed. New York: Cambridge University Press, 1993.

Sinnot-Armstrong, Walter. *Moral Dilemmas.* Oxford: Basil Blackwell, 1988.

Sumner, L. W., and Boyle, J. *Philosophical Perspectives on Bioethics.* Toronto: University of Toronto Press, 1996.

RELATIVISM AND DISAGREEMENT

Brandt, Richard B. "Ethical Relativism." In Paul Edwards, ed. *Encyclopedia of Philosophy.* Vol. 3. New York: Macmillan, 1967, 75–78.

Buchanan, Allen. "Judging the Past." *Hastings Center Report* 26 (May-June 1996), 25–30.

Gert, Bernard, Culver, Charles, and Clouser, K. Danner. *Bioethics: A Return to Fundamentals.* New York: Oxford University Press, 1997.

Harman, Gilbert, and Thomson, Judith Jarvis. *Moral Relativism and Moral Objectivity.* Cambridge, MA: Blackwell, 1996.

Krausz, Michael, ed. *Relativism: Interpretation and Confrontation.* Notre Dame, IN: University of Notre Dame Press, 1989.

Taylor, Charles, and Gutmann, Amy, eds. *Multiculturalism: Examining the Politics of Recognition.* Princeton, NJ: Princeton University Press, 1994.

JUSTIFICATION

Brandt, R. B. *Morality, Utilitarianism, and Rights.* Cambridge: Cambridge University Press, 1992.

Copp, David. "Explanation and Justification in Ethics." *Ethics* 100 (1990), 237–58.

Dancy, Jonathan. *Moral Reasons.* Cambridge: Blackwell, 1993.

Daniels, N. *Justice and Justification.* Cambridge: Cambridge University Press, 1996.

———. "Wide Reflective Equilibrium in Practice." In L. W. Sumner and J. Boyle, eds. *Philosophical Perspectives on Bioethics.* Toronto: University of Toronto Press, 1996, 96–114.

DePaul, Michael R. *Balance and Refinement: Beyond Coherence Models of Moral Inquiry.* London: Routledge, 1993.

Gert, Bernard. *Morality: A New Justification of the Moral Rules.* 2nd ed. New York: Oxford University Press, 1988.

The Monist 71 (July 1988). Special issue on "Justification."

Sinnot-Armstrong, Walter, and Timmons, Mark, eds. *Moral Knowledge? New Readings in Moral Epistemology.* Oxford: Oxford University Press, 1996.

UTILITARIANISM

Bailey, James Wood. *Utilitarianism, Institutions, and Justice.* New York: Oxford University Press, 1997.

Bentham, Jeremy. *Introduction to the Principles of Morals and Legislation* (1789). In W. Harrison, ed. *A Fragment on Government.* Oxford: Hafner Press, 1948.

Crisp, Roger. *Routledge Philosophy Guidebook to Mill on Utilitarianism.* New York: Routledge, 1997.

Frey, R. G., ed. *Utility and Rights.* Minneapolis, MN: University of Minnesota Press, 1984.

Gorovitz, Samuel, ed. *Mill: Utilitarianism, with Critical Essays.* New York: Bobbs-Merrill, 1971.

Griffin, James. *Well-Being: Its Meaning, Measurement and Moral Importance.* Oxford: Clarendon Press, 1986.

Kagan, Shelly. *The Limits of Morality.* Oxford: Clarendon Press, 1989.

Lyons, David, ed. *Mill's Utilitarianism: Critical Essays.* Lanham, MD: Rowman & Littlefield, 1997.

Mill, John Stuart. *Collected Works of John Stuart Mill.* Toronto: University of Toronto Press, 1969– .

Scarre, Geoffrey. *Utilitarianism.* New York: Routledge, 1996.

Scheffler, Samuel, ed. *Consequentialism and Its Critics.* Oxford: Oxford University Press, 1988.

Skorupski, John, ed. *The Cambridge Companion to Mill.* New York: Cambridge University Press, 1998.

KANTIAN AND DEONTOLOGICAL THEORIES

Baron, Marcia. *Kantian Ethics Almost without Apology.* Ithaca, NY: Cornell University Press, 1995.

Cummiskey, David. *Kantian Consequentialism.* New York: Oxford University Press, 1996.

Donagan, Alan. *The Theory of Morality.* Chicago: University of Chicago Press, 1977.

Gowans, Christopher W. "Intimacy, Freedom, and Unique Value: A 'Kantian' Account of the Irreplaceable and Incomparable Value of Persons." *American Philosophical Quarterly* 33 (January 1996), 75–89.

Guyer, Paul, ed. *The Cambridge Companion to Kant.* Cambridge: Cambridge University Press, 1992.

Herman Barbara. *The Practice of Moral Judgment.* Cambridge, MA: Harvard University Press, 1993.

Hill, Thomas E., Jr. *Dignity and Practical Reason in Kant's Moral Theory.* Ithaca, NY: Cornell University Press, 1992.

Kant, Immanuel. *Ethical Philosophy.* J. Ellington, ed. Indianapolis: Hackett, 1983.

Korsgaard, Christine M. *Creating the Kingdom of Ends.* Cambridge: Cambridge University Press, 1996.

Louden, Robert. *Kant's Impure Ethics: From Rational Beings to Human Beings.* New York: Oxford University Press, 1999.

Mulholland, Leslie A. *Kant's System of Rights.* New York: Columbia University Press, 1990.

Rawls, John. "Themes in Kant's Moral Philosophy." In Eckart Förster, ed. *Kant's Transcendental Deductions.* Stanford: Stanford University Press, 1989.

ETHICS OF CARE

Blustein, Jeffrey. *Care and Commitment: Taking the Personal Point of View.* New York: Oxford University Press, 1991.

Carse, Alisa L. "Impartial Principle and Moral Context: Securing a Place for the Particular in Ethical Theory." *Journal of Medicine and Philosophy* 23 (1998), 153–69.

———, and Nelson Hilde Lindemann. "Rehabilitating Care." *Kennedy Institute of Ethics Journal* 6 (1996), 19–35.

Carse, Alisa. "The Voice of Care: Implications for Bioethical Education." *Journal of Medicine and Philosophy* 16 (1991), 5–28.

Held, Virginia, ed., *Justice and Care: Essential Readings in Feminist Ethics.* Boulder, CO: Westview Press, 1995.

Holmes, Helen Bequaert, and Purdy, Laura M., eds. *Feminist Perspectives in Medical Ethics.* Bloomington, IN: Indiana University Press, 1992.

Kuhse, Helga. *Caring: Nurses, Women and Ethics.* Oxford: Blackwell, 1997.

Larrabee, Mary Jeanne, ed. *An Ethic of Care: Feminist and Interdisciplinary Perspectives.* New York: Routledge, 1993.

Little, Margaret Olivia. "Care From Theory to Orientation and Back." *Journal of Medicine and Philosophy* 23 (1998), 190–209.

Manning, Rita C. "A Care Approach." In Helga Kuhse and Peter Singer, eds. *A Companion to Bioethics.* Malden, MA: Blackwell, 1998, 98–105.

Sherwin, Susan. *No Longer Patient: Feminist Ethics and Health Care.* Philadelphia: Temple University Press, 1992.

Gilligan, Carol. *In a Different Voice.* Cambridge, MA: Harvard University Press, 1982.

Noddings, Nel. *Caring: A Feminine Approach to Ethics and Moral Education.* Berkeley: University of California Press, 1984.

Wolf, Susan, ed. *Feminism & Bioethics.* New York: Oxford, 1996.

VIRTUE ETHICS

Aristotle, *Nicomachean Ethics.* Terence Irwin, trans. Indianapolis, IN: Hackett, 1985.

Baron, Marcia W., Pettit, Philip, and Slote, Michael. *Three Methods of Ethics: A Debate.* Cambridge: Blackwell, 1997.

Crisp, Roger, and Slote, Michael, eds. *Virtue Ethics.* Oxford: Oxford University Press, 1997.

Hursthouse, Rosalind. *On Virtue Ethics.* New York: Oxford University Press, 1999.

Hursthouse, Rosalind, Lawrence, Gavin, and Quinn, Warren, eds. *Virtues and Reasons: Philippa Foot and Moral Theory.* Oxford: Clarendon Press, 1995.

French, Peter A., Uehling, Theodore E., Jr., and Wettstein, Howard K. *Midwest Studies in Philosophy. Vol. 13, Ethical Theory: Character and Virtue.* Notre Dame, IN: University of Notre Dame Press, 1988.

Sherman, Nancy. *The Fabric of Character: Aristotle's Theory of Virtue.* Oxford: Clarendon Press, 1989.

MacIntyre, Alasdair. *After Virtue.* 2nd ed. Notre Dame, IN: University of Notre Dame Press, 1984.

Nussbaum, Martha. *Love's Knowledge.* Oxford: Oxford University Press, 1990.

CASUISTRY

Arras, John. "Getting Down to Cases: The Revival of Casuistry in Bioethics." *Journal of Medicine and Philosophy* 16 (1991), 29–51.

Arras, John. "Principles and Particularity: The Role of Cases in Bioethics." *Indiana Law Journal* 69 (1994), 983–1014.

Jonsen, Albert. "Casuistry as Methodology in Clinical Ethics." *Theoretical Medicine* 12 (1991), 299–302.

———. "Morally Appreciated Circumstances: A Theoretical Problem for Casuistry." In L. W. Sumner and J. Boyle, eds. *Philosophical Perspectives on Bioethics.* Toronto: University of Toronto Press, 1996, 37–49.

Jonsen, Albert, and Toulmin, Stephen. *The Abuse of Casuistry: A History of Moral Reasoning.* Berkeley: University of California Press, 1988.

Toulmin, Stephen. "The Tyranny of Principles." *Hastings Center Report* 11 (December 1981), 31–39.

MORAL PRINCIPLES

Beauchamp, Tom L., and Childress, James F. *Principles of Biomedical Ethics.* 5th ed. New York: Oxford University Press, 2001, chaps. 3–6.

Clouser, K. Danner, and Gert, Bernard. "A Critique of Principlism." *The Journal of Medicine and Philosophy* 15 (1990), 219–36.

———. "Morality vs. Principlism." In R. Gillon and A. Lloyd, eds., *Principles of Health Care Ethics.* London: John Wiley & Sons, 1994, 251–66.

Clouser, K. Danner. "Common Morality as an Alternative to Principlism." *Journal of the Kennedy Institute of Ethics* 5 (1995), 219–36.

Davis, R. B. "The Principlism Debate: A Critical Overview." *Journal of Medicine and Philosophy* 20 (1995), 85–105.

DeGrazia, David. "Moving Forward in Bioethical Theory: Theories, Cases, and Specified Principlism." *Journal of Medicine and Philosophy* 17 (1992), 511–39.

Engelhardt, H. Tristram, Jr. *The Foundations of Bioethics.* 2nd ed. New York: Oxford University Press, 1996.

Kennedy Institute of Ethics Journal 5 (1995). Special issue on "Principlism."

Gillon, Raanan, and Lloyd, Ann, eds. *Principles of Health Care Ethics.* London: John Wiley & Sons, 1994.

Levi, B. H. "Four Approaches to Doing Ethics." *Journal of Medicine and Philosophy* 21 (1996), 7–39.

Pellegrino, Edmund, and Thomasma, David. *For the Patient's Good: The Restoration of Beneficence in Health Care.* New York: Oxford University Press, 1988.

Richardson, Henry. "Specifying Norms as a Way to Resolve Concrete Ethical Problems." *Philosophy & Public Affairs* 19 (1990), 279–310.

Veatch, Robert M. *A. Theory of Medical Ethics.* New York: Basic Books, 1981.

ETHICS AND PUBLIC POLICY

Areen, Judith, et al. *Law, Science, and Medicine.* Mineola, NY: Foundation Press, 1984. Supplementary volume, 1987.

Brock, Dan W. "Truth or Consequences: The Role of Philosophers in Policy-Making." *Ethics* 97 (1987), 786–91.

Thompson, Dennis. "Philosophy and Policy." *Philosophy & Public Affairs* 14 (1985), 205–18.

Weisbard, Alan J. "The Role of Philosophers in the Public Policy Process." *Ethics* 97 (1987), 776–85.

MORALITY AND LAW

Dworkin, Ronald. *Taking Rights Seriously.* Cambridge, MA: Harvard University Press, 1977.

Feinberg, Joel. *The Moral Limits of the Criminal Law.* 4 vols. New York: Oxford University Press, 1984–1987.

George, Robert, ed. *Natural Law, Liberalism, and Morality.* New York: Oxford University Press, 1996.

Lyons, David. *Ethics and the Rule of Law.* Cambridge: Cambridge University Press, 1984.

Meyer, Michael J., and Parent, W. A., eds. *The Constitution of Rights.* Ithaca, NY: Cornell University Press, 1992.

Rawls, John. *Political Liberalism.* New York: Columbia University Press, 1996.

Simmonds, N. E. "Law and Morality." In Edward Craig, ed., *Routledge Encyclopedia of Philosophy.* Vol. 5. London: Routledge, 1998, 438–42.

Winston, Morton E., ed. *The Philosophy of Human Rights.* Belmont, CA: Wadsworth, 1989.

LIBERTY, AUTHORITY, AND PATERNALISM

Arneson, Richard. "Paternalism." In Edward Craig, ed. *Routledge Encyclopedia of Philosophy.* Vol. 7. London: Routledge, 1998, 250–52.

Beauchamp, Tom L., and McCullough, Laurence B. *Medical Ethics.* Englewood Cliffs, NJ: Prentice-Hall, 1984, chap. 4.

Epstein, Richard. *Principles for a Free Society: Reconciling Individual Liberty with the Common Good.* Reading, MA: Perseus Books, 1998.

Feinberg, Joel. *The Moral Limits of the Criminal Law.* New York: Oxford University Press, 1984–87. Esp. Vol. 3, *Harm to Self.*

———. "Paternalism." In Donald M. Borchert, ed. *Encyclopedia of Philosophy.* Supplement. New York: Macmillan, 1996, 390–92.

Kleinig, John. *Paternalism.* Totowa, NJ: Rowman and Allenheld, 1983.

Kultgen, John H. *Autonomy and Intervention: Parentalism in the Caring Life.* Oxford, England, Oxford University Press, 1995.

Sartorius, Rolf, ed. *Paternalism.* Minneapolis: University of Minnesota Press, 1983.

VanDeVeer, Donald. *Paternalistic Intervention: The Moral Bounds on Benevolence.* Princeton, NJ: Princeton University Press, 1986.

BIBLIOGRAPHIES AND ENCYCLOPEDIAS WITH BIBLIOGRAPHIES

Encyclopedia of Bioethics, ed. Warren Reich. 2nd ed. New York: Macmillan, 1995.

Encyclopedia of Ethics, ed. Lawrence Becker and Charlotte Becker. New York: Garland, 1992.

Routledge Encyclopedia of Philosophy. 10 vols., ed. Edward Craig. London: Routledge, 1998.

Lineback, Richard H., ed. *Philosopher's Index.* Vols. 1– . Bowling Green, OH: Philosophy Documentation Center, Bowling Green State University. Issued quarterly.

Several leading journals are devoted to philosophical ethics and bioethics. See *Philosophy and Public Affairs, Bioethics, Public Affairs Quarterly, The Journal of Medicine and Philosophy, The Kennedy Institute of Ethics Journal, Hastings Center Report, American Journal of Bioethics,* and *Ethics.*

Part II
JUSTICE AND AUTONOMY IN HEALTH CARE

2. Justice in Access to Health Care

INTRODUCTION

Health care costs have continued to rise dramatically for several decades. These costs have been studied by government agencies worldwide. Many have concluded that their payment policies fuel unacceptable increases in expenditures for health care services. The basic *economic problem* is how to control costs and efficiently distribute resources in order to satisfy human needs and desires. The basic *ethical problem* is how to structure a health care system that fairly distributes resources and provides equitable access to health care. These economic and ethical problems are intertwined in the formation of health policy.

The proper role of government lies at the center of these health policy discussions. It is widely agreed that government is constituted to protect citizens against risks from the environment, risks from external invasion, risks from crime, risks from fire, risks from highway accidents, and the like. But the idea that certain kinds of health care should be similarly provided as a government service is more controversial, and even if it is agreed in a country that the government has an obligation to provide health care, there seem to be severe limits on what government can and should do.

THE ALLOCATION OF HEALTH CARE RESOURCES

Public health policies allocate resources, as do private sector policies such as health insurance provided as an employee benefit. To *allocate* is to distribute goods, services, or financial resources according to a system or principle. The distribution scheme need not be established or controlled by governments. For example, charitable organizations often distribute health care and the free market distributes health care goods and services through exchanges made by free agents acting in their own interests.

When a decision is social or governmental, in contrast to individual, decisions fall into two broad types: macroallocation and microallocation. In *macroallocation,* social decisions are made about how much will be expended for health care resources as well as how it will be distributed. These decisions are taken by legislatures, health organizations, private foundations, and health insurance companies. At the *microallocation* level, decisions are made by specific institutions or health professionals about who shall obtain available resources—for example, which of several potential patients will be admitted to the last available bed in the intensive care unit. This chapter emphasizes issues of fairness in systems of macroallocation.

Two primary considerations are involved in macroallocation decisions about health care and research: (1) What percentage of the total available resources should be allotted to biomedicine, an area that must compete for funding with other social projects such as defense, education, and transportation? (2) How much budgeted to biomedicine should go to each specific area—for example, how much to cancer research, to preventive medicine, and to the production of technology for treatment facilities? An example of the second problem is whether funding for *preventive* medicine should take priority over funding for *crisis* medicine. The prevention of disease by improvements in unsanitary environments and dissemination of health information is often cheaper and more efficient in raising health levels and saving lives than are kidney dialysis, heart transplantation, and intensive care units. From another perspective, however, a concentrated preventive approach seems morally unsatisfactory if it leads to the neglect of sick and injured persons who could directly benefit from available resources.

These problems of macroallocation are handled differently by competing systems of distribution. Which is the fairest?

DISTRIBUTIVE JUSTICE IN REDISTRIBUTING RESOURCES

In Chapter 1 we surveyed competing theories of justice. We will now examine how these same theories might be used to gauge the justice of health care systems, including macroallocation decisions.

Egalitarian Theory. In Chapter 1 we noted that John Rawls's *A Theory of Justice* has been a particularly influential work on social justice in the egalitarian tradition. Rawls argues that a social arrangement is a communal effort to advance the good of all in the society. Because inequalities of birth, historical circumstance, and natural endowment are undeserved, persons in a cooperative society should aim to make the unequal situation of naturally disadvantaged members more equal. Evening out disabilities in this way, Rawls claims, is a fundamental part of our shared conception of justice. His recognition of a positive societal obligation to eliminate or reduce barriers that prevent fair opportunity and that correct or compensate for various disadvantages has clear implications for discussions of justice in health care. Indeed, Rawls's analysis of justice has deeply influenced the articles in this chapter by Norman Daniels and Robert Veatch.

In his first article in this chapter, Daniels addresses the question, "Is there a right to health care?" He proposes that we conceptualize this right as a requirement of justice and then considers how we might interpret the commitments of various theories of justice to health care rights. He interprets Rawls's theory, in particular, as an account of protecting equality of opportunity; and he uses this theory it to clarify the many complexities surrounding the idea of a right to health care.

Veatch begins with a somewhat different interpretation of Rawls and egalitarian theory. He argues that those individuals who are worst off in a society (that is, are at the minimum level) should be guaranteed access to a certain level of health care. In this way, the society improves the conditions of the least fortunate by increasing the level of care available to them.

Utilitarian Theory. One need not be an egalitarian to believe in an equitable social system that redistributes resources to improve the health care needs of all citizens. Utilitarians believe that society has obligations to assist its members by preventing harms such as sickness. In the distribution of health care, utilitarians commonly view justice as involving tradeoffs and partial allocations that strike a balance. In devising a system of public funding for health care, we must balance public and private benefit, predicted cost savings, the probability of failure, the magnitude of risks, and the like. In his essay, Daniels considers whether utilitarians can provide a basis for recognizing rights to health care, and, if so, what the scope of utilitarian rights would be.

Although no author in this chapter explicitly defends a utilitarian system of distribution for health care, it is worth noting that many governments around the world adopt roughly a utilitarian approach to health policy. Their policies reflect the view that government has an obligation to maximize social resources in determining how best to relieve suffering and prevent premature death. This general utilitarian outlook can be and has been implemented in more than one way. Some utilitarians endorse a system of universal access to health care; others argue for a two-tiered system of health care in which persons are free to purchase more than can be provided by a public scheme of health insurance. Both approaches are utilitarian because the fundamental goal is to maximize social welfare.

Libertarian Theory. A perennial problem associated with the distribution of health care is whether *justice requires* that societies adopt an explicit distribution plan for health care. Robert Nozick has raised the following question about our shared conception of justice:

> Hearing the term "distribution," most people presume that some thing or mechanism uses some principle or criterion to give out a supply of things. . . . So it is an open question, at least, whether *re*distribution [of resources] should take place; whether we should do again what has already been done once.[1]

In Chapter 1 we examine the libertarian theory of justice, for which Nozick is a spokesperson. Proponents of this theory reject the conclusion that egalitarian and utilitarian patterns of distribution represent an appropriate normative ideal for distributing health care. People may be equal in many morally significant respects, they say, but *justice* does not demand the collection and redistribution of economic resources that are required to fund government-distributed health care goods and services. For a libertarian, just distributions flow from free market procedures of acquiring property and legitimately transferring that property. A libertarian therefore prefers a system in which health care insurance is privately and voluntarily purchased by individual or group initiative. In this system no one has had property coercively extracted by the state in order to benefit someone else.

A libertarian theory is defended in this chapter by H. Tristram Engelhardt, Jr., who relies on the principle of rights of free choice rather than a substantive principle of justice. Engelhardt argues that a theory of justice should work to protect our right not to be coerced; it should not propound a doctrine intended to distribute resources with a particular outcome. Use of the tax code to effect social goals such as saving lives with advanced medical technologies is a matter of social *choice,* not social justice. Some disadvantages created by ill health, Engelhardt argues, are merely *unfortunate,* whereas injury and illness caused by another person are correctly viewed as *unfair.* From this perspective, one will call a halt to the demands of justice where one draws the distinction between the unfair (and therefore obligatory in justice to correct) and the merely unfortunate.

THE RIGHT TO HEALTH CARE

These debates about justice and fair macroallocation have implications for the idea of a right to health care. If this right exists, national allocations for health care would presumably be based (as Daniels notes) on demands of justice, not merely on charity, compassion, or benevolence. In this context a "right" is understood as an *entitlement* to some measure of health care; rights are contrasted with privileges, ideals, and acts of charity.

In many nations there is a firmly established legal right to health care goods and services for all citizens. The legal situation in the United States, by contrast, involves entitlements for a few, but not for most. In 1965 Congress created Medicare to provide coverage for health care costs in populations that could not afford adequate coverage, especially the elderly. Medicare conferred a right to health care on a particularly vulnerable population and thereby stimulated discussion of whether all citizens have, or at least should have, a right to health care under similar conditions of need.

There is, then, no *legal* basis to support entitlements to health care in the United States, but this fact does not mean there is no *moral* basis. As noted previously, Daniels's concern is with a moral right to health care and how it might be implemented in health policy; he is not concerned with whether the law provides an entitlement, only with whether it should provide such an entitlement. His Rawlsian account also does not give individuals a right to have all their health care needs met. Instead, he outlines how a health care system can be constructed to protect equality of opportunity through entitlements to certain kinds of health care services. Daniels argues that any social system that denies access to services that promote normal functioning does an injustice to those who cannot obtain the services.

It is often asked whether moral arguments like that proposed by Daniels can support what has been called a right to a "decent minimum" of health care. Proponents of a right of this description (Daniels being an apparent example) assert that each person should have equal access to an adequate (though not maximal) level or "tier" of health care for all available types of services. The distribution proceeds on the basis of need, and needs are met by fair access to adequate services. Better services, such as luxury hospital rooms and expensive but optional dental work, can then be made available for purchase at personal expense by those who are able to and wish to do so.

Allen Buchanan argues (in his article in the first section of this chapter) that we have no *right* to this decent minimum of care but that there is nonetheless a social *obligation* to provide this level of care to the needy. By contrast, Engelhardt concludes that there is no right and no social obligation, although a society may *freely choose* to enact such a policy. From his perspective and Buchanan's, if needs are unfortunate they may be ameliorated by benevolence or compassion, but only if they are unfair does the obligation of justice justify compensation to the disadvantaged by using state force to tax and redistribute resources.

Veatch defends a different conclusion. He defends a right even stronger than the right to a decent minimum. He proposes the distribution of health care based on the individual's health care needs using the yardstick of an "equal right to health care." The result is that "people have a right to needed health care to provide an opportunity for a level of health equal as far as possible to the health of other people." This application of the principle of justice to health care would result in a health care delivery system with only one class of services available rather than a two-tiered system.

Even if one does not support either moral rights to health care or political obligations to supply it, one can still support legal entitlements to health care on grounds of charity, beneficence, or a sense of moral excellence in a community. Appeals other than those to moral *rights* can therefore be used to defend public distributions that confer legal rights, as Buchanan argues in his essay.

MANAGED CARE AND ACCESS TO CARE

It is difficult to predict the outcome of the spirited debate in the United States about health care reform, but it is virtually certain that changes will occur in forms of access to care and in the system of managed care. Of special interest is how to arrange insurance and manage care so that all subscribers have access to it at an affordable price. Many ethical issues derive from unequal resources, unequal access to care, and incentives in the system to reduce costs.

Several obstacles stand in the way of a more efficient, fair, and comprehensive system of access to health care in the United States. Roughly 40 million U.S. citizens (including 8.5 million children, or approximately 14 percent of the total population), annually lack all health care insurance, largely because of the high cost of health insurance and a system in which access is generally obtained through an employer-based health plan. (Roughly 64 percent of the U.S. population is covered by a health plan related to employment.) Despite the fact that approximately 14 percent of the gross national product is spent annually for health care in the United States, the poor and the uninsured often cannot afford or find access to even minimally adequate care. Even counting the existing Medicaid program, approximately 30 percent of all poor people have no health insurance of any type.

Many U.S. citizens are uninsurable because they cannot pass physical examinations, present the kind of medical histories required for insurance, or are excluded because of their occupation. There is also a problem of underinsurance for over 20 million U.S. citizens. Costs require limiting coverage even in employer-based plans, and exclusionary clauses often deny access for types of treatment as well as for specific diseases, injuries, or organ systems. A few people are uninsured at times and underinsured at other times. They experience gaps in insurance coverage that cannot be bridged because they move quickly from job to job or suffer from temporary but lengthy layoffs. More than a million laborers lose their insurance for some period of time during the year while they are unemployed, and more than one-quarter of the entire U.S. population changes insurance, with a resulting coverage gap, during the course of each year.

The problem of rising costs and underinsurance afflicts many countries other than the United States. Most countries are now facing problems of serious undercoverage for their citizens. Each country is adjusting its system to meet the problems of health care costs and distribution, and each faces somewhat different issues. In the United States, concern has recently been focused primarily on managed care—the system that was introduced to provide health insurance together with delivery of care for specific populations of enrollees and in which clinical decision making is designed to control costs and boost efficiency and productivity. Managed competition among providers of care adds another dimension in which the system of health care is cost driven.

Managed care was originally devised to provide greater availability of care, but it was quickly noticed that there is potentially a deep conflict between the goal of reducing costs and the traditional ethics of medicine. Everyone lauds the prevention of unnecessary care, but a cost-driven system is by definition not a patient-centered system. A core worry is that managed care creates a situation of physicians with a divided loyalty: Loyalty to institutional goals of economic efficiency competes with loyalty to the patient. This divided loyalty may function to undermine trust in physicians if they cannot be relied on to act in the best interests of patients. If physicians cannot profess fidelity to the patient above other interests, a pivotal principle of traditional medical ethics has been lost.

Some systems of managed care heighten this concern through a structure of financial incentives that links remuneration or job security for physicians to efficiency and productivity, as determined by managed care institutions. This system has been criticized for prematurely discharging hospital patients, ordering cheaper but less effective drugs and devices, postponing expensive medical tests, not providing experimental treatments that constitute last-chance treatments for some patients, using less skilled physicians for some services, disallowing or discontinuing coverage for very sick patients, and the like.

Each author in the second section of this chapter deals with some of these questions about managed care. In the first article, Lawrence Gostin is concerned with a recent overemphasis on the economic effects of health care. He thinks that this concern is in part responsible for the turn to market theory and managed care. Gostin thinks that cost concerns have caused many to overlook even more fundamental values of maintaining the health of individuals and populations. His thesis is that the failure to provide universal coverage in the United States through reasonable levels of resource allocation itself has adverse effects on the economy, American business, and American health. He thinks that these adverse effects are as high or higher under the present system than they would be under a system in which the government assured universal coverage.

In the second selection in this section, Madison Powers focuses on this country's embrace of managed care in the absence of the kind of systematic and comprehensive health care reform endorsed by Gostin. Powers argues that what survives of the traditional free market system in the United States is managed care, but he thinks it shows no promise of either managed competition or universal access. He argues that this system works against the public interest, for two reasons. First, the system of incentives does not promote medical innovation, and this loss does not seem to be offset by a substantial increase of equity in the distribution of health care. Second, managed care plans are not structured to address needs for long-term accountability (e.g., responsibility for the lifetime health outcomes of the population served). In effect, Powers finds that the current system of diverse managed care plans does not face up to the most important moral and political questions of an efficient and just system of health care.

In the final essay in this section, Allen Buchanan considers three common moral criticisms of managed-care organizations, each of which he thinks misses the one truly significant problem of managed care. The three criticisms of managed-care organizations are: (1) that they "skim the cream" of the healthiest patient populations while denying access to other populations; (2) that, through rationing, they deprive patients of care to which they are entitled; and (3) that, through rationing, they interfere with physicians' fulfillment of the fiduciary obligation to provide the best care to each patient. Buchanan finds each criticism misconceived. The first criticism wrongly assumes that the system of health care insurance has ever been structured so that it creates obligations to cover less healthy groups of persons; and the second and third wrongly assume that the U.S. health care system provides clear standards of care so that we can objectively say that they are violated by the rules and procedures that have been adopted by managed-care organizations. Finally, the central criticism that Buchanan thinks ought to be directed at managed care is that it operates within a health care system in which no connection has been or can be made between rationing and the basic requirements of justice.

If Buchanan is right, rationing itself has become a central topic in the quest for a just health care system.

RATIONING

In the face of rising costs of health care and other welfare needs such as education and environmental protection, it has become apparent that governments and their citizens cannot afford all medically beneficial resources. It appears inevitable that limits must be placed how much is spent for health care. That is, rationing seems inevitable. But what does it mean to ration, and how can we do so in a manner that does not discriminate against the sick and the poor?

Unfortunately, the term *rationing* has acquired more than one meaning in discussions of the allocation of health care. This term often suggests financially stringent and medically extenuating circumstances in which some persons receive care and others are excluded from care. However, the original meaning of *rationing* did not suggest austerity, emergency, or exclusion. It meant a form of allowance, share, or portion, as when food is divided into rations in the military. Only recently has this term been tied to limited resources, the setting of priorities in the health care budget, and the inclusion of some to the exclusion of others.

Rationing has come to have at least three meanings, all centered on the notion of a *limiting of resources*. The first sense is "denial as a result of lack of resources." In a market economy, for example, many types of health care are to some extent rationed by ability to pay. A good or service is limited to those persons who can pay for it. A second sense is "limited as a result of a government determination of an allowance or allotment" (i.e., some individuals are denied access to some good or service beyond an allotment amount). This is limitation through social policy rather than through market ceilings. Rationing gasoline and certain types of food during a war is a well-known example, and health care could be structured to follow this same pattern. A third sense combines the first two: An allowance or allotment is determined and distributed equitably, and only those who can afford additional goods are not denied access beyond the allotted amount. In this third sense, public policy fixes an allowance, but those who can afford additional units are not denied access beyond the allowance.

The article by Peter A. Ubel and Susan Dorr Goold in this section deals in a nuanced way with how best to define this troublesome term. They note that this term generally carries a negative connotation in the United States, suggesting crisis decisions carrying potentially tragic consequences. Ubel and Goold explore the most significant definitions of *rationing* and provide a schematic way of understanding these definitions. Some definitions turn on whether mechanisms of rationing are both explicit and implicit, how the scarcity of resources is understood, and the nature of the services that are denied. Ubel and Goold themselves argue for a broad interpretation of rationing encompassing any explicit or implicit measure that causes or allows persons to go without beneficial health care services. They maintain that this broad sense has advantages over other definitions, the most important advantage being that it points directly to the frequency with which patients are allowed to go without beneficial health care services because of their cost.

If poor insurance coverage and inability to pay are ways of eliminating those who are uninsured from access to health care, then much of the U.S. health care system involves rationing by level of personal resources. However, many other forms of rationing are also already in place, including forms of government reimbursement to hospitals, various forms of cost containment, restriction of the elderly to certain forms of care, and methods for disseminating new medical technologies.

A closely watched attempt to implement a policy of rationing has taken place for more than a decade in the state of Oregon. Faced with skyrocketing costs and a restive population demanding more efficient and fairer access to quality health care, Oregon established a state committee in 1989 charged to rank hundreds of medical procedures for Medicaid, from most to least important, based in part on data about quality of well-being. State officials sought to extend coverage to a larger percentage of its citizens through its allocated Medicaid funds, and to do so both efficiently and fairly. The goal was to fund as many top priority–ranked services as possible.

The Oregon plan was implemented for its Medicaid population in 1994. By 2000 it had expanded health care coverage to well over 100,000 additional Oregonians, decreased the percentage of the uninsured, and reduced cost shifting. Although such outcomes make it appear that the Oregon system has been a major success, the plan does also explicitly deny health services to thousands of Oregonians. Moreover, ethical issues of fairness and comprehensiveness in coverage have long been raised about it. Problems of rationing stemming from the Oregon plan—but not limited to that plan—are treated in the selections by Daniels and Leonard M. Fleck. Daniels discusses troublesome questions about fairness that would have to be addressed in any system of rationing. He focuses on four general rationing problems that he thinks remain unresolved in bioethics and that also have plagued Oregon's rationing plan. In the course of a reply to Daniels, Fleck argues in the third selection that our national efforts at health reform ought to be informed by several lessons learned from Oregon. Specifically, he thinks that we can learn that rationing is inevitable and that it must be public and visible. The kind of hidden rationing that occurs in the present system therefore must be eliminated.

T.L.B.

NOTE

1. Robert Nozick, *Anarchy, State, and Utopia* (New York: Basic Books, 1974), pp. 149–50.

Just Health Care and the Right to Health Care

NORMAN DANIELS

Is There a Right to Health Care and, If So, What Does It Encompass?

Norman Daniels is Goldthwaite Professor of Philosophy at Tufts University and professor of medical ethics at Tufts Medical School. He has written widely in the philosophy of science, ethics, political and social philosophy, and medical ethics. Among his books are *Seeking Fair Treatment: From the AIDS Epidemic to National Health Care Reform* (Oxford) and (with Donald Light and Ronald Caplan) *Benchmarks of Fairness for Health Care Reform* (Oxford). He is currently working on *Just Health,* a substantial revision and expansion of his earlier book *Just Health Care.*

IS THERE A RIGHT TO HEALTH CARE?

LEGAL VS. MORAL RIGHTS TO HEALTH CARE

One way to answer this question is to adopt the stance of legal positivists, who claim that there are no rights except those that are embodied in actual institutions through law. We would then be able to reply that in nearly every advanced industrial democracy in the world, there is a right to health care, since institutions exist in them that assure everyone access to needed services regardless of ability to pay. The notable exception is the United States, where many poor and near poor people have no insurance coverage for, and thus no assured access to, medically necessary services, although by law they cannot be denied emergency services.

The legal right to health care is embodied in a wide variety of types of health-care systems. These range from national health services, where the government is the provider of services, as in Great Britain, to pub-

From Norman Daniels, "Is there a right to healthcare and, if so, what does it encompass?" in *A Companion to Bioethics,* eds. Helga Kuhse and Peter Singer, Blackwell Publishers © 1998, pp. 316–25. Reprinted by permission.

lic insurance schemes, where the government finances services, as in Canada, to mixed public and private insurance schemes, as in Germany and the Netherlands. Despite these differences in the design of systems, there is a broad overlap in the scope or content of the legal right to health care in these countries. Most cover "medically necessary" services, including a broad range or preventive, curative, rehabilitative and long-term care for physical and mental diseases, disorders and disabilities. Most exclude uses of medical technologies that enhance otherwise normal functioning or appearance, such as purely cosmetic surgery. The legal rights vary in significant ways, however, for example, in the degree to which they cover new reproductive technologies, or in the types of mental health and long-term care services that are offered.

In the context of rising costs and the rapid dissemination of new technologies, there is growing debate in many countries about how to set limits on the scope of a right to health care. This debate about the scope of rights to health care pushes moral deliberation about such a right into the forefront, even where a legal right is recognized. Legal entitlements, most people believe, should reflect what society is morally obliged to provide by way of medical services. What, then, is the basis and scope of a moral right to health care?

POSITIVE VS. NEGATIVE RIGHTS

A right to health care is a *positive* as opposed to a *negative* right. Put quite simply, a positive right requires others to do something beneficial or enabling for right-bearers, whereas a negative right requires others to refrain from doing something, usually harmful or restrictive, to right-bearers. To say that others are required to do something or to refrain from doing something is to say they must so act or refrain even if they could produce more good or improve the world by not doing so (Thomson, 1990). For example, a negative right to free expression requires others to refrain from censuring the expression of the right-bearer even if censuring this speech would make a better world. Some public-health measures that protect people against interference with their health, such as environmental protections that protect people against polluters of air, water and food sources, might be construed as requirements of a negative right. More generally, however, a right to health care imposes an obligation on others to assist the right-bearers in obtaining needed and appropriate services. Specifically, claiming a right to health care includes these other claims: society has the duty to its members to allocate an adequate share of its total resources to health-related needs; society has the duty to provide a just allocation of different types of health care services, taking into account the competing claims of different types of health-care needs; each person is entitled to a fair share of such services, where a "fair share" includes an answer to the question, who should pay for the services? (Daniels, 1985). Health-care rights thus form a part of a broader family of positive 'welfare' rights that includes rights to education and to income support. Because positive rights require other people to contribute their resources or skills to benefit right-bearers, rather than merely refraining from interfering with them, they have often been thought more difficult to justify than negative rights, and their scope and limits have been harder to characterize.

THEORIES OF JUSTICE AND RIGHTS TO HEALTH CARE

If we are to think of a right to health care as a requirement of justice, then we should look to more general theories of justice as a way to specify the scope and limits of that right. On some theories of justice, however, there is little basis for requiring people to assist others by meeting their health care or other needs. Libertarians, for example, believe that fundamental rights to property, including rights to personal assets, such as talents and skills, are violated if society coerces individuals into providing "needed" resources or skills (Nozick, 1974). Libertarians generally recognize an "imperfect" duty to act beneficently or charitably, but this duty involves discretion. It can be discharged in different ways that are matters of choice. People denied charity have no right to it and have no complaint against people who act charitably in other ways. Though some have argued that the difficulty of coordinating the delivery of charitable assistance might justify coercive measures (Buchanan, 1984), and others have tried to show that even libertarians must recognize some forms of welfare rights (Sterba, 1985), most libertarians resist any weakening of the property rights at the core of their view (Brennan and Friedman, 1981).

A spectre sometimes raised by libertarians against the idea of a right to health care is that such a right is a "bottomless pit." Since new technologies continuously expand the scope of "medical needs," a right to health care would give rise to unlimited claims on the resources of others (Fried, 1969; Engelhardt, 1986).

Protecting such an expansive right to health care would thus not be compatible with the function of a libertarian "minimal state" to assure the non-violation of rights to liberty and property.

Though there remains controversy about whether utilitarians can provide a basis for recognizing true moral rights, there are strong utilitarian arguments in favour of governments assuring access to at least some broad range of effective medical services. Preventing or curing disease or disability reduces suffering and enables people to function in ways that contribute to aggregate welfare. In addition, knowing that health-care services are available increases personal security and strengthens the ties of community. Utilitarians can also justify redistributing the burden of delivering these benefits to society as a whole, citing the decreasing marginal utility of money to support progressive financing of health-care services (Brandt, 1979).

Beneath these quite general arguments, however, there lies a more specific controversy about the scope of utilitarian entitlements to health care. There seems to be little utilitarian justification for investing resources in health care if those resources would produce more net welfare when invested in other things, yet many people believe they have moral obligations to assist others with their health-care needs even at a net cost in utility. For example, some highly expensive and effective medical treatments that most people believe should be offered to people might not be "cost beneficial" and thus not defensible on utilitarian grounds. Similarly, many forms of long-term care, especially for those who cannot be restored to productive social activity, are also difficult to defend on utilitarian grounds, yet we insist our health-care systems are obliged to provide such services.

Lack of moral acceptance of the distributive implications of utilitarianism makes many uncomfortable with the use of methods, such as cost-effectiveness analysis, that are intended to guide decisions about resource allocation in health care. For example, an assumption of cost-effectiveness analysis is that a unit of health benefit, such as a quality-adjusted life year (QALY), is of equal value or importance regardless of where it is distributed. But this assumption does not capture the concerns many people have about how much priority to give to the sickest patients, or when aggregating modest benefits to large numbers of people it outweighs the moral importance of delivering more significant benefits to fewer people (Nord, 1993; Daniels, 1993).

Two points about a utilitarian framework for a right to health care are worth noting. Recognizing a right to health care is compatible with recognizing limits on entitlements that result from resource scarcity and the fact that there are competing uses of those resources. Consequently, recognizing a right to health care need not open a bottomless pit. Second, just what entitlements to services follow from a right to health care cannot be specified outside the context of a *system* properly designed to deliver health care in a way that promotes aggregate utility. For the utilitarian, entitlements are *system-relative.* The same two points apply to other accounts of the foundations and limits of a right to health care.

Because many people reject the utilitarian rationales for health care (and other welfare) rights, theorists have explored other ways to ground such rights. Some claim that these rights are presupposed as enabling conditions for the exercise of other rights or liberties, or as practical presuppositions of all views of justice (Braybrooke, 1987) or as a way of avoiding vulnerability and exploitation (Goodin, 1988). One approach that has been developed in some detail views a right to health care as a special case of a right to equality of opportunity (Daniels, 1985). This approach shows how the most important contractarian theory of justice, Rawls' (1971) account of justice as fairness, can be extended to the problem of health care, since that theory gives prominence to a principle protecting equality of opportunity (Rawls, 1993). Without endorsing that account here, we shall use it to illustrate further the complexity surrounding the concept of a right to health care.

EQUAL OPPORTUNITY AND A RIGHT TO HEALTH CARE

The central observation underlying this account of a right to health care is that disease and disability restrict the range of opportunities that would otherwise be open to individuals. This is true whether they shorten our lives or impair our ability to function, including through pain and suffering. Health care in all its forms, whether public health or medical, preventive or acute or chronic, aims to keep people functioning as close to normally as possible. Since we are complex social creatures, our normal functional capabilities include our capabilities for emotional and cognitive functioning and not just physical capabilities.

Health care thus preserves for us the range of opportunities we would have, were we not ill or disabled, given our talents and skills.

The significant contribution health care makes to protecting the range of opportunities open to individuals is nevertheless *limited* in two important ways. It is limited because other things, such as the distribution of wealth and income and education, also profoundly affect equality of opportunity. It is also limited because health care, by restricting its aim to protecting normal functioning, leaves the normal distribution of talents and skills unmodified. It aims to help us function as "normal" competitors, not strictly equal ones.

Some argue that an equal opportunity account of health care should abandon the limit set by a focus on normal functioning (see Arneson, 1988; G. A. Cohen, 1989; Sen, 1992). They claim our concerns about equality, including equality of opportunity, require us to use health-care technologies whenever doing so would equalize opportunity for welfare or equalizes capabilities. For example, if through medical intervention we can "enhance" the otherwise normal capabilities of those who are at a competitive disadvantage, then our commitment to equality of opportunity requires us to do so. Obviously, this version of an equal opportunity account would vastly expand the moral requirements on medicine, yielding a right to health care much more expansive than any now embodied in actual systems and, arguably, one that would make administration of a health-care system unwieldy (Sabin and Daniels, 1994).

This expansive version of the appeal to equal opportunity ignores an important fact about justice: our concern for equality must be reconciled with considerations of liberty and efficiency in arriving at the overall requirements of justice (see Sen, 1992; Cohen, 1995; Daniels, 1996). Such a reconciliation seems to underlie the limits we commonly accept when we appeal to equality of opportunity. We generally believe that rights to equal opportunity are violated only if unfair social practices or preventable or curable diseases or disabilities interfere with the pursuit of reasonable plans of life within our society by making us lose competitive advantage. We accept, however, the fact that the natural distribution of talents and skills, working in an efficient market for them, will both enhance the social product and lead to inequalities in social outcomes. A just society will try to mitigate the effects of these inequalities in competitive advantage in others ways than by eliminating all eliminable differences in capabilities. For example, on Rawls' account, transfers that make the worst off as well off as they can be mitigate the effects on equality of allowing the natural distribution of talents and skills to enhance productivity. In what follows, the account of a right to health care rests on a more limited appeal to equal opportunity, one that takes the maintenance of normal functioning as a reasonable limit.

WHAT DOES A RIGHT TO HEALTH CARE INCLUDE?

SYSTEM-RELATIVE ENTITLEMENTS

By making the right to health care a special case of rights to equality of opportunity, we arrive at a reasonable, albeit incomplete and imperfect, way of restricting its scope while still recognizing its importance. The account does not give individuals a basic right to have all of their health-care needs met. At the same time, there are social obligations to design a health-care system that protects opportunity through an appropriate set of health-care services. If social obligations to provide appropriate health care are not met, then individuals are definitely wronged. For example, if people are denied access—because of discrimination or inability to pay—to a basic tier of services adequate to protect normal functioning, injustice is done to them. If the basic tier available to people omits important categories of services without consideration of their effects on normal functioning, for example, whole categories of mental health or long-term care or preventive services, their rights are violated.

Still, not every medical need gives rise to an entitlement to services. The scope and limits of rights to health care, that is, the entitlements they actually carry with them, will be relative to certain facts about a given system. For example, a health-care system can protect opportunity only within the limits imposed by resource scarcity and technological development within a society. We cannot make a direct inference from the fact that an individual has a right to health care to the conclusion that this person is entitled to some specific health-care service, even if the service would meet a health-care need. Rather the individual is entitled to a specific service only if, in the light of facts about a society's technological capabilities and resource limitations, it should be a part of a system that appropriately protects fair equality of opportunity. The equal opportunity account of a right to health care, like the utilitarian account, makes entitlements to health care system-relative.

EFFECTIVE TREATMENT OF DISEASE AND DISABILITY

The health care we have strongest claim to is care that effectively promotes normal functioning by reducing the impact of disease and disability, thus protecting the range of opportunities that would otherwise be open to us. Just what counts as "effective," however? And what should we do about hard cases on the boundary between treatment of disease or disability and enhancement of capabilities?

It is a common feature of public and private insurance systems to limit care to treatments that are not "experimental" and have some "proven effectiveness." Unfortunately, many services that count as standard treatment have little direct evidence about outcomes to support their use (Hadorn, 1992). They are often just customary treatment. Furthermore, it is often controversial just when new treatments or technologies should count as "safe and efficacious." What counts as "reasonably effective" is then a matter of judgement and depends on the kind of condition and the consequences of not correcting it. We might, for example, want to lower our standards for effectiveness when we face a treatment of last resort, or raise them if resource scarcity is very great. On the other hand, we do not owe people a chance to obtain miracles through whatever unproven procedures they prefer to try.

By focusing a right to health care on the maintenance of normal functioning, a line is drawn between uses of medical technologies that count as legitimate "treatments" and those that we may want but which do not meet our "health-care needs." Although we may want medical services that can enhance our appearance, like cosmetic (as opposed to reconstructive) plastic surgery, or that can optimize our otherwise normal functioning, like some forms of counselling or some uses of Prozac, we do not truly need these services to maintain normal functioning. We are obliged to help others achieve normal functioning, but we do not "owe" each other whatever it takes to make us more beautiful or strong or completely happy (Daniels, 1985).

Though this line is widely used in both public and private insurance practices, it leaves us with hard cases. Some of the hardest issues involve reproductive technologies. Abortion, where there is no preventive or therapeutic need, does not count as "treatment" because an unwanted pregnancy is not a disease or disability. Some nevertheless insist that requirements of justice, including a right to control one's body, means that non-therapeutic abortion should be included as an entitlement in a health-care system. Some national health-insurance schemes do not cover infertility services. Yet infertility is a departure from normal functioning, even if some people never want to bear children. Controversy may remain about how much social obligation we have to correct this form of impaired opportunity, especially where the costs of some interventions, such as *in vitro* fertilization, are high and their effectiveness is modest. Different societies will judge this question differently, in part because they may place different values on the rearing of biologically related children or on the experience of childbearing.

Hard cases involve non-reproductive technologies as well. In the United States, for example, many insurers will cover growth hormone treatment only for children deficient in growth hormone, not for those who are equally short but without any pathology. Yet the children denied therapy will suffer just as much as those who are eligible. Similar difficulties are involved in drawing a line between covered and non-covered uses of mental health services (Sabin and Daniels, 1994). As in the cases of reproductive technologies, there is room for different societies to "construct" the concept of mental disorder somewhat differently, with resulting variation in decisions about insurance coverage.

RIGHTS AND LIMITS ON EFFECTIVE TREATMENTS

Even when some health-care service is reasonably effective at meeting a medical need, not all such needs are equally important. When a disease or disability has little impact on the range of opportunities open to someone, it is not as morally important to treat as other conditions that more seriously impair opportunity. The effect on opportunity thus gives us some guidance in thinking about resource allocation priorities.

Unfortunately, the impact on our range of opportunities gives only a crude and incomplete measure of the importance or priority we should give to a need or service. In making decisions about priorities for purposes of resource allocation in health care, we face difficult questions about distributive fairness that are not answered by this measure of importance. For example, we must sometimes make a choice between investing in a technology that delivers a significant benefit to few people or one that delivers a more modest benefit to a larger number of people. Sometimes we must make a choice between investing in a service that helps the sickest, most impaired patients or one that helps those whose functioning is less impaired. Sometimes we must decide between the fairness of giving a scarce resource to those who derive the largest benefit or giving a broader range of people some chance at getting a benefit. In all of these cases, we lack clear principles for deciding how to make our choices, and the account of a right to health care we are discussing does not provide those principles either (Daniels, 1993). Some methodologies, like cost-effectiveness analysis, are intended to help us make appropriate resource allocation decisions in these kinds of cases. But these methodologies may themselves embody controversial moral assumptions about distributive fairness. This means they cannot serve as decision procedures for making these choices and can at best serve as aids to decision-makers who must be explicit about the moral reasoning that determines the distributive choices they make (Gold et al., 1996).

In any health-care system, then, some choices will have to be made by a fair, publicly accountable, decision-making process. Just what constitutes a fair decision-making procedure for resolving moral disputes about health care entitlements is itself a matter of controversy. It is a problem that has been addressed little in the literature. Our rights are not violated, however, if the choices that are made through fair decision-making procedures turn out to be ones that do not happen to meet our personal needs, but instead meet needs of others that are judged more important (Daniels and Sabin, 1997).

HOW EQUAL MUST OUR RIGHTS TO HEALTH CARE BE?

How equal must our rights to health care be? Specifically, must everyone receive exactly the same kinds of health-care services and coverage, or is fairness in health care compatible with a "tiered" system? Around the world, even countries that offer universal health insurance differ in their answers to this question. In Canada and Norway, for example, no supplementary insurance is permitted. Everyone is served solely by the national health-insurance schemes, though people who seek additional services or more rapid service may go elsewhere, as some Canadians do by crossing the border. In Britain, supplementary private insurance allows about 10 per cent of the population to gain quicker access to services for which there is extensive queuing in the public system. Basing a right to health care on an obligation to protect equality of opportunity is compatible with the sort of tiering the British have, but it does not require it, and it imposes some constraints on the kind of tiering allowed.

The primary social obligation is to assure everyone access to a tier of services that effectively promotes normal functioning and thus protects equality of opportunity. Since health care is not the only important good, resources to be invested in the basic tier are appropriately and reasonably limited, for example, by democratic decisions about how much to invest in education or job training as opposed to health care. Because of their very high "opportunity costs," there will be some beneficial medical services that it will be reasonable not to provide in the basic tier, or to provide only on a limited basis, for example, with queuing. To say that these services have "high opportunity costs" means that providing them consumes resources that would produce greater health benefits and protect opportunity more if used in other ways.

In a society that permits significant income and wealth inequalities, some people will want to buy coverage for these additional services. Why not let them? After all, we allow people to use their after-tax income and wealth as they see fit to pursue the "quality of life" and opportunities they prefer. The rich can buy special security systems for their homes. They can buy safer cars. They can buy private schooling for their children. Why not allow them to buy supplementary health care for their families?

One objection to allowing a supplementary tier is that its existence might undermine the basic tier either economically or politically. It might attract better-quality providers away from the basic tier, or raise costs in the basic tier, reducing the ability of society to meet its social obligations. The supplementary tier might undermine political support for the basic tier, for example, by undercutting the social solidarity needed if people are to remain committed to protecting opportunity for all. These objections are serious, and where a supplementary tier undermines the basic tier in either way, economically or politically, priority must be given to protecting the basic tier. In principle, however, it seems possible to design a system in which the supplementary tier does not undermine the basic one. If that can be done, then a system that permits tiering avoids restricting liberty in ways that some find seriously objectionable.

A second objection is not to tiering itself but to the structure of inequality that results. Compare two scenarios. In one, most people are adequately served by the basic tier and only the best-off groups in society have the means and see the need to purchase supplementary insurance. That is the case in Great Britain. In the other, the basic tier serves only the poorest groups in society and most other people buy supplementary insurance. The Oregon plan to expand Medicaid eligibility partly through rationing the services it covers has aspects of this structure of inequality, since most people are covered by plans that avoid these restrictions (Daniels, 1991). The first scenario seems preferable to the second on grounds of fairness. In the second, the poorest groups can complain that they are left behind by others in society even in the protection of their health. In the first, the majority has less grounds for reasonable resentment or regret.

If the basic tier is not undermined by higher tiers, and if the structure of the inequality that results is not objectionable, then it is difficult to see why some tiering should not be allowed. There is a basic conflict here between concerns about equality and concerns about liberty, between wanting to make sure everyone is treated properly with regard to health care and wanting to give people the liberty to use their resources (after tax) to improve their lives as they see fit. In practice, the crucial constraint on the liberty we allow people seems to depend on the magnitude of the benefit available in the supplementary tier and unavailable in the basic tier. Highly visible forms of saving lives and improving function would be difficult to exclude from the basic tier while we make them available in a supplementary tier. In principle, however, some forms of tiering will not be unfair even when they involve medical benefits not available to everyone.

REFERENCES

Arneson, Richard (1988). Equality and equal opportunity for welfare. *Philosophical Studies,* 54, 79–95.

Brandt, Richard (1979). *A Theory of the Good and the Right.* Oxford: Oxford University Press.

Braybrooke, David (1987). *Meeting Needs.* Princeton, NJ: Princeton University Press.

Brennan, Geoffrey and Friedman, David (1981). A libertarian perspective on welfare. In Peter G. Brown, Conrad Johnson and Paul Vernier (eds). *Income Support: Conceptual and policy issues.* Totowa, NJ: Rowman and Littlefield.

Buchanan, Allen (1984). The right to a decent minimum of health care. *Philosophy and Public Affairs,* 13, 55–78.

Cohen, G. A. (1989). On the currency of egalitarian justice. *Ethics,* 99, 906–44.

Cohen, Joshua (1995). Amartya Sen: *Inequality Reexamined. Journal of Philosophy,* 92/5, 275–88.

Daniels, N. (1985). *Just Health Care.* Cambridge: Cambridge University Press.

——— (1991). Is the Oregon rationing plan fair? *Journal of the American Medical Association,* 265, 2232–5.

——— (1993). Rationing fairly: programmatic considerations. *Bioethics,* 7, 224–33.

——— (1996). *Justice and Justification: reflective equilibrium in theory and practice.* Cambridge: Cambridge University Press.

Daniels, N. and Sabin, J. (1997). Limits to health care: fair procedures, democratic deliberation, and the legitimacy problem for insurers. *Philosophy and Public Affairs,* 26/4, 303–50.

Engelhardt, H. Tristram (1986). *The Foundations of Bioethics.* Oxford: Oxford University Press.

Fried, Charles (1969). *An Anatomy of Value.* Cambridge, MA: Harvard University Press.

Gold, Marthe, Siegel, Joanna, Russell, Louise, and Weinstein, Milton (eds) (1996). *Cost-Effectiveness in Health and Medicine: recommendations of the Panel on -Effectiveness in Health and Medicine.* New York: Oxford University Press.

Goodin, Robert (1988). *Reasons for Welfare.* Princeton, NJ: Princeton University Press.

Hadorn, David (ed.) (1992). *Basic Benefits and Clinical Guidelines.* Boulder, CO: Westview Press.

Nord, Eric (1993). The relevance of health state after treatment in prioritizing between different patients. *Journal of Medical Ethics,* 19, 37–42.

Nozick, R. (1974). *Anarchy, State, and Utopia.* New York: Basic Books.

Rawls, J. (1971). *A Theory of Justice.* Cambridge, MA: Harvard University Press.

——— (1993). *Political Liberalism.* New York: Columbia University Press.

Sabin, James and Daniels, Norman (1994). Determining "medical necessity" in mental health practice. *Hastings Center Report,* 24/6, 5–13.

Sen, Amartya (1992). *Inequality Reexamined.* Cambridge, MA: Harvard University Press.

Sterba, James (1985). From liberty to welfare. *Social Theory and Practice,* 11, 285–305.

Thomson, Judith (1990). *The Realm of Rights.* Cambridge, MA: Harvard University Press.

ROBERT M. VEATCH

Justice, the Basic Social Contract, and Health Care

Robert M. Veatch is professor of medical ethics and the former director of the Kennedy Institute of Ethics at Georgetown University. His recent books include *The Basics of Bioethics, Case Studies in Pharmacy Ethics,* and the second editions of *Case Studies in Nursing Ethics, Cross Cultural Perspectives in Medical Ethics,* and *Transplant Ethics.* His current research focuses on the history of professional medical ethics and its relation to philosophical and religious ethics.

The principle that each person's welfare should count equally is crucial if the community generated is to be a moral community. The moral community is one of impartiality. If the community employed an impartial perspective to draw up the basic principles or practices for the society, the principles would be generated without reference to individual talents, skills, abilities, or good fortune. Another way of formulating this condition is to say that the basic principles or practices established must meet the test of reversibility. That is, they must be acceptable to one standing on either the giving or the receiving end of a transaction.[1] The general notion is that the contractors must take equal account of all persons. . . .

The most intriguing contractual theory of ethics that makes this commitment to impartiality or reversibility is that espoused by John Rawls.[2] In his version of social contract theory, Rawls asks us to envision ourselves in what he calls the original position. He does not pretend that such a position exists or ever could exist. Rather, it is a device for making "vivid to ourselves the restrictions that it seems reasonable to impose on arguments for principles of justice, and therefore on these principles themselves."[3] The restrictions on the original position are that no one should be advantaged or disadvantaged in the choice of principles either by natural fortune or social circumstances. Persons in the original position are equal. To help us imagine such a situation, he asks us to impose what he calls a "veil of ignorance," under which "no one knows his place in society, his class position or social status, nor does any one know his fortune in the distribution of natural assets and abilities, his intelligence, strength, and the like."[4]

From that position one can derive impartially a set of principles or practices that provide the moral foundations for a society. Even if we cannot discover a universal basis for ethical decisions, perhaps we can create a community that accepts rules such as respect for freedom and the impartial consideration of interests; that is, one that adopts the moral point of view and thereby provides a common foundation for deciding what is ethical. Those who take this view believe it possible to generate some commonly agreed upon principles or practices for a society. The creation of a contractual framework could then provide a basis for making medical ethical decisions that would be commonly recognized as legitimate. . . .

There is . . . a moral community constituted symbolically by the metaphor of the contract or covenant. There is a convergence between the vision of people coming together to discover a preexisting moral order—an order that takes equally into account the welfare of all—and the vision of people coming together to invent a moral order that as well takes equally into account the welfare of all. The members of the moral community thus generated are bound together by bonds of mutual loyalty and trust. There is a fundamental equality and reciprocity in the relationship,

From *A Theory of Medical Ethics,* © 1981. Reprinted by permission of the Kennedy Institute of Ethics.

something missing in the philanthropic condescension of professional code ethics. . . .

THE MAXIMIN THEORY

Some say that reasonable people considering alternative policies or principles for a society would not opt to maximize the aggregate benefits that exist in the society. Rather, they say that at least for basic social practices that determine the welfare of members of the moral community, they would opt for a strategy that attempts to assure fundamentally that the least well off person would do as well as possible. . . .

The implication is that those having the greatest burden have some claim on the society independent of whether responding to their needs is the most efficient way of producing the greatest net aggregate benefit. Holders of this view say that the commitment of a principle of justice is to maximize not net aggregate benefit, but the position of the least advantaged members of the society. If the principle of justice is a right-making characteristic of actions, a principle that reasonable people would accept as part of the basic social contract independent of the principle of beneficence, it probably incorporated some moral notion that the distribution of benefits and burdens counts as well as the aggregate amount of them. One plausible alternative is to concentrate, insofar as we are concerned about justice, on the welfare of the least well off. This is part of those principles of justice defended by Rawls as derived from his version of social contract theory. . . .

Since Rawls's scheme is designed to provide insights into only the basic practices and social institutions, it is very hard to discern what the implications are for specific problems of resource distribution such as the allocation of health care resources. Some have argued that no direct implications can be read from the Rawlsian principles. That seems, however, to overstate the case. At the least, basic social practices and institutional arrangements must be subject to the test of the principles of justice.

It appears, then, that this view will not justify inequalities in the basic health care institutions and practices simply because they produce the greatest net aggregate benefit. Its notion of justice, concentrating on improving the lot of the least advantaged, is much more egalitarian in this sense than the utilitarian system. It would distribute health care resources to the least well off rather than just on the aggregate amount of benefit.

There is no obvious reason why our hypothetical contractors articulating the basic principles for a society would favor a principle that maximized aggregate utility any more than one that maximized minimum utility. Our contract model, as an epistemological device for discovering the basic principles, views them, after all, as committed to the moral point of view, as evaluating equally the welfare of each individual from a veil of ignorance, to use the Rawlsian language. This perspective retains the notion of individuals as identifiable, unique personalities, as noncommensurable human beings, rather than simply as components of an aggregate mass. Faced with a forced choice, it seems plausible that one would opt for maximizing the welfare of individuals, especially the least well-off individuals, rather than maximizing the aggregate.

Nevertheless, the interpretation of justice that attempts to maximize the minimum position in the society (and is hence sometimes called the "maximin" position), still permits inequalities and even labels them as just. What, for example, of basic health care institutional arrangements that systematically single out elites with unique natural talents for developing medical skill and services and gives these individuals high salaries as incentives to serve the interests of the least well off? What if a special health care system were institutionalized to make sure these people were always in the best of health, were cared for first in catastrophies, and were inconvenienced least by the normal bureaucratic nuisances of a health care system?

It is conceivable that such an institutional arrangement would be favored by reasonable people taking the moral point of view. They could justify the special gains that would come to the elites by the improved chances thus created for the rest of the population (who would not have as great a gain as the favored ones, but would at least be better off than if the elite were not so favored). The benefits, in lesser amounts, would trickle down in this plan to the consumers of health care so that all, or at least the least advantaged, would gain. The gap between the elite of the health profession and the masses could potentially increase by such a social arrangement, but at least all would be better off in absolute terms.

So it is conceivable that reasonable people considering equally both the health professionals and the masses would favor such an arrangement, but it is not obvious. Critics of the Rawlsian principles of justice say that in some cases alternative principles of distribution would be preferred. Brian Barry, for example, argues that rational choosers would look not just at the welfare of the least advantaged, but also at the average or aggregate welfare of alternative policies.[5] On the other hand, Barry and many others suggest that in some circumstances, rational choosers might opt for the principle that would maximize equality of outcome.[6] At most, considering the institutionalization of advantages for a health care elite, they would be supported as a prudent sacrifice of the demands of justice in order to serve some other justifiable moral end.

From this perspective, favoring elites with special monetary and social incentives in order to benefit the poor might be a prudent compromise.[7] It might mediate between the demands that see justice as requiring equality of outcome (subject to numerous qualifications) and the demands of the principle of beneficence requiring maximum efficiency in producing good consequences. If that is the case, though, then there is still a fourth interpretation of the principle of justice that must be considered, one that is more radically egalitarian than the maximin strategy.

THE EGALITARIAN THEORY

Those who see the maximin strategy as a compromise between the concern for justice and the concern for efficient production of good consequences must feel that justice requires a stricter focus on equality than the maximin understanding of the principle of justice. The maximin principle is concerned about the distribution of benefits. It justifies inequalities only if they benefit the least well off. But it does justify inequalities—and it does so in the name of justice.

Rawls recognizes that there is an important difference between a right action and a just or a fair action. Fairness is a principle applying to individuals along with beneficence, noninjury, mutual respect, and fidelity. The list is not far removed from the basic principles I have identified. But, given this important difference between what is right in this full, inclusive sense and what is fair, if one is convinced that incentives and advantages for medical elites are justified, why would one claim that the justification is one based on the principle of fairness? One might instead maintain that they are right on balance because they are a necessary compromise with the principle of fairness (or justice) in order to promote efficiently the welfare of a disadvantaged group. It is to be assumed, given the range of basic principles in an ethical system, that conflicts will often emerge so that one principle will be sacrificed, upon occasion, for the sake of another.

The egalitarian understanding of the principle of justice is one that sees justice as requiring (subject to certain important qualifications) equality of net welfare for individuals.[8] . . .

Everyone, according to the principle of egalitarian justice, ought to end up over a lifetime with an equal amount of net welfare (or, as we shall see shortly, a chance for that welfare). Some may have a great deal of benefit offset by large amounts of unhappiness or disutility, while others will have relatively less of both. What we would call "just" under this principle is a basic social practice or policy that contributes to the same extent to greater equality of outcome (subject to restrictions to be discussed). I am suggesting that reasonable people who are committed to a contract model for discovering, inventing, or otherwise articulating the basic principles will want to add to their list the notion that one of the right-making characteristics of a society would be the equality of welfare among the members of the moral community.

THE EQUALITY OF PERSONS

The choice of this interpretation of the principle of justice will depend upon how the contractors understand the commitment to the moral point of view—the commitment to impartiality that takes the point of view of all equally into account. We certainly are not asserting the equality of ability or even the equality of the merit of individual claims. . . .

If this is what is meant by the moral point of view, taking into account equally the individuality of each member of the community, then in addition to the right-making characteristics or principles of beneficence, promise keeping, autonomy, truth telling, and avoiding killing, the principle of justice as equality of net welfare must be added to the list. The principle might be articulated as affirming that people have a claim on having the total net welfare in their lives equal insofar as possible to the welfare in the lives of others.

Of course, no reasonable person, even an egalitarian, is going to insist upon or even desire that all the features of people's lives be identical.[9] It seems obvious that the most that anyone would want is that the total net welfare for each person be comparable. . . .

If this egalitarian understanding of the principle of justice would be acceptable to reasonable people taking the moral point of view, it provides a solution to the dilemma of the tension between focusing exclusively on the patient and opening the doors to considerations of social consequences such as in classical utilitarianism. The principle of justice provides another basis for taking into account a limited set of impacts on certain other parties. If the distribution of benefits as well as the aggregate amount is morally relevant, then certain impacts on other parties may be morally more relevant than others. A benefit that accrues to a person who is or predictably will be in a least well-off group would count as a consideration of justice while a benefit of equal size that accrued to other persons not in the least well-off group would not. The hypothetical benefits of a Nazi-type experiment would not accrue to a least well-off group (while the harms of the experiment presumably would). They are thus morally different from, in fact diametrically opposed to, a redistribution scheme that produced benefits for only the least advantaged group.

EQUALITY AND ENVY

Critics of the egalitarian view of justice have argued that the only way to account for such a position is by attributing it to a psychology of envy.[10] Freud accounted for a sense of justice in this way.[11] They feel the only conceivable reason to strive for equality is the psychological explanation that the less well off envy the better off, and they hold that contractors take that psychological fact into account. Since they believe that envy is not an adequate justification for a commitment to equal outcome, they opt instead for an alternative theory of justice. . . .

The egalitarian holds that there is something fundamentally wrong with gross inequalities, with gross differences in net welfare. The problem is encountered when people of unequal means must interact, say, when representatives of an impoverished community apply to an elite foundation for funds to support a neighborhood health program. There is no way that real communication can take place between the elites of the foundation and the members of the low-income community. It is not simply that the poor envy the foundation executives or that the executives feel resentful of the poor. Rather, as anyone who has been in such a relationship knows, the sense of community is fractured. Not only do the less well off feel that they cannot express themselves with self-respect, but the elites realize that there is no way the messages they receive can be disentangled from the status and welfare differentials. Neither can engage in any true interaction. A moral relationship is virtually impossible. . . .

THE IMPLICATIONS OF THE EGALITARIAN FORMULA

It turns out that incorporating health care into this system of total welfare will be extremely difficult. Let us begin, temporarily, therefore, by considering a simpler system dealing only with food, clothing, and shelter. Fairness could mean, according to the egalitarian formula, that each person had to have an equal amount of each of these. No reasonable person, however, would find that necessary or attractive. Rather, what the egalitarian has in mind with his concept of justice is that the net of welfare, summed across all three of these goods, be as similar as possible. We could arbitrarily fix the amount of resources in each category, but nothing seems wrong with permitting people to trade some food for clothing, or clothing for shelter. If one person preferred a large house and minimal food and could find someone with the opposite tastes, nothing seems wrong with permitting a trade. The assumption is that the need of people for food, clothing, and shelter is about the same in everybody and that marginal utilities in the trades will be about the same. If so, then permitting people to trade around would increase the welfare of each person without radically distorting the equality of net overall welfare. Up to this point, then, the egalitarian principle of justice says that it is just (though not necessarily right) to strive in social practices for equality of net welfare. . . .

For health care and education, however, the situation is much different. Here it is reasonable to assume that human needs vary enormously. Nothing could be more foolish than to distribute health care or even the money for health care equally. The result would be unequal overall well-being for those who were unfortunate in the natural lottery for health, objectively much worse off than others. If the goal of justice is to produce a chance for equal, objective net welfare, then the starting point for consideration of health care distribution should be the need for it. Education (or the resources to buy education) initially would be distributed in the same way. The amount added to the resources for food, clothing, and shelter should then be in proportion to an "unhealthiness status index" plus another amount proportional to an "educational needs index."

However, that proposal raises two additional questions: Should people be permitted to use the resources set aside for health care in some other way? And who should bear the responsibility if people have an opportunity to be healthy and do not take advantage of it?

Even for the egalitarian it is not obvious why society ought to strive for an equal right to health care. Certainly it ought not to be interested in obtaining the same amount of health care for everyone. To do so would require forcing those in need of great amounts of care to go without or those who have the good fortune to be healthy to consume uselessly. But it is not even obvious that we should end up with a right to health care equal in proportion to need, though that is the conclusion that many, especially egalitarians, are reaching. . . .

Is there any reason to believe that health care is any more basic than, say, food or protection from the elements? All are absolutely essential to human survival, at least up to some minimum for subsistence. All are necessary conditions for the exercise of liberty, self-respect, or any other functioning as part of the human moral community. Furthermore, while the bare minimum of health care is as necessary as food and shelter, in all cases these may not really be "necessities" at the margin. If trades are to be tolerated between marginal food and clothing, is there any reason why someone placing relatively low value on health care should not be permitted to trade, say, his annual checkups for someone else's monthly allotment of steak dinners? Or, if we shall make trading easier by distributing money fairly rather than distributing rations of these specific goods, is there any reason why, based on an "unhealthiness index," we could not distribute a fair portion of funds for health care as well as for other necessities? Individuals could then buy the health care (or health care insurance) that they need, employing individual discretion about where their limit for health care is in comparison with steak dinners. Those at a high health risk would be charged high amounts for health care (or high premiums for insurance), but those costs would be exactly offset by the money supplement based on the index.

Perhaps we cannot make a case for equal access to health care on the basis that it is more fundamental than other goods. There may still be reasons, though, why reasonable people would structure the basic institutions of society to provide a right to equal health care in the sense I am using the term, that is a right equal in proportion to need.

Our response will depend somewhat upon whether we are planning a health care distribution for a just world or one with the present inequities in the distribution of net welfare. . . .

But obviously we do not live in a perfectly just world. The problem becomes more complex. How do we arrange the health care system, which all would agree is fundamental to human well-being at least at some basic level, in order to get as close as possible to equality of welfare as the outcome? Pragmatic considerations may, at this point, override the abstract, theoretical argument allowing trades of health care for other goods even at the margin.

Often defenders of free-market and partial free-market solutions to the allocation of health care resources assume that if fixed in-kind services such as health care are not distributed, money will be. . . .

There is a more subtle case for an equal right to health care (in proportion to need) in an unfair world. Bargaining strengths are likely to be very unequal in a world where resources are distributed unfairly. Those with great resources, perhaps because of natural talents or naturally occurring good health or both, are in an invincible position. The needy, for example those with little earning power because of congenital health problems, may be forced to use what resources they have in order to buy immediate necessities, withholding on health care investment; particularly preventive health care and health insurance, while gambling that they will be able to survive without those services.

It is not clear what our moral response should be to those forced into this position of bargainers from weakness. If the just principle of distribution were Pareto optimality (where bargains were acceptable, regardless of the weaknesses of the parties, provided all gained in the transaction), we would accept the fact that some would bargain from weakness and be forced to trade their long-term health care needs for short-term necessities. If the principle of justice that reasonable people would accept taking the moral point of view, however, is something like the maximin position or the egalitarian position, then perhaps such trades of health care should be prohibited. The answer will depend on how one should behave in planning social policies in an unjust world. The fact that resources are not distributed fairly generates pressures on the least well off (assuming they act rationally) to make choices they would not have to make in a more fair world. If unfairness in the general distribution of resources is a given, we are forced into a choice between two unattractive options: We could opt for the rule that will permit the least well off to maximize their position under the existing conditions or we could pick the rule that would arrange resources as closely as possible to the way they would be arranged in a just world. In our present, unjust society distributing health care equally is a closer approximation to the way it would be distributed in a just society than giving a general resource like money or permitting trades. . . .

I see justice not just as a way to efficiently improve the lot of the least well off by permitting them trades (even though those trades end up increasing the gap between the haves and the have-nots). That might be efficient and might preserve autonomy, but it would not be justice. If I were an original contractor I would cast my vote in favor of the egalitarian principle of justice, applying it so that there would be a right to health care equal in proportion to health care need. The principle of justice for health care could, then, be stated as follows: People have a right to needed health care to provide an opportunity for a level of health equal as far as possible to the health of other people.

The principle of justice for health care is a pragmatic derivative from the general principle of justice requiring equality of objective net welfare. The result would be a uniform health care system with one class of service available for all. Practical problems would still exist, especially at the margins. The principle, for example, does not establish what percentage of total resources would go for health care. The goal would be to arrange resources so that health care needs would, in general, be met about as well as other needs. This means that a society would rather arbitrarily set some fixed amount of the total resources for health care. Every nation currently spends somewhere between five and ten percent of its gross national product (GNP) in this area, with the wealthier societies opting for the higher percentages. Presumably the arbitrary choice would fall in that range.

With such a budget fixed, reasonable people will come together to decide what health care services can be covered under it. The task will not be as great as it seems. The vast majority of services will easily be sorted into or out of the health care system. Only a small percentage at the margin will be the cause of any real debate. The choice will at times be arbitrary, but the standard applied will at least be clear. People should have services necessary to give them a chance to be as close as possible to being as healthy as other people. Those choices will be made while striving to emulate the position of original contractors taking the moral point of view. The decision-making panels will not differ in task greatly from the decision makers who currently sort health care services in and out of insurance coverage lists. However, panels will be committed to a principle of justice and will take the moral point of view, whereas the self-interested insurers try to maximize profits or efficiency or a bargaining position against weak, unorganized consumers.

NOTES

1. Kurt Baier, *The Moral Point of View: A Rational Basis of Ethics* (New York: Random House, 1965), p. 108.

2. John Rawls, *A Theory of Justice* (Cambridge, Mass.: Harvard University Press, 1971).

3. Ibid., p. 18.

4. Ibid., p. 12; cf. pp. 136–42.

5. Brian Barry, *The Liberal Theory of Justice: A Critical Examination of the Principal Doctrines in "A Theory of Justice" by John Rawls* (Oxford: Clarendon Press, 1973), p. 109; see also Robert L. Cunningham, "Justice: Efficiency or Fairness?" *Personalist* 52 (Spring 1971): 253–81.

6. Barry, *The Liberal Theory;* idem. "Reflections on 'Justice as Fairness,'" in Justice and Equality, ed. H. Bedau (Englewood Cliffs, N.J.: Prentice-Hall, 1971), pp. 103–115; Bernard Williams, "The Idea of Equality," reprinted in Bedau, *Justice and Equality,* pp. 116–137; Christopher Ake, "Justice as Equality," *Philosophy and Public Affairs* 5 (Fall 1975): 69–89; Robert M. Veatch, "What Is 'Just' Health Care Delivery?" in *Ethics and Health Policy,* ed. R. M. Veatch and R. Branson (Cambridge, Mass.: Ballinger, 1976), pp. 127–153.

7. Barry, "Reflections," p. 113.

8. See Ake, "Justice as Equality," for a careful development of the notion.

9. Hugo A. Bedau, "Radical Egalitarianism," in *Justice and Equality,* ed. H. A. Bedau, p. 168.

10. Rawls, *A Theory of Justice,* p. 538, note 9.

11. Sigmund Freud, *Group Psychology and the Analysis of the Ego,* rev. ed., trans. James Strachey (London: Hogarth Press, 1959), pp. 51f. (as cited in Rawls, *A Theory of Justice,* p. 439).

ALLEN E. BUCHANAN

The Right to a Decent Minimum of Health Care

Allen Buchanan is professor of philosophy at Duke University. He publishes mainly in bioethics and political philosophy and currently serves as a member of the Advisory Council for the Human Genome Research Institute on goals and funding priorities for genomic research. Among his books are *Ethics, Efficiency, and the Market* (1985) and (with Dan Brock) *Deciding for Others: The Ethics of Surrogate Decision Making* (1989).

THE ASSUMPTION THAT THERE IS A RIGHT TO A DECENT MINIMUM

A consensus that there is (at least) a right to a decent minimum of health care pervades recent policy debates and much of the philosophical literature on health care. Disagreement centers on two issues. Is there a more extensive right than the right to a decent minimum of health care? What is included in the decent minimum to which there is a right?

PRELIMINARY CLARIFICATION OF THE CONCEPT

Different theories of distributive justice may yield different answers both to the question "Is there a right to a decent minimum?" and to the question "What comprises the decent minimum?" The justification a particular theory provides for the claim that there is a right to a decent minimum must at least cohere with the justifications it provides for other right-claims. Moreover, the character of this justification will determine, at least in part, the way in which the decent minimum is specified, since it will include an account of the nature and significance of health-care needs. To the extent that the concept of a decent minimum is theory-dependent, then, it would be naive to assume that a mere analysis of the concept of a decent minimum would tell us whether there is such a right and what its content is. Nonetheless, before we proceed to an examination of various theoretical attempts to ground and specify a right to a decent minimum, a preliminary analysis will be helpful.

From President's Commission, *Securing Access to Health Care,* vol. 2. Washington, DC: U.S. Government Printing Office, 1983.

Sometimes the notion of a decent minimum is applied not to health care but to health itself, the claim being that everyone is entitled to some minimal level, or welfare floor, of health. I shall not explore this variant of the decent minimum idea because I think its implausibility is obvious. The main difficulty is that assuring any significant level of health for all is simply not within the domain of social control. If the alleged right is understood instead as the right to everything which can be done to achieve some significant level of health for all, then the claim that there is such a right becomes implausible simply because it ignores the fact that in circumstances of scarcity the total social expenditure on health must be constrained by the need to allocate resources for other goods.

Though the concept of a right is complex and controversial, for our purposes a partial sketch will do. To say that person A has a right to something, X, is first of all to say that A is entitled to X, that X is due to him or her. This is not equivalent to saying that if A were granted X it would be a good thing, even a morally good thing, or that X is desired by or desirable for A. Second, it is usually held that valid right-claims, at least in the case of basic rights, may be backed by sanctions, including coercion if necessary (unless doing so would produce extremely great disutility or grave moral evil), and that (except in such highly exceptional circumstances) failure of an appropriate authority to apply the needed sanctions is itself an injustice. Recent rights-theorists have also emphasized a third feature of rights, or at least of basic rights or rights in the strict sense: valid right-claims "trump" appeals to what would maximize utility, whether it be the utility of the right-holder, or social utility. In other words, if A has a right to X, then the mere fact that infringing A's right would maximize overall utility or even A's utility is not itself a sufficient reason for infringing it.[1] Finally, a universal (or general) right is one which applies to all persons, not just to certain individuals or classes because of their involvement in special actions, relationships, or agreements.

The second feature—enforceability—is of crucial importance for those who assume or argue that there is a universal right to a decent minimum of health care. For, once it is granted that there is such a right and that such a right may be enforced (absent any extremely weighty reason against enforcement), the claim that there is a universal right provides the moral basis for using the coercive power of the state to assure a decent minimum for all. Indeed, the surprising absence of attempts to justify a coercively backed decent minimum policy by arguments that do *not* aim at establishing a universal right suggests the following hypothesis: advocates of a coercively backed decent minimum have operated on the assumption that such a policy must be based on a universal right to a decent minimum. The chief aim of this article is to show that this assumption is false.

I think it is fair to say that many who confidently assume there is a (universal) right to a decent minimum of health care have failed to appreciate the significance of the first feature of our sketch of the concept of a right. It is crucial to observe that the claim that there is a right to a decent minimum is much stronger than the claim that everyone *ought* to have access to such a minimum, or that if they did it would be a good thing, or that any society which is capable, without great sacrifice, of providing a decent minimum but fails to do so is deeply morally defective. None of the latter assertions implies the existence of a right, if this is understood as a moral entitlement which ought to be established by the coercive power of the state if necessary. . . .

THE ATTRACTIONS OF THE IDEA OF A DECENT MINIMUM

There are at least three features widely associated with the idea of a right to a decent minimum which, together with the facile consensus that vagueness promotes, help explain its popularity over competing conceptions of the right to health care. First, it is usually, and quite reasonably, assumed that the idea of a decent minimum is to be understood in a society-relative sense. Surely it is plausible to assume that, as with other rights to goods or services, the content of the right must depend upon the resources available in a given society and perhaps also upon a certain consensus of expectations among its members. So the first advantage of the idea of a decent minimum, as it is usually understood, is that it allows us to adjust the level of services to be provided as a matter of right to relevant social conditions and also allows for the possibility that as a society becomes more affluent the floor provided by the decent minimum should be raised.

Second, the idea of a decent minimum avoids the excesses of what has been called the strong equal access principle, while still acknowledging a substantive universal right. According to the strong equal access principle, everyone has an equal right to the best health-care services available. Aside from the weakness of the justifications offered in support of it, the most implausible feature of the strong equal access principle is that it forces us to choose between two unpalatable alternatives. We can either set the publicly guaranteed level of health care lower than the level that is technically possible or we can set it as high as is technically possible. In the former case, we shall be committed to the uncomfortable conclusion that no matter how many resources have been expended to guarantee equal access to that level, individuals are forbidden to spend any of their resources for services not available to all. Granted that individuals are allowed to spend their after-tax incomes on more frivolous items, why shouldn't they be allowed to spend it on health? If the answer is that they should be so allowed, as long as this does not interfere with the provision of an adequate package of health-care services for everyone, then we have retreated from the strong equal access principle to something very like the principle of a decent minimum. If, on the other hand, we set the level of services guaranteed for all so high as to eliminate the problem of persons seeking extra care beyond this level, this would produce a huge drain on total resources, foreclosing opportunities for producing important goods other than health care.

So both the recognition that health care must compete with other goods and the conviction that beyond some less than maximal level of publicly guaranteed services individuals should be free to purchase additional services point toward a more limited right than the strong access principle asserts. Thus, the endorsement of a right to a decent minimum may be more of a recognition of the implausibility of the stronger right to equal access than a sign of any definite position on the content of the right to health care.

A third attraction of the idea of a decent minimum is that since the right to health care must be limited in scope (to avoid the consequences of a strong equal access right), it should be limited to the "most basic" services, those normally "adequate" for health, or for a "decent" or "tolerable" life. However, although this aspect of the idea of a decent minimum is useful because it calls attention to the fact that health-care needs are heterogeneous and must be assigned some order of priority, it does not itself provide any basis for determining which are most important.

THE NEED FOR A SUPPORTING THEORY

In spite of these attractions, the concept of a right to a decent minimum of health care is inadequate as a moral basis for a coercively backed decent minimum policy in the absence of a coherent and defensible theory of justice. Indeed, when taken together they do not even imply that there is a right to a decent minimum. Rather, they only support the weaker conditional claim that if there is a right to health care, then it is one that is more limited than a right of strong equal access, and is one whose content depends upon available resources and some scheme of priorities which shows certain health services to be more basic than others. It appears, then, that a theoretical grounding for the right to a decent minimum of health care is indispensable. . . .

My suggestion is that the combined weight of arguments from special (as opposed to universal) rights to health care, harm-prevention, prudential arguments of the sort used to justify public health measures, and two arguments that show that effective charity shares features of public goods (in the technical sense) is sufficient to do the work of an alleged universal right to a decent minimum of health care.

ARGUMENTS FROM SPECIAL RIGHTS

The right-claim we have been examining (and find unsupported) has been a *universal* right-claim: one that attributes the same right to all persons. *Special* right-claims, in contrast, restrict the right in question to certain individuals or groups.

There are at least three types of arguments that can be given for special rights to health care. First, there are arguments from the requirements of rectifying past or present institutional injustices. It can be argued, for example, that American blacks and native Americans are entitled to a certain core set of health-care services owing to their history of unjust treatment by government or other social institutions, on the grounds that these injustices have directly or indirectly had detrimental effects on the health of the groups in question. Second, there are arguments from the requirements of compensation to those who have suffered unjust harm or who have been unjustly exposed to health risks by the assignable actions of private individuals or corporations—for instance, those who have suffered neurological damage from the effects of chemical pollutants.

Third, a strong moral case can be made for special rights to health care for those who have undergone exceptional sacrifices for the good of society as a whole—in particular those whose health has been adversely affected through military service. The most obvious candidates for such compensatory special rights are soldiers wounded in combat.

ARGUMENTS FROM THE PREVENTION OF HARM

The content of the right to a decent minimum is typically understood as being more extensive than those traditional public health services that are usually justified on the grounds that they are required to protect the citizenry from certain harms arising from the interactions of persons living together in large numbers. Yet such services have been a major factor—if not *the* major factor—in reducing morbidity and mortality rates. Examples include sanitation and immunization. The moral justification of such measures, which constitute an important element in a decent minimum of health care, rests upon the widely accepted Harm (Prevention) Principle, not upon a right to health care.

The Harm Prevention argument for traditional public health services, however, may be elaborated in a way that brings them closer to arguments for a universal right to health care. With some plausibility one might contend that once the case has been made for expending public resources on public health measures, there is a moral (and perhaps Constitutional) obligation to achieve some standard of *equal protection* from the harms these measures are designed to prevent. Such an argument, if it could be made out, would imply that the availability of basic public health services should not vary greatly across different racial, ethnic, or geographic groups within the country.

PRUDENTIAL ARGUMENTS

Prudent arguments for health-care services typically emphasize benefits rather than the prevention of harm. It has often been argued, in particular, that the availability of certain basic forms of health care make for a more productive labor force or improve the fitness of the citizenry for national defense. This type of argument, too, does not assume that individuals have moral rights (whether special or universal) to the services in question.

It seems very likely that the combined scope of the various special health-care rights discussed above, when taken together with harm prevention and prudential arguments for basic health services and an argument from equal protection through public health measures, would do a great deal toward satisfying the health-care needs which those who advocate a universal right to a decent minimum are most concerned about. In other words, once the strength of a more pluralistic approach is appreciated, we may come to question the popular dogma that policy initiatives designed to achieve a decent minimum of health care for all must be grounded in a universal moral right to a decent minimum. This suggestion is worth considering because it again brings home the importance of the methodological difficulty encountered earlier. Even if, for instance, there is wide consensus on the considered judgment that the lower health prospects of inner city blacks are not only morally unacceptable but an injustice, it does not follow that this injustice consists of the infringement of a universal right to a decent minimum of health care. Instead, the injustice might lie in the failure to rectify past injustices or in the failure to achieve public health arrangements that meet a reasonable standard of equal protection for all.

TWO ARGUMENTS FOR ENFORCED BENEFICENCE

The pluralistic moral case for a legal entitlement to a decent minimum of health care (in the absence of a universal moral right) may be strengthened further by nonrights-based arguments from the principle of beneficence.[2] The possibility of making out such arguments depends upon the assumption that some principles may be justifiably enforced even if they are not principles specifying valid right-claims. There is at least one widely recognized class of such principles requiring contribution to the production of "public goods" in the technical sense (for example, tax laws requiring contribution to national defense). It is characteristic of public goods that each individual has an incentive to withhold his contribution to the collective goal even though the net result is that the goal will not be achieved. Enforcement of a principle requiring all individuals to contribute to the goal is necessary to overcome the individual's incentive to withhold contribution by imposing penalties for his own failure to contribute and by assuring him that others will contribute. There is a special subclass of principles whose enforcement is justified not only by the need to overcome the individual's incentive to withhold compliance with the principle but also to ensure that individuals' efforts are appropriately *coordinated.* For example, enforcing the rule of the road to drive only on the right not only ensures a joint effort toward the goal of safe driving but also coordinates individuals' efforts so as to make the attainment of that goal possible. Indeed, in the case of the 'rule of the road' a certain kind of coordinated joint effort is the public good whose attainment justifies enforcement. But regardless of whether the production of a public good requires the solution of a coordination problem or not, there may be no *right* that is the correlative of the coercively backed obligation specified by the principle. There are two arguments for enforced beneficence, and they each depend upon both the idea of coordination and on certain aspects of the concept of a public good.

Both arguments begin with an assumption reasonable libertarians accept: there is a basic moral obligation of charity or beneficence to those in need. In a society that has the resources and technical knowledge to improve health or at least to ameliorate important health defects, the application of this requirement of beneficence includes the provision of resources for at least certain forms of health care. If we are sincere, we will be concerned with the efficacy of our charitable or beneficent impulses. It is all well and good for the libertarian to say that voluntary giving *can* replace the existing array of government entitlement programs, but this *possibility* will be cold comfort to the needy if, for any of several reasons, voluntary giving falters.

Social critics on the left often argue that in a highly competitive acquisitive society such as ours it is naive to think that the sense of beneficence will win out over the urgent promptings of self-interest. One need not argue, however, that voluntary giving fails from weakness of the will. Instead one can argue that even if each individual recognizes a moral duty to contribute to the aid of others and is motivationally capable of acting on that duty, some important forms of beneficence will not be forthcoming because each individual will rationally conclude that he should not contribute.

Many important forms of health care, especially those involving large-scale capital investment for technology, cannot be provided except through the contributions of large numbers of persons. This is also true of the most important forms of medical research. But if so, then the beneficent individual will not be able to act effectively, in isolation. What is needed is a coordinated joint effort.

First argument. There are many ways in which I might help others in need. Granted the importance of health, providing a decent minimum of health care for all, through large-scale collective efforts, will be a more important form of beneficence than the various charitable acts A, B, and C, which I might perform *independently,* that is, whose success does not depend upon the contributions of others. Nonetheless, if I am rationally beneficent I will reason as follows: either enough others will contribute to the decent minimum project to achieve this goal, even if I do not contribute to it; or not enough others will contribute to achieve a decent minimum, even if I do contribute. In either case, my contribution will be wasted. In other words, granted the scale of the investment required and the virtually negligible size of my own contribution, I can disregard the minute possibility that my contribution might make the difference between success and failure. But if so, then the rationally beneficent thing for me to do is not to waste my contribution on the project of ensuring a decent minimum but instead to undertake an independent act of beneficence; A, B, or C—where I know my efforts will be needed and efficacious. But if everyone, or even many people, reason in this way, then what we each recognize as the most effective form of beneficence will not come about. Enforcement of a principle requiring contributions to ensuring a decent minimum is needed.

The first argument is of the same form as standard public goods arguments for enforced contributions to national defense, energy conservation, and many other goods, with this exception. In standard public goods arguments, it is usually assumed that the individual's incentive for not contributing is self-interest and that it is in his interest not to contribute because he will be able to partake of the good, if it is produced, even if he does not contribute. In the case at hand, however, the individual's incentive for not contributing to the joint effort is not self-interest, but rather his desire to maximize the good he can do for others with a given amount of his resources. Thus if he contributes but the goal of achieving a decent minimum for all would have been achieved without his contribution, then he has still failed to use his resources in a maximally beneficent way relative to the options of either contributing or not to the joint project, even though the goal of achieving a decent minimum is attained. The rationally beneficent thing to do, then, is not to contribute, even though the result of everyone's acting in a rationally beneficent way will be a relatively ineffective patchwork of small-scale individual acts of beneficence rather than a large-scale, coordinated effort.

Second argument. I believe that ensuring a decent minimum of health care for all is more important than projects A, B, or C, and I am willing to contribute to the decent minimum project, but only if I have assurance that enough others will contribute to achieve the threshold of investment necessary for success. Unless I have this assurance, I will conclude that it is less than rational—and perhaps even morally irresponsible—to contribute my resources to the decent minimum project. For my contribution will be wasted if not enough others contribute. If I lack assurance of sufficient contributions by others, the rationally beneficent thing for me to do is to expend my "beneficence budget" on some less-than-optimal project A, B, or C, whose success does not depend on the contribution of others. But without enforcement, I cannot be assured that enough others will contribute, and if others reason as I do, then what we all believe to be the most effective form of beneficence will not be forthcoming. Others may fail to contribute either because the promptings of self-interest overpower their sense of beneficence, or because they reason as I did in the First Argument, or for some other reason.

Both arguments conclude that an enforced decent minimum principle is needed to achieve coordinated joint effort. However, there is this difference. The Second Argument focuses on the *assurance problem,* while the first does not. In the Second Argument all that is needed is the assumption that rational beneficence requires assurance that enough others will contribute. In the First Argument the individual's reason for not contributing is not that he lacks assurance that enough others will contribute, but rather that it is better for him not to contribute regardless of whether others do or not.

Neither argument depends on an assumption of conflict between the individual's moral motivation of beneficence and his inclination of self-interest. Instead the difficulty is that in the absence of enforcement, individuals who strive to make their beneficence most effective will thereby fail to benefit the needy as much as they might.

A standard response to those paradoxes of rationality known as public goods problems is to introduce a coercive mechanism which attaches penalties to noncontribution and thereby provides each individual with the assurance that enough others will reciprocate so that his contribution will not be wasted and an effective incentive for him to contribute even if he has reason to believe that enough others will contribute to achieve the goal without his contribution. My suggestion is that the same type of argument that is widely accepted as a justification for enforced principles requiring contributions toward familiar public goods provides support for a coercively backed principle specifying a certain list of health programs for the needy and requiring those who possess the needed resources to contribute to the establishment of such programs, even if the needy have no *right* to the services those programs provide. Such an arrangement would serve a dual function: it would coordinate charitable efforts by focusing them on one set of services among the indefinitely large constellation of possible expressions of beneficence, and it would ensure that the decision to allocate resources to these services will become effective. . . .

NOTES

1. Ronald Dworkin, *Taking Rights Seriously* (Cambridge, MA: Harvard University Press, 1977), pp. 184–205.

2. For an exploration of various arguments for a duty of beneficence and an examination of the relationship between justice and beneficence, in general and in health care, see Allen E. Buchanan, "Philosophical Foundations of Beneficence," *Beneficence and Health Care,* ed. Earl E. Shelp (Dordrecht, Holland: Reidel Publishing Co., 1982).

H. TRISTRAM ENGELHARDT, JR.

Rights to Health Care, Social Justice, and Fairness in Health Care Allocations: Frustrations in the Face of Finitude

H. Tristram Engelhardt, Jr., is a professor of bioethics, medicine, and community medicine at the Baylor College of Medicine. His areas of scholarship are bioethics, philosophy of medicine, and continental philosophy. Among his books are *Foundations of Bioethics* (Oxford) and *Bioethics and Secular Humanism* (Trinity Press International).

The imposition of a single-tier, all-encompassing health care system is morally unjustifiable. It is a coercive act of totalitarian ideological zeal, which fails to recognize the diversity of moral visions that frame interests in health care, the secular moral limits of state authority, and the authority of individuals over themselves and their own property. It is an act of secular immorality.

A basic human secular moral right to health care does not exist—not even to a "decent minimum of health care." Such rights must be created.

The difficulty with supposed right to health care, as well as with many claims regarding justice or fairness in access to health care, should be apparent. Since the secular moral authority for common action is derived from permission or consent, it is difficult (indeed, for a large-scale society, materially impossi-

From *Foundations of Bioethics,* 2d ed., by H. Tristram Engelhardt, Jr. Reprinted by permission of Oxford University Press, 1996.

ble) to gain moral legitimacy for the thoroughgoing imposition on health care of one among the many views of beneficence and justice. There are, after all, as many accounts of beneficence, justice, and fairness as there are major religions.

Most significantly, there is a tension between the foundations of general secular morality and the various particular positive claims founded in particular visions of beneficence and justice. It is materially impossible both to respect the freedom of all and to achieve their long-range best interests. . . .

Rights to health care constitute claims on services and goods. Unlike rights to forbearance, which require others to refrain from interfering, which show the unity of the authority to use others, rights to beneficence are rights grounded in particular theories or accounts of the good. For general authority, they require others to participate actively in a particular understanding of the good life or justice. Without an appeal to the principle of permission, to advance such rights is to claim that one may press others into labor or confiscate their property. Rights to health care, unless they are derived from special contractual agreements, depend on particular understandings of beneficence rather than on authorizing permission. They may therefore conflict with the decisions of individuals who may not wish to participate in, and may indeed be morally opposed to, realizing a particular system of health care. Individuals always have the secular moral authority to use their own resources in ways that collide with fashionable understandings of justice or the prevailing consensus regarding fairness.

HEALTH CARE POLICY: THE IDEOLOGY OF EQUAL, OPTIMAL CARE

It is fashionable to affirm an impossible commitment in health care delivery, as, for example, in the following four widely embraced health care policy goals, which are at loggerheads:

1. The best possible care is to be provided for all.
2. Equal care should be guaranteed.
3. Freedom of choice on the part of health care provider and consumer should be maintained.
4. Health care costs are to be contained.

One cannot provide the best possible health care for all and contain health care costs. One cannot provide equal health care for all and respect the freedom of individuals peaceably to pursue with others their own visions of health care or to use their own resources and energies as they decide. For that matter, one cannot maintain freedom in the choice of health care services while containing the costs of health care. One may also not be able to provide all with equal health care that is at the same time the very best care because of limits on the resources themselves. That few openly address these foundational moral tensions at the roots of contemporary health care policy suggests that the problems are shrouded in a collective illusion, a false consciousness, an established ideology within which certain facts are politically unacceptable.

These difficulties spring not only from a conflict between freedom and beneficence, but from a tension among competing views of what it means to pursue and achieve the good in health care (e.g., is it more important to provide equal care to all or the best possible health care to the least-well-off class?). . . .

Only a prevailing collective illusion can account for the assumption in U.S. policy that health care may be provided (1) while containing costs (2) without setting a price on saving lives and preventing suffering when using communal funds and at the same time (3) ignoring the morally unavoidable inequalities due to private resources and human freedom. This false consciousness shaped the deceptions central to the Clinton health care proposal, as it was introduced in 1994. It was advanced to support a health care system purportedly able to provide all with (1) the best of care and (2) equal care, while achieving (3) cost containment, and still (4) allowing those who wish the liberty to purchase fee-for-service health care.[1] While not acknowledging the presence of rationing, the proposal required silent rationing in order to contain costs by limiting access to high-cost, low-yield treatments that a National Health Board would exclude from the "guaranteed benefit package."[2] In addition, it advanced mechanisms to slow technological innovation so as further to reduce the visibility of rationing choices.[3] One does not have to ration that which is not available. There has been a failure to acknowledge the moral inevitability of inequalities in health care due to the limits of secular governmental authority, human freedom, and the existence of private property, however little that may be. There was also the failure to acknowledge the need to ration health care within communal programs if costs are to be contained. It has been ideologically unacceptable to recognize these circumstances. . . .

JUSTICE, FREEDOM, AND INEQUALITY

Interests in justice as beneficence are motivated in part by inequalities and in part by needs. That some have so little while others have so much properly evokes moral concerns of beneficence. Still, . . . the moral authority to use force to set such inequalities aside is limited. These limitations are in part due to the circumstance that the resources one could use to aid those in need are already owned by other people. One must establish whether and when inequalities and needs generate rights or claims against others.

THE NATURAL AND SOCIAL LOTTERIES

"Natural lottery" is used to identify changes in fortune that result from natural forces, not directly from the actions of persons. The natural lottery shapes the distribution of both naturally and socially conditioned assets. The natural lottery contrasts with the social lottery, which is used to identify changes in fortune that are not the result of natural forces but the actions of persons. The social lottery shapes the distribution of social and natural assets. The natural and social lotteries, along with one's own free decisions, determine the distribution of natural and social assets. The social lottery is termed a lottery, though it is the outcome of personal actions, because of the complex and unpredictable interplay of personal choices and because of the unpredictable character of the outcomes, which do not conform to an ideal pattern, and because the outcomes are the results of social forces, not the immediate choices of those subject to them.

All individuals are exposed to the vicissitudes of nature. Some are born healthy and by luck remain so for a long life, free of disease and major suffering. Others are born with serious congenital or genetic diseases, others contract serious crippling fatal illnesses early in life, and yet others are injured and maimed. Those who win the natural lottery will for most of their lives not be in need of medical care. They will live full lives and die painless and peaceful deaths. Those who lost the natural lottery will be in need of health care to blunt their sufferings and, where possible, to cure their diseases and to restore function. There will be a spectrum of losses, ranging from minor problems such as having teeth with cavities to major tragedies such as developing childhood leukemia, inheriting Huntington's chorea, or developing amyelotrophic lateral sclerosis.

These tragic outcomes are the deliverances of nature, for which no one, without some special view of accountability or responsibility, is responsible (unless, that is, one recognizes them as the results of the Fall or as divine chastisements). The circumstance that individuals are injured by hurricanes, storms, and earthquakes is often simply no one's fault. When no one is to blame, no one may be charged with the responsibility of making whole those who lose the natural lottery on the ground of accountability for the harm. One will need an argument dependent on a particular sense of fairness to show that the readers of this volume should submit to the forcible redistribution of their resources to provide health care for those injured by nature. It may very well be unfeeling, unsympathetic, or uncharitable not to provide such help. One may face eternal hellfires for failing to provide aid.[4] But it is another thing to show in general secular moral terms that individuals owe others such help in a way that would morally authorize state force to redistribute their private resources and energies or to constrain their free choices with others. To be in dire need does not by itself create a secular moral right to be rescued from that need. The natural lottery creates inequalities and places individuals at disadvantage without creating a straightforward secular moral obligation on the part of others to aid those in need.

Individuals differ in their resources not simply because of outcomes of the natural lottery, but also due to the actions of others. Some deny themselves immediate pleasures in order to accumulate wealth or to leave inheritances; through a complex web of love, affection, and mutual interest, individuals convey resources, one to another, so that those who are favored prosper and those who are ignored languish. Some as a consequence grow wealthy and others grow poor, not through anyone's malevolent actions or omissions, but simply because they were not favored by the love, friendship, collegiality, and associations through which fortunes develop and individuals prosper. In such cases there will be neither fairness nor unfairness, but simply good and bad fortune.

In addition, some will be advantaged or disadvantaged, made rich, poor, ill, diseased, deformed, or disabled because of the malevolent and blameworthy actions and omissions of others. Such will be unfair circumstances, which just and beneficent states should try to prevent and to rectify through legitimate police protection, forced restitution, and charitable programs. Insofar as an injured party has a claim against an injurer to be made whole, not against society, the outcome is unfortunate from the perspective of society's obligations and obligations of innocent citizens to make restitution. Restitution is owed by the injurer, not society or others. There will be outcomes of the social lottery that are on the one hand blameworthy in the sense of resulting from the culpable actions of others, though on the other hand a society has no obligation to rectify them. The social lottery includes the exposure to the immoral and unjust actions of others. Again, one will need an argument dependent on a particular sense of fairness to show that the readers of this volume should submit to the forcible redistribution of their resources to provide health care to those injured by others.

When individuals come to purchase health care, some who lose the natural lottery will be able at least in part to compensate for those losses through their winnings at the social lottery. They will be able to afford expensive health care needed to restore health and to regain function. On the other hand, those who lose in both the natural and the social lottery will be in need of health care, but without the resources to acquire it.

THE RICH AND THE POOR: DIFFERENCES IN ENTITLEMENTS

If one owns property by virtue of just acquisition or just transfer, then one's title to that property will not be undercut by the tragedies and needs of others. One will simply own one's property. On the other hand, if one owns property because such ownership is justified within a system that ensures a beneficent distribution of goods (e.g., the achievement of the greatest balance of benefits over harms for the greatest number or the greatest advantage for the least-well-off class), one's ownership will be affected by the needs of others. . . . Property is in part privately owned in a strong sense that cannot be undercut by the needs of others. In addition, all have a general right to the fruits of the earth, which constitutes the basis for a form of taxation as rent to provide fungible payments to individuals, whether or not they are in need. Finally, there are likely to be resources held in common by groups that may establish bases for their distribution to meet health care concerns. The first two forms of entitlement or ownership exist unconstrained by medical or other needs. The last form of entitlement or ownership, through the decision of a community, may be conditioned by need.

The existence of any amount of private resources can be the basis for inequalities that secular moral authority may not set aside. Insofar as people own things, they will have a right to them, even if others need them. Because the presence of permission is cardinal, the test of whether one must transfer one's goods to others will not be whether such a redistribution will not prove onerous or excessive for the person subjected to the distribution, but whether the resources belong to that individual. Consider that you may be reading this book next to a person in great need. The test of whether a third person may take resources from you to help that individual in need will not be whether you will suffer from the transfer, but rather whether you have consented—at least this is the case if the principle of permission functions in general secular morality. . . . The principle of permission is the source of authority when moral strangers collaborate, because they do not share a common understanding of fairness or of the good. As a consequence, goal-oriented approaches to the just distribution of resources must be restricted to commonly owned goods, where there is authority to create programs for their use.

Therefore, one must qualify the conclusions of the 1983 American President's Commission for the Study of Ethical Problems that suggest that excessive burdens should determine the amount of tax persons should pay to sustain an adequate level of health care for those in need.[5] Further, one will have strong grounds for morally condemning systems that attempt to impose an all-encompassing health care plan that would require "equality of care [in the sense of avoiding] the creation of a tiered system [by] providing care based only on differences of need, not individual or group characteristics."[6] Those who are rich are always at secular moral liberty to purchase more and better health care.

DRAWING THE LINE BETWEEN THE UNFORTUNATE AND THE UNFAIR

How one regards the moral significance of the natural and social lotteries and the moral force of private ownership will determine how one draws the line between circumstances that are simply unfortunate and those that are unfortunate and in addition unfair in the sense of constituting a claim on the resources of others.

Life in general, and health care in particular, reveal circumstances of enormous tragedy, suffering, and deprivation. The pains and sufferings of illness, disability, and disease, as well as the limitations of deformity, call on the sympathy of all to provide aid and give comfort. Injuries, disabilities, and diseases due to the forces of nature are unfortunate. Injuries, disabilities, and diseases due to the unconsented-to actions of others are unfair. Still, outcomes of the unfair actions of others are not necessarily society's fault and are in this sense unfortunate. The horrible injuries that come every night to the emergency rooms of major hospitals may be someone's fault, even if they are not the fault of society, much less that of uninvolved citizens. Such outcomes, though unfair with regard to the relationship of the injured with the injurer, may be simply unfortunate with respect to society and other citizens (and may licitly be financially exploited). One is thus faced with distinguishing the difficult line between acts of God, as well as immoral acts of individuals that do not constitute a basis for societal retribution on the one hand, and injuries that provide such a basis on the other.

A line must be created between those losses that will be made whole through public funds and those that will not. Such a line was drawn in 1980 by Patricia Harris, the then secretary of the Department of Health, Education, and Welfare, when she ruled that heart transplantations should be considered experimental and therefore not reimbursable through Medicare.[7] To be in need of a heart transplant and not have the funds available would be an unfortunate circumstance but not unfair. One was not eligible for a heart transplant even if another person had intentionally damaged one's heart. From a moral point of view, things would have been different if the federal government had in some culpable fashion injured one's heart. So, too, if promises of treatment had been made. For example, to suffer from appendicitis or pneumonia and not as a qualifying patient receive treatment guaranteed through a particular governmental or private insurance system would be unfair, not simply unfortunate.

Drawing the line between the unfair and the unfortunate is unavoidable because it is impossible in general secular moral terms to translate all needs into rights, into claims against the resources of others. One must with care decide where the line is to be drawn. To distinguish needs from mere desires, one must endorse one among the many competing visions of morality and human flourishing. One is forced to draw a line between those needs (or desires) that constitute claims on the aid of others and those that do not. The line distinguishing unfortunate from unfair circumstances justifies by default certain social and economic inequalities in the sense of determining who, if any one, is obliged in general secular immorality to remedy such circumstances or achieve equality. Is the request of an individual to have life extended through a heart transplant at great cost, and perhaps only for a few years, a desire for an inordinate extension of life? Or is it a need to be secure against a premature death? . . . Outside a particular view of the good life, needs do not create rights to the services or goods of others.[8] Indeed, outside of a particular moral vision there is no canonical means for distinguishing desires from needs.

There is a practical difficulty in regarding major losses at the natural and social lotteries as generating claims to health care: attempts to restore health indefinitely can deplete societal resources in the pursuit of ever-more incremental extensions of life of marginal quality. A relatively limited amount of food and shelter is required to preserve the lives of individuals. But an indefinite amount of resources can in medicine be committed to the further preservation of human life, the marginal postponement of death, and the marginal alleviation of human suffering and disability. Losses at the natural lottery with regard to health can consume major resources with little return. Often one can only purchase a little relief, and that only at great costs. Still, more decisive than the problem of avoiding the possibly overwhelming costs involved in satisfying certain health care desires (e.g., postponing death for a while through the use of critical care) is the problem of selecting the correct content-full account of justice in order canonically to distinguish between needs and desires and to translate needs into rights.

BEYOND EQUALITY: AN EGALITARIANISM OF ALTRUISM VERSUS AN EGALITARIANISM OF ENVY

The equal distribution of health care is itself problematic, a circumstance recognized in *Securing Access to Health Care,* the 1983 report of the President's Commission.[9] The difficulties are multiple:

1. Although in theory, at least, one can envisage providing all with equal levels of decent shelter, one cannot restore all to or preserve all in an equal state of health. Many health needs cannot be satisfied in the same way one can address most needs for food and shelter.
2. If one provided all with the same amount of

funds to purchase health care or the same amount of services, the amount provided would be far too much for some and much too little for others who could have benefited from more investment in treatment and research.

3. If one attempts to provide equal health care in the sense of allowing individuals to select health care only from a predetermined list of available therapies, or through some managed health care plan such as accountable (to the government) health care plans or regional health alliances, which would be provided to all so as to prevent the rich from having access to better health care than the poor, one would have immorally confiscated private property and have restricted the freedom of individuals to join in voluntary relationships and associations.

That some are fortunate in having more resources is neither more nor less arbitrary or unfair than some having better health, better looks, or more talents. In any event, the translation of unfortunate circumstances into unfair circumstances, other than with regard to violations of the principle of permission, requires the imposition of a particular vision of beneficence or justice.

The pursuit of equality faces both moral and practical difficulties. If significant restrictions were placed on the ability to purchase special treatment with one's resources, one would need not only to anticipate that a black market would inevitably develop in health care services, but also acknowledge that such a black market would be a special bastion of liberty and freedom of association justified in general secular moral terms. . . .

CONFLICTING MODELS OF JUSTICE: FROM CONTENT TO PROCEDURE

John Rawls's *A Theory of Justice* and Robert Nozick's *Anarchy, State, and Utopia* offer contrasting understandings of what should count as justice or fairness. They sustain differing suggestions regarding the nature of justice in health care. They provide a contrast between justice as primarily structural, a pattern of distributions that is amenable to rational disclosure, versus justice as primarily procedural, a matter of fair negotiation.[10] In *A Theory of Justice* Rawls forwards an expository device of an ahistorical perspective from which to discover the proper pattern for the distribution of resources, and therefore presumably for the distribution of health care resources. In this understanding, it is assumed that societally based entitlements have moral priority. Nozick, in contrast, advances a historical account of just distributions within which justice depends on what individuals have agreed to do with and for each other. Nozick holds that individually based entitlements are morally prior to societally based entitlements. In contrast with Rawls, who argues that one can discover a proper pattern for the allocation of resources, Nozick argues that such a pattern cannot be discovered and that instead one can only identify the characteristics of a just process for fashioning rights to health care. . . .

The differences between Nozick of *Anarchy, State, and Utopia* and Rawls of *A Theory of Justice* express themselves in different accounts of entitlements and ownership, and in different understandings of non-principled fortune and misfortune. For Rawls, one has justifiable title to goods if such a title is part of a system that ensures the greatest benefit to the least advantaged, consistent with a just-savings principle, and with offices and positions open to all under conditions of fair equality and opportunity, and where each person has an equal right to the most extensive total system of equal basic liberties compatible with a similar system of liberty for all. In contrast, for Nozick, one simply owns things: "Things come into the world already attached to people having entitlements over them."[11] If one really owns things, there will be freedom-based limitations on principles of distributive justice. One may not use people or the property without their permission or authorization. The needs of others will not erase one's property rights. The readers of this book should consider that they may be wearing wedding rings or other jewelry not essential to their lives, which could be sold to buy antibiotics to save identifiable lives in the third world. Those who keep such baubles may in part be acting in agreement with Nozick's account and claiming that "it is my right to keep my wedding ring for myself, even though the proceeds from its sale could save the lives of individuals in dire need."

Nozick's account requires a distinction between someone's secular moral rights and what is right, good, or proper to do. At times, selling some (perhaps all) of one's property to support the health care of those in need will be the right thing to do, even though one has a secular moral right to refuse to sell. This contrast derives from the distinction Nozick makes between *freedom as a side constraint,* as the very condition for the possibility of a secular moral community, and *freedom as one value among others*. This contrast can be understood as a distinction between those claims of justice based on the very possibility of a moral community, versus those claims of justice that turn on interests in particular goods and values, albeit interests recognized in the original position. . . .

This contrast between Rawls and Nozick can be appreciated more generally as a contrast between two quite different principles of justice, each of which has strikingly different implications for the allocation of health care resources.

1. Freedom- or permission-based justice is concerned with distributions of goods made in accord with the notion of the secular moral community as a peaceable social structure binding moral strangers, members of diverse concrete moral communities. Such justice will therefore require the consent of the individuals involved in a historical nexus of justice-regarding institutions understood in conformity with the principle of permission. The principle of beneficence may be pursued only within constraints set by the principle of permission.
2. Goals-based justice is concerned with the achievement of the good of individuals in society, where the pursuit of beneficence is not constrained by a strong principle of permission, but driven by some particular understanding of morality, justice, or fairness. Such justice will vary in substance as one attempts, for example, to (a) give each person an equal share; (b) give each person what that person needs; (c) give each person a distribution as a part of a system designed to achieve the greatest balance of benefits over harms for the greatest number of persons; (d) give each person a distribution as a part of a system designed to maximize the advantage of the least-well-off class with conditions of equal liberty for all and of fair opportunity.

Allocations of health care in accord with freedom- or permission-based justice must occur within the constraint to respect the free choices of persons, including their exercise of their property rights. Allocations of health care in accord with goals-based justice will need to establish what it means to provide a just pattern of health care, and what constitutes true needs, not mere desires, and how to rank the various health goals among themselves and in comparison with non-health goals. Such approaches to justice in health care will require a way of ahistorically discovering the proper pattern for the distribution of resources.

Permission-based and goals-based approaches to justice in health care contrast because they offer competing interpretations of the maxim, "Justitia est constans et perpetua voluntas jus suum cuique tribuens" (Justice is the constant and perpetual will to render everyone his due).[12] A permission-based approach holds that justice is first and foremost giving to each the right to be respected as a free individual as the source of secular moral authority, in the disposition of personal services and private goods: that which is due *(ius)* to individuals is respect of their authority over themselves and their possessions. In contrast, a goals-based approach holds that justice is receiving a share of the goods, which is fair by an appeal to a set of ahistorical criteria specifying what a fair share should be, that is, what share is due to each individual. Since there are various senses of a fair share (e.g., an equal share, a share in accordance with the system that maximizes the balance of benefits over harms, etc.), there will be various competing senses of justice in health care under the rubric of goals-based justice. . . .

THE MORAL INEVITABILITY OF A MULTITIER HEALTH CARE SYSTEM

. . . In the face of unavoidable tragedies and contrary moral intuitions, a multitiered system of health care is in many respects a compromise. On the one hand, it provides some amount of health care for all, while on the other hand allowing those with resources to purchase additional or better services. It can endorse the use of communal resources for the provision of a decent minimal or basic amount of health care for all, while acknowledging the existence of private resources at the disposal of some individuals to purchase better basic as well as luxury care. While the propensity to seek more than equal treatment for oneself or loved ones is made into a vicious disposition in an egalitarian system, a multitier system allows for the expression of individual love and the pursuit of private advantage, though still supporting a general social sympathy for those in need. Whereas an egalitarian system must suppress the widespread human inclination to devote private resources to the purchase of the best care for those whom one loves, a multitier system can recognize a legitimate place for the expression of such inclinations. A multitier system

(1) should support individual providers and consumers against attempts to interfere in their free association and their use of their own resources, though (2) it may allow positive rights to health care to be created for individuals who have not been advantaged by the social lottery.

The serious task is to decide how to define and provide a decent minimum or basic level of care as a floor of support for all members of society, while allowing money and free choice to fashion special tiers of services for the affluent. In addressing this general issue of defining what is to be meant by a decent minimum basic level or a minimum adequate amount of health care, the American President's Commission in 1983 suggested that in great measure content is to be created rather than discovered by democratic processes, as well as by the forces of the market. "In a democracy, the appropriate values to be assigned to the consequences of policies must ultimately be determined by people expressing their values through social and political processes as well as in the marketplace."[13] The Commission, however, also suggested that the concept of adequacy could in part be discovered by an appeal to that amount of care that would meet the standards of sound medical practice. "Adequacy does require that everyone receive care that meets standards of sound medical practice."[14] But what one means by "sound medical practice" is itself dependent on particular understandings within particular cultures. Criteria for sound medical practice are as much created as discovered. The moral inevitability of multiple tiers of care brings with it multiple standards of proper or sound medical practice and undermines the moral plausibility of various obiter dicta concerning the centralized allocation of medical resources. . . .

Concepts of adequate care are not discoverable outside of particular views of the good life and of proper medical practice. In nations encompassing diverse moral communities, an understanding of what one will mean by an adequate level or a decent minimum of health care will need to be fashioned, if it can indeed be agreed to, through open discussion and by fair negotiation. . . .

NOTES

1. The White House Domestic Policy Council, *The President's Health Security Plan* (New York: Times Books, 1993).

2. The White House Domestic Policy Council, *The President's Health Security Plan,* p. 43.

3. Innovation would be discouraged as drug prices are subject to review as reasonable. The White House Domestic Policy Council, *The President's Health Security Plan,* p. 45.

4. In considering how to respond to the plight of the impecunious, one might consider the story Jesus tells of the rich man who fails to give alms to "a certain beggar named Lazarus, full of sores, who was laid at his gate, desiring to be fed with the crumbs which fell from the rich man's table" (Luke 16:20–21). The rich man, who was not forthcoming with alms, was condemned eternally to a hell of excruciating torment.

5. President's Commission for the Study of Ethical Problems in Medicine and Biomedical and Behavioral Research, *Securing Access to Health Care* (Washington, D.C.: U.S. Government Printing Office, 1983), vol. 1, pp. 43–46.

6. The White House Domestic Policy Council, "Ethical Foundations of Health Reform," in *The President's Health Security Plan,* p. 11.

7. H. Newman, "Exclusion of Heart Transplantation Procedures from Medicare Coverage." *Federal Register* 45 (Aug. 6, 1980): 52296. See also H. Newman, "Medicare Program: Solicitation of Hospitals and Medical Centers to Participate in a Study of Heart Transplants," *Federal Register* 46 (Jan. 22, 1981): 7072–75.

8. The reader should understand that the author holds that almsgiving is one of the proper responses to human suffering (in addition to being an appropriate expression of repentance, an act of repentance to which surely the author is obligated). It is just that the author acknowledges the limited secular moral authority of the state to compel charity coercively.

9. President's Commission, *Securing Access to Health Care,* vol. 1, pp. 18–19.

10. John Rawls, *A Theory of Justice* (Cambridge, Mass.: Harvard University Press, 1971), and Robert Nozick, *Anarchy, State, and Utopia* (New York: Basic Books, 1974).

11. Nozick, *Anarchy, State, and Utopia,* p. 160.

12. Flavius Petrus Sabbatius Justinianus, *The Institutes of Justinian,* trans. Thomas C. Sandars (1922; repr. Westport, Conn,: Greenwood Press, 1970), 1.1, p. 5.

13. President's Commission, *Securing Access to Health Care,* vol. 1, p. 37.

14. Ibid.

Managed Care and Access to Care

LAWRENCE O. GOSTIN

Securing Health or Just Health Care? The Effect of the Health Care System on the Health of America

Lawrence Gostin is professor of law at Georgetown University and professor of public health at the Johns Hopkins University. He is also director of the Center for Law and the Public's Health and editor of the Health Law and Ethics section of the *Journal of the American Medical Association.* His latest book is *Public Health Law: Power, Duty, Restraint* (University of California Press and the Milbank Memorial Fund).

. . . Given the emphasis on financial costs and personal burdens, it is not surprising that political debate and academic discourse on health care reform focused so intensely on market structures and the economic effects on major segments of commercial society. Consequently, the linguistics of health care reform was market-oriented: managed competition, small and large insurance markets, employer mandates, tax credits and other market incentives. The overarching concern was the economic impact on the predominate players in the market: large employers, small businesses, insurers, and health care providers.

Manifestly, the effects of reform on the buying and selling of health care as a commodity, and its economic effects on American business (including the business of health care) are weighty concerns. It is not misguided, then, that so much focus was placed on the effects of health care reform on the economy. Yet, it is striking that so little attention was given to a still more fundamental value—the effect of the health care system on the health of individuals and populations. It is my thesis that promotion of the health of the population is the most important objective of health care reform; that reasonable levels of resource allocation are warranted to achieve this purpose; and that the adverse effects on the economy, American business, and citizens are as high, or higher, under the status quo than they would be if government assured universal coverage for health care. . . .

From *Saint Louis University Law Journal* 39, no. 1 (Fall 1994), 7–43. Reprinted by permission.

I. THE PREEMINENCE OF THE VALUE OF HEALTH

. . . In this article, I make no claim to a right to health. The government cannot be expected to take responsibility for assuring the health of each member of the population, and the concept of a right to health is too broad to have legal meaning. Nor do I claim a constitutional right to any level of health care that a person may want. An unfettered constitutional right to health care is not currently tenable. Further, the government could not be expected to respond to all demands and preferences for health care, irrespective of the cost or effectiveness.

My claim is simply that the prevention of disease or disability and the promotion of health, within reasonable resource constraints, provides the preeminent justification for the government to act for the welfare of society. In determining the allocation of resources in society, the transcending public value must be based upon improved health outcomes for the population, based upon objective measures of morbidity and mortality. Despite marked increases in spending for personal medical services and advances in bio-medical technology, the decade 1980–90 showed little improvement in numerous objective health indicators such as maternal and child health, nutrition, sexually transmitted diseases, and occupational health and safety. Health promotion is measured not only by increased longevity or life extension. Rather, health promotion is measured by improvement in the quality of life, "compression" of morbidity and suffering, and extension of active or well-functioning life expectancy.

The very purpose of government is to attain through collective action human goods that individuals acting alone could not realistically achieve. Chief among those human goods is the assurance of the conditions under which people can be healthy. While the government cannot assure health, it can, within the reasonable limits of its resources, organize its activities in ways that best prevent illness and disability, and promote health among its population. . . .

II. THE IMPORTANCE OF UNIVERSAL ACCESS TO HEALTH CARE SERVICES

It is not necessary to demonstrate which is the more fundamental governmental activity—public health or personal medical services. What is important is that both are essential to the health of individuals and populations, and both systems are functioning badly. Consequently, an assessment of the inadequacies in the personal health care system shows many people receiving insufficient and inequitable access to medical services.

Most countries with advanced economies in the world concentrate their resources in one health insurance system that provides universal coverage to their populations.[1] The United States, however, provides a fragmented array of private and public programs that results in a substantial portion of the population without health insurance coverage or with highly inadequate coverage. The American public, while purporting to support universal coverage,[2] appears highly ambivalent about whether health insurance is a social good, of which the costs should be borne collectively, or an economic enterprise that effectively should be governed by market forces.[3]

Whatever vision of health care that the public may prefer, the system itself has become market-oriented. By the nature of markets those who are unable or unwilling to pay the price of the commodity are left out. Not being included in a commodities market that trades in durable goods and services may be justified on economic grounds, but exclusion from the market in health care presents profoundly different considerations.

The number and profile of those who have been left out of the health insurance market, juxtaposed with current national health expenditures, is illuminating. The United States spent approximately $900 billion dollars on health care in 1993.[4] This represented approximately 14% of the nation's gross domestic product.[5] Health care expenditures are expected to reach $1.7 trillion, between 16% and 18% of the gross domestic product, by the end of the decade if effective controls are not instituted.[6]

Despite the inordinate national expenditures on health care, many Americans lack health insurance. At any given time during the last year, approximately 37 to 40 million people were without health insurance,[7] about 15–18% of all children and adults.[8] While different methods of counting the uninsured have allowed critics of health care reform to obfuscate its true dimensions, any dispassionate assessment reveals a considerable and enduring national problem.[9] Thus, while the census reported 33.5 million uninsured in 1992 based on monthly averages, others calculated that 50[10] to 58 million[11] lacked health insurance for at least one month in that year.

It is suggested by market-oriented analysts that the alleged 37 million uninsured is a "big lie"[12] that "wilts under analysis."[13] These analysts claim that the chronically uninsured amount to fewer than 10 million, and that the number of uninsured persons could be reduced dramatically by introducing medical savings accounts.[14] These claims are based on data suggesting that the median spell length of persons without insurance is six months, and that 70% of all spells end within nine months.[15] However, a deeper examination of the pool of uninsured persons demonstrates the intransigence and severity of the problem. At least 28% of all uninsured spells last for more than one year, and 15–18% last more than two years. For over 20 million people in 1993, being without health insurance was not a temporary or transient phase in their lives.[16] Professor Swartz, the scholar who originally reported these insurance data, concludes that the point-in-time estimate of 37 million uninsured actually refers to at least 21 million long-term uninsured plus nearly 16 million with spells lasting less than one year.[17] . . .

The uninsured are not the only persons in the population with difficulties in obtaining access to health care. An additional 20 million people are thought to be underinsured. Under-insurance is a concept that is hard to define or quantify. Persons may have inadequate access to health care because of insufficient overall insurance coverage (e.g., capitations on coverage based on limits on cost or hospital stays);

exemptions for certain conditions (e.g., pre-existing coverage, waiting periods, mental health or childbirth services); or low reimbursement schedules for the payment of physicians, which results in denials of service (e.g., Medicaid patients in certain geographic areas or seeking certain kinds of services). . . .

The demographics of the uninsured population reveal the deep interconnections between the absence of health insurance and socio-economic status, race, and age. The uninsured population is disproportionately poor or near-poor, African-American or Hispanic, young, and unemployed.[18] . . .

There is certainly an inter-connectedness to each of the primary barriers to access—financial, structural, personal and cultural. It is clear, however, that without dismantling financial barriers, access to health care will continue to be highly adequate; the Institute of Medicine recently "reaffirmed that lack of health care coverage is, to a great extent, a good proxy for access."[19]

It is commonly believed that patients without health insurance are not so much denied access, but are diverted to emergency rooms and other public clinics for their care. It is, therefore, important to inquire whether the absence of insurance leads to delayed or insufficient access of such seriousness that it actually affects health outcomes. The data show that lack of access is closely associated not only with underutilization of services but, more importantly, with poorer health outcomes.[20] Although health insurance coverage is not the sole determinant of health status, it is a key factor. . . .

Those who reject the view that health is the foremost objective of a health care system may instead prefer to focus attention to the finance system, administrative efficiency, or a favorable cost-benefit ratio. Health care is only one of many possible goods that government can provide. It is, therefore, not unreasonable to suggest that if health care could be provided more efficiently and less expensively, government could spend on other worthwhile social programs such as housing, poverty, hunger, or education.

As explained previously, the expenditure on health care in the United States represents approximately 14% of the nation's gross domestic product.[21] Health care expenditures are expected to reach $1.7 trillion, between sixteen and eighteen percent of the gross domestic product, by the end of the decade if effective controls are not instituted.[22] These figures stand in stark contrast to the percentage of the gross national product (GNP) that is devoted to health care in countries that offer their citizens virtually universal health coverage such as Canada, Germany, Great Britain, and Japan; these countries devote from 5.8% to 8.7% of their GNP to health care.[23] In 1990, while the United Kingdom, Japan, and Germany spent between $909 and $1,287 on each person for health care, the United States spent $2,566;[24] for every $1 per capita spent in England, the United States spends $3 per capita.[25] The high per capita expenditures on health care in the United States relative to other countries is not all spent on personal care services. It is estimated that 19% to 24% of health care expenditures goes toward administrative expenses, including those of the nation's insurance companies.[26]

In summary, whether the U.S. health care system is measured in terms of infant mortality or life expectancy, utilization rates, or cost effectiveness, it appears to lag well behind other developed countries in North America and Europe.

III. INEQUITABLE ACCESS TO HEALTH CARE

There is another perspective on how to measure the quality of a health care system. All else held constant, it is possible to argue that if health care resources are distributed equitably, the system provides consistent and fair benefits for all citizens. Some may even be willing to sacrifice certain benefits of health care to achieve greater equity. If a society does very well in health outcomes for some of its citizens, say those who are in higher socioeconomic classes and within majority racial populations, and others do very poorly, is that society worth emulating? Under Rawlsian theory, if individuals could not pre-determine whether they would be born into a favored or the disfavored class, most people would choose to be in a country that provides roughly equal access to health care for all classes.[27] . . .

A. SCRUTINY OF THE "EQUITY" PRINCIPLE

Before examining the substantial disparities in access to health care and health status among various classes in the United States, it is necessary to ask two interrelated questions: what ethical values support the claim of equity in the distribution of health services, and what exactly is the equity claim being made? To many, it is not intuitively obvious that equity is a principle that deserves general recognition in society. Americans are prepared to tolerate significant and pervasive inequalities in wealth and in the distribution of most social goods. A theory of equity in health care must provide an account of why health care deserves special treatment, unless the advocate is prepared to defend a considerably broader view of distributive justice for all goods and services.

One theory of equity in health care . . . relies on the special importance of health care in providing a necessary condition for the fulfillment of human opportunity. Professor Daniels observes that pain and disability, limitation of function, and premature loss of life all restrict human opportunities.[28] If it is accepted that a certain level of health services is a precondition to affording human beings reasonable life opportunities, then some equitable access to those services is warranted.

Government is prepared to provide a public education to all children of school age. Access to education is presumably justified by the importance of education in furnishing fair opportunities for all children, irrespective of their social or economic class. Like education, a certain level of health care is essential to a person's ability to pursue life's opportunities on some roughly equitable basis. Health care, at least in some fundamental ways, is as important to equal opportunity as education. While health care does not provide opportunities by facilitating basic knowledge and skill, it does so by enabling the person to function mentally and physically in the application of that knowledge and skill.

More equitable access to health care is supported by collective, as well as individual goods. Health care does not only enable individuals to gain life opportunities for themselves, it also allows individuals to contribute to society. A healthy population, like an educated population, is much more likely to be socially and economically productive, and less dependent. A multi-tiered system of health care, in which those in the lower tiers receive clearly inferior and lower-quality services, perpetuates inequalities among individuals and groups. These inequalities occur not only in attaining health but, indirectly, in attaining status, acceptance, and livelihood in society. As various inequalities among individuals and groups expand, society must deal with the consequences of social unrest, alienation, and dissatisfaction. Strikingly disparate standards of health care for different social, economic and racial groups, then, is unjust for individuals who lose indispensable life opportunities and harmful for society generally which loses much productive activity and risks greater disaffection among major segments of the population.

Professor Daniels makes the following claim to equity in health care: "*if* an acceptable theory of justice includes a principle providing for fair equality of opportunity, then health care institutions should be among those governed by it."[29] But to suggest that health care institutions ought to be governed by the principle of fair equality of opportunity, is not the same as stating precisely the claim being made. For reasons explained earlier, no claim to health, let alone equal health, is feasible since the vast variabilities in health are to a great extent biologically, socially, and behaviorally determined. Nor do I make a claim for *equal* health care or even equal access to health care. Such a claim would not only require a fundamental redistribution of health care resources, but also would require restrictions on discretionary spending. Very few health care systems in developed countries restrict access to private health insurers, providers, and technology for people who can afford them, irrespective of the fact that these amenities are effectively inaccessible to the poor or near poor. Even in education, families are not restricted in their access to private educational opportunities of many kinds that are of better quality than public education. Nor is public education itself equal in quality, but is often superior in more affluent neighborhoods.

Rather than defending the broad re-distributive agenda implied in the principle of *equality* so that health care must be the same, I urge the modest claim of greater *equity,* so that health care is distributed more fairly. I do not even expect society to achieve anywhere near complete equity in the sense that health care is distributed in a totally impartial or unbiased way. But it is reasonable to expect society to set a goal of a more equitable system by reducing inordinately wide disparities in health care. The claim of equitable or fair access applies especially to those health services that most effectively help prevent illness, disease, disability, and premature death, and which best care for and treat persons in ill-health.

B. DISPARITIES IN ACCESS TO HEALTH CARE AMONG POPULATIONS

Access to health care is measured by the use of health services, the quality of those services, and health outcomes. The test of equity involves a determination of whether there are systematic differences in access, and whether these differences result from financial or other barriers to health care. Using these objective measures of equitable access to health care, researchers have been able to demonstrate persistent and sometimes remarkable differences among groups in the United States.

There is a powerful and growing literature on inequitable access to health care. On each of the three dimensions just discussed—use, quality, and health outcomes—considerable data exist to demonstrate significant differences among groups based upon their personal, social, and economic status. The disparities in access to care are particularly sharp and enduring for persons with low socioeconomic status (the poor or near poor, the uninsured, and those in public programs such as Medicaid) and persons in minority racial and ethnic groups.

The relationships between low socioeconomic status and poor health are deep and enduring. In 1991, there were 35.7 million persons below the official poverty level,[30] accounting for 14.2% of the population.[31] If alternative methods of valuation were used that excluded non-cash benefits such as Medicaid and food stamps, there would have been 54.8 million persons in official poverty, accounting for 21.8% of the population.[32] From 1977 to 1990, the poorest 20% of the population suffered a 15% loss in real income, while the wealthiest one percent had a 110% after-tax rise in income.[33] . . .

The subgroups that are over-represented in the poverty population are precisely those groups that are most affected by lack of health insurance and poor health. In 1991, nearly one-third (32.7%) of all African-Americans and more than one quarter of Hispanics (28.7%) were living under the poverty line.[34] One half of the nation's poor were either children or the elderly.[35] One-fourth of all children and one half of all African-American children were below the poverty line.[36]

Health disparities between poor people and those with higher incomes are almost universal for all dimensions of health. . . .

The association between economic disadvantage and ill-health is manifested most strongly in strikingly poor pregnancy outcomes (e.g., prematurity, low birth weight, birth defects) and higher infant mortality; the limitations in life activities due to ill health; and elevated mortality rates. Low income people have death rates that are twice the rates for people with incomes above the poverty level.

Compared to other groups in society, African-Americans and other racial and ethnic minorities are three times more likely to live in poverty and to lack health insurance. They also are subject to discrimination in health care. The effects of these burdens are borne out by poorer utilization of services, outcomes, and health status "virtually across the board." . . .

IV. HEALTH CARE AND MARKETS

• • •

A. THE APPLICABILITY OF MARKET THEORY TO HEALTH CARE

Competition is widely thought to be an effective mechanism for lowering the price and increasing the quality of goods and services in the marketplace. The question, however, is whether competition is an appropriate theory, or the marketplace is the appropriate approach, to the cost effective allocation of health care services. Competition in health care can occur at least on two levels—health care plans can compete for subscribers, and individual providers can compete in offering service to patients. Each level of competition presents its own set of opportunities for reducing cost and its own set of theoretical and practical problems.

Competition among health care plans, which is the organizing theory behind managed competition, is vehemently put forward as a strategy for cost containment. Managed competition remains a proposal constructed in theory, not practice. No health care system outside of the United States has demonstrated the worth of managed competition in promoting quality and constraining medical inflation.

The theory of managed competition assumes that a sufficient number of health care plans exist to sustain competition in the market. A study by one of managed competition's original proponents suggests that populations large enough to support three or more competing health plans exist only in middle-sized to large metropolitan areas.[37] Professor Kronick and his colleagues assume that a minimum of three competing health plans is necessary for the system to work effectively, however, no empirical evidence exists to rely on this number to foster competition. Would players in the market truly compete or would they collude to maintain prices? What economic conditions and/or antitrust arrangements would have to exist to ensure genuine competition? . . .

Predicting the economic effects of managed competition on national health spending is fraught with complexity. Managed competition is not based on empirical evidence, and since the elements of proposals are diverse, it is exceedingly difficult to determine the probable economic effects. Estimates of the economic impact of managed competition on national health care expenditures vary significantly, "rang[ing] from *increased spending* of $47.9 billion in 1993 to *decreased spending* of $21.8 billion in 1994."[38] Given the totality of the evidence, competition among health care plans has theoretical potential for impeding the rise in health care spending, but the potential is unproven and would be unlikely to produce significant reductions in national health expenditures.

Would greater competition among health care plans help achieve the primary good of increased access or equity? Managed competition theorists argue that the savings from their program might be used to fund subsidies for increased access, but no assurance exists as to when, or if, savings would occur. Even if savings do occur, much of the economic benefit will accrue to the private sector; it is unclear to what extent, if any, government would benefit or whether government would use any cost savings to subsidize health care for the poor. Competition at the level of the health plan, in and of itself, promises little to increase access to health services for the currently uninsured or under-insured.

Competition can also occur at the level of the individual provider who competes in offering services to patients. The implicit assumption behind competition is that consumers purchase health care in the same way they buy durable goods or personal services. Good reasons exist, however, for believing that consumers view health care rather differently than most other goods and services. Health services are unique because they can relieve unremitting pain or suffering, restore normal functioning, or prevent premature death. If a medical service could provide a small chance of an improved quality of life or a longer life, most people would be prepared to pay an inordinate price for the service. It is precisely because health is a preeminent human value that markets cannot determine the worth of medical services to individuals in need of care.

Additionally, when persons become ill they are more appropriately seen in the subservient position of a patient rather than of an educated consumer. Patients who are suffering seldom are able to make the clear-headed economic judgments society expects of consumers in the marketplace. They are unable to accurately assess the quality of the "product" or to make reasoned judgments about alternatives.

Even if it were accurately assumed that the market would behave as theorized when buying and selling health services, the result of a well functioning market would be the opposite of that which is desirable. The essential characteristic of the marketplace is that it allocates goods and services on the basis of the ability to pay rather than on the basis of the need for the service. The market, therefore, excludes those who are unable to afford the service being sold. Seen in this way, it is not surprising that the U.S. health care system has exhibited two notable trends, both harmful to the social fabric—steadily increasing prices and greater numbers of persons unable to afford medical services. If it is true that health care is a precious and sought after commodity, the demand for services would be expected to rise. As demand increases, so should price. It would be similarly expected that individuals in poorer income groups would have a decreasing ability to purchase the product as the price rises. Since poverty is often associated with poorer health for a variety of environmental, nutritional and behavioral reasons, those who need the service most would be least likely to afford access.

Free market scholars acknowledge that the market has not worked efficiently. Rather than abandoning the idea, they choose to "fix" the health services market through greater deregulation. The results of these efforts, however, are likely to exacerbate existing problems precisely because inaccessibility and inequity are inherent concerns with competition in all markets. . . .

At least from the time of President Truman to the present day, reform of the health care system at the national level has been very much a part of the public and scholarly discourse in the United States. Yet comprehensive reform of the health care system has become, for now and the immediate future, unattainable. The country appears caught in a paradox. We value the choice and quality in the current health care system, but recognize the harm to the economy of escalating costs and the harm to the social fabric from inadequate access and inequitable distribution of services. . . .

Those in our society who tolerate significant numbers of their fellow men, women, and children going without health care coverage have a burden of carefully explaining the values that underlie their position and demonstrating why they take precedence over the health of the wider community.

NOTES

1. John K. Iglehart, *The American Health Care System,* 326 New Engl. J. Med. 962, 962 (1992).

2. *See, e.g.,* Robert J. Blendon et al., *The American Public and the Critical Choices for Health Reform,* 271 JAMA 1540 (1994).

3. Iglehart, *supra* note 1, at 962.

4. *See* Sally T. Burner et al., *National Health Expenditures Projections Through 2030,* 11 Health Care Finance Rev. at 1, 14, 20 (1992) (estimates).

5. Office of Technology Assessment, U.S. Congress, Understanding Estimates of National Health Expenditures Under Health Reform 1 (1994) [hereinafter Understanding Estimates].

6. *See* id. at 1–3 (figures 1–2); Sally T. Sonnenfield et al., *Projections of National Health Expenditures Through the Year 2000,* Health Care Finance Rev., Fall 1991, at 1, 4, 22. *See also* Congressional Budget Office, Projections of National Health Expenditures 14 (1992) [hereinafter Health Expenditures] (table).

7. Sarah C. Snyder, *Who Are the Medically Uninsured in the United States?, Stat. Bull.,* 20, 21 (1994) (38.9 million had no private or public health insurance during 1992); BNA, *Number of Uninsured Persons Increases to 36.6 million in 1991,* Daily Labor Rep., Jan. 12, 1993, *available in* LEXIS, BNA Library, DLABRT File.

8. Emily Friedman, *The Uninsured: From Dilemma to Crisis,* 265 JAMA 2491, 2491 (1991).

9. *See How Many Americans Are Uninsured?,* 111 Archives of Ophthalmology 309, 309 (1993) (number of uninsured Americans varies with the method of surveying, giving a variety of numbers).

10. Bureau of the Census, U.S. Dep't of Commerce, Health Insurance Coverage: 1987-1990: Selected Data From the Survey of Income and Program Participation 3 (1992); Friedman, *supra* note 59, at 2491 (noting that 63.6 million lacked insurance for at least one month from 1986 to 1988).

11. Families USA Foundation, Half of US: Families Priced Out of Health Protection 3 (1993).

12. Alan Reynolds, *Another Big Lie,* Forbes, June 22, 1992, at 241, 241.

13. *Medical Reform Simplified,* Wall St. J., Oct. 18, 1993, at A16.

14. See id.

15. Katherine Swartz & Timothy McBride, *Spells with Health Insurance: Distributions of Durations and Their Link to Point-in-Time Estimates of the Uninsured,* 27 Inquiry 281, 283 (1990).

16. Katherine Swartz, *Dynamics of People Without Health Insurance: Don't Let the Numbers Fool You,* 271 JAMA 64, 65 (1994) (estimating that at least 21 million people were uninsured all of 1992).

17. Id..

18. Howard E. Freeman et al., Abstract, *Uninsured Working-age Adults: Characteristics and Consequences,* 265 JAMA 2474, 2474 (1991) (noting that "the uninsured are most likely to be poor or near poor, Hispanic, young, unmarried and unemployed.")

19. *See* Commission on Monitoring Access to Personal Health Care Services, Institute of Medicine, Access to Health Care in America 2 (Michael Millman ed., 1993) at 17 (hereinafter Access to Health Care] (noting that population-based strategies in such areas as the environment, pollutants, health education, occupational health, and injury control could potentially "save more lives and have a greater impact on quality of life than programs to extend health services.").

20. Id. at 3 (indicators that measure health outcomes suggest that low income persons with no health insurance experience profoundly different health outcomes).

21. Understanding Estimates, *supra* note 5, at 1.

22. Id. at 1–3 (figures 1–2); Sally T. Sonnenfield, *supra* note 6 at 1, 4, 22. *See also* Health Expenditures, *supra* note 6, at 14 (table).

23. George J. Schieber et al., *Health Care Systems in Twenty-Four Countries,* 10 Health Aff. 22, 24 (Fall 1991). *See* Timothy S. Jost & Sandra J. Tanenbaum, *Selling Cost Containment,* 19 Am. J. L., & Med. 95, 96–97 (1993).

24. *See generally* Organized for Economic and Community Development, Health Data: Comparative Analysis of Health Care Systems (1991) [hereinafter Comparative Analysis]: William C. Hsiao, *Comparing Health Care Systems: What Nations Can Learn from One Another,* 17 J. Health Pol., Pol'y & L. 613, 626–29 (1992).

25. Victor R. Fuchs, *The Best Health Care System in the World?,* 268 JAMA 916, 917 (1992).

26. Steffie Woolhandler & David U. Himmelstein, *The Deteriorating Administrative Efficiency of the U.S. Health Care System,* 324 New Eng. J. Med. 1253, 1255–56 (1991).

27. *See* John Rawls, A Theory of Justice 95–100 (1971).

28. *See generally* Norman Daniels, *Health-Care Needs and Distributive Justice,* 10 Phil., & Pub. Aff. 146 (1981); Norman Daniels, *Health Care Needs and Distributive Justice,* in In Search of Equity: Health Needs and the Health Care System 1 (Ronald Bayer et al. eds., 1983); Norman Daniels, Just Health Care (1985).

29. Norman Daniels, *Health Care Needs and Distributive Justice,* in In Search of Equity: Health Needs and the Health Care System 115 (Ronald Bayer et al. eds., 1983). (emphasis added).

30. The poverty line was set in 1993 at the low level of $11,890 for a family of three. This leaves many families living just above the poverty line who have difficulty affording housing, food, and clothing. *See* Victor W. Sidel et al., *The Resurgence of Tuberculosis in the United States: Societal Origins and Societal Responses,* 21 J. L., Med. & Ethics 303, 307 (1993).

31. *See* Eleanor Baugher, *Poverty,* in Bureau of the Census, U.S. Dep't of Commerce, Population Profile of the United States 1993, at 28 (1994).

32. Id. at 29.

33. Sidel, *supra* note 30, at 308 (citing Steffie Woolhandler & David U. Himmelstein, The National Health Program Chartbook 24 (1992)).

34. Bureau of the Census, U.S. Dep't of Commerce, Population Profile of the United States 1993, at 29 (1994).

35. Id.

36. Sidel, *supra* note 30, at 307.

37. Richard Kronick et al., *The Marketplace in Health Care Reform: The Demographic Limitations of Managed Competition,* 328 New Eng. J. Med. 148 (1993).

38. Office of Technology Assessment, U.S. Congress, An Inconsistent Picture: A Compilation of Analyses of Economic Impacts of Competing Approaches to Health Care Reform by Experts and Stakeholders 34 (1993) (emphasis added).

MADISON POWERS

Managed Care: How Economic Incentive Reforms Went Wrong

Madison Powers is a lawyer with a doctorate in philosophy from University College, Oxford. His research interests include political and legal philosophy, especially issues of distributive justice. Dr. Powers has taught at the Vanderbilt School of Law and the Johns Hopkins School of Public Health; he is currently director and senior research scholar at the Kennedy Institute of Ethics at Georgetown University. He is coeditor, with Ruth Faden and Gail Geller, of *AIDS, Women and the Next Generation* (Oxford). With Ruth Faden he is now completing a book entitled *The Job of Justice*.

MANAGED CARE AND INCENTIVE REFORM

In May 1991, *Journal of the American Medical Association* editor George Lundberg noted that an "aura of inevitability is upon us." What seemed inevitable to Lundberg and to almost every other knowledgeable observer at the time was the enactment of comprehensive national health care reform. The next two years were remarkable for the degree of political consensus that emerged on both the nature of the problem and the preferred solution. Surveys of both patients and physicians identified the two main deficiencies in the American health care system as uncontrollable costs and lack of universal access (Harvey 1990 and 1991). Economists Alain Enthoven and Richard Kronick (1991) labeled the problem as the "paradox of excess and deprivation."

Indeed, virtually all major parties to the debate accepted the premise that the twin problems of access and costs needed to be addressed in tandem. The Pepper Commission, for example, opined that political success in the battle for universal access required effective mechanisms for controlling costs (Rockefeller 1991). Health economists warned that universal access would remain an elusive goal without significant cost savings.

The available policy options were limited. The publicly financed and administered systems of Canada and Europe had demonstrated an ability to control costs and provide universal access. These systems provide health care to all, and they operate within the constraints of a fixed sum of money to be allocated for the benefit of an entire population. Setting a global budget or cap on aggregate expenditure made cost a primary consideration for health care decision makers. Implicit in a cost-driven system are the assumptions that not all beneficial care can be provided and that, accordingly, tradeoffs are necessary.

The incentive structure governing the United States health care system at the time was just the opposite. Fee-for-service medicine, combined with indemnity health insurance, virtually guaranteed that considerations of potential medical benefit would eclipse cost considerations. Rapid innovations in technology fueled increased demand for costly new services and whatever was perceived to be the latest and the best had a way of becoming the standard of medical care. The result was inadequate incentives for curbing the public appetite for expensive medical care, even when expected medical gains were modest or unproven.

Despite their successes, the centralized tax-based systems of Europe and Canada found little support among American political leaders. The consensus was that a distinctively American solution was needed, one built upon the existing mechanisms of private insurance companies, employer-provided health benefits, and the decentralized web of health care providers

From *Kennedy Institute of Ethics Journal* 7, no. 4 (1997), 353–360. Copyright © 1997 by The Johns Hopkins University Press. Reprinted by permission.

already in place. Presidential candidate Bill Clinton made health care reform a centerpiece of his campaign, and by late September 1992, he had embraced the key concepts of managed care and managed competition championed by the health economists in the Jackson Hole Group and by many of the nation's business leaders (Skocpol 1996).

Managed care arrangements were meant to control costs by mimicking a key component of European models. Like publicly controlled health authorities in Europe, managed care organizations (MCOs) would have the responsibility for maintaining the health of a defined population, and individual treatment decisions would be made within budget constraints that limit the total resources available for services for everyone in the plan.

Managed care alone, however, was not viewed as the complete solution. Instead of relying on global budgets set directly by the state, a managed competition model would make room for MCOs to compete for the business of cost-conscious consumers. Although specific plans differed in important respects, the main outlines of the theory were widely accepted. MCOs would put together an integrated system of health care providers and medical facilities needed for an efficient provision of services to its enrollees for a fixed per capita annual premium. Individuals would have a choice among managed care plans, and their choices would be based on price and quality of care. Employers and other sponsoring organizations—health care alliances, as they were called under the Clinton plan—would function as "market makers" (Newman 1995). They would perform an initial screening of the plans to be made available to their employees or members. All three parties—consumers, providers, and employers—would have powerful economic incentives for cost containment.

The goal of universal access would be achieved by a combination of legal requirements mandating employer-sponsored insurance and government financing for those not covered by employer sponsors. Under some managed competition proposals, additional fiscal discipline would be achieved by instituting global budgets for all sponsored plans operating in each geographic region. Employers and other health care purchasing alliances therefore would negotiate prices for health care with integrated MCOs under conditions in which aggregate expenditures either were capped by government regulation or by economic pressure that would keep expenditures within a targeted level (Enthoven 1993).

Managed competition, however, never became a reality. The Clinton legislation stalled, and public support for reform eroded (Skocpol 1996). Nonetheless, managed care—without managed competition, employer mandates, or universal access—grew by leaps and bounds in the 1990s. In the place of Enthoven's "set of economic principles which aim to focus incentives for these organizations to do the right thing" (Newman 1995), managed care developed into a system of incentives that bear faint resemblance to those Enthoven and others favored as a means of solving problems of access and cost control.

In the following sections, I identify two problems inherent in the incentive structure of MCOs developed without comprehensive health care reform, and I show how these incentives work against the public interest.

THE EQUITY-INNOVATION TRADEOFF

A central aim of managed care is to create greater downward pressure on medical costs by slowing the pace of medical innovation, especially the incorporation of high-cost, high-technology medical interventions into clinical practice. Those who worry that quality of care may be reduced too much will ask what benefit society gets in return for such a sharp reduction?

On the European model, the nature of the bargain is well understood. Tradeoffs in medical innovation and quality of care are usually made for the sake of greater equity (Reinhardt 1994). Cost savings derived from limiting expensive treatments are used to provide medical benefits for others in the population. Because the dominant incentive in public systems is the need for maintaining a broad political constituency, distributive principles resulting in the paradox of excess and deprivation are politically unpalatable. As one British physician puts it, the consensus on the appropriate tradeoffs is "bread for all before caviar for some" (Shaw 1994).

However, downward pressures on medical innovation exerted by MCOs result from very different incentives, and they involve a very different kind of tradeoff. Most MCOs are accountable first and foremost to their shareholders or governing boards. Because greater profit, or competitive advantage, not greater equity in the distribution of medical care, is the dominant incentive for MCOs, cost savings that lessen quality of care are not directly connected to a need to serve the public interest in greater equity of access.

Moreover, while uncontrollable health care costs virtually guarantee that many people will lack adequate access to health care, no knowledgeable observer thinks that the savings can lower insurance prices enough to make health care affordable to all. Indeed, nothing in the new medical marketplace offers incentives for MCOs to open their doors to the medically most expensive members of society. In fact, the intense competitive atmosphere increases market incentives for MCOs to exclude more costly enrollees from their plans. A recent study funded by the Robert Wood Johnson Foundation, for example, estimates that increasingly fierce competition in health care over the next few years will cause the number of uninsured Americans to rise from the current level of 40 million (already 6 to 9 million more than at the time of the Clinton health reform debate in 1992–93) to 67 million (Robert Wood Johnson Foundation 1996).

From a societal perspective, managed care does not serve an important element of the public interest as long as large (perhaps even larger) segments of the population lack health care even after costs have been cut and the pressure for medical innovation has been dampened. A system of managed care by itself provides no reliable mechanism for ensuring that potential sacrifices of innovation are offset by gains in equity. In short, bringing the medical arms race to an end does not guarantee how the peace dividend will be spent.

Some observers, however, may be less pessimistic, arguing that MCOs will respond to increased consumer demand for higher quality health care. They predict that quality, measured in terms of the richness of plan benefits, will join price as an important desideratum in choice of health plans, and they might point to increased marketing of plans offering direct access to medical specialists and other expanded consumer choices—e.g., point of service options—as evidence of the existence of strong market incentives for maintaining and improving quality of care.

Presently, however, there is little incentive for considerations of quality of care to figure in health plan purchase decisions. Most Americans get health coverage as a benefit of employment, and surveys of benefits managers reveal that most employers are interested chiefly in cost savings, not quality and that there are severe obstacles to assessment of differences in quality of care (Jensen et al. 1997). More importantly, most employees lack significant choice among health plans, and the trend is toward employers offering less choice among health plans. Roughly half of American workers have only one option and another quarter have only two (Etheredge, Jones, and Lewin 1996, p. 94). Absent legislation or a resurgence of the labor movement, this situation is unlikely to change. Employer incentives to cut down on costly negotiations and administrative overhead, and to deliver a large pool of enrollees to one MCO in return for substantial premium savings, are just too strong to resist.

Even if the optimists are right in supposing that there are enough available incentives to limit some of the erosion of quality of care, there may be negative implications for equity. Where the vast majority of employees once had a range of health care options, now only the more fortunate have such choices. Those who continue to have choices tend to be persons with superior bargaining position in the workplace. Thus, any change in consumer behavior toward more quality-based choice among plans is likely to come at the price of greater stratification between the health care haves and the health care have-nots.

To summarize the first dilemma of managed care: Where medical innovation is a casualty of managed care, there is little reason to expect that sacrifice will be offset by greater equity. Not only can we expect that some will continue to have caviar before there is bread for all, many of those who have had bread can expect less in the future. Managed care, divorced from its theoretical roots in a comprehensive approach to the problems of access and cost control, offers sacrifice without the promise of greater equity in return.

LONG-TERM ACCOUNTABILITY

A second problem inherent in the incentive structure of MCOs developed without comprehensive health care reform is the failure of such MCOs to address the problem of long-term accountability. Public plans in Europe operate with the expectation that they will have financial responsibility for the lifetime health outcomes of the population they serve. This expectation puts plan managers in a position to make rational and fair decisions about which treatments get priority, whether prevention will be preferred over acute care, how much, if any, to spend for research or the clinical application of new therapies, whether the claims of the young or the old are most pressing, and the like.

In the United States, however, most MCOs have no reason to expect enrollees to be their responsibility for more than a few years. People move in and out of plans, often because employers shift to new plans for reasons of cost (Jensen et al. 1997). This expectation of short-term responsibility, coupled with the ability to limit the coverage of those who enter the plan after leaving other MCOs, limits the incentives for plan managers to invest resources sufficient to maintain the long-term health of their enrollees. Hence, they lack the responsibility for making the hard choices that European plan managers must shoulder.

A more significant contributor to the long-term accountability problem is the role of Medicare and other programs for elderly health care in affecting the incentives surrounding MCO decisions. As long as MCOs can turn the burden of expensive senior care over to Medicare, the long-term care program under Medicaid, or another MCO carved out for seniors only, neither MCO plan managers concerned with their pre-65-year-old population, nor individuals concerned about prudent use of resources over their own lifetimes, nor the social institutions charged with making collective social policy are required to address questions of fair allocation among the generations.

The current arrangement is the antithesis of what proponents of managed competition advocated. The aim was to make individuals more cost-conscious consumers by forcing them to set priorities for their own care over the course of their lifetimes. The expectation was that people would forgo marginally beneficial care now provided near the end of life or in old age and that consumer demand in turn would make public and private institutional decision makers more accountable for the long-term health outcomes of the populations they serve. However, the current system of market segregation, or population-specific carve-out arrangements based on age, undermines any efforts to encourage individuals or institutional decision makers to think seriously about health care priorities over a complete lifetime.

CONCLUSION

What we are left with after the failure of the Clinton plan are small scale or incremental proposals either for preserving quality and innovation in medical care or for curbing some of the most unpopular (although not necessarily for worst) inequities of managed care. These approaches merely put off facing up to the moral and political questions raised by the equity/innovation tradeoff and long-term accountability problems.

The managed competition approach, whatever its shortcomings (and I think there are many), was a significant attempt to devise a comprehensive American alternative to European methods of addressing the twin problems of access and cost control. In its stead we have managed care, stripped of its central role for consumer choice and its commitment to universal coverage. Managed care alone, however, was never envisioned either as the right way to control costs or as a solution to the problem of access. Reformers sought to change the structure of incentives by giving individual consumers enhanced choice among competing plans and by removing market incentives for excluding persons from insurance coverage. In the present managed care environment, however, the problem of access has only worsened, and the role of consumer choice as a vehicle for controlling cost and ensuring quality of care is on its way to extinction. Individual consumers now have decreased ability to choose among competing plans or to disenroll from plans if they become dissatisfied with price, coverage, or quality of care. The kinds of incentives dominating the new medical marketplace are not what the reformers had in mind.

REFERENCES

Enthoven, Alain. 1993. The History and Principles of Managed Competition. *Health Affairs* 12: 24–46.

———, and Kronick, Richard. 1991. Universal Health Insurance Through Incentives Reform. *Journal of the American Medical Association* 265: 2532–36.

Etheredge, Lynn; Jones, Stanley; and Lewin, Lawrence. 1996. What Is Driving Health System Change? *Health Affairs* 15: 93–103.

Harvey, L. K. 1990 and 1991. *AMA Survey of Public and Physician's Opinions on Health Care Issues.* Chicago: American Medical Association.

Jensen, Gail; Morrisey, Michael; Gaffney, Shannon; and Liston, Derek. 1997. The New Dominance of Managed Care: Insurance Trends in the 1990s. *Health Affairs* 16: 125–35.

Lundberg, George. 1991. National Health Care Reform: An Aura of Inevitability is Upon Us. *Journal of the American Medical Association* 265: 2566–67.

Newman, Penny. 1995. Interview with Alain Enthoven: Is There Convergence between Britain and the United States in the Organization of Health Services? *British Medical Journal* 310: 1652–55.

Reinhardt, Uwe. 1994. Managed Competition in Health Care Reform: Just Another Dream, or the Perfect Solution? *Journal of Law, Medicine & Ethics* 22: 106–20.

Robert Wood Johnson Foundation. 1996. *Advances: The Quarterly Journal of the Robert Wood Johnson Foundation* (Issue no. 1).

Rockefeller, Jay. 1991. A Call for Action: The Pepper Commission's Blueprint for Health Care Reform. *Journal of the American Medical Association* 265:2507–10.

Shaw, A. B. 1994. In Defense of Ageism. *Journal of Medical Ethics* 20: 188–91.

Skocpol, Theda. 1996. *Boomerang: The Health Security Effort and the Anti-Government Turn in U.S. Politics.* New York: W. W. Norton.

ALLEN BUCHANAN

Managed Care: Rationing without Justice, But Not Unjustly

ETHICAL CRITICISMS OF MANAGED CARE

Managed care, the latest manifestation of efforts to privatize health care, is often passionately criticized on *ethical* grounds. The ethical criticisms most frequently voiced are these: (1) by "skimming the cream" of the patient population, managed care organizations fail to discharge their obligations to improve (or at least to not worsen) the access problem; (2) in order to contain costs, managed care organizations engage in rationing techniques that withhold some types of beneficial care and that reduce the quality of care, depriving patients of care to which they are entitled; and (3) by pressuring physicians to ration care, managed care organizations interfere with physicians fulfilling their professional fiduciary obligation to provide the best care for each patient (Council 1995; Emanuel and Dubler 1995; Rodwin 1993: 135–153; Spece, Shimm, and Buchanan 1996: 1–11).

I shall argue that each of these allegations is radically misconceived. The first criticism is misconceived because it rests on a false assumption: that the health care system within which managed care operates includes a workable division of responsibility for achieving access to care for all, and that this division of responsibility assigns obligations concerning access to managed care organizations. The second and third criticisms are misguided because they wrongly assume that we in the United States have taken the first step toward ensuring equitable access to care for all, namely, articulating a standard for what counts as the "adequate level" or "decent minimum" of care to which all are entitled. Because the current U.S. system provides no basis for assigning obligations concerning access to managed care organizations, these organizations cannot be said to violate any obligations when they act in ways that reduce access. Because no authoritative standard has been determined for what constitutes the types and quality of care to which everyone could be said to be entitled, complaints that patients are treated unethically when they are denied care or when they receive care of less than the highest quality are groundless. Because there is no authoritative standard for the care to which everyone is entitled, there is no benchmark for determining what the physician's fiduciary obligation to the patient is, once we acknowledge that in any system in which resources are not infinite, physicians cannot be expected to provide all of the highest quality care that is of any net benefit.

The three misguided criticisms stated above obscure the most fundamental ethical flaw of managed care: the fact that it operates in an institutional setting in which no connection can be made between the activity of rationing and the requirements of justice.

WHAT MANAGED CARE IS

For our purposes a simple characterization of managed care will suffice. A managed care organization *combines* health care *insurance* and the *delivery* of a broad range of integrated health care services for *populations* of plan enrollees, financing the services *prospectively* from a predicted, limited budget. At present the following cost-containment techniques are often identified with managed care: (1) payment limits (e.g., diagnosis-related grouping [DRGs] for Medicare hospital fees); (2) requirement of preauthorization for certain services (e.g., surgeries); (3) the use of primary care physicians as "gatekeepers" to control referral to specialists; (4) so-called "deskilling" (using less highly trained providers for certain services than was customary during the pre-managed care, third-party fee-for-service era); and (5) financial incentives for physicians to limit

From *Journal of Health Politics, Policy and Law,* 23, no. 4 (August 1998), 617–634. Copyright © 1998 by Duke University Press. All rights reserved. Reprinted by permission.

utilization of care (e.g., year-end bonuses or hold-backs of payments that physicians receive only if they do not exceed specified utilization limits). . . .

WHY MANAGED CARE ORGANIZATIONS HAVE NO OBLIGATIONS OF JUSTICE TO ENSURE ACCESS

Although they seem oblivious to the fact, those who currently criticize managed care organizations for marketing strategies and benefit designs that "skim the cream" of the patient population and exclude those with costly health conditions are simply repeating a fundamental mistake that the opponents of the first wave of privatization made a decade ago. In the mid-1980s, privatization of health care in the United States took the form of the rapid growth of for-profit hospitals. Critics complained that for-profit hospitals were shunning uninsured or underinsured patients and that this had the effect of dumping such patients on already financially precarious public hospitals, thereby worsening the access problem.

That such behavior on the part of for-profits has made it harder for public hospitals to serve the medically indigent is probably true. But it does not follow that in behaving in this way, for-profit hospitals are violating their obligations to help ensure access to care. They would only be guilty of violating obligations to help ensure access if they had such obligations, but they do not.

To understand why they do not, it is important to draw a distinction between two models for how access to a decent minimum or adequate level of health care for all might be achieved through the combined operation of the private sector and government entities (Buchanan 1992: 235–250). According to the first model, a private health care insurance market is expected to provide adequate care at affordable prices for a substantial portion (perhaps even a majority) of the total population, and government recognizes and acts on a commitment to fill whatever gaps in access remain. Private commercial entities, whether they are for-profit hospitals or managed care organizations, have no obligations to help ensure access. They are under no obligation to provide care that is not profitable for them to provide.

According to the second model, there is an institutionally prescribed *division of obligations to secure access* between the private and public sectors. Political processes at the highest level assign private-sector entities determinate obligations regarding access. In the first model, the role of government is to fill whatever gaps in access remain after the market has done its job, but commercial entities in the private sector have no obligations regarding access. In the second model, private-sector entities are not simply agents in the market; they have special obligations to act in ways they would not act if they simply acted as agents in the market.

Those who charge that managed care organizations are violating ethical obligations when they engage in practices that exclude especially costly patients from coverage altogether (and thereby increase the financial strain on public providers) are implicitly assuming that in doing so, these organizations are not bearing their fair share of the burden of securing access for all. But this last assumption would only be true if the United States had adopted the second model, that is, if it actually had an institutional division of labor that assigned obligations concerning access to private commercial entities. It does not. Nor does it have a government that is willing to play the gap-filling role required by the first model (nor, apparently, is there a majority of citizens that is willing and able to demand that their representatives act so as to make government play that role).

In the absence of a political assignment of obligations to private-sector entities such as for-profit hospitals or managed care organizations, there is no more reason to assume that such entities have obligations regarding access than there is to assume that grocers have obligations to supply the poor with food or that home builders are obligated to furnish free housing (Brock and Buchanan 1986: 224–249). It will not do to say that health care is unique. Food and shelter are also essential for life. . . .

It should be clear at this point that the chief *conceptual* mistake that prevents the U.S. public and policy makers from dealing with the primary access problem (and from even framing the ethical issues of managed care in a coherent and fruitful way) is that we overlook the unpleasant fact that our system is neither an instance of model one nor of model two. My point is not that we have an access problem due to a purely conceptual mistake. Rather, what I am suggesting is that this conceptual mistake aids and abets both our unwillingness to confront the primary access problem and our confusion about what the real ethical problems of current arrangements are. This is nowhere clearer than in the muddled terms with which the debate over rationing in managed care is framed.

The lack of (1) a societal agreement on what the entitlement to health care includes and of (2) concrete institutional arrangements for seeing that all have access to a decent minimum of care through the combined operations of the private and public sectors (the implementation of either model one or model two of a mixed private-public system) undercuts the very assumptions under which the current ethical debate about rationing in managed care is conducted. This fundamental point will become clearer as we examine the controversy over rationing in managed care. . . .

WHY THE DENIAL OF CARE IN MANAGED CARE IS NOT SUBSTANTIVELY UNJUST

There are three chief ways in which rationing practices may be unethical. Rationing practices are (1) *contractually unjust* if they violate the special rights of enrollees that are generated through the contract offering the plan. Rationing practices are (2) *procedurally unjust* if there is discrimination (say, on the basis of sex or race), if the rules for limiting care are applied inconsistently, or if there are no reasonable institutional mechanisms for informing patients that rationing choices are being made and giving them opportunities to appeal decisions they believe to be unfair. Rationing practices are (3) *substantively unjust* if the principles of rationing upon which they rely are themselves unjust, even when applied consistently, without discrimination, and under conditions of adequate disclosure and due process.

Sometimes the complaint about managed care rationing practices is that they are contractually or procedurally unjust, but often it is stated or implied that they are substantively unjust. For example, there has been considerable public outrage (and several lawsuits) in response to the fact that some patients who might have benefited from autologous bone marrow transplant have been denied this treatment for breast cancer by their HMOs. In some cases, the complaint has been that denial of such care violates contractually generated rights. However, even here there is often the suggestion that contractual language concerning the provision of "comprehensive care" is to be interpreted ultimately by reference to the notion of an adequate level or decent minimum of care to which the individual is supposed to be entitled. The complaint about denial of care is then based on the assumption that the care denied falls within the adequate level or decent minimum to which each individual is entitled and that ultimately defines the "comprehensive care" that HMOs promise to deliver.

If such complaints about denial of care are understood as charges of substantive injustice, as opposed to procedural or contractual injustice, then they must rest upon an assumption that the form of treatment being denied is included in the array of services to which the individual is entitled, independently of the particular nature of the plan contract. But we have already seen that at present in the United States there is no authoritative standard for defining the scope of this entitlement. For this reason an individual who is denied some service cannot plausibly argue that the rationing practice of the organization commits an injustice by excluding a service that ought to be immune from exclusion. In the absence of an authoritative determination of what is included in the adequate level or decent minimum, virtually *no* service is in principle immune from exclusion.

It would be quite different if there were an authoritative political determination or even a rough but deep societal consensus on what the adequate level or decent minimum includes. Then disputes about whether a particular service may be denied would in principle be resolvable. But in the United States we have not settled on a standard because we have not been forced to do so as a prerequisite of trying to implement a commitment to provide universal access. Yet in the absence of a societal agreement about what services the individual is entitled to, we cannot say that a managed care organization rations unfairly when it refuses to pay for a particular form of care (unless doing so is contractually or procedurally unjust). So, unless they are construed narrowly as disagreements about contractual rights or procedural injustice, charges that managed care wrongs patients by denying certain services are simply muddled. . . .

The further we proceed into the "managed care revolution," the less convincing it is to claim that enrollees have a reasonable expectation that there will be no limits on care. If contracts and policies are reasonably clear, if rationing policies are applied in a nondiscriminatory way, if marketing does not misrepresent coverage, and if a reasonable person should know that managed care means limits, there is no basis for inferring that injustice has occurred simply because a patient does not get some beneficial care or receives care of less than the highest quality. Efforts at ethical reform within the managed care system should focus on procedural and contractual injustices and on educating patients so that their expectations are realistic, not based on imagined substantive injustices.

WHY THE REDUCTION ON QUALITY OF CARE IN MANAGED CARE IS NOT IN ITSELF UNETHICAL

The situation is similar in the case of allegations that managed care is undermining the *quality* of care. The lack of an institutional commitment to securing access to an adequate level of care for all deprives us of any rational basis for saying that anyone is *wronged* by reductions in quality for the sake of cost containment, so long as contractual rights are respected and procedural justice is observed. For example, frequently there are complaints that managed care organizations are reducing the quality of care by so-called de-skilling—using less highly trained individuals to perform certain services (e.g., having nurses do some tasks physicians have customarily performed or using social workers to do what psychiatrists used to do). Or, to take another common example, there are complaints that some HMOs are using cheaper medications that have more side effects or that are less efficacious than the best drugs available for the condition in question (e.g., using older generation tricyclic antidepressants rather than the newer serotonin-uptake inhibitors).

Using a drug that is less efficacious or that has more side effects or using a provider with lesser skills may indeed reduce the quality of care. But it does not follow that there is anything unjust or in any way unethical about doing so. Rationing practices that reduce quality of care are only unethical if they are contractually unjust, procedurally unjust, or substantively unjust. Suppose for a moment that neither of our two examples of rationing-produced reductions in care quality involve violations of contractual obligations or of the requirements of procedural justice. Is there anything unethical per se about reducing quality to reduce costs?

The answer must be no, unless one of two assumptions is granted: (1) that every patient is entitled to the highest quality care that is technically feasible, regardless of cost; or (2) that these particular reductions in quality result in the care provided falling below the level of quality that is included in the adequate level or decent minimum of care to which every individual is entitled.

At this stage of the debate over health care costs, the falsity of the first assumption should be obvious to everyone. Providing the highest quality of care for everyone all the time is neither politically feasible nor required by any reasonable theory of just health care. Only if one denies that resources are scarce (or fails to understand that there are other goods in life besides health care) would one assume that everyone is entitled to the highest quality of care that is technically feasible, without regard to cost.

So if lower quality care is substantively unjust, it must be because it falls below the adequate level or decent minimum of care to which all are entitled. But as we have already seen, there is no societal consensus on what this is and political processes have yielded no authoritative determination of it. Of course, there may be some services that are so inexpensive and so efficacious in preventing or curing serious diseases that we can assume that they would be included in any reasonable societal consensus. But many reductions in quality wrought by managed care organizations will not fall within this uncontroversial core. For these latter quality reductions, there is no basis for saying that the organizations that effect them are acting wrongly, or that their enrollees are being deprived of something to which they are entitled.

WHY THE DENIAL OF CARE AND LOWER QUALITY ARE NOT INCOMPATIBLE WITH ETHICAL BEHAVIOR ON THE PART OF PROVIDERS

It is often said that participation in the rationing practices of managed care is incompatible with ethical behavior on the part of physicians (and nurses, etc.). The most vigorous critics seem to assume that it is unethical for physicians to provide anything other than all services that are expected to be of any benefit for the patient at the highest level of quality that is technically feasible.

This assumption, however, is indefensible. In any system, but especially in a system in which coverage is primarily financed by private employers, there must be limits on which services are provided and on the quality with which they are delivered. It is simply wishful thinking to assume that cost containment in managed care can succeed in controlling health care costs without having a negative impact on coverage and quality. (It is worth noting that some managed care organizations have explicitly acknowledged that reductions in quality are sometimes justified by emphasizing that they seek to maximize *value,* where value is understood as a function of quality and cost.)

So, in itself the fact that managed care rationing denies services and lowers quality provides no basis for saying that these organizations are requiring physicians to act unethically. In the absence of an authoritative standard for what counts as adequate care, such behavior on the part of physicians would only be unethical if physicians were obligated to provide all beneficial care and to provide only care of the highest quality. Of course, some assume that physicians have this obligation simply by virtue of being medical professionals. But if a realistic appreciation of the need to control costs in health care is to count for anything, such an understanding of the role of physicians must be rejected. There is every reason to believe that effective cost containment can only be achieved if physicians refrain from insisting on the highest quality care that is expected to be of any benefit, regardless of costs and regardless of the ratio of costs to benefits.

If this is so, then the alternatives are stark but simple: Either we hold fast to the assumption that medical professionalism is incompatible with physicians providing anything less than the highest quality care in every case, but must conclude that a system that effectively controls costs has no place for medical professionals; or we rethink our conception of medical professionalism to make room for the idea that providing less than the highest quality of care is sometimes acceptable.

The former alternative is unacceptable. There is no reason why cost control in our health care system should be held hostage to an indefensible "essentialist" conception of medical professionalism that, in effect, says that a physician cannot be a true physician or an ethical physician unless he ignores the fact that resources are scarce. None of this is to deny that physicians face serious ethical challenges in managed care. It is only to reject the groundless claim that whenever physicians do not provide all beneficial care or provide less than the highest quality care, they act wrongly. Once this point is appreciated, it becomes clear just how debilitating the absence of a standard for adequate care is. In the absence of such a standard for what patients are entitled to there is no answer to the question, "Which denials of care and how much reduction in quality is acceptable?" And there is no answer to the question: "When does the physician's participation in efforts at cost containment violate his or her fiduciary obligation to the patient?"

A disclaimer is in order at this point. My contention is not that no standards of ethical behavior apply to the actions of physicians in managed care, nor that everything physicians are asked to do by managed care organizations is ethically permissible. I have only argued that the fact that physicians do not provide potentially beneficial care, or that they provide care that is not of the highest quality, does not in itself constitute a breach of their obligations. There are other ways that physicians can go wrong ethically in the managed care environment, however. For example, if physicians encourage their patients to believe that they are acting solely as advocates for the patient's best interests, but in fact make decisions that do not maximize the patient's interests, then they act wrongly. Similarly, given the pervasive and longstanding cultural expectation that physicians are to give their patients all reasonable information about alternatives for treatment, "gag clauses" that prohibit physicians from informing their patients of potentially beneficial treatments available elsewhere that are not provided by the patient's managed care organization are unethical.

THE POVERTY OF ETHICAL THEORY

At this point it might be objected that even if there is no societal consensus or authoritative political determination of what constitutes an adequate level of care, and no existing institutional division of responsibilities for access, an appropriate conception of the moral right to health care can tell us what we need to know. The problem, however, is that no available general ethical theory or theory of justice in health care can in itself tell us what the appropriate division of labor between private and public entities for securing equitable access to health care is in a particular society at a particular point in its history. Empirical premises are needed—premises predicting what will actually work and which concrete institutional arrangements will effectively implement the right to health care, as the various theories understand this right. Moreover, there is no reason to believe that there is only one set of institutional arrangements that would secure access for all. What is needed is not only a conception of justice but also a political choice among the feasible alternatives for implementing it (White 1995: 290–291; Health Care Study Group 1994).

Similarly, no available general ethical theory or theory of justice in health care by itself can tell us what the concrete *content* of the right to health care is for a particular society at a particular time. With the exception of libertarian theories (which deny that there is a right to health care), the most influential theories of distributive justice converge on the notion that the right to health care is a limited right—a right to a decent minimum or adequate level of care, not a right to all care that would be of any benefit (President's Commission 1983; Buchanan 1996: 349–351). However, none of these theories seems capable of articulating the content of this right with sufficient specificity to provide a basis for saying which denials of care and which reductions in quality of care fall below the adequate level, even if we could assume that we actually have an institutional division of obligations that assigns managed care organizations the task of providing an adequate level of care to their enrollees.

This point about the limitations of ethical theory can best be illustrated by reference to what many believe is the most thoroughly developed account of justice in health care, Norman Daniels's adaptation of Rawls's theory. According to Daniels, the right to health care is based on the right to equal opportunity. The distinctive contribution to equal opportunity that health care makes is to prevent, restore, or compensate for adverse departures from "normal species functioning" (Daniels 1985: 26–31). Daniels's theory does give us some guidance in prioritizing various health care services: generally speaking, those that are more effective in addressing the more serious adverse departures from normal species functioning are more important.

However, as I argued some time ago, and as Daniels now acknowledges, neither his theory of justice in health care nor Rawls's general theory of distributive justice can tell us how to prioritize among the needs of different individuals (Buchanan 1983; Daniels 1993). For example, these theories provide no answer to the question, "Should we devote all or most of our health care resources to attempts to improve the conditions of those who are farthest from normal species functioning, or should some resources also be allocated for those whose departures from normal species functioning are not so serious?" In short, even the most systematic and best thought-out theory of the right to health care does not provide an answer to the question, "What is included in the adequate level or decent minimum of care to which all are entitled?"

It seems likely that ethical theory alone will not be able to provide a substantive account of what health care everyone is entitled to. Some ethical theories, such as Daniels's, may provide useful guidance on how to formulate an adequate level or decent minimum of care, but how generous the entitlement should be depends in part on the available resources in the society in question, and perhaps even on how much health care is generally valued compared to other goods. Above all, it is clear that in any pluralistic society there will be disagreements about the proper content of the right to health care that can only be resolved ultimately by procedurally just, democratic political processes, not by abstract theory. . . .

THE ILLUSION OF TECHNIQUE

In spite of the ethical complaints, managed care finds a number of supporters because it holds the promise of a technocratic solution to the problem of providing affordable, high-quality care. Managed care is not just a change in the structure of health care organizations—it is an effort to reshape the very way in which medicine is practiced, making it more scientific by fostering greater reliance on population-based outcome studies to determine which treatment modalities are most effective. However, no amount of outcome data and no improvements in the efficiency of the organization and delivery of care can answer the question, "What is the decent minimum of care to which all are entitled?" This is an unavoidably ethical question. At most, reasoning about efficiency can tell us how best to achieve the decent minimum for all and can help us make informed judgments about how generous the minimum should be, in light of trade-offs for other socially desirable goods for which the same resources might be used.

Furthermore, to the extent that its techniques are rooted in cost-benefit or cost-effectiveness methodologies and focus on the health of populations, managed care is likely to exhibit an uncritical and unarticulated bias toward purely consequentialist (utilitarian) decision making. But purely consequentialist decision making can only reveal what maximizes utility for a given group (whether it is society as a whole or the enrollees of a managed care organization); and maximizing utility for the group may come at the price of depriving some individuals of even the most basic goods. The enthusiasm for technique that characterizes managed care thus not only fails to address the fundamental issue of what the standard for care should be; it may even encourage modes of reasoning that tacitly legitimate rationing practices that compromise the commitment to treating each individual as a legitimate subject of entitlements.

CONCLUSION

I began this essay by noting that the problems of managed care seem to have eclipsed the primary access problem in the United States—the fact that over 40 million people lack health insurance (along with at least another 20 million who are radically underinsured). Before we become excessively preoccupied with the ethical dilemmas of managed care, we should pause to note that all the parties to the controversy over managed care are the "haves"—the insured population that worries about denial of beneficial care, the payers who want to control costs, and the providers who fear losing their professional autonomy and forfeiting patient trust. Conspicuously absent from this triad are the millions of uninsured. If my analysis is correct, the "haves" cannot so easily escape the "have nots"—that is, the ethics of managed care will remain a confused muddle of blame-shifting until the primary access problem is addressed. For until a societal consensus emerges on what forms of health care at what level of quality all are entitled to, and until an authoritative and realistic division of responsibilities for access is institutionalized in our mixed private-public system, the ethical debate about rationing and quality of care *in* managed care will continue to be confused and sterile. . . .

What is most ethically problematic about managed care is not that it denies beneficial care, reduces quality, and pressures physicians to act as rationers. What is most ethically problematic about managed care is the system of which it is a part, for whose most basic ethical flaw it provides, and can provide, no remedy.

REFERENCES

Brock, Dan W., and Allen Buchanan. 1986. Ethical Issues in For-Profit Health Care. In *For-Profit Enterprise in Health Care,* ed. Bradford H. Gray. Washington, DC: National Academy.

Buchanan, Allen. 1983. The Right to a "Decent Minimum" of Health Care. *Philosophy and Public Affairs* 13(2):55–78.

———. 1992. Private and Public Responsibilities in the U.S. Health Care System. In *Changing to National Health Care,* ed. Robert P. Huefner and Margaret P. Battin. Salt Lake City: University of Utah Press.

———. 1996. Health Care Delivery and Resource Allocation. In *Medical Ethics,* 2d ed., ed. Robert M. Veatch. Boston: Bartlett and Jones.

Council on Ethical and Judicial Affairs, American Medical Association. 1995. Ethical Issues in Managed Care. *Journal of the American Medical Association* 273(4):330–335.

Daniels, Norman. 1985. *Just Health Care.* Cambridge: Cambridge University Press.

———. 1986. Why Saying No to Patients in the United States Is So Hard. *New England Journal of Medicine* 314(21): 1380–1383.

———. 1993. Rationing Fairly: Programmatic Considerations. *Bioethics* 7(2–3):224–233.

Emanuel, Ezekiel J., and Nancy Neveloff Dubler. 1995. Preserving the Physician-Patient Relationship in the Era of Managed Care. *Journal of the American Medical Association* 273(4):323–329.

Health Care Study Group. 1994. Understanding the Choices in Health Care Reform. *Journal of Health Politics, Policy and Law* 19(3):499–541.

President's Commission for the Study of Ethical Problems in Medicine and Biomedical and Behavioral Research. 1983. *Securing Access to Health Care,* vol. 2. Washington, DC: U.S. Government Printing Office.

Rodwin, Marc. 1983. *Medicine, Money, and Morals: Physicians' Conflicts of Interest.* New York: Oxford University Press.

Spece, Roy G., Jr., David S. Shimm, and Allen Buchanan, eds. 1996. *Conflicts of Interest in Clinical Practice and Research.* New York: Oxford University Press.

White, Joseph. 1995. *Competing Solutions: American Health Care Proposals and International Experience.* Washington, DC: Brookings Institution.

PETER A. UBEL AND SUSAN DORR GOOLD

"Rationing" Health Care: Not All Definitions Are Created Equal

Peter Ubel is a member of the faculty of the University of Pennsylvania's Division of General Internal Medicine. His research interests focus on the allocation of scarce health care resources and on the psychology of moral decision making. His book *Pricing Life: Why It's Time for Health Care Rationing* was published by MIT Press.

Susan Dorr Goold teaches internal medicine and is associate director for Ethics and Health Policy in the Program in Society and Medicine at the University of Michigan Medical School. Dr. Goold's research interests include ethics and managed care, finances and the doctor-patient relationship, and allocating scarce medical resources. She has published on limiting treatment, cost-utility analysis, bedside rationing, and organizational ethics consultation.

Despite consensus among most experts that health care costs need to be contained, there is great controversy about whether it is ever acceptable to ration health care. Part of this controversy results from disagreement about whether health care costs can be adequately contained by eliminating waste, rather than by rationing health care. Another part of this controversy, however, may arise from disagreement about what it means to ration health care. To the extent that this is true, people may have similar views about what health care services ought to be offered to patients, while vehemently disagreeing about the appropriateness of rationing. . . .

In this article, we explore various definitions of health care rationing and provide a simple schematic to understand and categorize these definitions. We argue that not all these definitions are equally acceptable. Instead, we favor a broad interpretation of health care rationing, whereby rationing encompasses any explicit or implicit measures that allow people to go without beneficial health care services. We argue that this broad view of health care rationing has several advantages, most important being that it highlights the frequency with which we allow patients to go without beneficial health care services because of their cost.

DEFINITIONS OF RATIONING

. . . Rationing definitions differ in several ways. First, they differ according to whether something has to be explicit to qualify as rationing. Some argue that rationing includes only conscious decisions taken at an administrative level that make a service unavailable to some people. In contrast, others say that nonexplicit mechanisms, such as allocating goods by the free market, also qualify as rationing.

Second, they differ according to whether a resource must be absolutely scarce before its distribution qualifies as rationing. Some people think rationing is limited to the distribution of absolutely scarce resources, such as transplantable organs, while others think rationing can also refer to the allocation of nonscarce resources, such as access to subspecialists or prescriptions for expensive medicines.

Third, they differ according to whether rationing

From *Archives of Internal Medicine* 158 (Feb. 9 1998), 209–214. Footnotes renumbered.

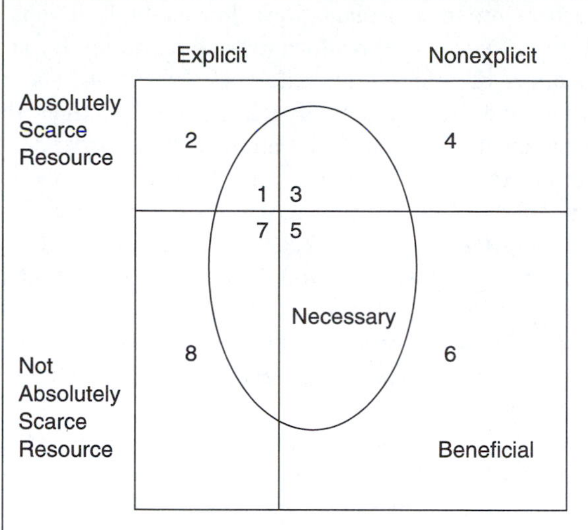

Distinctions among rationing definitions. The vertical line separates medical services that are being limited explicitly versus those limited nonexplicitly. The horizontal line separates absolutely scarce resource from those not absolutely scarce.

only involves limits on necessary services, or whether limits on any beneficial services qualify as health care rationing. By some definitions, rationing only involves withholding necessary medical services, such as dialysis for patients with end-stage renal disease. By other definitions, rationing also includes withholding beneficial (but unnecessary) services, such as the low-osmolar contrast agent described earlier.

The **figure** captures these 3 distinctions among rationing definitions. In the figure, the vertical line separates medical services that are being limited explicitly vs those that are being limited nonexplicitly. This line is to the left of the midpoint to suggest that more services are withheld nonexplicitly than explicitly, although the exact ratio of explicit-to-nonexplicit limitations is not represented. The horizontal line separates absolutely scarce resources from those that are not absolutely scarce. The horizontal line is above the midpoint of the diagram to suggest that few resources are absolutely scarce, although the exact ratio of scarce-to-nonscarce resources is not represented. Finally, within the figure is a circle. Inside the circle are those health care services believed to be necessary; outside the circle are those health care services that are believed to be beneficial but not necessary.

The figure is helpful in illustrating differences among various definitions of health care rationing. For example, the view that rationing only includes the explicit distribution of absolutely scarce and necessary resources, such as life-saving transplantations, is represented by section 1 of the figure. The slightly less restrictive view, that rationing includes explicit distribution of absolutely scarce resources that are either necessary or beneficial, is represented by sections 1 and 2. And our view, that rationing includes any mechanism that allows people to go without beneficial health care services, is represented by sections 1 through 8. Nevertheless, as we discuss later, the 8 areas delineated by this figure are not always distinct from each other. Instead, the lines between absolutely scarce and not absolutely scarce, between explicit and nonexplicit, and between necessary and beneficial are often fuzzy.

NOT ALL DEFINITIONS ARE CREATED EQUAL

. . . In the context of health care, the term *rationing* has gained largely negative connotations in this country. When politicians say a health care policy is an example of rationing they are not intending to compliment their opponents. *Health care rationing* is a morally charged term, suggesting difficult decisions with potentially tragic consequences. An ideal definition of rationing should recognize these powerful moral connotations. With this in mind, it is worthwhile to explore various definitions of rationing to see which are best at framing the difficult moral challenges facing our health care system.

IS HEALTH CARE RATIONING LIMITED TO EXPLICIT MECHANISMS?

Some authors define rationing as the explicit denial of health care services to people who could benefit from them. By this view, rationing involves explicit decisions about how many health care goods and what type of health care goods people will receive. This definition is reminiscent of U.S. government practices during World War II, when it limited the amount of gasoline and aluminum foil, for example, that people received.

It is important to understand that, according to this definition, the explicit denial of health care services to people is not merely an example of rationing, but it is the only example of rationing. That is, for something to qualify as rationing it must involve the explicit denial of health care services to people who could benefit from them.

There is little doubt that explicitly denying health

care services to people qualifies as rationing. What is in question is whether it encompasses all of rationing. To an economist, who would view rationing broadly to include any mechanisms that limit how many goods people receive, society rations BMW cars by requiring people to pay for them. According to the explicit definition of rationing, limiting the availability of health care services by ability to pay is not an example of rationing.

If common usage were determining the best definition of health care rationing, the explicit view of rationing would win out over the economists' broader view of rationing. People do not generally think that BMW cars are rationed by ability to pay. However, people do not think about health care the way they think about automobiles or videocassette recorders. Suppose, for example, that a health care policy made life-saving bypass surgery available only to those able to pay for it. It is likely that most people would consider this policy to be an example of health care rationing. People do not think about health care goods the same way they think about other goods. Some health care services are necessary and vitally important in a way that BMWs and videocassette recorders are not.

In summary, explicit programs to deny health care services to people are appropriately classified as rationing. But, when thinking about health care rationing, we should not limit it only to such explicit mechanisms. Some health care services are so important that limiting their distribution by ability to pay can result in a type of deprivation and hardship commonly associated with rationing. Furthermore, by only calling rationing that which is explicit, one is encouraging the development and use of implicit mechanisms, or hidden rationing. Since openness (or publicity) is a vital criterion for fairness, explicit mechanisms may be preferable. Thus, while explicit mechanisms to distribute health care resources are examples of health care rationing, they are not the only things that qualify as health care rationing. Implicit mechanisms, such as market mechanisms that influence the availability of health care resources, are also examples of health care rationing.

DOES HEALTH CARE RATIONING OCCUR ONLY WHEN RESOURCES ARE ABSOLUTELY SCARCE?

Some people limit the meaning of health care rationing to apply to the distribution of scarce resources, such as organ transplantations. For example, Evans[1] distinguishes between allocation and rationing. By allocation, he refers to aggregate level decisions about what type and amount of health care resources to make available, such as the number of intensive care beds or magnetic resonance imaging (MRI) scanners. By rationing, in contrast, he refers to "the process by which criteria are applied to selectively discriminate among patients who are eligible for resources that had been previously allocated to various programs."

By this view, rationing involves divvying up the health care pie, whereas allocation involves deciding how many pies to bake.

Evans' distinction between allocation and rationing is reminiscent of the distinction by Calabresi and Bobbit[2] between "first-order" and "second-order" tragic choices. Their book, *Tragic Choices,* explores the painful choices that become necessary when goods are scarce. First-order tragic choices determine how much of a particular item will be available, for example, the number of dialysis machines in the United States. Second-order tragic choices involve deciding who should receive available resources. . . .

By calling both first-order and second-order decisions tragic choices, Calabresi and Bobbit are able to highlight the moral significance of both kinds of decisions. Evans' distinction between allocation and rationing suggests a stronger separation than exists. Even Calabresi and Bobbitt admit that their distinction between first- and second-order decisions is an oversimplification. Rather, there are multiple levels of rationing decisions, and influence can travel from higher levels to lower levels or vice versa. Higher level decisions generally affect more people than lower level ones. For example, a public policy decision to base health care on a free market has a huge effect on almost everyone, and a corresponding decision to link health insurance with employment has a large effect on unemployed people, who have less insurance than others. At a lower level, a managed care organization's decision not to hire a pediatric surgeon would mainly affect children in the plan who need surgery, although it may free up more resources for other patients in the managed care plan. At the lowest level, a decision by a physician that a specific health care resource is not medically necessary would primarily affect the individual patient in question. But even these lowest level decisions influence, in a small way, higher levels. The number of MRIs available to physicians, for example, influences their decisions about who needs an MRI, while physicians' collective decisions about who needs an MRI influence higher level decisions about whether to purchase additional MRIs. All these decisions, whether implicit or explicit, whether involving absolutely scarce resources or relatively scarce resources, have important implications for health care rationing. All layers may involve tragic choices.

IMPLICATIONS FOR WHETHER HEALTH CARE RATIONING INVOLVES WITHHOLDING OR DISTRIBUTING SERVICES

If health care rationing occurred only when resources were absolutely scarce, then rationing would not primarily involve the withholding of these resources, but would involve the distribution of these scarce resources to those who could benefit from them. Some people would get the scarce resources and others would not. In such a scenario, it would make sense to talk about the resource being rationed to some people and rationed from others. . . .

In situations where resources are not absolutely scarce, health care rationing generally involves the withholding of services from patients. For example, if a physician decides not to order an MRI scan for a patient because the benefits are not worth the cost of an MRI, that MRI scan has been rationed from the patient. In contrast, if a physician decides to order an MRI scan for the patient because it is the most beneficial thing to do, it is not an example of health care rationing; the physician did not ration the MRI scan to the patient. Instead, there was no rationing in this case, because the patient received the most beneficial thing available. This decision may have rationing implications; the cost of the MRI may make fewer resources available for other patients. But unless this relationship between using one resource to the detriment of another is fairly direct, it makes little sense to describe this physician's decision to order an MRI scan as an example of rationing.

In summary, while it makes sense in some contexts to talk about rationing health care to patients rather than from patients, in most contexts, and in most discussions of health care rationing, attention is focused on withholding resources from patients. Thus, our discussion focuses on definitions of health care rationing that center on allowing patients to go without health care resources.

DOES HEALTH CARE RATIONING OCCUR ONLY WHEN WITHHELD SERVICES ARE NECESSARY?

. . . The phrase "beneficial health care service" does not have the strong implications that "necessary health care service" does for resource allocation decisions. Necessary services seem, almost by definition, to be necessary. We must provide them. Beneficial services, on the other hand, do not have to be provided. In fact, most people are probably willing to admit that cosmetic surgery is beneficial for fashion models while not wanting to make it part of any basic benefits package.

Determining which health care services are beneficial also requires difficult value judgments. For example, how do we decide when an unproved but theoretically promising treatment is beneficial? Nevertheless, determinations of which services are beneficial are less value laden than are the determinations of which services are necessary, because they do not involve cost-worthiness judgments. If yearly Pap smears bring more medical benefit than Pap smears every 3 years, then yearly Pap smears are beneficial, regardless of their financial cost. Expert panels deciding which necessary services to include in a basic benefits package must decide whether the additional costs of yearly Pap smears are justified. In contrast, panels deciding whether the intervention is beneficial do not have to make such cost-worthiness judgments. For this reason, some argue that decisions about determining basic benefits packages should not be made by expert panels, but instead by more representative bodies.

A great advantage of defining rationing as the withholding of beneficial services is that it will point out that it is no longer possible, if it ever was, to offer people every potentially beneficial medical service. Instead, determinations of which services are beneficial will often identify beneficial services that are unaffordable. Difficult judgments about whether to offer these benefits will no longer be made to look like scientific judgments about whether the benefits are truly necessary. Instead, people will recognize the need to make value judgments about whether specific beneficial services can be offered to everyone.

In addition, by equating rationing with the withholding of any beneficial medical service, we can use the word's negative connotations to draw attention to difficult moral decisions about which benefits are worth pursuing. By focusing attention on our inability to offer beneficial services to all who need them, we can highlight morally questionable health care policies that create inequitable access to beneficial health care. For example, it is not difficult to convince the public that allowing millions of people to be uninsured or underinsured is an example health care rationing. . . .

People do not like rationing. They should not like a health care system that allows so many people to live without adequate insurance. By equating rationing with the withholding of beneficial care, we can highlight the terrible consequences of having so many uninsured and underinsured people.

CHOOSING A BROAD DEFINITION OF HEALTH CARE RATIONING

We content that health care rationing is best defined as implicitly or explicitly allowing people to go without beneficial health care services. By arguing for this broad definition of health care rationing, we do not suggest that there is only 1 meaning of the term *health care rationing.* Instead, we argue that a broad definition of health care rationing is a more useful starting point for debates about health care policy and health care priority setting. . . .

As mentioned earlier, the dividing lines illustrated in the figure, between absolutely scarce and nonscarce resources, between explicitly and implicitly withheld resources, and between necessary and beneficial resources, are not nearly as sharp as the figure suggests. Where, for example, is the line between beneficial and necessary health care services? Given the fuzziness of these distinctions, it seems arbitrary to limit rationing to any of the narrow definitions that rely on maintaining these distinctions. Instead, a broad definition of rationing, by acknowledging the arbitrariness of these distinctions, focuses our attention less on distinctions and more on whether particular health care services are appropriate to withhold from patients. While we could debate whether cosmetic surgery is necessary or beneficial, it is much more important to decide whether all patients who want a specific type of cosmetic surgery should receive it.

Our broad definition of rationing will include many occurrences that do not strike most people as morally problematic and will include others where it is clearly wrong to withhold services from patients. It will force people to deal with the gray areas in moral debates about what patients ought to receive and what they should be allowed to live without. This broad definition of rationing forces us to deal with the moral issues in their full and troubling complexity.

By choosing this broad definition of health care rationing, we create room for many types of rationing, a number of which are suggested by the distinctions discussed earlier. For example, there is explicit rationing and implicit rationing, rationing of absolutely scarce resources and of fiscally scarce resources, and rationing of necessary resources and of beneficial but unnecessary resources. Similarly, it is highly likely that there are more and less justifiable types of rationing. By this broad definition of health care rationing, rationing is not defined as de facto inappropriate. Indeed, a major advantage of this broad view of rationing is that it forces us to decide when it is acceptable to allow particular patients to go without beneficial health care services.

It should be understood that this broad view of rationing is not without problems. There is no consensus, for example, about what constitutes beneficial health care. As discussed earlier, some of this debate occurs because many health care services have not been studied enough to show whether they are beneficial. Other parts of this debate occur because of more irresolvable controversies. What should we do, for example, about therapies that are beneficial for some subgroups of patients but, when used in aggregate, are not beneficial? These issues are beyond the scope of this article, but are clearly where much of the debate about health care policy ought to focus.

REFERENCES

1. Evans RW. Health care technology and the inevitability of resource allocation and rationing decisions. *JAMA* 1983;249: 2208–2219.

2. Calabresi G, Bobbit P. *Tragic Choices: the Conflicts Society Confronts in the Allocation of Tragically Scarce Resources.* New York, NY: WW Norton & Co Inc; 1978.

NORMAN DANIELS

Rationing Fairly: Programmatic Considerations

Despite its necessity, rationing raises troublesome questions about fairness. We ration in situations in which losers, as well as winners, have plausible claims to have their needs met. When we knowingly and deliberately refrain from meeting some legitimate needs, we had better have justification for the distributive choices we make. Not surprisingly, health planners and legislators appeal to bioethicists for help, asking what justice requires here. Can we help them? I think we are not ready to yet, and I will support this claim by noting four general rationing problems that we remain unsure how to solve, illustrating how they plague Oregon's rationing plan.

Before turning to the four problems, I want to make several preliminary remarks. First, philosophers (including me) have traditionally underestimated the importance of rationing, thinking of it as a peripheral, not central problem. Since we simply cannot afford, for example, to educate, treat medically, or protect legally people in all the ways their needs for these goods require or the accepted distributive principles seem to demand, rationing is clearly pervasive, not peripheral.

Rationing decisions share three key features. First, the goods we often must provide—legal services, health care, educational benefits—are not divisible without loss of benefit, unlike money. We thus cannot avoid unequal or "lumpy" distributions. Meeting the educational, health care or legal needs of some people, for example, will mean that the requirements of others will go unsatisfied. Second, when we ration, we deny benefits to some individuals who can plausibly claim they are owed them in principle. They can cite an accepted principle of distributive justice that governs their situation and should protect them. Third, the general distributive principles appealed to by claimants as well as by rationers do not by themselves provide adequate reasons for choosing among claimants: they are too schematic. This point was driven home to me by the way in which my "fair equality of opportunity" account of just health care (Daniels 1985, 1988) fails to yield specific solutions to the rationing problems I shall survey. Finally, even the best work in the general theory of justice has not squarely faced the problems raised by the indeterminacy of distributive principles. Rawls (1971), for example, suggests that the problem of fleshing out the content of principles of distributive justice is ultimately procedural, falling to the legislature. Perhaps, but the claim that we must in general turn to a fair democratic procedure should not be an assumption, but the conclusion, either of a general argument or of a failed search for appropriate moral constraints on rationing. If however, there are substantive principles governing rationing, then the theory of justice is incomplete in a way we have not noticed. This point cuts across the debates between proponents of "local justice" (Walzer 1983; Elster 1992) and "global justice" (Rawls 1971; Gauthier 1986), and between liberalism and communitarianism (cf. Emanuel 1991; Daniels 1992).

FOUR UNSOLVED RATIONING PROBLEMS: ILLUSTRATIONS FROM OREGON

THE FAIR CHANCES/BEST OUTCOMES PROBLEM

Before seeing how the fair chances/best outcomes problem arises in Oregon's macrorationing plan, consider its more familiar microrationing form: Which of several equally needy individuals should get a scarce resource, such as a heart transplant? Suppose, for example, that Alice and Betty are the same age, have waited on queue the same time, and that each will live only one week without a transplant. With the

From *Bioethics* 7 (1993), 224–233. Copyright © 1993 Basil Blackwell Ltd. Reprinted by permission.

transplant, however, Alice is expected to live two years and Betty twenty. Who should get the transplant (cf. Kamm 1989)? Giving priority to producing best outcomes, a priority built into some point systems for awarding organs, would mean that Betty gets the organ and Alice dies (assuming persistent scarcity of organs, as Brock (1988) notes). But Alice might complain, "Why should I give up my only chance at survival—and two years of survival is not insignificant—just because Betty has a chance to longer? It is not fair that I give up everything that is valuable to me just so Betty can have more of what is valuable to her." Alice demands a lottery that gives her an equal chance with Betty.

Some people agree with Alice's complaint and agree with her demand for a lottery. Few would agree with her, however, if she had very little chance at survival; more would agree if her outcomes were only somewhat worse than Betty's. Still, at the level of intuitions, there is much disagreement about when and how much to favor best outcomes. Brock (1988), like Broome (1987), proposes breaking this deadlock by giving Alice and Betty chances proportional to the benefits they can get (e.g., by assigning Alice one side of a ten sided die). Kamm (1989, 1993) notes that Brock's proposal must be amended once we allow differences in urgency or need among patients. She favors assigning multiplicative weights to the degree of need or urgency. Then, the neediest might end up with no chance to receive a transplant if their outcomes were very poor, but, compared to Brock's "proportional chances" proposal, they would have greater opportunity to get an organ if their outcomes were reasonably high. Both Brock's and Kamm's suggestions seem ad hoc. That there is some force to each of Alice's and Betty's demands does not, as Brock would have it, mean the force is clearly equal; similarly, assigning weights to more factors, as Kamm does, seems to add an element of precision lacking in our intuitions about these cases. Our intuitions may fall short of giving us clear, orderly principles here.

We might try to break the deadlock at the level of intuitions by appealing to more theoretical considerations. For example, we might respond to Alice that she already has lost a "natural" lottery; she might have been the one with twenty years expected survival, but it turned out to be Betty instead. After the fact, however, Alice is unlikely to agree that there were no prior differences in access to care and so on. To undercut Alice's demand for a new lottery, we would have to persuade her that the proper perspective for everyone to adopt is *ex ante,* not *ex post* information about her condition (cf. Menzel 1989). But what should Alice know about herself *ex ante?* If Alice knows about her family history of heart disease, she might well not favor giving complete priority to best outcomes. Perhaps Alice should agree it is reasonable to adopt more radical *ex ante* position, one that denies her all information about herself, a thick "veil of ignorance." Controversy persists. Behind such a veil, some would argue that it would be irrational to forego the greater expected payoff that would result from giving priority to best outcomes. Citing Rawls's adoption of a maximin strategy, Kamm (1993) argues against such "gambling" behind the veil. Alternatively, she appeals to Scanlon (1982): if Alice would "reasonably regret" losing to Betty, then she should not be held to a scheme that favors best outcomes. Unclear about our intuitions, we are also stymied by a controversy at the deepest theoretical levels.

The best outcomes problem arises in macrorationing as well. Consider HSS Secretary Louis Sullivan's (1992) recent refusal to grant a Medicaid waiver to Oregon's rationing plan. Sullivan's main criticism of the Oregon plan is that in preferring treatments that provide greater net benefits the plan discriminates against the disabled. The clearest example of such discrimination would be this: Two groups of patients, both in need of a treatment that can give them a net benefit of a given magnitude; because one group has a disability, e.g., difficulty walking, that would not be affected by the treatment, we deny them the treatment. Neither Sullivan nor the NLC give an example, even hypothetical, of how this situation could arise in the Oregon scheme. The denial of coverage for aggressive treatment of very low birthweight (<500 gr) neonates, which they do cite as an example of discrimination, is not an appropriate example, because the denial is premised on the lack of benefit produced by aggressive treatment of such neonates.

Consider an example suggestive of the Oregon scheme. Suppose two treatments, T1 and T2, can benefit different groups of patients, G1 and G2 as follows. T1 preserves life for G1's (or provides some other major benefit), but it does not restore a particular function, such as walking, to G1s. T2 not only preserves life for G2s (or provides some other major benefit), but it also enables them to walk again. The Oregon Health Service Commission ranks T2 as a more important service than T1 because it produces a greater net benefit (I ignore the OTA (1991) argument that net benefit is not a major contributor to rank). Sullivan says that it is discriminatory to deny G1s T1, even though a single person would clearly consider relative benefit in deciding between T1 and T2.

The Sullivan/NLCMDD objection can, with charity, be interpreted as a version of Alice's complaint that favoring best outcomes denies her a fair chance at a benefit. Interpreted this way, the Sullivan/NLCMDD objection is that we cannot rule out giving G1s any chance at the benefit treatment would bring them simply because G2s would benefit more from the use of our limited resources. In effect, they seem to be saying we should give no weight to best outcomes. As I noted earlier, this extreme position does not seem to match our intuitions in the microrationing case. But neither does the alternative extreme position, that we must always give priority to better outcomes. The point is that a rationing approach that ranks services by net benefit, whether it turns out to be Oregon's scheme or simply Hadorn's (1991) alternative proposal, thus carries with it unsolved moral issues. To justify ranking by net benefit we must be prepared to address those underlying issues.

THE PRIORITIES PROBLEM

Oregon's (intended) methodology of ranking by net benefit also ignores the moral issues I group here as the priorities problem. Suppose that two treatment condition pairs give equal net benefits. (Remember, this [does] not generally mean they produce the same health outcomes, only the same net benefits). Then the OHSC should rank them equal in importance. But now suppose that people with C1 are more seriously impaired by their disease or disability than people with C2. Though T1 and T2 produce equivalent net gains in benefit, people with C2 will end up better off than people with C1, since they started out better off. Nothing in the method of ranking treatment/condition pairs by net benefit responds to this difference between C1s and C2s. Nevertheless, most of us would judge it more important to give services to C1s than it is to give them to C2s under these conditions. We feel at least some inclination to help those worse off than those better off. For example, if C1s after treatment were no better off than C2s before treatment, we are more strongly inclined to give priority to the worse off. Our concern to respect that priority might decline if the effect of treating C1s but not C2s is that C1s end up better off than C2s. How troubled we would be by this outcome might depend on how great the

new equality turned out to be, or on how significant the residual impairment of C2s was.

Suppose now that there is greater net benefit from giving T2 to C2s than there is from giving T1 to C1s. If C1s are sufficiently worse off to start with than T2s, and if C1s end up worse off or not significantly better off than C2s, then our concern about priorities may compel us to forego the greater net benefit that results from giving T2 to C2s. But how much priority we give to the worst off still remains unclear. If we can only give a very modest improvement to the worst off, but we must forego a very significant improvement to those initially better off, then we may overrule our concern for the worst off. Our intuitions do not pull us toward a strict priority for the worst off.

Just what the structure of our concern about priority is, however, remains unclear. The unsolved priorities problem not only affects a methodology that ranks by net benefit or by net QLY's. It affects cost/benefit and cost/effectiveness rankings, including Eddy's (1991a) "willingness to pay" methodology. So too does the aggregation problem, to which I now briefly turn.

THE AGGREGATION PROBLEM

In June of 1990, the Oregon Health Services Commission released a list of treatment/condition pairs ranked by a cost/benefit calculation. Critics were quick to seize on rankings that seemed completely counterintuitive. For example, as Hadorn noted (1991), toothcapping was ranked higher than appendectomy. The reason was simple: an appendectomy cost about $4,000, many times the cost of capping a tooth. Simply aggregating the net medical benefit of many capped teeth yielded a net benefit greater than that produced by one appendectomy.

Eddy (1991b) points out that our intuitions in these cases are largely based on comparing treatment/condition pairs for their importance on a one:one basis. One appendectomy is more important than one toothcapping because it saves a life rather than merely reduces pain and preserves dental function. But our intuitions are much less developed when it comes to making one:many comparisons (though we can establish indifference curves that capture trades we are willing to make; cf. Nord 1992). When does saving more lives through one technology mean we should forego saving fewer through another? The complex debate about whether "numbers count" has a bearing on rationing problems. How many legs should we be willing to forego saving in order to save one life? How many eyes? How many teeth? Can we aggregate *any* small benefits, or only those that are in some clear way significant, when we want to weigh these benefits against clearly significant benefits (e.g. saving a life) to a few? Kamm (1987, 1993) argues persuasively that we should not favor saving one life and curing a sore throat over saving a different life, because curing a sore throat is not a "competitor" with saving a life. She also argues that benefits that someone is morally not required to sacrifice in order to save another's life also have significant standing and can be aggregated. If we are not required to sacrifice an arm in order to save someone's life, then we can aggregate arms saved and weigh them against lives saved. She suggests that our judgments about aggregation differ if we are in contexts where saving lives rather than inducing harms (positive vs. negative duties) are at issue.

Kamm shows that we are not straightforward aggregators of all benefits and that our moral views are both complex and difficult to explicate in terms of well-ordered principles. These views are not compatible with the straightforward aggregation (sum ranking) that is presupposed by the dominant methodologies derived from welfare economics. Yet we do permit, indeed require, some forms of aggregation. Our philosophical task is to specify which principles governing aggregation have the strongest justification. If it appears there is no plausible, principled account of aggregation, then we have strong reason to rely instead on fair procedures and an obligation to give any of them.

THE DEMOCRACY PROBLEM

When Sullivan rejected Oregon's application for a Medicaid waiver, he complained that the methodology for assessing net medical benefit drew on biased or discriminatory public attitudes toward disabilities. Adapting Kaplan's (Kaplan and Anderson 1990) "quality of wellbeing" scale for use in measuring the benefit of medical treatments, Oregon surveyed residents, asking them to judge on a scale of 0 (death) to 100 (perfect health) what the impact would be of having to live the rest of one's life with some physical or mental impairment or symptom; for example, wearing eyeglasses was rated 95 out of 100, for a weighting of −0.05. Many of these judgments seem downright bizarre, whether or not they reflect bias. For example, having to wear eyeglasses was rated slightly worse than the −0.046 weighting assigned to not being able to drive a car or use public transportation or the −0.049 assigned to having to stay at a hospital or nursing home. Other weightings clearly reflected cultural attitudes and possibly bias: having trouble with drugs or alcohol was given the second most negative weighting (−0.455) of all conditions, much worse than, for example, having a bad burn over large areas of your body (−0.372) or being so impaired that one needs help to eat or go to the bathroom (−0.106). Having to use a walker or wheelchair under your own control was weighted as much worse (−0.373) than having losses of consciousness from seizures, blackouts or coma (−0.114).

Claiming that people who experience a disabling condition, like being unable to walk, tend to give less negative ratings to them than people who have experienced them, Sullivan argued Oregon was likely to underestimate the benefit of a treatment that left people with such disabilities. Excluding such treatments would thus be the result of public bias.[1] His complaint carries over to other methodologies, e.g., Eddy's (1991) willingness-to-pay approach and the use of QLY's in cost-effectiveness or cost-benefit analyses.

Sullivan's complaint raises an interesting question: Whose judgments about the effects of a condition should be used? Those who do not have a disabling condition may suffer from cultural biases, overestimating the impact of disability. But those who have the condition may rate it as less serious because they have modified their preferences, goals, and values in order to make a "healthy adjustment" to their condition. Their overall dissatisfaction—tapped by these methodologies—may not reflect the impact that would be captured by a measure more directly attuned to the range of capabilities they retain. Still, insisting on the more objective measure has a high political cost and may even seem paternalistic.

Sullivan simply assumes that we must give priority to the judgments made by those experiencing the condition, but that is not so obvious. Clearly, there is something attractive about the idea, embedded in all these methodologies, of assessing the relative impact of conditions on people by asking them what they think about that impact (cf. Menzel 1992). Should we give people what they actually want? Or should we give them what they should want, correcting for various defects in their judgment? What corrections to expressed preferences are plausible?

The democracy problem arises at another level in procedures that purport to be directly democratic. The Oregon plan called for the OHSC to respect "community values" in its ranking of services. Because prevention and family planning services were frequently discussed in community meetings, the OHSC assigned the categories including those services very high ranking. Consequently, in Oregon, vasectomies are ranked more important than hip replacements. Remember the priority and aggregation problems: it would seem more important to restore mobility to someone who cannot walk than to improve the convenience of birth control through vasectomy in several people. But, assuming that the Commissioners properly interpreted the wishes of Oregonians, that is not what Oregonians wanted the rankings to be. Should we treat this as error? Or must we abide by whatever the democratic process yields?

Thus far I have characterized the problem of democracy as a problem of error: a fair democratic process, or a methodology that rests in part on expressions of preferences, leads to judgments that deviate from either intuitive or theoretically based judgments about the relative importance of certain health outcomes or services. The problem is how much weight to give the intuitive or theoretically based judgments as opposed to the expressed preferences. The point should be put in another way as well. Should we in the end think of the democratic process as a matter of pure procedural justice? If so, then we have no way to correct the judgment made through the process, for what it determines to be fair is what counts as fair. Or should we really consider the democratic process as an impure and imperfect form of procedural justice? Then it is one that can be corrected by appeal to some prior notion of what constitutes a fair outcome of rationing. I suggest that we do not yet know the answer to this question, and we will not be able to answer it until we work harder at providing a theory of rationing.

CONCLUSION

I conclude with a plea against provincialism. The four problems I illustrated have their analogues in the rationing of goods other than health care. To flesh out a principle that says "people are equal before the law" will involve decisions about how to allocate legal services among all people who can make plausible claims to need them by citing that principle. Similarly, to give content to a principle that assumes equal educational opportunity will involve decisions about resource allocation very much like those involved in rationing health care. Being provincial about health care rationing will prevent us from seeing the relationships among these rationing problems. Conversely, a rationing theory will have greater force if it derives from consideration of common types of problems that are independent of the kinds of goods whose distribution is in question. I am suggesting that exploring a theory of rationing in this way is a prolegomenon to serious work in "applied ethics."

REFERENCES

Brock, Dan. 1988. "Ethical Issues in Recipient Selection for Organ Transplantation." In D. Mathieu (ed.) *Organ Substitution Technology: Ethical, Legal, and Public Policy Issues*. Boulder: Westview. pp. 86–99.

Broome, John. 1987. "Fairness and the Random Distribution of Goods." (Unpublished manuscript.)

Capron, Alexander. 1992. "Oregon's Disability: Principles or Politics?" *Hastings Center Report* 22: 6 (November-December): 18–20.

Daniels, Norman. 1985. *Just Health Care*. Cambridge: Cambridge University Press.

Daniels, Norman. 1988. *Am I My Parents' Keeper? An Essay on Justice Between the Young and the Old*. New York: Oxford University Press.

Daniels, Norman. 1992. "Liberalism and Medical Ethics," *Hastings Center Report*. 22: 6 (November-December): 41–3.

Eddy, D. 1991a. "Rationing by Patient Choice," *JAMA* 265: 1 (January 2): 105–08.

Eddy, D. 1991b. "Oregon's Methods: Did Cost-Effectiveness Analysis Fail?" *JAMA* 266: 15 (October 16): 2135–41.

Elster, John. 1992. *Local Justice: How Institutions Allocate Scarce Goods and Necessary Burdens*. New York: Russel Sage.

Emanuel, Ezekiel. 1991. *The Ends of Human Life: Medical Ethics in a Liberal Polity*. Cambridge, MA: Harvard University Press.

Gauthier, D. 1986. *Morals By Agreement*. Oxford: Oxford University Press.

Hadorn, David. 1992. "The Problem of Discrimination in Health Care Priority Setting," *JAMA* 268: 11 (16 September): 1454–59.

Kamm, Frances. 1987. "Choosing Between People: Commonsense Morality and Doctors' Choices," *Bioethics* 1: 255–71.

Kamm, Frances. 1989. "The Report of the US Task Force on Organ Transplantation: Criticisms and Alternatives," *Mount Sinai Journal of Medicine* 56: 207–20.

Kamm, Frances. 1993. *Morality and Mortality*, Vol. 1. Oxford: Oxford University Press.

Kaplan, R.M. Anderson, J.P. 1990. "The General Health Policy Model: An Integrated Approach." In B. Spilker (ed.) *Quality of Life Assessments in Clinical Trials*. New York: Raven Press.

Menzel, Paul. 1989. *Strong Medicine*. New York: Oxford University Press.

Menzel, Paul. 1992. "Oregon's Denial: Disabilities and Quality of Life," *Hastings Center Report* 22: 6 (November-December): 21–25.

National Legal Center for the Medically Dependent and Disabled. 1991. Letter to Representative Christopher H. Smith.

Nord, Eric. 1992. "The Relevance of Health State After Treatment in Prioritising Between Different Patients," *Journal of Medical Ethics*. (forthcoming).

Office of Technology Assessment. 1991. *Evaluation of the Oregon Medicaid Proposal*. U.S. Congress (final draft in press).

Oregon Health Services Commission. 1991. *Prioritization of Health Services: A Report to the Governor and Legislature.*

Rawls, John. 1971. *A Theory of Justice*. Cambridge, MA: Harvard University Press.

Scanlon, Thomas. 1982. "Contractualism and Utilitarianism." In Amartya Sen and Bernard Williams, eds. *Utilitarianism and Beyond*, pp. 103–28. Cambridge: Cambridge University Press.

Sullivan, Louis. 1992. Press Release (August 3, 1992). Health and Human Services Press Office.

Walzer, Michael. 1983. *Spheres of Justice*. New York: Basic.

NOTE

1. The OTA (1991) notes that men gave dismenorhea a greater negative weight than women. The effect of this weighting is that greater net benefit, and thus higher rank accrues to treating dismenorhea if we include the judgments of men than if we counted only the judgments of women.

LEONARD M. FLECK

Just Caring: Oregon, Health Care Rationing, and Informed Democratic Deliberation

Leonard M. Fleck is currently professor of philosophy and medical ethics at Michigan State University. Dr. Fleck's main areas of teaching and research are medical ethics, health care policy, and social and political philosophy. His most recent major research project has been the book *Just Caring: The Moral and Political Challenges of Health Reform and Health Care Rationing*.

What does it mean to be a just and caring society when we have only limited resources and virtually unlimited health care needs that must be met? This is the problem of health care rationing. This is *the* central problem of health reform for the foreseeable future. Oregon has taken the lead in addressing this problem. Health care rationing is a ubiquitous phenomenon, though few recognize that, because rationing is accomplished for the most part in invisible ways that effectively hide the practice from critical scrutiny.

What is distinctive of Oregon is that its citizens chose to make explicit, visible, systematic rationing decisions that would be a product of democratic deliberations that were morally and rationally justifiable. For its efforts Oregon has been subjected to intense moral and political criticism, claiming that it is the politically weak, sick poor who will bear the burden of health care rationing. . . .

From *Journal of Medicine and Philosophy* 19 (1994), 367–388.
Copyright © Swets & Zeitlinger Publishers. Used with permission.

I. IS THE OREGON RATIONING PLAN FAIR?

We begin with two preliminary claims. First, the problems of health reform in general, and health care rationing in particular, are fundamentally moral and political problems, and only secondarily economic or organizational problems. . . . Health care services are not simply commodities in the market, like VCRs, that can be justifiably distributed in accord with individual ability to pay. As Daniels has argued, access to needed and effective health care is essential to protecting fair equality of opportunity in our society. Thus, health care ought to be thought of as a public good, as a public interest, and hence, as a legitimate object of public policy.

Our second preliminary claim is that *justice,* not beneficence, is the fundamental moral value that ought to govern the debates about health reform options. . . . What I have in mind is a Rawlsian, moderately egalitarian contractarian conception of justice congruent with our liberal democratic commitments. . . (Rawls, 1993). However, there are morally distinctive features of health care that require the articulation of a conception of "health care justice" (Fleck, 1989b). In this essay our goal is to articulate some considered judgments of just health care rationing.

Oregon sought to achieve two health policy objectives simultaneously: (1) expand access to needed health care for the uninsured, and (2) control health care costs for the state. . . . What is noteworthy is that these policies were justified by a very explicit appeal to moral principles. John Kitzhaber, physician-president of the Oregon Senate, has listed eight publicly approved principles behind this legislation (Kitzhaber, 1990). The first of these required "universal access for the state's citizens to a basic level of health care" while the fourth asserted that it is "the obligation of society to provide sufficient resources to finance a basic level of care for those who cannot pay for it themselves" (Kitzhaber, 1990).

Note that it is not *equal access* to health care that Oregon feels morally obligated to guarantee to the poor and uninsured. For Oregon the poor and uninsured do not have a moral claim to a middle class standard of care, but to *basic care*. There are *limits* to society's obligation to assure access to needed health care because, according to Oregon's eighth principle, "allocations for health care must be part of a broader allocation policy which recognizes that health can only be maintained if investments in a number of related areas are balanced" (Kitzhaber, 1990). These include housing, education, and highways, all of which are important public goods, all of which have legitimate claims on public resources, but none of which have unlimited claims on these resources. Granting this, how can we determine fairly and rationally what will count as basic health care that must be guaranteed to all citizens?

Oregon's response to our question was that there was no perfectly objective, uniquely rational, or indisputably fair way of answering it. At bottom, however, this was a process question that would have to be resolved through open, democratic dialogue whose outcome would be shaped both by social value judgments and medical information. The goal of the dialogue would be a prioritization of health services, a ranking of 709 medical-condition/treatment pairs, from those that were most effective in addressing a given medical problem and yielding substantial benefit at a reasonable cost, to those that were marginally effective at best and yielded only small benefits at often unreasonable costs.

Though the public dialogue initially shaped this prioritization process, the ultimate responsibility for the final rankings fell to a Commission comprised of eleven individuals. Then the legislature chose a funding level. The legislature was barred from tinkering with the rankings. All the services above that line constituted the basic package of health services guaranteed to all citizens in Oregon; the services below the line would not be funded. Morally speaking, services below the line did not represent futile or medically inappropriate or non-beneficial care. Rather, they represented marginally beneficial care, where the benefits were very uncertain or relatively small, especially in relationship to costs. This is health care rationing.

The well-known case of Coby Howard put a human face on the practice of rationing. Howard's death came about when it did and as it did because of a deliberate social choice not to fund bone marrow transplants. Middle class children in Oregon in the same medical circumstances as Coby did receive bone marrow transplants paid for by their parents' health insurance. Is it morally right that middle class children should have an opportunity for survival denied to poor *children?* . . .

II. THE INESCAPABILITY OF HEALTH CARE RATIONING

It is by now a truism that escalating health care costs are socially problematic. However, rising costs do not, of themselves, yield the conclusion that rationing is necessary, morally or politically, as a policy response. There are compelling reasons for resisting rationing as a cost containment strategy if there are other viable cost containment approaches. Rationing seems morally objectionable because: (1) needed, potentially beneficial health care is directly denied an identifiable individual; (2) the denial of these benefits is coercively imposed, not freely chosen; (3) the benefits that they are denied may be very substantial, such as life itself, and often irreplaceable and uncompensatable; (4) the individuals denied these benefits are sick and vulnerable; (5) the denial of benefits to individuals will appear to be arbitrary because the primary reason for the denial will be economic; (6) the ultimate source of the rationing decision disadvantaging this individual will be government, and government is supposed to protect equally the rights of all; and (7) the proximate source of the rationing decision will often be an individual's personal physician, ideally a loyal and uncompromised advocate for that individual.

The above paragraph represents the first premise in the anti-rationing argument. The second premise is that there are alternative ways of effectively controlling health costs that do not have the morally objectionable features associated with rationing. The unholy trinity of waste, fraud, and abuse are usually cited, and proposed remedies include: more effective utilization review (Angell, 1985), better technology assessment, banning self-referral by physicians (Rodwin, 1993), and reducing administrative waste (Himmelstein and Woolhandler, 1994). This list fairly represents premise two in the anti-rationing argument, which concludes that rationing is unnecessary given all these morally legitimate, barely tried alternatives to health care cost containment.

Note that critics of rationing construe the concept very narrowly. The most critical defining features seem to be that an identified individual is denied needed health care through a coercive government policy, and this seems to violate the social values of compassion and respect for individual liberty.

One implication of this narrow construal of rationing is that it will appear to be conceptually inappropriate to speak of "rationing by ability to pay." Markets distribute by ability to pay, but this seems to be done in a wholly impartial, mechanical manner that is wholly indifferent to the welfare of any identified individual. However, this is a dodge. One of the features of markets is that they do diffuse responsibility for bad outcomes, often creating the impression that these outcomes are a product of chance and the workings of specific markets. . . .

Angell (1985), Brown (1991) and Relman (1991a; 1991b) imagine that more rational and efficient overall management of health care system and the use of health services will result in cost containment without rationing. Health planning, technology assessment, utilization review and practice protocols are recommended to control health costs without the objectionable moral consequences associated with rationing. Yet all these cost containment methods will in various circumstances result in "preventable" deaths and harms. But these deaths and harms will be mixed so thoroughly with non-preventable, natural deaths and harms from assorted medical problems that they will all appear equally fated and equally unfortunate, whereas death or harm to someone like Coby Howard that is the product of an explicit rationing decision will appear to be uncaring and unjust and preventable. Is this in fact a morally correct judgment? I do not believe it is.

Implicit rationing is, first, a pervasive feature of our approaches to health care cost containment, and it is at least as morally problematic as Oregon's explicit approach to health care rationing. Second, that there are *identifiable* individuals who are the "victims" of health care rationing is morally and conceptually irrelevant. Here I disagree with Hadorn (1991b). What is conceptually essential to rationing is that someone makes a judgment regarding kinds of health care that are judged to be non-costworthy and marginally beneficial. Once that judgment is made there will always be individuals who will bear the consequences of that decision. Third, there is nothing intrinsically immoral about any rationing decision. The real moral question is whether a particular individual has a just claim to the health care that he will be denied. But, fourth, what is presumptively morally problematic about *implicit* forms of rationing is that all manner of arbitrary, discriminatory, and clearly unjust rationing decisions can be effectively hidden from moral scrutiny by anyone, including the individuals who are the victims of these choices. Hence, for its commitment to explicit rationing Oregon deserves moral commendation, not condemnation. Fifth, Oregon did make a moral mistake in the Coby Howard case, for it represented piecemeal, uncoordinated rationing, which will always be morally difficult to justify. Oregon's subsequent efforts at rationing and priority setting in a more comprehensive, rational, systematic fashion are immune to such criticism. But the many forms of implicit rationing that are pervasive features of most of our current approaches to health care cost containment continue to be morally objectionable because they are piecemeal and uncoordinated. This reflects our highly fragmented approach to health care financing, which both permits and encourages irresponsible cost-shifting. . . .

III. OREGON AND HEALTH CARE RATIONING: KEY MORAL LESSONS

We will draw eleven key moral lessons from Oregon's experience with health care rationing, explicate them, then respond to the moral criticisms directed at Oregon's efforts.

Lesson One: Rationing decisions made in a piecemeal, uncoordinated fashion are very likely to be arbitrary and unjust. Fair rationing decisions must be a product of comprehensive, systematic, rational deliberation. This is the main lesson of the Coby Howard case. Rationing decisions always imply trade-offs. Health resources will be denied to some health needs because there are other health needs that have a stronger just claim to those resources. When rationing is done systematically and explicitly, then we know what trade-offs we have endorsed, and those trade-offs are open to rational and moral assessment.

Lesson Two: Rationing decisions made publicly are open to critical assessment and correction, and are more likely to be just. Oregon was not the first state to permit the denial of life-sustaining medical care to a Medicaid patient. This is surely a routine occurrence in Medicaid programs and for patients who are without health insurance (Hadley, 1991; Lurie, 1984). But denials are effected subtly and are essentially hidden from the public scrutiny, as well as scrutiny by the patient himself which means there is ample opportunity for invidious discrimination.

Lesson Three: The whole process of health reform and health rationing must be guided by explicit moral considerations, such as health care justice, and only secondarily be economic or managerial or organizational considerations. There are thousands of children and adults like Coby Howard, whose lives are threatened by a deadly illness and whose lives could be prolonged if they had access to some expensive life-prolonging medical technology, such as a bone marrow transplant. Whether they have a just claim to that technology will not be settled by an economic equation or organizational theory or more clinical data. We need to address that issue directly as a moral problem. Further, allocational problems caused by advancing medical technology are not an oddity in our health care system; they are at the heart of twentieth-century technological medicine.

Lesson Four: Fair rationing decisions ought to be a product of informed democratic decisionmaking processes that include all who will be affected by the decision.

Lesson Five: If all who will be affected by rationing decisions have a fair opportunity to shape these decisions, then these rationing decisions will be freely self-imposed, which is an essential feature of just rationing decisions.

Lesson Six: Stable community membership over the course of a life is essential to preserving the fairness of the rationing process. Individuals cannot have the option of enjoying the benefits of health reform in a given community only to exit the community when the burdens of rationing fall upon them.

Lessons four through six comprise our "principle of community" for health care rationing. All of us as citizens must take responsibility for health reform; experts alone will not do. Expert knowledge is essential for intelligent rationing decisions, but expert knowledge is not a suitable replacement for public moral judgment and public moral responsibility for fair rationing judgments.

Moreover, rationing decisions are more likely to be fair if they are decisions that are self-imposed rather than being imposed by some (healthy individuals) on others (sick and vulnerable individuals). Note that for a liberal society embedded in this principle of community must be a principle of autonomy with respect to health care rationing: just rationing decisions must be freely self-imposed. These two principles must be inextricably linked with one another as a practical matter and as a moral matter. . . .

What the Oregon approach recognizes is that a budget for meeting health needs must be communally agreed to. As noted earlier, there is no perfectly objective way of identifying health needs because there are value considerations necessarily bound up with that determination, and because emerging medical technologies are constantly adding "new" health needs. This means there is no perfectly objective way of determining that communal health budget. That will require a balancing judgment that takes into account other important social needs. In a democratic society all should have the opportunity to participate in the making of that balancing judgment since all will be affected by the results of that judgment.

In order for such impartial circumstances to yield actually fair health priorities and rationing protocols all who have a voice in shaping those protocols and priorities must be ongoing members of that community so that all are more or less equally at risk of having to accept the burdens of rationing. . . .

Lesson Seven: Justice requires that there be limits that health care makes on total societal resources, and that these limits be expressed in the form of hard budgets. The moral virtue of hard budgets is that they make clear and visible the trade-offs that must be made among competing health needs.

Lesson Eight: Hard budgets give structure and coherence to a process of prioritizing health needs/services. A process of prioritizing that is explicit, rationally determined, and freely agreed to protects fairness against special pleading.

Lesson Nine: Those who are least well off healthwise have presumptively stronger moral claims to needed health resources so long as they are able to benefit sufficiently from those resources, and so long as their health needs are fairly judged as being of sufficiently high priority from the larger social perspective embodied in the prioritization process. No individual has a right to unlimited health care; and no individual has a moral right to have their health needs met at the expense of the more just (higher priority) health claims of others.

Lesson Ten: Physicians are more likely to protect their own moral integrity as loyal advocates of their patients' best interests and as fair rationers of societal resources if they make their rationing decisions within the framework of a fixed global budget and a system of health priorities that have been freely agreed to by all who are part of that health care system. This is the perspective that allows physicians to be just and compassionate to patients over the course of their life.

Lesson Eleven: Equity and efficiency must be achieved together. We will not have fair or effective or affordable or stable health reform if we attempt to maximize either of these social values at the expense of the other.

Oregon is less than a perfect exemplar of the moral lessons regarding just health care rationing sketched above. The most frequently voiced criticism of Oregon is that the poor were exploited to achieve health reform. That is, Oregon committed itself to achieving nearly universal access to health care and hoped to pay for it by imposing a rationing system on the poor, that is, those who were least well off. The objective was clearly laudable, but the means to the objective were unjust (Daniels, 1991, p. 2232). I have defended Oregon on this point at some length (Fleck, 1990c). I argue that this policy choice must be assessed from the perspective of non-ideal justice. More precisely, Oregon can justifiably argue that the poor as a class are better off under the reform proposal than they are under the current Medicaid program, which covers only 58% of the poor. All the poor can now be assured access to a basic package of health services. It is also morally relevant that rational poor persons, suitably informed, would autonomously choose this reform package over the current Medicaid program.

Daniels readily concedes that Oregon has achieved a more equitable health care system. However, he adds that "even greater reductions in inequality are possible if other groups sacrifice instead of Medicaid recipients. It is unfair for current Medicaid recipients to bear a burden that others could bear much better, especially since inequality would then be even further reduced" (1991, pp. 2232–33). Better-off Oregonians, for example, could pay more taxes in support of the Medicaid program. Indeed, an actual attempt was made to cover all state employees with the same benefit package and rationing protocols as the Medicaid population, but that measure was soundly defeated in the state legislature. Morally, this outcome is bothersome. Moreover, it is not consistent with the principle of community discussed above, since it appears that the healthy and powerful are imposing rationing protocols on the sick and poor, who are not in a fair bargaining position. . . .

IV. JUSTICE, RATIONING, AND DEMOCRATIC DELIBERATION

We now turn to a consideration of rational democratic deliberation as an approach to health care rationing. There are two criticisms of this process I will address. First, the poor were not fairly represented in the democratic forums in Oregon integral to priority-setting and were the ones who ended up having to bear the risks and burdens of rationing. Prima facie, this looks like a morally insensitive middle class majority imposing its will on the politically weak, sick poor.

This first criticism can be addressed if the following conditions are met: (1) We must all belong to one or another Accountable Health Plan. . . . Alternatively, we must all belong to the same single-payer health care system, where "all belong" means that there is no potentially morally objectionable sorting of individuals according to socio-economic status or health status. (2) Belonging to the plan must mean that there is a single health budget to purchase all health services for plan members. (3) We must know the budget cannot cover all likely demands for health services. (4) We must limit demands on the budget through a priority-setting process and mutually agreed upon rationing protocols that apply equally to all members of the plan. (5) We must be largely ignorant of our future health care needs, which is largely true for most of us most of the time. If these conditions are met, then the likelihood is that the rationing protocols and health priorities that emerge from a rationally informed process of democratic deliberation will be "just enough" or "fair enough." This is to concede that there will be future individuals who will die "prematurely" because they will have been denied the only medical intervention that promised them some additional opportunity for prolonged life for no better reason than that it was the informed and impartial judgment of the community that the benefits promised by these interventions were too small, too costly, and too uncertain. The essential fairness of the process is secure because any member of that community, given the right circumstances, could be the individual denied particular interventions.

A second critical objection is the democracy problem (Daniels, 1993). Democracy is about respecting expressed preferences. Daniels points out that Oregonians in community meetings were very concerned about assured access to family planning services. As a result vasectomies were rated more highly in the priority setting process than hip replacements for the elderly. Daniels asks whether we must abide by whatever the democratic process yields? If we see this as a matter of pure procedural justice, then there is no correcting of results that seem counter-intuitive. But if it can be corrected by an appeal to some prior notion of what counts as a fair rationing outcome, then we might wonder what the point of the democratic process is.

Yet another rationing problem is the "fair chances/best outcome" problem (Daniels, 1993, p. 225), which I see as related to the democracy problem. Daniels borrows the following example from Frances Kamm (1989). Alice and Betty are both in need of a liver transplant; both are the same age and have waited the same period of time for a transplant; both will be dead in a week without the transplant. With the transplant Alice will live only two years while Betty will live twenty. Who should get the transplant? We get the best outcome, maximum number of quality-adjusted life years saved, by saving Betty. But Alice wants a lottery, in effect arguing that each has an equal right to life, however long the rest of their life might be. Both have reasonable and morally compelling considerations on their side. Oregon's democratic deliberations favored the net benefit approach. The critical issue is whether Alice has a moral right to be aggrieved as this result. Has she been harmed in a morally significant sense, and does this undermine the moral authority of the democratic deliberative process for yielding just results?

In responding I want to sketch a somewhat idealized version of just rational democratic deliberation. We begin with the assumption that no matter how fine-grained a conception of health care justice we develop, it will never be fine-grained enough to generate a uniquely correct complete set of just rationing protocols. There are innumerable reasonable, morally permissible trade-offs that might be made in articulating some set of rationing protocols. I will refer to this moral space as "the domain of the just democratic decisionmaking." Again, within this space we have no reason to believe that we could identify something that could justifiably be called the "most just" set of rationing protocols possible for our society. Many possible trade-off patterns will be "just enough," all things considered, especially when we recall that there are other values besides justice that are a legitimate part of the overall moral equation.

There are two critical conditions that elicit and justify the need for a democratic deliberative process of decisionmaking. The first is that we cannot simply allow individual liberty to resolve this particular rationing decision. For if we did allow medical or administrative or consumer discretion to be ultimately determinative, the result would be the potential for arbitrary or discriminatory results that would be unjust. . . .

Our second condition for appealing to the rational democratic deliberative process is that there are these plural choice possibilities, all of which have prima facie moral and political legitimacy, but none of which are unequivocally superior from a moral, political, or rational perspective. This is the situation we are faced with regard to Alice and Betty. A good case can be made for going with a decision rule that might favor a lottery in this situation, or going with net benefits. There are any number of very complex decisions rules we might adopt, especially if we vary morally relevant case facts, such as the ages of the individuals, the gap between likelihood of survival for each, morally permissible quality of life consideration, and so on. What is morally important is that whatever decision rule we adopt through the democratic deliberative process is one that is applied consistently over time to all members of that society/health plan. So long as that decision rule is in place and was, in fact, approved by both Alice and Betty (or their democratic representatives) at some prior point in time when they did not know that their future medical circumstances, neither one will have just cause for moral complaint, no matter what the outcome. Again, one of the other assumptions we have to work with is that individual participants in this democratic process are ongoing members of this community so that the trade-offs they agree to, some specific distribution of benefits and burdens, or benefits and risks, is a distribution that they are imposing on themselves. That is, in many cases of rationing, say, with reference to the health care needs of the elderly (our future elderly selves), the distribution of benefits and burdens do not occur simultaneously with respect to any individual. It would clearly be unfair for a younger individual to derive the benefits of rationing health care for the elderly, then have the option of exiting that health plan as an older person to escape the risks/burdens of rationing for the elderly.

Two other large points must be made with respect to understanding the moral and political legitimacy of rational democratic decisionmaking. The first is that this "democratic space" should be thought of as being bounded and structured by principles of health care justice. These principles have emerged and will emerge through the same process of moral discourse that has generated medical ethics as we know it today. These principles should be thought of as having a status akin to constitutional principles, which is to say that any proposed rationing protocol that violated one of these principles would have to be rejected.

Among such principles, I would include: (1) a Publicity Principle, aimed at eliminating invisible rationing; (2) a Fair Equality of Opportunity Principle; (3) an Equality Principle, the intent of which is to assure each citizen equal moral consideration; (4) an Autonomy Principle: (5) a Just Maximizing Principle; (6) Need-Identification Principles, to distinguish health needs from health preferences; (7) Priority-Setting Principles; and (8) a Neutrality Principle aimed at protecting the liberal character of our society with respect to choosing health services in our benefit package. . . .

In concluding, Oregon failed to meet important requirements of just democratic decisionmaking. But it was an instructive failure. Oregon should not be thought of as being morally culpable for its failures; we however, would be morally culpable if we failed to learn the lessons of Oregon.

REFERENCES

Aaron, H.: 1992, "The Oregon experiment," in *Rationing America's Medical Care: The Oregon Plan and Beyond,* M. Strosberg *et al.* (eds.), The Brookings Institution, Washington, D.C., pp. 107–11.

Angell, M.: 1985, "Cost containment and the physician," *Journal of the American Medical Association* 254, 1203–07.

Brown, L.: 1991, "The national politics of Oregon's rationing plan," *Health Affairs* 10 (Summer), 28–51.

Daniels, N.: 1991, "Is the Oregon rationing plan fair?" *Journal of the American Medical Association* 265, 2232–35.

Daniels, N.: 1993, "Rationing fairly: programmatic considerations," *Bioethics* 7, 224–33.

Fleck, L. M.: 1990c, "The Oregon medicaid experiment: is it just enough?" *Business and Professional Ethics Journal* 9 (Fall) 201–17.

Hadley, J. et al.: 1991, "Comparison of uninsured and privately insured hospital patients: condition on admission, resource use, and outcome," *Journal of the American Medical Association* 265, 274–78.

Hadorn, D. C.: 1991a, "Oregon priority-seeting exercise: quality of life and public policy," *The Hastings Center Report* 19 (May/June), S11–16.

Hadorn, D. C.: 1991b, "Setting health care priorities in Oregon: cost-effectiveness meets the rule of rescue," *Journal of the American Medical Association* 265, 2218–25.

Himmelstein, D. U. and Woolhandler, S.: 1994, *The National Health Program Book: A Source Guide for Advocates,* Common Courage Press, Monroe, Maine.

Kamm, F.: 1993, *Morality, Mortality: Death and Whom to Save From It,* Volume 1, Oxford University Press, Oxford, England.

Kitzhaber, J.: 1990, "Rationing health care: the Oregon model," *The Center Report,* The Center for Public Policy and contemporary Issues (Denver) 2 (Winter), 3–4.

Lurie, N. *et al.*: 1984, "Termination from Medi-Cal—does it affect health?" *The New England Journal of Medicine* 311, 480–84.

Oregon Health Services Commission: 1991, *Prioritization of Health Services: A Report to the Governor and the Legislature,* Salem, Oregon.

Rawls, J.: 1993, *Political Liberalism,* Columbia University Press, New York.

Relman, A.: 1991a, "Is rationing inevitable?" *The New England Journal of Medicine* 322, 1809–10.

Relman, A.: 1991b, "The trouble with rationing," *The New England Journal of Medicine* 323, 911–12.

Rodwin, M.: 1993, *Money, Medicine, and Morals,* Oxford University Press, Oxford, England.

SUGGESTED READINGS FOR CHAPTER 2

Acheson, Sir Donald (Chairperson). *Independent Inquiry into Inequalities in Health: Report.* London: The Stationery Office, published for the Department of Health, 1998.

American Journal of Bioethics 1 (Spring 2001). Special issue on "Justice, Health, and Healthcare."

Benatar, Solomon R. "Health Care Reform in the New South Africa." *New England Journal of Medicine* 336 (March 20, 1997), 891–95.

Bodenheimer, Thomas. "The Oregon Health Plan—Lessons for the Nation." *New England Journal of Medicine* 337, nos. 9, 10 (1997), 651–56, 720–24.

Bole, Thomas J., and Bondeson, William B., eds. *Rights to Health Care.* Boston: Kluwer, 1991.

Brock, Dan W. "Justice, Health Care, and the Elderly." *Philosophy & Public Affairs* 18 (1989), 297–312.

———. "Justice and the ADA: Does Prioritizing and Rationing Health Care Discriminate against the Disabled?" *Social Philosophy and Policy* 12 (1995), 159–85.

Buchanan, Allen. "Health-Care Delivery and Resource Allocation." In Robert M. Veatch, ed., *Medical Ethics,* 2d ed. Boston: Jones and Bartlett, 1997, 321–61.

———. "Trust in Managed Care Organizations." *Kennedy Institute of Ethics Journal* 10 (2000), 189–212.

Callahan, Daniel. "Managed Care and the Goals of Medicine." *Journal of American Geriatrics Society* 46 (March 1998), 385–88.

———. *Setting Limits: Medical Goals in an Aging Society.* New York: Simon & Schuster, 1987.

———. *What Kind of Life: The Limits of Medical Progress.* New York: Simon & Schuster, 1990.

Chapman, Audrey R., ed. *Health Care Reform: A Human Rights Approach.* Washington, DC: Georgetown University, 1994.

Churchill, Larry M. *Self-Interest and Universal Health Care: Why Well-Insured Americans Should Support Coverage for Everyone.* Cambridge, MA: Harvard University Press, 1994.

Daniels, Norman. *Just Health Care.* New York: Cambridge University Press, 1985.

———. *Justice and Justification: Reflective Equilibrium in Theory and Practice.* New York: Cambridge University Press, 1997.

———. "National Health-Care Reform." In Robert M. Veatch, ed., *Medical Ethics,* 2d ed. Boston: Jones and Bartlett, 1997, 415–41.

———. "Rationing Fairly: Programmatic Considerations." *Bioethics* 7 (1993), 224–33.

———. *Seeking Fair Treatment: From the AIDS Epidemic to National Health Care Reform.* New York: Oxford University Press, 1995.

Daniels, Norman, Kennedy, Bruce P., and Kawachi, Ichiro. "Why Justice Is Good for Our Health: The Social Determinants of Health Inequalities." *Daedalus* 128 (Fall 1999): 215–25.

Daniels, Norman, Light, Donald W., and Caplan, Ronald L. *Benchmarks of Fairness for Health Care Reform.* New York: Oxford University Press, 1996.

Daniels, Norman, and Sabin, James E. "Closure, Fair Procedures, and Setting Limits within Managed Care Organizations." *Journal of the American Geriatrics Society* 46 (1998), 351–54.

———. "Last Chance Therapies and Managed Care." *Hastings Center Report* 28 (March/Apr. 1998), 27–41.

DeGrazia, David. "Why the United States Should Adopt a Single-Payer System of Health Care Finance." *Kennedy Institute of Ethics Journal* 6 (1996), 145–60.

Dougherty, Charles J. "And Still the Only Advanced Nation without Universal Health Coverage." *Hastings Center Report* 27 (July-August 1997), 39–41.

———. *Back to Reform: Values, Markets, and the Health Care System.* New York: Oxford University Press, 1996.

Elster, Jon. *Local Justice: How Institutions Allocate Scarce Goods and Necessary Burdens.* New York: Russell Sage Foundation, 1992.

Emanuel, Ezekiel J. *The Ends of Human Life: Medical Ethics in a Liberal Polity.* Cambridge, MA: Harvard University Press, 1991.

———, and Dubler, Nancy N. "Preserving the Physician-Patient Relationship in the Era of Managed Care." *Journal of the American Medical Association* 273 (1995), 323–29.

Engelhardt, H. Tristram. "Freedom and Moral Diversity: The Moral Failures of Health Care in the Welfare State." *Social Philosophy & Policy* 14 (1997), 180–96.

Epstein, Richard. *Mortal Peril: Our Inalienable Right to Health Care?* Reading, MA: Addison-Wesley, 1997.

Fleck, Leonard M. "Justice, HMOs, and the Invisible Rationing of Health Care Resources." *Bioethics* 4 (1990), 97–120.

Goold, Susan D. "Allocating Health Care: Cost-Utility Analysis, Informed Democratic Decision Making, or the Veil of Ignorance?" *Journal of Health Politics, Policy, and Law* 21 (1996), 69–98.

Hall, Mark A. *Making Medical Spending Decisions: The Law, Ethics, and Economics of Rationing Mechanisms.* New York: Oxford University Press, 1997.

———. "The Problem with Rule-Based Rationing." *The Journal of Medicine and Philosophy* 19 (1994), 315–32.

Health Affairs 10 (1991). Special issue on "Rationing."

Journal of the American Geriatrics Society 40 (1992). Special issue on "Ethics and Rationing."

Journal of Health Politics, Policy and Law 24 (February 1999). "Special Reports from the Field on The Oregon Plan."

Journal of Medicine and Philosophy 19 (August 1994). Special issue on the "Oregon Health Plan."

Journal of Medicine and Philosophy 26 (April 2001). Special issue on "Children and a Fair Share of Health and Dental Care."

Kitzhaber, John A. "The Oregon Health Plan: A Process for Reform." *Annals of Emergency Medicine* 23 (February 1994), 330–33.

Mechanic, David. "Dilemmas in Rationing Health Care Services: The Case for Implicit Rationing." *British Medical Journal* 310 (1995), 1655–59.

Menzel, Paul T. "Equality, Autonomy, and Efficiency: What Health Care System Should We Have?" *Journal of Medicine & Philosophy* 17 (1992), 33–57.

———. *Strong Medicine: The Ethical Rationing of Health Care.* New York: Oxford University Press, 1990.

Moreno, Jonathan D. "Recapturing Justice in the Managed Care Era." *Cambridge Quarterly of Healthcare Ethics* 5 (1996), 493–99.

Nord, Erik. *Cost-Value Analysis in Health Care: Making Sense Out of QALYs.* Cambridge: Cambridge University Press, 1999.

Nord, Erik, et al. "Incorporating Societal Concerns for Fairness in Numerical Valuations of Health Programmes." *Health Economics* 8 (1999), 25–39.

Orentlicher, David. "Destructuring Disability: Rationing of Health Care and Unfair Discrimination against the Sick." *Harvard Civil Rights-Civil Liberties Law Review* 31 (1996): 49–87.

———. "Health Care Reform and the Patient-Physician Relationship." *Health Matrix: Journal of Law-Medicine* 5 (1995), 141–80.

Patrick, Donald L., and Erickson, Pennifer. *Health Status and Health Policy.* New York: Oxford University Press, 1993.

Pellegrino, Edmund. "Managed Care and Managed Competition: Some Ethical Reflections." *Calyx* 4 (Fall 1994): 1–5.

Powers, Madison. "Justice and the Market for Health Insurance." *Kennedy Institute of Ethics Journal* 1 (1991), 307–23.

———, and Faden, Ruth. "Inequalities in Health, Inequalities in Health Care: Four Generations of Discussion about Justice and Cost-Effectiveness Analysis." *Kennedy Institute of Ethics Journal* 10 (June 2000), 109–27.

President's Commission for the Study of Ethical Problems in Medicine and Biomedical and Behavioral Research. *Securing Access to Health Care.* Vols. 1–3. Washington, DC: U.S. Government Printing Office, 1983.

Rawls, John. *The Law of Peoples.* Cambridge, MA: Harvard University Press, 1999.

Reinhardt, Uwe E. "Reforming the Health Care System: The Universal Dilemma." *American Journal of Law and Medicine* 19 (1993), 21–36.

Relman, Arnold S. "The Trouble with Rationing." *New England Journal of Medicine* 323 (September 27, 1990), 911–13.

Ubel, Peter A. "The Challenge of Measuring Community Values in Ways Appropriate for Setting Health Care Priorities." *Kennedy Institute of Ethics Journal* 9 (1999): 263–84.

Veatch, Robert M. "Single Payers and Multiple Lists: Must Everyone Get the Same Coverage in a Universal Health Plan?" *Kennedy Institute of Ethics Journal* 7 (1997), 153–69.

Weinstein, Milton C., and Stason, William B. "Allocating Resources: The Case of Hypertension." *Hastings Center Report* 7 (October 1977), 24–29.

World Health Organization. *The World Health Report 2000—Health Systems: Improving Performance.* Geneva: World Health Organization, 2000.

Yarborough, Mark. "The Private Health Insurance Industry: The Real Barrier to Healthcare Access?" *Cambridge Quarterly of Healthcare Ethics* 3 (1994), 99–107.

BIBLIOGRAPHIES AND REFERENCE WORKS

Curran, William J., et al. *Health Care Law and Ethics.* New York: Aspen Law & Business, Inc., 1998. (Includes bibliographical references.)

Becker, Lawrence, and Charlotte Becker, eds. *Encyclopedia of Ethics,* New York: Garland, 1992.

Leatt, Peggy, et al. *Perspectives on Physician Involvement in Resource Allocation and Utilization Management: An Annotated Bibliography.* Toronto: University of Toronto, 1991.

Lineback, Richard H., ed. *Philosopher's Index.* Vols. 1–. Bowling Green, OH: Philosophy Documentation Center, Bowling Green State University. Issued quarterly. Also CD Rom.

National Library of Medicine (NLM) Gateway. http://gateway.nlm.nih.gov.

Reich, Warren, ed. *Encyclopedia of Bioethics,* 2d ed., New York: Macmillan, 1995.

Walters, LeRoy, and Kahn, Tamar Joy, eds. *Bibliography of Bioethics.* Vols. 1–. New York: Free Press. Issued annually.

3.
Autonomy Rights and Medical Information

INTRODUCTION

The problems investigated in this chapter are (1) the conditions under which patients and related parties should have control over medical information and decisionmaking, and (2) how health professionals should manage and protect medical information.

MEDICAL CONFIDENTIALITY

The section on medical confidentiality in this chapter provides a strong link to traditional medical ethics, where rules of confidentiality have played a significant role since the Hippocratic Oath. There the physician vows: "What I may see or hear in the course of treatment or even outside of the treatment in regard to the life of men . . . I will keep to myself."

In the first selection in this chapter, Mark Siegler questions whether the tradition of confidentiality has been reduced to a "decrepit" concept of more symbolic than real value. Siegler maintains that traditional medical confidentiality has been systematically compromised in the course of modern bureaucratic health care and data storage systems that allow informational access to a large number of persons. He argues that infringements of confidentiality have become routine events in medical practice—the rule rather than the exception.

Siegler's article raises the question of whether medical confidentiality is an especially strict duty, a relic of the past, or a requirement in need of reconstruction. In addressing this question, we can begin by asking what would justify a practice of maintaining medical confidentiality in a profession in which access to vital information may mean the difference between life and death. Two general types of justification have been proposed for the confidentiality principle. The first type of justification appeals to the principle of respect for autonomy. The argument is that the health professional does not show proper respect for the patient's autonomy and privacy if he or she does not uphold the confidentiality of the professional-patient relationship. A variant of this approach asserts that there is an implied promise of confidentiality inherent in the professional-patient relationship, whether the professional explicitly recognizes the promise or not. In the absence of an explicit acknowledgment that confidentiality does *not* hold, the patient would always be entitled to assume that it does hold.

A second justification is that confidentiality should be maintained because it is a necessary condition of properly doing the work of a physician (or nurse or hospital). If confidentiality were ignored in medical practice, patients would be unwilling to reveal sensitive information to health professionals. This unwillingness would render diagnosis and cure more difficult and, in the long run, would be detrimental to the health of patients. The assumption is that the physician-patient relationship rests on a basis of trust that would be imperiled if physicians were not under an obligation to maintain confidence.

The second justification appeals to the positive *consequences* of confidentiality, whereas the first looks to a moral violation that would be wrong irrespective of the kinds of consequences envisaged in the second. That is, the first justification maintains that breaches of trust, broken promises, and failures to keep contractual obligations are themselves wrong, whereas the second looks not at what is intrinsically wrong but instead at whether the balance of the consequences supports maintaining confidentiality.

The second justification has been at the center of recent controversy about confidentiality. Its consequentialist commitments require that we compare the benefits of keeping confidences with the benefits of revealing confidential information in circumstances in which the information is desperately needed by another party. If through this comparison it turns out that there is an overriding duty to warn persons who might be seriously harmed if confidentiality were maintained, then confidentiality is not an absolute duty. Yet many have long held that confidentiality is an absolute duty.

A now classic case of conflict between the obligation of confidentiality and the obligation to protect others from harm occurred in *Tarasoff v. Regents of the University of California* (the second selection in this chapter). In this case a patient confided to his psychologist that he intended to kill a third party. The psychologist then faced the choice of preserving the confidentiality of the patient or of infringing his right of confidentiality to warn a young woman that her life might be in danger. The court finds that health care professionals have a duty to weigh a peril to the public that a patient discloses in confidence against the duty of maintaining confidentiality. But how is the one duty to be weighed against the other? How can we be confident that warning potential victims of a dangerous patient's disclosures will not undermine the benefits of a medical system that motivates disturbed individuals to seek help? As the *Tarasoff* opinion itself indicates, it is difficult to verify which alternative produces a better outcome for society.

One way out of this problem is to take the first justification very seriously and allow rights of patient autonomy to override the utilitarian social benefits of disclosing confidential information. There is a loss, however, by giving such stringent weight to rights of autonomy: The benefits of disclosure under desperate circumstances are lost if we allow no violations of confidentiality whatever. For example, physicians would not be able to report contagious diseases, child abuse, gunshot wounds, epilepsy (to a motor vehicle department), and the like.

To meet this challenge, perhaps one could support a *firm* rule of confidentiality without supporting an *absolute* rule. Using this approach, one could recognize a range of exceptions under which disclosure of clearly confidential information is permitted. One example of this problem is found in the contemporary discussion of the conditions under which confidential information about AIDS patients may be disclosed, especially when the disclosure constitutes a warning to persons such as health professionals of imminent danger.

Morton Winston considers a range of problems about AIDS and the limits of medical confidentiality in the final article in this section. He notes that rights of autonomy can often be limited by the *harm principle,* which requires persons to refrain from causing preventable wrongful harm to innocent others. This principle has special force when persons are vulnerable and dependent upon others. Winston uses these premises to argue that breaches of confidentiality can be justified in a range of cases in which each of the following conditions is satisfied: (1) persons would be placed at risk of contracting AIDS, (2) carriers will not freely disclose their status, and (3) the identity and status of the carrier is known to a health professional.

Not all examples of the problem of confidentiality are so dramatic or socially significant as those discussed in the Tarasoff case and the Winston article. More troublesome and pervasive problems concern how much of a patient's medical record can be fed into a widely accessed "public" data bank, how much information about a patient's genetic makeup may be revealed to a sexual partner if there is a substantial likelihood of the couple's producing genetically handicapped children, what information employers and insurance companies should and should not receive, and to whom in a family the full range of test results in genetic screening should be disclosed. These are some of the many issues about confidentiality currently under discussion.

TRUTH TELLING AND THE DISCLOSURE OF BAD NEWS

In modern medicine the nature and quality of the physician-patient relationship varies with prior contact, the mental or physical state of the patient, the manner in which the physician relates to the family, and problems in patient-family interactions. The patient's right to know the truth and the physician's obligation to tell it are contingent on these and other factors in the relationship.

Most writers in the history of medical ethics have held that departures from the general principle of truth telling are justified when information disclosure itself carries serious risks for patients. They view truth telling as limited by the Hippocratic principle that they should do no harm to patients in difficult circumstances by revealing upsetting conditions. If disclosure of a diagnosis of cancer, for example, would cause the patient anxiety or lead to an act of self-destruction, they believe that medical ethics requires that the physician carefully monitor and, at times, withhold the information that could cause additional harm. A common thesis is that in cases in which risks of harm from nondisclosure are low and benefits of nondisclosure to the patient are substantial, a physician may legitimately deceive or underdisclose the truth, and sometimes lie.

Deception is sometimes said to be easier to justify than blatant lying, because deception does not necessarily threaten the relationship of trust. Underdisclosure and nondisclosure are also thought to be more easily justified than lying. Those who share this perspective argue that it is important not to conflate duties, not to lie, not to deceive, and to disclose as if they were a single duty of veracity.

These justifications of nondisclosure seem especially plausible in cases in which bad news must be delivered to fragile patients or to strangers. Nevertheless, almost all authorities now agree that there is a strong duty of veracity in medicine because of respect for autonomous patients. Can these views about justified disclosure and justified nondisclosure be rendered consistent?

In the first essay in this chapter, David Thomasma explains both why truth telling is important and when truth telling rules might plausibly be overridden in the clinical setting. Thomasma defends the controversial thesis that "truth is a secondary good . . . [and] other primary values take precedence over the truth." Moreover, he says, "the only values that can trump the truth are recipient survival, community survival, and the ability to absorb the full impact of the truth at a particular time."

Using a very different analysis, Garry Sigman and colleagues analyze cases in which parents of children and adolescents request nondisclosure of a diagnosis. They use a case study to help identify specific clinical factors that are important when deciding whether to make truthful disclosures to children after their parents object to the disclosures. They analyze disclosure duties, disease specific factors, patient factors, and family factors—arguing for a context specific approach to truth telling in which lying to the patient and hiding information may occasionally be justified in light of all the factors at work.

Despite the mitigating conditions mentioned by Thomasma and Sigman and colleagues, many writers in contemporary bioethics believe that all intentional suppression of pertinent information violates a patient's autonomy rights and violates the fundamental duties of the health professional. Here the duty of veracity is derived from obligations of respect for the autonomy of persons. This thesis has been especially prominent in the recent literature on informed consent.

INFORMED CONSENT

It is now widely believed that the physician has a moral obligation not only to tell patients the truth, but also to help them decide important matters that affect their health. This ability to make an educated decision is dependent upon the availability of truthful information and the patient's capacity to handle the information. For this reason it is often said that before a physician performs a medical procedure on a competent patient, he or she has an obligation to obtain the patient's informed consent and to engage in mutual decision making with the patient.

The history of informed consent is not ancient. Prior to the 1950s, there was no firm ground in which a commitment to informed consent could take root. This is not to say that there is no relevant history of the physician's management of medical information in the encounter with patients. However, with few exceptions, no serious consideration was given to issues of either consent or self-determination by patients and research subjects. Proper principles, practices, and virtues of "truthfulness" in disclosure were occasionally discussed, but the perspective was largely one of how to make disclosures without harming patients by revealing their condition too abruptly and starkly.

Because of the vagueness that surrounds the term *informed consent,* some writers have been interested in analyzing the concept so that its meaning is as clear as possible. If overdemanding criteria such as "full disclosure and complete understanding" are adopted, an informed consent becomes impossible to obtain. Conversely, if underdemanding criteria such as "the patient signed the form" are used, an informed consent becomes too easy to obtain and the term loses all moral significance. Many interactions between a physician and a patient or an investigator and a subject that have been called informed consents have been so labelled only because they rest on underdemanding criteria; they are inappropriately referred to as informed consents. For example, a physician's truthful disclosure to a patient has often been declared the essence of informed consent, as if a patient's silence following disclosure could add up to an informed consent.

Jay Katz has been at the forefront of this effort to analyze the concept of informed consent. He argues that *informed consent* and *shared decision making* should be treated as virtually synonymous terms. His basic moral conviction is that the primary goal of informed consent in medical care and in research is to enable potential subjects and patients to make autonomous decisions about whether to grant or refuse authorization for medical and research interventions.

Ruth Faden and Tom Beauchamp agree that there is a historical relationship between shared decision making and informed consent but believe it is confusing to treat them as *synonymous.* They argue that decision making should be distinguished from a subject's or patient's act of knowledgeably *authorizing* the intervention, that is, giving an informed consent. The essence of an informed consent, on this analysis, is an autonomous authorization. Such an authorization requires more than merely acquiescing in, yielding to, or complying with an arrangement or a proposal made by a physician or investigator.

One crucial question addressed in the articles on informed consent in this chapter is whether a valid informed consent can be given if a patient or subject does *not* autonomously authorize an intervention. The authors in this chapter all appear to answer "No" to this question. Yet most of the "consents" obtained in health care institutions at the present time probably do not constitute autonomous authorizations, in the sense of autonomy discussed in Chapter 1. That is, it is doubtful that a patient substantially understands the circumstances, makes a decision absent coercion, and intentionally authorizes a professional to proceed with a medical or research intervention. This situation opens up a range of questions about the validity of the practices of consent currently at work in contemporary medicine and research.

Another problem addressed in these articles concerns adequate standards of disclosure in informed consent contexts. Legal history reveals an evolving doctrine of informed consent from a 1767 case to the 1972 *Canterbury v. Spence* case (and its aftermath). *Canterbury* was the first and most influential of the recent landmark informed consent cases. In *Canterbury,* surgery on the patient's back and a subsequent accident in the hospital led to further injuries and unexpected paralysis, the possibility of which had not yet been disclosed. Judge Spottswood Robinson's opinion focuses on the needs of the reasonable person and the right to self-determination. As for sufficiency of information, the court holds: "The patient's right of self-decision shapes the boundaries of the duty to reveal. That right can be effectively exercised only if the patient possesses enough information to enable an intelligent choice." Katz delivers a blistering attack on the development of these standards in the precedent legal cases, especially *Canterbury.*

Many have challenged whether any legal standard could be adequate for clinical ethics (as distinct from a standard in law), since the law is almost uniformly directed at adequate *disclosures.* In recent bioethics the focus on informed consent has turned somewhat away from disclosure duties and more toward the quality of understanding and consent in the patient. Much has been made of Katz's claim that the key to effective communication is to invite participation by patients or subjects in an exchange of information and dialogue. Asking questions, eliciting the concerns and interests of the patient or subject, and establishing a climate that encourages the patient or subject to ask questions seems to be more important for medical ethics than the full body of requirements of disclosed information in law.

In the final selection in this section, Robert Levine discusses why the Western model of informed consent is unsuitable in much of the remainder of the world, where he thinks the concept of "person" differs substantially from that in Western societies. Levine concludes that we would be better off if we used a procedural solution to these problems when they are encountered rather than insisting on rules of obtaining consent. Levine's treatment also suggests how we might handle the growing problem of cultural diversity in Western nations when patients from non-Western countries present to health professionals.

REFUSAL OF TREATMENT

The subject of the fourth section of this chapter is refusal of treatment by a patient or a duly authorized representative of the patient (when a patient is incompetent or seriously ill). The major question is, "Under what conditions, if any, is it permissible for patients, health professionals, and surrogate decision makers to forgo treatment with the foreknowledge that there may be serious health consequences for the patient (such as death or disability)?"

It is now generally agreed, in both law and ethics, that a competent patient has an autonomy right to forgo treatment at any time, including the right to refuse medical nutrition and hydration. Indeed, refusals in medical settings have a moral power lacking in mere requests for assistance: A physician is morally and legally required to comply with a refusal. However, competent persons sometimes exercise their rights in a way inconsistent with the beliefs of other members of their family or inconsistent with the commitments of a health care institution—a problem that arises in this chapter in the case of Elizabeth Bouvia. She suffered from cerebral palsy that left her with virtually no motor function in her limbs or skeletal muscles, but she was unaffected cognitively. The court asserts that patients like Bouvia have a moral and constitutional right to refuse treatment even if its exercise creates a "life-threatening condition" of which physicians disapprove and consider against standards of practice.

Several celebrated legal cases have centered on whether formerly competent patients have some kind of right to refuse treatment despite their present incompetence. Among the best known cases, and the only one to reach the U.S. Supreme Court, is that of Nancy Cruzan. The 25-year-old Ms. Cruzan was in a persistent vegetative state for over three years. Her parents then petitioned for permission to remove the feeding tube, knowing that, by doing so, their daughter would die. A lower court's authorization of termination of treatment was reversed by the Missouri Supreme Court, which ruled that no one may order an end to life-sustaining treatment for an incompetent person in the absence of a valid living will or clear and convincing evidence of the patient's wishes.

This decision was appealed to the U.S. Supreme Court, which handed down its decision in 1990. The majority opinion—the second selection in this section—holds that a state may constitutionally require "clear and convincing evidence" whenever surrogates claim to represent a patient's autonomous wishes about continuing or refusing life-sustaining treatment. The majority insists that its findings rest on a judgment by society that it is better to err in preserving life in a vegetative state than to err through a decision that leads directly to death. The dissenting justices express a particularly vigorous disagreement with this majority opinion. Justices Brennan, Marshall, and Blackmun find that "Nancy Cruzan has a fundamental right to be free of unwanted artificial nutrition and hydration"—a direct challenge to the line of argument in the majority opinion.

Whether the Court's opinion is adequate to protect the autonomy interests of patients is still under discussion. One of the major issues raised by *Cruzan* is whether a protected autonomy interest in refusing medical treatment can be meaningfully exercised only by competent patients or also by incompetent patients, either through their surrogates or through some forms of advance directive to health care authorities. These questions have fostered an active discussion of the role of advance directives in health care—our final topic in this chapter.

ADVANCE DIRECTIVES

In an advance directive—a device intended to implement patients' rights of autonomy—a person, while competent, either writes a directive for health care professionals or selects a surrogate to make decisions about treatments during periods of incompetence. Two types of advance directive have been recognized: *living wills,* which are substantive directives regarding medical procedures that should be provided or forgone in specific circumstances, and *durable powers of attorney* (DPA) for health care. A durable power of attorney is a legal document in which one person assigns another person as authority to perform specified actions on behalf of the signer.

Both kinds of advance directive can reduce stress for individuals, families, and health professionals who fear wrong outcomes or decisions, but they also generate practical and moral problems. First, relatively few persons compose them or leave explicit instructions. Second, a designated decision maker might be unavailable when needed, might be incompetent to make good decisions for the patient, or might have a conflict of interest. Third, laws often severely restrict the use of advance directives. For example, advance directives have legal effect in some states if and only if the patient is terminally ill and death is imminent. But decisions must be made in some cases when death is not imminent or the medical condition cannot appropriately be described as a terminal illness. Fourth, in the case of living wills, individuals have difficulty in specifying decisions or guidelines that adequately anticipate the full range of medical situations that might occur. The directive given may provide no basis for health professionals to overturn instructions that turn out not to be in the patient's best medical interest, although the patient could not have reasonably anticipated this circumstance while competent. Surrogate decision makers also make decisions with which physicians sharply disagree.

Despite these problems, the advance directive is widely recognized as a promising and valid way for competent persons to exercise their autonomy. On December 1, 1991, the Patient Self-Determination Act—a federal law known as PSDA—went into effect in the United States. This law requires health care facilities certified by Medicare or Medicaid to notify competent adult patients of their right to accept or refuse medical treatment and their right to execute an advance directive. This law gave powerful legal effect to advance directives in the United States.

The intent of this law—and of almost all rules and regulations pertaining to advance directives—is to allow patients to take control of their medical fate, on the grounds that their interests will ultimately be best served by making their own decisions, rather than having the decisions made for them. In their article in this chapter, Linda Emanuel and colleagues attempt to provide a practically oriented set of basic steps and skills for advance care planning. Their model of advance care planning *as a process* should be viewed as augmenting and updating (rather than replacing) executed advance directive forms. They identify several steps of providing information, facilitating discussion, recording statements, reviewing directives, and implementing decisions. They argue that their model will minimize risks and maximize benefits for patients and health professionals alike.

In the final article in this chapter, Ben A. Rich assesses advance directives as a form of anticipatory decision making that moves "beyond informed consent and refusal." Rich distinguishes between and assesses oral directives, living wills, and the durable power of attorney. He points to several flaws and limitations in these forms of advance planning, especially living wills and durable powers of attorney. He also discusses why there has been so much physician inattention to advance directives. Rich concludes that it is not the concept of advance directives that is flawed, but rather "our fledgling efforts at crafting them." He provides some reasons for optimism that "the next generation of advance directives will succeed where the others have failed."

T.L.B.

MARK SIEGLER

Confidentiality in Medicine—A Decrepit Concept

Mark Siegler, MD, is director of the MacLean Center for Clinical Medical Ethics and a professor in the Department of Medicine at the University of Chicago. With Albert Jonsen and William Winslade, he published *Clinical Ethics,* which is widely consulted by health professionals. Among his many articles in bioethics are "The External Control of Private Medical Decisions: A Major Change in the Doctor-Patient Relationship," *Journal of American Geriatrics Society* and a collaboration entitled "A Procedure for Balancing the Rights of Patients and the Responsibilities of Physicians," *The Law-Medicine Relation: A Philosophical Exploration*.

Medical confidentiality, as it has traditionally been understood by patients and doctors, no longer exists. This ancient medical principle, which has been included in every physician's oath and code of ethics since Hippocratic times, has become old, worn-out, and useless; it is a decrepit concept. Efforts to preserve it appear doomed to failure and often give rise to more problems than solutions. Psychiatrists have tacitly acknowledged the impossibility of ensuring the confidentiality of medical records by choosing to establish a separate, more secret record. The following case illustrates how the confidentiality principle is compromised systematically in the course of routine medical care.

A patient of mine with mild chronic obstructive pulmonary disease was transferred from the surgical intensive-care unit to a surgical nursing floor two days after an elective cholecystectomy. On the day of transfer, the patient saw a respiratory therapist writing in his medical chart (the therapist was recording the results of an arterial blood gas analysis) and became concerned about the confidentiality of his hospital records. The patient threatened to leave the hospital prematurely unless I could guarantee that the confidentiality of his hospital record would be respected.

This patient's complaint prompted me to enumerate the number of persons who had both access to his hospital record and a reason to examine it. I was amazed to learn that at least 25 and possibly as many as 100 health professionals and administrative personnel at our university hospital had access to the patient's record and that all of them had a legitimate need, indeed a professional responsibility, to open and use that chart. These persons included 6 attending physicians (the primary physician, the surgeon, the pulmonary consultant, and others); 12 house officers (medical, surgical, intensive-care unit, and "covering" house staff); 20 nursing personnel (on three shifts); 6 respiratory therapists; 3 nutritionists; 2 clinical pharmacists; 15 students (from medicine, nursing, respiratory therapy, and clinical pharmacy); 4 unit secretaries; 4 hospital financial officers; and 4 chart reviewers (utilization review, quality assurance review, tissue review, and insurance auditor). It is of interest that this patient's problem was straightforward, and he therefore did not require many other technical and support services that the modern hospital provides. For example, he did not need multiple consultants and fellows, such specialized procedures as dialysis, or social workers, chaplains, physical therapists, occupational therapists, and the like.

Upon completing my survey I reported to the patient that I estimated that at least 75 health professionals and hospital personnel had access to his med-

Reprinted by permission of *New England Journal of Medicine,* vol. 307. Copyright © 1982 Massachusetts Medical Society.

ical record. I suggested to the patient that these people were all involved in providing or supporting his health care services. They were, I assured him, working for him. Despite my reassurances the patient was obviously distressed and retorted, "I always believed that medical confidentiality was part of a doctor's code of ethics. Perhaps you should tell me just what you people mean by 'confidentiality'!"

TWO ASPECTS OF MEDICAL CONFIDENTIALITY

CONFIDENTIALITY AND THIRD-PARTY INTERESTS

Previous discussions of medical confidentiality usually have focused on the tension between a physician's responsibility to keep information divulged by patients secret and a physician's legal and moral duty, on occasion, to reveal such confidences to third parties, such as families, employers, public-health authorities, or police authorities. In all these instances, the central question relates to the stringency of the physician's obligation to maintain patient confidentiality when the health, well-being, and safety of identifiable others or of society in general would be threatened by a failure to reveal information about the patient. The tension in such cases is between the good of the patient and the good of others.

CONFIDENTIALITY AND THE PATIENT'S INTEREST

As the example above illustrates, further challenges to confidentiality arise because the patient's personal interest in maintaining confidentiality comes into conflict with his personal interest in receiving the best possible health care. Modern high-technology health care is available principally in hospitals (often, teaching hospitals), requires many trained and specialized workers (a "health-care team"), and is very costly. The existence of such teams means that information that previously had been held in confidence by an individual physician will now necessarily be disseminated to many members of the team. Furthermore, since health-care teams are expensive and few patients can afford to pay such costs directly, it becomes essential to grant access to the patient's medical record to persons who are responsible for obtaining third-party payment. These persons include chart reviewers, financial officers, insurance auditors, and quality-of-care assessors. Finally, as medicine expands from a narrow, disease-based model to a model that encompasses psychological, social, and economic problems, not only will the size of the health-care team and medical costs increase, but more sensitive information (such as one's personal habits and financial condition) will now be included in the medical record and will no longer be confidential.

The point I wish to establish is that hospital medicine, the rise of health-care teams, the existence of third-party insurance programs, and the expanding limits of medicine will appear to be responses to the wishes of people for better and more comprehensive medical care. But each of these developments necessarily modifies our traditional understanding of medical confidentiality.

THE ROLE OF CONFIDENTIALITY IN MEDICINE

Confidentiality serves a dual purpose in medicine. In the first place, it acknowledges respect for the patient's sense of individuality and privacy. The patient's most personal physical and psychological secrets are kept confidential in order to decrease a sense of shame and vulnerability. Secondly, confidentiality is important in improving the patient's health care—a basic goal of medicine. The promise of confidentiality permits people to trust (i.e., have confidence) that information revealed to a physician in the course of a medical encounter will not be disseminated further. In this way patients are encouraged to communicate honestly and forthrightly with their doctors. This bond of trust between patient and doctor is vitally important both in the diagnostic process (which relies on an accurate history) and subsequently in the treatment phase, which often depends as much on the patient's trust in the physician as it does on medications and surgery. These two important functions of confidentiality are as important now as they were in the past. They will not be supplanted entirely either by improvements in medical technology or by recent changes in relations between some patients and doctors toward a rights-based, consumerist model.

POSSIBLE SOLUTIONS TO THE CONFIDENTIALITY PROBLEM

First of all, in all nonbureaucratic, noninstitutional medical encounters—that is, in the millions of doctor–patient encounters that take place in physician's offices, where more privacy can be preserved—meticulous care should be taken to guarantee that patients' medical and personal information will be kept confidential.

Secondly, in such settings as hospitals or large-scale group practices, where many persons have opportunities to examine the medical record, we should aim to provide access only to those who have "a need to know." This could be accomplished through such administrative changes as dividing the entire record into several sections—for example, a medical and financial section—and permitting only health professionals access to the medical information.

The approach favored by many psychiatrists—that of keeping a psychiatric record separate from the general medical record—is an understandable strategy but one that is not entirely satisfactory and that should not be generalized. The keeping of separate psychiatric records implies that psychiatry and medicine are different undertakings and thus drives deeper the wedge between them and between physical and psychological illness. Furthermore, it is often vitally important for internists or surgeons to know that a patient is being seen by a psychiatrist or is taking a particular medication. When separate records are kept, this information may not be available. Finally, if generalized, the practice of keeping a separate psychiatric record could lead to the unacceptable consequence of having a separate record for each type of medical problem.

Patients should be informed about what is meant by "medical confidentiality." We should establish the distinction between information about the patient that generally will be kept confidential regardless of the interest of third parties and information that will be exchanged among members of the health-care team in order to provide care for the patient. Patients should be made aware of the large number of persons in the modern hospital who require access to the medical record in order to serve the patient's medical and financial interests.

Finally, at some point most patients should have an opportunity to review their medical record and to make informed choices about whether their entire record is to be available to everyone or whether certain portions of the record are privileged and should be accessible only to their principal physician or to others designated explicitly by the patient. This approach would rely on traditional informed-consent procedural standards and might permit the patient to balance the personal value of medical confidentiality against the personal value of high-technology, team health care. There is no reason that the same procedure should not be used with psychiatric records instead of the arbitrary system now employed, in which everything related to psychiatry is kept secret.

AFTERTHOUGHT: CONFIDENTIALITY AND INDISCRETION

There is one additional aspect of confidentiality that is rarely included in discussions of the subject. I am referring here to the wanton, often inadvertent, but avoidable exchanges of confidential information that occur frequently in hospital rooms, elevators, cafeterias, doctors' offices, and at cocktail parties. Of course, as more people have access to medical information about the patient the potential for this irresponsible abuse of confidentiality increases geometrically.

Such mundane breaches of confidentiality are probably of greater concern to most patients than the broader issues of whether their medical records may be entered into a computerized data bank or whether a respiratory therapist is reviewing the results of an arterial blood gas determination. Somehow, privacy is violated and a sense of shame is heightened when intimate secrets are revealed to people one knows or is close to—friends, neighbors, acquaintances, or hospital roommates—rather than when they are disclosed to an anonymous bureaucrat sitting at a computer terminal in a distant city or to a health professional who is acting in an official capacity.

I suspect that the principles of medical confidentiality, particularly those reflected in most medical codes of ethics, were designed principally to prevent just this sort of embarrassing personal indiscretion rather than to maintain (for social, political, or economic reasons) the absolute secrecy of doctor–patient communications. In this regard, it is worth noting that Percival's Code of Medical Ethics (1803) includes the following admonition: "Patients should be interrogated concerning their complaint in a tone of voice which cannot be overheard."* We in the medical profession frequently neglect these simple courtesies.

CONCLUSION

The principle of medical confidentiality described in medical codes of ethics and still believed in by patients no longer exists. In this respect, it is a decrepit concept. Rather than perpetuate the myth of confidentiality and invest energy vainly to preserve it, the public and the profession would be better served if they devoted their attention to determining which aspects of the original principle of confidentiality are worth retaining. Efforts could then be directed to salvaging those.

*Leake C. D., ed. Percival's medical ethics. Baltimore: Williams & Wilkins, 1927.

CALIFORNIA SUPREME COURT

Tarasoff v. Regents of the University of California

TOBRINER, Justice

On October 27, 1969, Prosenjit Poddar killed Tatiana Tarasoff. Plaintiffs, Tatiana's parents, allege that two months earlier Poddar confided his intention to kill Tatiana to Dr. Lawrence Moore, a psychologist employed by the Cowell Memorial Hospital at the University of California at Berkeley. They allege that on Moore's request, the campus police briefly detained Poddar, but released him when he appeared rational. They further claim that Dr. Harvey Powelson, Moore's superior, then directed that no further action be taken to detain Poddar. No one warned plaintiffs of Tatiana's peril. . . .

We shall explain that defendant therapists cannot escape liability merely because Tatiana herself was not their patient. When a therapist determines, or pursuant to the standards of his profession should determine, that his patient presents a serious danger of violence to another, he incurs an obligation to use reasonable care to protect the intended victim against such danger. The discharge of this duty may require the therapist to take one or more of various steps, depending upon the nature of the case. Thus it may call for him to warn the intended victim or others likely to apprise the victim of the danger, to notify the police, or to take whatever other steps are reasonably necessary under the circumstances. . . .

1. PLAINTIFFS' COMPLAINTS

Plaintiffs, Tatiana's mother and father, filed separate but virtually identical second amended complaints. The issue before us on this appeal is whether those complaints now state, or can be amended to state, causes of action against defendants. We therefore begin by setting forth the pertinent allegations of the complaints.

Plaintiffs' first cause of action, entitled "Failure to Detain a Dangerous Patient," alleges that on August 20, 1969, Poddar was a voluntary outpatient receiving therapy at Cowell Memorial Hospital. Poddar informed Moore, his therapist, that he was going to kill an unnamed girl, readily identifiable as Tatiana, when she returned home from spending the summer in Brazil. Moore, with the concurrence of Dr. Gold, who had initially examined Poddar, and Dr. Yandell, assistant to the director of the department of psychiatry, decided that Poddar should be committed for observation in a mental hospital. Moore orally notified Officers Atkinson and Teel of the campus police that he would request commitment. He then sent a letter to Police Chief William Beall requesting the assistance of the police department in securing Poddar's confinement.

Officers Atkinson, Brownrigg, and Halleran took Poddar into custody, but, satisfied that Poddar was rational, released him on his promise to stay away from Tatiana. Powelson, director of the department of psychiatry at Cowell Memorial Hospital, then asked the police to return Moore's letter, directed that all copies of the letter and notes that Moore had taken as therapist be destroyed, and "ordered no action to place Prosenjit Poddar in 72-hour treatment and evaluation facility."

Plaintiffs' second cause of action, entitled "Failure to Warn On a Dangerous Patient," incorporates the allegations of the first cause of action, but adds the assertion that defendants negligently permitted Poddar to be released from police custody without "notifying the parents of Tatiana Tarasoff that their daughter was in grave danger from Prosenjit Poddar." Poddar

From 131 *California Reporter* 14. Decided July 1, 1976. All footnotes and numerous references in the text of the decision and a dissent have been omitted.

persuaded Tatiana's brother to share an apartment with him near Tatiana's residence; shortly after her return from Brazil, Poddar went to her residence and killed her. . . .

2. PLAINTIFFS CAN STATE A CAUSE OF ACTION AGAINST DEFENDANT THERAPISTS FOR NEGLIGENT FAILURE TO PROTECT TATIANA

The second cause of action can be amended to allege that Tatiana's death proximately resulted from defendants' negligent failure to warn Tatiana or others likely to apprise her of her danger. Plaintiffs contend that as amended, such allegations of negligence and proximate causation, with resulting damages, establish a cause of action. Defendants, however, contend that in the circumstances of the present case they owed no duty of care to Tatiana or her parents and that, in the absence of such duty, they were free to act in careless disregard of Tatiana's life and safety. . . .

In the landmark case of *Rowland v. Christian* (1968), Justice Peters recognized that liability should be imposed "for an injury occasioned to another by his want of ordinary care or skill" as expressed in section 1714 of the Civil Code. Thus, Justice Peters, quoting from *Heaven v. Pender* (1883) stated: " 'whenever one person is by circumstances placed in such a position with regard to another . . . that if he did not use ordinary care and skill in his own conduct . . . he would cause danger of injury to the person or property of the other, a duty arises to use ordinary care and skill to avoid such danger.' "

We depart from "this fundamental principle" only upon the "balancing of a number of considerations"; major ones "are the foreseeability of harm to the plaintiff, the degree of certainty that the plaintiff suffered injury, the closeness of the connection between the defendant's conduct and the injury suffered, the moral blame attached to the defendant's conduct, the policy of preventing future harm, the extent of the burden to the defendant and consequences to the community of imposing a duty to exercise care with resulting liability for breach, and the availability, cost and prevalence of insurance for the risk involved."

The most important of these considerations in establishing duty is foreseeability. As a general principle, a "defendant owes a duty of care to all persons who are foreseeably endangered by his conduct, with respect to all risks which make the conduct unreasonably dangerous."

As we shall explain, however, when the avoidance of foreseeable harm requires a defendant to control the conduct of another person, or to warn of such conduct, the common law has traditionally imposed liability only if the defendant bears some special relationship to the dangerous person or to the potential victim. Since the relationship between a therapist and his patient satisfies this requirement, we need not here decide whether foreseeability alone is sufficient to create a duty to exercise reasonable care to protect a potential victim of another's conduct. . . .

A relationship of defendant therapists to either Tatiana or Poddar will suffice to establish a duty of care; as explained in section 315 of the Restatement Second of Torts, a duty of care may arise from either "(a) a special relation . . . between the actor and the third person which imposes a duty upon the actor to control the third person's conduct, or (b) a special relation . . . between the actor and the other which gives to the other a right of protection." . . .

The courts hold that a doctor is liable to persons infected by his patient if he negligently fails to diagnose a contagious disease, or, having diagnosed the illness, fails to warn members of the patient's family.

Since it involved a dangerous mental patient, the decision in *Merchants Nat. Bank & Trust Co. of Fargo v. United States* (1967) comes closer to the issue. The Veterans Administration arranged for the patient to work on a local farm, but did not inform the farmer of the man's background. The farmer consequently permitted the patient to come and go freely during non-working hours; the patient borrowed a car, drove to his wife's residence and killed her. Notwithstanding the lack of any "special relationship" between the Veterans Administration and the wife, the court found the Veterans Administration liable for the wrongful death of the wife.

In their summary of the relevant rulings Fleming and Maximov conclude that the "case law should dispel any notion that to impose on the therapists a duty to take precautions for the safety of persons threatened by a patient, where due care so requires, is in any way opposed to contemporary ground rules on the duty relationship. On the contrary, there now seems to be sufficient authority to support the conclusion that by entering into a doctor-patient relationship the therapist becomes sufficiently involved to assume some responsibility for the safety, not only of the patient himself, but also of any third person whom the doctor knows to be threatened by the patient." (Fleming & Maximov, *The Patient or His Victim: The Therapist's Dilemma* [1974] 62 Cal.L.Rev. 1025, 1030.)

Defendants contend, however, that imposition of a duty to exercise reasonable care to protect third persons is unworkable because therapists cannot accurately predict whether or not a patient will resort to violence. In support of this argument amicus representing the American Psychiatric Association and other professional societies cites numerous articles which indicate that therapists, in the present state of the art, are unable reliably to predict violent acts; their forecasts, amicus claims, tend consistently to overpredict violence, and indeed are more often wrong than right. Since predictions of violence are often erroneous, amicus concludes, the courts should not render rulings that predicate the liability of therapists upon the validity of such predictions. . . .

We recognize the difficulty that a therapist encounters in attempting to forecast whether a patient presents a serious danger of violence. Obviously we do not require that the therapist, in making that determination, render a perfect performance; the therapist need only exercise "that reasonable degree of skill, knowledge, and care ordinarily possessed and exercised by members of [that professional specialty] under similar circumstances." Within the broad range of reasonable practice and treatment in which professional opinion and judgment may differ, the therapist is free to exercise his or her own best judgment without liability; proof, aided by hindsight, that he or she judged wrongly is insufficient to establish negligence.

In the instant case, however, the pleadings do not raise any question as to failure of defendant therapists to predict that Poddar presented a serious danger of violence. On the contrary, the present complaints allege that defendant therapists did in fact predict that Poddar would kill, but were negligent in failing to warn.

Amicus contends, however, that even when a therapist does in fact predict that a patient poses a serious danger of violence to others, the therapist should be absolved of any responsibility for failing to act to protect the potential victim. In our view, however, once a therapist does in fact determine, or under applicable professional standards reasonably should have determined, that a patient poses a serious danger of violence to others, he bears a duty to exercise reasonable care to protect the foreseeable victim of that danger.

While the discharge of this duty of due care will necessarily vary with the facts of each case, in each instance the adequacy of the therapist's conduct must be measured against the traditional negligence standard of the rendition of reasonable care under the circumstances. As explained in Fleming and Maximov, *The Patient or His Victim: The Therapist's Dilemma* (1974) 62 Cal.L.Rev. 1025, 1967: ". . . the ultimate question of resolving the tension between the conflicting interests of patient and potential victim is one of social policy, not professional expertise. . . . In sum, the therapist owes a legal duty not only to his patient, but also to his patient's would-be victim and is subject in both respects to scrutiny by judge and jury." . . .

The risk that unnecessary warning may be given is a reasonable price to pay for the lives of possible victims that may be saved. We could hesitate to hold that the therapist who is aware that his patient expects to attempt to assassinate the President of the United States would not be obligated to warn the authorities because the therapist cannot predict with accuracy that his patient will commit the crime.

Defendants further argue that free and open communication is essential to psychotherapy, that "Unless a patient . . . is assured that . . . information [revealed to him] can and will be held in utmost confidence, he will be reluctant to make the full disclosure upon which diagnosis and treatment . . . depends." The giving of a warning, defendants contend, constitutes a breach of trust which entails the revelation of confidential communications.

We recognize the public interest in supporting effective treatment of mental illness and in protecting the rights of patients to privacy, and the consequent public importance of safeguarding the confidential character of psychotherapeutic communication. Against this interest, however, we must weigh the public interest in safety from violent assault. . . .

We realize that the open and confidential character of psychotherapeutic dialogue encourages patients to express threats of violence, few of which are ever executed. Certainly a therapist should not be encouraged routinely to reveal such threats; such disclosures could seriously disrupt the patient's relationship with his therapist and with the persons threatened. To the contrary, the therapist's obligations to his patient require that he not disclose a confidence unless such disclosure is necessary to avert danger to others, and even then that he do so discretely, and in a fashion that would preserve the privacy of his patient to the fullest extent compatible with the prevention of the threatened danger.

The revelation of a communication under the above circumstances is not a breach of trust or a violation of professional ethics; as stated in the Principles of Medical Ethics of the American Medical Association (1957), section 9: "A physician may not reveal the confidence entrusted to him in the course of medical attendance . . . *unless he is required to do so by law or unless it becomes necessary in order to protect the welfare of the individual or of the community.*" (Emphasis added.) We conclude that the public policy favoring protection of the confidential character of patient–psychotherapist communications must yield to the extent to which disclosure is essential to avert danger to others. The protective privilege ends where the public peril begins. . . .

For the foregoing reasons, we find that plaintiffs' complaints can be amended to state a cause of action against defendants Moore, Powelson, Gold, and Yandell and against the Regents as their employer, for breach of a duty to exercise reasonable care to protect Tatiana.

• • •

CLARK, Justice (dissenting).

Until today's majority opinion, both legal and medical authorities have agreed that confidentiality is essential to effectively treat the mentally ill, and that imposing a duty on doctors to disclose patient threats to potential victims would greatly impair treatment. Further, recognizing that effective treatment and society's safety are necessarily intertwined, the Legislature has already decided effective and confidential treatment is preferred over imposition of a duty to warn.

The issue of whether effective treatment for the mentally ill should be sacrificed to a system of warnings is, in my opinion, properly one for the Legislature, and we are bound by its judgment. Moreover, even in the absence of clear legislative direction, we must reach the same conclusion because imposing the majority's new duty is certain to result in a net increase in violence. . . .

Overwhelming policy considerations weigh against imposing a duty on psychotherapists to warn a potential victim against harm. While offering virtually no benefit to society, such a duty will frustrate psychiatric treatment, invade fundamental patient rights and increase violence.

The importance of psychiatric treatment and its need for confidentiality have been recognized by this court. "It is clearly recognized that the very practice of psychiatry vitally depends upon the reputation in the community that the psychiatrist will not tell." (Slovenko, *Psychiatry and a Second Look at the Medical Privilege* (1960) 6 Wayne L.Rev. 175, 188.)

Assurance of confidentiality is important for three reasons.

DETERRENCE FROM TREATMENT

First, without substantial assurance of confidentiality, those requiring treatment will be deterred from seeking assistance. It remains an unfortunate fact in our society that people seeking psychiatric guidance tend to become stigmatized. Apprehension of such stigma—apparently increased by the propensity of people considering treatment to see themselves in the worst possible light—creates a well-recognized reluctance to seek aid. This reluctance is alleviated by the psychiatrist's assurance of confidentiality.

FULL DISCLOSURE

Second, the guarantee of confidentiality is essential in eliciting the full disclosure necessary for effective treatment. The psychiatric patient approaches treatment with conscious and unconscious inhibitions against revealing his innermost thoughts. "Every person, however well-motivated, has to overcome resistances to therapeutic exploration. These resistances seek support from every possible source and the possibility of disclosure would easily be employed in the service of resistance." (Goldstein & Katz, 36 Conn. Bar J. 175, 179.) Until a patient can trust his psychiatrist not to violate their confidential relationship, "the unconscious psychological control mechanism of repression will prevent the recall of past experiences." (Butler, *Psychotherapy and Griswold: Is Confidentiality a Privilege or a Right?* (1971) 3 Conn.L.Rev. 599, 604.)

SUCCESSFUL TREATMENT

Third, even if the patient fully discloses his thoughts, assurance that the confidential relationship will not be breached is necessary to maintain his trust in his psychiatrist—the very means by which treatment is effected. "[T]he essence of much psychotherapy is the contribution of trust in the external world and ultimately in the self, modelled upon the trusting relationship established during therapy." (Dawidoff, *The Malpractice of Psychiatrists,* 1966 Duke L.J. 696, 704.) Patients will be helped only if they can form a trusting relationship with the psychiatrist. All authorities appear to agree that if the trust relationship cannot be developed because of collusive communication between the psychiatrist and others, treatment will be frustrated.

Given the importance of confidentiality to the practice of psychiatry, it becomes clear the duty to warn imposed by the majority will cripple the use and effectiveness of psychiatry. Many people, potentially violent—yet susceptible to treatment—will be deterred from seeking it; those seeking it will be inhibited from making revelations necessary to effective treatment; and, forcing the psychiatrist to violate the patient's trust will destroy the interpersonal relationship by which treatment is effected.

VIOLENCE AND CIVIL COMMITMENT

By imposing a duty to warn, the majority contributes to the danger to society of violence by the mentally ill and greatly increases the risk of civil commitment—the total deprivation of liberty—of those who should not be confined. The impairment of treatment and risk of improper commitment resulting from the new duty to warn will not be limited to a few patients but will extend to a large number of the mentally ill. Although under existing psychiatric procedures only a relatively few receiving treatment will ever present a risk of violence, the number making threats is huge, and it is the latter group—not just the former—whose treatment will be impaired and whose risk of commitment will be increased.

Both the legal and psychiatric communities recognize that the process of determining potential violence in a patient is far from exact, being fraught with complexity and uncertainty. In fact precision has not even been attained in predicting who of those having already committed violent acts will again become violent, a task recognized to be of much simpler proportions.

This predictive uncertainty means that the number of disclosures will necessarily be large. As noted above, psychiatric patients are encouraged to discuss all thoughts of violence, and they often express such thoughts. However, unlike this court, the psychiatrist does not enjoy the benefit of overwhelming hindsight in seeing which few, if any, of his patients will ultimately become violent. Now, confronted by the majority's new duty, the psychiatrist must instantaneously calculate potential violence from each patient on each visit. The difficulties researchers have encountered in accurately predicting violence will be heightened for the practicing psychiatrist dealing for brief periods in his office with heretofore nonviolent patients. And, given the decision not to warn or commit must always be made at the psychiatrist's civil peril, one can expect most doubts will be resolved in favor of the psychiatrist protecting himself.

MORTON E. WINSTON

AIDS, Confidentiality, and The Right to Know

Morton Winston is professor of philosophy at the College of New Jersey. His work has focused on applied ethics, human rights, cognitive science, and philosophy of the mind. He is also a former chair of the board of directors of Amnesty International. Recently he coauthored *Society, Ethics, and Technology* (Wadsworth) as well as *Global Ethics: Human Rights and Responsibilities* (University of Pennsylvania).

In June of 1987, a young woman who was nine months pregnant was shot with an arrow fired from a hunting bow on a Baltimore street by a man who was engaged in an argument with another person. Emergency workers from the city fire fighting unit were called to the scene, administered resuscitation to the profusely bleeding woman and took her to a local hospital where she died shortly afterwards. Her child, delivered by emergency Caesarian section, died the next day.

This tragedy would have been quickly forgotten as yet another incident of random urban violence if it had not been later learned that the woman was infected with the AIDS virus. A nurse at the hospital decided on her own initiative that the rescue workers who had brought the woman to the emergency room should be informed that they had been exposed to HIV-infected blood and contacted them directly. Several days after this story hit the newspapers two state legislators introduced a bill adding AIDS to the list of diseases that hospitals would be required to inform workers about. A hospital spokeswoman was quoted in the newspaper as opposing the proposed legislation on the grounds that it would violate patient confidentiality and that, "People taking care of patients should assume that everyone is a potential AIDS patient and take precautions. The burden is on you to take care of yourself.[1]"

This case, and others like it, raises difficult and weighty ethical and public policy issues. What are the limits of medical confidentiality? Who, if anyone, has a right to know that they may have been exposed to AIDS or other dangerous infectious diseases? Whose responsibility is it to inform the sexual contacts of AIDS patients or others who may have been exposed to the infection? Can public health policies be framed which will effectively prevent the spread of the epidemic while also protecting the civil and human rights of its victims?

I. THE LIMITS OF CONFIDENTIALITY

The rule of medical confidentiality enjoins physicians, nurses, and health care workers from revealing to third parties information about a patient obtained in the course of medical treatment. The rule protecting a patient's secrets is firmly entrenched in medical practice, in medical education, and receives explicit mention in all major medical oaths and codes of medical ethics. Sissela Bok has argued that the ethical justification for confidentiality rests on four arguments.[2]

The first and most powerful justification for the rule of confidentiality derives from the individual's right, flowing from autonomy, to control personal information and to protect privacy. The right of individuals to control access to sensitive information about themselves is particularly important in cases where revelation of such information would subject the individual to invidious discrimination, deprivation of rights, or physical or emotional harm. Since persons who are HIV-infected or who have AIDS or ARC (AIDS-Related Complex), are often subjected to discrimination, loss of employment, refusal of housing and insurance, many physicians believe that the confidentiality of HIV antibody test results and diagnoses

From *Public Affairs Quarterly* 2, no. 2 (April 1988), 91–104. Footnotes renumbered.

of AIDS should be safeguarded under all circumstances. Since many infected persons and AIDS patients are members of groups which have traditionally been subject to discrimination or social disapproval—homosexuals, drug users, or prostitutes—the protection of confidentiality of patients who belong to these groups is especially indicated.

The second and third arguments for confidentiality concern the special moral relationship which exists between physicians and their patients. Medical practice requires that patients reveal intimate personal secrets to their physicians, and that physicians live up to the trust that is required on the part of patients to reveal such information; to fail to do so would violate the physician's duty of fidelity. Additionally, since medical practice is normally conducted under a tacit promise of confidentiality, physicians would violate this expectation by revealing their patients' secrets.

The fourth argument for confidentiality is based on utilitarian or broadly pragmatic considerations. Without a guarantee of confidentiality, potential patients in need of medical care would be deterred from seeking medical assistance from fear that sensitive personal information will be revealed to third parties thereby exposing the individual to the risk of unjust discrimination or other harm. Many physicians who work with AIDS patients find such pragmatic arguments particularly compelling, believing, perhaps correctly, that breaches of medical confidentiality concerning antibody status or a diagnosis of AIDS, would have a "chilling effect" preventing people in high-risk groups from seeking voluntary antibody testing and counselling. . . .

Bok believes that confidentiality is at best a prima facie obligation, one that while generally justified, can be overridden in certain situations by more compelling moral obligations. Among the situations which license breaches of confidentiality Bok cites are: cases involving a minor child or incompetent patient who would be harmed if sensitive information were not disclosed to a parent or guardian, cases involving threats of violence against identifiable third parties, cases involving contagious sexually transmitted diseases, and other cases where identifiable third parties would be harmed or placed at risk unknowingly by failure to disclose information known to a physician obtained through therapeutic communication.

In general, personal autonomy, and the derivative right of individuals to control personal information, is limited by the "Harm Principle" [HP], which requires moral agents to refrain from acts and omissions which would foreseeably result in preventable wrongful harm to innocent others. Bok argues that when HP (or a related ethical principle which I will discuss shortly) comes into play, "the prima facie premises supporting confidentiality are overridden" . . .[3] If this argument is correct, then the strict observance of confidentiality cannot be ethically justified in all cases, and physicians and nurses who invoke the rule of confidentiality in order to justify their not disclosing information concerning threats or risks to innocent third parties, may be guilt of negligence.

Before accepting this conclusion, however, it is necessary that we clarify the force of HP in the context of the ethics of AIDS, and refine the analysis of the conditions under which breaches of confidentiality pertaining to a patient's antibody status or a diagnosis of AIDS may be ethically justifiable.

II. VULNERABILITY, DISEASE CONTROL, AND DISCRIMINATION

Defenders of HP typically hold that all moral agents have a general moral obligation with respect to all moral patients to (a) avoid harm, (b) prevent or protect against harm, and (c) remove harm. One problem with HP is that not all acts and omissions which result in harm to others appear to be wrong. For instance, if I buy the last pint of Haagen-Daz coffee ice cream in the store, then I have, in some sense, harmed the next customer who wants to buy this good. Similarly, if one baseball team defeats another, then they have harmed the other team. But neither of these cases represent *wrongful* harms. Why then are some harms wrongful and others not?

Robert Goodin has recently developed a theory which provides at least a partial answer to this question. According to Goodin, the duty to protect against harm tends to arise most strongly in contexts in which someone is specially dependent on others or in some way specially vulnerable to their choices and actions.[4] He dubs this the Vulnerability Principle [VP]. Vulnerability, implying risk or susceptibility to harm, should be understood in a relational sense: being vulnerable to another is a condition which involves both a relative inability of the vulnerable party to protect themselves from harm or risk, and a correlative ability of another individual to act (or refrain from actions) which would foreseeably place the vulnerable party in a position of harm or risk or remove them from such a position. . . .

The Vulnerability Principle is related to the Harm Principle in giving a more precise analysis of the circumstances in which a strict duty to protect others arises. For example, under HP it might be thought that individuals, qua moral agents, have a duty to insure that persons be inoculated against contagious, preventable diseases, such as polio. However, while we have no strong obligations under HP to ensure that other adults have been inoculated, we *do* have a strong general obligation under VP to see to it that all young children are inoculated, and I have a special duty as a parent to see that my own children are inoculated. Children, as a class, are especially vulnerable and lack the ability to protect themselves. Being a parent *intensifies* the duty to prevent harm to children, by focusing the duty to protect the vulnerable on individuals who are specially responsible for the care of children. For other adults, on the other hand, I have no strong duty to protect, since I may generally assume that mature moral agents have both the ability and the responsibility to protect themselves.

Viewed in this light, the remarks quoted earlier by the hospital spokeswoman take on new meaning and relevance. She argued that it is the responsibility of health care workers to protect themselves by taking appropriate infection control measures in situations in which they may be exposed to blood infected with HIV. This argument might be a good one if people who occupy these professional roles are trained in such measures and are equipped to use them when appropriate. If they were so equipped, then in the Baltimore case, the nurse who later informed the rescue workers of the patient's antibody status was *not* specially responsible to prevent harm; the paramedics were responsible for their own safety.

The main problem with this argument is that it is not always possible to assume that emergency workers and others who provide direct care to AIDS patients or HIV-infected individuals are properly trained and equipped in infection control, nor, even if they are, that it is always feasible for them to employ these procedures in emergency situations. The scene of an emergency is not a controlled environment, and while emergency and public safety workers may take precautions such as wearing gloves and masks, these measures can be rendered ineffective, say, if a glove is torn and the worker cut while wrestling someone from a mass of twisted metal that was a car. While *post hoc* notification of the antibody status of people whom public safety workers have handled may not prevent them from contracting infection, it can alert them to the need to be tested, and thus can prevent them from spreading the infection (if they are in fact infected) to others, e.g. their spouses.

Health care workers, public safety workers, paramedics, and others who come into direct contact with blood which may be infected with the AIDS virus represent a class of persons for whom the Vulnerability Principle suggests a special "duty to protect" is appropriate. It is appropriate in these cases because such workers are routinely exposed to blood in the course of their professional activities, and exposure to infected blood is one way in which people can become infected with the AIDS virus. Such workers could protect themselves by simply refusing to handle anyone whom they suspected of harboring the infection. Doing this, however, would mean violating their professional responsibility to provide care. Hence, morally, they can only protect themselves by reducing their risk of exposure, in this case, by employing infection control measures and being careful. In this respect, health care workers, whether they work inside or outside of the hospital, are in a relevantly different moral situation than ordinary people who are not routinely exposed to blood and who have no special duty to provide care, and this makes them specially vulnerable. It thus appears that the nurse who informed the emergency workers of their risk of exposure did the right thing in informing them, since in doing so she was discharging a duty to protect the vulnerable.

But do similar conclusions follow with respect to "ordinary" persons who need not expose themselves to infection in the course of their professional activities? Consider the case in which a patient who is known to have a positive antibody status informs his physician that he does not intend to break off having sexual relations and that he will not tell his fiancée that he is infected with the AIDS virus.

In this case, we have a known, unsuspecting party, the fiancée, who will be placed at risk by failure to discharge a duty to protect. The fiancée is vulnerable in this case to the infected patient, since it is primarily *his* actions or omissions which place her at risk. According to HP + VP, the patient has a strong special responsibility to protect those with whom he has or will have sexual relations against infection. There are a number of ways in which he can discharge this duty. For instance, he can break off the relationship, abstain from sexual intercourse, practice "safe sex," or he can inform his fiancée of his antibody status.

This last option protects the fiancée by alerting her to the need to protect herself. But does the physician in this case also have a special responsibility to protect the fiancée?

She does, in this case, if she has good reason to believe that her patient will not discharge his responsibility to protect his fiancée or inform her of his positive antibody status. Since the physician possesses the information which would alert her patient's fiancée to a special need to protect herself, and the only other person who has this information will not reveal it, the fiancée is specially dependent upon the physician's choices and actions. Were she to fail to attempt to persuade her patient to reveal the information, or if he still refused to do so, to see to it that the patient's fiancée was informed, she would be acting in complicity with a patient who was violating his duty to prevent harm, and so would also be acting unethically under the Vulnerability Principle.

It thus appears that the rule of confidentiality protecting a patient's HIV antibody status cannot be regarded as absolute. There are several sorts of cases where HP + VP override the rule of confidentiality. However, finding there are justified exceptions to a generally justified rule of practice does not allow for unrestricted disclosure of antibody status to all and sundry. The basic question which must be answered in considering revealing confidential information concerning a patient's HIV antibody status is: *Is the individual to be notified someone who is specially vulnerable? That is, are they someone who faces a significant risk of exposure to the infection, and, will revealing confidential information to them assist them in reducing this risk to themselves or others?*

Answering this question is not always going to be easy, and applying HP + VP and balancing its claims against those of confidentiality will require an extraordinary degree of moral sensitivity and discretion. Because the rule of confidentiality describes a valid prima facie moral responsibility of physicians, the burden of proof must always fall on those who would violate it in order to accommodate the claims of an opposing ethical principle. Perhaps this is why physicians tend to assume that if the rule of confidentiality is not absolute, it might as well be treated as such. Physicians, nurses, and others who are privy to information about patients' antibody status, by and large, are likely to lack the relevant degree of ethical sensitivity to discriminate the cases in which confidentiality can be justifiably violated from those where it cannot. So if we must err, the argument goes, it is better to err on the side of confidentiality.

Aside from underestimating the moral sensitivity of members of these professional groups, this argument fails to take into account that there are two ways of erring—one can err by wrongfully disclosing confidential information to those who have no right to know it, and one can err by failing to disclose confidential information to those who do have a right to know it. The harm that can result from errors of the first kind are often significant, and sometimes irreparable. But so are the harms that result from errors of the second kind. While the burden of proof should be placed on those who would breach the prima facie rule of confidentiality, it should sometimes be possible for persons to satisfy this burden and act in accordance with HP + VP without moral fault.

The strength of conviction with which many physicians in the forefront of AIDS research and treatment argue for the protection of confidentiality can be explained partly by recognizing that they view themselves as having a special responsibility to prevent harm to AIDS patients. The harm which they seek to prevent, however, is not only harm to their patient's health. It is also social harm caused by discrimination that these physicians are trying to prevent. This is yet a different application of HP + VP in the context of AIDS which merits close attention. . . .

Medical personnel and public health authorities who take the position that confidentiality is absolute in order to shield their patients from discrimination, will increasingly find themselves in the uncomfortable position of being accomplices to the irresponsible behavior of known noncompliant positives. What is needed, then, is a finely drawn public policy that includes strong and effective anti-discrimination standards, a public education program which encourages individual and professional responsibility, and a set of clear effective guidelines for public health authorities concerning when and to whom confidential information necessary for disease control and the protection of those at risk may be revealed.

III. WHO HAS A RIGHT TO KNOW?

The Vulnerability Principle suggests that breaches of confidentiality may be justified in cases where the following conditions obtain: (1) there is an identifiable person or an identifiable group of people who are "at risk" of contracting AIDS from a known carrier,

(2) the carrier has not or will not disclose his/her antibody status to those persons whom he/she has placed or will place at risk, and (3) the identity of the carrier and his/her antibody status is known to a physician, nurse, health care worker, public health authority, or another person privileged to this information. It is justifiable, under these circumstances, to reveal information which might enable others to identify an AIDS patient or HIV-infected person. Revelation of confidential information is justified under this rule by the fact that others are vulnerable to infection, or may be unknowingly infecting others, and the information to be revealed may serve as an effective means of protecting those at risk.

NOTES

1. *The Baltimore Sun,* June 11, 1987, p. D1.
2. Sissela Bok, *Secrets: On the Ethics of Concealment and Revelation* (New York: Vintage Books, 1983); Chapter IX.
3. Bok, Op. Cit., pp. 129–130.
4. Robert E. Goodin, *Protecting the Vulnerable: A Reanalysis of Our Social Responsibilities* (Chicago: The University of Chicago Press, 1985).

Truth Telling and Disclosing Bad News

DAVID C. THOMASMA

Telling the Truth to Patients: A Clinical Ethics Exploration

David Thomasma was professor of medical ethics in the Neiswanger Institute for Bioethics and Health Policy at Loyola University Chicago Medical Center, where until recently he directed the Medical Humanities Program. His many publications focused heavily on the Doctor-Patient Relationship. His collaborations with Dr. Ed Pellegrino long produced several books, including *For the Patient's Good: The Restoration of Beneficence in Health Care* (Oxford).

REASONS FOR TELLING THE TRUTH

. . . In all human relationships, the truth is told for a myriad of reasons. A summary of the prominent reasons are that it is a right, a utility, and a kindness.

It is a right to be told the truth because respect for the person demands it. As Kant argued, human society would soon collapse without truth telling, because it is the basis of interpersonal trust, covenants, contracts, and promises.

The truth is a utility as well, because persons need to make informed judgments about their actions. It is a mark of maturity that individuals advance and grow morally by becoming more and more self-aware of their needs, their motives, and their limitations. All these steps toward maturity require honest and forthright communication, first from parents and later also from siblings, friends, lovers, spouses, children, colleagues, co-workers, and caregivers.[1]

Finally, it is a kindness to be told the truth, a kindness rooted in virtue precisely because persons to whom lies are told will of necessity withdraw from important, sometimes life-sustaining and life-saving relationships. Similarly, those who tell lies poison not only their relationships but themselves, rendering themselves incapable of virtue and moral growth.[2] . . .

From *Cambridge Quarterly of Healthcare Ethics* 3 (1994), 375–82. Copyright © 1994 Cambridge University Press. Reprinted with the permission of Cambridge University Press.

. . . Not all of us act rationally and autonomously at all times. Sometimes we are under sufficient stress that others must act to protect us from harm. This is called necessary paternalism. Should we become seriously ill, others must step in and rescue us if we are incapable of doing it ourselves. . . .

IN GENERAL RELATIONSHIPS

In each of the three main reasons why the truth must be told, as a right, a utility, and a kindness, lurk values that may from time to time become more important than the truth. When this occurs, the rule of truth telling is trumped, that is, overridden by a temporarily more important principle. The ultimate value in all instances is the survival of the community and/or the well-being of the individual. Does this mean for paternalistic reasons, without the person's consent, the right to the truth, the utility, and the kindness, can be shunted aside? The answer is "yes." The truth in a relationship responds to a multivariate complexity of values, the context for which helps determine which values in that relationship should predominate.

Nothing I have said thus far suggests that the truth may be treated in a cavalier fashion or that it can be withheld from those who deserve it for frivolous reasons. The only values that can trump the truth are recipient survival, community survival, and the ability to absorb the full impact of the truth at a particular time. All these are only temporary trump cards in any event. They only can be played under certain limited conditions because respect for persons is a foundational value in all relationships.

IN HEALTHCARE RELATIONSHIPS

It is time to look more carefully at one particular form of human relationship, the relationship between the doctor and the patient or sometimes between other healthcare providers and the patient.

Early in the 1960s, studies were done that revealed the majority of physicians would not disclose a diagnosis of cancer to a patient. Reasons cited were mostly those that derived from nonmaleficence. Physicians were concerned that such a diagnosis might disturb the equanimity of a patient and might lead to desperate acts. Primarily physicians did not want to destroy their patients' hope. By the middle 1970s, however, repeat studies brought to light a radical shift in physician attitudes. Unlike earlier views, physicians now emphasized patient autonomy and informed consent over paternalism. In the doctor–patient relation, this meant the majority of physicians stressed the patient's right to full disclosure of diagnosis and prognosis.

One might be tempted to ascribe this shift of attitudes to the growing patients' rights and autonomy movements in the philosophy of medicine and in public affairs. No doubt some of the change can be attributed to this movement. But also treatment interventions for cancer led to greater optimism about modalities that could offer some hope to patients. Thus, to offer them full disclosure of their diagnosis no longer was equivalent to a death sentence. Former powerlessness of the healer was supplanted with technological and pharmaceutical potentialities.

A more philosophical analysis of the reasons for a shift comes from a consideration of the goal of medicine. The goal of all healthcare relations is to receive/provide help for an illness such that no further harm is done to the patient, especially in that patient's vulnerable state.[3] The vulnerability arises because of increased dependency. Presumably, the doctor will not take advantage of this vulnerable condition by adding to it through inappropriate use of power or the lack of compassion. Instead, the vulnerable person should be assisted back to a state of human equality, if possible, free from the prior dependency.[4]

First, the goal of the healthcare giver–patient relation is essentially to restore the patient's autonomy. Thus, respect for the right of the patient to the truth is measured against this goal. If nothing toward that goal can be gained by telling the truth at a particular time, still it must be told for other reasons. Yet, if the truth would impair the restoration of autonomy, then it may be withheld on grounds of potential harm. Thus the goal of the healing relationship enters into the calculus of values that are to be protected.

Second, most healthcare relationships of an interventionist character are temporary, whereas relationships involving primary care, prevention, and chronic or dying care are more permanent. These differences also have a bearing on truth telling. During a short encounter with healthcare strangers, patients and healthcare providers will of necessity require the truth more readily than during a long-term relation among near friends. In the short term, decisions, often dramatically important ones, need to be made in a compressed period. There is less opportunity to maneuver or delay for other reasons, even if there are concerns about the truth's impact on the person.

Over a longer period, the truth may be withheld for

compassionate reasons more readily. Here, the patient and physician or nurse know one another. They are more likely to have shared some of their values. In this context, it is more justifiable to withhold the truth temporarily in favor of more important long-term values, which are known in the relationship.

Finally, the goal of healthcare relations is treatment of an illness. An illness is far broader than its subset, disease. Illness can be viewed as a disturbance in the life of an individual, perhaps due to many nonmedical factors. A disease, by contrast, is a medically caused event that may respond to more interventionist strategies.[5]

Helping one through an illness is a far greater personal task than doing so for a disease. A greater, more enduring bond is formed. The strength of this bond may justify withholding the truth as well, although in the end "the truth will always out."

CLINICAL CASE CATEGORIES

The general principles about truth telling have been reviewed, as well as possible modifications formed from the particularities of the healthcare professional–patient relationship. Now I turn to some contemporary examples of how clinical ethics might analyze the hierarchy of values surrounding truth telling.

There are at least five clinical case categories in which truth telling becomes problematic: intervention cases, long-term care cases, cases of dying patients, prevention cases, and nonintervention cases.

INTERVENTION CASES

Of all clinically difficult times to tell the truth, two typical cases stand out. The first usually involves a mother of advanced age with cancer. The family might beg the surgeon not to tell her what has been discovered for fear that "Mom might just go off the deep end." The movie *Dad,* starring Jack Lemmon, had as its centerpiece the notion that Dad could not tolerate the idea of cancer. Once told, he went into a psychotic shock that ruptured standard relationships with the doctors, the hospital, and the family. However, because this diagnosis requires patient participation for chemotherapeutic interventions and the time is short, the truth must be faced directly. Only if there is not to be intervention might one withhold the truth from the patient for a while, at the family's request, until the patient is able to cope with the reality. A contract about the time allowed before telling the truth might be a good idea.

The second case is that of ambiguous genitalia. A woman, 19 years old, comes for a checkup because she plans to get married and has not yet had a period. She is very mildly retarded. It turns out that she has no vagina, uterus, or ovaries but does have an undescended testicle in her abdomen. She is actually a he. Should she be told this fundamental truth about herself? Those who argue for the truth do so on grounds that she will eventually find out, and more of her subsequent life will have been ruined by the lies and disingenuousness of others. Those who argue against the truth usually prevail. National standards exist in this regard. The young woman is told that she has something like a "gonadal mass" in her abdomen that might turn into cancer if not removed, and an operation is performed. She is assisted to remain a female.

More complicated still is a case of a young Hispanic woman, a trauma accident victim, who is gradually coming out of a coma. She responds only to commands such as "move your toes." Because she is now incompetent, her mother and father are making all care decisions in her case. Her boyfriend is a welcome addition to the large, extended family. However, the physicians discover that she is pregnant. The fetus is about 5 weeks old. Eventually, if she does not recover, her surrogate decision makers will have to be told about the pregnancy, because they will be involved in the terrible decisions about continuing the life of the fetus even if it is a risk to the mother's recovery from the coma. This revelation will almost certainly disrupt current family relationships and the role of the boyfriend. Further, if the mother is incompetent to decide, should not the boyfriend, as presumed father, have a say in the decision about his own child?

In this case, revelation of the truth must be carefully managed. The pregnancy should be revealed only on a "need to know" basis, that is, only when the survival of the young woman becomes critical. She is still progressing moderately towards a stable state.

LONG-TERM CASES

Rehabilitation medicine provides one problem of truth telling in this category. If a young man has been paralyzed by a football accident, his recovery to some level of function will depend upon holding out hope. As he struggles to strengthen himself, the motivation might be a hope that caregivers know to be false, that he may someday be able to walk again. Yet this falsehood is not corrected, lest he slip into despair. Hence, because this is a long-term relationship, the truth will be gradually discovered by the patient under the aegis of encouragement by his physical therapists, nurses, and physicians, who enter his life as near friends.

CASES OF DYING PATIENTS

Sometimes, during the dying process, the patient asks directly, "Doctor, am I dying?" Physicians are frequently reluctant to "play God" and tell the patient how many days or months or years they have left. This reluctance sometimes bleeds over into a less-than-forthright answer to the question just asked. A surgeon with whom I make rounds once answered this question posed by a terminally ill cancer patient by telling her that she did not have to worry about her insurance running out!

Yet in every case of dying patients, the truth can be gradually revealed such that the patient learns about dying even before the family or others who are resisting telling the truth. Sometimes, without directly saying "you are dying," we are able to use interpretative truth and comfort the patient. If a car driver who has been in an accident and is dying asks about other family members in the car who are already dead, there is no necessity to tell him the truth. Instead, he can be told that "they are being cared for" and that the important thing right now is that he be comfortable and not in pain. One avoids the awful truth because he may feel responsible and guilt ridden during his own dying hours if he knew that the rest of his family were already dead.

PREVENTION CASES

A good example of problems associated with truth telling in preventive medicine might come from screening. The high prevalence of prostate cancer among men over 50 years old may suggest the utility of cancer screening. An annual checkup for men over 40 years old is recommended. Latent and asymptomatic prostate cancer is often clinically unsuspected and is present in approximately 30% of men over 50 years of age. If screening were to take place, about 16.5 million men in the United States alone would be diagnosed with prostate cancer, or about 2.4 million men each year. As of now, only 120,000 cases are newly diagnosed each year. Thus, as Timothy Moon noted in a recent sketch of the disease, "a majority of patients with prostate cancer that is not clinically diagnosed will experience a benign course throughout their lifetime."[6]

The high incidence of prostate cancer coupled with a very low malignant potential would entail a whole host of problems if subjected to screening. Detection would force patients and physicians to make very difficult and life-altering treatment decisions. Among them are removal of the gland (with impotence a possible outcome), radiation treatment, and most effective of all, surgical removal of the gonads (orchiectomy). But why consider these rather violent interventions if the probable outcome of neglect will overwhelmingly be benign? For this reason the U.S. Preventive Services Task Force does not recommend either for or against screening for prostate cancer.[7] Quality-of-life issues would take precedence over the need to know.

NONINTERVENTION CASES

This last example more closely approximates the kind of information one might receive as a result of gene mapping. This information could tell you of the likelihood or probability of encountering a number of diseases through genetic heritage, for example, adult onset or type II diabetes, but could not offer major interventions for most of them (unlike a probability for diabetes).

Some evidence exists from recent studies that the principle of truth telling now predominates in the doctor–patient relationship. Doctors were asked about revealing diagnosis for Huntington's disease and multiple sclerosis, neither of which is subject to a cure at present. An overwhelming majority would consider full disclosure. This means that, even in the face of diseases for which we have no cure, truth telling seems to take precedence over protecting the patient from imagined harms.

The question of full disclosure acquires greater poignancy in today's medicine, especially with respect to Alzheimer's disease and genetic disorders that may be diagnosed in utero. There are times when our own scientific endeavors lack a sufficient conceptual and cultural framework around which to assemble facts. The facts can overwhelm us without such conceptual frameworks. The future of genetics poses just such a problem. In consideration of the new genetics, this might be the time to stress values over the truth.

CONCLUSION

Truth in the clinical relationship is factored in with knowledge and values.

First, truth is contextual. Its revelation depends

upon the nature of the relationship between the doctor and patient and the duration of that relationship.

Second, truth is a secondary good. Although important, other primary values take precedence over the truth. The most important of these values is survival of the individual and the community. A close second would be preservation of the relationship itself.

Third, truth is essential for healing an illness. It may not be as important for curing a disease. That is why, for example, we might withhold the truth from the woman with ambiguous genitalia, curing her disease (having a gonad) in favor of maintaining her health (being a woman).

Fourth, withholding the truth is only a temporary measure. *In vino, veritas* it is said. The truth will eventually come out, even if in a slip of the tongue. Its revelation, if it is to be controlled, must always aim at the good of the patient for the moment.

At all times, the default mode should be that the truth is told. If, for some important reason, it is not to be immediately revealed in a particular case, a truth-management protocol should be instituted so that all caregivers on the team understand how the truth will eventually be revealed.

NOTES

1. Bok S. *Lying: Moral Choice in Public and Personal Life.* New York: Vintage Books, 1989.

2. Pellegrino E. D., Thomasma D. C. *The Virtues in Medical Practice*. New York: Oxford University Press, 1993.

3. Cassell E. The nature of suffering and the goals of medicine. *New England Journal of Medicine* 1982; 306(11):639–45.

4. See Nordenfelt L., issue editor. Concepts of health and their consequences for health care. *Theoretical Medicine* 1993; 14(4).

5. Moon T. D. Prostate cancer. *Journal of the American Geriatrics Society* 1992; 40:622–7 (quote from 626).

6. See note 5. Moon. 1992; 40:622–7.

GARRY S. SIGMAN, JEROME KRAUT, AND JOHN LA PUMA

Disclosure of a Diagnosis to Children and Adolescents When Parents Object

Garry S. Sigman, MD, practices adolescent medicine at Lutheran General Children's Hospital (Park Ridge, Illinois) and teaches in the Department of Pediatrics at Northwestern University in Chicago. In addition to serving as the director of adolescent medicine programs, he has served on institutional ethics committees. His collaborative publications include "Ethical Issues in Research on Adolescents," *Adolescent Medicine* and "Confidential Health Care for Adolescents," *Journal of Adolescent Health*.

Jerome R. Kraut, MD, is director of the Pediatric Resident Program and an attending physician at the Lutheran General Children's Hospital, Park Ridge, Illinois. He also has served as clinical associate professor of pediatrics at the University of Chicago, Department of Pediatrics, and as lecturer at the Northwestern University School of Medicine. In addition to his service on ethics committees and advisory committees, he has also published several medical works in the field of pediatrics and ethics.

John La Puma, MD, was formerly a clinical associate professor at the University of Chicago and is now professor of nutrition at Kendall College and School of Culinary Arts in Evanston, Illinois. Following a postgraduate fellowship in medical ethics at the University of Chicago, he has published in the fields of medical ethics, alternative medicine, and nutrition. He has served as the national spokesperson for the Harvard DASH (Dietary Approaches to Stop Hypertension) eating plan and is also the founder and executive director of Alternative Medicine Alert.

Parents of children and adolescents occasionally request that the physician not disclose a diagnosis or prognosis to the young patient. Such a request creates an ethical dilemma for the practitioner: the conflict between a duty to respect parents' wishes as well as a duty to tell the truth to the child.

The authority of parents to direct the flow of information to the child and to organize and provide appropriate systems of emotional support is well recognized in pediatric care. Parents are regarded as moral agents for their children; pediatricians perceive that the integrity of the patient's family is necessary to sustain and nurture the child.

Still, parental authority cannot be absolute. A "best interest" standard that extends beyond parents' wishes is recognized in nontreatment decisions in severely ill neonates and children,[1] in relationship to the treatment of children whose parents have religious objection to usual care,[2] and in relationship to the confidential care of adolescents.[3]

Reprinted by permission of the publisher from *American Journal of Diseases of Children* 147 (1993), 764–768. Copyright © 1993, American Medical Association.

Several cases exploring the physicians' duties to tell the truth to children have been reported.[4–6] We attempt to advance the discussion by using an extraordinary case to identify the clinical circumstances that are important in the decision regarding truthful disclosure to children when parents object.

REPORT OF A CASE

The patient, aged 19 years, was first seen by her current physician, a specialist in the treatment of cystic fibrosis (CF) at age 9 years. After a normal pregnancy, labor, and delivery, the newborn developed irritability, vomiting, and frequent foul stools soon after discharge. At age 4 months, failure to thrive prompted a sweat test that was diagnostic for CF.

Both parents were born in Italy and moved to the United States as adults. The father, aged 48 years, owns a barber shop and is a postal worker. The mother, aged 39 years, cares for her family in the home. The now 6-year-old sister does not have CF.

The parents recall feeling devastated when told that CF is a lethal disease that usually results in early death. They said that nothing could be more horrible than their child knowing of her fatal disease. They agreed at the time of diagnosis that they would never tell her or her extended family of her disease and would not allow health care professionals to disclose the diagnosis and prognosis to their daughter. . . .

By age 15, the patient had grown into a normal-appearing teenager who did well in school and had a normal social life and good relationship with her parents. The physician felt increasingly guilty about participation in the nondisclosure, not because the patient was asking questions (she was not), but simply because she was getting older. In another conference, he and the social worker tried again to convince the parents to change their minds. The parents remained committed to their decision and made it clear that it was not negotiable. The parents agreed to counseling but did not see the benefits of telling their daughter her diagnosis and refused to make that a goal of counseling. They did not follow through with this treatment. . . .

Just after her 18th birthday, the patient developed another pulmonary exacerbation and was seen in the office prior to hospitalization. The physician explained the secrecy oath and the diagnosis and prognosis to the patient, with her parents present. Her mother tried to remove her daughter from the office, but the father gently calmed the mother and allowed the first discussion their daughter ever had about her disease. She reacted calmly and asked questions.

After the session the patient said that she had no idea that she had CF and had not felt the need to question her parents or physician. She thought she had allergies, asthma, and "weak lungs." The patient denied any anger toward her parents or the physician about the secrecy. She has had no further admissions, is doing well to date, understands her disease, and is involved in self-care . . .

ANALYZING DISCLOSURE DUTIES

If there is a moral justification for lying to the patient, or willfully hiding the truth, it must have a strength that overrides the principle of veracity, derived from basic human respect.[7(p31)] People deserve to be told the truth; and circumstances must be morally persuasive when considering deviating from this basic moral duty.

Physician factors, disease-specific factors, patient factors, and family factors are each important in the decision regarding disclosure to pediatric patients (see the table). The strength of the individual factors will ultimately determine the "right" action for the physician regarding disclosure. The factors' relative importance is not implied by their order in the text; all or one may be important in individual cases. Indeed, the relative value of each clinical factor will be different in each case; each clinical decision is context specific. Decisions about disclosure must be made by consid-

Clinical Factors to Be Considered Regarding Truthful Disclosure to Pediatric Patients

Physician factors
- Personal value system
- Societal, legal, and economic influences on medical decision making
- Professional codes of behavior

Disease-specific factors
- Natural history of disease
- Factors relating to provision of care
- Public health considerations

Patient factors
- Development and maturation
- Personality traits
- Psychiatric risk factors and symptoms

Family factors
- Cultural considerations
- Family dynamics and support mechanisms
- Family dysfunction and disease

ering the specific details of the case; they are decisions that must be made by a particular physician, regarding a particular disease, for and with a particular child from a particular family.

PHYSICIAN FACTORS

Physicians differ in their approaches to disclosure decisions. For example, individual differences exist in physicians' personal value systems. Some physicians view deception as therapeutic and therefore a justifiable alternative in certain clinical settings.[8] For them, truth telling is not a moral imperative, but a virtue with variable consequences for the patient's health.[9] For other physicians, any deception is wrong, no matter what the consequence. These physicians may consider nontruthful disclosure destructive of the physician's effectiveness with patients.[7(p238–241)] Even though they are unable to formally consent, the assent of children in medical decisions is increasingly recognized as morally and clinically important;[10] the lack of truthful disclosure would be antithetical to such a moral stance.

Internal personal values are derived from religious, social, and familial influences and affect physician attitudes regarding physician-assisted suicide,[11] withholding and withdrawing life-sustaining treatment,[12,13] and drug testing.[14] Some physicians find that, despite rational ethical arguments favoring certain decisions, they cannot make them because "it's against my conscience," an expression of personal values.

In addition, societal, economic, and legal phenomena also influence physicians' management of truth-telling dilemmas. Societal movements supporting individual rights and self-determination have become important and current during the last 25 years. Physicians have correspondingly altered their practices in favor of truthful disclosure, in recognition of patients' right of self-determination.[15,16]

Codes of professional behavior might influence physicians' ethical decisions. The American Medical Association's code of professional responsibility is not specific about truthful disclosure of diagnoses, although principle 2 of the preamble states, "A physician shall deal honestly with patients and colleagues."[17] The code's requirement for informed consent might be taken to apply to truthful disclosure, but the code does not address such issues regarding minors whose parents object to disclosure. To the best of our knowledge, the American Academy of Pediatrics has not published policies regarding truthful disclosure.

Suggesting that physicians differ on disclosure does not imply a moral relativism that leaves us unable to resolve any moral dilemmas. It does suggest that the medical profession, instead of mandating by code or standard of practice, has allowed decisions about disclosure to be left to each physician's assessment of the clinical circumstances.

DISEASE-SPECIFIC FACTORS

A strong argument for disclosure exists if a child's knowledge of the disease positively affects its course and prognosis. There are diseases in which self-care and survival would be impossible without a patient's knowledge of the disease and performance of daily self-care. Examples include diabetes mellitus, chronic renal failure, and severe CF.

Considering only physical aspects of disease does not address the question of whether knowing affects adjustment and prognosis. For CF, it appears that psychological adjustment to the disease is adequate for most adolescents and young adults who know their diagnosis and prognosis,[18–20] although gender differences in coping style have been reported. Girls have more difficulty integrating the presence of the disease with their self-concept.[21] Considering only adolescent identity formation and coping considerations, delay in learning of a CF diagnosis in a mild case may not be harmful in certain patients.

In addition, patients must know the facts of their disease to plan their lives. In CF, premature death and infertility (for most) are generally certain. Patients with CF should be made aware of the effects of the disease on reproduction, "when he or she is sexually and emotionally mature."[22] All young people who have a potential desire to procreate and who are sexually active should have access to genetic counseling. These facts about CF strengthen the need for a patient's decision making. A pediatrician might accede to parents who wish to raise a child in a particular way, but not to parents who usurp a child's future life decisions.

As with many chronic diseases, care for patients with CF is provided by a team approach. Nondisclosure, even if justified, cannot be carried out without a significant alteration in the normal patterns of team communication.[23] Such a "conspiracy" may have an effect on collective care givers that negatively impacts on morale and care provision. Medical education as well may be adversely affected if students and residents perceive that lying to the patient is okay as long as the parents insist.

Do patients with chronic diseases do better if they meet and interact with others with the disease? This cannot be empirically studied since this is standard for patients with CF. Nevertheless, a patient unable to attend a special disease of specialty-based clinic might be unable to take advantage of new diagnostic or treatment opportunities that are on the cutting edge.

The duty to disclose to the patient, despite parental objection, increases with the potential threat to the public health. While no such threats exist for CF, the diagnosis for youth who have human immunodeficiency virus infection, for example, cannot be hidden because of the potential for unwitting transmission. This also applies to truthful disclosure of other chronic transmissible infections, such as hepatitis B or genital herpes simplex.

PATIENT FACTORS

The duty to respect a patient by allowing him or her to make decisions is altered by the patient's inability to make such a decision. At young ages, children cannot do so and are dependent; parents are, of necessity, the primary decision makers. A parent's request to shield a young child from specific knowledge is less morally objectionable than such a request for a child or adolescent of greater maturity.

As a child matures, his or her ability and need to understand increases so that surrogate decision makers are less necessary.[24] As maturity progresses, an emerging adult takes on the moral authority to think, speak, and act for himself or herself.[25,26] The patient's advancing maturity confers an increasing duty to value the patient's right to know personal information above a parent's right to control that information.

The desire for self-determination and decision making varies among pediatric patients. These individual differences are a result of developmental maturity, personality factors, and environmental influences. Children differ in regard to the degree of control they believe that they have (and want) over their lives and their illnesses.[27]

Does a physician have a duty to disclose to a mature patient unrequested information? Just as it might be considered paternalistic on the part of parents to require secrecy, it is also paternalistic on the part of physicians to assume that truth is "good for the patient" if it is unrequested. The fact that patients do not ask does not mean that they do not desire more information. Families of patients with chronic diseases and fatal prognoses sometimes have unspoken agreements of silence about the prognosis; it is taboo to bring the reality of a child's impending death into the open.[28] This is recognized as a family defense mechanism and supports an emotional equilibrium in the family.[29]

An adolescent patient might emerge from a system of overwhelming family secrecy and demonstrate personal needs and desires if given a chance to speak confidentially to care givers. The physician must form a hypothesis about the patient's desire for autonomy in self-care and the ability to cope. It is a physician's duty to ask directly whether more information is requested. If the physician perceives that the patient wishes to achieve more control over decision making, helping the patient to become more autonomous is required. If the patient express no such wishes, the physician can respect the silence and allow others to decide, while making ongoing inquiries of the patient about his or her own desires.[30]

Finally, the patient's mental health must be considered. When a parent fears that the result of a disclosure might cause psychological harm, the physician should carefully consider the (generally remote) possibility of triggering psychiatric symptoms. Suicide has been reported in adolescents with chronic or fatal illnesses, but this is rare. Physicians should consider whether the history and examination demonstrate clinical features that might suggest a high risk for psychiatric symptoms when considering how, when, and whether disclosure should occur.[31]

FAMILY FACTORS

Just as every patient is different, so is every family; cultural backgrounds and beliefs of families differ. Kleinman et al.[32] have written, "Illness behavior is a normative experience governed by cultural rules." Whether disclosure is right for a patient must be interpreted in light of a family's particular cultural background.[33,34] Otherwise, a physician might simply impose his or her own cultural value of "truth" or "autonomy" and thereby breach a boundary of paternalism. He or she might also do harm by upsetting a stable system of social support provided by the family.

The strength and consistency of parental authority differs between families, regardless of how it is derived. Families differ in how, when, and where they make decisions. Physicians must discern and respect unique decision-making practices in families when faced with dilemmas of disclosure and truth telling.

Family psychosocial dysfunction may account for

the request of parents to not disclose a diagnosis. One or both parents may be delusional, guilt ridden, or otherwise unable to cope with a child's chronic illness. Psychiatric or psychological consultation may be helpful to determine whether the potential for harm to the child and the dysfunctional family member exists if their child is given information they wish him or her not to have.

CLINICAL FACTORS AND THE PRESENT CASE

The clinical factors described above apply specifically to the present case as follows:

PHYSICIAN FACTORS

The personal value system of the CF specialist in this case allowed him to care for the patient, even after deciding not to disclose the diagnosis. This decision was based on his belief that as long as the patient's medical needs were being met, the parents had a right to control medical information. No legal requirement mandated disclosure, and none was suggested by a professional code. The physician's personal reservations about adhering to the parents' demands were overridden by other factors.

DISEASE-SPECIFIC FACTORS

At the beginning of the patient's disease course, prognosis and care needs probably were not altered by her ignorance of the diagnosis. In practical terms, the only difference in her therapy would have been attending the CF clinic, taking pancreatic enzymes, and receiving more frequent chest physiotherapy. There will never be full scientific evidence to prove or disprove the long-term effectiveness of chest physiotherapy[35] since it is one of many treatment modalities that cannot be evaluated singly. It is generally accepted as standard therapy, so one must assume that the lack of it was a deficiency in the care of this patient. All other prescribed treatments were faithfully carried out by the parents, including the administration of medications when necessary.

It is not certain that the patient's treatment was of poorer quality than it would have been had she known about her disease. It cannot be shown that she suffered physically or psychologically by not knowing her diagnosis. For her parents, who did not accept the overriding "right" of autonomy and self-determination of their daughter, it was difficult to accept the physician's argument that improved health would likely result if he told the patient her diagnosis. . . .

PATIENT FACTORS

Adolescent development and the maturing of cognitive processes created an increasing responsibility for the physician to seek out the patient's autonomous wishes. Even in her middle and late teenage years, however, she did not demonstrate initiative in discovering more than what she was told. Her lack of curiosity and general acceptance of all medical prescriptions suggested no desire to alter or rebel against the authority of her parents. A striving for independence and self-actualization did not appear as she aged, at least in regard to her medical care. She questioned neither her parents nor the physician.

It is possible that the patient had perceived a "secret" that must not be discussed and wished to respect this boundary. She did not seem to challenge any such "taboo" and did not seem to seek help from the physician in challenging it. The long-term deception may have prevented her from expressing her choices and her physician from discerning them.

In summary, patient factors were significant in the final decision to disclose, but were not compelling early in the physician's involvement with her. Without evidence of patient psychopathology, the physician did not fear harming the patient by disclosure. The secrecy so firmly demanded by the parents prevented the physician from determining or even guessing what information the patient wanted.

FAMILY FACTORS

. . . The patient was aware of and respected a parent-dominated social structure in which parents made all medical and most nonmedical decisions for their children. Beyond the special characteristics of many first-generation Italian families, however, the persistence of the parents' refusal to tell their daughter the truth, the rigidity of their position, and their resistance to change as the daughter matured can be interpreted as an indication of a dysfunctional family process.[36] The parents unfortunately recognized neither a need for therapy nor any dysfunction in themselves or their daughter.

CONCLUSION

. . . The answer to the problem of disclosure depends on the clinical context that defines the patient's best interests and the physician's values and attitudes. Decisions about truth telling are context specific; they should be continually examined as the clinical situation changes. Patients' needs change with the natural history of their disease and as their developmental capabilities evolve. It is appropriate that models are developed for clinical ethics that embody this evolution.

NOTES

1. Walters J. W. Approaches to ethical decision making in the neonatal intensive care unit. *AJDC*. 1988;142:825–830.

2. Ackerman T. F. The limits of beneficence: Jehovah's Witness and childhood cancer. *Hasting Cent Rep*. 1980;10:13–18.

3. Forman E. N., Ladd R. E. Treating adolescents: when is a child an adult? In: *Ethical Dilemmas in Pediatrics: A Case Study Approach*. New York, NY: Springer Verlag NY Inc; 1991:111–128.

4. Leiken S. L. An ethical issue in pediatric cancer care: nondisclosure of a fatal prognosis. *Pediatr Ann*. 1981;10:37–46.

5. Truth telling in pediatrics. In: Ganos D., Lipson R. E., Warren G., Weil B. J., eds. *Difficult Decisions in Medical Ethics*. New York, NY: Alan R. Liss Inc; 1983:171–196.

6. Higgs, R., ed. A father says, 'Don't tell my son the truth.' *J Med Ethics*. 1985;11:153–158.

7. Bok S. *Lying: Moral Choice in Public and Private Life*. New York, NY: Vintage Books; 1978.

8. Novack D. H., Detering B. J., Arnold R., Forrow L., Ladinsky M., Pezzullo J. C. Physicians' attitudes toward using deception to resolve difficult ethical problems. *JAMA*. 1989;261:2980–2985.

9. Pernick M. S. Childhood death and medical ethics: an historical perspective on truth-telling in pediatrics. In: Ganos D., Lipson R.E., Warren G., Weil B. J., eds. *Difficult Decisions in Medical Ethics*. New York, NY: Alan R. Liss Inc; 1983:173–188.

10. Bartholome W. G. A new understanding of consent in pediatric practice. *Pediatr Ann*. 1989;18:262–265.

11. Klagsbrun S. C. Physician-assisted suicide: a double dilemma. *J Pain Symptom Manage*. 1991;6(special issue):325–328.

12. Paris J., Lantos J. The case of baby L. *N Engl J Med*. 1990;322:1012–1014.

13. Cranford R. E. Helga Wanglie's ventilator. *Hastings Cent Rep*. 1991;21:23–24.

14. Linn L. S., Yager J., Leake B. Professional vs personal factors related to physicians' attitudes toward drug testing. *J Drug Educ*. 1990;20:95–109.

15. Pellegrino E. D., Thomasma D. C. *For the Patient's Good*. New York, NY: Oxford University Press Inc; 1988:4.

16. Novack D. H., Plumer R., Smith R. L., Ochitill H., Morrow G. R., Bennet J. M. Changes in physicians' attitudes toward telling the cancer patient. *JAMA* 1979;241:897–900.

17. American Medical Association. *Principles of Medical Ethics and Current Opinions of the Council on Ethical and Judicial Affairs*. Chicago, Ill: American Medical Association; 1989:ix.

18. Kashani J. H., Barbero G. J., Wifley D. E., Morris D. A., Sheppard J.A. Psychological concomitants of cystic fibrosis in children and adolescents. *Adolescence*. 1988;23:873–880.

19. Mador J. A., Smith D. H. The psychological adaptation of adolescents with cystic fibrosis: a review of the literature. *J Adolesc Health Care*. 1988;10:136–142.

20. Shepard S. L., Hovell M. F., Harwood I. R., et al. A comparative study of the psychosocial assets of adults with cystic fibrosis and their healthy peers. *Chest*. 1990;97:1310–1316.

21. Simmons R., Corey M., Cowen L., Keenan N., Robertson J., Levinson H. Emotional adjustment of early adolescents with cystic fibrosis. *Psychosom Med*. 1985;47:111–122.

22. Levine S. B., Stern R. C. Sexual function in cystic fibrosis. *Chest*. 1982;81:422–428.

23. Matthews L. W., Droter D. Cystic fibrosis: A challenging long-term chronic disease. *Pediatr Clin North Am*. 1984;31: 133–151.

24. Moreno J. D. Treating the adolescent patient: an ethical analysis. *J Adolesc Health Care*. 1989;10:454–459.

25. Lantos J. D., Miles S. H. Autonomy in adolescent medicine. *J Adolesc Health Care*. 1989;10:460–466.

26. Chesler M. A., Paris J., Barbarin O. A. 'Telling' the child with cancer: parental choices to share information with ill children. *J Pediatr Psychol*. 1986;2:497–515.

27. Sanger M. S., Sandler-Howard K., Perrin E. C. Concepts of illness and perception of control in healthy children and in children with chronic illnesses. *J Dev Behav Pediatr*. 1988;9:252–256.

28. Bluebond-Langer M. *The Private Worlds of Dying Children*. Princeton, NJ: Princeton University Press; 1978:198–230.

29. Silber T. J. Ethical considerations in the care of the chronically ill adolescent. In: Blum R. W., ed. *Chronic Illness and Disabilities in Childhood and Adolescence*. Philadelphia, Pa: Grune & Stratton; 1984:17–27.

30. Childress J. F. The place of autonomy in bioethics. *Hastings Cent Rep*. 1990;20:12–17.

31. Gunther M. S. Acute-onset serious chronic organic illness in adolescence: some critical issues. *Adolesc Psychiatry*. 1985;12:58–76.

32. Kleinman A. M., Eisenberg L., Good B. Culture, illness and care: clinical lessons from anthropologic and cross-cultural research. *Ann Intern Medical*. 1978;88:251–258.

33. Surbone A. Truth telling to the patient. *JAMA*. 1992;268: 1661–1662.

34. Pellegrino E. D. Is truth telling to the patient a cultural artifact? *JAMA*. 1992;268:1734–1735.

35. MacLusky I., Levison H. Cystic fibrosis. In: Chernick V., Kendig E. L., eds. *Kendig's Disorders of the Respiratory Tract in Children*. 5th ed. Philadelphia, Pa: WB Saunders Co; 1990:711.

36. Andolfi M., Angelo C., Menghi P., Nicolo-Carigliano A. M. *Behind the Family Mask: Therapeutic Change in Rigid Family Systems*. New York, NY: Brunner/Mazel Publishers; 1983:13–14.

Informed Consent

CANTERBURY V. SPENCE

United States Court of Appeals

SPOTTSWOOD W. ROBINSON, III, Circuit Judge

Suits charging failure by a physician adequately to disclose the risks and alternatives of proposed treatment are not innovations in American law. They date back a good half-century, and in the last decade they have multiplied rapidly. There is, nonetheless, disagreement among the courts and the commentators on many major questions, and there is no precedent of our own directly in point. For the tools enabling resolution of the issues on this appeal, we are forced to begin at first principles.

The root premise is the concept, fundamental in American jurisprudence, that "[e]very human being of adult years and sound mind has a right to determine what shall be done with his own body. . . ." True consent to what happens to one's self is the informed exercise of a choice, and that entails an opportunity to evaluate knowledgeably the options available and the risks attendant upon each. The average patient has little or no understanding of the medical arts, and ordinarily has only his physician to whom he can look for enlightenment with which to reach an intelligent decision. From these almost axiomatic considerations springs the need, and in turn the requirement, of a reasonable divulgence by physician to patient to make such a decision possible.

• • •

Once the circumstances give rise to a duty on the physician's part to inform his patient, the next inquiry is the scope of the disclosure the physician is legally obliged to make. The courts have frequently confronted this problem, but no uniform standard defining the adequacy of the divulgence emerges from the decisions. Some have said "full" disclosure,[1] a norm we are unwilling to adopt literally. It seems obviously prohibitive and unrealistic to expect physicians to discuss with their patients every risk of proposed treatment—no matter how small or remote—and generally unnecessary from the patient's viewpoint as well. Indeed, the cases speaking in terms of "full" disclosure appear to envision something less than total disclosure,[2] leaving unanswered the question of just how much.

The larger number of courts, as might be expected, have applied tests framed with reference to prevailing fashion within the medical profession. Some have measured the disclosure by "good medical practice," others by what a reasonable practitioner would have bared under the circumstances, and still others by what medical custom in the community would demand. We have explored this rather considerable body of law but are unprepared to follow it. The duty to disclose, we have reasoned, arises from phenomena apart from medical custom and practice. The latter, we think, should no more establish the scope of the duty than its existence. Any definition of scope in terms purely of a professional standard is at odds with the patient's prerogative to decide on projected therapy himself. That prerogative, we have said, is at the very foundation of the duty to disclose, and both the patient's right to know and the physician's correlative obligation to tell him are diluted to the extent that its compass is dictated by the medical profession.

In our view, the patient's right of self-decision shapes the boundaries of the duty to reveal. That right can be effectively exercised only if the patient

No. 22099, U.S. Court of Appeals, District of Columbia Circuit, May 19, 1972. 464 Federal Reporter, 2nd Series, 772.

possesses enough information to enable an intelligent choice. The scope of the physician's communications to the patient, then, must be measured by the patient's need, and that need is the information material to the decision. Thus the test for determining whether a particular peril must be divulged is its materiality to the patient's decision: all risks potentially affecting the decision must be unmasked. And to safeguard the patient's interest in achieving his own determination on treatment, the law must itself set the standard for adequate disclosure.

Optimally for the patient, exposure of a risk would be mandatory whenever the patient would deem it significant to his decision, either singly or in combination with other risks. Such a requirement, however, would summon the physician to second-guess the patient, whose ideas on materiality could hardly be known to the physician. That would make an undue demand upon medical practitioners, whose conduct, like that of others, is to be measured in terms of reasonableness. Consonantly with orthodox negligence doctrine, the physician's liability for nondisclosure is to be determined on the basis of foresight, not hindsight; no less than any other aspect of negligence, the issue of nondisclosure must be approached from the viewpoint of the reasonableness of the physician's divulgence in terms of what he knows or should know to be the patient's informational needs. If, but only if, the fact-finder can say that the physician's communication was unreasonably inadequate is an imposition of liability legally or morally justified.

Of necessity, the content of the disclosure rests in the first instance with the physician. Ordinarily it is only he who is in a position to identify particular dangers; always he must make a judgment, in terms of materiality, as to whether and to what extent revelation to the patient is called for. He cannot know with complete exactitude what the patient would consider important to his decision, but on the basis of his medical training and experience he can sense how the average, reasonable patient expectably would react. Indeed, with knowledge of, or ability to learn, his patient's background and current condition, he is in a position superior to that of most others—attorneys, for example—who are called upon to make judgments on pain of liability in damages for unreasonable miscalculation.

From these considerations we derive the breadth of the disclosure of risks legally to be required. The scope of the standard is not subjective as to either the physician or the patient; it remains objective with due regard for the patient's informational needs and with suitable leeway for the physician's situation. In broad outline, we agreed that "[a] risk is thus material when a reasonable person, in what the physician knows or should know to be the patient's position, would be likely to attach significance to the risk or cluster of risks in deciding whether or not to forgo the proposed therapy."[3]

The topics importantly demanding a communication of information are the inherent and potential hazards of the proposed treatment, the alternatives to that treatment, if any, and the results likely if the patient remains untreated. The factors contributing significance to the dangerousness of a medical technique are, of course, the incidence of injury and the degree of the harm threatened. A very small chance of death or serious disablement may well be significant; a potential disability which dramatically outweighs the potential benefit of the therapy or the detriments of the existing malady may summon discussion with the patient.

There is no bright line separating the significant from the insignificant; the answer in any case must abide a rule of reason. Some dangers—infection, for example—are inherent in any operation; there is no obligation to communicate those of which persons of average sophistication are aware. Even more clearly, the physician bears no responsibility for discussion of hazards the patient has already discovered, or those having no apparent materiality to patients' decision on therapy. The disclosure doctrine, like others marking lines between permissible and impermissible behavior in medical practice, is in essence a requirement of conduct prudent under the circumstances. Whenever nondisclosure of particular risk information is open to debate by reasonable-minded men, the issue is for the finder of the facts.

Two exceptions to the general rule of disclosure have been noted by the courts. Each is in the nature of a physician's privilege not to disclose, and the reasoning underlying them is appealing. Each, indeed, is but a recognition that, as important as is the patient's right to know, it is greatly outweighed by the magnitudinous circumstances giving rise to the privilege. The first comes into play when the patient is unconscious or otherwise incapable of consenting, and harm from a failure to treat is imminent and outweighs any harm threatened by the proposed treatment. When a genuine emergency of that sort arises, it is settled that the impracticality of conferring with the patient dispenses with need for it. Even in situations of that character the physician should, as current law requires, attempt to secure a relative's consent if possible. But if time is too short to accommodate discussion obviously the physician should proceed with the treatment.

The second exception obtains when risk-disclosure poses such a threat of detriment to the patient as to become unfeasible or contraindicated from a medical point of view. It is recognized that patients occasionally become so ill or emotionally distraught on disclosure as to foreclose a rational decision, or complicate or hinder the treatment, or perhaps even pose psychological damage to the patient. Where that is so, the cases have generally held that the physician is armed with a privilege to keep the information from the patient, and we think it clear that portents of that type may justify the physician in action he deems medically warranted. The critical inquiry is whether the physician responded to a sound medical judgment that communication of the risk information would present a threat to the patient's well-being.

The physician's privilege to withhold information for therapeutic reasons must be carefully circumscribed, however, for otherwise it might devour the disclosure rule itself. The privilege does not accept the paternalistic notion that the physician may remain silent simply because divulgence might prompt the patient to forgo therapy the physician feels the patient really needs. That attitude presumes instability or perversity for even the normal patient, and runs counter to the foundation principle that the patient should and ordinarily can make the choice for himself. Nor does the privilege contemplate operation save where the patient's reaction to risk information, as reasonably foreseen by the physician, is menacing. And even in a situation of that kind, disclosure to a close relative with a view to securing consent to the proposed treatment may be the only alternative open to the physician.

NOTES

1. *E.g., Salgo v. Leland Stanford Jr. Univ. Bd. of Trustees,* 154 Cal. App. 2d 560, 317 P.2d 170, 181 (1975); *Woods v. Brumlop, supra* note 13 [in original text], 377 P.2d at 524–525.

2. See, Comment, Informed Consent in Medical Malpractice, 55 Calif. L. Rv. 1396, 1402–03 (1967).

3. Waltz and Scheuneman, Informed Consent to Therapy, 64, Nw. U.L. Rev. 628, 640 (1970).

JAY KATZ

Physicians and Patients: A History of Silence

Jay Katz, MD, is Elizabeth K. Dollard Professor Emeritus of Law, Medicine, and Psychiatry, as well as Harvey L. Karp Professorial Lecturer in Law and Psychoanalysis at Yale Law School. In the field of bioethics, he published two foundational works in the field: the edited work *Experimentation with Human Beings* (Russell Sage Foundation) and the authored work *The Silent World of Doctor and Patient* (Johns Hopkins University Press).

Disclosure and consent, except in the most rudimentary fashion, are obligations alien to medical thinking and practice. Disclosure in medicine has served the function of getting patients to "consent" to what physicians wanted them to agree to in the first place. "Good" patients follow doctor's orders without question. Therefore, disclosure becomes relevant only with recalcitrant patients. Since they are "bad" and "ungrateful," one does not need to bother much with them. Hippocrates once said, "Life is short, the Art long, Opportunity fleeting, Experiment treacherous, Judgment difficult. The physician must be ready, not only to do his duty himself, but also to secure the cooperation of the patient, of the attendants and of

Reprinted by permission of the author.

externals." These were, and still are, the lonely obligations of physicians: to wrestle as best they can with life, art, opportunity, experiment and judgment. Sharing with patients the vagaries of available opportunities, however perilous or safe, or the rationale underlying judgments, however difficult or easy, is not part of the Hippocratic task. For doing that, the Art is too long and Life too short.

Physicians have always maintained that patients are only in need of caring custody. Doctors felt that in order to accomplish that objective they were obligated to attend to their patients' physical and emotional needs and to do so on their own authority, without consulting with their patients about the decisions that needed to be made. Indeed, doctors intuitively believed that such consultations were inimical to good patient care. The idea that patients may also be entitled to liberty, to sharing the burdens of decision with their doctors, was never part of the ethos of medicine. Being unaware of the idea of patient liberty, physicians did not address the possible conflict between notions of custody and liberty. When, however, in recent decades courts were confronted with allegations that professionals had deprived citizen-patients of freedom of choice, the conflict did emerge. Anglo-American law has, at least in theory, a long-standing tradition of preferring liberty over custody; and however much judges tried to sidestep law's preferences and to side with physicians' traditional beliefs, the conflict remained and has ever since begged for a resolution. . . .

The legal doctrine remained limited in scope, in part, because judges believed or wished to believe that their pronouncements on informed consent gave legal force to what good physicians customarily did; therefore they felt that they could defer to the disclosure practices of "reasonable medical practitioners." Judges did not appreciate how deeply rooted the tradition of silence was and thus did not recognize the revolutionary, alien implications of their appeal for patient "self-determination." In fact, precisely because of the appeal's strange and bewildering novelty, physicians misinterpreted it as being more far-reaching than courts intended it to be.

Physicians did not realize how much their opposition to informed consent was influenced by suddenly encountering obligations divorced from their history, their clinical experience, or medical education. Had they appreciated that even the doctrine's modest appeal to patient self-determination represented a radical break with medical practices, as transmitted from teacher to student during more than two thousand years of recorded medical history, they might have been less embarrassed by standing so unpreparedly, so nakedly before this new obligation. They might then perhaps have realized that their silence had been until most recently a historical necessity, dictated not only by the inadequacy of medical knowledge but also by physicians' incapacity to discriminate between therapeutic effectiveness based on their actual physical interventions and benefits that must be ascribed to other causes. They might also have argued that the practice of silence was part of a long and venerable tradition that deserved not to be dismissed lightly. . . .

When I speak of silence I do not mean to suggest that physicians have not talked to their patients at all. Of course, they have conversed with patients about all kinds of matters, but they have not, except inadvertently, employed words to invite patients' participation in sharing the burden of making joint decisions. . . .

Judges have made impassioned pleas for patient self-determination, and then have undercut them by giving physicians considerable latitude to practice according to their own lights, exhorting them only to treat each patient with the utmost care. Judges could readily advance this more limited plea because generally doctors do treat their patients with solicitude. The affirmation of physicians' commitment to patients' physical needs, however, has failed to address physicians' lack of commitment to patients' decision making needs. These tensions have led judges to fashion a doctrine of informed consent that has secured for patients the right to better custody but not to liberty—the right to choose how to be treated. . . .

CANTERBURY V. SPENCE (1972)

Judge Robinson, of the D.C. Court of Appeals, who authored the . . . last landmark informed consent decision, also had good intentions. . . . The lesson to be learned from a study of *Canterbury* [is that]: The strong commitment to self-determination at the beginning of the opinion gets weaker as the opinion moves from jurisprudential theory to the realities of hospital and courtroom life. By the end, the opinion has only obscured the issue it intended to address: the nature of the relationship between the court's doctrine of informed consent, as ultimately construed, and its root premise of self-determination. . . .

> Respect for the patient's right of self-determination on particular therapy demands a standard set by law for physicians rather than one which physicians may or may not impose upon themselves.

For this apparently bold move, *Canterbury* has been widely celebrated, as well as followed in many jurisdictions.

The new rule of law laid down in *Canterbury,* however, is far from clear. Judge Robinson, returning to basic principles of expert testimony, simply said that there is "no basis for operation of the special medical standard where the physician's activity does not bring his medical knowledge and skills peculiarly into play," and that ordinarily disclosure is not such a situation. But he left room for such situations by adding: "When medical judgment enters the picture and for that reason the special standard controls, prevailing medical practice must be given its *just due.*" He did not spell out the meaning of *"just due."*

Both standards tend to confuse the need for *medical knowledge* to elucidate the risks of and alternatives to a proposed procedure in the light of professional experience with the need for *medical judgment* to establish the limits of appropriate disclosure to patients. The difference is crucial to the clarification of the law of informed consent. In *Natanson* and many subsequent cases, judges lumped the two together uncritically, relying solely on current medical practice to resolve the question of reasonableness of disclosure. In *Canterbury,* the distinction was formally recognized. The plaintiff was required to present expert evidence of the applicable medical knowledge, while the defendant had to raise the issue of medical judgment to limit disclosure in defense. But even *Canterbury* did not undertake a detailed judicial analysis of the nature of medical judgment required, precisely because judges were hesitant to make rules in an area that doctors strongly believed was solely the province of medicine.

In *Canterbury,* Dr. Spence claimed that "communication of that risk (paralysis) to the patient is not good medical practice because it might deter patients from undergoing needed surgery and might produce adverse psychological reactions which could preclude the success of the operation." Such claims will almost invariably be raised by physicians since they are derived from deeply held tenets of medical practice. Judge Robinson's enigmatic phrase of "just due" certainly suggests that the medical professional standard would be applicable in such a case, raising profound questions about the extent to which the novel legal standard has been swallowed up by the traditional and venerable medical standard.

In fact, medical judgment was given its "just due" twice. It could also be invoked under the "therapeutic privilege" not to disclose, which Judge Robinson retained as a defense to disclosure:

> It is recognized that patients occasionally become so ill or emotionally distraught on disclosure as to foreclose a rational decision, or complicate or hinder the treatment, or perhaps even pose psychological damage to the patient. . . . The critical inquiry is whether the physician responded to a sound medical judgment that communication of the risk information would present a threat to the patient's well-being.

The therapeutic privilege not to disclose is merely a procedurally different way of invoking the professional standard of care. . . .

Since the court wished to depart from medical custom as the standard, it had to give some indication as to the information it expected physicians to disclose. The court said that "the test for determining whether a particular peril must be divulged is its materiality to the patient's decision: all risks potentially affecting the decision must be unmasked." It added that physicians must similarly disclose alternatives to the proposed treatment and the "results likely if the patient remains untreated."

But then the court chose to adopt an "objective" test for disclosure of risks and alternatives—what a [reasonable] *prudent* person in the patient's position would have decided if suitably informed"—and rejected a "subjective" test of materiality—"what an *individual* patient would have considered a significant risk." In opting for an "objective" standard, self-determination was given unnecessarily short shrift. The whole point of the inquiry was to safeguard the right of *individual* choice, even where it may appear idiosyncratic. Although law generally does not protect a person's right to be unreasonable and requires reasonably prudent conduct where injury to another may occur, it remains ambiguous about the extent to which prudence can be legally enforced where the potential injury is largely confined to the individual decision maker. For example, courts have split on the question of whether society may require the wearing of motorcycle helmets and whether an adult patient may be compelled to undergo unwanted blood transfusions.

The "objective" standard for disclosure contradicts the right of each individual to decide what will be done with his or her body. The belief that there is one "reasonable" or "prudent" response to every situation inviting medical intervention is nonsense, from the point of view of both the physician and the patient. The most cursory examination of medical practices demonstrates that what is reasonable to the internist may appear unreasonable to the surgeon or even to other internists and, more significantly, that the value preferences of physicians may not coincide with those of their patients. For example, doctors generally place a higher value on physical longevity than their patients do. But physical longevity is not the only touchstone of prudence. Why should not informed consent law countenance a wide range of potentially reasonable responses by patients to their medical condition based on other value preferences? . . .

Ascertaining patients' informational needs is difficult. Answers do not lie in guessing or "sensing" patients' particular concerns or in obliterating the "subjective" person in an "objective" mass of persons. The "objective" test of materiality only tempts doctors to introduce their own unwarranted subjectivity into the disclosure process. It would have been far better if the court had not committed itself prematurely to the labels "objective" and "subjective." Instead it should have considered more the patients' plight and required physicians to learn new skills: how to inquire openly about their patients' *individual* informational needs and patients' concerns, doubts, and misconceptions about treatment—its risks, benefits, and alternatives. Safeguarding self-determination requires assessing whether patients' informational needs have been satisfied by asking them whether they understand what has been explained to them. Physicians should not try to "second-guess" patients or "sense" how they will react. Instead, they need to explore what questions require further explanation. Taking such unaccustomed obligations seriously is not easy. . . .

SUMMING UP

The legal life of "informed consent," if quality of human life is measured not merely by improvements in physical custody but also by advancement of liberty, was over almost as soon as it was born. Except for the . . . law promulgated in a handful of jurisdictions and the more generally espoused dicta about "self-determination" and "freedom of choice," this is substantially true. Judges toyed briefly with the idea of patients' right to self-determination and largely cast it aside. . . .

Treatment decisions are extremely complex and require a more sustained dialogue, one in which patients are viewed as participants in medical decisions affecting their lives. This is not the view of most physicians, who believe instead that patients are too ignorant to make decisions on their own behalf, that disclosure increases patients' fears and reinforces "foolish" decisions, and that informing them about the uncertainties of medical interventions in many instances seriously undermines faith so essential to the success of therapy. Therefore, physicians asserted that they must be the ultimate decision makers. Judges did not probe these contentions in depth but were persuaded to refrain from interfering significantly with traditional medical practices.

I have not modified my earlier assessment of law's informed consent vision:

> [T]he law of informed consent is substantially mythic and fairy tale-like as far as advancing patients' rights to self-decisionmaking is concerned. It conveys in its dicta about such rights a fairy tale-like optimism about human capacities for "intelligent" choice and for being respectful of other persons' choices; yet in its implementation of dicta, it conveys a mythic pessimism of human capacities to be choice-makers. The resulting tensions have had a significant impact on the law of informed consent which only has made a bow toward a commitment to patients' self-determination, perhaps in an attempt to resolve these tensions by a belief that it is "less important that this commitment be total than that we believe it to be there."

Whether fairy tale and myth can and should be reconciled more satisfactorily with reality remains to be seen. If judges contemplate such a reconciliation, they must acquire first a more profound understanding and appreciation of medicine's vision of patients and professional practice, of the capacities of physicians and patients for autonomous choice, and of the limits of professional knowledge. Such understanding cannot readily be acquired in courts of law, during disputes in which inquiry is generally constrained by claims and counter-claims that seek to assure victory for one side.

The call to liberty, embedded in the doctrine of informed consent, has only created an atmosphere in which freedom has the potential to survive and grow. The doctrine has not as yet provided a meaningful blueprint for implementing patient self-determination.

The message . . . is this: Those committed to greater patient self-determination can, if they look hard enough, find inspiration in the common law of informed consent, and so can those, and more easily, who seek to perpetuate medical paternalism. Those who look for evidence of committed implementation will be sadly disappointed. The legal vision of informed consent, based on *self-determination,* is still largely a mirage. Yet a mirage, since it not only deceives but also can sustain hope, is better than no vision at all. . . .

RUTH R. FADEN AND TOM L. BEAUCHAMP

The Concept of Informed Consent

Ruth R. Faden is Philip Franklin Wagley Professor of Biomedical Ethics and executive director of the Bioethics Institute at the Johns Hopkins University. She is also a senior research scholar at the Kennedy Institute, Georgetown University and former chair of the President's Advisory Committee on Human Radiation Experiments. Among her books are *AIDS, Women and the Next Generation* (Oxford), edited with Gail Geller and Madison Powers, *A History and Theory of Informed Consent* (Oxford), written with Tom Beauchamp, and *HIV, AIDS, and Childbearing* (Oxford), edited with Nancy Kass.

Tom L. Beauchamp is professor of philosophy and senior research scholar at the Kennedy Institute, Georgetown University. He has written widely in applied ethics, concentrating in research ethics and medical ethics, and also specializes in the philosophy of David Hume. Among his books are *Principles of Biomedical Ethics* (Oxford), written with James Childress, and *A History and Theory of Informed Consent* (Oxford), written with Ruth Faden. He has published two volumes in the Clarendon Hume (a critical edition of Hume's *Works*) and is currently working on two more volumes.

What is an informed consent? Answering this question is complicated because there are two common, entrenched, and starkly different meanings of "informed consent." That is, the term is analyzable in two profoundly different ways—not because of mere subtle differences of connotation that appear in different contexts, but because two different *conceptions* of informed consent have emerged from its history and are still at work, however unnoticed, in literature on the subject.

In one sense, which we label *sense*$_1$, "informed consent" is analyzable as a particular kind of action by individual patients and subjects: an autonomous authorization. In the second sense, *sense*$_2$, informed consent is analyzable in terms of the web of cultural and policy rules and requirements of consent that collectively form the social practice of informed consent in institutional contexts where *groups* of patients and subjects must be treated in accordance with rules, policies, and standard practices. Here, informed consents are not always *autonomous* acts, nor are they always in any meaningful respect *authorizations*.

SENSE$_1$: INFORMED CONSENT AS AUTONOMOUS AUTHORIZATION

The idea of an informed consent suggests that a patient or subject does more than express agreement with, acquiesce in, yield to, or comply with an

From *A History and Theory of Informed Consent* by Ruth R. Faden and Tom L. Beauchamp. Copyright © 1986 by Oxford University Press, Inc. Reprinted by permission.

arrangement or a proposal. He or she actively *authorizes* the proposal in the act of consent. John may *assent* to a treatment plan without authorizing it. The assent may be a mere submission to the doctor's authoritative order, in which case John does not call on his own authority in order to give permission, and thus does not authorize the plan. Instead, he acts like a child who submits, yields, or assents to the school principal's spanking and in no way gives permission for or authorizes the spanking. Just as the child merely submits to an authority in a system where the lines of authority are quite clear, so often do patients.

Accordingly, an informed consent in $sense_1$ should be defined as follows: An informed consent is an autonomous action by a subject or a patient that authorizes a professional either to involve the subject in research or to initiate a medical plan for the patient (or both). We can whittle down this definition by saying that an informed consent in $sense_1$ is given if a patient or subject with (1) substantial understanding and (2) in substantial absence of control by others (3) intentionally (4) authorizes a professional (to do intervention I).

All substantially autonomous acts satisfy conditions 1–3; but it does not follow from that analysis alone that all such acts satisfy 4. The fourth condition is what distinguishes informed consent as one *kind* of autonomous action. (Note also that the definition restricts the kinds of authorization to medical and research contexts.) A person whose act satisfies conditions 1–3 but who refuses an intervention gives an *informed refusal.*

The Problem of Shared Decisionmaking. This analysis of informed consent in $sense_1$ is deliberately silent on the question of how the authorizer and agent(s) being authorized *arrive at an agreement* about the performance of "I." Recent commentators on informed consent in clinical medicine, notably Jay Katz and the President's Commission, have tended to equate the idea of informed consent with a model of "shared decisionmaking" between doctor and patient. The President's Commission titles the first chapter of its report on informed consent in the patient-practitioner relationship "Informed Consent as Active, Shared Decision Making," while in Katz's work "the idea of informed consent" and "mutual decisionmaking" are treated as virtually synonymous terms.[1]

There is of course an historical relationship in clinical medicine between medical decisionmaking and informed consent. The emergence of the legal doctrine of informed consent was instrumental in drawing attention to issues of decisionmaking as well as authority in the doctor-patient relationship. Nevertheless, it is a confusion to treat informed consent and shared decisionmaking as anything like *synonymous.* For one thing, informed consent is not restricted to clinical medicine. It is a term that applies equally to biomedical and behavioral research contexts where a model of shared decisionmaking is frequently inappropriate. Even in clinical contexts, the social and psychological dynamics involved in selecting medical interventions should be distinguished from the patient's *authorization.*

We endorse Katz's view that effective communication between professional and patient or subject is often instrumental in obtaining informed consents ($sense_1$), but we resist his conviction that the idea of informed consent entails that the patient and physician "share decisionmaking," or "reason together," or reach a consensus about what is in the patient's best interest. This is a manipulation of the concept from a too singular and defined moral perspective on the practice of medicine that is in effect a moral program for changing the practice. Although the patient and physician *may* reach a decision together, they need not. It is the essence of informed consent in $sense_1$ only that the patient or subject *authorizes autonomously;* it is a matter of indifference where or how the proposal being authorized originates.

For example, one might advocate a model of shared decisionmaking for the doctor-patient relationship without simultaneously advocating that every medical procedure requires the consent of patients. Even relationships characterized by an ample slice of shared decisionmaking, mutual trust, and respect would and should permit many decisions about routine and low-risk aspects of the patient's medical treatment to remain the exclusive province of the physician, and thus some decisions are likely always to remain subject exclusively to the physician's authorization. Moreover, in the uncommon situation, a patient could autonomously authorize the physician to make *all* decisions about medical treatment, thus giving his or her informed consent to an arrangement that scarcely resembles the sharing of decisionmaking between doctor and patient.

Authorization. In authorizing, one both assumes responsibility for what one has authorized and transfers to another one's authority to implement it. There is no informed consent unless one *understands* these features of the act and *intends* to perform that act. That is, one must understand that one is assuming responsibility and warranting another to proceed.

To say that one assumes responsibility does not quite locate the essence of the matter, however, because a *transfer* of responsibility as well as of authority also occurs. The crucial element in an authorization is that the person who authorizes uses whatever right, power, or control he or she possesses in the situation to endow another with the right to act. In so doing, the authorizer assumes some responsibility for the actions taken by the other person. Here one could either authorize *broadly* so that a person can act in accordance with general guidelines, or *narrowly* so as to authorize only a particular, carefully circumscribed procedure.

SENSE$_2$: INFORMED CONSENT AS EFFECTIVE CONSENT

By contrast to sense$_1$, sense$_2$, or *effective* consent, is a policy-oriented sense whose conditions are not derivable solely from analyses of autonomy and authorization, or even from broad notions of respect for autonomy. "Informed consent" in this second sense does not refer to *autonomous* authorization, but to a legally or institutionally *effective* (sometimes misleadingly called *valid*) authorization from a patient or a subject. Such an authorization is "effective" because it has been obtained through procedures that satisfy the rules and requirements defining a specific institutional practice in health care or in research.

The social and legal practice of requiring professionals to obtain informed consent emerged in institutional contexts, where conformity to operative rules was and still is the sole necessary and sufficient condition of informed consent. Any consent is an informed consent in sense$_2$ if it satisfies whatever operative rules apply to the practice of informed consent. Sense$_2$ requirements for informed consent typically do not focus on the autonomy of the act of giving consent (as sense$_1$ does), but rather on regulating the behavior of the *consent-seeker* and on establishing *procedures and rules* for the context of consent. Such requirements of professional behavior and procedure are obviously more readily monitored and enforced by institutions.

However, because formal institutional rules such as federal regulations and hospital policies govern whether an act of authorizing is effective, a patient or subject can autonomously authorize an intervention, and so give an informed consent in sense$_1$, and yet *not effectively authorize* that intervention in sense$_2$.

Consider the following example. Carol and Martie are nineteen-year-old, identical twins attending the same university. Martie was born with multiple birth defects, and has only one kidney. When both sisters are involved in an automobile accident, Carol is not badly hurt, but her sister is seriously injured. It is quickly determined that Martie desperately needs a kidney transplant. After detailed discussions with the transplant team and with friends, Carol consents to be the donor. There is no question that Carol's authorization of the transplant surgery is substantially autonomous. She is well informed and has long anticipated being in just such a circumstance. She has had ample opportunity over the years to consider what she would do were she faced with such a decision. Unfortunately, Carol's parents, who were in Nepal at the time of the accident, do not approve of her decision. Furious that they were not consulted, they decide to sue the transplant team and the hospital for having performed an unauthorized surgery on their minor daughter. (In this state the legal age to consent to surgical procedures is twenty-one.)

According to our analysis, Carol gave her informed consent in sense$_1$ to the surgery, but she did not give her informed consent in sense$_2$. That is, she autonomously authorized the transplant and thereby gave an informed consent in sense$_1$ but did not give a consent that was effective under the operative legal and institutional policy, which in this case required that the person consenting be a legally authorized agent. Examples of other policies that can define sense$_2$ informed consent (but not sense$_1$) include rules that consent be witnessed by an auditor or that there be a one-day waiting period between solicitation of consent and implementation of the intervention in order for the person's authorization to be effective. Such rules can and do vary, both within the United States by jurisdiction and institution, and across the countries of the world.

Medical and research codes, as well as case law and federal regulations, have developed models of informed consent that are delineated entirely in a sense$_2$ format, although they have sometimes attempted to justify the rules by appeal to something like sense$_1$. For example, disclosure conditions for informed consent are central to the history of "informed consent" in sense$_2$, because disclosure has traditionally been a *necessary* condition of effective informed consent (and sometimes a *sufficient* condition!). The legal doctrine of informed consent is primarily a law of disclosure; satisfaction of disclosure rules virtually consumes "informed consent" in law. This should come as no surprise, because the legal system needs a generally applicable informed consent mechanism by which injury and responsibility can be readily and fairly assessed in court. These disclosure requirements in the legal and regulatory contexts are not conditions of "informed consent" in sense$_1$; indeed disclosure may be entirely irrelevant to giving an informed consent in sense$_1$. If a person has an adequate *understanding* of relevant information without benefit of a disclosure, then it makes no difference whether someone *discloses* that information.

Other sense$_2$ rules besides those of disclosure have been enforced. These include rules requiring evidence of adequate comprehension of information and the aforementioned rules requiring the presence of auditor witnesses and mandatory waiting periods. Sense$_2$ informed consent requirements generally take the form of rules focusing on disclosure, comprehension, the minimization of potentially controlling influences, and competence. These requirements express the present-day mainstream conception in the federal government of the United States. They are also typical of international documents and state regulations, which all reflect a sense$_2$ orientation.

THE RELATIONSHIP BETWEEN SENSE$_1$ AND SENSE$_2$

A sense$_1$ "informed consent" can fail to be an informed consent in sense$_2$ by a lack of conformity to applicable rules and requirements. Similarly, an informed consent in sense$_2$ may not be an informed consent in sense$_1$. The rules and requirements that determine sense$_2$ consents need not result in autonomous authorizations at all in order to qualify as informed consents.

Such peculiarities in informed consent law have led Jay Katz to argue that the legal doctrine of "informed consent" bears a "name" that "promises much more than its construction in case law has delivered." He has argued insightfully that the courts have, in effect, imposed a mere duty to warn on physicians, an obligation confined to risk disclosures and statements of proposed interventions. He maintains that "This judicially imposed obligation must be distinguished from the *idea* of informed consent, namely, that patients have a decisive role to play in the medical decision-making process. The idea of informed consent, though alluded to also in case law, cannot be implemented, as courts have attempted, by only expanding the disclosure requirements." By their actions and declarations, Katz believes, the courts have made informed consent a "cruel hoax" and have allowed "the idea of informed consent . . . to wither on the vine."[2]

The most plausible interpretation of Katz's contentions is through the sense$_1$/sense$_2$ distinction. If a physician obtains a consent under the courts' criteria, then an informed consent (sense$_2$) has been obtained. But it does not follow that the courts are using the *right* standards, or *sufficiently rigorous* standards in light of a stricter autonomy-based model—or "idea" as Katz puts it—of informed consent (sense$_1$).[3] If Katz is correct that the courts have made a mockery of informed consent and of its moral justification in respect for autonomy, then of course his criticisms are thoroughly justified. At the same time, it should be recognized that people can proffer legally or institutionally effective authorizations under prevailing rules even if they fall far short of the standards implicit in sense$_1$.

Despite the differences between sense$_1$ and sense$_2$, a definition of informed consent need not fall into one or the other class of definitions. It may conform to both. Many definitions of informed consent in policy contexts reflect at least a strong and definite reliance on informed consent in sense$_1$. Although the conditions of sense$_1$ are not logically necessary conditions for sense$_2$, we take it as morally axiomatic that they *ought* to serve—and in fact have served—as the benchmark or model against which the moral adequacy of a definition framed for sense$_2$ purposes is to be evaluated. This position is, roughly speaking, Katz's position.

A defense of the moral viewpoint that policies governing informed consent in sense$_2$ *should* be formulated to conform to the standards of informed consent in sense$_1$ is not hard to express. The goal of informed consent in medical care and in research—that is, the purpose behind the obligation to obtain informed consent—is to enable potential subjects and patients to make autonomous decisions about whether to grant or refuse authorization for medical and research interventions. Accordingly, embedded in the reason for having the social institution of informed consent is the idea that institutional requirements for informed consent in $sense_2$ *should* be intended to maximize the likelihood that the conditions of informed consent in $sense_1$ will be satisfied.

A major problem at the policy level, where rules and requirements must be developed and applied in the aggregate, is the following: The obligations imposed to enable patients and subjects to make authorization decisions must be evaluated not only in terms of the demands of a set of abstract conditions of "true" or $sense_1$ informed consent, but also in terms of the impact of imposing such obligations or requirements on various institutions with their concrete concerns and priorities. One must take account of what is fair and reasonable to require of health care professionals and researchers, the effect of alternative consent requirements on efficiency and effectiveness in the delivery of health care and the advancement of science, and—particularly in medical care—the effect of requirements on the welfare of patients. Also relevant are considerations peculiar to the particular social context, such as proof, precedent, or liability theory in case law, or regulatory authority and due process in the development of federal regulations and IRB consent policies.

Moreover, at the $sense_2$ level, one must resolve not only which requirements will define effective consent; one must also settle on the rules stipulating the conditions under which effective consents must be obtained. In some cases, hard decisions must be made about whether requirements of informed consent (in $sense_2$) should be imposed at all, even though informed consent (in $sense_1$) *could* realistically and meaningfully be obtained in the circumstances and could serve as a model for institutional rules. For example, should there be any consent requirements in the cases of minimal risk medical procedures and research activities?

This need to balance is not a problem for informed consent in $sense_1$, which is not policy oriented. Thus, it is possible to have a *morally acceptable* set of requirements for informed consent in $sense_2$ that deviates considerably from the conditions of informed consent in $sense_1$. However, the burden of moral proof rests with those who defend such deviations since the primary moral justification of the obligation to obtain informed consent is respect for autonomous action.

NOTES

1. President's Commission, *Making Health Care Decisions,* Vol. 1, 15 and Jay Katz, *The Silent World of Doctor and Patient* (New York: The Free Press, 1984), 87 and "The Regulation of Human Research—Reflections and Proposals," *Clinical Research* 21 (1973): 758–91. Katz does not provide a sustained analysis of joint or shared decisionmaking, and it is unclear precisely how he would relate this notion to informed consent.

2. Jay Katz, "Disclosure and Consent," in A. Milunsky and G. Annas, eds., *Genetics and the Law II* (New York: Plenum Press, 1980), 122, 128.

3. We have already noted that Katz's "idea" of informed consent—as the active involvement of patients in the medical decisionmaking process—is different from our $sense_1$.

ROBERT J. LEVINE

Informed Consent: Some Challenges to the Universal Validity of the Western Model

Robert J. Levine, MD, is professor of medicine, lecturer in pharmacology, and chairman of the Human Investigation Committee (an IRB) at the Yale University School of Medicine. He has served as president of the American Society of Law, Medicine, and Ethics and as a fellow at both the Hastings Center and the American College of Physicians. Dr. Levine's focus in bioethics is research ethics. His works include "The Need to Revise the Declaration of Helsinki" (*New England Journal of Medicine*), "Ethics of Clinical Trials: Do They Help the Patient?" (*Cancer*), and the influential textbook *Ethics and Regulation of Clinical Research* (Urban & Schwarzenberg).

INFORMED CONSENT

Informed consent holds a central place in the ethical justification of research involving human subjects. This position is signaled by the fact that it is the first-stated and, by far, the longest principle of the Nuremberg Code.[1]

> I. The voluntary consent of the human subject is absolutely essential. This means that the person involved should have the legal capacity to give consent; should be so situated as to be able to exercise free power of choice, without the intervention of any element of force, fraud, deceit, duress, overreaching, or other ulterior form of constraint or coercion; and should have sufficient knowledge and comprehension of the elements of the subject matter involved as to enable him to make an understanding and enlightened decision. This latter element requires that before the acceptance of an affirmative decision by the experimental subject there should be made known to him the nature, duration, and purpose of the experiment; the method and means by which it is to be conducted; all inconveniences and hazards reasonably to be expected; and the effects upon his health or person which may possibly come from his participation in the experiment. . . .

The Nuremberg Code identifies four attributes of consent without which consent cannot be considered valid: consent must be "voluntary," "legally competent," "informed," and "comprehending." These four attributes stand essentially unchanged to this day. Although there has been extensive commentary on the meaning of each of these attributes and how they are to be interpreted in specific contexts, there has been no authoritative agreement reached that any of them may be omitted or that there should be any additional attribute elevated to the status of the original four. . . .

The National Commission grounded the requirement for informed consent in the ethical principle of respect for persons which it defined as follows:

> Respect for persons incorporates at least two basic ethical convictions: First, that individuals should be treated as autonomous agents, and second, that persons with diminished autonomy and thus in need of protection are entitled to such protections.

The National Commission defined an "autonomous person" as ". . . an individual capable of deliberation about personal goals and of acting under the direction of such deliberation." To show respect for autonomous persons requires that we leave them alone, even to the point of allowing them to choose activities that might be harmful, unless they agree or consent that we may do otherwise. We are not to touch them or to encroach upon their private spaces unless such touching or encroachment is in accord with their wishes. Our actions

From *Law, Medicine, and Health Care* 19(1991), 207–13. Reprinted with permission of the American Society of Law, Medicine & Ethics.

should be designed to affirm their authority and enhance their capacity to be self-determining; we are not to obstruct their actions unless they are clearly detrimental to others. We show disrespect for autonomous persons when we either repudiate their considered judgments or deny them the freedom to act on those judgments in the absence of compelling reasons to do so.

The National Commission's discussion of an autonomous person is consistent with the prevailing perception of the nature of the "moral agent" in Western civilization. A moral agent is an individual who is capable of forming a rational plan of life, capable of rational deliberation about alternative plans of action with the aim of making choices that are compatible with his or her life plan and who assumes responsibility for the consequences of his or her choices.

Although the National Commission did not cite either of the following sources as authoritative in developing its definition of respect for persons, it is clear to this observer that they found them influential: The first is the statement of the principle of respect for persons as articulated by the German philosopher, Immanuel Kant: "So act as to treat humanity, whether in thine own person or in that of any other, in every case as an end withal, never as a means only." A second influential statement is that of the American judge, Benjamin Cardozo: "Every human being of adult years and sound mind has the right to determine what will be done with his own body . . ."

. . . In the actual process of negotiating informed consent and in the reviews of plans for informed consent conducted by Institutional Review Boards (IRBs), there is a tendency to concentrate on the information to be presented to the prospective subject. Among the IRB's principal concerns are the following questions: Is there a full statement of each of the elements of informed consent? Is the information presented in a style of language that one could expect the prospective subject to understand? Implicit in this is a vision of informed consent as a two step process. First, information is presented to the subject by the investigator. Secondly, the subject satisfies himself or herself that he or she understands, and based upon this understanding either agrees or refuses to participate in the research project. . . .

In the paper I presented at an earlier CIOMS conference[2] I concluded:

> This brief survey of descriptions of relationships between health professionals and patients in three disparate cultures leads me to conclude that the informed consent standards of the Declaration of Helsinki are not universally valid. Imposition of these standards as they are now written will not accomplish their purposes; i.e., they will not guide physicians in their efforts to show respect for persons because they do not reflect adequately the views held in these cultures of the nature of the person in his or her relationship to society.

This conclusion was based on a review of observations of the doctor–patient relationship, subject–investigator relationship and perspectives on the nature of disease in three cultures: Western Africa, China, and a Central American Mayan Indian culture.

The concept of personhood as it exists in various cultures has been addressed in an excellent paper by Willy De Craemer.[3] De Craemer is a cross-cultural sociologist with extensive experience in the field in, among other places, Central Africa and Japan.

In this paper he makes it clear that the Western vision of the person is a minority viewpoint in the world. The majority viewpoint manifest in most other societies, both technologically developing (e.g., Central Africa) and technologically developed (e.g., Japan), does not reflect the American perspective of radical individualism. . . .

Although I commend to the readers' attention De Craemer's entire essay, I shall here excerpt some passages from his description of the Japanese vision of the person. I do this because Japan is unquestionably a highly developed society technologically as well as in other respects. Thus, it is less easy to dismiss its vision of the person as exotic, as could be done with some of the examples examined in my earlier paper: . . .

> The special status that the Japanese accord to human relationships, with its emphasis on the empathic and solidary interdependence of many individuals, rather than on the autonomous independence of the individual person, includes within it several other core attributes. To begin with, the kind of reciprocity (*on*) that underlies human relationships means that both concretely and symbolically what anthropologist Marcel Mauss . . . termed "the theme of the gift" is one of its dominant motifs. A continuous, gift-exchange-structured flow of material and nonmaterial "goods" and "services" takes place between the members of the enclosed human nexus to which each individual belongs. Through a never-ending process of mutual giving, receiving, and repaying . . . a web of relations develops that binds donors and recipients together in diffuse, deeply personal, and overlapping creditor-debtor ways. Generalized benevolence is

> involved, but so is generalized obligation, both of which take into account another crucial parameter of Japanese culture: the importance attached to status, rank, and hierarchical order in interpersonal relationships, and to . . . "proper-place occupancy" within them. The triple obligation to give, receive, and repay are tightly regulated by this status-formalism and sense of propriety. . . .

It is not difficult to imagine how a research ethics committee in the Western world—particularly in the United States—would evaluate the custom of exchange of gifts—both material and immaterial—in a system that recognized the legitimacy of "status, rank, and hierarchical order." Attention would soon be focused on the problems of "conflicts of interest." Questions would be raised as to whether consent would be invalidated by "undue inducement," or what the Nuremberg Code calls "other ulterior form(s) of constraint or coercion." In my views, it is impossible to evaluate the meaning of cash payments, provision of free services, and other "inducements" without a full appreciation of the cultural significance of such matters.

It is against this backdrop that I have been asked by the CIOMS Conference Programme Committee to "provide a definition [of informed consent] which is widely applicable to different countries and cultures." Given that the purpose of informed consent is to show respect for persons, in recognition of the vastly different perspectives of the nature of "person," I cannot do this. Since I cannot provide a substantive definition of informed consent, I shall suggest a procedural approach to dealing with the problem.

As an American I am firmly committed to the Western vision of the person and deeply influenced by my experience with the American variant of this vision. . . .

Thus, it would not be prudent to trust an American to provide a universally applicable definition of informed consent. I suggest further, that it would not be prudent to rely on any person situated in any culture to provide a universally applicable definition of informed consent.

Before proceeding, I wish to comment on the continuing controversy on the topic of ethical justification of research that crosses national boundaries. There are those who contend that all research, wherever it is conducted, should be justified according to universally applicable standards; I refer to them as "universalists." Those opposed to the universalist position, whom I call "pluralists," accept some standards as universal, but argue that other standards must be adapted to accommodate the mores of particular cultures. Pluralists commonly refer to the universalist position as "ethical imperialism," while universalists often call that of their opponents, "ethical relativism."

Universalists correctly point out that most therapeutic innovations are developed in industrialized nations. Investigators from these countries may go to technologically developing countries to test their innovations for various reasons; some of these reasons are good and some of them are not (e.g., to save money and to take advantage of the less complex and sophisticated regulatory systems typical to technologically developing countries). Moreover, universalists observe that, once the innovations have been proved safe and effective, economic factors often limit their availability to citizens of the country in which they were tested. Requiring investigators to conform to the ethical standards of their own country when conducting research abroad is one way to restrain exploitation of this type. Universalists also point to the Declaration of Helsinki as a widely accepted universal standard for biomedical research that has been endorsed by most countries, including those labeled "technologically developing." This gives weight to their claim that research must be conducted according to universal principles. Furthermore, the complex regulations characteristic of technologically developed countries are, in general, patterned after the Declaration of Helsinki.

Marcia Angell, in a particularly incisive exposition of the universalists' position, suggests this analogy[4]

> Does apartheid offend universal standards of justice, or does it instead simply represent the South African custom that should be seen as morally neutral? If the latter view is accepted, then ethical principles are not much more than a description of the mores of a society. I believe they must have more meaning than that. There must be a core of human rights that we would wish to see honored universally, despite local variations in their superficial aspects . . . The force of local custom or law cannot justify abuses of certain fundamental rights, and the right of self-determination, on which the doctrine of informed consent is based, is one of them.

Pluralists join with universalists in condemning economic exploitation of technologically developing countries and their citizens.[5] Unlike the universalists, however, they see the imposition of ethical standards for the conduct of research by a powerful country on a developing country as another form of exploitation. In their view, it is tantamount to saying, "No, you may not participate in this development of technology, no matter how much you desire it, unless you permit us to replace your ethical standards with our own." Pluralists call attention to the fact that the Declaration of Helsinki, although widely endorsed by the nations of the world, reflects a uniquely Western view of the nature of the person; as such it does not adequately guide investigators in ways to show respect for all persons in the world.

An example of pluralism may be found in the diversity of national policies regarding blind HIV-seroprevalence studies. The United States Centers for Disease Control are now conducting anonymous tests of leftover blood drawn for other purposes without notification in studies designed to "determine the level of HIV-seroprevalence in a nationwide sample of hospital patients and clients at family planning, sexually transmitted disease, tuberculosis, and drug treatment clinics. . . ." No personal identifiers are kept.[6] Although there seems to be widespread agreement among US commentators that such anonymous testing without notification is ethically justified, different judgments have been reached in other countries, most notably in the United Kingdom and in the Netherlands.[7] Who is to say which of these nations has the correct ethical perspective that should be made part of the "universal standard?"

The legitimacy of the pluralists' position is recognized implicitly in U.S. policy on whether research subjects are required to be informed of the results of HIV antibody testing.[8] In general, this policy requires that all individuals "whose test results are associated with personal identifiers must be informed of their own test results . . . individuals may not be given the option 'not to know' the result. . . ." This policy permits several narrowly defined exceptions. One of these provides that research "conducted at foreign sites should be carefully evaluated to account for cultural norms, the health resource capability and official health policies of the host country." Then "the reviewing IRB must consider if any modification to the policy is significantly justified by the risk/benefit evaluation of the research."

WHO/CIOMS Proposed International Guidelines provide specific guidance for the conduct of research in which an investigator or an institution in a technologically developed country serves as the "external sponsor" of research conducted in a technologically developing "host country."[9] In my judgment these guidelines strike a sensitive balance between the universalist and pluralist perspectives. They require that "the research protocol should be submitted to ethical review by the initiating agency. The ethical standards applied should be no less exacting than they would be for research carried out within the initiating country" (Article 28). They also provide for accommodation to the mores of the culture within the "host country." For example:

> Where individual members of a community do not have the necessary awareness of the implications of participation in an experiment to give adequately informed consent directly to the investigators, it is desirable that the decision whether or not to participate should be elicited through the intermediary of a trusted community leader. (Article 15).

The conduct of research involving human subjects must not violate any universally applicable ethical standards. Although I endorse certain forms of cultural relativism, there are limits to how much cultural relativism ought to be tolerated. Certain behaviors ought to be condemned by the world community even though they are sponsored by a nation's leaders and seem to have wide support of its citizens. For example, the Nuremberg tribunal appealed to universally valid principles in order to determine the guilt of the physicians (war criminals) who had conducted research according to standards approved by their nation's leaders.

I suggest that the principle of respect for persons is one of the universally applicable ethical standards. It is universally applicable when stated at the level of formality employed by Immanuel Kant: "So act as to treat humanity, whether in thine own person or in that of any other, in every case as an end withal, never as a means only." The key concept is that persons are never to be treated only or merely as means to another's ends. When one goes beyond this level of formality or abstraction, the principle begins to lose its universality. When one restates the principle of respect for persons in a form that reflects a peculiarly Western view of the person, it begins to lose its relevance to some people in Central Africa, Japan, Central America, and so on.

The Conference Programme Committee asked me to address the problem "of obtaining consent in cultures where non-dominant persons traditionally do not give consent, such as a wife." Having subscribed to the Western vision of the meaning of person, I believe that all persons should be treated as autonomous agents, wives included. Thus, I believe that we should show respect for wives in the context of research by soliciting their informed consent. But, if this is not permitted within a particular culture, would I exclude wives from participation in research?

Not necessarily. If there is a strong possibility either that the wife could benefit from participation in the research or that the class of women of which she is a representative could benefit (and there is a reasonable balance of risks and potential benefits), I would offer her an opportunity to participate. To do otherwise would not accomplish anything of value (e.g., her entitlement to self-determination); it would merely deprive her of a chance to secure the benefits of participation in the research. I would, of course, offer her an opportunity to decline participation, understanding that in some cultures she would consider such refusal "unthinkable."

. . . Finally, the Conference Programme Committee has asked me to consider "the special problems of obtaining consent when populations are uneducated or illiterate." Lack of education in and of itself presents no problems that are unfamiliar to those experienced with negotiating informed consent with prospective subjects. These are barriers to comprehension which are not generally insurmountable. Greater problems are presented by those who hold beliefs about health and illness that are inconsistent with the concepts of Western medicine. It may, for example, be difficult to explain the purpose of vaccination to a person who believes that disease is caused by forces that Western civilization dismisses as supernatural or magical.[10] The meaning of such familiar (in the Western world) procedures as blood-letting may be vastly different and very disturbing in some societies.[11] Problems with such explanations can, I believe, be dealt with best by local ethical review committees.

Illiteracy, in and of itself, presents no problems to the process of informed consent which, when conducted properly, entails talking rather than reading. Rather, it presents problems with the documentation of informed consent. The process of informed consent, designed to show respect for persons, fosters their interests by empowering them to pursue and protect their own interests. The consent form, by contrast, is an instrument designed to protect the interests of investigators and their institutions and to defend them against civil or criminal liability. If it is necessary to have such protection of investigators, subjects may be asked to make their mark on a consent document and a witness may be required to countersign and attest to the fact that the subject received the information.

A PROCEDURAL RESOLUTION

In "Proposal Guidelines for International Testing of Vaccines and Drugs Against HIV Infection and AIDS" (hereafter referred to as "Proposed HIV Guidelines"), reference is made to an ethical review system.[12] This system is based on that set forth in the WHO/CIOMS Proposed International Guidelines for Biomedical Research Involving Human Subjects. In the Proposed HIV Guidelines, there are suggestions for divisions of responsibility for ethical review. Here I shall elaborate how responsibilities should be divided for determining the adequacy of informed consent procedures.

This proposal presupposes the existence of an international standard for informed consent. I suggest that the standards for informed consent as set forth in the WHO/CIOMS Proposed International Guidelines and as elaborated in the Proposed HIV Guidelines, be recognized as the international standard for informed consent.

1. All plans to conduct research involving human subjects should be reviewed and approved by a research ethics committee (REC). Ideally the REC should be based in the community in which the research is to be conducted. However, as noted in CIOMS/WHO Proposed International Guidelines, under some circumstances regional or national committees may be adequate for these purposes. In such cases it is essential that regional or national committees have as members or consultants individuals who are highly familiar with the customs of the community in which the research is to be done.

The authority of the REC to approve research should be limited to proposals in which the plans for informed consent conform either to the international standard or to a modification of the international standard that has been authorized by a national ethical review body.

2. Proposals to employ consent procedures that do not conform to the international standard should be justified by the researcher and submitted for review and approval by a national ethical review body. Earlier in this paper I identified some conditions or

circumstances that could justify such omissions or modifications.

The role of the national ethical review body is to authorize consent procedures that deviate from the international standard. The responsibility for review and approval of the entire protocol (with the modified consent procedure) remains with the REC. Specific details of consent procedures that conform to the international standard or to a modified version of the international standard approved by the national ethical review body should be reviewed and approved by the local ethical review committee.

3. There should be established an international ethical review body to provide advice, consultation and guidance to national ethical review bodies when such is requested by the latter.

4. In the case of externally sponsored research: Ethical review should be conducted in the initiating country. Although it may and should provide advice to the host country, its approval should be based on its finding that plans for informed consent are consistent with the international standard. If there has been a modification of consent procedures approved by the national ethical review body in the host country, the initiating country may either endorse the modification or seek consultation with the international review body.

NOTES

1. Reprinted in R. J. Levine: *Ethics and Regulation of Clinical Research.* Urban & Schwarzenberg, Baltimore & Munich, Second Edition, 1986.

2. R. J. Levine, "Validity of Consent Procedures in Technologically Developing Countries". In: *Human Experimentation and Medical Ethics*. Ed. by Z. Bankowski and N. Howard-Jones, Council for International Organizations of Medical Sciences, Geneva, 1982, pp. 16–30.

3. W. De Craemer, "A Cross-Cultural Perspective on Personhood," *Milbank Memorial Fund Quarterly* 61:19–34, Winter 1983.

4. M. Angell, "Ethical Imperialism? Ethics in International Collaborative Clinical Research." *New England Journal of Medicine* 319:1081–1083, 1988.

5. M. Barry, "Ethical Considerations of Human Investigation in Developing Countries: The AIDS Dilemma." *New England Journal of Medicine* 319:1083–1086, 1988; N. A. Christakis, "Responding to a Pandemic: International Interests in AIDS Control." *Daedalus* 118 (No. 2):113–114, 1989; and N. A. Christakis, "Ethical Design of an AIDS Vaccine Trial in Africa." *Hastings Center Report* 18 (No. 3):31–37, June/July, 1988.

6. M. Pappaioanou et al., "The Family of HIV Seroprevalence Studies: Objectives, Methods and Uses of Sentinel Surveillance in the United States." *Public Health Reports* 105(2):113–119, 1990.

7. R. Bayer, L. H. Lumey, and L. Wan, "The American, British and Dutch Responses to Unlinked Anonymous HIV Seroprevalence Studies: An International Comparison." *AIDS* 4:283–290, 1990, reprinted in this issue of *Law, Medicine and Health Care,* 19:3–4.

8. R. E. Windom, Assistant Secretary for Health, policy on informing those tested about HIV serostatus, letter to PHS agency heads, Washington, DC, May 9, 1988.

9. Proposed International Guidelines for Biomedical Research Involving Human Subjects, A Joint Project of the World Health Organization and the Council for International Organizations of Medical Sciences, CIOMS, Geneva, 1982.

10. See De Craemer, *supra* note 3 and Levine, *supra* note 2.

11. A. J. Hall, "Public Health Trials in West Africa: Logistics and Ethics," *IRB: A Review of Human Subjects Research* 11 (No. 5):8–10, Sept/Oct 1989. See also Christakis, *supra* note 5.

12. R. J. Levine, and W. K. Mariner, "Proposed Guidelines for International Testing of Vaccines and Drugs Against HIV Infection and AIDS," prepared at the request of WHO, Global Programme on AIDS and submitted January 5, 1990.

Refusal of Treatment

CALIFORNIA COURT OF APPEALS, SECOND DISTRICT

Bouvia v. Superior Court

OPINION AND ORDER FOR A PEREMPTORY WRIT OF MANDATE
BEACH, Associate Justice

Petitioner, Elizabeth Bouvia, a patient in a public hospital seeks the removal from her body of a nasogastric tube inserted and maintained against her will and without her consent by physicians who so placed it for the purpose of keeping her alive through involuntary forced feeding. . . .

The trial court denied petitioner's request for the immediate relief she sought. It concluded that leaving the tube in place was necessary to prolong petitioner's life, and that it would, in fact, do so. With the tube in place petitioner probably will survive the time required to prepare for trial, a trial itself and an appeal, if one proved necessary. The real party physicians also assert, and the trial court agreed, that physically petitioner tolerates the tube reasonably well and thus is not in great physical discomfort. . . .

FACTUAL BACKGROUND

Petitioner is a 28-year-old woman. Since birth she has been afflicted with and suffered from severe cerebral palsy. She is quadriplegic. She is now a patient at a public hospital maintained by one of the real parties in interest, the County of Los Angeles. . . . Petitioner's physical handicaps of palsy and quadriplegia have progressed to the point where she is completely bedridden. Except for a few fingers of one hand and some slight head and facial movements, she is immobile. She is physically helpless and wholly unable to care for herself. She is totally dependent upon others for all of her needs. These include feeding, washing, cleaning, toileting, turning, and helping her with elimination and other bodily functions. She cannot stand or sit upright in bed or in a wheelchair. She lies flat in bed and must do so the rest of her life. She suffers also from degenerative and severely crippling arthritis. She is in continual pain. Another tube permanently attached to her chest automatically injects her with periodic doses of morphine which relieves some, but not all of her physical pain and discomfort.

She is intelligent, very mentally competent. She earned a college degree. She was married but her husband has left her. She suffered a miscarriage. She lived with her parents until her father told her that they could no longer care for her. She has stayed intermittently with friends and at public facilities. A search for a permanent place to live where she might receive the constant care which she needs has been unsuccessful. She is without financial means to support herself and, therefore, must accept public assistance for medical and other care.

She has on several occasions expressed the desire to die. In 1983 she sought the right to be cared for in a public hospital in Riverside County while she intentionally "starved herself to death." A court in that county denied her judicial assistance to accomplish that goal. She later abandoned an appeal from that ruling. Thereafter, friends took her to several different facilities, both public and private, arriving finally at her present location. . . .

Petitioner must be spoon fed in order to eat. Her present medical and dietary staff have determined that she is not consuming a sufficient amount of nutrients. Petitioner stops eating when she feels she cannot

Reprinted from the *California Reporter,* 225 Cal.Rptr. 297 (Cal. App. 2 Dist.).

orally swallow more, without nausea and vomiting. As she cannot now retain solids, she is fed soft liquid-like food. Because of her previously announced resolve to starve herself, the medical staff feared her weight loss might reach a life-threatening level. Her weight since admission to real parties' facility seems to hover between 65 and 70 pounds. Accordingly, they inserted the subject tube against her will and contrary to her express written instruction. . . .

THE RIGHT TO REFUSE MEDICAL TREATMENT

"[A] person of adult years and in sound mind has the right, in the exercise of control over his own body, to determine whether or not to submit to lawful medical treatment." (*Cobbs v. Grant* (1972) 8 Cal.3d 229, 242, 104 Cal.Rptr. 505, 502 P.2d 1.) It follows that such a patient has the right to refuse *any* medical treatment, even that which may save or prolong her life. (*Barber v. Superior Court* (1983) 147 Cal. App.3d 1006, 195 Cal.Rptr. 484; *Bartling v. Superior Court* (1984) 163 Cal.App.3d 186, 209 Cal.Rptr. 220.) In our view the foregoing authorities are dispositive of the case at bench. Nonetheless, the County and its medical staff contend that for reasons unique to this case, Elizabeth Bouvia may not exercise the right available to others. Accordingly, we again briefly discuss the rule in the light of real parties' contentions.

The right to refuse medical treatment is basic and fundamental. It is recognized as a part of the right of privacy protected by both the state and federal constitutions. . . . Its exercise requires no one's approval. It is not merely one vote subject to being overridden by medical opinion.

In *Barber v. Superior Court, supra,* 147 Cal.App.3d 1006, 195 Cal.Rptr. 484, we considered this same issue although in a different context. Writing on behalf of this division, Justice Compton thoroughly analyzed and reviewed the issue of withdrawal of life-support systems beginning with the seminal case of the *Matter of Quinlan* (N.J. 1976) 355 A.2d 647, *cert. den.* 429 U.S. 922, 97 S.Ct. 319, 50 L.Ed.2d 289, and continuing on to the then recent enactment of the California Natural Death Act (Health & Saf. Code. §§ 7185–7195). His opinion clearly and repeatedly stresses the fundamental underpinning of its conclusion, i.e., the patient's right to decide: 147 Cal.App.3d at page 1015, 195 Cal.Rptr. 484, "In this state a clearly recognized legal right to control one's own medical treatment predated the Natural Death Act. A long line of cases, approved by the Supreme Court in *Cobbs v. Grant* (1972) 8 Cal.3d 229 [104 Cal.Rptr. 505, 502 P.2d 1] . . . have held that where a doctor performs treatment in the absence of an informed consent, there is an actionable battery. The obvious corollary to this principle is that *"a competent adult patient has the legal right to refuse medical treatment."* . . .

Bartling v. Superior Court, supra, 163 Cal.App.3d 186, 209 Cal.Rptr. 220, was factually much like the case at bench. Although not totally identical in all respects, the issue there centered on the same question here present: i.e., "May the patient refuse even life continuing treatment?" Justice Hastings, writing for another division of this court, explained: "In this case we are called upon to decide whether a competent adult patient, with serious illness which are probably incurable but have not been diagnosed as terminal, has the right, over the objection of his physicians and the hospital, to have life-support equipment disconnected despite the fact that withdrawal of such devices will surely hasten his death." (At p. 189, 209 Cal.Rptr. 220.) . . .

The description of Mr. Bartling's condition fits that of Elizabeth Bouvia. The holding of that case applies here and compels real parties to respect her decision even though she is not "terminally" ill. . . .

THE CLAIMED EXCEPTIONS TO THE PATIENT'S RIGHT TO CHOOSE ARE INAPPLICABLE

. . . At bench the trial court concluded that with sufficient feeding petitioner could live an additional 15 to 20 years; therefore, the preservation of petitioner's life for that period outweighed her right to decide. In so holding the trial court mistakenly attached undue importance to the *amount of time* possibly available to petitioner, and failed to give equal weight and consideration for the *quality* of that life; an equal, if not more significant, consideration.

All decisions permitting cessation of medical treatment or life-support procedures to some degree hastened the arrival of death. In part, at least, this was permitted because the quality of life during the time remaining in those cases had been terribly diminished. In Elizabeth Bouvia's view, the quality of her life has been diminished to the point of hopelessness, uselessness, unenjoyability and frustration. She, as the patient, lying helplessly in bed, unable to care for herself, may consider her existence meaningless. . . .

Here Elizabeth Bouvia's decision to forego medical treatment or life-support through a mechanical means belongs to her. It is not a medical decision for her physicians to make. Neither is it a legal question whose soundness is to be resolved by lawyers or judges. It is not a conditional right subject to approval by ethics committees or courts of law. It is a moral and philosophical decision that, being a competent adult, is hers alone. . . .

Here, if force fed, petitioner faces 15 to 20 years of a painful existence, endurable only by the constant administrations of morphine. Her condition is irreversible. There is no cure for her palsy or arthritis. Petitioner would have to be fed, cleaned, turned, bedded, toileted by others for 15 to 20 years! Although alert, bright, sensitive, perhaps even brave and feisty, she must lie immobile, unable to exist except through physical acts of others. Her mind and spirit may be free to take great flights but she herself is imprisoned and must lie physically helpless subject to the ignominy, embarrassment, humiliation, and dehumanizing aspects created by her helplessness. We do not believe it is the policy of this State that all and every life must be preserved against the will of the sufferer. It is incongruous, if not monstrous, for medical practitioners to assert their right to preserve a life that someone else must live, or, more accurately, endure, for "15 to 20 years." We cannot conceive it to be the policy of this State to inflict such an ordeal upon anyone.

It is, therefore, immaterial that the removal of the nasogastric tube will hasten or cause Bouvia's eventual death. Being competent she has the right to live out the remainder of her natural life in dignity and peace. It is precisely the aim and purpose of the many decisions upholding the withdrawal of life-support systems to accord and provide a large measure of dignity, respect and comfort as possible to every patient for the remainder of his days, whatever be their number. This goal is not to hasten death, though its earlier arrival may be an expected and understood likelihood. . . .

It is not necessary to here define or dwell at length upon what constitutes suicide. Our Supreme Court dealt with the matter in the case of *In re Joseph G.* (1983) 34 Cal.3d 429, 194 Cal.Rptr. 163, 667 P.2d 1176, wherein declaring that the State has an interest in preserving and recognizing the sanctity of life, it observed that it is a crime to aid in suicide. But it is significant that the instances and the means there discussed all involved affirmative, assertive, proximate, direct conduct such as furnishing a gun, poison, knife, or other instrumentality or usable means by which another could physically and immediately inflict some death-producing injury upon himself. Such situations are far different than the mere presence of a doctor during the exercise of his patient's constitutional rights.

This is the teaching of *Bartling* and *Barber*. No criminal or civil liability attaches to honoring a competent, informed patient's refusal of medical service.

We do not purport to establish what will constitute proper medical practice in all other cases or even other aspects of the care to be provided petitioner. We hold only that her right to refuse medical treatment even of the life-sustaining variety, entitles her to the immediate removal of the nasogastric tube that has been involuntarily inserted into her body. The hospital and medical staff are still free to perform a substantial, if not the greater part of their duty, i.e., that of trying to alleviate Bouvia's pain and suffering.

Petitioner is without means to go to a private hospital and, apparently, real parties' hospital as a public facility was required to accept her. Having done so it may not deny her relief from pain and suffering merely because she has chosen to exercise her fundamental right to protect what little privacy remains to her. . . .

IT IS ORDERED

Let a peremptory writ of mandate issue commanding the Los Angeles Superior Court immediately upon receipt thereof, to make and enter a new and different order granting Elizabeth Bouvia's request for a preliminary injunction, and the relief prayed for therein; in particular to make an order (1) directing real parties in interest forthwith to remove the nasogastric tube from petitioner, Elizabeth Bouvia's, body, and (2) prohibiting any and all of the real parties in interest from replacing or aiding in replacing said tube or any other or similar device in or on petitioner without her consent. . . .

COMPTON, ASSOCIATE JUSTICE, CONCURRING OPINION

I have no doubt that Elizabeth Bouvia wants to die; and if she had the full use of even one hand, could probably find a way to end her life—in a word—commit suicide. In order to seek the assistance which she needs in ending her life by the only means she sees available—starvation—she has had to stultify her position before this court by disavowing her desire to end her life in such a fashion and proclaiming that she will eat all that she can physically tolerate. Even the majority opinion here must necessarily "dance" around the issue.

Elizabeth apparently has made a conscious and informed choice that she prefers death to continued existence in her helpless and, to her, intolerable condition. I believe she has an absolute right to effectuate that decision. This state and the medical profession instead of frustrating her desire, should be attempting to relieve her suffering by permitting and in fact assisting her to die with ease and dignity. The fact that she is forced to suffer the ordeal of self-starvation to achieve her objective is in itself inhumane.

The right to die is an integral part of our right to control our own destinies so long as the rights of others are not affected. That right should, in my opinion, include the ability to enlist assistance from others, including the medical profession, in making death as painless and quick as possible. . . .

UNITED STATES SUPREME COURT

Cruzan v. Director, Missouri Department of Health

ARGUED DECEMBER 6, 1989.
DECIDED JUNE 25, 1990.

OPINION OF THE COURT

CHIEF JUSTICE REHNQUIST delivered the opinion of the Court.

Petitioner Nancy Beth Cruzan was rendered incompetent as a result of severe injuries sustained during an automobile accident. Co-petitioners Lester and Joyce Cruzan, Nancy's parents and co-guardians, sought a court order directing the withdrawal of their daughter's artificial feeding and hydration equipment after it became apparent that she had virtually no chance of recovering her cognitive faculties. The Supreme Court of Missouri held that because there was no clear and convincing evidence of Nancy's desire to have life-sustaining treatment withdrawn under such circumstances, her parents lacked authority to effectuate such a request. . . .

She now lies in a Missouri state hospital in what is commonly referred to as a persistent vegetative state: generally, a condition in which a person exhibits motor reflexes but evinces no indications of significant cognitive function. The State of Missouri is bearing the cost of her care.

From *United States [Supreme Court] Reports* 497 (1990), 261–357 (excerpts). Footnotes and some references omitted.

After it had become apparent that Nancy Cruzan had virtually no chance of regaining her mental facilities her parents asked hospital employees to terminate the artificial nutrition and hydration procedures. All agree that such a removal would cause her death. The employees refused to honor the request without court approval. The parents then sought and received authorization from the state trial court for termination. The court found that a person in Nancy's condition had a fundamental right under the State and Federal Constitutions to refuse or direct the withdrawal of "death prolonging procedures." App to Pet for Cert A99. The court also found that Nancy's "expressed thoughts at age twenty-five in somewhat serious conversation with a housemate friend that if sick or injured she would not wish to continue her life unless she could live at least halfway normally suggest that given her present condition she would not wish to continue with her nutrition and hydration." Id., at A97–A98.

The Supreme Court of Missouri reversed by a divided vote. The court recognized a right to refuse treatment embodied in the common-law doctrine of informed consent, but expressed skepticism about the application of that doctrine in the circumstances of this case. *Cruzan v. Harmon,* 760 SW2d 408, 416–417 (Mo 1988) (en banc). The court also declined to read a broad right of privacy into the State Constitution which would "support the right of a person to refuse medical treatment in every circumstance," and expressed doubt as to whether such a right existed under the United States Constitution. Id., at 417–418. It then decided that the Missouri Living Will statue, Mo Rev Stat § 459.010 et seq. (1986), embodied a state policy strongly favoring the preservation of life. 760 SW2d, at 419–420. The court found that Cruzan's statements to her roommate regarding her desire to live or die under certain conditions were "unreliable for the purpose of determining her intent," id., at 424, "and thus insufficient to support the co-guardians claim to exercise substituted judgment on Nancy's behalf." Id., at 426. It rejected the argument that Cruzan's parents were entitled to order the termination of her medical treatment, concluding that "no person can assume that choice for an incompetent in the absence of the formalities required under Missouri's Living Will statutes or the clear and convincing, inherently reliable evidence absent here." Id., at 425. The court also expressed its view that "[b]road policy questions bearing on life and death are more properly addressed by representative assemblies" than judicial bodies. Id., at 426. . . .

The common-law doctrine of informed consent is viewed as generally encompassing the right of a competent individual to refuse medical treatment. Beyond that, [court] decisions demonstrate both similarity and diversity in their approach to decision of what all agree is a perplexing question with unusual strong moral and ethical overtones. State courts have available to them for decision a number of sources—state constitutions, statutes, and common law—which are not available to us. In this Court, the question is simply and starkly whether the United States Constitution prohibits Missouri from choosing the rule of decision which it did. This is the first case in which we have been squarely presented with the issue of whether the United States Constitution grants what is in common parlance referred to as a "right to die." . . .

The Fourteenth Amendment provides that no State shall "deprive any person of life, liberty, or property, without due process of law." The principle that a competent person has a constitutionally protected liberty interest in refusing unwanted medical treatment may be inferred from our prior decisions. . . .

But determining that a person has a "liberty interest" under the Due Process Clause does not end the inquiry; "whether respondent's constitutional rights have been violated must be determined by balancing his liberty interests against the relevant state interests." *Youngberg v. Romeo,* 457 US 307, 321 (1982). See also *Mills v. Rogers,* 457 US 291, 299 (1982).

Petitioners insist that under the general holdings of our cases, the forced administration of life-sustaining medical treatment, and even of artificially delivered food and water essential to life, would implicate a competent person's liberty interest. . . . The dramatic consequences involved in refusal of treatment would inform the inquiry as to whether the deprivation of the interest is constitutionally permissible. But for purposes of this case, we assume that the United States Constitution would grant a competent person a constitutionally protected right to refuse lifesaving hydration and nutrition.

Petitioners go on to assert that an incompetent person should possess the same right in this respect as is possessed by a competent person. . . .

The difficulty with petitioners' claim is that in a sense it begs the question: an incompetent person is not able to make an informed and voluntary choice to exercise a hypothetical right to refuse treatment or any other right. Such a "right" must be exercised for her, if at all, by some sort of surrogate. Here, Missouri has in effect recognized that under certain circumstances a surrogate may act for the patient in electing to have hydration and nutrition withdrawn in such a way as to cause death, but it has established a procedural safeguard to assure that the action of the surrogate conforms as best it may to the wishes expressed by the patient while competent. Missouri requires that evidence of the incompetent's wishes as to the withdrawal of treatment be proved by clear and convincing evidence. The question, then, is whether the United States Constitution forbids the establishment of this procedural requirement by the State. We hold that it does not.

Whether or not Missouri's clear and convincing evidence requirement comports with the United States Constitution depends in part on what interests the State may properly seek to protect in this situation. Missouri relies on its interest in the protection and preservation of human life, and there can be no gainsaying this interest. . . .

But in the context presented here, a State has more particular interests at stake. The choice between life and death is a deeply personal decision of obvious and overwhelming finality. We believe Missouri may legitimately seek to safeguard the personal element of this choice through the imposition of heightened evidentiary requirements. It cannot be disputed that the

Due Process Clause protects an interest in life as well as an interest in refusing life-sustaining medical treatment. Not all incompetent patients will have loved ones available to serve as surrogate decision makers. And even where family members are present "[t]here will, of course, be some unfortunate situations in which family members will not act to protect a patient." . . . Finally, we think a State may properly decline to make judgments about the "quality" of life that a particular individual may enjoy, and simply assert an unqualified interest in the preservation of human life to be weighed against the constitutionally protected interests of the individual.

In our view, Missouri has permissibly sought to advance these interests through the adoption of a "clear and convincing" standard of proof to govern such proceedings. "The function of a standard of proof, as that concept is embodied in the Due Process Clause and in the realm of factfinding, is to 'instruct the factfinder concerning the degree of confidence our society thinks he should have in the correctness of factual conclusions for a particular type of adjudication.' " . . .

There is no doubt that statutes requiring wills to be in writing, and statutes of frauds which require that a contract to make a will be in writing, on occasion frustrate the effectuation of the intent of a particular decedent, just as Missouri's requirement of proof in this case may have frustrated the effectuation of the not-fully-expressed desires of Nancy Cruzan. But the Constitution does not require general rules to work faultlessly; no general rule can. . . .

The Supreme Court of Missouri held that in this case the testimony adduced at trial did not amount to clear and convincing proof of the patient's desire to have hydration and nutrition withdrawn. In so doing, it reversed a decision of the Missouri trial court which had found that the evidence "suggest[ed]" Nancy Cruzan would not have desired to continue such measures, App to Pet for Cert A98, but which had not adopted the standard of "clear and convincing evidence" enunciated by the Supreme Court. The testimony adduced at trial consisted primarily of Nancy Cruzan's statements made to a housemate about a year before her accident that she would not want to live should she face life as a "vegetable," and other observations to the same effect. The observations did not deal in terms with withdrawal of medical treatment or of hydration and nutrition. We cannot say that the Supreme Court of Missouri committed constitutional error in reaching the conclusion that it did. . . .

No doubt is engendered by anything in this record but that Nancy Cruzan's mother and father are loving and caring parents. If the States were required by the United States Constitution to repose a right of "substituted judgment" with anyone, the Cruzans would surely qualify. But we do not think the Due Process Clause requires the State to repose judgment on these matters with anyone but the patient herself. Close family members may have a strong feeling—a feeling not at all ignoble or unworthy, but not entirely disinterested, either—that they do not wish to witness the continuation of the life of a loved one which they regard as hopeless, meaningless, and even degrading. But there is no automatic assurance that the view of close family members will necessarily be the same as the patient's would have been had she been confronted with the prospect of her situation while competent. All of the reasons previously discussed for allowing Missouri to require clear and convincing evidence of the patient's wishes lead us to conclude that the State may choose to defer only to those wishes, rather than confide the decision to close family members.

The judgment of the Supreme Court of Missouri is affirmed.

SEPARATE OPINIONS

JUSTICE O'CONNOR, concurring.

[T]he Court does not today decide the issue whether a State must also give effect to the decisions of a surrogate decisionmaker. . . . In my view, such a duty may well be constitutionally required to protect the patient's liberty interest in refusing medical treatment. Few individuals provide explicit oral or written instructions regarding their intent to refuse medical treatment should they become incompetent. States which decline to consider any evidence other than such instructions may frequently fail to honor a patient's intent. Such failures might be avoided if the State considered an equally probative source of evidence: the patient's appointment of a proxy to make health care decisions on her behalf. Delegating the authority to make medical decisions to a family member or friend is becoming a common method of planning for the future. . . .

Today's decision, holding only that the Constitution permits a State to require clear and convincing evidence of Nancy Cruzan's desire to have artificial hydration and nutrition withdrawn, does not preclude a future determination that the Constitution requires the States to implement the decisions of a patient's duly appointed surrogate. Nor does it prevent States from developing other approaches for protecting an incompetent individual's liberty interest in refusing medical treatment. As is evident from the Court's survey of state court decisions . . . no national consensus has yet emerged on the best solution for this difficult and sensitive problem. Today we decide only that one State's practice does not violate the Constitution; the more challenging task of crafting appropriate procedures for safeguarding incompetents' liberty interests is entrusted to the "laboratory" of the States, *New State Ice Co. v. Liebmann,* 285 US 262, 311 (1932) (Brandeis, J., dissenting), in the first instance.

Justice Brennan, with whom Justice Marshall and Justice Blackmun join, dissenting.

A grown woman at the time of the accident, Nancy had previously expressed her wish to forgo continuing medical care under circumstances such as these. Her family and her friends are convinced that this is what she would want. A guardian ad litem appointed by the trial court is also convinced that this is what Nancy would want. See 760 SW2d at 444 (Higgins, J., dissenting from denial of rehearing). Yet the Missouri Supreme Court, alone among state courts deciding such a question, has determined that an irreversibly vegetative patient will remain a passive prisoner of medical technology—for Nancy, perhaps for the next 30 years. . . . Because I believe that Nancy Cruzan has a fundamental right to be free of unwanted artificial nutrition and hydration, which right is not outweighed by any interests of the State, and because I find that the improperly biased procedural obstacles imposed by the Missouri Supreme Court impermissibly burden that right, I respectfully dissent. Nancy Cruzan is entitled to choose to die with dignity. . . .

I

. . . The right to be free from medical attention without consent, to determine what shall be done with one's own body, *is* deeply rooted in this Nation's traditions, as the majority acknowledges. . . . This right has long been "firmly entrenched in American tort law" and is securely grounded in the earliest common law. . . . " 'Anglo-American law starts with the premise of thoroughgoing self determination. It follows that each man is considered to be master of his own body, and he may, if he be of sound mind, expressly prohibit the performance of lifesaving surgery, or other medical treatment.' " *Natanson v. Kline,* 186 Kan 393, 406–407, 350 P2d 1093, 1104 (1960). . . .

No material distinction can be drawn between the treatment to which Nancy Cruzan continues to be subject—artificial nutrition and hydration—and any other medical treatment. . . .

Artificial delivery of food and water is regarded as medical treatment by the medical profession and the Federal Government. According to the American Academy of Neurology, "[t]he artificial provision of nutrition and hydration is a form of medical treatment . . . analogous to other forms of life-sustaining treatment, such as the use of the respirator. When a patient is unconscious, both a respirator and an artificial feeding device serve to support or replace normal bodily functions that are compromised as a result of the patient's illness." . . .

II

A

The right to be free from unwanted medical attention is a right to evaluate the potential benefit of treatment and its possible consequences according to one's own values and to make a personal decision whether to subject oneself to the intrusion. For a patient like Nancy Cruzan, the sole benefit of medical treatment is being kept metabolically alive. . . .

There are also affirmative reasons why someone like Nancy might choose to forgo artificial nutrition and hydration under these circumstances. Dying is personal. And it is profound. For many, the thought of an ignoble end, steeped in decay, is abhorrent. A quiet, proud death, bodily integrity intact, is a matter of extreme consequence. "In certain, thankfully rare, circumstances the burden of maintaining the corporeal existence degrades the very humanity it was meant to serve." *Brophy v. New England Sinai Hospital, Inc.* 398 Mass 417, 434, 497 NE2d 626, 635–636 (1986). . . .

Such conditions are, for many, humiliating to contemplate, as is visiting a prolonged and anguished vigil on one's parents, spouse, and children. A long, drawn-out death can have a debilitating effect on family members. . . .

B

Although the right to be free of unwanted medical intervention, like other constitutionally protected interests, may not be absolute, no State interest could outweigh the rights of an individual in Nancy Cruzan's position. Whatever a State's possible interests in mandating life-support treatment under other circumstances, there is no good to be obtained here by Missouri's insistence that Nancy Cruzan remain on life-support systems if it is indeed her wish not to do so. Missouri does not claim, nor could it, that society as a whole will be benefited by Nancy's receiving medical treatment. No third party's situation will be improved and no harm to others will be averted. Cf, nn 6 and 8, supra.

The only state interest asserted here is a general interest in the preservation of life. But the State has no legitimate general interest in someone's life, completely abstracted from the interest of the person living that life, that could outweigh the person's choice to avoid medical treatment. . . . Thus, the State's general interest in life must accede to Nancy Cruzan's particularized and intense interest in self-determination in her choice of medical treatment. There is simply nothing legitimately within the State's purview to be gained by superseding her decision. . . .

III

Missouri may constitutionally impose only those procedural requirements that serve to enhance the accuracy of a determination of Nancy Cruzan's wishes or are at least consistent with an accurate determination. The Missouri "safeguard" that the Court upholds today does not meet that standard. The determination needed in this context is whether the incompetent person would choose to live in a persistent vegetative state on life-support or to avoid this medical treatment. Missouri's rule of decision imposes a markedly asymmetrical evidentiary burden. Only evidence of specific statements of treatment choice made by the patient when competent is admissible to support a finding that the patient, now in a persistent vegetative state, would wish to avoid further medical treatment. Moreover, this evidence must be clear and convincing. No proof is required to support a finding that the incompetent person would wish to continue treatment. . . .

Even more than its heightened evidentiary standard, the Missouri court's categorical exclusion of relevant evidence dispenses with any semblance of accurate factfinding. The court adverted to no evidence supporting its decision, but held that no clear and convincing, inherently reliable evidence had been presented to show that Nancy would want to avoid further treatment. In doing so, the court failed to consider statements Nancy had made to family members and a close friend. The court also failed to consider testimony from Nancy's mother and sister that they were certain that Nancy would want to discontinue artificial nutrition and hydration, even after the court found that Nancy's family was loving and without malignant motive. See 760 SW2d, at 412. The court also failed to consider the conclusions of the guardian ad litem, appointed by the trial court, that there was clear and convincing evidence that Nancy would want to discontinue medical treatment and that this was in her best interests. Id., at 444 (Higgins, J., dissenting from denial of rehearing); Brief for Respondent Guardian Ad Litem 2–3. The court did not specifically define what kind of evidence it would consider clear and convincing, but its general discussion suggests that only a living will or equivalently formal directive from the patient when competent would meet this standard. Seed 760 SW2d, at 424–425. . . .

The Missouri Court's disdain for Nancy's statements in serious conversations not long before her accident, for the opinions of Nancy's family and friends as to her values, beliefs and certain choice, and even for the opinion of an outside objective factfinder appointed by the State evinces a disdain for Nancy Cruzan's own right to choose. The rules by which an incompetent person's wishes are determined must represent every effort to determine those wishes. The rule that the Missouri court adopted and that this Court upholds, however, skews the result away from a determination that as accurately as possible reflects the individual's own preferences and beliefs. It is a rule that transforms human beings into passive subjects of medical technology. . . .

That Missouri and this Court may truly be motivated only by concern for incompetent patients makes no matter. As one of our most prominent jurists warned us decades ago: "Experience should teach us to be most on our guard to protect liberty when the government's purposes are beneficent. . . . The greatest dangers to liberty lurk in insidious encroachment by men of zeal, well meaning but without understanding." *Olmstead v. United States,* 277 US 438, 479 (1928) (Brandeis, J., dissenting).

I respectfully dissent.

Advance Directives

LINDA A. EMANUEL, MARION DANIS, ROBERT A. PEARLMAN, AND PETER A. SINGER

Advance Care Planning as a Process: Structuring the Discussions in Practice

Linda A. Emanuel, MD, is professor of medicine at Northwestern University Medical School as well as the founder and principal of the Education for Physicians in End-of-Life Care (EPEC) Project. She trained at Cambridge University, University College–Oxford, and Harvard Medical School. She also pursued studies in both medical and professional ethics. Former Vice President of Ethics Standards and head of the Institute for Ethics at the American Medical Association, she has published extensively in the field of bioethics, with particular attention to end-of-life care, the doctor-patient relationship, academic integrity, and organizational ethics.

Marion Danis, MD, is chief of the Bioethics Consultation Service and head of the Section on Ethics and Health Policy in the Department of Clinical Bioethics in the Clinical Center of the National Institutes of Health. In this position, she has focused on the connection between ethical values and health policy. Some of her other articles on advanced directives include "Following Advance Directives," *Hastings Center Report* and "A Prospective Study of Advance Directives for Life-Sustaining Care," *New England Journal of Medicine*.

Robert A. Pearlman, MD, is located at the VA Puget Sound Health Care System, where he has served as chair of the Ethics Advisory Committee. He is also a professor of medicine, specializing in geriatric medicine and gerontology, at the University of Washington School of Medicine as well as adjunct professor in the program in Medical History and Ethics at the University of Washington. He has published extensively on issues of consent, advance care planning, the quality of life, and empirical research in clinical ethics.

Peter A. Singer, MD, holds the Sun Life Chair in Bioethics at the University of Toronto and is director of the University of Toronto Joint Centre for Bioethics. He is professor in the Department of Medicine and is extensively involved in bioethics in Canada. In addition to his longstanding interests in advance directives, he has worked on problems of euthanasia and physician-assisted suicide, global health ethics, and research ethics.

From *The American Geriatrics Society* 43 (1995), 440–446.
Reprinted by permission.

FACILITATING A STRUCTURED DISCUSSION

The structured discussion should be aimed at framing the issues, and tentatively identifying wishes. It need not aim to resolve all issues or come to final determination of all prior wishes. Neither should it aim to be a deep personal revelation seeking perfect knowledge of the patient's core self; this is unrealistic and unnecessary. Nevertheless, this step is the core of all advanced planning processes.

The skills required of the professional for this stage are those of communicating pertinent medical understanding and of supportive elicitation of the patient's wishes, as in most ideal informed consent discussions. Specific training sessions may be needed to acquire the information, skills, and judgment involved in this critical part of the process of advance plan-ning because, unlike most medical decisions, in this case patients' preferences are cast forward into future scenarios.

Initial Decisions about the Mode of Advance Planning. An early part of the discussion may focus on whether proxy designation, instructional directives, or both are most suitable for the particular patient. Most patients should be advised to combine the two forms of planning so that the proxy may be guided by the patient's stated prior wishes. Thus, the conversation might continue as follows:

"Ms/r. X, I suggest we start by considering a few examples as a way of getting to know your thinking. I will use examples that I use for everyone."

If, in the physician's judgment, a particular patient proves not competent to make prior directives, he or she might nevertheless be competent to designate a proxy decision-maker. In such a case the conversation might go rather differently. For example, the physician might proceed as follows:

"These decisions may be hard to think about when they are not even relevant right now. You have had a long and trusting relationship with Ms/r. Y. You might even have had discussions like this before with her/him. Would you want to give Ms/r. Y, or someone else you trust, the authority to make decisions for you in case of need?"

Understanding the Patient's Goals for Treatment in a Range of Scenarios. When instructional directives are suitable, we believe that the physician should help the patient articulate abstract values, goals of treatment, and concrete examples of treatment preferences in order to provide all the major components of decision-making. Discussions can be well structured by going through an illustrative predrafted document together; this approach can prevent long confusing and overwhelming encounters. With such structuring, this portion of advance planning can be informative, accessible to patients with a wide range of educational levels, and still quite brief. Many documents that can be used for structuring discussions are available; however, a properly validated document should be chosen to maximize the chance that patients are accurately representing their wishes.

Scenarios representative of the range of prognosis and of the range of disability usually encountered in circumstances of incompetence should be presented to the patient. The physician might start like this:

"So, let's try to imagine several circumstances. We will go through four and then perhaps another one or two. First imagine you were in a coma with no awareness. Assume there was a chance that you might wake up and be yourself again, but it wasn't likely. Some people would want us to withdraw treatment and let them die, others would want us to attempt everything possible, and yet others would want us to try to restore health but stop treatment and allow death if it was not working. What do you think you would want?"

After a standard set of scenarios, tailored scenarios can be considered. When a patient has a serious diagnosis with a predictable outcome involving incompetence that is not covered in the standard document, the physician might continue:

"We should also consider the situations that your particular illness can cause; that way you can be sure we will do what you want. For sure, all people are different and you may never face these circumstances. Nevertheless, let's imagine . . ."

While illness scenarios may be difficult for people to imagine, we suggest that preferences arrived at without illness scenarios are unlikely to be accurate or realistic wishes; a treatment preference without a specified illness circumstance is meaningless.

A patient considering illness scenarios also may be able to articulate which states, if any, are greatly feared and/or are felt to be *worse than death* for them. So, for example, the physician may go on:

"People often think about circumstances they have seen someone in or heard about in the news. Some may seem worse than death. Do you have such concerns?"

When a range of scenarios have been considered it

is often possible to go back and identify the scenario(s) in which the patient's goals changed from "treat" to "don't treat." This can provide a useful personal threshold to guide the physician and proxy later. The physician may also use it to check back at the time with the patient that his or her wishes are properly reflected, saying, for example:

"Well, we've gone through several scenarios now. It seems to me that you feel particularly strongly about . . . Indeed, you move from wanting intervention to wanting to be allowed to die in peace at the point when . . . Do I speak for you correctly if I say that your personal threshold for deciding to let go is . . . ?"

Raising Specific Examples and Asking About General Values. In any scenario after the patient's response about goals, specific examples may be used:

"So, let us take an example to be sure I understand you, not only in general but also in specific. Say you were in a coma with a very small chance of recovery, and you had pneumonia; to cure the pneumonia we would have to put you on a breathing machine. Would you want us to use the breathing machine and try to cure; allow the pneumonia to cause death; or perhaps try the treatment, withdrawing the breathing machine if you did not get better?"

Checking and specifying a patient's views by providing concrete examples may be a useful way to reduce the incidence of clinically unrealistic choices by patients. So, for example, a patient who declines intubation but wants resuscitation may need more information on resuscitation and a suggestion as to how his or her wishes may be translated into a clinically reasonable decision.

The preceding discussion about goals for treatment and specific choices may be usefully combined with an open ended question about the patient's reasons for particular decisions and the *values* that pertain to such decisions.

"I think you have given a good picture of particular decisions you would want. Can you also say something about the values or beliefs that you hold? Understanding your more general views can be an important part of getting specific decisions right."

Patients' statements might refer to their wish to act in accord with the positions of their religious denomination, or to their views on the sanctity of life or dignity of death, or they might articulate their disposition to take a chance or to favor a secure choice.

Including the Proxy. The proxy, if already known at this point, should be encouraged to attend this discussion. Much understanding of the patient's wishes can be gained from hearing this part of the process. The clinician can guide the proxy to adopt a listening role; the proxy may ask clarifying questions but should avoid biasing the patient's expressions. Sometimes the proxy can be following the conversation with a predrafted document in hand, noting down the patient's statements. The ground can be set for future discussions between any of the patient, physician, and proxy. The proxy becomes part of the working team, and future interactions between proxy and physician, if the patient does become incompetent, are likely to go more smoothly than they might without such prior discussions.

At this stage, the advance directive should be, at most, pencilled in. The tentative draft can be taken home by the patient for further reflection and review with other involved parties, such as the proxy, family, friends, or pastor. This step can be a useful mechanism for dealing with difference among the parties ahead of time. The structured discussion should be brief and followed by a subsequent meeting when a directive may be finalized. Physicians will initially take longer in these interviews, but with training in the requisite skills and with experience, time will be reduced.

COMPLETING AN ADVISORY DIRECTIVE AND RECORDING IT

. . . The professional's main required skill here is to ascertain whether the patient has reached resolution and is ready to articulate well considered preferences. Any facet of the first two steps not yet complete should be completed at this step. Even if a patient has reached resolution, there should be a reminder that advance directives can be revised if his/her wishes are changed. If the proxy has not been present at previous stages, the physician should particularly encourage the proxy to enter the process at this point. The proxy should again be encouraged to adopt a listening and clarifying role, avoiding undue influence on the patient. It can be helpful for the physician to co-sign the document at this stage to endorse physician involvement and to document the primary physician for ease of future follow up.

REVIEWING AND UPDATING DIRECTIVES

Along with other regular check-ups and screening tests, patients should be told to expect periodic review of their directives. The clinician may re-introduce the topic.

"Ms/r. X, a year has gone by since we completed your advance care plans, and in that time a lot has happened. People do sometimes change their wishes so let's review the wishes you wrote down a year ago."

Competent people are often known to change their minds about all matters, whether they are of great import or not. Reasonable but imperfect consistency has also been found in advance planning decisions by competent individuals. Physicians should be aware of this and should review directives with the patient periodically. Physicians should check which decisions a patient maintains and which are changed. Changed positions should prompt the physician to pay particular attention to the source of change; some changes will be well reasoned, and others will be markers for misunderstandings that need to be clarified. Some people will be generally changeable; the physician should address this observation to the patient, inquiring after the reason. If supportive guidance and education do not permit the patient to reach reasonable stability in his or her advance directives, more emphasis must be placed on proxy decision-making for the patient. The physician will often be able to come to this decision jointly with the patient and proxy:

"Your choices changed on several decisions both times when we reviewed your statement, even though we have discussed the issues a lot. You have already said that you want Ms/r. Y to be your proxy. Would you prefer to give these decisions over to Ms/r. Y to decide according to what she/he thinks would be in your best interests?"

Some changed decisions may occur after the onset of incompetence. There is continuing debate on how to deal with such circumstances. The physician should be careful to evaluate the exact nature of the patient's incompetence; some patients will be globally incompetent while others will be competent to make some decisions and incompetent for other decisions. The role of the proxy and possibly a further adjudicating party may be crucial in such circumstances.

The skills that physicians require for this portion of advance planning are not as yet matched by detailed understanding of how patients might make or can be encouraged to make valid and enduring decisions, or the type of circumstances that tend to prompt changes. It is reasonable to expect that researchers will continue to study how best to elicit patient's enduring and valid wishes.

APPLICATION OF PRIOR DIRECTIVES TO ACTUAL CIRCUMSTANCES

Clinicians will require both interpersonal and interpretive skills in this difficult final step. Patients will often end up in need of decisions that are not accurately specified in their advance directive. The physicians and proxy, then, must work from the information they have to make a good guess as to what the patient would have wanted. Knowledge of the patient's values, goals, choices in a range of scenarios, and thresholds for withholding or withdrawing specific interventions can all be helpful. Choices in scenarios can often provide very accurate predictors.

The spirit as much as the letter of the directive should be the focus of the physician and the proxy. Documents that are given as an advisory statement rather than a legal imperative are less likely to lead to blind application of irrelevant decisions. So, for example, if a patient has a poorly drafted document stating only that he or she does not want to be on a respirator, the physicians should try to clarify what circumstances this preference applies to; the patient may have intended the statement to apply to circumstances of hopeless prognosis, but may actually be facing a reversible life threatening illness. The physicians and proxy would need to "override" the simple statement in order to honor the true wishes of the patient in such a case; they would be interpreting simple statements to match presumed true wishes, not trumping the patient's wishes. The full responsibility of this interpretive process and the risks of misusing it in parentalistic judgments should be clear to the physician and proxy.

When the physician writes orders for the incompetent patient's care they should be as detailed as the advance directive permits. Thus a "Do Not Resuscitate" order can usually be supplemented with orders such as "evaluate and treat infection," "do not intubate," "provide full comfort care," and so forth. They can be gathered together in a series of orders altogether intended to translate the directive into doctors orders. Life threatening illness often prompts a change in health care facility or attending physician and will, therefore, entail transfer of advance directives from the physician who has guided the process to a new physician. At a minimum, physicians, patients, proxies, and institutions should all be aware of the need to transfer advance care documents with the patient to the new facility and physician. However, transmittal of accurate portrayals of a patient's wishes will rarely be adequately completed by simply passing on a document; whenever possible, the earlier physician should remain available as a key resource as the patient's prior wishes are brought to bear on specific decisions. It is likely that the physician and proxy who have undertaken the entire process of advance planning with the patient will have a more accurate sense of the patient's actual wishes than those who were simply presented with a document after patient incompetence has already occurred. Those who attempt substituted judgments in the absence of specific patient guidance are known to have discrepancies in their decisions compared with the wishes of the patient, and it is reasonable to assume that explicit communication on the matter should reduce the gap.

Decision-making, especially when there is a proxy involved, is a collaborative matter. The physician and the proxy have distinct roles that should be understood. The physician's role is to diagnose the condition and convey information, opinions, and judgment, and then to discuss them with the proxy, as would ordinarily occur with the patient. The proxy's role is to attempt substituted judgments and speak for the patient wherever possible, or to make best interest judgments as a second best approach if there is no way of surmising what the patient would have wanted. Unless the patient or the local state statutes say otherwise, the proxy should take on the "voice" of the patient and assume equal levels of authority—nor more or less—that would have been the patient's.

FURTHER CONCERNS

ARE ADVANCED DIRECTIVES FOR EVERYONE?

Time constraints and other practical considerations may lead physicians to target their sicker and older patients. However, younger and healthier patients are often quite interested in the approach. Furthermore, advance planning for those who suffer an accident or sudden illness may be most helpful. Advance planning may be considered as a branch of preventive medicine.

There will be a proportion of patients who should not be advised to undertake advance care planning. For example, there are people with no one they wish to choose as a proxy who also have limited ability to imagine future hypothetical situations. Others might find the notion so dissonant with the type of care relationship they want that they do not wish to consider the process. This latter group of patients should still have sufficient discussion to permit understanding of how decisions get made in the absence of directives. For example, the different powers of proxy and next of kin should be clear, as should the occasional role of a guardian ad lidum, and the limited ability of substituted decisions to match the patient's prior wishes in the absence of guidance from the patient. Neither physician nor patient should allow themselves the assumption that this is a topic they need not even raise. If the patient and physician are explicitly content with the hitherto more traditional approaches to decision-making at the end of life, this is acceptable.

A considerable proportion of people have no primary care physician or health professional, and the only educational materials that reach them will be through the public media. Some of these people are able to have a physician; they should seek out a physician for the purposes of advance planning if they wish to undertake it. They should be aware that many directives are highly dependent on medical knowledge and understanding of the individual patient's medical circumstances; decisions made in the absence of medical expertise may be inaccurate reflections of the person's true preferences.

People who face limited access to the health care system should not be discouraged from advance care planning if they are inclined toward it. However, people who complete directives without talking to a physician should be encouraged to discuss their views in as much depth as possible with their next-of-kin or proxy so that ultimately someone will be able to discuss with a physician how the patient's known prior wishes relate to actual circumstances and treatment decisions. Publicly provided information or work sheets to guide persons and their proxy in such discussions can be helpful.

WHEN AND WHERE SHOULD ADVANCE DIRECTIVES BE DISCUSSED?

Advanced care planning should ideally be initiated in the outpatient setting, where such discussions are known to be well received. Then, when the topic is raised on admission to the hospital, as required by the Patient Self Determination Act, it is likely to be less threatening. Inquiry can be continued to an indepth inpatient discussion in selected cases. For example, it is appropriate with patients who are at risk of needing life-sustaining intervention soon, and discussions in this setting can be well conducted, providing guidance and welcome coordination of goals and expectations for all concerned. Although judgment of need for such intervention is known to be difficult, physicians may be guided in part by published criteria. For those with a completed directive, review during an admission may also be advisable. Other patients with a good prognosis who want to complete directives should first be advised of the merits of deferring the process to an outpatient setting. While there is little data on the question, we fear that those patients who complete directives for the first time in the hospital setting risk making more unstable decisions because of the emotional turbulence of the moment. For those who do complete a directive for the first time during hospital admission, review of the directives after health has stabilized may be particularly important.

TIME CONSTRAINTS

No step in the process of advance care planning needs to take longer than standard doctor-patient encounters. Furthermore, advance care planning probably reduces difficult and time-consuming decisions made in the absence of such planning and should, therefore, be understood as a wise investment of time. Like any other clinical process, skill and experience will make the planning process more time-efficient.

WHAT IS THE ROLE FOR NONPHYSICIAN HEALTHCARE PROFESSIONALS?

Decision-making for incompetent patients has always been among the central tasks of the physician. We regard the facilitation of a structured discussion as the central step in the process of advance planning and, therefore, as particularly dependent on physician involvement. Nevertheless, time constraints and the different communication styles of physicians will make it inevitable that some, and perhaps many, physicians will not include all the steps of advance planning in the routine activities that are the core of good doctoring. Thus, there is likely to be a need for other healthcare professionals to engage in the process of advance planning. Some facilities may form interdisciplinary source groups or consult services that will be available to physicians or patients who seek extra help. Other facilities may train nursing staff in advance planning. Social workers may have a role in facilitating communication around these difficult concepts. However, we view it as essential that the physician, who must ultimately take responsibility for life-sustaining treatment decisions, communicate with the patient at some point and at least check with the pa-

tient for possible misunderstandings' unrealistic expectations, or wishes for treatment that the physician would find contrary to standards of medical practice or contrary to his or her conscience. Omission of this step risks discovery of advance directives which have internal inconsistencies or other major problems when it is too late to correct the problem. If the physician cannot participate in this step of advance planning, then another appropriate point may be at the next step of completing a signed advisory statement.

HELPING PROXIES UNDERSTAND THEIR ROLE

The proxy will need to distinguish his or her emotional and personal motives from concerns appropriate to their role as a proxy. Some will have emotional connections with the patient or personal views of their own that will drive them toward more aggressive intervention; others may have monetary or other concerns which may cause a conflict of interest and motivate them toward less aggressive intervention than the patient would have wanted. The physician should be sensitive to these and related possibilities and be able to help the proxy disentangle and understand the relevant motivations, both during the planning process and when making actual decisions. Complex or destructive cases may require further professional counseling and support. Together, the physician and proxy should deliberate the various therapeutic options available. The goal is to avoid any need for one party to assert authority over the other and to achieve consensus instead.

RISKS OF PLACING THE ADVANCE DIRECTIVE IN THE PATIENT'S CHART

Concerns have arisen about how to record the statement in such a fashion that it is least likely to result in inappropriate care and most likely to be available when it becomes relevant. Advance directives placed in hospital records may run the same risk as "Do Not Resuscitate" orders, which are known to sometimes result in inappropriate cessation of other therapies. Education of health professionals on the matter is clearly necessary. Detailed doctors orders can help too. In addition, sections in the medical records for advance directives may be prominently stamped with a statement to the effect that prior directives are (1) intended as an extension of patient autonomy beyond *wishlessness,* (2) may be for the purposes of requesting as well as declining treatment, and (3) have no relevance to care before incompetence.

Copies of the advisory statement and statutory document are best kept not only by the physician but also the proxy and any other person likely to be in early contact in the event of changed medical circumstances. The physician's copy should be recorded as part of the patient's medical records.

DEALING WITH LEGAL CONCERNS

Advance planning statements with physicians should be considered as advisory statements rather than adversarial challenges. (We use the term "advisory statement" in order to distinguish planning devices from narrower statutory documents, which have different legal purposes.) Physicians should make it clear to patients that the advisory statement is the area where medical counsel is most relevant and that the advisory statement is one of the best means of expressing their wishes. An advisory statement can be considered a portrait of a patient's wishes, a profile that should be interpreted to fit with whatever circumstances ultimately pertain. Such a statement can be interpreted with the flexibility needed to meet the complexities of medical decision-making and uncertainties of human decision-making.

Clinicians should be reassured that it has been well argued that such advisory statements will be honored under Common, Statutory, or Constitutional Law, even if they are not part of a statutory document. We nevertheless urge health care professionals to be less concerned with legal issues and more concerned with the medical task of translating a patient's deepest wishes into sound medical decisions. Usually, an advisory statement does not need to raise legal issues because its primary purpose is to provide a valid description of the patient's wishes. However, points of legal concern such as whether living will and proxy statutes in other states are significantly different, may require legal expertise; in such a case the physician should avoid offering unauthorized legal advice and refer to a lawyer.

Physicians may encourage simultaneous use of statutory documents, i.e., predrafted statements designed for specific state statutes, because this is what gives physicians most legal immunity from prosecution when the physician carries out the patient's or proxy's directions. Some statutory documents may contain an advisory section. If not, the advisory and statutory documents may be combined or filed together.

BEN A. RICH

Advance Directives: The Next Generation

Ben A. Rich teaches in the Bioethics Program at the University of California–Davis Medical Center. He is also visiting professor at the U.C. Davis School of Law. As a lawyer, he specialized in litigation and health law. Later in his career he focused his interests on bioethics. He has published numerous works on pain management and advance directives, including *Strange Bedfellows: How Medical Jurisprudence has Influenced Medical Ethics and Medical Practice* (Kluwer Academic/Plenum Publishers).

PROSPECTIVE AUTONOMY AND THE RECOGNITION OF ADVANCE DIRECTIVES

• • •

BEYOND INFORMED CONSENT AND REFUSAL

The doctrine of informed consent, in respecting the individual autonomy of the patient, presupposes that the person has present decisional capacity. Thus, the circumstances of diagnosis, prognosis, and proposed treatment are directly and immediately confronting the patient and are ripe for decisionmaking. When the patient gives or refuses consent to a recommended procedure or a course of treatment, it is one that is deemed by the physician to be appropriate given the patient's present and/or immediately anticipated circumstances. While there is always a certain amount of speculation or uncertainty involved, it is probably as low as it ever will be.

When, on the other hand, a healthy person states preferences for treatment or nontreatment of a hypothetical condition that might arise during some possible future period of decisional incapacity, the level of potential uncertainty is greatly increased. The question then arises whether the uncertainty is so great that, as a matter of ethics, law, and public policy, it is reasonable to honor such declarations. Perhaps we can best consider this question in the context of a few judicial decisions involving oral directives. In doing so, we also can begin to appreciate why a movement in support of statutorily recognized written directives developed.

From *The Journal of Legal Medicine,* 19 (1998), 63–97. Copyright © 1998 Taylor & Francis. Footnotes renumbered.

ORAL DIRECTIVES

It is not uncommon for people, when reflecting upon serious illness or disabling injury, to share with relatives and close friends their views on how they would wish to be cared for under such circumstances. If, at some future time, the individual does become a victim of such an illness or disability, and is also decisionally incapacitated, then the concern is whether the person, when making those statements, actually intended such expressions to dictate subsequent treatment or nontreatment.

The case of *In re Eichner*[1] presented such a scenario. Brother Fox, the member of a Catholic religious order, had discussed the highly publicized case of Karen Ann Quinlan with other members of the order. He indicated that he did not wish to have his life sustained if he were to become, as she was, permanently unconscious. Some years later, during a surgical procedure, Brother Fox suffered cardiac arrest. Although he was resuscitated, he remained in a persistent vegetative state with no reasonable prospect of regaining consciousness. Father Eichner, acting on behalf of Brother Fox, petitioned the court for an order directing the hospital to remove all life support.

The testimony was uncontroverted that Brother Fox, in his prior statements, had fortuitously addressed precisely the medical contingency that had now befallen him—permanent unconsciousness, which might be prolonged indefinitely through medical interventions. The decision of the court turned upon the seriousness with which Brother Fox had made the statement. The continuum along which such statements run appears to be that of "casual remarks" at one end and "solemn pronouncements" at the other. The court concluded that Brother Fox's statements constituted solemn pronouncements, and therefore met the clear and convincing evidence standard applied in such cases.[2] . . .

[In *In re Martin,*][3] Michael Martin had a tremendous fear of becoming and remaining severely debilitated and disabled, regardless of whether it was mental, physical, or both. He discussed this profound concern on several occasions with his wife, indicating that he would not wish to have his life sustained by medical interventions if he were incapable of performing various functions such as walking, conversing with others, dressing and bathing himself, or tending to his basic needs. For example, after a conversation about frail and demented patients in long-term care facilities who were completely dependent upon others, Michael Martin's wife quoted him as saying: "I would never want to live like that. Please don't ever let me exist that way because those people don't even have their dignity."[4] On another occasion, after viewing the motion picture "Brian's Song," the story of an athlete with a terminal illness, Michael Martin said to his wife: "If I ever get sick don't put me on any machines to keep me going if there is no hope of getting better." He then said to her, in an obvious effort to emphasize the point, that if she ever did that to him: "I'll always haunt you, Mary."[5] On still another occasion, Michael Martin, who was an avid hunter, indicated to his wife that, if he were to become the victim of a hunting accident in which he was seriously and permanently injured, so that he would never again be the same person, then he would not want to go on living. To further reinforce his point, he said to his wife: "Mary, promise me you wouldn't let me live like that if I can't be the person I am right now, because if you do, believe me I'll haunt you every day of your life."[6]

Within months after the last in a series of conversations of this nature with his wife, Michael Martin sustained grave injuries in an automobile accident. As a result of these injuries, he was rendered decisionally incapacitated, unable to walk or talk, and dependent upon a colostomy tube for elimination and a gastrostomy tube for nutrition and hydration. His wife was appointed his guardian, and respecting his repeatedly expressed views, she sought to have his life-sustaining interventions withdrawn. The ethics committee of the institution where he was being treated reviewed the case and concluded that withdrawing his nutritional support was both medically and ethically appropriate, but suggested that prior judicial authorization should be obtained.[7] When Mary Martin filed a petition in the probate court requesting such authorization, Michael Martin's mother and sister opposed the petition and sought to have Mary removed as Michael's guardian. Remarkably, the probate court ruled that, although clear and convincing evidence had been presented that Michael's present condition was one in which he had indicated he would not wish to have his life maintained, his wishes could not be considered because they were never expressed in writing. The court also declined to remove Mary as Michael's guardian.[8]

Following the remand by the appellate court for additional evidentiary proceedings, the trial court found that nutritional support could be withdrawn by the guardian based upon the clear and convincing evidence that Michael's present, irreversible condition was one in which he had indicated he would not wish to be maintained. The appellate court affirmed, based upon the determination that Michael Martin's present condition fell within the parameters that he had described when competent.

The Michigan Supreme Court, in a fashion reminiscent of the Missouri Supreme Court in the case of Nancy Cruzan,[9] disagreed on the weight and sufficiency of the evidence as determined by the trial court, and reversed on the grounds that the majority was not satisfied that the evidence in the record is "so clear, direct, weighty and convincing as to enable [the fact finder] to come to a clear conviction, without hesitancy, of the truth of the precise facts in issue."[10] The majority cites with favor the following language from the brief filed by the respondents regarding the various remarks made by Michael Martin:

> [the remarks] were remote in time and place from his present circumstances. At the time the remarks were supposedly made, Michael was young and healthy. The remarks were general, vague and casual, because Mr. Martin was not presently experiencing and likely had never experi-

enced the form of "helplessness" he supposedly disliked, and thus he could not bring to bear his specific views about specific circumstances of which he was intimately knowledgeable. Not being informed by his actual experience, Michael's purported remarks thus were "no different than those that many of us might make after witnessing an agonizing death of another."[11]

The implications of this proposition for the exercise of prospective autonomy are immense and profoundly negative. A few of them are discussed here. First, young and healthy persons would be precluded from issuing directives (that such courts will honor) refusing treatment in the event of grave and permanent injury because (1) they have never experienced life under such circumstances, and (2) the occurrence of such catastrophic illness or injury may come years later. Second, and more significant, no competent person may ever prospectively decline treatment for a future period of incompetence because the person will have no first-hand experience of what life is like as an incompetent individual. Their refusal, from this point of view, is fatally uninformed and therefore need not be respected. Followed to its natural conclusion, 20 years of public policy in support of advance care planning would be completely annihilated.

Because Michigan, like New York, is one of the few jurisdictions that refuses to apply a best interests approach in the absence (real or purported) of clear and convincing evidence, there was no basis upon which the petitioner could argue for withdrawal of nutritional support. Again echoing the Missouri Supreme Court in *Cruzan,* the Michigan Supreme Court asserted: "Our determination is consistent with the furtherance of this state's interest in preserving the sanctity of life and does not abridge Mr. Martin's right to refuse life-sustaining medical treatment."[12] This facile and self-serving observation by the court to the contrary notwithstanding, the conclusion for the citizens of Michigan is inescapable: if you wish your views on withholding or withdrawing life-sustaining treatment to overcome the almost insurmountable burdens imposed by the clear and convincing evidence standard (as interpreted by the state's highest court) and the state's strong interest in preserving the sanctity of life (regardless of its quality or the disproportion between the burdens and benefits of continued existence to the individual), then you must express those views in a formal written directive. Furthermore, do not just state your views so that anyone can understand them, state them so that no one can misunderstand them.

Cases such as those considered in this section help to explain why citizens concerned about their ability to exercise a purported right to prospective autonomy turned to the state legislatures for redress.

THE LIVING WILL

The first type of written advance directive to be recognized by law was the living will. It is the most well known, to the extent that it has (problematically) become in common parlance a generic term for any type of directive. A living will is usually a declaration that, under certain medical conditions, the declarant would not wish to have his or her life sustained through major medical interventions such as artificial respiration, nutrition or hydration, or cardiopulmonary resuscitation. Living wills were designed to prevent the use of medical technology that could not cure disease or reverse an ultimately terminal condition, and thus might reasonably be viewed as merely prolonging the dying process rather than saving life.

What is both interesting and ironic about living wills is that the most significant impetus for their development came from highly publicized cases such as that of Karen Ann Quinlan, a woman in her early twenties whose life was sustained for years while she remained in a persistent vegetative state (PVS) with no hope of recovery to a competent, sapient state.[13] Many of the people who executed living wills believed that, in so doing, they were ensuring they would avoid Karen Quinlan's fate. However, many state living will statutes require, before the will can take effect, that an attending and one other physician certify in writing not only that the patient is unconscious, comatose, or otherwise decisionally incapacitated, but also that the patient's condition is terminal (that is, will result in the patient's death within six months). Many physicians do not consider a PVS to be terminal, because with proper care, such patients may live for many years. Thus, the fate worse than death, which those executing living wills sought to avoid (being kept alive biologically with no hope of regaining consciousness), was something from which those directives could not protect them.

The other ironic aspect of the *Quinlan* case as an impetus for the use of living wills is that, as previously noted, Quinlan was a very young and otherwise healthy woman when she entered a PVS. Yet it is rarely the case that people in their twenties or even thirties execute living wills. Similarly, even those physicians who have become proponents of living wills acknowledge that they do not make a practice of discussing these instruments with their young, healthy patients, even though they are perhaps most at risk of severe brain injury through trauma.

Another difficulty with the terminal illness requirement is that it means different things to different physicians. If the statute recognizing living wills defines terminal condition, then it may characterize it as an irreversible condition from which the patient will die in six months. Medicine is not good at making such predictions except for patients who are only a few hours or at most a few days away from death, regardless of the medical interventions they receive. This is another fact confirmed by SUPPORT. If the statute does not define terminal illness in terms of a maximum life expectancy, then there is likely to be wide variation among physicians as to when they would be willing to certify in writing that a condition is terminal. A conservative view may reject the terminal label until death is imminent (a matter of hours), thereby essentially nullifying the living will. A liberal view may take the position that any irreversible condition that ultimately will result in the patient's death should be deemed a terminal condition, including a PVS.

The other common limitation of living will statutes is that certain types of interventions are specifically excluded. The Missouri living will statute, which was discussed by the Missouri Supreme Court (with highly questionable relevance) in the *Cruzan* case, provides a dramatic example. One of the dissenting judges in that case described the Missouri Living Will Act as "a fraud on Missourians who believe we have been given a right to execute a living will, and to die naturally, respectably, and in peace."[14] The Missouri Living Will Act excludes from the phrase "death-prolonging procedure" comfort care, artificial nutrition and hydration, or the administration of any medication (presumably even antibiotics in the case of pneumonia). Even statutes that do not completely exclude certain procedures from the ambit of living will declarations may, as is the case in Colorado, require that declarants specifically state that they do not wish to receive artificial nutrition and hydration if they are decisionally incapacitated and suffering from a terminal condition.

THE DURABLE POWER OF ATTORNEY FOR HEALTH CARE

The primary purpose of this type of advance directive is the designation of a particular individual as the attorney-in-fact for the making of surrogate health care decisions. To be valid, a health care power of attorney need not contain any indication of the person's views about life, death, life-sustaining medical interventions, or other information that might be informative and helpful to the designated surrogate or treating physicians. There seems to be an assumption, which may not necessarily be accurate, that the person executing the health care power of attorney has made his or her wishes with regard to various forms of treatment, and the medical interventions they might entail, known to the attorney-in-fact and perhaps the individual's primary care physician as well. Such an assumption may be nothing more than wishful thinking, however.

In many states, the health care power of attorney constitutes a means by which to avoid the serious limitations that characterize the living will. Typically, the statutes recognizing this form of directive require only the decisional incapacity of the patient in order for the power of attorney to take effect. Similarly, most statutes do not single out any particular intervention (such as artificial nutrition and hydration), which the attorney-in-fact may not reject or reject only when certain conditions have been met. Consequently, the attorney-in-fact has the same, virtually unlimited, authority to reject any or all medical procedures, including those necessary to sustain the life of the patient, as the patient has when competent.

Although the durable power of attorney for health care can be viewed as a significant improvement on the living will in terms of the exercise of prospective autonomy, use of this form of directive carries potential risks for the declarant. An often-repeated critique of advance directives generally, which was noted in *Martin,* is that no one who is competent and reasonably healthy can anticipate accurately how he or she might feel about major medical interventions, especially potentially life-saving ones, during a later period of incompetence and grave illness. To the extent that this critique is valid, it can be asserted even more strongly with regard to a surrogate decisionmaker. Particularly in those situations in which the document contains no personal statement, and the declarant and the attorney-in-fact have not had extensive discussions on this subject, there exists a considerable risk that the surrogate, in making health care decisions for the incompetent patient, will project his or her own views onto the patient. Indeed, health care professionals often (wittingly or unwittingly) encourage such behaviors on the part of surrogates by posing the critical question to them in terms such as: "What do you want us to do for the patient?" rather than using the more appropriate phraseology: "Knowing the patient as you do, what do you believe that he/she would want us to do under the circumstances as we have described them?"

When the person executing the durable power of attorney provides explicit indications of the kinds of interventions he or she would wish to receive in particular situations, as well as those the person would not wish, an objective standard can be said to have been applied by the attorney-in-fact acting as the duly appointed surrogate decisionmaker. However, when explicit indications are not provided in the durable power, and the author simply trusts that the designated attorney-in-fact will know the right thing to do, then a subjective standard will have to be applied. The practice of referring to the standard of decisionmaking under these circumstances as one of "substituted judgment" can be misleading. Courts using such terminology state that the surrogate substitutes his or her judgment for that of the incompetent patient. Typically, however, when a person designates another to be a health care proxy, it is not because that person has demonstrated a capacity to make good decisions in general. Rather, the proxy is selected because he or she knows the patient well, and based upon that familiarity will be in the best position to know, or at least intuit, what the now incompetent patient would decide if he or she were still competent and had been apprised fully of the circumstances.

A person who wishes to create a durable power of attorney for health care that provides the designated proxy (attorney-in-fact), and the health care professionals with whom the proxy will interact on behalf of the incompetent patient, with reasonably explicit guidance on the values and preferences that should inform the decisionmaking process, must expend some significant amount of time and effort. Personal views and wishes on these matters must be assessed accurately and clearly expressed in the directive as well as in discussions with the individual's primary care physician, designated attorney-in-fact, and one or more alternate surrogates in the event that the primary surrogate is no longer available at the critical time. The more out of the mainstream the patient's views are with regard to desired treatment or nontreatment during grave or terminal illness, the greater will be the need to document those views. Otherwise, physicians responsible for the incompetent patient's care reasonably may believe that the proxy is not acting in good faith and in pursuit of the patient's best interests.

A health care proxy document that is neither too general nor too specific presents a genuine challenge in draftsmanship. If too general, then the document will not provide the attorney-in-fact with sufficient guidance or documentation of views that may have been previously expressed in conversation. If too specific, then the document may be viewed as addressing only the situations actually mentioned, thereby suggesting that any other circumstance, no matter how similar, was not intended to be governed by it. One solution for the version that errs on the side of specificity is to include the phrase "by way of example and not limitation" in conjunction with the discussion of particular medical conditions or interventions. Another solution is to utilize one of the next generation of advance care planning documents discussed later in this article. . . .

• • •

CONCLUSION

A common explanation for physician inattention to advance directives is the lack of time and reimbursement for such discussions. However, in the era of cost containment, such an attitude is counterproductive. Most patients who engage in advance care planning choose to limit care at the end of life rather than demand care that would be described as "futile." Thus, the time spent in assisting patients in carefully and clearly constraining the use of heroic measures in their care ultimately will produce significant reductions in the cost of care, not to mention stress and anxiety on the part of caregivers. A health care system that seeks to contain costs and minimize inappropriate care (which certainly should include within its ambit care the patient would not want) has every reason to embrace wholeheartedly all forms of advance care planning.

Patients, physicians, hospitals, and health plans all can benefit immensely from the utilization of some combination of health care proxies, medical directives, and a values history. The emphasis should be upon the creation of a clear, cogent, yet concise record of patient wishes and preferences, including the identity of surrogate decisionmakers. In addition to the tangible benefits discussed, engaging in the process of creating and reviewing the next generation of directives offers the intangible benefit of countering the increasingly common patient perception that physicians are cold, impersonal, and more interested in moving on to the next case than in relating to them as a unique individual.

As we move into our new millennium, we would do well to learn from the past, lest we repeat it. It is not the concept of advance directives that is flawed and unworkable, but merely our fledgling efforts at crafting them. The next generation of advance directives will succeed where the others have failed. They will do so, in significant part, because they remedy the fatal flaw of the earlier versions—removal of the physician from a fundamental aspect of the professional relationship, which is to provide guidance, counsel, and moral support in planning for care at the end of life.

NOTES

1. 420 N.E.2d 64 (N.Y. 1981).
2. *Id.* at 72.
3. *In re* Martin, 538 N.W.2d 399 (Mich. 1995).
4. *Id.* at 412.
5. *Id.*
6. *Id.*
7. *Id.* at 402.
8. *Id.* at 403.
9. Cruzan v. Harmon, 760 S.W.2d 408 (Mo. 1988) (en banc).
10. *Martin,* 538 N.W.2d at 413.
11. *Id.* at 411.
12. *Id.* at 413.
13. *In re* Quinlan, 355 A.2d 647 (N.J. 1976).
14. *Cruzan,* 760 S.W.2d at 442 (Welliver, J., dissenting).

SUGGESTED READINGS FOR CHAPTER 3

CONFIDENTIALITY

Bayer, Ronald, and Toomey, Kathleen E. "HIV Prevention and the Two Faces of Partner Notification." *American Journal of Public Health* 82 (August 1992), 1158–64.

Beauchamp, Tom L., and Childress, James F. *Principles of Biomedical Ethics,* 5th ed. New York: Oxford University Press, 2001, chaps. 3 and 7.

Beck, James C., ed. *Confidentiality versus the Duty to Protect: Foreseeable Harm in the Practice of Psychiatry.* Washington, DC: American Psychiatry Press, 1990.

Black, Sir Douglas. "Absolute Confidentiality?" In Raanan Gillon, ed. *Principles of Health Care Ethics.* London: John Wiley & Sons, 1994.

Bok, Sissela. *Secrets: On the Ethics of Concealment and Revelation.* New York: Pantheon Books, 1983.

Gostin, Lawrence O. "Genetic Privacy." *Journal of Law, Medicine & Ethics* 23 (1995), 320–30.

———. "Health Information Privacy." *Cornell Law Review* 80 (1995), 451–528.

——— et al. "Privacy and Security of Personal Information in a New Health Care System." *Journal of the American Medical Association* 270 (November 24, 1993), 2487–93.

Hall, Robert. "Confidentiality as an Organizational Ethics Issue." *The Journal of Clinical Ethics* 10 (Fall 1999), 230–36.

Kottow, Michael H. "Medical Confidentiality: An Intransigent and Absolute Obligation." *Journal of Medical Ethics* 12 (1986), 117–22.

Powers, Madison. "Privacy and the Control of Genetic Information." In Mark S. Frankel and Albert Teich, eds. *The Genetic Frontier: Ethics, Law, and Policy.* Washington: AAAS, 1994, 77–100.

Roback, Howard B., et al. "Confidentiality Dilemmas in Group Psychotherapy with Substance-Dependent Physicians." *American Journal of Psychiatry* 153 (1996), 1250–60.

TRUTH TELLING AND THE MANAGEMENT OF BAD NEWS

Akabayashi, A., et al. "Truth Telling in the Case of a Pessimistic Diagnosis in Japan." *The Lancet* 354 (October 1999), 1263.

Asai, Atsushi. "Should Physicians Tell Patients the Truth?" *Western Journal of Medicine* 163 (1995), 36–39.

Bok, Sissela. *Lying: Moral Choice in Public and Private Life.* New York: Pantheon Books, 1978.

Buckman, R. F. *How to Break Bad News.* Baltimore: Johns Hopkins University Press, 1992.

Burack, Jeffrey H., Back, Anthony L., and Pearlman, Robert A. "Provoking Nonepileptic Seizures: The Ethics of Deceptive Diagnostic Testing." *Hastings Center Report* 27 (July-August 1997), 24–33.

Cabot, Richard C. "The Use of Truth and Falsehood in Medicine," as edited by Jay Katz from the 1909 version. *Connecticut Medicine* 42 (1978), 189–94.

Erde, Edmund L., Drickamer, Margaret A., and Lachs, Mark S. "Should Patients with Alzheimer's Disease Be Told Their Diagnosis?" *New England Journal of Medicine* 326 (April 1992), 947–51.

Fallowfield, L. "Giving Sad and Bad News." *The Lancet* 341 (February 1993), 476–78.

Gillon, Raanan. "Is There an Important Moral Distinction for Medical Ethics between Lying and Other Forms of Deception?" *Journal of Medical Ethics* 19 (1993), 131–32.

Jackson, Jennifer. "Telling the Truth." *Journal of Medical Ethics* 17 (1991), 5–9.

Orona, Celia J., Koenig, Barbara A., and Davis, Anne J. "Cultural Aspects of Nondisclosure." *Cambridge Quarterly of Healthcare Ethics* 3 (1994), 338–46.

Potter, Nancy. "Discretionary Power, Lies, and Broken Trust." *Theoretical Medicine* 17 (1996), 329–52.

Ptacek, J. T., and Eberhardt, Tara L. "Breaking Bad News: A Review of the Literature." *Journal of the American Medical Association* 276 (August 14, 1996), 496–502.

INFORMED CONSENT

American Psychiatric Association. Council on Psychiatry and Law. "American Psychiatric Association Resource Document on Principles of Informed Consent in Psychiatry." *Journal of the*

American Academy of Psychiatry and the Law 25 (1997), 121–25.

American Society of Human Genetics. "ASHG Report: Statement on Informed Consent for Genetic Research." *American Journal of Human Genetics* 59 (1996), 471–74.

Beauchamp, Tom L., and Childress, James F. *Principles of Biomedical Ethics,* 5th ed. New York: Oxford University Press, 2001, chap. 3.

Berg, Jessica W., Applebaum, Paul S., Lidz, Charles W., and Parker, Lisa S. *Informed Consent: Legal Theory and Clinical Practice,* 2d ed. New York: Oxford University Press, 2001.

Bok, Sissela. "Shading the Truth in Seeking Informed Consent." *Kennedy Institute of Ethics Journal* 5 (1995), 1–17.

Buchanan, Allen E., and Brock, Dan W. *Deciding for Others: The Ethics of Surrogate Decision Making.* Cambridge: Cambridge University Press, 1989.

Cocking, Dean, and Oakley, Justin. "Medical Experimentation, Informed Consent and Using People." *Bioethics* 8 (1994), 293–311.

Faden, Ruth R. "Informed Consent and Clinical Research." *Kennedy Institute of Ethics Journal* 6 (1996), 356–59.

———, and Beauchamp, Tom L. *A History and Theory of Informed Consent.* New York: Oxford University Press, 1986.

Geller, Gail, Strauss, Misha, Bernhardt, Barbara A., and Holtzman, Neil A. " 'Decoding' Informed Consent: Insights from Women Regarding Breast Cancer Susceptibility Testing." *Hastings Center Report* 27 (March-April 1997), 28–33.

Gostin, Lawrence O. "Informed Consent, Cultural Sensitivity, and Respect for Persons." *Journal of American Medical Association* 274 (September 13, 1995), 844–45.

Gunderson, Martin, Mayo, David, and Rhame, Frank. "Routine HIV Testing of Hospital Patients and Pregnant Women: Informed Consent in the Real World." *Kennedy Institute of Ethics Journal* 6 (1996), 161–82.

Hewlett, Sarah. "Consent to Clinical Research—Adequately Voluntary or Substantially Influenced?" *Journal of Medical Ethics* 22 (1996), 232–37.

Howe, Edmund G. "Leaving Laputa: What Doctors Aren't Taught about Informed Consent." *The Journal of Clinical Ethics* 11 (Spring 2000), 3–13.

Katz, Jay. *The Silent World of Doctor and Patient.* New York: Free Press, 1984.

Kondo, Douglas G., Bishop, F. Marian, and Jacobson, Jay A. "Residents' and Patients' Perspectives on Informed Consent in Primary Care Clinics." *The Journal of Clinical Ethics* 11 (Spring 2000), 39–48.

Meisel, Alan. "The Legal Consensus about Forgoing Life-Sustaining Treatment: Its Status and its Prospects." *Kennedy Institute of Ethics Journal* 2 (1992): 309–345.

Meisel, Alan, and Kuczewski, Mark. "Legal and Ethical Myths About Informed Consent." *Archives of Internal Medicine* 156 (December 1996), 2521–26.

Veatch, Robert M. "Abandoning Informed Consent." *Hastings Center Report* 25 (March-April 1995), 5–12.

White, Becky Cox, and Zimbelman, Joe. "Abandoning Informed Consent: An Idea Whose Time Has Not Yet Come." *Journal of Medicine and Philosophy* 23 (1998), 477–99.

REFUSAL OF TREATMENT

Beauchamp, Tom L., and Veatch, Robert, eds. *Ethical Issues in Death and Dying.* Upper Saddle River, NJ: Prentice-Hall, 1996.

DeGrazia, David. "On the Right of 'Nondangerous' Incompetent Patients to Leave Psychiatric Units Against Medical Advice." *Contemporary Philosophy* 14 (September 1992), 1–5.

Elliston, Sarah. "If You Know What's Good For You: Refusal of Consent to Medical Treatment by Children." In Sheila A. M. McLean, ed. *Contemporary Issues in Law, Medicine and Ethics.* Brookfield, VT: Dartmouth, 1996, 29–55.

Gostin, Lawrence O. "Life and Death Choices after *Cruzan.*" *Law, Medicine & Health Care* 19 (1991), 9–12.

Hewson, Barbara. "The Law on Managing Patients Who Deliberately Harm Themselves and Refuse Treatment." *British Medical Journal* 319 (October 1999), 905–07.

Kliever, Lonnie D., ed. *Dax's Case: Essays in Medical Ethics and Human Meaning.* Dallas, TX: Southern Methodist University Press, 1989.

Powell, Tia, and Lowenstein, Bruce. "Refusing Life-Sustaining Treatment after Catastrophic Injury: Ethical Implications." *Journal of Law, Medicine and Ethics* 24 (Spring 1996), 54–61.

President's Commission for the Study of Ethical Problems in Medicine and Biomedical and Behavioral Research. *Deciding to Forego Life-Sustaining Treatment.* Washington, DC: U.S. Government Printing Office, 1983.

Ross, Lainie Friedman. *Children, Families, and Health Care Decision Making.* New York: Oxford University Press, 1998.

Sullivan, Mark D., and Youngner, Stuart J. "Depression, Competence, and The Right to Refuse Lifesaving Medical Treatment." *American Journal of Psychiatry* 151 (July 1994), 971–78.

Wear, A. N., and Brahams, D. "To Treat or Not to Treat: The Legal, Ethical and Therapeutic Implications of Treatment Refusal." *Journal of Medical Ethics* 17 (September 1991), 131–35.

Weir, Robert F., and Peters, Charles. "Affirming the Decisions Adolescents Make about Life and Death." *Hastings Center Report* 27 (November-December 1997), 29–40.

Youngner, Stuart J. "Competence To Refuse Life-Sustaining Treatment." In Maurice D. Steinberg, and Stuart J. Youngner, eds. *End-of-Life Decisions: A Psychosocial Perspective.* Washington, DC: American Psychiatric Press, 1998, 19–54.

ADVANCE DIRECTIVES

Ackerman, Terrence F. "Forsaking the Spirit for the Letter of the Law: Advance Directives in Nursing Homes." *Journal of the American Geriatrics Society* 45 (1997), 114–16.

Bradley, Elizabeth H., and Rizzo, John A. "Public Information and Private Search: Evaluating the Patient Self-Determination Act." *Journal of Health Politics, Policy and Law* 24 (April 1999), 239–73.

Brock, Dan W. "A Proposal for The Use of Advance Directives in the Treatment of Incompetent Mentally Ill Persons." *Bioethics* 7 (April 1993), 247–56.

———. "What Is the Moral Authority of Family Members to Act as Surrogates for Incompetent Patients?" *Milbank Quarterly* 74 (1996), 599–618.

Celesia, Gastone G. "Persistent Vegetative State: Clinical and Ethical Issues." *Theoretical Medicine* 18 (1997), 221–36.

Dresser, Rebecca. "Confronting the 'Near Irrelevance' of Advance Directives." *Journal of Clinical Ethics* 5 (1994), 55–56.

Engel, John D., et al. "The Patient Self-Determination Act and Advance Directives: Snapshots of Activities in a Tertiary Health Care Center." *Journal of Medical Humanities* 18 (1997), 193–208.

King, Nancy. *Making Sense of Advance Directives.* Dordrecht: Kluwer Academic Publishers, 1991.

May, Thomas. "Reassessing the Reliability of Advance Directives." *Cambridge Quarterly of Healthcare Ethics* 6 (1997), 325–38.

Olick, Robert S. *Taking Advance Directives Seriously: Prospective Autonomy and Decisions Near the End of Life.* Washington: Georgetown University Press, 2001.

Ritchie, Janet, Sklar, Ron, and Steiner, Warren. "Advance Directives in Psychiatry: Resolving Issues of Autonomy and Competence." *International Journal of Law and Psychiatry* 21 (1998), 245–60.

Sehgal, A., et al. "How Strictly Do Dialysis Patients Want Their Advance Directives Followed?" *Journal of the American Medical Association* 267 (January 1, 1992), 59–63.

Teno, Joan M., and Lynn, Joanne, et al. "Do Formal Advance Directives Affect Resuscitation Decisions and the Use of Resources for Seriously Ill Patients?" *Journal of Clinical Ethics* 5 (1994), 23–30 [with following commentary].

BIBLIOGRAPHIES AND REFERENCE WORKS

Curran, William J., et al. *Health Care Law and Ethics.* New York: Aspen Law & Business, 1998. [Includes bibliographical references.]

Harman, Laurinda Beebe. *Ethical Challenges in the Management of Health Information.* Gaithersburg, MD: Aspen Publishers, 2001.

Lineback, Richard H., ed. *Philosopher's Index.* Vols. 1–. Bowling Green, OH: Philosophy Documentation Center, Bowling Green State University. Issued quarterly.

National Library of Medicine (NLM) Gateway, http://gateway.nlm.nih.gov.

Reich, Warren, ed. *Encyclopedia of Bioethics.* New York: Macmillan, 1995.

Walters, LeRoy, and Kahn, Tamar Joy, eds. *Bibliography of Bioethics.* Vols. 1–. New York: Free Press. Issued annually.

Part III
LIFE AND DEATH

4.
End-of-Life Decision Making

INTRODUCTION

There is no stronger or more enduring prohibition in medicine than the rule against killing or intentionally causing the death of patients. Yet many writers in bioethics now suggest a need to rethink this prohibition in both law and medicine. This challenge is addressed in the present chapter.

KEY TERMS AND DISTINCTIONS

Physicians and nurses have long worried that if they withdraw treatment and a patient dies, they will be accused of killing the patient and will be subject to criminal liability. A parallel concern exists that patients who refuse life-sustaining treatment are killing themselves and that health professionals assist in the suicide if they acknowledge the refusal. A related concern is that physicians who help patients hasten the time of their deaths are involved either in physician-assisted suicide or euthanasia.

We will later look at the *ethical* issues that surround these worries. However, we need first to define some central terms. What do key words like *killing, letting die, euthanasia,* and *physician-assisted suicide* mean in the context of these controversies?

The Distinction between Killing and Letting Die. In its ordinary language meaning, *killing* is any form of deprivation or destruction of life, including animal and plant life. *Killing* represents a family of ideas whose central condition is direct causation of another's death, whereas *letting die* represents another family of ideas whose central condition is intentional avoidance of causal intervention so that a natural death is caused by disease or injury.

However, this way of distinguishing killing and letting die has problems. A person can be killed, it seems, by intentionally letting him or her die of a "natural" condition of disease when the death should have been prevented by a physician. Is this circumstance a killing, a letting die, or both? Can an act be both? What are we to say about a circumstance in which a physician prescribes a lethal medication at a patient's request, which the patient then voluntarily ingests and dies. Is this a killing, a letting die, or neither?

Even if one can provide a clear distinction between killing and letting die that answers these questions, the term *killing* cannot be said to entail a wrongful act or a crime. Standard justifications of killing, such as killing in self-defense, killing to rescue a person endangered by other persons' immoral acts, and killing by misadventure (accidental, nonnegligent killing while engaged in a lawful act), prevent us from prejudging an action as wrong merely because it is a killing. To correctly apply the label *killing* or the label *letting die* to an action will therefore fail to determine whether it is acceptable or unacceptable.

Euthanasia. Euthanasia is the act or practice of ending a person's life in order to release the person from an incurable disease, intolerable suffering, or undignified death. Originally, *euthanasia* was derived from two Greek roots meaning "good death." Today the term is used to refer both to painlessly causing death and to failing to prevent death from natural causes for merciful reasons.

Two main types of euthanasia are commonly distinguished: active euthanasia and passive euthanasia. Using this distinction, four subtypes of euthanasia can be represented schematically as follows:

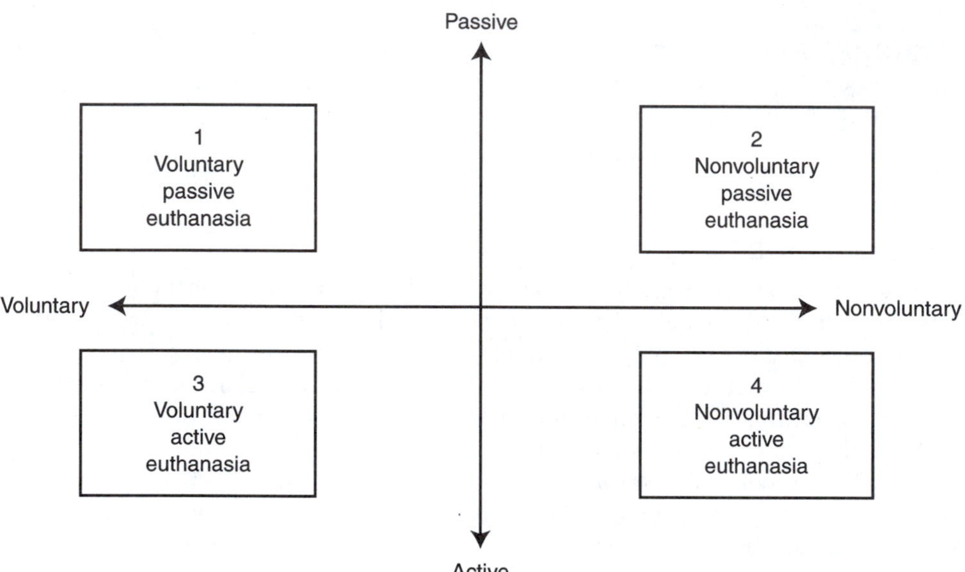

If a person requests the termination of his or her life, the action is called *voluntary euthanasia.* (See the introduction to Dan Brock's essay in this chapter.) If the person is not mentally competent to make an informed request, the action is called *nonvoluntary euthanasia.* Both forms should be distinguished from *involuntary euthanasia,* in which a person capable of making an informed request has not done so. Involuntary euthanasia has been universally condemned and is not under discussion in this chapter. Articles in this chapter are concerned primarily with subtype 3: *voluntary active euthanasia* (VAE).

Physician-Assisted Suicide. Physician-assisted suicide is a patient's voluntary choice of death (suicide) with the assistance of a physician. Unlike voluntary active euthanasia, physician-assisted suicide does not entail that the person who dies be acutely suffering or terminally ill, though these conditions are usually the reasons for electing suicide. The persons who die are themselves the ultimate cause of death; the physician merely assists.

Physician-assisted suicide can be difficult to distinguish from both treatment withdrawals and physician assistance to control pain. Like suicides, patients who refuse a treatment often *intend* to end their lives because of their grim prospects, not because they seek death as an end in itself. From this perspective, their deaths are self-produced. In other cases, physicians heavily sedate dying patients and the drugs have the *unintended* though *foreseen* effect of causing death. From this perspective, an act of controlling pain causes the death, under the foreknowledge that death might be the outcome.

THE RIGHT TO DIE

Several issues about killing, letting die, and physician-assisted death have been discussed under the general heading of the "right to die"—itself a controversial idea because it implies that there *is* a right to die. But is there a right to die? If so, what is it.

We saw in Chapter 1 that a right is a valid claim to a liberty or to a benefit. The notion of a right to die, in particular, points to a liberty right. It derives historically in the U.S. from a series of landmark "right-to-die" cases dating from *in re Quinlan* (1976). These cases include the Cruzan and Bouvia cases considered previously in Chapter 3 (see pp. 168–171, 171–75). Prior to the Quinlan case, few judicial cases and effectively no public policy set the contours of decision-making rights for seriously ill or injured patients. In *Quinlan,* the New Jersey Supreme Court held that it is permissible for a guardian to direct a physician and hospital to discontinue all extraordinary measures. The court asserted that the patient's rights and autonomous judgment are to prevail over the physician's judgment in decisions at the end of life.

The main ethical issue soon became whether all medical treatments, depending on the circumstances, can be construed as optional: Are artificial nutrition and hydration and all other medical technologies subject to the same standards of evaluation? The answer was decided by increasing the scope of the right to make autonomous choices. These legal developments joined with a developing ethics literature and increased public interest to produce a social consensus in the 1990s: A passive letting die at a patient's or family's request is generally acceptable, but an active hastening of death or killing is not. Accordingly, it became the established rule that there is a right to refuse treatment, but no right to request (or perform) an intentionally hastened death.

Leading legal decisions have raised questions about precisely what one has a right to decide and what one does not have a right to decide in the circumstance of one's own death. Over time, the idea of the right to die has evolved from a recognition of a purely negative right against intrusive medical procedures to a positive right to determine the actual manner of one's dying. From this perspective, the right to die has historically not been one thing, but a gradually developing set of autonomy rights giving patients more control over the dying process.

These developments have led to questions of whether the right to die includes the right to request that physicians assist in one's dying. Many physicians (including Leon Kass in this chapter) have been concerned that an expansive, positive right to die may restructure or redefine the physician's role so that the physician is obligated to assist the patient in committing suicide when requested to do so. Some physicians even worry that what began as an effort to give patients the right to be free from unwanted control by physicians will eventually lead to patients having a right to control physicians. However, proponents of a right to die have always insisted that the right includes only a right to request assistance, not a right to compel it.

The two opening articles in the chapter exhibit the sharply different opinions that surround these questions. F. M. Kamm discusses whether death can be a benefit, whether there is a right to choose the end of one's life, whether a doctor has a duty to relieve suffering even if it foreseeably makes the doctor a killer, and whether a patient can waive the right to live, thereby releasing others from the duty not to kill him or her. Kamm believes that a patient would sometimes do no wrong in intending or causing his or her death. She argues that if it is permissible to treat persons in their best interests when we foresee that the treatment will rapidly cause death, then it is permissible to intentionally kill or assist in killing someone when the death is in the person's best interest. Kamm therefore concludes that both euthanasia and physician-assisted suicide are justified under some circumstances.

In the second essay in this section, Leon Kass raises questions about both the coherence and the consequences of the right to die. Noting that the language of rights was introduced into political discourse by Hobbes and Locke, Kass argues that the right to die betrays the excessive individualism of its intellectual forebears. Kass questions whether the right-to-die notion applies equally well to contexts in which treatment is refused with uncertain consequences and to situations in which treatment is refused in order to achieve the result of the patient's death. He suspects that the right to die is at times cynically asserted on behalf of others by healthy people who fervently hope that the unproductive, the incurable, and the repulsive will die sooner rather than later.

THE LEGAL BACKGROUND IN THE UNITED STATES

It is one thing to attempt to justify particular acts of causing death to seriously ill or injured patients and quite another to justify general practices or social policies. Particular acts of assisted suicide may in some circumstances be humane, compassionate, and in a person's best interest, but a social policy that authorizes such acts in medicine, it is often argued, would weaken moral restraints that we cannot replace, threatening practices that provide a basis of trust between patients and health care professionals. Should we, then, *legalize* physician-assisted death?

The right-to-die movement has exerted pressure to reform current laws so that physicians are allowed to play a more extensive role in facilitating the wishes of patients. A major initiative was accepted by the majority of citizens in the state of Oregon. A ballot measure (Measure 16) was first approved by voters in that state in November 1994. It allows physicians to prescribe lethal drugs for those terminally ill patients who wish to escape unbearable suffering. Under the provisions of the Oregon Death with Dignity Act, which is reprinted in this chapter, physicians are legally allowed to prescribe death-inducing drugs for terminally ill patients (so declared by two physicians) when they wish to escape unbearable suffering. These patients must three times request a physician's prescription for lethal drugs.

This Oregon legislation was upheld as a result of two 1997 U.S. Supreme Court decisions: *Vacco v. Quill* and *Washington v. Glucksberg,* both reprinted in this chapter. The Supreme Court reviewed two decisions in circuit courts (both of which are discussed by John Arras in this chapter). These decisions had endorsed a constitutional right to limited physician-assisted suicide. The decisions of these lower courts were reversed by the Supreme Court, which found that there are no constitutional rights to physician aid in dying, but that each state may set its own policy. By returning the issue to the states, the Supreme Court effectively recognized the legal validity of statutes that allow physician-assisted death as well as those that disallow it.

Chief Justice Rehnquist maintains in these opinions that a doctor may provide "aggressive palliative care" that "hastens a patient's death" if the doctor's intent is "only to ease his patient's pain." This doctor is presumably distinguished from the doctor who has the intention of assisting in a suicide because, according to Justice Rehnquist, doctors involved in physician-assisted suicide "must, necessarily and indubitably, intend primarily that the patient be made dead." The Chief Justice appears to be using intention to distinguish between killing and letting die, while assuming that the former is unwarranted and the latter permissible.

This approach has generated controversy. The doctor who prescribes a fatal medication with the intention of giving the patient the choice of using or not using it need have no ill intention; the physician may even try to convince the patient not to use the medication. The doctor's intention may be a benevolent one of easing the patient's anxiety about a loss of control while giving the patient an option he or she has requested. This raises the question of whether the physician's intention is an important consideration in assessing the morality of the physician's action.

Despite Rehnquist's reservations about physician-assisted suicide, the U.S. Supreme Court decision had the effect of clearing the way for a right to physician-assisted death to be enacted by individual states, which then occurred in Oregon in 1997. The Oregon law appears to reflect the new frontier of issues about whether society should expand autonomy rights to control the moment of death. The cutting edge of the right-to-die movement seems, from this perspective, to have shifted from *refusal* of treatment to *request* for aid. On November 6, 2001, however, U.S. Attorney General John Ashcroft attempted to trump the Oregon law. He issued a directive to the Drug Enforcement Agency to investigate physicians who prescribe federally controlled substances and to revoke their license to prescribe the very drugs used in Oregon. The state of Oregon, in turn, sued the U.S. government. The state challenged Ashcroft's authority to limit the practice of medicine under Oregon law.

The final opinion in this chapter on the legal background is *Wendland v. Wendland,* an opinion of the California Supreme Court. In this case, the Court considered whether a patient's conservator (a person designated to protect the interests of an incompetent) can validly withhold artificial nutrition and hydration from a patient even though the patient is not terminally ill, comatose, or in a persistent vegetative state. The patient, Robert Wendland, sustained a severe injury to the brain that left him conscious but severely disabled, both mentally and physically. He had not left an advance directive or appointed a surrogate decision maker. Wendland's wife proposed to direct his physician to remove his feeding tube and allow him to die, but Wendland's mother and sister objected. They saw the act as *killing* Robert, not *allowing him to die.* A twenty-member hospital ethics committee supported the wife's decision, but without speaking with Robert's mother or sister. The court finds that the conservator may not withhold artificial nutrition and hydration absent a clear and convincing statement by the patient or clear and convincing evidence that the act is in the best interest of the patient.

THE MORAL FOUNDATIONS OF PUBLIC POLICY

The legal developments just examined have encouraged the belief that the most pressing moral questions about physician-assisted death is whether it should be *legalized.* This issue will now be framed in terms of the moral foundations of public policy.

Many who are opposed to the legalization of killing or any form of intentional hastening of death appeal not to the intrinsic moral wrongness of helping someone die, but to the social consequences that would result from a public policy that supports physician-assisted dying. A prominent argument in this discussion is the *slippery slope argument.* It proceeds roughly as follows: Although particular acts of active killing are sometimes morally justified, the social consequences of sanctioning practices of killing would run serious risks of abuse and misuse and, on balance, would cause more harm than benefit. The argument is not that these negative consequences will occur immediately, but that they will grow incrementally over time. Although society might start by carefully restricting the number of patients who qualify for assistance in suicide or homicide, these restrictions would be revised and expanded over time, with an ever-increasing risk of unjustified killing. Unscrupulous persons would learn how to abuse the system, just as they do with methods of tax evasion. Slippery slope arguments are discussed in this chapter by several authors, including Brock, John Arras, and the authors of the articles on the Netherlands (see later).

Supporters of a public policy that permits physician-assisted death argue that there are cases in which respect for the rights of patients obligates society to respect the decisions of those who elect this course. Brock supports this position. He and others note that competent patients have a legal and moral right to refuse treatment that brings about their deaths. Why, then, they ask, should there not be a similar right to arrange for death by an active means? Proponents of assisted death like Brock emphasize circumstances in which a condition has become overwhelmingly burdensome for a patient, pain management for the patient is inadequate, and only a physician seems capable of bringing relief.

Brock argues that the "central ethical argument" for voluntary active euthanasia is that it promotes patient autonomy and well-being in circumstances in which persons have a strong need to be in control of their lives. Brock does not balk at the thesis that euthanasia involves intentionally killing the innocent, but he argues that such killing is justified under certain circumstances. Brock views the argument against euthanasia at the policy level as stronger than the argument against it at the level of individual cases, but he maintains that the objections are unpersuasive at both levels.

In the next selection in this section, Arras considers slippery slope arguments with the intention of showing that the legalization of physician-assisted suicide would pose serious and predictable social harms, but he also allows for democratic deliberation on the issue. The natural home for this sort of discussion he finds in legislatures rather than the courts in which so many discussions of the treatment of the dying have appeared in the past. Arras argues that physician-assisted suicide poses a "tragic choice" for society in that there will be victims of any policy that is ultimately adopted. The best public policy, he suggests, is one that limits social harms by erecting legal barriers to assisted death while vigorously addressing the medical and social problems that prompt requests for an early death.

If dire consequences will flow from the legal legitimation of assisted suicide or voluntary active euthanasia, then it would appear that such practices should be legally prohibited, as Arras recommends. But, Brock and others ask, how accurate is the evidence that such dire consequences will occur? Is there a sufficient reason to think that we cannot provide safeguards and maintain control over a public policy of assisted death?

PHYSICIAN-ASSISTED DEATH IN THE NETHERLANDS

As the controversy over assisted death has increased, its practice in the Netherlands has become ever more closely watched. Many in the Netherlands, both inside and outside the medical profession, believe that physician-administered death (killing) in cases of seriously ill and dying patients can be morally and legally justified. However, opponents of the Dutch system have argued that loose state controls have led to an almost unregulated and dangerous social practice.

Dutch euthanasia practices and reporting requirements are addressed first in this chapter by Henk Jochemsen and John Keown. They discuss statistical findings about current practices and consider whether these findings show that voluntary euthanasia is under effective control in the Netherlands. They conclude that although there has been significant improvement in compliance with reporting and other procedural requirements, the practice of voluntary euthanasia remains beyond effective controls and that safeguards in the Dutch system have largely failed. They are concerned that the situation has led to a precarious slippery slope in which Dutch physicians have failed to act on the promise to involve only last resort cases.

In a response, Johannes J. M. van Delden argues three main points. First, he argues that it is not always inappropriate to use euthanasia when palliative care might have been used instead. Such cases do not provide evidence of a slippery slope, he maintains, because patients made their own autonomous judgments about the best way to end their lives. Second, he argues that no significant data show that a slippery slope has occurred in the Netherlands in the sense that *nonvoluntary* euthanasia has become a threat in the system. Finally, he argues that the Dutch reporting system has now been altered to address problems of underreporting. He agrees that many questions remain about needed reforms, but he thinks that the Dutch are now diligent in addressing these questions.

ALTERNATIVES TO PHYSICIAN-ASSISTED DEATH

The two final articles in this chapter discuss several alternatives to physician-assisted suicide that either increase the range of patient autonomy or offer better end-of-life care. In the first, Bernard Gert, Charles M. Culver, and K. Danner Clouser argue that no patient should feel constrainted by the system to stay alive, because every patient can refuse hydration and nutrition, which will ultimately cause death—a form of *passive* euthanasia. All patients therefore already have the right to control their own destinies, and there is no need to rush to physician-assisted suicide or voluntary *active* euthanasia. These authors maintain that key questions turn on whether a competent patient has rationally refused treatment. What makes something a case of letting a competent person die is the patient's refusal, not an omission by the physician. Therefore, the distinction between killing and letting die should be retained, but should be based on the difference between patients' *requests* and patients' *refusals:* Dying by starvation is, on this analysis, a case of letting die, not of killing, despite the fact that the physician cares for the patient during the dying process.

In the final article in this chapter, Timothy Quill, Bernard Lo, and Dan Brock discuss four options that might be presented to patients, so that they can choose how they will die. These authors argue that both terminal sedation and voluntarily stopping eating and drinking would allow physicians to be responsive to the suffering of certain types of patients, but they argue that these strategies are ethically and clinically far closer to physician-assisted suicide and voluntary active euthanasia than has generally been appreciated. These authors propose safeguards for a system in which patients can choose to die as they wish. They also maintain that explicit public policy allowing these alternatives (rather than leaving them hidden, as is now often the case) would reassure many patients who fear a bad death in their future. Unlike Gert and colleagues, these authors consider physician-assisted suicide as one among the four viable options for patients, the other three being improved palliative care, terminal sedation, and refusal of hydration and nutrition.

Whatever options are made available to patients, it should not be presumed that physicians face large numbers of desperately ill patients who wish to be assisted through voluntary active euthanasia or physician-assisted suicide. Virtually all parties to these controversies believe that pain management has made circumstances at least bearable for many of today's patients, reducing the need for physician-assisted death and increasing the need for adequate medical facilities, training, and hospice programs. Nonetheless, as Quill, Lo, and Brock point out, some patients cannot be satisfactorily relieved and experience intolerable suffering. If physicians can benefit patients of this description in ways other than by palliation, terminal sedation, or the withholding of food and fluids, should they be restricted by law or morals from doing so? This question remains at the center of the contemporary discussion.

T.L.B.

F. M. KAMM

A Right to Choose Death?

Frances Myrna Kamm is professor of philosophy at NYU and of medicine and affiliated faculty at the NYU School of Law. She is a member of the editorial boards of *Utilitas* and *Legal Theory,* and the advisory board of the Routledge International Library of Philosophy. Her publications include *Creation and Abortion* (1992) and *Morality, Mortality, vols. 1 and 2* (1996).

. . . [T]he debate about the right to choose death may appear to present a stand-off between people who endorse life's intrinsic value, and those who think life's value depends on the interests, judgments, and choices of the person whose life it is.

This picture of irreconcilable moral conflict is, I believe, too despairing about the powers of moral argument. To make headway, however, we may need to pay closer attention to the complexities of cases and the specific moral terrain they occupy: to think about people on medication, being treated by physicians, sometimes relying on technical means to stay alive, trying to decide how to live out what remains of their lives. I will explore this terrain in *moral,* not legal, terms: I will be asking you to consult your moral judgments about cases, and follow out the implications of those judgments. Though this moral argument bears on constitutional argument and on appropriate legislation, I will not propose laws or rules for judges, doctors, or hospital administrators to consult, or worry about slippery slopes created by legally hard cases. The moral landscape affords firmer footing, and does not, I will suggest, permit a blanket ban on euthanasia and physician-assisted suicide: Though both involve intentionally ending human lives, both are sometimes morally permissible. I will conclude by discussing a different argument for such permissibility offered by a distinguished group of moral philosophers in a recent amicus brief to the Supreme Court.

I. LOGICAL TROUBLES?

Before getting to the issue of moral permissibility, we need to overcome a preliminary hurdle. I said that euthanasia and physician-assisted suicide are intended to benefit the patient. Some may object that these ideas make no sense. How is it possible for death to benefit the person who dies? Death eliminates the person—how can we produce a benefit if we eliminate the potential beneficiary?

To see how, consider the parallel question about death as a harm: Can a person be harmed by her own death even though death means that she is no longer around to suffer the harm? Suppose Schubert's life would have included even greater musical achievement had he not died so young. Because musical achievement is an important good, Schubert had a less good life overall than he would have had if he lived longer. But living a less good life is a harm. By excluding those achievements, then, Schubert's death harmed him: it prevented the better life. Now come back to the original concern about how death might be a benefit. Suppose a person's life would go on containing only misery and pain with no compensating goods. That person will be better off living a shorter life containing fewer such uncompensated-for bad things rather than a longer one containing more of them. But living a better life is a benefit. By interfering with the important bads, the person's death benefits him; it prevents the worse life.

From *Boston Review* (Summer 1997), 20–23. An earlier version of this paper was given as a talk at the Plenary Session of the American Academy of Forensic Sciences in New York, in February 1997.

It is possible, in short, to benefit a person by ending his life. The concept of euthanasia is, therefore, at least not simply logically confused; similarly for the idea that physician-assisted suicide may be aimed at the good of the patient. But conceptual coherence does not imply moral permissibility. So let's turn now to the moral question: Is it ever morally permissible to benefit a person by hastening his death, even when he requests it?

II. A RIGHT TO CHOOSE

Suppose a doctor is treating a terminally ill patient in severe pain. Suppose, too, that the pain can only be managed with morphine, but that giving the morphine is certain to hasten the patient's death. With the patient's consent, the doctor may nevertheless give the morphine. Why so? Because, in this particular case, the greater good for the patient is relief of pain, and the lesser evil is loss of life: after all, the patient is terminally ill, and in severe pain, so life would end soon anyway and is not of very good quality. So the patient is overall benefited by having a shorter pain-free life rather than a longer, even more painful life. (Notice that this could be true even if the morphine put the patient in a deep unconscious state from which he never awoke, so that he never consciously experienced pain-free time.)

In giving morphine to produce pain relief, the doctor foresees with certainty (let's assume) that the patient will die soon. Still, death is a side-effect of the medication, not the doctor's goal or reason for giving it: the doctor, that is, is not *intending* the patient's death, and would give the medication even if he thought death would not result. (If I have a drink to soothe my nerves and foresee a hangover, it does not follow that I intend the hangover.) Because the intended death is not present, we don't yet have a case of euthanasia or physician-assisted suicide. At the same time, in giving morphine for pain relief, the doctor is not simply letting the patient die as the disease runs its course; he administers a drug which causes death. So I think this should be understood as a case of killing, even though the doctor does not intend the death. (In other cases we have no trouble seeing that it is possible to kill without intending death: consider a driver who runs someone over while speeding.)

Now suppose the morphine loses its power to reduce the intensity of the patient's pain, but that administering it would still shorten the patient's life and thus limit the duration of his pain. Suppose, too, that the patient requests the morphine; fully aware of its effects, he wants to take it so that it will end his pain by killing him. In short, we now have a case of *morphine for death* rather than *morphine for pain relief*. Is it still morally permissible to give the morphine? Some people say that we may not kill in this case. They do not deny that relief of pain is still the greater good and death the lesser evil: they know that the consequences are essentially the same as in the case of morphine for pain relief. The problem, they say, lies in a difference of intent. In the case of giving morphine for pain relief, we intend the pain relief, and merely foresee the death; but in the case of giving morphine for death, we intend the death (which is the lesser evil): we would not give the morphine if we did not expect the death. But some people think it is impermissible to act with the intent to produce an evil. They support what is called the *Doctrine of Double Effect,* according to which there is a large moral difference between acting with the foresight that one's conduct will have some evil consequence and acting with the intent to produce that same evil (even as part of or means to a greater good). So whereas killing the patient by giving morphine for pain relief is permissible, killing the patient by giving morphine for death is impermissible.

The distinction between intending an evil and merely foreseeing it sometimes makes a moral difference. But does it provide a reason to refrain from performing euthanasia or assisting in suicide? I think not. On many occasions already, doctors (with a patient's consent) *intend the lesser evil* to a person in order *to produce his own greater good*. For example, a doctor may intentionally amputate a healthy leg (the lesser evil) in order to get at and remove a cancerous tumor, thereby saving the patient's life (the greater good). Or, he may intentionally cause blindness in a patient if seeing would somehow, for example, destroy the patient's brain, or cause him to die. Furthermore, he may intentionally cause someone pain, thereby acting contrary to a duty to relieve suffering, if this helps to save the person's life. The duty to save life sometimes just outweighs the other duty. Why then is it impermissible for doctors to intend death when it is the lesser evil, in order to produce the greater good of no pain; why is it morally wrong to benefit the patient by giving her a shorter, less painful life rather than having her endure a longer, more painful one? Recall that in the case of morphine for pain relief, it was assumed that death would be the lesser evil and pain relief the greater good. That was one reason we could give the morphine. Why is it wrong, then, for doctors sometimes to act against a duty to preserve life in order to relive pain, just as they could sometimes act against a duty not to intend pain in order to save a life?

To summarize, I have constructed a three-step argument for physician-assisted suicide and euthanasia. Assuming patient consent:

1. We may permissibly cause death as a side effect if it relieves pain, because sometimes death is a lesser evil and pain relief a greater good.
2. We may permissibly intend other lesser evils to the patient, for the sake of her greater good.
3. Therefore, when death is a lesser evil, it is sometimes permissible for us to intend death in order to stop pain.

Thus, suppose we accept that it is sometimes permissible to *knowingly* shorten a life by giving pain-relieving medication, and agree, too, that it is sometimes permissible for a doctor to *intend* a lesser evil in order to produce a greater good. How, then, can it be wrong to *intentionally* shorten a life when that will produce the greater good?[1]

I don't expect that everyone will immediately find this argument compelling. I suspect that many—including some who are inclined to agree with the conclusion—will feel that death is different, so to speak. While they agree that we may intend pain, if it is a lesser evil, in order to save a life, they think it is impermissible to intentionally hasten death in order to relieve pain. I will address this concern later. But first I want to add another set of considerations that support euthanasia and physician-assisted suicide.

III. AN ARGUMENT FOR DUTY

According to the three-step argument, a doctor is *permitted* to give morphine for pain relief, even though he knows it will expedite the patient's death, if death is the lesser evil. But I think we can say more. Suppose, as I have stipulated, that giving morphine is the only way for a doctor to relieve a patient's suffering. A doctor, I assume, has a duty to relieve a patient's suffering. I conclude that the doctor has a *duty* to relieve suffering by giving the morphine, if the patient requests this. He cannot refuse to give the morphine on the ground that he will be a killer if he does.

If doctors have a duty to relieve pain, and even being a killer does not override this duty when the patient requests morphine for pain relief, then perhaps they also have a duty, not merely a permission, to kill their patients, or aid in their being killed, intending their deaths in order to relieve suffering. Now we have a new argument. Assuming patient consent:

1. There is a duty to treat pain even if it foreseeably makes one a killer, when death is the lesser evil and no pain is the greater good.
2. There is a duty to intend the other lesser evils (e.g., amputation) for a patient's own greater good.
3. There is a duty to kill the patient, or assist in his being killed, intending his death when this is the lesser evil and pain relief the greater good.

I think this argument, too, is compelling, but will concentrate here on the case for permissibility.

IV. IS KILLING SPECIAL?

As I indicated earlier, a natural rejoinder to the three-step argument for euthanasia and physician-assisted suicide is to emphasize that "death is different." But how precisely is it different, and why is the difference morally important?

Perhaps it will be said, simply, that the doctor who intends the death of his patient is *killing*. Even if intending a lesser evil for a greater good is often permissible, it might be condemned when it involves killing. Killing, it might be said, is not on a par with other lesser evils.

But this does not suffice to upset the three-step argument. For giving a lethal injection of morphine to relieve pain also involves killing and we approve of giving the morphine. To be sure, a patient's right to life includes a right not to be killed. But that right gives us a protected option whether to live or die, an option with which others cannot legitimately interfere; it does not give one a duty to live. If a patient decides to die, he is waiving his right to live. By waiving his right, he releases others (perhaps a specific other person) from a duty not to kill him, at least insofar as that duty stems from his right to live.[2] The duty not to kill him may also stem from their duty not to harm him, even if he so wishes; but I have stipulated that the doctor is to kill only when death is the lesser evil.

A more compelling version of the objection is, however, waiting in the wings. This one points not merely to the fact of killing, but to intentional killing. It claims that there is something distinctive about intending death, and that this distinction makes a large moral difference. In particular, acting with the intention to bring about death as a lesser evil requires that we treat ourselves or other persons as available to be used for achieving certain goods—in particular, the reduction of suffering. In euthanasia and physician-assisted suicide, we intentionally terminate a being with a rational nature—a being that judges, aims at goals, and evaluates how to act.[3] We have no such intention to use a person as a mere means when we aim at such lesser evils as destruction of a leg. Indeed, one of the things that seems odd about killing someone only if he is capable of voluntarily deciding in a reasonable way to end his life is that one is thereby ensuring that what is destroyed is a reasoning, thinking being, and therefore a being of great worth. This will not be so if the person is unconscious or vegetative or otherwise no longer functioning as a rational being. Obviously, people take control of their lives and devote their rational natures to the pursuit of certain goals within those lives; but, it is claimed, when this is appropriate, they do not aim to interfere with or destroy their personhood but set it in one direction or another.

The idea that there are limits on what we may do to ourselves as persons derives from Immanuel Kant. In his moral writings, Kant said that rational humanity, as embodied in ourselves and others, is—and should be treated as—*an end in itself, and not a mere means* to happiness or other goals. The fact that one is a judging, aiming, evaluating rational agent has worth in itself. To have this value as a person is more like an honor to us (Kant called it "dignity") than a benefit that answers to some interest of ours. Thus my life may have worth, even if my life is not a benefit to me (and my death would benefit me) because goods *other than* being a person are outweighed by bads. The worth of my life is not measured solely by its worth to me in satisfying my desires, or its worth to others in satisfying theirs. According to Kant, then, it is wrong for others to treat me as a mere means for their ends, but equally wrong for me to treat myself as a mere means for my own ends: As others should respect my dignity as a person by not using me merely as a means for their purposes, I should have proper regard for my own dignity as a person, and not simply use myself as a means for my own purposes. But that is precisely what I do when I aim at my own death as a way to eliminate pain. So I ought not to pursue that aim, and therefore ought not to consent to a morphine injection aiming at death, or give one to a patient who has consented.

Before assessing this Kantian argument, I want to justify focusing it on intentional killing rather than other ways of intentionally contributing to a death. Consider a patient who intends his own death and therefore wants life support of any sort removed. Suppose, for the sake of argument, that we disapprove of this intention. Suppose, too, that we disapprove of a doctor's agreeing to remove treatment because he also intends this patient's death. But while we may disapprove of the intentions and conduct, acting on that disapproval would require us to *force* life support on the patient, and he has a right that we not do this. Our opposition to his intentions and the doctor's is trumped by our opposition to forced invasion of the patient. So we permit the patient and doctor to act—to remove treatment—intending death. Consider, in contrast, a patient who intends his own death and, therefore, requests a lethal injection or pills. Suppose, once more, that we disapprove of this intention. Acting on our opposition would require us to refrain from invading him with a lethal injection or refuse the pills. But it seems clear that the right not to be invaded with treatment against one's will is stronger than the right simply to be invaded (with a lethal injection) or given pills. So the fact that we must terminate treatment, even when the patient and doctor intend the patient's death, does not show that it is permissible to kill the patient or assist him in killing when he and his doctor intend his death. Correspondingly, an objection to intentional killing need not imply an objection to terminating treatment for someone who intends his own death.[4]

I turn now to the Kantian-style argument against aiming at one's death (or aiming at another's death with his consent). In assessing this argument, we must distinguish three different ways in which one may treat a person as a mere means:

1. Calculating the worth of living on in a way which gives insufficient weight to the worth of being a person.
2. Treating the nonexistence of persons as a means to a goal (e.g., no pain).
3. Using persons in order to bring about their own end.

The first idea is that being a person has worth in itself and is not merely a means to an overall balance of other goods over evils in the person's life. On this interpretation, we treat persons as a mere means if we give inadequate weight in our decisions to the value of our existence as persons; if we do, then death may seem a lesser evil. But even when there are few goods in life besides the capacity to be a rational agent, the loss of life—and therefore the loss of that capacity—may still be a greater evil than pain.

Though I do not doubt that this idea has force, it can equally well be given as a reason for not terminating a course of treatment, even when one merely foresees one's death. Because this way of treating a person as a mere means does not distinguish the *morality of intending death* from the *morality of merely foreseeing death,* it cannot be used to explain why intentional killing in particular is impermissible.[5] . . .

What, then, about the second and third interpretations of the idea of using persons as mere means? To see the difference between them, consider an analogy: My radio is a device for getting good sounds and filtering out bad sounds. It is a means to a balance of good sounds over bad ones. Suppose it stops performing well, that it only produces static, but cannot be turned off. I can wait until its batteries run down and not replace them, or I can smash it now, thus using the radio itself to stop the noise it produces. Either way, I would see its death as I saw its life, as a means to a better balance of good over bad sounds. While I have always seen my radio as a mere means to an end if I smash it, I use it as a means to its end (termination): This is sense (3).[6] If I let the radio run down, intending its demise, but do not smash it—I see it wasting away and do not replace its parts—then I do not see it as a means to its own end, but I do see *its end as a means* to a better balance of sounds. This is sense (2).

Active suicide is analogous to smashing the radio: the person uses himself as a means to his own death. Some people find this complete taking control of one's life particularly morally inappropriate, perhaps because they think our bodies belong to God and that we have no right to achieve the goal of our own death by manipulating a "tool" that is not ours (or intending that others manipulate it). This objection is not present if—here we have sense (2)—we terminate medical assistance with the intention that the system run down, aiming at its death. For then we achieve the goal of death by interfering with what is ours (the medication), not God's. Here we have another reason why someone may object to killing but not to terminating treatment, even if accompanied by the intention that the system run down; unlike intentional killing, terminating treatment does not involve using persons to bring about their own end. Some say, though, that this way of using persons as means is also more objectionable than merely foreseeing the death. They say that if we terminate medical assistance, intending death, we do not merely treat our life as a means to greater good over bad, but treat *our death (the end of our life)* as a means to greater good over bad.

How much weight, then, should be placed on the second and third senses of "using a person as a means"? Should they really stand in our way? I believe not. It cannot be argued, at least in secular moral terms, that one's body belongs to someone else and that one cannot, therefore, use it as a means to achieve death. Notice also that if your body belonged to someone else, it isn't clear why you should be permitted to use it by administering morphine to stop your pain when you merely foresee that this will destroy the body. We aren't usually permitted to treat other people's property in this way either. Nor does it seem that treating one's death as available for one's purposes (i.e., being rid of pain) is necessarily a morally inappropriate attitude to take to oneself—so long as there is not failure to properly value the importance of just being a person. If this is right, then, at least sometimes, a patient would do no wrong in intending or causing his death. At least sometimes, a doctor who helped him by giving pills would also do no wrong merely because he killed, or assisted killing, aiming at death.

The strongest case for such conduct can be made, I believe, if the overriding aim is to end physical pain. The need to do this may be rare with modern techniques of pain control, but still the patient has a "disjunctive" right: either to adequate pain control or the assistance in suicide of a willing doctor. Psychological suffering which is a reaction to one's knowledge or beliefs about a state of affairs is a weaker case. The test I suggest here is: Would we give a drug to treat psychological suffering if we *foresaw* that it would rapidly kill as a side effect? If not, then giving pills to a patient intending that they kill him in order to end psychological suffering would not be permissible. This same test can be applied to other reasons that might be offered for seeking death by euthanasia or physician-assisted suicide. For example, would we allow a patient to use a drug that will rapidly cause death (rather than a safer one) if it will save him money? If not, then we may not perform euthanasia or physician-assisted suicide to stop the drain on his family finances. Would we give a demented patient a drug that unraveled the tangled neurons that caused his dementia but which we foresaw would rapidly kill him as a side effect? If not, then why should we be permitted to give him pills, intending his death? Of course, the application of this test may yield positive responses rather than negative ones to these questions.

NOTES

1. I first presented this argument in *Creation and Abortion* (New York: Oxford University Press, 1992), pp. 33–35, and again in *Morality, Mortality,* Vol. II (New York: Oxford University Press, 1996), pp. 194–98.

2. Notice that this waiver seems to be morally necessary even when the doctor wishes to give morphine that will kill as a foreseen side effect. This means doctors should get permission for giving the morphine for pain relief as well as for giving it to deliberately kill. (I do not believe they always do so.)

3. We also terminate human life considered independently of whether it is the life of a rational being. It may seem harder to justify destroying a person than a human life that lacks qualities required for personhood—for example, a functioning brain. But I will assume that one could substitute "human life" for "person" in the argument I give against intentional killing and in my response to that argument.

4. In contrast, suppose that a patient who intends his own death is also suffering great pain that only morphine will stop. He asks for the morphine, not because it will stop the pain, but because he knows it will kill him. If it would not kill him, he would not ask for it. Does he have a right that the doctor give him the morphine? If he does, then the doctor is not at liberty to refuse simply because of the *patient's intention,* any more than he could refuse to terminate treatment because of the patient's intention. Indeed we might not be permitted to interfere with the doctor's giving morphine in this case even if he gave it only because *he* intended death. I owe this case to Timothy Hall.

5. Kant thought we had a duty to actively preserve rational humanity and hence we should not too lightly do what we foresee will lead to its end. Still, he allows that we may sometimes engage in conduct though we foresee it will result in our deaths, but we may never aim at our deaths.

6. If I see someone else destroy it and do not interfere, I may be intending its use as a means to its own end, though I do not myself use it.

LEON R. KASS

Is There a Right to Die?

Leon Kass is Addie Clark Harding Professor in the Committee on Social Thought and the College of the University of Chicago. Kass has served as a surgeon for the U.S. Public Health Service and has held positions in the field of medical ethics at the National Academy of Sciences, St. John's College, and the Kennedy Institute of Ethics of Georgetown University. Among his books are *Toward a More Natural Science: Biology and Human Affairs* (1998) and *The Hungry Soul: Eating and the Perfecting of Our Nature* (1994). In August 2001, Kass was named chair of a new Council on Bioethics by President George W. Bush.

It has been fashionable for some time now and in many aspects of American public life for people to demand what they want or need as a matter of rights. During the past few decades we have heard claims of a right to health or health care, a right to education or employment, a right to privacy (embracing also a right to abort or to enjoy pornography, or to commit suicide or sodomy), a right to clean air, a right to dance naked, a right to be born, and a right not to have been born. Most recently we have been presented with the ultimate new rights claim, a "right to die."

This claim has surfaced in the context of changed circumstances and burgeoning concerns regarding the end of life. Thanks in part to the power of medicine to preserve and prolong life, many of us are fated to end our once-flourishing lives in years of debility,

From *Hastings Center Report* 23 (January–February 1993), 34–40, 41–43. Copyright © 1993. Leon R. Kass. Reprinted by permission of the author.

dependence, and disgrace. Thanks to the respirator and other powerful technologies that can, all by themselves, hold comatose and other severely debilitated patients on this side of the line between life and death, many who would be dead are alive only because of sustained mechanical intervention. Of the 2.2 million annual deaths in the United States, 80 percent occur in health care facilities; in roughly 1.5 million of these cases, death is preceded by some explicit decision about stopping or not starting medical treatment. Thus, death in America is not only medically managed, but its timing is also increasingly subject to deliberate choice. It is from this background that the claims of a right to die emerge.

I do not think that the language and approach of rights are well suited either to sound personal decision-making or to sensible public policy in this very difficult and troubling matter. In most of the heartrending end-of-life situations, it is hard enough for practical wisdom to try to figure out what is morally right and humanly good, without having to contend with intransigent and absolute demands of a legal or moral right to die. And, on both philosophical and legal grounds, I am inclined to believe that there can be no such thing as a *right* to die—that the notion is groundless and perhaps even logically incoherent. Even its proponents usually put "right to die" in quotation marks, acknowledging that it is at best a misnomer.

Nevertheless, we cannot simply dismiss this claim, for it raises important and interesting practical and philosophical questions. Practically, a right to die is increasingly asserted and gaining popular strength; increasingly, we see it in print without the quotation marks. The former Euthanasia Society of America, shedding the Nazi-tainted and easily criticized "E" word, changed its name to the more politically correct Society for the Right to Die before becoming Choice In Dying. End-of-life cases coming before the courts, nearly always making their arguments in terms of rights, have gained support for some sort of "right to die." The one case to be decided by a conservative Supreme Court, the *Cruzan* case, has advanced the cause. . . .

The voter initiatives to legalize physician-assisted suicide and euthanasia in Washington and California were narrowly defeated, in part because they were badly drafted laws; yet the proponents of such practices seem to be winning the larger social battle over principle. According to several public opinion polls, most Americans now believe that "if life is miserable, one has the right to get out, actively and with help if necessary." Though the burden of philosophical proof for establishing new rights (especially one as bizarre as a "right to die") should always fall on the proponents, the social burden of proof has shifted to those who would oppose the voluntary choice of death through assisted suicide. Thus it has become politically necessary—and at the same time exceedingly difficult—to make principled arguments about why doctors must not kill, about why euthanasia is not the proper human response to human finitude, and about why there is no right to die, natural or constitutional. This is not a merely academic matter: our society's willingness and ability to protect vulnerable life hang in the balance.

An examination of "right to die" is even more interesting philosophically. It reveals the dangers and the limits of the liberal—that is, rights-based—political philosophy and jurisprudence to which we Americans are wedded. As the ultimate new right, grounded neither in nature nor in reason, it demonstrates the nihilistic implication of a new ("postliberal") doctrine of rights, rooted in the self-creating will. And as liberal society's response to the bittersweet victories of the medical project to conquer death, it reveals in pure form the tragic meaning of the entire modern project, both scientific and political.

The claim of a right to die is made only in Western liberal societies—not surprisingly, for only in Western liberal societies do human beings look first to the rights of individuals. Also, only here do we find the high-tech medicine capable of keeping people from dying when they might wish. Yet the claim of a right to die is also a profoundly strange claim, especially in a liberal society founded on the primacy of the right to life. We Americans hold as a self-evident truth that governments exist to secure inalienable rights, first of all, to self-preservation; now we are being encouraged to use government to secure a putative right of self-destruction. A "right to die" is surely strange and unprecedented, and hardly innocent. Accordingly, we need to consider carefully what it could possibly mean, why it is being asserted, and whether it really exists—that is, whether it can be given a principled grounding or defense.

A *RIGHT* TO DIE

Though the major ambiguity concerns the substance of the right—namely, to die—we begin by reminding ourselves of what it means, in general, to say that someone has a right to something. I depart for now from the original notion of *natural* rights, and indeed abstract altogether from the question of the source of rights. I focus instead on our contemporary usage, for it is only in contemporary usage that this current claim of a right to die can be understood.

A right, whether legal or moral, is not identical to a need or a desire or an interest or a capacity. I may have both a need and a desire for, and also an interest in, the possessions of another, and the capacity or power to take them by force or stealth—yet I can hardly be said to have a right to them. A right, to begin with, is a species of liberty. Thomas Hobbes, the first teacher of rights, held a right to be a *blameless* liberty. Not everything we are free to do, morally or legally, do we have a right to do: I may be at liberty to wear offensive perfumes or to sass my parents or to engage in unnatural sex, but it does not follow that I have a right to do so. Even the decriminalization of a once-forbidden act does not yet establish a legal right, not even if I can give reasons for doing it. Thus, the freedom to take my life—"I have inclination, means, reasons, opportunity, and you cannot stop me, and it is not against the law"—does not suffice to establish the *right* to take my life. A true right would be at least a blameless or permitted liberty, at best a praiseworthy or even rightful liberty, to do or not to do, without anyone else's interference or opposition.

Historically, the likelihood of outside interference and opposition was in fact the necessary condition for the assertion of rights. Rights were and are, to begin with, *political* creatures, the first principles of liberal politics. The rhetoric of claiming rights, which are in principle always absolute and unconditional, performs an important function of defense, but only because the sphere of life in which they are asserted is limited. Rights are asserted to protect, by deeming them blameless or rightful, certain liberties that others are denying or threatening to curtail. Rights are claimed to defend the safety and dignity of the individual against the dominion of tyrant, king, or prelate, and against those high-minded moralizers and zealous meddlers who seek to save man's soul or to preserve his honor at the cost of his life and liberty.

To these more classical, negative rights against interference with our liberties, modern thought has sought to add certain so-called welfare rights—rights that entitle us to certain opportunities or goods to which, it is argued, we have a rightful claim on others, usually government, to provide. The rhetoric of welfare rights extends the power of absolute and unqualified claims beyond the goals of defense against tyranny and beyond the limited sphere of endangered liberties; for these reasons their legitimacy as rights is often questioned. Yet even these ever-expanding lists of rights are not unlimited. I cannot be said to have a right to be loved by those who I hope will love me, or a right to become wise. There are many good things that I may rightfully possess and enjoy, but to which I have no claim if they are lacking. Most generally, then, having a right means having a *justified* claim against others that they act in a fitting manner: either that they refrain from interfering or that they deliver what is justly owed. It goes without saying that the mere assertion of a claim or demand, or the stipulation of a right, is insufficient to establish it; making a claim and actually having a rightful claim to make are not identical. In considering an alleged right to die, we must be careful to look for a *justifiable* liberty or claim, and not merely a desire, interest, power, or demand.

Rights seem to entail obligations: one person's right, whether to noninterference or to some entitled good or service, necessarily implies another person's obligation. It will be important later to consider what obligations on others might be entailed by enshrining a right to die.

A RIGHT *TO DIE*

Taken literally, a right to die would denote merely a right to the inevitable; the certainty of death for all that lives is the touchstone of fated inevitability. Why claim a right to what is not only unavoidable, but is even, generally speaking, an evil? Is death in danger of losing its inevitability? Are we in danger of bodily immortality? Has death, for us, become a good to be claimed rather than an evil to be shunned or conquered?

Not exactly and not yet, though these questions posed by the literal reading of "right to die" are surely germane. They hint at our growing disenchantment with the biomedical project, which seeks, in principle, to prolong life indefinitely. It is the already available means to sustain life for prolonged periods—not indefinitely, but far longer than is in many cases reasonable or desirable—that has made death so untimely late as to seem less than inevitable, that has made death, when it finally does occur, appear to be a blessing.

For we now have medical "treatments" (that is, interventions) that do not treat (that is, cure or ameliorate) specific diseases, but do nothing more than keep people alive by sustaining vital functions. The most notorious such device is the respirator. Others include simple yet still artificial devices for supplying food and water and the kidney dialysis machine for removing wastes. And, in the future, we shall have the artificial heart. These devices, backed by aggressive institutional policies favoring their use, are capable of keeping people alive, even when comatose, often for decades. The "right to die," in today's discourse, often refers to—and certainly is meant to embrace—a right to refuse such life-sustaining medical treatment.

But the "right to die" usually embraces also something more. The ambiguity of the term blurs over the difference in content and intention between the already well-established common-law right to refuse surgery or other unwanted medical treatments and hospitalization and the newly alleged "right to die." The former permits the refusal of therapy, even a respirator, even if it means accepting an increased risk of death. The latter permits the refusal of therapy, such as renal dialysis or the feeding tube, *so that* death *will* occur. The former seems more concerned with choosing how to live while dying; the latter seems mainly concerned with a choice *for death*. In this sense the claimed "right to die" is not a misnomer.

Still less is it a misnomer when we consider that some people who are claiming it demand not merely the discontinuance of treatment but positive assistance in bringing about their deaths. Here the right to die embraces the (welfare!) right to a lethal injection or an overdose of pills administered by oneself, by one's physician, or by someone else. This "right to die" would better be called a right to assisted suicide or a right to be mercifully killed—in short, a right *to become dead,* by assistance if necessary.

This, of course, looks a lot like a claim to a right to commit suicide, which need not have any connection to the problems of dying or medical technology. Some people in fact argue that the "right to die" through euthanasia or medically assisted suicide grows not from a right to refuse medical treatment but rather from this putative right to commit suicide (suicide is now decriminalized in most states). There does seem to be a world of moral difference between submitting to death (when the time has come) and killing yourself (in or out of season), or between permitting to die and causing death. But the boundary becomes fuzzy with the alleged right to refuse food and water, artificially delivered. Though few proponents of a right to die want the taint of a general defense of suicide (which though decriminalized remains in bad odor), they in fact presuppose its permissibility and go well beyond it. They claim not only a right to attempt suicide but a right to succeed, and this means, in practice, a *right to the deadly assistance of others.* It is thus certainly proper to understand the "right to die" in its most radical sense, namely, as a right to become or to be made dead, by whatever means.

This way of putting the matter will not sit well with those who see the right to die less as a matter of life and death, more as a matter of autonomy or dignity. For them the right to die means the right to continue, despite disability, to exercise control over one's own destiny. It means, in one formulation, not the right to become dead, but the right to choose the manner, the timing, and the circumstances of one's death, or the right to choose what one regards as the most humane or dignified way to finish out one's life. Here the right to die means either the right to self-command or the right to death with dignity—claims that would oblige others, at a minimum, to stop interfering, but also, quite commonly, to "assist self-command" or to "provide dignity" by participating in bringing one's life to an end, according to plan. In the end, these proper and high-minded demands for autonomy and dignity turn out in most cases to embrace also a right to become dead, with assistance if necessary.

This analysis of current usage shows why one might be properly confused about the meaning of the term "right to die." In public discourse today, it merges all the aforementioned meanings: right to refuse treatment even if, or so that, death may occur; right to be killed or to become dead; right to control one's own dying; right to die with dignity; right to assistance in death. Some of this confusion inheres in the term; some of it is deliberately fostered by proponents of all these "rights," who hope thereby to gain assent to the more extreme claims by merging them with the more modest ones. Partly for this reason, however, we do well to regard the "right to die" at its most radical—and I will do so in this essay—as a right to become dead, by active means and if necessary with the assistance of others. In this way we take seriously and do justice to the novelty and boldness of the claim, a claim that intends to go beyond both the existing common-law right to refuse unwanted medical treatment and the so-called right to commit suicide all by oneself. (The first right is indisputable, the second, while debatable, will not be contested in this essay.

What concerns us here is those aspects of the "right to die" that go beyond a right to attempt suicide and a right to refuse treatment.)

Having sought to clarify the meaning of "right to die," we face next the even greater confusion about who it is that allegedly has such a right. Is it only those who are "certifiably" terminally ill and irreversibly dying, with or without medical treatment? Also those who are incurably ill and severely incapacitated, although definitely not dying? Everyone, mentally competent or not? Does a senile person have a "right to die" if he is incapable of claiming it for himself? Do I need to be able to claim *and act* on such a right in order to have it, or can proxies be designated to exercise my right to die on my behalf? If the right to die is essentially an expression of my autonomy, how can anyone else exercise it for me?

Equally puzzling is the question, Against whom or what is a right to die being asserted? Is it a liberty right mainly against those officious meddlers who keep me from dying—against those doctors, nurses, hospitals, right-to-life groups, and district attorneys who interfere either with my ability to die (by machinery and hospitalization) or with my ability to gain help in ending my life (by criminal sanctions against assisting suicide)? If it is a right to become dead, is it not also a welfare right claimed against those who do not yet assist—a right demanding also the provision of the poison that I have permission to take? (Compare the liberty right to seek an abortion with the welfare right to obtain one.) Or is it, at bottom, a demand asserted also *against nature,* which has dealt me a bad hand by keeping me alive, beyond my wishes and beneath my dignity, and alas without terminal illness, too senile or enfeebled to make matters right?

The most radical formulations, whether in the form of "a right to become dead" or "a right to control my destiny" or "a right to dignity," are, I am convinced, the complaint of human pride against what our tyrannical tendencies lead us to experience as "cosmic injustice, directed against me." Here the ill-fated demand a right not to be ill-fated; those who want to die, but cannot, claim a right to die, which becomes, as Harvey Mansfield has put it, a tort claim against nature. It thus becomes the business of the well-fated to correct nature's mistreatment of the ill-fated by *making them dead.* Thus would the same act that was only yesterday declared a crime against humanity become a mandated act, not only of compassionate charity but of compensatory justice!

WHY ASSERT A RIGHT TO DIE?

Before proceeding to the more challenging question of the existence and ground of a "right to die," it would be useful briefly to consider why such a right is being asserted, and by whom. Some of the reasons have already been noted in passing:

- fear of prolongation of dying due to medical intervention; hence, a right to refuse treatment or hospitalization, even if death occurs as a result;
- fear of living too long, without fatal illness to carry one off; hence, a right to assisted suicide;
- fear of the degradations of senility and dependence; hence, a right to death with dignity;
- fear of loss of control; hence, a right to choose the time and manner of one's death.

Equally important for many people is the fear of becoming a burden to others—financial, psychic, social. Few parents, however eager or willing they might be to stay alive, are pleased by the prospect that they might thereby destroy their children's and grandchildren's opportunities for happiness. Indeed, my own greatest weakening on the subject of euthanasia is precisely this: I would confess a strong temptation to remove myself from life to spare my children the anguish of years of attending my demented self and the horrible likelihood that they will come, hatefully to themselves, to resent my continued existence. Such reasons in favor of death might even lead me to think I had a *duty* to die—they do not, however, establish for me any right to become dead.[1]

But the advocates of a "right to die" are not always so generous. On the contrary, much dishonesty and mischief are afoot. Many people have seen the advantage of using the language of individual rights, implying voluntary action, to shift the national attitudes regarding life and death, to prepare the way for the practice of terminating "useless" lives.[2]

Many who argue for a right to die mean for people not merely to have it but to exercise it with dispatch, so as to decrease the mounting socioeconomic costs of caring for the irreversibly ill and dying. In fact, most of the people now agitating for a "right to die" are themselves neither ill nor dying. Children looking at parents who are not dying fast enough, hospital administrators and health economists concerned about cost-cutting and waste, doctors disgusted with caring for incurables, people with eugenic or aesthetic interests who are repelled by the prospect of a society in which the young and vigorous expend enormous energy to keep alive the virtually dead—all these want to change our hard-won ethic in favor of life.

But they are either too ashamed or too shrewd to state their true intentions. Much better to trumpet a right to die, and encourage people to exercise it. These advocates understand all too well that the present American climate requires one to talk of rights if one wishes to have one's way in such moral matters. Consider the analogous use of arguments for abortion rights by organizations which hope thereby to get women—especially the poor, the unmarried, and the nonwhite—to exercise their "right to choose," to do their supposed duty toward limiting population growth and the size of the underclass.

This is not to say that all reasons for promoting a "right to die" are suspect. Nor do I mean to suggest that it would never be right or good for someone to elect to die. But it might be dangerous folly to circumvent the grave need for prudence in these matters by substituting the confused yet absolutized principle of a "right to die," especially given the mixed motives and dangerous purposes of some of its proponents.

Truth to tell, public discourse about moral matters in the United States is much impoverished by our eagerness to transform questions of the right and the good into questions about individual rights. Partly, this is a legacy of modern liberalism, the political philosophy on which the genius of the American republic mainly rests. But it is augmented by American self-assertion and individualism, increasingly so in an age when family and other mediating institutions are in decline and the naked individual is left face to face with the bureaucratic state.

But the language of rights gained a tremendous boost from the moral absolutism of the 1960s, with the discovery that the nonnegotiable and absolutized character of all rights claims provides the most durable battering ram against the status quo. Never mind that it fuels resentments and breeds hatreds, that it ignores the consequences to society, or that it short-circuits a political process that is more amenable to working out a balanced view of the common good. Never mind all that: go to court and demand your rights. And the courts have been all too willing to oblige, finding or inventing new rights in the process.

These sociocultural changes, having nothing to do with death and dying, surely are part of the reason we are now confronted with vociferous claims of a right to die. These changes are also part of the reason why, despite its notorious difficulties, a right to die is the leading moral concept advanced to address these most complicated and delicate human matters at the end of life. Yet the reasons for the assertion, even if suspect, do not settle the question of truth, to which, at long last, we finally turn. Let us examine whether philosophically . . . we can truly speak of a right to die.

IS THERE A RIGHT TO DIE?

Philosophically speaking, it makes sense to take our bearings from those great thinkers of modernity who are the originators and most thoughtful exponents of our rights-based thinking. They above all are likely to have understood the purpose, character, grounds, and limits for the assertion of rights. If a newly asserted right, such as the right to die, cannot be established on the natural or rational ground for rights offered by these thinkers, the burden of proof must fall on the proponents of novel rights, to provide a new yet equally solid ground in support of their novel claims.

If we start at the beginning, with the great philosophical teachers of natural rights, the very notion of a right to die would be nonsensical. As we learn from Hobbes and from John Locke, all the rights of man, given by nature, presuppose our self-interested attachment to our own lives. All natural rights trace home to the primary right to life, or better, the right to self-preservation—itself rooted in the powerful, self-loving impulses and passions that seek our own continuance, and asserted first against deadly, oppressive policies or against those who might insist that morality requires me to turn the other cheek when my life is threatened. Mansfield summarizes the classical position elegantly:

> Rights are given to men by nature, but they are needed because men are also subject to nature's improvidence. Since life is in danger, men's equal rights would be to life, to the liberty that protects life, and to the pursuit of the happiness with which life, or a tenuous life, is occupied.
>
> In practice, the pursuit of happiness will be the pursuit of property, for even though property is less valuable than life or liberty, it serves as guard for them. Quite apart from the pleasures of being rich, having secure property shows that one has liberty secure from invasion either by the government or by others; and secure liberty is the best sign of a secure life.[3]

Because death, my extinction, is the evil whose avoidance is the condition of the possibility of my having any and all of my goods, my right to secure my life against death—that is, my rightful liberty to self-preservative conduct—is the bedrock of all other rights and of all politically relevant morality. Even Hans Jonas, writing to defend "the right to die," acknowledges that it stands alone, and concedes that "every other right ever argued, claimed, granted, or denied can be viewed as an extension of this primary right [to life], since every particular right concerns the exercise of some faculty of life, the access to some necessity of life, the satisfaction of some aspiration of life."[4] It is obvious that one cannot found on this rock any right to die or right to become dead. Life loves to live, and it needs all the help it can get.

This is not to say that these early modern thinkers were unaware that men might tire of life or might come to find existence burdensome. But the decline in the will to live did not for them drive out or nullify the right to life, much less lead to a trumping new right, a right to die. For the right to life is a matter of nature, not will. Locke addresses and rejects a natural right to suicide, in his discussion of the state of nature:

> But though this be a state of liberty, yet it is not a state of license; though man in that state has an uncontrollable liberty to dispose of his person or possessions, yet he has not liberty to destroy himself, or so much as any creature in his possession, but where some nobler use than its bare preservation calls for it. The state of nature has a law of nature to govern it, which obliges everyone; and reason, which is that law, teaches all mankind who will but consult it, that, being all equal and independent, no one ought to harm another in his life, health, liberty, or possessions.[5]

Admittedly, the argument here turns explicitly theological—we are said to be our wise Maker's property. But the argument against a man's willful "quitting of his station" seems, for Locke, to be a corollary of the natural inclination and right of self-preservation.

Some try to argue, wrongly in my view, that Locke's teaching on property rests on a principle of self-ownership, which can then be used to justify self-destruction: since I own my body and my life, I may do with them as I please. As this argument has much currency, it is worth examining in greater detail. Locke does indeed say something that seems at first glance to suggest self-ownership:

> Though the earth and all inferior creatures be common to all men, *yet every man has a property in his own person;* this nobody has a right to but himself. The labor of his body and the work of his hands we may say are properly his.[6]

But the context defines and constricts the claim. Unlike the property rights in the fruits of his labor, the property a man has in his own person is inalienable: a man cannot transfer title to himself by selling himself into slavery. The "property in his own person" is less a metaphysical statement declaring self-ownership, more a political statement denying ownership by another. This right removes each and every human being from the commons available to all human beings for appropriation and use. My body and my life are my property *only in the limited sense* that they are *not yours*. They are different from my alienable property—my house, my car, my shoes. My body and my life, while mine to use, are not mine to dispose of. In the deepest sense, my body is nobody's body, not even mine.[7]

Even if one continues, against reason, to hold to strict self-ownership and self-disposability, there is a further argument, one that is decisive. Self-ownership might enable one at most to justify *attempting* suicide; it cannot justify a right to succeed or, more important, a right to the assistance of others. The designated potential assistant-in-death has neither a natural duty nor a natural right to become an actual assistant-in-death, and the liberal state, instituted above all to protect life, can never countenance such a right to kill, even on request. A right to become dead or to be made dead cannot be sustained on classical liberal grounds.

Later thinkers in the liberal tradition, including those who prized freedom above preservation, also make no room for a "right to die." Jean-Jacques Rousseau's complaints about the ills of civil society centered especially and most powerfully on the threats to life and limb from a social order whose main purpose should have been to protect them.[8] And Immanuel Kant, for whom rights are founded not in nature but in reason, holds that the self-willed act of self-destruction is simply self-contradictory.

> It seems absurd that a man can injure himself (*volenti non fit injuria* [Injury cannot happen to one who is willing]). The Stoic therefore considered it a prerogative of his personality as a wise man to walk out of his life with an undisturbed mind whenever he liked (as out of a smoke-filled room), not because he was afflicted by actual or anticipated ills, but simply because he could make use of nothing more in this life. And yet this very courage, this strength of mind—of not fearing death and of knowing of something which man can prize more highly than his life—ought to have been an ever so much greater motive for him not to

destroy himself, a being having such authoritative superiority over the strongest sensible incentives; consequently, it ought to have been a motive for him not to deprive himself of life.

Man cannot deprive himself of his personhood so long as one speaks of duties, thus so long as he lives. That man ought to have the authorization to withdraw himself from all obligation, i.e., to be free to act as if no authorization at all were required for this withdrawal, involves a contradiction. To destroy the subject of morality in his own person is tantamount to obliterating from the world, as far as he can, the very existence of morality itself; but morality is, nevertheless, an end in itself. Accordingly, to dispose of oneself as a mere means to some end of one's own liking is to degrade the humanity in one's person *(homo noumenon)*, which, after all, was entrusted to man *(homo phoenomenon)* to preserve.[9]

It is a heavy irony that it should be autonomy, the moral notion that the world owes mainly to Kant, that is now invoked as the justifying ground of a right to die. For Kant, autonomy, which literally means self-legislation, requires acting in accordance with one's true self—that is, with one's rational will determined by a universalizable, that is, rational, maxim. Being autonomous means not being a slave to instinct, impulse, or whim, but rather doing as one ought, as a rational being. But autonomy has now come to mean "doing as you please," compatible no less with self-indulgence than with self-control. Herewith one sees clearly the triumph of the Nietzschean self, who finds reason just as enslaving as blind instinct and who finds his true "self" rather in unconditioned acts of pure creative will.

Yet even in its willful modern meaning, "autonomy" cannot ground a right to die. First, one cannot establish on this basis a right to have *someone else's* assistance in committing suicide—a right, by the way, that would impose an obligation on someone else and thereby restrict *his* autonomy. Second, even if my choice for death were "reasonable" and my chosen assistant freely willing, my autonomy cannot ground *his right* to kill me, and, hence, it cannot ground my right to become dead. Third, a liberty right to an assisted death (that is, a right against interference) can at most approve assisted suicide or euthanasia for the mentally competent and alert—a restriction that would prohibit effecting the deaths of the mentally incompetent or comatose patients who have not left explicit instructions regarding their treatment. It is, by the way, a long philosophical question whether all such instructions must be obeyed, for the person who gave them long ago may no longer be "the same person" when they become relevant. Can my fifty-three-year-old self truly prescribe today the best interests for my seventy-five-year-old and senile self?

In contrast to arguments presented in recent court cases, it is self-contradictory to assert that a proxy not chosen by the patient can exercise the patient's rights of autonomy. Can a citizen have a right to vote that would be irrevocably exercised "on his behalf," and in the name of his autonomy, by the government?[10] Finally, if autonomy and dignity lie in the free exercise of will and choice, it is at least paradoxical to say that our autonomy licenses an act that puts our autonomy permanently out of business.

It is precisely this paradox that appeals to the Nietzschean creative self, the bearer of so many of this century's "new rights." As Mansfield brilliantly shows, the creative ones are not bound by normality or good sense:

Creative beings are open-ended. They are open-ended in fact and not merely in their formal potentialities. Such beings do not have interests; for who can say what is in the interest of a being that is becoming something unknown? Thus the society of new rights is characterized by a loss of predictability and normality: no one knows what to expect, even from his closest companions.[11]

The most authentic self-creative self revels in the unpredictable, the extreme, the perverse. He does not even flinch before self-contradiction; indeed, he can display the triumph of his will most especially in self-negation. And though it may revolt us, who are we to deny him this form of self-expression? Supremely tolerant of the rights of others to their own eccentricities, we avert our glance and turn the other moral cheek. Here at last is the only possible philosophical ground for a right to die: arbitrary will, backed by moral relativism. Which is to say, no ground at all.

• • •

THE TRAGIC MEANING OF "RIGHT TO DIE"

The claim of a "right to die," asserted especially against physicians bent on prolonging life, clearly exposes certain deep difficulties in the foundations of modern society. Modern liberal, technological society rests especially upon two philosophical pillars raised first in the seventeenth century, at the beginning of the modern era: the preeminence of the human individual, embodied in the doctrine of natural rights as espoused first by Hobbes and Locke; and the idea of mastery of nature, attained through a radically new science of nature as proposed by Francis Bacon and René Descartes.

Both ideas were responses to the perceived partial inhospitality of nature to human need. Both encouraged man's opposition to nature, the first through the flight from the state of nature into civil society for the purpose of safeguarding the precarious rights to life and liberty; the second through the subduing of nature for the purpose of making life longer, healthier, and more commodious. One might even say that it is especially an opposition to death that grounds these twin responses. Politically, the fear of violent death at the hands of warring men requires law and legitimate authority to secure natural rights, especially life. Technologically, the fear of death as such at the hands of unfriendly nature inspires a bolder approach, namely, a scientific medicine to wage war against disease and even against death itself, ultimately with a promise of bodily immortality.

Drunk on its political and scientific successes, modern thought and practice have abandoned the modest and moderate beginnings of political modernity. In civil society the natural rights of self-preservation, secured through active but moderate self-assertion, have given way to the non-natural rights of self-creation and self-expression; the new rights have no connection to nature or to reason, but appear as the rights of the untrammeled will. The "self" that here asserts itself is not a natural self, with the predictable interests given it by a universal human nature with its bodily needs, but a uniquely individuated and self-made self. Its authentic selfhood is demonstrated by its ability to say no to the needs of the body, the rules of society, and the dictates of reason. For such a self, self-negation through suicide and the right to die can be the ultimate form of self-assertion.

In medical science, the unlimited battle against death has found nature unwilling to roll over and play dead. The successes of medicine so far are partial at best and the victory incomplete, to say the least. The welcome triumphs against disease have been purchased at the price of the medicalized dehumanization of the end of life: to put it starkly, once we lick cancer and stroke, we can all live long enough to get Alzheimer's disease. And if the insurance holds out, we can die in the intensive care unit, suitably intubated. Fear of the very medical power we engaged to do battle against death now leads us to demand that it give us poison.

Finally, both the triumph of individualism and our reliance on technology (not only in medicine) and on government to satisfy our new wants-demanded-as-rights have weakened our more natural human associations—especially the family, on which we all need to rely when our pretense to autonomy and mastery is eventually exposed by unavoidable decline. Old age and death have been taken out of the bosom of family life and turned over to state-supported nursing homes and hospitals. Not the clergyman but the doctor (in truth, the nurse) presides over the end of life, in sterile surroundings that make no concessions to our finitude. Both the autonomous will and the will's partner in pride, the death-denying doctor, ignore the unavoidable limits on will and technique that nature insists on. Failure to recognize these limits now threatens the entire venture, for rebellion against the project through a "right to die" will only radicalize its difficulties. Vulnerable life will no longer be protected by the state, medicine will become a death-dealing profession, and isolated individuals will be technically dispatched to avoid the troubles of finding human ways to keep company with them in their time of ultimate need.

• • •

Nothing I have said should be taken to mean that I believe life should be extended under all circumstances and at all costs. Far from it. I continue, with fear and trembling, to defend the practice of allowing to die while opposing the practice of deliberately killing—despite the blurring of this morally bright line implicit in the artificial food and water cases, and despite the slide toward the retailing of death that continues on the sled of a right to refuse treatment. I welcome efforts to give patients as much choice as possible in how they are to live out the end of their lives. I continue to applaud those courageous patients and family members and those conscientious physicians who try prudently to discern, in each case, just what form of treatment or nontreatment is truly good for the patient, even if it embraces an increased likelihood of death. But I continue to insist that we cannot serve the patient's good by deliberately eliminating the patient. And if we have no right to do this to another, we have no right to have others do this to ourselves. There is, when all is said and done, no defensible right to die.

A CODA: ABOUT RIGHTS

The rhetoric of rights still performs today the noble, time-honored function of protecting individual life and liberty, a function now perhaps even more necessary than the originators of such rhetoric could have imagined, given the tyrannical possibilities of the modern bureaucratic and technologically competent state. But with the claim of a "right to die," as with so many of the novel rights being asserted in recent years, we face an extension of this rhetoric into areas where it no longer relates to that protective function, and beyond the limited area of life in which rights claims are clearly appropriate and indeed crucial. As a result, we face a number of serious and potentially dangerous distortions in our thought and in our practice. We distort our understanding of rights and weaken their respect-ability in their proper sphere by allowing them to be invented—without ground in nature or in reason—in response to moral questions that lie outside the limited domain of rights. We distort our understanding of moral deliberation and the moral life by reducing all complicated questions of right and good to questions of individual rights. We subvert the primacy and necessity of prudence by pretending that the assertion of rights will produce the best—and most moral—results. In trying to batter our way through the human condition with the bludgeon of personal rights, we allow ourselves to be deceived about the most fundamental matters: about death and dying, about our unavoidable finitude, and about the sustaining interdependencies of our lives.

Let us, by all means, continue to deliberate about whether and when and why it might make sense for someone to give up on his life, or even actively to choose death. But let us call a halt to all this dangerous thoughtlessness about rights. Let us refuse to talk any longer about a "right to die."

NOTES

1. For my "generosity" to succeed, I would, of course, have to commit suicide without assistance and without anyone's discovering it—i.e., well before I were demented. I would not want my children to believe that I suspected them of being incapable of loving me through my inevitable decline. There is another still more powerful reason for resisting this temptation: is it not unreasonably paternalistic of me to try to order the world so as to free my children from the usual intergenerational experiences, ties, obligations, and burdens? What principle of family life am I enacting and endorsing with my "altruistic suicide"?

2. Here is a recent example from a professor of sociology who objected to my condemnation of Derek Humphry's *Final Exit:*

> Is Mr. Kass absolutely opposed to suicide? Would he have dissuaded Hitler? Would he disapprove of suicide by Pol Pot? . . . If we would welcome suicide by certain figures on limited occasions, should we prolong the lives of people who lived useless, degrading or dehumanized lives; who inflicted these indignities upon others; or who led vital lives but were reduced to uselessness and degradation by incurable disease? (*Commentary,* May 1992, p. 12).

3. Harvey C. Mansfield, Jr., "The Old Rights and the New: Responsibility vs. Self-Expression," in *Old Rights and New,* ed. Robert A. Licht (Washington: American Enterprise Institute, 1993), in press.

4. Hans Jonas, "The Right to Die," *Hastings Center Report* 8, no. 4 (1978): 31–36, at 31.

5. John Locke, *Second Treatise on Civil Government,* ch. 2, "Of the State of Nature," para. 6.

6. Locke, *Second Treatise,* ch. 5, "Of Property," para. 27. Emphasis added.

7. Later, in discussing the extent of legislative power, Locke denies to the legislative, though it be the supreme power in every commonwealth, arbitrary power over the individual and, in particular, power to destroy his life. "For nobody can transfer to another more power than he has in himself; and nobody has an absolute arbitrary power over himself or over any other to destroy his own life, or take away the life or property of another." *Second Treatise,* ch. 9, "Of the Extent of the Legislative Power," para. 135. Because the state's power derives from the people's power, the person's lack of arbitrary power over himself is the ground for restricting the state's power to kill him.

8. See, for example, Rousseau, *Discourse on the Origin and Foundations of Inequality among Men,* note 9, especially paragraphs four and five.

9. Immanuel Kant, *The Metaphysical Principles of Virtue,* trans. James Ellington (Indianapolis: Bobbs-Merrill, 1964), pp. 83–84. My purpose in citing Kant here is not to defend Kantian morality—and I am not myself a Kantian—but simply to show that the thinker who thought most deeply about rights in relation to *reason* and *autonomy* would have found the idea of a "right to die" utterly indefensible on these grounds.

10. The attempt to ground a right to die in the so-called right to privacy fails for the same reasons. A right to make independent judgments regarding one's body in one's private sphere, free of governmental inference, cannot be the basis of the right of someone else, appointed by or protected by government, to put an end to one's bodily life.

11. Mansfield, "The Old Rights and the New." This permanent instability of "the self" defeats the main benefit of a rights-based politics, which knows how to respect individual rights precisely because they are understood to be rooted in a common human nature, with reliable common interests, both natural and rational. The self-determining self, because it is variable, also turns out to be an embarrassment for attempts to respect prior acts of self-determination, as in the case of living wills. For if the "self" is truly constantly being recreated, there is no reason to honor today "its" prescriptions of yesterday, for the two selves are not the same.

The Legal Background in the United States

The Oregon Death with Dignity Act

ALLOWS TERMINALLY ILL ADULTS
TO OBTAIN PRESCRIPTION
FOR LETHAL DRUGS

Question. Shall law allow terminally ill adult patients voluntary informed choice to obtain physician's prescription for drugs to end life?

Summary. Adopts law. Allows terminally ill adult Oregon residents voluntary informed choice to obtain physician's prescription for drugs to end life. Removes criminal penalties for qualifying physician-assisted suicide. Applies when physicians predict patient's death within 6 months. Requires:

15-day waiting period;

2 oral, 1 written request;

second physician's opinion;

counseling if either physician believes patient has mental disorder, impaired judgment from depression.

Person has choice whether to notify next of kin. Health care providers immune from civil, criminal liability for good faith compliance. . . .

SECTION 2: WRITTEN REQUEST FOR MEDICATION TO END ONE'S LIFE IN A HUMANE AND DIGNIFIED MANNER

§ 2.01 WHO MAY INITIATE A WRITTEN REQUEST FOR MEDICATION

An adult who is capable, is a resident of Oregon, and has been determined by the attending physician and consulting physician to be suffering from a terminal disease, and who has voluntarily expressed his or her wish to die, may make a written request for medication for the purpose of ending his or her life in a humane and dignified manner in accordance with this Act. . . .

SECTION 3: SAFEGUARDS

§ 3.01 ATTENDING PHYSICIAN RESPONSIBILITIES

The attending physician shall:

1. Make the initial determination of whether a patient has a terminal disease, is capable, and has made the request voluntarily;
2. Inform the patient of:
   (a) his or her medical diagnosis;
   (b) his or her prognosis;
   (c) the potential risks associated with taking the medication to be prescribed;
   (d) the probable result of taking the medication to be prescribed;
   (e) the feasible alternatives, including, but not limited to, comfort care, hospice care and pain control.
3. Refer the patient to a consulting physician for medical confirmation of the diagnosis, and for a determination that the patient is capable and acting voluntarily;
4. Refer the patient for counseling if appropriate pursuant to Section 3.03;
5. Request that the patient notify next of kin;
6. Inform the patient that he or she has an opportunity to rescind the request at any time and in any manner, and offer the patient an opportunity to rescind at the end of the 15-day waiting period pursuant to Section 3.06;
7. Verify, immediately prior to writing the prescription for medication under this Act, that the patient is making an informed decision;
8. Fulfill the medical record documentation requirements of Section 3.09;
9. Ensure that all appropriate steps are carried out in accordance with this Act prior to writing a prescription for medication to enable a qualified patient to end his or her life in a humane and dignified manner.

§ 3.02 CONSULTING PHYSICIAN CONFIRMATION

Before a patient is qualified under this Act, a consulting physician shall examine the patient and his or her relevant medical records and confirm, in writing, the attending physician's diagnosis that the patient is suffering from a terminal disease, and verify that the patient is capable, is acting voluntarily and has made an informed decision.

§ 3.03 COUNSELING REFERRAL

If in the opinion of the attending physician or the consulting physician a patient may be suffering from a psychiatric or psychological disorder, or depression causing impaired judgment, either physician shall refer the patient for counseling. No medication to end a patient's life in a humane and dignified manner shall be prescribed until the person performing the counseling determines that the patient is not suffering from a psychiatric or psychological disorder, or depression causing impaired judgment.

§ 3.04 INFORMED DECISION

No person shall receive a prescription for medication to end his or her life in a humane and dignified manner unless he or she has made an informed decision as defined in Section 1.01(7). Immediately prior to writing a prescription for medication under this Act, the attending physician shall verify that the patient is making an informed decision.

§ 3.05 FAMILY NOTIFICATION

The attending physician shall ask the patient to notify next of kin of his or her request for medication pursuant to this Act. A patient who declines or is unable to notify next of kin shall not have his or her request denied for that reason.

§ 3.06 WRITTEN AND ORAL REQUESTS

In order to receive a prescription for medication to end his or her life in a humane and dignified manner, a qualified patient shall have made an oral request and a written request, and reiterate the oral request to his or her attending physician no less than fifteen (15) days after making the initial oral request. At the time the qualified patient makes his or her second oral request, the attending physician shall offer the patient an opportunity to rescind the request.

§ 3.07 RIGHT TO RESCIND REQUEST

A patient may rescind his or her request at any time and in any manner without regard to his or her mental state. No prescription for medication under this Act may be written without the attending physician offering the qualified patient an opportunity to rescind the request.

§ 3.08 WAITING PERIODS

No less than fifteen (15) days shall elapse between the patient's initial oral request and the writing of a prescription under this Act. No less than 48 hours shall elapse between the patient's written request and the writing of a prescription under the Act.

§ 3.09 MEDICAL RECORD DOCUMENTATION REQUIREMENTS

The following shall be documented or filed in the patient's medical record:

1. All oral requests by a patient for medication to end his or her life in a humane and dignified manner;
2. All written requests by a patient for medication to end his or her life in a humane and dignified manner;
3. The attending physician's diagnosis and prognosis, determination that the patient is capable, acting voluntarily and has made an informed decision;
4. The consulting physician's diagnosis and prognosis, and verification that the patient is capable, acting voluntarily and has made an informed decision;
5. A report of the outcome and determinations made during counseling, if performed;
6. The attending physician's offer to the patient to rescind his or her request at the time of the patient's second oral request pursuant to Section 3.06; and
7. A note by the attending physician indicating that all requirements under this Act have been met and indicating the steps taken to carry out the request, including a notation of the medication prescribed.

§ 3.10 RESIDENCY REQUIREMENTS

Only requests made by Oregon residents, under this Act, shall be granted.

§ 3.11 REPORTING REQUIREMENTS

1. The Health Division shall annually review a sample of records maintained pursuant to this Act.
2. The Health Division shall make rules to facili-

tate the collection of information regarding compliance with this Act. The information collected shall not be a public record and may not be made available for inspection by the public.

3. The Health Division shall generate and make available to the public an annual statistical report of information collected under Section 3.11(2) of this Act.

§ 3.12 EFFECT ON CONSTRUCTION OF WILLS, CONTRACTS, AND STATUTES

1. No provision in a contract, will or other agreement, whether written or oral, to the extent the provision would affect whether a person may make or rescind a request for medication to end his or her life in a humane and dignified manner, shall be valid.
2. No obligation owing under any currently existing contract shall be conditioned or affected by the making or rescinding of a request, by a person, for medication to end his or her life in a humane and dignified manner.

§ 3.13 INSURANCE OR ANNUITY POLICIES

The sale, procurement, or issuance of any life, health, or accident insurance or annuity policy or the rate charged for any policy shall not be conditioned upon or affected by the making or rescinding of a request, by a person, for medication to end his or her life in a humane and dignified manner. Neither shall a qualified patient's act of ingesting medication to end his her life in a humane and dignified manner have an effect upon a life, health, or accident insurance or annuity policy.

§ 3.14 CONSTRUCTION OF ACT

Nothing in this Act shall be construed to authorize a physician or any other person to end a patient's life by lethal injection, mercy killing or active euthanasia. Actions taken in accordance with this Act shall not, for any purpose, constitute suicide, assisted suicide, mercy killing or homicide, under the law.

SECTION 4: IMMUNITIES AND LIABILITIES

§ 4.01 IMMUNITIES

Except as provided in Section 4.02:

1. No person shall be subject to civil or criminal liability or professional disciplinary action for participating in good faith compliance with this Act. This includes being present when a qualified patient takes the prescribed medication to end his or her life in a humane and dignified manner.
2. No professional organization or association, or health care provider, may subject a person to censure, discipline, suspension, loss of license, loss of privileges, loss of membership or other penalty for participating or refusing to participate in good faith compliance with this Act.
3. No request by a patient for or provision by an attending physician of medication in good faith compliance with the provisions of this Act shall constitute neglect for any purpose of law or provide the sole basis for the appointment of a guardian or conservator.
4. No health care provider shall be under any duty, whether by contract, by statute or by any other legal requirement to participate in the provision to a qualified patient of medication to end his or her life in a humane and dignified manner. If a health care provider is unable or unwilling to carry out a patient's request under this Act, and the patient transfers his or her care to a new health care provider, the prior health care provider shall transfer, upon request, a copy of the patient's relevant medical records to the new health care provider.

§ 4.02 LIABILITIES

1. A person who without authorization of the patient willfully alters or forges a request for medication or conceals or destroys a rescission of that request with the intent or effect of causing the patient's death shall be guilty of a Class A felony.
2. A person who coerces or exerts undue influence on a patient to request medication for the purpose of ending the patient's life, or to destroy a rescission of such a request, shall be guilty of a Class A felony. . . .

SECTION 6: FORM OF THE REQUEST

§ 6.01 FORM OF THE REQUEST

A request for medication as authorized by this act shall be in substantially the [boxed] form.

REQUEST FOR MEDICATION TO END MY LIFE IN A HUMANE AND DIGNIFIED MANNER

I, ____________________________, am an adult of sound mind.

I am suffering from ___________________________, which my attending physician has determined is a terminal disease and which has been medically confirmed by a consulting physician.

I have been fully informed of my diagnosis, prognosis, the nature of medication to be prescribed and potential associated risks, the expected result, and the feasible alternatives, including comfort care, hospice care and pain control.

I request that my attending physician prescribe medication that will end my life in a humane and dignified manner.

INITIAL ONE:

_____ I have informed my family of my decision and taken their opinions into consideration.
_____ I have decided not to inform my family of my decision.
_____ I have no family to inform of my decision.

I understand that I have the right to rescind this request at any time.
I understand the full import of this request and I expect to die when I take the medication to be prescribed.
I make this request voluntarily and without reservation, and I accept full moral responsibility for my actions.

Signed:____

Dated:____

DECLARATION OF WITNESSES

We declare that the person signing this request:

(a) Is personally known to us or has provided proof of identity;
(b) Signed this request in our presence;
(c) Appears to be of sound mind and not under duress, fraud or undue influence;
(d) Is not a patient for whom either of us is attending physician.

____________________________________Witness 1/Date

____________________________________Witness 2/Date

NOTE: one witness shall not be a relative (by blood, marriage or adoption) of the person signing this request, shall not be entitled to any portion of the person's estate upon death and shall not own, operate or be employed at a health care facility where the person is a patient or resident. If the patient is an inpatient at a health care facility, one of the witnesses shall be an individual designated by the facility.

UNITED STATES SUPREME COURT

Dennis C. Vacco, Attorney General of New York, et al., Petitioners v. Timothy E. Quill et al.

On Writ of Certiorari to the United States Court of Appeals for the Second Circuit

CHIEF JUSTICE REHNQUIST delivered the opinion of the Court.

In New York, as in most States, it is a crime to aid another to commit or attempt suicide, but patients may refuse even lifesaving medical treatment. The question presented by this case is whether New York's prohibition on assisting suicide therefore violates the Equal Protection Clause of the Fourteenth Amendment. We hold that it does not. . . .

The Equal Protection Clause commands that no State shall "deny to any person within its jurisdiction the equal protection of the laws." This provision creates no substantive rights. . . . Instead, it embodies a general rule that States must treat like cases alike but may treat unlike cases accordingly. . . .

On their faces, neither New York's ban on assisting suicide nor its statutes permitting patients to refuse medical treatment treat anyone differently than anyone else or draw any distinction between persons. *Everyone,* regardless of physical condition, is entitled, if competent, to refuse unwanted lifesaving medical treatment; *no one* is permitted to assist a suicide. Generally speaking, laws that apply evenhandedly to all "unquestionably comply" with the Equal Protection Clause. . . .

The Court of Appeals, however, concluded that some terminally ill people—those who are on life-support systems—are treated differently than those who are not, in that the former may "hasten death" by ending treatment, but the latter may not "hasten death" through physician-assisted suicide. 80 F. 3d, at 729. This conclusion depends on the submission that ending or refusing lifesaving medical treatment "is nothing more nor less than assisted suicide." *Ibid.* Unlike the Court of Appeals, we think the distinction between assisting suicide and withdrawing life-sustaining treatment, a distinction widely recognized and endorsed in the medical profession and in our legal traditions, is both important and logical; it is certainly rational. . . .

The distinction comports with fundamental legal principles of causation and intent. First, when a patient refuses life-sustaining medical treatment, he dies from an underlying fatal disease of pathology; but if a patient ingests lethal medication prescribed by a physician, he is killed by that medication. . . .

Furthermore, a physician who withdraws, or honors a patient's refusal to begin, life-sustaining medical treatment purposefully intends, or may so intend, only to respect his patient's wishes and "to cease doing useless and futile or degrading things to the patient when [the patient] no longer stands to benefit from them." Assisted Suicide in the United States, Hearing before the Subcommittee on the Constitution of the House Committee on the Judiciary, 104th Cong., 2d Sess., 368 (1996) (testimony of Dr. Leon R. Kass). The same is true when a doctor provides aggressive palliative care; in some cases, painkilling drugs may hasten a patient's death, but the physician's purpose and intent is, or may be, only to ease his patient's pain. A doctor who assists a suicide, however, "must,

521 U.S. 793; 117 S. Ct. 2293; 138 L. Ed. 2d 834; 1997 U.S. LEXIS 4038; 65 U.S.L.W. 4695; 97 Cal. Daily Op. Service 5027; 97 Daily Journal DAR 8122; 11 Fla. L. Weekly Fed. S 174

necessarily and indubitably, intend primarily that the patient be made dead." *Id.*, at 367. Similarly, a patient who commits suicide with a doctor's aid necessarily has the specific intent to end his or her own life, while a patient who refuses or discontinues treatment might not. . . .

The law has long used actors' intent or purpose to distinguish between two acts that may have the same result. See, *e.g., United States v. Bailey,* 444 U.S. 394, 403–406 (1980) ("[T]he . . . common law of homicide often distinguishes . . . between a person who knows that another person will be killed as the result of his conduct and a person who acts with the specific purpose of taking another's life"). . . . M. Hale, 1 Pleas of the Crown 412 (1847) ("If A., with an intent to prevent gangrene beginning in his hand doth without any advice cut off his hand, by which he dies, he is not thereby *felo de se* for tho it was a voluntary act, yet it was not with an intent to kill himself"). Put differently, the law distinguishes actions taken "because of" a given end from actions taken "in spite of" their unintended but foreseen consequences. *Feeney,* 442 U.S., at 279; *Compassion in Dying v. Washington,* 79 F. 3d 790, 858 (CA9 1996) (Kleinfeld, J., dissenting) ("When General Eisenhower ordered American soldiers onto the beaches of Normandy, he knew that he was sending many American soldiers to certain death. . . . His purpose, though, was to . . . liberate Europe from the Nazis").

Given these general principles, it is not surprising that many courts, including New York courts, have carefully distinguished refusing life-sustaining treatment from suicide. See, *e.g., Fosmire v. Nicoleau,* 75 N.Y. 2d 218, 227, and n. 2, 551 N.E. 2d 77, 82, and n. 2 (1990) ("[M]erely declining medical . . . care is not considered a suicidal act").[1] In fact, the first state-court decision explicitly to authorize withdrawing lifesaving treatment noted the "real distinction between the self-infliction of deadly harm and a self-determination against artificial life support." *In re Quinlan,* 70 N.J. 10, 43, 52. . . .

Similarly, the overwhelming majority of state legislatures have drawn a clear line between assisting suicide and withdrawing or permitting the refusal of unwanted lifesaving medical treatment by prohibiting the former and permitting the latter. And "nearly all states expressly disapprove of suicide and assisted suicide either in statutes dealing with durable powers of attorney in health-care situations, or in 'living will' statutes." *Kevorkian,* 447 Mich., at 478–479, and nn. 53–54, 527 N.W 2d, at 731–732, and nn. 53–54. Thus, even as the States move to protect and promote patients' dignity at the end of life, they remain opposed to physician-assisted suicide. . . .

This Court has also recognized, at least implicitly, the distinction between letting a patient die and making that patient die. In *Cruzan v. Director, Mo. Dept. of Health,* 497 U.S. 261, 278 (1990), we concluded that "[t]he principle that a competent person has a constitutionally protected liberty interest in refusing unwanted medical treatment may be inferred from our prior decisions," and we assumed the existence of such a right for purposes of that case, *id.*, at 279. But our assumption of a right to refuse treatment was grounded not, as the Court of Appeals supposed, on the proposition that patients have a general and abstract "right to hasten death," 80 F, 3d at 727–728, but on well established, traditional rights to bodily integrity and freedom from unwanted touching, *Cruzan,* 497 U.S., at 278–279; *id.*, at 287–288. (O'Connor, J., concurring). In fact, we observed that "the majority of States in this country have laws imposing criminal penalties on one who assists another to commit suicide." *Id.*, at 280. *Cruzan* therefore provides no support for the notion that refusing life-sustaining medical treatment is "nothing more nor less than suicide."

For all these reasons, we disagree with respondents' claim that the distinction between refusing lifesaving medical treatment and assisted suicide is "arbitrary" and "irrational." Brief for Respondents 44. Granted, in some cases, the line between the two may not be clear, but certainty is not required, even were it possible. Logic and contemporary practice support New York's judgment that the two acts are different, and New York may therefore, consistent with the Constitution, treat them differently. By permitting everyone to refuse unwanted medical treatment while prohibiting anyone from assisting a suicide, New York law follows a longstanding and rational distinction.

New York's reasons for recognizing and acting on this distinction—including prohibiting intentional killing and preserving life; preventing suicide; maintaining physicians' role as their patients' healers; protecting vulnerable people from indifference, prejudice, and psychological and financial pressure to end their lives; and avoiding a possible slide towards euthanasia—are discussed in greater detail in our opinion in *Glucksberg, ante*. These valid and important public interests easily satisfy the constitutional requirement that a legislative classification bear a rational relation to some legitimate end.

The judgment of the Court of Appeals is reversed.

It is so ordered.

NOTE

1. Thus, the Second Circuit erred in reading New York law as creating a "right to hasten death"; instead, the authorities cited by the court recognize a right to refuse treatment, and nowhere equate the exercise of this right with suicide. *Schloendorff v. Society of New York Hospital,* 211 N.Y. 125, 129–130, 105 N.E. 92, 93 (1914), which contains Justice Cardozo's famous statement that "[e]very human being of adult years and sound mind has a right to determine what shall be done with his own body," was simply an informed-consent case. . . .

UNITED STATES SUPREME COURT

Washington, et al., Petitioners v. Harold Glucksberg et al.

On Writ of Certiorari to the United States Court of Appeals for the Ninth Circuit

CHIEF JUSTICE REHNQUIST delivered the opinion of the Court.

The question presented in this case is whether Washington's prohibition against "caus[ing]" or "aid[ing]" a suicide offends the Fourteenth Amendment to the United States Constitution. We hold that it does not. . . .

In almost every State—indeed, in almost every western democracy—it is a crime to assist a suicide. The States' assisted-suicide bans are not innovations. Rather, they are longstanding expressions of the States' commitment to the protection and preservation of all human life. . . . Indeed, opposition to and condemnation of suicide—and, therefore, of assisting suicide—are consistent and enduring themes of our philosophical, legal, and cultural heritages. . . .

Because of advances in medicine and technology, Americans today are increasingly likely to die in institutions, from chronic illnesses. President's Comm'n for the Study of Ethical Problems in Medicine and Biomedical and Behavioral Research, Deciding to Forego Life-Sustaining Treatment 16–18 (1983). Public concern and democratic action are therefore sharply focused on how best to protect dignity and independence at the end of life, with the result that there have been many significant changes in state laws and in the attitudes these laws reflect. . . .

Thus, the States are currently engaged in serious, thoughtful examinations of physician-assisted suicide and other similar issues. For example, New York State's Task Force on Life and the Law—an ongoing, blue-ribbon commission composed of doctors, ethicists, lawyers, religious leaders, and interested laymen—was convened in 1984 and commissioned with "a broad mandate to recommend public policy on issues raised by medical advances." New York Task Force vii. . . .

Attitudes toward suicide itself have changed . . . but our laws have consistently condemned, and continue to prohibit, assisting suicide. Despite changes in medical technology and notwithstanding an increased emphasis on the importance of end-of-life decision-making, we have not retreated from this prohibition. Against this backdrop of history, tradition, and

521 U.S. 702; 117 S. Ct. 2258; 117 S. Ct. 2302; 138 L. Ed. 2d 772; 1997 U.S. LEXIS 4039; 65 U.S.L.W. 4669; 97 Cal. Daily Op. Service 5008; 97 Daily Journal DAR 8150; 11 Fla. L. Weekly Fed. S 190

practice, we now turn to respondents' constitutional claim.

II

The Due Process Clause guarantees more than fair process, and the liberty" it protects includes more than the absence of physical restraint. . . . The Clause also provides heightened protection against government interference with certain fundamental rights and liberty interests. . . . We have . . . assumed, and strongly suggested, that the Due Process Clause protects the traditional right to refuse unwanted lifesaving medical treatment. *Cruzan,* 497 U.S., at 278–279.

But we "ha[ve] always been reluctant to expand the concept of substantive due process because guideposts for responsible decisionmaking in this unchartered area are scarce and open-ended." *Collins,* 503 U.S., at 125. By extending constitutional protection to an asserted right or liberty interest, we, to a great extent, place the matter outside the arena of public debate and legislative action. . . .

Our established method of substantive-due-process analysis has two primary features: First, we have regularly observed that the Due Process Clause specially protects those fundamental rights and liberties which are, objectively, "deeply rooted in this Nation's history and tradition," *id.,* at 503 (plurality opinion); . . . Second, we have required in substantive-due-process cases a "careful description" of the asserted fundamental liberty interest. . . .

The Washington statute at issue in this case prohibits "aid[ing] another person to attempt suicide," Wash. Rev. Code §9A.36.060(1) (1994), and, thus, the question before us is whether the "liberty" specially protected by the Due Process Clause includes a right to commit suicide which itself includes a right to assistance in doing so.

We now inquire whether this asserted right has any place in our Nation's traditions. Here, as discussed above . . . we are confronted with a consistent and almost universal tradition that has long rejected the asserted right . . .

Respondents contend, however, that the liberty interest they assert *is* consistent with this Court's substantive-due-process line of cases, if not with this Nation's history and practice. Pointing to *Casey* and *Cruzan,* respondents read our jurisprudence in this area as reflecting a general tradition of "self-sovereignty," Brief of Respondents 12, and as teaching that the "liberty" protected by the Due Process Clause includes "basic and intimate exercises of personal autonomy," *id.,* at 10; see *Casey,* 505 U.S., at 847 ("It is a promise of the Constitution that there is a realm of personal liberty which the government may not enter"). According to respondents, our liberty jurisprudence, and the broad, individualistic principles it reflects, protects the "liberty of competent, terminally ill adults to make end-of-life decisions free of undue government interference." Brief for Respondents 10. . . .

The decision to commit suicide with the assistance of another may be just as personal and profound as the decision to refuse unwanted medical treatment, but it has never enjoyed similar legal protection. Indeed, the two acts are widely and reasonably regarded as quite distinct. See *Quill v. Vacco, post,* at 5–13. In *Cruzan* itself, we recognized that most States outlawed assisted suicide—and even more do today—and we certainly gave no intimation that the right to refuse unwanted medical treatment could be somehow transmuted into a right to assistance in committing suicide. 497 U.S., at 280. . . .

[O]ur decisions lead us to conclude that the asserted "right" to assistance in committing suicide is not a fundamental liberty interest protected by the Due Process Clause. The Constitution also requires, however, that Washington's assisted-suicide ban be rationally related to legitimate government interests. . . . This requirement is unquestionably met here. As the court below recognized, 79 F. 3d, at 816–817,[1] Washington's assisted-suicide ban implicates a number of state interests.[2] . . .

First, Washington has an "unqualified interest in the preservation of human life." *Cruzan,* 497 U.S., at 282. The State's prohibition on assisted suicide, like all homicide laws, both reflects and advances its commitment to this interest. . . .

The State also has an interest in protecting the integrity and ethics of the medical profession. In contrast to the Court of Appeals' conclusion that "the integrity of the medical profession would [not] be threatened in any way by [physician-assisted suicide]," 79 F. 3d, at 827, the American Medical Association, like many other medical and physicians' groups, has concluded that "[p]hysician-assisted suicide is fundamentally incompatible with the physician's role as healer." American Medical Association, Code of Ethics §2.211 (1994); see Council on Ethical and Judicial Affairs, Decisions Near the End of Life, 267 JAMA 2229, 2233 (1992) ("[T]he societal risks of involving physicians in medical interventions to cause patients' deaths is too great"); New York Task Force 103–109 (discussing physicians' views). And physician-assisted suicide could, it is argued, undermine the trust that is essential to the doctor–patient relationship by blurring the time-honored line between healing and harming. . . .

Next, the State has an interest in protecting vulnerable groups—including the poor, the elderly, and disabled persons—from abuse, neglect, and mistakes. The Court of Appeals dismissed the State's concern that disadvantaged persons might be pressured into physician-assisted suicide as "ludicrous on its face." 79 F. 3d, at 825. We have recognized, however, the real risk of subtle coercion and undue influence in end-of-life situations. *Cruzan,* 497 U.S., at 281. Similarly, the New York Task Force warned that "[l]egalizing physician-assisted suicide would pose profound risks to many individuals who are ill and vulnerable. . . . The risk of harm is greatest for the many individuals in our society whose autonomy and well-being are already compromised by poverty, lack of access to good medical care, advanced age, or membership in a stigmatized social group." New York Task Force 120. . . .

Finally, the State may fear that permitting assisted suicide will start it down the path to voluntary and perhaps even involuntary euthanasia. . . .

We need not weigh exactingly the relative strengths of these various interests. They are unquestionably important and legitimate, and Washington's ban on assisted suicide is at least reasonably related to their promotion and protection. We therefore hold that Wash. Rev. Code §9A.36.060(1) (1994) does not violate the Fourteenth Amendment, either on its face or "as applied to competent, terminally ill adults who wish to hasten their deaths by obtaining medication prescribed by their doctors." 79 F. 3d, at 838.

• • •

Throughout the Nation, Americans are engaged in an earnest and profound debate about the morality, legality, and practicality of physician-assisted suicide. Our holding permits this debate to continue, as it should in a democratic society. The decision of the en banc Court of Appeals is reversed, and the case is remanded for further proceedings consistent with this opinion.

It is so ordered.

JUSTICE STEVENS, concurring in the judgments. . . .

A State, like Washington, that has authorized the death penalty and thereby has concluded that the sanctity of human life does not require that it always be preserved, must acknowledge that there are situations in which an interest in hastening death is legitimate. Indeed, not only is that interest sometimes legitimate, I am also convinced that there are times when it is entitled to constitutional protection.

• • •

The state interests supporting a general rule banning the practice of physician-assisted suicide do not have the same force in all cases. . . . That interest not only justifies—it commands—maximum protection of every individual's interest in remaining alive, which in turn commands the same protection for decisions about whether to commence or to terminate life-support systems or to administer pain medication that may hasten death. Properly viewed, however, this interest is not a collective interest that should always outweigh the interests of a person who because of pain, incapacity, or sedation finds her life intolerable, but rather, an aspect of individual freedom. . . .

Although as a general matter the State's interest in the contributions each person may make to society outweighs the person's interest in ending her life, this interest does not have the same force for a terminally ill patient faced not with the choice of whether to live, only of how to die. Allowing the individual, rather than the State, to make judgments " 'about the "quality" of life that a particular individual may enjoy.'" *ante,* at 25 (quoting *Cruzan,* 497 U.S., at 282), does not mean that the lives of terminally-ill, disabled people have less value than the lives of those who are healthy, see *ante,* at 28. Rather, it gives proper recognition to the individual's interest in choosing a final chapter that accords with her life story, rather than one that demeans her values and poisons memories of her. . . .

Similarly, the State's legitimate interests in preventing suicide, protecting the vulnerable from coercion and abuse, and preventing euthanasia are less significant in this context. I agree that the State has a compelling interest in preventing persons from committing suicide because of depression, or coercion by third parties. But the State's legitimate interest in preventing abuse does not apply to an individual who is not victimized by abuse, who is not suffering from depression, and who makes a rational and voluntary decision to seek assistance in dying. . . .

Relatedly, the State and *amici* express the concern that patients whose physical pain is inadequately treated will be more likely to request assisted suicide. Encouraging the development and ensuring the availability of adequate pain treatment is of utmost importance; palliative care, however, cannot alleviate all pain and suffering. . . . An individual adequately informed of the care alternatives thus might make a rational choice for assisted suicide. For such an individual, the State's interest in preventing potential abuse and mistake is only minimally implicated.

The final major interest asserted by the State is its interest in preserving the traditional integrity of the medical profession. The fear is that a rule permitting physicians to assist in suicide is inconsistent with the perception that they serve their patients solely as healers. But for some patients, it would be a physician's refusal to dispense medication to ease their suffering and make their death tolerable and dignified that would be inconsistent with the healing role. . . . For doctors who have long-standing relationships with their patients, who have given their patients advice on alternative treatments, who are attentive to their patient's individualized needs, and who are knowledgeable about pain symptom management and palliative care options, see Quill, Death and Dignity, A Case of Individualized Decision Making, 324 New England J. of Med. 691–694 (1991), heeding a patient's desire to assist in her suicide would not serve to harm the physician–patient relationship. Furthermore, because physicians are already involved in making decisions that hasten the death of terminally ill patients—through termination of life support, withholding of medical treatment, and terminal sedation—there is in fact significant tension between the traditional view of the physician's role and the actual practice in a growing number of cases. . . .

I agree that the distinction between permitting death to ensue from an underlying fatal disease and causing it to occur by the administration of medication or other means provides a constitutionally sufficient basis for the State's classification. Unlike the Court, however, . . . I am not persuaded that in all cases there will in fact be a significant difference between the intent of the physicians, the patients or the families in the two situations.

There may be little distinction between the intent of a terminally-ill patient who decides to remove her life-support and one who seeks the assistance of a doctor in ending her life; in both situations, the patient is seeking to hasten a certain, impending death. The doctor's intent might also be the same in prescribing lethal medication as it is in terminating life support. A doctor who fails to administer medical treatment to one who is dying from a disease could be doing so with an intent to harm or kill that patient. Conversely, a doctor who prescribes lethal medication does not necessarily intend the patient's death—rather that doctor may seek simply to ease the patient's suffering and to comply with her wishes. The illusory character of any differences in intent or causation is confirmed by the fact that the American Medical Association unequivocally endorses the practice of terminal sedation—the administration of sufficient dosages of pain-killing medication to terminally ill patients to protect them from excruciating pain even when it is clear that the time of death will be advanced. The purpose of terminal sedation is to ease the suffering of the patient and comply with her wishes, and the actual cause of death is the administration of heavy doses of lethal sedatives. This same intent and causation may exist when a doctor complies with a patient's request for lethal medication to hasten her death.

Thus, although the differences the majority notes in causation and intent between terminating life-support and assisting in suicide support the Court's rejection of the respondents' facial challenge, these distinctions may be inapplicable to particular terminally ill patients and their doctors. Our holding today in *Vacco v. Quill* that the Equal Protection Clause is not violated by New York's classification, just like our holding in *Washington v. Glucksberg* that the Washington statue is not invalid on its face, does not foreclose the possibility that some applications of the New York statute may impose an intolerable intrusion on the patient's freedom.

There remains room for vigorous debate about the outcome of particular cases that are not necessarily resolved by the opinions announced today. How such cases may be decided will depend on their specific facts. In my judgment, however, it is clear that the so-called "unqualified interest in the preservation of human life," *Cruzan,* 497 U.S., at 282, *Glucksberg, ante,* at 24, is not itself sufficient to outweigh the interest in liberty that may justify the only possible means of preserving a dying patient's dignity and alleviating her intolerable suffering. . . .

JUSTICE O'CONNOR, concurring.*

Death will be different for each of us. For many, the last days will be spent in physical pain and perhaps the despair that accompanies physical deterioration and a loss of control of basic bodily and mental functions. Some will seek medication to alleviate that pain and other symptoms.

The Court frames the issues in this case as whether the Due Process Clause of the Constitution protects a "right to commit suicide, which itself includes a right to assistance in doing so," . . . and concludes that our Nation's history, legal traditions, and practices do not support the existence of such a right. I join the Court's opinions because I agree that there is no generalized right to "commit suicide." But respondents urge us to address the narrower question whether a mentally competent person who is experiencing great suffering has a constitutionally cognizable interest in controlling the circumstances of his or her imminent death. I see no need to reach that question in the context of the facial challenges to the New York and Washington laws at issue here. . . . The parties and *amici* agree that in these States a patient who is suffering from a terminal illness and who is experiencing great pain has no legal barriers to obtaining medication, from qualified physicians, to alleviate that suffering, even to the point of causing unconsciousness and hastening death. . . . In this light, even assuming that we would recognize such an interest, I agree that the State's interests in protecting those who are not truly competent or facing imminent death, or those whose decisions to hasten death would not truly be voluntary, are sufficiently weighty to justify a prohibition against physician-assisted suicide. . . .

Every one of us at some point may be affected by our own or a family member's terminal illness. There is no reason to think the democratic process will not strike the proper balance between the interests of terminally ill, mentally competent individuals who would seek to end their suffering and the State's interests in protecting those who might seek to end life mistakenly or under pressure. As the Court recognizes, States are presently undertaking extensive and serious evaluation of physician-assisted suicide and other related issues. . . . In such circumstances, "the . . . challenging task of crafting appropriate procedures for safeguarding . . . liberty interests is entrusted to the 'laboratory' of the States . . . in the first instance." *Cruzan v. Director, Mo. Dept. of Health,* 497 U.S. 261, 292 (1990) (O'CONNOR, J., concurring) (citing *New State Ice Co. v. Liebmann,* 285 U.S. 262, 311 (1932)).

In sum, there is no need to address the question whether suffering patients have a constitutionally cognizable interest in obtaining relief from the suffering that they may experience in the last days of their lives. There is no dispute that dying patients in Washington and New York can obtain palliative care, even when doing so would hasten their deaths. The difficulty in defining terminal illness and the risk that a dying patient's request for assistance in ending his or her life might not be truly voluntary justifies the prohibitions on assisted suicide we uphold here.

*JUSTICE GINSBURG concurs in the Court's judgments substantially for the reasons stated in this opinion. JUSTICE BREYER joins this opinion except insofar as it joins the opinion of the Court.

NOTES

1. The court identified and discussed six state interests: (1) preserving life; (2) preventing suicide; (3) avoiding the involvement of third parties and use of arbitrary, unfair, or undue influence; (4) protecting family members and loved ones; (5) protecting the integrity of the medical profession; and (6) avoiding future movement toward euthanasia and other abuses. 79 F. 3d, at 816–832.

2. Respondents also admit the existence of these interests, Brief for Respondents 28–39, but contend that Washington could better promote and protect them through regulation, rather than prohibition, of physician-assisted suicide. Our inquiry, however, is limited to the question whether the State's prohibition is rationally related to legitimate state interests.

THE SUPREME COURT OF CALIFORNIA

Rose Wendland v. Florence Wendland et al.

In this case we consider whether a conservator of the person may withhold artificial nutrition and hydration from a conscious conservatee who is not terminally ill, comatose, or in a persistent vegetative state, and who has not left formal instructions for health care or appointed an agent or surrogate for health care decisions. Interpreting Probate Code section 2355 in light of the relevant provisions of the California Constitution, we conclude a conservator may not withhold artificial nutrition and hydration from such a person absent clear and convincing evidence the conservator's decision is in accordance with either the conservatee's own wishes or best interest.

The trial court in the case before us, applying the clear and convincing evidence standard, found the evidence on both points insufficient and, thus, denied the conservator's request for authority to withhold artificial nutrition and hydration. The Court of Appeal, which believed the trial court was required to defer to the conservator's good faith decision, reversed. We reverse the decision of the Court of Appeal.

I. FACTS AND PROCEDURAL HISTORY

On September 29, 1993, Robert Wendland rolled his truck at high speed in a solo accident while driving under the influence of alcohol. The accident injured Robert's brain, leaving him conscious yet severely disabled, both mentally and physically, and dependent on artificial nutrition and hydration. Two years later Rose Wendland, Robert's wife and conservator, proposed to direct his physician to remove his feeding tube and allow him to die. Florence Wendland and Rebekah Vinson (respectively Robert's mother and sister) objected to the conservator's decision. This proceeding arose under the provisions of the Probate Code authorizing courts to settle such disputes. (Prob. Code, §§ 2355, 2359.)

Following the accident, Robert remained in a coma, totally unresponsive, for several months. During this period Rose visited him daily, often with their children, and authorized treatment as necessary to maintain his health.

Robert eventually regained consciousness. . . .

After Robert regained consciousness and while he was undergoing therapy, Rose authorized surgery three times to replace dislodged feeding tubes. When physicians sought her permission a fourth time, she declined. She discussed the decision with her daughters and with Robert's brother Michael, all of whom believed that Robert would not have approved the procedure even if necessary to sustain his life. Rose also discussed the decision with Robert's treating physician, Dr. Kass, other physicians, and the hospital's ombudsman, all of whom apparently supported her decision. Dr. Kass, however, inserted a nasogastric feeding tube to keep Robert alive pending input from the hospital's ethics committee.

Eventually, the 20-member ethics committee unanimously approved Rose's decision. In the course of their deliberations, however, the committee did not speak with Robert's mother or sister. Florence learned, apparently through an anonymous telephone call, that Dr. Kass planned to remove Robert's feeding tube. Florence and Rebekah applied for a temporary restraining order to bar him from so doing, and the court granted the motion ex parte.

Rose immediately thereafter petitioned for appointment as Robert's conservator. In the petition, she asked the court to determine that Robert lacked the capacity to give informed consent for medical treatment and to confirm her authority "to withdraw and/or withhold medical treatment and/or life-sustaining treatment, including, but not limited to, withholding nutrition and hydration." Florence and Rebekah (hereafter sometimes objectors) opposed the petition. . . .

Robert's wife, brother and daughter recounted pre-accident statements Robert had made about his attitude towards life-sustaining health care. Robert's wife recounted specific statements on two occasions. The first occasion was Rose's decision whether to turn off a respirator sustaining the life of her father, who was near death from gangrene. Rose recalls Robert saying: "I would never want to live like that, and I wouldn't want my children to see me like that and look at the hurt you're going through as an adult seeing your father like that." On cross-examination, Rose acknowledged Robert said on this occasion that Rose's father "wouldn't want to live like a vegetable" and "wouldn't want to live in a comatose state." . . .

II. DISCUSSION

A. THE RELEVANT LEGAL PRINCIPLES

The ultimate focus of our analysis must be section 2355, the statute under which the conservator has claimed the authority to end the conservatee's life and the only statute under which such authority might plausibly be found. . . .

Effective July 1, 2000, the Health Care Decisions Law (Stats. 1999, ch. 658) gives competent adults extremely broad power to direct all aspects of their health care in the event they become incompetent. The new law permits a competent person to execute an advance directive about "any aspect" of health care. (§ 4701). Among other things, a person may direct that life-sustaining treatment be withheld or withdrawn under conditions specified by the person and not limited to terminal illness, permanent coma, or persistent vegetative state. A competent person may still use a power of attorney for health care to give an agent the power to make health care decisions (§ 4683), but a patient may also orally designate a surrogate to make such decisions by personally informing the patient's supervising health care provider. (§ 4711.) Under the new law, agents and surrogates are required to make health care decisions "in accordance with the principal's individual health care instructions, if any, and other wishes to the extent known to the agent." . . .

The ultimate focus of our analysis, as mentioned at the outset, must be section 2355, the statute under which the conservator claims the authority to end the conservatee's life. . . .

Historical evidence is lacking, however, that the Legislature . . . actually contemplated that the statute would be understood as authorizing a conservator to deliberately end the life of a conservatee by withholding artificially delivered food and water. Such authority, if it indeed existed, would have been merely implicit, as a consequence of the statute's broad language. The claim that section 2355 conferred that authority was first considered and accepted in 1988 by the court in *Drabick,* 200 Cal.App.3d 185.

The *Drabick* court also read former section 2355 as severely restricting the role of courts in supervising conservators' treatment decisions. "[W]e do not believe," the court wrote, "that it is the [trial] court's role to substitute its judgment for the conservator's. Instead, when the conservator or another interested person has requested the court's approval the court should confine its involvement to ensuring that the conservator has made the type of decision for which the Probate Code expressly calls: a 'good faith' decision 'based on medical advice' whether treatment is 'necessary.' " (*Drabick,* 200 Cal.App.3d 185, 200, quoting former § 2355.) The required decision, the court explained, is the *conservator's* assessment of the conservatee's best interests. . . .

In 1990, the Legislature repealed and reenacted former section 2355 without change while reorganizing the Probate Code. But in 1999, section 2355 changed significantly with the Legislature's adoption of the Health Care Decisions Law (§ 4600 et seq., added by Stats. 1999, ch. 658). That law took effect on July 1, 2000, about four months after the Court of Appeal filed the opinion on review. Many of the new law's provisions, as already noted, are the same as, or drawn from, the Uniform Health-Care Decisions Act. (See Cal. Law Revision Com. Rep., at p. 49.) Section 2355, as a statute addressing medical treatment decisions, was revised to conform to the new law.

The main purpose of the Health Care Decisions Law is to provide "procedures and standards" governing "health care decisions to be made for adults at a time when they are incapable of making decisions on their own and [to] provide "mechanisms for directing their health care in anticipation of a time when they may become incapacitated." (Cal. Law Revision Com. Rep., at p. 6.) . . .

B. THE PRESENT CASE

This background illuminates the parties' arguments, which reduce in essence to this: The conservator has claimed the power under section 2355, as she interprets it, to direct the conservatee's health care providers to cease providing artificial nutrition and hydration. In opposition, the objectors have contended the statute violates the conservatee's rights to privacy and life under the facts of this case if the conservator's interpretation of the statute is correct.

1. The primary standard: a decision in accordance with the conservatee's wishes. The conservator asserts she offered sufficient evidence at trial to satisfy the primary statutory standard, which contemplates a decision "in accordance with the conservatee's . . . wishes. . . ." (§ 2355, subd. (a).) The trial court, however, determined the evidence on this point was insufficient. The conservator did "not [meet] her duty and burden," the court expressly found, "to show by clear and convincing evidence that [the] conservatee . . . , who is not in a persistent vegetative state nor suffering from a terminal illness would, under the circumstances, want to die." . . .

The objectors, in opposition, argue that section 2355 would be unconstitutional if construed to permit a conservator to end the life of a conscious conservatee based on a finding by the low preponderance of the evidence standard that the latter would not want to live. We see no basis for holding the statute unconstitutional on its face. We do, however, find merit in the objectors' argument. We therefore construe the statute to minimize the possibility of its unconstitutional application by requiring clear and convincing evidence of a conscious conservatee's wish to refuse life-sustaining treatment when the conservator relies on that asserted wish to justify withholding life-sustaining treatment. This construction does not entail a deviation from the language of the statute and constitutes only a partial rejection of the Law Revision Commission's understanding that the preponderance of the evidence standard would apply; we see no constitutional reason to apply the higher evidentiary standard to the majority of health care decisions made by conservators not contemplating a conscious conservatee's death. Our reasons are as follows:

At the time the Legislature was considering the present version of section 2355, no court had interpreted any prior version of the statute as permitting a conservator deliberately to end the life of a *conscious* conservatee. Even today, only the decision on review so holds. . . .

In amending section 2355 in 1999, neither the Legislature, nor the Law Revision Commission in its official report to the Legislature, alluded to the possibility that the statute might be invoked to justify withholding artificial nutrition and hydration from a conscious patient. The conservator sees evidence of specific legislative authority for such a decision in the findings that accompanied the Health Care Decisions Law, but we do not. . . .

One must acknowledge that the primary standard for decisionmaking set out in section 2355 does articulate what will in some cases form a constitutional basis for a conservator's decision to end the life of a conscious patient: deference to the patient's own wishes. This standard also appears in the new provisions governing decisions by agents and surrogates designated by competent adults. (§§ 4684, 4714). As applied in that context, the requirement that decisions be made "in accordance with the principal's individual health care instructions . . . and other wishes" (§ 4684) merely respects the principal-agent relationship and gives effect to the properly expressed wishes of a competent adult. Because a competent adult may refuse life-sustaining treatment (see *ante,* at p. 11 et seq.), it follows that an agent properly and voluntarily designated by the principal may refuse treatment on the principal's behalf unless, of course, such authority is revoked. (See, e.g., §§ 4682, 4689, 4695 [providing various ways in which the authority of an agent for health care decisions may be revoked or the agent's instructions countermanded].)

The only apparent purpose of requiring conservators to make decisions in accordance with the conservatee's wishes, when those wishes are known, is to enforce the fundamental principle of personal autonomy. The same requirement, as applied to agents and surrogates freely designated by competent persons, enforces the principles of agency. A reasonable person presumably will designate for such purposes only a person in whom the former reposes the highest degree of confidence. A conservator, in contrast, is *not* an agent of the conservatee, and unlike a freely designated agent cannot be presumed to have special knowledge of the conservatee's health care wishes. A person with "sufficient capacity . . . to form an intelligent preference" may nominate his or her own conservator (§ 1810), but the nomination is not binding because the appointment remains "solely in the discretion of the court" (§ 1812, subd. (a)). Furthermore, while statutory law gives preference to spouses and other persons related to the conservatee (*id.,* subd. (b)), who might know something of the conservatee's health care preferences, the law also permits the court in its sole discretion to appoint unrelated persons and even public conservators *(ibid.).* While it may be constitutionally permissible to assume that an agent freely designated by a formerly competent person to make all health care decisions, including life-ending ones, will resolve such questions "in accordance with the principal's . . . wishes" (§ 4684), one cannot apply the same assumption to conservators and conservatees (cf. § 2355, subd, (a)). For this reason, when the legal premise of a conservator's decision to end a conservatee's life by withholding medical care is that the conservatee would refuse such care, to apply a high standard of proof will help to ensure the reliability of the decision. . . .

In this case, the importance of the ultimate decision and the risk of error are manifest. So too should be the degree of confidence required in the necessary findings of fact. The ultimate decision is whether a conservatee lives or dies, and the risk is that a conservator, claiming statutory authority to end a conscious conservatee's life "in accordance with the conservatee's . . . wishes" (§ 2355, subd. (a)) by withdrawing artificial nutrition and hydration, will make a decision with which the conservatee subjectively disagrees and which subjects the conservatee to starvation, dehydration, and death. This would represent the gravest possible affront to a conservatee's state constitutional right to privacy, in the sense of freedom from unwanted bodily intrusions, and to life. While the practical ability to make autonomous health care decisions does not survive incompetence, the ability to perceive unwanted intrusions may. Certainly it is possible, as the conservator here urges, that an incompetent and uncommunicative but conscious conservatee might perceive the efforts to keep him alive as unwanted intrusion and the withdrawal of those efforts as welcome release. But the decision to treat is reversible. The decision to withdraw treatment is not. The role of a high evidentiary standard in such a case is to adjust the risk of error to favor the less perilous result. . . .

In conclusion, to interpret section 2355 to permit a conservator to withdraw artificial nutrition and hydration from a conscious conservatee based on a finding, by a mere preponderance of the evidence, that the conservatee would refuse treatment creates a serious risk that the law will be unconstitutionally applied in some cases, with grave injury to fundamental rights. . . .

III. CONCLUSION

For the reasons set out above, we conclude the superior court correctly required the conservator to prove, by clear and convincing evidence, either that the conservatee wished to refuse life-sustaining treatment or that to withhold such treatment would have been in his best interest; lacking such evidence, the superior court correctly denied the conservator's request for permission to withdraw artificial hydration and nutrition. We emphasize, however, that the clear and convincing evidence standard does not apply to the vast majority of health care decisions made by conservators under section 2355. Only the decision to withdraw life-sustaining treatment, because of its effect on a conscious conservatee's fundamental rights, justifies imposing that high standard of proof. Therefore, our decision today affects only a narrow class of persons: conscious conservatees who have not left formal directions for health care and whose conservators propose to withhold life-sustaining treatment for the purpose of causing their conservatees' deaths. Our conclusion does not affect permanently unconscious patients, including those who are comatose or in a persistent vegetative state (see generally *Conservatorship of Morrison,* 206 Cal.App.3d 304; *Drabick, supra,* 200 Cal.App.3d 185; *Barber,* 147 Cal.App.3d 1006), persons who have left legally cognizable instructions for health care (see §§ 4670, 4673, 4700), persons who have designated agents or other surrogates for health care (see §§ 4671, 4680, 4711), or conservatees for whom conservators have made medical decisions other than those intended to bring about the death of a conscious conservatee.

The decision of the Court of Appeal is reversed.

WERDEGAR. J.

WE CONCUR:

GEORGE, C.J.
KENNARD, J.
BAXTER, J.
CHIN, J.
BROWN, J.

The Moral Foundations of Public Policy on Physician-Assisted Death

DAN W. BROCK

Voluntary Active Euthanasia

Dan W. Brock was, until recently Charles C. Tillinghast, Jr., University Professor, professor of philosophy and biomedical ethics, and director of the Center for Biomedical Ethics at Brown University. He is a former staff philosopher on the President's Commission for the Study of Ethical Problems in Medicine. His books include *Life and Death: Philosophical Essays in Biomedical Ethics,* and (with Allen Buchanan) *Deciding for Others: The Ethics of Surrogate Decision Making*. Brock is currently at the National Institutes of Health (NIH).

In the recent bioethics literature some have endorsed physician-assisted suicide but not euthanasia. Are they sufficiently different that the moral arguments for one often do not apply to the other? A paradigm case of physician-assisted suicide is a patient's ending his or her life with a lethal dose of a medication requested of and provided by a physician for that purpose. A paradigm case of voluntary active euthanasia is a physician's administering the lethal dose, often because the patient is unable to do so. The only difference that need exist between the two is the person who actually administers the lethal dose—the physician or the patient. In each, the physician plays an active and necessary causal role.

In physician-assisted suicide the patient acts last (for example, Janet Adkins herself pushed the button after Dr. Kevorkian hooked her up to his suicide machine), whereas in euthanasia the physician acts last by performing the physical equivalent of pushing the button. In both cases, however, the choice rests fully with the patient. In both the patient acts last in the sense of retaining the right to change his or her mind until the point at which the lethal process becomes irreversible. How could there be a substantial moral difference between the two based only on this small difference in the part played by the physician in the causal process resulting in death? Of course, it might be held that the moral difference is clear and important—in euthanasia the physician kills the patient whereas in physician-assisted suicide the patient kills him- or herself. But this is misleading at best. In assisted suicide the physician and patient together kill the patient. To see this, suppose a physician supplied a lethal dose to a patient with the knowledge and intent that the patient will wrongfully administer it to another. We would have no difficulty in morality or the law recognizing this as a case of joint action to kill for which both are responsible.

If there is no significant, intrinsic moral difference between the two, it is also difficult to see why public or legal policy should permit one but not the other; worries about abuse or about giving anyone dominion over the lives of others apply equally to either. As a result, I will take the arguments evaluated below to apply to both and will focus on euthanasia.

My concern here will be with *voluntary* euthanasia only—that is, with the case in which a clearly competent patient makes a fully voluntary and persistent request for aid in dying. Involuntary euthanasia, in which a competent patient explicitly refuses or opposes receiving euthanasia, and nonvoluntary euthanasia, in which a patient is incompetent and unable to express his or her wishes about euthanasia, will be considered here only as potential unwanted side-effects of permitting voluntary euthanasia. I emphasize as well that I am concerned with *active* euthanasia, not withholding or withdrawing life-sustaining

From "Voluntary Active Euthanasia," *Hastings Center Report* 22, no. 2 (March/April 1992), 10–22 (edited). Reprinted by permission of the publisher.

treatment, which some commentators characterize as "passive euthanasia." . . .

THE CENTRAL ETHICAL ARGUMENT FOR VOLUNTARY ACTIVE EUTHANASIA

The central ethical argument for euthanasia is familiar. It is that the very same two fundamental ethical values supporting the consensus on patient's rights to decide about life-sustaining treatment also support the ethical permissibility of euthanasia. These values are individual self-determination or autonomy and individual well-being. By self-determination as it bears on euthanasia, I mean people's interest in making important decisions about their lives for themselves according to their own values or conceptions of a good life, and in being left free to act on those decisions. Self-determination is valuable because it permits people to form and live in accordance with their own conception of a good life, at least within the bounds of justice and consistent with others doing so as well. In exercising self-determination people take responsibility for their lives and for the kinds of persons they become. A central aspect of human dignity lies in people's capacity to direct their lives in this way. The value of exercising self-determination presupposes some minimum of decisionmaking capacities or competence, which thus limits the scope of euthanasia supported by self-determination; it cannot justifiably be administered, for example, in cases of serious dementia or treatable clinical depression.

Does the value of individual self-determination extend to the time and manner of one's death? Most people are very concerned about the nature of the last stage of their lives. This reflects not just a fear of experiencing substantial suffering when dying, but also a desire to retain dignity and control during this last period of life. Death is today increasingly preceded by a long period of significant physical and mental decline, due in part to the technological interventions of modern medicine. Many people adjust to these disabilities and find meaning and value in new activities and ways. Others find the impairments and burdens in the last stage of their lives at some point sufficiently great to make life no longer worth living. For many patients near death, maintaining the quality of one's life, avoiding great suffering, maintaining one's dignity, and insuring that others remember us as we wish them to become of paramount importance and outweigh merely extending one's life. But there is no single, objectively correct answer for everyone as to when, if at all, one's life becomes all things considered a burden and unwanted. If self-determination is a fundamental value, then the great variability among people on this question makes it especially important that individuals control the manner, circumstances, and timing of their dying and death.

The other main value that supports euthanasia is individual well-being. It might seem that individual well-being conflicts with a person's self-determination when the person requests euthanasia. Life itself is commonly taken to be a central good for persons, often valued for its own sake, as well as necessary for pursuit of all other goods within a life. But when a competent patient decides to forgo all further life-sustaining treatment then the patient, either explicitly or implicitly, commonly decides that the best life possible for him or her with treatment is of sufficiently poor quality that it is worse than no further life at all. Life is no longer considered a benefit by the patient, but has now become a burden. The same judgment underlies a request for euthanasia: continued life is seen by the patient as no longer a benefit, but now a burden. Especially in the often severely compromised and debilitated states of many critically ill or dying patients, there is no objective standard, but only the competent patient's judgment of whether continued life is no longer a benefit. . . .

Most opponents do not deny that there are some cases in which the values of patient self-determination and well-being support euthanasia. Instead, they commonly offer two kinds of arguments against it that on their view outweigh or override this support. The first kind of argument is that in any individual case where considerations of the patient's self-determination and well-being do support euthanasia, it is nevertheless always ethically wrong or impermissible. The second kind of argument grants that in some individual cases euthanasia may *not* be ethically wrong, but maintains nonetheless that public and legal policy should never permit it. The first kind of argument focuses on features of any individual case of euthanasia, while the second kind focuses on social or legal policy. In the next section I consider the first kind of argument.

EUTHANASIA IS THE DELIBERATE KILLING OF AN INNOCENT PERSON

The claim that any individual instance of euthanasia is a case of deliberate killing of an innocent person is, with only minor qualifications, correct. Unlike forgoing life-sustaining treatment, commonly understood as allowing to die, euthanasia is clearly killing, defined as depriving of life or causing the death of a living being. While providing morphine for pain relief at doses where the risk of respiratory depression and an earlier death may be a foreseen but unintended side effect of treating the patient's pain, in a case of euthanasia the patient's death is deliberate or intended even if in both the physician's ultimate end may be respecting the patient's wishes. If the deliberate killing of an innocent person is wrong, euthanasia would be nearly always impermissible.

In the context of medicine, the ethical prohibition against deliberately killing the innocent derives some of its plausibility from the belief that nothing in the currently accepted practice of medicine is deliberate killing. Thus, in commenting on the "It's Over, Debbie" case, four prominent physicians and bioethicists could entitle their paper "Doctors Must Not Kill."[1] The belief that doctors do not in fact kill requires the corollary belief that forgoing life-sustaining treatment, whether by not starting or by stopping treatment, is allowing to die, not killing. Common though this view is, I shall argue that it is confused and mistaken.

Why is the common view mistaken? Consider the case of a patient terminally ill with ALS disease. She is completely respirator dependent with no hope of ever being weaned. She is unquestionably competent but finds her condition intolerable and persistently requests to be removed from the respirator and allowed to die. Most people and physicians would agree that the patient's physician should respect the patient's wishes and remove her from the respirator, though this will certainly cause the patient's death. The common understanding is that the physician thereby allows the patient to die. But is that correct?

Suppose the patient has a greedy and hostile son who mistakenly believes that his mother will never decide to stop her life-sustaining treatment and that even if she did her physician would not remove her from the respirator. Afraid that his inheritance will be dissipated by a long and expensive hospitalization, he enters his mother's room while she is sedated, extubates her, and she dies. Shortly thereafter the medical staff discovers what he has done and confronts the son. He replies, "I didn't kill her, I merely allowed her to die. It was her ALS disease that caused her death." I think this would rightly be dismissed as transparent sophistry—the son went into his mother's room and deliberately killed her. But, of course, the son performed just the same physical actions, did just the same thing, that the physician would have done. If that is so, then doesn't the physician also kill the patient when he extubates her? . . .

I have argued elsewhere that this alternative account is deeply problematic, in part because it commits us to accepting that what the greedy son does is to allow to die, not kill. Here, I want to note two other reasons why the conclusion that stopping life support is killing is resisted.

The first reason is that killing is often understood, especially within medicine, as unjustified causing of death; in medicine it is thought to be done only accidentally or negligently. It is also increasingly widely accepted that a physician is ethically justified in stopping life support in a case like that of the ALS patient. But if these two beliefs are correct, then what the physician does cannot be killing, and so must be allowing to die. Killing patients is not, to put it flippantly, understood to be part of physicians' job description. What is mistaken in this line of reasoning is the assumption that all killings are *unjustified* causings of death. Instead, some killings are ethically justified, including many instances of stopping life support.

Another reason for resisting the conclusion that stopping life support is often killing is that it is psychologically uncomfortable. Suppose the physician had stopped the ALS patient's respirator and had made the son's claim, "I didn't kill her, I merely allowed her to die. It was her ALS disease that caused her death." The clue to the psychological role here is how naturally the "merely" modifies "allowed her to die." The characterization as allowing to die is meant to shift felt responsibility away from the agent—the physician—and to the lethal disease process. Other language common in death and dying contexts plays a similar role; "letting nature take its course" or "stopping prolonging the dying process" both seem to shift responsibility from the physician who stops life support to the fatal disease process. However psychologically helpful these conceptualizations may be in making the difficult responsibility of a physician's role in the patient's death bearable, they nevertheless are confusions. Both physicians and family members can instead be helped to understand that it is the patient's decision and consent to stopping treatment that limits their responsibility for the patient's death and that shifts that responsibility to the patient. . . .

Suppose both my arguments are mistaken. Suppose that killing is worse than allowing to die and that withdrawing life support is not killing, although euthanasia is. Euthanasia still need not for that reason be morally wrong. To see this, we need to determine the basic principle for the moral evaluation of killing persons. What is it that makes paradigm cases of wrongful killing wrongful? One very plausible answer is that killing denies the victim something that he or she values greatly—continued life or a future. Moreover, since continued life is necessary for pursuing any of a person's plans and purposes, killing brings the frustration of all of these plans and desires as well. In a nutshell, wrongful killing deprives a person of a valued future, and of all the person wanted and planned to do in that future.

A natural expression of this account of the wrongness of killing is that people have a moral right not to be killed. But in this account of the wrongness of killing, the right not to be killed, like other rights, should be waivable when the person makes a competent decision that continued life is no longer wanted or a good, but is instead worse than no further life at all. In this view, euthanasia is properly understood as a case of a person having waived his or her right not to be killed.

This rights view of the wrongness of killing is not, of course, universally shared. Many people's moral views about killing have their origins in religious views that human life comes from God and cannot be justifiably destroyed or taken away, either by the person whose life it is or by another. But in a pluralistic society like our own with a strong commitment to freedom of religion, public policy should not be grounded in religious beliefs which many in that society reject. I turn now to the general evaluation of public policy on euthanasia.

WOULD THE BAD CONSEQUENCES OF EUTHANASIA OUTWEIGH THE GOOD?

The argument against euthanasia at the policy level is stronger than at the level of individual cases, though even here I believe the case is ultimately unpersuasive, or at best indecisive. The policy level is the place where the main issues lie, however, and where moral considerations that might override arguments in favor of euthanasia will be found, if they are found anywhere. It is important to note two kinds of disagreement about the consequences for public policy of permitting euthanasia. First, there is empirical or factual disagreement about what the consequences would be. This disagreement is greatly exacerbated by the lack of firm data on the issue. Second, since on any reasonable assessment there would be both good and bad consequences, there are moral disagreements about the relative importance of different effects. In addition to these two sources of disagreement, there is also no single, well-specified policy proposal for legalizing euthanasia on which policy assessments can focus. But without such specification, and especially without explicit procedures for protecting against well-intentioned misuse and ill-intentioned abuse, the consequences for policy are largely speculative. Despite these difficulties, a preliminary account of the main likely good and bad consequences is possible. This should help clarify where better data or more moral analysis and argument are needed, as well as where policy safeguards must be developed.

POTENTIAL GOOD CONSEQUENCES OF PERMITTING EUTHANASIA

What are the likely good consequences? First, if euthanasia were permitted it would be possible to respect the self-determination of competent patients who want it, but now cannot get it because of its illegality. . . .

One important factor substantially affecting the number of persons who would seek euthanasia is the extent to which an alternative is available. The widespread acceptance in the law, social policy, and medical practice of the right of a competent patient to forgo life-sustaining treatment suggests that the number of competent persons in the United States who would want euthanasia if it were permitted is probably relatively small.

A second good consequence of making euthanasia legally permissible benefits a much larger group. Polls have shown that a majority of the American public believes that people should have a right to obtain euthanasia if they want it.[2] No doubt the vast majority of those who support this right to euthanasia will never in fact come to want euthanasia for themselves. Nevertheless, making it legally permissible would reassure many people that if they ever do want euthanasia they would be able to obtain it. This reassurance would supplement the broader control over the process of dying given by the right to decide about life-sustaining treatment. . . .

A third good consequence of the legalization of euthanasia concerns patients whose dying is filled with severe and unrelievable pain or suffering. When there is a life-sustaining treatment that, if forgone, will lead relatively quickly to death, then doing so can bring an end to these patients' suffering without recourse to euthanasia. For patients receiving no such treatment, however, euthanasia may be the only release from their otherwise prolonged suffering and agony. This argument from mercy has always been the strongest argument for euthanasia in those cases to which it applies.[3]

The importance of relieving pain and suffering is less controversial than is the frequency with which patients are forced to undergo untreatable agony that only euthanasia could relieve. If we focus first on suffering caused by physical pain, it is crucial to distinguish pain that *could* be adequately relieved with modern methods of pain control, though it in fact is not, from pain that is relievable only by death.[4] For a variety of reasons, including some physicians' fear of hastening the patient's death, as well as the lack of a publicly accessible means for assessing the amount of the patient's pain, many patients suffer pain that could be, but is not, relieved.

Specialists in pain control, as for example the pain of terminally ill cancer patients, argue that there are very few patients whose pain could not be adequately controlled, though sometimes at the cost of so sedating them that they are effectively unable to interact with other people or their environment. Thus, the argument from mercy in cases of physical pain can probably be met in a large majority of cases by providing adequate measures of pain relief. This should be a high priority, whatever our legal policy on euthanasia—the relief of pain and suffering has long been, quite properly, one of the central goals of medicine. Those cases in which pain could be effectively relieved, but in fact is not, should only count significantly in favor of legalizing euthanasia if all reasonable efforts to change pain management techniques have been tried and have failed.

Dying patients often undergo substantial psychological suffering that is not fully or even principally the result of physical pain.[5] The knowledge about how to relieve this suffering is much more limited than in the case of relieving pain, and efforts to do so are probably more often unsuccessful. If the argument from mercy is extended to patients experiencing great and unrelievable psychological suffering, the numbers of patients to which it applies are much greater.

One last good consequence of legalizing euthanasia is that once death has been accepted, it is often more humane to end life quickly and peacefully, when that is what the patient wants. Such a death will often be seen as better than a more prolonged one. People who suffer a sudden and unexpected death, for example by dying quickly or in their sleep from a heart attack or stroke, are often considered lucky to have died in this way. We care about how we die in part because we care about how others remember us, and we hope they will remember us as we were in "good times" with them and not as we might be when disease has robbed us of our dignity as human beings. . . .

POTENTIAL BAD CONSEQUENCES OF PERMITTING EUTHANASIA

Some of the arguments against permitting euthanasia are aimed specifically against physicians, while others are aimed against anyone being permitted to perform it. I shall first consider one argument of the former sort. Permitting physicians to perform euthanasia, it is said, would be incompatible with their fundamental moral and professional commitment as healers to care for patients and to protect life. Moreover, if euthanasia by physicians became common, patients would come to fear that a medication was intended not to treat or care, but instead to kill, and would thus lose trust in their physicians. This position was forcefully stated in a paper by Willard Gaylin and his colleagues:

> The very soul of medicine is on trial. This issue touches medicine at its moral center; if this moral center collapses, if physicians become killers or are even licensed to kill, the profession—and, therewith, each physician—will never again be worthy of trust and respect as healer and comforter and protector of life in all its frailty.

These authors go on to make clear that, while they oppose permitting anyone to perform euthanasia, their special concern is with physicians doing so:

> We call on fellow physicians to say that they will not deliberately kill. We must also say to each of our fellow physicians that we will not tolerate killing of patients and that we shall take disciplinary action against doctors who kill. And we must say to the broader community that if it insists on tolerating or legalizing active euthanasia, it will have to find nonphysicians to do its killing.[6]

If permitting physicians to kill would undermine the very "moral center" of medicine, then almost certainly physicians should not be permitted to perform euthanasia. But how persuasive is this claim? Patients should not fear, as a consequence of permitting *voluntary* active euthanasia, that their physicians will substitute a lethal injection for what patients want and believe is part of their care. If active euthanasia is restricted to cases in which it is truly voluntary, then no patient should fear getting it unless she or he has voluntarily requested it. (The fear that we might in time also come to accept nonvoluntary, or even involuntary, active euthanasia is a slippery slope worry I address below.) Patients' trust of their physicians could be increased, not eroded, by knowledge that physicians will provide aid in dying when patients seek it. . . .

A second bad consequence that some foresee is that permitting euthanasia would weaken society's commitment to provide optimal care for dying patients. We live at a time in which the control of health care costs has become, and is likely to continue to be, the dominant focus of health care policy. If euthanasia is seen as a cheaper alternative to adequate care and treatment, then we might become less scrupulous about providing sometimes costly support and other services to dying patients. Particularly if our society comes to embrace deeper and more explicit rationing of health care, frail, elderly, and dying patients will need to be strong and effective advocates for their own health care and other needs, although they are hardly in a position to do this. We should do nothing to weaken their ability to obtain adequate care and services.

This second worry is difficult to assess because there is little firm evidence about the likelihood of the feared erosion in the care of dying patients. There are at least two reasons, however, for skepticism about this argument. The first is that the same worry could have been directed at recognizing patients' or surrogates' rights to forgo life-sustaining treatment, yet there is no persuasive evidence that recognizing the right to refuse treatment has caused a serious erosion in the quality of care of dying patients. The second reason for skepticism about this worry is that only a very small proportion of deaths would occur from euthanasia if it were permitted. In the Netherlands, where euthanasia under specified circumstances is permitted by the courts, though not authorized by statute, the best estimate of the proportion of overall deaths that result from it is about 2 percent.[7] Thus, the vast majority of critically ill and dying patients will not request it, and so will still have to be cared for by physicians, families, and others. Permitting euthanasia should not diminish people's commitment and concern to maintain and improve the care of these patients.

A third possible bad consequence of permitting euthanasia (or even a public discourse in which strong support for euthanasia is evident) is to threaten the progress made in securing the rights of patients or their surrogates to decide about and to refuse life-sustaining treatment.[8] This progress has been made against the backdrop of a clear and firm legal prohibition of euthanasia, which has provided a relatively bright line limiting the dominion of others over patients' lives. It has therefore been an important reassurance to concerns about how the authority to take steps ending life might be misused, abused, or wrongly extended.

Many supporters of the right of patients or their surrogates to refuse treatment strongly oppose euthanasia, and if forced to choose might well withdraw their support of the right to refuse treatment rather than accept euthanasia. Public policy in the last fifteen years has generally let life-sustaining treatment decisions be made in health care settings between physicians and patients or their surrogates, and without the involvement of the courts. However, if euthanasia is made legally permissible greater involvement of the courts is likely, which could in turn extend to a greater court involvement in life-sustaining treatment decisions. Most agree, however, that increased involvement of the courts in these decisions would be undesirable, as it would make sound decisionmaking more cumbersome and difficult without sufficient compensating benefits.

As with the second potential bad consequence of permitting euthanasia, this third consideration too is speculative and difficult to assess. The feared erosion of patients' or surrogates' rights to decide about life-sustaining treatment, together with greater court involvement in those decisions, are both possible. However, I believe there is reason to discount this general worry. The legal rights of competent patients and, to a lesser degree, surrogates of incompetent patients to decide about treatment are very firmly embedded in a long line of informed consent and life-sustaining treatment cases, and are not likely to be eroded by a debate over, or even acceptance of, euthanasia. It will not be accepted without safeguards that reassure the public about abuse, and if that debate shows the need for similar safeguards for some life-sustaining treatment decisions they should be adopted there as well. In neither case are the only possible safeguards greater court involvement, as the recent growth of institutional ethics committees shows.

The fourth potential bad consequence of permitting euthanasia has been developed by David Velleman and turns on the subtle point that making a new option or choice available to people can sometimes make them worse off, even if once they have the choice they go on to choose what is best for them.[9] Ordinarily, people's continued existence is viewed by them as given, a fixed condition with which they must cope. Making euthanasia available to people as an option denies them the alternative of staying alive by default. If people are offered the option of euthanasia, their continued existence is now a choice for which they can be held responsible and which they can be asked by others to justify. We care, and are right to care, about being able to justify ourselves to others. To the extent that our society is unsympathetic to justifying a severely dependent or impaired existence, a heavy psychological burden of proof may be placed on patients who think their terminal illness or chronic infirmity is not a sufficient reason for dying. Even if they otherwise view their life as worth living, the opinion of others around them that it is not can threaten their reason for living and make euthanasia a rational choice. Thus the existence of the option becomes a subtle pressure to request it.

This argument correctly identifies the reason why offering some patients the option of euthanasia would not benefit them. Velleman takes it not as a reason for opposing all euthanasia, but for restricting it to circumstances where there are "unmistakable and overpowering reasons for persons to want the option of euthanasia," and for denying the option in all other cases. But there are at least three reasons why such restriction may not be warranted. First, polls and other evidence support that most Americans believe euthanasia should be permitted (though the recent defeat of the referendum to permit it in the state of Washington raises some doubt about this support). Thus, many more people seem to want the choice than would be made worse off by getting it. Second, if giving people the option of ending their life really makes them worse off, then we should not only prohibit euthanasia, but also take back from people the right they now have to decide about life-sustaining treatment. The feared harmful effect should already have occurred from securing people's right to refuse life-sustaining treatment, yet there is no evidence of any such widespread harm or any broad public desire to rescind that right. Third, since there is a wide range of conditions in which reasonable people can and do disagree about whether they would want continued life, it is not possible to restrict the permissibility of euthanasia as narrowly as Velleman suggests without thereby denying it to most persons who would want it; to permit it only in cases in which virtually everyone would want it would be to deny it to most who would want it.

A fifth potential bad consequence of making euthanasia legally permissible is that it might weaken the general legal prohibition of homicide. This prohibition is so fundamental to civilized society, it is argued, that we should do nothing that erodes it. If most cases of stopping life support are killing, as I have already argued, then the court cases permitting such killing have already in effect weakened this prohibition. However, neither the courts nor most people have seen these cases as killing and so as challenging the prohibition of homicide. The courts have usually grounded patients' or their surrogates' rights to refuse life-sustaining treatment in rights to privacy, liberty, self-determination, or bodily integrity, not in exceptions to homicide laws.

Legal permission for physicians or others to perform euthanasia could not be grounded in patients' rights to decide about medical treatment. Permitting euthanasia would require qualifying, at least in effect, the legal prohibition against homicide, a prohibition that in general does not allow the consent of the victim to justify or excuse the act. Nevertheless, the very same fundamental basis of the right to decide about life-sustaining treatment—respecting a person's self-determination—does support euthanasia as well. Individual self-determination has long been a well-entrenched and fundamental value in the law, and so extending it to euthanasia would not require appeal to novel legal values or principles. That suicide or attempted suicide is no longer a criminal offense in virtually all states indicates an acceptance of individual self-determination in the taking of one's own life analogous to that required for voluntary active euthanasia. The legal prohibition (in most states) of assisting in suicide and the refusal in the law to accept the consent of the victim as a possible justification of homicide are both arguably a result of difficulties in the legal process of establishing the consent of the victim after the fact. If procedures can be designed that clearly establish the voluntariness of the person's request for euthanasia, it would under those procedures represent a carefully circumscribed qualification on the legal prohibition of homicide. Nevertheless, some remaining worries about this weakening can be captured in the final potential bad consequence, to which I will now turn.

This final potential bad consequence is the central concern of many opponents of euthanasia and, I believe, is the most serious objection to a legal policy permitting it. According to this "slippery slope" worry, although active euthanasia may be morally permissible in cases in which it is unequivocally voluntary and the patient finds his or her condition unbearable, a legal policy permitting euthanasia would inevitably lead to active euthanasia being performed in many other cases in which it would be morally wrong. To prevent those other wrongful cases of euthanasia we should not permit even morally justified performance of it.

Slippery slope arguments of this form are problematic and difficult to evaluate.[10] From one perspective, they are the last refuge of conservative defenders of the status quo. When all the opponent's objections to the wrongness of euthanasia itself have been met, the opponent then shifts ground and acknowledges both that it is not in itself wrong and that a legal policy which resulted only in its being performed would not be bad. Nevertheless, the opponent maintains, it should still not be permitted because doing so would result in its being performed in other cases in which it is not voluntary and would be wrong. In this argument's most extreme form, permitting euthanasia is the first and fateful step down the slippery slope to Nazism. Once on the slope we will be unable to get off.

Now it cannot be denied that it is *possible* that permitting euthanasia could have these fateful consequences, but that cannot be enough to warrant prohibiting it if it is otherwise justified. A similar *possible* slippery slope worry could have been raised to securing competent patients' rights to decide about life support, but recent history shows such a worry would have been unfounded. It must be relevant how likely it is that we will end with horrendous consequences and an unjustified practice of euthanasia. How *likely* and *widespread* would the abuses and unwarranted extensions of permitting it be? By abuses, I mean the performance of euthanasia that fails to satisfy the conditions required for voluntary active euthanasia, for example, if the patient has been subtly pressured to accept it. By unwarranted extensions of policy, I mean

later changes in legal policy to permit not just voluntary euthanasia, but also euthanasia in cases in which, for example, it need not be fully voluntary. Opponents of voluntary euthanasia on slippery slope grounds have not provided the data or evidence necessary to turn their speculative concerns into well-grounded likelihoods.

It is at least clear, however, that both the character and likelihood of abuses of a legal policy permitting euthanasia depend in significant part on the procedures put in place to protect against them. I will not try to detail fully what such procedures might be, but will just give some examples of what they might include:

1. The patient should be provided with all relevant information about his or her medical condition, current prognosis, available alternative treatments, and the prognosis of each.
2. Procedures should ensure that the patient's request for euthanasia is stable or enduring (a brief waiting period could be required) and fully voluntary (an advocate for the patient might be appointed to ensure this).
3. All reasonable alternatives must have been explored for improving the patient's quality of life and relieving any pain or suffering.
4. A psychiatric evaluation should ensure that the patient's request is not the result of a treatable psychological impairment such as depression.[11]

These examples of procedural safeguards are all designed to ensure that the patient's choice is fully informed, voluntary, and competent, and so a true exercise of self-determination. Other proposals for euthanasia would restrict its permissibility further—for example, to the terminally ill—a restriction that cannot be supported by self-determination. Such additional restrictions might, however, be justified by concern for limiting potential harms from abuse. At the same time, it is important not to impose procedural or substantive safeguards so restrictive as to make euthanasia impermissible or practically infeasible in a wide range of justified cases.

These examples of procedural safeguards make clear that it is possible to substantially reduce, though not to eliminate, the potential for abuse of a policy permitting voluntary active euthanasia. Any legalization of the practice should be accompanied by a well-considered set of procedural safeguards together with an ongoing evaluation of its use. Introducing euthanasia into only a few states could be a form of carefully limited and controlled social experiment that would give us evidence about the benefits and harms of the practice. Even then firm and uncontroversial data may remain elusive, as the continuing controversy over what has taken place in the Netherlands in recent years indicates.[12]

THE SLIP INTO NONVOLUNTARY ACTIVE EUTHANASIA

While I believe slippery slope worries can largely be limited by making necessary distinctions both in principle and in practice, one slippery slope concern is legitimate. There is reason to expect that legalization of voluntary active euthanasia might soon be followed by strong pressure to legalize some nonvoluntary euthanasia of incompetent patients unable to express their own wishes. Respecting a person's self-determination and recognizing that continued life is not always of value to a person can support not only voluntary active euthanasia, but some nonvoluntary euthanasia as well. These are the same values that ground competent patients' right to refuse life-sustaining treatment. Recent history here is instructive. In the medical ethics literature, in the courts since Quinlan, and in norms of medical practice, that right has been extended to incompetent patients and exercised by a surrogate who is to decide as the patient would have decided in the circumstances if competent.[13] It has been held unreasonable to continue life-sustaining treatment that the patient would not have wanted just because the patient now lacks the capacity to tell us that. Life-sustaining treatment for incompetent patients is today frequently forgone on the basis of a surrogate's decision, or less frequently on the basis of an advance directive executed by the patient while still competent. The very same logic that has extended the right to refuse life-sustaining treatment from a competent patient to the surrogate of an incompetent patient (acting with or without a formal advance directive from the patient) may well extend the scope of active euthanasia. The argument will be, Why continue to force unwanted life on patients just because they have now lost the capacity to request euthanasia from us? . . .

Even if voluntary active euthanasia should slip into nonvoluntary active euthanasia, with surrogates acting for incompetent patients, the ethical evaluation is more complex than many opponents of euthanasia allow. Just as in the case of surrogates' decisions to forgo life-sustaining treatment for incompetent patients, so also surrogates' decisions to request euthanasia for incompetent persons would often accurately reflect what the incompetent person would have wanted and would deny the person nothing that he or she would have considered worth having. Making nonvoluntary active euthanasia legally permissible, however, would greatly enlarge the number of patients on whom it might be performed and substantially enlarge the potential for misuse and abuse. As noted above, frail and debilitated elderly people, often demented or otherwise incompetent and thereby unable to defend and assert their own interests, may be especially vulnerable to unwanted euthanasia.

For some people, this risk is more than sufficient reason to oppose the legalization of voluntary euthanasia. But while we should in general be cautious about inferring much from the experience in the Netherlands to what our own experience in the United States might be, there may be one important lesson that we can learn from them. One commentator has noted that in the Netherlands families of incompetent patients have less authority than do families in the United States to act as surrogates for incompetent patients in making decisions to forgo life-sustaining treatment.[14] From the Dutch perspective, it may be we in the United States who are *already* on the slippery slope in having given surrogates broad authority to forgo life-sustaining treatment for incompetent persons. In this view, the more important moral divide, and the more important with regard to potential for abuse, is not between forgoing life-sustaining treatment and euthanasia, but instead between voluntary and nonvoluntary performance of either. If this is correct, then the more important issue is ensuring the appropriate principles and procedural safeguards for the exercise of decisionmaking authority by surrogates for incompetent persons in *all* decisions at the end of life. This may be the correct response to slippery slope worries about euthanasia. . . .

NOTES

1. Willard Gaylin, Leon R. Kass, Edmund D. Pellegrino, and Mark Siegler, "Doctors Must Not Kill," *JAMA* 259 (1988): 2139–40.

2. P. Painton and E. Taylor, "Love or Let Die," *Time,* 19 March 1990, pp. 62–71; *Boston Globe*/Harvard University Poll, *Boston Globe,* 3 November 1991.

3. James Rachels, *The End of Life* (Oxford: Oxford University Press, 1986).

4. Marcia Angell, "The Quality of Mercy," *NEJM* 306 (1982): 98–99; M. Donovan, P. Dillon, and L. Mcguire, "Incidence and

Characteristics of Pain in a Sample of Medical-Surgical Inpatients," *Pain* 30 (1987): 69–78.

5. Eric Cassell, *The Nature of Suffering and the Goals of Medicine* (New York: Oxford University Press, 1991).

6. Gaylin et al., "Doctors Must Not Kill."

7. Paul J. Van der Maas et al., "Euthanasia and Other Medical Decisions Concerning the End of Life," *Lancet* 338 (1991): 669–674.

8. Susan M. Wolf, "Holding the Line on Euthanasia," Special Supplement, *Hastings Center Report* 19, no. 1 (1989): 13–15.

9. My formulation of this argument derives from David Velleman's statement of it in his commentary on an earlier version of this paper delivered at the American Philosophical Association Central Division meetings; a similar point was made to me by Elisha Milgram in discussion on another occasion.

10. Frederick Schauer, "Slippery Slopes," *Harvard Law Review* 99 (1985): 361–83; Wibren van der Burg, "The Slippery Slope Argument," *Ethics* 102 (October 1991): 42–65.

11. There is evidence that physicians commonly fail to diagnose depression. See Robert I. Misbin, "Physicians Aid in Dying," *NEJM* 325 (1991): 1304–7.

12. Richard Fenigsen, "A Case against Dutch Euthanasia," Special Supplement, *Hastings Center Report* 19, no. 1 (1989): 22–30.

13. Allen E. Buchanan and Dan W. Brock, *Deciding for Others: The Ethics of Surrogate Decisionmaking* (Cambridge: Cambridge University Press, 1989).

14. Margaret P. Battin, "Seven Caveats Concerning the Discussion of Euthanasia in Holland," *American Philosophical Association Newsletter on Philosophy and Medicine* 89, no. 2 (1990).

JOHN D. ARRAS

Physician-Assisted Suicide: A Tragic View

John Arras is the Porterfield Professor of Biomedical Ethics, professor of philosophy, and director of the Undergraduate Program in Bioethics at the University of Virginia. He was for fourteen years a professor of bioethics at Montefiore Medical Center/Albert Einstein College of Medicine and adjunct professor of philosophy at Barnard College, Columbia University. A former member of the New York State Task Force on Life and Law, Dr. Arras is the editor (with Bonnie Steinbock) of *Ethical Issues in Modern Medicine, 4th ed.*, and *Bringing the Hospital Home: Ethical and Social Implications of High Technology Home Care,* and the author of numerous articles on bioethics.

For many decades now, the calls the PAS and euthanasia have been perennial lost causes in American society. Each generation has thrown up an assortment of earnest reformers and cranks who, after attracting their fifteen minutes of fame, inevitably have been defeated by the combined weight of traditional law and morality. Incredibly, two recent federal appellate court decisions suddenly changed the legal landscape in this area, making the various states within their respective jurisdictions the first governments in world history, excepting perhaps the Nazi regime in Germany, to officially sanction PAS. Within the space of a month, both an eight-to-three majority of the United States Court of Appeals for the Ninth Circuit[1] on the West Coast, and a three-judge panel in the United States Court of Appeals for the Second Circuit,[2] in the Northeast, struck down long-standing state laws forbidding physicians to aid or abet their patients in acts of suicide. Within a virtual blink of an eye, the unthinkable had come to pass: PAS and euthanasia had emerged from their exile beyond the pale of law to occupy center stage in a dramatic public debate that eventually culminated in the United States Supreme Court's unanimous reversal of both lower court decisions in June 1997.[3]

From Margaret P. Battin, Rosamond Rhodes, and Anita Silvers, *Physician Assisted Suicide: Expanding the Debate.* New York and London: Routledge 1998, 279–300. Footnotes renumbered.

Judge Reinhardt, writing for a majority of an *en banc* decision of the Ninth Circuit,[4] held that competent, terminally ill patients have a powerful "liberty interest," what used to be called a Constitutional right, to enlist the aid of their physicians in hastening death via prescriptions for lethal drugs.[5] He argued that, just as the right to privacy guarantees women the right to choose an abortion, this liberty interest protects a right to choose the time and manner of one's death.[6] . . .

Writing for the Second Circuit in striking down a similar New York statute, Judge Miner explicitly rejected the claim of the Second Circuit majority that a "substantive due process" right of PAS exists in the Constitution. While presciently conceding that the Supreme Court was unlikely to extend the boundaries of the so-called right to privacy, Judge Miner found nevertheless that the statute violated the equal protection clause of the Constitution. . . .

The Supreme Court has finally left little doubt about where it stands on these questions. In a set of majority and concurring opinions remarkable for their ideological restraint, compassion, and thoughtfulness, the various Justices have concluded that extant state laws barring PAS and euthanasia violate neither the Fourteenth Amendment protection of liberty nor the Fifth Amendment's due process provision.[8] While thus issuing a painful rebuke to the partisans of liberalization, each of the Justices tempered his or her final judgment with the recognition that their collective decision would by no means end public debate, but would rather displace it onto the agendas of the fifty state legislatures.

As a firm believer in patient autonomy, I find myself to be deeply sympathetic to the central values motivating the case for PAS and euthanasia; I have concluded, however, that these practices pose too great a threat to the rights and welfare of too many people to be legalized in this country at the present time. Central to my argument in this essay will be the claim that the recently overturned decisions of the circuit courts employ a form of case-based reasoning that is ill-suited to the development of sound social policy in this area. I shall argue that in order to do justice to the very real threats posed by the widespread social practices of PAS and euthanasia, we need to adopt precisely the kind of policy perspective that the circuit courts rejected on principle. Thus, this essay presents the case for a forward-looking, legislative approach to PAS and euthanasia, as opposed to an essentially backward-looking, judicial or constitutional approach. Although I suggest below that the soundest legislative policy at the present time would be to extend the legal prohibition of PAS into the near future, I remain open to the possibility that a given legislature, presented with sufficient evidence of the reliability of various safeguards, might come to a different conclusion. . . .

OBJECTIONS TO PAS/EUTHANASIA

Opponents of PAS and euthanasia can be grouped into three main factions. One strongly condemns both practices as inherently immoral, as violations of the moral rule against killing the innocent. Most members of this group tend to harbor distinctly religious objections to suicide and euthanasia, viewing them as violations of God's dominion over human life.[9] They argue that killing is simply wrong in itself, whether or not it is done out of respect for the patient's autonomy or out of concern for her suffering. Whether or not this position ultimately is justifiable from a theological point of view, its imposition on believers and nonbelievers alike is incompatible with the basic premises of a secular, pluralistic political order.

A second faction primarily objects to the fact that physicians are being called upon to do the killing. While conceding that killing the terminally ill or assisting in their suicides might not always be morally wrong for others to do, this group maintains that the participation of physicians in such practices undermines their role as healers and fatally compromises the physician-patient relationship.[10]

Finally, a third faction readily grants that neither PAS nor active euthanasia, practiced by ordinary citizens or by physicians, are always morally wrong. On the contrary, this faction believes that in certain rare instances early release from a painful or intolerably degrading existence might constitute both a positive good and an important exercise of personal autonomy for the individual. Indeed, many members of this faction concede that should such a terrible fate befall them, they would hope to find a thoughtful, compassionate, and courageous physician to release them from their misery. But in spite of these important concessions, the members of this faction shrink from endorsing or regulating PAS and active euthanasia due to fears bearing on the social consequences of liberalization. This view is based on two distinct kinds of so-called "slippery slope" arguments. One bears on the inability to cabin PAS/euthanasia within the confines envisioned by its proponents; the other focuses on the likelihood of abuse, neglect, and mistake.

The first version of the slippery slope argument contends that a socially sanctioned practice of PAS would in all likelihood prove difficult, if not impossible, to cabin within its originally anticipated boundaries. Proponents of legalization usually begin with a wholesomely modest policy agenda, limiting their suggested reforms to a narrow and highly specified range of potential candidates and practices.[11] "Give us PAS," they ask, "not the more controversial practice of active euthanasia, for presently competent patients who are terminally ill and suffering unbearable pain." But the logic of the case for PAS, based as it is upon the twin pillars of patient autonomy and mercy, makes it highly unlikely that society could stop with this modest proposal once it had ventured out on the slope. As numerous other critics have pointed out, if autonomy is the prime consideration, then additional constraints based upon terminal illness or unbearable pain, or both, would appear hard to justify.[12] Indeed, if autonomy is crucial, the requirement of unbearable suffering would appear to be entirely subjective. Who is to say, other than the patient herself, how much suffering is too much? Likewise, the requirement of terminal illness seems an arbitrary standard against which to judge patients' own subjective evaluation of their quality of life. If my life is no longer worth living, why should a terminally ill cancer patient be granted PAS but not me, merely because my suffering is due to my "nonterminal" arterio-lateral sclerosis ("ALS") or intractable psychiatric disorder?[13]

Alternatively, if pain and suffering are deemed crucial to the justification of legalization, it is hard to see how the proposed barrier of contemporaneous consent of competent patients could withstand serious erosion. If the logic of PAS is at all similar to that of forgoing life-sustaining treatments, and we have every reason to think it so, then it would seem almost inevitable that a case soon would be made to permit PAS for incompetent patients who had left advance directives. That would then be followed by a "substituted judgment" test for patients who "would have wanted" PAS, and finally an "objective" test would be developed for patients (including newborns) whose best interests would be served by PAS or active euthanasia even in the absence of any subjective intent.[14]

In the same way, the joint justification of autonomy and mercy combine to undermine the plausibility of a line drawn between PAS and active euthanasia. As the authors of one highly publicized proposal have come to see, the logic of justification for active euthanasia is identical to that of PAS.[15] Legalizing PAS, while continuing to ban active euthanasia, would serve only to discriminate unfairly against patients who are suffering and wish to end their lives, but cannot do so because of some physical impairment. Surely these patients, it will be said, are "the worst off group," and therefore they are the most in need of the assistance of others who will do for them what they can no longer accomplish on their own.

None of these initial slippery slope considerations amount to knock-down objections to further liberalization of our laws and practices. After all, it is not obvious that each of these highly predictable shifts (e.g., from terminal to "merely" incurable, from contemporaneous consent to best interests, and from PAS to active euthanasia), are patently immoral and unjustifiable. Still, in pointing out this likely slippage, the consequentialist opponents of PAS/euthanasia are calling on society to think about the likely consequences of taking the first tentative step onto the slope. If all of the extended practices predicted above pose substantially greater risks for vulnerable patients than the more highly circumscribed initial liberalization proposals, then we need to factor in these additional risks even as we ponder the more modest proposals.

THE LIKELIHOOD OF ABUSE

The second prong of the slippery slope argument argues that whatever criteria for justifiable PAS and active euthanasia ultimately are chosen, abuse of the system is highly likely to follow. In other words, patients who fall outside the ambit of our justifiable criteria will soon be candidates for death. This prong resembles what I have elsewhere called an "empirical slope" argument, as it is based not on the close logical resemblance of concepts or justifications, but rather on an empirical prediction of what is likely to happen when we insert a particular social practice into our existing social system.[16]

In order to reassure skeptics, the proponents of PAS/euthanasia concur that any potentially justifiable social policy in this area must meet at least the following three requirements.[17] The policy would have to insist: first, that all requests for death be truly voluntary; second, that all reasonable alternatives to PAS and active euthanasia must be explored before acceding to a patient's wishes; and, third, that a reliable system of reporting all cases must be establishes in order to effectively monitor these practices and respond to abuses. As a social pessimist on these matters, I believe, given social reality as we know it, that all three assumptions are problematic.

With regard to the voluntariness requirement, we pessimists contend that many requests would not be sufficiently voluntary. In addition to the subtly coercive influences of physicians and family members, perhaps the most slippery aspect of this slope is the highly predictable failure of most physicians to diagnose reliably and treat reversible clinical depression, particularly in the elderly population. As one geriatric psychiatrist testified before the New York Task Force, we now live in the "golden age" of treating depression, but the "lead age" of diagnosing it.[18] We have the tools, but physicians are not adequately trained and motivated to use them. Unless dramatic changes are effected in the practice of medicine, we can predict with confidence that many instances of PAS and active euthanasia will fail the test of voluntariness.

Second, there is the lingering fear that any legislative proposal or judicial mandate would have to be implemented within the present social system, one marked by deep and pervasive discrimination against the poor and members of minority groups. We have every reason to expect that a policy that worked tolerably well in an affluent community like Scarsdale or Beverly Hills might not work so well in a community like Bedford-Stuyvesant or Watts, where your average citizen has little or no access to basic primary care, let alone sophisticated care for chronic pain at home or in the hospital. There is also reason to worry about any policy of PAS initiated within our growing system of managed care, capitation, and physician incentives for delivering less care.[19] Expert palliative care no doubt is an expensive and time-consuming proposition, requiring more, rather than less, time spent just talking with patients and providing them with humane comfort. It is highly doubtful that the context of physician-patient conversation within this new dispensation of "turnstile medicine" will be at all conducive to humane decisions untainted by subtle economic coercion.

In addition, given the abysmal and shameful track record of physicians in responding adequately to pain and suffering, we also can confidently predict that in many cases all reasonable alternatives will *not* have been exhausted. Instead of vigorously addressing the pharmacological and psychosocial needs of such patients, physicians no doubt will continue to ignore, undertreat, or treat many of their patients in an impersonal manner. The result is likely to be more depression, desperation, and requests for physician-assisted death from patients who could have been successfully treated. The root causes of this predictable failure are manifold, but high on the list is the inaccessibility of decent primary care to over thirty-seven million Americans. Other notable causes include an appalling lack of training in palliative care among primary care physicians and cancer specialists alike; discrimination in the delivery of pain control and other medical treatments on the basis of race and economic status; various myths shared by both physicians and patients about the supposed ill effects of pain medications; and restrictive state laws on access to opioids.

Finally, with regard to the third requirement, pessimists doubt that any reporting system would adequately monitor these practices. A great deal depends here on the extent to which patients and practitioners will regard these practices as essentially *private* matters to be discussed and acted upon within the privacy of the doctor-patient relationship. As the Dutch experience has conclusively demonstrated, physicians will be extremely loath to report instances of PAS and active euthanasia to public authorities, largely for fear of bringing the harsh glare of publicity upon the patients' families at a time when privacy is most needed. The likely result of this predictable lack of oversight will be society's inability to respond appropriately to disturbing incidents and long-term trends. In other words, the practice most likely will not be as amenable to regulation as the proponents contend.

The moral of this story is that deeply seated inadequacies in physicians' training, combined with structural flaws in our healthcare system, can be reliably predicted to secure the premature deaths of many people who would in theory be excluded by the criteria of most leading proposals to legalize PAS. If this characterization of the status quo is at all accurate, then the problem will not be solved by well-meaning assurances that abuses will not be tolerated, or that patients will, of course, be offered the full range of palliative care options before any decision for PAS is ratified. . . .

We come now to the difficult task of assessing the capacity of various social policy approaches to address adequately all of the conflicting values implicated in this debate. This section shall contrast a forward-looking, policy-oriented legislative approach to the backward-looking, case-oriented judicial approach taken in the *Compassion in Dying* and *Vacco* cases. Before coming to that comparison, however, a crucial preliminary point must be noted. Central to any serious evaluation of competing policy approaches to PAS and euthanasia is the distinction between the morality of individual acts and the wisdom of social policy. Much of the debate in the popular media is driven by the depiction of especially dramatic and poignant instances of suffering humanity, desperate for release from the painful thrall of terminal illness. Understandably, many of us are prompted to respond: "Should such a terrible fate ever befall me, I certainly would not want to suffer interminably; I would want the option of an early exit and the help of my trusted physician in securing it." The problem, however, lies in getting from such compelling individual cases to social policy. The issue is not simply, "What should I want?" but rather, what is the best social policy, all things considered. Social pessimists warn that we cannot make this jump from individual case to policy without endangering the autonomy and the very lives of others, many of whom are numbered among our most vulnerable citizens.

A JUDGE-MADE POLICY BASED ON CONSTITUTIONAL LAW

Appellate judges in the Ninth and Second Circuits authored powerful opinions giving constitutional protection to PAS for competent patients facing terminal illness. While these opinions fully vindicated patients' important stake in having a freely chosen and pain-free death, they seriously and fatally discounted the states' important interests in preventing the kinds of slippage and abuse catalogued above.

Dismissal of Social Consequences. The opinion of the Ninth Circuit, *Compassion in Dying,* authored by Judge Reinhardt, is particularly troubling with regard to the dismissal of social consequences. In response to the objection that legalizing PAS inevitably will prove "infinitely expansive," the court acknowledged the difficulty that it may be hard to distinguish the moral logic of PAS from that animating the call for direct physician-administered euthanasia. He further conceded that in some cases, patients will need the help of a physician in carrying out their choice of an autonomous and painless death. Instead of carefully weighing this sobering possibility in the balance, or asking whether this likelihood of slippage should make us hesitate in taking the first step onto the slope, the court immediately dismissed it as a problem for future cases, not this one, noting that, "here we decide only the issue before us."[20] For those who worry that direct euthanasia carried out by physicians might impose too great a risk in the current social climate, the dictum will prove less than comforting, especially in view of the judge's confession that "it [is] less important who administers the medication than who determines whether the terminally ill person's life shall end."[21]

Thus, although we have argued that this kind of forward-looking, policy-oriented perspective is crucial for adequately assessing the individual benefits and social risks involved in the proposal to legalize PAS, the judicial approach to the problem operates fully equipped with social blinders, and willfully dismisses the very real dangers lurking further down the slope, all in the name of individual rights. Indeed, at one point Judge Reinhardt implied that a refusal to contemplate such dangers is demanded by the judicial role itself.[22] To put it mildly and most charitably, this rights-oriented mind-set does not put us in a learning mode. When life and death are at stake, we need to base our social policy on a more comprehensive picture of the likely benefits and risks.

Judge Reinhardt's grasp of the clinical realities of depression and the ubiquitous absence of adequate pain control was no more impressive than the scope of his social vision. In response to the objection that the legalization of PAS eventually would lead physicians to treat requests to die in a routine and impersonal manner, Judge Reinhardt reassured us, in the face of massive evidence to the contrary, that "doctors would not assist a terminally ill patient to hasten his death as long as there were any reasonable chance of alleviating the patient's suffering or enabling him to live under tolerable conditions."[23] Judge Reinhardt's faith in professional and governmental regulations to ensure that all requests truly are voluntary (i.e., not due to depression), and free from the taint of untreated pain and suffering, is perhaps refreshing in the age of governmental regulation-bashing, but it is a naive and dangerous faith in all the same.

Equal Protection and the Fate of Responsible Regulation. The ability of a constitutional right to assisted suicide to provide adequately for safeguards against abuse, neglect, and mistake is especially problematic within the context of the Second Circuit's equal protection analysis in *Vacco.* That court's assertion of the moral and legal equivalence of withholding life-sustaining treatments, the provision of potentially death-hastening analgesics, and assisted suicide raised extremely troubling questions about the constitutionality of a wide variety of possibly effective regulations. The basic question is: If we have a constitutionally protected liberty interest in determining the time and manner of our deaths, then to what extent will various regulatory schemes cut too deeply into our personal choices?

We actually have seen this script played out before in the context of abortion law. Prior to *Roe v. Wade,* many states already had begun liberalizing their statutes to allow women to opt for abortion under specified conditions. One regulatory constraint that had been placed on women's choice in some jurisdictions was mandatory review by a hospital-based committee. Now, whether or not we think that such committee review was a good idea in the context of abortion—I do not think it was—it is still interesting to note that this regulatory mechanism, along with a host of others, was discarded unceremoniously by the Supreme Court in *Doe v. Bolton,*[24] the companion case to *Roe v. Wade.* In sum, the Court held that such mechanisms only serve to encumber the woman's choice, which really belongs to her (and perhaps also her doctor) alone.

Now, if the Second Circuit's equal protection analysis had prevailed, and had the Supreme Court come to see no cognizable legal or moral differences between "allowing to die" and assisted suicide, then presumably the regulatory mechanisms surrounding the two sets of practices would have been subjected to identical standards of moral analysis and judicial review. This kind of legally mandated parity would have had two likely consequences. First, all the paraphernalia of surrogate decision-making that currently surrounds decisions to forgo treatment would have been extended to PAS. Just as most states presently allow family or close friends to make life-and-death decisions for loved ones on the basis of so-called "substituted judgment" ("What would the patient have wanted?") or best-interests or reasonable-person determinations, so we would have to allow family members the same role in those cases in which suicide "would have been chosen" by the patient or "would have been" in his best interest. Obviously, this implication of the equal protection approach would have required proponents of PAS to bite a very large bullet indeed regarding the charge of indefinite expansion.

The second implication of the equal protection analysis is that a broad range of possibly helpful regulatory mechanisms, including waiting periods, committee review, second opinions, mandatory reporting, and perhaps even the requirement of terminal illness, might well have been swept aside in the name of individual liberty. Currently, we do not require these kinds of substantive and procedural constraints for most decisions to forgo life-sustaining treatments by competent, terminally ill patients. If, however, there is really no moral or legal difference between "allowing to die" and "assisting suicide"—if, as Judge Miner opines, adding PAS to our repertoire of choices would not add one iota of additional risk to individuals or society over and above those we already countenance—then encumbering the choice for PAS with all sorts of extra protective devices would seemingly lack constitutional validity. In sum, then, the equal protection analysis championed in the Second Circuit threatened precisely those braking mechanisms that arguably might make the slippery slope a far safer place on which to practice physician-assisted death.

The Conflation of Killing and Allowing to Die. Proceeding directly to the fulcrum of Judge Miner's analysis, we now consider the denial of a significant moral or legal difference between allowing a patient to die by means of forgoing life-sustaining treatments and assisting a patient in committing suicide. According to both circuit court opinions, there is no significant difference between withdrawing a ventilator, discontinuing a feeding tube, administering pain-killing but (potentially) life-shortening opioids, and prescribing a lethal dose of barbiturates.[25] In all these cases, the judges alleged, the intention is the same (i.e., to hasten death), the cause of death is the same (an *act* attributable to human agency), and the social risks of mistake and abuse are the same (e.g., misdiagnosis, undue pressure, etc.). Consequently, Judge Reinhardt concluded that PAS poses no greater threat to the state's interests in preventing suicide and in safeguarding the integrity of the medical profession than the already accepted practice of forgoing life-sustaining treatment. For identical reasons Judge Miner saw no point in a more restrictive public policy towards PAS and based his entire Constitutional argument upon the purported identity of the intentions and effects of these two social practices.[26]

Along with a majority of the Supreme Court, I wish to uphold, for purposes of social policy analysis, the distinction between forgoing treatment and assisting suicide. Although the boundaries between these two practices at times are admittedly quite fuzzy, overlooking relevant differences between them leads proponents of legalization to ignore the very real social risks inherent in the judicial approach to policy.[27]

Whatever the outcome of our long-standing conceptual skirmishes bearing on the "intrinsic" distinctions between PAS, direct euthanasia, and forgoing life-sustaining treatments, the crucial question remains whether any of the purported distinctions between these activities constitute important differences for purposes of social policy. As a slippery slope opponent of PAS and euthanasia, I have already conceded that individual acts involving either PAS or active euthanasia can be morally justified under certain circumstances. Having thus conceded that certain individual actions can be morally appropriate even when the intent is simply and unambiguously to end the patient's life, and even when "the cause" of death is simply and unambiguously attributable to the action of the physician, the crucial question is whether there are any remaining distinctions between allowing to die and actively killing (or assisting in a suicide) that might illuminate the negative policy implications of PAS and euthanasia.

Two points can be made in this connection. First, as the New York Task Force pointed out, the social consequences of not honoring requests to forgo treatment are very different from the consequences of failing to honor requests for PAS and euthanasia. When society fails to honor requests to prescribe or deliver a lethal dose, the results can admittedly be very onerous for individual patients. The patient may face a prolonged period of deterioration before death, with increased pain and decreased dignity, contrary to what they otherwise would have wished. It is important to note, however, that in many such cases there are alternatives to prolonged and painful deaths. Under the present legal regime it is still permissible for a patient to seek out effective and compassionate hospice care, to refuse further administration of life-sustaining treatments, to request "terminal sedation" (inducing a loss of consciousness until death), and even to starve to death with the aid of a physician. It is also legal for an individual truly to take matters into his own hands and to kill himself, perhaps with the guidance of a popular "self-help" book. Finally, it is possible for many patients with good and trusting relationships with compassionate physicians to achieve their objectives within the bounds of private and discreet relationships, but without the cover and consolations of law.

By contrast, were society, systematically and as a matter of policy, to refuse to honor requests to forgo life-sustaining treatments in order to curb possible abuses, then everyone would have to submit to the imposition of unwanted and often invasive measures. Whereas the refusal to honor a request for PAS or direct euthanasia amounts to a refusal of a positive benefit or assistance, the imposition of medical treatment against one's will represents a violation of personal autonomy and physical integrity totally incompatible with the deepest meaning of our traditional respect for liberty. Such a refusal would entail the virtual imprisonment of the entire population of terminally ill and dying patients. While the failure to offer a deadly drug to a dying patient represents a failure of mercy requiring moral justification, the forced imposition of medical treatment against a patient's will arguably constitutes a trespass, or technically a legal battery, so profound that it simply cannot be justified, especially at the level of broad-gauged social policy.

Without trying to sound especially hyperbolical, we can say that the practice of forgoing treatment is by now so deeply embedded in our social and medical practices that a reversal of policy on this point would throw most of our major medical institutions into a state approaching chaos. The same cannot be said of a refusal to honor requests for PAS and euthanasia. Thus, while there may well be many overlapping similarities between withholding treatment and participating in PAS or euthanasia, their respective denial at the level of social policy would entail vastly different individual and social consequences. If our goal is to reduce the level of social risk surrounding all practices involving the treatment of incurable and/or dying patients, a blanket prohibition of PAS can arguably advance this goal without totally unacceptable moral, legal, and social consequences. The same cannot be said of a blanket prohibition of forgoing life-sustaining treatments.

The second point in this connection is that the practice of PAS and/or active euthanasia would be bound to implicate many more persons than the practice of forgoing treatment. While we should definitely worry about the possibility of error, neglect, and abuse in the context of allowing patients to die, it is at least somewhat comforting to realize that just about every patient in this category must be very badly off indeed. By the time that physicians discuss forgoing treatment with a patient or family, the patient is usually well into the process of dying.

With regard to PAS and euthanasia, however, we can expect that many candidates will be perfectly ambulatory and far from the dreaded scene of painful terminal illness depicted by advocates. Depending on how great the social slippage, this category may well come to encompass those with an incurable condition but who are not presently "terminal," such as persons in the early stages of HIV infection or Alzheimer's disease. It also may come to encompass patients suffering from prolonged and intractable depression who exhibit no other symptoms of physical illness. Although one important legislative proposal specifically excludes patients whose only symptoms are psychiatric in nature, this reluctance was likely motivated in no small measure by political considerations.[28] Once PAS or active euthanasia, or both, are firmly in place, however, it will be extremely difficult to withhold them from persons whose suffering is every bit as real but whose source is entirely psychological rather than physical. That, Judge Miner and many others would surely object, would constitute an invidious distinction and thus a form of unconstitutional discrimination against the mentally ill.

IF THE STATES ARE THE LABORATORY, WHAT'S THE EXPERIMENT?

Although the Ninth Circuit was prepared to grant that states have a legitimate interest in avoiding the possibly adverse social consequences of PAS, the court insisted that regulation, rather than prohibition, is the only constitutionally permissible means of so doing.[29] Toward that end, it would have assigned the challenging task of crafting appropriate regulations to the "laboratory of the states." In view of the very real possibility that the social and individual harms attendant upon the legalization of PAS eventually would prove disproportionate to their benefits, this division of labor between the judiciary and the state legislatures is highly problematic. Had the Supreme Court affirmed the Ninth Circuit's reasoning in granting constitutional protection to the liberty interest in choosing death, states would have been deprived of their ability to put a stop to the widespread practice of PAS even if credible studies were to demonstrate that abuses were rampant and highly resistant to procedural safeguards. Short of a Constitutional amendment, there would have been no turning back had the right to PAS been guaranteed by either the due process or equal protection clauses.

Instead of putting ourselves into this precarious position, we should assign a different and more fundamental task to the laboratory of the states. Given the very real possibilities for extension and abuse of this liberty interest, state legislatures should be entrusted with the basic questions of whether, when, and under what circumstances such a risky social experiment should be attempted in the first place. State legislatures are in a better position than federal judges to study the social and clinical facts and come to a reasonable conclusion on the likely balance of individual benefit and social risks. Given the social and medical realities of this country, I would hope that most states would follow the lead of the New York Task Force in refusing to countenance the legalization and routinization of PAS at this time. However, even if some states do decide to run these risks as a social experiment, i.e., to determine for themselves on the basis of empirical evidence and moral judgment whether more good than harm will come from legalizing PAS, they would have the flexibility, absent rigidly defined constitutional mandates, both to impose very strict regulations and, if necessary, to stop the experiment cold in the face of disconcerting evidence of serious moral slippage. Such an approach is, I believe, much better suited to asking the relevant policy questions and taking appropriate and prudent action.

In addition to being safer, the legislative approach is also, at least potentially, much more democratic than the judicial, rights-based orientation. The legislature is the traditional site in this country for the resolution of most difficult and divisive questions of social policy, especially those marked by deep moral questions and highly troubling empirical uncertainties involving the lives and welfare of many citizens. A court-mandated solution to the question of PAS would, I believe, have secured a decisive and irrevocable victory for one side of this controversy before a thorough and robust public debate had taken place. One significant merit of a legislative approach is that, while it would not guarantee such a debate, it would at least be compatible with large-scale efforts at the state and local levels to foster a more democratically deliberative public dialogue on this matter. Such efforts could give citizens a chance to weigh the nature and value of the liberties at stake against the extent and probability of the social dangers posed by PAS. They could thus serve as a valuable *via media* between the judicial approach, which can often short circuit public debate, and decision-making by public referendum, which is more democratic in theory but often lacks an explicitly deliberative dimension that would allow citizens a deeper understanding of the issues involved before their legislatures took action.

TOWARD A POLICY OF PRUDENT (LEGAL) RESTRAINT AND AGGRESSIVE (MEDICAL) INTERVENTION

In contrast to the judicial approach, which totally vindicates the value of patient autonomy at the expense of protecting the vulnerable, my own preferred approach to a social policy of PAS and euthanasia conceives of this debate as posing essentially a "tragic choice." It frankly acknowledges that whatever choice we make, whether we opt for a reaffirmation of the current legal restraints or for a policy of legitimation and regulation, there are bound to be victims. The victims of the current policy are easy to identify: They are on the news, the talk shows, the documentaries, and often on Dr. Kevorkian's roster of so-called "patient." The victims of legalization, by contrast, will be largely hidden from view; they will include the clinically depressed eighty-year-old man who could have lived for another year of good quality if only he had been adequately treated, and the fifty-year-old woman who asks for death because doctors in her financially stretched HMO cannot, or will not, effectively treat her unrelenting, but mysterious, pelvic pain. Perhaps eventually, if we slide far enough down the slope, the uncommunicative stroke victim, whose distant children deem an earlier death to be a better death, will fall victim. There will be others besides these, many coming from the ranks of the uninsured and the poor. To the extent that minorities and the poor already suffer from the effects of discrimination in our healthcare system, it is reasonable to expect that any system of PAS and euthanasia will exhibit similar effects, such as failure to access adequate primary care, pain management, and psychiatric diagnosis and treatment. Unlike Dr. Kevorkian's "patients," these victims will not get their pictures in the papers, but they all will have faces and they will all be cheated of good months or perhaps even years.

This "tragic choice" approach to social policy on PAS/euthanasia takes the form of the following argument formulated at the legislative level. First, the number of "genuine cases" justifying PAS, active euthanasia, or both, will be relatively small. Patients who receive good personal care, good pain relief, treatment for depression, and adequate psychosocial supports tend not to persist in their desire to die.

Second, the social risks of legalization are serious and highly predictable. They include the expansion of these practices to nonvoluntary cases, the advent of active euthanasia, and the widespread failure to pursue readily available alternatives to suicide motivated by pain, depression, hopelessness, and lack of access to good primary medical care.

Third, rather than propose a momentous and dangerous policy shift for a relatively small number of "genuine cases"—a shift that would surely involve a great deal of persistent social division and strife analogous to that involved in the abortion controversy—we should instead attempt to redirect the public debate toward a goal on which we can and should all agree, namely the manifest and urgent need to reform the way we die in America. Instead of pursuing a highly divisive and dangerous campaign for PAS, we should attack the problem at its root with an ambitious program of reform in the areas of access to primary care and the education of physicians in palliative care. . . .

CONCLUSION

Instead of conceiving this momentous debate as a choice between, on the one hand, legalization and regulation with all of their attendant risks, and on the other hand, the callous abandonment of patients to their pain and suffering, enlightened opponents must recommend a positive program of clinical and social reforms. On the clinical level, physicians must learn how to really listen to their patients, to unflinchingly engage them in sensitive discussions of their needs and the meaning of their requests for assisted death, to deliver appropriate palliative care, to distinguish fact from fiction in the ethics and law of pain relief, to diagnose and treat clinical depression, and finally, to ascertain and respect their patients' wishes for control regarding the forgoing of life-sustaining treatments. On the social level, opponents of PAS must aggressively promote major initiatives in medical and public education regarding pain control, in the sensitization of insurance companies and licensing agencies to issues of the quality of dying, and in the reform of state laws that currently hinder access to pain relieving medications.

In the absence of an ambitious effort in the direction of aggressive medical and social reform, I fear that the medical and nursing professions will have lost whatever moral warrant and credibility they might still have in continuing to oppose physician-assisted suicide and active euthanasia. As soon as these reforms are in place, however, we might then wish to proceed slowly and cautiously with experiments in various states to test the overall benefits of a policy of legalization. Until that time, however, we are not well served as a society by court decisions allowing for legalization of PAS. The Supreme Court has thus reached a sound decision in ruling out a constitutional right to PAS. As the Justices acknowledged, however, this momentous decision will not end the moral debate over PAS and euthanasia. Indeed, it should and hopefully will intensify it.

NOTES

1. *Compassion in Dying v. Washington,* 79 F. 3d 790, 838 (9th Cir. 1996).

2. *Quill v. Vacco,* 80 F. 3d 716, 731 (2nd Cir. 1996).

3. *Vacco, Attorney General of New York, et al. v. Quill et al.,* certiorari to the United States Court of Appeals for the second circuit, No. 95–1858. Argued January 8, 1997—Decided June 26, 1997. *Washington et al. v. Glucksberg et al.,* certiorari to the United States Court of Appeals for the ninth circuit, No. 96–110. Argued January 8, 1997—Decided June 26, 1997.

4. See *Compassion in Dying,* 79 F. 3d at 790.

5. Ibid., 816.

6. Ibid., 813–14.

7. *Vacco v. Quill,* 80 F. 3d 716, 724–25 (2nd Cir. 1996).

8. *Washington v. Glucksberg,* 117 Sup. Ct. 2258 (1997). *Vacco v. Quill,* 117 Sup. Ct. 2293 (1997).

9. For religious objections to suicide and euthanasia, see St. Thomas Aquinas, "Whether It Is Lawful to Kill Oneself," in Tom L. Beauchamp and Robert Veatch, eds., *Ethical Issues in Death and Dying,* 2nd ed. (1996), pp. 119–21.

10. Willard Gaylin et al., "Doctors Must Not Kill," *Journal of the American Medical Association* 259 (1988): 2139–40. See also David Orentlicher, "Physician Participation in Assisted Suicide," *Journal of the American Medical Association* 262 (1989): 1844–45.

11. See Christine Cassel et al., "Care of the Hopelessly Ill: Proposed Clinical Criteria for Physician-Assisted Suicide," *New England Journal of Medicine* 327 (1992): 1380–84 (approving of PAS but not of active euthanasia because it poses excessive social risks).

12. See Daniel Callahan, *The Troubled Dream of Life: Living With Mortality* (New York: Simon and Schuster, 1993). See also Yale Kamisar, "Against Assisted Suicide-Even a Very Limited Form," *University of Detroit-Mercy Law Review* 72 (1995): 735.

13. ALS also is known as Lou Gehrig's disease.

14. *In re Conroy,* 486 A. 2d 1209 (1985) (summarizing the logic of foregoing life-sustaining treatments).

15. Cassel et al., "Care of the Hopelessly Ill," 1380–84. See also Franklin G. Miller et al., "Regulating Physician-Assisted Death," *New England Journal of Medicine* 331 (1994): 199–23 (conceding the untenability of the previous distinction).

16. John Arras, "The Right to Die on the Slippery Slope," *Social Theory and Practice* 8 (1982): 285 (describing the "slippery slope" argument in favor of PAS).

17. See, e.g., Cassel et al., "Care of the Hopelessly Ill"; Miller et al., "Regulating Physician-Assisted Death"; Charles H. Baron et al., "Statute A Model State Act to Authorize and Regulate Physician-Assisted Suicide," *Harvard Journal of Legislation* 33 (1996): 1.

18. Dr. Gary Kennedy, Division of Geriatrics, Montefiore Medical Center, Albert Einstein College of Medicine, Testimony before the New York Task Force on Life and the Law.

19. Susan M. Wolf, "Physician-Assisted Suicide in the Context of Managed Care," *Duquesne Law Review* 35 (1996): 455.

20. *Compassion in Dying v. Washington,* 79 F. 3d 790, 830–32 (9th Cir. 1996).

21. *Compassion in Dying,* 79 F. 3d 832.

22. Ibid., 831.

23. Ibid., 827.

24. 410 U.S. 179 (1973).

25. *Quill v. Vacco,* 80 F. 3d 716, 729 (2nd Cir. 1996); see also *Compassion in Dying v. Washington,* 79 F. 3d 790, 822–24 (9th Cir. 1996).

26. *Quill v. Vacco,* 80 F. 3d 716, 729 (2nd Cir. 1996).

27. Dan Brock, "Voluntary Active Euthanasia," *Hastings Center Report* 22 (1992): 10. See also Brock, "Borderline Cases of Morally Justified Taking Life in Medicine," in Tom Beauchamp, ed., *Intending Death: The Ethics of Assisted Suicide and Euthanasia* (Upper Saddle River, NJ: Prentice Hall, 1996): 131–49.

28. Baron et al., "A Model State Act to Authorize and Regulate Physician-Assisted Suicide,""11.

29. *Compassion in Dying v. Washington,* 79 F. 3d 790, 832–33, 836–37 (9th Cir. 1996).

Public Policy in the Netherlands on Physician-Assisted Death

HENK JOCHEMSEN AND JOHN KEOWN

Voluntary Euthanasia under Control? Further Empirical Evidence from the Netherlands

Henk Jochemsen is director of the Lindeboom Institute in the Netherlands and has held the Lindeboom Chair of Medical Ethics at the Free University in Amsterdam since 1998. He is a member of the Ethics Commission of the Federation of Associations of Patients with Congenital Disease and from 1992 to 1996 was a member of the Board of Administration of the European Association of Centres of Medical Ethics. Currently he is an Advisory Board member of the Center for Bioethics and Human Dignity and a member of the European editorial board of the journal *Ethics and Medicine*.

John Keown is senior lecturer in the Law and Ethics of Medicine at the University of Cambridge and a senior research fellow at Churchill College, Cambridge. He has served as a member of the Medical Ethics Committee of the British Medical Association and as a member of the board of the Human Values in Health Care Forum. Dr. Keown has also served as governor and vice-chairman of the Linacre Centre for Health Care Ethics, vice-chairman of the Centre for Bioethics and Public Policy, and manager of the Ver Heyden de Lancey Fund for Medico-Legal Studies at the University of Cambridge. His books include *Abortion, Doctors and the Law: Some Aspects of the Legal Regulation of Abortion in England from 1803 to 1982* and the edited collection *Euthanasia Examined: Ethical, Clinical and Legal Perspectives*.

INTRODUCTION

Worldwide, the euthanasia debate continues to intensity. In 1997, the Australian parliament voted to repeal euthanasia legislation in the Northern Territory and the US Supreme Court upheld the constitutionality of legislation prohibiting "physician-assisted suicide."[1] In deciding whether euthanasia or assisted suicide should be permitted in principle, and whether they can be controlled in practice, the experience of the Netherlands, where they have been officially tolerated and widely practised for well over a decade, is clearly of profound importance.

Nineteen ninety-one saw the publication of the results of an important survey, by Professor P.I. van der Maas, into end-of-life decision making by Dutch doctors in the year 1990.[2] Despite claims to the contrary by supporters of Dutch euthanasia, this survey helped to cast serious doubt on Dutch claims that their guidelines were sufficiently strict effectively to control the practice of voluntary euthanasia (the intentional termination of patients' lives at their request) and to prevent non-voluntary euthanasia (the intentional termination of the lives of patients incapable of making a request).

The survey disclosed the widespread practice of non-voluntary euthanasia; the use of euthanasia even

From *Journal of Medical Science* 25, no. 1 (February 1999), 16–21. Footnotes renumbered.

Table 1. End-of-Life Decisions by Doctors in the Netherlands, 1990–1995

	1990	1995
Deaths in the Netherlands	129000 (100%)	135500 (100%)
Requests for euthanasia	8900 (7%)	9700 (7.1%)
Euthanasia	2300 (1.8%)	3200 (2.4%)
Assisted suicide	400 (0.3%)	400 (0.3%)
Life-terminating acts without explicit request	1000 (0.8%)	900 (0.7%)
Intensification of pain and symptom treatment	22500 (17.5%)	20000 (14.8%)
a. Explicitly intended to shorten life	1350 (1%)	2000 (1.5%)
b. Partly intended to shorten life	6750 (5.2%)	2850 (2.1%)
c. Taking into account the probability that life will be shortened	14400 (11.3%)	15150 (11.1%)
Withdrawal/withholding treatment (incl. tube-feeding)	22500 (17.5%)	27300 (20.1%)
a. At the explicit request of the patient	5800 (4.5%)	5200 (3.8%)
b. Without the explicit request of the patient		
b1. Explicitly intended to short life	2670 (2.1%)	14200 (10.5%)
b2. Partly intended to shorten life	3170 (2.5%)	—
b3. Taking into account the probability that life will be shortened	10850 (8.4%)	7900 (5.8%)
Intentional termination of neonates		
a. Without withholding/withdrawing treatment	—	10.00
b. Withholding/withdrawing treatment plus administration of medication explicitly to shorten life	—	80.00
Assisted suicide of psychiatric patients	—	2–5

when doctors thought that palliative care was a viable alternative, and the common practice by doctors of illegally certifying euthanasia deaths as deaths by "natural causes" instead of reporting them, as required by the guidelines, to the authorities.[3]

In 1996, Van der Maas and Van der Wal published the results of an extensive survey into end-of-life decisions by Dutch doctors in the year 1995.[4] Do the results of this survey show any improvement in the degree of control over euthanasia?

I. THE SURVEY

The survey sought particularly to ascertain the incidence of intentional life-shortening by doctors; the extent to which they complied with their duty to report such cases (in accordance with a procedure dating from late 1990 which was given statutory force in June 1994), and the quality of their reporting. The main purpose of the reporting procedure is to provide for possible scrutiny of the intentional termination of life by doctors and to promote careful decision making in such cases. The most important quantitative data generated by the survey are reproduced in Table 1. . . .

1. EUTHANASIA AND ASSISTED SUICIDE

Between 1990 and 1995 the number of requests for euthanasia increased, as did the number of requests granted. Cases of euthanasia and assisted suicide rose from 2,700 cases in 1990 to 3,600 in 1995, or from 2.1% to 2.7% of all deaths.

According to the attending physicians, there were treatment alternatives in 17% of these cases but in almost all the patients did not want them. However, in 1994, the Dutch Supreme Court held that doctors should not hasten death whenever the alternative of palliative treatment was available, at least in cases of mental suffering and the ministers of justice and health, and the Royal Dutch Medical Association (KNMG), have decided that the same restriction should apply in cases of somatic suffering. The above cases appear, therefore, to have breached this guideline.

Life was shortened by one to four weeks in 31% of euthanasia cases and 45% of assisted suicides and by more than a month in 7% of cases of euthanasia and in 30% of assisted suicides.

Physicians stated that the main reason why patients requested euthanasia was "intolerable suffering without prospect of improvement" (74%), which has become the standard terminology to describe the seriousness of the condition required by the law. But the next most common reasons were "to prevent loss of dignity" (56%) and "to prevent further suffering" (47%). It must surely be doubted whether either of these reasons, by itself, satisfies the requirement of unbearable suffering.

Interestingly, one of the most important reasons for rejecting a request for euthanasia (cited by 35% of physicians) was the physician's opinion that the patient's suffering was not intolerable. This suggests that, despite the emphasis placed by the advocates of euthanasia on patient autonomy, the application of euthanasia is more a function of the *physician's judgment about the quality of the patient's life* than of respect for the patient's autonomy. This suggestion is fortified by the evidence about the extent to which Dutch doctors continue to terminate the lives of patients without an explicit request.

2. LIFE-TERMINATING ACTIONS WITHOUT EXPLICIT REQUEST

The survey confirms that the intentional shortening of patients' lives without explicit request remains far from uncommon. Nine hundred patients had their lives ended without explicit request in 1995, representing 0.7% of all deaths, only a slight decrease on the 0.8% so terminated in 1990. In other words, of the 4,500 (3,200 + 400 +900) cases in which doctors admitted they actively and intentionally terminated life, one in five involved no explicit request.

The main reason for not discussing the issue with the patient was stated to be the patient's incompetence (due, for example, to dementia). But not all patients whose lives were terminated without an explicit request were incompetent. In 15% of cases where no discussion took place but could have, the doctor did not discuss the termination of life because the doctor thought that the termination of the patient's life was clearly in the patient's best interests.

Furthermore, in a third of the 900 cases, there had been a discussion with the patient about the possible termination of life, and some 50% of these patients were fully competent, yet their lives were terminated without an explicit request.

Moreover, in 17% of the 900 cases, treatment alternatives were thought to be available by the attending physician.

The physicians thought that life was shortened by

one to four weeks in 3% of cases but by more than a month in 6%. Finally, physicians had not discussed their action with a colleague in 40% of cases, with a close relative in 30% of cases, and with anyone at all in 5%.

3. INTENSIFICATION OF PAIN AND SYMPTOM TREATMENT

In 20,000 cases (according to the physician interviews) or 25,800 cases (according to the death certificate survey), palliative drugs were administered in doses which almost certainly shortened life. In some 2,000 of these cases the doctor explicitly intended, and in a further 2,850 cases, partly intended, to shorten life. The researchers estimate that the grey area between intending to alleviate pain and symptoms and intending to shorten life is about 2% of all deaths, the same as in 1990.

Where doctors administered palliative drugs partly in order to shorten life, they had discussed it with the patient in just over half of the cases (52%) and in only 36% of the cases was there an explicit request for life-shortening doses by the patient. The physicians stated that 86 patients (3%) with whom they had not discussed this treatment were fully competent. Moreover, in only 36% of the cases had the doctors consulted a colleague. Life was shortened by an estimated one to four weeks in 7% of cases but by more than a month in 1%.

4. WITHHOLDING/WITHDRAWING TREATMENT

In some 27,300 cases a treatment was withheld or withdrawn (in 5,200 cases at the patient's explicit request) taking into account a probable shortening of life.

However, in 18,000 of these cases (14,200 of which involved no explicit request by the patient) it was the physician's explicit intention to shorten life (though the survey does not state in how many cases the treatment was disproportionate, in which case doctors could, had they wished, have properly withdrawn it for that reason and without intending to shorten life.

In the majority of cases in which no discussion with the patient had taken place, the physicians stated that the patient was either incompetent or only partly competent. However, in 1% of these cases (140 patients) the physician considered the patient fully competent.

In cases where treatment was withheld or withdrawn with the explicit intent to shorten life, the physician estimated that life was shortened by one to seven days in 34% of cases, by one to four weeks in 18% and by more than a month in 9%.

5. NEONATES

The survey reports that over 1,000 newborns die in the Netherlands before their first birthday and estimates that the lives of about 15 are actively and intentionally terminated by doctors. The figure of 15 seems, however, a significant underestimate.

The survey shows that in ten cases (1%) doctors administered a drug with the explicit intention of shortening life. But it also reveals a further 80 cases in which, also with the explicit intention of shortening life, doctors administered a drug and withdrew or withheld a life-prolonging treatment. In total, therefore, it appears to have been the explicit intention of doctors to shorten the lives of 90 neonates, not 15.

Moreover, in no fewer than 41% of the 1,000 cases, treatment was withdrawn or withheld with the explicit intention of shortening life. In a significant proportion of these cases, life was terminated because the babies' lives were not thought bearable. Forty-five per cent of these babies expected to live more than four weeks, and some of them more than half a year.

In around a fifth of cases in which doctors intentionally withheld or withdrew treatment with the explicit purpose of shortening life because the baby's life was thought unbearable, there had been no discussion with the parents. Doctors said that in most cases this was because the situation was so clear that discussion was unnecessary or because there was no time, though these reasons are not elaborated.

Finally, doctors reported hardly any cases of the intentional shortening of neonatal life to the authorities.

6. ASSISTED SUICIDE OF PSYCHIATRIC PATIENTS

Based on the replies of psychiatrists in respect of the year 1995, the survey estimates that although some 320 psychiatric patients explicitly request assistance in suicide annually, only two to five are assisted to commit suicide by psychiatrists. Among psychiatrists who would never grant a request for assisted suicide on the basis of mental suffering (almost 1/3 of the respondents) "professional opinion" was cited by 88% as the most important reason. Only 2% of psychiatrists had ever assisted suicide.

This relatively restrictive approach of psychiatrists may owe not a little to the controversy generated by the case of Dr. Chabot, a psychiatrist criticised by a medical disciplinary court for assisting in the suicide of a 50-year-old woman who suffered grief after the loss of her two sons.

Disclosing statistics which support a restrictive approach, the survey also indicates that of those patients not assisted in suicide, 16% committed suicide without assistance by a physician and that, of those patients still living, 35% no longer wished for death and that the death wish in a further 10% had diminished.

7. CONSULTATION

The guidelines for permissible euthanasia and assisted suicide require the doctor, before agreeing to either, to engage in a formal consultation *(consultatie),* and not merely an informal discussion *(overleg),* with a colleague.

In cases of euthanasia and assisted suicide 92% of doctors had, according to the survey, discussed the case with a colleague. In 13% of these cases, however, the discussion did not amount to a formal consultation. Consultation took place, therefore, in 79% of cases. However, other figures in the survey suggest that consultation occurred in a significantly smaller percentage of cases. For the survey indicates that consultation occurred in 99% of reported cases but in only 18% of unreported cases and that almost 60% of all cases of euthanasia and assisted suicide were not reported, from which it seems that consultation occurred in only around half of all cases.

In the cases of life-termination without explicit request, a discussion occurred in 43% of cases but in 40% this did not amount to consultation. Consequently, there was no consultation in 97% of such cases.

Moreover, even when consultation did take place, it was usually with a physician living locally and the most important reasons given for consulting such a physician were his views on life-ending decisions and his living nearby: expertise in palliative care was hardly mentioned. Further, in the overwhelming majority of cases, the first doctor had made his mind up before consulting and the doctor consulted disagreed in only 7% of cases. In short, the requirement of consultation, even when it is satisfied, hardly operates as a rigorous check on decision making.

8. REPORTING

In 1995 41% of cases of euthanasia and assisted suicide were reported to the local medical examiner, as required by the reporting procedure. While this is an improvement on the figure of 18% reported in 1990, it means that a clear majority of cases, almost 60%, still go unreported. Moreover, the survey confirms that the legal requirements are breached more frequently in unreported cases, in which there is less often a written request by the patient, a written record by the doctor, or consultation by the doctor.

The most important reasons given by doctors for failing to report in 1995 were (as in 1990), the wish to avoid the inconvenience (for the doctor and/or the relatives) of an investigation by the authorities, and to avoid the risk of prosecution (though, as the consistently tiny number of prosecutions indicates, this risk is negligible). Thirty per cent of doctors stated that they did not report because they had failed to observe the requirements for permissible euthanasia and 12% because they considered euthanasia was a private matter between doctor and patient.

II. DISCUSSION

The second survey confirms at least three disturbing findings of the first survey.

1. INCIDENCE OF INTENTIONAL LIFE-SHORTENING WITH AND WITHOUT EXPLICIT REQUEST

Like the first survey, the second indicates a sizeable incidence of intentional life-shortening by Dutch doctors. Even adopting the unusually narrow Dutch definition of euthanasia as active, voluntary euthanasia there were no fewer than 3,200 cases in 1995 (2.4% of all deaths), an increase of almost a thousand on the 1990 total of 2,300 (1.8% of all deaths).

But if *all* cases in which doctors explicitly intended to shorten life (whether by act or omission, and whether with or without the patient's request) are included, the total rises steeply. Adding the cases of assisted suicide (400); life-termination without explicit request (900) and the intensification of pain and symptom treatment with the explicit intent to shorten life (2,000), the total more than doubles from 3,200 to 6,500.

And if to this number are added the cases of withholding or withdrawing treatment with the explicit intent to shorten life (18,000); cases in which neonates were intentionally terminated (90 cases) and psychiatric patients assisted in suicide (two to five cases), the total rises to over 24,500 cases.

2. EUTHANASIA AS AN ALTERNATIVE TO PALLIATIVE CARE

The survey's comment that "the quality of medical treatment near the end of life has improved" might not unreasonably be thought to display a certain complacency, particularly in a country which has some way to go in the provision of adequate palliative care. The high incidence of intentional life-shortening disclosed by the survey and the relative weakness of the reasons for euthanasia given in many cases by the doctors tend to suggest that euthanasia is not confined to cases of "last resort" and is at least sometimes used as an alternative to palliative care. The case of Dr. Chabot, in which the defendant doctor assisted a grieving woman, whom he did not consider to be physically or mentally ill, to kill herself, and in which the Supreme Court held that such suffering could indeed justify assisted suicide, illustrates the elasticity of the requirement of "unbearable suffering."

The survey confirms that, even when doctors believe that treatment alternatives are available, they not infrequently resort to euthanasia. The opinion of the Supreme Court, the ministers of justice and health, and the KNMG, that euthanasia is impermissible when treatment alternatives are available, even if the patient refuses them, has clearly not prevented its administration in such circumstances. In a move that would make the prospect of prosecution even more remote, the then minister of justice appeared to reverse her earlier position and instructed the attorneys general that the refusal by the patient of available treatment alternatives does not render euthanasia unlawful.

3. WIDESPREAD BREACH OF THE REQUIREMENT TO REPORT

Although 41% of cases (1,466) were reported in 1995 as opposed to 18% (486) in 1990, it remains true that in both years, as in every year in between, a clear majority of cases has gone unreported. There was, in short, no official control whatever over the majority of cases of euthanasia, assisted suicide or the termination of life without explicit request.

Nor should the alleged increase in reporting be accepted uncritically. First, the second survey records an increase in cases of euthanasia between 1990 and 1995 (900 cases) almost as large as the increase in cases reported (980 cases). Secondly, if the total of 6,500 cases of active, intentional life-shortening is used, then the proportion of unreported cases rises from 59% to 77%. On the total of 24,500 cases, the proportion unreported reaches 94%.

It will be recalled that the purpose of the reporting procedure is to allow for scrutiny of the intentional termination of life by doctors and to promote observance of the legal and professional requirements for euthanasia. The undisputed fact that a clear majority of cases (59% according to the survey, at least 77% on our calculations) still goes unreported, serves only to reinforce doubts about the ability of the procedure to fulfil its purpose and to undermine Dutch claims of effective regulation, scrutiny and control. Further, even those cases which *are* reported are reported by the doctor, and one may wonder whether the doctor's report is any more likely to disclose evidence of wrongdoing than is a tax return to disclose evidence of undeclared earnings.

CONCLUSIONS

With the publication of the first Van der Maas survey in 1991 it became clear that the so-called "strict safeguards" laid down in 1984 by the courts and the Royal Dutch Medical Association had largely failed. The survey cast doubt on central assurances which had been given by the advocates of voluntary euthanasia: that euthanasia would be performed only at the patient's explicit request and that doctors terminating life without request would be prosecuted for murder; that euthanasia would be used only in cases of "last resort" and not as an alternative to palliative care; and that cases would be openly reported and duly scrutinised. The Dutch reaction to the survey's findings was also revealing: the cases of nonvoluntary euthanasia it disclosed, far from being criticised, were largely condoned. In short, the survey indicated that, in less than a decade, the Dutch had slid down the slippery slope.

It is therefore surprising that an American commentator should observe that the similarity between the findings in respect of 1990 and 1995 shows that the Dutch are apparently *not* descending a slippery slope.[5] This observation quite overlooks the fact that the first survey showed that the descent had already occurred by 1990: the second survey, far from showing that there has been no *de*scent from 1984 to 1995 shows merely that there has been no significant *as*cent from 1990 to 1995.

The second survey is little more reassuring than the first. Dutch proponents of voluntary euthanasia claimed that tolerating voluntary euthanasia, subject to "safeguards," would allow it to be "brought into the open" and effectively controlled. As the valuable surveys by Van der Maas and Van der Wal disclose, and as several expert commentators have now concluded,[6] the reality is that a clear majority of cases of euthanasia, both with and without request, go unreported and unchecked. In the face of the undisputed fact that in a clear majority of cases there is not even an opportunity for official scrutiny, Dutch claims of effective regulation ring hollow.

REFERENCES AND NOTES

1. *Washington v. Glucksberg* (1997) 117 S Ct 2258; *Vacco v. Quill* (1997) 117 S Ct 2293.

2. Maas PJ van der *et al. Medische beslissingen rond het levenseinde.* s-Gravenhage: SDU Uitgeverij Plantijnstraat, 1991 (published in translation as *Euthanasia and other medical decisions concerning the end of life.* Amsterdam: Elsevier, 1992).

3. See for example Jochemsen H. Euthanasia in Holland: an ethical critique of the new law. *Journal of Medical Ethics* 1994;**20:**212; Keown J. Euthanasia in the Netherlands: sliding down the slippery slope? In: Keown J, ed. *Euthanasia examined.* Cambridge: Cambridge University Press, 1995: ch. 16.

4. Wal G van der, Maas PJ van der. *Euthanasie en andere medische beslissingen rond het levenseinde. De praktijk en de meldingsprocedure. (Euthanasia and other medical decision concerning the end of life. Practice and reporting procedure.)* Den Haag: SDU uitgevers, 1996.

5. See for example Angell M. Euthanasia in the Netherlands—good news or bad? *New England Journal of Medicine* 1996;**335:**1677.

6. See for example Gomez C. *Regulating death.* New York: Free Press, 1991; see reference 8: Hendin; see reference 3: Jochemsen; see reference 3; Keown.

JOHANNES J. M. VAN DELDEN

Slippery Slopes in Flat Countries—A Response

Johannes van Delden is a senior fellow at the Center for Bioethics and Health Law at Utrecht University in the Netherlands and a nursing home physician. Dr. van Delden serves as the Secretary of the International Association of Bioethics and was a principal investigator of the Remmelink Committee, which was established by the Dutch Government's Ministers of Justice and Public Health to investigate euthanasia in the Netherlands. His publications include (with Paul J. van der Maas and Loes Pijnenborg) "Changes in Dutch Opinions on Active Euthanasia," *Journal of the American Medical Association* and (with Paul J. van der Maas, Loes Pijnenborg, and C.W. Looman) "Deciding Not to Resuscitate in Dutch Hospitals," *Journal of Medical Ethics*.

I would like to . . . further the discussion by trying to analyse the Dutch situation in response to the points put forward by Jochemsen and Keown. . . .

Jochemsen and Keown have three major worries:

- the use of euthanasia even when doctors thought that palliative care was a viable alternative;
- the incidence of non-voluntary euthanasia;
- the underreporting of the euthanasia cases.

The reports that lead to these worries are not disputed, by either Jochemsen and Keown, or by me. Like them, I will use the term "euthanasia" in the Dutch way: euthanasia is the intentional ending of a patient's life at the patient's explicit request. My point, however, is that I think a more interesting analysis of the problem can be given than by repeating the ominous and incriminating slippery slope metaphor.

EUTHANASIA AND PALLIATIVE CARE

The Netherlands are often criticised for their presumed lack of palliative care. The existence of only very few hospices in the Netherlands, for example, is often interpreted as proof of a neglect of palliative care. Although much of this criticism is based on misunderstanding and much effort is made to improve palliative care at present, Jochemsen and Keown are right when they say that the Netherlands "have some way to go in the provision of adequate palliative care." Which is, of course, also true for many other countries. But what does this mean for a moral evaluation of euthanasia?

By and large there appear to be three ways of dealing with the issue of euthanasia. The first is to reject it on the grounds that it is forbidden by the principle of respect for life. Proponents of this view often also claim that euthanasia is not necessary at all. They believe that by paying sincere and close attention to the person who requests euthanasia the "question behind the question" will surely be revealed to be something other than a request for death, and that with good palliative care extreme suffering need not remain unanswered. In this view euthanasia and palliative care are incompatible.

An alternative response to the euthanasia issue stresses the importance of compassion. From this point of view, respect for life is of paramount importance as is good palliative care. Sometimes however, supporters of this view admit that sometimes illness and dying come with such suffering that life is reduced to pointless surviving. If all other palliative measures fail, then euthanasia may be justified. The result of this view of euthanasia is the medicalisation of the end of life, since whether euthanasia is justifiable

From *Journal of Medical Ethics* 25, no. 1 (February 1999), 22–24. Footnotes renumbered.

becomes largely a matter of medical discretion.

These two responses appear to differ primarily in their answer to the question: "Does intractable excruciating suffering exist?" However, even palliative care specialists will state that, unfortunately, it does. The real difference therefore, will be whether one allows the principle of respect for life to be overridden by other considerations in special circumstances.

Most proposals to regulate euthanasia follow the second view. This is also true for the official legal position in the Netherlands where a conflict of the physician's duties is the basis for not prosecuting him or her, not the granting of a patient's right. There is no right to die in the Netherlands, nor is there an obligation for the physician to comply with the request of a competent patient to die even if certain conditions are met. From an official and legal point of view, therefore, euthanasia is only tolerated as a last resort.

The reality of the Dutch euthanasia practice, however, seems to be developing in another direction, with increasing emphasis on respect for patient autonomy. This could lead to a shift to a third approach in which euthanasia is seen as a choice. Some patients do not want to live through suffering and decline even if pain can be controlled. They want autonomously to decide about how and when to die and they want their relatives to remember them as they were when they were more or less healthy. They want to step out of life before the terminal phase really starts and they want a doctor to do the lethal work.

This development is reflected in the data produced in all major studies in the Netherlands. The first nationwide study of end-of-life decisions showed that pain hardly ever was the sole reason for requesting euthanasia.[1] In 1992 an independent study by Van der Wal showed that in 56% of cases of euthanasia, requests were made because patients thought suffering to be pointless and in 46% because they feared the decline.[2] And the 1996 report showed that many patients asked for euthanasia to prevent more suffering. . . .

One may also predict (as an aside) that this emphasis on patient autonomy will lead to a change in the medical circumstances in euthanasia cases. At this moment cancer is by far the predominant diagnosis. The shift towards autonomy-based decisions, however, will lead to an increase in the prevalence of situations characterised by a loss of autonomy (such as in dementia or after a stroke).

This emerging sense that one does have a right to die means that more palliative care does not necessarily lead to a decreasing incidence of euthanasia. From a sociological point of view one may be tempted to interpret the shift towards autonomy-based requests for euthanasia as a byproduct of a liberal society, with its emphasis on self-government, control and rational choice. A moral evaluation of this development, however, will depend largely on one's normative views. Jochemsen and Keown will presume that they can rest their case: their prediction of the slippery slope has come true. Others will say that more emphasis on patient autonomy fits perfectly into the process of emancipation of the patient that has been going on since the beginning of the 1970s. They might say that it is about time to start thinking about patient decisions concerning the end of life, instead of about medical ones.

THE CASES OF NON-VOLUNTARY EUTHANASIA

The cases of non-voluntary euthanasia, described both in the 1991 and the 1996 reports, created a new dimension in the Dutch euthanasia debate. Since the middle of the 1980s, this debate had been focused on euthanasia and assisted suicide with the explicit request of the patient as central feature. This in part had been a deliberate narrowing of the discussion because it was felt that consensus was greatest for these cases. The Dutch even changed their definition of euthanasia to mean only the cases in which there was an explicit request by the patient. Thus, a possibly justifying feature (the request) was turned into a necessary condition.

The description of the non-voluntary cases has broadened the discussion again. But what does their appearance in the reports mean? Does this prove the slippery slope? For many years Dutch commentators on euthanasia only talked about cases on request and non-voluntary cases only recently became known. Thus, the impression may have risen that the Dutch began with hastening the end of life on request and ended up with non-voluntary cases.

This, however, is not necessarily true. We simply do not know whether non-voluntary euthanasia occurred less or more often in the past. What we do know is that the occurrence of non-voluntary euthanasia did not increase in the Netherlands between 1991 and 1996, and also that its prevalence is much higher in another country (Australia), which did not slide down the slope by tolerating euthanasia for years and years.[3]

But even if they do not prove the existence of the slippery slope, the non-voluntary euthanasia cases do form a very serious problem. They are obviously not justified by the principle of respect for patient autonomy as in the third view described above, and therefore can only be tolerated (if at all) in extreme situations where life termination is really a last resort and non-voluntary euthanasia becomes "mercy-killing." It is very unlikely that this was the case in all cases described in the Dutch reports.

UNDERREPORTING

To accept euthanasia in an individual case is one thing, to accept it on a public policy level is quite something else. It is often argued that proposals to legalise euthanasia can never contain absolute safeguards.[4] I think this is true: there is no rule that cannot (and will not) be broken. By the way, this goes for the prohibition of drunk-driving as well. The question is whether this justifies a prohibition of euthanasia in an individual case. The Dutch tried to have it both ways by creating a public policy based on individual cases. The least one can say is that this resulted in an unsatisfactory situation of accepting and prohibiting at the same time. This created uncertainty and unclarity both for patients and physicians and probably contributed to some extent to the critical reports such as the one commented upon here.

Persuading the physician to bring euthanasia cases to the knowledge of the authorities is a problem for any euthanasia policy. The Dutch notification procedure helped to raise the notification rate to 41% in 1995.[5] . . . The government has tried to diminish further the number of unreported cases by developing a new notification procedure, in which much of the assessment is done "outside of" the legal system. Since November 1, 1998, five regional multidisciplinary assessment committees have to advise the public prosecutor in all reported cases of euthanasia. The effect of this change in procedure is not clear yet.

Cuperus-Bosma et al. hope that reducing the role of the public prosecution will lead to fewer differences in assessment and more legal equality. However, one may ask why would these committees differ less in their assessment of cases. Their strength is their opportunity to communicate with the reporting physician in a decriminalised setting and, by so doing, influence practice. Uniformity should not be their main concern.

CONCLUSION

You cannot do ethics until you know the facts. Therefore, the need for empirical research in ethics is very clear. One of its tasks is to describe the morally relevant facts. Another task may be to verify empirical claims (as in the slippery slope argument and as in many consequentialist claims) and to provide insight into the effects of cultural differences on certain practices. Thus, facts provide the ethicist with the information she needs. However, facts will not settle a moral debate. When it comes to the euthanasia issue there is much to be learned from studies that the Dutch have performed. But the interpretation of these facts remains largely dependent upon our moral views. Not vice versa.

REFERENCES

1. Maas P.I. van der, Delden J.J.M. van, Pijnenborg L. *Euthanasia and other medical decisions concerning the end of life.* Amsterdam: Elsevier, 1992.
2. Wal G. van der, Eijk J.Th.M. van, Spreeuwenberg C. Euthanasia and assisted suicide. II. Do Dutch family doctors act prudently? *Family Practice* 1992;**9:**135–40.
3. Kuhse H., Singer P., Baume P., Clark M., Rickard M. End-of-life decisions in Australian medical practice. *Medical Journal of Australia* 1997;**166:**191–6.
4. Miles S., Pappas D., Koepp R. Considerations of safeguards proposed in laws and guidelines to legalize assisted suicide. In: Weir Robert E., ed. *Physician-assisted suicide.* Bloomington: Indiana University Press, 1997.
5. Wal G. van der, Maas P.J. van der. *Euthanasie en andere medische beslissingen rond het levenseinde.* Den Haag: SDU uitgevers, 1996: 57.

BERNARD GERT, CHARLES M. CULVER, AND K. DANNER CLOUSER

An Alternative to Physician-Assisted Suicide

Bernard Gert is the Stone Professor of Intellectual and Moral Philosophy at Dartmouth College and adjunct professor and psychiatry at Dartmouth Medical School. He is the editor of *Man and Citizen* (1972, 1991) by Thomas Hobbes, first author of *Morality and the New Genetics* (1996), and (with Charles M. Culver and K. Danner Clouser) *Bioethics: A Return to Fundamentals* (1997). He is also author of *Morality: Its Nature and Justification* (1998), a systematic work in ethical theory.

Charles Culver is a professor of medical education, director of Didactic Education, and chair of the Admissions Committee at Barry University. He is a psychiatrist who has coauthored (with Bernard Gert and K. Danner Clouser) *Bioethics: A Return to Fundamentals* (1997). Dr. Culver is also the coauthor of *Philosophy in Medicine: Conceptual and Ethical Problems in Medicine and Psychiatry* and editor of *Ethics at the Bedside*.

The late K. Danner Clouser was University Professor of Humanities at the Penn State College of Medicine from 1968 until his retirement in 1996. He was instrumental in building the first humanities department ever established at any medical school and was a pioneer in the newly emerging field of bioethics. His publications include (with Bernard Gert and Charles M. Culver) *Bioethics: A Return to Fundamentals* (1997) and *Teaching Bioethics: Strategies, Problems, and Resources*. His work was critically examined in a book edited by Loretta M. Kopelman, entitled *Building Bioethics: Conversations with Clouser and Friends on Medical Ethics*.

Two tasks are necessary in order to determine whether physician-assisted suicide should be legalized. The first is to clarify the meaning of the phrase "physician-assisted suicide" (PAS) so that one can be precise about what procedures are correctly specified by the phrase. The second task is to inquire into the moral acceptability of doctors' carrying out those procedures that are appropriately labeled as PAS. It is essential to settle the conceptual task before deciding about PAS's moral acceptability. Once conceptual matters are clarified and the moral acceptability of PAS is determined, disagreements about the social consequences of legalizing PAS continue to make it an issue on which reasonable people can take either side. However, we shall show that awareness of an alternative to PAS, namely, the refusal of food and fluids, significantly weakens the arguments in favor of legalizing PAS.

It may seem odd to claim that there is a problem in clarifying what is meant by PAS. The prototypical example of PAS, and the way it is almost always practiced, is for a doctor to provide a lethal quantity of sedating medication to a patient who subsequently ingests it and dies. Everyone agrees that the doctor who carries out such an action has engaged in PAS. The conceptual problem arises not with the prototypical

From Margaret P. Battin, Rosamond Rhodes, and Anita Silvers, *Physician-Assisted Suicide: Expanding the Debate*. New York and London: Routledge, 1998, 182–202.

example but with the conceptual analyses that some philosophers and some courts have made in commenting on whether PAS is morally justified, or is legally sanctioned or forbidden. One philosopher, for example, has claimed that there is no morally significant difference between killing a patient (voluntary, active euthanasia; VAE) and helping a patient commit suicide (PAS).[1] One circuit court has argued that performing PAS is exactly the same as withdrawing life support and rendering palliative care as a patient dies.[2] Thus PAS has been identified both as the same as killing a patient (VAE) and the same as allowing a patient to die (voluntary, passive euthanasia; VPE). We believe that the three alternatives, 1) PAS; 2) killing a patient (VAE); and 3) allowing a patient to die (VPE), are quite distinct from one another conceptually and morally.

ACTIVE AND PASSIVE EUTHANASIA

To understand how PAS, VAE, and VPE differ, it is useful to begin with the distinction between VAE and VPE. A distinction between these two has traditionally been made and accepted both by clinicians and by philosophers. VAE is killing and, even if requested by a competent patient, is illegal and has been historically prohibited by the American Medical Association. VPE is "allowing to die" and, if requested by a competent patient, it is legally permitted and morally acceptable.

None of the standard attempts to describe the conceptual distinction between VAE and VPE have gained wide acceptance. These attempts have involved the following concepts and issues: 1) acts versus omissions, 2) stopping treatment (withdrawing) versus not starting treatment (withholding), 3) ordinary care versus extraordinary care, and 4) whether the patient's death is due to an underlying malady. However none of these four ways of making the distinction has any clear moral significance and all are inadequate because they all fail to appreciate the moral significance of the *kind of decision* the patient makes, in particular whether it is a request or a refusal.[3] It is this failure that leads to the mistaken conclusion that there is no morally significant distinction between VAE and VPE.

First, a terminological matter needs to be clarified. It is perfectly standard English to use the term "request" when talking about a refusal. Thus one can say that a patient requests that a treatment (such as ventilation) be stopped. The patient is, in fact, refusing continued use of the respirator. Unfortunately, this perfectly correct and common way of talking obscures the crucial moral distinction between patients' refusals and requests. When combined with the use of the terms "choice" and "decision," which also can be applied to both requests and refusals, the language fosters the false conclusion that all patient decisions or choices, whether refusals or requests, generate the same moral obligation for physicians.

This confusion is compounded because the most common use of the terms "decision" and "choice" with regard to a patient involves neither refusals nor requests, but rather the patient's picking one of the options that her physician has presented to her during the process of informed consent. However, when dealing with patients who want to die, this most common use of "decision" or "choice" is not relevant. Rather a patient is either 1) refusing life-sustaining treatment (VPE), or 2) requesting that the physician kill her (VAE), or 3) requesting that the physician provide the medical means for the patient to kill herself (PAS). Thus talking of a patient's decision or choice to die can be extremely ambiguous. Furthermore, refusals of treatment and requests for treatment, whether or not death is a foreseeable result, have very different moral and legal implications.[4]

• • •

REFUSAL OF TREATMENT AND THE DUTIES OF A PHYSICIAN

Overruling a competent informed patient's rational refusal of treatment, including life preserving treatment, always involves depriving the patient of freedom, and usually involves causing him pain. No impartial rational person would publicly allow these kinds of paternalistic actions and so they are morally unacceptable. Since it is morally unacceptable to overrule the rational refusal of a competent informed patient, it cannot be the duty of a physician to do so. Theoretically, the situation does not change when lack of treatment will result in the patient's death, but as a practical matter, it does make a difference. Death is such a serious harm that it is never irrational to choose any other harm in order to prevent death. Even though it is sometimes rational to choose death over other harms, choosing death may be, and often is, irrational. Further, people are usually ambivalent about choosing death, often changing their minds several times, but death is permanent, and once it occurs, no further change of mind is possible.

The seriousness of death requires physicians to make certain that patients realize that death will result from failure to receive the life sustaining treatment. It also requires physicians to make sure a patient's desire to die is not due to suffering that can be relieved by palliative care. The physician also must make certain that a patient's desire to die, and hence his request to die, is not primarily the result of a treatable depression and, more generally, that a patient's unavoidable suffering is sufficient to make it rational for him to prefer death to continuing to live. When patients have terminal diseases, however, it is generally the case that when they want to die, it is rational for them to choose death. Further, although there is often some ambivalence, in our experience, their desire to die usually remains their dominant desire. When an informed competent patient makes a rational decision to stop life-prolonging treatment, a physician cannot have a duty to overrule his refusal of treatment, even though normally a physician has a duty to prevent death.

We have shown that physicians cannot have a duty to preserve the lives of their competent patients when those patients want to die and their desires are informed and rational. When prolonging a person's life requires unjustifiably depriving him of freedom, it is morally unacceptable to do so. We have thus established that physicians do not and cannot have a duty to prolong the lives of their patients when their patients have a rational desire to die. We are not suggesting that whenever a patient with a terminal disease makes any tentative suggestion that treatment be stopped, the physician should, with no question, immediately do so. It is part of the duty of a physician to make sure both that the refusal is rational and that it is the informed, considered, and noncoerced preference of the patient. When, however, it is clear that a patient really does want to die and the refusal is rational, then it is morally unacceptable for the physician to administer life prolonging treatment.

KILLING VERSUS ALLOWING TO DIE

Having shown that a physician does not have a duty to prolong the lives of patients who rationally prefer to die, the next issue to be settled is whether not treating such patients counts as killing them. If it does count as killing them, then the conclusions of the previous section may have to be revised. In the previous section not treating was taken as simply not prolonging the life of a competent patient when he rationally refuses treatment. However, not treating is sometimes correctly regarded as killing. If a physician turns off the respirator of a competent patient who does not want to die, with the result that the patient dies, the physician has killed him. The same is true if the physician discontinues antibiotics, or food and fluids. It may even count as killing if the physician refuses to start any of these treatments for his patient when the patient wants the treatment started and there is no medical reason for not starting it. Just as parents whose children die because of not being fed can be regarded as having killed their children, physicians who have a duty to provide life-saving treatment for their patients can be regarded as killing them if they do not provide that treatment. However, we have shown that a physician does not have a duty to provide life-saving treatment when a competent patient rationally refuses such treatment. Not treating counts as killing only when there is a duty to treat; in the absence of such a duty, not treating does not count as killing.[5]

If the patient refuses treatment and there is no duty to treat, then it does not make any moral difference whether the physician stops treating by an act, e.g., turning off the respirator, or an omission, e.g., not giving antibiotics. It also makes no moral difference whether the physician stops some treatment that has already started, e.g., turning off the respirator or discontinuing antibiotics, or simply does not start such treatment. . . .

STOPPING FOOD AND FLUIDS

. . . Since the point of dying sooner is to avoid the pain and suffering of a terminal illness, stopping only food while continuing fluids is not a good method of dying because it takes a long time, often more than a month. However, when fluids are also stopped, dying is much quicker; usually unconsciousness occurs within a week and death less than a week later. Further, contrary to what is widely assumed, dying because of lack of food and fluids is not physically unpleasant or painful if there is even minimal nursing care.[6] When there is no medical treatment keeping the patient alive, stopping food and fluids may be the best way of allowing a patient to die. It is usually painless, it takes long enough for the patient to have the opportunity to change his mind, but is short enough that significant relief from pain and suffering is gained. However, because of the psychological difficulties involved in a longer dying process, some patients may still prefer PAS to discontinuing food and fluids.

It may be thought that, if complying with a patient's refusal of treatment requires the physician to perform some identifiable act, e.g., turning off a respirator, which is the act that results in the patient's death, then regardless of what was said before, the doctor has killed the patient. This seems to have the support of the *Oxford English Dictionary* which says that to kill is simply to deprive of life. One may accept that a doctor is morally and legally required to turn off the respirator and thus is justified in killing her patient, but still maintain that she has killed him. Even those who accept the death penalty and hold that some prison official is morally and legally required to execute the prisoner do not deny that the official has killed the prisoner. Killing in self-defense is both morally and legally allowed, yet no one denies that it is killing. Similarly, one could agree that the doctor is doing nothing morally or legally unacceptable by turning off the respirator and even that the doctor is morally and legally required to do so, yet claim that in doing so the doctor is killing the patient.

If one accepts this analysis, then it might also seem plausible to say that an identifiable decision to omit a life-prolonging treatment, even if such an omission is morally and legally required, also counts as killing the patient. One could simply stipulate that doctors are sometimes morally and legally required to kill their patients, namely, when their action or omission is the result of a competent patient rationally refusing to start or to continue a life-prolonging treatment. Thus it would seem that the important point is that the doctor is morally and legally required to act as she does, not whether what she does is appropriately called killing. However, it is still significant whether such an action should be regarded as killing because having a too simple account of killing can cause numerous problems.

Many doctors do not want to regard themselves as killing their patients, even justifiably killing them. More importantly, all killing requires a justification or an excuse. If all the morally relevant features are the same, the justification or excuse that is not adequate for one way of killing will not be adequate for all other ways of killing either. Thus, if a justification is not publicly allowed for injecting a lethal dose of morphine, then it will not be publicly allowed for disconnecting the patient from the respirator. Since even advocates of VAE do not propose that doctors should ever be morally and legally required to kill their patients, even justifiably, doctors would not be required to comply with rational refusals of treatment by competent patients. It might even come to be thought justifiable to prohibit physicians from honoring the rational refusals of life-sustaining treatments of competent patients. Thus changing the way killing is understood (i.e., counting complying with a patient's rational refusal as killing him) would have unfortunate implications.

Those who favor legalizing VAE do not want to require doctors to kill their patients; they merely want to allow those doctors who are willing to kill, to do so. Similarly for PAS, no one has yet suggested that a doctor be required to comply with a patient's request for a lethal prescription. On the other hand, since doctors are morally and legally required to comply with a competent patient's rational refusal of life-sustaining treatment, complying with such a refusal has not been regarded as killing. Providing palliative care to a patient who refuses life-sustaining treatment is not morally controversial either. Killing a competent patient on his rational request or assisting him to commit suicide are morally controversial. No one claims that doctors are morally and legally required to do either. Thus it is clear that complying with a competent patient's rational refusal of treatment is not normally regarded as killing, nor does providing palliative care to such a patient count as assisting suicide.

Part of the problem is that insufficient attention is paid to the way in which the term "kill" is actually used. Killing is not as simple a concept as it is often taken to be. Killing is causing death, but what counts as causing death or any other harm is a complex matter. If the harm that results from one's action, or omission, needs to be justified or excused, then one is regarded as having caused that harm. Of course, causing harm often can be completely justified or excused, so that one can cause a harm and be completely free of any unfavorable moral judgment. So killing, taken as causing death, may be completely justified, perhaps even morally required.

All acts that are done in order to bring about someone's death count as causing the person's death, or killing them, for all such intentional actions need justification. Also, if the act which results in death is the kind of act which is morally unacceptable such as deceiving, breaking a promise, cheating, breaking the law, or neglecting one's duty, knowingly performing the act or omission needs justification and so counts as killing. For example, if I lie to someone, telling him that a mushroom that I know to be intensely poisonous is safe to eat, then if he eats the mushroom and dies, I have caused his death. Or if a child dies because her parents did not feed her, they have killed her, because parents have a duty to feed their children. This analysis shows why it is important to make clear that doctors have no duty to treat, or even feed, patients who refuse treatment or food. However, if one does not intend, but only knows, that one's act will result in someone's death, and the act is the kind of act that is morally acceptable, (such as giving a patient sufficient analgesia to control her severe pain) then even though this act results in the person's death, it may not count as causing his death.

When complying with the rational refusal of a competent patient, the doctor's intention is not to kill the patient, but rather to honor the patient's refusal even though she knows that the result will be that the patient dies. Even if the doctor agrees that it is best for the patient to die, her honoring that refusal does not count as intentionally causing his death. Of course, an individual doctor can want her patient to die, but her intention in these circumstances is not determined by whether she wants her patient to die. Rather, the intention is determined by what facts account for her deciding to act in one way rather than another. If she would cease treatment even if she did not want the patient to die and would not cease it if the patient had not refused such treatment, then her intention is not to kill the patient but to comply with the patient's refusal. Further, most doctors do not want to kill their patients, even if such actions were morally and legally justified, so clearly their intentions are simply to honor their patients' rational refusals. . . .

That our society does not regard death resulting from complying with a competent patient's rational refusal, even a refusal of food and fluids, as killing, is shown by the fact that almost all states have advance directives that explicitly require a physician to stop treatment, even food and fluids, if the patient has the appropriate advance directive. They also allow a presently competent patient to refuse treatment and food and fluids. None of these states allow a physician to kill a patient, under any circumstances. Most of these states do not even allow physicians to assist suicide, which strongly suggests that turning off a respirator, is not regarded even as assisting suicide when doing so is required by the rational refusal of a competent patient.

Thus, complying with a competent patient's rational refusal of treatment is not killing or assisting suicide, and it may even be misleading to say that a physician is allowing the patient to die. To talk of a physician allowing the patient to die suggests that the physician has a choice, that it is up to her to decide whether or not to save the patient's life. When a competent patient has rationally refused treatment, however, a physician has no choice. It is morally and legally prohibited to overrule the patient's refusal. The physician allows her patient to die only in the sense that it is physically possible for her to save her patient and she does not. Complying with the rational refusal of life-saving treatment by a competent patient is not merely morally acceptable, it is morally required. Overruling such a refusal is itself a morally unacceptable deprivation of freedom. . . .

IS THE REFUSAL OF LIFE-SUSTAINING TREATMENT SUICIDE?

If suicide is regarded simply as killing oneself, then the analysis of killing should apply to it in a fairly straightforward fashion. An action or an omission which is intended to result in the death of a patient and which does result in his death counts as killing. Therefore, one might argue that the refusal of treatment or of food and fluids that is intended by the patient to result in his own death and which does result in his death, should count as suicide. And if "assisting suicide" simply means doing those acts which help the person commit suicide, then physicians who provide palliative care to patients who are refusing life sustaining treatments are assisting suicide. Accepting this analysis would make providing palliative care to such patients a kind of assisted suicide.

However, it is not clear that the view that suicide is simply killing oneself should be accepted. Partly, this may be because "killing oneself" does not seem to need a justification or excuse as much as killing another person. This may be because our society, with some limitations, regards each person as allowed to do anything he wants to himself, as long as no one else is harmed. Indeed, it seems that any act which one does not intend but only knows will result in one's own death does not count as suicide. (It is only in an extended sense that someone who continues to smoke or drink or eat too much, when he knows that it may result in his death, could be said to be, slowly committing suicide.) It also seems that our society does not count as suicide any death that results from omissions, at least omissions stemming from rational decisions to omit or to stop treatment. Rather only those positive acts that are done in order to bring about one's own death immediately count as suicide, since those acts so closely resemble the paradigms of killing. Patients who take some pills to bring about their own death are committing suicide, but those who have the respirator removed or who refuse food and fluids are usually not regarded as committing suicide.[7]

This more complex analysis of suicide explains why the law has never regarded providing palliative care to those who are refusing treatment as assisting suicide. Even those states which explicitly forbid assisting suicide do not prohibit providing palliative care to those who are refusing treatment or food and fluids. Of course those who support legalizing PAS favor the simpler account of suicide because they can then claim that some PAS is already allowed, and hence that it is simply inconsistent not to allow other quicker and less painful suicides. That our society does not count refusals of treatment as suicide and hence does not count palliative care for patients who refuse treatment as assisting suicide is not intended by us as an argument against legalizing PAS. However, it does show that one argument for legalizing PAS, namely, that PAS is already allowed in the provision of palliative care for those who are refusing life-prolonging treatment, is based on a misunderstanding of how our society regards providing such palliative care.

Our argument places PAS much closer to VPE than to VAE, and so allowing PAS, one could argue, need not lead to allowing VAE. It is compatible with our analyses so far that one can either be for or against legalizing PAS. However, we believe that recognition of the option of refusing treatment or food and fluids makes much stronger the major argument against legalizing PAS, namely, that doing so will not have sufficient benefits to compensate for the risks involved. But we are also aware that different people can rank and weigh these benefits and risks differently. . . .

IS KILLING PATIENTS EVER JUSTIFIED?

Stopping food and fluids is often the best way of allowing a patient to die, but it may be claimed that killing is sometimes better. Given present knowledge and technology, one can kill a patient or allow a patient to kill herself absolutely painlessly within a matter of minutes. If patients have a rational desire to die, why wait several days or weeks for them to die; why not kill them or let them kill themselves quickly and painlessly in a matter of minutes? We have provided no argument against allowing patients to kill themselves or even killing patients who want to die that applies to an ideal world where there are never any misunderstandings between people and everyone is completely moral and trustworthy. In such a world, if one could provide a patient with pills or inject the patient with appropriate drugs so that the patient dies painlessly and almost instantaneously, there would be no need to worry about the distinction between refusals and requests, or between killing, assisting suicide, and allowing to die. But in the real world, there are misunderstandings and not everyone is completely moral and trustworthy. In the real world no one even proposes that PAS or VAE be allowed without elaborate procedural safeguards, which almost always require at least two weeks. So, on a practical level, legalizing PAS or VAE would not result in a quicker death than simply complying with a refusal of food and fluids.

On our account, VPE is complying with the rational refusal of life-saving treatment or food and fluids by a competent patient. Since there is no duty to overrule a rational refusal by a competent patient, complying with this refusal does not count as killing. Further, failing to comply with such a refusal is itself morally prohibited, for it is an unjustified deprivation of the patient's freedom. Also, in some newer codes of medical ethics, e.g., that of the American College of Physicians, respecting patients' refusals is now listed as a duty. Physicians are not merely morally allowed to practice VPE, they are morally required to do so. VAE is killing; it is complying with the rational request of a competent patient to be killed. Although PAS is not killing, it does involve active intervention by the physician that is more than merely stopping treatment. It is not simply complying with a patient's desire to be left alone; it is providing the patient with some substance that causes his death, when one has no duty to do so.

VAE is killing and so needs to be justified. This contrasts quite sharply with VPE, and even with PAS, which may not even need to be morally justified. When a patient refuses treatment or food and fluids, it is not the complying with a patient's refusal but rather the overruling of the refusal that needs to be justified. But, as noted earlier, physicians may cause pain to their patients and be completely justified, because they do so at their patients' request, or at least with their consent, and do it in order to prevent what the patient takes to be a greater harm, e.g., disability or death. VAE could be regarded as no different than any other instance of a doctor being morally justified in doing a morally unacceptable *kind of act* with regard to a patient at the patient's request, in order to prevent what the patient takes to be a greater harm. In VAE the patient takes death to be a lesser harm than suffering pain and requests that the moral rule prohibiting killing be violated with regard to himself.

If causing pain can be justified, why is killing not justified when all of the other morally relevant features are the same? The answer is that killing needs a stronger justification because of a special feature of death that distinguishes it from all of the other serious harms. The special feature is that, after death, the person killed no longer exists and so cannot protest that he did not want to be killed. All impartial rational persons would advocate that violations against causing pain be publicly allowed when the person toward whom the rule is being violated rationally prefers to suffer that pain rather than suffer some other harm, e.g., disability or death. It is uncertain how many impartial rational persons would advocate that killing be publicly allowed when the person being killed rationally prefers to be killed rather than to continue to suffer pain. This uncertainty stems from taking seriously the two features that are essential to morality, the public character of morality and the fallibility of persons.

Causing pain with valid consent can be publicly allowed without any significant anxiety being caused thereby. Patients can usually correct a mistake rather quickly by ordering a stop to the painful treatment. Also physicians have a constant incentive to be careful not to cause pain by mistake, for patients will complain if they did not really want the pain caused. Killing, even with valid consent, being publicly allowed may create significant anxiety. Patients may fear that they will be mistakenly killed and that they will have no opportunity to correct that mistake. That a patient will not be around to complain if they are mistakenly killed removes a strong safeguard against mistaken violations. But it is not merely mistakes about which a patient would not be able to complain. If a physician tries to take advantage of legalized killing and intentionally kills a patient, complaint would not be possible. Taking advantage of causing pain being publicly allowed does not pose similar problems.

Legalizing PAS might prevent some pain and suffering that could not be prevented by greater education concerning refusing food and fluids, but it would also be likely to create significant anxiety and some unwanted deaths. Impartial rational persons can therefore disagree on whether they would advocate legalizing PAS. Once it is recognized that withholding food and fluids 1) can be painless; 2) usually results in unconsciousness in one week and death in two weeks; and 3) allows for patients to change their minds, the need for PAS significantly diminishes.

Unlike others who argue against legalizing PAS, we do not claim that PAS is in itself morally unacceptable, only that it may create a serious risk of unwanted deaths. Since impartial rational persons can rank these risks as outweighing the benefits of legalization, legalizing PAS is controversial. If the goal is to allow a patient to choose her own time of dying and also dying to be accomplished relatively painlessly, there seems to be little need for PAS. If patient refusal of treatment, including refusal of food and fluids, were not sufficient for a relatively quick and painless death for the overwhelming number of terminally ill patients, then we would favor PAS, although we would still have serious objections to VAE. However, since VPE, especially when this includes refusing food and fluids, is available together with appropriate palliative care, it seems far more difficult to justify controversial methods like PAS. The harms prevented by PAS are no longer the long term suffering of patients who have no other way to die, they are only the one week of suffering that may be present while the patient is refusing food and fluids, and this suffering can be almost completely controlled by appropriate palliative care. This is an excellent example of why the presence of an alternative is a morally relevant feature.

Given the alternative of refusing food and fluids, very little additional harm seems to be prevented by PAS. The presence of an alternative is a morally relevant feature and makes it questionable whether it has sufficient benefits to justify the risks involved in legalizing it. There are good reasons for believing that the advantages of refusing food and fluids together with adequate palliative care make it preferable to legalizing PAS. This is especially true in a multicultural society where doctors and patients sometimes do not even speak the same language. There are a small number of cases in which refusal of food and fluids might be difficult, but it is necessary to weigh the benefit to this relatively small number of people against the harm that might be suffered by a great number of people by the legalizing of PAS. . . .

SUMMARY

. . . We believe that the strongest argument against PAS is that, given the alternatives available, it does not provide sufficient benefit to individual patients to justify the societal risks. Patients already have the alternative of refusing treatment and food and fluids, and of receiving palliative care while they are refusing that treatment. If physicians were to educate patients about these matters and to make clear that they will support their choices and continue to care for them if they choose to refuse treatment, there might be little, if any, call for PAS. Because of the time involved, patients seem far less likely to be pressured into refusing treatment or food and fluids than they are to avail themselves of PAS. There would also be far fewer opportunities for abuse. PAS provides less incentive to be concerned with palliative care. And finally, given the bureaucratic safeguards that most regard as necessary with PAS, death can come as soon or sooner with refusal of treatment or refusal of food and fluids than it would with PAS.[8]

A PRACTICAL PROPOSAL FOR STATE LEGISLATORS

In order to avoid the serious societal risks of legalizing physician-assisted suicide, while still providing a method for allowing seriously ill patients to determine the timing of their deaths, we think that states should consider passing legislation based on language such as the following. This language is completely consistent with the statement of the United States Supreme Court that, "Just as a State may prohibit assisting suicide while permitting patients to refuse unwanted lifesaving treatment, it may permit palliative care related to that refusal, which may have the foreseen but unintended 'double effect' of hastening the patient's death."

If a competent patient is terminally ill or suffering from a condition involving severe chronic pain or serious permanent disability, that patient's refusal of treatment, or refusal or food and fluids, shall not count as suicide, even though the patient knows that death will result from not starting or from stopping that treatment. All physicians and other healthcare workers shall be informed that they are legally prohibited from overruling any rational refusal of a competent patient, including refusal of food and fluids, even though it is known that death will result. All patients will be in-

formed that they are allowed to refuse any treatment, or to refuse food and fluids, even though it is known that death will result, and that physicians and other healthcare workers are legally prohibited from overruling any such rational refusal by a competent patient.

Further, there shall be no prohibition placed upon any physician who provides pain relief in any form, in order to relieve the pain and suffering of the patient who has refused treatment, or food and fluids. In particular, providing pain medication shall not be considered as assisting suicide, and there shall be no liability for the physician who provides such pain medication for the purpose of relieving pain and suffering. The physician shall not provide such medication for the purpose of hastening the time of death, but is not prohibited from providing medication which is consistent with adequate pain relief even if he knows that such medication will hasten the time of death. Physicians are required to rigorously follow the accepted standards of medical practice in determining the competence of patients who refuse any treatment, or who refuse food and fluids, when they know that death will result from complying with that refusal.

NOTES

1. Dan W. Brock, "Voluntary Active Euthanasia," *Hastings Center Report* 22 (2): 10–22 (1992).

2. *Quill v. Vacco,* the U.S. Court of Appeals for the Second Circuit.

3. See James L. Bernat, Bernard Gert, and R. Peter Mogielnicki, "Patient Refusal of Hydration and Nutrition: An Alternative to Physician Assisted Suicide or Voluntary Euthanasia," *Archives of Internal Medicine* 153: 2723–28 (December 27, 1993).

4. See Bernard Gert, James L. Bernat, and R. Peter Mogielnicki, "Distinguishing between Patients' Refusals and Requests," *The Hastings Center Report* 24 (4): 13–15 (July–August 1994).

5. See K. Danner Clouser, "Allowing or Causing: Another Look," *Annals of Internal Medicine* 87: 622–24 (1977).

6. See Kathleen M. Foley, M.D., "The Relationship of Pain and Symptom Management to Patient Requests for Physician-Assisted Suicide," *Journal of Pain and Symptom Management* 6 (5): 289–297 (July 1991).

7. This view is not held by all. Some, especially those with religious views, regard refusing treatment and especially refusing food and fluids when treatment, or food and fluids would sustain life for a long time, as committing suicide. But this is not the prevailing view, nor is it the view that governs the legal classification of the act. However, a terminally ill patient who intentionally goes into the woods in order to stop eating and drinking, does so, and thereby dies, would be regarded by most as having committed suicide. For a sensitive analysis of the difficulty of formulating a precise definition of "suicide," see Tom L. Beauchamp, "Suicide" in Tom Regan, ed., *Matters of Life and Death,* 2nd ed. (New York: Random House, 1986), pp. 77–89.

8. See K. Danner Clouser, "The Challenge for Future Debate on Euthanasia," *The Journal of Pain and Symptom Management* 6 (5): 306–311 (July 1991).

TIMOTHY E. QUILL, BERNARD LO, AND DAN W. BROCK

A Comparison of Voluntarily Stopping Eating and Drinking, Terminal Sedation, Physician-Assisted Suicide, and Voluntary Active Euthanasia

Timothy Quill is associate chief of Medicine at the Genesee Hospital, a professor of medicine and psychiatry at the University of Rochester School of Medicine and Dentistry, and a primary care internist in Rochester, New York. He also directs the University of Rochester's Program for Biopsychosocial Studies. His publications include *Death and Dignity: Making Choices and Taking Charge* and *A Midwife Through the Dying Process: Stories of Healing and Hard Choices in Life*.

Bernard Lo is director of the Center for AIDS Prevention Studies Ethics Core and a professor of medicine and director of the Program in Medical Ethics at UCSF. He is a member of the Board of Health Sciences Policy, the Institute of Medicine, the Board of Directors of the American Society of Law, Medicine, and Ethics, and the National Bioethics Advisory Commission. His publications include (with A. Alpers) "Physician-Assisted Suicide in Oregon: A Bold Experiment," in *Resolving Ethical Dilemmas: A Guide for Clinicians* (2000).

Palliative care is the standard of care when terminally ill patients find that the burdens of continued life-prolonging treatment outweigh the benefits.[1–4] To better relieve suffering near the end of life, physicians need to improve their skills in palliative care and to routinely discuss it earlier in the course of terminal illness. In addition, access to palliative care needs to be improved, particularly for those Americans who lack health insurance. However, even the highest-quality palliative care fails or becomes unacceptable for some patients, some of whom request help hastening death. Between 10% and 50% of patients in programs devoted to palliative care still report significant pain 1 week before death.[1,5–7] Furthermore, patients request a hastened death not simply because of unrelieved pain, but because of a wide variety of unrelieved physical symptoms in combination with loss of meaning, dignity, and independence.[8,9]

How should physicians respond when competent, terminally ill patients whose suffering is not relieved by palliative care request help in hastening death? If the patient is receiving life-prolonging interventions, the physician should discontinue them, in accordance with the patient's wishes. Some patients may voluntarily stop eating and drinking (VSED). If the patient has unrelieved pain or other symptoms and accepts sedation, the physician may legally administer terminal sedation (TS). However, it is generally legally impermissible for physicians to participate in physician-assisted suicide (PAS) or voluntary active euthanasia (VAE) in response to such patient requests. The recent Supreme Court decisions that determined that there is no constitutional right to PAS placed great emphasis on the importance of relieving pain and suffering near the end of life.[10,11] The Court acknowledged the legal acceptability of providing pain relief, even to the point

From *Journal of the American Medical Association* 278, no. 23 (December 17, 1997), 2099–2104.

of hastening death if necessary, and left open the possibility that states might choose to legalize PAS under some circumstances.

In this article, we compare VSED, TS, PAS, and VAE as potential interventions of last resort for competent, terminally ill patients who are suffering intolerably in spite of intensive efforts to palliate and who desire a hastened death. Some clinicians and patients may find some of the differences between these practices to be ethically and psychologically critical, whereas others perceive the differences as inconsequential. We will define and compare the practices, examine underlying ethical justifications, and consider appropriate categories of safeguards for whichever practices our society eventually condones.

DEFINITIONS AND CLINICAL COMPARISONS

With VSED, a patient who is otherwise physically capable of taking nourishment makes an active decision to discontinue all oral intake and then is gradually "allowed to die," primarily of dehydration or some intervening complication.[12–14] Depending on the patient's preexisting condition, the process will usually take 1 to 3 weeks or longer if the patient continues to take some fluids. Voluntarily stopping eating and drinking has several advantages. Many patients lose their appetites and stop eating and drinking in the final stages of many illnesses. Ethically and legally, the right of competent, informed patients to refuse life-prolonging interventions, including artificial hydration and nutrition, is firmly established, and voluntary cessation of "natural" eating and drinking could be considered an extension of that right. Because VSED requires considerable patient resolve, the voluntary nature of the action should be clear. Voluntarily stopping eating and drinking also protects patient privacy and independence, so much so that it potentially requires no participation by a physician.

The main disadvantages of VSED are that it may last for weeks and may initially increase suffering because the patient may experience thirst and hunger. Subtle coercion to proceed with the process may occur if patients are not regularly offered the opportunity to eat and drink, yet such offers may be viewed as undermining the patient's resolve. Some patients, family members, physicians, or nurses may find the notion of "dehydrating" or "starving" a patient to death to be morally repugnant. For patients whose current suffering is severe and unrelievable, the process would be unacceptable without sedation and analgesia. If physicians are not involved, palliation of symptoms may be inadequate, the decision to forgo eating and drinking may not be informed, and cases of treatable depression may be missed. Patients are likely to lose mental clarity toward the end of this process, which may undermine their sense of personal integrity or raise questions about whether the action remains voluntary.

Although several articles,[12,13] including a moving personal narrative,[14] have proposed VSED as an alternative to other forms of hastened death, there are no data about how frequently such decisions are made or how acceptable they are to patients, families, physician, or nurses.

With TS, the suffering patient is sedated to unconsciousness, usually through ongoing administration of barbiturates or benzodiazepines. The patient then dies of dehydration, starvation, or some other intervening complication, as all life-sustaining interventions are withheld.[15–18] Although death is inevitable, it usually does not take place for days or even weeks, depending on clinical circumstances. Because patients are deeply sedated during this terminal period, they are believed to be free of suffering.

It can be argued that death with TS is "foreseen" but not "intended" and that the sedation itself is not causing death.[15–18] The sedation is intended to relieve suffering, a long-standing and uncontroversial aim of medicine, and the subsequent withholding of life-sustaining therapy has wide legal and ethical acceptance. Thus, TS probably requires no change in the law. The recent Supreme Court decision gave strong support to TS, saying that pain in terminally ill patients should be treated, even to the point of rendering the patient unconscious or hastening death.[10,11] Terminal sedation is already openly practiced by some palliative care and hospice groups in cases of unrelieved suffering, with a reported frequency from 0% to 44% of cases.[1,6,7,15–20]

Terminal sedation has other practical advantages. It can be carried out in patients with severe physical limitations. The time delay between initiation of TS and death permits second-guessing and reassessment by the health care team and the family. Because the health care team must administer medications and monitor effects, physicians can ensure that the patient's decision is informed and voluntary before beginning TS. In addition, many proponents believe that it is appropriate to use TS in patients who lack decision-making capacity but appear to be suffering intolerably, provided that the patient's suffering is extreme and otherwise unrelievable, and the surrogate or family agrees.

Nonetheless, TS remains controversial[21–23] and has many of the same risks associated with VAE and PAS. Like VAE, the final actors are the clinicians, not the patient. Terminal sedation could therefore be carried out without explicit discussions with alert patients who appear to be suffering intolerably or even against their wishes. Some competent, terminally ill patients reject TS. They believe that their dignity would be violated if they had to be unconscious for a prolonged time before they die, or that their families would suffer unnecessarily while waiting for them to die. Patients who wish to die in their own homes may not be able to arrange TS because it probably requires admission to a health care facility. There is some controversy in the anesthesia literature about whether heavily sedated persons are actually free of suffering or simply unable to report or remember it.[24–26] In some clinical situations, TS cannot relieve the patient's symptoms, as when a patient is bleeding uncontrollably from an eroding lesion or a refractory coagulation disorder, cannot swallow secretions because of widespread oropharyngeal cancer, or has refractory diarrhea from the acquired immunodeficiency syndrome (AIDS). Although such patients are probably not conscious of their condition once sedated, their death is unlikely to be dignified or remembered as peaceful by their families. Finally, and perhaps most critically, there may be confusion about the physician's ethical responsibility for contributing to the patient's death.[21,22]

With PAS, the physician provides the means, usually a prescription of a large dose of barbiturates, by which a patient can end his or her life.[1,3,27] Although the physician is morally responsible for this assistance, the patient has to carry out the final act. Physician-assisted suicide has several advantages. For some patients, access to a lethal dose of medication may give them the freedom and reassurance to continue living, knowing they can escape if and when they choose.[28,29] Because patients have to ingest the drug by their own hand, their action is likely to be voluntary. Physicians report being more comfortable with PAS than VAE,[30–32] presumably because their participation is indirect.

Opponents of PAS believe that it violates traditional moral and professional prohibitions against intentionally contributing to a patient's death. Physician-assisted suicide also has several practical disadvantages. Self-administration does not guarantee competence or voluntariness. The patient may have impaired judgment at the time of the request or the act or may be influenced by external pressures. Physician-assisted suicide is limited to patients who are physically capable of taking the medication themselves. It is not always effective,[33,34] so families may be faced with a patient who is vomiting, aspirating, or cognitively impaired, but not dying. Patients brought to the emergency department after ineffective attempts are likely to receive unwanted life-prolonging treatment. Requiring physicians to be present when patients ingest the medication could coerce an ambivalent patient to proceed, yet their absence may leave families to respond to medical complications alone.

Physician-assisted suicide is illegal in most states, but no physicians have ever been successfully prosecuted for their participation.[3] Several studies have documented a secret practice of PAS in the United States. In Washington State, 12% of physicians responding to a survey had received genuine requests for PAS within the year studied.[8] Twenty-four percent of requests were acceded to, and over half of those patients died as a result. An Oregon study showed similar results.[35] Physician-assisted suicide is usually conducted covertly, without consultation, guidelines, or documentation. Public controversy about legalizing PAS continues in the United States. After narrow defeats of referenda in the states of Washington and California, an Oregon referendum was passed in 1994 that legalized PAS, subject to certain safeguards.[36] After a series of legal challenges, the Oregon legislature required that the referendum be resubmitted to the electorate this November before implementation, and it was repassed this November by a margin of 60% to 40%. The US Supreme Court ruled that laws in the states of Washington and New York prohibiting PAS were not unconstitutional, but the Court simultaneously encouraged public discussion and state experimentation through the legislative and referendum processes.[10,11,37,38]

With VAE, the physician not only provides the means, but is the final actor by administering a lethal injection at the patient's request.[1,3,25] As practiced in the Netherlands, the patient is sedated to unconsciousness and then given a lethal injection of a muscle-paralyzing agent like curare. For patients who are prepared to die because their suffering in intolerable, VAE has the advantages of being quick and effective. Patients need not have manual dexterity, the ability to swallow, or an intact gastrointestinal system. Voluntary active euthanasia also requires active and direct physician participation. Physicians can ensure the patient's competence and voluntariness at the time of the act, support the family, and respond to complications. The directness of the act makes the physician's moral responsibility clear.

On the other hand, VAE explicitly and directly conflicts with traditional medical prohibitions against intentionally causing death.[39] Although intended to relieve suffering, VAE achieves this goal by causing death. Furthermore, VAE could be conducted without explicit patient consent.[40,41] If abused, VAE could then be used on patients who appear to be suffering severely or posing extreme burdens to physician, family, or society, but have lost the mental capacity to make informed decisions.

The Netherlands is the only country where VAE and PAS are openly practiced, regulated, and studied, although the practices remain technically illegal. According to the Remmelink reports,[9,42,43] VAE accounts for 1.8% to 2.4% of all deaths, and PAS, another 0.2% to 0.4%. In 0.7% to 0.8% of deaths, active euthanasia was performed on patients who had lost the capacity to consent, raising concern about whether guidelines restricting VAE is competent patients can be enforced in practice.[44]

United States laws prohibiting VAE, however, are stricter than those governing PAS and more likely to be prosecuted. Physicians are also more reluctant to participate in VAE even if it were legalized.[30,31] Even less is known about the secret practice of VAE than of PAS in the United States. The recent Washington State study showed that 4% of physicians had received a genuine request for VAE within the year studied, and 24% of those responded by administering a lethal injection.[8] Voluntary active euthanasia was recently legalized in a province of Australia, but this legalization was subsequently reversed by the legislature.[45]

ETHICAL COMPARISONS BETWEEN THE PRACTICES

Many normative ethical analyses use the doctrine of double effect and the distinction between active and passive assistance to distinguish between currently permissible acts that may hasten death (forgoing life-sustaining treatment and high-dose pain medications) and those that are impermissible (PAS and VAE).[1,2,4,46,47] Both TS and VSED have been argued to be ethically preferable alternatives to PAS and VAE

on the basis of similar arguments.[12,13,16,19] In this section, we will critically examine these analyses. We also discuss the issues of voluntariness, proportionality, and conflict of duties, which may ultimately be more central to the ethical evaluation of these options. We suggest that there are more problems with the doctrine of double effect and the active/passive distinction than are ordinarily acknowledged and that TS and VSED are more complex and less easily distinguished ethically from PAS and VAE than proponents seem to realize. Our discussion in this section will be restricted to the potential ethical permissibility of these actions and not the public policy implications.

DOCTRINE OF DOUBLE EFFECT

When evaluating an action, the doctrine of double effect distinguishes between effects that a person intends (both the end sought and the means taken to the end) and consequences that are foreseen but unintended.[21,22,48,49] As long as the physician's intentions are good, it is permissible to perform actions with foreseeable consequences that it would be wrong to intend. In this view, intentionally causing death is morally impermissible, even if desired by a competent patient whose suffering could not otherwise be relieved. But if death comes unintentionally as the consequence of an otherwise well-intentioned intervention, even if foreseen with a high probability, the physician's action can be morally acceptable. The unintended but foreseen bad effect must also be proportional to the intended good effects.

The doctrine of double effect has been important in justifying the use of sufficient pain medications to relieve suffering near the end of life.[1,2,4,46,47] When high-dose opioids are used to treat pain, neither the patient nor the physician intends to accelerate death, but they accept the risk of unintentionally hastening death in order to relieve the pain. The doctrine of double effect has also been used to distinguish TS from PAS and VAE.[15,16,18,19] Relief of suffering is intended in all 3 options, but death is argued to be intended with PAS and VAE but is merely foreseen with TS. Yet to us it seems implausible to claim that death is unintended when a patient who wants to die is sedated to the point of coma, and intravenous fluids and artificial nutrition are withheld, making death certain.[21,22,50] Although the overarching intention of the sedation is to relieve the patient's suffering, the additional step of withholding fluids and nutrition is not needed to relieve pain, but is typically taken to hasten the patient's wished-for death. In contrast, when patients are similarly sedated to treat conditions like status epilepticus, therapies such as fluids and mechanical ventilation are continued with the goal of prolonging life.

According to the doctrine of double effect, intentionally taking life is always morally impermissible, whereas doing so foreseeably but unintentionally can be permissible when it produces a proportionate good. As applied to end-of-life medical decision making, the intentions of the physician are given more moral weight than the wishes and circumstances of the patient. An alternative view is that it is morally wrong to take the life of a person who wants to live, whether doing so intentionally or foreseeably. In this view, what can make TS morally permissible is that the patient gives informed consent to it, not that the physician only foresees but does not intend the patient's inevitable death.

The issue of intention is particularly complicated because the determination of what is intended by the patient or physician is often difficult to verify and because practices that are universally accepted may involve the intention to hasten death in some cases.[21,51] Death is not always intended or sought when competent patients forgo life support; sometimes patients simply do not want to continue a particular treatment, but hope nevertheless that they can live without it. But some patients find their circumstances intolerable, even with the best of care, and refuse further life support with the intent of bringing about their death. There is broad agreement that physicians must respect such refusals, even when the patient's intention is to die.[1–4,46,47,51] However, such practices are highly problematic when analyzed according to the doctrine of double effect.

THE ACTIVE/PASSIVE DISTINCTION

According to many normative ethical analyses, active measures that hasten death are unacceptable, whereas passive or indirect measures that achieve the same ends would be permitted.[1,2,4,46,47,52] However, how the active/passive distinction applies to these 4 practices remains controversial.[21,27] Voluntary active euthanasia is active assistance in dying, because the physician's actions directly cause the patient's death. Stopping life-sustaining therapies is typically considered passive assistance in dying, and the patient is said to die of the underlying disease no matter how proximate the physician's action and the patient's death. Physicians, however, sometimes experience stopping life-sustaining interventions as very active.[53] For example, there is nothing psychologically or physically passive about taking someone off a mechanical ventilator who is incapable of breathing on his or her own. Voluntarily stopping eating and drinking is argued to be a variant of stopping life-sustaining therapy, and the patient is said to die of the underlying disease.[12,13] However, the notion that VSED is passively "letting nature take its course" is unpersuasive, because patients with no underlying disease would also die if they stopped eating and drinking. Death is more a result of the patient's will and resolve than an inevitable consequence of his disease. Furthermore, even if the physician's role in hastening death is generally passive or indirect, most would argue that it is desirable to have physicians involved to ensure the patient is fully informed and to actively palliate symptoms.

Both PAS and TS are challenging to evaluate according to the active/passive distinction. Physician-assisted suicide is active in that the physician provides the means whereby the patient may take his or her life and thereby contributes to a new and different cause of death than the patient's disease. However, the physician's role in PAS is passive or indirect because the patient administers the lethal medication. The psychological and temporal distance between the prescribing and the act may also make PAS seem indirect and thereby more acceptable to physicians than VAE.[30–32] These ambiguities may allow the physi-cian to characterize his or her actions as passive or indirect.[21,50]

Terminal sedation is passive because the administration of sedation does not directly cause the patient's death and because the withholding of artificial feedings and fluids is commonly considered passively allowing the patient to die.[15,16,19] However, some physicians and nurses may consider it very active to sedate to unconsciousness someone who is seeking death and then to withhold life-prolonging interventions. Furthermore, the notion that TS is merely "letting nature take its course" is problematic, because often the patient dies of dehydration from the withholding of fluids, not of the underlying disease.

The application and the moral importance of both the active/passive distinction and the doctrine of double effect are notoriously controversial and should not serve as the primary basis of determining the morality of these practices.

VOLUNTARINESS

We suggest that the patient's wishes and competent consent are more ethically important than whether the acts are categorized as active or passive or whether death is intended or unintended by the physician.[54–56] With competent patients, none of these acts would be morally permissible without the patient's voluntary and informed consent. Any of these actions would violate a competent patient's autonomy and would be both immoral and illegal if the patient did not understand that death was the inevitable consequence of the action or if the decision was coerced or contrary to the patient's wishes. The ethical principle of autonomy focuses on patients' rights to make important decisions about their lives, including what happens to their bodies, and may support genuinely autonomous forms of these acts.[27,52]

However, because most of these acts require cooperation from physicians and, in the case of TS, the health care team, the autonomy of participating medical professionals also warrants consideration. Because TS, VSED, PAS, and VAE are not part of usual medical practice and they all result in a hastened death, clinicians should have the right to determine the nature and extent of their own participation. All physicians should respect patients' decisions to forgo life-sustaining treatment, including artificial hydration and nutrition, and provide standard palliative care, including skillful pain and symptom management. If society permits some or all of these practices (currently TS and VSED are openly tolerated), physicians who choose not to participate because of personal moral considerations should at a minimum discuss all available alternatives in the spirit of informed consent and respect for patient autonomy. Physicians are free to express their own objections to these practices as part of the informing process, to propose alternative approaches, and to transfer care to another physician if the patient continues to request actions to hasten death that they find unacceptable.

PROPORTIONALITY

The principles of beneficence and nonmaleficence obligate the physician to act in the patient's best interests and to avoid causing net harm.[52] The concept of proportionality requires that the risk of causing harm must bear a direct relationship to the danger and immediacy of the patient's clinical situation and the expected benefit of the intervention.[52,57] The greater the patient's suffering, the greater risk the physician can take of potentially contributing to the patient's death, so long as the patient understands and accepts that risk. For a patient with lung cancer who is anxious and short of breath, the risk of small doses of morphine or anxiolytics is warranted. At a later time, if the patient is near death and gasping for air, more aggressive sedation is warranted, even in doses that may well cause respiratory depression. Although proportionality is an important element of the doctrine of double effect, proportionality can be applied independently of this doctrine. Sometimes a patient's suffering cannot be relieved despite optimal palliative care, and continuing to live causes torment that can end only with death.[58] Such extreme circumstances sometimes warrant extraordinary medical actions, and the forms of hastening death under consideration in this article may satisfy the requirement of proportionality. The requirement of proportionality, which all health care interventions should meet, does not support any principled ethical distinction between these 4 options.

CONFLICT OF DUTIES

Unrelievable, intolerable suffering by patients at the end of life may create for physicians an explicit conflict between their ethical and professional duty to relieve suffering and their understanding of their ethical and professional duty not to use at least some means of deliberately hastening death.[57,59] Physicians who believe they should respond to such suffering by acceding to the patient's request for a hastened death may find themselves caught between their duty to the patient as a caregiver and their duty to obey the law as a citizen.[58] Solutions often can be found in the intensive application of palliative care, or within the currently legitimized options of forgoing life supports, VSED, or TS. Situations in which VSED or TS may not be adequate include terminally ill patients with uncontrolled bleeding, obstruction from nasopharyngeal cancer, and refractory AIDS diarrhea or patients who believe that spending their last days iatrogenically sedated would be meaningless, frightening, or degrading. Clearly the physician has a moral obligation not to abandon patients with refractory suffering[60]; hence, those physicians who could not provide some or all of these options because of moral or legal reservations should be required to search assiduously with the patient for mutually acceptable solutions.

SAFEGUARDS

In the United States, health care is undergoing radical reform driven more by market forces than by commitments to quality of care,[61,62] and 42 million persons are currently uninsured. Capitated reimbursement could provide financial incentives to encourage terminally ill patients to hasten their deaths. Physicians' participation in hastening death by any of these methods can be justified only as a last resort when standard palliative measures are ineffective or unacceptable to the patient.

Safeguards to protect vulnerable patients from the risk of error, abuse, or coercion must be constructed for any of these practices that are ultimately accepted. These risks, which have been extensively cited in the debates about PAS and VAE,[39–41] also exist for TS and VSED. Both TS and VSED could be carried out without ensuring that optimal palliative care has been provided. This risk may be particularly great if VSED is carried out without physician involvement. In TS, physicians who unreflectively believe that death is unintended or that it is not their explicit purpose may fail to acknowledge the inevitable consequences of their action or their responsibility.

The typical safeguards proposed for regulating VAE and PAS[63–66] are intended to allow physicians to respond to unrelieved suffering, while ensuring that adequate palliative measures have been attempted and that patient decisions are autonomous. These safeguards need to balance respect for patient privacy with the need to adequately oversee these interventions. Similar professional safeguards should be considered for TS and VSED, even if these practices are already sanctioned by the law. The challenge of safeguards is to be flexible enough to be responsive to individual patient dilemmas and rigorous enough to protect vulnerable persons.

Categories of safeguards include the following.

1. Palliative care ineffective: Excellent palliative care must be available, yet insufficient to relieve intolerable suffering for a particular patient.

2. Informed consent: Patients must be fully informed about and capable of understanding their condition and treatment alternatives (and their risks and benefits). Requests for a hastened death must be patient initiated, free of undue influence, and enduring. Waiting periods must be flexible, depending on the nearness of inevitable death and the severity of immediate suffering.

3. Diagnostic and prognostic clarity: Patients must have a clearly diagnosed disease with known lethality. The prognosis must be understood, including the degree of uncertainty about outcomes (ie, how long the patient might live).

4. Independent second opinion: A consultant with expertise in palliative care should review the case. Specialists should also review any questions about the patient's diagnosis or prognosis. A psychiatrist should consult if there is uncertainty about treatable depression or about the patient's mental capacity.

5. Documentation and review: Explicit processes for documentation, reporting, and review should be in place to ensure accountability.

The restriction of any of these methods to the terminally ill involves a trade-off. Some patients who suffer greatly from incurable, but not terminal, illnesses and who are unresponsive to palliative measures will be denied access to a hastened death and forced to continue suffering against their will. Other patients whose request for a hastened death is denied will avoid a premature death because their suffering can subsequently be relieved with more intensive palliative care. Some methods (e.g., PAS, VAE, TS) might be restricted to the terminally ill because of current inequities of access, concerns about errors and abuse, and lack of experience with the process. Others (e.g., VSED) might be allowed for those who are incurably ill, but not imminently dying, if they meet all other criteria, because of the inherent waiting period, the great resolve that they require, and the opportunity for reconsideration. If any methods are extended to the incurably, but not terminally, ill, safeguards should be more stringent, including substantial waiting periods and mandatory assessment by psychiatrists and specialists, because the risk and consequences of error are increased.

We believe that clinical, ethical, and policy differences and similarities among these 4 practices need to be debated openly, both publicly and within the medical profession. Some may worry that a discussion of the similarities between VSED and TS on the one hand and PAS and VAE on the other may undermine the desired goal of optimal relief of suffering at the end of life.[40,41] Others may worry that a critical analysis of the principle of double effect or the active/passive distinction as applied to VSED and

TS may undermine efforts to improve pain relief or to ensure that patient's or surrogate's decisions to forgo unwanted life-sustaining therapy are respected.[67] However, hidden, ambiguous practices, inconsistent justifications, and failure to acknowledge the risks of accepted practices may also undermine the quality of terminal care and put patients at unwarranted risk.

Allowing a hastened death only in the context of access to good palliative care puts it in its proper perspective as a small but important facet of comprehensive care for all dying patients.[1–4] Currently, TS and VSED are probably legal and are widely accepted by hospice and palliative care physicians. However, they may not be readily available because some physicians may continue to have moral objections and legal fears about these options. Physician-assisted suicide is illegal in most states, but may be difficult, if not impossible, to successfully prosecute if it is carried out at the request of an informed patient. Voluntary active euthanasia is illegal and more likely to be aggressively prosecuted if uncovered. In the United States, there is an underground, erratically available practice of PAS and even VAE that is quietly condoned.

Explicit public policies about which of these 4 practices are permissible and under what circumstances could have important benefits. Those who fear a bad death would face the end of life knowing that their physicians could respond openly if their worst fears materialize. For most, reassurance will be all that is needed, because good palliative care is generally effective. Explicit guidelines for the practices that are deemed permissible can also encourage clinicians to explore why a patient requests hastening of death, to search for palliative care alternatives, and to respond to those whose suffering is greatest.[58,60,68–70]

REFERENCES

1. Foley K. M. Pain, physician-assisted suicide, and euthanasia. *Pain Forum.* 1995;4:163–178.

2. Council on Scientific Affairs, American Medical Association. Good care of the dying patient. *JAMA* 1996;275: 474–478.

3. Quill T. E.: *Death and Dignity: Making Choices and Taking Charge.* New York, NY: WW Norton & Co; 1993:1–255.

4. American Board of Internal Medicine End of Life Patient Care Project Committee. *Caring for the Dying: Identification and Promotion of Physician Competency.* Philadelphia, Pa: American Board of Internal Medicine; 1996.

5. Kasting G. A.: The nonnecessity of euthanasia. In: Humber J. D., Almeder R. F., Kasting G. A., eds. *Physician-Assisted Death.* Totowa, NJ: Humana Press; 1993:25–43.

6. Coyle N., Adelhardt J., Foley K. M., Portenoy R. K. Character of terminal illness in the advance cancer patient. *J Pain Symptom Manage.* 1990;5:83–93.

7. Ingham J., Portenoy R. Symptom assessment. *Hematol Oncol Clin North Am.* 1996;10:21–39.

8. Back A. L., Wallace J. I., Starks H. E., Pearlman R. A. Physician-assisted suicide and euthanasia in Washington State. *JAMA.* 1996;275:919–925.

9. vanderMaas P. J., van Delden J. J. M., Pijnenborg L. *Euthanasia and Other Medical Decisions Concerning the End of Life.* Amsterdam, the Netherlands: Elsevier, 1992.

10. *Vacco v. Quill,* 117 SCt 2293 (1997).

11. *Washington v. Glucksberg,* 117 SCt 2258 (1997).

12. Bernat J. L., Gert B., Mogielnicki R. P. Patient refusal of hydration and nutrition. *Arch Intern Med.* 1993;153:2723–2727.

13. Printz L. A. Terminal dehydration, a compassionate treatment. *Arch Intern Med* 1992;152:697–700.

14. Eddy D. M. A conversation with my mother. *JAMA.* 1994;272:179–181.

15. Cherney N. I., Portenoy R. K. Sedation in the management of refractory symptoms: guidelines for evaluation and treatment. *J Palliat Care.* 1994;10:31–38.

16. Truog R. D., Berde D. B., Mitchell C., Grier H.E. Barbiturates in the care of the terminally ill. *N Engl J Med.* 1991;327:1678–1681.

17. Enck R. E. *The Medical Care of Terminally Ill Patients.* Baltimore, Md: Johns Hopkins University Press; 1994.

18. Saunders C., Sykes N. *The Management of Terminal Malignant Disease.* 3rd ed. London, England: Hodder Headline Group; 1993:1–305.

19. Byock I. R. Consciously walking the fine line: thoughts on a hospice response to assisted suicide and euthanasia. *J Palliat Care.* 1993;9:25–58.

20. Ventrafridda B., Ripamonti C., DeConno F., et al. Symptom prevalence and control during cancer patients' last days of life. *J Palliat Care* 1990;6:7–11.

21. Brody H. Causing, intending, and assisting death. *J Clin Ethics.* 1993;4:112–117.

22. Billings J. A. Slow euthanasia. *J Palliat Care.* 1996; 12:21–30.

23. Orentlicher D. The Supreme Court and physician-assisted suicide: rejecting assisted suicide but embracing euthanasia. *N Engl J Med.* 1997;337:1236–1239.

24. Moerman N., Bonke B., Oosting J. Awareness and recall during general anesthesia: facts and feelings. *Anesthesiology.* 1993;79:454–464.

25. Utting J. E. Awareness: clinical aspects; consciousness, awareness, and pain. In: Rosen M, Linn JN. *General Anesthesia.* London, England: Butterworths; 1987:171–179.

26. Evans J. M. Patient's experience of awareness during general anesthesia; consciousness, awareness and pain. In: Rosen M, Linn JN. *General Anesthesia.* London, England: Butterworths; 1987:184–192.

27. Brock D. W. Voluntary active euthanasia. *Hastings Cent Rep.* 1992;22:10–22.

28. Quill T. E. Death and dignity. *N Engl J Med.* 1991; 324:691–694.

29. Rollin B. *Last Wish.* New York, NY: Warner Books, 1985.

30. Cohen J. S., Fihn S. D., Boyko E. J., et al. Attitudes toward assisted suicide and euthanasia among physicians in Washington State. *N Engl J Med.* 1994;331:89–94.

31. Bachman J. G., Alchser K. H., Koukas D. J., et al. Attitudes of Michigan physicians and the public toward legalizing physician-assisted suicide and voluntary euthanasia. *N Engl J Med.* 1996;334:303–309.

32. Duberstein P. R, Conwell Y., Cox C., et al. Attitudes toward self-determined death. *J Am Geriatr Soc.* 1995;43:395–400.

33. Preston T. A., Mero R. Observations concerning terminally-ill patients who choose suicide. *J Pharm Care Pain Symptom Control.* 1996;1:183–192.

34. Admiraal P. V. Toepassing van euthanatica (the use of euthanatics). *Ned Tijdschr Geneeskd.* 1995;139:265–268.

35. Lee M. A., Nelson H. D., Tilden V. P., Ganzini L., Schmidt T. A., Tolle S. W. Legalizing assisted suicide: views of physicians in Oregon. *N Engl J Med.* 1996;334:310–315.

36. Alpers A., Lo B. Physician-assisted suicide in Oregon: a bold experiment. *JAMA.* 1995;274:483–487.

37. *Compassion in Dying v Washington,* No. 94-35534, 1966 WL 94848 (9th Cir, Mar 6, 1996).

38. *Quill v. Vacco,* No. 95-7028 (2d Cir. April 9, 1996).

39. Gaylin W., Kass L. R., Pellegrino E. D., Siegler M. Doctors must not kill. *JAMA.* 1988;259:2139–2140.

40. Teno J., Lynn J. Voluntary active euthanasia: the individual case and public policy. *J Am Geriatr Soc.* 1991;39:827–830.

41. Kamisar Y. Against assisted suicide—even a very limited form. *Univ Detroit Mercy Law Rev.* 1995;72:735–769.

42. vanderMaas P. J, vanderWal G., Haverkate I., et al. Euthanasia, physician-assisted suicide and other medical practices involving the end of life in the Netherlands, 1990–1995. *N Engl J Med.* 1996;335:1699–1705.

43. van der Wal G., van der Maas P. J., Bosma J. M., et al. Evaluation of the notification procedure for physician-assisted death in the Netherlands. *N Engl J Med.* 1996;335:1706–1711.

44. Hendin H. Seduced by death. *Issues Law Med.* 1994;10:123–168.

45. Ryan C. J., Kaye M. Euthanasia in Australia: the Northern Territory rights of the terminally ill act. *N Engl J Med.* 1996;334:326–328.

46. President's Commission for the Study of Ethical Problems in Medicine and Biomedical and Behavioral Research. *Deciding to Forego Life-Sustaining Treatment: Ethical, Medical and Legal Issues in Treatment Decisions.* Washington, DC: US Government Printing Office; 1982.

47. The Hastings Center Report. *Guidelines on the Termination of Life-Sustaining Treatment and the Care of the Dying.* Briarcliff Manor, NY: Hastings Center, 1987.

48. Marquis D. B. Four versions of the double effect. *J Med Philos.* 1991;16:515–544.

49. Kamm F. The doctrine of double effect. *J Med Philos.* 1991:16:571–585.

50. Quill T. E. The ambiguity of clinical intentions. *N Engl J Med.* 1993;329:1039–1040.

51. Alpers A., Lo B. Does it make clinical sense to equate terminally ill patients who require life-sustaining interventions with those who do not? *JAMA.* 1997;277:1705–1708.

52. Beauchamp T. L., Childress J. F. *Principles of Biomedical Ethics.* 4th ed. New York, NY: Oxford University Press; 1994.

53. Edwards M. J., Tolle S. W. Disconnecting a ventilator at the request of a patient who knows he will die. *Ann Intern Med.* 1992;117:254–256.

54. Orentlicher D. The legalization of physician-assisted suicide. *N Engl J Med.* 1996;335:663–667.

55. Drickamer M. A., Lee Ganzini L. Practical issues in physician-assisted suicide. *Ann Intern Med.* 1997;126:146–151.

56. Angell M. The Supreme Court and physician-assisted suicide: the ultimate right. *N Engl J Med.* 1997;336:50–53.

57. de Wachter M. A. M. Active euthanasia in the Netherlands. *JAMA.* 1989;262:3316–3319.

58. Quill T. E., Brody R. V. 'You promised me I wouldn't die like this': a bad death as a medical emergency. *Arch Intern Med.* 1995;155:1250–1254.

59. Welie J. V. M. The medical exception: physicians, euthanasia and the Dutch criminal law. *J Med Philos.* 1992;17:419–437.

60. Quill T. E., Cassel C. K. Nonabandonment: a central obligation for physicians. *Ann Intern Med.* 1995;122:368–374.

61. Emanuel E. J., Brett A. S. Managed competition and the patient-physician relationship. *N Engl J Med.* 1993;329:879–882.

62. Morrison R. S., Meier D. E. Managed care at the end of life. *Trends Health Care Law Ethics.* 1995;10:91–96.

63. Quill T. E., Cassel C. K., Meier D. E. Care of the hopelessly ill: proposed criteria for physician-assisted suicide. *N Engl J Med* 1992;327:1380–1384.

64. Brody H. Assisted death. *N Engl J Med.* 1992;327: 1284–1388.

65. Miller F. G., Quill T. E., Brody H., et al. Regulating physician-assisted death. *N Engl J Med.* 1994;331:119–123.

66. Baron C. H., Bergstresser C., Brock D. W., et al. Statute: a model state act to authorize and regulate physician-assisted suicide. *Harvard J Legislation* 1996;33:1–34.

67. Mount B., Flanders E. M. Morphine drips, terminal sedation, and slow euthanasia: definition and facts, not anecdotes. *J Palliat Care.* 1996;12:31–37.

68. Lee M. A., Tolle S. W. Oregon's assisted-suicide vote: the silver lining. *Ann Intern Med.* 1996;124:267–269.

69. Block S. D., Billings A. Patient requests to hasten death: evaluation and management in terminal care. *Arch Intern Med.* 1994;154:2039–2047.

70. Quill T. E., Doctor, I want to die: will you help me? *JAMA.* 1993;270:870–873.

SUGGESTED READINGS FOR CHAPTER 4

Angell, Marcia. "The Supreme Court and Physician-Assisted Suicide—the Ultimate Right." *New England Journal of Medicine* 336 (1997), 50–53.

Annas, George J., and Grodin, Michael, eds. *The Nazi Doctors and the Nuremberg Code.* New York: Oxford University Press, 1992.

Battin, Margaret P., Rhodes, Rosamond, and Silvers, Anita, eds. *Physician Assisted Suicide: Expanding the Debate.* New York, NY: Routledge, 1998.

Beauchamp, Tom L., ed. *Intending Death: The Ethics of Assisted Suicide and Euthanasia.* Upper Saddle River, NJ: Prentice-Hall, 1996.

Beauchamp, Tom L., and Veatch, Robert, eds. *Ethical Issues in Death and Dying.* Upper Saddle River, NJ: Prentice-Hall, 1997.

Beauchamp, Tom L., and Childress, James F. *Principles of Biomedical Ethics,* 5th ed. New York: Oxford University Press, 2001, chap. 4.

Bernat, James L., Gert, Bernard, and Mogielnicki, R. Peter. "Patient Refusal of Hydration and Nutrition: An Alternative to Physician-Assisted Suicide or Voluntary Active Euthanasia." *Archives of Internal Medicine* 153 (December 27, 1993), 2723–28.

Brock, Dan W. "A Critique of Three Objectives to Physician-Assisted Suicide." *Ethics* 109 (April 1999), 519–47.

———. "Death and Dying." In Robert M. Veatch, ed. *Medical Ethics,* 2d ed. Boston: Jones and Bartlett, 1997.

———. "Medical Decisions at the End of Life." In Helga Kuhse and Peter Singer, eds. *A Companion to Bioethics.* Malden, MA: Blackwell, 1998, 231–41.

Brody, Baruch A. *Suicide and Euthanasia: Historical and Contemporary Themes.* Dordrecht, Holland: Kluwer Academic Publishers, 1989.

Callahan, Daniel. "Pursuing a Peaceful Death." *Hastings Center Report* 23 (1993), 32–38.

———. *The Troubled Dream of Life: Living with Mortality.* New York: Simon & Schuster, 1993.

Cantor, Norman L. "Glucksberg, the Putative Right to Adequate Pain Relief, and Death with Dignity." *Journal of Health Law* 34 (2001), 301–33.

Caplan, Arthur, and Blank, Robert H, eds. *Compassion: Government Intervention in the Treatment of Critically Ill Newborns.* Totowa, NJ: Humana Press, 1992.

Cassel, Christine K. "Physician-Assisted Suicide: Are We Asking the Right Questions?" *Second Opinion* 18 (October 1992), 95–98.

Cavanaugh, Thomas A. "Currently Accepted Practices That Are Known to Lead to Death, and PAS: Is There an Ethically Relevant Difference?" *Cambridge Quarterly of Healthcare Ethics* 7 (Fall 1998), 375–81.

Dworkin, Ronald. *Life's Dominion: An Argument about Abortion, Euthanasia, and Individual Freedom.* New York: Knopf, 1993.

Dworkin, Gerald, Frey, Raymond G., and Bok, Sissela. *Euthanasia and Physician-Assisted Suicide: For and Against.* New York: Cambridge University Press, 1998.

Emanuel, Ezekiel J. "What Is the Great Benefit of Legalizing Euthanasia or Physician-Assisted Suicide?" *Ethics* 109 (April 1999), 629–42.

———, et al. "The Practice of Euthanasia and Physician-Assisted Suicide in the United States: Adherence to Proposed Safeguards and Effects on Physicians." *Journal of the American Medical Association* 280 (August 1998), 507–13.

Emanuel, Linda L., ed. *Regulating How We Die: The Ethical, Medical, and Legal Issues Surrounding Physician-Assisted Suicide.* Cambridge, MA: Harvard University Press, 1998.

Gert, Bernard, Culver, Charles M., and Clouser, K. Danner, *Bioethics: A Return to Fundamentals.* New York: Oxford, 1997, chaps. 11–12.

Glover, Jonathan. *Causing Death and Saving Lives.* New York: Penguin Books, 1977.

Gomez, Carlos. *Regulating Death: Euthanasia and the Case of the Netherlands.* New York: Free Press, 1991.

Gostin, Lawrence O. "Deciding Life and Death in the Courtroom: From *Quinlan* to *Cruzan, Glucksberg,* and *Vacco*—A Brief History and Analysis of Constitutional Protection of the 'Right to Die.' " *Journal of the American Medical Association* 278 (November 1997), 1523–28.

Kadish Sanford H. "Authorizing Death." In Jules Coleman, and Allen Buchanan, eds. *Harm's Way.* Cambridge: Cambridge University Press, 1993.

Kamm, Frances M. "Physician-Assisted Suicide, The Doctrine of Double Effect, and the Ground of Value." *Ethics* 109 (April 1999), 586–605.

Koop, C. Everett, and Grant, Edward R. "The 'Small Beginnings' of Euthanasia." *Journal of Law, Ethics & Public Policy* 2 (1986), 607–32.

Leenen, H. J. J., and Ciesielski-Carlucci, Chris. "*Force majeure* (Legal Necessity): Justification for Active Termination of Life in the Case of Severely Handicapped Newborns after Forgoing Treatment." *Cambridge Quarterly of Healthcare Ethics* 2 (Summer 1993), 271–74.

Lifton, Robert J. *The Nazi Doctors: Medical Killing and the Psychology of Genocide.* New York: Basic Books, 1986.

McMillan, Richard C., Engelhardt, H. Tristram, Jr., and Spicker, Stuart F., eds. *Euthanasia and the Newborn: Conflicts Regarding Saving Lives.* Dordrecht: D. Reidel, 1987.

Meier, Diane E., et al. "A National Survey of Physician-Assisted Suicide and Euthanasia in the United States." *New England Journal of Medicine* 338 (April 23, 1998), 1193–1201.

Meisel, Alan. *The Right to Die,* 2d ed. New York: John Wiley and Sons, 1995.

———, Jernigan, Jan C., and Youngner, Stuart J. "Prosecutors and End-of-Life Decision Making." *Archives of Internal Medicine* 159 (May 1999), 1089–95.

Miller, Franklin G., et al. "Regulating Physician-Assisted Death." *New England Journal of Medicine* 331 (1994), 119–23.

———, Fins, Joseph J., and Snyder, Lois. "Assisted Suicide Compared with Refusal of Treatment: A Valid Distinction?" *Annals of Internal Medicine* 132 (March 2000), 470–75.

New York State Task Force on Life and the Law. *When Death Is Sought: Assisted Suicide and Euthanasia in the Medical Context.* New York: New York State Task Force, 1994.

Orentlicher, David. "The Legalization of Physician Assisted Suicide: A Very Modest Revolution." *Boston College Law Review* 28 (1997), 443–75.

Perrett, Roy W. "Killing, Letting Die and the Bare Difference Argument." *Bioethics* 10 (1996), 131–39.

Quill, Timothy E. "Death and Dignity: A Case of Individualized Decision Making." *New England Journal of Medicine* 324 (March 7, 1991), 691–94.

———. *Death and Dignity: Making Choices and Taking Charge.* New York: W. W. Norton, 1993.

———, et al. "The Debate over Physician-Assisted Suicide: Empirical Data and Convergent Views." *Annals of Internal Medicine* 128 (April 1998), 552–58.

———, et al. "Palliative Treatments of Last Resort: Choosing the Least Harmful Alternative." *Annals of Internal Medicine* 132 (March 2000), 488–93.

———, and Byock, Ira R. "Responding to Intractable Terminal Suffering: The Role of Terminal Sedation and Voluntary Refusal of Food and Fluids: Position Paper." *Annals of Internal Medicine* 132 (March 2000), 408–14.

Rachels, James. "Active and Passive Euthanasia." *New England Journal of Medicine* 292 (January 9, 1975), 78–80.

———. *The End of Life: Euthanasia and Morality.* Oxford: Oxford University Press, 1986.

Regan, Tom, ed. *Matters of Life and Death,* 3d ed. New York: Random House, 1992.

Salem, Tania. "Physician-Assisted Suicide: Promoting Autonomy—or Medicalizing Suicide? *Hastings Center Report* 29 (May–June 1999), 30–36.

Schaffner, Kenneth F. "Recognizing the Tragic Choice: Food, Water, and the Right to Assisted Suicide." *Critical Care Medicine* 16 (October 1988), 1063–68.

Stead, William W., et al. "Terminal Dehydration as an Alternative to Physician-Assisted Suicide." [Letters and responses]. *Annals of Internal Medicine* 129 (December 1998), 1080–82.

Thomasma, David C. "When Physicians Choose to Participate in the Death of Their Patients." *Journal of Law, Medicine & Ethics* 24 (1996), 183–97.

———, and Graber, Glenn C. *Euthanasia: Toward an Ethical Social Policy.* New York: Continuum, 1990.

Truog, Robert, and Berde, Charles B. "Pain, Euthanasia, and Anesthesiologists." *Anesthesiology* 78 (February 1993), 353–60.

———, et al. "Barbiturates in the Care of the Terminally Ill." *New England Journal of Medicine* 327 (December 3, 1992), 1678–82.

Thomson, Judith Jarvis. "Physician-Assisted Suicide: Two Moral Arguments." *Ethics* 109 (April 1999), 497–518.

van Delden, Johannes J. M., et al. "The Remmelink Study: Two Years Later." *Hastings Center Report* 23 (1993), 24–27.

van der Maas, Paul J, et al. "Euthanasia and Other Medical Decisions Concerning the End of Life." *Lancet* 338 (1991), 669–74.

Velleman, J. David. "A Right to Self-Termination?" *Ethics* 109 (April 1999), 606–28.

Wanzer, S. H., et al. "The Physician's Responsibility toward Hopelessly Ill Patients: A Second Look." *New England Journal of Medicine* 320 (1989), 844–49.

Willems, Dick L., et al. "Attitudes and Practices Concerning the End of Life: A Comparison Between Physicians from the United States and from the Netherlands." *Archives of Internal Medicine* 160 (January 2000), 63–68.

Wolf, Susan. "Holding the Life on Euthanasia." *Hastings Center Report* 19 (1989), S13–S15.

BIBLIOGRAPHIES AND REFERENCE WORKS

Becker, Lawrence, and Becker, Charlotte, eds. *Encyclopedia of Ethics.* New York: Garland Publishing Inc., 1992.

Curran, William J., et al. *Health Care Law and Ethics.* New York: Aspen Law & Business, 1998. [Includes bibliographical references.]

Lineback, Richard H., ed. *Philosopher's Index.* Vols. 1–. Bowling Green, OH: Philosophy Documentation Center, Bowling Green State University. Issued quarterly. Also CD Rom.

National Library of Medicine (NLM) Gateway, http://gateway.nlm.nih.gov.

Reich, Warren, ed. *Encyclopedia of Bioethics,* 2d ed. New York: Macmillan, 1995.

Walters, LeRoy, and Kahn, Tamar Joy, eds. *Bibliography of Bioethics.* Vols. 1–. New York: Free Press. Issued annually.

5.
Abortion and Maternal-Fetal Relations

INTRODUCTION

Despite the fact that abortion is legal in many Western nations, questions of its ethical acceptability continue to be widely debated. In this chapter contemporary issues about both abortion and maternal-fetal relations are examined.

THE PROBLEM OF MORAL JUSTIFICATION

Abortions are sought for many reasons: psychological trauma, pregnancy caused by rape, the inadvertent use of fetus-deforming drugs, genetic predisposition to disease, prenatally diagnosed birth defects, and many personal and family reasons such as the financial burden of a child. These circumstances explain why abortions are obtained. But an *explanation* of this sort does not address the problem of *justification* (see Chapter 1, pp. 11–12): What reasons, if any, are sufficient to justify the act of aborting a human fetus?

Some contend that abortion is never acceptable or, at most, is permissible only if it is necessary to bring about a moral good such as saving a pregnant woman's life. This view is commonly called the *conservative theory of abortion* because it emphasizes conserving life. Roman Catholics are well-known proponents of this approach, but they are by no means its only advocates. A philosophical case for this point of view is presented in this chapter by Don Marquis, who does not rely on any form of religious claim to defend his views.

The opposed view is that abortion is always permissible, whatever the state of fetal development. This outlook is commonly termed the *liberal theory of abortion* because it emphasizes freedom of choice and the right of a woman to make decisions that affect her body. Mary Anne Warren defends this approach in this chapter.

Many writers defend theories that are intermediate between liberal and conservative approaches. They hold that abortion is ethically permissible up to a specified stage of fetal development or for moral reasons that warrant abortions under limited circumstances (such as pregnancy from rape and pregnancy that presents a risk of death to the woman). Baruch Brody presents an intermediate theory that leans toward conservatism, while Judith Thomson's essay suggests an intermediate theory that leans toward liberalism.

THE ONTOLOGICAL STATUS OF THE FETUS

Recent controversies about abortion focus on ethical problems of our obligations to fetuses and on what rights, if any, fetuses possess. One basic issue concerns the *kind of entities* fetuses are. This is the problem of the *ontological status* of the fetus.

Several layers of questions can be distinguished about ontological status: (1) Is the fetus an individual organism? (2) Is the fetus biologically a human being? (3) Is the fetus psychologically a human being? and (4) Is the fetus a person? It is widely agreed that one attributes a more significant status to the fetus by granting that it is fully a human being (biologically and psychologically), rather than merely saying that it is an individual organism, and that one enhances its status still further by attributing personhood to the fetus.

Many are willing to concede that an individual life begins at fertilization but not willing to concede that a psychological human being or a person exists at fertilization.

Others claim that the fetus is human biologically and psychologically at fertilization but not a person. Still others grant full personhood at fertilization. Those who espouse these views sometimes differ because they define one or more central terms differently. Other critical differences derive from theories of humanity or personhood.

THE CONCEPT OF HUMANITY

The concept of human life has long been at the center of the abortion discussion. It is a complicated notion, because "human life" carries two very different meanings. On one hand, it can mean *biological human life,* that group of biological characteristics that set the human species apart from nonhuman species. On the other hand, "human life" can be used to mean *life that is distinctively human*—that is, a life characterized by psychological rather than biological properties. For example, the ability to use symbols, to imagine, to love, and to perform higher intellectual skills are among the most distinctive human properties.

A simple example illustrates the differences between these two senses of "human life": Some infants with extreme disabilities die shortly after birth. They are born of human parents, and they are biologically human; but they never exhibit the distinctively human psychological traits mentioned above and (in many cases) have no potential to do so. For these individuals it is not possible to make human life in the biological sense human life in the psychological sense. It is noteworthy that we do not differentiate these two aspects of life in discourse about any other animal species. We do not, for example, speak of making feline life more distinctively feline. But we do meaningfully speak of making human life more human, and this usage makes sense because of the dual meaning just mentioned.

In discussions of abortion, it is important to be clear about which meaning is being employed when using the expression "the taking of human life."

THE CONCEPT OF PERSONHOOD

The concept of personhood may or may not be different from either the biological sense or the psychological sense of human life. That is, it could be argued that what it means to be a person is simply to have some properties that make an organism human in one or both of these senses. However, many writers have suggested a list of more demanding criteria for being a person. They have suggested that an entity is a person if and only if it possesses certain *cognitive* properties, not merely *human* properties. Cognitive conditions of personhood similar to the following have been promoted by several writers, among them Warren:

1. Self-consciousness (of oneself as existing over time)
2. Capacity to act on reasons
3. Capacity to communicate with others using a language
4. Capacity to act freely
5. Rationality

Sometimes it is said by those who propose such a list that in order to be a person an individual need only satisfy one of the aforementioned criteria—for example, bona fide linguistic behavior (condition 3)—but need not also satisfy the other conditions (nos. 1–2, 4–5). Others say that all of these conditions must be satisfied. In theories in which more than one of these criteria is necessary to qualify as a person, it is usually said to follow that fetuses, newborns, profoundly brain-damaged persons, and most if not all animals fail one of the criteria, and so do not have the moral standing conferred by the category of person. Here the critical question is whether any list approximating criteria 1–5 is acceptable. Marquis, Brody, and Thomson (unlike Warren) seem not to view the core problems of abortion as turning on the acceptance or rejection of any such list.

The problem of ontological status is further complicated by a factor related to the biological development of the fetus. It is important, in some theories, to be able to specify the point during development at which an entity achieves the status of a human or a person. Locating this point of development is a central task in Brody's essay and also in the opinions in *Roe v. Wade* and *Planned Parenthood v. Casey* of the U.S. Supreme Court. Many positions have been advanced on how to establish this point of development. Moderate theories draw the line somewhere between the extremes of conception and birth. For example, the line may be drawn at quickening, at viability, or when brain waves are first present, as Brody argues.

A very different position is that the fetus fails to satisfy any of the criteria mentioned above and therefore has *no ontological status* (of any moral importance). Warren defends this view. The opposite position is that the fetus always has *full ontological status* in regard to all of the significant measures of status. Marquis supports a version of this view, but one closely tied to what will now be discussed as "the moral status of the fetus."

THE MORAL STATUS OF THE FETUS

Philosophers have explicated the notion of *moral status* in several ways. In a weak sense, this term refers to a standing, grade, or rank of moral importance or of moral value. In a stronger and more common sense, *status* means to have rights, or the functional equivalent of rights, in the form of having protected interests and being positioned to make valid claims (or to have them asserted on one's behalf). Thus, having moral status is to qualify under some range of moral protections. If fetuses have *full moral status* then they possess the same rights as those who have been born. Brody holds this thesis for at least some periods of fetal development, and Marquis's analysis suggests it for all periods.

By contrast, many writers hold that fetuses have only a *partial moral status* and therefore only a partial set of rights, and some maintain that fetuses possess no moral status and therefore no rights, as Warren maintains. If Warren's account is accepted, then the fetus has no more right to life than a body cell or a tumor, and an abortion is no more morally objectionable than surgery to remove the tumor. But if the full-status view is accepted, fetuses possess the rights possessed by all human beings, and an abortion is as objectionable as any common killing of an innocent person.

Theories of moral status have direct links to theories of ontological status. Many writers in philosophy, religion, science, and popular culture have suggested that some special properties of persons, such as self-consciousness and rationality, confer a unique moral standing on those individuals who possess it (though many others have been skeptical that such a property or set of properties does or even could confer moral status).

A typical conservative thesis is that because the line between the human and the nonhuman is properly drawn at conception, the fetus has full ontological status and, therefore, full moral status. A typical liberal claim is that the line between the human and the nonhuman must be drawn at birth; the fetus has no significant ontological status and, therefore, no significant moral status. Some liberals argue that even though the fetus is biologically human, it is nonetheless not human in an ontologically significant sense and, therefore, has no significant moral status. This claim is usually accompanied by the thesis that *only* persons have a significant ontological status, and because fetuses are not persons they have no moral status (see Warren).

Moderates use a diverse mixture of arguments, which sometimes do and sometimes do not combine an ontological account with a moral one. Typical of moderate views is the claim that the line between the human and the nonhuman or the line between persons and nonpersons should be drawn at some point between conception and birth. Therefore, the fetus has no significant moral status during some stages of growth but does have significant moral status beginning at some later stage. For example, the line may be drawn at viability, with the result that the fetus is given either full moral status or partial moral status at viability. Some arguments in U.S. Supreme Court cases involve a similar (although not identical) premise about the role of viability.

PROBLEMS OF CONFLICTING RIGHTS

If either the liberal or the conservative view of the moral status of the fetus is adopted, the problem of morally justifying abortion may seem straightforward. If one holds that a fetus does not have human rights, abortions do not seem morally reprehensible and are prudentially justified just as surgical procedures are. In contrast, if one accepts that a fetus at any stage of development is a human life with full moral status, then the equation "abortion is murder" (at the designated stage of development) seems to follow.

However, establishing a position on abortion is not this straightforward. Even on a conservative theory there may be cases of justified abortion. For example, it has been argued by many writers that a pregnant woman may legitimately abort the fetus in "self-defense" if both will die unless the life of the fetus is terminated. In order to claim that abortion is always wrong, one must justify the claim that the fetus's "right to life" always overrides the pregnant woman's rights to life and liberty. Even if a theory held that human fetuses are owed equal consideration or have equal rights, these rights might not always override all other moral rights. Here rights are *conflicting:* The unborn possess some rights (including a right to life) and pregnant women also possess rights (including a right to life). Those who possess the rights have a (prima facie) moral claim to be treated in accordance with their rights. But what happens when the rights conflict?

This problem is also present for many moderate theories of the moral status of the fetus. These theories provide moral grounds against arbitrary termination of fetal life (the fetus has some claim to protection against the actions of others) yet do not grant to the fetus (at least in some stages of development) the same rights to life possessed by persons. Advocates of these theories are faced with the problem of specifying which rights should take precedence in situations of conflict. Does the woman's right to decide what happens to her body justify abortion? Does pregnancy resulting from rape justify abortion? Does self-defense justify abortion? Does psychological damage justify abortion? Does knowledge of a grossly deformed fetus justify abortion? And further, does the fetus have a right to a "minimum quality of life," that is, to protection against wrongful life? Some of these issues about conflicting rights are raised by Thomson, who is then criticized by both Brody and Warren.

LEGAL ISSUES

The 1973 U.S. Supreme Court case of *Roe v. Wade* set a precedent for how abortion legislation may and may not be formulated in the United States. In the opinion of the Court, the majority held that the right to privacy implicit in the Fourteenth Amendment is broad enough to encompass a woman's decision to have an abortion. This right overrides all other concerns until the fetus reaches the point of viability. After that point, the Court finds that states have a legitimate interest in protecting the life of the fetus, even if the protection afforded directly competes with the woman's interest in liberty.

The Court's arguments in *Roe v. Wade* have often come under attack. Even some Supreme Court justices have expressed significant disagreement with this opinion. Justice

Sandra Day O'Connor presented an influential criticism in the case of *City of Akron v. Center for Reproductive Health.* She attacked the framework of *Roe,* maintaining that the Court's reasoning was not sufficient to justify its fundamental analytical framework of "stages" of pregnancy. She also argued that the notion of compelling interests in maternal and fetal health will change as medical technology changes. O'Connor envisioned the following possibility: As the point of viability is pushed back to earlier stages of development by technological advancement, the point at which abortion is legally allowed must also be pushed back; as medical practices improve, the need to protect maternal health will also be reduced. She concluded that the *Roe* framework is unworkable and "on a collision course with itself."

In *Planned Parenthood v. Casey,* which appears as the second reading in the legal section of this chapter, O'Connor and two other justices join forces in reaffirming the essential holding in *Roe* that a woman has a legal right to seek an abortion prior to fetal viability, but they strip *Roe* of what they consider its untenable parts, especially the "trimester" conception of three stages of pregnancy. They argue that an undue burden test should replace the trimester framework in evaluating legal restrictions placed on access to abortion prior to viability. They also maintain that certain restrictions do not constitute undue burdens, including requirements of informed consent, parental notification and consent, and a 24-hour waiting period. However, they argue that a spousal notification provision would place an undue burden on a woman, and they therefore declare it legally invalid.

In the third legal opinion in this section, *Carhart v. Stenberg,* the central issue is a Nebraska statute that banned "partial birth abortion." In this type of abortion procedure, a "substantial portion" of the fetus is extracted from the uterus prior to being killed. A physician, Dr. LeRoy Carhart, challenged the constitutionality of the Nebraska statute. In response, the state of Nebraska argued that the *Roe* and *Casey* decisions apply exclusively to the *unborn,* thereby leaving room for a statute that protects *partially born* human beings (those "more outside of the uterus than inside"). However, the U.S. Court of Appeals, Eighth Circuit, found that there was no relevant difference between this type of abortion and other types and that *Roe* and *Casey* therefore were applicable to this type of abortion. The Court also found that the Nebraska statute imposed an undue burden on a woman's right to choose to have an abortion.

MATERNAL-FETAL RELATIONSHIPS AND RIGHTS

We previously discussed the problem of conflicting rights when the fetus's rights and the pregnant woman's rights conflict. Under the assumption that both have rights, we discussed whose rights should prevail if the woman seeks an abortion. Now we are positioned to extend this discussion beyond abortion to problems of maternal-fetal relationships that arise not from the desire to end pregnancy, but from the condition of pregnancy itself.

In order to protect the fetus, various laws and court decisions have attempted to restrict or otherwise control the behavior of pregnant women and, in some cases, women who have the potential to become pregnant. In some influential cases, U.S. courts have held that women cannot legitimately be excluded from employment while pregnant merely because they are pregnant. More untested in the courts are circumstances in which corporations, municipalities, states, and institutions such as hospitals adopt laws or policies that involve the exclusion, coercion, detention, or incarceration of pregnant women for alcohol and drug abuse (or other forms of abuse) during pregnancy. In a few cases, physicians or courts have imposed or attempted to impose surgical or other medical interventions on women who do not consent to recommended procedures that are intended to protect their fetuses. These interventions include forced surgical procedures such as caesarean sections, forced medication such as penicillin, and incarceration to reduce the threat of harm. The motives are sometimes paternalistic—to protect the women—but in virtually all cases there is a motive to protect the fetus.

It is not disputed that pregnant women have moral obligations to protect their fetuses from harmful abuses, but it is contested whether other persons gain a right to limit the liberty of pregnant women when they fail to live up to this obligation. Areas of controversy have centered on (1) what constitutes a risk of harm to the fetus that is sufficiently grave to justify limitation of a woman's liberty, and (2) what constitutes a legitimate reason for women not to take steps to prevent harm. Regarding the first question, the possibility of harm is sometimes remote, whereas in other circumstances it is virtually certain that harm will occur. Regarding the second question, women sometimes have reasons for their actions that are recognized in other contexts as valid grounds for refusing medical treatment, such as religious beliefs that lead to refusing a surgical intervention requiring blood transfusions.

The larger question at issue is, "What constitutes a sufficient reason for legal coercion of pregnant women?" Many believe that it is fundamentally wrong to transform any *moral* obligation to prevent harm to or promote the health of the fetus into a *legal* obligation that allows institutions and courts to coerce pregnant women. Several reasons have been offered in support of this view. One is the right of all competent persons to refuse medical interventions, and another is that an action is normally made a legal violation only if one person has actually caused harm to another, not because there is merely a risk that harm may be caused.

Other arguments focus on negative consequences that will occur if laws restrict a pregnant woman's liberty. For example, some writers argue that: (1) women who are most likely to harm a fetus by their behavior will stay away from prenatal care (where their abuse must by law be reported), thereby increasing rather than decreasing risk to the fetus; (2) many women will become skeptical and distrustful of their physicians; and (3) society and the fetus will be worse off rather than better off by placing pregnant women in correctional facilities, which typically offer poor health care. In effect, the argument is that the negative consequences of these policies outweigh any positive consequences.

Persons who defend rights of fetuses are unpersuaded by these arguments about negative social consequences of public policies. They regard the fetus no less than the woman as a patient to be helped, and they see fetal abuse as a cause of avoidable deaths and serious birth defects. These violations, they argue, are wrong irrespective of the consequences, and should be declared both legal and moral wrongs. From their perspective, to prosecute a woman who abuses a fetus or to remove a child at birth from the woman's care is justifiable in order to protect the fetus from unnecessary harm.

The opening selection dealing with these issues—the U.S. Supreme Court opinion in *Automobile Workers v. Johnson Controls, Inc.*—illustrates one facet of these problems, and the one that has been most decisively handled in the courts. The problem in this case first came to the public's attention in the 1980s, when it was reported in leading newspapers that fertile women workers were, in increasing numbers, electing to undergo voluntary sterilization rather than give up high-paying jobs involving exposure to chemicals that are potentially harmful to a developing fetus. This disclosure precipitated discussion of a new civil rights issue: Is a company unjustifiably discriminating against a woman in order to protect her unborn child?

At issue in *Johnson Controls* was a corporation's Fetal Protection Program. It held that women must be excluded unless they can prove sterility and that women of childbearing capacity would not be hired for positions that exposed them to unacceptable lead contamination or for positions from which they could transfer to such jobs. The reasons for corporate policies excluding women from hazardous workplaces is straightforward: Of the thousands of toxic substances listed by the National Institute of Occupational Safety and Health (NIOSH), over fifty are animal mutagens (that is, they cause chromosomal damage to either the ova or the sperm cells), and over five hundred are animal teratogens (that is, they can cause deformations in a developing fetus). Corporations sought to protect the fetus against these effects of chemicals in the workplace by banning pregnant and potentially pregnant women from jobs with exposure to known mutagens and teratogens.

However, the U.S. Supreme Court found that employers cannot legally adopt fetal protection policies that exclude women of childbearing age from a hazardous workplace. The Court held that these policies involve illegal sex discrimination. As a result of this decision, most U.S. corporations no longer have policies to protect fetuses that involve the actual exclusion of women, although prior to 1990 policies of exclusion had been the industry standard. Instead, corporations now simply notify employees of potential harm. Still at issue is whether these notification policies adequately protect the fetus.

The second court opinion in this section focuses on forced caesarean sections. In the much discussed case of *In re A. C.*, a 28-year old, terminally ill woman named Angela Carder was forced by a court order to undergo a caesarean section in a failed attempt to save her 26½-week-old fetus. Her premature infant was born but died within three hours. The patient had agreed to a caesarean at 28 weeks, but not at 26½ weeks. The family wanted Carder to be allowed to die in peace, but the hospital requested legal intervention, and a court allowed an emergency caesarean to be performed. The patient had expressly, though perhaps incompetently, refused to consent to the intervention. Testimony indicated that, at the critical time of the patient's decision, the patient was too heavily medicated to be able to respond to questions, and that the medication could not be reduced without threatening to reduce her survival time.

However, the District of Columbia Court of Appeals held that the trial judge was in error in authorizing the caesarean. The appellate court vacated the decision of the lower court, holding that there had been an incorrect weighing of Carder's interests against the state's interests in her fetus and also an error in attempting to determine if Carder was competent. This opinion broke with a judicial trend of ordering women to submit to caesarean sections at the request of physicians. However, the court left unaddressed many questions about a woman's rights in pregnancy when her behavior presents substantial risk to the fetus.

The final two selections in this section consider other risks in maternal-fetal relations. The article by Alexander Capron is a general introduction to the question of what society should do when women expose their fetuses to avoidable risks. He treats, in particular, (1) the dangers of potent fertility drugs (which can produce "multiple births") and (2) addicted mothers (especially crack cocaine users) who produce addicted babies. Capron is principally concerned with the moral culpability of those who place the fetus at risk and the role of physicians in guiding their patients to morally responsible behavior. Capron concludes that physicians need to do much more than they traditionally have done to help women adjust their goals and lifestyles to give their children "a better start in life."

Kenneth DeVille and Loretta Kopelman consider how society should respond to potential mothers who place their fetuses at risk through alcohol or drug abuse. They reject coercive and punitive actions by the state on grounds that they may involve gender bias or racial bias and also because they may worsen the health status of fetuses. They anticipate that coercive and punitive actions directed at pregnant women will be less successful than a policy of voluntary outpatient substance abuse education, counseling, and treatment.

These problems of maternal-fetal relations present challenges to health care centers and clinicians. If women and fetuses are both patients, clinicians must decide who the primary patient is and whose rights have priority. "When does the fetus become a significant patient?" is a question that looks very much like the question, "When does the fetus gain significant status?" Problems of ontological and moral status, then, may underlie moral problems of maternal-fetal relationships no less than moral problems of abortion.

T.L.B.

The Problem of Justifying Abortion

DON MARQUIS

Why Abortion is Immoral

Donald Marquis, professor of philosophy at the University of Kansas, has maintained active interests in the history of ethics as well as problems of abortion, social ethics, and research ethics. Representative publications include: "Leaving Therapy to Chance: An Impasse in the Ethics of Randomized Clinical Trials," *The Hastings Center Report,* "An Ethical Problem Concerning Recent Therapeutic Research on Breast Cancer," *Hypatia,* and "Four Versions of Double Effect," *The Journal of Medicine and Philosophy*.

The view that abortion is, with rare exceptions, seriously immoral has received little support in the recent philosophical literature. No doubt most philosophers affiliated with secular institutions of higher education believe that the anti-abortion position is either a symptom of irrational religious dogma or a conclusion generated by seriously confused philosophical argument. The purpose of this essay is to undermine this general belief. This essay sets out an argument that purports to show, as well as any argument in ethics can show, that abortion is, except possibly in rare cases, seriously immoral, that it is in the same moral category as killing an innocent adult human being.

The argument is based on a major assumption. Many of the most insightful and careful writers on the ethics of abortion . . . believe that whether or not abortion is morally permissible stands or falls on whether or not a fetus is the sort of being whose life it is seriously wrong to end. The argument of this essay will assume, but not argue, that they are correct.

Also, this essay will neglect issues of great importance to a complete ethics of abortion. Some anti-abortionists will allow that certain abortions, such as abortion before implantation or abortion when the life of a woman is threatened by a pregnancy or abortion

From *Journal of Philosophy* 86, no. 4 (April 1989): 470–486. Footnotes renumbered.

after rape, may be morally permissible. This essay will not explore the casuistry of these hard cases. The purpose of this essay is to develop a general argument for the claim that the overwhelming majority of deliberate abortions are seriously immoral. . . .

I.

Passions in the abortion debate run high. There are both plausibilities and difficulties with the standard positions. Accordingly, it is hardly surprising that partisans of either side embrace with fervor the moral generalizations that support the conclusions they preanalytically favor, and reject with disdain the moral generalizations of their opponents as being subject to inescapable difficulties. It is easy to believe that the counterexamples to one's own moral principles are merely temporary difficulties that will dissolve in the wake of further philosophical research, and that the counterexamples to the principles of one's opponents are as straightforward as the contradiction between *A* and *O* propositions in traditional logic. This might suggest to an impartial observer (if there are any) that the abortion issue is unresolvable.

There is a way out of this apparent dialectical quandary. The moral generalizations of both sides are not quite correct. The generalizations hold for the most part, for the usual cases. This suggests that they are all *accidental* generalizations, that the moral claims made by those on both sides of the dispute do not touch on the *essence* of the matter.

This use of the distinction between essence and accident is not meant to invoke obscure metaphysical categories. Rather, it is intended to reflect the rather atheoretical nature of the abortion discussion. If the generalization a partisan in the abortion dispute adopts were derived from the reason why ending the life of a human being is wrong, then there could not be exceptions to that generalization unless some special case obtains in which there are even more powerful countervailing reasons. Such generalizations would not be merely accidental generalizations; they would point to, or be based upon, the essence of the wrongness of killing, what it is that makes killing wrong. All this suggests that a necessary condition of resolving the abortion controversy is a more theoretical account of the wrongness of killing. After all, if we merely believe, but do not understand, why killing adult human beings such as ourselves is wrong, how could we conceivably show that abortion is either immoral or permissible?

II.

In order to develop such an account, we can start from the following unproblematic assumption concerning our own case: It is wrong to kill *us*. Why is it wrong? Some answers can be easily eliminated. It might be said that what makes killing us wrong is that a killing brutalizes the one who kills. But the brutalization consists of being inured to the performance of an act that is hideously immoral; hence, the brutalization does not explain the immorality. It might be said that what makes killing us wrong is the great loss others would experience due to our absence. Although such hubris is understandable, such an explanation does not account for the wrongness of killing hermits, or those whose lives are relatively independent and whose friends find it easy to make new friends.

A more obvious answer is better. What primarily makes killing wrong is neither its effect on the murderer nor its effect on the victim's friends and relatives, but its effect on the victim. The loss of one's life is one of the greatest losses one can suffer. The loss of one's life deprives one of all the experiences, activities, projects, and enjoyments that would otherwise have constituted one's future. Therefore, killing someone is wrong, primarily because the killing inflicts (one of) the greatest possible losses on the victim. To describe this as the loss of life can be misleading, however. The change in my biological state does not by itself make killing me wrong. The effect of the loss of my biological life is the loss to me of all those activities, projects, experiences, and enjoyments which would otherwise have constituted my future personal life. These activities, projects, experiences, and enjoyments are either valuable for their own sakes or are means to something else that is valuable for its own sake. Some parts of my future are not valued by me now, but will come to be valued by me as I grow older and as my values and capacities change. When I am killed, I am deprived both of what I now value which would have been part of my future personal life, but also what I would come to value. Therefore, when I die, I am deprived of all of the value of my future. Inflicting this loss on me is ultimately what makes killing me wrong. This being the case, it would seem that what makes killing *any* adult human being prima facie seriously wrong is the loss of his or her future.

How should this rudimentary theory of the wrongness of killing be evaluated? It cannot be faulted for deriving an "ought" from an "is," for it does not. The analysis assumes that killing me (or you, reader) is prima facie seriously wrong. The point of the analysis is to establish which natural property ultimately explains the wrongness of the killing, given that it is wrong. A natural property will ultimately explain the wrongness of killing, only if (1) the explanation fits with our intuitions about the matter and (2) there is no other natural property that provides the basis for a better explanation of the wrongness of killing. This analysis rests on the intuition that what makes killing a particular human or animal wrong is what it does to that particular human or animal. What makes killing wrong is some natural effect or other of the killing. Some would deny this. For instance, a divine-command theorist in ethics would deny it. Surely this denial is, however, one of those features of divine-command theory which renders it so implausible.

The claim that what makes killing wrong is the loss of the victim's future is directly supported by two considerations. In the first place, this theory explains why we regard killing as one of the worst of crimes. Killing is especially wrong, because it deprives the victim of more than perhaps any other crime. In the second place, people with AIDS or cancer who know they are dying believe, of course, that dying is a very bad thing for them. They believe that the loss of a future to them that they would otherwise have experienced is what makes their premature death a very bad thing for them. A better theory of the wrongness of killing would require a different natural property associated with killing which better fits with the attitudes of the dying. What could it be?

The view that what makes killing wrong is the loss to the victim of the value of the victim's future gains additional support when some of its implications are examined. In the first place, it is incompatible with the view that it is wrong to kill only beings who are biologically human. It is possible that there exists a different species from another planet whose members have a future like ours. Since having a future like that is what makes killing someone wrong, this theory entails that it would be wrong to kill members of such a species. Hence, this theory is opposed to the claim that only life that is biologically human has great moral worth, a claim which many anti-abortionists have seemed to adopt. This opposition, which this theory has in common with personhood theories, seems to be a merit of the theory.

In the second place, the claim that the loss of one's future is the wrong-making feature of one's being killed entails the possibility that the futures of some actual nonhuman mammals on our own planet are sufficiently like ours that it is seriously wrong to kill them also. Whether some animals do have the same right to life as human beings depends on adding to the account of the wrongness of killing some additional account of just what it is about my future or the futures of other adult human beings which makes it wrong to kill us. No such additional account will be offered in this essay. Undoubtedly, the provision of such an account would be a very difficult matter. Undoubtedly, any such account would be quite controversial. Hence, it surely should not reflect badly on this sketch of an elementary theory of the wrongness of killing that it is indeterminate with respect to some very difficult issues regarding animal rights.

In the third place, the claim that the loss of one's future is the wrong-making feature of one's being killed does not entail, as sanctity of human life theories do, that active euthanasia is wrong. Persons who are severely and incurably ill, who face a future of pain and despair, and who wish to die will not have suffered a loss if they are killed. It is, strictly speaking, the value of a human's future which makes killing wrong in this theory. This being so, killing does not necessarily wrong some persons who are sick and dying. Of course, there may be other reasons for a prohibition of active euthanasia, but that is another matter. Sanctity-of-human-life theories seem to hold that active euthanasia is seriously wrong even in an individual case where there seems to be good reason for it independently of public policy considerations. This consequence is most implausible, and it is a plus for the claim that the loss of a future of value is what makes killing wrong that it does not share this consequence.

In the fourth place, the account of the wrongness of killing defended in this essay does straightforwardly entail that it is prima facie seriously wrong to kill children and infants, for we do presume that they have futures of value. Since we do believe that it is wrong to kill defenseless little babies, it is important that a theory of the wrongness of killing easily account for this. Personhood theories of the wrongness of killing, on the other hand, cannot straightforwardly account for the wrongness of killing infants and young children. Hence, such theories must add special ad hoc accounts of the wrongness of killing the young. The plausibility of such ad hoc theories seems to be a function of how desperately one wants such theories to work. The claim that the primary wrong-making feature of a killing is the loss to the victim of the value of its future accounts for the wrongness of killing young children and infants directly; it makes the wrongness of such acts as obvious as we actually think it is. This is a further merit of this theory. Accordingly, it seems that this value of a future-like-ours theory of the wrongness of killing shares strengths of both sanctity-of-life and personhood accounts while avoiding weaknesses of both. In addition, it meshes with a central intuition concerning what makes killing wrong.

The claim that the primary wrong-making feature of a killing is the loss to the victim of the value of its future has obvious consequences for the ethics of abortion. The future of a standard fetus includes a set of experiences, projects, activities, and such which are identical with the futures of adult human beings and are identical with the futures of young children. Since the reason that is sufficient to explain why it is wrong to kill human beings after the time of birth is a reason that also applies to fetuses, it follows that abortion is prima facie seriously morally wrong.

This argument does not rely on the invalid inference that, since it is wrong to kill persons, it is wrong to kill potential persons also. The category that is morally central to this analysis is the category of having a valuable future like ours; it is not the category of personhood. The argument to the conclusion that abortion is prima facie seriously morally wrong proceeded independently of the notion of person or potential person or any equivalent. Someone may wish to start with this analysis in terms of the value of a human future, conclude that abortion is, except perhaps in rare circumstances, seriously morally wrong, infer that fetuses have the right to life, and then call fetuses "persons" as a result of their having the right to life. Clearly, in this case, the category of person is being used to state the *conclusion* of the analysis rather than to generate the *argument* of the analysis.

The structure of this anti-abortion argument can be both illuminated and defended by comparing it to what appears to be the best argument for the wrongness of the wanton infliction of pain on animals. This latter argument is based on the assumption that it is prima facie wrong to inflict pain on me (or you, reader). What is the natural property associated with the infliction of pain which makes such infliction wrong? The obvious answer seems to be that the infliction of pain causes suffering and that suffering is a misfortune. The suffering caused by the infliction of pain is what makes the wanton infliction of pain on me wrong. The wanton infliction of pain on other adult humans causes suffering. The wanton infliction of pain on animals causes suffering. Since causing suffering is what makes the wanton infliction of pain wrong and since the wanton infliction of pain on animals causes suffering, it follows that the wanton infliction of pain on animals is wrong.

This argument for the wrongness of the wanton infliction of pain on animals shares a number of structural features with the argument for the serious prima facie wrongness of abortion. Both arguments start with an obvious assumption concerning what it is wrong to do to me (or you, reader). Both then look for the characteristic or the consequence of the wrong action which makes the action wrong. Both recognize that the wrong-making feature of these immoral actions is a property of actions sometimes directed at individuals other than postnatal human beings. If the structure of the argument for the wrongness of the wanton infliction of pain on animals is sound, then the structure of the argument for the prima facie serious wrongness of abortion is also sound, for the structure of the two arguments is the same. The structure common to both is the key to the explanation of how the wrongness of abortion can be demonstrated without recourse to the category of person. In neither argument is that category crucial.

This defense of an argument for the wrongness of abortion in terms of a structurally similar argument for the wrongness of the wanton infliction of pain on animals succeeds only if the account regarding animals is the correct account. Is it? In the first place, it seems plausible. In the second place, its major competition is Kant's account. Kant believed that we do not have direct duties to animals at all, because they are not persons. Hence, Kant had to explain and justify the wrongness of inflicting pain on animals on the grounds that "he who is hard in his dealings with animals becomes hard also in his dealing with men."[1] The problem with Kant's account is that there seems to be no reason for accepting this latter claim unless Kant's account is rejected. If the alternative to Kant's account is accepted, then it is easy to understand why someone who is indifferent to inflicting pain on animals is also indifferent to inflicting pain on humans, for one is indifferent to what makes inflicting pain wrong in both cases. But, if Kant's account is accepted, there is no intelligible reason why one who is hard in his dealings with animals (or crabgrass or stones) should also be hard in his dealings with men. After all, men are persons: animals are no more persons than crabgrass or stones. Persons are Kant's crucial moral category. Why, in short, should a Kantian accept the basic claim in Kant's argument?

Hence, Kant's argument for the wrongness of inflicting pain on animals rests on a claim that, in a world of Kantian moral agents, is demonstrably false. Therefore, the alternative analysis, being more plausible anyway, should be accepted. Since this alternative analysis has the same structure of the anti-abortion argument being defended here, we have further support for the argument for the immorality of abortion being defended in this essay.

Of course, this value of a future-like-ours argument, if sound, shows only that abortion is prima facie wrong, not that it is wrong in any and all circumstances. Since the loss of the future to a standard fetus, if killed, is, however, at least as great a loss as the loss of the future to a standard adult human being who is killed, abortion, like ordinary killing, could be justified only by the most compelling reasons. The loss of one's life is almost the greatest misfortune that can happen to one. Presumably abortion could be justified in some circumstances, only if the loss consequent on failing to abort would be at least as great. Accordingly, morally permissible abortions will be rare indeed unless, perhaps, they occur so early in pregnancy that a fetus is not yet definitely an individual. Hence, this argument should be taken as showing that abortion is presumptively very seriously wrong, where the presumption is very strong—as strong as the presumption that killing another adult human being is wrong.

III.

How complete an account of the wrongness of killing does the value of a future-like-ours account have to be in order that the wrongness of abortion is a consequence? This account does not have to be an account of the necessary conditions for the wrongness of killing. Some persons in nursing homes may lack valuable human futures, yet it may be wrong to kill them for other reasons. Furthermore, this account does not obviously have to be the sole reason killing is wrong where the victim did have a valuable future. This analysis claims only that, for any killing where the victim did have a valuable future like ours, having that future by itself is sufficient to create the strong presumption that the killing is seriously wrong.

One way to overturn the value of a future-like-ours argument would be to find some account of the wrongness of killing which is at least as intelligible and which has different implications for the ethics of abortion. Two rival accounts possess at least some degree of plausibility. One account is based on the obvious fact that people value the experience of living and wish for that valuable experience to continue. Therefore, it might be said, what makes killing wrong is the discontinuation of that experience for the victim. Let us call this the *discontinuation account*. Another rival account is based upon the obvious fact that people strongly desire to continue to live. This suggests that what makes killing us so wrong is that it interferes with the fulfillment of a strong and fundamental desire, the fulfillment of which is necessary for the fulfillment of any other desires we might have. Let us call this the *desire account*.[2]

Consider first the desire account as a rival account of the ethics of killing which would provide the basis for rejecting the anti-abortion position. Such an account will have to be stronger than the value of a future-like-ours account of the wrongness of abortion if it is to do the job expected of it. To entail the wrongness of abortion, the value of a future-like-ours account has only to provide a sufficient, but not a necessary, condition for the wrongness of killing. The desire account, on the other hand, must provide us also with a necessary condition for the wrongness of killing in order to generate a pro-choice conclusion on abortion. The reason for this is that presumably the argument from the desire account moves from the claim that what makes killing wrong is interference with a very strong desire to the claim that abortion is not wrong because the fetus lacks a strong desire to live. Obviously, this inference fails if someone's having the desire to live is not a necessary condition of its being wrong to kill that individual.

One problem with the desire account is that we do regard it as seriously wrong to kill persons who have little desire to live or who have no desire to live or, indeed, have a desire not to live. We believe it is seriously wrong to kill the unconscious, the sleeping, those who are tired of life, and those who are suicidal. The value-of-a-human-future account renders standard morality intelligible in these cases; these cases appear to be incompatible with the desire account.

The desire account is subject to a deeper difficulty. We desire life, because we value the goods of this life. The goodness of life is not secondary to our desire for it. If this were not so, the pain of one's own premature death could be done away with merely by an appropriate alteration in the configuration of one's desires. This is absurd. Hence, it would seem that it is the loss of the goods of one's future, not the interference with the fulfillment of a strong desire to live, which accounts ultimately for the wrongness of killing.

It is worth noting that, if the desire account is modified so that it does not provide a necessary, but only a sufficient, condition for the wrongness of killing, the desire account is compatible with the value of a future-like-ours account. The combined accounts will yield an anti-abortion ethic. This suggests that one can retain what is intuitively plausible about the desire account without a challenge to the basic argument of this paper.

It is also worth noting that, if future desires have moral force in a modified desire account of the wrongness of killing, one can find support for an anti-abortion ethic even in the absence of a value of a future-like-ours account. If one decides that a morally relevant property, the possession of which is sufficient to make it wrong to kill some individual, is the desire at some future time to live—one might decide to justify one's refusal to kill suicidal teenagers on these grounds, for example—then, since typical fetuses will have the desire in the future to live, it is wrong to kill typical fetuses. Accordingly, it does not seem that a desire account of the wrongness of killing can provide a justification of a pro-choice ethic of abortion which is nearly as adequate as the value of a human-future justification of an anti-abortion ethic.

The discontinuation account looks more promising as an account of the wrongness of killing. It seems just as intelligible as the value of a future-like-ours account, but it does not justify an anti-abortion position. Obviously, if it is the continuation of one's activities, experiences, and projects, the loss of which makes killing wrong, then it is not wrong to kill fetuses for that reason, for fetuses do not have experiences, activities, and projects to be continued or discontinued. Accordingly, the discontinuation account does not have the anti-abortion consequences that the value of a future-like-ours account has. Yet it seems as intelligible as the value of a future-like-ours account, for when we think of what would be wrong with our being killed, it does seem as if it is the discontinuation of what makes our lives worthwhile which makes killing us wrong.

Is the discontinuation account just as good an account as the value of a future-like-ours account? The discontinuation account will not be adequate at all, if it does not refer to the *value* of the experience that may be discontinued. One does not want the discontinuation account to make it wrong to kill a patient who begs for death and who is in severe pain that cannot be relieved short of killing. (I leave open the question of whether it is wrong for other reasons.) Accordingly, the discontinuation account must be more than a bare discontinuation account. It must make some reference to the positive value of the patient's experiences. But, by the same token, the value of a future-like-ours account cannot be a bare future account either. Just having a future surely does not itself rule out killing the above patient. This account must make some reference to the value of the patient's future experiences and projects also. Hence, both accounts involve the value of experiences, projects, and activities. So far we still have symmetry between the accounts.

The symmetry fades, however, when we focus on the time period of the value of the experiences, etc., which has moral consequences. Although both accounts leave open the possibility that the patient in our example may be killed, this possibility is left open only in virtue of the utterly bleak future for the patient. It makes no difference whether the patient's immediate past contains intolerable pain, or consists in being in a coma (which we can imagine is a situation of indifference), or consists in a life of value. If the patient's future is a future of value, we want our account to make it wrong to kill the patient. If the patient's future is intolerable, whatever his or her immediate past, we want our account to allow killing the patient. Obviously, then, it is the value of that patient's future which is doing the work in rendering the morality of killing the patient intelligible.

This being the case, it seems clear that whether one has immediate past experiences or not does no work in the explanation of what makes killing wrong. The addition the discontinuation account makes to the value of a human future account is otiose. Its addition to the value-of-a-future account plays no role at all in rendering intelligible the wrongness of killing. Therefore, it can be discarded with the discontinuation account of which it is a part.

IV.

The analysis of the previous section suggests that alternative general accounts of the wrongness of killing are either inadequate or unsuccessful in getting around the anti-abortion consequences of the value of a future-like-ours argument. A different strategy for avoiding these anti-abortion consequences involves limiting the scope of the value of a future argument. More precisely, the strategy involves arguing that fetuses lack a property that is essential for the value-of-a-future argument (or for any anti-abortion argument) to apply to them.

One move of this sort is based upon the claim that a necessary condition of one's future being valuable is that one values it. Value implies a valuer. Given this, one might argue that, since fetuses cannot value their futures, their futures are not valuable to them. Hence, it does not seriously wrong them deliberately to end their lives.

This move fails, however, because of some ambiguities. Let us assume that something cannot be of value unless it is valued by someone. This does not entail that my life is of no value unless it is valued by me. I may think, in a period of despair, that my future is of no worth whatsoever, but I may be wrong because others rightly see value—even great value—in it. Furthermore, my future can be valuable to me even if I do not value it. This is the case when a young person attempts suicide, but is rescued and goes on to significant human achievements. Such young people's futures are ultimately valuable to them, even though such futures do not seem to be valuable to them at the moment of attempted suicide. A fetus's future can be valuable to it in the same way. Accordingly, this attempt to limit the anti-abortion argument fails.

Another similar attempt to reject the anti-abortion position is based on Tooley's claim that an entity cannot possess the right to life unless it has the capacity to desire its continued existence. It follows that, since fetuses lack the conceptual capacity to desire to continue to live, they lack the right to life. Accordingly, Tooley concludes that abortion cannot be seriously prima facie wrong (*op. cit.,* pp. 46/7). . . .

One might attempt to defend Tooley's basic claim on the grounds that, because a fetus cannot apprehend continued life as a benefit, its continued life cannot be a benefit or cannot be something it has a right to or cannot be something that is in its interest. This might be defended in terms of the general proposition that, if an individual is literally incapable of caring about or taking an interest in some *X,* then one does not have a right to *X* or *X* is not a benefit or *X* is not something that is in one's interest.[3]

Each member of this family of claims seems to be open to objections. . . . As Tooley himself has pointed out, persons who have been indoctrinated, or drugged, or rendered temporarily unconscious may be literally incapable or caring about or taking an interest in something that is in their interest or is something to which they have a right, or is something that benefits them. Hence, the Tooley claim that would restrict the scope of the value of a future-like-ours argument is undermined by counterexamples.[4]

Finally, Paul Bassen[5] has argued that, even though the prospects of an embryo might seem to be a basis for the wrongness of abortion, an embryo cannot be a victim and therefore cannot be wronged. An embryo cannot be a victim, he says, because it lacks sentience. His central argument for this seems to be that, even though plants and the permanently unconscious are alive, they clearly cannot be victims. What is the explanation of this? Bassen claims that the explanation is that their lives consist of mere metabolism and mere metabolism is not enough to ground victimizability. Mentation is required.

The problem with this attempt to establish the absence of victimizability is that both plants and the permanently unconscious clearly lack what Bassen calls "prospects" or what I have called "a future life like ours." Hence, it is surely open to one to argue that the real reason we believe plants and the permanently unconscious cannot be victims is that killing them cannot deprive them of a future life like ours; the real reason is not their absence of present mentation. . . .

V.

In this essay, it has been argued that the correct ethic of the wrongness of killing can be extended to fetal life and used to show that there is a strong presumption that any abortion is morally impermissible. If the ethic of killing adopted here entails, however, that contraception is also seriously immoral, then there would appear to be a difficulty with the analysis of this essay.

But this analysis does not entail that contraception is wrong. Of course, contraception prevents the actualization of a possible future of value. Hence, it follows from the claim that futures of value should be maximized that contraception is prima facie immoral.

This obligation to maximize does not exist, however; furthermore, nothing in the ethics of killing in this paper entails that it does. The ethics of killing in this essay would entail that contraception is wrong only if something were denied a human future of value by contraception. Nothing at all is denied such a future by contraception, however.

Candidates for a subject of harm by contraception fall into four categories: (1) some sperm or other, (2) some ovum or other, (3) a sperm and an ovum separately, and (4) a sperm and an ovum together. Assigning the harm to some sperm is utterly arbitrary, for no reason can be given for making a sperm the subject of harm rather than an ovum. Assigning the harm to some ovum is utterly arbitrary, for no reason can be given for making an ovum the subject of harm rather than a sperm. One might attempt to avoid these problems by insisting that contraception deprives both the sperm and the ovum separately of a valuable future like ours. On this alternative, too many futures are lost. Contraception was supposed to be wrong, because it deprived us of one future of value, not two. One might attempt to avoid this problem by holding that contraception deprives the combination of sperm and ovum of a valuable future like ours. But here the definite article misleads. At the time of contraception, there are hundreds of millions of sperm, one (released) ovum and millions of possible combinations of all of these. There is no actual combination at all. Is the subject of the loss to be a merely possible combination? Which one? This alternative does not yield an actual subject of harm either. Accordingly, the immorality of contraception is not entailed by the loss of a future-like-ours argument simply because there is no nonarbitrarily identifiable subject of the loss in the case of contraception.

VI.

The purpose of this essay has been to set out an argument for the serious presumptive wrongness of abortion subject to the assumption that the moral permissibility of abortion stands or falls on the moral status of the fetus. Since a fetus possesses a property, the possession of which in adult human beings is sufficient to make killing an adult human being wrong, abortion is wrong. This way of dealing with the problem of abortion seems superior to other approaches to the ethics of abortion, because it rests on an ethics of killing which is close to self-evident, because the crucial morally relevant property clearly applies to fetuses, and because the argument avoids the usual equivocations on "human life," "human being," or "person." The argument rests neither on religious claims nor on Papal dogma. It is not subject to the objection of "speciesism." Its soundness is compatible with the moral permissibility of euthanasia and contraception. It deals with our intuitions concerning young children.

Finally, this analysis can be viewed as resolving a standard problem—indeed, *the* standard problem—concerning the ethics of abortion. Clearly, it is wrong to kill adult human beings. Clearly, it is not wrong to end the life of some arbitrarily chosen single human cell. Fetuses seem to be like arbitrarily chosen human cells in some respects and like adult humans in other respects. The problem of the ethics of abortion is the problem of determining the fetal property that settles this moral controversy. The thesis of this essay is that the problem of the ethics of abortion, so understood, is solvable.

NOTES

1. "Duties to Animals and Spirits," in *Lectures on Ethics,* Louis Infeld, trans. (New York: Harper, 1963), p. 239.

2. Presumably a preference utilitarian would press such an objection. Tooley once suggested that his account has such a theoretical underpinning. See his "Abortion and Infanticide," *Philosophy and Public Affairs* 2 (1972), pp. 44–5.

3. Donald VanDeVeer seems to think this self-evident. See his "Whither Baby Doe?" in *Matters of Life and Death,* p. 233.

4. See Tooley again in "Abortion and Infanticide," pp. 47–49.

5. "Present Sakes and Future Prospects: The Status of Early Abortion," *Philosophy and Public Affairs,* XI, 4 (1982):322–326.

JUDITH JARVIS THOMSON

A Defense of Abortion[1]

Judith Jarvis Thomson, professor of philosophy at the Massachusetts Institute of Technology, works in both ethics and metaphysics. Her book *Realm of Rights* is a comprehensive theory of the subject. Representative publications include "Self-Defense," *Philosophy and Public Affairs,* "On Some Ways in which a Thing Can Be Good," *Social Philosophy and Policy,* and "Physician-Assisted Suicide: Two Moral Arguments," *Ethics*.

Most opposition to abortion relies on the premise that the fetus is a human being, a person, from the moment of conception. The premise is argued for, but, as I think, not well. Take, for example, the most common argument. We are asked to notice that the development of a human being from conception through birth into childhood is continuous; then it is said that to draw a line, to choose a point in this development and say "before this point the thing is not a person, after this point it is a person" is to make an arbitrary choice, a choice for which in the nature of things no good reason can be given. It is concluded that the fetus is, or anyway that we had better say it is, a person from the moment of conception. But this conclusion does not follow. Similar things might be said about the development of an acorn into an oak tree, and it does not follow that acorns are oak trees, or that we had better say they are. Arguments of this form are sometimes called "slippery slope arguments"—the phrase is perhaps self-explanatory—and it is dismaying that opponents of abortion rely on them so heavily and uncritically.

I am inclined to agree, however, that the prospects for "drawing a line" in the development of the fetus look dim. I am inclined to think also that we shall probably have to agree that the fetus has already become a human person well before birth. Indeed, it comes as a surprise when one first learns how early in its life it begins to acquire human characteristics. By the tenth week, for example, it already has a face, arms and legs, fingers and toes; it has internal organs, and brain activity is detectable.[2] On the other hand, I think that the premise is false, that the fetus is not a person from the moment of conception. A newly fertilized ovum, a newly implanted clump of cells, is no more a person than an acorn is an oak tree. But I shall not discuss any of this. For it seems to me to be of great interest to ask what happens if, for the sake of argument, we allow the premise. How, precisely, are we supposed to get from there to the conclusion that abortion is morally impermissible? Opponents of abortion commonly spend most of their time establishing that the fetus is a person, and hardly any time explaining the step from there to the impermissibility of abortion. Perhaps they think the step too simple and obvious to require much comment. Or perhaps instead they are simply being economical in argument. Many of those who defend abortion rely on the premise that the fetus is not a person, but only a bit of tissue that will become a person at birth; and why pay out more arguments than you have to? Whatever the explanation, I suggest that the step they take is neither easy nor obvious, that it calls for closer examination than it is commonly given, and that when we do give it this closer examination we shall feel inclined to reject it.

I propose, then, that we grant that the fetus is a person from the moment of conception. How does the argument go from here? Something like this, I take it. Every person has a right to life. So the fetus has a

Reprinted with permission of the publisher from *Philosophy and Public Affairs* 1, no. 1 (1971): 47–66. Copyright © 1971 by Princeton University Press.

right to life. No doubt the mother has a right to decide what shall happen in and to her body; everyone would grant that. But surely a person's right to life is stronger and more stringent than the mother's right to decide what happens in and to her body, and so outweighs it. So the fetus may not be killed; an abortion may not be performed.

It sounds plausible. But now let me ask you to imagine this. You wake up in the morning and find yourself back to back in bed with an unconscious violinist. A famous unconscious violinist. He has been found to have a fatal kidney ailment, and the Society of Music Lovers has canvassed all the available medical records and found that you alone have the right blood type to help. They have therefore kidnapped you, and last night the violinist's circulatory system was plugged into yours, so that your kidneys can be used to extract poisons from his blood as well as your own. The director of the hospital now tells you, "Look, we're sorry the Society of Music Lovers did this to you—we would never have permitted it if we had known. But still, they did it, and the violinist now is plugged into you. To unplug you would be to kill him. But never mind, it's only for nine months. By then he will have recovered from his ailment, and can safely be unplugged from you." Is it morally incumbent on you to accede to this situation? No doubt it would be very nice of you if you did, a great kindness. But do you *have* to accede to it? What if it were not nine months, but nine years? Or longer still? What if the director of the hospital says, "Tough luck, I agree, but you've now got to stay in bed, with the violinist plugged into you, for the rest of your life. Because remember this. All persons have a right to life, and violinists are persons. Granted you have a right to decide what happens in and to your body, but a person's right to life outweighs your right to decide what happens in and to your body. So you cannot ever be unplugged from him." I imagine you would regard this as outrageous, which suggests that something really is wrong with that plausible-sounding argument I mentioned a moment ago.

In this case, of course, you were kidnapped; you didn't volunteer for the operation that plugged the violinist into your kidneys. Can those who oppose abortion on the ground I mentioned make an exception for a pregnancy due to rape? Certainly. They can say that persons have a right to life only if they didn't come into existence because of rape; or they can say that all persons have a right to life, but that some have less of a right to life than others, in particular, that those who came into existence because of rape have less. But these statements have a rather unpleasant sound. Surely the question of whether you have a right to life at all, or how much of it you have, shouldn't turn on the question of whether or not you are the product of a rape. And in fact the people who oppose abortion on the ground I mentioned do not make this distinction, and hence do not make an exception in case of rape.

Nor do they make an exception for a case in which the mother has to spend the nine months of her pregnancy in bed. They would agree that would be a great pity, and hard on the mother; but all the same, all persons have a right to life, the fetus is a person, and so on. I suspect, in fact, that they would not make an exception for a case in which, miraculously enough, the pregnancy went on for nine years, or even the rest of the mother's life.

Some won't even make an exception for a case in which continuation of the pregnancy is likely to shorten the mother's life; they regard abortion as impermissible even to save the mother's life. Such cases are nowadays very rare, and many opponents of abortion do not accept this extreme view. All the same, it is a good place to begin: a number of points of interest come out in respect to it.

1. Let us call the view that abortion is impermissible even to save the mother's life "the extreme view." I want to suggest first that it does not issue from the argument I mentioned earlier without the addition of some fairly powerful premises. Suppose a woman has become pregnant, and now learns that she has a cardiac condition such that she will die if she carries the baby to term. What may be done for her? The fetus, being a person, has a right to life, but as the mother is a person too, so has she a right to life. Presumably they have an equal right to life. How is it supposed to come out that an abortion may not be performed? If mother and child have an equal right to life, shouldn't we perhaps flip a coin? Or should we add to the mother's right to life her right to decide what happens in and to her body, which everybody seems to be ready to grant—the sum of her rights now outweighing the fetus's right to life?

The most familiar argument here is the following. We are told that performing the abortion would be directly killing[3] the child, whereas doing nothing would not be killing the mother, but only letting her die. Moreover, in killing the child, one would be killing an innocent person, for the child has committed no crime, and is not aiming at his mother's death. And then there are a variety of ways in which this might be continued. (a) But as directly killing an innocent person is always and absolutely impermissible, an abortion may not be performed. Or, (b) as directly killing an innocent person is murder, and murder is always and absolutely impermissible, an abortion may not be performed.[4] Or, (c) as one's duty to refrain from directly killing an innocent person is more stringent than one's duty to keep a person from dying, an abortion may not be performed. Or, (d) if one's only options are directly killing an innocent person or letting a person die, one must prefer letting the person die, and thus an abortion may not be performed.[5]

Some people seem to have thought that these are not further premises which must be added if the conclusion is to be reached, but that they follow from the very fact that an innocent person has a right to life.[6] But this seems to me to be a mistake, and perhaps the simplest way to show this is to bring out that while we must certainly grant that innocent persons have a right to life, the theses in (a) through (d) are all false. Take (b), for example. If directly killing an innocent person is murder, and thus is impermissible, then the mother's directly killing the innocent person inside her is murder, and thus is impermissible. But it cannot seriously be thought to be murder if the mother performs an abortion on herself to save her life. It cannot seriously be said that she *must* refrain, that she *must* sit passively by and wait for her death. Let us look again at the case of you and the violinist. There you are, in bed with the violinist, and the director of the hospital says to you, "It's all most distressing, and I deeply sympathize, but you see this is putting an additional strain on your kidneys, and you'll be dead within the month. But you *have* to stay where you are all the same. Because unplugging you would be directly killing an innocent violinist, and that's murder, and that's impermissible." If anything in the world is true, it is that you do not commit murder, you do not do what is impermissible, if you reach around to your back and unplug yourself from that violinist to save your life.

The main focus of attention in writings on abortion has been on what a third party may or may not do in answer to a request from a woman for an abortion. This is in a way understandable. Things being as they are, there isn't much a woman can safely do to abort herself. So the question asked is what a third party may do, and what the mother may do, if it is mentioned at all, is deduced, almost as an afterthought, from what it is concluded that third parties may do. But it seems to me that to treat the matter in this way is to refuse to grant to the mother that very status of person which is so firmly insisted on for the fetus. For we cannot simply read off what a person may do from what a third party may do. Suppose you find yourself trapped in a tiny house with a growing child. I mean a very tiny house, and a rapidly growing child—you are already up against the wall of the house and in a few minutes you'll be crushed to death. The child on the other hand won't be crushed to death; if nothing is done to stop him from growing he'll be hurt, but in the end he'll simply burst open the house and walk out a free man. Now I could well understand it if a bystander were to say, "There's nothing we can do for you. We cannot choose between your life and his, we cannot be the ones to decide who is to live, we cannot intervene." But it cannot be concluded that you too can do nothing, that you cannot attack it to save your life. However innocent the child may be, you do not have to wait passively while it crushes you to death. Perhaps a pregnant woman is vaguely felt to have the status of house, to which we don't allow the right of self-defense. But if the woman houses the child, it should be remembered that she is a person who houses it.

I should perhaps stop to say explicitly that I am not claiming that people have a right to do anything whatever to save their lives. I think, rather, that there are drastic limits to the right of self-defense. If someone threatens you with death unless you torture someone else to death, I think you have not the right, even to save your life, to do so. But the case under consideration here is very different. In our case there are only two people involved, one whose life is threatened, and one who threatens it. Both are innocent: the one who is threatened is not threatened because of any fault, the one who threatens does not threaten because of any fault. For this reason we may feel that we bystanders cannot intervene. But the person threatened can.

In sum, a woman surely can defend her life against the threat to it posed by the unborn child, even if doing so involves its death. And this shows not merely that the theses in (a) through (d) are false; it shows also that the extreme view of abortion is false, and so we need not canvass any other possible ways of arriving at it from the argument I mentioned at the outset.

2. The extreme view could of course be weakened to say that while abortion is permissible to save the

mother's life, it may not be performed by a third party, but only by the mother herself. But this cannot be right either. For what we have to keep in mind is that the mother and the unborn child are not like two tenants in a small house which has, by an unfortunate mistake, been rented to both: the mother *owns* the house. The fact that she does adds to the offensiveness of deducing that the mother can do nothing from the supposition that third parties can do nothing. But it does more than this: it casts a bright light on the supposition that third parties can do nothing. Certainly it lets us see that a third party who says "I cannot choose between you" is fooling himself if he thinks this is impartiality. If Jones has found and fastened on a certain coat, which he needs to keep him from freezing, but which Smith also needs to keep him from freezing, then it is not impartiality that says "I cannot choose between you" when Smith owns the coat. Women have said again and again "This body is *my* body!" and they have reason to feel angry, reason to feel that it has been like shouting into the wind. Smith, after all, is hardly likely to bless us if we say to him, "Of course it's your coat, anybody would grant that it is. But no one may choose between you and Jones who is to have it."

We should really ask what it is that says "no one may choose" in the face of the fact that the body that houses the child is the mother's body. It may be simply a failure to appreciate this fact. But it may be something more interesting, namely, the sense that one has a right to refuse to lay hands on people, even where it would be just and fair to do so, even where justice seems to require that somebody do so. Thus justice might call for somebody to get Smith's coat back from Jones, and yet you have a right to refuse to be the one to lay hands on Jones, a right to refuse to do physical violence to him. This, I think, must be granted. But then what should be said is not "no one may choose," but only "*I* cannot choose," and indeed not even this, but "*I* will not *act,*" leaving it open that somebody else can or should, and in particular that anyone in a position of authority, with the job of securing people's rights, both can and should. So this is no difficulty. I have not been arguing that any given third party must accede to the mother's request that he perform an abortion to save her life, but only that he may.

I suppose that in some views of human life the mother's body is only on loan to her, the loan not being one which gives her any prior claim to it. One who held this view might well think it impartiality to say "I cannot choose." But I shall simply ignore this possibility. My own view is that if a human being has any just, prior claim to anything at all, he has a just, prior claim to his own body. And perhaps this needn't be argued for here anyway, since, as I mentioned, the arguments against abortion we are looking at do grant that the woman has a right to decide what happens in and to her body.

But although they do grant it, I have tried to show that they do not take seriously what is done in granting it. I suggest the same thing will reappear even more clearly when we turn away from cases in which the mother's life is at stake, and attend, as I propose we now do, to the vastly more common cases in which a woman wants an abortion for some less weighty reason than preserving her own life.

3. Where the mother's life is not at stake, the argument I mentioned at the outset seems to have a much stronger pull. "Everyone has a right to life, so the unborn person has a right to life." And isn't the child's right to life weightier than anything other than the mother's own right to life, which she might put forward as ground for an abortion?

This argument treats the right to life as if it were unproblematic. It is not, and this seems to me to be precisely the source of the mistake.

For we should now, at long last, ask what it comes to, to have a right to life. In some views having a right to life includes having a right to be given at least the bare minimum one needs for continued life. But suppose that what in fact *is* the bare minimum a man needs for continued life is something he has no right at all to be given. If I am sick unto death, and the only thing that will save my life is the touch of Henry Fonda's cool hand on my fevered brow, then all the same, I have no right to be given the touch of Henry Fonda's cool hand on my fevered brow. It would be frightfully nice of him to fly in from the West Coast to provide it. It would be less nice, though no doubt well meant, if my friends flew out to the West Coast and carried Henry Fonda back with them. But I have no right at all against anybody that he should do this for me. Or again, to return to the story I told earlier, the fact that for continued life that violinist needs the continued use of your kidneys does not establish that he has a right to be given the continued use of your kidneys. He certainly has no right against you that *you* should give him continued use of your kidneys. For nobody has any right to use your kidneys unless you give him such a right; and nobody has the right against you that you shall give him this right—if you do allow him to go on using your kidneys, this is a kindness on your part, and not something he can claim from you as his due. Nor has he any right against anybody else that they should give him continued use of your kidneys. Certainly he had no right against the Society of Music Lovers that *they* should plug him into you in the first place. And if you now start to unplug yourself, having learned that you will otherwise have to spend nine years in bed with him, there is nobody in the world who must try to prevent you, in order to see to it that he is given something he has a right to be given.

Some people are rather stricter about the right to life. In their view, it does not include the right to be given anything, but amounts to, and only to, the right not to be killed by anybody. But here a related difficulty arises. If everybody is to refrain from killing that violinist, then everybody must refrain from doing a great many different sorts of things. Everybody must refrain from slitting his throat, everybody must refrain from shooting him—and everybody must refrain from unplugging you from him. But does he have a right against everybody that they shall refrain from unplugging you from him? To refrain from doing this is to allow him to continue to use your kidneys. It could be argued that he has a right against us that we should allow him to continue to use your kidneys. That is, while he had no right against us that we should give him the use of your kidneys, it might be argued that he anyway has a right against us that we shall not now intervene and deprive him of the use of your kidneys. I shall come back to third-party interventions later. But certainly the violinist has no right against you that *you* shall allow him to continue to use your kidneys. As I said, if you do allow him to use them, it is a kindness on your part, and not something you owe him.

The difficulty I point to here is not peculiar to the right to life. It reappears in connection with all the other natural rights; and it is something which an adequate account of rights must deal with. For present purposes it is enough just to draw attention to it. But I would stress that I am not arguing that people do not have a right to life—quite to the contrary, it seems to me that the primary control we must place on the acceptability of an account of rights is that it should turn out in that account to be a truth that all persons have a right to life. I am arguing only that having a right to life does not guarantee having either a right to be given the use of or a right to be allowed continued use of another person's body—even if one needs it for life itself. So the right to life will not serve the opponents of abortion in the very simple and clear way in which they seem to have thought it would.

4. There is another way to bring out the difficulty. In the most ordinary sort of case, to deprive someone of what he has a right to is to treat him unjustly. Suppose a boy and his small brother are jointly given a box of chocolates for Christmas. If the older boy takes the box and refuses to give his brother any of the chocolates, he is unjust to him, for the brother has been given a right to half of them. But suppose that, having learned that otherwise it means nine years in bed with that violinist, you unplug yourself from him. You surely are not being unjust to him for you gave him no right to use your kidneys, and no one else can have given him any such right. But we have to notice that in unplugging yourself, you are killing him; and violinists, like everybody else, have a right to life, and thus in the view we were considering just now, the right not to be killed. So here you do what he supposedly has a right you shall not do, but you do not act unjustly to him in doing it.

The emendation which may be made at this point is this: the right to life consists not in the right not to be killed, but rather in the right not to be killed unjustly. This runs a risk of circularity, but never mind: it would enable us to square the fact that the violinist has a right to life with the fact that you do not act unjustly toward him in unplugging yourself, thereby killing him. For if you do not kill him unjustly, you do not violate his right to life, and so it is no wonder you do him no injustice.

But if this emendation is accepted, the gap in the argument against abortion stares us plainly in the face: It is by no means enough to show that the fetus is a person, and to remind us that all persons have a right to life—we need to be shown also that killing the fetus violates its right to life, i.e., that abortion is unjust killing. And is it?

I suppose we may take it as a datum that in a case of pregnancy due to rape the mother has not given the unborn person a right to the use of her body for food and shelter. Indeed, in what pregnancy could it be supposed that the mother has given the unborn person such a right? It is not as if there were unborn persons drifting about the world, to whom a woman who wants a child says "I invite you in."

But it might be argued that there are other ways one can have acquired a right to the use of another person's body than by having been invited to use it by that person. Suppose a woman voluntarily indulges in intercourse, knowing of the chance it will issue in pregnancy, and then she does become pregnant; is she not in part responsible for the presence, in fact the very existence, of the unborn person inside her? No doubt she did not invite it in. But doesn't her partial responsibility for its being there itself give it a right to the use of her body?[7] If so, then her aborting it would be more like the boy's taking away the chocolates, and less like your unplugging yourself from the violinist—doing so would be depriving it of what it does have a right to, and thus would be doing it an injustice.

And then, too, it might be asked whether or not she can kill it even to save her own life: If she voluntarily called it into existence, how can she now kill it, even in self-defense?

The first thing to be said about this is that it is something new. Opponents of abortion have been so concerned to make out the independence of the fetus, in order to establish that it has a right to life, just as its mother does, that they have tended to overlook the possible support they might gain from making out that the fetus is *dependent* on the mother, in order to establish that she has a special kind of responsibility for it, a responsibility that gives it rights against her which are not possessed by any independent person—such as an ailing violinist who is a stranger to her.

On the other hand, this argument would give the unborn person a right to its mother's body only if her pregnancy resulted from a voluntary act, undertaken in full knowledge of the chance a pregnancy might result from it. It would leave out entirely the unborn person whose existence is due to rape. Pending the availability of some further argument, then, we would be left with the conclusion that unborn persons whose existence is due to rape have no right to the use of their mothers' bodies, and thus that aborting them is not depriving them of anything they have a right to and hence is not unjust killing.

And we should also notice that it is not at all plain that this argument really does go even as far as it purports to. For there are cases and cases, and the details make a difference. If the room is stuffy, and I therefore open a window to air it, and a burglar climbs in, it would be absurd to say, "Ah, now he can stay, she's given him a right to the use of her house—for she is partially responsible for his presence there, having voluntarily done what enabled him to get in, in full knowledge that there are such things as burglars, and that burglars burgle." It would be still more absurd to say this if I had had bars installed outside my windows, precisely to prevent burglars from getting in, and a burglar got in only because of a defect in the bars. It remains equally absurd if we imagine it is not a burglar who climbs in, but an innocent person who blunders or falls in. Again, suppose it were like this: people-seeds drift about in the air like pollen, and if you open your windows, one may drift in and take root in your carpets or upholstery. You don't want children, so you fix up your windows with fine mesh screens, the very best you can buy. As can happen, however, and on very, very rare occasions does happen, one of the screens is defective; and a seed drifts in and takes root. Does the person-plant who now develops have a right to the use of your house? Surely not—despite the fact that you voluntarily opened your windows, you knowingly kept carpets and upholstered furniture, and you knew that screens were sometimes defective. Someone may argue that you are responsible for its rooting, that it does have a right to your house, because after all you *could* have lived out your life with bare floors and furniture, or with sealed windows and doors. But this won't do—for by the same token anyone can avoid a pregnancy due to rape by having a hysterectomy, or anyway by never leaving home without a (reliable!) army.

It seems to me that the argument we were looking at can establish at most that there are *some* cases in which the unborn person has a right to the use of its mother's body, and therefore *some* cases in which abortion is unjust killing. There is room for much discussion and argument as to precisely which, if any. But I think we should sidestep this issue and leave it open, for at any rate the argument certainly does not establish that all abortion is unjust killing.

5. There is room for yet another argument here, however. We surely must all grant that there may be cases in which it would be morally indecent to detach a person from your body at the cost of his life. Suppose you learn that what the violinist needs is not nine years of your life, but only one hour. All you need do to save his life is to spend one hour in that bed with him. Suppose also that letting him use your kidneys for that one hour would not affect your health in the slightest. Admittedly you were kidnapped. Admittedly you did not give anyone permission to plug him into

you. Nevertheless it seems to me plain you *ought* to allow him to use your kidneys for that hour—it would be indecent to refuse.

Again, suppose pregnancy lasted only an hour, and constituted no threat to life or health. And suppose that a woman becomes pregnant as a result of rape. Admittedly she did not voluntarily do anything to bring about the existence of a child. Admittedly she did nothing at all which would give the unborn person a right to the use of her body. All the same it might well be said, as in the newly emended violinist story, that she *ought* to allow it to remain for that hour—that it would be indecent in her to refuse.

Now some people are inclined to use the term "right" in such a way that it follows from the fact that you ought to allow a person to use your body for the hour he needs, that he has a right to use your body for the hour he needs, even though he has not been given that right by any person or act. They may say that it follows also that if you refuse, you act unjustly toward him. This use of the term is perhaps so common that it cannot be called wrong; nevertheless it seems to me to be an unfortunate loosening of what we would do better to keep a tight rein on. Suppose that box of chocolates I mentioned earlier had not been given to both boys jointly, but was given only to the older boy. There he sits, stolidly eating his way through the box, his small brother watching enviously. Here we are likely to say "You ought not to be so mean. You ought to give your brother some of those chocolates." My own view is that it just does not follow from the truth of this that the brother has any right to any of the chocolates. If the boy refuses to give his brother any, he is greedy, stingy, callous—but not unjust. I suppose that the people I have in mind will say it does follow that the brother has a right to some of the chocolates, and thus that the boy does act unjustly if he refuses to give his brother any. But the effect of saying this is to obscure what we should keep distinct, namely the difference between the boy's refusal in this case and the boy's refusal in the earlier case, in which the box was given to both boys jointly, and in which the small brother thus had what was from any point of view clear title to half.

A further objection to so using the term "right" that from the fact that A ought to do a thing for B, it follows that B has a right against A that A do it for him, is that it is going to make the question of whether or not a man has a right to a thing turn on how easy it is to provide him with it; and this seems not merely unfortunate, but morally unacceptable. Take the case of Henry Fonda again. I said earlier that I had no right to the touch of his cool hand on my fevered brow, even though I needed it to save my life. I said it would be frightfully nice of him to fly in from the West Coast to provide me with it, but that I had no right against him that he should do so. But suppose he isn't on the West Coast. Suppose he has only to walk across the room, place a hand briefly on my brow—and lo, my life is saved. Then surely he ought to do it, it would be indecent to refuse. Is it to be said "Ah well, it follows that in this case she has a right to the touch of his hand on her brow, and so it would be an injustice in him to refuse"? So that I have a right to it when it is easy for him to provide it, though no right when it's hard? It's rather a shocking idea that anyone's right should fade away and disappear as it gets harder and harder to accord them to him.

So my own view is that even though you ought to let the violinist use your kidneys for the one hour he needs, we should not conclude that he has a right to do so—we would say that if you refuse, you are, like the boy who owns all the chocolates and will give none away, self-centered and callous, indecent in fact, but not unjust. And similarly, that even supposing a case in which a woman pregnant due to rape ought to allow the unborn person to use her body for the hour he needs, we should not conclude that he has a right to do so; we should conclude that she is self-centered, callous, indecent, but not unjust, if she refuses. The complaints are no less grave; they are just different. However, there is no need to insist on this point. If anyone does wish to deduce "he has a right" from "you ought," then all the same he must surely grant that there are cases in which it is not morally required of you that you allow that violinist to use your kidneys, and in which he does not have a right to use them, and in which you do not do him an injustice if you refuse. And so also for mother and unborn child. Except in such cases as the unborn person has a right to demand it—and we were leaving open the possibility that there may be such cases—nobody is morally *required* to make large sacrifices, of health, of all other interests and concerns, of all other duties and commitments, for nine years, or even for nine months, in order to keep another person alive.

6. We have in fact to distinguish between two kinds of Samaritan: the Good Samaritan and what we might call the Minimally Decent Samaritan. The story of the Good Samaritan, you will remember, goes like this:

> A certain man went down from Jerusalem to Jericho, and fell among thieves, which stripped him of his raiment, and wounded him, and departed, leaving him half dead.
>
> And by chance there came down a certain priest that way; and when he saw him, he passed by on the other side.
>
> And likewise a Levite, when he was at the place, came and looked on him, and passed by on the other side.
>
> But a certain Samaritan, as he journeyed, came where he was; and when he saw him he had compassion on him.
>
> And went to him, and bound up his wounds, pouring in oil and wine, and set him on his own beast, and brought him to an inn, and took care of him.
>
> And on the morrow, when he departed, he took out two pence, and gave them to the host, and said unto him, "Take care of him; and whatsoever thou spendest more, when I come again, I will repay thee."
>
> (Luke 10:30–35)

The Good Samaritan went out of his way, at some cost to himself, to help one in need of it. We are not told what the options were, that is, whether or not the priest and the Levite could have helped by doing less than the Good Samaritan did, but assuming they could have, then the fact they did nothing at all shows they were not even Minimally Decent Samaritans, not because they were not Samaritans, but because they were not even minimally decent.

These things are a matter of degree, of course, but there is a difference, and it comes out perhaps most clearly in the story of Kitty Genovese, who, as you will remember, was murdered while thirty-eight people watched or listened, and did nothing at all to help her. A Good Samaritan would have rushed out to give direct assistance against the murderer. Or perhaps we had better allow that it would have been a Splendid Samaritan who did this, on the ground that it would have involved a risk of death for himself. But the thirty-eight not only did not do this, they did not even trouble to pick up a phone to call the police. Minimally Decent Samaritanism would call for doing at least that, and their not having done it was monstrous.

After telling the story of the Good Samaritan, Jesus said, "Go, and do thou likewise." Perhaps he meant that we are morally required to act as the Good Samaritan did. Perhaps he was urging people to do more than is morally required of them. At all events it seems plain that it was not morally required of any of the thirty-eight that he rush out to give direct assistance at the risk of his own life, and that it is not morally required of anyone that he give long stretches of his life—nine years or nine months—to sustaining the life of a person who has no special right (we were leaving open the possibility of this) to demand it.

Indeed, with one rather striking class of exceptions, no one in any country in the world is *legally* required to do anywhere near as much as this for anyone else. The class of exceptions is obvious. My main concern here is not the state of the law in respect to abortion, but it is worth drawing attention to the fact that in no state in this country is any man compelled by law to be even a Minimally Decent Samaritan to any person; there is no law under which charges could be brought against the thirty-eight who stood by while Kitty Genovese died. By contrast, in most states in this country women are compelled by law to be not merely Minimally Decent Samaritans, but Good Samaritans to unborn persons inside them. This doesn't by itself settle anything one way or the other, because it may well be argued that there should be laws in this country—as there are in many European countries—compelling at least Minimally Decent Samaritanism.[8] But it does show that there is a gross injustice in the existing state of the law. And it shows also that the groups currently working against liberalization of abortion laws, in fact working toward having it declared unconstitutional for a state to permit abortion, had better start working for the adoption of Good Samaritan laws generally, or earn the charge that they are acting in bad faith.

I should think, myself, that Minimally Decent Samaritan laws would be one thing, Good Samaritan laws quite another, and in fact highly improper. But we are not here concerned with the law. What we should ask is not whether anybody should be compelled by law to be a Good Samaritan, but whether we must accede to a situation in which somebody is being compelled—by nature, perhaps—to be a Good Samaritan. We have, in other words, to look now at third-party interventions. I have been arguing that no person is morally required to make large sacrifices to sustain the life of another who has no right to demand them, and this even where the sacrifices do not include life itself; we are not morally required to be Good Samaritans or anyway Very Good Samaritans to one another. But what if a man cannot extricate himself from such a situation? What if he appeals to us to extricate him? It seems to me plain that there are cases in which we can, cases in which a Good Samaritan would extricate him. There you are, you were kidnapped, and nine years in bed with that violinist lie ahead of you. You have your own life to lead. You are sorry, but you simply cannot see giving up so much of your life to the sustaining of his. You cannot extricate yourself, and ask us to do so. I should have thought that—in light of his having no right to the use of your body—it was obvious that we do not have to accede to your being forced to give up so much. We can do what you ask. There is no injustice to the violinist in our doing so.

7. Following the lead of the opponents of abortion, I have throughout been speaking of the fetus merely as a person, and what I have been asking is whether or not the argument we began with, which proceeds only from the fetus's being a person, really does establish its conclusion. I have argued that it does not.

But of course there are arguments and arguments, and it may be said that I have simply fastened on the wrong one. It may be said that what is important is not merely the fact that the fetus is a person, but that it is a person for whom the woman has a special kind of responsibility issuing from the fact that she is its mother. And it might be argued that all my analogies are therefore irrelevant—for you do not have that special kind of responsibility for that violinist, Henry Fonda does not have that special kind of responsibility for me. And our attention might be drawn to the fact that men and women both *are* compelled by law to provide support for their children.

I have in effect dealt (briefly) with this argument in section 4 above; but a (still briefer) recapitulation now may be in order. Surely we do not have any such "special responsibility" for a person unless we have assumed it, explicitly or implicitly. If a set of parents do not try to prevent pregnancy, do not obtain an abortion, and then at the time of birth of the child do not put it out for adoption, but rather take it home with them, then they have assumed responsibility for it, they have given it rights, and they cannot *now* withdraw support from it at the cost of its life because they now find it difficult to go on providing for it. But if they have taken all reasonable precautions against having a child, they do not simply by virtue of their biological relationship to the child who comes into existence have a special responsibility for it. They may wish to assume responsibility for it, or they may not wish to. And I am suggesting that if assuming responsibility for it would require large sacrifices, then they may refuse. A good Samaritan would not refuse—or anyway, a Splendid Samaritan, if the sacrifices that had to be made were enormous. But then so would a Good Samaritan assume responsibility for that violinist; so would Henry Fonda, if he is a Good Samaritan, fly in from the West Coast and assume responsibility for me.

8. My argument will be found unsatisfactory on two counts by many of those who want to regard abortion as morally permissible. First, while I do argue that abortion is not impermissible, I do not argue that it is always permissible. There may well be cases in which carrying the child to term requires only Minimally Decent Samaritanism of the mother, and this is a standard we must not fall below. I am inclined to think it a merit of my account precisely that it does *not* give a general yes or a general no. It allows for and supports our sense that, for example, a sick and desperately frightened fourteen-year-old schoolgirl, pregnant due to rape, may *of course* choose abortion, and that any law which rules this out is an insane law. And it also allows for and supports our sense that in other cases resort to abortion is even positively indecent. It would be indecent in the woman to request an abortion, and indecent in a doctor to perform it, if she is in her seventh month and wants the abortion just to avoid the nuisance of postponing a trip abroad. The very fact that the arguments I have been drawing attention to treat all cases of abortion, or even all cases of abortion in which the mother's life is not at stake, as morally on a par ought to have made them suspect at the outset.

Secondly, while I am arguing for the permissibility of abortion in some cases, I am not arguing for the right to secure the death of the unborn child. It is easy to confuse these two things in that up to a certain point in the life of the fetus it is not able to survive outside the mother's body; hence removing it from her body guarantees its death. But they are importantly different. I have argued that you are not morally required to spend nine months in bed, sustaining the life of that violinist; but to say this is by no means to say that if, when you unplug yourself, there is a miracle and he survives, you then have a right to turn around and slit his throat. You may detach yourself even if this costs him his life; you have no right to be guaranteed his death, by some other means, if unplugging yourself does not kill him. There are some people who will feel dissatisfied by this feature of my argument. A woman may be utterly devastated by the thought of a child, a bit of herself, put out for adoption and never seen or heard of again. She may therefore want not merely that the child be detached from her, but more, that it die. Some opponents of abortion are inclined to regard this as beneath contempt—

thereby showing insensitivity to what is surely a powerful source of despair. All the same, I agree that the desire for the child's death is not one which anybody may gratify, should it turn out to be possible to detach the child alive.

At this place, however, it should be remembered that we have only been pretending throughout that the fetus is a human being from the moment of conception. A very early abortion is surely not the killing of a person, and so is not dealt with by anything I have said here.

NOTES

1. I am very much indebted to James Thomson for discussion, criticism, and many helpful suggestions.

2. Daniel Callahan, *Abortion: Law, Choice and Morality* (New York, 1970), p. 373. This book gives a fascinating survey of the available information on abortion. The Jewish tradition is surveyed in David M. Feldman, *Birth Control in Jewish Law* (New York, 1968), Part 5; the Catholic tradition in John T. Noonan, Jr., "An Almost Absolute Value in History," in *The Morality of Abortion,* ed. John T. Noonan, Jr. (Cambridge, Mass., 1970).

3. The term "direct" in the arguments I refer to is a technical one. Roughly, what is meant by "direct killing" is either killing as an end in itself, or killing as a means to some end, for example, the end of saving someone else's life. See note 6, below, for an example of its use.

4. Cf. *Encyclical Letter of Pope Pius XI on Christian Marriage,* St. Paul Editions (Boston, n.d.), p. 32: "however much we may pity the mother whose health and even life is gravely imperiled in the performance of the duty allotted to her by nature, nevertheless what could ever be a sufficient reason for excusing in any way the direct murder of the innocent? This is precisely what we are dealing with here." Noonan (*The Morality of Abortion,* p. 43) reads this as follows: "What cause can ever avail to excuse in any way the direct killing of the innocent? For it is a question of that."

5. The thesis in (d) is in an interesting way weaker than those in (a), (b), and they rule out abortion even in cases in which both mother and child will die if the abortion is not performed. By contrast, one who held the view expressed in (d) could consistently say that one needn't prefer letting two persons die to killing one.

6. Cf. the following passage from Pius XII, *Address to the Italian Catholic Society of Midwives:* "The baby in the maternal breast has the right to life immediately from God.—Hence there is no man, no human authority, no science, no medical eugenic, social, economic or moral 'indication' which can establish or grant a valid juridical ground for a direct deliberate disposition of an innocent human life, that is a disposition which looks to its destruction either as an end or as a means to another end perhaps in itself not illicit.—The baby, still not born, is a man in the same degree and for the same reason as the mother" (quoted in Noonan, *The Morality of Abortion,* p. 45).

7. The need for a discussion of this argument was brought home to me by members of the Society for Ethical and Legal Philosophy, to whom this paper was originally presented.

8. For a discussion of the difficulties involved, and a survey of the European experience with such laws, see *The Good Samaritan and the Law,* ed. James M. Ratcliffe (New York, 1966).

BARUCH BRODY

The Morality of Abortion

Baruch Brody is Leon Jaworski Professor of Biomedical Ethics, director of the Center for Medical Ethics and Health Policy at the Baylor College of Medicine, professor of philosophy at Rice University, and director of the Ethics Program at Methodist Hospital. Brody is a prolific writer in many areas of bioethics. Representative works include *The Sanctity of Human Life, The Ethics of Biomedical Research* and *Life and Death Decision-Making*.

THE WOMAN'S RIGHT TO HER BODY

It is a common claim that a woman ought to be in control of what happens to her body to the greatest extent possible, that she ought to be able to use her body in ways that she wants to and refrain from using it in ways that she does not want to. This right is particularly pressed where certain uses of her body have deep and lasting effects upon the character of her life, personal, social, and economic. Therefore, it is argued, a woman should be free either to carry her fetus to term, thereby using her body to support it, or to abort the fetus, thereby not using her body for that purpose.

In some contexts in which this argument is advanced, it is clear that it is not addressed to the issue of the morality of abortion at all. Rather, it is made in opposition to laws against abortion on the ground that the choice to abort or not is a moral decision that should belong only to the mother. But that specific direction of the argument is irrelevant to our present purposes; I will consider it [later] when I deal with the issues raised by laws prohibiting abortions. For the moment, I am concerned solely with the use of this principle as a putative ground tending to show the permissibility of abortion, with the claim that because it is the woman's body that carries the fetus and upon which the fetus depends, she has certain rights to abort the fetus that no one else may have.

We may begin by remarking that it is obviously correct that, as carrier of the fetus, the mother has it within her power to choose whether or not to abort the fetus. And, as an autonomous and responsible agent, she must make this choice. But let us notice that this in no way entails either that whatever choice she makes is morally right or that no one else has the right to evaluate the decision that she makes.

• • •

At first glance, it would seem that this argument cannot be used by anyone who supposes, as we do for the moment, that there is a point in fetal development from which time on the fetus is a human being. After all, people do not have the right to do anything whatsoever that may be necessary for them to retain control over the uses of their bodies. In particular, it would seem wrong for them to kill another human being in order to do so.

In a recent article,[1] Professor Judith Thomson has, in effect, argued that this simple view is mistaken. How does Professor Thomson defend her claim that the mother has a right to abort the fetus, even if it is a human being, whether or not her life is threatened and whether or not she has consented to the act of intercourse in which the fetus is conceived? At one point,[2] discussing just the case in which the mother's life is threatened, she makes the following suggestion:

From *Abortion and the Sanctity of Human Life: A Philosophical View* (Cambridge, MA: MIT Press, 1975), pp. 26–32, 37–39, 44–47, 123–129, 131, and "Fetal Humanity and the Theory of Essentialism," in *Philosophy and Sex,* Robert Baker and Frederick Elliston, eds. (Buffalo, NY: Prometheus Books, 1975), pp. 348–352. (Some parts of these essays were later revised by Professor Brody.) Reprinted by permission.

> In [abortion], there are only two people involved, one whose life is threatened and one who threatens it. Both are innocent: the one who is threatened is not threatened because of any fault, the one who threatens does not threaten because of any fault. For this reason, we may feel that we bystanders cannot intervene. But the person threatened can.

But surely this description is equally applicable to the following case: *A* and *B* are adrift on a lifeboat, *B* has a disease that he can survive, but *A*, if he contracts it, will die, and the only way that *A* can avoid that is by killing *B* and pushing him overboard. Surely, *A* has no right to do this. So there must be some special reason why the mother has, if she does, the right to abort the fetus.

There is, to be sure, an important difference between our lifeboat case and abortion, one that leads us to the heart of Professor Thomson's argument. In the case that we envisaged, both *A* and *B* have equal rights to be in the lifeboat, but the mother's body is hers and not the fetus's and she has first rights to its use. The primacy of these rights allows an abortion whether or not her life is threatened. Professor Thomson summarizes this argument in the following way:[3]

> I am arguing only that having a right to life does not guarantee having either a right to be given the use of, or a right to be allowed continued use of, another person's body—even if one needs it for life itself.

One part of this claim is clearly correct. I have no duty to *X* to save *X*'s life by giving him the use of my body (or my life savings, or the only home I have, and so on), and *X* has no right, even to save his life, to any of those things. Thus, the fetus conceived in the laboratory that will perish unless it is implanted into a woman's body has in fact no right to any woman's body. But this portion of the claim is irrelevant to the abortion issue, for in abortion of the fetus that is a human being the mother must kill *X* to get back the sole use of her body, and that is an entirely different matter.

This point can also be put as follows: . . . we must distinguish the taking of *X*'s life from the saving of *X*'s life, even if we assume that one has a duty not to do the former and to do the latter. Now that latter duty, if it exists at all, is much weaker than the first duty; many circumstances may relieve us from the latter duty that will not relieve us from the former one. Thus, I am certainly relieved from my duty to save *X*'s life by the fact that fulfilling it means the loss of my life savings. It may be noble for me to save *X*'s life at the cost of everything I have, but I certainly have no duty to do that. And the same observation may be made about cases in which I can save *X*'s life by giving him the use of my body for an extended period of time. However, I am not relieved of my duty not to take *X*'s life by the fact that fulfilling it means the loss of everything I have and not even by the fact that fulfilling it means the loss of my life. . . .

At one point in her paper, Professor Thomson does consider this objection. She has previously imagined the following case: a famous violinist, who is dying from a kidney ailment, has been, without your consent, plugged into you for a period of time so that his body can use your kidneys:

> Some people are rather stricter about the right to life. In their view, it does not include the right to be given anything, but amounts to, and only to, the right not to be killed by anybody. But here a related difficulty arises. If everybody is to refrain from killing that violinist, then everybody must refrain from doing a great many different sorts of things . . . everybody must refrain from unplugging you from him. But does he have a right against everybody that they shall refrain from unplugging you from him? To refrain from doing this is to allow him to continue to use your kidneys . . . certainly the violinist has no right against you that you shall allow him to continue to use your kidneys.

Applying this argument to the case of abortion, we can see that Professor Thomson's argument would run as follows:

a. Assume that the fetus's right to life includes the right not to be killed by the woman carrying him.
b. But to refrain from killing the fetus is to allow him the continued use of the woman's body.
c. So our first assumption entails that the fetus's right to life includes the right to the continued use of the woman's body.
d. But we all grant that the fetus does not have the right to the continued use of the woman's body.
e. Therefore, the fetus's right to life cannot include the right not to be killed by the woman in question.

And it is also now clear what is wrong with this argument. When we granted that the fetus has no right to the continued use of the woman's body, all that we meant was that he does not have this right merely because the continued use saves his life. But, of course, there may be other reasons why he has this right. One would be that the only way to take the use of the woman's body away from the fetus is by killing him, and that is something that neither she nor we have the right to do. So, I submit, the way in which Assumption d is true is irrelevant, and cannot be used by Professor Thomson, for Assumption d is true only in cases where the saving of the life of the fetus is at stake and not in cases where the taking of his life is at stake.

I conclude therefore that Professor Thomson has not established the truth of her claims about abortion, primarily because she has not sufficiently attended to the distinction between our duty to save *X*'s life and our duty not to take it. Once one attends to that distinction, it would seem that the mother, in order to regain control over her body, has no right to abort the fetus from the point at which it becomes a human being.

It may also be useful to say a few words about the larger and less rigorous context of the argument that the woman has a right to her own body. It is surely true that one way in which women have been oppressed is by their being denied authority over their own bodies. But it seems to me that, as the struggle is carried on for meaningful amelioration of such oppression, it ought not to be carried so far that it violates the steady responsibilities all people have to one another. Parents may not desert their children, one class may not oppress another, one race or nation may not exploit another. For parents, powerful groups in society, races or nations in ascendancy, there are penalties for refraining from these wrong actions, but those penalties can in no way be taken as the justification for such wrong actions. Similarly, if the fetus is a human being, the penalty of carrying it cannot, I believe, be used as the justification for destroying it.

• • •

THE MODEL PENAL CODE CASES

All of the arguments that we have looked at so far are attempts to show that there is something special about abortion that justifies its being treated differently from other cases of the taking of human life. We shall now consider claims that are confined to certain special cases of abortion: the case in which the mother has been raped, the case in which bearing the child would be harmful to her health, and the case in which having the child may cause a problem for the rest of her family (the latter case is a particular case of the societal argument). In addressing these issues, we shall see whether there is any point to the permissibility of abortions in some of the cases covered by the Model Penal Code[4] proposals.

When the expectant mother has conceived after being raped, there are two different sorts of considerations that might support the claim that she has the right to take the life of the fetus. They are the following: (A) the woman in question has already suffered immensely from the act of rape and the physical and/or psychological aftereffects of that act. It would be particularly unjust, the argument runs, for her to have to live through an unwanted pregnancy owing to that act of rape. Therefore, even if we are at a stage at which the fetus is a human being, the mother has the right to abort it; (B) the fetus in question has no right to be in that woman. It was put there as a result of an act of aggression upon her by the rapist, and its continued presence is an act of aggression against the mother. She has a right to repel that aggression by aborting the fetus.

The first argument is very compelling. We can all agree that a terrible injustice has been committed on the woman who is raped. The question that we have to consider, however, is whether it follows that it is morally permissible for her to abort the fetus. We must make that consideration reflecting that, however unjust the act of rape, it was not the fetus who committed or commissioned it. The injustice of the act, then, should in no way impinge upon the rights of the fetus, for it is innocent. What remains is the initial misfortune of the mother (and the injustice of her having to pass through the pregnancy, and, further, to assume responsibility of at least giving the child over for adoption or assuming the burden of its care). However unfortunate that circumstance, however unjust, the misfortune and the injustice are not sufficient cause to justify the taking of the life of an innocent human being as a means of mitigation.

It is at this point that Argument B comes in, for its whole point is that the fetus, by its mere presence in the mother, is committing an act of aggression against her, one over and above the one committed by the rapist, and one that the mother has a right to repel by abortion. But . . . (1) the fetus is certainly innocent (in the sense of not responsible) for any act of aggression against the mother and . . . (2) the mere presence of the fetus in the mother, no matter how unfortunate for her, does not constitute an act of aggression by the fetus against the mother. Argument B fails then at just that point at which Argument A needs its support, and we can therefore conclude that the fact that pregnancy is the result of rape does not give the mother the right to abort the fetus.

We turn next to the case in which the continued existence of the fetus would threaten the mental and/or physical health but not necessarily the life of the mother. Again, . . . the fact that the fetus's continued existence poses a threat to the life of the mother does not justify her aborting it.* It would seem to be true, a fortiori, that the fact that the fetus's continued existence poses a threat to the mental and/or physical health of the mother does not justify her aborting it either.

We come finally to those cases in which the continuation of the pregnancy would cause serious problems for the rest of the family. There are a variety of cases that we have to consider here together. Perhaps the health of the mother will be affected in such a way that she cannot function effectively as a wife and mother during, or even after, the pregnancy. Or perhaps the expenses incurred as a result of the pregnancy would be utterly beyond the financial resources of the family. The important point is that the continuation of the pregnancy raises a serious problem for other innocent people involved besides the mother and the fetus, and it may be argued that the mother has the right to abort the fetus to avoid that problem.

By now, the difficulties with this argument should be apparent. We have seen earlier that the mere fact that the continued existence of the fetus threatens to harm the mother does not, by itself, justify the aborting of the fetus. Why should anything be changed by the fact that the threatened harm will accrue to the other members of the family and not to the mother? Of course, it would be different if the fetus were committing an act of aggression against the other members of the family. But, once more, this is certainly not the case.

We conclude, therefore, that none of these special circumstances justifies an abortion from that point at which the fetus is a human being.

• • •

FETAL HUMANITY AND BRAIN FUNCTION

The question which we must now consider is the question of fetal humanity. Some have argued that the fetus is a human being with a right to life (or, for convenience, just a human being) from the moment of conception. Others have argued that the fetus only becomes a human being at the moment of birth. Many positions in between these two extremes have also been suggested. How are we to decide which is correct?

The analysis which we will propose here rests upon certain metaphysical assumptions which I have defended elsewhere. These assumptions are: (a) the question is when has the fetus acquired all the properties essential (necessary) for being a human being, for when it has, it is a human being; (b) these properties are such that the loss of any one of them means that the human being in question has gone out of existence and not merely stopped being a human being; (c) human beings go out of existence when they die. It follows from these assumptions that the fetus becomes a human being when it acquires all those characteristics which are such that the loss of any one of them would result in the fetus's being dead. We must, therefore, turn to the analysis of death.

• • •

We will first consider the question of what properties are essential to being human if we suppose that death and the passing out of existence occur only if there has been an irreparable cessation of brain function (keeping in mind that that condition itself, as we have noted, is a matter of medical judgment). We shall then consider the same question on the supposition that [Paul] Ramsey's more complicated theory of death (the modified traditional view) is correct.

According to what is called the brain-death theory,

**Ed. note:* Professor Brody provided a lengthy argument to this effect in a chapter not here excerpted. His summary of that argument is as follows: "Is it permissible, as an act of killing a pursuer, to abort the fetus in order to save the mother? The first thing that we should note is that Pope Pius's objection to aborting the fetus as a permissible act of killing a pursuer is mistaken. His objection is that the fetus shows no knowledge or intention in his attempt to take the life of the mother, that the fetus is, in a word, innocent. But that only means that the condition of guilt is not satisfied, and we have seen that its satisfaction is not necessary."

"Is, then, the aborting of the fetus, when necessary to save the life of the mother, a permissible act of killing a pursuer? It is true that in such cases the fetus is a danger to the mother. But it is also clear that the condition of attempt is not satisfied. The fetus has neither the beliefs nor the intention to which we have referred. Furthermore, there is on the part of the fetus no action that threatens the life of the mother. So not even the condition of action is satisfied. It seems to follow, therefore, that aborting the fetus could not be a permissible act of killing a pursuer."

as long as there has not been an irreparable cessation of brain function the person in question continues to exist, no matter what else has happened to him. If so, it seems to follow that there is only one property—leaving aside those entailed by this one property—that is essential to humanity, namely, the possession of a brain that has not suffered an irreparable cessation of function.

Several consequences follow immediately from this conclusion. We can see that a variety of often advanced claims about the essence of humanity are false. For example, the claim that movement, or perhaps just the ability to move, is essential for being human is false. A human being who has stopped moving, and even one who has lost the ability to move, has not therefore stopped existing. Being able to move, and a fortiori moving, are not essential properties of human beings and therefore are not essential to being human. Similarly, the claim that being perceivable by other human beings is essential for being human is also false. A human being who has stopped being perceivable by other humans (for example, someone isolated on the other side of the moon, out of reach even of radio communication) has not stopped existing. Being perceivable by other human beings is not an essential property of human beings and is not essential to being human. And the same point can be made about the claims that viability is essential for being human, that independent existence is essential for being human, and that actual interaction with other human beings is essential for being human. The loss of any of these properties would not mean that the human being in question had gone out of existence, so none of them can be essential to that human being and none of them can be essential for being human.

Let us now look at the following argument: (1) A functioning brain (or at least, a brain that, if not functioning, is susceptible of function) is a property that every human being must have because it is essential for being human. (2) By the time an entity acquires that property, it has all the other properties that are essential for being human. Therefore, when the fetus acquires that property it becomes a human being. It is clear that the property in question is, according to the brain-death theory, one that is had essentially by all human beings. The question that we have to consider is whether the second premise is true. It might appear that its truth does follow from the brain-death theory. After all, we did see that the theory entails that only one property (together with those entailed by it) is essential for being human. Nevertheless, rather than relying solely on my earlier argument, I shall adopt an alternative approach to strengthen the conviction that this second premise is true: I shall note the important ways in which the fetus resembles and differs from an ordinary human being by the time it definitely has a functioning brain (about the end of the sixth week of development). It shall then be evident, in light of our theory of essentialism, that none of these differences involves the lack of some property in the fetus that is essential for its being human.

Structurally, there are few features of the human being that are not fully present by the end of the sixth week. Not only are the familiar external features and all the internal organs present, but the contours of the body are nicely rounded. More important, the body is functioning. Not only is the brain functioning, but the heart is beating sturdily (the fetus by this time has its own completely developed vascular system), the stomach is producing digestive juices, the liver is manufacturing blood cells, the kidney is extracting uric acid from the blood, and the nerves and muscles are operating in concert, so that reflex reactions can begin.

What are the properties that a fetus acquires after the sixth week of its development? Certain structures do appear later. These include the fingernails (which appear in the third month), the completed vocal chords (which also appear then), taste buds and salivary glands (again, in the third month), and hair and eyelashes (in the fifth month). In addition, certain functions begin later than the sixth week. The fetus begins to urinate (in the third month), to move spontaneously (in the third month), to respond to external stimuli (at least in the fifth month), and to breathe (in the sixth month). Moreover, there is a constant growth in size. And finally, at the time of birth the fetus ceases to receive its oxygen and food through the placenta and starts receiving them through the mouth and nose.

I will not examine each of these properties (structures and functions) to show that they are not essential for being human. The procedure would be essentially the one used previously to show that various essentialist claims are in error. We might, therefore, conclude, on the supposition that the brain-death theory is correct, that the fetus becomes a human being about the end of the sixth week after its development.

There is, however, one complication that should be noted here. There are, after all, progressive stages in the physical development and in the functioning of the brain. For example, the fetal brain (and nervous system) does not develop sufficiently to support spontaneous motion until some time in the third month after conception. There is, of course, no doubt that that stage of development is sufficient for the fetus to be human. No one would be likely to maintain that a spontaneously moving human being has died; and similarly, a spontaneously moving fetus would seem to have become human. One might, however, want to claim that the fetus does not become a human being until the point of spontaneous movement. So then, on the supposition that the brain-death theory of death is correct, one ought to conclude that the fetus becomes a human being at some time between the sixth and twelfth week after its conception.

But what if we reject the brain-death theory, and replace it with its equally plausible contender, Ramsey's theory of death? According to that theory—which we can call the brain, heart, and lung theory of death—the human being does not die, does not go out of existence, until such time as the brain, heart and lungs have irreparably ceased functioning naturally. What are the essential features of being human according to this theory?

Actually, the adoption of Ramsey's theory requires no major modifications. According to that theory, what is essential to being human, what each human being must retain if he is to continue to exist, is the possession of a functioning (actually or potentially) heart, lung, or brain. It is only when a human being possesses none of these that he dies and goes out of existence; and the fetus comes into humanity, so to speak, when he acquires one of these.

On Ramsey's theory, the argument would now run as follows: (1) The property of having a functioning brain, heart, or lungs (or at least organs of the kind that, if not functioning, are susceptible of function) is one that every human being must have because it is essential for being human. (2) By the time that an entity acquires that property it has all the other properties that are essential for being human. Therefore, when the fetus acquires that property it becomes a human being. There remains, once more, the problem of the second premise. Since the fetal heart starts operating rather early, it is not clear that the second premise is correct. Many systems are not yet operating, and many structures are not yet present. Still, following our theory of essentialism, we should conclude that the fetus becomes a human being when it acquires a functioning heart (the first of the organs to function in the fetus).

There is, however, a further complication here, and it is analogous to the one encountered if we adopt the brain-death theory: When may we properly say that the fetal heart begins to function? At two weeks, when occasional contractions of the primitive fetal heart are present? In the fourth to fifth week, when the heart, although incomplete, is beating regularly and pumping blood cells through a closed vascular system, and when the tracings obtained by an ECG exhibit the classical elements of an adult tracing? Or after the end of the seventh week, when the fetal heart is functionally complete and "normal"?

We have not reached a precise conclusion in our study of the question of when the fetus becomes a human being. We do know that it does so some time between the end of the second week and the end of the third month. But it surely is not a human being at the moment of conception and it surely is one by the end of the third month. Though we have not come to a final answer to our question, we have narrowed the range of acceptable answers considerably.

[In summary] we have argued that the fetus becomes a human being with a right to life some time between the second and twelfth week after conception. We have also argued that abortions are morally impermissible after that point except in rather unusual circumstances. What is crucial to note is that neither of these arguments appeal to any theological considerations. We conclude, therefore, that there is a human-rights basis for moral opposition to abortions.

• • •

LAW AND SOCIETY IN A DEMOCRACY

Before turning to such considerations, however, we must first examine several important assertions about law and society that, if true, would justify the joint assertion of the principles that abortion is murder but nevertheless should be or remain legal. The first is the assertion that citizens of a pluralistic society must forgo the use of the law as a method of enforcing what are their private moralities. It might well be argued that in our pluralistic society, in which there are serious disagreements about the status of the fetus and about the rightness and wrongness of abortion in consequence, it would be wrong (or inappropriate) to legislate against abortion.

Such assertions about a pluralistic society are difficult to evaluate because of their imprecision. So let us first try to formulate some version of them more carefully. Consider the following general principle: Principle [1]. When the citizens of a society strongly disagree about the rightness and wrongness of a given action, and a considerable number think that such an action is right (or, at least, permissible), then it is wrong (or inappropriate) for that society to prohibit that action by law, even if the majority of citizens believe such an action to be wrong.

There are a variety of arguments that can be offered in support of the principle. One appeals to the right of the minority to follow its own conscience rather than being compelled to follow the conscience of the majority. That right has a theoretical political justification, but it also is practically implicit in the inappropriateness in the members of the majority imposing this kind of enforcement upon the minority that would be opposed were they the minority and were the enforcement being imposed upon them. Another argument appeals to the detrimental consequences to a society of the sense on the part of a significant minority that the law is being used by the majority to coerce. Such considerations make it seem that a principle like [1] is true.

If Principle [1] is true, it is easy to offer a defense of the joint assertion of the principles that abortion is murder but nevertheless should be or remain legal. All we need are the additional obvious assumptions that the citizens of our society strongly disagree about the morality of abortion and that at least a significant minority of individuals believe that there are many cases in which abortion is permissible. From these assumptions and Principle [1] it follows that abortions should be or remain legal even if they are murders.

The trouble with this argument is that it depends upon Principle [1]. I agree that, because of the considerations mentioned already, something like Principle [1] must be true. But Principle [1] as formulated is much too broad to be defensible. Consider, after all, a society in which a significant number of citizens think that it is morally permissible, and perhaps even obligatory, to kill Blacks or Jews, for example, because they are seen as being something less than fully human. It would seem to follow from Principle [1] that the law should not prohibit such actions. Surely this consequence of Principle [1] is wrong. Even if a pluralistic society should forgo passing many laws out of deference to the views of those who think that the actions that would thereby be prevented are not wrong, there remain some cases in which the force of the law should be applied because of the evil of the actions it is intended to prevent. If such actions produce very harmful results and infringe upon the rights of a sufficiently large number of individuals, then the possible benefits that may be derived from passing and enforcing a law preventing those actions may well override the rights of the minority (or even of the majority) to follow its conscience.

Principle [1] must therefore be modified as follows: Principle [2]. When the citizens of a society strongly disagree about the rightness and wrongness of a given action, and a considerable number think that such an action is right (or, at least, permissible), then it is wrong (or inappropriate) for that society to prohibit that action by law, even if the majority of citizens believe such an action to be wrong, unless the action in question is so evil that the desirability of legal prohibition outweighs the desirability of granting to the minority the right to follow its own conscience.

Principle [2] is, of course, rather vague. In particular, its last clause needs further clarification. But Principle [2] is clear enough for us to see that it cannot be used to justify the joint assertibility of the principles that abortion is murder but should nevertheless be or remain legal. Principle [2], conjoined with the obvious truths that the citizens of our society strongly disagree about the rightness and wrongness of abortion and that a significant number of citizens believe that, in certain circumstances, the right (or, at least, a permissible) thing to do is to have an abortion, does not yield the conclusion that abortion should be or remain legal if abortion is murder. After all, if abortion is murder, then the action in question is the unjustifiable taking of a human life and may well fall under the last clause of Principle [2]. The destruction of a fetus may not be unlike the killing of a Black or Jew. They may all be cases of the unjust taking of a human life.

• • •

THE DECISION IN *ROE V. WADE*

Two decisions were announced by the [U.S. Supreme] Court on January 22 [1973]. The first *(Roe v. Wade)* involved a challenge to a Texas law prohibiting all abortions not necessary to save the life of the mother. The second *(Doe v. Bolton)* tested a Georgia law incorporating many of the recommendations of the Model Penal Code as to the circumstances under which abortion should be allowed (in the case of rape and of a defective fetus, as well as when the pregnancy threatens the life or health of the mother), together with provisions regulating the place where abortions can be performed, the number of doctors that must concur, and other factors.

Of these two decisions, the more fundamental was *Roe v. Wade*. It was in this case that the Court came to grips with the central legal issue, namely, the extent to which it is legitimate for the state to prohibit or regulate abortion. In *Doe v. Bolton,* the Court was more concerned with subsidiary issues involving the legitimacy of particular types of regulations.

The Court summarized its decision in *Roe v. Wade* as follows:[5]

> (a) For the stage prior to approximately the end of the first trimester/three months the abortion decision and its effectuation must be left to the medical judgment of the pregnant woman's attending physician.
>
> (b) For the stage subsequent to approximately the end of the first trimester, the state, in promoting its interest in the health of the mother, may, if it chooses, regulate the abortion procedure in ways that are reasonably related to maternal health.
>
> (c) For the stage subsequent to viability, the state, in promoting its interest in the potentiality of human life, may, if it chooses, regulate, and even proscribe, abortion except where it is necessary, in appropriate medical judgment, for the preservation of the life or health of the mother.

In short, the Court ruled that abortion can be prohibited only after viability and then only if the life or health of the mother is not threatened. Before viability, abortions cannot be prohibited, but they can be regulated after the first trimester if the regulations are reasonably related to maternal health. This last clause is taken very seriously by the Court. In *Doe v. Bolton,* instances of regulation in the Georgia code were found unconstitutional on the ground that they were not reasonably related to maternal health.

How did the Court arrive at this decision? In Sections V and VII of the decision, it set out the claims on both sides. Jane Roe's argument was summarized in these words:[6]

> The principal thrust of appellant's attack on the Texas statutes is that they improperly invade a right, said to be possessed by the pregnant woman, to choose to determine her pregnancy.

On the other hand, the Court saw as possible legitimate interests of the state the regulation of abortion, like other medical procedures, so as to ensure maximum safety for the patient and the protection of prenatal life. At this point in the decision, the Court added the following very significant remark:[7]

> Logically, of course, a legitimate state interest in this area need not stand or fall on acceptance of the belief that life begins at conception or at some other point prior to live birth. In assessing the state's interest, recognition may be given to the less rigid claim that as long as at least potential life is involved, the state may assert interests beyond the protection of the pregnant woman alone.

In Sections VIII to X, the Court stated its conclusion. It viewed this case as one presenting a conflict of interests, and it saw itself as weighing these interests. It began by agreeing that the woman's right to privacy did encompass her right to decide whether or not to terminate her pregnancy. But it argued that this right is not absolute, since the state's interests must also be considered:[8]

> We therefore conclude that the right of personal privacy includes the abortion decision, but that this right is not unqualified and must be considered against important state interests in regulation.

The Court had no hesitation in ruling that the woman's right can be limited after the first trimester because of the state's interest in preserving and protecting maternal health. But the Court was less prepared to agree that the woman's right can be limited because of the state's interest in protecting prenatal life. Indeed, the Court rejected Texas's strong claim that life begins at conception, and that the state therefore has a right to protect such life by prohibiting abortion. The first reason advanced for rejecting that claim was phrased in this way:[9]

> We need not resolve the difficult question of when life begins. When those trained in the respective disciplines of medicine, philosophy, and theology are unable to arrive at any consensus, the judiciary, at this point in the development of man's knowledge, is not in a position to speculate as to the answer.

Its second reason was that[10]

> In areas other than criminal abortion, the law has been reluctant to endorse any theory that life, as we recognize it, begins before live birth or to accord legal rights to the unborn except in narrowly defined situations and except when the rights are contingent upon live birth.

The Court accepted the weaker claim that the state has an interest in protecting the potential of life. But when does that interest become compelling enough to enable the state to prohibit abortion? The Court said:[11]

> . . . the compelling point is at viability. This is so because the fetus then has the capacity of meaningful life outside the mother's womb. State regulation protective of fetal life after viability thus has both logical and biological justifications. If the state is interested in protecting fetal life after viability, it may go so far as to proscribe abortion during that period except where it is necessary to preserve the life or health of the mother.

THE COURT ON POTENTIAL LIFE

I want to begin by considering that part of the Court's decision that allows Texas to proscribe abortions after viability so as to protect its interest in potential life. I note that it is difficult to evaluate that important part of the decision because the Court had little to say in defense of it other than the paragraph just quoted.

There are three very dubious elements of this ruling:

1. Why is the state prohibited from proscribing abortions when the life or health of the mother is threatened? Perhaps the following argument may be offered in the case of threat to maternal life: the mother is actually alive but the fetus is only potentially alive, and the protection of actual life takes precedence over the protection of potential life. Even if we grant this argument, why is the state prevented from prohibiting abortion when only maternal health is threatened? What is the argument against the claim that protecting potential life takes precedence in that case?

2. Why does the interest in potential life become compelling only when the stage of viability is reached? The Court's whole argument for this claim is[12]

> This is so because the fetus then presumably has the capacity of meaningful life outside the mother's womb.

There is, no doubt, an important type of potential for life, the capacity of meaningful life outside the mother's womb, that the fetus acquires only at the time of viability. But there are other types of potential for life that it acquires earlier. At conception, for example, the fertilized cell has the potential for life in the sense that it will, in the normal course of events, develop into a human being. A six-week-old fetus has the potential for life in the stronger sense that all of the major organs it needs for life are already functioning. Why then does the state's interest in protecting potential life become compelling only at the point of viability? The Court failed to answer that question.

3. It can fairly be said that those trained in the respective disciplines of medicine, philosophy, and theology are unlikely to be able to arrive at any consensus on the question of when the fetus becomes potentially alive and when the state's interest in protecting this potential life becomes compelling enough to outweigh the rights of the mother. Why then did not the Court conclude, as it did when it considered the question of fetal humanity, that the judiciary cannot rule on such a question?

In pursuit of this last point, we approach the Court's more fundamental arguments against prohibiting abortion before viability.

THE COURT ON ACTUAL LIFE

The crucial claim in the Court's decision is that laws prohibiting abortion cannot be justified on the ground that the state has an interest in protecting the life of the fetus who is a human being. The Court offered two reasons for this claim: that the law has never yet accorded the fetus this status, and that the matter of fetal humanity is not one about which it is appropriate for the courts to speculate.

The first of the Court's reasons is not particularly strong. Whatever force we want to ascribe to precedent in the law, the Court has in the past modified its previous decisions in light of newer information and insights. In a matter as important as the conflict between the fetus's right to life and the rights of the mother, it would have seemed particularly necessary to deal with the issues rather than relying upon precedent.

In its second argument, the Court did deal with those issues by adopting the following principle:

1. It is inappropriate for the Court to speculate about the answer to questions about which relevant professional specialists cannot arrive at a consensus.

This principle seems irrelevant. The issue before the Court was whether the Texas legislature could make a determination in light of the best available evidence and legislate on the basis of it. Justice White, in his dissent, raised this point:[13]

> The upshot is that the people and legislatures of the fifty states are constitutionally disentitled to weigh the relative importance of the continued existence and development of the fetus on the one hand against the spectrum of possible impacts on the mother on the other hand.

This objection could be met, however, if we modified the Court's principle in the following way:

2. It is inappropriate for a legislature to write law upon the basis of its best belief when the relevant professional specialists cannot agree that that belief is correct.

On the basis of such a principle, the Court could argue that Texas had no right to protect by law the right of the fetus to life, thereby acknowledging it to be a human being with such a right, because the relevant specialists do not agree that the fetus has that right. As it stands, however, Principle 2 is questionable. In a large number of areas, legislatures regularly do (and must) act upon issues upon which there is a wide diversity of opinion among professional specialists. So Principle 2 has to be modified to deal with only certain cases, and the obvious suggestion is:

3. It is inappropriate for the legislature, on the ground of belief, to write law in such a way as to violate the basic rights of some individuals, when professional specialists do not agree that that belief is correct.

This principle could be used to defend the Court's decision. But is there any reason to accept it as true? Two arguments for this principle immediately suggest themselves: (a) If the relevant professional specialists do not agree, then there cannot be any proof that the answer in question is the correct one. But a legislature should not infringe the rights of people on the basis of unproved belief. (b) When the professional specialists do not agree, there must be legitimate and reasonable alternatives of belief, and we ought to respect the rights of believers in each of these alternatives to act on their own judgments.

• • •

We have already discussed . . . the principles that lie behind these arguments. We saw . . . that neither of these arguments, as applied to abortion, is acceptable if the fetus is a human being. To employ these arguments correctly, the Court must presuppose that the fetus is not a human being. And that, of course, it cannot do, since the aim of its logic is the view that courts and legislatures, at least at this juncture, should remain neutral on the issue of fetal humanity.

There is a second point that should be noted about Principles 1 to 3. There are cases in which, by failing to deal with an issue, an implicit, inevitable decision is in fact reached. We have before us such a case. The Court was considering Texas's claim that it had the right to prohibit abortion in order to protect the fetus. The Court conceded that if the fetus had a protectable right to life, Texas could prohibit abortions. But when the Court concluded that it (and, by implication, Texas) could not decide whether the fetus is a human being with the right to life, Texas was compelled to act as if the fetus had no such right that Texas could protect. Why should Principles like 1 to 3 be accepted if the result is the effective endorsement of one disputed claim over another?[14]

There is an alternative to the Court's approach. It is that each of the legislatures should consider the vexing problems surrounding abortions, weigh all of the relevant factors, and write law on the basis of its conclusions. The legislature would, undoubtedly, have to consider the question of fetal humanity, but, I submit, the Court is wrong in supposing that there is a way in which that question can be avoided.

• • •

CONCLUSION

The Supreme Court has ruled, and the principal legal issues in this country are, at least for now, resolved. I have tried to show, however, that the Court's ruling was in error, that it failed to grapple with the crucial issues surrounding the laws prohibiting abortion. The serious public debate about abortion must, and certainly will, continue.

NOTES

1. J. Thomson, "A Defense of Abortion," *Philosophy and Public Affairs,* Vol. 1 (1971), pp. 47–66.
2. Ibid., p. 53.
3. Ibid., p. 56.
4. On the Model Penal Code provisions, see American Law Institute, *Model Penal Code:* Tentative Draft No. 9 (1959).
5. *Roe v. Wade,* 41 *LW* 4229.
6. *Roe,* 41 *LW* 4218.
7. *Roe,* 41 *LW* 4224.
8. *Roe,* 41 *LW* 4226.
9. *Roe,* 41 *LW* 4227.
10. *Roe,* 41 *LW* 4228.
11. *Roe,* 41 *LW* 4228–4229.
12. Ibid.
13. *Roe,* 41 *LW* 4246.
14. This argument is derived from one used (for very different purposes) by William James in *The Will to Believe,* reprinted in William James, *The Will to Believe and Other Essays on Popular Philosophy* (New York: Dover, 1956), pp. 1–31.

MARY ANNE WARREN

On the Moral and Legal Status of Abortion

Mary Anne Warren is professor of philosophy at San Francisco State University. She has written on many topics concerning abortion and feminism. Representative publications include "The Abortion Struggle in America," *Bioethics, Moral Status: Obligations to Persons and Other Living Things, Gendercide: The Implications of Sex Selection,* and *The Nature of Woman: An Encyclopedia & Guide to the Literature.*

We will be concerned with both the moral status of abortion, which for our purposes we may define as the act which a woman performs in voluntarily terminating, or allowing another person to terminate, her pregnancy, and the legal status which is appropriate for this act. I will argue that, while it is not possible to produce a satisfactory defense of a woman's right to obtain an abortion without showing that a fetus is not a human being, in the morally relevant sense of that term, we ought not to conclude that the difficulties involved in determining whether or not a fetus is human make it impossible to produce any satisfactory solution to the problem of the moral status of abortion. For it is possible to show that, on the basis of intuitions which we may expect even the opponents of abortion to share, a fetus is not a person, and hence not the sort of entity to which it is proper to ascribe full moral rights.

Of course, while some philosophers would deny the possibility of any such proof,[1] others will deny that there is any need for it, since the moral permissibility of abortion appears to them to be too obvious to require proof. But the inadequacy of this attitude should be evident from the fact that both the friends and the foes of abortion consider their position to be morally self-evident. Because proabortionists have never adequately come to grips with the conceptual issues surrounding abortion, most, if not all, of the arguments which they advance in opposition to laws restricting access to abortion fail to refute or even weaken the traditional antiabortion argument, i.e., that a fetus is a human being, and therefore abortion is murder.

These arguments are typically of one of two sorts. Either they point to the terrible side effects of the restrictive laws, e.g., the deaths due to illegal abortions, and the fact that it is poor women who suffer the most as a result of these laws, or else they state that to deny a woman access to abortion is to deprive her of her right to control her own body. Unfortunately, however, the fact that restricting access to abortion has tragic side effects does not, in itself, show that the restrictions are unjustified, since murder is wrong regardless of the consequences of prohibiting it; and the appeal to the right to control one's body, which is generally construed as a property right, is at best a rather feeble argument for the permissibility of abortion. Mere ownership does not give me the right to kill innocent people whom I find on my property, and indeed I am apt to be held responsible if such people injure themselves while on my property. It is equally unclear that I have any moral right to expel an innocent person from my property when I know that doing so will result in his death.

Furthermore, it is probably inappropriate to describe a woman's body as her property, since it seems natural to hold that a person is something distinct from her property, but not from her body. Even those who would object to the identification of a person with his body, or with the conjunction of his body and his mind, must admit that it would be very odd to de-

Reprinted from *The Monist* 57, no. 1 (January 1973) with the permission of the publisher. Copyright © 1973, *The Monist.*

scribe, say, breaking a leg, as damaging one's property, and much more appropriate to describe it as injuring one*self*. Thus it is probably a mistake to argue that the right to obtain an abortion is in any way derived from the right to own and regulate property.

But however we wish to construe the right to abortion, we cannot hope to convince those who consider abortion a form of murder of the existence of any such right unless we are able to produce a clear and convincing refutation of the traditional antiabortion argument, and this has not, to my knowledge, been done. With respect to the two most vital issues which that argument involves, i.e., the humanity of the fetus and its implication for the moral status of abortion, confusion has prevailed on both sides of the dispute.

Thus, both proabortionists and antiabortionists have tended to abstract the question of whether abortion is wrong to that of whether it is wrong to destroy a fetus, just as though the rights of another person were not necessarily involved. This mistaken abstraction has led to the almost universal assumption that if a fetus is a human being, with a right to life, then it follows immediately that abortion is wrong (except perhaps when necessary to save the woman's life), and that it ought to be prohibited. It has also been generally assumed that unless the question about the status of the fetus is answered, the moral status of abortion cannot possibly be determined.

Two recent papers, one by B. A. Brody,[2] and one by Judith Thomson,[3] have attempted to settle the question of whether abortion ought to be prohibited apart from the question of whether or not the fetus is human. Brody examines the possibility that the following two statements are compatible: (1) that abortion is the taking of innocent human life, and therefore wrong; and (2) that nevertheless it ought not to be prohibited by law, at least under the present circumstances.[4] Not surprisingly, Brody finds it impossible to reconcile these two statements since, as he rightly argues, none of the unfortunate side effects of the prohibition of abortion is bad enough to justify legalizing the *wrongful* taking of human life. He is mistaken, however, in concluding that the incompatibility of (1) and (2), in itself, shows that "the legal problem about abortion cannot be resolved independently of the status of the fetus problem" (p. 369).

What Brody fails to realize is that (1) embodies the questionable assumption that if a fetus is a human being, then of course abortion is morally wrong, and that an attack on *this* assumption is more promising, as a way of reconciling the humanity of the fetus with the claim that laws prohibiting abortion are unjustified, than is an attack on the assumption that if abortion is the wrongful killing of innocent human beings then it ought to be prohibited. He thus overlooks the possibility that a fetus may have a right to life and abortion still be morally permissible, in that the right of a woman to terminate an unwanted pregnancy might override the right of the fetus to be kept alive. The immorality of abortion is no more demonstrated by the humanity of the fetus, in itself, than the immorality of killing in self-defense is demonstrated by the fact that the assailant is a human being. Neither is it demonstrated by the *innocence* of the fetus, since there may be situations in which the killing of innocent human beings is justified.

It is perhaps not surprising that Brody fails to spot this assumption, since it has been accepted with little or no argument by nearly everyone who has written on the morality of abortion. John Noonan is correct in saying that "the fundamental question in the long history of abortion is, How do you determine the humanity of a being?"[5] He summarizes his own antiabortion argument, which is a version of the official position of the Catholic Church, as follows:

> . . . it is wrong to kill humans, however poor, weak, defenseless, and lacking in opportunity to develop their potential they may be. It is therefore morally wrong to kill Biafrans. Similarly, it is morally wrong to kill embryos.[6]

Noonan bases his claim that fetuses are human upon what he calls the theologians' criterion of humanity: that whoever is conceived of human beings is human. But although he argues at length for the appropriateness of this criterion, he never questions the assumption that if a fetus is human then abortion is wrong for exactly the same reason that murder is wrong.

Judith Thomson is, in fact, the only writer I am aware of who has seriously questioned this assumption; she has argued that, even if we grant the antiabortionist his claim that a fetus is a human being, with the same right to life as any other human being, we can still demonstrate that, in at least some and perhaps most cases, a woman is under no moral obligation to complete an unwanted pregnancy.[7] Her argument is worth examining, since if it holds up it may enable us to establish the moral permissibility of abortion without becoming involved in problems about what entitles an entity to be considered human, and accorded full moral rights. To be able to do this would be a great gain in the power and simplicity of the proabortion position, since, although I will argue that these problems can be solved at least as decisively as can any other moral problem, we should certainly be pleased to be able to avoid having to solve them as part of the justification of abortion.

On the other hand, even if Thomson's argument does not hold up, her insight, i.e., that it requires *argument* to show that if fetuses are human then abortion is properly classified as murder, is an extremely valuable one. The assumption she attacks is particularly invidious, for it amounts to the decision that it is appropriate, in deciding the moral status of abortion, to leave the rights of the pregnant woman out of consideration entirely, except possibly when her life is threatened. Obviously, this will not do; determining what moral rights, if any, a fetus possesses is only the first step in determining the moral status of abortion. Step two, which is at least equally essential, is finding a just solution to the conflict between whatever rights the fetus may have, and the rights of the woman who is unwillingly pregnant. While the historical error has been to pay far too little attention to the second step, Ms. Thomson's suggestion is that if we look at the second step first we may find that a woman has a right to obtain an abortion *regardless* of what rights the fetus has.

Our own inquiry will also have two stages. In Section I, we will consider whether or not it is possible to establish that abortion is morally permissible even on the assumption that a fetus is an entity with a full-fledged right to life. I will argue that in fact this cannot be established, at least not with the conclusiveness which is essential to our hopes of convincing those who are skeptical about the morality of abortion, and that we therefore cannot avoid dealing with the question of whether or not a fetus really does have the same right to life as a (more fully developed) human being.

In Section II, I will propose an answer to this question, namely, that a fetus cannot be considered a member of the moral community, the set of beings with full and equal moral rights, for the simple reason that it is not a person, and that it is personhood, and not genetic humanity, i.e., humanity as defined by Noonan, which is the basis for membership in this community. I will argue that a fetus, whatever its stage of development, satisfies none of the basic criteria of personhood, and is not even enough *like* a person to be accorded even some of the same rights on the basis of this resemblance. Nor, as we will see, is a fetus's *potential* personhood a threat to the morality of abortion, since, whatever the rights of potential people may be, they are invariably overridden in any conflict with the moral rights of actual people.

I

We turn now to Professor Thomson's case for the claim that even if a fetus has full moral rights, abortion is still morally permissible, at least sometimes, and for some reasons other than to save the woman's life. Her argument is based upon a clever, but I think faulty, analogy. She asks us to picture ourselves waking up one day, in bed with a famous violinist. Imagine that you have been kidnapped, and your bloodstream hooked up to that of the violinist, who happens to have an ailment which will certainly kill him unless he is permitted to share your kidneys for a period of nine months. No one else can save him, since you alone have the right type of blood. He will be unconscious all that time, and you will have to stay in bed with him, but after the nine months are over he may be unplugged, completely cured, that is, provided that you have cooperated.

Now then, she continues, what are your obligations in this situation? The antiabortionist, if he is consistent, will have to say that you are obligated to stay in bed with the violinist: for all people have a right to life, and violinists are people, and therefore it would be murder for you to disconnect yourself from him and let him die (p. 49). But this is outrageous, and so there must be something wrong with the same argument when it is applied to abortion. It would certainly be commendable of you to agree to save the violinist, but it is absurd to suggest that your refusal to do so would be murder. His right to life does not obligate you to do whatever is required to keep him alive; nor does it justify anyone else in forcing you to do so. A law which required you to stay in bed with the violinist would clearly be an unjust law, since it is no proper function of the law to force unwilling people to make huge sacrifices for the sake of other people toward whom they have no such prior obligation.

Thomson concludes that, if this analogy is an apt one, then we can grant the antiabortionist his claim that a fetus is a human being, and still hold that it is at least sometimes the case that a pregnant woman has the right to refuse to be a Good Samaritan towards the fetus, i.e., to obtain an abortion. For there is a great gap between the claim that x has a right to life, and the claim that y is obligated to do whatever is necessary to keep x alive, let alone that he ought to be forced to do so. It is y's duty to keep x alive only if he has somehow contracted a *special* obligation to do so; and a woman who is unwillingly pregnant, e.g., who was raped, has done nothing which obligates her to make the enormous sacrifice which is necessary to preserve the conceptus.

This argument is initially quite plausible, and in the extreme case of pregnancy due to rape it is probably conclusive. Difficulties arise, however, when we try to specify more exactly the range of cases in which abortion is clearly justifiable even on the assumption that the fetus is human. Professor Thomson considers it a virtue of her argument that it does not enable us to conclude that abortion is *always* permissible. It would, she says, be "indecent" for a woman in her seventh month to obtain an abortion just to avoid having to postpone a trip to Europe. On the other hand, her argument enables us to see that "a sick and desperately frightened schoolgirl pregnant due to rape may *of course* choose abortion, and that any law which rules this out is an insane law" (p. 65). So far, so good; but what are we to say about the woman who becomes pregnant not through rape but as a result of her own carelessness, or because of contraceptive failure, or who gets pregnant intentionally and then changes her mind about wanting a child? With respect to such cases, the violinist analogy is of much less use to the defender of the woman's right to obtain an abortion.

Indeed, the choice of a pregnancy due to rape, as an example of a case in which abortion is permissible even if a fetus is considered a human being, is extremely significant; for it is only in the case of pregnancy due to rape that the woman's situation is adequately analogous to the violinist case for our intuitions about the latter to transfer convincingly. The crucial difference between a pregnancy due to rape and the *normal* case of an unwanted pregnancy is that in the normal case we cannot claim that the woman is in no way responsible for her predicament; she could have remained chaste, or taken her pills more faithfully, or abstained on dangerous days, and so on. If, on the other hand, you are kidnapped by strangers, and hooked up to a strange violinist, then you are free of any shred of responsibility for the situation, on the basis of which it would be argued that you are obligated to keep the violinist alive. Only when her pregnancy is due to rape is a woman clearly just as nonresponsible.[8]

Consequently, there is room for the antiabortionist to argue that in the normal case of unwanted pregnancy a woman has, by her own actions, assumed responsibility for the fetus. For if x behaves in a way which he could have avoided, and which he knows involves, let us say, a 1 percent chance of bringing into existence a human being, with a right to life, and does so knowing that if this should happen then that human being will perish unless x does certain things to keep him alive, then it is by no means clear that when it does happen x is free of any obligation to what he knew in advance would be required to keep that human being alive.

The plausibility of such an argument is enough to show that the Thomson analogy can provide a clear and persuasive defense of a woman's right to obtain an abortion only with respect to those cases in which the woman is in no way responsible for her pregnancy, e.g., where it is due to rape. In all other cases, we would almost certainly conclude that it was necessary to look carefully at the particular circumstances in order to determine the extent of the woman's responsibility, and hence the extent of her obligation. This is an extremely unsatisfactory outcome, from the viewpoint of the opponents of restrictive abortion laws, most of whom are convinced that a woman has a right to obtain an abortion regardless of how and why she got pregnant.

Of course a supporter of the violinist analogy might point out that it is absurd to suggest that forgetting her pill one day might be sufficient to obligate a woman to complete an unwanted pregnancy. And indeed it *is* absurd to suggest this. As we shall see, the moral right to obtain an abortion is not in the least dependent upon the extent to which the woman is responsible for her pregnancy. But unfortunately, once we allow the assumption that a fetus has full moral rights, we cannot avoid taking this absurd suggestion seriously. Perhaps we can make this point more clear by altering the violinist story just enough to make it more analogous to a normal unwanted pregnancy and less to a pregnancy due to rape, and then seeing whether it is still obvious that you are not obligated to stay in bed with the fellow.

Suppose, then, that violinists are peculiarly prone to the sort of illness the only cure for which is the use of someone else's bloodstream for nine months, and that because of this there has been formed a society of music lovers who agree that whenever a violinist is stricken they will draw lots and the loser will, by some means, be made the one and only person capable of saving him. Now then, would you be obligated to cooperate in curing the violinist if you had voluntarily joined this society, knowing the possible consequences, and then your name had been drawn and you had been kidnapped? Admittedly, you did not promise ahead of time that you would, but you did deliberately place yourself in a position in which it might happen that a human life would be lost if you did not. Surely this is at least a prima facie reason for supposing that you have an obligation to stay in bed with the violinist. Suppose that you had gotten your name drawn deliberately; surely *that* would be quite a strong reason for thinking that you had such an obligation.

It might be suggested that there is one important disanalogy between the modified violinist case and the case of an unwanted pregnancy, which makes the woman's responsibility significantly less, namely, the fact that the fetus *comes into existence* as the result of the woman's actions. This fact might give her a right to refuse to keep it alive, whereas she would not have had this right had it existed previously, independently, and then as a result of her actions become dependent upon her for its survival.

My own intuition, however, is that *x* has no more right to bring into existence, either deliberately or as a foreseeable result of actions he could have avoided, a being with full moral rights *(y)*, and then refuse to do what he knew beforehand would be required to keep that being alive, than he has to enter into an agreement with an existing person, whereby he may be called upon to save that person's life, and then refuse to do so when so called upon. Thus, *x*'s responsibility for *y*'s existence does not seem to lessen his obligation to keep *y* alive, if he is also responsible for *y*'s being in a situation in which only he can save him.

Whether or not this intuition is entirely correct, it brings us back once again to the conclusion that once we allow the assumption that a fetus has full moral rights it becomes an extremely complex and difficult question whether and when abortion is justifiable. Thus the Thomson analogy cannot help us produce a clear and persuasive proof of the moral permissibility of abortion. Nor will the opponents of the restrictive laws thank us for anything less; for their conviction (for the most part) is that abortion is obviously *not* a morally serious and extremely unfortunate, even though sometimes justified act, comparable to killing in self-defense or to letting the violinist die, but rather is closer to being a morally neutral act, like cutting one's hair.

The basis of this conviction, I believe, is the realization that a fetus is not a person, and thus does not have a full-fledged right to life. Perhaps the reason why this claim has been so inadequately defended is that it seems self-evident to those who accept it. And so it is, insofar as it follows from what I take to be perfectly obvious claims about the nature of personhood, and about the proper grounds for ascribing moral rights, claims which ought, indeed, to be obvious to both the friends and foes of abortion. Nevertheless, it is worth examining these claims, and showing how they demonstrate the moral innocuousness of abortion, since this apparently has not been adequately done before.

II

The question which we must answer in order to produce a satisfactory solution to the problem of the moral status of abortion is this: How are we to define the moral community, the set of beings with full and equal moral rights, such that we can decide whether a human fetus is a member of this community or not? What sort of entity, exactly, has the inalienable rights to life, liberty, and the pursuit of happiness? Jefferson attributed these rights to all *men,* and it may or may not be fair to suggest that he intended to attribute them *only* to men. Perhaps he ought to have attributed them to all human beings. If so, then we arrive, first, at Noonan's problem of defining what makes a being human, and second, at the equally vital question which Noonan does not consider, namely, What reason is there for identifying the moral community with the set of all human beings, in whatever way we have chosen to define that term?

ON THE DEFINITION OF "HUMAN"

One reason why this vital second question is so frequently overlooked in the debate over the moral status of abortion is that the term "human" has two distinct, but not often distinguished, senses. This fact results in a slide of meaning, which serves to conceal the fallaciousness of the traditional argument that since (1) it is wrong to kill innocent human beings, and (2) fetuses are innocent human beings, then (3) it is wrong to kill fetuses. For if "human" is used in the same sense in both (1) and (2) then, whichever of the two senses is meant, one of these premises is question-begging. And if it is used in two different senses, then of course the conclusion doesn't follow.

Thus, (1) is a self-evident moral truth,[9] and avoids begging the question about abortion, only if "human being" is used to mean something like "a full-fledged member of the moral community." (It may or may not also be meant to refer exclusively to members of the species *Homo sapiens*.) We may call this the *moral* sense of "human." It is not to be confused with what we will call the *genetic* sense, i.e., the sense in which any member of the species is a human being, and no member of any other species could be. If (1) is acceptable only if the moral sense is intended, (2) is non-question-begging only if what is intended is the genetic sense.

In "Deciding Who Is Human," Noonan argues for the classification of fetuses with human beings by pointing to the presence of the full genetic code, and the potential capacity for rational thought (p. 135). It is clear that what he needs to show, for his version of the traditional argument to be valid, is that fetuses are human in the moral sense, the sense in which it is analytically true that all human beings have full moral rights. But, in the absence of any argument showing that whatever is genetically human is also morally human, and he gives none, nothing more than genetic humanity can be demonstrated by the presence of the human genetic code. And, as we will see, the *potential* capacity for rational thought can at most show that an entity has the potential for *becoming* human in the moral sense.

DEFINING THE MORAL COMMUNITY

Can it be established that genetic humanity is sufficient for moral humanity? I think that there are very good reasons for not defining the moral community in this way. I would like to suggest an alternative way of defining the moral community, which I will argue for only to the extent of explaining why it is, or should be, self-evident. The suggestion is simply that the moral community consists of all and only *people*, rather than all and only human beings;[10] and probably the best way of demonstrating its self-evidence is by considering the concept of personhood, to see what sorts of entity are and are not persons, and what the decision that a being is or is not a person implies about its moral rights.

What moral characteristics entitle an entity to be considered a person? This is obviously not the place to attempt a complete analysis of the concept of personhood, but we do not need such a fully adequate analysis just to determine whether and why a fetus is or isn't a person. All we need is a rough and approximate list of the most basic criteria of personhood, and some idea of which, or how many, of these an entity must satisfy in order to properly be considered a person.

In searching for such criteria, it is useful to look beyond the set of people with whom we are acquainted, and ask how we would decide whether a totally alien being was a person or not. (For we have no right to assume that genetic humanity is necessary for personhood.) Imagine a space traveler who lands on an unknown planet and encounters a race of beings utterly unlike any he has ever seen or heard of. If he wants to be sure of behaving morally toward these beings, he has to somehow decide whether they are people, and hence have full moral rights, or whether they are the sort of thing which he need not feel guilty about treating as, for example, a source of food.

How should he go about making this decision? If he has some anthropological background he might look for such things as religion, art, and the manufacturing of tools, weapons, or shelters, since these factors have been used to distinguish our human from our prehuman ancestors, in what seems to be closer to the moral than the genetic sense of "human." And no doubt he would be right to consider the presence of such factors as good evidence that the alien beings were people, and morally human. It would, however, be overly anthropocentric of him to take the absence of these things as adequate evidence that they were not, since we can imagine people who have progressed beyond, or evolved without ever developing, these cultural characteristics.

I suggest that the traits which are most central to the concept of personhood, or humanity in the moral sense, are, very roughly, the following:

1. Consciousness (of objects and events external and/or internal to the being), and in particular the capacity to feel pain;
2. Reasoning (the *developed* capacity to solve new and relatively complex problems);
3. Self-motivated activity (activity which is relatively independent of either genetic or direct external control);
4. The capacity to communicate, by whatever means, messages of an indefinite variety of types, that is, not just with an indefinite number

of possible contents, but on indefinitely many possible topics;

5. The presence of self-concepts, and self-awareness, either individual or racial, or both.

Admittedly, there are apt to be a great many problems involved in formulating precise definitions of these criteria, let alone in developing universally valid behavioral criteria for deciding when they apply. But I will assume that both we and our explorer know approximately what (1)–(5) mean, and that he is also able to determine whether or not they apply. How, then, should he use his findings to decide whether or not the alien beings are people? We needn't suppose that an entity must have *all* of these attributes to be properly considered a person; (1) and (2) alone may well be sufficient for personhood, and quite probably (1)–(3) are sufficient. Neither do we need to insist that any one of these criteria is *necessary* for personhood, although once again (1) and (2) look like fairly good candidates for necessary conditions, as does (3), if "activity" is construed so as to include the activity of reasoning.

All we need to claim, to demonstrate that a fetus is not a person, is that any being which satisfies *none* of (1)–(5) is certainly not a person. I consider this claim to be so obvious that I think anyone who denied it, and claimed that a being which satisfied none of (1)–(5) was a person all the same, would thereby demonstrate that he had no notion at all of what a person is—perhaps because he had confused the concept of a person with that of genetic humanity. If the opponents of abortion were to deny the appropriateness of these five criteria, I do not know what further arguments would convince them. We would probably have to admit that our conceptual schemes were indeed irreconcilably different, and that our dispute could not be settled objectively.

I do not expect this to happen, however, since I think that the concept of a person is one which is very nearly universal (to people), and that it is common to both proabortionists and antiabortionists, even though neither group has fully realized the relevance of this concept to the resolution of their dispute. Furthermore, I think that on reflection even the antiabortionists ought to agree not only that (1)–(5) are central to the concept of personhood, but also that it is a part of this concept that all and only people have full moral rights. The concept of a person is in part a moral concept; once we have admitted that *x* is a person we have recognized, even if we have not agreed to respect, *x*'s right to be treated as a member of the moral community. It is true that the claim that *x* is a *human being* is more commonly voiced as part of an appeal to treat *x* decently than is the claim that *x* is a person, but this is either because "human being" is here used in the sense which implies personhood, or because the genetic and moral senses of "human" have been confused.

Now if (1)–(5) are indeed the primary criteria of personhood, then it is clear that genetic humanity is neither necessary nor sufficient for establishing that an entity is a person. Some human beings are not people, and there may well be people who are not human beings. A man or woman whose consciousness has been permanently obliterated but who remains alive is a human being which is no longer a person; defective human beings, with no appreciable mental capacity, are not and presumably never will be people; and a fetus is a human being which is not yet a person, and which therefore cannot coherently be said to have full moral rights. Citizens of the next century should be prepared to recognize highly advanced, self-aware robots or computers, should such be developed, and intelligent inhabitants of other worlds, should such be found, as people in the fullest sense, and to respect their moral rights. But to ascribe full moral rights to an entity which is not a person is as absurd as to ascribe moral obligations and responsibilities to such an entity.

FETAL DEVELOPMENT AND THE RIGHT TO LIFE

Two problems arise in the application of these suggestions for the definition of the moral community to the determination of the precise moral status of a human fetus. Given that the paradigm example of a person is a normal adult being, then (1) How like this paradigm, in particular how far advanced since conception, does a human being need to be before it begins to have a right to life by virtue, not of being fully a person as of yet, but of being *like* a person? and (2) To what extent, if any, does the fact that a fetus has the *potential* for becoming a person endow it with some of the same rights? Each of these questions requires some comment.

In answering the first question, we need not attempt a detailed consideration of the moral rights of organisms which are not developed enough, aware enough, intelligent enough, etc., to be considered people, but which resemble people in some respects. It does seem reasonable to suggest that the more like a person, in the relevant aspects, a being is, the stronger is the case for regarding it as having a right to life, and indeed the stronger its right to life is. Thus we ought to take seriously the suggestion that, insofar as "the human individual develops biologically in a continuous fashion . . . the rights of a human person might develop in the same way."[11] But we must keep in mind that the attributes which are relevant in determining whether or not an entity is enough like a person to be regarded as having some of the same moral rights are no different from those which are relevant to determining whether or not it is fully a person—i.e., are not different from (1)–(5)—and that being genetically human, or having recognizably human facial and other physical features, or detectable brain activity, or the capacity to survive outside the uterus, are simply not among these relevant attributes.

Thus it is clear that even though a seven- or eight-month fetus has features which make it apt to arouse in us almost the same powerful protective instinct as is commonly aroused by a small infant, nevertheless it is not significantly more personlike than is a very small embryo. It is *somewhat* more personlike; it can apparently feel and respond to pain, and it may even have a rudimentary form of consciousness, insofar as its brain is quite active. Nevertheless, it seems safe to say that it is not fully conscious, in the way that an infant of a few months is, and that it cannot reason, or communicate messages of indefinitely many sorts, does not engage in self-motivated activity, and has no self-awareness. Thus, in the *relevant* respects, a fetus, even a fully developed one, is considerably less personlike than is the average mature mammal, indeed the average fish. And I think that a rational person must conclude that if the right to life of a fetus is to be based upon its resemblance to a person, then it cannot be said to have any more right to life than, let us say, a newborn guppy (which also seems to be capable of feeling pain), and that a right of that magnitude could never override a woman's right to obtain an abortion, at any stage of her pregnancy.

There may, of course, be other arguments in favor of placing legal limits upon the stage of pregnancy in which an abortion may be performed. Given the relative safety of the new techniques of artificially inducing labor during the third trimester, the danger to the woman's life or health is no longer such an argument. Neither is the fact that people tend to respond to the thought of abortion in the later stages of pregnancy with emotional repulsion, since mere emotional responses cannot take the place of moral reasoning in determining what ought to be permitted. Nor, finally, is the frequently heard argument that legalizing abortion, especially late in the pregnancy, may erode the level of respect for human life, leading, perhaps to an increase in unjustified euthanasia and other crimes. For this threat, if it is a threat, can be better met by educating people to the kinds of moral distinctions which we are making here than by limiting access to abortion (which limitation may, in its disregard for the rights of women, be just as damaging to the level of respect for human rights).

Thus, since the fact that even a fully developed fetus is not personlike enough to have any significant right to life on the basis of its person-likeness shows that no legal restrictions upon the stage of pregnancy in which an abortion may be performed can be justified on the grounds that we should protect the rights of the older fetus; and since there is no other apparent justification for such restrictions, we may conclude that they are entirely unjustified. Whether or not it would be *indecent* (whatever that means) for a woman in her seventh month to obtain an abortion just to avoid having to postpone a trip to Europe, it would not, in itself, be *immoral,* and therefore it ought to be permitted.

POTENTIAL PERSONHOOD AND THE RIGHT TO LIFE

We have seen that a fetus does not resemble a person in any way which can support the claim that it has even some of the same rights. But what about its *potential,* the fact that if nurtured and allowed to develop naturally it will very probably become a person? Doesn't that alone give it at least some right to life? It is hard to deny that the fact that an entity is a potential person is a strong prima facie reason for not destroying it; but we need not conclude from this that a potential person has a right to life, by virtue of that potential. It may be that our feeling that it is better, other things being equal, not to destroy a potential person is better explained by the fact that potential people are still (felt to be) an invaluable resource, not to be lightly squandered. Surely, if every speck of dust were a potential person, we would be much less apt to conclude that every potential person has a right to become actual.

Still, we do not need to insist that a potential person has no right to life whatever. There may well be something immoral, and not just imprudent, about wantonly destroying potential people, when doing so isn't necessary to protect anyone's rights. But even if a potential person does have some prima facie right to life, such a right could not possibly outweigh the right of a woman to obtain an abortion, since the rights of any actual person invariably outweigh those of any potential person, whenever the two conflict. Since this may not be immediately obvious in the case of a human fetus, let us look at another case.

Suppose that our space explorer falls into the hands of an alien culture, whose scientists decide to create a few hundred thousand or more human beings, by breaking his body into its component cells, and using these to create fully developed human beings, with, of course, his genetic code. We may imagine that each of these newly created men will have all of the original man's abilities, skills, knowledge, and so on, and also have an individual self-concept, in short that each of them will be a bona fide (though hardly unique) person. Imagine that the whole project will take only seconds, and that its chances of success are extremely high, and that our explorer knows all of this, and also knows that these people will be treated fairly. I maintain that in such a situation he would have every right to escape if he could, and thus to deprive all of these potential people of their potential lives; for his right to life outweighs all of theirs together, in spite of the fact that they are all genetically human, all innocent, and all have a very high probability of becoming people very soon, if only he refrains from action.

Indeed, I think he would have a right to escape even if it were not his life which the alien scientists planned to take, but only a year of his freedom, or, indeed, only a day. Nor would he be obligated to stay if he had gotten captured (thus bringing all these people-potentials into existence) because of his own carelessness, or even if he had done so deliberately, knowing the consequences. Regardless of how he got captured, he is not morally obligated to remain in captivity for *any* period of time for the sake of permitting any number of potential people to come into actuality, so great is the margin by which one actual person's right to liberty outweighs whatever rights to life even a hundred thousand potential people have. And it seems reasonable to conclude that the rights of a woman will outweigh by a similar margin whatever right to life a fetus may have by virtue of its potential personhood.

Thus, neither a fetus's resemblance to a person, nor its potential for becoming a person provides any basis whatever for the claim that it has any significant right to life. Consequently, a woman's right to protect her health, happiness, freedom, and even her life,[12] by terminating an unwanted pregnancy will always override whatever right to life it may be appropriate to ascribe to a fetus, even a fully developed one. And thus, in the absence of any overwhelming social need for every possible child, the laws which restrict the right to an abortion, or limit the period of pregnancy during which an abortion may be performed, are a wholly unjustified violation of a woman's most basic moral and constitutional rights.[13]

POSTSCRIPT ON INFANTICIDE

Since the publication of this [essay], many people have written to point out that my argument appears to justify not only abortion, but infanticide as well. For a new-born infant is not significantly more person-like than an advanced fetus, and consequently it would seem that if the destruction of the latter is permissible so too must be that of the former. Inasmuch as most people, regardless of how they feel about the morality of abortion, consider infanticide a form of murder, this might appear to represent a serious flaw in my argument.

Now, if I am right in holding that it is only people who have a full-fledged right to life, and who can be murdered, and if the criteria of personhood are as I have described them, then it obviously follows that killing a new-born infant isn't murder. It does *not* follow, however, that infanticide is permissible, for two reasons. In the first place, it would be wrong, at least in this country and in this period of history, and other things being equal, to kill a new-born infant, because even if its parents do not want it and would not suffer from its destruction, there are other people who would like to have it, and would, in all probability, be deprived of a great deal of pleasure by its destruction. Thus, infanticide is wrong for reasons analogous to those which make it wrong to wantonly destroy natural resources, or great works of art.

Secondly, most people, at least in this country, value infants and would much prefer that they be preserved, even if foster parents are not immediately available. Most of us would rather be taxed to support orphanages than allow unwanted infants to be destroyed. So long as there are people who want an infant preserved, and who are willing and able to provide the means of caring for it, under reasonably humane conditions, it is, *certeris paribus,* wrong to destroy it.

But, it might be replied, if this argument shows that infanticide is wrong, at least at this time and in this country, doesn't it also show that abortion is wrong? After all, many people value fetuses, are disturbed by their destruction, and would much prefer that they be preserved, even at some cost to themselves. Furthermore, as a potential source of pleasure to some foster family, a fetus is just as valuable as an infant. There is, however, a crucial difference between the two cases: so long as the fetus is unborn, its preservation, contrary to the wishes of the pregnant woman, violates her rights to freedom, happiness, and self-determination. Her rights override the rights of those who would like the fetus preserved, just as if someone's life or limb is threatened by a wild animal, his right to protect himself by destroying the animal overrides the rights of those who would prefer that the animal not be harmed.

The minute the infant is born, however, its preservation no longer violates any of its mother's rights, even if she wants it destroyed, because she is free to put it up for adoption. Consequently, while the moment of birth does not mark any sharp discontinuity in the degree to which an infant possesses the right to life, it does mark the end of its mother's right to determine its fate. Indeed, if abortion could be performed without killing the fetus, she would never possess the right to have the fetus destroyed, for the same reasons that she has no right to have an infant destroyed.

On the other hand, it follows from my argument that when an unwanted or defective infant is born into a society which cannot afford and/or is not willing to care for it, then its destruction is permissible. This conclusion will, no doubt, strike many people as heartless and immoral; but remember that the very existence of people who feel this way, and who are willing and able to provide care for unwanted infants, is reason enough to conclude that they should be preserved.

NOTES

1. For example, Roger Wertheimer, who in "Understanding the Abortion Argument" (*Philosophy and Public Affairs,* 1, No. 1 [Fall, 1971], 67–95), argues that the problem of the moral status of abortion is insoluble, in that the dispute over the status of the fetus is not a question of fact at all, but only a question of how one responds to the facts.

2. B. A. Brody, "Abortion and the Law," *The Journal of Philosophy,* 68, No. 12 (June 17, 1971), 357–69.

3. Judith Thomson, "A Defense of Abortion," *Philosophy and Public Affairs,* 1, No. 1 (Fall, 1971), 47–66.

4. I have abbreviated these statements somewhat, but not in a way which affects the argument.

5. John Noonan, "Abortion and the Catholic Church: A Summary History," *Natural Law Forum,* 12 (1967), 125.

6. John Noonan, "Deciding Who Is Human," *Natural Law Forum,* 13 (1968), 134.

7. "A Defense of Abortion."

8. We may safely ignore the fact that she might have avoided getting raped, e.g., by carrying a gun, since by similar means you might likewise have avoided getting kidnapped, and in neither case does the victim's failure to take all possible precautions against a highly unlikely event (as opposed to reasonable precautions against a rather likely event) mean that he is morally responsible for what happens.

9. Of course, the principle that it is (always) wrong to kill innocent human beings is in need of many other modifications, e.g., that it may be permissible to do so to save a greater number of other innocent human beings, but we may safely ignore these complications here.

10. From here on, we will use "human" to mean genetically human, since the moral sense seems closely connected to, and perhaps derived from, the assumption that genetic humanity is sufficient for membership in the moral community.

11. Thomas L. Hayes, "A Biological View," *Commonweal,* 85 (March 17, 1967), 677–78; quoted by Daniel Callahan, in *Abortion, Law, Choice, and Morality* (London: Macmillan & Co., 1970).

12. That is, insofar as the death rate, for the woman, is higher for childbirth than for early abortion.

13. My thanks to the following people, who were kind enough to read and criticize an earlier version of this paper: Herbert Gold, Gene Glass, Anne Lauterbach, Judith Thomson, Mary Mothersill, and Timothy Binkley.

UNITED STATES SUPREME COURT

Roe v. Wade: Majority Opinion and Dissent

[JUSTICE BLACKMUN delivered the opinion of the Court.]

It is . . . apparent that at common law, at the time of the adoption of our Constitution, and throughout the major portion of the nineteenth century, abortion was viewed with less disfavor than under most American statutes currently in effect. Phrasing it another way, a woman enjoyed a substantially broader right to terminate a pregnancy than she does in most states today. At least with respect to the early stage of pregnancy, and very possibly without such a limitation, the opportunity to make this choice was present in this country well into the nineteenth century. Even later, the law continued for some time to treat less punitively an abortion procured in early pregnancy. . . .

Three reasons have been advanced to explain historically the enactment of criminal abortion laws in the nineteenth century and to justify their continued existence.

It has been argued occasionally that these laws were the product of a Victorian social concern to discourage illicit sexual conduct. Texas, however, does not advance this justification in the present case, and it appears that no court or commentator has taken the argument seriously. . . .

A second reason is concerned with abortion as a medical procedure. When most criminal abortion laws were first enacted, the procedure was a hazardous one for the woman. This was particularly true prior to the development of antisepsis. Antiseptic techniques, of course, were based on discoveries by Lister, Pasteur, and others first announced in 1867, but were not generally accepted and employed until about the turn of the century. Abortion mortality was high. Even after 1900, and perhaps until as late as the development of antibiotics in the 1940s, standard modern techniques such as dilation and curettage were not nearly so safe as they are today. Thus it has been argued that a state's real concern in enacting a criminal abortion law was to protect the pregnant woman, that is, to restrain her from submitting to a procedure that placed her life in serious jeopardy.

Modern medical techniques have altered this situation. Appellants and various *amici* refer to medical data indicating that abortion in early pregnancy, that is, prior to the end of first trimester, although not without its risk, is now relatively safe. Mortality rates for women undergoing early abortions, where the procedure is legal, appear to be as low as or lower than the rates for normal childbirth. Consequently, any interest of the state in protecting the woman from an inherently hazardous procedure, except when it would be equally dangerous for her to forgo it, has largely disappeared. Of course, important state interests in the area of health and medical standards do remain. The state has a legitimate interest in seeing to it that abortion, like any other medical procedure, is performed under circumstances that insure maximum safety for the patient. This interest obviously extends at least to the performing physician and his staff, to the facilities involved, to the availability of after-care, and to adequate provision for any complication or emergency that might arise. The prevalence of high mortality rates at illegal "abortion mills" strengthens, rather than weakens, the state's interest in regulating the conditions under which abortions are performed. Moreover, the risk to the woman increases as her pregnancy continues. Thus the state retains a definite in-

Reprinted from 410 *United States Reports* 113; decided January 22, 1973.

terest in protecting the woman's own health and safety when an abortion is performed at a late stage of pregnancy.

The third reason is the state's interest—some phrase it in terms of duty—in protecting prenatal life. Some of the argument for this justification rests on the theory that a new human life is present from the moment of conception. The state's interest and general obligation to protect life then extends, it is argued, to prenatal life. Only when the life of the pregnant mother herself is at stake, balanced against the life she carries within her, should the interest of the embryo or fetus not prevail. Logically, of course, a legitimate state interest in this area need not stand or fall on acceptance of the belief that life begins at conception or at some other point prior to live birth. In assessing the state's interest, recognition may be given to the less rigid claim that as long as at least *potential* life is involved, the state may assert interests beyond the protection of the pregnant woman alone.

Parties challenging state abortion laws have sharply disputed in some courts the contention that a purpose of these laws, when enacted, was to protect prenatal life. Pointing to the absence of legislative history to support the contention, they claim that most state laws were designed solely to protect the woman. Because medical advances have lessened this concern, at least with respect to abortion in early pregnancy, they argue that with respect to such abortions the laws can no longer be justified by any state interest. There is some scholarly support for this view of original purpose. The few states courts called upon to interpret their laws in the late nineteenth and early twentieth centuries did focus on the state's interest in protecting the woman's health rather than in preserving the embryo and fetus. . . .

The Constitution does not explicitly mention any right of privacy. In a line of decisions, however, going back perhaps as far as *Union Pacific R. Co. v. Botsford* (1891), the Court has recognized that a right of personal privacy, or a guarantee of certain areas or zones of privacy, does exist under the Constitution. In varying contexts the Court or individual Justices have indeed found at least the roots of that right in the First Amendment, . . . in the Fourth and Fifth Amendments, . . . in the penumbras of the Bill of Rights, . . . in the Ninth Amendment, . . . or in the concept of liberty guaranteed by the first section of the Fourteenth Amendment. . . . These decisions make it clear that only personal rights that can be deemed "fundamental" or "implicit in the concept of ordered liberty" . . .

are included in this guarantee of personal privacy. They also make it clear that the right has some extension to activities relating to marriage, . . . procreation, . . . contraception, . . . family relationships, . . . and child rearing and education. . . .

This right of privacy, whether it be founded in the Fourteenth Amendment's concept of personal liberty and restrictions upon state action, as we feel it is, or, as the District Court determined, in the Ninth Amendment's reservation of rights to the people, is broad enough to encompass a woman's decision whether or not to terminate her pregnancy. . . .

Appellants and some *amici* argue that the woman's right is absolute and that she is entitled to terminate her pregnancy at whatever time, in whatever way, and for whatever reason she alone chooses. With this we do not agree. Appellants' arguments that Texas either has no valid interest at all in regulating the abortion decision, or no interest strong enough to support any limitation upon the woman's sole determination, is unpersuasive. The Court's decisions recognizing a right of privacy also acknowledge that some state regulation in areas protected by that right is appropriate. As noted above, a state may properly assert important interests in safeguarding health, in maintaining medical standards, and in protecting potential life. At some point in pregnancy, these respective interests become sufficiently compelling to sustain regulation of the factors that govern the abortion decision. The privacy rights involved, therefore, cannot be said to be absolute. . . .

We therefore conclude that the right of personal privacy includes the abortion decision, but that this right is not unqualified and must be considered against important state interests in regulation.

We note that those federal and state courts that have recently considered abortion law challenges have reached the same conclusion. . . .

Although the results are divided, most of these courts have agreed that the right of privacy, however based, is broad enough to cover the abortion decision; that the right, nonetheless, is not absolute and is subject to some limitations; and that at some point the state interests as to protection of health, medical standards, and prenatal life, become dominant. We agree with this approach. . . .

The appellee and certain *amici* argue that the fetus is a "person" within the language and meaning of the Fourteenth Amendment. In support of this they outline at length and in detail the well-known facts of fetal development. If this suggestion of personhood is established, the appellant's case, of course, collapses, for the fetus's right to life is then guaranteed specifically by the Amendment. The appellant conceded as much on reargument. On the other hand, the appellee conceded on reargument that no case could be cited that holds that a fetus is a person within the meaning of the Fourteenth Amendment. . . .

All this, together with our observation, *supra,* that throughout the major portion of the nineteenth century prevailing legal abortion practices were far freer than they are today, persuades us that the word "person," as used in the Fourteenth Amendment, does not include the unborn. . . . Indeed, our decision in *United States v. Vuitch* (1971), inferentially is to the same effect, for we there would not have indulged in statutory interpretation favorable to abortion in specified circumstances if the necessary consequence was the termination of life entitled to Fourteenth Amendment protection.

. . . As we have intimated above, it is reasonable and appropriate for a state to decide that at some point in time another interest, that of health of the mother or that of potential human life, becomes significantly involved. The woman's privacy is no longer sole and any right of privacy she possesses must be measured accordingly.

Texas urges that, apart from the Fourteenth Amendment, life begins at conception and is present throughout pregnancy, and that, therefore, the state has a compelling interest in protecting that life from and after conception. We need not resolve the difficult question of when life begins. When those trained in the respective disciplines of medicine, philosophy, and theology are unable to arrive at any consensus, the judiciary, at this point in the development of man's knowledge, is not in a position to speculate as to the answer.

It should be sufficient to note briefly the wide divergence of thinking on this most sensitive and difficult question. There has always been strong support for the view that life does not begin until live birth. This was the belief of the Stoics. It appears to be the predominant, though not the unanimous, attitude of the Jewish faith. It may be taken to represent also the position of a large segment of the Protestant community, insofar as that can be ascertained; organized groups that have taken a formal position on the abortion issue have generally regarded abortion as a matter for the conscience of the individual and her family. As we have noted, the common law found greater significance in quickening. Physicians and their scientific colleagues have regarded that event with less interest and have tended to focus either upon conception or upon live birth or upon the interim point at which the fetus becomes "viable," that is, potentially able to live outside the mother's womb, albeit with artificial aid. Viability is usually placed at about seven months (28 weeks) but may occur earlier, even at 24 weeks. . . .

In areas other than criminal abortion the law has been reluctant to endorse any theory that life, as we recognize it, begins before live birth or to accord legal rights to the unborn except in narrowly defined situations and except when the rights are contingent upon live birth. . . . In short, the unborn have never been recognized in the law as persons in the whole sense.

In view of all this, we do not agree that, by adopting one theory of life, Texas may override the rights of the pregnant woman that are at stake. We repeat, however, that the state does have an important and legitimate interest in preserving and protecting the health of the pregnant woman, whether she be a resident of the state or a nonresident who seeks medical consultation and treatment there, and that it has still *another* important and legitimate interest in protecting the potentiality of human life. These interests are separate and distinct. Each grows in substantiality as the woman approaches term and, at a point during pregnancy, each becomes "compelling."

With respect to the state's important and legitimate interest in the health of the mother, the "compelling" point, in the light of present medical knowledge, is at approximately the end of the first trimester. This is so because of the now established medical fact . . . that until the end of the first trimester mortality in abortion is less than mortality in normal childbirth. It follows that, from and after this point, a state may regulate the abortion procedure to the extent that the regulation reasonably relates to the preservation and protection of maternal health. Examples of permissible state regulation in this area are requirements as to the qualifications of the person who is to perform the abortion; as to the licensure of that person; as to the facility in which the procedure is to be performed, that is, whether it must be a hospital or may be a clinic or some other place of less-than-hospital status; as to the licensing of the facility; and the like.

This means, on the other hand, that, for the period of pregnancy prior to this "compelling" point, the attending physician, in consultation with his patient, is free to determine, without regulation by the state, that in his medical judgment the patient's pregnancy should be terminated. If that decision is reached, the judgment may be effectuated by an abortion free of interference by the state.

With respect to the state's important and legitimate interest in potential life, the "compelling" point is at viability. This is so because the fetus then presumably has the capability of meaningful life outside the mother's womb. State regulation protective of fetal life after viability thus has both logical and biological justifications. If the state is interested in protecting fetal life after viability, it may go so far as to proscribe abortion during that period except when it is necessary to preserve the life or health of the mother. . . .

To summarize and repeat:

1. A state criminal abortion statute of the current Texas type, that excepts from criminality only a *lifesaving* procedure on behalf of the mother, without regard to pregnancy stage and without recognition of the other interests involved, is violative of the Due Process Clause of the Fourteenth Amendment.

(a) For the stage prior to approximately the end of the first trimester, the abortion decision and its effectuation must be left to the medical judgment of the pregnant woman's attending physician.

(b) For the stage subsequent to approximately the end of the first trimester, the state, in promoting its interest in the health of the mother, may, if it chooses, regulate the abortion procedure in ways that are reasonably related to maternal health.

(c) For the stage subsequent to viability the state, in promoting its interest in the potentiality of human life, may, if it chooses, regulate, and even proscribe, abortion except where it is necessary, in appropriate medical judgment, for the preservation of the life or health of the mother.

2. The state may define the term "physician" . . . to mean only a physician currently licensed by the state, and may proscribe any abortion by a person who is not a physician as so defined.

. . . The decision leaves the state free to place increasing restrictions on abortion as the period of pregnancy lengthens, so long as those restrictions are tailored to the recognized state interests. The decision vindicates the right of the physician to administer medical treatment according to his professional judgment up to the points where important state interests provide compelling justifications for intervention. Up to those points the abortion decision in all its aspects is inherently, and primarily, a medical decision, and basic responsibility for it must rest with the physician. If an individual practitioner abuses the privilege of exercising proper medical judgment, the usual remedies, judicial and intraprofessional, are available. . . .

[JUSTICE WHITE, with whom Justice Rehnquist joins, dissenting.]

At the heart of the controversy in these cases are those recurring pregnancies that pose no danger whatsoever to the life or health of the mother but are, nevertheless, unwanted for any one or more of a variety of reasons—convenience, family planning, economics, dislike of children, the embarrassment of illegitimacy, etc. The common claim before us is that for any one of such reasons, or for no reason at all, and without asserting or claiming any threat to life or health, any woman is entitled to an abortion at her request if she is able to find a medical advisor willing to undertake the procedure.

The Court for the most part sustains this position: During the period prior to the time the fetus becomes viable, the Constitution of the United States values the convenience, whim, or caprice of the putative mother more than the life or potential life of the fetus; the Constitution, therefore, guarantees the right to an abortion as against any state law or policy seeking to protect the fetus from an abortion not prompted by more compelling reasons of the mother.

With all due respect, I dissent. I find nothing in the language or history of the Constitution to support the Court's judgment. The Court simply fashions and announces a new constitutional right for pregnant mothers and, with scarcely any reason or authority for its action, invests that right with sufficient substance to override most existing state abortion statutes. The upshot is that the people and the legislatures of the 50 states are constitutionally disentitled to weigh the relative importance of the continued existence and development of the fetus, on the one hand, against a spectrum of possible impacts on the mother, on the other hand. As an exercise of raw judicial power, the

Court perhaps has authority to do what it does today; but in my view its judgment is an improvident and extravagant exercise of the power of judicial review that the Constitution extends to this Court.

The Court apparently values the convenience of the pregnant mother more than the continued existence and development of the life or potential life that she carries. Whether or not I might agree with that marshaling of values, I can in no event join the Court's judgment because I find no constitutional warrant for imposing such an order of priorities on the people and legislatures of the states. In a sensitive area such as this, involving as it does issues over which reasonable men may easily and heatedly differ, I cannot accept the Court's exercise of its clear power of choice by interposing a constitutional barrier to state efforts to protect human life and by investing mothers and doctors with the constitutionally protected right to exterminate it. This issue, for the most part, should be left with the people and to the political processes the people have devised to govern their affairs.

It is my view, therefore, that the Texas statute is not constitutionally infirm because it denies abortions to those who seek to serve only their convenience rather than to protect their life or health. Nor is this plaintiff, who claims no threat to her mental or physical health, entitled to assert the possible rights of those women whose pregnancy assertedly implicated their health. This, together with *United States v. Vuitch,* 402 U.S. 62 (1971), dictates reversal of the judgment of the District Court.

UNITED STATES SUPREME COURT

Planned Parenthood of Southeastern Pennsylvania v. Robert P. Casey, et al., etc.

[JUSTICE O'CONNOR, JUSTICE KENNEDY, and JUSTICE SOUTER announced the judgment of the Court and delivered the opinion of the Court.]

I

Liberty finds no refuge in a jurisprudence of doubt. Yet 19 years after our holding that the Constitution protects a woman's right to terminate her pregnancy in its early stages, *Roe v. Wade,* 410 U.S. 113 (1973), that definition of liberty is still questioned. Joining the respondents as *amicus curiae,* the United States, as it has done in five other cases in the last decade, again asks us to overrule *Roe*. . . .

At issue in these cases are five provisions of the Pennsylvania Abortion Control Act of 1982 as amended in 1988 and 1989. . . . The Act requires that a woman seeking an abortion give her informed consent prior to the abortion procedure, and specifies that she be provided with certain information at least 24 hours before the abortion is performed. For a minor to obtain an abortion, the Act requires the informed consent of one of her parents, but provides for a judicial bypass option if the minor does not wish to or cannot obtain a parent's consent. Another provision of the Act requires that, unless certain exceptions apply, a married woman seeking an abortion must sign a statement indicating that she has notified her husband of her intended abortion. The Act exempts compliance with these three requirements in the event of a "medical emergency," which is defined in § 3203 of the Act. In addition to the above provisions regulating the performance of abortions, the Act imposes certain reporting requirements on facilities that provide abortion services. . . .

We find it imperative to review once more the principles that define the rights of the woman and the legitimate authority of the State respecting the termination of pregnancies by abortion procedures.

Slip Opinion, Docket No. 91–744, 29 June 1992.

After considering the fundamental constitutional questions resolved by *Roe,* principles of institutional integrity, and the rule of *stare decisis,* we are led to conclude this: the essential holding of *Roe v. Wade* should be retained and once again reaffirmed.

It must be stated at the outset and with clarity that *Roe*'s essential holding, the holding we reaffirm, has three parts. First is a recognition of the right of the woman to choose to have an abortion before viability and to obtain it without undue interference from the State. Before viability, the State's interests are not strong enough to support a prohibition of abortion or the imposition of a substantial obstacle to the woman's effective right to elect the procedure. Second is a confirmation of the State's power to restrict abortions after fetal viability, if the law contains exceptions for pregnancies which endanger a woman's life or health. And third is the principle that the State has legitimate interests from the outset of the pregnancy in protecting the health of the woman and the life of the fetus that may become a child. These principles do not contradict one another; and we adhere to each.

II

Constitutional protection of the woman's decision to terminate her pregnancy derives from the Due Process Clause of the Fourteenth Amendment. It declares that no State shall "deprive any person of life, liberty, or property, without due process of law." The controlling word in the case before us is "liberty." . . .

It is a promise of the Constitution that there is a realm of personal liberty which the government may not enter. We have vindicated this principle before. Marriage is mentioned nowhere in the Bill of Rights and interracial marriage was illegal in most States in the 19th century, but the Court was no doubt correct in finding it to be an aspect of liberty protected against state interference by the substantive component of the Due Process Clause. . . .

In *Griswold,* we held that the Constitution does not permit a State to forbid a married couple to use contraceptives. That same freedom was later guaranteed, under the Equal Protection Clause, for unmarried couples. See *Eisenstadt v. Baird,* 405 U.S. 438 (1972). Constitutional protection was extended to the sale and distribution of contraceptives in *Carey v. Population Services International,* supra. It is settled now, as it was when the Court heard arguments in *Roe v. Wade,* that the Constitution places limits on a State's right to interfere with a person's most basic decisions about family and parenthood. . . .

The inescapable fact is that adjudication of substantive due process claims may call upon the Court in interpreting the Constitution to exercise that same capacity which by tradition courts always have exercised: reasoned judgment. Its boundaries are not susceptible of expression as a simple rule. That does not mean we are free to invalidate state policy choices with which we disagree; yet neither does it permit us to shrink from the duties of our office. . . .

It should be recognized, moreover, that in some critical respects the abortion decision is of the same character as the decision to use contraception, to which *Griswold v. Connecticut, Eisenstadt v. Baird,* and *Carey v. Population Services International,* afford constitutional protection. We have no doubt as to the correctness of those decisions. They support the reasoning in *Roe* relating to the woman's liberty because they involve personal decisions concerning not only the meaning of procreation but also human responsibility and respect for it. As with abortion, reasonable people will have differences of opinion about these matters. One view is based on such reverence for the wonder of creation that any pregnancy ought to be welcomed and carried to full term no matter how difficult it will be to provide for the child and ensure its well-being. Another is that the inability to provide for the nurture and care of the infant is a cruelty to the child and an anguish to the parent. These are intimate views with infinite variations, and their deep, personal character underlay our decisions in *Griswold, Eisenstadt,* and *Carey*. The same concerns are present where the woman confronts the reality that, perhaps despite her attempts to avoid it, she has become pregnant. . . .

III

. . . No evolution of legal principle has left *Roe*'s doctrinal footings weaker than they were in 1973. No development of constitutional law since the case was decided has implicitly or explicitly left *Roe* behind as a mere survivor of obsolete constitutional thinking. . . .

The *Roe* Court itself placed its holding in the succession of cases most prominently exemplified by *Griswold v. Connecticut,* 381 U.S. 479 (1965), see *Roe,* 410 U.S., at 152–153. When it is so seen, *Roe* is clearly in no jeopardy, since subsequent constitutional developments have neither disturbed, nor do they threaten to diminish, the scope of recognized protection accorded to the liberty relating to intimate relationships, the family, and decisions about whether or not to beget or bear a child. . . .

[However], time has overtaken some of *Roe*'s factual assumptions: advances in maternal health care allow for abortions safe to the mother later in pregnancy than was true in 1973, see *Akron I, supra,* at 429, n. 11, and advances in neonatal care have advanced viability to a point somewhat earlier. . . . But these facts go only to the scheme of time limits on the realization of competing interests, and the divergences from the factual premises of 1973 have no bearing on the validity of *Roe*'s central holding, that viability marks the earliest point at which the State's interest in fetal life is constitutionally adequate to justify a legislative ban on nontherapeutic abortions. The soundness or unsoundness of that constitutional judgment in no sense turns on whether viability occurs at approximately 28 weeks, as was usual at the time of *Roe,* at 23 to 24 weeks, as it sometimes does today, or at some moment even slightly earlier in pregnancy, as it may if fetal respiratory capacity can somehow be enhanced in the future. Whenever it may occur, the attainment of viability may continue to serve as the critical fact, just as it has done since *Roe* was decided; which is to say that no change in *Roe's* factual underpinning has left its central holding obsolete, and none supports an argument for overruling it. . . .

. . . Liberty must not be extinguished for want of a line that is clear. And it falls to us to give some real substance to the woman's liberty to determine whether to carry her pregnancy to full term.

We conclude the line should be drawn at viability, so that before that time the woman has a right to choose to terminate her pregnancy. We adhere to this principle for two reasons. First . . . is the doctrine of *stare decisis*. Any judicial act of line-drawing may seem somewhat arbitrary, but *Roe* was a reasoned statement, elaborated with great care. We have twice reaffirmed it in the face of great opposition. . . .

The second reason is that the concept of viability, as we noted in *Roe,* is the time at which there is a realistic possibility of maintaining and nourishing a life outside the womb, so that the independent existence of a second life can in reason and all fairness be the object of state protection that now overrides the rights of the woman. See *Roe v. Wade,* 410 U.S., at 163. Consistent with other constitutional norms, legislatures may draw lines which appear arbitrary without the necessity of offering a justification. But courts may not. We must justify the lines we draw. And there is no line other than viability which is more workable. To be sure, as we have said, there may be some medical developments that affect the precise point of viability, but this is an imprecision within tolerable limits given that the medical community and all those who must apply its discoveries will continue to explore the matter. The viability line also has, as a practical matter, an element of fairness. In some broad sense it might be said that a woman who fails to act before viability has consented to the State's intervention on behalf of the developing child.

The woman's right to terminate her pregnancy before viability is the most central principle of *Roe v. Wade*. It is a rule of law and a component of liberty we cannot renounce.

On the other side of the equation is the interest of the State in the protection of potential life. The *Roe* Court recognized the State's "important and legitimate interest in protecting the potentiality of human life." *Roe, supra,* at 162. The weight to be given this state interest, not the strength of the woman's interest, was the difficult question faced in *Roe*. We do not need to say whether each of us, had we been Members of the Court when the valuation of the State interest came before it as an original matter, would have concluded, as the *Roe* Court did, that its weight is insufficient to justify a ban on abortions prior to viability even when it is subject to certain exceptions. The matter is not before us in the first instance, and coming as it does after nearly 20 years of litigation in *Roe*'s wake we are satisfied that the immediate question is not the soundness of *Roe*'s resolution of the issue, but the precedential force that must be accorded to its holding. And we have concluded that the essential holding of *Roe* should be reaffirmed.

Yet it must be remembered that *Roe v. Wade* speaks with clarity in establishing not only the woman's liberty but also the State's "important and legitimate interest in potential life." *Roe, supra,* at 163. That portion of the decision in *Roe* has been given too little acknowledgement and implementation by the Court in its subsequent cases. . . .

Roe established a trimester framework to govern abortion regulations. Under this elaborate but rigid construct, almost no regulation at all is permitted during the first trimester of pregnancy; regulations designed to protect the woman's health, but not to further the State's interest in potential life, are permitted during the second trimester; and during the third trimester, when the fetus is viable, prohibitions are permitted provided the life or health of the mother is not at stake. *Roe v. Wade, supra,* at 163–166. Most of our cases since *Roe* have involved the application of rules derived from the trimester framework. . . .

The trimester framework no doubt was erected to ensure that the woman's right to choose not become so subordinate to the State's interest in promoting fetal life that her choice exists in theory but not in fact. We do not agree, however, that the trimester approach is necessary to accomplish this objective. A framework of this rigidity was unnecessary and in its later interpretation sometimes contradicted the State's permissible exercise of its powers.

Though the woman has a right to choose to terminate or continue her pregnancy before viability, it does not at all follow that the State is prohibited from taking steps to ensure that this choice is thoughtful and informed. Even in the earliest stages of pregnancy, the State may enact rules and regulations designed to encourage her to know that there are philosophic and social arguments of great weight that can be brought to bear in favor of continuing the pregnancy to full term and that there are procedures and institutions to allow adoption of unwanted children as well as a certain degree of state assistance if the mother chooses to raise the child herself. . . .

Numerous forms of state regulation might have the incidental effect of increasing the cost or decreasing the availability of medical care, whether for abortion or any other medical procedure. The fact that a law which serves a valid purpose, one not designed to strike at the right itself, has the incidental effect of making it more difficult or more expensive to procure an abortion cannot be enough to invalidate it. Only where state regulation imposes an undue burden on a woman's ability to make this decision does the power of the State reach into the heart of the liberty protected by the Due Process Clause. . . .

These considerations of the nature of the abortion right illustrate that it is an overstatement to describe it as a right to decide whether to have an abortion "without interference from the State," *Planned Parenthood of Central Mo. v. Danforth,* 428 U.S. 52, 61 (1976). All abortion regulations interfere to some degree with a woman's ability to decide whether to terminate her pregnancy. . . .

Roe v. Wade was express in its recognition of the State's "important and legitimate interest[s] in preserving and protecting the health of the pregnant woman [and] in protecting the potentiality of human life." 410 U.S., at 162. The trimester framework, however, does not fulfill *Roe*'s own promise that the State has an interest in protecting fetal life or potential life. *Roe* began the contradiction by using the trimester framework to forbid any regulation of abortion designed to advance that interest before viability. *Id.,* at 163. Before viability, *Roe* and subsequent cases treat all governmental attempts to influence a woman's decision on behalf of the potential life within her as unwarranted. This treatment is, in our judgment, incompatible with the recognition that there is a substantial state interest in potential life throughout pregnancy. Cf. *Webster,* 492 U.S., at 519 (opinion of Rehnquist, C. J.); *Akron I, supra,* at 461 (O'Connor, J., dissenting).

The very notion that the State has a substantial interest in potential life leads to the conclusion that not all regulations must be deemed unwarranted. Not all burdens on the right to decide whether to terminate a pregnancy will be undue. In our view, the undue burden standard is the appropriate means of reconciling the State's interest with the woman's constitutionally protected liberty. . . .

A finding of an undue burden is a shorthand for the conclusion that a state regulation has the purpose or effect of placing a substantial obstacle in the path of a woman seeking an abortion of a nonviable fetus. A statute with this purpose is invalid because the means chosen by the State to further the interest in potential life must be calculated to inform the woman's free choice, not hinder it. . . . That is to be expected in the application of any legal standard which must accommodate life's complexity. We do not expect it to be otherwise with respect to the undue burden standard. We give this summary:

(a) To protect the central right recognized by *Roe v. Wade* while at the same time accommodating the State's profound interest in potential life, we will employ the undue burden analysis as explained in this opinion. An undue burden exists, and therefore a provision of law is invalid, if its purpose or effect is to place a substantial obstacle in the path of a woman seeking an abortion before the fetus attains viability.

(b) We reject the rigid trimester framework of *Roe v. Wade.* To promote the State's profound interest in potential life, throughout pregnancy the State may take measures to ensure that the woman's choice is informed, and measures designed to advance this interest will not be invalidated as long as their purpose is to persuade the woman to choose childbirth over abortion. These measures must not be an undue burden on the right.

(c) As with any medical procedure, the State may enact regulations to further the health or safety of a woman seeking an abortion. Unnecessary health regulations that have the purpose or effect of presenting a substantial obstacle to a woman seeking an abortion impose an undue burden on the right.

(d) Our adoption of the undue burden analysis does not disturb the central holding of *Roe v. Wade,* and we reaffirm that holding. Regardless of whether exceptions are made for particular circumstances, a State may not prohibit any woman from making the ultimate decision to terminate her pregnancy before viability.

(e) We also reaffirm *Roe*'s holding that "subsequent to viability, the State in promoting its interest in the potentiality of human life may, if it chooses, regulate, and even proscribe, abortion except where it is necessary, in appropriate medical judgment, for the preservation of the life or health of the mother." *Roe v. Wade,* 410 U.S., at 164–165.

These principles control our assessment of the Pennsylvania statute, and we now turn to the issue of the validity of its challenged provisions.

V

The Court of Appeals applied what it believed to be the undue burden standard and upheld each of the provisions except for the husband notification requirement. We agree generally with this conclusion, but refine the undue burden analysis in accordance with the principles articulated above. . .

B

We next consider the informed consent requirement. 18 Pa. Cons. Stat. Ann. § 3205. Except in a medical emergency, the statute requires that at least 24 hours before performing an abortion a physician inform the woman of the nature of the procedure, the health risks of the abortion and of childbirth, and the "probable gestational age of the unborn child." The physician or a qualified nonphysician must inform the woman of the availability of printed materials published by the State describing the fetus and providing information about medical assistance for childbirth, information about child support from the father, and a list of agencies which provide adoption and other services as alternatives to abortion. An abortion may not be performed unless the woman certifies in writing that she has been informed of the availability of these printed materials and has been provided them if she chooses to view them.

Our prior decisions establish that as with any medical procedure, the State may require a woman to give her written informed consent to an abortion. . . .

In *Akron I,* 462 U.S. 416 (1983), we invalidated an ordinance which required that a woman seeking an abortion be provided by her physician with specific information "designed to influence the woman's informed choice between abortion or childbirth." *Id.,* at 444. As we later described the *Akron I* holding in *Thornburgh v. American College of Obstetricians and Gynecologists,* 476 U.S., at 762, there were two purported flaws in the Akron ordinance: the information was designed to dissuade the woman from having an abortion and the ordinance imposed "a rigid requirement that a specific body of information be given in all cases, irrespective of the particular needs of the patient. . . ." *Ibid.* . . .

In attempting to ensure that a woman apprehend the full consequences of her decision, the State furthers the legitimate purpose of reducing the risk that a woman may elect an abortion, only to discover later, with devastating psychological consequences, that her decision was not fully informed. If the information the State requires to be made available to the woman is truthful and not misleading, the requirement may be permissible.

We also see no reason why the State may not require doctors to inform a woman seeking an abortion of the availability of materials relating to the consequences to the fetus, even when those consequences have no direct relation to her health. An example illustrates the point. We would think it constitutional for the State to require that in order for there to be informed consent to a kidney transplant operation the recipient must be supplied with information about risks to the donor as well as risks to himself or herself. . . .

Whether the mandatory 24-hour waiting period is nonetheless invalid because in practice it is a substantial obstacle to a woman's choice to terminate her pregnancy is a closer question. The findings of fact by the District Court indicate that because of the distances many women must travel to reach an abortion provider, the practical effect will often be a delay of much more than a day because the waiting period requires that a woman seeking an abortion make at least two visits to the doctor. The District Court also found that in many instances this will increase the exposure of women seeking abortions to "the harassment and hostility of anti-abortion protestors demonstrating outside a clinic." 744 F. Supp., at 1351. As a result, the District Court found that for those women who have the fewest financial resources, those who must travel long distances, and those who have difficulty explaining their whereabouts to husbands, employers, or others, the 24-hour waiting period will be "particularly burdensome." . . .

We are left with the argument that the various aspects of the informed consent requirement are unconstitutional because they place barriers in the way of abortion on demand. Even the broadest reading of *Roe,* however, has not suggested that there is a constitutional right to abortion on demand. See, *e.g., Doe v. Bolton,* 410 U.S., at 189. Rather, the right protected by *Roe* is a right to decide to terminate a pregnancy free of undue interference by the State. Because the informed consent requirement facilitates the wise exercise of that right it cannot be classified as an interference with the right *Roe* protects. The informed consent requirement is not an undue burden on that right.

C

Section 3209 of Pennsylvania's abortion law provides, except in cases of medical emergency, that no physician shall perform an abortion on a married woman without receiving a signed statement from the woman that she has notified her spouse that she is about to undergo an abortion. The woman has the option of providing an alternative signed statement certifying that her husband is not the man who impregnated her; that her husband could not be located; that the pregnancy is the result of spousal sexual assault which she has reported; or that the woman believes that notifying her husband will cause him or someone else to inflict bodily injury upon her. A physician who performs an abortion on a married woman without receiving the appropriate signed statement will have his or her license revoked, and is liable to the husband for damages. . . .

The American Medical Association (AMA) has published a summary of the recent research in this field, which indicates that in an average 12-month period in this country, approximately two million women are the victims of severe assaults by their male partners. In a 1985 survey, women reported that nearly one of every eight husbands had assaulted their wives during the past year. The AMA views these figures as "marked underestimates," because the nature of these incidents discourages women from reporting them, and because surveys typically exclude the very poor, those who do not speak English well, and women who are homeless or in institutions or hospitals when the survey is conducted. According to the AMA, "[r]esearchers on family violence agree that the true incidence of partner violence is probably *double* the above estimates; or four million severely assaulted women per year. Studies suggest that from one-fifth to one-third of all women will be physically assaulted by a partner or ex-partner during their lifetime." AMA Council on Scientific Affairs, Violence Against Women 7 (1991) (emphasis in original). Thus on an average day in the United States, nearly 11,000 women are severely assaulted by their male partners. Many of these incidents involve sexual assault. . . . In families where wife-beating takes place, moreover, child abuse is often present as well. . . .

In well-functioning marriages, spouses discuss important intimate decisions such as whether to bear a child. But there are millions of women in this country who are the victims of regular physical and psychological abuse at the hands of their husbands. Should these women become pregnant, they may have very good reasons for not wishing to inform their husbands of their decision to obtain an abortion. Many may have justifiable fears of physical abuse, but may be no less fearful of the consequences of reporting prior abuse to the Commonwealth of Pennsylvania. Many may have a reasonable fear that notifying their husbands will provoke further instances of child abuse; these women are not exempt from § 3209's notification requirement. . . . If anything in this field is certain, it is that victims of spousal sexual assault are extremely reluctant to report the abuse to the government; hence, a great many spousal rape victims will not be exempt from the notification requirement imposed by § 3209.

The spousal notification requirement is thus likely to prevent a significant number of women from obtaining an abortion. It does not merely make abortions a little more difficult or expensive to obtain; for many women, it will impose a substantial obstacle. We must not blind ourselves to the fact that the significant number of women who fear for their safety and the safety of their children are likely to be deterred from procuring an abortion as surely as if the Commonwealth had outlawed abortion in all cases. . . .

This conclusion is in no way inconsistent with our

decisions upholding parental notification or consent requirements. See, *e.g., Akron II*. Those enactments, and our judgment that they are constitutional, are based on the quite reasonable assumption that minors will benefit from consultation with their parents and that children will often not realize that their parents have their best interests at heart. We cannot adopt a parallel assumption about adult women. . . .

Our cases establish, and we reaffirm today, that a State may require a minor seeking an abortion to obtain the consent of a parent or guardian, provided that there is an adequate judicial bypass procedure. See, *e.g., Akron II*. Under these precedents, in our view, the one-parent consent requirement and judicial bypass procedure are constitutional. . . .

VI

Our Constitution is a covenant running from the first generation of Americans to us and then to future generations. It is a coherent succession. Each generation must learn anew that the Constitution's written terms embody ideas and aspirations that must survive more ages than one. We accept our responsibility not to retreat from interpreting the full meaning of the covenant in light of all of our precedents. We invoke it once again to define the freedom guaranteed by the Constitution's own promise, the promise of liberty.

• • •

The judgment in No. 91–902 is affirmed. The judgment in No. 91–744 is affirmed in part and reversed in part, and the case is remanded for proceedings consistent with this opinion, including consideration of the question of severability.

It is so ordered.

UNITED STATES COURT OF APPEALS, EIGHTH CIRCUIT

LeRoy H. CARHART v. Donald STENBERG

• • •

RICHARD S. ARNOLD, Circuit Judge

The State of Nebraska appeals a District Court decision holding a Nebraska statute banning "partial-birth abortion" unconstitutional. . . . For the following reasons, we affirm the judgment of the District Court.

It is important to have in mind that we deal here with a particular legal question: the validity, under the Constitution of the United States, of a certain Nebraska law. The law refers to "partial-birth abortion," but this term, though widely used by lawmakers and in the popular press, has no fixed medical or legal content. The closest thing we have to a medical definition comes from the American College of Obstetricians and Gynecologists (ACOG). The ACOG definition describes a method of abortion (commonly called dilation and extraction, or D&X) involving extraction, from the uterus and into the vagina, of all of the body of a fetus except the head, following which the fetus is killed by extracting the contents of the skull. Thereafter, the dead but otherwise intact fetus is taken from the mother's body. Certainly this medical description is within the definition of "partial-birth abortion" contained in the Nebraska statute before us. The difficulty is that the statute covers a great deal more. It would

Submitted April 19, 1999. Decided September 24, 1999.

also prohibit, in many circumstances, the most common method of second-trimester abortion, called a dilation and evacuation (D&E). Under the controlling precedents laid down by the Supreme Court, such a prohibition places an undue burden on the right of women to choose whether to have an abortion. It is therefore our duty to declare the statute invalid.

I

On June 9, 1997, Nebraska's Governor signs into law Legislative Bill 23, a bill enacted by the Nebraska Legislature prohibiting "partial-birth abortion." The statute provides:

> No partial-birth abortion shall be performed in this state, unless such procedure is necessary to save the life of the mother whose life is endangered by a physical disorder, physical illness, or physical injury, including a life-endangering physical condition caused by or arising from the pregnancy itself.

Neb.Rev.Stat. § 28–328(1) (1998). "Partial-birth abortion" is defined in the statute as:

> an abortion procedure in which the person performing the abortion partially delivers vaginally a living unborn child before killing the unborn child and completing the delivery. For purposes of this subdivision, the term partially delivers vaginally a living unborn child before killing the unborn child means deliberately and intentionally delivering into the vagina a living unborn child, or a substantial portion thereof, for the purpose of performing a procedure that the person performing such procedure knows will kill the unborn child and does kill the unborn child.

Id. § 28–326(9). The intentional and knowing performance of an unlawful "partial-birth abortion" is a Class III felony. See *id.* § 28–328(2). A physician who intentionally and knowingly performs an unlawful "partial-birth abortion" will automatically have his license to practice medicine in Nebraska suspended and revoked. See *id.* § 28–328(4).

Shortly after the passage of LB 23, Dr. LeRoy Carhart filed a complaint challenging the constitutionality of the statute. In response to the complaint, the District Court granted a temporary restraining order, followed by a preliminary injunction, suspending enforcement of the statute. After a trial on the merits, the District Court issued its final judgment, holding LB 23 unconstitutional, and permanently enjoining enforcement of LB 23 against Dr. Carhart, his patients, and other similarly situated individuals.

Dr. Carhart challenged the constitutionality of LB 23 on two separate grounds. He argued that LB 23 imposed an undue burden on himself and his patients in two ways. First, because the D&X procedure is the safest procedure for some women in certain circumstances, banning that procedure places an undue burden on women seeking an abortion. Second, because LB 23 prohibits vaginally delivering a "substantial portion" of a fetus as part of an abortion procedure, the law bans the dilation and evacuation (D&E) procedure as well. Because the D&E procedure is the most widely used second-trimester abortion procedure, this ban also places an undue burden on women seeking to have an abortion. Dr. Carhart also challenged the law as being vague, arguing that it was unclear what "substantial portion" meant. The District Court agreed, holding both that the law created an undue burden for Dr. Carhart and his patients, and that the law was void for vagueness. *Carhart v. Stenberg,* 11 F.Supp.2d 1099 (D.Neb. 1998).

II

We state the facts as found by the District Court. . . . Dr. Carhart operates a family medical practice with a specialized abortion facility in Bellevue, Nebraska. He is licensed to practice medicine in Nebraska, as well as in seven other states. Dr. Carhart performs abortions in a clinic setting from a gestational age of three weeks until fetal viability. The abortion procedures Dr. Carhart performs vary depending on the gestational age of the fetus as well as on various other medical factors. As we shall explain, two of the procedures Dr. Carhart performs are directly affected by LB 23's ban; dilation and evacuation (D&E) and intact dilation and evacuation or dilation and extraction (D&X). Both are procedures for second-trimester abortions. LB 23 affects not only Dr. Carhart, but any doctor in Nebraska who performs the D&E or the D&X procedure, as well as that doctor's patients.

The most common method of abortion during the second trimester is the D&E procedure. A physician performing a D&E procedure gradually dilates the cervix and then removes the fetus and other products of conception. A report by the American Medical Association describes the D&E procedure used from thirteen to fifteen weeks' gestation as follows: . . . Instruments are inserted through the cervix into the uterus to remove fetal and placental tissue. Because fetal tissue is friable and easily broken, the fetus may not be removed intact. The walls of the uterus are scraped with a curette to ensure that no tissue remains. . . . Because the fetus is larger [from sixteen to twenty-four weeks gestation] (particularly the head), and because bones are more rigid, dismemberment or other destructive procedures are more likely to be required than at earlier gestational ages to remove fetal and placental tissue. . . .

When dismemberment occurs during a D&E procedure it does not occur in utero. Dr. Carhart explained that during the D&E procedure, the dismemberment occurs after a part of the fetus has been pulled through the cervix, into the vagina. . . .

In some circumstances, a physician performing a D&E procedure may attempt to remove the fetus intact. This procedure, known as an intact dilation and evacuation (intact D&E) or a dilation and extraction (D&X) can be used in abortions performed from sixteen to twenty-four weeks' gestation. . . . The physician generally brings all of the fetus, except for the head, out of the uterus into the vagina. Trial Tr. 35–36; J.A. 1150. Because the cervix is not dilated enough to allow the head to pass through, the physician inserts an instrument into the fetal skull and evacuates the contents, collapsing the skull and allowing removal of an intact fetus. Trial Tr. 35–36, 716; J.A. 1150.

. . . In both procedures, the physician brings a part of a living fetus out of the uterus into the vagina. . . . In either procedure, fetal demise will generally occur within a matter of minutes, and after part of the fetus has been brought out of the uterus into the vagina. *Id.* at 112–13, 118–19.

III

[1–3] The Supreme Court has held that a woman has a constitutional right to choose whether to terminate a pregnancy. *Roe v. Wade,* 410 U.S. 113, 153, 93 S.Ct. 705, 35 L.Ed.2d 147 (1973). Although a state cannot prohibit a woman from choosing to have an abortion, the state can promote the interest in potential human life and, after fetal viability, "regulate, and even proscribe, abortion except where it is necessary, in appropriate medical judgment, for the preservation of the life or health of the mother." *Roe,* 410 U.S. at 164–65, 93 S.Ct. 705. A state can also enact abortion regulations at the pre-viability stage, so long as there is no "undue burden" placed on the woman seeking to have an abortion. *Planned Parenthood of Southeastern Pennsylvania v. Casey.* A regulation which "has the purpose or effect of placing a substantial obstacle in the path of a woman seeking an abortion of a nonviable fetus" creates an undue burden and is invalid.

Several states have enacted statutes seeking to ban "partial-birth abortion." The precise wording of the statutes, and how far the statutes go in their attempts to regulate pre-viability abortions, differ from state to state. The results from constitutional challenges to the statutes, however, have been almost unvarying in most of the cases that reached the federal courts, the courts have held the statutes unconstitutional. . . .

If the regulation operates "as a substantial obstacle to a woman's choice to undergo an abortion 'in a large fraction of the cases in which [it] is relevant . . . [i]t is an undue burden, and therefore invalid.' " (quoting *Casey,* 505 U.S. at 895, 112 S.Ct. 2791).

The District Court determined that LB 23 created an undue burden because in many instances it would ban the most common procedure for second-trimester abortions, the D&E. The State argues that LB 23's ban on partial-birth abortion prohibits only the D&X procedure, and not the D&E. . . . The State argues that the Nebraska Legislature's intent was to ban only the D&X procedure. The language of the statute, however, describes a procedure which encompasses more than just D&X.

[6–8] In interpreting the statute, it is our duty to give it a construction, if reasonably possible, that would avoid constitutional doubts. We cannot, however, twist the words of the law and give them a meaning they cannot reasonably bear. The crucial problem is the term "substantial portion," which is nowhere defined in the statute. What the term means for the purposes of LB 23 has been debated at length, both in the record before us and on the floor of the Nebraska Legislature. But if "substantial portion" means an arm or a leg—and surely it must—then the ban created by LB 23 encompasses both the D&E and the D&X procedures. We agree with the District Court's assessment that "[i]n any sensible and ordinary reading of the word, a leg or arm is 'substantial.' " *Carhart v. Stenberg,* 11 F.Supp.2d 1099, 1129 (D.Neb. 1998). In the D&E procedure, the physician often inserts forceps into the uterus, grasps a part of the living fetus, and pulls that part of the fetus through the cervix. That part of the fetus is commonly an arm or a leg. Prelim.Inj.Tr. 117–18; Trial Tr. 31. LB 23 bars intentionally bringing a substantial portion of a living fetus into the vagina for purposes of performing a procedure that will kill the fetus. A physician who brings an arm or a leg into the vagina as part of the D&E procedure therefore violates the statute. . . .

Additionally, the person performing the procedure must do so with the purpose of performing a procedure that the person knows "will kill the unborn child and does kill the unborn child." Neb.Rev.Stat. § 28–326(9) (1998). In any abortion procedure the physician performing the procedure does so knowing, and with the purpose, that the procedure will kill the fetus. The language of LB 23 describes a method of abortion that includes the D&E procedure, and the intent requirement of the statute does not work to protect physicians who perform the D&E procedure from violating the statute LB 23 not only prohibits the D&X procedure, but the D&E procedure as well.

V

Having determined that LB 23 bans the D&E procedure, we turn now to the question of whether such a ban imposes an undue burden on women seeking second-trimester abortions.

. . . LB 23 does not limit all second-trimester abortions. It does, however, prohibit the most common procedure for second-trimester abortions and, in doing so, imposes an undue burden on a woman's right to choose to have an abortion.

VI

[11] In its final argument, the State suggests that *Roe* and *Casey* do not apply to LB 23 because *Roe* and *Casey* apply only to the "unborn" and do not prohibit states from protecting partially born human beings. The State argues that "the Supreme Court has left protection in place for the partially born." Appellant's Br. 71. The State also suggests that because the partial-birth abortion procedure involves a fetus which is more outside of the uterus than inside, the fetus is not unborn, sufficiently distinguishing this case from *Roe* and *Casey*. The phrase "partially born" is new to us. Apparently the State uses it to describe a process in which the fetus is killed when it is more outside the womb than inside. If we assume that there is such a legal category, and that, as the State argues, the rule of *Roe v. Wade* does not apply to it, the argument is still unavailing on the record before us in this case. As we have explained, the Nebraska statute is violated when an arm or a leg of a fetus that is still alive is pulled out of the womb as part of the D&E abortion procedure. In such a situation, although a substantial part of the fetus, as defined by the Nebraska law, has been extracted from the uterus, it cannot be said that the fetus as a whole is more outside the uterus than inside. In addition, we think that the word "born" refers most naturally to a viable fetus, one that is capable of surviving outside the mother. The Nebraska statute is not limited to viable fetuses. Indeed, as we have observed, both the proof and the legal arguments in this case seem to be exclusively about nonviable fetuses. So if there is a separate legal category for the "partially born," and we express no view on that question, we do not see how it could be relevant to the present case.

• • •

[VII.]

For the foregoing reasons, we affirm the judgment of the District Court.

UNITED STATES SUPREME COURT

Automobile Workers v. Johnson Controls, Inc.

[JUSTICE BLACKMUN delivered the opinion of the Court.]

In this case we are concerned with an employer's gender-based fetal-protection policy. May an employer exclude a fertile female employee from certain jobs because of its concern for the health of the fetus the woman might conceive?

I

Respondent Johnson Controls, Inc., manufactures batteries. In the manufacturing process, the element lead is a primary ingredient. Occupational exposure to lead entails health risks, including the risk of harm to any fetus carried by a female employee.

Before the Civil Rights Act of 1964, 78 Stat. 241, became law, Johnson Controls did not employ any woman in a battery-manufacturing job. In June 1977, however, it announced its first official policy concerning its employment of women in lead-exposure work. . . .

Johnson Controls "stopped short of excluding women capable of bearing children from lead exposure," *id.,* at 138, but emphasized that a woman who expected to have a child should not choose a job in which she would have such exposure. The company also required a woman who wished to be considered for employment to sign a statement that she had been advised of the risk of having a child while she was exposed to lead. . . .

Five years later, in 1982, Johnson Controls shifted from a policy of warning to a policy of exclusion. Between 1979 and 1983, eight employees became pregnant while maintaining blood lead levels in excess of 30 micrograms per deciliter. Tr. of Oral Arg. 25, 34. This appeared to be the critical level noted by the Occupational Health and Safety Administration (OSHA) for a worker who was planning to have a family. See 29 CFR § 1910.1025 (1989). The company responded by announcing a broad exclusion of women from jobs that exposed them to lead:

> ". . . [I]t is [Johnson Controls'] policy that women who are pregnant or who are capable of bearing children will not be placed into jobs involving lead exposure or which could expose them to lead through the exercise of job bidding, bumping, transfer or promotion rights." App. 85–86.

The policy defined "women . . . capable of bearing children" as "[a]ll women except those whose inability to bear children is medically documented." *Id.,* at 81. It further stated that an unacceptable work station was one where, "over the past year," an employee had recorded a blood lead level of more than 30 micrograms per deciliter or the work site had yielded an air sample containing a lead level in excess of 30 micrograms per cubic meter. *Ibid.*

II

In April 1984, petitioners filed in the United States District Court for the Eastern District of Wisconsin a class action challenging Johnson Controls' fetal-protection policy as sex discrimination that violated Title VII of the Civil Rights Act of 1964, as amended, 42 U. S. C. § 2000e *et seq.* Among the individual plaintiffs were petitioners Mary Craig, who had chosen to be sterilized in order to avoid losing her job. . . .

III

The bias in Johnson Controls' policy is obvious. Fertile men, but not fertile women, are given a choice as

Supreme Court Reporter 111, 1196–1217, March 20, 1991.

to whether they wish to risk their reproductive health for a particular job. Section 703(a) of the Civil Rights Act of 1964, 78 Stat. 255, as amended, 42 U. S. C. § 2000e-2(a), prohibits sex-based classifications in terms and conditions of employment, in hiring and discharging decisions, and in other employment decisions that adversely affect an employee's status. Respondent's fetal-protection policy explicitly discriminates against women on the basis of their sex. The policy excludes women with childbearing capacity from lead-exposed jobs and so creates a facial classification based on gender. Respondent assumes as much in its brief before this Court. Brief for Respondent 17, n. 24.

Nevertheless, the Court of Appeals assumed, as did the two appellate courts who already had confronted the issue, that sex-specific fetal-protection policies do not involve facial discrimination. . . .

. . . The court assumed that because the asserted reason for the sex-based exclusion (protecting women's unconceived offspring) was ostensibly benign, the policy was not sex-based discrimination. That assumption, however, was incorrect.

First, Johnson Controls' policy classifies on the basis of gender and childbearing capacity, rather than fertility alone. Respondent does not seek to protect the unconceived children of all its employees. Despite evidence in the record about the debilitating effect of lead exposure on the male reproductive system, Johnson Controls is concerned only with the harms that may befall the unborn offspring of its female employees. . . . Johnson Controls' policy is facially discriminatory because it requires only a female employee to produce proof that she is not capable of reproducing.

Our conclusion is bolstered by the Pregnancy Discrimination Act of 1978 (PDA), 92 Stat. 2076, 42 U. S. C. § 2000e(k), in which Congress explicitly provided that, for purposes of Title VII, discrimination "on the basis of sex" includes discrimination "because of or on the basis of pregnancy, childbirth, or related medical conditions." "The Pregnancy Discrimination Act has now made clear that, for all Title VII purposes, discrimination based on a woman's pregnancy is, on its face, discrimination because of her sex." *Newport News Shipbuilding & Dry Dock Co. v. EEOC,* 462 U. S. 669, 684 (1983). In its use of the words "capable of bearing children" in the 1982 policy statement as the criterion for exclusion, Johnson Controls explicitly classifies on the basis of potential for pregnancy. Under the PDA, such a classification must be regarded, for Title VII purposes, in the same light as explicit sex discrimination. Respondent has chosen to treat all its female employees as potentially pregnant; that choice evinces discrimination on the basis of sex. . . .

The beneficence of an employer's purpose does not undermine the conclusion that an explicit gender-based policy is sex discrimination under § 703(a) and thus may be defended only as a BFOQ [bona fide occupational qualification].

The enforcement policy of the Equal Employment Opportunity Commission accords with this conclusion. On January 24, 1990, the EEOC issued a Policy Guidance in the light of the Seventh Circuit's decision in the present case. . . .

In sum, Johnson Controls' policy "does not pass the simple test of whether the evidence shows 'treatment of a person in a manner which but for that person's sex would be different.' " . . .

IV

Under § 703(e)(1) of Title VII, an employer may discriminate on the basis of "religion, sex, or national origin in those certain instances where religion, sex, or national origin is a bona fide occupational qualification reasonably necessary to the normal operation of that particular business or enterprise." 42 U. S. C. § 2000e-2(e)(1). We therefore turn to the question whether Johnson Controls' fetal-protection policy is one of those "certain instances" that come within the BFOQ exception. . . .

The PDA's amendment to Title VII contains a BFOQ standard of its own: unless pregnant employees differ from others "in their ability or inability to work," they must be "treated the same" as other employees "for all employment-related purposes." 42 U. S. C. § 2000e(k). This language clearly sets forth Congress' remedy for discrimination on the basis of pregnancy and potential pregnancy. Women who are either pregnant or potentially pregnant must be treated like others "similar in their ability . . . to work." *Ibid.* In other words, women as capable of doing their jobs as their male counterparts may not be forced to choose between having a child and having a job. . . .

V

We have no difficulty concluding that Johnson Controls cannot establish a BFOQ. Fertile women, as far as appears in the record, participate in the manufacture of batteries as efficiently as anyone else. Johnson Controls' professed moral and ethical concerns about the welfare of the next generation do not suffice to establish a BFOQ of female sterility. Decisions about the welfare of future children must be left to the parents who conceive, bear, support, and raise them rather than to the employers who hire those parents. Congress has mandated this choice through Title VII, as amended by the Pregnancy Discrimination Act. Johnson Controls has attempted to exclude women because of their reproductive capacity. Title VII and the PDA simply do not allow a woman's dismissal because of her failure to submit to sterilization.

Nor can concerns about the welfare of the next generation be considered a part of the "essence" of Johnson Controls' business. . . .

Johnson Controls argues that it must exclude all fertile women because it is impossible to tell which women will become pregnant while working with lead. This argument is somewhat academic in light of our conclusion that the company may not exclude fertile women at all; it perhaps is worth noting, however, that Johnson Controls has shown no "factual basis for believing that all or substantially all women would be unable to perform safely and efficiently the duties of the job involved." *Weeks v. Southern Bell Tel. & Tel. Co.,* 408 F. 2d 228, 235 (CA5 1969), quoted with approval in *Dothard,* 433 U. S., at 333. Even on this sparse record, it is apparent that Johnson Controls is concerned about only a small minority of women. Of the eight pregnancies reported among the female employees, it has not been shown that any of the babies have birth defects or other abnormalities. The record does not reveal the birth rate for Johnson Controls' female workers but national statistics show that approximately nine percent of all fertile women become pregnant each year. The birthrate drops to two percent for blue collar workers over age 30. See Becker, 53 U. Chi. L. Rev., at 1233. Johnson Controls' fear of prenatal injury, no matter how sincere, does not begin to show that substantially all of its fertile women employees are incapable of doing their jobs. . . .

It is no more appropriate for the courts than it is for individual employers to decide whether a woman's reproductive role is more important to herself and her family than her economic role. Congress has left this choice to the woman as hers to make.

The judgment of the Court of Appeals is reversed and the case is remanded for further proceedings consistent with this opinion.

It is so ordered.

DISTRICT OF COLUMBIA COURT OF APPEALS

In Re A. C.

On Hearing en Banc

TERRY, ASSOCIATE JUDGE:

This case comes before the court for the second time. In *In re A. C.,* 533 A.2d 611 (D.C. 1987), a three-judge motions division denied a motion to stay an order of the trial court which had authorized a hospital to perform a caesarean section on a dying woman in an effort to save the life of her unborn child. The operation was performed, but both the mother and the child died. A few months later, the court ordered the case heard en banc and vacated the opinion of the motions division. *In re A. C.,* 539 A.2d 203 (D.C.1988). Although the motions division recognized that, as a practical matter, it "decided the entire matter when [it] denied the stay," 533 A.2d at 613, the en banc court has nevertheless heard the full case on the merits.

District of Columbia Court of Appeals. 573 A.2d 1235 (D.C. App. 1990).

We are confronted here with two profoundly difficult and complex issues. First, we must determine who has the right to decide the course of medical treatment for a patient who, although near death, is pregnant with a viable fetus. Second, we must establish how that decision should be made if the patient cannot make it for herself—more specifically, how a court should proceed when faced with a pregnant patient, *in extremis,* who is apparently incapable of making an informed decision regarding medical care for herself and her fetus. We hold that in virtually all cases the question of what is to be done is to be decided by the patient—the pregnant woman—on behalf of herself and the fetus. If the patient is incompetent or otherwise unable to give an informed consent to a proposed course of medical treatment, then her decision must be ascertained through the procedure known as substituted judgment. Because the trial court did not follow that procedure, we vacate its order and remand the case for further proceedings.

This case came before the trial court when George Washington University Hospital petitioned the emergency judge in chambers for declaratory relief as to how it should treat its patient, A.C., who was close to death from cancer and was twenty-six and one-half weeks pregnant with a viable fetus. After a hearing lasting approximately three hours, which was held at the hospital (though not in A.C.'s room), the court ordered that a caesarean section be performed on A.C. to deliver the fetus. Counsel for A.C. immediately sought a stay in this court, which was unanimously denied by a hastily assembled division of three judges. *In re A. C.,* 533 A.2d 611 (D.C. 1987). The caesarean was performed, and a baby girl, L.M.C., was delivered. Tragically, the child died within two and one-half hours, and the mother died two days later.

Counsel for A.C. now maintain that A.C. was competent and that she made an informed choice not to have the caesarean performed. Given this view of the facts, they argue that it was error for the trial court to weigh the state's interest in preserving the potential life of a viable fetus against A.C.'s interest in having her decision respected. They argue further that, even if the substituted judgment procedure had been followed, the evidence would necessarily show that A.C. would not have wanted the caesarean section. . . .

A.C. was first diagnosed as suffering from cancer at the age of thirteen. In the ensuing years she underwent major surgery several times, together with multiple radiation treatments and chemotherapy. A.C. married when she was twenty-seven, during a period of remission, and soon thereafter she became pregnant. . . .

On Tuesday, June 9, 1987, when A.C. was approximately twenty-five weeks pregnant, she went to the hospital for a scheduled check-up. Because she was experiencing pain in her back and shortness of breath, an x-ray was taken, revealing an apparently inoperable tumor which nearly filled her right lung. On Thursday, June 11, A.C. was admitted to the hospital as a patient. By Friday her condition had temporarily improved, and when asked if she really wanted to have her baby, she replied that she did.

Over the weekend A.C.'s condition worsened considerably. Accordingly, on Monday, June 15, members of the medical staff treating A.C. assembled, along with her family, in A.C.'s room. The doctors then informed her that her illness was terminal, and A.C. agreed to palliative treatment designed to extend her life until at least her twenty-eighth week of pregnancy. The "potential outcome [for] the fetus," according to the doctors, would be much better at twenty-eight weeks than at twenty-six weeks if it were necessary to "intervene." A.C. knew that the palliative treatment she had chosen presented some increased risk to the fetus, but she opted for this course both to prolong her life for at least another two weeks and to maintain her own comfort. When asked if she still wanted to have the baby, A.C. was somewhat equivocal, saying "something to the effect of 'I don't know, I think so.'" As the day moved toward evening, A.C.'s condition grew still worse, and at about 7:00 or 8:00 p.m. she consented to intubation to facilitate her breathing.

The next morning, June 16, the trial court convened a hearing at the hospital . . . and the District of Columbia was permitted to intervene for the fetus as *parens patriae*. The court heard testimony . . . that the chances of survival for a twenty-six-week fetus delivered at the hospital might be as high as eighty percent, but that this particular fetus, because of the mother's medical history, had only a fifty to sixty percent chance of survival. . . .

Regarding A.C.'s ability to respond to questioning and her prognosis, Dr. Louis Hamner, another treating obstetrician, testified that A.C. would probably die within twenty-four hours "if absolutely nothing else is done. . . . As far as her ability to interact, she has been heavily sedated in order to maintain her ventilatory function. She will open her eyes sometimes when you are in the room, but as far as her being able to . . . carry on a meaningful-type conversation . . . at this point, I don't think that is reasonable." . . .

There was no evidence before the court showing that A.C. consented to, or even contemplated, a caesarean section before her twenty-eighth week of pregnancy. There was, in fact, considerable dispute as to whether she would have consented to an immediate caesarean delivery at the time the hearing was held. A.C.'s mother opposed surgical intervention, testifying that A.C. wanted "to live long enough to hold that baby" and that she expected to do so, "even though she knew she was terminal." Dr. Hamner testified that, given A.C.'s medical problems, he did not think she would have chosen to deliver a child with a substantial degree of impairment. . . .

After hearing this testimony and the arguments of counsel, the trial court made oral findings of fact. It found, first, that A.C. would probably die, according to uncontroverted medical testimony, "within the next twenty-four to forty-eight hours"; second, that A.C. was "pregnant with a twenty-six and a half week viable fetus who, based upon uncontroverted medical testimony, has approximately a fifty to sixty percent chance to survive if a caesarean section is performed as soon as possible"; third, that because the fetus was viable, "the state has [an] important and legitimate interest in protecting the potentiality of human life"; and fourth, that there had been some testimony that the operation "may very well hasten the death of [A.C.]," but that there had also been testimony that delay would greatly increase the risk to the fetus and that "the prognosis is not great for the fetus to be delivered post-mortem. . . ." Most significantly, the court found:

> The court is of the view that it does not clearly know what [A.C.'s] present views are with respect to the issue of whether or not the child should live or die. . . .

Having made these findings of fact and conclusions of law, the court ordered that a caesarean section be performed to deliver A.C.'s child.

The court's decision was then relayed to A.C., who had regained consciousness. When the hearing reconvened later in the day, Dr. Hamner told the court:

> I explained to her essentially what was going on. . . . I said it's been deemed we should intervene on behalf of the baby by caesarean section and it would give it the only possible chance of it living. Would you agree to this procedure? *She said yes*. I said, do you realize that you may not survive the surgical procedure? *She said yes.* And I repeated the two questions to her again [and] asked her did she understand. *She said yes*. [Emphasis added.]

When the court suggested moving the hearing to A.C.'s bedside, Dr. Hamner discouraged the court from doing so, but he and Dr. Weingold, together with A.C.'s mother and husband, went to A.C.'s room to confirm her consent to the procedure. . . .

[A.C.] then seemed to pause for a few moments and then very clearly mouthed words several times, *I don't want it done. I don't want it done.*

[Dr. Weingold testified:]

> I would obviously state the obvious and that is this is an environment in which, from my perspective as a physician, this would not be an informed consent one way or the other. She's under tremendous stress with the family on both sides, but I'm satisfied that I heard clearly what she said. . . .

Dr. Weingold later qualified his opinion as to A.C.'s ability to give an informed consent, stating that he thought the environment for an informed consent was non-existent because A.C. was in intensive care, flanked by a weeping husband and mother. . . .

After hearing this new evidence, the court found that it was "still not clear what her intent is" and again ordered that a caesarean section be performed. A.C.'s counsel sought a stay in this court, which was denied. *In re A. C.*, 533 A.2d 611, 613 (D.C. 1987). The operation took place, but the baby lived for only a few hours, and A.C. succumbed to cancer two days later. . . .

It has been suggested that fetal cases are different [from other duty-to-aid cases] because a woman who "has chosen to lend her body to bring [a] child into the world" has an enhanced duty to assure the welfare of the fetus, sufficient even to require her to undergo caesarean surgery. Robertson, *Procreative Liberty,* 69 Va.L.Rev. at 456. Surely, however, a fetus cannot have rights in this respect superior to those of a person who has already been born. . . .

This court has recognized as well that, above and beyond common law protections, the right to accept or forego medical treatment is of constitutional magnitude. . . .

What we distill from the [precedent] cases is that every person has the right, under the common law and the Constitution, to accept or refuse medical treatment. This right of bodily integrity belongs equally to persons who are competent and persons who are not. Further, it matters not what the quality of a patient's life may be; the right of bodily integrity is not extinguished simply because someone is ill, or even at death's door. To protect that right against intrusion by others—family members, doctors, hospitals, or anyone else, however well-intentioned—we hold that a court must determine the patient's wishes by any means available, and must abide by those wishes unless there are truly extraordinary or compelling reasons to override them. . . .

From the record before us, we simply cannot tell whether A.C. was ever competent, after being sedated, to make an informed decision one way or the other regarding the proposed caesarean section. The trial court never made any finding about A.C.'s competency to decide. Undoubtedly, during most of the proceedings below, A.C. was incompetent to make a treatment decision; that is, she was unable to give an informed consent based on her assessment of the risks and benefits of the contemplated surgery. . . .

We have no reason to believe that, if competent, A.C. would or would not have refused consent to a caesarean. We hold, however, that without a competent refusal from A.C. to go forward with the surgery, and without a finding through substituted judgment that A.C. would not have consented to the surgery, it was error for the trial court to proceed to a balancing analysis, weighing the rights of A.C. against the interests of the state. . . .

The court should also consider previous decisions of the patient concerning medical treatment, especially when there may be a discernibly consistent pattern of conduct or of thought. . . . Thus in a case such as this it would be highly relevant that A.C. had consented to intrusive and dangerous surgeries in the past, and that she chose to become pregnant and to protect her pregnancy by seeking treatment at the hospital's high-risk pregnancy clinic. It would also be relevant that she accepted a plan of treatment which contemplated caesarean intervention at the twenty-eighth week of pregnancy, even though the possibility of a caesarean during the twenty-sixth week was apparently unforeseen. On the other hand, A.C. agreed to a plan of palliative treatment which posed a greater danger to the fetus than would have been necessary if she were unconcerned about her own continuing care. Further, when A.C. was informed of the fatal nature of her illness, she was equivocal about her desire to have the baby.

Courts in substituted judgment cases have also acknowledged the importance of probing the patient's value system as an aid in discerning what the patient would choose. We agree with this approach. . . . Most people do not foresee what calamities may befall them; much less do they consider, or even think about, treatment alternatives in varying situations. The court in a substituted judgment case, therefore, should pay special attention to the known values and goals of the incapacitated patient, and should strive, if possible, to extrapolate from those values and goals what the patient's decision would be. . . .

After reviewing the transcript of the hearing and the court's oral findings, it is clear to us that the trial court did not follow the substituted judgment procedure. . . .

The court did not go on, as it should have done, to make a finding as to what A.C. would have chosen to do if she were competent. Instead, the court undertook to balance the state's and L.M.C.'s interests in surgical intervention against A.C.'s perceived interest in not having the caesarean performed.

After A.C. was informed of the court's decision, she consented to the caesarean; moments later, however, she withdrew her consent. The trial court did not then make a finding as to whether A.C. was competent to make the medical decision or whether she had made an informed decision one way or the other. Nor did the court then make a substituted judgment for A.C. Instead, the court said that it was "still not clear what her intent is" and again ordered the caesarean.

It is that order which we must now set aside. What a trial court must do in a case such as this is to determine, if possible, whether the patient is capable of making an informed decision about the course of her medical treatment. If she is, and if she makes such a decision, her wishes will control in virtually all cases. . . .

Accordingly, we vacate the order of the trial court and remand the case for such further proceedings as may be appropriate. We note, in doing so, that the trial court's order allowing the hospital to perform the caesarean section was presumptively valid from the date it was entered until today. What the legal effect of that order may have been during its lifetime is a matter on which we express no opinion here.

Vacated and remanded.

BELSON, ASSOCIATE JUDGE, concurring in part and dissenting in part:

I agree with much of the majority opinion, but I

disagree with its ultimate ruling that the trial court's order must be set aside, and with the narrow view it takes of the state's interest in preserving life and the unborn child's interest in life. . . .

The state's interest in preserving human life and the viable unborn child's interest in survival are entitled, I think, to more weight than I find them assigned by the majority when it states that "in virtually all cases the decision of the patient . . . will control." Majority opinion at 1252. I would hold that in those instances, fortunately rare, in which the viable unborn child's interest in living and the state's parallel interest in protecting human life come into conflict with the mother's decision to forgo a procedure such as a caesarean section, a balancing should be struck in which the unborn child's and the state's interests are entitled to substantial weight.

It was acknowledged in *Roe v. Wade,* 410 U.S. 113, 93 S.Ct. 705, 35 L.Ed.2d 147 (1973), that the state's interest in potential human life becomes compelling at the point of viability. Even before viability, the state has an "important and legitimate interest in protecting the potentiality of human life." . . .

We are dealing with the situation that exists when a woman has carried an unborn child to viability. When the unborn child reaches the state of viability, the child becomes a party whose interests must be considered. . . .

[In] *Bonbrest v. Kotz,* 65 F.Supp. 138 (D.D.C. 1946) . . . the court . . . stated:

> It has, if viable, its own bodily form and members, manifests all the anatomical characteristics of individuality, possesses its own circulatory, vascular and excretory systems and is capable *now* of being ushered into the visible world.

Id. at 141 (footnote omitted).

Bonbrest proved to be a landmark case. In *Greater Southeast Hospital v. Williams,* 482 A.2d 394 (D.C. 1984), this court noted that "every jurisdiction in the United States has followed *Bonbrest* in recognizing a cause of action for prenatal injury, at least when the injury is to a viable infant later born alive." *Id.* at 396. We went on to hold in *Greater Southeast Hospital* that a viable unborn child *is a person* within the coverage of the wrongful death statute, D.C.Code § 16-2701 (1981):

> Inherent in our adoption of *Bonbrest* is the recognition that a viable fetus is an independent person with the right to be free of prenatal injury. The liability for prenatal injury recognized in *Bonbrest* arises at the time of the injury. If a viable fetus is a "person injured" at the time of the injury, then perforce the fetus is a "person" when he dies of those injuries, and it can make no difference in liability under the wrongful death and survival statutes whether the fetus dies of the injuries just prior to or just after birth. . . .

A viable unborn child is a *person* at common law who has legal rights that are entitled to the protection of the courts. In a case like the one before us, the unborn child is a patient of both the hospital and any treating physician, and the hospital or physician may be liable to the child for the child's prenatal injury or death if caused by their negligence. . . .

The balancing test should be applied in instances in which women become pregnant and carry an unborn child to the point of viability. This is not an unreasonable classification because, I submit, a woman who carries a child to viability is in fact a member of a unique category of persons. Her circumstances differ fundamentally from those of other potential patients for medical procedures that will aid another person, for example, a potential donor of bone marrow for transplant. This is so because she has undertaken to bear another human being, and has carried an unborn child to viability. Another unique feature of the situation we address arises from the singular nature of the dependency of the unborn child upon the mother. A woman carrying a viable unborn child is not in the same category as a relative, friend, or stranger called upon to donate bone marrow or an organ for transplant. Rather, the expectant mother has placed herself in a special class of persons who are bringing another person into existence, and upon whom that other person's life is totally dependent. Also, uniquely, the viable unborn child is literally captive within the mother's body. No other potential beneficiary of a surgical procedure on another is in that position.

For all of these reasons, a balancing becomes appropriate in those few cases where the interests we are discussing come into conflict. To so state is in no sense to fail to recognize the extremely strong interest of each individual person, including of course the expectant mother, in her bodily integrity, her privacy, and, where involved, her religious beliefs.

Thus, I cannot agree with the conclusion of the majority opinion that while we "do not quite foreclose the possibility that a conflicting state interest may be so compelling that the patient's wishes must yield . . .

we anticipate that such cases will be extremely rare and truly exceptional." Majority opinion at 1252. While it is, fortunately, true that such cases will be rare in the sense that such conflicts between mother and viable unborn child are rare, I cannot agree that in cases where a viable unborn child is in the picture, it would be extremely rare, within that universe, to require that the mother accede to the vital needs of the viable unborn child. . . .

I next address the sensitive question of how to balance the competing rights and interests of the viable unborn child and the state against those of the rare expectant mother who elects not to have a caesarean section necessary to save the life of her child. The indisputable view that a woman carrying a viable child has an extremely strong interest in her own life, health, bodily integrity, privacy, and religious beliefs necessarily requires that her election be given correspondingly great weight in the balancing process. In a case, however, where the court in an exercise of a substituted judgment has concluded that the patient would probably opt against a caesarean section, the court should vary the weight to be given this factor in proportion to the confidence the court has in the accuracy of its conclusion. Thus, in a case where the indicia of the incompetent patient's judgment are equivocal, the court should accord this factor correspondingly less weight. The appropriate weight to be given other factors will have to be worked out by the development of law in this area, and cannot be prescribed in a single court opinion. Some considerations obviously merit special attention in the balancing process. One such consideration is any danger to the mother's life or health, physical or mental, including the relatively small but still significant danger that necessarily inheres in any caesarean delivery, and including especially any danger that exceeds that level. The mother's religious beliefs as they relate to the operation would appear to deserve inclusion in the balancing process.

On the other side of the analysis, it is appropriate to look to the relative likelihood of the unborn child's survival. . . . The child's interest in being born with as little impairment as possible should also be considered. This may weigh in favor of a delivery sooner rather than later. The most important factor on this side of the scale, however, is life itself, because the viable unborn child that dies because of the mother's refusal to have a caesarean delivery is deprived, entirely and irrevocably, of the life on which the child was about to embark.

. . . Also to be considered in the balance was the rather minimal, but nevertheless undisputable, additional risk that caesarean delivery presented for the mother.

Turning to the interest of the unborn child in living and the parallel interest of the state in protecting that life, the evidence indicated that the child had a fifty to sixty percent chance of survival and a less than twenty percent chance of entering life with a serious handicap such as cerebral palsy or mental retardation. The evidence also showed that a delay in delivering the child would have increased the likelihood of a handicap. In view of the record before Judge Sullivan, and on the basis that there had been no plain error in not applying the sort of substituted judgment analysis that we for the first time mandate in today's ruling, I think it cannot be said that he abused his discretion in the way he struck the balance between the considerations that favored the procedure and those that went against it.

For the reasons stated above, I would affirm.

ALEXANDER MORGAN CAPRON

Punishing Mothers

Alexander Capron is Henry W. Bruce Professor of Law, University Professor of Law and Medicine, and codirector of the Pacific Center for Health Policy and Ethics at the University of Southern California. Capron has served on a number of boards and commissions, including the National Council on Death and Dying and the Biomedical Ethics Advisory Committee of the U.S. Congress. Representative publications include "Genetics and Insurance: Accessing and Using Private Information," *Social Philosophy and Policy* and "What Contributions Have Social Science and the Law Made to the Development of Policy on Bioethics?" *Journal of the American Academy of Arts and Sciences.*

What should society do when a woman, in producing children, exposes them to avoidable risks? That recurring question—which plunges one quickly and deeply into the murky waters of child protection, women's rights, and the far reaches of medical science—has been back on the front pages recently. Two very different stories illustrate how context affects our answer.

MULTIPLE BIRTHS

[In the fall of 1997] the international media cast the bright, warm glow of an approving spotlight on Carlisle, Iowa, the home of Kenny and Bobbi McCaughey, who gave birth to four boys and three girls on 20 November. The babies, who were born two months premature and ranged from 2.5 to 3.4 pounds, seem to be doing well, making them the first surviving septuplets in the world. With the use of fertility drugs and in vitro fertilization, multiple births are becoming more frequent; for example, fifty-seven quintuplets were born in the United States in 1995. A few months before the McCaugheys' babies, septuplets were born in Saudi Arabia but six died, and in May 1985 an American woman carrying seven fetuses gave birth to six (the seventh was stillborn) but lost three within nineteen days.

From *Hastings Center Report* (January/February 1998), 31–33.

Most media coverage was supportive of the McCaugheys, as were friends and neighbors in their small town, the governor of Iowa, and numerous business enterprises, which promised a new house (to replace the two bedroom home the couple had shared with their two-year-old daughter, Mikayla), an extra-large van, and life-time supplies of such items as disposable diapers. While parents who had experienced the heavy demands of multiple births warned of everything from sleepless nights to bankruptcy, the general sentiment was summed up by the septuplets' maternal grandfather Robert Hepworth, who termed their births "a miracle."

Still, a few objections were voiced by physicians as well as ethicists. Fertility specialists in Britain, where artificial reproduction (but not the use of fertility drugs) is closely regulated, raised "serious questions about whether such a multiple pregnancy should have been allowed to happen," viewing it less as a triumph of medicine than as a "medical disaster."[1]

Though most critics did not go so far as to argue that the McCaugheys should not have used fertility drugs unless they were willing to undergo "selective reduction" early in the pregnancy (in which the number of fetuses would have been reduced from seven to at most two or three), Gregory Pence did suggest that they had made an unethical choice. Rather than claiming it was "God's will," the McCaugheys should take responsibility for the choice they made. "They took bad odds and hoped that all seven would be healthy, and in so doing, they took the risk of having seven disabled or dead babies."[2]

More frequently, the criticism focused instead on the physicians involved. Through ultrasound scans and other means of monitoring, fertility specialists can tell when their interventions will lead to the release of a dangerously high number of eggs, so the woman can avoid conceiving that month or can undergo egg harvesting and in vitro fertilization, with only a few of the resulting embryos being transferred to the uterus and the rest frozen for later use if needed. Peter Brinsden, medical director at Bourn Hall in Cambridge where Louise Brown, the first test-tube baby, was born in 1978, chided physicians who do not use their medical powers responsibly. "The aim of fertility treatment should be to give couples one or two children at most."

Besides the stress that multiple births place on parents (and on their marriage) after the children are born, the general experience with such pregnancies is that they are very dangerous for mother and fetuses alike. Overstimulation of the ovaries can lead in rare cases to heart failure, and carrying many fetuses is associated with potentially fatal blood clots and miscarriages.

Even when such fetuses survive their crowded uterine environment, they will almost certainly be born many weeks early and small, conditions that give rise to a litany of medical and developmental risks, such as chronic lung disease, mental retardation, and blindness. If, like the McCaughey babies, they succeed in weathering the risks of pregnancy, prematurity, and low birth weight, and emerge relatively intact from weeks of vigorous and very expensive care in a neonatal intensive care unit (NICU), such children still face an elevated risk of child abuse.

ADDICTED BABIES

Direct charges of child neglect lay at the heart of another recent motherhood story, as recounted in a decision handed down by the Supreme Court of South Carolina less than a month before the McCaughey septuplets' birth.[3] The spotlight of public attention that shone on Cornelia Whitner after she gave birth in Pickens County several years ago was certainly less intense but also much less warm than that which greeted the birth of the McCaughey septuplets in Des Moines.

Ms. Whitner's baby was born with cocaine metabolites in his system, and she admitted using crack cocaine during the third trimester of her pregnancy. Charged with criminal child neglect under S.C. Code §20-7-50, Ms. Whitner pled guilty and was sentenced to eight years in prison.

Rather than appealing her conviction, Ms. Whitner filed a petition for Post Conviction Relief, arguing that §20-7-50 covered children but not fetuses. Thus, she claimed, she had received ineffective assistance of her trial counsel, who failed to advise her that the statute might not apply to prenatal drug abuse, and the trial court lacked jurisdiction to accept a guilty plea to a nonexistent offense. After her petition was granted on both grounds, the state appealed to the Supreme Court of South Carolina.

The South Carolina Children's Code provides that "Any person having the legal custody of any child . . . who shall, without lawful excuse, refuse or neglect to provide . . . the proper care and attention for such child . . . so that the life, health or comfort of such child . . . is endangered or is likely to be endangered, shall be guilty of a misdemeanor." Another provision of the code defines "child" as a "a person under the age of eighteen."

Is a fetus a "person" for the purposes of the children's code? Looking to the language of the statute (in light of comparable language in other contexts) as well as to the policy behind the law, the state supreme court answered "yes." It thus reached a different conclusion from other courts in similar prosecutions over the past dozen years around the country.

As the abuse of illegal drugs—particularly but not exclusively crack cocaine—swelled in the late 1980s to epidemic levels, physicians became concerned about the growing number of babies who had been exposed to these drugs prenatally. Though early medical reports—magnified through the lens of the popular media into a picture of NICUs filled with the Charles Mansons of the future—probably overstated the physical and behavioral consequences of prenatal drug exposure, studies have by now established that many babies whose mothers used cocaine and other drugs during pregnancy will have been harmed, in ways that are not always remediable.

Thus, it is hardly surprising that public officials took steps to deter maternal drug abuse and to punish women whose use of drugs exposed their children to harm before birth. Prosecutions took two forms. In some cases, women were charged under statutes forbidding delivery or distribution of illicit substances, in other cases, under statutes that punish child endangerment. Yet in decision after decision in the early 1990s, state occurs rejected these prosecutions and held the statutes inapplicable to pregnant women's drug use insofar as the harm alleged occurred before a child's birth.

THE *WHITNER* DECISION

The South Carolina Supreme Court reached a different conclusion in the *Whitner* case. Since the case involved only a child endangerment provision, the court did not need to deal with the issue of how "delivery" of a drug would be established under a statute forbidding drug distribution. And the court found "no question" that "Whitner endangered the life, health, and comfort of her child" when she ingested crack cocaine in the third trimester of the pregnancy.

Nor did the court have much difficulty in interpreting its statute to include a fetus within the meaning of "child" because, unlike most of the other states that had rejected prosecutions for prenatal drug abuse, South Carolina had substantial case law construing "person" to include a viable fetus.

The earlier cases dealt with two situations. Going back to 1960, South Carolina's courts have allowed wrongful death actions arising from injuries sustained prenatally by a viable fetus, whether born alive or (after a 1964 decision) stillborn. The second context first arose in a homicide prosecution of a man who stabbed his nine-months-pregnant wife in the neck, arms, and abdomen. Despite an attempted caesarean delivery, the child died while still in utero, and the defendant was convicted of voluntary manslaughter.[4] Proclaiming a desire to be consistent with its holdings in the civil cases, the state supreme court upheld the conviction and recognized the crime of feticide, at least as to fetuses who were capable of surviving outside the womb.

In light of these earlier holdings, the *Whitner* court felt there was no "rational basis for finding a viable fetus is not a 'person' in the . . . context" of the child endangerment statute. In this ruling, it departed from the conclusion reached by a Massachusetts court that refused to recognize criminal liability of a pregnant woman for transmitting cocaine to her viable fetus, even though that state, like South Carolina, allows wrongful death actions for viable fetuses injured in utero and homicide prosecutions of third parties who kill viable fetuses. While the Massachusetts court had read its precedents as limited to cases in which the "mother's or parents' interest in the potentiality of life, not the state's interest, are sought to be vindicated,"[5] the South Carolina court held that the state may protect the interests of a viable fetus even from its mother.

MATERNAL LIABILITY

Since South Carolina is not unusual in vindicating the interests of children for prenatal injuries in torts cases, adoption of the *Whitner* court's reasoning by other courts would have profound implications for state regulation of the behavior of expectant mothers.

First, the implication of the decision—though nowhere directly addressed—is that it is acceptable for the state to monitor the status of pregnant women and of their babies, such as by doing tests for illicit drugs without consent. If toxicology screening requires informed consent, then women who know that such tests will label them child abusers will refuse permission.

Conversely, if such screening is seen as acceptable without consent, under some general public health doctrine, then pregnant addicts may avoid routine prenatal care so as not to be arrested and incarcerated, and they may even seek to deliver their children outside usual medical settings—all to the detriment of their health and that of their child-to-be. Further, some pregnant addicts might seek late-term abortions, rather than deliver a baby with telltale signs of drug usage.[6]

It is also hard to believe that the court's holding in *Whitner* will stay confined to viable fetuses. While the courts may feel constrained to limit feticide prosecutions to cases where the victim is viable, civil damages are awarded for injuries that occur not just before viability but even before conception and are then manifested after birth. A similar reading of the child endangerment statute can be expected, especially in light of the medical evidence that the developing fetus is probably at greater risk of injury from maternal drug abuse in the first few months of gestation than in the final months.

While the *Whitner* court repeatedly emphasized that it was only addressing the situation before it—a pregnant woman's abuse of an illegal substance—there is nothing in the child protection law that limits the range of acts for which prosecution is possible. The focus of §20-7-30 is on preventing action or inaction that endangers a child's "life, health or comfort." While the statute excepts acts done with "lawful excuse," it is not clear that anything short of necessity would provide such an excuse—certainly not the mere comfort or convenience of an expectant mother.

The conduct that would therefore be most likely to lead to prosecution would be maternal drinking, since the link between fetal harm and prenatal exposure to alcohol is, if anything, even better documented than the link to prenatal exposure to illegal drugs. Alcoholic beverages carry warnings of this risk, and obstetricians routinely warn their patients to refrain from drinking even before their pregnancies are confirmed. Failure to follow such advice, or medical advice either to take or to refrain from taking prescription drugs or following other medical regimes, could thus lay the basis for a child endangerment prosecution if shown to have led to serious harm to a child.

Indeed, in the words of the South Carolina court, there does not appear to be "any rational basis" for limiting the wrongful acts that could form the basis for a prosecution, whether the conduct occurred previability or was otherwise legal for a woman who was not pregnant. And, to return to the Iowa septuplets, application of the *Whitner* doctrine would appear to expose to prosecution any woman who decided to initiate a pregnancy following fertility treatment if she was informed about the great risks of multiple births.

Of course, future Bobbi McCaugheys are unlikely to give much thought to such matters, and for good reason, as society regards the decision to proceed with a multiple pregnancy very differently from the abuse of illegal drugs. Yet both are situations in which children are exposed to the risk of death or severe handicaps, and both are situations in which the medical profession needs to do much more to help women (and their partners) to adjust their behavior in ways that offer their children a better start in life.

REFERENCES

1. Chris Mihill and Sarah Boseley, "Multiple Births: When the Shine Wears Off a Miracle." *The Guardian* (London), 21 November 1997, p. 17.

2. Gregory Pence, "McCaughey Septuplets: God's Will or Human Choice?" *Birmingham Sunday News,* 30 November 1997, p. C1.

3. Whitner v. State, 1997 W.L. 680091 (S.C.), filed 15 July 1997 and amended and refiled on grant of rehearing 27 October 1997.

4. State v. Horne, 282 S.C. 444, 319 S.E.2d 703 (1984).

5. Commonwealth v. Pellegrini, No. 87970 (Mass. Super. Ct., 15 October 1990), slip op. at 11.

6. The *Whitner* court rejected the argument that the pressure to take this step amounted to a penalty on the decision to carry a pregnancy to term in violation of the woman's right of privacy recognized in Cleveland Board of Education v. LaFleur, 414 U.S. 632 (1974).

KENNETH A. DEVILLE
AND LORETTA M. KOPELMAN

Moral and Social Issues Regarding Pregnant Women Who Use and Abuse Drugs

Kenneth De Ville is professor in the department of Medical Humanities at the Brody Medical School at East Carolina University and is "of counsel" at a law firm in Raleigh, North Carolina. He is the author of numerous articles and books. Representative publications include *Medical Malpractice in Nineteenth Century America: Origins and Legacy* and *Physician-Assisted Suicide: What Are the Issues?*, co-edited with Loretta Kopelman.

Loretta Kopelman is a member of the Department of Medical Humanities at the Brody Medical School at East Carolina University. She has held numerous national offices, including founding president of the American Society for Bioethics and Humanities and many NIH study sections and editorial boards. She has published over a hundred books, articles, and commentaries. Representative publications include "Bioethics and Humanities: What Makes Us One Field?" *Journal of Medicine and Philosophy* and "Values and Virtues: How Should They Be Taught?" *Academic Medicine*.

How should society respond to pregnant women using recreational or additive drugs that may harm their future children? During the past three decades, medical science has become increasingly aware of the potential impact of maternal lifestyle choices on fetal well-being. Beginning in the early 1980s, a series of studies regarding fetal health and substance use and abuse surfaced and helped to inspire the unprecedented attempt to improve fetal outcomes by monitoring, controlling, and sanctioning the actions of pregnant women. In 1988 a national study found that 5 million women confirmed the use of an illegal substance in the month before they delivered a child.[4,20] The following year, researchers found that 11% of the women who delivered infants in the hospital in the study had used illegal drugs sometime during their pregnancy. Moreover, evidence is accumulating that fetuses may be damaged by maternal use of a variety of substances, including heroin, methadone, amphetamines, prescription and over-the-counter drugs, tobacco, marihuana, cocaine, and alcohol; but the evidence for each substance varies in reliability and relevance. For example, marihuana use during pregnancy, although almost certainly unwise, is incompletely studied and has not been correlated definitively with fetal growth retardation or neurologic behavioral changes in infants.[2]

The pregnant woman's use of cocaine generates the most attention and concern. Such use has been linked to somewhat increased risk of a variety of fetal teratogenic effects, including intestinal atresia, cardiac malformations, genitourinary anomalies, limb defects, and brain and skull deformations.[2] One study found that 16% of newborns who had been exposed to cocaine during pregnancy sustained microcephaly in comparison with 6% of the controls. Similarly, maternal cocaine use has been correlated with low birth weight, small-for-gestational age and premature births,[46] tremors, seizures, irritability, hypertension,

From *Obstetrics and Gynecology Clinics of North America* 25, no. 1 (March 1998), 235–254.

abnormal reflex behavior, depressed interactive abilities, sudden infant death syndrome, and slow development in the first 6 months to 2 years of life.[18,19] However, methodologic difficulties plague demonstrations of direct causal links between cocaine and some of these observed effects. One study identified cognitive and behavioral delays in 40% of children who had been exposed to drugs in utero, but a similar percentage of delays was observed in children with no drug exposure who lived in underprivileged environments.[25] Moreover, neonatal neurologic syndrome may be temporary, with only a minority of cocaine-exposed neonates sustaining significant injury.[46] Maternal cocaine use is potentially destructive and represents a documented danger to fetuses, but the nature of that risk is unclear.[32] Limited data outline the impact of low doses of maternal cocaine use.

Despite the public attention focused on cocaine use, the damaging effects of alcohol taken during pregnancy are better documented and more dramatic.[2] Fetal alcohol syndrome is the most common recognizable cause of mental retardation. Alcohol consumption has been correlated with an increase in spontaneous abortion, fetal growth retardation, premature delivery, abruptio placentae, and breech presentations. Alcohol is also a proven teratogen, and heavy maternal use has been associated with a variety of congenital defects including microcephaly and other cerebral and craniofacial abnormalities. Some studies have found such defects present in as many as 80% of the children of heavy drinkers. Typically, heavy alcohol use in the first trimester is associated with morphologic defects, whereas alcohol use later in the pregnancy is accompanied by growth retardation and neurobehavioral disturbances. Moderate amounts of alcohol use during pregnancy have been correlated with behavioral features such as distractibility, excitability, and disciplinary problems, as well as autism, learning disabilities, and lowered intellectual capabilities. Although the neurobehavioral effects of lower levels of prenatal alcohol exposure seem to dissipate slowly as the child develops, the impact of moderate and high alcohol use may last much longer and even into adulthood.[2]

Although many tragic cases associated with substance use during pregnancy are preventable, most of the data on this problem remain equivocal and are rendered problematic by several confounding factors. Polydrug and multiple substance use may make it difficult to delineate with precision the fetal toxic affects of each discrete substance. In addition, it is difficult for investigators to determine both the amount of the substance or substances ingested and when in the course of the pregnancy they were used. Other factors, such as socioeconomic status, the availability of prenatal care, and individual patient pathophysiology, frequently have an important role in suboptimal fetal outcomes.[2] The public, clinicians, and policy makers sometimes unconsciously inflate the degree and certitude of risk represented by maternal substance use or tend to direct the focus of their attention and efforts to one substance to the exclusion of other equally hazardous toxins.

PUNITIVE OR COERCIVE STATE INTERVENTIONS

Social responses to prevent substance abuse damage to the future child fall into two general classes. One group of responses is voluntary and nonpunitive, such as educational and drug treatment programs; the other actions are coercive and punitive. . . . This section describes punitive or coercive state interventions designed to stop pregnant women from taking recreational or addictive drugs that may harm their future children. In subsequent sections it is argued that such actions raise serious moral and social problems.

One type of intervention represents an attempt to prevent damage or further damage from occurring to a fetus while it is still in utero. A judge in Washington, DC, sentenced a pregnant, drug-using woman to jail for the duration of her pregnancy, presumably to protect the fetus from drug-induced damage.[35] A New York hospital petitioned a court to commit civilly a pregnant woman under the state mental health law for mandatory substance abuse treatment because she was 8 months pregnant and known to have used crack cocaine.[12] Frequently, even when the request for a legal detention order is ultimately denied or overturned, the woman has already been held against her will during the course of the legal proceedings. For example, a Wisconsin court used the state's existing child abuse statute to rule that a pregnant woman who had tested positive for drugs could be held against her will and treated for substance abuse. The court justified the action as an attempt to take the fetus into protective custody.[41] Although the state supreme court ultimately condemned such use of the statute, the woman was successfully detained for the duration of her pregnancy.

A second type of intervention attempts to invoke criminal sanctions for women who give birth to injured infants or who have used substances during pregnancy.[35] These interventions are typically punitive in nature and are motivated by the hope that such punishments, if publicized, will deter future substance abuse during pregnancy. In 1993 an Indiana woman was arrested, jailed, and charged with reckless homicide after she reportedly used drugs and gave birth to a 22-week-old baby who died after 4 days.[9] Similarly, prosecutors in California, New Jersey, and other jurisdictions have attempted to use their states' homicide statutes to prosecute women who deliver stillborn and mortally injured infants prematurely after using illegal substances, usually cocaine.[17] Women who have used cocaine, alcohol, and other substances have been charged with criminal mistreatment of a child,[16] reckless endangerment,[10] child abuse,[6,7] and child neglect.[13] In an especially innovative series of cases, prosecutors have charged pregnant women who use drugs with the delivery or distribution of drugs to a minor, in some instances, through the medium of the umbilicus during the instant after delivery but before the cord was severed by the physician.

For the most part, these prosecutions have failed. Most courts have dismissed or overturned fetal protection prosecutions not on constitutional grounds (although such a defense may be viable) but rather on the statutory construction of words such as "delivery" and "distribution" in the controlled substances prosecutions, and of "child," "human being," and "person" in the abuse and homicide prosecutions. In refusing to interpret these terms broadly, courts have typically concluded that current statutes were not intended by the legislature to apply to fetuses.[22,23,28,36,37,42] That conclusion, however, is not foreordained. The Supreme Court of South Carolina, for example, recently affirmed the child abuse conviction of a woman who tested positive for cocaine during a prenatal care visit and whose child was later born unharmed but with cocaine metabolites in his blood stream. The woman was sentenced to 8 years in prison.[48]

Despite the court decision in South Carolina, it seems likely that most state court judges will refuse to allow prosecutors to pursue pregnant women who use or abuse drugs and alcohol through existing homicide, controlled substance, and child abuse statutes. The failure of these prosecutions under existing remedies has been followed by the introduction of scores of fetal protection bills in state legislatures. These bills take on a variety of forms but typically include proposed legislation to permit explicitly the prosecution of women for child abuse if they test positive for a controlled substance. Other bills would create the legal presumption that a woman who uses drugs while pregnant is likely to abuse her child in the future, thereby justifying state custody proceedings or expanding the definition of the terms *child* and *human being* in abuse and homicide statutes in an attempt to hold pregnant women who use drugs and alcohol criminally liable.[11,14,15] . . .

MATERNAL RIGHTS, INTERESTS, AND DUTIES

. . . Moral duties to future children are not absolute. People have a variety of obligations, and no one is expected to set aside all other duties and interests for any one else, even a future child. Women may have duties to themselves, relating to their jobs or health, that may override benefits to someone else or a future child. . . .

Thus, even when there is a moral duty to the future child, pregnant women are not required to subrogate all other duties or interests during pregnancy to prevent harm to the child. Moral obligations of the pregnant woman in regards to her future child do not demand that she subject herself to great personal risks, ignore all other duties, or forgo all pleasures to do what is absolutely best for the fetus. Rather, the woman is morally obligated to give due consideration to the future child's interests in balancing the child's claims with other duties and interests.[43] What is an unreasonable harm depends upon (1) the likelihood the harm will occur; (2) the gravity of the harm to the future child if it materializes; and (3) the degree and importance of the interests and pleasures that the woman must compromise to prevent that harm.

In egregious cases of substance abuse, the moral analysis offers clear and uncontroversial examples of violations of the pregnant woman's moral duty to give due consideration the interests of her future child. The scientific evidence regarding the impact of heavy smoking, heavy drinking, and habitual use of cocaine on the fetus represents potential harms of significant probability and magnitude. Therefore, the pregnant woman who has decided to carry to term has a moral duty to avoid egregious abuse of substances during the course of her pregnancy.[31] Indeed, she and other family members may have similar duties even after the child is delivered.

A woman who did not intend to become pregnant and who is denied access to abortion by legal restrictions or financial or other limitations still has a moral obligation to consider the claims of her offspring. Some scholars, however, argue that this obligation has less moral force when a woman involuntarily carries the fetus to term.[24] The moral duties of the woman who is bearing a child against her will might more closely resemble those of the third-party stranger who has a generalized duty not to harm others, rather than the greater duty of a parent. Although this suggestion is controversial, it underscores the difficulty in evaluating precisely the nature of a pregnant woman's moral duty toward her future child and highlights one of the many difficulties inherent in any attempt to enshrine moral duty into law and policy. . . .

FAIRNESS, SOCIAL POLICY, AND THE LIMITS OF LIBERTY

Given that pregnant women have some moral duty to protect the children they intend to deliver, and that they have interests in avoiding harm, what is the status of current fetal protection policies in terms of prudence, fairness, justice, and morality? Society clearly possesses some duties and rights to promote the health and flourishing of its future citizens, for example, by providing prenatal programs and removing environmental hazards causing birth defects. Is it a natural extension of those commitments to frame laws and adopt policies that force pregnant women to refrain from the use of recreational or addictive drugs that may harm the conceptus or fetus or to punish them for such behavior?

A comprehensive moral assessment of a fetal protection policy must taken into account the interests of future children and the interests of society in protecting its members. It must also include, however, a full appreciation and respect of the rights and interests of pregnant women as well as an assessment of whether such policies are effective. In Western society, individuals are presumed to possess rights to liberty and autonomy—the right to be left alone. Moreover, the pregnant woman is typically considered the presumptive decision maker for her child-who-will-be-born. . . .

The case for coercive state measures is strongest when serious injury is most likely to befall the child-who-will-be-born. However, as the probability and magnitude of these harms diminish, it becomes increasingly difficult to justify punitive or coercive state measures. The moderate or high use of alcohol, tobacco, and narcotics has been correlated with lower intelligence quotients, fetal immaturity, and lower birth rates, and thus a case may be made in regards to such use. These types of injuries, however, occur less frequently with moderate-to-low use, can often be overcome as the child ages, and may be attributable to other causal factors. Some maternal behavior is linked to great fetal injury, but most substance use probably falls into the class of low-to-moderate use that poses possible but uncertain or low risk to the fetus.

A morally justifiable fetal protection policy would have to resolve the profoundly difficult issue of setting the threshold of probability and magnitude of harm that is sufficient to outweigh the other interests and duties of the expectant mother. Such a determination is made more problematic by the fact that, as the result of biologic variability, virtually identical behavior by pregnant women will result in different fetal outcomes. The calculus that is required to determine the magnitude of a pregnant women's duty to her child-who-will-be-born is complex, uncertain, and value-laden. Striking a balance between duties and interests is complicated furthermore because not all pregnant women choose pregnancy and consciously and voluntarily eliminate abortion as an option. Indeed, it would be an ironic twist if a policy intended to protect the health and well-being of future children scared targeted women into terminating their pregnancies by abortion because they feared punitive or coercive state action. Therefore, there are well-established moral and parental duties to refrain from behavior that will cause the child-who-will-be-born harm and a limited societal duty to prevent such harm. It is questionable whether these duties justify broad coercive or punitive social policies of detention, forced treatment, or criminal sanctions to protect the fetus.

FAIRNESS AND GENDER BIAS

In an effort to protect children from prenatal harm, public concern, proposed fetal protection policies, and enforcement efforts currently focus predominantly on the actions and lifestyle choices of the pregnant woman. Equality before the law, however, is a fundamental political and a constitutional principle in democratic societies.[26] As a result, the public, policy makers, enforcement agents, and physicians should be inherently skeptical of any approach that reserves restrictive and punitive measures for one segment of society while neglecting analogous wrongs perpetrated by another segment of society. Irresponsible actions on the part of men can have a significant impact on the health of the fetus and the well-being of the resulting child. Although the literature is not as fully developed as that regarding substance abuse and the pregnant woman, preliminary evidence suggests that male abuse of alcohol, tobacco, and illegal drugs may damage the sperm in ways that might lead to fetal abnormalities. Similarly, exposure to toxic materials in the workplace can damage the sperm prior to fertilization.[39] Yet, little societal concern and virtually no official action are directed at the potential impact of male substance abuse on the health of future children. . . .

Society and public policy have failed in other ways to appreciate fully and regulate male responsibilities during pregnancy. For example, there is growing evidence, statistical and anecdotal, that pregnant women are at a greater risk for physical abuse than are other women,[5] and that domestic violence remains a highly underreported and underprosecuted phenomenon. Physical assaults pose a danger not only to the female and pregnant victim but also to her future child. Future fathers also have a duty to safeguard the interests of the child-to-be-born. The often cited case of Pamela Rae Stewart is instructive. Stewart was charged with child neglect after she reportedly, and against the advice of physicians, eschewed bed rest and prescribed medication, engaged in sexual intercourse, used marihuana and amphetamines, and did not contact her physician when she began bleeding. It is often overlooked that Stewart's husband also had a duty to their future child and also heard the physician's advice. He reportedly used drugs with her, had sex with her, assaulted her, and failed to call physicians when she began bleeding yet, unlike his wife, was never charged with child neglect.[40] Fathers and other men can have a central role in encouraging drug or alcohol use by pregnant women and are arguably culpable in any damage caused to future children. In addition, second-hand exposure to crack, marihuana, and tobacco smoke may present at least marginal potential dangers to pregnant women and their fetuses.[40]

Despite the variety of ways in which the actions of the male partner during pregnancy can wrong the child-who-will-be-born, public scrutiny remains focused on the pregnant woman. Although the pregnant woman's actions frequently pose a greater immediate risk of harm, in some instances this is not true. It is likely that the issues of fetal protection focus on women because our culture still views child-bearing and child-rearing as largely female responsibilities.[39] Even if these cultural expectations underlie current fetal protection efforts, they are insufficient justification in a society based on the aspiration that all citizens should be treated equally by law.

FAIRNESS AND RACIAL BIAS

Similarly, fetal protection policies have disproportionately focused on poor women, especially those of color. Although studies have suggested that the rate of alcohol and drug use among white and black pregnant women is comparable, reporting and enforcement practices have the effect of singling out women of color. In one institution, black women who used alcohol or illegal drugs during pregnancy were 10 times as likely to be reported to child protection services and law enforcement agencies in comparison with white women who used such substances during pregnancy.[20] Virtually all of the women arrested for child abuse under South Carolina's maternal drug prevention program have been African-American.[8] Other studies reveal similar figures.[27] This disparity may be explained in a variety of ways, including thinly veiled racism. Fetal protection, reporting, and enforcement policies typically focus on public clinics and prenatal cocaine use, especially crack use, making poor women of color the more likely target of enforcement efforts. Such highly selective enforcement policies make women of a particular ethnic and socioeconomic identity the more likely targets of fetal protection policies. Upper and middle class women are more likely to receive their prenatal care from a private physician than from a clinic and may be less likely to abuse cocaine during their pregnancies. They are, however, equally likely to abuse other potentially harmful drugs such as tobacco and alcohol during pregnancy. Such practices probably account for as much or more fetal injury than does cocaine. Even if a draconian fetal protection policy could be defended in the abstract, it would still be suspect. Current attempts to protect fetuses from maternal lifestyle choices reflect stark racial and socioeconomic disparities. Such policies are also antithetical to the constitutional and political ethos that all persons be treated equally under the law. Universal and broad enforcement of fetal protection policies without regard to race or economic status might be one way to meet this criticism. Given the existing social biases, such a color-blind, class-neutral policy would probably be politically tricky, difficult to craft, and objectionable on other grounds.

The most egregious cases of maternal irresponsibility and the tragic plight and prospects of the newborn seriously injured by prenatal substance abuse seem to cry out for action. The state has an interest in promoting and protecting the health of future citizens. Children who have been injured or disadvantaged by prenatal substance abuse represent an unnecessary burden on society's medical, educational, and social services. The economic costs of fetal alcohol syndrome in the United States have been estimated to be $321 million each year for all affected children less than 21 years of age. The lifetime societal costs of a permanently disabled citizen may be even higher.[44] Individuals in society have a duty to prevent unnecessary harm to others, including children-who-will-be-born; a woman who decides to carry a fetus to term may have a heightened duty of care. Although most women who abuse substances during pregnancy may acknowledge and accept this duty, they may be unable to help themselves because of the realities of substance addiction or social and economic dependency.

Despite the foregoing arguments, these policies remain problematic. Unless such measures can be justified, jail detention or hospital commitment of a pregnant woman who is using or abusing substances intrudes upon the most revered and protected right in Western culture—the right to liberty and the freedom from bodily restraint. Although the state may sometimes infringe upon the rights of individuals, it may only justifiably do so in highly circumscribed situations, such as when great public harm is threatened, when other less onerous alternatives are unavailable, or when the risk of harm to other individuals is both severe and likely.

In most cases, the confinement and treatment of pregnant women who use substances does not meet these standards for limiting liberty. In most cases, other less coercive means exist. Voluntary outpatient substance abuse education, counseling, and treatment do not infringe on the pregnant woman's right of liberty, are profoundly less restrictive, and would most likely be more successful in reducing drug and alcohol use during pregnancy.[21] Individuals who voluntarily submit to substance abuse treatment are likely to be more committed and to be faithful to a substance-free lifestyle and pregnancy and thus are more responsive to therapy. In general, mandated substance abuse programs are less successful than voluntary ones. . . .

It is also illegitimate to limit an individual's liberty without substantial evidence concerning the nature, probability, and magnitude of the harm to be avoided. Even though substance abuse poses a risk of fetal harm, that risk and its intensity are highly unpredictable. Heavy alcohol use throughout pregnancy yields clear and significant fetal damage in a high percentage of, but not all, resulting births. The results of lower levels of usage are more ambiguous, as is the relative impact of alcohol use at differing points during pregnancy. The evidence involving cocaine, marihuana, and other controlled substances is even more equivocal. A vast majority of children born to women who use or abuse controlled substances during pregnancy sustain little or no long-term injury. Thus, the endemic uncertainty of maternal alcohol and drug use on the health of newborns makes it a slender reed upon which to justify the profound intrusion on individual liberty that is represented by confinement and mandatory treatment.

The relevant liberty in this instance is not the right to use illegal substances or abuse alcohol, rather, it is the right to move about freely in the world as one wishes and to refuse treatment that one does not desire. Although it may be irresponsible and even immoral to abuse substances when one is pregnant, a just public policy should intervene only in important individual liberties when there is a clear risk of serious harm to third parties or society. Confinement during pregnancy and mandatory treatment do not meet this standard. Although such policies may prevent serious damage to newborns in some cases, they unnecessarily and unjustifiably violate the almost transcendent liberties of women in many others.

In addition, fetal protection strategies must not offend or undermine the professional ethos of the physicians and health care professionals who are, by necessity, integrally involved in the implementation of the various policies. Thus, even when there is a moral duty for women to avoid the use of substances that pose a risk to the child-who-will-be-born, there may be no legal policy devised that is morally justifiable, clinically and socially efficacious, and nondiscriminatory.

EVALUATING PUNISHMENTS AFTER DELIVERY

During the past decade, many women have been charged with child abuse, manslaughter, and the delivery of drugs to minors. . . . Postbirth prosecutions are justified on the grounds that newborn infants do not deserve to be burdened for life by the irresponsible behavior of others, especially their mothers. Society, they assert, should not be forced to bear the economic and social burdens represented by the child who is unnecessarily injured prenatally. Such supporters contend that women who continue to abuse drugs and alcohol during pregnancy are obviously not responding to available education and counseling and thereby should be subject to stronger, punitive measures.

Despite these arguments forwarded by fetal-protection advocates, sanctions applied after delivery are probably unjust, unwarranted, and unlikely to accomplish any goal beyond the punishment of women who have used illegal substances during their pregnancies. Moreover, the argument for such sanctions does not apply to other more dangerous behaviors such as alcohol consumption. The focus on punitive measures for using illegal substances does nothing to stop or assuage the damage that has already occurred to children exposed during gestation or to help the mother gain control of her life. The proposed role of these sanctions in preventing harm to children born and unborn is also only speculative. It is unclear that the prosecution and imprisonment of women is the most effective means to bring maternal drug and alcohol use to a halt. Substance abusers are not likely to calculate rationally the cost and benefits of their behaviors. More likely, the prospect of prosecution may encourage women to bypass vital prenatal care and available counseling in an attempt to evade potential detection of maternal drug use. Such a course of action is more likely to lead to higher levels of neonatal morbidity rather than lower, as the proposed legislation presumably intends. Some studies have suggested that voluntary education and counseling tend to have a more lasting benefit in comparison with coercive programs.[21]

Imposing criminal sanctions for prenatal drug use following a positive urine test during pregnancy or the discovery of cocaine metabolites in cord blood represents an unjust use of criminal law. Even though substance abuse during pregnancy represents a known and preventable risk of harm to the child-who-will-be-born, such use results in injury to the child in a minority of cases only. Law, both criminal and civil, typically imposes sanctions on individuals for wrongs and harms, and not for creating the risk of wrongs and harms. Negligent behavior does not generate civil damages unless damage results. Individuals with criminal intent are not prosecuted and punished until that intent results in a socially defined injury. The woman who uses drugs or alcohol during pregnancy may risk harming her child-to-be-born, but that harm does not always come to fruition.

Criminal fetal protection sanctions, however, penalize women regardless of the resulting harm. The woman in South Carolina who received an 8-year sentence for child abuse after repeat positive tests for cocaine gave birth to an uninjured, healthy child.[48] Newly framed child abuse, drug delivery, and homicide statutes that apply to fetuses, if they are confirmed by legislatures, will punish many, even most women for behavior that results in no harm to the newborn child. . . . Criminal fetal protection statutes, if enacted, stand almost alone in Anglo-American law as examples of serious punishment meted out even in the absence of showing harm to the putative victim.

Punishment in the form of imprisonment or automatic loss of child custody may be difficult to justify even when injury has occurred. In some cases, it is relatively easy to determine that conscious, prenatal abuse of substances has caused a particular injury or deficiency in a newborn. However, those cases are probably in the minority. In most instances, any number of potential comorbidity factors ranging from congenital to economic to environmental blur the causal link between the maternal use of substances and the deficiency or harm sustained by the infant. Typically, proposed fetal protection statutes ignore this murky causal link between maternal action and fetal injury. The criminal punishment of individuals is usually justified by society's interest in deterrence, restraint, rehabilitation, education, and retribution.[30]

As discussed earlier, little evidence suggests that any of these objectives, except retribution, are better served by punitive measures than they would be by less expensive and less intrusive voluntary education, treatment, and counseling opportunities.[1]. . .

CONCLUSIONS

. . . The evaluation of fetal protection policies is inescapably a discussion involving individual liberty and the degree to which it should be limited. It is also an issue of pragmatism. The most successful approach to the problem of substance use and abuse during pregnancy recognizes that the woman's, the child's, and society's interests are usually consonant. All would be better served by a comprehensive approach to the challenge of fetal health that would respect not only individual liberty but also recognize and address the social and economic context within which disadvantaged children are born.

REFERENCES

1. American Academy of Pediatrics, Committee on Substance Abuse: Drug-exposed infants. Pediatrics 96:364-366, 1995.

2. Bell G.L., Lau K.: Perinatal and neonatal issues of substance abuse. Pediatr Clin North Am 42:261–281, 1995.

3. Brody B.: Fetal humanity and brain function. *In* Bioethics: Readings and Cases. Englewood Cliffs, NJ, Prentice-Hall, 1987, pp 143–146.

4. Campbell D.E., Fleischman A.R.: Ethical challenges in medical care for the pregnant substance abuser. Clin Obstet Gynecol 35:803–812, 1995.

5. Campbell J.C., Poland M.M.L., Waller J.B., et al: Correlates of battering during pregnancy. Res Nurs Health 15:219–226, 1992.

6. Center for Reproductive Law & Policy: Charges dropped against woman for allegedly drinking while pregnant. Reproductive Freedom News 2(13):6, July 2, 1993.

7. Center for Reproductive Law & Policy: South Carolina court asked to overturn conviction of jailed woman wrongly charged. Reproductive Freedom News 2(20):5–6, November 5, 1993.

8. Center for Reproductive Law & Policy: South Carolina hospital subject of rights investigation. Reproductive Freedom News 3(3):4–5, February 11, 1994.

9. Center for Reproductive Law & Policy: Judge dismisses homicide charges against Indiana woman. Reproductive Freedom News 3(4):4–5, February 25, 1994.

10. Center for Reproductive Law & Policy: Pennsylvania court rejects punishment for actions during pregnancy. Reproductive Freedom News 3(5):3, March 11, 1994.

11. Center for Reproductive Law & Policy: In the states. Reproductive Freedom News 3(12):7, June 24, 1994.

12. Center for Reproductive Law & Policy: In the states. Reproductive Freedom News 4(6):3, March 24, 1995.

13. Center for Reproductive Law & Policy: New York High court rules that positive drug test is not sufficient evidence of newborn's neglect. Reproductive Freedom News 5(2):5, January 26, 1996.

14. Center for Reproductive Law & Policy: Legislation punishing women for prenatal conduct threatens women's health and children's interests. Reproductive Freedom News 5(5):4–5, March 8, 1996.

15. Center for Reproductive Law & Policy: In the states. Reproductive Freedom News 3(5):6, March 11, 1996.

16. Center for Reproductive Law & Policy: Washington appeals panel affirms dismissal of charges against woman for behavior during pregnancy. Reproductive Freedom News 5(11):3, June 28, 1996.

17. Center for Reproductive Law & Policy: New Jersey dismisses criminal charges brought against woman for conduct during pregnancy. Reproductive Freedom News 6(1):6, January 17, 1997.

18. Chasnoff I.J., Burns W.J., Schnoll S.H., et al: Cocaine use in pregnancy. N Engl J Med 313:666–669, 1985.

19. Chasnoff I.J., Griffith D., MacGregor S., et al: Temporal patterns of cocaine use in pregnancy. JAMA 261:1741–1744, 1989.

20. Chasnoff I.J., Landress H.J., Barret M.E.: The prevalence of illicit-drug or alcohol use during pregnancy and discrepancies in

mandatory reporting in Pinellas County, Florida. N Engl J Med 322:1202–1206, 1990.

21. Chavkin W.: Mandatory treatment for drug use during pregnancy. JAMA 266(11):1556–1561, 1991.

22. *Commonwealth v Kemp,* 642 A2d 705 (Pa Super Ct 1994).

23. *Commonwealth v Welch,* 864 SW2d 280 (Ky 1993).

24. Draper H: Women, forced caesareans and antenatal responsibilities. J Med Ethics 22:327–333, 1996.

25. Franck E.J.: Prenatally drug-exposed children in out-of-home care: Are we looking at the whole picture? Child Welfare 75(1):19–33, 1996.

26. Graber M.A.: Rethinking Abortion: Equal Choice, the Constitution, and Reproductive Politics. Princeton, NJ, Princeton University Press, 1966.

27. Johnson D.E.: Maternal-fetal relationship: Legal and regulatory issues. *In* Reich WT (ed): Encyclopedia of Bioethics. New York, Simon & Schuster Macmillan, 1995, pp 1413–1418.

28. *Johnson v State,* 602 So2d 1288 (Fla 1992).

29. Kopelman L.M.: Children: Health care and research. *In* Encyclopedia of Bioethics. New York, MacMillan, 1995, pp 357–368.

30. LaFave W.R., Scott A.W.: Criminal Law. St. Paul, MN, West Publishing, 1972, pp 21–25.

31. Mathieu D.: Preventing Prenatal Harm: Should the State Intervene? Washington, DC, Georgetown University Press, 1996.

32. Mayes L., Granger R., Bornstein M., et al: The problem of prenatal cocaine exposure. JAMA 267:406–408, 1992.

33. Mill J.S.: On Liberty. Great Britain, Penguin, 1974.

34. Noonan J.T.: An almost absolute value in history. *In* Arras JD, Rhoden N.K. (eds): Ethical Issues in Modern Medicine, ed 3. Mountain View, CA, Mayfield Publishing, 1989, pp 261–265.

35. Note: Medical technology and the law. Harvard Law Review 103:1519–1676, 1990, at 1573.

36. *People v. Hardy,* 469 NW2d 50 (Mich Ct App 1991).

37. *Reyes v State,* 75 Cal App3d 214 (1977).

38. Robertson J.A., Schulman J.D.: Pregnancy and prenatal harm to offspring: The case of mothers with PKU. Hastings Center Report 17(4):23–32, 1987.

39. Schroedel J.R., Pretz P.: A gender analysis of policy formation: The case of fetal abuse. J Health Polit Policy Law 19:335–360, 1994.

40. Solomon R.I.: Future fear: Prenatal duties imposed by private parties. Am J Law Med 17:411–434, 1991.

41. *State ex rel Angela MW v Kruzicki,* S41 NW 2d 482 (ct App 1995).

42. *State v Gray,* 584 NE2d 710 (Ohio 1992).

43. Steinbock B.: Life Before Birth. New York, Oxford University Press, 1992.

44. Streissguth M.E., Andresko M, Stryker J, et al: Fetal alcohol syndrome in adolescents and adults. JAMA 265:1961–1967, 1991.

45. Tooley M.: Abortion and Infanticide. Oxford, Clarendon Press, 1983.

46. Volpe J.J.: Effect of cocaine use on the fetus. N Engl J Med 327:399–407, 1992.

47. Warren M.A.: Abortion. *In* Companion to Ethics. Oxford, Basil Blackwell, 1991, pp 306–313.

48. *Whitner v State,* SC Sup Crt, July 15, 1996.

SUGGESTED READINGS FOR CHAPTER 5

American Medical Association. Board of Trustees. "Legal Interventions during Pregnancy: Court-Ordered Medical Treatments and Legal Penalties for Potentially Harmful Behavior by Pregnant Women." *Journal of the American Medical Association* 264 (November 1990), 2663–70.

Bopp, James, Jr., and Cook, Curtis R. "Partial-Birth Abortion: The Final Frontier of Abortion Jurisprudence." *Issues in Law & Medicine* 14 (1998), 3–57.

Brandt, Richard B. "The Morality of Abortion." *The Monist* 36 (1972), 503–26.

Callahan, Daniel, and Callahan, Sidney, eds. *Abortion: Understanding Differences.* New York: Plenum Press, 1984.

Callahan, Joan. "Ensuring a Stillborn: The Ethics of Fetal Lethal Injection in Late Abortion." *Journal of Clinical Ethics* 6 (1995), 254–63.

Chervenak, Frank A., and McCullough, Laurence B.: "Inadequacies with the ACOG and AAP Statements on Managing Ethical Conflict During the Intrapartum Period." *Journal of Clinical Ethics* 2 (Spring 1991), 23–24.

Colker, Ruth. *Abortion and Dialogue: Prochoice, Prolife, and American Law.* Bloomington and Indianapolis: Indiana University Press, 1992.

Connery, John R. *Abortion: The Development of the Roman Catholic Perspective.* Chicago: Loyola University Press, 1977.

Cook, Rebecca J., Dickens, Bernard M., and Bliss, Laura E. "International Developments in Abortion Law from 1988 to 1998." *American Journal of Public Health* 89 (April 1999), 579–86.

Cudd, Ann E. "Sensationalized Philosophy: A Reply to Marquis's 'Why Abortion Is Immoral.'" *Journal of Philosophy* 87 (1990), 262–64.

Davis, Michael. "Fetuses, Famous Violinists, and the Right to Continued Aid." *Philosophical Quarterly* 33 (1983), 259–78.

Davis, Nancy (Ann). "Abortion and Self-Defense." *Philosophy & Public Affairs* 13 (1984), 175–207.

———. "The Abortion Debate: The Search for Common Ground." Parts 1–2. *Ethics* 103 (1993), 516–39, 731–78.

De Ville, Kenneth A., and Kopelman, Loretta M. "Fetal Protection in Wisconsin's Revised Child Abuse Law: Right Goal, Wrong Remedy." *Journal of Law, Medicine & Ethics* 27 (1999), 332–42.

Destro, Robert A. "Is *Roe v. Wade* Obsolete?" *The Human Life Review* 24 (Summer 1998), 55–70.

Druker, Dan. *Abortion Decisions of the Supreme Court, 1973–1989.* Jefferson, NC: McFarland, 1990.

Dworkin, Ronald. *Life's Dominion: An Argument about Abortion, Euthanasia and Individual Freedom.* New York: Knopf, 1993.

Dwyer, Susan, and Feinberg, Joel, ed. *The Problem of Abortion,* 3rd ed. Belmont, CA: Wadsworth, 1997.

Engelhardt, H. Tristram. *The Foundations of Bioethics.* 2d ed. New York: Oxford University Press, 1996, chap. 6.

English, Jane. "Abortion and the Concept of a Person." *Canadian Journal of Philosophy* 5 (1975), 233–43.

Fagot-Largeault, Anne. "Abortion and Arguments from Potential." In Raanan Gillon, ed. *Principles of Health Care Ethics.* Chichester, Wiley, 1994, 577–86.

Finnis, John. "Abortion and Health Care Ethics." In Raanan Gillon, ed. *Principles of Health Care Ethics.* Chichester: Wiley, 1994, 547–57.

———. "The Rights and Wrongs of Abortion: A Reply to Judith Thomson." *Philosophy & Public Affairs* 2 (1973), 117–45.

Gert, Heather J. "Viability." *International Journal of Philosophical Studies* 3 (1995), 133–42.

Gevers, Sjef. "Third Trimester Abortion for Fetal Abnormality." *Bioethics* 13 (1999), 306–13.

Ginsburg, Ruth Bader. "Some Thoughts on Autonomy and Equality in Relation to *Roe v. Wade.*" *North Carolina Law Review* 63 (1985), 375–86.

Goldberg, Susan. "Medical Choices during Pregnancy: Whose Decision Is It, Anyway?" *Rutgers Law Review* 41 (1989), 591–623.

Graber, M. A. *Rethinking Abortion: Equal Choice, the Constitution, and Reproductive Politics.* Princeton: Princeton University Press, 1996.

Hare, R. M. "Abortion and the Golden Rule." *Philosophy & Public Affairs* 4 (1975), 201–22.

Harris, John. "The Concept of the Person and the Value of Life." *Kennedy Institute of Ethics Journal* 9 (December 1999), 293–308.

Hasnas, John. "From Cannibalism to Caesareans: Two Conceptions of Fundamental Rights." *Northwestern University Law Review* 89 (1995), 900–41.

Hursthouse, Rosalind. *Beginning Lives.* Oxford: Basil Blackwell, 1987.

———. "Virtue Theory and Abortion." *Philosophy & Public Affairs* 20 (1991), 223–46.

Kamm, Frances M. *Creation and Abortion.* New York: Oxford University Press, 1992.

Kennedy Institute of Ethics Journal 9 (December 1999). Special Issue on Persons, ed. Gerhold K. Becker.

King, Patricia A. "The Juridical Status of the Fetus: A Proposal for Legal Protection of the Unborn." *Michigan Law Review* 77 (1979), 1647–87.

Little, Margaret. *Abortion, Intimacy, and Responsibilities to Gestate.* Oxford: Clarendon Press, 2003.

———. "The Morality of Abortion." *Blackwell Companion to Applied Ethics.* Oxford: Blackwell, 2002.

Loewy, Arnold H. "Why *Roe v. Wade* Should be Overruled." *North Carolina Law Review* 67 (1989), 939–48.

MacKenzie, Catriona. "Abortion and Embodiment." *Australasian Journal of Philosophy* 70 (1992), 136–55.

Mathieu, Deborah. *Preventing Prenatal Harm: Should the State Intervene?* 2d ed. Washington: Georgetown University Press, 1996.

McMahan, Jeff. "The Right to Choose an Abortion." *Philosophy & Public Affairs* 22 (1993), 331–48.

Noonan, John T., Jr., ed. *The Morality of Abortion: Legal and Historical Perspectives.* Cambridge, MA: Harvard University Press, 1970.

Overall, Christine. "Mother/Fetus/State Conflicts." *Health Law in Canada* 9 (1989), 101–03, 122.

Persson, Ingmar. "Harming the Non-Conscious." *Bioethics* 13 (1999), 294–305.

Plessinger, M. A., and Woods, J. R. "Cocaine in Pregnancy: Recent Data on Maternal and Fetal Risks," *Obstetrics and Gynecology Clinics of North America* 25 (1998), 99–112.

Pojman, Louis P., and Beckwith, Francis J., eds. *The Abortion Controversy.* Boston: Jones and Bartlett, 1994.

Purdy, Laura M. "Are Pregnant Women Fetal Containers?" *Bioethics* 4 (1990), 273–91.

Quinn, Warren. "Abortion: Identity and Loss." *Philosophy & Public Affairs* 13 (1984), 24–54.

Regan, Tom, ed. *Matters of Life and Death.* 3rd ed. New York: Random House, 1992.

Rhoden, Nancy K. "Cesareans and Samaritans." *Law, Medicine & Health Care* 15 (Fall 1987), 118–25.

———. "The Judge in the Delivery Room: The Emergence of Court-Ordered Caesareans." *California Law Review* 74 (1986), 1951–2030.

———. "A Compromise on Abortion." *Hastings Center Report* 19 (1989), 32–37.

Rubin, Eva R., ed. *The Abortion Controversy: A Documentary History.* Westport, CT: Greenwood Press, 1994.

Seymour, John. "A Pregnant Woman's Decision to Decline Treatment: How Should the Law Respond?" *Journal of Law and Medicine* 2 (1994), 27–37.

Singer, Peter. *Practical Ethics.* Cambridge: Cambridge University Press, 1993.

Solomon, Renee I. "Future Fear: Prenatal Duties Imposed by Private Parties." *American Journal of Law and Medicine* 17 (1991), 411–34.

Stein, Ellen J. "Maternal-Fetal Conflict: Reformulating the Equation." In Andrew Grubb, ed. *Challenges in Medical Care.* New York: Wiley, 1992, 91–108.

Steinbock, Bonnie. *Life before Birth.* New York: Oxford University Press, 1992.

Sumner, L. W. *Abortion and Moral Theory.* Princeton, NJ: Princeton University Press, 1981.

Thomson, Judith Jarvis. "Rights and Deaths." *Philosophy & Public Affairs* 2 (1973), 146–55.

Tooley, Michael. *Abortion and Infanticide.* Oxford: Oxford University Press, 1983.

Tribe, Laurence H. *Abortion: The Clash of Absolutes.* New York: Norton, 1990.

Warren, Mary Anne. "Abortion." In Peter Singer, ed. *A Companion to Ethics.* Cambridge, MA: Blackwell Reference, 1991, 303–14.

———. *Moral Status: Obligations to Persons and Other Living Things.* New York: Oxford University Press, 1997.

Women's Health Issues 1 (Fall 1990). Special issue on "Maternal-Fetal Relations."

BIBLIOGRAPHIES AND REFERENCE WORKS

Curran, William J., et al. *Health Care Law and Ethics.* New York: Aspen Law & Business, 1998. [Includes bibliographical references.]

Becker, Lawrence, and Becker, Charlotte, eds. *Encyclopedia of Ethics.* 1992.

Lineback, Richard H., ed. *Philosopher's Index.* Vols. 1–. Bowling Green, OH: Philosophy Documentation Center, Bowling Green State University. Issued quarterly. Also CD Rom.

National Library of Medicine (NLM) Gateway, http://gateway.nlm.nih.gov.

Reich, Warren, ed. *Encyclopedia of Bioethics,* 2d ed., New York: Macmillan, 1995.

Walters, LeRoy, and Kahn, Tamar Joy, eds. *Bibliography of Bioethics.* Vols. 1–. Washington, DC: Kennedy Institute of Ethics.

Part IV
BIOMEDICAL RESEARCH AND TECHNOLOGY

6.
Research Involving Human and Animal Subjects

INTRODUCTION

Since the early 1990s there has been a renaissance of interest in research ethics. This new interest has been sparked in part by new historical research on past abuses of human research subjects, especially the (often unwitting) subjects of U.S. radiation experiments. However, the field of bioethics has also devoted substantial attention to international research ethics and to the new questions that arise as the locus of much research moves from academic to commercial, or at least semicommercial, settings. While there is widespread agreement on the general ethical guidelines that should govern human research, there are lingering disagreements about the best oversight system for such research, about research in Third World settings, and about the use of placebo controls in clinical trials. Meanwhile, on a parallel track, bioethicists, policy makers, and the public have also focused renewed attention on the welfare of animals in research. Here there is much less consensus than in the realm of human research, with at least two polar positions being argued vigorously by their advocates and with thoughtful scholars attempting to articulate new positions that mediate between the extremes.

CONCEPTUAL QUESTIONS

The definition of *research* can perhaps be best approached by way of considering the concepts of *therapy* and *research*. In the biomedical and behavioral fields, *therapy* refers to a class of activities designed solely to benefit an individual or the members of a group. Therapy may take several forms: It may be a treatment for a disease, or it may consist of diagnostic procedures or even preventive measures. In contrast, *research* refers to a class of scientific activities designed to develop or contribute to generalizable knowledge. Examples of research are a study of alternative methods for training pigeons, a comparison of two drugs for treating AIDS, and a review of patient charts in an effort to detect a correlation between smoking and lung cancer.

Two subtypes of research involving human or animal subjects can be identified. On one hand, research can be combined with the diagnosis, treatment, or prevention of illness in the subjects themselves; that is, it can be aimed directly toward discovering better methods of diagnosing or treating the condition from which human or animal patients are suffering or toward preventing disease in susceptible humans or animals. A study of a new polio vaccine in children at risk for contracting polio would be an example of such research. This kind of inquiry is often designated as *clinical research.* Randomized clinical trials are an important subtype of clinical research. On the other hand, research can be unrelated (or at least not directly related) to an illness or susceptibility of the subjects involved. For example, healthy human volunteers can be involved in studies that examine how long a new drug remains in the bodies of people who receive a certain dose of the drug. Similarly, healthy nonhuman animals are frequently involved in research that aims to understand disease processes in human beings. Thus, coronary arteries may be obstructed in canine subjects so that researchers can better understand what happens to the human heart in a myocardial infraction (heart attack). There is no simple or widely accepted term that applies to all the various kinds of nonclinical research.

There is one category of research that, at first glance, seems to straddle the line between clinical and nonclinical research. It is research on human patients that is unrelated to diagnosing or treating the patients' illnesses. This type of research deserves special mention because it was a prominent feature in the Tuskegee syphilis study and in the human radiation experiments conducted by the U.S. Atomic Energy Commission. In terms of the distinctions developed in the preceding paragraph, this kind of research should be categorized as nonclinical because it is not designed to benefit the patients being studied—even though the research may be conducted in a clinic.

Because of the ambiguities that have surrounded notions like *clinical* and especially *nontherapeutic* in connection with research, some commentators have recommended that these and similar terms be applied only to specific *procedures* or *interventions* rather than to research protocols as a whole. For example, in a clinical trial that compares a standard drug with an investigational new drug, the administration of each drug can reasonably be described as *therapeutic* in intent. The researchers also hope that both drugs will be therapeutic in its outcome for the subjects participating in the study. However, the study protocol will also require types of monitoring for the subjects and, in most cases, additional diagnostic tests that would not be required of patients receiving the standard drug in the typical clinical setting. In addition, subjects in a research protocol may be asked to begin their participation in a study by going through a washout period during which some or all current medications are stopped. These procedures, which differ from the usual practice of administering therapy to patients, can be designated as *nontherapeutic* procedures.

A BRIEF HISTORY OF HUMAN AND ANIMAL RESEARCH

Systematic research on living animals is a relatively recent phenomenon in the history of science. The first important results of animal research were achieved in the seventeenth century when William Harvey demonstrated the circulation of the blood and Robert Hooke explored the mechanism of respiration.[1] Both researchers employed living animals in their work. Similar physiological research continued during the eighteenth century but achieved special prominence in nineteenth-century France, especially in the pioneering studies of François Magendie and his student, Claude Bernard.[2] Late in life Bernard wrote an extended defense of animal research, often called *vivisection* by its critics, in the book entitled *An Introduction to the Study of Experimental Medicine.*[3] During the twentieth century basic physiological research involving animals has continued, even as new modes of applied research in animals have been developed—for example, innovations in surgical technique and the preclinical testing of drugs and biological agents like vaccines.

Systematic research in human beings is also a relatively recent phenomenon. One of the earliest well-documented studies was Dr. Zabdiel Boylston's attempt, during the early years of the eighteenth century, to protect Boston's children against smallpox through inoculation. Boylston's feasibility study, conducted in 1703, involved inoculating his son and two of his slaves with small doses of infectious material.[4] At mid-century a Scottish-born physician, James Lind, demonstrated in a small clinical trial that citrus fruits prevented scurvy in sailors.[5] Toward the end of the eighteenth century, in 1789, Edward Jenner attempted to immunize several children against smallpox by using swinepox and cowpox injections. His own son and several orphan children were among the first subjects.[6]

The involvement of human subjects in research has increased steadily since 1800. During the nineteenth century the French physiological approach that had produced such striking results in animal studies was also applied to human beings. Once again, Claude Bernard was a pioneer.[7] Bernard's countrymen, Pierre Louis and Louis Pasteur, also made important contributions to biomedical knowledge.[8] At the turn of the century U.S. Army Major Walter Reed recruited more than a dozen human volunteers in his effort to demonstrate that yellow fever was transmitted through the bites of mosquitoes.[9] Large-scale clinical trials are primarily a post–World War II phenomenon, with Sir Bradford Hill's 1948 randomized study of streptomycin in the treatment of pulmonary tuberculosis being one of the first clear examples.[10]

ETHICAL ISSUES IN HUMAN RESEARCH

THE MORAL JUSTIFICATION

The general justification for human research is that a human organism responds to biomedical interventions or other stimuli in ways that could not be predicted on the basis of studies with human cells or nonhuman animals. In other words, human physiology involves complex interactions among genes, cells, and organs that cannot be modeled by computer simulations or in other biological systems. In some research—for example, psychological research on reaction times or the capacity to recall words—the goal of the research is simply the acquisition of new knowledge about how human beings function. In much of biomedical research the aim is to find new ways to diagnose or treat disease.

In the literature on human research, including codes of research ethics, surprisingly little attention is paid to the general justification for involving human subjects in biomedical research. This silence at the most general level of justification is particularly striking when one considers that the traditional ethic of medicine has been exclusively a patient-benefit ethic. The motto *primum non nocere* (do no harm) has generally been interpreted to mean, "Do nothing that is not intended for the direct benefit of the patient." One must ask, then, whether good reasons can be given for deviating in any way from therapy, as that term was defined earlier.

The primary argument in favor of human research appeals to the principle of beneficence (as described in Chapter 1). It asserts that the social benefits to be gained from such research are substantial and that the harms resulting from the cessation of such investigations would be exceedingly grave. Proponents of carefully controlled human research have argued that the therapeutic value of many reputed "therapies" is in fact unknown; indeed, these treatments may be no more useful than the bloodletting technique so much in vogue during the eighteenth and nineteenth centuries. On this view, the only alternative to a perpetual plague of medically induced illness is the vigorous pursuit of biomedical research, including research involving human subjects.[11]

A second approach to the justification of human research is based on a joint appeal to the principles of beneficence and justice. According to this view, beneficence requires that each of us make at least a modest positive contribution to the good of our fellow citizens or the society as a whole. If our participation in research promises significant benefit to others, at little or no risk to ourselves, then such participation may be a duty of beneficence. In addition, if we fail to fulfill this modest duty while most of our contemporaries perform it, we may be acting unjustly, since we are not performing our fair share of a communal task.

The justice argument can be further elaborated by reference to the past. Every person currently alive is the beneficiary of earlier human subjects' involvement in research. To be more specific, the willingness of past human volunteers to take part in studies of antibiotics (such as penicillin) and vaccines (such as polio vaccine) has contributed to the health of us all. Accordingly, it seems unfair for us to reap the benefits of already performed research without making a similar contribution to the alleviation of disability and disease for future generations.

Several commentators on the moral justification of research involving human subjects have vigorously contested both of these approaches to the general justification of human research. In answer to the consequential argument, they assert that while human research generally contributes to medical progress, most research involving human subjects is not *essential* to the well-being or survival of the human species. These critics, most notably Hans Jonas,[12] have also rejected the thesis that there is a general moral duty to participate in biomedical research. On this view, there is no injustice involved in people's not volunteering to take part in the production of generalizable knowledge. Nonparticipants in research are simply being less altruistic than their fellow citizens who volunteer for this type of community service.[13]

Within the past decade, a paradigm shift has occurred in the debate about the moral justification of research involving human subjects. The view that participation in clinical research entails a sacrifice for human subjects has been replaced, or at least complemented, by the notion that participation in many kinds of clinical trials is, on balance, beneficial to the subjects themselves. The development of new therapies for AIDS and HIV infection was the first context in which this new emphasis appeared. More recently, commentators on the ethics of human research have called for expanded access by women, including pregnant women, and children to clinical trials.[14]

GENERAL CRITERIA FOR THE ETHICAL CONDUCT OF HUMAN RESEARCH

The codes and guidelines that have been developed for research involving human subjects can be construed as efforts to identify what philosophers term *necessary and sufficient conditions* for proper conduct. These guidelines can also be viewed as examples of what was identified in Chapter 1 as the common morality. That is, there is little disagreement about the general principles and rules that should govern human research, although there may be differences of opinion on the interpretation of some guidelines and uncertainties about how to apply the guidelines in particular circumstances.

The two central conditions identified by the U.S. National Bioethics Advisory Commission for ethical conduct in research are (1) independent review of proposed research to assess its potential benefits and harms for research subjects, and (2) the opportunity for potential subjects to decide freely whether to become participants in the proposed research. Other commentators have proposed more extensive lists of conditions. For example, in an influential article that is not reprinted here, Ezekiel Emanuel, David Wendler, and Christine Grady have suggested seven conditions that make clinical research ethical:

1. Social or scientific value
2. Scientific validity
3. Fair subject selection
4. A favorable risk-benefit ratio (involving either a risk-benefit or a risk-knowledge calculus)
5. Independent review
6. Informed consent by subjects or their proxies
7. Respect for potential and enrolled subjects.[15]

According to the authors, "Fulfilling all 7 requirements is necessary and sufficient to make clinical research ethical."[16]

ETHICAL ISSUES IN ADVANCED INDUSTRIALIZED SOCIETIES

At the conclusion of its five-year existence, the U.S. National Bioethics Advisory Commission (NBAC) performed an audit of the oversight system for human research conducted in the United States. A summary of this audit is included in this chapter under the title "Protecting Research Participants—A Time for Change." While expressing appreciation for progress that has been made since the 1960s and 1970s, the members of NBAC suggest that major, perhaps even radical, changes are required to protect participants in human research. According to the commission, the guidelines for the conduct of research in the United States present a confusing patchwork of sometimes conflicting rules, depending on whether the research is funded by federal government agencies or by commercial firms. In response, the commission proposes the establishment of a new national office—perhaps analogous to the Federal Trade Commission—to oversee all human research in the United States, without regard to funding source. This new agency should, in the commission's view, enforce a uniform set of standards for the ethical conduct of research. NBAC also suggests ways to enhance the work of local research review committees because such committees are, in many ways, the linchpin of the current system for protecting human subjects.

The essay by Ezekiel Emanuel and Franklin Miller tackles a controversial issue in human research ethics—the use of placebos (inactive substances like sugar pills) in clinical research. The authors note that the debate about placebo use has become increasingly polarized, with advocates of placebo orthodoxy arguing that only the widespread use of placebos can preserve the scientific validity of many studies. In contrast, advocates of active-control orthodoxy argue that if a standard therapy is available, placebo controls should never be used. In their analysis Emanuel and Miller point out practical problems that can occur with active-control designs while at the same time acknowledging that placebo controls have sometimes been employed in ways that caused serious, avoidable discomfort to human subjects. The authors' mediating proposal would exclude placebo controls in all but a carefully delimited group of research protocols.

ETHICAL ISSUES IN INTERNATIONAL SETTINGS

The last two essays in the section on ethical issues in human research ask readers to expand their focus to problems in research that is sponsored by developed countries but conducted in less-developed countries. Harold Shapiro and Eric Meslin, chair and executive director, respectively, of the National Bioethics Advisory Commission when they wrote their essay, clearly draw upon NBAC's extensive discussions of research in the Third World. The authors emphasize the importance of having Third World research that responds to Third World needs rather than serving as a less expensive way to develop information that will be used primarily in well-to-do countries. Shapiro and Meslin also argue for an ongoing commitment to the participants in Third World clinical trials by trial sponsors. Solomon Benatar would undoubtedly agree with many of the arguments put forward by his North American counterparts. However, from his Third World perspective in Cape Town, South Africa, Benatar formulates a much more radical critique of spending priorities in the wealthiest nations. In his view, the developed countries are guilty of gross moral negligence, if not criminal neglect, in ignoring the health needs of Third World countries. Citing statistics published in 1990, Benatar notes that in the United States 90 percent of spending for health-related research is dedicated to diseases that cause only 10 percent of the global disease burden. Benatar's proposed solutions would go far beyond the revision of spending priorities in biomedical research and would include a fundamental restructuring of the relationship between the developed and less developed worlds.

(Several issues raised by Benatar are discussed in greater detail in Chapter 9 of this book, in the context of the global AIDS epidemic.)

PAST ABUSES OF HUMAN RESEARCH SUBJECTS

The current chapter includes three accounts of gross abuses committed against human subjects during the course of the twentieth century. The first example—the Tuskegee syphilis study—was more a study in the natural history of disease in African-American men than an experiment in the strict sense. President William Clinton formally apologized for the U.S. government's sponsorship of this study in 1997. A second example of unethical research is much less well known. During the 1930s and 1940s, Japanese soldiers who occupied China and Manchuria—in collaboration with physicians and scientists—deliberately exposed hapless civilians from the occupied countries to a panoply of infectious diseases. Finally, the United States government also sponsored several thousand human radiation experiments, many of them performed on unsuspecting human subjects, during the years between 1944 and 1974. These studies were first described in detail by a presidential advisory committee in 1995.

RESEARCH INVOLVING ANIMALS

The first question to be clarified in any discussion of animal research is: Which animals are to be included within the scope of consideration? Books and articles on the ethics of animal research have devoted surprisingly little attention to this question. One can usually infer from these writings that nonhuman mammals—such as monkeys, dogs, and rats—are to be included in the protected group. Indeed, in his extensive writings on the topic of animal research, Tom Regan explicitly limits his argument to "all species of mammalian animals."[17] A somewhat broader class would be all vertebrates—that is, mammals plus birds, reptiles, amphibians, and fish. In the discussion that follows, it is assumed that the term *animals* refers to nonhuman vertebrates.

Statistics from two countries that closely monitor the use of animals in research may serve to make the notion of animal research more concrete. In the United Kingdom, approximately 2.7 million research procedures involving animals were performed in the year 2000. Approximately 21 percent of the procedures were performed in genetically modified animals. Rodents were the research subjects in 82 percent of the cases; fish, amphibians, reptiles, and birds comprised another 14 percent of the subjects.[18] Data from Canada indicate that 1,746,606 animals were used in scientific research, testing, and education in 1999. This number represents a 17.5 percent reduction from the number used in 1992, which was 2,115,006. Of the animals used in 1999, approximately 917,200, or 52.5 percent were rats and mice. Scientific research accounted for 83 percent of the total use of animals.[19]

The European Biomedical Research Association annually reports comprehensive statistics on the numbers of animals used for research in France, the United Kingdom, Germany, the Netherlands, Spain, Denmark, Portugal, Greece, and Ireland.[20] In contrast, U.S. reporting on animal research is grossly deficient. Current regulations adopted pursuant to the Animal Welfare Act do not require public reporting on the number of mice, rats, and birds used in research each year. Thus, the most recent report from the Department of Agriculture indicates that in fiscal year 2000, 1,416,643 animals were used in research. It seems reasonable, as animal welfare advocate Barbara Orlans has suggested, to multiply this number by 10 to achieve numbers that are comparable to those of Canada and many European countries.[21] Thus, the number of animals used in U.S. research in fiscal year 2001 is likely to have been approximately 14 million. Even these figures are probably underestimates. Harvard Medical School alone estimated in 1999 that it would likely double its annual use of mice within the next five years to 1 million mice per year.[22]

The four authors whose essays are reprinted in this chapter all represent mediating, or intermediate, positions in the debate about animal research. That is, none of the authors agrees with the abolitionists, on one hand, or with research proponents who deny that our treatment of animals raises moral questions, on the other. In his historical review, Andrew Rowan notes that theological and philosophical traditions have reached radically different conclusions about the moral status of animals. Rowan advocates a nuanced position that takes into account what he calls "a tapestry of characteristics," including "the possession of life," "the possession of sentience," "the possession of desires," and "the possession of self-awareness." He clearly thinks that some research involving the infliction of pain on animals is morally justified, yet he acknowledges that there is room for improvement in research designs and the development of alternatives to animal research.

The essays by David DeGrazia and Baruch Brody analyze two competing views on the moral status of animals. The first view argues that nonhuman animals and their interests deserve equal consideration to human beings and their interests. According to the alternative view, animal interests should always be taken into account, but they are less important than human interests. DeGrazia speaks of a "sliding scale" that can be used in evaluating animal interests—a scale that is based on the animals' "cognitive, affective, and social complexity." In contrast, Brody employs an economic metaphor: the interests of nonhuman animals can be "discounted." Both authors criticize views that are regularly put forward by biomedical research proponents, especially in the United States. DeGrazia complains about a "party line" among biomedical researchers, a position and a rhetorical style that attempt to depict animal welfare advocates as extremists. Brody rejects the position that human interests *always* trump animal interests; he finds this human-priority position clearly articulated in most U.S. guidelines for animal research but less clearly present in comparable European guidelines.

According to Brody, the interests of animals may justifiably be discounted in two ways. First, in principle, human interests are more important than animal interests. Second, special roles or obligations to one's fellow human beings can justify an even deeper discounting of animal interests. The challenge for future ethical analysis will be to demonstrate exactly how the discounting procedure works in practice and to specify whether there are some types or levels of pain, distress, or suffering that should never be inflicted on animals, regardless of the good consequences that could be expected for human health or well-being.

A specific case that deserves further ethical analysis is what is called "unrelieved pain and distress" in laboratory animals. Animal welfare advocates are deeply concerned about research that causes such animal pain and distress.[23] U.S. Department of Agriculture regulations require that all procedures that inflict unrelieved pain and distress on animals be reported to the Department annually. In fiscal year 2000, such procedures occurred in more than 7 percent of reported animals and affected 104,202 animals.[24] However, as noted earlier, current regulations exclude bird and purpose-bred rats and mice. Thus, it is likely that the total number of laboratory animals experiencing unrelieved pain and distress is approximately one million per year in the United States alone.[25]

The concluding essay by Richard Smith reports on progress with the three Rs—replacement, reduction, and refinement—that has occurred in the United Kingdom since the introduction of the Animals (Scientific Procedures) Act of 1986. Smith reports a 25 percent reduction in the number of animal procedures performed in the United Kingdom during the twenty years following the enactment of the new law and reports on European efforts to develop substitutes for the use of live animals in research. He warns, however, that excessive refinement can have the unintended effect of making scientific results less sound, "so possibly rendering the animal's suffering worthless."

CODES AND GUIDELINES

The codes and guidelines reprinted in this chapter illustrate a gradual evolution in standards for the proper conduct of research involving human and animal subjects. The central affirmation of the Nuremberg Code, that the voluntary consent of every human subject is a *sine qua non* for the subject's participation, has gradually been supplemented by other important emphases. For example, the Declaration of Helsinki adds to Nuremberg's accent on consent the distinction between research involving patients and research involving healthy volunteers. Helsinki also advocates prior review of research protocols by an "independent committee," as well as making explicit provision for participation in research by legally-incompetent persons. In the most recent revision of the Helsinki Declaration, adopted in 2000, the appropriate setting for the use of placebo-controlled trials was a hotly contested topic. The formulation contained in Article 29 was clarified in a supplementary statement issued a year later. The CIOMS guidelines for human and animal research illustrate the global character of research with both human and animal subjects and the substantial international consensus that exists, especially on the ethics of human research. In addition, the 1993 CIOMS guidelines are attentive to the issues that may arise when human research is conducted in Third World settings.

In the essay that concludes the first section of this chapter, Baruch Brody illustrates the both the extent and limits of ethical agreement on research ethics. For research involving competent adult human subjects, Brody discovers near-unanimity on ethical standards throughout the world. Ethical guidelines for research involving animals reveal areas of disagreement, while the views of various nations and expert advisory groups on research with preimplantation human embryos are sharply divided. Brody notes that conflicting presuppositions about the moral, and even metaphysical, status of animals and early human embryos underlie at least some of the disagreements about research involving these two types of subjects.

L.W.

NOTES

1. Baruch A. Brody, *The Ethics of Biomedical Research: An International Perspective* (New York: Oxford University Press, 1998), 12.
2. *Ibid.*
3. Claude Bernard, *An Introduction to the Study of Experimental Medicine,* trans. H. C. Greene (New York: Dover, 1957).
4. Gert H. Brieger, "Human Experimentation: History," in Warren T. Reich, ed., *Encyclopedia of Bioethics* (New York: Free Press, 1978), 686.
5. *Ibid.*
6. Albert R. Jonsen, *The Birth of Bioethics* (New York: Oxford University Press, 1998), 126.
7. *Ibid.,* 127.
8. Leon Eisenberg, "The Social Imperatives of Medical Research." *Science* 198 (December 16, 1977), 1105–1110.
9. Brieger, "Human Experimentation," 687–88.
10. Brody, *Ethics of Biomedical Research,* 140.
11. For a classic statement of this argument, see Eisenberg, "The Social Imperatives of Medical Research."
12. Hans Jonas, "Philosophical Reflections on Experimenting with Human Subjects," *Daedalus* 98 (Spring 1969), 219–47.
13. *Ibid.,* 223–24, 231–33.

14. See, for example, Anna C. Mastroianni, Ruth Faden, and Daniel Federman, eds., *Women and Health Research: Ethical and Legal Issues of Including Women in Clinical Studies,* 2 vols. (Washington, DC: National Academy Press, 1994).

15. Ezekiel J. Emanuel, David Wendler, and Christine Grady, "What Makes Clinical Research Ethical?" *Journal of the American Medical Association* 283, (2000), 2701–11.

16. *Ibid.,* 2701.

17. Tom Regan, *The Case for Animal Rights* (Berkeley: University of California Press, 1983).

18. U.K. Home Office, *Statistics of Scientific Procedures on Living Animals—Great Britain, 2000* (London: Her Majesty's Stationery Office, July 2001), 24–37. [http://www.archive.official-documents.co.uk/document/cm52/5244/524401.htm

19. Canadian Council on Animal Care, Animal Use Survey for 1999, "Facts & Figures"; online report. [http://www.ccac.ca/english/survey/aus99.htm]

20. European Biomedical Research Association, "European Statistics," primarily from the year 1991. [hhtp://www.ebra.org/stats/index.html]

21. F. Barbara Orlans, "Research on Animals, Law, Legislative, and Welfare Issues in the Use of Animals for Genetic Engineering and Xenotransplantation," in Thomas H. Murray and Maxwell J. Mehlman, eds., *Encyclopedia of Ethical, Legal, and Policy Issues in Biotechnology,* 2 vols. (New York: John Wiley and Sons, 2000), 1024–25.

22. John F. Lauerman, "Animal Research," *Harvard Magazine* 101 (January–February 1999), 48–57. [http://www.harvardmagazine.com/issues/jf99/mice.html]

23. See for example, William S. Stokes, "Introduction: Reducing Unrelieved Pain and Distress in Laboratory Animals Using Humane Endpoints," *ILAR Journal* 41 (2000), 59–61. [http://www4.nationalacademies.org/ijhome.nsf/web/ilar_journal_online?OpenDocument]

24. U.S. Department of Agriculture, *Animal Welfare Report: Fiscal Year 2002* (Washington, DC: USDA, July 2001), 38–39. [http://www.aphis.usda.gov/ac/publications.html]

25. *Ibid.*

Codes and Guidelines

The Nuremberg Code (1947)

The great weight of the evidence before us is to the effect that certain types of medical experiments on human beings, when kept within reasonably well-defined bounds, conform to the ethics of the medical profession generally. The protagonists of the practice of human experimentation justify their views on the basis that such experiments yield results for the good of society that are unprocurable by other methods or means of study. All agree, however, that certain basic principles must be observed in order to satisfy moral, ethical and legal concepts.

1. The voluntary consent of the human subject is absolutely essential.

This means that the person involved should have legal capacity to give consent; should be so situated as to be able to exercise free power of choice, without the intervention of any element of force, fraud, deceit, duress, overreaching, or other ulterior form of constraint or coercion; and should have sufficient knowledge and comprehension of the elements of the subject matter involved as to enable him to make an understanding and enlightened decision. This latter element requires that before the acceptance of an affirmative decision by the experimental subject there should be made known to him the nature, duration, and purpose of the experiment; the method and means by which it is to be conducted; all inconveniences and hazards reasonably to be expected; and the effects upon his health or person which may possibly come from his participation in the experiment.

The duty and responsibility for ascertaining the quality of the consent rests upon each individual who initiates, directs or engages in the experiment. It is a personal duty and responsibility which may not be delegated to another with impunity.

2. The experiment should be such as to yield fruitful results for the good of society, unprocurable by other methods or means of study, and not random and unnecessary in nature.

3. The experiment should be so designed and based on the results of animal experimentation and a knowledge of the natural history of the disease or other problems under study that the anticipated results will justify the performance of the experiment.

4. The experiment should be so conducted as to avoid all unnecessary physical and mental suffering and injury.

5. No experiment should be conducted where there is an *a priori* reason to believe that death or disabling injury will occur; except perhaps, in those experiments where the experimental physicians also serve as subjects.

6. The degree of risk to be taken should never exceed that determined by the humanitarian importance of the problem to be solved by the experiment.

7. Proper preparations should be made and adequate facilities provided to protect the experimental subject against even remote possibilities of injury, disability, or death.

8. The experiment should be conducted only by scientifically qualified persons. The highest degree of skill and care should be required through all stages of the experiment of those who conduct or engage in the experiment.

9. During the course of the experiment the human subject should be at liberty to bring the experiment to an end if he has reached the physical or mental state where continuation of the experiment seems to him to be impossible.

10. During the course of the experiment the scientist in charge must be prepared to terminate the experiment at any stage, if he has probable cause to believe, in the exercise of the good faith, superior skill and careful judgment required of him that a continuation of the experiment is likely to result in injury, disability, or death to the experimental subject.

From *Trials of War. Criminals before the Nuremberg Military Tribunals under Control Council Law No. 10.* Vol. 2. Nuremberg, October 1946–April 1949.

WORLD MEDICAL ASSOCIATION

Declaration of Helsinki
Ethical Principles for Medical Research Involving Human Subjects

A. INTRODUCTION

1. The World Medical Association has developed the Declaration of Helsinki as a statement of ethical principles to provide guidance to physicians and other participants in medical research involving human subjects. Medical research involving human subjects includes research on identifiable human material or identifiable data.
2. It is the duty of the physician to promote and safeguard the health of the people. The physician's knowledge and conscience are dedicated to the fulfillment of this duty.
3. The Declaration of Geneva of the World Medical Association binds the physician with the words, "The health of my patient will be my first consideration," and the International Code of Medical Ethics declares that, "A physician shall act only in the patient's interest when providing medical care which might have the effect of weakening the physical and mental condition of the patient."
4. Medical progress is based on research which ultimately must rest in part on experimentation involving human subjects.
5. In medical research on human subjects, considerations related to the well-being of the human subject should take precedence over the interests of science and society.
6. The primary purpose of medical research involving human subjects is to improve prophylactic, diagnostic and therapeutic procedures and the understanding of the aetiology and pathogenesis of disease. Even the best proven prophylactic, diagnostic, and therapeutic methods must continuously be challenged through research for their effectiveness, efficiency, accessibility and quality.
7. In current medical practice and in medical research, most prophylactic, diagnostic and therapeutic procedures involve risks and burdens.
8. Medical research is subject to ethical standards that promote respect for all human beings and protect their health and rights. Some research populations are vulnerable and need special protection. The particular needs of the economically and medically disadvantaged must be recognized. Special attention is also required for those who cannot give or refuse consent for themselves, for those who may be subject to giving consent under duress, for those who will not benefit personally from the research and for those for whom the research is combined with care.
9. Research Investigators should be aware of the ethical, legal and regulatory requirements for research on human subjects in their own countries as well as applicable international requirements. No national ethical, legal or regulatory requirement should be allowed to reduce or eliminate any of the protections for human subjects set forth in this Declaration.

Adopted by the 18th WMA General Assembly
Helsinki, Finland, June 1964 and amended by the 29th WMA General Assembly, Tokyo, Japan, October 1975; 35th WMA General Assembly, Venice, Italy, October 1983; 41st WMA General Assembly, Hong Kong, September 1989; 48th WMA General Assembly, Somerset West, Republic of South Africa, October 1996; and the 52nd WMA General Assembly, Edinburgh, Scotland, October 2000.

B. BASIC PRINCIPLES FOR ALL MEDICAL RESEARCH

10. It is the duty of the physician in medical research to protect the life, health, privacy, and dignity of the human subject.
11. Medical research involving human subjects must conform to generally accepted scientific principles, be based on a thorough knowledge of the scientific literature, other relevant sources of information, and on adequate laboratory and, where appropriate, animal experimentation.
12. Appropriate caution must be exercised in the conduct of research which may affect the environment, and the welfare of animals used for research must be respected.
13. The design and performance of each experimental procedure involving human subjects should be clearly formulated in an experimental protocol. This protocol should be submitted for consideration, comment, guidance, and where appropriate, approval to a specially appointed ethical review committee, which must be independent of the investigator, the sponsor or any other kind of undue influence. This independent committee should be in conformity with the laws and regulations of the country in which the research experiment is performed. The committee has the right to monitor ongoing trials. The researcher has the obligation to provide monitoring information to the committee, especially any serious adverse events. The researcher should also submit to the committee, for review, information regarding funding, sponsors, institutional affiliations, other potential conflicts of interest and incentives for subjects.
14. The research protocol should always contain a statement of the ethical considerations involved and should indicate that there is compliance with the principles enunciated in this Declaration.
15. Medical research involving human subjects should be conducted only by scientifically qualified persons and under the supervision of a clinically competent medical person. The responsibility for the human subject must always rest with a medically qualified person and never rest on the subject of the research, even though the subject has given consent.
16. Every medical research project involving human subjects should be preceded by careful assessment of predictable risks and burdens in comparison with foreseeable benefits to the subject or to others. This does not preclude the participation of healthy volunteers in medical research. The design of all studies should be publicly available.
17. Physicians should abstain from engaging in research projects involving human subjects unless they are confident that the risks involved have been adequately assessed and can be satisfactorily managed. Physicians should cease any investigation if the risks are found to outweigh the potential benefits or if there is conclusive proof of positive and beneficial results.
18. Medical research involving human subjects should only be conducted if the importance of the objective outweighs the inherent risks and burdens to the subject. This is especially important when the human subjects are healthy volunteers.
19. Medical research is only justified if there is a reasonable likelihood that the populations in which the research is carried out stand to benefit from the results of the research.
20. The subjects must be volunteers and informed participants in the research project.
21. The right of research subjects to safeguard their integrity must always be respected. Every precaution should be taken to respect the privacy of the subject, the confidentiality of the patient's information and to minimize the impact of the study on the subject's physical and mental integrity and on the personality of the subject.
22. In any research on human beings, each potential subject must be adequately informed of the aims, methods, sources of funding, any possible conflicts of interest, institutional affiliations of the researcher, the anticipated benefits and potential risks of the study and the discomfort it may entail. The subject should be informed of the right to abstain from participation in the study or to withdraw consent to participate at any time without reprisal. After ensuring that the subject has understood the information, the physician should then obtain the subject's freely-given informed consent, preferably in writing. If the consent cannot be obtained in writing, the non-written consent must be formally documented and witnessed.

23. When obtaining informed consent for the research project, the physician should be particularly cautious if the subject is in a dependent relationship with the physician or may consent under duress. In that case the informed consent should be obtained by a well-informed physician who is not engaged in the investigation and who is completely independent of this relationship.
24. For a research subject who is legally incompetent, physically or mentally incapable of giving consent or is a legally incompetent minor, the investigator must obtain informed consent from the legally authorized representative in accordance with applicable law. These groups should not be included in research unless the research is necessary to promote the health of the population represented and this research cannot instead be performed on legally competent persons.
25. When a subject deemed legally incompetent, such as a minor child, is able to give assent to decisions about participation in research, the investigator must obtain that assent in addition to the consent of the legally authorized representative.
26. Research on individuals from whom it is not possible to obtain consent, including proxy or advance consent, should be done only if the physical/mental condition that prevents obtaining informed consent is a necessary characteristic of the research population. The specific reasons for involving research subjects with a condition that renders them unable to give informed consent should be stated in the experimental protocol for consideration and approval of the review committee. The protocol should state that consent to remain in the research should be obtained as soon as possible from the individual or a legally authorized surrogate.
27. Both authors and publishers have ethical obligations. In publication of the results of research, the investigators are obliged to preserve the accuracy of the results. Negative as well as positive results should be published or otherwise publicly available. Sources of funding, institutional affiliations and any possible conflicts of interest should be declared in the publication. Reports of experimentation not in accordance with the principles laid down in this Declaration should not be accepted for publication.

C. ADDITIONAL PRINCIPLES FOR MEDICAL RESEARCH COMBINED WITH MEDICAL CARE

28. The physician may combine medical research with medical care, only to the extent that the research is justified by its potential prophylactic, diagnostic or therapeutic value. When medical research is combined with medical care, additional standards apply to protect the patients who are research subjects.
29. The benefits, risks, burdens and effectiveness of a new method should be tested against those of the best current prophylactic, diagnostic, and therapeutic methods. This does not exclude the use of placebo, or no treatment, in studies where no proven prophylactic, diagnostic or therapeutic method exists.

To further clarify the WMA position on the use of placebo controlled trials, the WMA Council issued, during October 2001, a note of clarification on article 29 [see below].

30. At the conclusion of the study, every patient entered into the study should be assured of access to the best proven prophylactic, diagnostic and therapeutic methods identified by the study.
31. The physician should fully inform the patient which aspects of the care are related to the research. The refusal of a patient to participate in a study must never interfere with the patient-physician relationship.
32. In the treatment of a patient, where proven prophylactic, diagnostic and therapeutic methods do not exist or have been ineffective, the physician, with informed consent from the patient, must be free to use unproven or new prophylactic, diagnostic and therapeutic measures, if in the physician's judgement it offers hope of saving life, re-establishing health or alleviating suffering. Where possible, these measures should be made the object of research, designed to evaluate their safety and efficacy. In all cases, new information should be recorded and, where appropriate, published. The other relevant guidelines of this Declaration should be followed.

NOTE OF CLARIFICATION ON PARAGRAPH 29 OF THE WMA DECLARATION OF HELSINKI

The WMA is concerned that paragraph 29 of the revised Declaration of Helsinki (October 2000) has led to diverse interpretations and possible confusion. It hereby reaffirms its position that extreme care must be taken in making use of a placebo-controlled trial and that in general this methodology should only be used in the absence of existing proven therapy. However, a placebo-controlled trial may be ethically acceptable, even if proven therapy is available, under the following circumstances:

- Where for compelling and scientifically sound methodological reasons its use is necessary to determine the efficacy or safety of a prophylactic, diagnostic or therapeutic method; or
- Where a prophylactic, diagnostic or therapeutic method is being investigated for a minor condition and the patients who receive placebo will not be subject to any additional risk of serious or irreversible harm.

All other provisions of the Declaration of Helsinki must be adhered to, especially the need for appropriate ethical and scientific review.

COUNCIL FOR INTERNATIONAL ORGANIZATIONS OF MEDICAL SCIENCES (CIOMS) IN COLLABORATION WITH THE WORLD HEALTH ORGANIZATION (WHO)

International Ethical Guidelines for Biomedical Research Involving Human Subjects (1993)

• • •

GENERAL ETHICAL PRINCIPLES

All research involving human subjects should be conducted in accordance with three basic ethical principles, namely respect for persons, beneficence and justice. It is generally agreed that these principles, which in the abstract have equal moral force, guide the conscientious preparation of proposals for scientific studies. In varying circumstances they may be expressed differently and given different moral weight, and their application may lead to different decisions or courses of action. The present guidelines are directed at the application of these principles to research involving human subjects.

Reprinted from Z. Bankowski and R. J. Levine, eds., *Ethics and Research on Human Subjects: International Guidelines* (Geneva: CIOMS, 1993), pp. 1–45 (excerpts). Reprinted with the permission of CIOMS. These guidelines are being revised and updated, and the final version will be available in Summer, 2002.

Respect for persons incorporates at least two fundamental ethical considerations, namely:

a) respect for autonomy, which requires that those who are capable of deliberation about their personal choices should be treated with respect for their capacity for self-determination; and
b) protection of persons with impaired or diminished autonomy, which requires that those who are dependent or vulnerable be afforded security against harm or abuse.

Beneficence refers to the ethical obligation to maximize benefits and to minimize harms and wrongs. This principle gives rise to norms requiring that the risks of research be reasonable in the light of the expected benefits, that the research design be sound, and that the investigators be competent both to conduct the research and to safeguard the welfare of the research subjects. Beneficence further proscribes the deliberate infliction of harm on persons; this aspect of beneficence is sometimes expressed as a separate principle, **nonmaleficence** (do no harm).

Justice refers to the ethical obligation to treat each person in accordance with what is morally right and proper, to give each person what is due to him or her. In the ethics of research involving human subjects the principle refers primarily to **distributive justice,** which requires the equitable distribution of both the burdens and the benefits of participation in research. Differences in distribution of burdens and benefits are justifiable only if they are based on morally relevant distinctions between persons; one such distinction is vulnerability. "Vulnerability" refers to a substantial incapacity to protect one's own interests owing to such impediments as lack of capability to give informed consent, lack of alternative means of obtaining medical care or other expensive necessities, or being a junior or subordinate member of a hierarchical group. Accordingly, special provisions must be made for the protection of the rights and welfare of vulnerable persons.

PREAMBLE

The term "research" refers to a class of activities designed to develop or contribute to generalizable knowledge. Generalizable knowledge consists of theories, principles or relationships, or the accumulation of information on which they are based, that can be corroborated by accepted scientific methods of observation and inference. In the present context "research" includes both medical and behavioral studies pertaining to human health. Usually "research" is modified by the adjective "biomedical" to indicate that the reference is to health-related research.

Progress in medical care and disease prevention depends upon an understanding of physiological and pathological processes or epidemiological findings, and requires at some time research involving human subjects. The collection, analysis and interpretation of information obtained from research involving human beings contribute significantly to the improvement of human health.

Research involving human subjects includes that undertaken together with patient care (clinical research) and that undertaken on patients or other subjects, or with data pertaining to them, solely to contribute to generalizable knowledge (non-clinical biomedical research). Research is defined as "clinical" if one or more of its components is designed to be diagnostic, prophylactic or therapeutic for the individual subject of the research. Invariably, in clinical research, there are also components designed not to be diagnostic, prophylactic or therapeutic for the subject; examples include the administration of placebos and the performance of laboratory tests in addition to those required to serve the purposes of medical care. Hence the term "clinical research" is used here rather than "therapeutic research."

Research involving human subjects includes:

- studies of a physiological, biochemical or pathological process, or of the response to a specific intervention—whether physical, chemical or psychological—in healthy subjects or patients;
- controlled trials of diagnostic, preventive or therapeutic measures in larger groups of persons, designed to demonstrate a specific generalizable response to these measures against a background of individual biological variation;
- studies designed to determine the consequences for individuals and communities of specific preventive or therapeutic measures; and
- studies concerning human health-related behaviour in a variety of circumstances and environments.

Research involving human subjects may employ either observation or physical, chemical or psychological intervention; it may also either generate records or make use of existing records containing biomedical or other information about individuals who may or may not be identifiable from the records or information. The use of such records and the protection of the confidentiality of data obtained from those records are discussed in *International Guidelines for Ethical Review of Epidemiological Studies* (CIOMS, 1991).

Research involving human subjects includes also research in which environmental factors are manipulated in a way that could affect incidentally-exposed individuals. Research is defined in broad terms in order to embrace field studies of pathogenic organisms and toxic chemicals under investigation for health-related purposes.

Research involving human subjects is to be distinguished from the practice of medicine, public health and other forms of health care, which is designed to contribute directly to the health of individuals or communities. Prospective subjects may find it confusing when research and practice are to be conducted simultaneously, as when research is designed to obtain new information about the efficacy of a drug or other therapeutic, diagnostic or preventive modality.

Research involving human subjects should be carried out only by, or strictly supervised by, suitably qualified and experienced investigators and in accordance with a protocol that clearly states: the aim of the research; the reasons for proposing that it involve human subjects; the nature and degree of any known risks to the subjects; the sources from which it is proposed to recruit subjects; and the means proposed for ensuring that subjects' consent will be adequately informed and voluntary. The protocol should be scientifically and ethically appraised by one or more suitably constituted review bodies, independent of the investigators.

New vaccines and medicinal drugs, before being approved for general use must be tested on human subjects in clinical trials; such trials . . . constitute a substantial part of all research involving human subjects. . . .

THE GUIDELINES

INFORMED CONSENT OF SUBJECTS

Guideline 1: Individual Informed Consent. For all biomedical research involving human subjects, the investigator must obtain the informed consent of the prospective subject or, in the case of an individual who is not capable of giving informed consent, the proxy consent of a properly authorized representative.

• • •

Guideline 2: Essential Information for Prospective Research Subjects. Before requesting an individual's consent to participate in research, the investigator must provide the individual with the following information, in language that he or she is capable of understanding:

- that each individual is invited to participate as a subject in research, and the aims and methods of the research;
- the expected duration of the subject's participation;
- the benefits that might reasonably be expected to result to the subject or to others as an outcome of the research;
- any foreseeable risks or discomfort to the subject, associated with participation in the research;
- any alternative procedures or courses of treatment that might be as advantageous to the subject as the procedure or treatment being tested;
- the extent to which confidentiality of records in which the subject is identified will be maintained;
- the extent of the investigator's responsibility, if any, to provide medical services to the subject;
- that therapy will be provided free of charge for specified types of research-related injury;
- whether the subject or the subject's family or dependents will be compensated for disability or death resulting from such injury; and
- that the individual is free to refuse to participate and will be free to withdraw from the research at any time without penalty or loss of benefits to which he or she would otherwise be entitled.

• • •

Guideline 3: Obligations of Investigators Regarding Informed Consent. The investigator has a duty to:

- communicate to the prospective subject all the information necessary for adequately informed consent;
- give the prospective subject full opportunity and encouragement to ask questions;

- exclude the possibility of unjustified deception, undue influence and intimidation;
- seek consent only after the prospective subject has adequate knowledge of the relevant facts and of the consequences of participation, and has had sufficient opportunity to consider whether to participate;
- as a general rule, obtain from each prospective subject a signed form as evidence of informed consent; and
- renew the informed consent of each subject if there are material changes in the conditions or procedures of the research.

• • •

Guideline 4: Inducement to Participate. Subjects may be paid for inconvenience and time spent, and should be reimbursed for expenses incurred, in connection with their participation in research; they may also receive free medical services. However, the payments should not be so large or the medical services to extensive as to induce prospective subjects to consent to participate in the research against their better judgment ("undue inducement"). All payments, reimbursements and medical services to be provided to research subjects should be approved by an ethical review committee.

• • •

Guideline 5: Research Involving Children. Before undertaking research involving children, the investigator must ensure that:

- children will not be involved in research that might equally well be carried out with adults;
- the purpose of the research is to obtain knowledge relevant to the health needs of children;
- a parent or legal guardian of each child has given proxy consent;
- the consent of each child has been obtained to the extent of the child's capabilities;
- the child's refusal to participate in research must always be respected unless according to the research protocol the child would receive therapy for which there is no medically-acceptable alternative;
- the risk presented by interventions not intended to benefit the individual child-subject is low and commensurate with the importance of the knowledge to be gained; and
- interventions that are intended to provide therapeutic benefit are likely to be at least as advantageous to the individual child-subject as any available alternative.

• • •

Guideline 6: Research Involving Persons with Mental or Behavioral Disorders. Before undertaking research involving individuals who by reason of mental or behavioral disorders are not capable of giving adequately informed consent, the investigator must ensure that:

- such persons will not be subjects of research that might equally well be carried out on persons in full possession of their mental faculties;
- the purpose of the research is to obtain knowledge relevant to the particular health needs of persons with mental or behavioral disorders;
- the consent of each subject has been obtained to the extent of that subject's capabilities, and a prospective subject's refusal to participate in non-clinical research is always respected;
- in the case of incompetent subjects, informed consent is obtained from the legal guardian or other duly authorized person;
- the degree of risk attached to interventions that are not intended to benefit the individual subject is low and commensurate with the importance of the knowledge to be gained; and
- interventions that are intended to provide therapeutic benefit are likely to be at least as advantageous to the individual subject as any alternative.

• • •

Guideline 7: Research Involving Prisoners. Prisoners with serious illness or at risk of serious illness should not arbitrarily be denied access to investigational drugs, vaccines or other agents that show promise of therapeutic or preventive benefit.

• • •

Guideline 8: Research Involving Subjects in Underdeveloped Communities. Before undertaking research involving subjects in underdeveloped communities, whether in developed or developing countries, the investigator must ensure that:

- persons in underdeveloped communities will not ordinarily be involved in research that could be carried out reasonably well in developed communities;
- the research is responsive to the health needs and the priorities of the community in which it is to be carried out;
- every effort will be made to secure the ethical imperative that the consent of individual subjects be informed; and
- the proposals for the research have been reviewed and approved by an ethical review committee that has among its members or consultants persons who are thoroughly familiar with the customs and traditions of the community.

• • •

Guideline 9: Informed Consent in Epidemiological Studies. For several types of epidemiological research individual informed consent is either impracticable or inadvisable. In such cases the ethical review committee should determine whether it is ethically acceptable to proceed without individual informed consent and whether the investigator's plans to protect the safety and respect the privacy of research subjects and to maintain the confidentiality of the data are adequate.

• • •

SELECTION OF RESEARCH SUBJECTS

Guideline 10: Equitable Distribution of Burdens and Benefits. Individuals or communities to be invited to be subjects of research should be selected in such a way that the burdens and benefits of the research will be equitably distributed. Special justification is required for inviting vulnerable individuals and, if they are selected, the means of protecting their rights and welfare must be particularly strictly applied.

• • •

Guideline 11: Selection of Pregnant or Nursing (Breastfeeding) Women as Research Subjects. Pregnant or nursing women should in no circumstances be the subjects of non-clinical research unless the research carries no more than minimal risk to the fetus or nursing infant and the object of the research is to obtain new knowledge about pregnancy or lactation. As a general rule, pregnant or nursing women should not be subjects of any clinical trials except such trials as are designed to protect or advance the health of pregnant or nursing women or fetuses or nursing infants, and for which women who are not pregnant or nursing would not be suitable subjects.

• • •

CONFIDENTIALITY OF DATA

Guideline 12: Safeguarding Confidentiality. The investigator must establish secure safeguards of the confidentiality of research data. Subjects should be told of the limits to the investigators' ability to safeguard confidentiality and of the anticipated consequences of breaches of confidentiality.

• • •

COMPENSATION OF RESEARCH SUBJECTS FOR ACCIDENTAL INJURY

Guideline 13: Rights of Subjects to Compensation. Research subjects who suffer physical injury as a result of their participation are entitled to such financial or other assistance as would compensate them equitably for any temporary or permanent impairment or disability. In the case of death, their dependents are entitled to material compensation. The right to compensation may not be waived.

• • •

REVIEW PROCEDURES

Guideline 14: Constitution and Responsibilities of Ethical Review Committees. All proposals to conduct research involving human subjects must be submitted for review and approval to one or more independent ethical and scientific review committees. The investigator must obtain such approval of the proposal to conduct research before the research is begun.

• • •

Guideline 15: Obligations of Sponsoring and Host Countries. Externally sponsored research entails two ethical obligations:

- An external sponsoring agency should submit the research protocol to ethical and scientific review according to the standards of the country of the sponsoring agency, and the ethical standards applied should be no less exacting than they would be in the case of research carried out in that country.
- After scientific and ethical approval in the country of the sponsoring agency, the appropriate authorities of the host country, including a national or local ethical review committee or its equivalent, should satisfy themselves that the proposed research meets their own ethical requirements.

• • •

REFERENCE

CIOMS. 1991. *International Guidelines for Ethical Review of Epidemiological Studies.* Geneva.

COUNCIL FOR INTERNATIONAL ORGANIZATIONS OF MEDICAL SCIENCES

International Guiding Principles for Biomedical Research Involving Animals (1985)

PREAMBLE

Experimentation with animals has made possible major contributions to biological knowledge and to the welfare of man and animals, particularly in the treatment and prevention of diseases. Many important advances in medical science have had their origins in basic biological research not primarily directed to practical ends as well as from applied research designed to investigate specific medical problems. There is still an urgent need for basic and applied research that will lead to the discovery of methods for the prevention and treatment of diseases for which adequate control methods are not yet available—notably the noncommunicable diseases and the endemic communicable diseases of warm climates.

Past progress has depended, and further progress in the foreseeable future will depend, largely on animal experimentation which, in the broad field of human medicine, is the prelude to experimental trials on human beings of, for example, new therapeutic, prophylactic, or diagnostic substances, devices, or procedures.

There are two international ethical codes intended principally for the guidance of countries or institutions that have not yet formulated their own ethical requirements for human experimentation: The Tokyo revision of the *Declaration of Helsinki* of the World Medical Association (1975); and the *Proposed International Guidelines for Biomedical Research Involving Human Subjects* of the Council for International Organizations of Medical Sciences and the World Health Organization (1982). These codes recognize that while experiments involving human subjects are a *sine qua non* of medical progress, they must be subject to strict ethical requirements. In order to ensure that such ethical requirements are observed, national and institutional ethical codes have also been elaborated with a view to the protection of human subjects involved in biomedical (including behavioral) research.

Reprinted from Council for International Organizations of Medical Sciences, *International Guiding Principles for Biomedical Research Involving Animals* (Geneva: CIOMS, 1985), 17–19. Reprinted with the permission of CIOMS.

A major requirement both of national and international ethical codes for human experimentation, and of national legislation in many cases, is that new substances or devices should not be used for the first time on human beings unless previous tests on animals have provided a reasonable presumption of their safety.

The use of animals for predicting the probable effects of procedures on human beings entails responsibility for their welfare. In both human and veterinary medicine animals are used for behavioral, physiological, pathological, toxicological, and therapeutic research and for experimental surgery or surgical training and for testing drugs and biological preparations. The same responsibility toward the experimental animals prevails in all of these cases.

Because of differing legal systems and cultural backgrounds there are varying approaches to the use of animals for research, testing, or training in different countries. Nonetheless, their use should be always in accord with humane practices. The varying approaches in different countries to the use of animals for biomedical purposes, and the lack of relevant legislation or of formal self-regulatory mechanisms in some, point to the need for international guiding principles elaborated as a result of international and interdisciplinary consultations.

The guiding principles proposed here provide a framework for more specific national or institutional provisions. They apply not only to biomedical research but also to all uses of vertebrate animals for other biomedical purposes, including the production and testing of therapeutic, prophylactic, and diagnostic substances, the diagnosis of infections and intoxications in man and animals, and to any other procedures involving the use of intact live vertebrates.

BASIC PRINCIPLES

I. The advancement of biological knowledge and the development of improved means for the protection of the health and well-being both of man and of animals require recourse to experimentation on intact live animals of a wide variety of species.

II. Methods such as mathematical models, computer simulation and *in vitro* biological systems should be used wherever appropriate.

III. Animal experiments should be undertaken only after due consideration of their relevance for human or animal health and the advancement of biological knowledge.

IV. The animals selected for an experiment should be of an appropriate species and quality, and the minimum number required to obtain scientifically valid results.

V. Investigators and other personnel should never fail to treat animals as sentient, and should regard their proper care and use and the avoidance or minimization of discomfort, distress, or pain as ethical imperatives.

VI. Investigators should assume that procedures that would cause pain in human beings cause pain in other vertebrate species, although more needs to be known about the perception of pain in animals.

VII. Procedures with animals that may cause more than momentary or minimal pain or distress should be performed with appropriate sedation, analgesia, or anesthesia in accordance with accepted veterinary practice. Surgical or other painful procedures should not be performed on unanesthetized animals paralysed by chemical agents.

VIII. Where waivers are required in relation to the provisions of article VII, the decisions should not rest solely with the investigators directly concerned but should be made, with due regard to the provisions of articles IV, V, and VI, by a suitably constituted review body. Such waivers should not be made solely for the purpose of teaching or demonstration.

IX. At the end of, or, when appropriate, during an experiment, animals that would otherwise suffer severe or chronic pain, distress, discomfort, or disablement that cannot be relieved should be painlessly killed.

X. The best possible living conditions should be maintained for animals kept for biomedical purposes. Normally the care of animals should be under the supervision of veterinarians having experience in laboratory animal science. In any case, veterinary care should be available as required.

XI. It is the responsibility of the director of an institute or department using animals to ensure that investigators and personnel have appropriate qualifications or experience for conducting procedures on animals. Adequate opportunities shall be provided for in-service training, including the proper and humane concern for the animals under their care. . . .

BARUCH A. BRODY

Research Ethics: International Perspectives

Baruch Brody is Leon Jaworski Professor of Biomedical Ethics, Director of the Center for Medical Ethics and Health Policy at the Baylor College of Medicine, Professor of Philosophy at Rice University, and Director of the Ethics Program at Methodist Hospital in Houston, Texas. Brody is a prolific writer in many areas of bioethics. Representative works include *The Ethics of Biomedical Research: An International Perspective* (Oxford University Press) and *Life and Death Decision-Making* (Oxford University Press).

In recent years, bioethics has increasingly become an international area of inquiry, with major contributions being made not only in North America but also in Europe and in the Pacific Rim countries. This general observation is particularly true for research ethics. Little attention has been paid, however, to this internationalization of bioethics in general and research ethics in particular, and there are few studies comparing what has emerged in the different countries.

I have recently completed a book-length comparative study[1] of the official policies in various countries on a wide variety of issues in the ethics of research on subjects. It reveals that there is a wide variation ranging from substantial international agreement on some issues to major disagreement on other issues. An important question about the foundations of bioethics emerges: What makes some issues more amenable to the development of an international consensus in official national policies than other issues?

In this paper, I will briefly review three examples of issues in research ethics: research on competent adult subjects, research on animals, and research on embryos shortly after fertilization. I will show the existence of a broad consensus about principles in national policies on the first issue, of some disagreement about principles combined with substantial agreement on most principles in national policies on the second issue, and of total disagreement about fundamental principles among national policies on the third issue. I will also offer a hypothesis to explain the difference between these three areas, a hypothesis that relates this difference to certain traditional claims in cultural anthropology about cultural differences on ethical issues.

RESEARCH ON COMPETENT ADULT SUBJECTS: AN INTERNATIONAL CONSENSUS

The regulation of research on competent adult subjects grew out of a response to the horrors of German and Japanese research in World War II. It also grew out of a recognition that there were continuing real, even if more modest, abuses in research activities in democratic countries in the post World War II period.

Extensive international and national policies have been developed. The Declaration of Helsinki, first issued in 1964 but modified several times since then, represents the most important international response, although mention must also be made of the influential 1982 guidelines (modified in important ways in 1993) from the World Health Organization-Council for International Organizations of Medical Sciences. In the United States, there exist regulations from the National Institutes of Health (NIH) and the Food and Drug Administration (FDA) from the early 1980s combined with the federal Common Rule of 1991.[2] In Canada, there exist 1978 guidelines, revised in 1987, from the Medical Research Council.[3] Europe contributed in 1990 two major multinational guidelines,

Reprinted with the permission of the publisher from *Cambridge Quarterly of Healthcare Ethics* 6 (1997), 376–84. Copyright © 1997 Cambridge University Press.

the Recommendation of the Committee of Ministers of the Council of Europe[4] and the Guidelines on Good Clinical Trials from the Commission of the European Union.[5] These are supplemented by important national guidelines in Europe, including British reports (from the Royal College of Physicians in 1990, from the British Medical Association in 1993, and from the National Health Service in 1993),[6] French legislation (the 1988 Huriet-Serusclat Act, modified and supplemented several times in the 1990s),[7] German legislation (the 1994 Amendment to the German Drug Law,)[8] Swiss Guidelines (from the Swiss Academy of Medical Sciences in 1984), and the common Nordic Guidelines of 1989.[9] The National Medical and Research Council of Australia updated its earlier guidelines in 1992, as did the New Zealand Department of Health in 1991.[10]

It is possible to describe a consensus of basic principles embodied in all of this material. One basic and universal principle is the procedural principle that research on competent adult subjects needs to be articulated in a protocol that is approved in advance by a committee that is independent of researchers. Two other basic and universal principles are substantive: informed voluntary consent of the subjects must be obtained and the research protocol must minimize risks and must involve a favorable risk-benefit ratio. Other principles often mentioned are the protection of confidentiality and the equitable, nonexploitative selection of subjects.

This is not to say that there exist no disagreements in this area of research ethics. They do exist. Among the questions that have provoked some disagreement are the following: (1) What should be the composition of the independent review group? How much public representation should there be on that group? How can its independence from the researchers best be maintained? (2) Are there any occasions on which such research can be conducted without informed consent? What about emergency research when the subjects are temporarily incapable of consenting and surrogate consent cannot be obtained? What about research being conducted in societies in which individual informed consent would be culturally inappropriate? (3) How should informed voluntary consent be obtained and documented? Are some inducements to participate so great that they interfere with the voluntariness of the subject's choice? What information must be provided for the consent to be properly informed? Must the consent always be in writing? (4) Given that there will always be risks associated with the research process, what arrangements should be made to compensate those who suffer from their participation? (5) Are there groups of competent adult subjects (e.g., prisoners) who are vulnerable to exploitation in the research process and who must be protected from this exploitation? If so, how should they be protected? Alternatively, are there groups of competent adult subjects (e.g., women) who have been unfairly denied the benefits of participation in research and who are entitled to the elimination of that injustice? If so, what is the best way to eliminate it?

As one reviews this list of questions and others that have been raised, it is clear that their existence in no way challenges the broad international consensus about the ethical principles governing research on competent adult subjects. Most of them are disagreements about the details of how the principles of the consensus should be carried out; their existence presupposes the consensus rather than challenges it.

The only exceptions to this generalization are the issues raised under (2), the questions about the exceptions to informed consent. But even there, those who would allow emergency research without consent usually confine that exception to cases in which it is reasonable to suppose that the subjects would consent if they could. And those who allow for cultural exceptions to the informed consent requirement often say that this is justified because the subjects, as members of the cultural community in question, would neither expect nor want, if they could even understand, the insistence upon individual informed consent. In an important sense, then, they are arguing that the exceptions really are based on the values embodied in the normal requirement for informed consent. The critics of these exceptions are, of course, equally committed to the values in question, and do not see how they can be realized by making exceptions. At a deep level, then, this disagreement still presupposes the principles of the consensus.

I am not claiming that research practice in any country is fully in accord with the principles of the international consensus nor am I claiming that all the countries in question have been equally, even if imperfectly, successful in carrying out these principles. All I am claiming is that there exists in this area a remarkable consensus about principles in both national and international regulatory policies. We shall soon see that not all areas of research ethics have realized a similar consensus.

The regulation of the use of animals in research, which dates back to the British Act of 1876, predates the regulation of research using human subjects. It too arose as a response to abuses. In the case of animal research, it was opposition both to the public demonstrations by Magendie and Bernard on live animals of their physiological findings and to the perceived insensitivity of researchers in physiology to the pain experienced by their research subjects. As the use of live animals for research has increased, and the concern about animal interests and rights has also increased, extensive regulatory schemes have emerged in many countries.

The Council for International Organizations of Medical Sciences issued in 1985 a set of international guiding principles for biomedical research involving animals. The basic framework for much of the regulation in Europe, incorporating in many ways the international guiding principles, is provided by a 1986 directive from the Council of the European Communities (now the European Union). It is implemented in Great Britain by the Animals (Scientific Procedures) Act of 1986, in Germany by the 1986 Law on Animal Protection, in France by the 1987 decree on Animal Experimentation, and in Sweden by the 1988 Animal Protection Law. All of these recent European national policies replace and strengthen earlier policies.[11] In the same time period, the United States regulatory scheme was strengthened by 1986 regulations from the National Institutes of Health and by the 1985 Animal Welfare Act enforced by the Department of Agriculture.[12] The Canadian system of regulation dates back to the 1968 formation of the Canadian Council on Animal Care.[13] Finally, animal research in Australia is governed by a Code of Practice whose fifth edition was issued in 1990. While not quite as extensive as the national policies governing the use of human subjects, these national policies certainly represent an extensive effort deserving careful comparative analysis.

It is once more possible to describe a consensus of basic principles embodied in all of this material. Procedurally, all of these regulatory schemes involve some process for review of animal research by an external body that is independent of the researchers. Substantively, all of these regulatory schemes reject the human dominion view that maintains that animal interests may be totally disregarded as well as the animal equality view that maintains that animal interests and/or the rights of animals count as much as the interests of human beings. Put otherwise, they are schemes designed to minimize the burdens on animals while permitting human beings to continue to obtain the benefits from experimentation on [animal] subjects. They do this by mandating (1) improving the conditions in which animals used for research live, (2) lessening suffering in the actual research process (e.g., by the use, where possible, of analgesics and/or anesthesia), and (3) minimizing the number of animals used in research.

This is not to say that there are no disagreements in this area of research ethics. Among the issues about which official regulatory schemes disagree are the following: (a) Which animals should be protected by the regulatory schemes? Should they extend to all vertebrates? Should the protection of some vertebrates be given higher priority? Should a preference be shown for conducting research on animals bred for that purpose? Should any invertebrates be protected? (b) Should independent review and monitoring be conducted by governmental agencies or by review processes created by the institutions doing the research? Should research protocols be reviewed in advance? (c) Just how much expense must be incurred to improve research animal living conditions? Must attention be paid to psychological and emotional well-being or is it sufficient that physical needs be appropriately met? (d) Are there research protocols that involve so much unalleviable suffering that they should not be conducted regardless of the potential benefits?

As one reviews this list of issues, it is clear that their existence in no way challenges the existence of a broad international consensus on the principles governing research on animals. They presuppose the existence of the consensus and the attempt to resolve them is an attempt to elaborate on the meaning of the principles structuring the international consensus.

There is, however, one disagreement among the regulatory schemes that does involve a fundamental disagreement about principles. The 1986 British Act requires that the regulatory authority, in deciding whether to issue a license authorizing the conduct of a particular research project, must "weigh the likely adverse effects on the animals concerned against the benefit likely to accrue as a result of the programme to be specified in the license." I call this type of position a balancing position. On this position, animal interests count sufficiently, even if not equally with human interests, that they can outweigh human interests in the conduct of the research; in such cases, the research is not allowed. This should be differentiated from the human priority position that attempts to minimize animal suffering by modifying the conduct of the research but that does not allow that concern with animal suffering to prevent the research being conducted. As far as I can see, some of the European regulations (Great Britain, Switzerland, perhaps Germany) and the Australian regulations accept the balancing position, while the rest of the European regulations (following the Directive of the Council of the European Communities) do so at least in research involving severe pain or distress. On the other hand, the North American regulations, by making no reference to balancing judgments, seem to accept the human priority position.

This type of disagreement does represent a disagreement about fundamental principles; its existence means that there is a less than complete international consensus about the principles governing animal research.

What is this disagreement really about? It is a disagreement about the moral status of animals. The human dominion view gives animals no moral standing while the animal equality view gives animals the same moral standing as human beings. The various regulatory schemes, rejecting these two extreme positions, give animals some moral standing, but they disagree about what that standing is. For the human priority position, human interests take lexical priority over animal interests, so we do the research we need, while limiting animal suffering to the extent that we can. For the balancing position, there is no such lexical priority. As a result, if animal losses are sufficiently great, they can outweigh human gains. This is a subtle, but very real, difference in principle. When its implications are carefully explored, I believe it will become clear that this difference has substantial implications for what types of research on animals may be conducted.

It would be interesting to see whether these differences have already appeared in the actual conduct of research on animals in the different countries. For now, however, it suffices to say that the international consensus on principles is less than complete in this area of research ethics.

RESEARCH ON PREIMPLANTATION ZYGOTES: A COMPLETE LACK OF CONSENSUS

The development of regulations on preimplantation zygotes did not arise as a response to specific abuses; instead, it is nearly contemporaneous with the development of a new technology, in vitro fertilization, that makes such research possible. Such research could be conducted on 'spare zygotes', created to produce a pregnancy but not implanted; such zygotes would otherwise be disposed of or frozen for use in future attempts to create a pregnancy. Alternatively, such research could be conducted on zygotes specifically created for use in research (analogously to animals bred for use in research).

Two radically different approaches have developed in official regulatory schemes, a permissive approach and a restrictive approach. The permissive approach allows for such research subject to various restrictions, some of which are themselves matters of controversy. The restrictive approach prohibits all, or at least nearly all, such research. The permissive approach was adopted by Victoria in its 1984 Infertility (Medical Procedures) Act, by Great Britain in its 1990 Human Fertilization and Embryology Act,[14] and by Canada in a 1993 report of the Canadian Royal Commission on New Reproductive Technologies.[15] A number of other European countries have adopted it. It was recommended in the United States by an NIH advisory panel in 1994.[16] The restrictive approach was adopted by Germany in its 1990 Embryo Protection Law,[17] by France in its 1994 Bioethics statue,[18] by Norway in a 1990 report of its National Committee for Medical Research Ethics,[19] and by Victoria in a 1995 statute which repealed the 1984 statute.[20] The European Parliament of the Council of Europe adopted a restrictive approach in 1989 and insisted in 1995 that Article 15 of the proposed European Bioethics convention drop the provision allowing for such research in those countries that approve it.[21] In the United States, the advisory panel's report has not been implemented, and Congress has temporarily banned federal funding for such research.

The following are the main components of the permissive position: (a) it allows for research on preimplantation zygotes after consent without commercial inducements has been obtained from the donor and after an independent review board has approved the research; (b) it sets a time limit after fertilization on the conduct of such research. The Australian time limit is 7–14 days after fertilization, corresponding to the time [during] which implantation occurs. The British and Canadian time limit is 14 days, corresponding to the time at which the primitive streak appears and further division into two embryos is not possible. The NIH advisory panel allowed for some cases of research until 17–21 days, corresponding to the time of the beginning of the closure of the neural tube; (c) with the exception of the 1984 Victoria statute, it allows for the creation of zygotes for use in research, either because the emergence of freezing as a successful technique has limited the supply of spare zygotes or because some types of research (e.g., research on the safety of new drugs to induce ovulation) require the use of such zygotes; (d) it bans some types of research, most commonly cross-species research and research on post-cloning transfer of zygotes. The NIH panel, responding to important feminist concerns, also banned research on preimplantation gender selection.

It is of interest to note that several versions of the permissive position were specifically advocated by their proponents as attempts to fashion a compromise between those who advocated a ban on preimplantation zygote research and those who would be far more permissive. This is the explicit motivation of some of the recommendations in the Canadian report. It has also been advocated by some of the members of the NIH advisory panel. In light of the widespread adoption of the restrictive position, it is clear that this attempt to fashion a moral compromise as a basis for a regulatory consensus has not been successful.

There are a number of features of the restrictive position that need to be emphasized: (1) Not all preimplantation research is prohibited. Therapeutic research, designed to improve the likelihood of the zygote's developing normally, followed by an attempt to implant the zygote is explicitly allowed in the French statute and implicitly allowed for in the Norwegian report and the new Victorian statute, which only prohibit destructive research. This exception covers, of course, only a small portion of the research that has been proposed: (2) The basis of the opposition to preimplantation research is expressed in different terms in different sources. Some see the prohibition of nontherapeutic research on preimplanted zygotes as the protection of the rights of a human being with full rights deserving of protection. Some see this prohibition as an expression of respect for the value of human life in general. Some see it as an implementation of the principle of protecting the vulnerable from exploitation. (3) Particular opposition is expressed to the creation of zygotes for research purposes. This is very different from the case of research on animals, where the breeding of animals for use in research is seen as morally preferable.

Enough has been said to demonstrate that this is an area of research ethics in which official national policies are in sharp disagreement with each other. The only type of research that nearly every policy will permit is the very limited case of therapeutic research designed to improve the outcome for the particular zygote in question once it is implanted.

A HYPOTHESIS

In our examination of official policies in three areas of research ethics, we have found a significant international consensus in one area, a subtle but important disagreement in a second area, and major fundamental disagreements in a third area. In my forthcoming book, I demonstrate that this type of difference extends to other areas of research ethics; the extent of consensus in official policies is highly variable.

Can we explain this variability? A full explanation would require examining all of the different areas of research ethics, and that lies beyond the scope of this paper. For now, I would like to examine the differences demonstrated in this paper to see what can explain them.

There is a feature found in the case of research on animals and research on preimplantation zygotes that may explain why there is more disagreement in those areas. In both of those cases, there is continuing disagreement about the moral status of the subjects on which the research is conducted. Such disagreement is not found in the case of research on competent adult human subjects. My suggestion is that disagreements about the moral status of entities are harder to resolve than other moral disagreements and that it is this difficulty which explains the lack of an international consensus.

There is a long history of disagreement about the moral status of animals, about whether we are morally required to consider their interests. Some, such as Descartes, denied that they had the feelings which are prerequisites of having interests. On that account, we obviously do not need to consider their interests; in that way, they have no moral status. Others, such as Kant, did not deny them the requisite feelings, but did deny them moral status anyway. This is not to say that Kant allowed for wanton cruelty to animals. But he opposed such practices only because they hardened our feelings and might lead to indifference to human suffering. Since the rise of utilitarianism, with its emphasis on the moral significance of suffering, there has been more of a commitment to the moral status of animals, more of a commitment to the view that animal interests in avoiding suffering must be considered. Still, in a world in which animals are consumed for food after being produced in confining conditions, the animal equality position on the significance of animals interests is unlikely to be the basis for official policies; animals are not accorded that degree of moral status. So animals are treated as having a real but subordinate moral status; their interests count but not as much as human interests. This leaves room for considerable disagreement about the exact moral significance of protecting animal interests; it is just this type of disagreement that is reflected in the difference between the official policies that do and the policies that do not incorporate the balancing approach.

There is an equally long history of controversy about the moral status of zygotes, embryos, and fetuses, a controversy that is complicated when one considers the preimplantation status of preimplantation zygotes. There are those who would accord no moral status to any of these entities until birth (or even afterwards). At the other extreme, there are those who argue that such entities have full moral status from the moment of conception, even in vitro. Naturally, many in-between positions exist as well. Of particular importance is the view that the moral status of such entities is sufficiently close to the moral status of postbirth humans that a failure to respect the interests of these prebirth entities would seriously damage the basic respect for human life which is central to civilized societies. The permissive policies represent an attempt to fashion a national policy that is an adequate compromise between these views; the proponents of the restrictive policy insist that the compromises proposed are inadequate. This fundamental disagreement results in fundamentally different official policies.

Why are such disagreements so difficult to resolve? Earlier in this century, Edward Westermarck pointed out in his studies of ethical differences among societies[22] that the differences were not primarily about the content of the accepted moral rules; rather, they were primarily differences about the scope of the rules. Societies differed primarily over who was accorded moral status, about who was protected by the accepted moral rules. Some extended those rules only to favored groups within the society, others to all members of the society, others to larger groups (perhaps even to all human beings). The process of extending the scope is hard to justify rationally. It seems to involve an emotional recognition of similarities, rather than any rational argumentation. Think of how Huck Finn comes to recognize Jim as a fellow human being. Naturally, different individuals and/or different societies may not share in these recognitions. To be sure, some philosophical systems offer a systematic approach to the question of the scope of their moral principles. Classical utilitarianism, with its view that all who can experience pleasure and pain count, is the most clear-cut example. But official policies are rarely based upon philosophical systems. Not surprisingly, then, official policies are likely to vary when questions of moral status are involved.

I am not claiming that all fundamental differences between official policies in research ethics are due to differences in social attitudes toward the moral status of the subjects involved. Such a claim would have to be evaluated in light of a more comprehensive examination of all of the areas of research ethics. All that I am claiming is that this factor helps explain the variability [and] the extent of the differences in the three areas we have examined.

One final thought. Some might believe that a comparative study of official policies on research ethics would be a technical exploration of legal technicalities. I hope that this paper helps to undercut such a belief. The issues of research ethics are related to fundamental moral and metaphysical questions, and answers to those questions (even when they are not part of systematic theories) help shape official policies. A comparative study of those policies sheds much light upon how different societies answer those questions differently.

NOTES

1. Brody B. *Ethics of Biomedical Research: An International Perspective.* New York: Oxford University Press, 1998.

2. The NIH regulations are found in 45 *CFR* 46 and the FDA in 21 *CFR* 50. The Federal Common Rule was published in the 18 June 1991 issue of the *Federal Register,* pp. 28002–32.

3. Medical Research Council of Canada. *Guidelines on Research Involving Human Subjects.* Ottawa: Medical Research Council of Canada, 1987.

4. European guidance on medical research. *Bulletin of Medical Ethics* 1990;(56):9–10.

5. Guidelines in good clinical trials. *Bulletin of Medical Ethics* 1990;(60):18–23.

6. Foster CG. *Manual for Research Ethics Committees.* London: King's College, 1993.

7. Gromb S. *Le droit de l'experimentation sur l'homme.* Paris: Litec, 1992.

8. Graf HP, Cole D. Ethics committee authorization in Germany. *Journal of Medical Ethics* 1995;(21):229–33.

9. Nordic Council of Medicines. *Good Clinical Trial Practice: Nordic Guidelines.* Uppsala: Nordic Council on Medicines, 1989.

10. McNeil P. *The Ethics and Politics of Human Experimentation.* Cambridge: Cambridge University Press, 1993.

11. The European and the Australian material is conveniently collected in *Animals and their Legal Rights.* Washington (DC): Animal Welfare Institute, 1990.

12. The best source for the complex U.S. laws and regulations is Office for Protection Research Risks. *Institutional Animal Care and Use Committee Guidebook.* Washington (DC): National Institutes of Health, 1992.

13. *Guide to the Care and Use of Experimental Animals.* Ottawa: Canadian Council on Animal Care, 1993.

14. *Public General Acts* no. 2 (1990) 1471–1509.

15. *Proceed with Caution.* Ottawa: Minister of Government Services, 1993.

16. *Report of the Human Embryo Research Panel.* Washington (DC): National Institutes of Health, 1994.

17. *International Digest of Health Legislation* 1991:42;60–4.

18. *International Digest of Health Legislation* 1994:45;479.

19. *Research on Fetuses.* Oslo: National Committee for Medical Research Ethics, 1990.

20. A good discussion of the old and the new Victoria legislation is found in New Victoria IVF law changes pioneering legislation. *Monash Bioethics Review* 1995:14(3):6.

21. Rogers A, deBousingen DD. *Bioethics in Europe.* Strasbourg: Council of Europe Press, 1995.

22. Westermarck E. *Ethical Relativity.* [Westport, CT:] Greenwood Press: 1970 [1932].

Ethical Issues in Human Research

NATIONAL BIOETHICS ADVISORY COMMISSION

Protecting Research Participants—A Time for Change

INTRODUCTION

Protecting the rights and welfare of those who volunteer to participate in research is a fundamental tenet of ethical research. A great deal of progress has been made in recent decades in changing the culture of research to incorporate more fully this ethical responsibility into protocol design and implementation. In the 1960s and 1970s, a series of scandals concerning social science research and medical research conducted with the sick and the illiterate underlined the need to systematically and rigorously protect individuals in research (Beecher 1966; Faden and Beauchamp 1986; Jones 1981; Katz 1972; Tuskegee Syphilis Study Ad Hoc Advisory Panel 1973). However, the resulting system of protections that evolved out of these rising concerns—although an improvement over past practices—is no longer sufficient. It is a patchwork arrangement associated with the receipt of federal research funding or the regulatory review and approval of new drugs and devices. In addition, it depends on the voluntary cooperation of investigators, research institutions, and professional societies across a wide array of research disciplines. Increasingly, the current system is being viewed as uneven in its ability to

Reprinted from National Bioethics Advisory Commission, *Ethical and Policy Issues in Research Involving Human Participants: Summary* (Bethesda, MD: NBAC, August 2001), pp. i–ix.

simultaneously protect the rights and welfare of research participants and promote ethically responsible research.

Research involving human participants has become a vast academic and commercial activity, but this country's system for the protection of human participants has not kept pace with that growth. On the one hand, the system is too narrow in scope to protect all participants, while on the other hand, it is often so unnecessarily bureaucratic that it stifles responsible research. Although some reforms by particular federal agencies and professional societies are under way,[1] it will take the efforts of both the executive and legislative branches of government to put in place a streamlined, effective, responsive, and comprehensive system that achieves the protection of all human participants and encourages ethically responsible research.

Clearly, scientific investigation has extended and enhanced the quality of life and increased our understanding of ourselves, our relationships with others, and the natural world. It is one of the foundations of our society's material, intellectual, and social progress. For many citizens, scientific discoveries have alleviated the suffering caused by disease or disability. Nonetheless, the prospect of gaining such valuable scientific knowledge need not and should not be pursued at the expense of human rights or human dignity. In the words of philosopher Hans Jonas, "progress is an optional goal, not an unconditional commitment, and . . . its tempo . . . compulsive as it may become, has nothing sacred about it" (Jonas 1969, 245).

Since the 1974 formation of the National Commission for the Protection of Human Subjects of Biomedical and Behavioral Research and the activities in the early 1980s of the President's Commission for the Study of Ethical Problems in Medicine and Biomedical and Behavioral Research, American leaders have consistently tried to enhance the protections for human research participants. The research community has, in large part, supported the two essential protections for human participants: independent review of research to assess risks and potential benefits and an opportunity for people to voluntarily and knowledgeably decide whether to participate in a particular research protocol.

The charter of the National Bioethics Advisory Commission (NBAC), a presidential commission created in 1995, makes clear the Commission's focus: "As a first priority, NBAC shall direct its attention to consideration of protection of the rights and welfare of human research subjects." In our first five years, we focused on several issues concerning research involving human participants, issuing five reports and numerous recommendations that, when viewed as a whole, reflect our evolving appreciation of the numerous and complex challenges facing the implementation and oversight of any system of protections.[2] The concerns and recommendations addressed in these reports reflect our dual commitment to ensuring the protection of those who volunteer for research while supporting the continued advance of science and understanding of the human condition. This report views the oversight system as a whole, provides a rationale for change, and offers an interrelated set of recommendations to improve the protection of human participants and enable the oversight system to operate more efficiently.

RESPECTING RESEARCH PARTICIPANTS

Whether testing a new medical treatment, interviewing people about their personal habits, studying how people think and feel, or observing how they live within groups, research seeks to learn something new about the human condition. Unfortunately, history has also demonstrated that researchers sometimes treat participants not as persons but as mere objects of study. As Jonas observed: "Experimentation was originally sanctioned by natural science. There it is performed on inanimate objects, and this raises no moral questions. But as soon as animate, feeling beings become the subject of experiment . . . this innocence of the search for knowledge is lost and questions of conscience arise" (Jonas 1969, 219).

How, then, should people be studied? For over half a century, since the revelations of medical torture under the guise of medical experimentation were described at the Nuremberg Trials,[3] it has been agreed that people should participate in research only when the study addresses important questions, its risks are justifiable, and an individual's participation is voluntary and informed.

The principles underlying the *Belmont Report: Ethical Principles and Guidelines for the Protections of Human Subjects of Research (Belmont Report)* (National Commission 1979) have served for over 20 years as a leading source of guidance regarding the ethical standards that should govern research with human participants in the United States. The *Belmont Report* emphasized that research must respect the autonomy of participants, must be fair in both conception and implementation, and must maximize potential benefits while minimizing potential harms. The report's recommendations provided a coherent rationale for the federal policies and rules that created the current U.S. system of decentralized, independent research review coupled with some degree of federal oversight. But although the *Belmont Report* is rightly hailed as a key source of guidance on informed consent, assessment of risk, and the injustice of placing individuals (and groups) in situations of vulnerability, the principles the report espouses and the regulations adopted as federal policy 20 years ago have often fallen short in achieving their overarching goal of protecting human research participants. Moreover, since the *Belmont Report* was published, additional concerns have arisen that require much-needed attention today.

ENSURING INDEPENDENT REVIEW OF RISKS AND POTENTIAL BENEFITS

A central protection for research participants is the guarantee that someone other than the investigator will assess the risks of the proposed research. *No one should participate in research unless independent review concludes that the risks are reasonable in relation to the potential benefits.* In the United States, the Institutional Review Board, or IRB, has been the principal structure responsible for conducting such reviews.

Independent review of research is essential because it improves the likelihood that decisions are made free from inappropriate influences that could distort the central task of evaluating risks and potential benefits. Certainly, reviewers should not have a financial interest in the work, but social factors may be just as crucial. Reviewers may feel constrained because they are examining the work of their colleagues or their supervisors, and they should not participate in protocol review unless they are able to separate these concerns from their task. All reviewers who themselves are members of the research community should recognize that their familiarity with research and (perhaps) their predilection to support research are factors that could distort their judgment. Truly independent and sensitive review requires more involvement of individuals drawn from the ranks of potential research participants or those who can adequately represent the interests of potential research participants.

A critical purpose of independent review is to ensure that risks are reasonable in relation to potential personal and societal benefits. This is a precondition to offering people the opportunity to volunteer, since informed consent alone cannot justify enrollment. When reviewed for risks and potential benefits, research studies must be evaluated in their entirety. Studies often include different components, however, and the risks and potential benefits of each should also be examined separately, lest the possibility of great benefit or monetary enticement in one component cause potential participants or IRBs to minimize or overlook risk in another. No matter what potential benefit is offered to individual participants or society at large, the possibility of benefit from one element of a study should not be used to justify otherwise unacceptable elements.

In our view, IRBs should appreciate that for some components of a study, participants might incur risks with no personal potential benefit—for example, when a nondiagnostic survey is included among the components of a psychotherapy protocol or when placebos are given to some participants in a drug trial. For these elements, there should be some limitation on the amount of social and physical risk that can be imposed, regardless of the participants' willingness to participate or the monetary (or other) enticement being offered. Further, the possibility of some benefit from one element of a study should not be used to justify otherwise unacceptable elements of research whose potential benefits, if any, accrue, solely to society at large. If aspects of a study present unacceptable risks, protocols should not be approved until these elements are eliminated. If removing the risky component would impair the study as a whole, then the entire study should be redesigned so that each of its elements presents risks that are reasonable in relation to potential benefits.

Other parts of studies can obscure risks, such as when standard medical interventions are compared in a patient population, leading some participants and researchers to discount the risks because they are associated with known therapies. It is essential that participants and investigators not be led to believe that participating in research is tantamount to being in a traditional therapeutic relationship. Regardless of whether there is the possibility or even the likelihood of direct benefit from participation in research, such participation still alters the relationship between a professional and the participant by introducing another loyalty beyond that to the participant, to wit, loyalty to doing good science. It is too often forgotten that even though the researchers may consider participants' interests to be important, they also have a serious, and perhaps conflicting, obligation to science.

Years of experience with the current system of independent review have demonstrated that there are enduring questions about how to arrive at such impartial judgments and how to go about deciding when potential benefits justify risks that are incurred solely by participants or the community from which they come. In recent years, increasing strains on the system have undermined the practice of independent review. IRBs are overburdened by the volume of research coming before them, a strain that is compounded by concerns about training of IRB members and possible conflicts of interest. In addition, the constantly changing nature of research challenges existing notions about what constitutes risks and potential benefits.

Because IRBs are so central to the current oversight system, they need better guidance on how to review and monitor research, how to assess potential benefits to research participants and their communities, and how to distinguish among levels of risk. This report provides such guidance in the following areas: determining the type of review necessary for minimal risk research; ensuring that research participants are able to make voluntary decisions and are appropriately informed prior to giving consent; providing adequate protections for privacy and confidentiality; identifying appropriate measures needed when participants are susceptible to coercion or are otherwise placed in vulnerable situations; and monitoring ongoing research. In addition, the report recommends that IRB members and staff complete educational and certification programs on research ethics before being permitted to review research studies.

OBTAINING VOLUNTARY INFORMED CONSENT

Even when risks are reasonable, however, *no one should participate in research without giving voluntary informed consent (except in the case of an appropriate authorized representative or a waiver). Investigators must make appropriate disclosures and ensure that participants have a good understanding of the information and their choices, not only at the time of enrollment, but throughout the research.* Engaging in this process is one of the best ways researchers can demonstrate their concern and respect for those they aim to enroll in a study. It also serves as the best means for those who do not wish to participate to protect themselves.[4]

Recommendations from our previous reports are reinforced in this report, which emphasizes the *process* of providing information and ensuring comprehension rather than the form of documentation of the decision to give consent. Both the information and the way it is conveyed—while meeting full disclosure requirements—must be tailored to meet the needs of the participants in the particular research context. In addition, documentation requirements must be adapted for varying research settings, and the criteria for deciding when informed consent is not necessary must be clarified so that participants' rights and welfare are not endangered.

The decision to participate in research must not only be informed; it must be voluntary. Even when risks are reasonable and informed consent is obtained, it may nonetheless be wrong to solicit certain people as participants. Those who are not fully capable of resisting the request to become participants—such as prisoners and other institutionalized or otherwise vulnerable persons—should not be enrolled in studies merely because they are easily accessible or convenient. This historic emphasis on protecting people from being exploited as research participants, however, has failed to anticipate a time when, at least for some areas of medical research, people would be demanding to be included in certain studies because they might provide the only opportunity for receiving medical care for life-threatening diseases.

MAKING RESEARCH INCLUSIVE WHILE PROTECTING INDIVIDUALS AND CATEGORIZED AS VULNERABLE

Vulnerable individuals need additional protection in research. Although certain individuals and populations are more vulnerable as human participants than others, people whose circumstances render them vulnerable should not be arbitrarily excluded from research for this reason alone. This includes those viewed as more open to harm (e.g., children), more subject to coercion (e.g., institutionalized persons), more "complicated" (e.g., women, who are considered more biologically complicated than men), or more inconvenient (e.g., women with small children, who are viewed as less reliable research participants due to conflicting demands on time). Calling competent people intrinsically "vulnerable" can be both insulting and misleading. It is not their gender or other group designation that exposes them to injury or coercion, but rather their situation that can be exploited by ethically unacceptable research. That is, it is their circumstances, which are situational, that create the vulnerability. At other times it is the intrinsic characteristics of the person—for example, children or those with certain mental or developmental disorders—that make them generally vulnerable in the research setting.

The response, whenever possible, should not be to exclude people from research, but instead to change the research design so that it does not create situations in which people are unnecessarily harmed. To do otherwise is to risk developing knowledge that helps only a subset of the population. To the extent that the results are not generalizable, the potential societal benefits that justify doing the research are attenuated. *Research participants must be treated equally and with respect. Whenever possible, research should be designed to encourage the participation of all groups while protecting their rights and welfare.*

To accomplish this, we recommend that rather than focusing primarily on categorizing groups as vulnerable, investigators and IRBs should also recognize and avoid situations that create susceptibility to harm or coercion. Such situations may be as varied as patients being recruited by their own physicians; sick and desperate patients seeking enrollment in clinical trials; participants being recruited by those who teach or employ them; or studies involving participants with any characteristic that may make them less likely to receive care and respect from others (e.g., convicted criminals or intravenous drug users). In these circumstances, rather than excluding whole groups of people, researchers should design studies that reduce the risk of exploitation, whether by using a different method of recruitment, by using a recruiter who shares the participants' characteristics, or by some other technique. This is not always easy. It requires researchers to consider carefully their research design and the potential pool of participants. At times, it will mean anticipating that otherwise seemingly benign situations may become more complex because a particular participant or group of participants will be unusually susceptible to harm or manipulation. At other times, the nature of the vulnerability may require using a different research design. Ethical research does not avoid complexity. Rather, it acknowledges the full range and realities of the human condition.

COMPENSATING FOR HARMS

Despite all these precautions, however, some research participants might be harmed. *Participants who are harmed as a direct result of research should be cared for and compensated.* This is simple justice. The fact that they offered to participate in no way alters the view that mere decency calls for us to take care of these volunteers. Unfortunately, this is a greater challenge than it might appear. For those who endure harm while participating in research, it is often very difficult to separate injuries traceable to the research from those that stem from the underlying disease or social condition being studied. For others, appropriate care and compensation would be far beyond the means of the researchers, their sponsors, and their institutions. Two decades ago, the President's Commission for the Study of Ethical Problems in Medicine and Biomedical and Behavioral Research called for pilot studies of compensation programs—a recommendation that was not pursued. It is time to reconsider the need for some type of compensation program and to explore the possible mechanisms that could be used were one to be adopted. Regardless of individual motives, research participants are providing a service for society, and justice requires that they be treated with great respect and receive appropriate care for any related injuries. It should always be remembered that it is a privilege for any researcher to involve human participants in his or her research.

ESTABLISHING A COMPREHENSIVE, EFFECTIVE, AND STREAMLINED SYSTEM

In the United States, government regulations, professional guidelines, and the general principles highlighted in the *Belmont Report* (1979) form the basis of the current system of protections. In the earliest stages of adoption, the federal regulations were fragmented and confusing. Even today, they apply to most—but not all—research funded or conducted by the federal government, but have inconsistent and sometimes no direct application to research funded or conducted by state governments, foundations, or industry. They apply to medical drugs and devices and vaccines approved for interstate sale, but not to some medical innovations that would remain wholly within state borders. And they apply to other research only when the investigators and their institutions volunteer to abide by the rules.

A comprehensive and effective oversight system is essential to uniformly protect the rights and welfare of participants while permitting ethically and scientifically responsible research to proceed without undue delay. A fundamental flaw in the current oversight system is the ethically indefensible difference in the protection afforded participants in federally sponsored research and those in privately sponsored research that falls outside the jurisdiction of the Food and Drug Administration. As a result, people have been subjected to experimentation without their knowledge or informed consent in fields as diverse as plastic surgery, psychology, and infertility treatment. This is wrong. *Participants should be protected from avoidable harm, whether the research is publicly or privately financed.* We have repeated this assertion throughout our deliberations, and recommendations in this regard appear in four previous reports (NBAC 1997; NBAC 1999a; NBAC 1999b; NBAC 2001).

In this report, we recommend that the protections of an oversight system extend to the entire private sector for both domestic and international research. A credible, effective oversight system must apply to all research, and all people are entitled to the dignity that comes with freely and knowingly choosing whether to participate in research, as well as to protection from undue research risks. This is consistent with our 1997 resolution that no one should be enrolled in research absent the twin protections of independent review and voluntary informed consent.

Even when current protections apply, the interpretation of the federal regulations can vary unpredictably, depending on which federal agency oversees the research. Even the most basic, common elements of the federal rules took a decade to develop into regulations, because there was no single authority within the government to facilitate and demand cooperation and consistency. There still is no such single authority.[5] This has slowed the diffusion of basic protections and made it almost impossible to develop consistent interpretations of the basic protections or those relevant to especially problematic research, such as studies involving children or the decisionally impaired. Nor has there been a unified response to emerging areas of research, such as large-scale work on medical records and social science databases or on stored human biological materials.

Today's research protection system cannot react quickly to new developments. Efforts to develop rules for special situations, such as research on those who can no longer make decisions for themselves, have languished for decades in the face of bureaucratic hurdles, and there is no reason to believe that efforts to oversee other emerging research areas will be any more efficient. In addition, the current system leaves people vulnerable to new, virtually uncontrolled experimentation in emerging fields, such as some aspects of reproductive medicine and genetic research.

Indeed, some areas of research are not only uncontrolled, they are almost invisible. In an information age, poor management of research using medical records, human tissue, or personal interview data could lead to employment and insurance discrimination, social stigmatization, or even criminal prosecution.[6] The privacy and confidentiality concerns raised by this research are real, but the federal response has often been illusory. There is almost no guidance and certainly no coordination on these topics. The time has come to have a single source of guidance for these emerging areas, one that would be better positioned to effect change across all divisions of the government and private sector, as well as to facilitate development of specialized review bodies, as needed.

In this report *we propose a new independent oversight office that would have clear authority over all other segments of the federal government and extend protections to the entire private sector for both domestic and international research.* A single office would decide how to introduce consistency or reforms, and only that office would develop mechanisms to provide specialized review when needed. We recognize the challenges to such a proposal. For example, an independent office might lack the political support accorded an existing cabinet-level department. Although assigning one department, such as the Department of Health and Human Services, the role of "first among equals" would allow it to advocate forcefully for uniform rules across the government, without special provisions it would not have the authority to require other departments to comply, nor is it certain to escape the temptation to develop rules premised on a traditional, biomedical model rather than the wider range of research to be covered.

Federal research protections should be uniform across all government agencies, academe, and the private sector, but they should be flexible enough to be applied in widely different research settings or to emerging areas of research. Furthermore, any central coordinating body should be open to public input, have significant political or legal authority over research involving human participants—whether in the public or private sector—and have the support of the executive and legislative branches of government.

EDUCATION AS THE KEY TO PROMOTING LOCAL RESPONSIBILITY

Currently, federal protections depend on a decentralized oversight system involving IRBs, institutions, investigators, sponsors, and participants. We endorse the spirit and intent of this approach, specifically its contention that *the ethical obligation to protect participants lies first with researchers, their sponsors, and the IRBs that review their research.* Protecting research participants is a duty that researchers, research institutions, and sponsors cannot delegate completely to others or to the government. In addition, merely adhering to a set of rules and regulations does not fulfill this duty. Rather, it is accomplished by acting within a culture of concern and respect for research participants.

It is unrealistic to think that ethical obligations can be fully met without guidance and resources. *To help researchers and IRBs fulfill their responsibilities, the federal government should promote the development of education, certification, and accreditation systems that apply to all researchers, all IRB members and staff, and all institutions.* These tools should help researchers craft and IRBs review studies that pose few problems and to know when their work requires special oversight. Today, investigators and IRBs are rightly confused over issues as basic as which areas of inquiry should be reviewed and who constitutes a human participant.

Education is the foundation of the oversight system and is essential to protecting research participants. In all of our reports, we have highlighted the need to educate all those involved in research with human participants, including the public, investigators, IRB members, institutions, and federal agencies. In *Cloning Human Beings* (1997), we recommended federal support of public education in biomedical sciences that increasingly affect our cultural values. In *Research Involving Persons with Mental Disorders That May Affect Decisionmaking Capacity* (1998), we called for practice guidelines and ethics education on special concerns regarding this population. In *Ethical and Policy Issues in International Research: Clinical Trials in Developing Countries* (2001), we recommended measures to help developing countries build their capacity for designing and conducting clinical trials, for reviewing the ethics and science of proposed research, and for using research results after a trial is completed.

In this report, we again acknowledge the inadequacy of educational programs on research ethics in the United States. This deficiency begins at the highest level within the federal oversight system and extends to the local level at individual institutions. We recommend that investigators and IRB members and staff successfully complete educational programs on research ethics and become certified before they perform or review research, that research ethics be taught to the next generation of scientists, and that research ethics be included in continuing education programs.

CLARIFYING THE SCOPE OF OVERSIGHT

Many areas of scientific inquiry are "research," and many of these involve human participants, but only some need federal oversight, while others might be better regulated through professional ethics, social custom, or other state and federal law. For example, certain types of surveys and interviews are considered research, but they can be well managed to avoid harms without federal oversight, as the risks are few and participants are well situated to decide for themselves whether to participate. On the other hand, certain studies of medical records, databases, and discarded surgical tissue are often perceived as something other than human research, even when the information retrieved is traceable to an identifiable person. Such research does need oversight to avoid putting people at risk of identity disclosure or discrimination without their knowledge. *Federal policies should clearly identify the kinds of research that are subject to review and the types of research participants to whom protections should apply.* When research poses significant risks or when its risks are imposed on participants without their knowledge, it clearly requires oversight. However, meaningless or overly rigid oversight engenders disdain on the part of researchers, creates an impossible and pointless workload for IRBs, and deters ethically sound research from going forward.

ENSURING THAT THE LEVEL OF REVIEW CORRESPONDS TO THE LEVEL OF RISK

Even within areas of research that need oversight, many individual studies will involve little or no risk to participants. Although current federal policies allow for some distinction between research involving minimal risk and research involving more than minimal risk, the distinction operates mostly in terms of how the research will be reviewed—that is, how procedures are to be followed. But the distinction should be based on how the research is pursued, how the participants are treated, and how the work is monitored over time. Overall, the emphasis should be on knowing how to protect participants rather than on knowing how to navigate research regulations. Instead of focusing so much on the period during which a research design is reviewed, oversight should also include an ongoing system of education and certification that helps researchers to anticipate and minimize research risks. Oversight should also make it easier for researchers to collaborate with their colleagues here and abroad without the burden of redundant reviews. *Research review and monitoring should be intensified as the risk and complexity of the research increase and at all times should emphasize protecting participants rather than following rigid rules. In addition, the review process should facilitate rather than hinder collaborative research among institutions and across national boundaries, provided that participants are protected.*

PROVIDING RESOURCES FOR THE OVERSIGHT SYSTEM

Creating a system that protects the rights and welfare of participants and facilitates responsible research demands political and financial support from the federal government as well as the presence of a central coordinating body to provide guidance and oversee education and accreditation efforts. *The oversight system should be adequately funded at all levels to ensure that research continues in a manner that demonstrates respect and concern for the interests of research participants.*

CONCLUSIONS

The current system for protecting human participants in research is in need of reform. It does not protect all research participants, and where protection is offered, it is often burdened by excessive bureaucracy, confusing or conflicting interpretations of rules, and an inability to respond to emerging areas of research. We recommend that a new oversight system be adopted that is led by a responsive and authoritative federal office, that emphasizes researcher education and research design as the primary means to protect participants, and that encourages responsible research while protecting all research participants.

NOTES

1. For example, the Office for Human Research Protections is implementing a new process by which institutions assure future compliance with human participant protections. The Institute of Medicine has recently issued a report on accreditation standards for IRBs (IOM 2001). Public Responsibility in Medicine and Research has established training programs and has co-founded a new organization, the Association for the Accreditation of Human Research Protection Programs.

2. To date, NBAC has issued five reports: *Cloning Human Beings* (NBAC 1997), *Research Involving Persons with Mental Disorders That May Affect Decisionmaking Capacity* (NBAC 1998), *Ethical Issues in Human Stem Cell Research* (NBAC 1999a), *Research Involving Human Biological Materials: Ethical Issues and Policy Guidance* (NBAC 1999b), and *Ethical and Policy Issues in International Research: Clinical Trials in Developing Countries* (NBAC 2001).

3. *United States* v. *Karl Brandt* et al., Trials of War Criminals Before the Nuremberg Military Tribunals Under Control Council Law 10. Nuremberg, October 1946–April 1949. Volumes I–II. Washington, D.C.: U.S. Government Printing Office.

4. There are, of course, some circumstances in which consent cannot be obtained and in which an overly rigid adherence to this principle would preclude research that is either benign or potentially needed by the participant him- or herself. Thus, NBAC endorses the current exceptions for research that is of minimal risk to participants and for potentially beneficial research in emergency settings where no better alternative for the participants exists. NBAC also urges attention to emerging areas of record, database, and tissue bank research in which consent serves only as a sign of respect and in which alternative ways to respect participants do exist (NBAC 1999b; 21 CFR 50.24). In a previous report, the Commission made recommendations regarding persons who lack decisionmaking capacity and from whom informed consent cannot be obtained (NBAC 1998)

5. Porter, J., Testimony before NBAC. November 23, 1997. Bethesda, Maryland. See McCarthy, C.R., "Reflections on the Organizational Locus of the Office for Protection from Research Risks." This background paper was prepared for NBAC and is available in Volume II of this report.

6. See Goldman, J., and A. Choy, "Privacy and Confidentiality in Health Research" and Sieber, J., "Privacy and Confidentiality: As Related to Human Research in Social and Behavioral Science." These background papers were prepared for NBAC and are available in Volume II of this report. See also *Ferguson* v. *City of Charleston* 121 S. Ct. 1281. (2001).

REFERENCES

Beecher, H. K. 1966. "Ethics and Clinical Research." *New England Journal of Medicine* 274(24):1354–1360.

Faden, R. R., and T. L. Beauchamp. 1986. *A History and Theory of Informed Consent.* New York: Oxford University Press.

Institute of Medicine (IOM). 2001. *Preserving Public Trust: Accreditation and Human Research Participant Protection Programs.* Washington, D.C.: National Academy Press.

Jonas, H. 1969. "Philosophical Reflections on Experimenting with Human Subjects." *Daedalus* 98:219–247.

Jones, J. H. 1981. *Bad Blood: The Tuskegee Syphilis Experiment.* New York: The Free Press.

Katz, J. 1972. *Experimentation with Human Beings.* New York: Russell Sage Foundation.

National Bioethics Advisory Commission (NBAC). 1997. *Cloning Human Beings.* 2 vols. Rockville, MD: U.S. Government Printing Office.

———. 1998. *Research Involving Persons with Mental Disorders That May Affect Decisionmaking Capacity.* 2 vols. Rockville, MD: U.S. Government Printing Office.

———. 1999a. *Ethical Issues in Human Stem Cell Research.* 3 vols. Rockville, MD: U.S. Government Printing Office.

———. 1999b. *Research Involving Human Biological Materials: Ethical Issues and Policy Guidance.* 2 vols. Rockville, MD: U.S. Government Printing Office.

———. 2001. *Ethical and Policy Issues in International Research: Clinical Trials in Developing Countries.* 2 vols. Bethesda, MD: U.S. Government Printing Office.

National Commission for the Protection of Human Subjects of Biomedical and Behavioral Research (National Commission). 1979. *Belmont Report: Ethical Principles and Guidelines for the Protection of Human Subjects of Research.* Washington, D.C.: U.S. Government Printing Office.

Tuskegee Syphilis Study Ad Hoc Advisory Panel. 1973. *Final Report.* Washington, D.C.: U.S. Department of Health, Education, and Welfare.

EZEKIEL J. EMANUEL AND FRANKLIN G. MILLER

The Ethics of Placebo-Controlled Trials—A Middle Ground

Ezekiel J. Emanuel is the Chair of the Department of Clinical Bioethics at the Warren G. Magnuson Clinical Center, National Institutes of Health. His research interests include: end-of-life care, protecting communities in research, best ethical strategies for managed care and just allocation of health care resources. His book on medical ethics, *The Ends of Human Life* (Harvard University Press), has been widely praised and received honorable mention for the Rosenhaupt Memorial Book Award by the Woodrow Wilson Foundation.

Franklin G. Miller is a Special Expert in the Intramural Research Program of the National Institutes of Health and Department of Clinical Bioethics at the Warren Grant Magnuson Clinical Center. His research interests include ethical issues in psychiatric research and death and dying. He has published widely in bioethics and medical journals including *the New England Journal of Medicine, the Annals of Internal Medicine,* and *Archives of General Psychiatry.*

The first placebo-controlled trial was probably conducted in 1931, when sanocrysin was compared with distilled water for the treatment of tuberculosis.[1] Ever since then, placebo-controlled trials have been controversial, especially when patients randomly assigned to receive placebo have forgone effective treatments.[2–5] Recently, the debate has become polarized. One view, dubbed "placebo orthodoxy" by its opponents, is that methodologic considerations make placebo-controlled trials necessary.[6–11] The other view, which might be called "active-control orthodoxy," is that placebo orthodoxy sacrifices ethics and the rights and welfare of patients to presumed scientific rigor.[10–14] The latest revision of the Declaration of Helsinki, although controversial,[15,16] embraces the active-control orthodoxy.[17] Both views discount the ethical and methodologic complexities of clinical research. In this essay, we argue that placebo-controlled trials are permissible when proven therapies exist, but only if certain ethical and methodologic criteria are met.

From *New England Journal of Medicine* 345, no. 12 (September 20, 2001), 915–919. Copyright © 2001, Massachusetts Medical Society. All rights reserved.

PLACEBO ORTHODOXY

Advocates of placebo-controlled studies argue that it is ethical to conduct such trials even in the case of medical conditions for which there are interventions known to be effective, because of the methodologic limitations of trials in which active treatment is used as the control.[6–9] Sometimes therapies that are known to be effective are no better than placebo in particular trials because of variable responses to drugs in particular populations, unpredictable and small effects, and high rates of spontaneous improvement in patients. Consequently, without a placebo group to ensure validity, the finding that there is no difference between the investigational and standard treatments can be misleading or uninterpretable.[8,9] New treatments that are no better than existing treatments may still be clinically valuable if they have fewer side effects or are more effective for particular subgroups of patients.[18] However, no drug should be approved for use in patients unless it is clearly superior to placebo or no treatment. Despite the methodologic rigor of placebo-controlled trials, commentators acknowledge that they are unethical in some circumstances, especially when withholding an effective treatment might be life-threatening or might cause serious morbidity.[8,9]

There are serious problems with placebo orthodoxy. First, in our opinion, the criteria for ethical use of placebo controls are never precisely stated. In a recent review, for instance, Temple and Ellenberg[8,9] claimed that the use of placebo controls is ethical if the research participants who receive placebo will experience "no permanent adverse consequence," if there is a risk of "only temporary discomforts," or if they "will not be harmed." We think that these formulations are not equivalent. Since patients may be harmed by temporary but reversible conditions, the criterion of no harm would exclude many placebo-controlled trials that meet the criterion of no permanent adverse consequence.

Second, the criteria permit intolerable suffering on the part of study participants. This point is illustrated by trials of the antinausea medication ondansetron.[8] In 1981, research demonstrated clinically and statistically significant differences between metoclopramide and placebo for the treatment of vomiting induced by chemotherapy.[19] In the early 1990s, placebo-controlled trials of ondansetron for chemotherapy-induced vomiting, some of which involved patients who had not previously received chemotherapy, were reported.[20–22] These trials were unethical.[23,24] Although vomiting induced by chemotherapy, especially with highly emetic drugs such as cisplatin, is not life-threatening and does not cause irreversible disability, it causes serious, avoidable harm that is more than mere discomfort. Indeed, the need for better antiemetic medication had been justified in the first place by the argument that "uncontrolled nausea and vomiting [from chemotherapy] frequently results in poor nutritional intake, metabolic derangements, deterioration of physical and mental condition, as well as the possible rejection of potentially beneficial treatment."[22] Even in 1990, patients receiving the chemotherapeutic drugs evaluated in the ondansetron trials were routinely given antiemetic prophylaxis. Other trials conducted at the time used active controls.[25,26]

Finally, the proponents of placebo controls seem to focus on physical harm. In arguing for placebo-controlled trials of antidepressants, Temple and Ellenberg suggest that the only relevant harm is depression-induced suicide.[8,9] Psychological and social harms caused by depression—such as mental anguish, loss of employment, and disruption of relationships—are either not considered or dismissed. Yet psychological and social harms are invoked to justify the value of the research. This is contradictory. In evaluating the risk–benefit ratio, psychological and social harms must be addressed.

ACTIVE-CONTROL ORTHODOXY

Because of these problems, commentators have attacked placebo orthodoxy as unethical.[10–14] Proponents of active controls contend that whenever an effective intervention for a condition exists, it must be used in the control group. Furthermore, they argue that placebo controls are inappropriate because the clinically relevant question is not whether a new drug is better than nothing but whether it is better than standard treatments. To justify this approach, they cite the Declaration of Helsinki,[13,14,17] the most recent version of which states, "The benefits, risks, burdens and effectiveness of a new method should be tested against those of the best current prophylactic, diagnostic, and therapeutic methods. This does not exclude the use of placebo, or no treatment, in studies where no proven prophylactic, diagnostic or therapeutic method exists."[27] Advocates of active controls criticize placebo orthodoxy for placing the demands of science ahead of the rights and well-being of study participants.

Active-control orthodoxy also has several problems. First, the dichotomy between rigorous science and ethical protections is false. Scientific validity constitutes a fundamental ethical protection.[24] Scientifically invalid research cannot be ethical no matter how favorable the risk-benefit ratio for study participants.[24,28] If placebo controls are necessary or desirable for scientific reasons, that constitutes an ethical reason to use them, although it may not be a sufficient reason.

Second, in some cases, the harm and discomfort associated with the use of placebo controls are nonexistent or are so small that there can be no reasonable ethical requirement for new treatments to be tested only against standard treatments. Who could persuasively argue that for trials involving conditions such as baldness or some types of headaches, it is unethical to withhold effective treatments from some study participants and give them placebo instead?[29] There is no meaningful harm that stringent ethicists should worry about in letting a person who has given informed consent continue to suffer temporarily from a headache or untreated baldness as part of a clinical trial. Some critics of placebo controls contend that such trials are unethical because physicians owe medical care to patients who are seeking treatment for these ailments.[11] This argument conflates clinical research with clinical care. Clinicians frequently do not treat such ailments and patients often forgo treatment, indicating that there can be no ethical necessity to provide it.[9] The absolute prohibition against the use of placebo controls in every case in which an effective treatment exists is too broad; the magnitude of harm likely to be caused by using placebo must be part of the ethical consideration.

Third, opponents of placebo-controlled trials pay insufficient attention to the power of the placebo response. Substantial proportions of patients receiving placebo have measurable and clinically meaningful improvements—for example, 30 to 50 percent of patients with depression[30] and 30 to 80 percent of those with chronic stable angina.[31] A recent meta-analysis of randomized clinical trials with both placebo and no-treatment groups found little evidence of the therapeutic benefits of placebo over no treatment.[32] However, the patients given no treatment received clinical attention that may have contributed to observed improvements. This clinical attention may account for the placebo effect. Placebo-controlled trials in which patients receive potentially therapeutic clinical attention test whether an investigational treatment is better than this attention, not whether it is better than nothing.[33]

Most important, trials with active controls may expose more patients to harm than placebo-controlled trials. Equivalence trials, which evaluate the hypothesis that one drug is equivalent to another, typically require larger samples to achieve sufficient power, because the delta, or difference between the rates of response to the two drugs, is likely to be smaller than that between the rates of response to an investigational treatment and placebo.[18,34] Consider an equivalence trial in which an investigational drug is compared with a standard drug that is known to have a 60 percent response rate. With a delta of 10 percent (if they were equivalent, the difference between the standard and investigational drugs would be less than 10 percent) and a one-sided statistical test to show equivalence, each group must contain 297 participants. Conversely, if a placebo is hypothesized to have a 30 percent response rate and the investigational drug a 60 percent response rate, then only 48 participants are needed in each group.

With the sample required for the equivalence trial—larger by a factor of six than the sample required for the placebo-controlled trial—many more subjects will be exposed to an investigational drug that may be ineffective or even more toxic than the standard drug. Moreover, if it turns out that the rate of response to the investigational drug is 53 percent—still within the 10 percent range for equivalence—more participants will actually be harmed by not receiving the standard treatment than if a placebo-controlled trial were conducted instead. That is, in an equivalence trial of an investigational drug with a response rate of 53 percent, there will be 21 more subjects without a response in the group of 297 receiving the investigational drug than in the group of 297 receiving the standard drug with a known response rate of 60 percent. Conversely, consider a placebo-controlled trial with a 30 percent rate of response to placebo and a 53 percent rate of response to the investigational drug. Then, there will be 18 more subjects without a response in the group of 96 patients participating in the trial than if all 96 patients had received the standard drug. Indeed, the lower the rate of response to the investigational drug, the larger the number of participants in an equivalence trial who will be exposed to the harms associated with nonresponse. It is therefore simplistic to argue that placebo-controlled trials involving conditions for which the existing interventions are only partly effective necessarily sacrifice the well-being of patients.

A MIDDLE GROUND

For clinical research to be ethical, it must fulfill several universal requirements. Among other requirements, it must be scientifically valid and must minimize the risks to which the research participants are exposed.[24] When these requirements conflict, advocates of placebo controls opt for maintaining scientific validity, whereas advocates of active controls opt for minimizing risks. We believe these absolute positions are neither tenable nor defensible.

There is a middle ground. First, both sides agree that certain placebo-controlled trials are clearly unethical. If effective, life-saving, or at least life-prolonging treatment is available, and if patients assigned to receive placebo would be substantially more likely to suffer serious harm than those assigned to receive the investigational drug, a placebo-controlled trial should be prohibited. The efficacy of streptokinase in reducing morbidity and mortality after myocardial infarction made it unethical to conduct placebo-controlled trials of tissue plasminogen activator.[35]

Second, advocates of active controls should agree that for ailments that are not serious, if there is only a minimal chance that patients randomly assigned to receive placebo will suffer harm or even severe discomfort, the use of placebo controls is ethical.[36] A placebo-controlled trial of a new treatment for allergic rhinitis would be ethical because the moderate discomfort associated with allergic rhinitis typically does not impair health or cause severe discomfort.[29] Indeed, the risks associated with such trials are no greater than those deemed acceptable in natural-history and epidemiologic studies in which blood samples are obtained solely for research purposes and in pharmacokinetic studies in which medications are administered to healthy volunteers and blood samples obtained from them even though there is no prospect of a benefit to the study participants.

The disagreements center on whether it is ethical to use placebo controls when there is a treatment known to be effective and there is some potential for harm to participants receiving placebo. In this context, it is important to recognize that placebo-controlled trials and those in which active treatment is used as the control frequently have distinct objectives, and each type of trial may have a role in a sequential approach to evaluating new interventions. Whenever the risks of research with placebos are similar to the risks in these other types of studies, the use of placebo should be ethically justifiable. Placebo-controlled trials are often deemed important to determine the efficacy of a new treatment and to facilitate the design of larger trials in which the new treatment is compared with standard interventions. In addition, a trial comparing standard and new interventions may include a placebo group for internal validity when high placebo-response rates are anticipated.[32] However, proponents of active controls deem even these initial efficacy and three-group trials unethical when effective standard therapies exist. Placebo-controlled trials of treatments for angina and depression have been the focus of this disagreement, as have short-term trials designed to establish the efficacy of new treatments for asthma and hypertension before large, randomized trials are conducted to compare the new intervention with standard therapies.

When effective treatments exist, there must be compelling methodologic reasons to conduct a placebo-controlled trial. Proving that a new treatment has sufficient efficacy before large-scale equivalence trials are conducted is such a reason, whereas conducting a scientifically valid study with a smaller sample is not. A placebo-controlled trial has a sound scientific rationale if the following criteria are met: there is a high placebo-response rate; the condition is typically characterized by a waxing-and-waning course, frequent spontaneous remissions, or both; and existing therapies are only partly effective or have very serious side effects; or the low frequency of the condition means that an equivalence trial would have to be so large that it would reasonably prevent adequate enrollment and completion of the study.

If these methodologic criteria are met, then the risk of using a placebo control should be evaluated according to several criteria. Research participants in the placebo group should not be substantially more likely than those in the active-treatment group to die; to have irreversible morbidity or disability or to suffer other harm; to suffer reversible but serious harm; or to experience severe discomfort. There is no way of removing qualifying words such as "serious" or "severe" from these criteria, since ethical evaluation necessarily calls for contextualized judgments. Just as courts are empowered to make contextualized judgments about the standard of a separation between church and state, federal regulations empower institutional review boards to determine the levels of risk and severity of harm associated with research.

Although placebo-controlled trials that meet these

methodologic and ethical criteria may be justifiable even though the participants forgo therapies known to be effective, they remain worrisome because of the potential to cause suffering. Consequently, standard precautions must be scrupulously implemented for these trials. When such a trial is proposed, the institutional review board must ensure that the following safeguards are instituted to minimize harm: participants at increased risk of harm from nonresponse are excluded; the placebo period is limited to the minimum required for scientific validity; subjects will be carefully monitored, with inpatient observation when appropriate; rescue medications will be administered if serious symptoms develop; and there are explicit and specific criteria for the withdrawal of subjects who have adverse events. In addition, as part of the informed-consent process, the investigators must clearly disclose the rationale for using placebo, explain that subjects who are randomly assigned to the placebo group will not receive standard effective treatments, and state the risks associated with forgoing such treatments. The protocol should include provisions to ensure optimal treatment for participants who withdraw early or who remain symptomatic at the conclusion of the trial.

A CASE EXAMPLE

Chronic stable angina can cause substantial functional impairment and suffering. It is associated with a placebo-response rate of 30 to 80 percent.[31] Patients with chronic stable angina typically have fluctuating courses with spontaneous remissions, and for some patients, current therapies are partly effective at best. The long history of positive findings from open trials of cardiovascular treatments that have subsequently been disproved by blinded, placebo-controlled trials—including ligation of the internal mammary artery for angina,[37,38] chelation for claudication,[39] encainide and flecainide for arrhythmias,[40] and most recently, laser systems that create holes in cardiac tissue[41]—provides good scientific reasons for conducting placebo-controlled trials of treatments for chronic angina.

Even if it is methodologically sound, a placebo-controlled trial of a new treatment for chronic angina should satisfy the ethical criteria for an acceptable level of risk—that is, participation in the trial would not cause death, irreversible disability, reversible but serious harm, or severe discomfort. There is no evidence that medical management of chronic angina prolongs survival. Furthermore, a comprehensive review of double-blind, placebo-controlled, randomized trials of treatment for chronic angina showed that the risk of adverse events did not differ significantly between the drug and placebo groups.[42] The authors concluded that "withholding active treatment does not increase the risk of serious cardiac events." Nonetheless, patients at high risk for myocardial infarction and other cardiac events should be excluded from such trials, nitroglycerin should be provided for breakthrough anginal pain, and the period of treatment with placebo should be brief, usually less than 10 weeks. Patients should be contacted frequently to ensure careful monitoring of their condition, and those whose symptoms exceed an explicit threshold should be withdrawn from the trial. The informed-consent process must make it clear to patients that their angina may worsen and that they are free to withdraw from the trial at any time.

CONCLUSIONS

Placebo-controlled trials are caught in a battle between two orthodoxies. One is that placebo should be used as a control unless there is an increased risk of death or irreversible morbidity associated with its use. The other view is that if an effective therapy exists, the use of a placebo should be prohibited. These two positions are both absolute and indefensible. We propose a middle ground in which placebo-controlled trials are permitted but only when the methodologic reasons for their use are compelling, a strict ethical evaluation has made it clear that patients who receive placebo will not be subject to serious harm, and provisions have been made to minimize the risks associated with the receipt of placebo. This framework provides a basis for deliberation in difficult cases, with the recognition that reasonable people might make divergent judgments in a particular case.

REFERENCES

1. Lilienfeld A. M. The Fielding H. Garrison Lecture: *Ceteris paribus:* the evolution of the clinical trial. Bull Hist Med 1982;56:1–18.
2. Lasagna L., Mosteller F., von Felsinger J. M., Beecher H. K. A study of the placebo response. Am J Med 1954; 16:770–9.
3. Lasagna L. Placebos and controlled trials under attack. Eur J Clin Pharmacol 1979;15:373–4.
4. Feinstein A. R. Should placebo-controlled trials be abolished? Eur J Clin Pharmacol 1980;17:1–4.
5. Way W. L. Placebo controls. N Engl J Med 1984;311:413–4.
6. Temple R. Government viewpoint of clinical trials. Drug Inform J 1982;16:10–7.

7. *Idem.* Problems in interpreting active control equivalence trials. In: Accountability in research. Vol. 4. New York: Gordon and Breach, 1996:267–75.
8. Temple R, Ellenberg S. S. Placebo-controlled trials and active-control trials in the evaluation of new treatments. I. Ethical and scientific issues. Ann Intern Med 2000; 133:455–63.
9. Ellenberg S. S., Temple R. Placebo-controlled trials and active-control trials in the evaluation of new treatments. II. Practical issues and specific cases. Ann Intern Med 2000;133:464–70.
10. Freedman B., Weijer C., Glass K. C. Placebo orthodoxy in clinical research. I. Empirical and methodological myths. J Law Med Ethics 1996;24:243–51.
11. Freedman B., Glass K. C., Weijer C. Placebo orthodoxy in clinical research. II. Ethical, legal, and regulatory myths. J Law Med Ethics 1996; 24:252–9.
12. Freedman B. Placebo-controlled trials and the logic of clinical purpose. IRB 1990;12(6):1–6.
13. Rothman K. J., Michels K. B. The continuing unethical use of placebo controls. N Engl J Med 1994;331:394–8.
14. Rothman K. J. Declaration of Helsinki should be strengthened. BMJ 2000;321:442–5.
15. Shapiro H. T., Meslin E. M. Ethical issues in the design and conduct of clinical trials in developing countries. N Engl J Med 2001;345:139–42.
16. Koski G., Nightingale S. L. Research involving human subjects in developing countries. N Engl J Med 2001; 345:136–8.
17. Enserink M. Helsinki's new clinical rules: fewer placebos, more disclosure. Science 2000;290:418–9.
18. Active control equivalence studies. In: Senn S. Statistical issues in drug development. Chichester, England: John Wiley, 1997:207–17.
19. Gralla R. J., Itri L. M., Pisko S. E., et al. Antiemetic efficacy of high-dose metoclopramide: randomized trials with placebo and prochlorperazine in patients with chemotherapy-induced nausea and vomiting. N Engl J Med 1981;305: 905–9.
20. Cubeddu L. X., Hoffmann I. S., Fuenmayor N. T., Finn A. L. Efficacy of ondansetron (GR 38032F) and the role of serotonin in cisplatin-induced nausea and vomiting. N Engl J Med 1990;322:810–6.
21. Gandara D. R., Harvey W. H., Monaghan G. G., et al. The delayed-emesis syndrome from cisplatin: phase III evaluation of ondansetron versus placebo. Semin Oncol 1992; 19:67–71.
22. Beck T. M., Ciociola A. A., Jones S. E., et al. Efficacy of oral ondansetron in the prevention of emesis in outpatients receiving cyclophosphamide-based chemotherapy. Ann Intern Med 1993;118:407–13.
23. Hait W. N. Onadansetron and cisplatin-induced nausea and vomiting. N Engl J Med 1990;323:1485–6.
24. Emanuel E. J., Wendler D., Grady C. What makes clinical research ethical? JAMA 2000;283:2701–11.
25. Marty M., Pouillart P., Scholl S., et al. Comparison of the 5-hydroxy-tryptamine$_3$ (serotonin) antagonist ondansetron (GR 38032F) with high-dose metoclopramide in the control of cisplatin-induced emesis. N Engl J Med 1990; 322:816–21.
26. Hainsworth J., Harvey W., Pendergrass K., et al. A single-blind comparison of intravenous ondansetron, a selective serotonin antagonist, with intravenous metoclopramide in the prevention of nausea and vomiting associated with high-dose cisplatin chemotherapy. J Clin Oncol 1991;9:721–8.
27. World Medical Association Declaration of Helsinki: ethical principles for medical research involving human subjects. Edinburgh, Scotland: World Medical Association, October 2000. (Accessed August 31, 2001, at http://www.wma.net/e/policy/17-c_e.html.)
28. Rutstein D. D. The ethical design of human experiments. In: Freund PA, ed. Experimentation with human subjects. New York: George Braziller, 1970:383–401.
29. Senn S. The misunderstood placebo. Appl Clin Trials (May 2001), 40–46.
30. Khan A., Warner H. A., Brown W. A. Symptom reduction and suicide risk in patients treated with placebo in antidepressant clinical trials: an analysis of the Food and Drug Administration database. Arch Gen Psychiatry 2000; 57:311–7.
31. Bienenfeld L., Frishman W., Glasser S. P. The placebo effect in cardiovascular disease. Am Heart J 1996;132: 1207–21.
32. Hróbjartsson A., Gøtzsche P. C. Is the placebo powerless? An analysis of clinical trials comparing placebo with no treatment. N Engl J Med 2001; 344:1594–602.
33. Miller F. G. Placebo-controlled trials in psychiatric research: an ethical perspective. Biol Psychiatry 2000;47:707–16.
34. Leon A. C. Placebo protects subjects from nonresponse: a paradox of power. Arch Gen Psychiatry 2000;57:329–30.
35. Brody B. A. When are placebo-controlled trials no longer appropriate? Control Clin Trials 1997;18:602–12.
36. Vastag B. Helsinki discord? A controversial declaration. JAMA 2000;284:2983–5.
37. Dimond E. G., Kittle C. F., Crockett J. E. Evaluation of internal mammary artery ligation and sham procedure in angina pectoris. Circulation 1958;18:712–3.
38. Cobb L. A., Thomas G. I., Dillard D. H., Merendino K. A., Bruce R. A. An evaluation of internal-mammary-artery ligation by a double-blind technic. N Engl J Med 1959;260: 1115–8.
39. van Rij A. M., Solomon C., Packer S. G. K., Hopkins W. G. Chelation therapy for intermittent claudication: a double-blind, randomised, controlled trial. Circulation 1994;90: 1194–9.
40. The Cardiac Arrhythmia Suppression Trial (CAST) Investigators. Preliminary report: effect of encainide and flecainide on mortality in a randomized trial of arrhythmia suppression after myocardial infarction. N Engl J Med 1989;321:406–12.
41. Winslow R. Placebo study questions effectiveness of laser heart treatment. Wall Street Journal. October 19, 2000:B14.
42. Glasser S. P., Clark P. I., Lipicky R. J., Hubbard J. M., Yusuf S. Exposing patients with chronic, stable, exertional angina to placebo periods in drug trials. JAMA 1991;265: 1550–4.

HAROLD T. SHAPIRO
ERIC M. MESLIN

Ethical Issues in the Design and Conduct of Clinical Trials in Developing Countries

Harold T. Shapiro is emeritus President of Princeton University and Professor of Economics and Public Affairs. He chaired President Clinton's National Bioethics Advisory Commission, which issued the report *Cloning Human Beings* (1997). He holds memberships in the Conference Board Inc. and the Bretton Woods Committee.

Eric M. Meslin is Director of the Indiana University Center for Bioethics, Professor of Medicine and Assistant Dean for Bioethics at Indiana University School of Medicine, and Professor of Philosophy, at the Indiana University School of Liberal Arts. He was Executive Director of President Clinton's National Bioethics Advisory Commission and advised the White House and the federal government on a range of bioethics issues. He has authored (or co-authored) more than 75 articles and book chapters, including more than 30 publications in the peer-reviewed literature, with most focusing on various topics in research ethics, clinical ethics, and health policy.

There has been considerable controversy about the ethics of clinical trials that are sponsored or conducted by groups in industrialized countries but carried out in developing countries.[1–8] The National Bioethics Advisory Commission, of which we serve as chairman and executive director, respectively, has recently addressed these and related issues.[9] International collaborative research covers a broad spectrum of methods, topics, and research strategies. In this essay, we discuss ethical issues in the design and conduct of clinical trials in developing countries. In particular, we focus on phase 3 and other drug trials that, if successful, can lead to the use of effective new treatments.

Clinical trials should not exploit the subjects who agree to participate in them.[10] The United States is one of several countries that have developed substantive ethical standards (based on the principles of justice and individual autonomy) for conducting clinical research, as well as a required set of procedures for implementing the standards.

These standards and procedures are embodied in regulations developed over two decades ago—the "common rule"[11] and parallel regulations of the Food and Drug Administration (FDA)[12]—which apply to research involving human subjects that is funded by many federal agencies or regulated by the FDA. Despite some noticeable shortcomings and its limited scope, this system for the protection of human subjects has worked reasonably well for clinical research conducted in the United States. Unfortunately, not all research conducted in the United States is subject to the common rule or the FDA regulations (e.g., some studies conducted in physicians' offices and any type of research at academic institutions that do not receive federal funds). There is also continuing concern about the capacity of ethics committees to meet fully their critical responsibilities to protect human subjects and to provide oversight of studies.[13–15]

Reprinted with permission from the *New England Journal of Medicine* 345, (July 12, 2001), 139–42. Copyright © 2001 by the Massachusetts Medical Society. All rights reserved.

For clinical trials that are sponsored by the U.S. government and conducted in developing countries by U.S.-based researchers, or otherwise carried out within the federal regulatory framework, two associated questions arise. The first question is whether it is appropriate to apply the same set of ethical standards and procedures that is used for trials in the United States to trials conducted in developing countries, where the context may be different. The second is whether such clinical trials pose unique ethical issues that must be addressed.

EXPORTING ETHICAL STANDARDS

We believe that clinical trials conducted abroad should meet all the ethical standards for trials based in the United States, including prior review and approval by ethics review committees, the minimization of risk to the participants, a favorable risk–benefit ratio, and the provision of individual informed consent by all competent adult participants. Arguably, there should be additional standards to ensure that participants are drawn from a broad cross-section of the population and to ensure that there is adequate medical care of participants during the trial, with compensation for any injuries directly related to participation, even though these provisions are not required in the United States. Within the framework of these ethical standards, however, procedures could be adopted in developing countries that might differ from those in the United States and that might be more in line with local custom, conditions, and culture.

An important additional safeguard is needed to avoid the exploitation of potentially vulnerable populations in developing countries—namely, clinical trials sponsored or regulated by U.S. groups should be limited to those that are responsive to the host country's health needs. If the intervention being tested is not likely to be affordable in the host country or if the health care infrastructure cannot support its proper distribution and use, it is unethical to ask persons in that country to participate in the research, since they will not enjoy any of its potential benefits. Research participants in developing countries are less likely to have continued access to the intervention being evaluated than are participants in developed countries. This raises the ethical question of whether any health care benefits will ever reach the citizens of the host country.[6–8] In addition, there is always a concern that the developed country may be exploiting a country that is poorer, less powerful, and therefore more vulnerable. Although it has long been recognized that collaboration between peoples of different nations has great potential to generate substantial benefits for both sides, there is often controversy over the nature of the collaboration and whether the distribution of any benefits will be equitable.

Given these issues, researchers, sponsors, and ethics review committees in developed countries must take great care to ensure that the justification for conducting a trial in a developing country is adequately articulated. This is especially important if the trial is to be conducted in a country or region where the population may be vulnerable to exploitation because of pervasive poverty and disease or lack of understanding of the scientific issues surrounding the health problem and the role of the clinical trial in the search for a solution.

A trial in a developing country might be justified in a number of ways. The research might address an important health problem in that country, or it might represent a joint effort by the country sponsoring or conducting the study and the host country to address an important health problem in both countries. However, conducting a trial in a developing country because it is more convenient or efficient or less troublesome to do so is never a sufficient justification.

SPECIFIC ETHICAL ISSUES

There are specific ethical issues that arise when researchers from developed countries conduct clinical trials in developing countries. These issues are not unique—they pertain to all clinical research—but how they are interpreted and addressed may be unique.

THE PROCESS OF INFORMED CONSENT

The particular procedures for obtaining voluntary informed consent in developing countries may need to be tailored to local custom and culture, even though we share the view that the principle of informed consent applies throughout the world.[16] For example, U.S. regulatory procedures focus on the informed-consent document itself, rather than on the process of informed consent, and require written consent. Such procedures may be impossible to implement in some areas, because persons may be illiterate or because signing a form may be considered dangerous in countries with oppressive regimes. In any case, obtaining a signature on paper—in the United States or elsewhere—does not ensure that a participant understands the proposed research. Although signed forms make it easy to audit informed consent—one useful dividend of this process—there are other ways to ensure that it has been obtained. An ethically sound alternative to written consent is oral consent that has been witnessed and verified.

In many countries, it is important to obtain permission from local leaders for researchers to seek individual informed consent and to discuss other aspects of the research. Although it may be difficult to identify the members of the community who should be consulted and to determine the level of authority they should have in permitting researchers to approach potential participants, we believe that such consultations can be helpful in improving both the informed-consent process and the overall research design.

RESEARCH DESIGN AND ETHICS REVIEW

One of the most controversial issues in the conduct of clinical trials in developing countries is whether the control group must receive the same intervention as that which would be provided if the study were conducted in a developed country. For example, trials that compared a short course of zidovudine with placebo for the prevention of perinatal transmission of human immunodeficiency virus (HIV) infection generated considerable controversy.[17–19] It was already known that a longer course of zidovudine reduced perinatal transmission,[20] so some argued that the use of a placebo in subsequent studies was unethical.[19] In our view, an experimental intervention should normally be compared with an established, effective treatment (defined as a treatment that has widespread acceptance by the medical profession throughout the world and that is as effective as any alternative treatment for the disease or condition), whether or not that treatment is available in the host country. Therefore, the presumption is that a placebo control, or any other control that is less effective than an established, effective treatment, is not ethically acceptable.

However, we would permit an exception in a situation in which the only useful research design, from the host country's perspective, required a less effective intervention in the control group, if the condition being studied was not life-threatening and if the trial received approval from an ethics review committee in the host country as well as one in the United States. We recognize that the requirement of approval by an ethics review committee is not without its own challenges—in the United States and abroad—particularly if the committee lacks the independence or capacity to conduct a thorough review. The research investigators and sponsors must therefore assume considerable ethical responsibility in determining whether an exception to the standard is warranted. It may not be feasible to design a study that both answers a question that is relevant for the host country and that would be ethically acceptable if it were conducted in the United States. An exception should be limited and should not be extended to trials that fail to meet these requirements and qualifications. It would not apply to the treatment of life-threatening diseases such as HIV infection. If our standard were adopted, many trials currently under way or in the planning stages might have to be stopped or redesigned.

Some of these issues are illustrated by a recent case. Earlier this year, a U.S. biotechnology company submitted a proposal to the FDA for a study of a new surfactant drug in premature newborn infants with the respiratory distress syndrome—a potentially fatal condition.[3] The study, which was to be conducted in several Latin American countries, was designed to include three groups of infants: those receiving the new drug, those receiving an FDA-approved surfactant drug, and those receiving placebo. In studies of this kind—involving a disease that is life-threatening and one for which an established, effective treatment is available—a placebo control is not permissible. Moreover, such a trial is not ethical if patients in the developed country would be the primary beneficiaries and if it is not clear that the trial would be responsive to the health care needs of the host country. Surfactant treatment in infants with the respiratory distress syndrome is widely used in developed countries but not in developing countries. In April, the company that proposed the placebo control redesigned the study so that no infants would receive placebo.

These issues are also addressed in the recent revision of the Declaration of Helsinki.[21] It states, "The benefits, risks, burdens and effectiveness of the new method should be tested against those of the best current prophylactic, diagnostic and therapeutic methods." This statement may, in our view, be too rigid. It could undermine ethically sound attempts to address critical health issues, such as the treatment of a disease that is extraordinarily burdensome—for example, lower respiratory tract infections, perinatal disorders, or diarrheal conditions. In many developing countries, other ethical concerns may compete with the commitment to protect participants in research—for example, the need to prioritize access to medical interventions and to make the most of limited resources. The Helsinki standard for the control group should be the presumptive standard for trial design. Nonetheless, ethics review committees should be able to approve a deviation from this standard, but only if it is required in order to address an urgent health problem in the host country.

Prior review and approval of a proposed clinical trial by an independent ethics committee is an internationally accepted ethical standard for research involving human subjects.[21–23] A review by ethics committees in both the host and sponsoring countries does not guarantee that the trial will be carried out in an ethical manner but does help ensure that both the ethical aspects of the trial and the local context are considered. There should be greater efforts to make sure that local ethics committees have the necessary expertise to carry out their responsibilities.[24]

Finally, it has been suggested that it is unethical to conduct clinical trials in a country that does not share the democratic traditions of the United States. For example, an editorial in the *Washington Post* stated, "At the least, the FDA should not accept trials conducted in non-democratic countries. . . ."[25] We believe that the ethical obligations of the United States as a participant in international collaborative research are not limited to countries that share our democratic system. The same editorial went on to suggest that the FDA should not "allow the export of drugs for trials if they have been rejected for such use in the United States." We support in part the sentiment behind this suggestion, but in our judgment it is too rigid and, like the recent Helsinki revision, might prevent ethically sound research from being conducted.

POST-TRIAL BENEFITS

Ethical issues arise at the conclusion of all clinical trials. The Declaration of Helsinki states (Principle 30), "At the conclusion of the study, every patient entered into the study should be assured of access to the best proven prophylactic, diagnostic and therapeutic methods identified by the study." Other international documents either require similar post-trial provisions or call for the best efforts of sponsors and researchers to secure benefits for the participants in the trial and, in some cases, for other persons who might be candidates for the successful intervention.[21,24]

Making a successful new intervention available to participants after a trial is an especially important ethical obligation. There is a related obligation to ensure that participants are no worse off during the trial than they were before it. In addition, we believe that research participants should not be made worse off as a result of their inability to have continued access to the successful intervention after the trial has ended. Although the researcher–participant relationship is different from the doctor–patient relationship, trust in the medical profession is central to anyone's willingness to participate in a trial. Any sense of abandonment is difficult to address adequately in the informed-consent process.

A plan for the routine provision of a successful new intervention to participants after a trial has been completed is one way to ensure that the study is responsive to the health needs of the host country. The ethical obligation to provide the intervention to others in the community who might benefit from it is considerably less strong, but a plan to do so would help reduce the risk of exploitation.

CONCLUSIONS

The unprecedented international movement of people, goods, and ideas has made people in developed countries more aware of the imbalance in the global burden of disease. This is sometimes referred to as the "10/90 gap"—less than 10 percent of global health care expenditures are devoted to diseases that account for 90 percent of the global burden of disease.[26] Initiatives to reduce the burden of disease in developing countries are urgently needed. Clinical trials that are responsive to the health care needs of these countries constitute one such initiative, but it is neither necessary nor desirable to relax our ethical standards in order to achieve this goal. On the contrary, the standards should be maintained, with circumscribed adaptations to the needs of developing countries.

REFERENCES

1. Stephens J. The body hunters: as drug testing spreads, profits and lives hang in the balance. Washington Post. December 17, 2000:A1.
2. Flaherty M. P., Nelson D., Stephens J. The body hunters: overwhelming the watchdogs. Washington Post. December 18, 2000:A1.
3. Flaherty M., Stephens J. Pa. firm asks FDA to back experiment forbidden in U.S. Washington Post. February 23, 2001:A3.
4. Angell M. Investigators' responsibilities for human subjects in developing countries. N Engl J Med 2000; 342:967–9.
5. Loue S., Okello D. Research bioethics in the Ugandan context. II. Procedural and substantive reform. J Law Med Ethics 2000;28:165–73.

6. Benatar S. R., Singer P. A. A new look at international research ethics. BMJ 2000;321:824–6.
7. del Rio C. Is ethical research feasible in developed and developing countries? Bioethics 1998;12:328–30.
8. Glantz L. H., Annas G. J., Grodin M. A., Mariner W. K. Research in developing countries: taking "benefit" seriously. Hastings Cent Rep 1998;28(6):38–42.
9. Ethical and policy issues in international research: clinical trials in developing countries. Bethesda, Md.: National Bioethics Advisory Commission, 2001.
10. Gambia Government/Medical Research Council Joint Ethical Committee. Ethical issues facing medical research in developing countries. Lancet 1998;351:286–7.
11. 45 CFR 46 (Subpart A) (1981).
12. 21 CFR 56 (1981).
13. Advisory Committee on Human Radiation Experiments: final report. Washington, D.C.: Government Printing Office, 1995.
14. Scientific research: continued vigilance critical to protecting human subjects: report to the Ranking Minority Member, Committee on Governmental Affairs, U.S. Senate. Washington, D.C.: General Accounting Office, 1996.
15. Office of the Inspector General. Institutional review boards: a time for reform. Washington, D.C.: Department of Health and Human Services, 1998.
16. IJsselmuiden C. B., Faden R. R. Research and informed consent in Africa—another look. N Engl J Med 1992;326:830–4.
17. Angell M. The ethics of clinical research in the Third World. N Engl J Med 1997;337:847–9.
18. Varmus H., Satcher D. Ethical complexities of conducting research in developing countries. N Engl J Med 1997; 337:1003–5.
19. Lurie P., Wolfe S. M. Unethical trials of interventions to reduce perinatal transmission of the human immunodeficiency virus in developing countries. N Engl J Med 1997;337:853–6.
20. Connor E. M., Sperling R. S., Gelber R., et al. Reduction of maternal–infant transmission of human immunodeficiency virus type 1 with zidovudine treatment. N Engl J Med 1994;331:1173–80.
21. World Medical Association Declaration of Helsinki: ethical principles for medical research involving human subjects. Edinburgh, Scotland: World Medical Association, October 2000. Accessed June 22, 2001. (See http://www.wma.net/e/policy/17-c_3.html.)
22. International ethical guidelines for biomedical research involving human subjects. Geneva: Council for International Organizations of Medical Sciences (CIOMS), 1993.
23. Operational guidelines for ethics committees that review biomedical research. Geneva: World Health Organization, 2000. (Report no. TDR/PRD/ETHICS/2000.1.)
24. Ethical considerations in HIV preventive vaccine research: UNAIDS guidance document. Geneva: Joint United Nations Programme on HIV/AIDS (UNAIDS), 2001.
25. Testing drugs abroad. Washington Post. December 24, 2000:B6.
26. The 10/90 report on health research 2000. Geneva: Global Forum for Health Research, 2000.

SOLOMON R. BENATAR

Justice and Medical Research: A Global Perspective[1]

Solomon Benatar is Professor of Medicine and Director of the University of Cape Town Bioethics Centre; Visiting Professor in Public Health Sciences and Medicine at the University of Toronto's Joint Centre for Bioethics; and Chairperson of South Africa's Ministerial Committee on Health Research Ethics.

INTRODUCTION

When Harold Macmillan (then Prime Minister of Britain) visited Africa in 1960, he referred to the "wind of change" that he perceived blowing through Africa—in the wake of decades of colonialism and oppression.[2] The history of sub-Saharan Africa since then has been stormy. Initial encouraging advances made by many countries in the early years of their independence have been followed by subsequent retrogression due to both external and internal influences. External factors include the adverse effects of neo-liberal economics on trade and the incurring of debts, the subsequent structural adjustment programs imposed by the IMF and World Bank, and the impact of arms trading and 'Cold War' interference in Africa. Internal factors include corruption, political patronage, power struggles and poor governance. Adverse environmental conditions and the HIV/AIDS pandemic have posed additional massive burdens to progress.[3] The "wind of change" associated with emancipation from oppression in apartheid South Africa has culminated in a much admired peaceful transition in that country.[4] How this transition will play out in the face of the HIV/AIDS pandemic and in the context of a globalising world is of great importance.[5]

THE WORLD AT THE BEGINNING OF THE 21ST CENTURY

It is necessary to appreciate that the "wind of change" is now being felt throughout the world, as globalising forces create ever widening disparities in wealth, with important implications for health and well being.[6] Despite great progress in science, technology and communication during the 20th century, the world at the beginning of the new millennium is characterized by chaos and despair at many levels.[7] Escalating economic disparities, especially during the past 30 years, illustrate the impact of the "visible hand" of the market place and the "squeezed up" effect, that is, the funneling of resources upwards resulting in wider disparities in wealth and health between rich and poor than ever before—rather than the so much spoken about and praised "invisible hand" and "trickle down effect." Indeed more than half the world's population lives in poverty—25% in abject poverty.

The shift in the accumulation of capital from the nation state to multinational corporations, and the creation of unpayable third world debt, have impoverished third world countries and reduced annual per capita health care expenditures to less than $10 in most poor countries—where less than 50% of the population have access to even essential drugs. Health care services are rudimentary for many in a world in which 87% of annual global expenditure on health is directed to 16% of the world's population, who only bear 7% of the global burden of disease, and in which increasingly unethical, market driven research neglects many diseases.[8] Of all US $56 billion spent annually on medical research 90% is spent on those diseases causing only 10% of the global burden of disease.[9]

Meanwhile vast expenditure continues on the military. Many small wars, fuelled by trade in weapons, have resulted in unprecedented numbers of civilian

From *Bioethics* 15, (2001), 333–340. Copyright © Blackwell Publishers Ltd. 2001.

deaths and displacement of millions of people from their social roots, with profound disruption of their lives. In addition there is a world-wide movement of people, within and across national borders through urbanization, migration, tourism and illicit trading in drugs and people[10]—all favoring the rapid spread of infectious diseases. Growth of the world's population and massive increases in energy consumption (five and 30 fold increases respectively over the past 150 years) further threaten our ecology.[11]

New ecological niches created by these destructive social and environmental changes favor the emergence of many new infectious diseases, the worst being HIV/AIDS, and the recrudescence of old diseases such as tuberculosis and malaria that cause immense suffering and millions of premature deaths.[12] These and other infectious diseases that may emerge in the future challenge thinkers to better understand the world and how it could be improved.

HOW CAN THE WORLD BE EXPLAINED?

On the one hand the world can be considered as an unfortunate place in which most suffer disproportionately and unavoidably. On this account it is presumed that the manner and direction in which money flows, power is expressed, and social values develop are shaped by forces beyond the control of individuals or nations.

On the other hand an unjust world can be considered as one created by human activities, and one which can, and should be, changed. On this account the flow of money can be explained on the basis of national/international political forces and economic trends, and on such other aspects of globalization as advances in science and technology that have profoundly altered the nature of the global economy, as well as by exploitation at many levels (both overt–trade practices protecting the rich, and covert–debt trade and the arms trade as forms of enslavement). Some have used the term "global apartheid" for the processes that have promoted (and continue to aggravate) vast disparities between rich and poor across the world.[13] Others have described third world debt, an integral component of globalization, as analogous to slavery in its impact,[14] and have called for reflection on the magnificent achievements of the 20th century, and on how the human condition and health could be improved globally.[15]

CHALLENGES FOR INTERNATIONAL RESEARCH ETHICS

This brief review of the adverse effects of progress serves to locate the context in which the controversy about research ethics has arisen and the backdrop against which the goals of change need to be considered: how to construct universally valid guidelines for collaborative international medical research with the view to enhancing sensitivity to issues of justice and our common humanity. In brief, the rationale for embarking on this endeavor now more than ever before includes:

- The scale of injustice at a global level.
- Knowledge of the history of abuse of humans in medical research and the need to protect (vulnerable) research subjects.
- The need for research on diseases that know no boundaries and potentially threaten all—e.g., HIV/AIDS, and the diseases to which antimicrobial drug resistance is developing.
- Significant growth of research to promote the use of therapeutic drugs in a lucrative market.
- The attractiveness of doing research in developing countries: easy access to patients, reduced costs, and less stringent regulations—the "research sweat shop" equivalent.
- Understanding that researchers do not go to developing countries mainly for altruistic reasons.
- A perception by the vulnerable that they are being exploited.
- The need to balance the notion that solutions to disease and illness lie entirely in the realm of biomedicine with recognition that global forces promote emergence and resurgence of infectious diseases, and have many adverse effects on health.
- The goal of fostering empowerment through cooperation that may enhance human flourishing by making subjects essential partners in the research process.

The challenge to be faced in international research ethics is the development of universal rules for research world wide, at a time when health care is being delivered within very different health care systems (even within any single country) and in a multicultural world in which people live under radically different conditions—ranging from immense luxury to abject poverty. Variable trajectories of emancipation of individuals from communities have also given rise to a wide spectrum of how people view themselves, what it means to be ill and how health care systems should be structured.[16]With recognition of the role of social conditions in shaping the world, and how privileged people view the world and themselves, comes the realization that research cannot be considered in isolation. Medical research, health care, conditions of life around the world and how humans flourish may seem separate, but they are all interdependent. Taking such a comprehensive global perspective adds complexity to the task of crafting universal research ethics guidelines.

SOME SOLUTIONS TO THE CONTROVERSY ON RESEARCH ETHICS

Against this background of the context in which the controversy regarding alterations to the Helsinki Declaration and other guidelines for research ethics has arisen[17] a choice which can be made from several options. First, the status quo could be upheld in the hope that the progress of science and of economic growth will continue uninterrupted with beneficial effects for all even if disparities persist or grow. This would be the easiest choice as it presupposes no responsibility for global injustice. However, it would also be immoral as current injustices will be perpetuated and aggravated.

The second choice would be to make piecemeal changes at the margins—for example in international research by tinkering with the Helsinki Declaration and making some minor modifications. This course is also appealing to those who wish to make research easier and less accountable, but there is powerful and justified resistance to diluting protection for vulnerable research subjects and any progress made would in all probability be insufficient and temporary.[18]

Third, there could be acknowledgment of the need for a paradigm shift in thinking and action—towards reciprocal relationships between individuals, society, and the notion of rational self-interest and long term interdependence.[19] This is a more difficult decision and one that may have higher costs in the short term. It would, however, reflect recognition of the adverse impact of globalization and allow use of such desirable universal values as human rights to build a more widely achievable universalism. Such a decision could advance human relationships to the high moral ground, with the consequent best hope for long-term results. South Africa's peaceful transition through a negotiated revolution is an example. It is suggested that privileged people need to hold up a mirror to their lives, and try to see themselves from the perspective of the marginalised and weak in the world today and as historians in the future may see them in retrospect—as decadent and selfish.

Given the responsibility to use power and knowledge wisely, it is suggested that the deliberations at this meeting should include the possibility of introducing several new components into the Declaration of Helsinki and other international research guidelines—to extend and honor the concepts of justice and of integrity in the research endeavor:

- Vulnerable groups should be provided with increasing accessibility to research, and this should apply to the vulnerable within all countries.
- Exploitation of subjects, or their use as mere means to the ends of others, should be explicitly excluded by ensuring that the research is of relevance to the individuals participating in the research as well as their communities.
- The potential benefits of research should considerably outweigh potential risks or harms to vulnerable individuals and communities.
- Research subjects should be encouraged to participate in planning and conducting studies.
- Research in developing countries should be linked with capacity building in health care, and with economic and educational empowerment that has beneficial effects on the delivery of health care and on progress generally in the host country.

The first Global Forum on International Research, which opened discussion of all the topics listed on this agenda, was an enlightened first step forward. The second step would be to promote the addition of the newly proposed clauses to the Helsinki and other declarations. Third, there should be consideration of an expanded role for Institutional Review Boards (Research Ethics Committees)—taking them beyond mere review bodies to include duties of audit and education. Fourth, there is the need to influence mind sets—for example through societal marketing processes, rewards for compliance, wider publicity for and marginalisation of those doing unethical research, and by bringing bioethics and human rights programs closer to each other. Such actions could act as bridges, levers, and moral examples for the process of narrowing disparities. Education, the acquisition of self-knowledge coupled to activism, and moral example are all necessary for the promotion of a "global new deal."[20]

In summary support is provided here for the suggestion that to help the world's poorest, and indeed to foster the interests of all, the dialogue between rich and poor should be enhanced, the power of science and technology should be mobilized to address the problems of poor countries, new institutional alliances should be constructed, the concept of intellectual property rights should be re-evaluated to avoid "ripping off the poor," and long term financing should be planned for the international good necessary for human flourishing.[21] Herein lie the challenges to which the international research ethics endeavor could contribute.[22]

NOTES

1. Based on the opening address given by the author at the Fogarty International Global Research Ethics Forum Bethesda, Maryland. USA, November 1999.

2. H. Macmillan. "The wind of change is blowing through the continent. Whether we like it or not, this growth of national consciousness is a fact." Speech in the South African Parliament, Cape Town, February 3, 1960.

3. D. E. Logie, S. R. Benatar. Africa in the 21st century: can despair be turned to hope? *BMJ* 1997; 315: 1444–46. R. Sandbrook. 2000. *Closing the circle: democratization and development in Africa.* London. Zed Books.

4. H. Adam, K. Moodley, 1993. *The negotiated revolution: society and politics in post-apartheid South Africa.* Johannesburg. Jonathan Ball Publ.

5. K. Lee, A. B. Zwi. A global political economy approach to AIDS: ideology, interests and implications. *New Political Economy* 1996; 1: 355–73. S. R. Benatar. South Africa's transition in a globalising world: HIV/AIDS as a window and a mirror. *International Affairs* 2001; 77: 347–375.

6. S. R. Benatar. Global disparities in health and human rights. *American Journal of Public Health* 1998; 88: 295–300. J. Frenk et al., The new world order and international health. *BMJ,* 1997; 314: 1404–7.

7. E. Hobsbawm. 1994. *The age of extremes: a history of the world 1914–1991.* New York. Pantheon Books.

8. J. Iglehart. American health services: expenditure. *NEJM.* 1999; 340: 70–76.

9. Commission on Health Research for Development. 1990. *Health research: essential link to equity in development.* Oxford. Oxford University Press.

10. H. R. Friman, P. Andreas, (Eds). 1999. *Illicit global economy and state power.* New York. Rowan & Littlefield.

11. A. J. McMichael, *Planetary overload: global environmental change and the health of the human species.* Cambridge. Cambridge University Press.

12. WHO. *World health report 1996.* Geneva. K. Lee, A.B. Zwi. A global political economy approach to AIDS.

13. A. Richmond. 1994. *Global apartheid: refugees, racism and the new world order.* Oxford. Oxford University Press. T. Alexander. 1996. *Unraveling global apartheid.* Cambridge. Polity Press.

14. A. Pettifor. 1996. Debt, the most potent form of slavery. London, *Christian Aid Society. Jubilee 2000 Coalition,* 2000. "Kicking the habit: finding a lasting solution to addictive lending and borrowing—and its corrupting side effects." London.

15. The Jubilee 2000 campaign. www.jubilee2000.org

16. N. Smart. 1995. *World views: cross-cultural explorations of human beliefs.* New Jersey. Prentice Hall. R. Wilkinson. 1996. *Unhealthy societies: afflictions of inequality.* London. Routledge.

17. Revising the Declaration of Helsinki: a fresh start. *Bulletin of Medical Ethics.* 1999; 150: 3–44. Nuffield Council on Bioethics, 1999. *The ethics of clinical research in developing countries: a discussion paper.* London. D. Hellman. Trials on trial. *Report from the Institute for Philosophy and Public Policy.* 1998; 128: 142–147.

18. The Helsinki Declaration was modified at the 52nd World Medical Association (WMA) General Assembly in October 2000, Edinburgh, Scotland.

19. S. R. Benatar. 1997. Streams of global change. In: *Ethics, equity and health for all.* Z. Bankowski, J. H. Bryant, J. Gallagher (Eds). Geneva. CIOMS: 75–85. S. R. Benatar, P. A. Singer. A new look at international research ethics. *BMJ* 2000; 321: 824–26. A. Costello, A. Zumla. Moving to research partnerships in developing countries. *BMJ* 2000; 321: 827–29.

20. R. J. Barnett, J. Cavanagh. 1994. A global new deal. In: *Beyond Bretton Woods: alternatives to the new world order.* J. Cavanagh, D. Wysham, M. Arruda (Eds). London. Pluto Press. R. Falk. 1999. *Predatory globalization: a critique.* Cambridge. Polity Press. A. J. McMichael. 1997. *Planetary overload.* J. Rotblat (Ed) *World citizenship: allegiance to humanity.* London. MacMillan. G. Teeple. 2000. *Globalization and the decline of social reform.* 2nd ed. Aurora, Ontario. Garamond Press.

21. J. Sachs. Helping the world's poorest. *The Economist* 14 August, 1999: 17–20.

22. J. Stephens et al. The body hunters. A series of six articles in the *Washington Post* 17–21 December 2000, describing some of the horrors associated with the growing commercialization of drug research in developing countries.

GREGORY E. PENCE

The Tuskegee Study

Gregory E. Pence wrote *Who's Afraid of Human Cloning?* (Rowman & Littlefield) and has taught for twenty-three years at the University of Alabama at Birmingham, where he is a Professor in the Department of Philosophy and the School of Medicine. He is also the author of *Classic Cases in Medical Ethics: Accounts of the Cases That Have Shaped Medical Ethics* (McGraw-Hill) and editor of *Classic Works in Medical Ethics* (McGraw-Hill).

The Tuskegee study of syphilis began during the great depression—around 1930—and lasted for 42 years. Because of its long time span . . . some historical background is important for understanding the many issues raised by the Tuskegee research.

THE MEDICAL ENVIRONMENT: SYPHILIS

Syphilis is a chronic, contagious bacterial disease, often venereal and sometimes congenital. Its first symptom is a chancre; after this chancre subsides, the disease spreads silently for a time but then produces an outbreak of secondary symptoms such as fever, rash, and swollen lymph glands. Then the disease becomes latent for many years, after which it may reappear with a variety of symptoms in the nervous or circulatory systems. Today, syphilis is treated with penicillin or other antibiotics; but this treatment has been possible only since about 1946, when penicillin first became widely available.

Until relatively recently, then, the common fate of victims of syphilis—kings and queens, peasants and slaves—was simply to suffer the sequelae once the first symptoms had appeared. Victims who suffered this inevitable progress included Cleopatra, King Herod of Judea, Charlemagne, Henry VIII of England, Napoleon Bonaparte, Frederick the Great, Pope Sixtus IV, Pope Alexander VI, Pope Julius II, Catherine the Great, Christopher Columbus, Paul Gauguin, Franz Schubert, Albrecht Dürer, Johann Wolfgang von Goethe, Friedrich Nietzsche, John Keats, and James Joyce.[1]

It is generally believed that syphilis was brought to Europe from the new world during the 1490s, by Christopher Columbus's crews, but the disease may have appeared in Europe before that time. In any case, advances in transportation contributed greatly to the spread of syphilis. . . . For hundreds of years, syphilis was attributed to sin and was associated with prostitutes, though attempts to check its spread by expelling prostitutes failed because their customers were disregarded. Efforts to eradicate it by quarantine also failed.

In the eighteenth century, standing professional armies began to be established, and with them came a general acceptance of high rates of venereal disease. It is estimated, for instance, that around the year 1900, one-fifth of the British army had syphilis or gonorrhea.

Between 1900 and 1948, and especially during the two world wars, American reformers mounted what was called a *syphilophobia* campaign: the Social Hygiene Movement or Purity Crusade. Members of the campaign emphasized that syphilis was spread by prostitutes, and held that it was rapidly fatal; as an alternative to visiting a prostitute, they advocated clean, active sports (in today's terms, "Just say no"). According to the medical historian Allan Brandt, there were two splits resulting from disagreements within this reform movement: once during World War I, when

From Gregory E. Pence, *Classic Cases in Medical Ethics,* 2nd edition. Copyright © 1995 by McGraw-Hill. Reprinted by permission.

giving out condoms was controversial; and later during World War II, when giving out penicillin was at issue. In each of these conflicts, reformers whose basic intention was to reduce the physical harm of syphilis were on one side, whereas those who wanted to reduce illicit behavior were on the other side.[2]

The armed services during the world wars took a pragmatic position. Commanders who needed healthy troops overruled the moralists and ordered the release of condoms in the first war and penicillin in the second—and these continued to be used by returning troops after each war.

The spirochete (bacterium) which causes syphilis was discovered by Fritz Schaudinn in 1906. Syphilis is, classically, described in three stages:

- *Primary syphilis*—In this first stage, spirochetes mass and produce a primary lesion causing a *chancre* (pronounced "SHANK-er"). During the primary stage, syphilis is highly infectious.
- *Secondary syphilis*—In the second stage, spirochetes disseminate from the primary lesion throughout the body, producing systemic and widespread lesions, usually in internal organs and other internal sites. Externally, however—after the initial chancre subsides—syphilis spreads silently during a "latent" period lasting from 1 to 30 years, although secondary symptoms such as fever, rash, and swollen glands may appear. During the secondary stage, the symptoms of syphilis vary so widely that it is known as the "great imitator."
- *Tertiary syphilis*—In the third stage, chronic destructive lesions cause major damage to the cardiac system, the neurological system, or both, partly because immune responses decrease with age. During the tertiary stage, syphilis may produce paresis (slight or incomplete paralysis), gummas (gummy or rubbery tumors), altered gait, blindness, or lethal narrowing of the aorta.

Beginning in the sixteenth century, mercury—a heavy metal—was the common treatment for syphilis; it was applied to the back as a paste and absorbed through the skin. During the nineteenth century, this treatment alternated with bismuth, another heavy metal administered the same way. Neither mercury nor bismuth killed the spirochetes, though either could ameliorate symptoms.

In 1909, after the spirochete of syphilis had been identified, two researchers—a German, Paul Ehrlich, and a Japanese, S. Hata—tried 605 forms of arsenic and finally discovered what seemed to be a "magic bullet" against it: combination 606 of heavy metals including arsenic. Ehrlich called this *salvarsan* and patented it; the generic name is arsphenamine.[3] Salvarsan was administered as an intramuscular injection. After finding that it cured syphilis in rabbits, Ehrlich injected it into men with syphilis. (According to common practice, none of the men was asked to consent.)

At first, salvarsan seemed to work wonders, and during 1910 Ehrlich was receiving standing ovations at medical meetings. Later, however, syphilis recurred, fatally, in some patients who had been treated with salvarsan; furthermore, salvarsan itself apparently killed some patients. Ehrlich maintained that the drug had not been given correctly, but he also developed another form, neosalvarsan, which was less toxic and could be given more easily. Neosalvarsan also was injected intramuscularly—ideally, in 20 to 40 dosages given over 1 year.

Though better than salvarsan, neosalvarsan was (as described by a physician of the time) used erratically, and "generally without rhyme or reason—an injection now and then, possibly for a symptom, [for] some skin lesion, or when the patient had a ten-dollar bill."[4] It was also expensive. Moreover, neither salvarsan nor neosalvarsan was a "magic bullet" for patients with tertiary syphilis.

Another researcher, Caesar Boeck in Norway, took a different approach: from 1891 to 1910, he studied the natural course of untreated syphilis in 1,978 subjects. Boeck, a professor of dermatology at the University of Oslo, believed that heavy metals removed only the symptoms of syphilis rather than its underlying cause; he also thought that these metals suppressed what is today recognized as the immune system. He therefore decided that not treating patients at all might be an improvement over treatment with heavy metals.

In 1929, Boeck's student and successor, J. E. Bruusgaard, selected 473 of Boeck's subjects for further evaluation, in many cases examining their hospital charts.[5] This method had an obvious bias, since the more severely affected of Boeck's subjects would be most likely to have hospital records. Despite this bias, however, Bruusgaard was surprised to find that in 65 percent of these cases, either the subjects were externally symptom-free or there was no mention in their charts of the classic symptoms of syphilis. Of the subjects who had had syphilis for more than 20 years, 73 percent were asymptomatic.

Bruusgaard's findings contradicted the message of the syphilophobia campaign: they indicated that syphilis was not universally fatal, much less rapidly so. These results also suggested the possibility that some people with syphilis spirochetes would never develop any symptoms of the disease.

When the Tuskegee study began in 1932, Boeck's and Bruusgaard's work was the only existing study of the natural course of untreated syphilis.

THE RACIAL ENVIRONMENT

In the 1930s, American medicine was, and had long been, widely racist—certainly by our present standards and to some extent even by the standards of the time. For at least a century before the Tuskegee study began, most physicians condescended to African American patients, held stereotypes about them, and sometimes used them as subjects of nontherapeutic experiments.

The historian Todd Savitt, for example, has described how in the 1800s, J. Marion Sims, a pioneer in American gynecology, practiced techniques for closing vesical-vaginal fistulas on slave women.[6] John Brown, a former slave who wrote a book about his life under slavery, described how a physician in Georgia kept him in an open-pit oven to produce sunburns and to try out different remedies.

The best known account of the racial background of the Tuskegee study is James Jones's *Bad Blood* (1981; the significance of the title will become apparent below).[7] In the late nineteenth century, the United States was swept by social Darwinism, a popular corruption of Darwin's theory of evolution by natural selection. . . . Some whites predicted on this basis that the Negro race (to use the term then current) would be extinct by 1900: their idea was that Darwin's "survival of the fittest" implied a competition which Negroes would lose. (It bears repeating that this is a misconception and misapplication of Darwin's actual theory.) According to Jones, this popular belief was shared by white physicians, who thought that it was confirmed by defects in African Americans' anatomy and therefore became obsessed with the details of such presumed defects. Although comparable defects in white patients went unreported, defects in black patients were described in great detail in medical journals and became the basis for sweeping conclusions; to take one example, genital development and brain development were said to vary inversely.

In addition to social Darwinism, physicians shared many of the popular stereotypes of African Americans; well into the twentieth century, physicians often simply advanced such stereotypes as "facts." The following example appeared in *Journal of the American Medical Association* in 1914:

> The negro springs from a southern race, and as such his sexual appetite is strong; all of his environments stimulate this appetite, and as a general rule his emotional type of religion certainly does not decrease it.[8]

African Americans were also seen as dirty, shiftless, promiscuous, and incapable of practicing personal hygiene. Around the turn of the century, a physician in rural Georgia wrote, "Virtue in the negro race is like 'angels' visits'—few and far between. In a practice of sixteen years in the South, I have never examined a virgin over fourteen years of age."[9] In 1919, a medical professor in Chicago wrote that African American men were like bulls or elephants in *furor sexualis,* unable to refrain from copulation when in the presence of females.[10]

Ideas about syphilis reflected this racial environment. For white physicians at the time when the Tuskegee study began, syphilis was a natural consequence of the innately low character of African Americans, who were described by one white physician as a "notoriously syphilis-soaked race."[11] Moreover, it was simply assumed that African American men would not seek treatment for venereal disease.

The historian Allan Brandt has suggested that in the United States during the early 1900s, it was a rare white physician who was not a racist—and that this would have remained the case throughout many years of the Tuskegee study. He writes, "There can be little doubt that the Tuskegee researchers regarded their subjects as less than human."[12]

DEVELOPMENT OF THE TUSKEGEE CASE

A "STUDY IN NATURE" BEGINS

Studies in nature were distinguished from experiments in 1865 by a famous experimenter and physiologist, Claude Bernard: in an experiment, some factor is manipulated, whereas a *study in nature* merely observes what would happen anyway. For a century before the Tuskegee study, medicine considered it crucially important to discover the natural history of a disease and therefore relied extensively on studies in nature.

The great physician William Osler had said, "Know syphilis in all its manifestations and relations, and all others things clinical will be added unto you."[13] As late as 1932, however, the natural history of syphilis had not been conclusively documented (the only existing study, as noted above, was that of Boeck and Bruusgaard), and there was uncertainty about the inexorability of its course. The United States Public Health Service (USPHS) believed that a study in nature of syphilis was necessary because physicians needed to know its natural sequence of symptoms and final outcomes in order to recognize key changes during its course. This perceived need was one factor in the Tuskegee research.

A second factor was simply that USPHS found what it considered an opportunity for such a study. Around 1929, there were several counties in the United States where venereal disease was extraordinarily prevalent, and a philanthropical organization—the Julius Rosenwald Foundation in Philadelphia—started a project to eradicate it. With help from USPHS, the foundation originally intended to treat with neosalvarsan all syphilitics in six counties with rates of syphilis above 20 percent. In 1930, the foundation surveyed African American men in Macon County, Alabama, which was then 82 percent black; this was the home of the famous Tuskegee Institute. The survey found the highest rate of syphilis in the nation: 36 percent. The foundation planned a demonstration study in which these African American syphilitics would be treated with neosalvarsan, and it did treat or partially treat some of the 3,694 men who had been identified as having syphilis (estimates of how many received treatment or partial treatment range from less than half to 95 percent). However, 1929 was the year when the great depression began; as it ground on, funds for philanthropy plummeted, and the Rosenwald Foundation pulled out of Tuskegee, hoping that USPHS would continue the treatment program. (Funds available for public health were also dropping, though: USPHS would soon see its budget lowered from over $1 million before the depression to less than $60,000 in 1935.)

In 1931, USPHS repeated the foundation's survey in Macon County, testing 4,400 African American residents; USPHS found a 22 percent rate of syphilis in men, and a 62 percent rate of congenital syphilis. In this survey, 399 African American men were identified who had syphilis of several years' duration but had never been treated by the Rosenwald Foundation or in any other way. It was the identification of these 399 untreated men that USPHS saw as an ideal opportunity for a study in nature of syphilis. The surgeon general suggested that they should be merely observed rather than treated: this decision would become a moral crux of the study.

It is important to reemphasize that the USPHS research—it was undertaken in cooperation with the Tuskegee Institute and is called the *Tuskegee study* for that reason—was a study in nature. The Tuskegee physicians saw themselves as ecological biologists, simply observing what occurred regularly and naturally. In 1936, a paper in *Journal of the American Medical Association* by the surgeon general and his top assistants described the 1932–1933 phase of the Tuskegee study as "an unusual opportunity to study the untreated syphilitic patient from the beginning of the disease to the death of the infected person." It noted specifically that the study consisted of "399 syphilitic Negro males who had never received treatment."[14]

There are also two important points to emphasize about the subjects of the Tuskegee study. First, at the outset the 399 syphilitic subjects had *latent syphilis,* that is, secondary syphilis; most of them were probably in the early latent stage. During this stage, syphilis is largely noninfectious during sexual intercourse, although it can be passed easily through a blood transfusion (or, in a pregnant woman, through the placenta). However, latent or secondary syphilis (as noted above) has extremely variable symptoms and outcomes; and external lesions, which can be a source of infection during sex, do sometimes appear.

Second, these 399 syphilitic subjects were not divided into the typical experimental and control or "treatment" and "not treatment" groups: they were all simply to be observed. There was, however, another group of "controls," consisting of about 200 age-matched men who did not have syphilis. (Originally, there was also a third group, consisting of 275 syphilitic men who had been treated with small amounts of arsphenamine; these subjects were followed for a while but were dropped from the study in 1936—perhaps because funds were lacking, or perhaps because the researchers were by then interested only in the "study in nature" group.)

THE MIDDLE PHASE: "BAD BLOOD"

The Tuskegee study was hardly a model of scientific research or scientific method; and even on its own terms, as a study in nature, it was carried out rather haphazardly. Except for an African American nurse, Eunice Rivers, who was permanently assigned to the study, there was no continuity of medical personnel. There was no central supervision; there were no written protocols; no physician was in charge. Names of the subjects were not housed at any one location or facility. Most worked as sharecroppers or as small farmers and simply came into the town of Tuskegee when Eunice Rivers told them to do so (she would drive them into town in her car, a ride that several subjects described as making them feel important).

There were large gaps in the study. The "federal doctors," as the subjects called them, returned only every few years. Visits are documented in 1939 and then not again until 1948; 7 years passed between visits in 1963 and 1970. Only the nurse, Eunice Rivers, remained to hold the shaky study together. When the physicians did return to Tuskegee after a gap, they found it difficult to answer their own questions because the records were so poor.

Still, there were some rudimentary procedures. The physicians wanted to know, first, if they had a subject in the study group; and second, if so, how far his syphilis had progressed. To determine the progress of the disease, spinal punctures (called *taps*) were given to 271 of the 399 syphilitic subjects. In a spinal tap, a 10-inch needle is inserted between two vertebrae into the cerebrospinal fluid and a small amount of fluid is withdrawn—a delicate and uncomfortable process. The subjects were warned to lie very still, lest the needle swerve and puncture the fluid sac, causing infection and other complications.

Subjects were understandably reluctant to leave their farms, travel for miles over back roads to meet the physicians, and then undergo these painful taps, especially when they had no pressing medical problem. For this reason, the physicians offered inducements: free transportation, free hot lunches, free medicine for any disease other than syphilis, and free burials. (The free burials were important to poor subjects, who often died without enough money for even a pauper's grave; but USPHS couldn't keep this promise itself after its budget was reduced and had to be rescued by the Milbank Memorial Fund.) In return for these "benefits," the physicians got not only the spinal taps but, later, autopsies to see what damage syphilis had or had not done.

There seems no doubt that the researchers also resorted to deception. Subjects were told that they had "bad blood" and that the spinal taps were "treatment" for it; moreover, the researchers sensationalized the effects of untreated "bad blood." USPHS sent the subjects the following letter, under the imposing letterhead "Macon County Health Department," with the subheading "Alabama State Board of Health and U.S. Public Health Service Cooperating with Tuskegee Institute" (all of which participated in the study):

> Dear Sir:
>
> Some time ago you were given a thorough examination and since that time we hope you have gotten a great deal of treatment for bad blood. You will now be given your last chance to get a second examination. This examination is a very special one and after it is finished you will be given a special treatment if it is believed you are in a condition to stand it.[15]

The "special treatment" mentioned was simply the spinal tap for neurosyphilis, a diagnostic test. The subjects were instructed to meet the public health nurse for transportation to "Tuskegee Institute Hospital for this free treatment." The letter closed in capitals:

> REMEMBER THIS IS YOUR LAST CHANCE
> FOR SPECIAL FREE TREATMENT.
> BE SURE TO MEET THE NURSE.

To repeat, the researchers never treated the subjects for syphilis. In fact, during World War II, the researchers contacted the local draft board and prevented any eligible subject from being drafted—and hence from being treated for syphilis by the armed services. Although penicillin was developed around 1941–1943 and was widely available by 1946, the subjects in the Tuskegee study never received it, even during the 1960s or 1970s. However, as will be discussed below, it is not clear how much the subjects with late noninfectious syphilis were harmed by not getting penicillin.

THE FIRST INVESTIGATIONS

In 1966, Peter Buxtun, a recent college graduate, had just been hired by USPHS as a venereal disease investigator in San Francisco. After a few months, he learned of the Tuskegee study and began to question and criticize the USPHS officials who were still running it.[16] By this time, the physicians supervising the study and its data collection had been moved to the newly created Centers for Disease Control (CDC) in

Atlanta. CDC officials were annoyed by Buxtun's questions about the morality of the study; later in 1966, having invited him to Atlanta for a conference on syphilis, they harangued him and tried to get him to be silent. He expected to be fired from USPHS; he was not, though, and he continued to press CDC for 2 more years.

By 1969, Buxtun's inquiries and protests led to a meeting of a small group of physicians at CDC to consider the Tuskegee study. The group consisted of William J. Brown (Director of Venereal Diseases at CDC), David Sencer (Director of CDC), Ira Meyers (Alabama's State Health Officer from 1951 to 1986), Sidney Olansky (a physician at Emory Hospital who was knowledgeable about the early years of the study and had been in charge of it in 1951), Lawton Smith (an ophthalmologist from the University of Miami), and Gene Stollerman (chairman of medicine at the University of Tennessee). In general, this group avoided Buxtun's questions about the morality of the study and focused on whether continuing the study would harm the subjects. Meyers said of the Tuskegee subjects, "I haven't seen this group, but I don't think they would submit to treatment" if they were told what was going on.[17] Smith (the ophthalmologist) pressed hardest for continuing the study; only Stollerman repeatedly opposed continuing it, on both moral and therapeutic grounds. At the end, the committee overrode Stollerman and voted to continue the study.

Also in 1969, Ira Meyers told the physicians in the Macon County Medical Society about the Tuskegee study. These physicians did not object to the study; in fact, they were given a list of all the subjects and agreed not to give antibiotics to any subjects for any condition, if a subject came to one of their offices. It should be noted that although this medical society had been all-white in the 1930s, during the 1960s its membership was almost entirely African American.

In 1970, a monograph on syphilis was published, sponsored by the American Public Health Association, to give useful information to public health officials and venereal disease (VD) control officers. This monograph stated that treatment for late benign syphilis should consist of "6.0 to 9.0 million units of benzathine pencillin G given 3.0 million units at sessions seven days apart."[18] The first author listed on the monograph is William J. Brown, head of CDC's Tuskegee section from 1957 to 1971. Brown had been on the CDC panel in 1969 (when the monograph was probably written) and had argued for continuing the Tuskegee study, in which, of course, subjects with late benign syphilis received *no* penicillin.

THE STORY BREAKS

In July of 1972, Peter Buxtun, who had then been criticizing the Tuskegee research for 6 years and was disappointed by CDC's refusal to stop it, mentioned the Tuskegee study to a friend who was a reporter for the Associated Press (AP) on the west coast. Another AP reporter—Jean Heller, on the east coast—was assigned to the story, and on the morning of July 26, 1972, her report appeared on front pages of newspapers nationwide.[19]

Heller's story described a medical study run by the federal government in Tuskegee, Alabama, in which poor, uneducated African American men had been used as "guinea pigs." After noting the terrible effects of tertiary syphilis, the story said that in 1969 a CDC study of 276 of the untreated subjects had proved that at least 7 subjects died "as a direct result of syphilis."

Heller's story had an immediate effect. (It might have made even more of an impact, but it was competing with a political story which broke the same day—a report that the Democratic candidate for vice president, Thomas Eagleton, had received shock therapy for depression.) Some members of Congress were amazed to learn of the Tuskegee study, and Senator William Proxmire called it a "moral and ethical nightmare."

CDC, of course, responded. J. D. Millar, chief of Venereal Disease Control, said that the study "was never clandestine," pointing to 15 published articles in medical and scientific journals over a 30-years span. Millar also maintained that the subjects had been informed that they could get treatment for syphilis at any time. "Patients were not denied drugs," he said; "rather, they were not offered drugs." He also tried to emphasize that "the study began when attitudes were much different on treatment and experimentation."[20]

The public and the press, however, scorned Millar's explanations. One political cartoon, for instance, showed a frail African American man being studied under a huge microscope by a white man in a white coat with a sign in the background: "This is a NO-TREATMENT study by your Public Health Service."[21] Another cartoon showed ragged African American men walking past tombstones; the caption read: "Secret Tuskegee Study—free autopsy, free burial, plus

$100 bonus." Another showed a white physician standing near the body of an African American man, partially covered by a sheet; the chart at the foot of the hospital bed on which the body lay read "Ignore this syphilis patient (experiment in progress)"; in the background, a skeptical nurse holding a syringe asked, "*Now* can we give him penicillin?"

CDC and USPHS had always feared a "public relations problem" if the Tuskegee study became generally known, and now they had one. So did the Macon County Medical Society: when its president told the *Montgomery Advertiser* that the members had voted to identify remaining subjects and given them "appropriate therapy," USPHS in Atlanta flatly contradicted him, retorting that the local physicians—African American physicians—had accepted the Tuskegee study. The society then acknowledged that it had agreed to continuation of the study but had not agreed to withhold treatment from subjects who came to the offices of its members, whereupon USPHS documented the physicians' agreement to do exactly that.

THE AFTERMATH

Almost immediately after Heller's story appeared, Congress commissioned a special panel to investigate the Tuskegee study and issue a report. (The report was supposed to be ready by December 31, 1972; as we will see, however, it was late.)

Also almost at once, senators Sparkman and Allen of Alabama (both Democrats) sponsored a federal bill to give each of the Tuskegee subjects $25,000 in compensation. The southern African American electorate had been instrumental in electing these two senators and many southern members of Congress in the 1960s and 1970s, as well as presidents Kennedy and Johnson.

On November 16, 1972, Casper Weinberger, Secretary of Health, Education, and Welfare (HEW), officially terminated the Tuskegee study. At that time, CDC estimated that 28 of the original syphilitic group had died of syphilis during the study; after the study was ended, the remaining subjects received penicillin.

In February and March 1973, Senator Edward Kennedy's Subcommittee on Health of the Committee on Labor and Public Welfare held hearings on the Tuskegee study. Two of the Tuskegee subjects, Charles Pollard and Lester Scott, testified; one of them appeared to have been blinded by late-stage syphilis. These two men revealed more about the study: Pollard said they had not been told that they had syphilis; both said they thought "bad blood" meant something like low energy. Kennedy strongly condemned the study and proposed new regulations for medical experimentation.

In April 1973, the investigatory panel that had been commissioned when the Tuskegee story broke finally issued its report, which did not prove to be very useful. Moreover, for some reason this panel had met behind closed doors, and thus reporters had not been able to cover it.[22]

On July 23, 1973, Fred Gray, representing some of the Tuskegee subjects, filed a class-action suit against the federal government. Gray, a former Alabama legislator (in 1970, he had become the first African American Democrat elected in Alabama since Reconstruction), had been threatening to sue for compensation since Heller's story first broke, hoping for a settlement. He presented the suit as an issue of race, suing only the federal government and omitting the Tuskegee Institute, Rivers, the Tuskegee hospitals, and the Macon County Medical Society.

Eventually, the Justice Department decided that it couldn't win the suit in federal court, since the trail would have been held in nearby Montgomery, in the court of Frank Johnson, a liberal Alabama judge who had desegregated southern schools and upgraded mental institutions. Therefore, in December 1974 the government settled out of court.

According to the settlement, "living syphilitics" (subjects alive on July 23, 1973) received $37,500 each; "heirs of deceased syphilitics," $15,000 (since some children might have congenital syphilis); "living controls," $16,000; heirs of "deceased controls," $5,000. (Controls and their descendants were compensated because they had been prevented from getting antibiotics during the years of the study.) Also, the federal government agreed to provide free lifetime medical care for Tuskegee subjects, their wives, and their children. By September 1988, the government had paid $7.5 million for medical care for Tuskegee subjects. At that time, 21 of the original syphilitic subjects were still alive—each of whom had had syphilis for at least 57 years.[23] In addition, 41 wives and 19 children had evidence of syphilis and were receiving free medical care.

By the time this settlement was reached, more than 18 months had passed since Jean Heller's first story, and the Tuskegee issue was no longer front-page news: even the *New York Times* was giving it only an occasional short paragraph or two on inside pages. The issue was, after all, complicated; ethical standards had changed over the long course of the Tuskegee research; and, as noted above, the special panel commissioned to evaluate the study had met in secret. The public, therefore, had more or less forgotten about the Tuskegee study.

NOTES

1. Molly Selvin, "Changing Medical and Societal Attitudes toward Sexually Transmitted Diseases: A Historical Overview," in King K. Holmes et al., eds., *Sexually Transmitted Diseases,* McGraw-Hill, New York, 1984, pp. 3–19.

2. Allan Brandt, "Racism and Research: The Case of the Tuskegee Syphilis Study," *Hastings Center Report,* vol. 8, no. 6, December 1978, pp. 21–29.

3. Paul de Kruif, *Microbe Hunters,* Harcourt Brace, New York, 1926, p. 323.

4. R. H. Kampmeier, "The Tuskegee Study of Untreated Syphilis" (editorial), *Southern Medical Journal,* vol. 65, no. 10, October 1972, pp. 1247–51.

5. J. E. Bruusgaard, "Über das Schicksal der nicht spezifisch behandelten Luetiker" ("Fate of Syphilitics Who Are Not Given Specific Treatment") *Archives of Dermatology of Syphilis,* vol. 157, April 1929, pp. 309–32.

6. Todd Savitt, *Medicine and Slavery: The Disease and Health of Blacks in Antebellum Virginia,* University of Illinois Press, Champaign, 1978.

7. James Jones, *Bad Blood,* Free Press, New York, 1981.

8. H. H. Hazen, "Syphilis in the American Negro," *Journal of the American Medical Association,* vol. 63, August 8, 1914, p. 463.

9. Jones, op. cit., p. 74

10. Ibid.

11. Ibid.

12. Brandt, op. cit.

13. Quoted in E. Ramont, "Syphilis in the AIDS Era," *New England Journal of Medicine,* vol. 316, no. 25, June 18, 1987, pp. 600–601.

14. R. A. Vonderlehr, T. Clark, and J. R. Heller, "Untreated Syphilis in the Male Negro," *Journal of the American Medical Association,* pp. 107, no. 11, September 12, 1936.

15. Archives of National Library of Medicine; quoted in Jones, op. cit., p. 127.

16. Jones, op. cit., pp. 190–3.

17. Quoted ibid., p. 196.

18. W. J. Brown et al., *Syphilis and Other Venereal Diseases,* Harvard University Press, Cambridge, Mass., 1970, p. 34.

19. Jean Heller, "Syphilis Victims in the United States Study Went Untreated for 40 Years," *New York Times,* July 26, 1972, pp. 1, 8.

20. Ibid., p. 8.

21. Jones, op. cit., insert following p. 48.

22. Tuskegee Syphilis Study Ad Hoc Panel to Department of Health, Education, and Welfare, *Final Report,* Superintendent of Documents, Washington, D.C., 1973.

23. David Tase, "Tuskegee Syphilis Victims, Kin May Get $1.7 Million in Fiscal 1989," Associated Press, September 11, 1988.

WILLIAM J. CLINTON

In Apology for the Study Done in Tuskegee

William J. Clinton was elected Arkansas Attorney General in 1976 and won the governorship in 1978. He was elected the 42nd President of the United States in 1992 and served until 2001. More information can be found at www.whitehouse.gov/history/presidents.

. . . The eight men who are survivors of the syphilis study at Tuskegee are a living link to a time not so very long ago that many Americans would prefer not to remember, but we dare not forget. It was a time when our nation failed to live up to its ideals, when our nation broke the trust with our people that is the very foundation of our democracy. It is not only in remembering that shameful past that we can make amends and repair our nation, but it is in remembering that past that we can build a better present and a better future. And without remembering it, we cannot make amends and we cannot go forward.

So today America does remember the hundreds of men used in research without their knowledge and consent. We remember them and their family members. Men who were poor and African American, without resources and with few alternatives, they believed they had found hope when they were offered free medical care by the United States Public Health Service. They were betrayed.

Medical people are supposed to help when we need care, but even once a cure was discovered, they were denied help, and they were lied to by their government. Our government is supposed to protect the rights of its citizens; their rights were trampled upon. Forty years, hundreds of men betrayed, along with their wives and children, along with the community in Macon County, Alabama, the City of Tuskegee, the fine university there, and the larger African American community.

Washington, DC: The White House, Office of the Press Secretary, 1997 May 16; 3p. (Online). Available: http://clinton4.nara.gov/textonly/New/Remarks/Fri/19970516-898.html.

The United States government did something that was wrong—deeply, profoundly, morally wrong. It was an outrage to our commitment to integrity and equality for all our citizens.

To the survivors, to the wives and family members, the children and the grandchildren, I say what you know: No power on Earth can give you back the lives lost, the pain suffered, the years of internal torment and anguish. What was done cannot be undone. But we can end the silence. We can stop turning our heads away. We can look at you in the eye and finally say on behalf of the American people, what the United States government did was shameful, and I am sorry.

The American people are sorry—for the loss, for the years of hurt. You did nothing wrong, but you were grievously wronged. I apologize and I am sorry that this apology has been so long in coming.

To Macon County, to Tuskegee, to the doctors who have been wrongly associated with the events there, you have our apology, as well. To our African American citizens, I am sorry that your federal government orchestrated a study so clearly racist. That can never be allowed to happen again. It is against everything our country stands for and what we must stand against is what it was.

So let us resolve to hold forever in our hearts and minds the memory of a time not long ago in Macon County, Alabama, so that we can always see how adrift we can become when the rights of any citizens are neglected, ignored and betrayed. And let us resolve here and now to move forward together.

The legacy of the study at Tuskegee has reached far and deep, in ways that hurt our progress and divide our nation. We cannot be one America when a whole segment of our nation has no trust in America. An apology is the first step, and we take it with a commitment to rebuild that broken trust. We can begin by making sure there is never again another episode like this one. We need to do more to ensure that medical research practices are sound and ethical, and that researchers work more closely with communities.

Today I would like to announce several steps to help us achieve these goals. First, we will help to build that lasting memorial at Tuskegee. The school founded by Booker T. Washington, distinguished by the renowned scientist George Washington Carver and so many others who advanced the health and well-being of African Americans and all Americans, is a fitting site. The Department of Health and Human Services will award a planning grant so the school can pursue establishing a center for bioethics in research and health care. The center will serve as a museum of the study and support efforts to address its legacy and strengthen bioethics training.

Second, we commit to increase our community involvement so that we may begin restoring lost trust. The study at Tuskegee served to sow distrust of our medical institutions, especially where research is involved. Since the study was halted, abuses have been checked by making informed consent and local review mandatory in federally-funded and mandated research.

Still, 25 years later, many medical studies have little African American participation and African American organ donors are few. This impedes efforts to conduct promising research and to provide the best health care to all our people, including African Americans. So today, I'm directing the Secretary of Health and Human Services, Donna Shalala, to issue a report in 180 days about how we can best involve communities, especially minority communities, in research and health care. You must—every American group must be involved in medical research in ways that are positive. We have put the curse behind us; now we must bring the benefits to all Americans.

Third, we commit to strengthen researchers' training in bioethics. We are constantly working on making breakthroughs in protecting the health of our people and in vanquishing diseases. But all our people must be assured that their rights and dignity will be respected as new drugs, treatments and therapies are tested and used. So I am directing Secretary Shalala to work in partnership with higher education to prepare training materials for medical researchers. They will be available in a year. They will help researchers build on core ethical principles of respect for individuals, justice and informed consent, and advise them on how to use these principles effectively in diverse populations.

Fourth, to increase and broaden our understanding of ethical issues and clinical research, we commit to providing postgraduate fellowships to train bioethicists especially among African Americans and other minority groups. HHS will offer these fellowships beginning is September of 1998 to promising students enrolled in bioethics graduate programs.

And, finally, by executive order I am also today extending the charter of the National Bioethics Advisory Commission to October of 1999. The need for this commission is clear. We must be able to call on the thoughtful, collective wisdom of experts and community representatives to find ways to further strengthen our protections for subjects in human research.

We face a challenge in our time. Science and technology are rapidly changing our lives with the promise of making us much healthier, much more productive and more prosperous. But with these changes we must work harder to see that as we advance we don't leave behind our conscience. No ground is gained and, indeed, much is lost if we lose our moral bearings in the name of progress.

The people who ran the study at Tuskegee diminished the stature of man by abandoning the most basic ethical precepts. They forgot their pledge to heal and repair. They had the power to heal the survivors and all the others and they did not. Today, all we can do is apologize. But you have the power, for only you—Mr. Shaw, the others who are here, the family members who are with us in Tuskegee—only you have the power to forgive. Your presence here shows us that you have chosen a better path than your government did so long ago. You have not withheld the power to forgive. I hope today and tomorrow every American will remember your lesson and live by it.

Thank you, and God bless you.

SHELDON H. HARRIS

Factories of Death

Sheldon H. Harris is Professor of History emeritus at California State University, Northridge. Harris is interested in germ and chemical warfare. He authored *Factories of Death: Japanese Biological Warfare 1932–45, and the American Cover-Up* (Routledge). He has also written several other books and journal articles and has spoken extensively around the world.

The Manchurian village of Beiyinhe in 1933 was a non-descript community of perhaps twenty to thirty families. It was one of several tiny villages that collectively the locals called "Zhong Ma City." The inhabitants were simple illiterate peasants trying to produce sufficient food for themselves and to earn a few coins to purchase a necessity.

There was nothing special about Beiyinhe. Manchuria was dotted with thousands of tiny hamlets similar in composition to Beiyinhe. However, it did have one thing in its favor. Beiyinhe was located on the Beiyin River and adjacent to the Northeastern Lafa-Harbin Railroad line. It was only 2 *li* (less than one kilometer) from the railroad station. Harbin, Heilongjiang province's principal city, was little more than 100 kilometers north of the town. By train, Harbin could be reached in less than one and one half hours.[1]

One day in either July or August 1932,[2] several Japanese officers, along with supporting troops, roared into Beiyinhe, and ordered everyone to pack their belongings and to be prepared to leave the village within three days. Those who did not obey the orders would be killed on evacuation day, and their homes and belongings would be burned. The villagers, aware of the brutality of the Japanese occupation, complied reluctantly with the order.

The officer in charge to the Beiyinhe operation was a young major whom the Chinese called Zhijiang Silang, but who is better known as Ishii Shiro. Major Ishii had recently been posted to Manchuria. He was anxious to put into practice some novel ideas he had developed on modern warfare, and, he believed, what better place could there be to experiment with these concepts than in Manchuria, Japan's newest colony? Consequently, he is reported to have written to his superiors in Tokyo in late 1932 that "due to your great help we have already achieved a great deal in our bacteria research. It is time we start to experiment. We appeal to be sent to Manchukuo to develop new weapons."[3]

There were many miscreants who share responsibility for Japan's chemical and biological warfare programs. In fact, so many members of Japan's scientific establishment, along with virtually every military leader of note, either participated in chemical or biological warfare research, or supported these projects with men, money, and material, that it is difficult today to apportion exact blame or responsibility. But there is no doubt that the person most responsible for converting Manchuria into one huge biological warfare [BW] laboratory during the Japanese occupation was the young Army doctor, Major Ishii Shiro.

• • •

The Ping Fan project was an enormously complex and expensive undertaking. In reality, Ishii controlled a huge fiefdom in Ping Fan. He employed thousands of Chinese workers, both unskilled and craftsmen, in the construction and maintenance of his death factory. Many Japanese scientists and technicians were

From *Factories of Death: Japanese Biological Warfare, 1932–45, and the American Cover-Up* by Sheldon H. Harris, pp. 13–14, 39, 62–69, 76–82, 189, 242–243, 245, 250. Copyright © 1994 Routledge. Reprinted by permission.

brought to Ping Fan to work on various scientific projects under Ishii's direction. Hundreds of other Japanese served there in clerical and technical support roles. Delicate and intricate equipment, much of it coming from Europe and the United States, and costing tens of thousands of yen, was purchased for the facility.[4]

It was such a huge project that even arrogant Japanese administrators were forced to invent a cover story for Ping Fan. They were usually so contemptuous of, or indifferent to, Chinese public opinion, that the normal procedure was to ignore it. But Ping Fan was simply too large to ignore. Consequently, as an artifice, the local population was informed by Ishii's subordinates that the Japanese were constructing a lumber mill within the compound. And with the exquisite sarcastic "humor" for which Ishii and his colleagues were famous, they referred among themselves to their human subjects as *maruta,* or logs.[5]

• • •

Human experimentation followed three separate tracks. The most important of these were the laboratory experiments conducted at Ping Fan, at Anda and at the other Ishii Unit branches in Manchuria and occupied China. A second path was open-air experiments on humans at Anda that were conducted to discover the effectiveness of . . . prototype delivery systems. . . . And, finally, there were the field tests in which both civilian populations and military contingents were subject to pathogenic exposure.

Hundreds, if not thousands, of experiments were conducted on humans in the underground laboratories that were a characteristic of all the BW research installations constructed under Ishii's master plans. *Marutas* were dragged from their cells in buildings 7 and 8, or their smaller counterparts in the branch units, and led into the underground testing facilities. Here scientists injected victims with pathogens of differing dosages in order to determine the appropriate quantity of a specific germ to administer to individuals or to a general population. Tests were conducted on the "logs" with separate properties to learn whether certain foods, fabrics, tools, or utensils could be used as germ carriers. Human subjects were forced to eat different foods laced with specific germs. These included chocolates filled with anthrax, and cookies containing plague bacteria.[6] Other subjects were given various fluids (tea, coffee, milk, water, beer, spirits, etc.) to drink, with each liquid containing some specific dose of a pathogen.

Ishii found produce was a valuable conduit for spreading disease, and experimented with a number of viruses injected into different vegetables and fruits. Most of the fruit and vegetable studies were conducted at the Army Medical College in Tokyo under the direction of one of Ishii's brightest disciples, Naito Ryiochi.[7] Naito focused most of his research on "fugu toxin," which he obtained from the livers of blowfish. He reported success with developing a concentrate of toxin sufficient to kill mice, and he believed that he could secure excellent results for man if he were given enough time. However, the "degree of concentration" required to be effective with humans "was not obtained, and further efforts were interrupted by B-29 raids" over Tokyo in November 1944, and "ceased altogether with destruction, by fire, of the Army Medical College in April, 1945."[8]

Each laboratory at Ping Fan contained a large bulletin board that was displayed prominently on one wall. A technician recorded on the board every day data such as: "Specific date; 3 *maruta,* numbers so and so, were given injections of so and so, x cc; we need x number of hearts, or x number of livers, etc."[9] Laboratory technicians would then go to either building 7 or 8, order guards to provide the number of "logs" needed for the next experiment, and prepare the laboratory to receive victims. Some of the tests involved hanging "material" (humans) upside down, in order to determine the time necessary for a person to choke to death. Other experiments were conducted in which air was injected into the subjects to test the rate of onset of embolisms. Horse urine was injected into human kidneys in still other experiments. Mitomo Kazuo later recalled one experiment conducted in late August 1944, in which he

> put as much as a gram of heroin into some porridge to an arrested Chinese citizen . . . about thirty minutes later he lost consciousness and remained in that state until he died 15–16 hours later. . . . On some prisoners I experimented 5–6 times, testing the action of Korean bindweed, heroin, bactal and castor-oil seeds. . . . I was also present when gendarmes shot three prisoners on whom I had performed experiments.[10]

Some of the tests conducted by "scientists" and "medical doctors" defy imagination today.

"Logs" generally lasted a few weeks before either they succumbed to the experiments, or they were "sacrificed" because they were no longer viable test material. A few somehow remained alive for four to six months, but no longer. There was always a ready supply of fresh replacements.[11] Pathologists inherited the dead *maruta* almost immediately after the conclusion of the test. They would wheel the dead into one of the autopsy rooms, and would go to work by making a large "y"-shaped incision on the "material," and then performing the normal autopsy. After all tests were completed, the pathologists directed orderlies and guards to dispose of the carcasses in one of the several nearby crematoria.

Experiments covered every conceivable approach to spreading disease, and to prevention. A typical laboratory experiment with cholera was conducted in May and June 1940. Twenty prisoners, all between the ages of twenty and thirty, and in good health, were selected for the test. Eight persons were given cholera vaccine injections produced with ultrasonic equipment. Eight others were injected with cholera vaccine manufactured by a conventional method. Four experimentees were not inoculated. Twenty days later, all the victims were forced to drink copious quantities of cholera-infected milk. The four who received no immunization contracted cholera and died. Several of those tested who received conventional cholera injections also became ill and died. The eight who were vaccinated with ultrasonic cholera vaccine showed no cholera symptoms. A similar test with plague vaccines produced comparable results. Ishii then ordered his Vaccine Squad, renamed the "A Team" in 1940, to work only with ultrasonically produced vaccines.[12]

Ishii, Kitano, [Masaii], and the other Unit 731 researchers did not trumpet their activities throughout the scientific world, but neither did they shrink from publicly sharing some of their findings. They just disguised the human experimentation aspect. Researchers published or read more than one hundred scientific papers, both during the heyday of Unit 731's operation as well as in the postwar period. When dealing with humans, the researchers referred to experiments with "monkeys," or "Manchurian monkeys;" animal experiments were labeled with the animals' proper subspecies, such as "long-tailed monkey," "Taiwan monkey," or "Formosan monkey."[13] In "Japanese medical society," their human experiments "were known; that is, [were] an open secret."[14]

Under a cloak of immunity from possible prosecution, the "open secret" became detailed fact in 1946 and 1947. By that time, Unit 731 scientists did not have to resort to deceptive animal terms in describing their work to American scientists eager to gain precious information concerning human BW experiments. Perhaps they were not totally candid with the Americans, but they did provide them with specific details of some of their previous work in the course of lengthy interviews, and in written reports to investigators. The data were allegedly reconstructed from memory, since all records in Manchuria were supposedly destroyed during the Japanese retreat in 1945. However, the documents themselves suggest strongly that many of 731's records survived.[15]

Dugway, Utah, is approximately 10,000 miles from Ping Fan. Yet, here in the barren, windswept desert of western Utah is a United States Army chemical and biological warfare base which houses some of the remnants of Japanese BW research.[16] Among the many facilities to be found at Dugway Proving Grounds, a restricted research center that stretches over 840,911 acres of Utah desert, is a technical library that receives all the latest scientific publications that relate to CW and BW research, as well as general publications.[17] It also stores materials that other research centers no longer want, but that may contain useful intelligence for investigators. Tucked away in an unmarked box in the technical library are more than twenty reports compiled by American scientists from their postwar interviews with Ishii, Kitano, and other surviving Unit 731 authorities. This box contains also three extraordinary autopsy reports that cover glanders, plague, and anthrax. The autopsy reports range in length from 350 pages to more than 800 pages. Each autopsy report contains hundreds of pastel-colored artist drawings of human organs in various states of disintegration. At one time, these reports were designated as Top Secret, but advances in BW research make the findings obsolete, if not arcane. They were declassified in 1978.

At least two dozen BW scientists were interviewed, and the topics ranged from aerosols to typhus. The purpose of the exchanges was to "obtain information necessary to clarify reports submitted by Japanese personnel on the subject of B.W. . . . To examine human pathological material. . . . To obtain protocols necessary for understanding the significance of the pathological material."[18] What follows is a representative selection of the data Unit 731 researchers provided:

Dr. Futagi Hideo, in reporting on his experiments with tuberculosis, noted that in human tests with the Calmette bacillus (BCG) "All subjects recovered in this series," but in tests with the C1 Tuberculosis Hominis, "all doses produced military tuberculosis which was fatal within 1 month in those injected with 10.0 and 1.0 mg. The others were severely ill, lived longer but probably died later." In another test, "death at 1 month occurred following a stormy course with fever immediately post-injection." Futagi experimented with Manchurian children and achieved positive tuberculin results. He received the "original stock" of tuberculum germs from a "natural case. Virulence was maintained by passage through guinea pigs."[19] Dr Futagi Hideo's experiments were particularly hideous because tuberculosis is not an effective BW strategy. Usually it is too slow to have a BW impact. It is reasonable to conclude, therefore, that these experiments were carried out for purely academic purposes at the expense of the lives of those subjects tested.

Dr Tabei Kanau worked on typhoid experiments from 1938 until he was transferred in 1943. During that five-year period he tested perhaps several hundred subjects with different strains and dosages of typhoid germs. Some strains were mixed with sucrose, while others were stirred into milk. In one experiment, "Deaths occurred in 2 cases and 3 committed suicide." In another

> One subject was exposed to a bomb burst containing buckshot mixed with 10 mg bacilli and 10 gm of clay. The buckshot had grooves which were impregnated with the bacteria-clay mixture. Bomb burst 1 meter from the rear of the subject. He developed symptoms of typhoid fever with positive laboratory signs. Laboratory infections occurred in 2 Japanese investigators who seemed to be much sicker than Manchurians although none died. It was the impression of Dr. Tabei that Manchurians had more natural resistance than Japanese.[20]

Kitano dealt with many diseases, some of which were exotic, while others were of the common garden variety. His findings on songo fever, tick encephalitis, and typhus were especially welcomed by the Americans. They now could secure data on tick encephalitis that involved injecting mouse brain suspension in humans. One man, according to Kitano's protocol, "produced symptoms after an incubation of 7 days. Highest temperature was 39.8°C. This subject was sacrificed when fever was subsiding, about the 12th day." Another "received similar mouse brain emulsion i. n. in a dose of 1.0 cc. After an incubation period of 10 days the same symptoms appeared." The manifestations of the disease were grim:

> Fever is the first change. When the fever begins to subside, motor paralysis appears in the upper extremities, neck, face, eyelids, and respiratory muscles. There are no significant sensor changes. No paralysis is observed in the tongue, muscles of deglutition or lower extremities. After recovery, paralysis may be permanent. . . . Kitano observed it longer than 6 months.[21]

Ishii, as usual, was the star. He was interviewed on his work with human subjects that related to botulism, brucellosis, gas gangrene, glanders, influenza, meningococcus, plague, smallpox, tetanus, and tularemia.[22] Some of his findings were detailed, and covered many typescript pages. Others were as brief as: "Tularemia, Experiments in M were conducted with 10 subjects who were injected s.c. All developed fever lasting as long as 6 months. None died or were sacrificed."[23]

At least thirty-five reports involving human experiments were submitted by the Japanese scientists interviewed,[24] detailing tests conducted upon 801 "logs" plus 30 suicides.[25] This was remarkable, since the interviews took place within slightly more than a one-month period, November–December, in late 1947. Material obtained in such a limited time frame was a fraction of the information Japanese BW researchers realized in China and Manchuria, but even this paltry amount delighted their American counterparts. The Japanese apologetically acknowledged that they maintained autopsy reports on slightly less than 1000 sacrificed persons. Moreover, they regretted that "adequate material" for only 403[26] cases was still available.[27] This, too, was a patent understatement of the true facts, but American scientists rejoiced at their good fortune.

After completing a brief mission to Japan in November 1947, Edwin V. Hill, M.D., Chief, Basic Sciences, Camp Detrick, Maryland, observed, "Evidence gathered in this investigation has greatly supplemented and amplified previous aspects of this field." The data gathered by enemy scientists was secured "at the expenditure of many millions of dollars and years of work. . . . Such information could not be obtained in our own laboratories because of scruples attached to human experimentation." However, thanks to the Japanese, Hill observed the "data were secured with a total outlay of ¥250,000 to date, a mere pittance by comparison with the actual cost of the studies." Hill noted also that "the pathological material which has been collected constitutes the only material evidence of the nature of these experiments."[28]

The toll of sacrificed *maruta* was much greater than the figures provided to United States investigators. At the 1949 trial of Japanese prisoners in Khabarovsk, USSR, Major General Kawashima Kiyoshi, former head of Unit 731's First, Third, and Fourth Sections, testified that "I can say that the number of prisoners of Detachment 731 who died from the effects of experiments in infecting them with severe infectious diseases was no less than about 600 per annum."[29] Kawashima was stationed at Ping Fan from 1941 until the end of the war. Scholars, using Kawashima's figure of 600 deaths annually, concluded that 3000 people were killed in the BW experiments.[30]

Three thousand deaths is a gross underestimate of the actual number of men, women, and children slaughtered. It does not take into consideration those killed prior to 1941. Ishii, it must be remembered, began human experiments in Harbin in 1932. Hundreds, perhaps thousands, were destroyed during the Beiyinhe venture. Others were killed at Ping Fan from 1938 until Kawashima's arrival there in 1941. Still others were exterminated in the branch camps at Anda, Hailar, Linkow, Sunyu, and Dairen. Many more were murdered in Canton,[31] Peking (Beijing),[32] and, most probably, Shanghai and Singapore (Unit 9420).[33] At least 5000–6000 humans were annihilated in BW death factories not directly under Ishii's control (Mukden, Nanking, and Changchun) during the Japanese rampage in China. Nor does the count include the tens of thousands massacred in August 1945 in order to prevent their falling into the hands of the advancing Soviet or Chinese troops.[34]

• • •

The city of Anda lies directly due north of Harbin, roughly two hours by train from Ping Fan. Today it is a fairly prosperous community of 200,000 inhabitants that sits astride the Daqing oilfield. China's largest known petroleum deposit. From 1939 until 1945 Anda achieved another sort of distinction. Then little more than an expanse of empty pastureland interspersed with a handful of villages, Anda was the remote site for Unit 731's proving ground. When a new procedure appeared promising in the Ping Fan laboratory, it was submitted to further tests at Anda. Invariably, humans were used throughout the testing procedure, either in underground laboratories similar to those at Ping Fan, or, more frequently, in above-ground open-air trials. . . .

Scores of tests were conducted with hundreds of human guinea pigs at Anda during the Ishii-Kitano reign. Although there is no exact count of the number of proving-ground casualties, the scope of the enterprise can be gauged from some data disclosed during the postwar Soviet investigation of Japanese BW activities. For example, in the course of the annual inspection of the Anda facility in 1945, a probationary officer in the Quartermaster Corps was asked by a civilian employee for permission to discard some worn blankets. This request offers an important clue for a tally of sacrificed humans, since each year obsolete or worn equipment was replaced with new supplies, if the inspector gave his approval. The probationary officer noticed that "Dried blood was visible on them. These blankets were extremely tattered." There were some eighty badly frayed and blood-encrusted blankets in the pile shown to the quartermaster. When asked to account for the ragged condition of the blankets, the civilian employee replied that they "were used to protect the bodies of experimentees while experiments were being performed on them."[35] It is reasonable to conclude, therefore, that more than eighty persons were killed at the Anda proving grounds yearly during the period it existed.

Anda dealt with the usual laundry list of pathogens. It appears, though, that special emphasis was placed on testing the possibilities of plague,[36] anthrax and frostbite.[37] As early as June 1941, Anda tested plague-infested flea bombs on humans. Between ten and fifteen captives were fastened to stakes in the ground in one trial, and then an airplane dropped more than ten bombs on the site. The results are unknown, but they must have been promising, since other tests followed that summer.

In the next experiment, fifteen humans were fastened to stakes in the ground. "Flags and smoke signals were used to guide the planes." The planes took off from Ping Fan, and once over the site, dropped at least "two dozen bombs, which burst at about 100 or 200 meters from the ground." The fleas dispersed, and after waiting a sufficient length of time for the fleas to infect the prisoners, the victims were disinfected and taken back to Ping Fan for observation. Unfortunately, the tests were unsuccessful, disappointing the Colonel in charge of the experiment. He told a colleague that "the experiment did not yield good results." Evidently, the explosive force of the bombs' blasts caused excessively high temperatures, which in turn made the fleas "very sluggish."[38] Shrapnel bombs simply did not prove to be effective plague-dispersal vessels.[39]

Anthrax experiments were conducted periodically at Anda throughout 1943 and 1944. In general, scientists worked with ten *maruta* in each test. The head of Ping Fan's anthrax production team visited Anda on several occasions in 1943 and 1944 to supervise experiments, and observed that the *maruta* tested "looked like Chinese." They, too, as with the plague "logs," were tied to stakes in the ground. Then anthrax-filled bombs were exploded nearby. The anthrax expert did note with some professional pride that "some of the experimentees were infected with anthrax and, as I learned later, they died."[40] Nevertheless, experiments at Anda with anthrax were disappointing. Unit 731 experts failed to develop a viable anthrax delivery system by the end of the war.[41]

Since most germ bomb experiments ended in failure, Unit 731 scientists in 1944 conducted experiments with plague germ contamination through the respiratory tract. They hoped to develop a technique that would prove to be a feasible venue for BW. Accordingly, ten *maruta* were brought to Anda, and, as usual, were tied to stakes in the ground. Each *maruta* was stationed a prescribed number of meters away from his fellow "log." Test tubes filled with an emulsion of plague germs which were bred from the lymph, spleen, and hearts of plague-infected rats were scattered among the *maruta* at predetermined distances. The scientists arranged for the test tubes to burst, and their contents were distributed among the experimentees. The plague emulsion broke into tiny droplets which eventually were inhaled by the test subjects. Despite the hopes of the scientists involved in developing this technique, the test ended in failure. Still other respiratory tract experiments were conducted throughout 1944 and 1945, but they, too, ended in failure.[42]

• • •

. . . [Beginning in 1939,] Ishii expanded his field test operations to encompass all of Manchuria and both occupied and free China. From late 1939 through 1942, Unit 731 operatives conducted many tests against both enemy military forces and civilian populations. The logistics required for such extensive trials were so great that Ishii must have received approval to move forward from both the Kwantung Army leaders and area commanders of Japan's invading China forces. Logic suggests strongly that the top War Ministry officials in Tokyo were kept apprised of his operations, and approved them. They were so far-reaching that the devastation and carnage he unleashed brought an outcry from too many sources in China to be refuted as nothing more than lying Kuomintang propaganda.

The tests covered a host of insidious but imaginative artifices. Manchurian water wells were laced with typhoid germs that were remarkably effective killers. It is estimated that more than 1000 wells in and around Harbin were contaminated with typhoid bacilli in 1939 and 1940. Casualties ranged from single deaths to limited outbreaks of typhoid, which devastated entire villages. Mrs. Ada Pivo, a native of Harbin, remembered the day her eldest sister died of typhoid fever. The sister belonged to a Harbin Jewish Zionist youth group that went on a field trip in early summer 1940. The day was extremely warm, and on their return home, some of the forty-odd youngsters, thirteen to fifteen years old, bought bottles of lemonade in downtown Harbin. All children who drank the lemonade, which was bottled locally, and contained well-drawn water, contracted typhoid fever and subsequently died. The attending doctors traced the typhoid outbreak to the contaminated lemonade.[43]

Ishii, working with his Changchun counterpart,[44] caused a cholera outbreak in the Manchukuon capital. He descended upon the city in 1940, informed local authorities that cholera was moving in on their community, and that the general population must be inoculated. What he did not tell them was that the "vaccine" he intended to use was a solution containing cholera germs. Innocent people were lined up, given an injection, and possibly some liquid to drink or some contaminated food to eat. In any event, a cholera epidemic spread through metropolitan Changchun shortly after.[45]

In July 1942, Ishii led a BW expedition to Nanking, where he linked forces with local BW death factory personnel. Jointly, they distributed typhoid and paratyphoid germs from metal flasks and glass bottles, dumping the bacteria into wells, marshes, and houses of ordinary citizens. They could afford to be lavish with their dispensation, since Ishii brought along 130 kilograms of paratyphoid "A" and anthrax germs, and an unknown quantity of typhoid, all produced at Ping Fan.[46] Epidemics broke out in the region shortly afterwards, much to the delight of the researchers.

The Nanking trip yielded other benefits as well. Ishii, during his visit to the city, provided special treats for Chinese prisoners of war held in two nearby camps. In addition, he prepared an unusual delicacy for local youngsters, chocolates filled with anthrax bacteria.[47] Three thousand POWs were given, as a special holiday favor, dumplings that had been injected with either typhoid or paratyphoid. The prisoners were then released and sent home, where they acted as unwitting agents for spreading disease. The children gorged themselves on chocolates, with the unavoidable resulting side effects.

Sweet cakes, infused with typhoid and paratyphoid bacteria, were still another Ishii confectionery delight that he used in the Nanking expedition. Japanese soldiers were given 300–400 of the sweet cakes and ordered to leave them near fences and by trees. The idea was to create an impression that the soldiers forgot to take the food with them in the midst of a hasty retreat. It was expected that the local population, always short of food, would be delighted with the opportunity to feast on Japanese provisions. Inevitably, an outbreak of disease occurred shortly after the sweet cakes were ingested. Researchers concluded that "paratyphoid had proved to be the most effective"[48] of the pathogens tested.

In other field tests, Unit 731 saboteurs released, into densely populated areas, rats that were carrying plague-infested fleas. Researchers anticipated that the plague rats would breed with the local rat population, resulting in outbreaks of massive plague epidemics. Unit 731 men found also that germs implanted into expressly modified fountain pens and walking sticks were an effective method for disseminating BW. The germ-encrusted devices were dropped along dirt paths and paved roads, where either the curious or the needy would take them home. An epidemic would develop (plague generally), Japanese soldiers would rush to the affected area, order all villagers to evacuate, and then proceed to torch the villages in order to prevent outsiders from discovering what really took place. These sabotage techniques were so successful that Sir Joseph Needham, the great British scientist stationed in China at the time, noted:

> In the beginning, I felt great doubt about its credibility, but I believe now that the information collected by the Chinese Military Medical Bureau clearly indicates that the Japanese forces have been scattering and are continuing to scatter plague invested fleas in several areas.[49]

Massive BW testing actually commenced with an attack upon an innocent population in July 1940. Two months earlier, Ishii dispatched from Ping Fan a heavily guarded train. Its destination was Hangchow (Hangzhou), the beautiful holiday resort favored by Shanghai's wealthy. The train's cargo was 70 kilograms of typhoid bacterium, 50 kilos of cholera germs, and 5 kilos of plague-infested fleas. The BW target was Ning Bo, a community south of Hangchow. Ning Bo was an important Treaty Port in the nineteenth century, and the birthplace of Chiang Kai Shek.[50] For the next five months, Ning Bo and its environs were subjected to a series of BW attacks.

The methods for spreading disease in Ning Bo varied. Ishii and his researchers devised a host of delivery systems they planned to test on the simple residents of the area. Pathogens were dumped into water reservoirs, ponds, and individual residential water wells. Infected grains of wheat and millet were disseminated by aerial spraying in early October. Later that month, Ishii personally directed the scattering of contaminated wheat and cotton in and around Ning Bo. On 26 November, specially equipped Unit 731 aircraft flew over nearby Jin Hua county, dropping bombs which, on impact, gave off smoke-like objects that later turned a light yellow color.

The final results were that, as a consequence of the five-month campaign, cholera, typhus, and plague spread throughout Ning Bo and at least five surrounding counties. It is known that more than 1000 persons became ill with one or another of the Ishii-produced diseases, and that over 500 people succumbed.[51] Most alarming is that the diseases Ishii unleashed in summer and fall 1940 had long-term effects. Plague ravaged Ning Bo and nearby communities in 1941, 1946, and 1947. Casualties were high.[52]

• • •

All tests on humans, BW as well as the specialized non-BW experiments, were recorded carefully by the Unit 731 scientist or technician in charge of a specific project. The data compiled, both on paper and on film, indicate that Ishii's and Kitano's men recorded every conceivable reaction the human subjects developed during the course of the experiment, until the subject either perished from the effects of the tests, or was no longer a useful specimen and, therefore, was sacrificed. The records accumulated were of enormous quantity, and would prove alluring to both Soviet and

American scientists and intelligence authorities in the heyday of the Cold War.

• • •

By the end of 1947, if not earlier, the [American] authorities amassed enormous quantities of data suggesting strongly that a number of Japanese scientists—both military and civilian—had conducted BW experiments that involved the use of human guinea pigs. Much of their work constituted blatant human rights violations as defined by the charters governing both the Nuremburg and the Tokyo war crimes trials. The principals (Ishii, Wakamatsu, Kitano, et al.) tried to wriggle their way out from prosecution for their past conduct by lies, deceptions, evasions, and pleas of ignorance during repeated questioning. Still, some of their responses inadvertently damaged their cause. In addition, testimony by former colleagues convincingly branded them as being war criminals. So much evidence was compiled over a two-year investigation, linking the leaders to violations of international law, that any prosecutor could have taken their cases to the proper authorities and secured indictments and probable convictions. All that was required for such a scenario to take place was the desire of responsible officials to see justice done.

Unfortunately for Ishii's victims, the United States military had other priorities. The dominant American view in Tokyo was that the former commander of Ping Fan was too important a figure to be subjected to the criteria used for determining the issue of prosecuting an individual for war crimes. This attitude perhaps was best expressed by Lt. Colonel Robert McQuail of Army Intelligence (G-2). In a "Summary of Information" that McQuail prepared for his office in early January 1947, he noted that "A Confidential Informant claims that Ishii had his assistants inject bubonic plague bacilli into the bodies of some Americans in Mukden, Manchuria, as an experiment." McQuail, instead of being horrified, commented matter-of-factly that "Naturally, the results of these experiments are of the highest intelligence value."[53] Intelligence value, not war crimes, would be the dominant factor in all discussions concerning the Japanese BW experts.

NOTES

1. The account of the Beiyinhe facility is based on an interview I conducted with Mr Han Xiao, Deputy Director of the Unit 731 Memorial Museum in Ping Fan, Manchuria, 8 June 1989, and the following publications: Han Xiao and Zhou Deli, "Record of Actual Events of the Bacterial Factory in Ping Fan," *People's China,* vol. 3 (1971), translated by Ms Wang Qing Ling; Han Xiao, "Bacterial Factory in Beiyinhe, Zhong Ma City," *Harbin Historical Chronicle,* vol. 1 (1984), pp. 80–83, translated by Ms Lu Cheng; Dong Zhen Yu, "Kwantung Army Number 731," *Historical Material on Jilin History,* ed. by Jilin Branch of the Committee on Culture and History (Changchun), 1987, pp. 47–77, translated by Ms Wang Qing Ling.

2. The Chinese authorities are a little hazy on the exact date.

3. Quoted in Dong, "Kwantung Army Number 731" [see note 1].

4. Interview with John W. Powell, Jr., 28 February 1989.

5. Interview with Mr. Hao Yun Feng, Professor of Welding, Harbin Institute of Technology, 24 April 1984. Mr. Hao, a native of the Ping Fan area, was a teenager during Ping Fan's peak period of operation. He barely avoided being drafted to work in Ping Fan before the end of the war.

6. *Materials on the Trial of Former Servicemen of the Japanese Army Charged with Manufacturing and Employing Bacteriological Weapons* (Moscow: Foreign Languages Publishing House, 1950), p. 286; hereafter referred to as *Khabarovsk Trial.* Anthrax is not naturally transmitted in the fashion described at the Khabarovsk trial, and possibly it cannot infect via this route. The defendant testifying may have meant to name another disease that could be distributed in food. However, it should be remembered that Ishii's group was testing all possibilities shotgun style, and may have attempted to spread anthrax in the manner described above.

7. Lt. Colonel Naito would play an important role in the postwar United States interrogation of Japanese BW scientists. He ostensibly collaborated fully with the Americans. Once freed of the threat of war crimes prosecution, Naito would go on to an illustrious career in the "ethical drug" industry in the three decades after 1945.

8. Thompson, Arvo T., "Report on Japanese Biological Warfare (BW) Activities, 31 May 1946," Army Service Forces, Camp Detrick, Frederick, Md., p. 17, Fort Detrick Library Archives. Hereafter referred to as Thompson Report.

9. Dong, "Kwantung Army Number 731."

10. *Khabarovsk Trial,* p. 80.

11. Ibid

12. Han Xiao, "Compliation of Camp 731 Fascist Savage Acts," *Unforgettable History* (Harbin, 1985), translated by Ms Lu Cheng. . . .

13. See, as representative examples, [the] citations in footnotes 34, 35, 36, 37, 38, [in] Tsuneishi, Kei-ichi, "The Research Guarded by Military Secrecy—The Isolation of the E.H.F. Virus in [the] Japanese Bilogical Warfare Unit." *Historia Scientarium,* No. 30 (Tokyo), 1986, pp. 88–90; see also Tsuneishi, Kei-ichi, *The Germ Warfare Unit That Disappeared: Kwantung Army's 731st Unit* (Tokyo: Kai-mei-sha Publishers, 1981), pp. 164–165 in the English translation kindly furnished me by Mr Norman Covert. All citations hereafter are from the English translation, and the title will be cited as *The Germ Warfare Unit That Disappeared;* Morimura, Seiichi, *The Devil's Gluttony* (Tokyo: Kadokawa Shoten, Tokyo, 1983), vol. 3, Chapter 4.

14. Tsuneishi, "Research Guarded by Military Secrecy," p. 89.

15. See Thompson Report, pp. 11–12.

16. I want to thank United States Representative Wayne Owens (Dem., Utah) for his help in enabling me to visit Dugway Proving Grounds in November 1989.

17. Typescript copy, "Dugway Proving Grounds History"

(1987), provided by the Dugway Proving Grounds Public Information Office.

18. Edwin V. Hill to General Alden C. Waitt, 12 December 1947, Folder 56-5365, Dugway Proving Grounds Technical Library (hereafter cited as Dugway Library).

19. "Tuberculosis," Interview with Dr Hideo Futagi, 15 November 1947, Document 020, AA, Dugway Library. Futagi's data are unusual, since it usually takes a longer period of incubation for tuberculosis to have an impact on a subject.

20. "Typhoid," Interview with Dr. Tabei, 24 November 1947, Document 022, AC, Dugway Library.

21. "Tick Encephalitis," Information Furnished by Drs Yukio Kashara and Masaji Kitano, Document 019, Dugway Library.

22. Edwin V. Hill to General Alden C. Waitt, 12 December 1947, Dugway Library.

23. "Tularemia," Interview with Dr Shiro Ishii, 22 November 1947, Document 021, Dugway Library.

24. I have been unable to locate fifteen, or possibly more, reports allegedly submitted to American authorities. These documents may still be in other military archives, protected under some cloak of secrecy.

25. *Tulsa* (Okla.) *Tribune,* 29 February 1984, p. 13 A.

26. The Hill memo to General Waitt gives the figure as 401, but a tally of the data in his memo indicated that the correct figure is 403.

27. Only the three autopsy reports referred to earlier are in the Dugway Technical Library. Others no doubt exist, but their location at present is unknown.

28. Hill to General Alden C. Waitt, 12 December 1947, Dugway Library.

29. *Khabarovsk Trial,* p. 57. Kawashima committed suicide shortly before he was due to be repatriated to Japan in 1956. See the NHK Television documentary, *Modern History Scoop,* 13, 14 April 1992.

30. See, for representative statements, Tsuneishi, *The Germ Warfare Unit That Disappeared,* passim; Morimura, *Devil's Gluttony,* vol. 1; *Japan Times* (Tokyo), 1 August 1982, p. 1; and Pitter, C. and Yamamoto, R., *Gene Wars: Military Control over the New Genetic Technologies* (New York: Beach Books, William Morrow, 1988), p. 87.

31. At present, little is known of the Canton operation, except for the unit's designation, Unit 8604 (called Bo Zi in Chinese, or "Wave Unit"), and that it was housed until 1944 on a site that is today Sun Yat Sen University. Information provided me by Mr. Han Xiao in an interview on 10 June 1991.

32. The North China Army established Unit 1855 in Peking in 1938. The 2000-man unit was housed near the Temple of Heaven in Peking, and was headed by a Colonel Nishimura Yeni, who was a surgeon. Unit 1855 reported directly to Ishii. There is currently no published material in China on Unit 1855. However, a key authority estimates that the unit killed at least 1000 persons in experiments from 1938 until 1945. Information provided me by Mr. Han Xiao in an interview conducted on 10 June 1991.

33. At present, there is no concrete evidence concerning a purported BW unit in Shanghai. However, Kitano worked there from early 1945 until Japan's surrender. There are other tantalizing bits of information suggesting a Shanghai BW operation, but at the moment no substantial body of data has surfaced. For Singapore, see the Singapore *Straits Times,* 19 September 1991, pp. 1, 3; 25 September 1991, p. 1; 11 November 1991, pp. 1, 3; and Sidhu, H., *The Bamboo Fortress: True Singapore War Stories* (Singapore: Native Publications, 1991), pp. 160–184.

34. It was previously noted that Chinese authorities discovered a mass grave in Hailar containing more than ten thousand bodies. These people were killed in the closing days of the war. Many came from the BW facility in Hailar. Interview with Mr E. Er Dun in Hailar, 14 June 1991.

35. *Khabarovsk Trial,* p. 371.

36. "*Question:* What germs were tested most frequently on the proving ground? *Answer:* Plague germs." *Khabarovsk Trial,* p. 259.

37. See the discussion on pp. 28, 34, 69–71 for frostbite tests. [not reprinted]

38. *Khabarovsk Trial,* pp. 57, 259.

39. Tsuneishi, *The Germ Warfare Unit That Disappeared,* p. 133.

40. *Khabarovsk Trial,* p. 67.

41. Tsuneishi, *The Germ Warfare Unit That Disappeared,* pp. 130–133.

42. Ibid., pp. 131–132.

43. Interview with Mrs. Ada Pivo of Encino, California, 7 February 1989.

44. See Chapter 7. [not reprinted]

45. Han, "Compilation of Camp 731 Fascist Savage Acts."

46. *Khabarovsk Trial,* p. 66–67.

47. Ibid., pg. 286. . . .

48. Ibid. pp., 354–355.

49. Quoted in Tsuneishi, *The Germ Warfare Unit That Disappeared,* p. 148.

50. Chiang was born in a village near Ning Bo in 1887. See Spence, Jonathan D., *The Search for Modern China* (New York: W. W. Norton, 1990), p. 276–277.

51. Han Xiao and Zhou Deli, "Record of Actual Events of the Biological Factory in Ping Fan," *People's China,* vol. 3, 1971.

52. Ibid.

53. Summary of Information, Subject Ishii, Shiro. 10 Jan 47, Document 41, US Army Intelligence and Security Command Archive, Fort Meade, Md.

ADVISORY COMMITTEE ON HUMAN RADIATION EXPERIMENTS

Final Report

THE CREATION OF THE ADVISORY COMMITTEE

On January 15, 1994, President Clinton appointed the Advisory Committee on Human Radiation Experiments. The President created the Committee to investigate reports of possible unethical experiments funded by the government decades ago.

The members of the Advisory Committee were fourteen private citizens from around the country: a representative of the general public and thirteen experts in bioethics, radiation oncology and biology, nuclear medicine, epidemiology and biostatistics, public health, history of science and medicine, and law. . . .

The controversy surrounding the plutonium experiments and others like them brought basic questions to the fore: How many experiments were conducted or sponsored by the government, and why? How many were secret? Was anyone harmed? What was disclosed to those subjected to risk, and what opportunity did they have for consent? By what rules should the past be judged? What remedies are due those who were wronged or harmed by the government in the past? How well do federal rules that today govern human experimentation work? What lessons can be learned for application to the future? . . .

THE PRESIDENT'S CHARGE

The President directed the Advisory Committee to uncover the history of human radiation experiments during the period 1944 through 1974. It was in 1944 that the first known human radiation experiment of interest was planned, and in 1974 that the Department of Health, Education and Welfare adopted regulations governing the conduct of human research, a watershed event in the history of federal protections for human subjects.

In addition to asking us to investigate human radiation experiments, the President directed us to examine cases in which the government had intentionally released radiation into the environment for research purposes. He further charged us with identifying the ethical and scientific standards for evaluating these events, and with making recommendations to ensure that whatever wrongdoing may have occurred in the past cannot be repeated.

We were asked to address human experiments and intentional releases that involved radiation. The ethical issues we addressed and the moral framework we developed are, however, applicable to all research involving human subjects. . . .

THE COMMITTEE'S APPROACH

. . . As we began our search into the past, we quickly discovered that it was going to be extremely difficult to piece together a coherent picture. Many critical documents had long since been forgotten and were stored in obscure locations throughout the country. Often they were buried in collections that bore no obvious connection to human radiation experiments. There was no easy way to identify how many experiments had been conducted, where they took place, and which government agencies had sponsored them. Nor was there a quick way to learn what rules applied to these experiments for the period prior to the mid-1960s. With the assistance of hundreds of federal officials and agency staff, the Committee retrieved and reviewed hundreds of thousands of government documents. Some of the most important documents were secret and were declassified at our request. Even after this extraordinary effort, the historical record remains incomplete. Some potentially important collections could not be located and were evidently lost or destroyed years ago.

Nevertheless, the documents that were recovered

From United States Advisory Committee on Human Radiation Experiments, *Final Report: Executive Summary and Guide to Final Report* (Washington, DC: U.S. Government Printing Office, 1995), pp. 3–19.

enabled us to identify nearly 4,000 human radiation experiments sponsored by the federal government between 1944 and 1974. In the great majority of cases, only fragmentary data was locatable; the identity of subjects and the specific radiation exposures involved were typically unavailable. Given the constraints of information, even more so than time, it was impossible for the Committee to review all these experiments, nor could we evaluate the experiences of countless individual subjects. We thus decided to focus our investigation on representative case studies reflecting eight different categories of experiments that together addressed our charge and priorities. These case studies included:

- experiments with plutonium and other atomic bomb materials
- the Atomic Energy Commission's program of radioisotope distribution
- nontherapeutic research on children
- total body irradiation
- research on prisoners
- human experimentation in connection with nuclear weapons testing
- intentional environmental releases of radiation
- observational research involving uranium miners and residents of the Marshall Islands

In addition to assessing the ethics of human radiation experiments conducted decades ago, it was also important to explore the current conduct of human radiation research. Insofar as wrongdoing may have occurred in the past, we needed to examine the likelihood that such things could happen today. We therefore undertook three projects:

- A review of how each agency of the federal government that currently conducts or funds research involving human subjects regulates this activity and oversees it.
- An examination of the documents and consent forms of research projects that are today sponsored by the federal government in order to develop insight into the current status of protections for the rights and interests of human subjects.
- Interviews of nearly 1,900 patients receiving outpatient medical care in private hospitals and federal facilities throughout the country. We asked them whether they were currently, or had been, subjects of research, and why they had agreed to participate in research or had refused.

THE HISTORICAL CONTEXT

Since its discovery 100 years ago, radioactivity has been a basic tool of medical research and diagnosis. In addition to the many uses of the x ray, it was soon discovered that radiation could be used to treat cancer and that the introduction of "tracer" amounts of radioisotopes into the human body could help to diagnose disease and understand bodily processes. At the same time, the perils of overexposure to radiation were becoming apparent.

During World War II the new field of radiation science was at the center of one of the most ambitious and secret research efforts the world has known—the Manhattan Project. Human radiation experiments were undertaken in secret to help understand radiation risks to workers engaged in the development of the atomic bomb.

Following the war, the new Atomic Energy Commission used facilities built to make the atomic bomb to produce radioisotopes for medical research and other peacetime uses. This highly publicized program provided the radioisotopes that were used in thousands of human experiments conducted in research facilities throughout the country and the world. This research, in turn, was part of a larger postwar transformation of biomedical research through the infusion of substantial government monies and technical support.

The intersection of government and biomedical research brought with it new roles and new ethical questions for medical researchers. Many of these researchers were also physicians who operated within a tradition of medical ethics that enjoined them to put the interests of their patients first. When the doctor also was a researcher, however, the potential for conflict emerged between the advancement of science and the advancement of the patient's well-being.

Other ethical issues were posed as medical researchers were called on by government officials to play new roles in the development and testing of nuclear weapons. For example, as advisers they were asked to provide human research data that could reassure officials about the effects of radiation, but as scientists they were not always convinced that human research could provide scientifically useful data. Similarly, as scientists, they came from a tradition in which research results were freely debated. In their capacity as advisers to and officials of the government, however, these researchers found that the openness of science now needed to be constrained.

None of these tensions were unique to radiation research. Radiation represents just one of several examples of the exploration of the weapons potential of new scientific discoveries during and after World War II. Similarly, the tensions between clinical research and the treatment of patients were emerging throughout medical science, and were not found only in research involving radiation. Not only were these issues not unique to radiation, but they were not unique to the 1940s and 1950s. Today society still struggles with conflicts between the openness of science and the preservation of national security, as well as with conflicts between the advancement of medical science and the rights and interests of patients.

KEY FINDINGS

HUMAN RADIATION EXPERIMENTS

- Between 1944 and 1974 the federal government sponsored several thousand human radiation experiments. In the great majority of cases, the experiments were conducted to advance biomedical science; some experiments were conducted to advance national interests in defense or space exploration; and some experiments served both biomedical and defense or space exploration purposes. As noted, in the great majority of cases only fragmentary data are available.
- The majority of human radiation experiments identified by the Advisory Committee involved radioactive tracers administered in amounts that are likely to be similar to those used in research today. Most of these tracer studies involved adult subjects and are unlikely to have caused physical harm. However, in some nontherapeutic tracer studies involving children, radioisotope exposures were associated with increases in the potential lifetime risk for developing thyroid cancer that would be considered unacceptable today. The Advisory Committee also identified several studies in which patients died soon after receiving external radiation or radioisotope doses in the therapeutic range that were associated with acute radiation effects.
- Although the AEC, the Defense Department and the National Institutes of Health recognized at an early date that research should proceed only with the consent of the human subject, there is little evidence of rules or practices of consent except in research with healthy subjects. It was commonplace during the 1940s and 1950s for physicians to use patients as subjects of research without their awareness or consent. By contrast, the government and its researchers focused with substantial success on the minimization of risk in the conduct of experiments, particularly with respect to research involving radioisotopes. But little attention was paid during this period to issues of fairness in the selection of subjects.
- Government officials and investigators are blameworthy for not having had policies and practices in place to protect the rights and interests of human subjects who were used in research from which the subjects could not possibly derive direct medical benefit. To the extent that there was reason to believe that research might provide a direct medical benefit to subjects, government officials and biomedical professionals are less blameworthy for not having had such protections and practices in place.

INTENTIONAL RELEASES

- During the 1944–1974 period, the government conducted several hundred intentional releases of radiation into the environment for research purposes. Generally, these releases were not conducted for the purpose of studying the effects of radiation on humans. Instead they were usually conducted to test the operation of weapons, the safety of equipment, or the dispersal of radiation into the environment.
- For those intentional releases where dose reconstructions have been undertaken, it is unlikely that members of the public were directly harmed solely as a consequence of these tests. However, these releases were conducted in secret and despite continued requests from the public that stretch back well over a decade, some information about them was made public only during the life of the Advisory Committee.

URANIUM MINERS

- As a consequence of exposure to radon and its daughter products in underground uranium mines, at least several hundred miners died of lung cancer and surviving miners remain at elevated risk. These men, who were the subject of government study as they mined uranium for use in weapons manufacturing, were subject to radon exposures well in excess of levels known to be hazardous. The government failed to act to require the reduction of the hazard by ventilating the mines, and it failed to adequately warn the miners of the hazard to which they were being exposed.

SECRECY AND THE PUBLIC TRUST

- The greatest harm from past experiments and intentional releases may be the legacy of distrust they created. Hundreds of intentional releases took place in secret, and remained secret for decades. Important discussion of the policies to govern human experimentation also took place in secret. Information about human experiments was kept secret out of concern for embarrassment to the government, potential legal liability, and worry that public misunderstanding would jeopardize government programs.
- In a few instances, people used as experimental subjects and their families were denied the opportunity to pursue redress for possible wrongdoing because of actions taken by the government to keep the truth from them. Where programs were legitimately kept secret for national security reasons, the government often did not create or maintain adequate records, thereby preventing the public, and those most at risk, from learning the facts in a timely and complete fashion.

CONTEMPORARY HUMAN SUBJECTS RESEARCH

- Human research involving radioisotopes is currently subjected to more safeguards and levels of review than most other areas of research involving human subjects. There are no apparent differences between the treatment of human subjects of radiation research and human subjects of other biomedical research.
- Based on the Advisory Committee's review, it appears that much of human subjects research poses only minimal risk of harm to subjects. In our review of research documents that bear on human subjects issues, we found no problems or only minor problems in most of the minimal-risk studies we examined.
- Our review of documents identified examples of complicated, higher-risk studies in which human subjects issues were carefully and adequately addressed and that included excellent consent forms. In our interview project, there was little evidence that patient-subjects felt coerced or pressured by investigators to participate in research. We interviewed patients who had declined offers to become research subjects, reinforcing the impression that there are often contexts in which potential research subjects have a genuine choice.
- At the same time, however, we also found evidence suggesting serious deficiencies in aspects of the current system for the protection of the rights and interests of human subjects. For example, consent forms do not always provide adequate information and may be misleading about the impact of research participation on people's lives. Some patients with serious illnesses appear to have unrealistic expectations about the benefits of being subjects in research.

CURRENT REGULATIONS ON SECRECY IN HUMAN RESEARCH AND ENVIRONMENTAL RELEASES

- Human research can still be conducted in secret today, and under some conditions informed consent in secret research can be waived.
- Events that raise the same concerns as the intentional releases mentioned in the Committee's charter could take place in secret today under current environmental laws. . . .

KEY RECOMMENDATIONS

APOLOGIES AND COMPENSATION

The government should deliver a personal, individualized apology and provide financial compensation to those subjects of human radiation experiments, or their next of kin, in cases where:

- efforts were made by the government to keep information secret from these individuals or their families, or the public, for the purpose of avoiding embarrassment or potential legal liability, and where this secrecy had the effect of denying individuals the opportunity to pursue potential grievances.
- there was no prospect of direct medical benefit to the subjects, or interventions considered controversial at the time were presented as standard practice, and physical injury attributable to the experiment resulted.

- The Interagency Working Group, together with Congress, should give serious consideration to amending the provisions of the Radiation Exposure Compensation Act of 1990 relating to uranium miners in order to provide compensation to *all* miners who develop lung cancer after some minimal duration of employment underground (such as one year), without requiring a specific level of exposure. The act should also be reviewed to determine whether the documentation standards for compensation should be liberalized.

IMPROVED PROTECTION FOR HUMAN SUBJECTS

- The Committee found no differences between human radiation research and other areas of research with respect to human subjects issues, either in the past or the present. In comparison to the practices and policies of the 1940s and 1950s, there have been significant advances in the federal government's system for the protection of the rights and interests of human subjects. But deficiencies remain. Efforts should be undertaken on a national scale to ensure the centrality of ethics in the conduct of scientists whose research involves human subjects.
- One problem in need of immediate attention by the government and the biomedical research community is unrealistic expectations among some patients with serious illnesses about the prospect of direct medical benefit from participating in research. Also, among the consent forms we reviewed, some appear to be overly optimistic in portraying the likely benefits of research, to inadequately explain the impact of research procedures on quality of life and personal finances, and to be incomprehensible to lay people.
- A mechanism should be established to provide for continuing interpretation and application in an open and public forum of ethics rules and principles for the conduct of human subjects research. Three examples of policy issues in need of public resolution that the Advisory Committee confronted in our work are: (1) clarification of the meaning of minimal risk in research with healthy children; (2) regulations to cover the conduct of research with institutionalized children; and (3) guidelines for research with adults of questionable competence, particularly for research in which subjects are placed at more than minimal risk but are offered no prospect of direct medical benefit.

SECRECY: BALANCING NATIONAL SECURITY AND THE PUBLIC TRUST

Current policies do not adequately safeguard against the recurrence of the kinds of events we studied that fostered distrust. The Advisory Committee concludes that there may be special circumstances in which it may be necessary to conduct human research or intentional releases in secret. However, to the extent that the government conducts such activities with elements of secrecy, special protections of the rights and interests of individuals and the public are needed.

Research Involving Human Subjects. The Advisory Committee recommends the adoption of federal policies requiring:

- the informed consent of all human subjects of classified research. This requirement should not be subject to exemption or waiver.
- that classified research involving human subjects be permitted only after the review and approval of an independent panel of appropriate nongovernmental experts and citizen representatives, with all the necessary security clearances.

Environmental Releases. There must be independent review to assure that the action is needed, that risk is minimized, and that records will be kept to assure a proper accounting to the public at the earliest date consistent with legitimate national security concerns. Specifically, the Committee recommends that:

- Secret environmental releases of hazardous substances should be permitted only after the review and approval of an independent panel. This panel should consist of appropriate, nongovernmental experts and citizen representatives, all with the necessary security clearances.
- An appropriate government agency, such as the Environmental Protection Agency, should maintain a program directed at the oversight of classified programs, with suitably cleared personnel. . . .

Ethical Issues in Animal Research

DAVID DEGRAZIA

The Ethics of Animal Research: What Are the Prospects for Agreement?

David DeGrazia is Associate Professor of Philosophy at George Washington University. He is interested in such fields as ethical theory, biomedical ethics, and personal identity theory. He has authored *Taking Animals Seriously* and articles published in such journals as the *Hastings Center Report, Public Affairs Quarterly,* and *History of Philosophy Quarterly.*

Few human uses of nonhuman animals (hereafter simply "animals") have incited as much controversy as the use of animals in biomedical research. The political exchanges over this issue tend to produce much more heat than light, as representatives of both biomedicine and the animal protection community accuse opponents of being "Nazis," "terrorists," and the like. However, a healthy number of individuals within these two communities offer the possibility of a more illuminating discussion of the ethics of animal research.

One such individual is Henry Spira. Spira almost single-handedly convinced Avon, Revlon, and other major cosmetics companies to invest in the search for alternatives to animal testing. Largely due to his tactful but persistent engagement with these companies—and to their willingness to change—many consumers today look for such labels as "not tested on animals" and "cruelty free" on cosmetics they would like to buy.

Inspired by Spira, this paper seeks common ground between the positions of biomedicine and animal advocates. (The term "biomedicine" here refers to everyone who works in medicine or the life sciences, not just those conducting animal research. "Animal advocates" and "animal protection community" refer to those individuals who take a major interest in protecting the interests of animals and who believe that much current usage of animals is morally unjustified. The terms are not restricted to animal activists, because some individuals meet this definition without being politically active in seeking changes.) The paper begins with some background on the political and ethical debate over animal research. It then identifies important points of potential agreement between biomedicine and animal advocates; much of this common ground can be missed due to distraction by the fireworks of the current political exchange. Next, the paper enumerates issues on which continuing disagreement is likely. Finally, it concludes with concrete suggestions for building positively on the common ground.

From *Cambridge Quarterly of Healthcare Ethics* 8 (1999), 23–34. Copyright © 1999 Cambridge University Press. Reprinted with permission.

BACKGROUND ON THE DEBATE OVER ANIMAL RESEARCH

What is the current state of the debate over the ethics of animal research? Let us begin with the viewpoint of biomedicine. It seems fair to say that biomedicine has a "party line" on the ethics of animal research, conformity to which may feel like a political litmus test for full acceptability within the professional community. According to this party line, animal research is clearly justified because it is necessary for medical progress and therefore human health—and those who disagree are irrational, antiscience, misanthropic "extremists" whose views do not deserve serious attention. (Needless to say, despite considerable conformity, not everyone in biomedicine accepts this position.)

In at least some countries, biomedicine's leadership apparently values conformity to this party line more than freedom of thought and expression on the animal research issue. (In this paragraph, I will refer to the American situation to illustrate the point.) Hence the unwillingness of major medical journals, such as *JAMA* and *The New England Journal of Medicine,* to publish articles that are highly critical of animal research. Hence also the extraordinary similarity I have noticed in pro-research lectures by representatives of biomedicine. I used to be puzzled about why these lectures sounded so similar and why, for example, they consistently made some of the same philosophical and conceptual errors (such as dichotomizing animal welfare and animal rights, and taking the latter concept to imply identical rights for humans and animals). But that was before I learned of the "AMA [American Medical Association] Animal Research Action Plan" and the AMA's "White Paper." Promoting an aggressive pro-research campaign, these documents encourage AMA members to say and do certain things for public relations purposes, including the following: "Identify animal rights activists as anti-science and against medical progress"; "Combat emotion with emotion (eg [sic], 'fuzzy' animals contrasted with 'healing' children)"; and "Position the biomedical community as moderate—centrist—in the controversy, not as a polar opposite."[1]

It is a reasonable conjecture that biomedicine's party line was developed largely in reaction to fear—both of the most intimidating actions of some especially zealous animal advocates, such as telephoned threats and destruction of property, and of growing societal concern about animals. Unfortunately, biomedicine's reaction has created a political culture in which many or most animal researchers and their supporters do not engage in sustained, critical thinking about the moral status of animals and the basic justification (or lack thereof) for animal research. Few seem to recognize that there is significant merit to the opposing position, fewer have had any rigorous training in ethical reasoning, and hardly any have read much of the leading literature on animal ethics. The stultifying effect of this cultural phenomenon hit home with me at a small meeting of representatives of biomedicine, in which I had been invited to explain "the animal rights philosophy" (the invitation itself being exceptional and encouraging). After the talk, in which I presented ideas familiar to all who really know the literature and issues of animal ethics, several attendees pumped my hand and said something to this effect: "This is the first time I have heard such rational and lucid arguments for the other side. I didn't know there were any."

As for the animal protection community, there does not seem to be a shared viewpoint except at a very general level: significant interest in animal welfare and the belief that much current animal usage is unjustified. Beyond that, differences abound. For example, the Humane Society of the United States opposes factory farming but not humane forms of animal husbandry, rejects current levels of animal use in research but not animal research itself, and condemns most zoo exhibits but not those that adequately meet animals' needs and approximate their natural habitats.[2] Meanwhile, the Animal Liberation Front, a clandestine British organization, apparently opposes all animal husbandry, animal research, and the keeping of zoo animals.[3] Although there are extensive differences within the animal protection community, as far as our paper topic goes, it seems fair to say that almost everyone in this group opposes current levels of animal research.

That's a brief sketch of the perspectives of biomedicine and animal advocates on the issue of animal research. What about the state of animal ethics itself? The leading book-length works in this field exhibit a near consensus that the status quo of animal usage is ethically indefensible and that at least significant reductions in animal research are justified. Let me elaborate.

Defending strong animal rights positions in different ways, Tom Regan and Evelyn Pluhar advocate abolition of all research that involves harming animals.[4] Ray Frey and Peter Singer, by contrast, hold the use of animals to the very stringent utilitarian standard—accepting only those experiments whose benefits (factoring in the likelihood of achieving them) are expected to outweigh the harms and costs involved—where the interests of animal subjects (e.g., to avoid suffering) are given the same moral weight that we give comparable human interests.[5]

Without commiting either to a strong animal rights view or to utilitarianism, my own view shares with these theories the framework of equal consideration for animals: the principle that we must give equal moral weight to comparable interests, no matter who has those interests.[6] But unlike the aforementioned philosophers, I believe that the arguments for and against equal consideration are nearly equal in strength. I therefore have respect for progressive views that attribute moral standing to animals without giving them fully equal consideration. The unequal consideration view that I find most plausible gives moral weight to animals' comparable interests in accordance with the animals' cognitive, affective, and social complexity—a progressive, "sliding scale" view. Since I acknowledge that I might be mistaken about equal consideration, my approach tracks the practical implications both of equal consideration and of the alternative just described.

Arguing from pluralistic frameworks, which are developed in different ways, Steve Sapontzis, Rosemary Rodd, and Bernard Rollin support relatively little animal research in comparison with current levels.[7] Drawing significantly from feminist insights, Mary Midgley presents a view whose implications seem somewhat more accepting of the status quo of animal research but still fairly progressive.[8] Of the leading contributors to animal ethics, the only one who embraces the status quo of animal research and does not attribute significant moral status to animals is Peter Carruthers.[9] (It is ironic that while biomedicine characterizes those who are critical of animal research as irrational "extremists," nearly all of the most in-depth, scholarly, and respected work in animal ethics supports such a critical standpoint at a general level.)

In discussing the prospects for agreement between biomedicine and animal advocates, I will ignore political posturing and consider only serious ethical reflection. In considering the two sides of this debate, I will assume that the discussants are morally serious, intellectually honest, reflective, and well informed both about the facts of animal research and about the range of arguments that come into play in animal ethics. I will not have in mind, then, the researcher who urges audiences to dismiss "the animal rights view" or the animal activist who tolerates no dissent from an abolitionist position. The two representative interlocutors I will imagine differ on the issue of animal research, but their views result from honest, disciplined, well-informed ethical reflection. Clearly, their voices are worth hearing.

POINTS ON WHICH THE BIOMEDICAL AND ANIMAL PROTECTION COMMUNITIES CAN AGREE

The optimistic thesis of this paper is that the biomedical and animal protection communities can agree on a fair number of important points, and that much can be done to build upon this common ground. I will number and highlight (in italics) each potential point of agreement and then justify its inclusion by explaining how both sides can agree to it, without abandoning their basic positions, and why they should.

1. The use of animals in biomedical research raises ethical issues. Today very few people would disagree with this modest claim, and any who would are clearly in the wrong.[10] Most animal research involves harming animal subjects, provoking ethical concerns, and the leading goal of animal research, promotion of human health, is itself ethically important; even the expenditure of taxpayers' money on government-funded animal research raises ethical issues about the best use of such money. Although a very modest assertion, this point of agreement is important because it legitimates a process that is sometimes resisted: *discussing* the ethics of animal research.

It is worth noting a less obvious claim that probably enjoys strong majority support but not consensus: that animals (at least sentient ones, as defined below) have moral status. To say animals have moral status is to say that their interests have moral importance independently of effects on human interests. ('Interests' may be thought of as components of well-being. For example, sentient animals have an interest in avoiding pain, distress, and suffering.) If animals have moral status, then to brutalize a horse is wrong because of the harm inflicted on the horse, not simply because the horse is someone's property (if that is so) or because animal lovers' feelings may be hurt (if any animal lovers find out about the abuse). The idea is that gratuitously harming the horse *wrongs the horse.* Although nearly every leader in animal ethics holds that animals have moral status—and though most people, on reflection, are likely to find this idea commonsensical—Carruthers argues that it is mistaken.[11]

2. Sentient animals, a class that probably includes at least the vertebrates, deserve moral protection. Whether because they have moral status or because needlessly harming them strongly offends many people's sensibilities, sentient animals deserve some measure of moral protection. By way of definition, sentient animals are animals endowed with any sorts of feelings: (conscious) sensations such as pain or emotional states such as fear or suffering. But which animals are sentient? Addressing this complex issue implicates both the natural sciences and the philosophy of mind. Lately, strong support has emerged for the proposition that at least vertebrate animals are very likely sentient.[12] This proposition is implicitly endorsed by major statements of principles regarding the humane use of research animals, which often mention that they apply to vertebrates.[13] (Hereafter, the unqualified term "animals" will refer to sentient animals in particular.)

3. Many animals (at the very least, mammals) are capable of having a wide variety of aversive mental states, including pain, distress (whose forms include discomfort, boredom, and fear), and suffering. In biomedical circles, there has been some resistance to attributing suffering to animals, so government documents concerned with humane use of animals have often mentioned only pain, distress, and discomfort.[14] Because "suffering" refers to a *highly* unpleasant mental state (whereas pain, distress, and discomfort can be mild and transient), the attribution of suffering to animals is morally significant. An indication that resistance may be weakening is the attribution of suffering to sentient animals in the National Aeronautics and Space Administration's "Principles for the Ethical Care and Use of Animals."[15] Whatever government documents may say, the combined empirical and philosophical case for attributing suffering to a wide range of animals is very strong.[16]

4. Animals' experiential well-being (quality of life) deserves protection. If the use of animals raises ethical issues, meaning that their interests matter morally, we confront the question of what interests animals have. This question raises controversial issues. For example, do animals have an interest in remaining alive (life interests)? That is, does death itself—as opposed to any unpleasantness experienced in dying—harm an animal? A test case would be a scenario in which a contented dog in good health is painlessly and unwittingly killed in her sleep: Is she harmed?

Another difficult issue is whether animal well-being can be understood *entirely* in terms of experiential well-being—quality of life in the familiar sense in which (other things equal) pleasure is better than pain, enjoyment better than suffering, satisfaction better than frustration. Or does the exercise of an animal's natural capacities count positively toward well-being, even if quality of life is not enhanced? A test case would be a scenario in which conditioning, a drug, or brain surgery removes a bird's instinct and desire to fly without lowering quality of life: Does the bird's transformation to a new, nonflying existence represent a harm?

Whatever the answers to these and other issues connected with animal well-being, what is not controversial is that animals have an interest in experiential well-being, a good quality of life. That is why animal researchers are normally expected to use anesthesia or analgesia where these agents can reduce or eliminate animal subjects' pain, distress, or suffering.

5. Humane care of highly social animals requires extensive access to conspecifics. It is increasingly appreciated that animals have different needs based on what sorts of creatures they are. Highly social animals, such as apes, monkeys, and wolves, need social interactions with conspecifics (members of their own species). Under normal circumstances, they will develop social structures, such as hierarchies and alliances, and maintain long-term relationships with conspecifics. Because they have a strong instinct to seek such interactions and relationships, depriving them of the opportunity to gratify this instinct harms these animals. For example, in some species, lack of appropriate social interactions impedes normal development. Moreover, social companions can buffer the effects of stressful situations, reduce behavioral abnormalities, provide opportunities for exercise, and increase cognitive stimulation.[17] Thus in the case of any highly social animals used in research, providing them extensive access to conspecifics is an extremely high moral priority.

6. Some animals deserve very strong protections (as, for example, chimpanzees deserve not to be killed for the purpose of population control). Biomedicine and animal advocates are likely to disagree on many details of ethically justified uses of animals in research, as we will see in the next section. Still, discussants can agree that there is an obligation to protect not just the experiential well-being, but also the lives, of at least some animals. This claim might be supported by the (controversial) thesis that such animals have life interests. On the other hand, it might be supported by the goal of species preservation (in the case of an endangered species), or by the recognition that routine killing of such animals when they are no longer useful for research would seriously disturb many people.[18]

Without agreeing on all the specific justifications, members of the National Research Council's Committee on Long-Term Care of Chimpanzees were able to agree (with one dissent) that chimps should not be killed for the purpose of population control, although they could be killed if suffering greatly with no alternative means of relief.[19] This recommended protection of chimps' lives is exceptional, because animal research policies generally state no presumption against killing animal subjects, requiring only that killings be as painless as possible.[20] Since this committee represents expert opinion in biomedicine, it seems correct to infer that biomedicine and the animal protection community can agree that at least chimpanzees should receive some very strong protections—of their lives and of certain other components of their well-being, such as their needs for social interaction, reasonable freedom of movement, and stimulating environments.[21]

7. Alternatives should now be used whenever possible and research on alternatives should expand. Those who are most strongly opposed to animal research hold that alternatives such as mathematical models, computer simulations, and in vitro biological systems should replace nearly all use of animals in research. (I say "nearly all" because, as discussed below, few would condemn animal research that does not harm its subjects.) Even for those who see the animal research enterprise more favorably, there are good reasons to take an active interest in alternatives. Sometimes an alternative method is the most valid way to approach a particular scientific question; often alternatives are cheaper.[22] Their potential for reducing animal pain, distress, and suffering is, of course, another good reason. Finally, biomedicine may enjoy stronger public support if it responds to growing social concern about animal welfare with a very serious investment in nonanimal methods. This means not just using alternatives wherever they are currently feasible, but also aggressively researching the possibilities for expanding the use of such methods.

8. Promoting human health is an extremely important biomedical goal. No morally serious person would deny the great importance of human health, so its status as a worthy goal seems beyond question. What is sometimes forgotten, however, is that a worthy goal does not automatically justify all the means thereto. Surely it would be unethical to force large numbers of humans to serve as subjects in highly painful, eventually lethal research, even if its goal were to promote human health. The controversy over animal research focuses not on the worthiness of its principal goal—promoting human health—but rather on the means, involving animal subjects, taken in pursuit of that goal.

9. There are some morally significant differences between humans and other animals. Many people in biomedicine are not aware that the views of animal advocates are consistent with this judgment. Indeed, some animal advocates might not realize that their views are consistent with this judgment! So let me identify a couple of ideas, to which all should agree, that support it.

First, the principle of respect for autonomy applies to competent adult human beings, but to very few if any animals. This principle respects the self-regarding decisions of individuals who are capable of autonomous decisionmaking and action. Conversely, it opposes paternalism toward such individuals, who have the capacity to decide for themselves what is in their interests. Now, many sentient beings, including human children and at least most nonhuman animals, are not autonomous in the relevant sense and so are not covered by this principle.[23] Thus it is often appropriate to limit their liberty in ways that promote their best interests, say, preventing the human child from drinking alcohol, or forcing a pet dog to undergo a vaccination. We might say that where there is no autonomy to respect, the principles of beneficence (promoting best interests) and respect for autonomy cannot conflict; where there is autonomy to respect, paternalism becomes morally problematic.

Second, even if sentient animals have an interest, others things equal, in staying alive (as I believe), the moral presumption against taking human life is stronger than the presumption against killing at least some animals. Consider fish, who are apparently sentient yet cognitively extremely primitive in comparison with humans. I have a hard time imagining even very committed animal advocates maintaining that killing a fish is as serious a matter as killing a human being. Leaders in animal ethics consistently support—though in interestingly different ways—the idea that, ordinarily, killing humans is worse than killing at least some animals who have moral status. (It is almost too obvious to mention that it's worse to kill humans than to kill animals, such as amoebas, that *lack* moral status.[24])

The only notable exception seems to be Sapontzis, who tries to undermine the major arguments proffered to support such comparative claims. But the comparisons he opposes always involve humans and other mammals or birds.[25] The farther one goes down the phylogenetic scale, the more incredible it becomes to hold that it is equally prima facie wrong to kill humans and to kill other animals. At the very least, someone like Sapontzis will have to admit that killing humans tends to be worse than killing fish in that (1) humans tend to live much longer, so that untimely death generally robs them of more good years, and (2) untimely human death causes deep social sorrow and anguish to others in a way that is not paralleled in the fish world. So I believe that the comparative judgment I have made is well justified and embraceable by all parties to the present debate. There may be other morally interesting differences to which all should agree,[26] but these examples will suffice for present purposes.

10. Some animal research is justified. Many animal advocates would say that they disagree with this statement. But I'm not sure they do. Or, if they really do, they shouldn't. Let me explain by responding to the three likeliest reasons some animal advocates might take exception to the claim.

First, one might oppose all uses of animals that involve *harming them for the benefit of others* (even other animals)—as a matter of absolute principle—and overlook the fact that some animal research does not harm animal subjects at all. Although such nonharmful research represents a tiny sliver of the animal research enterprise, it exists. Examples are certain observational studies of animals in their natural habitats, some ape language studies, and possibly certain behavioral studies of other species that take place in laboratories but do not cause pain, distress, or suffering to the subjects. And if nonsentient animals cannot be harmed (in any morally relevant sense), as I would argue, then any research involving such animals falls under the penumbra of nonharming research.

Moreover, there is arguably no good reason to oppose research that imposes only *minimal* risk or harm on its animal subjects. After all, minimal risk research on certain human subjects who, like animals, cannot consent (namely, children) is permitted in many countries; in my view, this policy is justified. Such research might involve a minuscule likelihood of significant harm or the certainty of a slight, transient harm, such as the discomfort of having a blood sample taken.

Second, one might oppose all animal research because one believes that none of it actually benefits human beings. Due to physical differences between species, the argument goes, what happens to animal subjects when they undergo some biomedical intervention does not justify inferences about what will happen to humans who undergo that intervention. Furthermore, new drugs, therapies, and techniques must always be tried on human subjects before they can be accepted for clinical practice. Rather than tormenting animals in research, the argument continues, we should drop the useless animal models and proceed straight to human trials (with appropriate protections for human subjects, including requirements for informed or proxy consent).

Although I believe a considerable amount of current animal research has almost no chance of benefitting humans,[27] I find it very hard to believe that no animal research does. While it is true that human subjects must eventually be experimented on, evidence suggests that animal models sometimes furnish data relevant to human health.[28] If so, then the use of animal subjects can often decrease the risk to human subjects who are eventually involved in experiments that advance biomedicine, by helping to weed out harmful interventions. This by itself does not justify animal research, only the claim that it sometimes benefits humans (at the very least human subjects themselves and arguably the beneficiaries of biomedical advances as well).

Note that even if animal research never benefited humans, it would presumably sometimes benefit conspecifics of the animals tested, in sound veterinary research.[29] It can't be seriously argued that animal models provide no useful information about animals! Moreover, in successful *therapeutic* research (which aims to benefit the subjects themselves), certain animals benefit directly from research and are not simply used to benefit other animals. For that reason, blanket opposition to animal research, including the most promising therapeutic research in veterinary medicine, strikes me as almost unintelligible.

Almost unintelligible, but not quite, bringing us to the third possible reason for opposing all animal research. It might be argued that, whether or not it harms its subjects, all animal research involves *using animals (without their consent) for other's benefit,* since—qua research—it seeks *generalizable knowledge.* But to use animals in this way reduces them to *tools* (objects to be used), thereby *disrespecting* the animals.

Now the idea that we may never use nonconsenting individuals, even in benign ways, solely for the benefit of others strikes me as an implausibly strict ethical principle. But never mind. The fact that some veterinary research is intended to benefit the subjects themselves (as well as other animals or humans down the road) where no other way to help them is known shows that such research, on any reasonable view, is *not* disrespectful toward its subjects. Indeed, in such cases, the animals *would* consent to taking part, if they could, because taking part is in their interests. I fully grant that therapeutic veterinary research represents a minuscule portion of the animal research conducted today. But my arguments are put forward in the service of a goal that I think I have now achieved: demonstrating, beyond a shadow of a doubt, that some animal research is justified.

If animal advocates and representatives of biomedicine were aware of these ten points of potential agreement, they might perceive their opponents' views as less alien than they had previously taken them to be. This change in perception might, in turn, convince all parties that honest, open discussion of outstanding issues has a decent chance of repaying the effort.

POINTS ON WHICH AGREEMENT BETWEEN THE TWO SIDES IS UNLIKELY

Even if biomedicine and the animal protection community approach the animal research issue in good faith, become properly informed about animal ethics and the facts of research, and so forth, they are still likely to disagree on certain important issues. After all, their basic views differ. It may be worthwhile to enumerate several likely points of difference.

First, disagreement is likely on the issue of *the moral status of animals in comparison with humans.* While representatives of biomedicine may attribute moral status to animals, they hold that animals may justifiably be used in many experiments (most of which are nontherapeutic and harm the subjects) whose primary goal is to promote human health. But for animal advocates, it is not at all obvious that much animal research is justified. This suggests that animal advocates ascribe higher moral status to animals than biomedicine does.[30]

Second, disagreement is likely to continue on the issue of *the specific circumstances in which the worthy goal of promoting human health justifies harming animals.* Biomedicine generally tries to protect the status quo of animal research. Animal advocates generally treat not using animals in research as a presumption, any departures from which would require careful justification. Clearly, animal advocates will have many disagreements with biomedicine over when it is appropriate to conduct animal research.

Third, in a similar vein, continuing disagreement is likely on the issue of *whether current protections for research animals are more or less adequate.* Biomedicine would probably answer affirmatively, with relatively minor internal disagreements over specific issues (e.g., whether apes should ever be exposed to diseases in order to test vaccines). Animal advocates will tend to be much more critical of current protections for research animals. They will argue, for example, that animals are far too often made to suffer in pursuit of less than compelling objectives, such as learning about behavioral responses to stress or trauma.

In the United States, critics will argue that the basic principles that are supposed to guide the care and use of animals in federally funded research ultimately provide very weak protection for research animals. That is because the tenth and final principle begins with implicit permission to make exceptions to the previous nine: "Where exceptions are required in relation to the provisions of these Principles. . . ."[31] Since no limits are placed on permissible exceptions, this final principle precludes any absolute restraints on the harm that may be inflicted on research animals—an indefensible lack of safeguards from the perspective of animal advocates. (Although similar in several ways to these American principles, including some ways animal advocates would criticize, the International Guiding Principles for Biomedical Research Involving Animals avoids this pitfall of a global loophole. One of its relatively strong protections is Principle V: "Investigators and other personnel should never fail to treat animals as sentient, and should regard their proper care and use and the avoidance or minimization of discomfort, distress, or pain as ethical imperatives."[32])

Although protections of research animals are commonly thought of in terms of preventing unnecessary pain, distress, and suffering, they may also be thought of in terms of protecting animal life. A fourth likely area of disagreement concerns *whether animal life is morally protectable.* Return to a question raised earlier: whether a contented animal in good health is harmed by being painlessly killed in her sleep. Since government documents for the care and use of research animals generally require justification for causing pain or distress to animal subjects, but no justification for painless killing, it seems fair to infer that biomedicine generally does not attribute life interests to animals. Although I lack concrete evidence, I would guess that most animal advocates would see the matter quite differently, and would regard the killing of animals as a serious moral matter even if it is justified in some circumstances.

The four issues identified here as probable continuing points of difference are not intended to comprise an exhaustive list. But they show that despite the fact that the biomedical and animal protection communities can agree on an impressive range of major points, given their basic orientations they cannot be expected to agree on every fundamental question. Few will find this assertion surprising. But I also suggest, less obviously, that even if both sides cannot be entirely right in their positions, differences that remain after positions are refined through honest, open-minded, fully educated inquiry can be reasonable differences.

WHAT CAN BE DONE NOW TO BUILD UPON THE POINTS OF AGREEMENT

Let me close with a series of suggestions offered in the constructive yet critical-minded spirit of Henry Spira's work for how to build on the points of agreement identified above. For reasons of space, these suggestions will be stated somewhat tersely and without elaboration.

First, biomedical organizations and leaders in the profession can do the following: openly acknowledge that ethical issues involving animals are complex and important; educate themselves or acquire education about the ethical issues; tolerate views departing from the current party line; open up journals to more than one basic viewpoint; and stop disseminating one-sided propaganda.

Second, the more "militant" animal advocates can acknowledge that there can be reasonable disagreement on some of the relevant issues and stop intimidating people with whom they disagree.

Third, biomedicine can openly acknowledge, as NASA recently did in its principles, that animals can suffer and invite more serious consideration of animal suffering.

Fourth, the animal protection community can give credit to biomedicine where credit is due—for example, for efforts to minimize pain and distress, to improve housing conditions, and to refrain from killing old chimpanzees who are no longer useful for research but are expensive to maintain.

Fifth, animal researchers and members of animal protection organizations can be required by their organizations to take courses in ethical theory or animal ethics to promote knowledgeable, skilled, broad-minded discussion and reflection.

Sixth, the animal protection community can openly

acknowledge that some animal research is justified (perhaps giving examples to reduce the potential for misunderstanding).

Seventh, more animal research ethics committees can bring aboard at least one dedicated animal advocate who (unlike mainstream American veterinarians) seriously questions the value of most animal research.

Eighth, conditions of housing for research animals can be improved—for example, with greater enrichment and, for social animals, more access to conspecifics.

Ninth, all parties can endorse and support the goal of finding ways to *eliminate* animal subjects' pain, distress, and suffering.[33]

Tenth, and finally, governments can invest much more than they have to date in the development and use of alternatives to animal research, and all parties can give strong public support to the pursuit of alternatives.

NOTES

1. American Medical Association. Animal Research Action Plan. (June 1989), p.6. See also American Medical Association. White Paper (1988).

2. See the Humane Society of the United States (HSUS). *Farm Animals and Intensive Confinement.* Washington, D.C.: HSUS, 1994; *Animals in Biomedical Research.* Washington, D.C.: HSUS, revised 1989; and *Zoos: Information Packet.* Washington, D.C.: HSUS, 1995.

3. Animal Liberation Front. Animal Liberation Frontline Information Service: the A.L.F. Primer. (website)

4. Regan T. *The Case for Animal Rights.* Berkeley: University of California Press, 1983; Pluhar E. *Beyond Prejudice.* Durham, North Carolina: Duke University Press, 1995.

5. Frey R. G. *Interests and Rights.* Oxford: Clarendon, 1980; Singer P. *Animal Liberation,* 2d ed. New York: New York Review of Books, 1990.

6. DeGrazia D. *Taking Animals Seriously.* Cambridge: Cambridge University Press, 1996.

7. Sapontzis S. F. *Morals, Reason, and Animals.* Philadelphia: Temple University Press, 1987; Rodd R. *Biology, Ethics, and Animals.* Oxford: Clarendon, 1990; and Rollin B. E. *Animal Rights and Human Morality,* 2d ed. Buffalo, New York: Prometheus, 1992.

8. Midgley M. *Animals and Why They Matter.* Athens, Georgia: University of Georgia Press, 1983.

9. Carruthers P. *The Animals Issue.* Cambridge: Cambridge University Press, 1992.

10. In a letter to the editor, Robert White, a neurosurgeon well known for transplanting monkeys' heads, asserted that "[a]nimal usage is not a moral or ethical issue . . ." (White R. Animal ethics? [letter]. *Hastings Center Report* 1990;20(6):43). For a rebuttal to White, see my letter, *Hastings Center Report* 1991;21(5):45.

11. See note 9, Carruthers 1992. For an attempt to undermine Carruthers' arguments, see note 6, DeGrazia 1996:53–6.

12. See Rose M., Adams D. Evidence for pain and suffering in other animals. In: Langley G., ed. *Animal Experimentation.* New

York: Chapman and Hall, 1989:42–71; Smith J. A., Boyd K. M. *Lives in the Balance.* Oxford: Oxford University Press, 1991:ch. 4. See also note 7 Rodd 1990:ch. 3; and DeGrazia D., Rowan A. Pain, suffering, and anxiety in animals and humans. *Theoretical Medicine* 1991;12:193–211.

13. See, e.g., U.S. Government Principles for the Utilization and Care of Vertebrate Animals Used in Testing, Research, and Training. In: National Research Council. *Guide for the Care and Use of Laboratory Animals.* Washington, D.C.: National Academy Press, 1996:117–8; National Aeronautics and Space Administration. *Principles for the Ethical Care and Use of Animals.* NASA Policy Directive 8910.1, effective 23 March 1998; and Council for International Organizations of Medical Sciences. *International Guiding Principles for Biomedical Research Involving Animals.* Geneva: CIOMS, 1985:18. (Reprinted in this chapter)

14. See note 13, National Research Council 1996; CIOMS 1985.

15. See note 13, NASA 1998.

16. See note 12, Rose, Adams 1989; DeGrazia, Rowan 1991. And see note 7, Rodd 1990:ch. 3. There is also much evidence that at least mammals can experience anxiety. (See note 12, DeGrazia, Rowan 1991; note 12, Smith, Boyd 1991:ch. 4.)

17. See note 13, National Research Council 1996:37.

18. Note that the term "euthanasia," which means a death that is good for the one who dies, is inappropriate when animals are killed because they are costly to maintain or for similarly human-regarding reasons.

19. National Research Council Committee on Long-Term Care of Chimpanzees. *Chimpanzees in Research.* Washington, D.C.: National Academy Press, 1997:38.

20. Such policies typically state that animals who would otherwise experience severe or chronic pain or distress should be painlessly killed. See, e.g., note 13, National Research Council 1996:117; CIOMS 1985:19; and [British] Home Office. *Home Office Guidance on the Operation of the Animals [Scientific Procedures] Act 1986.* London: Home Office, 1986. Although this directive addresses what to do with animals who could survive only in agony, it does not state any presumption against killing animals who could live well following research.

21. The committee addresses these chimpanzee interests in note 19, National Research Council 1997:ch. 3.

22. See note 12, Smith, Boyd 1991:334.

23. See note 6, DeGrazia 1996:204–10.

24. Admittedly, some unusual individuals would claim that amoebas have moral status, either because they think amoebas are sentient or because they think that sentience is unnecessary for moral status. I know of no one, however, who would claim that killing amoebas is as serious a matter as killing humans.

25. See note 7, Sapontzis 1987:216–22.

26. For example, if I am right, just as the moral presumption against taking life can differ in strength across species, so can the presumption against confining members of different species (the interest at stake being freedom). See note 6, DeGrazia 1996:254–6.

27. That is, except those humans who benefit directly from the conduct of research, such as researchers and people who sell animals and laboratory equipment.

28. See, e.g., note 12, Smith, Boyd 1991:ch. 3.

29. Peter Singer reminded me of this important point.

30. The idea of differences of moral status can be left intuitive here. Any effort to make it more precise will invite controversy. (See note 6, DeGrazia 1996:256–7.)

31. See note 13, National Research Council 1996:118.

32. See note 13, CIOMS 1985:18.

33. This is the stated goal of a new initiative of the Humane Society of the United States, which expects the initiative to expand to Humane Society International.

BARUCH A. BRODY

Defending Animal Research: An International Perspective

I. INTRODUCTION

In a recent article, "The Ethics of Animal Research," philosopher David DeGrazia asks the very important question of whether or not there is room for at least some agreement between "biomedicine" and "animal advocates" on the issue of animal research.[1] This is an important question, but one on which we are unlikely to make any progress until the contents of both positions are clearly understood. This essay is devoted to better articulating the position which supports animal research, the position that DeGrazia labels the "biomedicine" position; I leave the analysis of the animal-advocacy position for other occasions.

My reason for adopting this strategy is as follows: There has been in recent years an extensive philo-

Reprinted by permission of Transaction Publishers. "Defending Animal Research: An International Perspective" by Baruch A. Brody in Ellen F. Paul and Jeffrey Paul, eds. *Why Animal Experimentation Matters.* Copyright © 2001 by Transaction Publishers.

sophical discussion of various versions of the animal-advocacy position, and the variations on this position have been analyzed by several authors.[2] Much less attention has been paid to development of the pro-research position. DeGrazia himself describes the articulation of that position in negative terms:

> It seems fair to say that biomedicine has a "party line" on the ethics of animal research, conformity to which may feel like a political litmus test for full acceptability within the professional community. According to this party line, animal research is clearly justified because it is necessary for medical progress and therefore human health. . . . [M]any or most animal researchers and their supporters do not engage in sustained, critical thinking about the moral status of animals and the basic justification (or lack thereof) for animal research.[3]

Whether or not this is fully accurate, this perception of the status of the pro-research position seems to be widespread. It therefore seems important to attempt a better articulation and defense of a reasonable version of that position.

What do I mean by a reasonable pro-research position on animal research, the type of position that I wish to defend? I understand such a position to be committed to at least the following propositions:

1. Animals have interests (at least the interest in not suffering, and perhaps others as well), which may be adversely affected either by research performed on them or by the conditions under which they live before, during, and after the research.
2. The adverse effect on animals' interests is morally relevant, and must be taken into account when deciding whether or not a particular program of animal research is justified or must be modified or abandoned.
3. The justification for conducting a research program on animals that would adversely affect them is the benefits that human beings would receive from the research in question.
4. In deciding whether or not the research in question is justified, human interests should be given greater significance than animal interests.

Some preliminary observations about these propositions are in order. Propositions (1) and (2) commit the reasonable pro-research position to a belief that animal interests are morally relevant, and that the adverse impact of animal research on these interests should not be disregarded. This distinguishes the position I am trying to articulate from positions (such as the classical Cartesian position) that maintain that animals have no interests or that those interests do not count morally.[4] In light of their ability to experience pleasures and pains, it is implausible to deny animals interests or to give those interests no moral significance at all. Propositions (3) and (4) distinguish the pro-research position from the animal-advocacy position by insisting that it is permissible for animals to be adversely affected by legitimate research—they do not have a trumping right not to be used adversely for human benefit.[5] Toward this end, proposition (4) asserts that human benefits have greater significance than harms to animals in determining the legitimacy of the research, as animals have less moral significance than humans.[6]

What is the nature of humans' greater significance? It seems to me that this is the crucial question that must be faced by any reasonable pro-research position, for it is the answer to this question that will determine when animal research that has an adverse impact on animal subjects is justified. Many pro-research positions are possible; these positions differ over the research they accept as justified precisely because they differ over the nature of the priority of human interests over animal interests. It seems to me, moreover, that this crucial question must be answered before one even begins any discussion of possible justifications for an actual pro-research position, since the justification of any specific pro-research position will have to involve justifying a specific view of the priority of human interests.

Another way of putting this point is as follows: The reasonable pro-research position is actually a family of positions that differ both theoretically (on their conceptions of the nature of the priority of human interests) and practically (on the resulting types of justified research). What is needed first is a full examination of this family of positions, an examination that explores the plausibility of different views on the priority of human interests. Once we can identify the more plausible of these views, we can begin the attempt to justify one of them.

It is this observation that structures this essay. In Section II, I will present two very different understandings of the priority of human interests. The first understanding is involved in official U.S. policies governing animal research; the second underlies some official European policies. In Section III, I will argue that the U.S. understanding is less plausible than the European one, and that defenders of the pro-research position should focus on trying to articulate and justify some version of the European position. In Section IV, I will show that there is an important structural analogy between the European position and certain familiar positions on the prerogative, and on the obligation, to give priority to the interests of some humans over the interests of others. This will suggest that the pro-research position is part of a larger family of positions that deny the thesis that all interests count equally; it will also suggest that the justification of the pro-research position is to be found in the arguments that are used to justify that larger family of positions. In the final section of this essay, I will raise a fundamental concern about this whole family of positions, designed not to challenge their validity but rather to open a new type of investigation into such positions.

II. THE U.S. AND EUROPEAN POSITIONS

The best statement of the U.S. policy on animal research is found in a 1986 document from the Public Health Service entitled "U.S. Government Principles for the Utilization and Care of Vertebrate Animals Used in Testing, Research, and Training."[7] This document plays the same role for animal research that the Belmont Report[8] does for research on human subjects, by identifying the principles that lie behind and justify the specific regulations governing the research. I want to highlight what is and is not present in the U.S. principles; they call upon researchers to:

- Use the "minimum number [of animals] required to obtain valid results"
- Consider alternatives such as "mathematical models, computer simulation, and in vitro biological systems"
- Practice the "avoidance or minimization of discomfort, distress or pain when consistent with sound scientific practices"
- Use "appropriate sedation, analgesia, or anesthesia"
- Kill animals painlessly after experiments when the animals "would otherwise suffer severe or chronic pain or distress that cannot be relieved"
- Provide living conditions that are "appropriate for their species and contribute to their health and comfort"[9]

All of these principles are compatible with the familiar program, developed by W. M. S. Russell and R. L. Burch in 1959, which has come to be called the 3R program.[10] This program calls for the *replacement* of animal experimentation with other research methods where possible; this is why the U.S. principles request the consideration of alternative research techniques. The program also calls for the *reduction* of the number of animals used; hence, the U.S. principles state a commitment to minimizing the number of animals used as much as is consistent with obtaining scientifically valid results. Finally, the 3R program calls for *refining* both the conduct of the research and the environment in which the research animals live; the aim is to minimize the animals' pain and suffering. This is why the U.S. principles talk about pain relief, euthanasia when necessary, and species-appropriate living conditions.

These U.S. principles are not the only place in which this 3R approach (without being officially designated by that name) is adopted as official U.S. policy. The 1993 National Institutes of Health (NIH) Revitalization Act calls upon the NIH to support research on using alternative models to animals, on reducing the number of animals used in research, on producing less pain and distress for these animals, and on using nonmammalian marine life as a research substitute for the use of more advanced animals. This research is to help establish "the validity and reliability" of these methods; for those "methods that have been found to be valid and reliable," the research is aimed at encouraging acceptance of those methods and at training scientists to use them.[11]

All of this is very much in the spirit of propositions (1) and (2) of my account of the responsible pro-research position on animal research. It is because animals have interests that may be adversely affected by the research—interests that count morally—that we are called upon to replace, reduce, and refine the use of animals in research. Proposition (3) is also explicitly part of the U.S. principles, which assert that "procedures involving animals should be designed and performed with due consideration of their relevance to human or animal health, the advancement of knowledge, or the good of society."[12] But what about proposition (4)? What sort of greater significance are human interests given over animal interests in the U.S. regulations?

In fact, that question is never directly addressed. This stands in sharp contrast to the U.S. regulations on human subjects in research. These regulations require the minimization of risks, but they also require that the minimized risks be "reasonable in relation to anticipated benefits, if any, to subjects, and the importance of the knowledge that may reasonably be expected to result."[13] Nothing like these strictures occurs in the U.S. principles and regulations governing animal research.

Something else can be inferred from the wording of the U.S. principles on animal research. Discomfort, distress, or pain of the animals should be minimized "when consistent with sound scientific practices." The number of animals used should be minimized to "the number required to obtain valid results." Unrelieved pain necessary to conduct the research is acceptable so long as the animal is euthanized after or during the procedure.[14] What this amounts to in the end is that whatever is required for the research is morally acceptable; the 3R principles are to be applied only as long as they are compatible with maintaining scientifically valid research. There is never the suggestion that the suffering of the animal might be so great—even when it is minimized as much as possible while still maintaining scientific validity—that its suffering might outweigh the benefits from the research. Even when these benefits are modest, the U.S. principles never morally require the abandonment of a research project.

This is a position that gives very strong priority to human interests over animal interests, especially to the human interests that are promoted by scientific research using animals as subjects. Given the wide variety of such animal research projects, which range from developing and testing new life-saving surgical techniques to developing and testing new cosmetics, the human interests that are given this strong priority over animal interests are very diverse. It is not clear if there are any human interests that are not given this priority. Whether or not this strong and broad priority is compatible with the adoption of the 3R principles is a question to which we will return later.

The European approach to these issues is quite different. It is not that the Europeans do not believe in the 3R principles; their regulations embody these principles. Rather, the Europeans find these principles incomplete and augment them with additional principles that give greater significance to animal interests by disallowing some research because the costs to the animal subjects are too great.

The 1986 Directive from the Council of the European Communities (now called the European Community) provides us with one example of this approach, directed to cases in which animals suffer severe, prolonged pain that cannot be relieved. The directive stipulates that the relevant authority "shall take appropriate judicial or administrative action if it is not satisfied that the experiment is of sufficient importance for meeting the essential needs of man or animal."[15] This is a limited provision, as it involves animal interests outweighing human interests only in the case of severe and prolonged pain. The provision does not clearly specify what the "appropriate" actions in such cases are, and it implies that even severe and prolonged pain is acceptable if the research is of "sufficient importance." Nevertheless, it goes beyond anything in the U.S. principles and regulations by giving somewhat greater significance to animal interests.

This approach is developed in national legislation in several European countries. In Great Britain, for example, the British Animals (Scientific Procedures) Act of 1986, which requires each project involving animal research to get a project license, stipulates that "in determining whether and on what terms to grant a project licence the Secretary of State shall weigh the likely adverse effects on the animals concerned against the benefit likely to accrue as a result of the programme to be specified in the licence."[16] This provision is broader than the provision in the E.C. directive because the British legislation is not limited to the case of severe prolonged pain. Furthermore, it is also more explicit in specifying that when animal interests are unduly affected, the appropriate regulatory action is to forbid the research from proceeding at all. A similar provision is found in a German statute that requires that "experiments may be carried out on vertebrates only if the pain, suffering, or harm which they can be expected to inflict upon the animals is ethically justifiable in relation to the purposes of the experiment."[17]

While these national provisions are both broader in application and more explicit in their implications than is the E.C. directive, they still leave a crucial question unanswered. Let me explain. All the European regulations assume that animal interests in avoiding the harmful consequences of being in a research project have enough moral significance—in comparison to human interests in conducting research—that in some cases the proposed research is ethically unacceptable. All involve a balancing of animal interests against human interests in a way that allows the protection of animal interests to be given priority in some cases. In this way, they all reject the American pro-research position, in which human interests seem to have priority in all cases. This may be due to European acceptance of the very strong animal-advocacy position that animal interests count equally with human interests. But one need not accept this extreme position, and I see no evidence for such a strong claim. To justify the European positions as found in their regulations, it would be sufficient to maintain that animal interests and human interests are comparable enough so that very significant animal interests can outweigh minimal human interests. Exactly how comparable these interests are is left unanswered by each of the European regulations.

Let me put this point another way. Consider a whole continuum of positions, ranging from the claim that animal interests and human interests count equally (the *equal-significance position*) to the claim that even though one may attend to animal interests, human interests always take precedence (the *human-priority position*). In moving from the first position to the second, the significance of animal interests in comparison to human interests is gradually discounted. The intermediate positions move from those that discount animal interests modestly (and are therefore increasingly close to the equal-significance position) to those that discount them significantly (and are therefore increasingly close to the human-priority position). The U.S. position is the human-priority end of this continuum, and the animal rights movement's rejection of proposition (4) of the pro-research position puts that movement at the other end. The European positions are somewhere in-between, but there is no way to tell from their regulations where they are on the continuum. This could best be ascertained by examining how their systems actually operate in practice. What sorts of research projects have they rejected that might have been acceptable in the United States? Unfortunately, no comparative study of this sort has been conducted on the actual operation of the various national systems of review of animal research. Therefore, at this point, one cannot tell from European practices where various nations stand on the continuum.

A country's position on the continuum is not merely of theoretical interest. Your place on the continuum determines which research you would disallow because of its adverse impact upon animal interests. My impression is that the very limited balancing in the E.C. directive—which rules out animal research only in cases of severe, prolonged pain, and then only when the research is not "of sufficient importance for meeting the essential needs of man or animal"—means that the E.C. position is pretty close to the U.S. end of the continuum. In contrast, the broader language in the British and German statutes suggests that they are further away from the American end of the continuum, that is, they discount animal interests to a lesser degree. But how far their positions are from the human-priority position is totally undetermined. In this respect, their positions are in need of much further articulation.

In short, we have seen that proposition (4) of the pro-research position, the principle of giving greater significance to human interests than to animal interests, is understood very differently in the United States and in Europe. For the United States, the proposition means that human interests in conducting research always take lexical priority over animal interests. This lexical priority is not characteristic of the European positions, which allow for some balancing of interests. But there is no evidence that the Europeans have rejected proposition (4) and adopted the equal-significance position that is characteristic of the animal-advocacy position. They seem, instead, to have adopted some discounting of animal interests in comparison to human interests, with the crucial discount rate being undetermined.

Are there any reasons for supposing that a lexical-priority approach is a more plausible articulation of proposition (4) than is a discounting approach (or vice versa)? This is the question I will examine in the next section of this essay.

III. LEXICAL PRIORITY VERSUS DISCOUNTING

There are two arguments I will consider in this section. The first argument, in favor of a lexical-priority approach to proposition (4), argues that the cross-species comparison of interests that is presupposed by the discounting approach is meaningless, and that the discounting approach must, therefore, be rejected in favor of a lexical-priority approach. The second argument, in favor of the discounting approach, asserts that lexical priority is incompatible with significant components of the 3R program, and that pro-research adherents of that program must, therefore, adopt the discounting approach.

The first argument begins by noting that there are three steps to the discounting approach. The first step is to identify and quantify the impact of the research on the animal subjects and on the human beneficiaries of the knowledge that might be gained. The second step is to discount the impact on the animals by whatever discount rate is adopted by the particular version of the discounting approach. The final step is to decide whether to allow the research to proceed, taking into consideration the full impact on the humans and the discounted impact on the animals. The quantification involved in the first step and the discounting involved in the second step must be on a common metric, or the third step becomes meaningless. It is the existence of this common metric that is challenged by the first argument.

This challenge of the first argument thus has two components. The first component is the claim that there is no basis for placing animal pain and pleasure (if one defines 'interests' hedonistically) or the satisfaction of animal preferences (if one defines 'interests' in terms of preference-satisfaction) on a common metric with human pain and pleasure or human preference-satisfaction. I will refer to this first component of the challenge as the *incommensurability claim.* The second component is the claim that even if there were such a basis, we do not know enough about the sensations or preferences of animals to make such comparisons; I will call this component the *cross-species ignorance claim.*

It should be noted that this two-pronged challenge, if sound, is as much an objection to the animal-advocacy equal-significance position as it is to the pro-research discounting approach. Both involve quantifying, on a common metric, the pains and pleasures or the preference-satisfactions of humans and animals; the two only differ on whether or not the animal quantifications should be discounted before we draw any conclusions about the total impact of the research on all the interests involved. If there is something problematic about performing the initial quantification, that casts doubt upon both approaches.

It is also important to note that even if one accepts this two-pronged challenge, it does not necessarily follow from this that we should adopt the lexical-priority approach to proposition (4). Those who oppose the lexical-priority approach on the intuitive grounds that it does not give sufficient significance to animal interests can simply conclude that some other approach, one which captures those intuitions, must be developed. All that does follow from the first argument's two-pronged challenge is that the lexical-priority approach to proposition (4) is more plausible than is the discounting approach (which, if the incommensurability claim is correct, has no plausibility at all).

But should we grant the challenge's components? I see no reason to accept the incommensurability claim. Human pain and pleasure is quantified on the basis of dimensions such as duration and intensity; animal pain and pleasure can also be quantified on those dimensions. Duration is certainly not conceptually different for different species, and no reason has been offered for why we should treat intensity as differing conceptually for different species. Thus, there is a basis for a common metric for hedonistic comparisons of the impact of research on human and animal interests. I think that the same is true for preference-satisfaction comparisons of the impact of research on human and animal interests, but it is hard to say that with the same degree of confidence, since we still have little understanding of the dimensions on which we quantify preference-satisfaction. The duration dimension is certainly the same, and the dimension of the importance of the preference may be the same as well, but that is the dimension we do not really understand. In short, then, the premises of the incommensurability claim are questionable.

The cross-species ignorance claim is more serious. We are not particularly good at measuring *human* pains, pleasures, and preference-satisfaction on the same metric, even for one person let alone many. These uncertainties can only be magnified when we do cross-species comparisons. How does the discounting approach intend to deal with this problem?

This issue has been faced most directly by a working party of the British Institute of Medical Ethics (an unofficial but respected interdisciplinary group of scholars) in a report published in 1991.[18] The working party's members took note of the fact that the quantification of interests on a common metric seems to be required by the British Animals Act, and that there are doubts as to whether this can be done. In response to these concerns, they make two observations, which seem to me to be the beginning of a good answer to these concerns. First, they note that not every reliable judgment must be based upon a mathematically quantifiable balancing of values: it is often sufficient to have confidence in "the procedures which have been used to arrive at that judgment, . . . upon whether [researchers] have taken into account all the known morally relevant factors, and whether they have shown themselves responsive to all the relevant moral interests."[19] Second, the working party claims that it is possible to identify the moral factors relevant to the assessment of animal research and the degree to which they are present in a given case; this knowledge would allow for reliable judgments about the moral acceptability of proposed protocols for animal research. In fact, the working party goes on to create such a scheme and to show by examples how it might work in a reliable fashion.[20]

I say that this is only the beginning of a good answer because the working party does not really note the issue of discounting and its implications for the approach that they are adopting. Thus, more work needs to be done on their approach in order to incorporate this crucial component of the pro-research position. Moreover, more work is needed in defense of this view that reliable judgments need not be based on mathematically quantifiable balancing. I have provided some of this defense in my own writings on pluralistic casuistry.[21] I believe, however, that those who support the discounting approach to proposition (4) of the pro-research position can feel confident that they need not abandon it and adopt the lexical-priority approach.

This brings me to the second argument of this section. There are, this second argument suggests, reasons for doubting that the lexical-priority approach is compatible with even the 3R approach to the reasonable pro-research position. Satisfying the 3R principles, even if done in a way that allows the proposed research to proceed, involves considerable costs. These costs mean that other human interests, in research or otherwise, will not be satisfied. If human interests truly take precedence over animal interests, this seems inappropriate. A lexical-priority approach, then, cannot support even the now widely accepted 3R approach to protecting animal interests; this, it seems to me, makes the lexical-priority interpretation of proposition (4) an implausible version of the pro-research position.

Consider, for example, that aspect of the 3R program's refinement plank that calls for modifications in the environment in which research animals live in order to make those environments species-appropriate and not a source of distress or discomfort. Those modifications, now widely required throughout the world, are often quite costly, and these costs are passed on to the researchers as a cost of doing research. Some poorly funded research never takes place because these extra costs cannot be absorbed. Other, better funded, research projects go on, but require extra funding. This extra funding may mean that other research projects are not funded, or that the funded research will not be as complete as originally envisioned. To avoid these outcomes, extra funding would have to be provided to research efforts in general, but this would compromise funding for other human interests. In these ways and others, the adoption of this aspect of the 3R program is not compatible with maintaining the full research effort and/or with meeting other human interests. Hence, human interests are not being given full priority, contrary to the basic premise of the lexical-priority position.

None of this, of course, is a problem for the discounting approach unless the discounting of animal interests is so significant that it approaches the lexical-priority position. If the discounting is not this extensive—if animal interests count a lot, even if not as much as the interests of humans—then it seems reasonable to suppose that the interests of the animals in living in a species-appropriate environment are sufficiently great to justify imposing these burdens on the research effort.

There are components of the 3R program that do not raise this problem for the lexical-priority approach. The most obvious of these is the requirement to reduce the number of animal subjects to the minimum necessary to maintain the scientific validity of the research. This demand may often be cost-saving, and is unlikely to ever be cost-increasing. The impact of the 3R program's replacement component is the hardest to be sure about, because the cost comparison between using animals and using other models will vary.

In short, then, those who want a reasonable pro-research position to incorporate the widely adopted 3R program should find the discounting approach more plausible than the lexical-priority approach. But what could possibly justify such a discounting of animal interests? We turn to that question in the next section.

IV. THE RATIONALE FOR DISCOUNTING

Before attempting to develop an approach to justifying discounting, it is important to be clear as to exactly what is claimed by discounting. I shall develop this point by using a hedonistic account of interests; the same point could be developed using other accounts of interests.

Consider a human being experiencing pain for a certain duration of time and at a certain level of intensity. Now suppose that an animal experiences pain of the same intensity for the same duration of time. Some will say that the animal's experience may count less, morally, because the human being anticipates the pain beforehand and remembers it afterwards in ways that the animal does not; these factors allegedly add to the total quantity of pain or distress experienced by the human being. This may or may not be true, but it is not what is at stake in the claim of discounting. To see this, suppose further that the pain is totally unanticipated and that both the human being and the animal are immediately given amnesiac drugs so that neither remembers anything about the painful experience. The claim of discounting is that the animal's pain would still count less, morally. Others may attempt to find additional associated mental states in the human being that add to the badness of the human pain and make it count more. Suppose further that none of these associated mental states is present in the case in question. The claim of discounting is that the animal's pain would *still* count less, morally. Discounting, then, is the claim that the same unit of pain counts less, morally, if it is experienced by an animal than it would if it is experienced by a human being, not because of the human's associated experiences but simply because of the species of the experiencer. Discounting directly denies the equal consideration of interests across species.

I am emphasizing this point to make it clear that *discounting* of animal interests is radically different than the *preference* for human interests that even animal advocates such as Peter Singer accept:

> There are many areas in which the superior mental powers of normal adult humans make a difference: anticipation, more detailed memory, greater knowledge of what is happening, and so on. These differences explain why a human dying from cancer is likely to suffer more than a mouse.[22]

But for Singer and other supporters of the equal-significance position, all that follows from this is that humans may suffer more and that this quantitative difference in the amount of suffering is morally relevant. What discounting affirms, and what they deny, is that even when there is no quantitative difference in the amount of suffering, the human suffering counts more morally.

With this understanding of the claim of discounting, we can easily understand why many would find its claims ethically unacceptable. Why should the moral significance of the same amount of suffering differ according to the species of the sufferer if there are no associated additional differences?

There have been many attempts to answer this question, and I certainly do not intend to review and critically analyze them here. I do want to note just a few points. Some of these attempts deny moral status to animals on the ground that they lack certain capacities. That approach is unavailable to adherents of the reasonable pro-research position who concede that animal interests count morally, and may even (in the discounting approach) outweigh human interests. Other attempts to justify the preference to human interests do so on religious/metaphysical grounds. Whatever the merit of such claims, they are unavailable to adherents of the reasonable pro-research position who want to use this position as the foundation of public policy on animal research.

I see no reasonable alternative for the adherent of the discounting position except to challenge the whole idea that we are, in general, morally committed to an equal consideration of interests. This is a plausible move, since equal consideration of interests has come under much challenge in contemporary moral philosophy, totally independently of the debate over the moral significance of the interests of animals. I would trace the beginning of the idea that we should not accept equal consideration of interests to W. D. Ross's contention, as early as 1930, that we have special obligations to ourselves, our family members, our friends, our fellow citizens, etc.[23] Recognizing these special obligations means, of course, giving higher priority to the interests of some (those to whom we have special obligations) than to the interests of others (those to whom we do not). Equally important is the emphasis in the 1980s on the idea that we have a morally permissible prerogative to pay special attention to our own interests in the fulfillment of some of our central projects.[24] Recognizing this prerogative means giving a higher priority to at least some of our interests over the interests of others. Each of these ideas, in separate ways, presupposes a denial of equal consideration of interests, and both are best understood as forms of the discounting of certain interests.

How should we understand the special obligations that we have? One good way of understanding them is that we have special obligations to some people to give a higher priority to their interests than we do to those of others. This may call upon us to promote their interests even at the cost of not promoting the greater interests of strangers. Note, by the way, that it is implausible to see this as a form of lexical priority favoring the interests of those people to whom we have special obligations. When their interests at stake are modest, and when the conflicting interests of strangers are great, we are not obliged to put the interests of those to whom we are specially obligated first; we may not even be permitted to do so. It would appear, then, that special obligations might well be understood as involving a requirement that we discount the interests of strangers when they compete with the interests of those to whom we have special obligations.

The same approach sheds much light upon our prerogative to pursue personal goals even at the cost of not aiding others (or even hindering them) in the pursuit of their interests. This is, once again, hardly a lexical priority. No matter how important a goal may be to me, I may be morally required to put it aside if the competing interests of others are especially great. Our prerogative may best be understood as involving only a permission to discount the interests of strangers when they compete with our interests in attaining our goals.

Note, by the way, that this means that we really have a whole family of theories about special obligations and about personal prerogatives. Different theories will differ on the acceptable discount rate.

Looked at from this perspective, the discounting approach to the animal research position no longer seems anomalous. Rather than involving a peculiar discounting of the interests of animals, in violation of the fundamental moral requirement of the equal consideration of interests, the approach represents one more example of the discounting of the interests of strangers, a feature that is pervasive in morality.

We can see another way of developing this point if we consider the difference between the following two questions:

1A. Why should the interests of my children count more than do those of others?
1B. Why should the interests of my children count more for me than do those of others?

The former question, asked from an impersonal perspective, is unanswerable. The latter question, which is asked from the personal perspective, is answerable. The same needs to be said about the following pair of questions:

2A. Why should the interests of humans count more than do those of animals?
2B: Why should the interests of humans count more for human beings than do those of animals?

As with the previous pair of questions, what is unanswerable from one perspective may be very answerable from the other perspective.

There is, of course, an important difference between special obligations, even to oneself, and personal prerogatives. The former *require* you to give certain interests priority, while the latter just *permit* you to do so. This difference is helpful in explaining a certain ambiguity in the reasonable pro-research position. While its adherents often seem to be attempting to justify only the permissibility of animal research, they sometimes talk as though they are arguing that such research is required. Consider, for example, the standard Food and Drug Administration requirement that new drugs be tested on animals before they are tested on humans. I would suggest the following: when adherents justify the permissibility of animal research, they are invoking the analogy to prerogatives, but when they want to require this research, they are invoking the analogy to special obligations. On the latter view, we have an obligation to human beings, as part of our special obligations to members of our species, to discount animal interests in comparison to human interests by testing new drugs on animals first.

This defense of animal research on the ground of species solidarity has been developed elsewhere by the British philosopher Mary Midgley, although her emphasis seems to me to be more on psychological bonds and less on the logical structure of the consideration of interests in moral thought.[25] It may be that the discounting of interests, which I endorse, is grounded in differential psychological and social bonds, but it may not be. For now, it is sufficient to note the discounting version of the pro-research position fits in with the general structure of the consideration of interests in moral thought. It will not do, as many have tried, to assert that the very definition of "thinking morally" requires we count all interests equally and that, therefore, the discounting of animal interests is morally unacceptable. Any definition of morality or conception of moral thinking that requires this conclusion is suspect for just that reason.

V. FURTHER ISSUES

My argument until now has been that a reasonable pro-research position should be formulated in terms of discounting animal interests rather than in terms of giving a lexical priority to human interests. The discounting approach is better able to incorporate the complete 3R program, and it allows for some balancing of human interests against discounted animal interests (as called for in some European regulations). While discounting does not accept the equal consideration of interests, that by itself is not problematic since much of common morality rejects that postulate anyway. There remain, of course, several aspects of the discounting approach that require fuller development. An appropriate discount rate is yet to be determined; the process of cross-species comparisons of gains and losses in interests must be refined; and the conditions under which discounting is merely permissible as opposed to when it is mandatory need to be defined.

In addition to these necessary developments, there is a fundamental challenge that still needs to be confronted. It is a variation on the issue of equal consideration of interests, and it requires much further theoretical reflection.

Recall that the basic objection to the discounting approach was that it violated the principle of the equal consideration of interests. That objection was met by the observation that this principle is not necessarily correct, because we seem to accept the permissibility of violating it in some cases and the requirement to violate it in others. However, there seem to be some violations of the principle that are clearly wrong. Discounting the interests of members of other races or of the other gender seems to be part of the wrong of racism and sexism. Might one not argue that discounting the interests of the members of other species is equally wrong? That is the wrong of "speciesism."

This point can also be put as follows: The charge of speciesism might just be the charge that discounting animal interests is wrong because it violates the principle of equal consideration of interests. This charge is severely weakened by the challenge to the legitimacy of the equal-consideration principle. But the charge might be the very different claim that discounting animal interests is wrong because it is a *discriminatory* version of discounting; this charge is not challenged by the general challenge to the principle of the equal consideration of interests. This version of the charge is articulated by DeGrazia in a critique of Midgley:

> Can appeals to social bondedness in justifying partiality towards humans be convincingly likened to family-based preferences but contrasted with bigotry? Why are racism and sexism unjustified, if species-based partiality is justified?[26]

It is of interest and importance to note that the examples DeGrazia invokes are of partiality toward family members, on the one hand, and toward members of our race or gender, on the other hand. Left out are partiality toward fellow citizens, fellow believers, and fellow members of an ethnic group. All of these seem, *as long as they are not excessive,* to be within the bounds of acceptable partially toward our fellows and of acceptable discounting of the interests of others. This is why it is appropriate that so much charitable giving is organized by religions and national groups. This is, also, why it is appropriate that nearly all redistribution is done at the individual-country level rather than at the international level. These examples are important in reminding us that the rejection of the equal consideration of interests principle in common morality is very broad and covers large-scale groups that are more analogous to species than to family members. Of course, this by itself is not a refutation of the discrimination charge leveled against the pro-research position. It does, however, place the position in the company of partialities and discountings that are widely accepted in moral theory and in public policy.

What my arguments foreshadow is the need for further ethical reflection on these controversial issues. We have seen that morality can legitimately involve the discounting of even other people's interests when one acts from a prerogative or a special obligation. A question that requires much more exploration is what differentiates legitimate discounting from discrimination? Only an answer to this question can fully justify the discounting-based, reasonable pro-research position that I have articulated in this essay.

NOTES

1. David DeGrazia, "The Ethics of Animal Research," *Cambridge Quarterly of Healthcare Ethics* 8, no. 1 (Winter 1999): 23–34.

2. For summaries of the extensive literature, see, for example, Tom Beauchamp, "The Moral Standing of Animals in Medical Research," *Law, Medicine, and Health Care* 20, nos. 1–2 (Spring/Summer 1992): 7–16; and David DeGrazia, "The Moral Status of Animals and Their Use in Research: A Philosophical Review," *Kennedy Institute of Ethics Journal* 1, no. 1 (March 1991): 48–70.

3. DeGrazia, "The Ethics of Animal Research," 23–24.

4. For a discussion of Descartes's position on these issues, see F. Barbara Orlans, *In the Name of Science: Issues in Responsible Animal Experimentation* (New York: Oxford University Press, 1993), 3–4.

5. This is in opposition to the position articulated in Tom Regan, *The Case for Animal Rights* (Berkeley: University of California Press, 1983).

6. This is in opposition to the position articulated in Peter Singer, *Practical Ethics,* 2d ed. (New York: Cambridge University Press, 1993).

7. National Institutes of Health—Office for Protection from Research Risks (NIH-OPRR), *Public Health Service Policy on Humane Care and Use of Laboratory Animals* (Bethesda, MD: NIH-OPRR, 1986).

8. National Commission for the Protection of Human Subjects of Biomedical and Behavioral Research (USNCPHS), *The Belmont Report: Ethical Principles and Guidelines for the Protection of Human Subjects of Research* (Washington, DC: USNCPHS, 1978).

9. NIH-OPRR, *Policy on Humane Care and Use of Laboratory Animals,* i.

10. W. M. S. Russell and R. L. Burch, *The Priniciples of Humane Experimental Technique* (London: Methuen, 1959).

11. *National Institutes of Health Revitalization Act of 1993,* 42 U.S.C.S. sec. 283e(a) (Law. Co-op. 1999).

12. NIH-OPRR, *Policy on Humane Care and Use of Laboratory Animals,* principle 2, p. i.

13. 45 C.F.R. sec. 46. 111 (1999).

14. NIH-OPRR, *Policy on Humane Care and Use of Laboratory Animals,* principles 3, 4, and 6, p. i.

15. Council Directive of November 24, 1986, art. 12, sec. 2, reprinted in Baruch Brody, *The Ethics of Biomedical Research: An International Perspective* (New York: Oxford University Press, 1998), 237–40.

16. *British Animals (Scientific Procedures) Act of 1986,* sec. 5(4), reprinted in Brody, *The Ethics of Biomedical Research,* 321–25.

17. Federal Republic of Germany, *Law on Animal Protection,* art. 7(3), reprinted in Animal Welfare Institute, *Animals and Their Legal Rights,* 4th ed. (Washington, DC: Animal Welfare Institute, 1990), 336–52.

18. Jane A. Smith and Kenneth M. Boyd, eds., *Lives in the Balance: The Ethics of Using Animals in Biomedical Research—The Report of a Working Party of the Institute of Medical Ethics* (Oxford: Oxford University Press, 1991).

19. Ibid., 141.

20. Ibid., 141–46.

21. See, most recently, Brody, *The Ethics of Biomedical Research,* chap. 10.

22. Singer, *Practical Ethics,* 60.

23. W. D. Ross, *The Right and the Good* (Oxford: Oxford University Press, 1930), chap. 2.

24. Samuel Scheffler, *The Rejection of Consequentialism* (Oxford: Oxford University Press, 1982), chap. 3.

25. Mary Midgley, *Animals and Why They Matter* (Hammondsworth, Middlesex: Penguin Books, 1983).

26. David DeGrazia, *Taking Animals Seriously: Mental Life and Moral Status* (New York: Cambridge University Press, 1996), 64.

ANDREW N. ROWAN

Formulation of Ethical Standards for Use of Animals in Medical Research

Andrew N. Rowan is Senior Vice-President for Research, Education and International Issues, Humane Society of the United States. He is on the Advisory Board for the Johns Hopkins University Center for Alternatives to Animal Testing. He is the author of *Of Mice, Models and Men* (State University of New York Press) and *The Animal Research Controversy* (Center for Animals and Public Policy, Tufts University School of Veterinary Medicine) and editor of *State of the Animals, 2001* (Humane Society Press). His publications include numerous scientific articles on the ethics of animal research, companion animal issues, and human-animal interactions.

• • •

THE MODERN CONTROVERSY

In the last 20 years, more has been written about the moral status of animals than in the previous 2000, but we seem to be no nearer to resolving some of the central arguments and controversies. For example, what grounds can be used to distinguish humans and animals as different in kind rather than degree? If we choose one [criterion] like reason or language, then what reasons should we give for excluding chimpanzees, while including humans who cannot talk or reason? Whatever criterion is chosen, there are either some animals that appear to meet it or some humans that do not. Moral theories that argue that only those who have duties can have rights[1] would exclude a significant number of humans, who are not deemed capable of having duties, from the category of "rights-holders."

If suffering is to be given a critical place in our moral theory, then how do we decide what animals are capable of suffering and is all suffering equivalent? Are humans, with their considerable capacity for abstract thought capable of more intense mental anguish than nonverbal animals? Are insects or other invertebrates capable of suffering given that most theories of suffering require the presence of significant cognitive abilities?

Despite the difficult questions, we may find that it is much easier to come to a broadly supported consensus on the ethics of animal research than the overblown rhetoric and ad hominem attacks in the media would seem to imply. First, however, it is desirable to examine some of the ethical positions[2] that are evident in the modern debate because the various protagonists, most of whom are not trained in the analytical tools of moral philosophy, often have difficulty in articulating their own positions regarding the moral status of animals. As such, it is hardly surprising that they are not aware of all the implications of either their own ethical positions or those of their opponents. The following positions do not represent an exhaustive list but they do provide a broad sweep of the arguments that are evident in the modern debate.

DIVINELY GRANTED DOMINION

People commonly refer to biblical authority to justify the position that we can use and kill animals as we wish provided we are not careless or malevolent. Some go further and suggest that there are no constraints whatever on our use of animals[3] but the prevailing view is that God-granted dominion falls far short of

Reprinted with the permission of the author and publisher from *Toxicology Letters* 68 (1993), 63–71. Copyright © 1993 Elsevier Science Publishers B. V.

domination and should be interpreted more as stewardship. One is then faced with questions about the extent of the obligations to animals that are required by this position of stewardship.

THE THOMIST/KANTIAN POSITION

Although Aquinas and Kant did not have much to say on the animal issue, they both argued that we should not abuse animals, not because of any inherent value that the animals hold, but because animal abusers are more likely to move on to abuse other humans. There is a strong thread of this philosophy apparent in humane education and in anticruelty laws.

Although research tends to support the link between animal abuse and subsequent aggressive behavior towards other humans,[4] it is also possible that the tendency of some individuals to abuse humans may be reduced by the opportunity to mistreat an animal. In this case, the counter-intuitive nature of the Thomist-Kantian position is evident. Imagine the public reaction if people were encouraged to engage in cruelty to animals as part of their psychotherapy!

UTILITARIANISM

Most of the American public probably rely heavily, albeit unknowingly, on Utilitarian arguments to support their moral behavior. Many laws and regulations are based on Utilitarian ideas of maximizing good and minimizing harm. Early Utilitarians, especially the 18th century British philosopher, Jeremy Bentham, identified suffering as a key harm. Bentham then extended his moral orbit to include animal suffering. Indeed, one of his passages is widely quoted in the animal movement's literature.

> It may come one day to be recognized, that the number of legs, the villosity of the skin, or the termination of the os sacrum, are reasons equally insufficient [as blackness of the skin among humans] for abandoning a sensitive being to the same fate. What else is it that should trace the insuperable line? Is it the faculty of reason, or perhaps the faculty of discourse? But a full-grown horse or dog is beyond comparison a more rational as well as more conversable animal, than an infant of a day, or a week, or even a month, old. But suppose the case were otherwise, what would it avail? The question is not Can they *reason*? nor Can they *talk*? but, Can they *suffer*?[5] (emphasis [in original]).

The rationality and linguistic skills of the individual being were not important to Bentham. If the creature could suffer and experience pleasure—that is, if it was sentient—then it would be entitled to have its suffering and pleasure compared and weighed against the similar suffering and pleasure of other sentient creatures, including humans. This does not imply that a chicken and a horse should be "treated" the same, just that their interests in not experiencing the same type of suffering are equal and should be "considered" equally.

In the area of animal research, Utilitarian arguments are very common. On the scientific side, people argue that animal research is justified because its benefits to humans and animals outweigh the harms to the laboratory animals. On the animal activist side, philosophers such as Singer[6] use Utilitarian arguments to attack the use of animals in research. One could characterize these two opposing positions as Permissive and Restrictive Utilitarianism. Clearly, the two sides are not arguing about the use of Utilitarian theory itself, but rather about the extent of human benefit and animal suffering. Singer holds that animal suffering in the laboratory is considerable and that most of the benefits are either too limited to warrant such suffering or, with sufficient effort, could be achieved without the use of animals. In addition, Singer places an animal's interests in not suffering on a virtually equal footing with a human's interests in not suffering. (Singer's arguments have been an important element in the upsurge of support for the animal movement over the past decade.) By contrast, scientists tend to maximize claims of benefit and argue that animal suffering is minimal or nonexistent.

There are several problems with the Utilitarian approach. For example, it is virtually impossible to develop the necessary calculations that permit a measured and rational balancing of harm against good. Frequently one has to attempt to balance very different outcomes. How, for example, does one compare the suffering of a certain number of rats with the increased understanding of a biological phenomenon? In the United Kingdom, where the law governing animal research requires a balancing of costs and benefits, nobody has yet produced a systematic way to compare them.[7] As in the United States, most of the attention is paid to reducing the costs (i.e., animal suffering).

It has also proved difficult to identify what groups of animals experience suffering and distress (do insects suffer?) and whether the suffering of rats is equivalent to that of dogs, or humans? Suffering is usually not defined but the usual implication is that it requires a minimum level of cognitive ability that may not be present in most invertebrates (the octopus being a possible exception). The concept appears to be like obscenity where everybody thinks they can recognize it but nobody can define it for regulatory purposes.

REVERENCE FOR LIFE

Albert Schweitzer argued that our moral concern should be extended beyond just those life forms capable of feeling or sensation (sentience). He held that all life exhibits a "will to live" and that it is "good to maintain and cherish . . . [and] . . . evil to destroy and check."[8] Nevertheless, his philosophy did not cause him to oppose all animal research, nor was he a vegetarian. His view was that any injury to life must be "necessary" and "unavoidable," but he did not spell out the conditions that make the sacrifice of animals in general, or research animals in particular, "necessary."[9] Many people make appeals as to the sanctity of life but such appeals are usually reserved for human life. The taking of animal life is usually considered to be acceptable provided little or no suffering is involved and the animal's death is necessary for some human end. The wanton killing of animals is usually not condoned. However, "reverence for life" is a common phrase in the lexicon of animal activists and, in its strong form, it usually implies no killing of animals for human benefit.

ANIMAL RIGHTS

Animal rights is not a new concept. People have talked of the rights of animals for centuries. In the 18th and 19th centuries a number of authors discussed the status of animals using the term "animal rights." These culminated in the 1892 book by Henry Salt, entitled *Animals' Rights,*[10] which presented a very modern exposition of the issues. Today, the concept of "animal rights" is a central issue in the clash between opponents and proponents of animal research. Unfortunately, the term animal rights now tends to cloud and confuse rather than clarify the issues because it has come to be used as a convenient hook on which to hang oneself or one's opponents! There are three contexts in which the term is used: (i) the "common sense," (ii) the political, and (iii) the philosophical—that are rarely distinguished nor identified in the course of debate and argument.

(i) *"Common sense."* Approximately 80% of the public believes that animals have rights. However, about 85 % of that same public believes that humans have the right to kill and eat animals.[11] Thus, whatever "rights" the public believes animals have claim to, they do not include the right to life. The concept of animal rights held by the general public probably amounts to no more than a vague and woolly idea that animals have the right to some, rather limited moral consideration.

(ii) *Political views.* In the developed world, there is a growing tendency to couch political claims in "rights" language. Thus, we talk of civil rights, women's rights, gay rights, and the like. Therefore, in the political arena, a rights claim carries significant political resonance. It is only to be expected that the animal movement would attempt to appropriate the power of rights language for its own cause. In this sense, the public campaign for animal rights also includes the animal welfare movement although there has been some attempt, both inside and outside the animal protection movement, to distinguish between animal welfare and animal rights organizations. Peter Singer who, as a Utilitarian, does not agree with rights language, has ironically accepted his identification with the animal rights movement (although he prefers the term "animal liberation") because he sees it as primarily a political movement with only loose ties to its philosophical roots.

(iii) *Philosophical arguments.* In philosophical circles, a right can be defined (simply and simplistically) as nothing more than a claim that cannot be overridden by claims to human utility. A rights claim can only be overridden by another rights claim. Thus, one has to determine just what is being claimed as a right. The fact that most of the philosophical arguments espousing animal rights have been radical challenges to current human use of animals—usually setting forth a claim that animals cannot be used solely as a means to a human end[12]—does not mean that all animal rights positions need be that radical.

The very strong Animal Rights argument—developed by Regan[12] and others—asserts that we cannot use animals merely as a means to our own ends. A weaker, but plausible Animal Rights argument is one where the assertion is made that animals have the right not to be caused to suffer. In both positions, the term "rights" is used simply to define a claim that cannot be over-ridden merely because it would be useful to do so.

Most rights-based arguments have to identify some characteristic or complex of characteristics that confer moral rights. Regan,[12] for example, suggests that animals that have beliefs and desires are the "subjects of a life" and this confers inherent worth that gives them the right not to be killed or used to satisfy human ends. He identifies adult mammals as having this capacity and would give the benefit of the doubt to birds and perhaps other vertebrates. Thus, Regan's animal rights philosophy tends to require a vegetarian life style and little or no animal use by humans.

Rights-based moral arguments have difficulties dealing with shades of grey. In Regan's philosophy, an animal either is a "subject-of-a-life" or it is not. It cannot half fulfill the requirements. This creates certain problems from an evolutionary perspective although it is conceivable that the capacity to have beliefs and desires is an all-or-none property. Nonetheless, Regan runs into difficulties when he argues (as he does in his book) that a human has a richer life than a dog and is therefore to be favored over a dog when faced with a direct conflict of competing rights.[12]

ANOTHER POSSIBLE APPROACH

Nearly every articulated argument on the moral status of animals has presented its arguments on the basis of a single morally relevant characteristic. For example, Schweitzer argues that possession of a life is "the" important characteristic. For Singer, it is sentience. For Regan, it is the possession of beliefs and desires. However, it is very likely that no single characteristic is sufficient to describe a complete ethical theory on animal treatment. The world is not that simple. One has to consider a tapestry of characteristics,[13] including the possession of life, the possession of sentience, the possession of beliefs and desires, the possession of self-awareness, and the like.[2]

One can develop a two-tiered approach to ethical thinking in which there are proscriptive obligations to animals based on the possession of life, sentience, purposiveness, self-awareness and personhood that establish baseline levels of moral consideration below which one cannot go. On this relatively complex edifice, one can add a layer of prescriptive obligations that are owed to beings with which one has established certain explicit or implicit contracts. Thus, one is required to treat one's family with greater consideration than a stranger but the stranger is owed certain basic obligations that cannot be voided.

This approach has strong Darwinian overtones in that the ranking of obligations tends to follow evolutionary paths. Thus, sentient vertebrates would be accorded more consideration than living, but not sentient coelenterates, and self-aware apes would be accorded more consideration than sentient, but (presumably) not self-aware frogs. The scheme also provides a place for the additional moral obligations incurred by explicit or implicit contracts between humans and animals. Thus, this scheme could explain why we might owe more to the family dog than to a purpose-bred laboratory beagle.

ESTABLISHING A MORAL FRAMEWORK

In actual fact, when one looks at the way that we come to decisions about the ethics of animal research, one finds that a variety of ethical approaches are used. For example, we place a high value on virtue in that we try to identify virtuous people who have high standards of ethical behavior to sit on our animal care and use committees. We also try to identify the values that should guide our decision-making and usually incorporate some mix of the following:

(a) reduce animal suffering as much as possible,
(b) reduce the number of animals required as far as possible,
(c) ensure that the science is properly planned and likely to achieve its goals, and
(d) ensure that those conducting the research are adequately trained so that they will be able to minimize animal suffering.

Finally, we have also established some rules of behavior that should guide our decision-making. Thus, conducting multiple surgeries on a single animal is not permitted unless it is part of the same protocol.

In other words, our every-day approach to moral conduct incorporates such supposedly disparate traditions in ethics as virtue, value, and deontological rules. Whatever the approach used, it is striking to note that nearly every philosopher who has addressed the question of the moral status of animals in the past 20 years has come to the conclusion that not only are the questions difficult but that society should also seriously consider upgrading the moral status of animals. Only a few have taken a contrary view. Fox produced a book justifying the use of animals in research[14] but then recanted his position shortly after the book was published and now argues that animals have rights that prohibit their use as research tools.[15] Cohen argues that not only can animal research be justified but that it is morally mandated.[1] He is one of the few professional philosophers who have come out in unquestioning support of the traditional position.

In conclusion, the issue of the appropriate moral status of animals is neither an easy nor a trivial question. It involves developing theories for the moral weight to be accorded to such qualities as life, sentience and suffering, self-awareness, and the like. It then requires a more sophisticated understanding of the concepts of sentience so that we can identify which animals might satisfy the requirements. In justifying biomedical research, one is faced with difficult questions about the value of basic knowledge and likely therapeutic benefit. Most of the public and many scientists consider the testing of cosmetics and toiletries on animals as an unjustifiable activity. However, people have been severely injured by unsafe personal care products in the past, so what should we do now about testing?

If we agree that animal use in research involves moral costs that need to be taken seriously (a widespread view despite recent tendencies by defenders of science to avoid "apologizing" for animal use in the media), then how much attention must be paid to the three "Rs" of Russell (replacement, reduction, and refinement) and Burch and the idea of alternatives? In toxicology, a broad public consensus on this issue is developing but there is still much suspicion of the concept of alternatives in the halls of the National Institutes of Health, neuroscience, and physiology. Nonetheless, much progress in attending to the moral issues related to animal research and testing is evident although there is still a great deal left to do. We will need wisdom, humor, and a good sense of proportion in the decades to come if we are to continue to make progress on these issues.

NOTES

1. Cohen, C. (1986) The case for the use of animals in biomedical research. *N. Engl. J. Med.* 315, 865–870.

2. Tannenbaum, J. and Rowan, A. N. (1985) Rethinking the morality of animal research. Hastings Center Rep. 15(5), 32–43.

3. White, R. J. (1990) Animal ethics? Hastings Center Rep. 20(6), 43.

4. Felthouse, A. R. and Kellert, S. R. (1987) Childhood cruelty to animals and later aggression against people: A review. Am J. Psychiatry 144, 710–717.

5. Bentham, J. (1962) The Works of Jeremy Bentham, J. Bowring (Ed.), Vol. 1, Russell and Russell, New York, pp. 142–143.

6. Singer, P. (1975) Animal Liberation. New York Review of Books/Random House, New York.

7. Smith, J. A. and Boyd, K. M. (1991) Lives in the Balance: The Ethics of Using Animals in Biomedical Research. Oxford University Press, Oxford.

8. Schweitzer, A. (1929) Civilization and Ethics, trans. C. Champion, Macmillan, New York, pp. 246–247.

9. Schweitzer, A. (1950) The Philosophy of Civilization, trans. C. Champion. Macmillan, New York, p. 318.

10. Salt, H. S. (1892) Animals' Rights. London. New edition issued by International Society for Animal Rights, Clarks Summit, PA, 1980.

11. Parents Magazine. (1989). Parents Poll on Animal Rights, Attractiveness, Television and Abortion. Kane and Parsons Associates, New York, Sept.–Oct., 1989.

12. Regan, T. (1983) The case for animal rights. University of California Press, Berkeley, CA.

13. Nozick, R. (1983) About mammals and people. New York Times Book Review, November 27, p. 11.

14. Fox, M. A. (1986) The Case for Animal Experimentation: An Evolutionary and Ethical Perspective. University of California Press. Berkeley, CA.

15. Fox, M. A. (1987) Animal experimentation; a philosopher's changing views. Between the Species 3(2), 55–60, 75, 80, 82.

RICHARD SMITH

Animal Research: The Need for a Middle Ground

Richard Smith is Editor of the *British Medical Journal,* Chief Executive of the BMJ Publishing Group, and Visiting Professor at the London School of Hygiene and Tropical Medicine. He was a founding member of the Committee on Publication Ethics (COPE).

Many countries, including Britain, suffer from grossly oversimplified debates on important issues like drugs, crime and punishment, genetically modified foods, and animal research. Are you for or against? Sign here. Yet none of these issues is moved forward by such polarised arguments. The British debate on animal research currently features people in ski masks using every tactic, including illegal and violent ones, to close down animal research institutes pitted against intimidated scientists arguing that no progress can be made in treating serious human diseases without animal research. We need more understanding of the complexities of animal research and a greater concentration on where we agree.

Can any of us imagine a world where animals were not used for food, clothing, or transport, where we had no pets, where rats and other vermin were not controlled, and where an ape, or even a fly, was regarded as the moral equal of the Archbishop of Canterbury? Most of us can't, and many people in Britain accept the need for some animal research.[1] Yet most of us would not tolerate a world where animals had no rights and could be exploited for whatever cause. We thus have to find some middle ground in our relationship with animals, and a world that tries to afford more rights to men and women will probably also try to give more to animals.

The arguments over animal research are so polarised because the two sides have completely different ways of thinking.[2] Opponents of research are concerned primarily with the rights and suffering of animals, whereas supporters are interested in the capacity of animal research to speed developments in understanding biology and preventing and treating disease. We need methods and ideas to promote agreement rather than disagreement, and the three Rs of animal research—replacement, reduction, and refinement—can do just that. They were first proposed by William Russell (zoologist, psychologist, and classical scholar) and Rex Burch (microbiologist) in 1959.[3] Replacement is "any scientific method employing non-sentient material which may . . . replace methods which use conscious, living vertebrates." Reduction is lowering "the number of animals needed to obtain information of a given account and precision." Refinement is any development that leads to a "decrease in the incidence or severity of inhumane procedures applied to those animals which have to be used."

The three Rs underpin most animal research policy and practice. They start with the assumption that there will be animal research but hold open the possibility that science might advance to a point where it would no longer be necessary. Replacement is the option that is most attractive to animals lovers and politicians and has been actively promoted by the Fund for Replacement of Animals in Medical Experimentation (www.frame-uk.demon.co.uk) and the European Centre for the Validation of Alternative Methods, which was set up by the European Union.[4,5] Replacement can be relative (using humane killing to provide cells, tissues, or organs), absolute (using permanent cul-

From *British Medical Journal* 322 (2001), 248–49. Reprinted with permission from the BMJ Publishing Group.

tures of cells or tissues), direct (using, for example, skin in vitro rather than in vivo), indirect (replacing, for example, the pyrogen test in rabbits with a test on whole human blood), total (using a human volunteer), or partial (using non-animal methods in prescreening of toxic compounds).[2]

The science of replacement is growing rapidly, but the Holy Grail of complete replacement of animals is as far off as ever.[2] The central problem is that molecular, cell, tissue, or organ models are highly simplified when compared with whole animals or humans. After 20 years of research there are only a handful of validated and genuine replacements for animal methods.

Reduction has not received the same attention as replacement, and seems to be still more difficult.[6] It depends primarily on better research and better statistical analysis, which will be brought about through improved education and training. Reduction can also compete with refinement in that using fewer animals to achieve the same level of precision might mean exposing animals to greater suffering. Nevertheless, the number of animals used in scientific procedures in Great Britain has fallen over the past 20 years. In 1998, 2.66 million procedures were carried out—a reduction of more than 25% since the introduction of the Animals (Scientific Procedures) Act in 1986.[7]

Refinement has also been neglected relative to replacement, but the notion has been broadened to include all aspects of the life of a laboratory animal—from birth to death. Researchers worry that refinement may make the science less sound (so possibly rendering the animal's suffering worthless), but a joint working group of the Royal Society for the Prevention of Cruelty to Animals, FRAME, the Universities Federation for Animal Welfare, and the British Veterinary Association Animal Welfare Foundation have made specific recommendations for advancing refinement.[8]

The beauty of the three Rs is that they provide a way for all parties to work together to advance the cause of both animals and humans. Nothing will be gained by forcing laboratories to close or by oversimplifying the debate. . . .

NOTES

1. Aldhous P. Animal experiments: where do you draw the line? *New Scientist* 1999;162:31–6. (www.animalexperiments.newscientist.com)
2. Grayson L. *Animals in research: for and against.* London: British Library, 2000.
3. Russell W. M. S., Burch R. L. *The principles of humane experimental technique.* London: Methuen, 1959. (www.users.dircon.co.uk/~ufaw3/)
4. Balls M. On keeping your eyes on the prize: Dorothy Hegarty and acceptance of the concept of replacement of laboratory animal procedures in research, education, and testing. *Alternatives to Laboratory Animals* 1996;23:756–74.
5. Balls M. Defining the role of ECVAM in the development, validation, and acceptance of alternative tests and testing strategies. *Toxicology in Vitro* 1995;9:863–9.
6. Festing M. F. W., and others. Reducing the use of laboratory animals in biomedical research: problems and possible solutions: ECVAM Workshop report 29. *Alternatives to Laboratory Animals* 1998;26:283–301.
7. www.homeoffice.gov.uk/animact/aspaf.htm (accessed 30 Jan 2001).
8. Morton D. B. and others. Removal of blood from laboratory mammals and birds: first report of the BVA/FRAME/RSPCA/UFAW Joint Working Group on Refinement. *Laboratory Animals* 1993;27:1–22.

SUGGESTED READINGS

CODES AND GUIDELINES

Annas, George J. and Grodin, Michael A., eds. *The Nazi Doctors and the Nuremberg Code: Human Rights in Human Experimentation.* Oxford: Oxford University Press, 1992.

Baker, Robert. "Bioethics and Human Rights: A Historical Perspective." *Cambridge Quarterly of Healthcare Ethics* 10 (2001), 241–52.

———. "A Theory of International Bioethics: Multiculturalism, Postmodernism, and the Bankruptcy of Fundamentalism." *Kennedy Institute of Ethics Journal* 8 (1998), 201–31.

———. "A Theory of International Bioethics: The Negotiable and the Non-Negotiable." *Kennedy Institute of Ethics Journal* 8 (1998), 233–73.

Bankowski, Zbigniew, and Levine, Robert J., eds. *Ethics and Research on Human Subjects: International Guidelines.* Geneva: Council for International Organizations of Medical Sciences, 1993.

Beran, Roy G. "The Ethics of Clinical Research and the Conduct of Clinical Drug Trials: International Comparisons and Codes of Conduct." *Medicine and Law* 19 (2000), 501–21.

Brody, Baruch A. *The Ethics of Biomedical Research : An International Perspective.* New York : Oxford University Press, 1998, Appendixes 1–4.

Canada. Medical Research Council of Canada, Natural Sciences and Engineering Research Council of Canada, and Social Sciences and Humanities Research Council of Canada. *Tri-Council Policy Statement: Ethical Conduct for Research Involving Human Subjects.* Ottowa: The Three Councils, August 1998.

Canadian Council on Animal Care. *Guide to the Care and Use of Experimental Animals.* Ottawa, Ontario, Canada: The Council, Vol. 1, 2nd ed., 1993, Vol. 2, 1984. [Online at http://www.ccac.ca]

Childress, James F. "Nuremberg's Legacy: Some Ethical Reflections." *Perspectives in Biology and Medicine* 43 (2000), 347–61.

Flanagin, Annette. "Who Wrote the Declaration of Helsinki?" *Journal of the American Medical Association* 277 (1997), 926.

Forster, Heidi P., Emanuel, Ezekiel, and Grady, Christine. "The 2000 Revision of the Declaration of Helsinki: A Step Forward or More Confusion?" *Lancet* 358 (2001), 1449–53.

Katz, Jay. "The Nuremberg Code and the Nuremberg Trial: A Reappraisal." *Journal of the American Medical Association* 276 (1996), 1662–66.

Knoppers, Bartha Maria, and Sprumont, Dominique. "Human Subjects Research, Ethics, and International Codes on Genetic Research." In Thomas H. Murray and Maxwell J. Mehlman, eds. *Ethical, Legal, and Policy Issues in Biotechnology.* 2 vols. New York: John Wiley & Sons, 2000, 566–76.

Levine, Robert J., and Gorovitz, Samuel, with James Gallagher, eds. *Biomedical Research Ethics: Updating International Guidelines—A Consultation.* Geneva: Council for International Organizations of Medical Sciences, 2000.

———. "International Codes and Guidelines for Research Ethics: A Critical Appraisal." In Harold Y. Vanderpool, ed. *The Ethics of Research Involving Human Subjects: Facing the 21st Century.* Frederick, MD: University Publishing Group, 1996, 235–39.

Lewis, John A., et al. "Placebo-Controlled Trials and the Declaration of Helsinki." *Lancet* 359 (2002), 1337–40.

Macklin, Ruth. "After Helsinki: Unresolved Issues in International Research." *Kennedy Institute of Ethics Journal* 11 (2001), 17–36.

Moreno, Jonathan D. " 'The Only Feasible Means': The Pentagon's Ambivalent Relationship with the Nuremberg Code." *Hastings Center Report* 26 (September–October 1996), 11–9.

———. "Reassessing the Influence of the Nuremberg Code on American Medical Ethics." *Journal of Contemporary Health Law and Policy* 13 (1997), 347–60.

Richter, Elihu D., et al. "Extending the Boundaries of the Declaration of Helsinki: A Case Study of an Unethical Experiment in a Non-Medical Setting." *Journal of Medical Ethics* 27 (2001), 126–29.

Rothman, Kenneth J., et al. "Declaration of Helsinki Should Be Strengthened." *British Medical Journal* 321 (2000), 442–45.

Shevell, Michael I. "Neurology's Witness to History: Part II—Leo Alexander's Contributions to the Nuremberg Code (1946–1947)," *Neurology* 50 (1998), 274–78.

Shuster, Evelyne. "Fifty Years Later: The Significance of the Nuremberg Code." *New England Journal of Medicine* 337 (1997), 1436–40.

Singer, Peter A. and Benatar, Solomon R. "Beyond Helsinki: A Vision for Global Health Ethics." *British Medical Journal* 322 (2001), 747–48.

Spicer, Carol Mason, ed. "Appendix: IV. Ethical Directives for Human Research." In Warren Thomas Reich, ed. *Encyclopedia of Bioethics.* Revised ed. New York: Simon & Schuster Macmillan, 1995, 2761–2800.

Tollman, Stephen M., et al. "What Are the Effects of the Fifth Revision of the Declaration of Helsinki?" *British Medical Journal* 323 (2001), 1417–23.

U. K., Home Office. *Draft Guidance on the Operation of the Animals (Scientific Procedures) Act 1986: Consultation* [Online-http://www.homeoffice.gov.uk/ccpd/cons.htm.]

U. S., National Bioethics Advisory Commission. *Ethical and Policy Issues in International Research: Clinical Trials in Developing Countries.* 2 vols. Washington, DC: U.S. Government Printing Office, 2001.

U. S., National Commission for the Protection of Research Subjects. *The Belmont Report: Ethical Principles and Guidelines for the Protection of Human Subjects of Research and Appendix.* 3 vols. Washington, DC: U.S. Government Printing Office, 1978. [Excerpts published in *Federal Register* 44 (1979), 23192–97.]

Vastag, Brian. "Helsinki Discord? A Controversial Declaration." *Journal of the American Medical Association* 284 (2000), 2983–86.

Weijer, Charles and Anderson, James A. "The Ethics Wars: Disputes Over International Research." *Hastings Center Report* 31 (2001), 18–20.

Wunder, Michael. "Medicine and Conscience: The Debate on Medical Ethics and Research in Germany 50 Years after Nuremberg." *Perspectives in Biology and Medicine* 43 (2000), 373–81.

Zion, Deborah, Gillam, Lynn, and Loff, Bebe. "The Declaration of Helsinki, CIOMS and the Ethics of Research on Vulnerable Populations." *Nature Medicine* 6 (2000), 615–17.

ETHICAL ISSUES IN HUMAN RESEARCH

Ackerman, Terrence L. "Human Subjects Research, Ethics, Compensation of Subjects for Injury." In Thomas H. Murray and Maxwell J. Mehlman, eds. *Ethical, Legal, and Policy Issues in Biotechnology.* 2 vols. New York: John Wiley & Sons, 2000, 585–95.

Altman, Douglas G., et al. "The Revised CONSORT Statement for Reporting Randomized Trials: Explanation and Elaboration." *Annals of Internal Medicine* 134 (2001), 663–94.

Angell, Marcia. "Investigators' Responsibilities for Human Subjects in Developing Countries." *New England Journal of Medicine* 342 (2000), 967–69.

———. "Is Academic Medicine for Sale?" *New England Journal of Medicine* 342 (2000), 1516–18.

Annas, George J., et al. *Informed Consent to Human Experimentation: The Subject's Dilemma.* Cambridge, MA: Ballinger, 1977.

Antman, Karen, et al. "Designing and Funding Clinical Trials of Novel Therapies." *New England Journal of Medicine* 344 (2001), 762–63.

Ashcroft, Richard and Pfeffer, Naomi. "Ethics Behind Closed Doors: Do Research Ethics Committees Need Secrecy?" *British Medical Journal* 322 (2001), 1294–96.

Association of American Medical Colleges. *Protecting Subjects, Preserving Trust, Promoting Progress—Policy and Guidelines for the Oversight of Individual Financial Interests in Human Subjects Research.* Washington, DC: Association of American Medical Colleges, 2001.

Avila, Matthew T., et al. "A Comparison of Symptom Provocation Procedures in Psychiatry and Other Areas of Medicine: Implications for Their Ethical Use in Research." *Biological Psychiatry* 50 (2001), 479–86.

Backlar, Patricia. "Human Subjects Research, Ethics, Research on Vulnerable Populations." In Thomas H. Murray and Maxwell J. Mehlman, eds. *Ethical, Legal, and Policy Issues in Biotechnology.* 2 vols. New York: John Wiley & Sons, 2000, 641–50.

Baram, Michael. "Making Clinical Trials Safer for Human Subjects." *American Journal of Law and Medicine* 27 (2001), 253–82.

Barber, Bernard. *Informed Consent in Medical Therapy and Research.* New Brunswick, NJ: Transaction Books, 1978.

Beauchamp, Tom L., et al., eds. *Ethical Issues in Social Science Research.* Baltimore, MD: Johns Hopkins University Press, 1982.

Beecher, Henry K. *Research and the Individual: Human Studies.* Boston: Little, Brown, 1970.

Benatar, Solomon R. and Singer, Peter A. "A New Look at International Research Ethics." *British Medical Journal* 321 (2000), 824–26.

Bhutta, Zulfiqar. "Ethics in International Health Research: A Perspective from the Developing World." *Bulletin of the World Health Organization* 80 (2002), 114–20.

Bodenheimer, Thomas. "Uneasy Alliance: Clinical Investigators and the Pharmaceutical Industry." *New England Journal of Medicine* 342 (2000), 1539–44

Brieger, Gert H. "Human Experimentation: History." In Warren T. Reich, ed. *Encyclopedia of Bioethics*. 4 vols. New York: Free Press, 1978, 684–92.

Brody, Baruch A. *Ethical Issues in Drug Testing, Approval, and Pricing: The Clot-Dissolving Drugs*. New York: Oxford University Press, 1995.

———. *The Ethics of Biomedical Research: An International Perspective*. New York Oxford University Press, 1998.

———. "When Are Placebo-Controlled Trials No Longer Appropriate?" *Controlled Clinical Trials* 18 (1997), 602–12.

Capron, Alexander M. "Ethical and Human Rights Issues in Research on Mental Disorders That May Affect Decisionmaking Capacity." *New England Journal of Medicine* 340 (1999), 1430–34.

———. "Human Experimentation." In Robert M. Veatch, ed. *Medical Ethics*. 2nd ed. Sudbury, MA: Jones and Bartlett, 1997, 135–84.

Chastain, Garvin, et al., eds. *Protecting Human Subjects: Departmental Subject Pools and Institutional Review Boards*. Washington, DC: American Psychological Association, 1999.

Childress, James F. "Compensating Injured Research Subjects: The Moral Argument." *Hastings Center Report* 6 (1976), 21–27.

Coughlan, Steven S., and Beauchamp, Tom L. *Ethics and Epidemiology*. New York: Oxford University Press, 1996.

Crigger, Bette-Jane. "What Does It Mean to 'Review' a Protocol?" *IRB: Ethics and Human Research* 23 (July–August 2001), 13–5.

Crouch, Robert A. "Eligibility, Extrapolation and Equipoise: Unlearned Lessons in the Ethical Analysis of Clinical Research." *IRB: Ethics and Human Research* 23 (July–August 2001), 6–8.

DeBruin, Debra A. "Justice and the Inclusion of Women in Clinical Studies." *Kennedy Institute of Ethics Journal* 4 (1994), 117–46.

De Deyn, Peter P., ed. *The Ethics of Animal and Human Experimentation*. London: John Libbey, 1994.

Dickens, Bernard M. "Human Research and the Medical Model: Legal and Ethical Issues." *Medicine and Law* 16 (1997), 687–703.

Dickert, Neal, et al. "Paying Research Subjects: An Analysis of Current Policies." *Annals of Internal Medicine* 136 (2002), 368–73.

Dresser, Rebecca. *When Science Offers Salvation: Patient Advocacy and Research Ethics*. New York: Oxford University Press, 2001.

Djulbegovic, Benjamin and Clarke, Mike. "Scientific and Ethical Issues in Equivalence Trials." *Journal of the American Medical Association* 285 (2001), 1206–08.

Eckenwiler, Lisa. "Moral Reasoning and the Review of Research Involving Human Subjects." *Kennedy Institute of Ethics Journal* 11 (2001), 37–69.

Edgar, Harold, and Rothman, David J. "The Institutional Review Board and Beyond: Future Challenges to the Ethics of Human Experimentation." *Milbank Quarterly* 73 (1995), 489–506.

Edwards, S. D. "An Argument against Research on People with Intellectual Difficulties." *Medicine, Health Care and Philosophy* 3 (2000), 69–73.

Eisenberg, Leon. "The Social Imperatives of Medical Research." *Science* 198 (1977), 1105–10.

Ellenberg, Susan; Fleming, Thomas; and DeMets, David. *Data Monitoring Committees in Clinical Trials: A Practical Perspective* (New York: John Wiley & Sons, 2002).

Emanuel, Ezekiel J.; Wendler, David; and Grady, Christine. "What Makes Clinical Research Ethical?" *Journal of the American Medical Association* 283 (2000), 2701–11.

Evans, Martyn. "Justified Deception? The Single Blind Placebo in Drug Research." *Journal of Medical Ethics* 26 (2000), 188–93.

Faden, Ruth R., Beauchamp, Tom L. with King, Nancy M. P. *A History and Theory of Informed Consent*. New York: Oxford University Press, 1986, Chapters 5–9.

Fleischman, Alan R. "Regulating Research Involving Adults Who Lack Decision Making Capacity." *Pharos* Spring (2001), 12–7.

Fox, Renée C. *Experiment Perilous: Physicians and Patients Facing the Unknown*. New Brunswick, NJ: Transaction Publishers, 1998.

Francis, Charles K. "Medical Ethos and Social Responsibility in Clinical Medicine." *Journal of Urban Health: Bulletin of the New York Academy of Medicine* 78 (2001), 29–45.

Freedman, Benjamin. "Equipoise and the Ethics of Clinical Research." *New England Journal of Medicine* 317 (1987), 141–45.

———. Placebo Orthodoxy in Clinical Research II: Ethical, Legal, and Regulatory Myths." *Journal of Law, Medicine and Ethics* 24 (1996), 252–59.

———; Weijer, Charles; and Glass, Kathleen Cranley. "Placebo Orthodoxy in Clinical Research I: Empirical and Methodological Myths." *Journal of Law, Medicine and Ethics* 24 (1996), 243–51.

Freedman, Ruth I. "Ethical Challenges in the Conduct of Research Involving Persons With Mental Retardation." *Mental Retardation* 39 (2001), 130–41.

Freund, Paul, ed. *Experimentation with Human Subjects*. New York: George Braziller, 1970.

Fried, Charles. *Medical Experimentation: Personal Integrity and Social Policy*. New York: American Elsevier, 1974.

Giffels, J. Joseph. *Clinical Trials: What You Should Know Before Volunteering to Be a Research Subject*. New York: Demos Medical Publishing, 1996.

Gifford, Fred. "Freedman's 'Clinical Equipoise' and 'Sliding-Scale All-Dimensions-Considered Equipoise'." *Journal of Medicine and Philosophy* 25 (2000), 399–426.

Gorman, Holly M., and Dane, Francis C. "Balancing Methodological Rigour and Ethical Treatment: The Necessity of Voluntary, Informed Consent." In P. P. De Deyn, ed. *The Ethics of Animal and Human Experimentation*. London: John Libbey, 1994, 35–41.

Gray, Bradford H. *Human Subjects in Medical Experimentation*. New York: Wiley, 1975.

———, et al. "Research Involving Human Subjects." *Science* 201 (1978), 1094–1101.

Grodin, Michael A, and Annas, George J. "Legacies of Nuremberg: Medical Ethics and Human Rights." *Journal of the American Medical Association* 276 (1996), 1682–83.

Grodin, Michael A, and Glantz, Leonard H., eds. *Children as Research Subjects: Science, Ethics, and Law*. New York: Oxford University Press, 1994.

Horton, Richard. "The Clinical Trial: Deceitful, Disputable, Unbelievable, Unhelpful, and Shameful—What Next?" *Controlled Clinical Trials* 22 (2001), 593–604.

Huston, Patricia and Peterson, Robert. "Withholding Proven Treatment in Clinical Research." *New England Journal of Medicine* 345 (2001), 912–14.

Institute of Medicine. *Preserving Public Trust: Accreditation and Human Research Participation Protection Programs*. Washington, DC: National Academy Press, 2001.

Ioannidis, John P. A. and Lau, Joseph. "Completeness of Safety Reporting in Randomized Trials." *Journal of the American Medical Association* 285 (2001), 437–43.

Jonas, Hans. "Philosophical Reflections on Experimenting with Human Subjects." In Jonas, Hans, *Philosophical Essays: From Current Creed to Technological Man*. Chicago: University of Chicago Press, 1980, 105–31.

Jones, Thomas C. "Call for a New Approach to the Process of Clinical Trials and Drug Registration." *British Medical Journal* 322 (2001), 920–23.

Juni, Peter, Altman, Douglas G., and Egger, Matthias. "Assessing the Quality of Controlled Clinical Trials." *British Medical Journal* 323 (2001), 42–46.

Kahn, Jeffrey P.; Mastroianni, Anna C.; and Sugarman, Jeremy, eds. *Beyond Consent: Seeking Justice in Research*. New York: Oxford University Press, 1998.

Kahn, Jeffrey, and Mastroianni, Anna C. "Doing Research Well By Doing Right." *Chronicle of Higher Education,* February 15, 2002, B24.

———. "Moving From Compliance to Conscience." *Archives of Internal Medicine* 161 (2001), 925–28.

Karlawish, Jason H. T, and Lantos, John. "Community Equipoise and the Architecture of Clinical Research." *Cambridge Quarterly of Healthcare Ethics* 6 (1997), 385–96.

Kass, Nancy E. "Human Subjects Research, Ethics, Informed Consent in Research." In Thomas H. Murray and Maxwell J. Mehlman, eds. *Ethical, Legal, and Policy Issues in Biotechnology.* 2 vols. New York: John Wiley & Sons, 2000, 611–22.

Katz, Jay. "Human Experimentation and Human Rights." *Saint Louis University Law Journal* 38 (1993): 7–54.

Kelch, Robert P. "Maintaining the Public Trust in Clinical Research." *New England Journal of Medicine* 346 (2002), 285–87.

Killen, Jack; Grady, Christine; Folkers, Gregory K.; and Fauci, Anthony S. "Ethics of Clinical Research in the Developing World." *Nature Reviews: Immunology* 2 (2002), 210–15.

King, Nancy M. P. "Defining and Describing Benefit Appropriately in Clinical Trials." *Journal of Law, Medicine and Ethics* 28 (2000), 332–43.

Kopelman, Loretta M. "Human Subjects Research, Ethics, and Research on Children." In Thomas H. Murray and Maxwell J. Mehlman, eds. *Ethical, Legal, and Policy Issues in Biotechnology.* 2 vols. New York: John Wiley & Sons, 2000, 576–85.

Koski, Greg and Nightingale, Stuart L. "Research Involving Human Subjects in Developing Countries." *New England Journal of Medicine* 345 (2001), 136–38.

Lackey, Douglas P. "Clinical Trials in Developing Countries: A Review of the Moral Issues." *Mount Sinai Journal of Medicine* 68 (2001), 4–12.

Lawrey, Robert P., and Anderson, Thomas W. "University-Industry Research Relationships, Ethics, Conflict of Interest." In Thomas H. Murray and Maxwell J. Mehlman, eds. *Ethical, Legal, and Policy Issues in Biotechnology*. 2 vols. New York: John Wiley & Sons, 2000, 1099–1106.

Levine, Robert J. *Ethics and Regulation of Human Research.* 2nd ed. Baltimore, MD: Urban and Schwarzenberg, 1986.

———. "Human Subjects Research, Ethics, Principles Governing Research with Human Subjects." In Thomas H. Murray and Maxwell J. Mehlman, eds. *Ethical, Legal, and Policy Issues in Biotechnology*. 2 vols. New York: John Wiley & Sons, 2000, 622–30.

———, and Ellenberg, Susan S. "Human Subjects Research, Ethics, Stopping Rules for Randomized Clinical Trials." In Thomas H. Murray and Maxwell J. Mehlman, eds. *Ethical, Legal, and Policy Issues in Biotechnology.* 2 vols. New York: John Wiley & Sons, 2000, 651–54.

Lilford, Richard J., et al. "Monitoring Clincial Trials—Interim Data Should Be Publicly Available." *British Medical Journal* 323 (2001), 441–2.

London, Alex John. "The Ambiguity and the Exigency: Clarifying 'Standard of Care' Arguments in International Research." *Journal of Medicine and Philosophy* 25 (2000), 379–97.

McCrary, S. Van, Anderson, Cheryl B., Jakovljevic, Jelena, Khan, Tonya, McCullough, Laurence B., Wray, Nelda P., and Brody, Baruch A. "A National Survey of Policies on Disclosure of Conflicts of Interest in Biomedical Research." *New England Journal of Medicine* 343 (2000): 1621–26.

Madsen, S. M., et al. "Ethical Aspects of Clinical Trials: the Attitudes of Participants in Two Non-Cancer Trials." *Journal of Internal Medicine* 248 (2000), 463–74.

Mastroianni, Anna C. and Kahn, Jeffrey. "Swinging on the Pendulum: Shifting Views of Justice in Human Subjects Research." *Hastings Center Report* (May–June 2001), 21–28.

Mastroianni, Anna C.; Faden, Ruth R.; and Federman, Daniel, eds. *Women and Health Research: Ethical and Legal Issues of Including Women in Clinical Studies*. 2 vols. Washington, DC: National Academy Press, 1994.

Meldrum, Marcia L. "A Brief History of the Randomized Controlled Trial." *Hematology/Oncology Clinics of North America* 14 (2000), 745–60.

Michels, Robert. "Are Research Ethics Bad for Our Mental Health?" *New England Journal of Medicine* 340 (1999), 1427–30.

Mishkin, Barbara. "Law and Public Policy in Human Studies Research." *Perspectives in Biology and Medicine* 43 (2000), 362–72.

Moher, David; Schulz, Kenneth F.; and Altman, Douglas G. "The CONSORT Statement: Revised Recommendations for Improving the Quality of Reports of Parallel-Group Randomized Trials." *Annals of Internal Medicine* 134 (2001), 657–62.

Moreno, Jonathan D. "Goodbye to All That: The End of Moderate Protectionism in Human Subjects Research." *Hastings Center Report* (May–June 2001), 9–17.

———. *Undue Risk: Secret State Experiments on Humans*. New York: Routledge, 2001.

Moreno, Jonathan D.; Caplan, Arthur L.; Wolpe, Paul Root; and the Human Research Ethics Group (University of Pennsylvania Health Systems, Center for Bioethics. Project on Informed Consent). "Updating Protections for Human Subjects Involved in Research." *Journal of the American Medical Association* 280 (1998), 1951–58.

Morin, Karine, et al. "Managing Conflicts of Interest in the Conduct of Clinical Trials." *Journal of the American Medical Association* 287 (2002), 78–84.

Morse, Michael A.; Califf, Robert A.; and Sugarman, Jeremy. "Monitoring and Ensuring Safety during Clinical Research." *Journal of the American Medical Association* 285 (2001), 1201–05.

Nuffield Council on Bioethics. *The Ethics of Research Related to Healthcare in Developing Countries*. London: the Council, 2002.

Pence, Gregory. *Classic Cases in Medical Ethics*. 3rd ed New York: McGraw-Hill, 2000, Chapters 10 and 14.

Pincus, Harold Alan; Lieberman, Jeffrey A. and Ferris, Sandy, eds. *Ethics in Psychiatric Research: A Resource Manual for Human Subjects Protection*. Washington, DC: American Psychiatric Association, 1999.

Pullman, Daryl, and Wang, Xikui. "Adaptive Designs, Informed Consent, and the Ethics of Research." *Controlled Clinical Trials* 22 (2001), 203–10.

Rettig, Richard A. "The Industrialization of Clinical Research." *Health Affairs* (March/April 2000), 129–46.

Roberts, Laura Weiss, et al. "Placebos and Paradoxes in Psychiatric Research: An Ethics Perspective." *Biological Psychiatry* 49 (2001), 887–93.

Roberts, Marc J., and Reich, Michael R. "Ethical Analysis in Public Health." *Lancet* 359 (2002), 1055–9.

Robertson, John A. "Compensating Injured Research Subjects: The Law." *Hastings Center Report* 6 (1976), 29–31.

Rothman, David J. "Research, Human: Historical Aspects." In Warren Thomas Reich, ed. *Encyclopedia of Bioethics*. Revised ed. New York: Simon & Schuster Macmillan, 1995: 2248–58.

———. "The Shame of Medical Research." *New York Review of Books*. November 30, 2000, 60–4.

———. *Strangers at the Bedside: A History of How Law and Bioethics Transformed Medical Decision Making.* New York: Basic Books, 1991.

Sales, Bruce D., and Folkman, Susan, eds. *Ethics in Research with Human Participants*. Washington, DC: American Psychological Association, 2000.

Schafer, Arthur. "The Ethics of the Randomized Clinical Trial." *New England Journal of Medicine* 307 (1982), 719–24.

Schuklenk, Udo and Ashcroft, Richard. "International Research Ethics." *Bioethics* 14 (2000), 158–72.

Shalala, Donna. "Protecting Research Subjects—What Must Be Done." *New England Journal of Medicine* 343 (2000), 808–10.

Shamoo, Adil E., ed. *Ethics in Neurobiological Research with Human Subjects: The Baltimore Conference on Ethics.* Amsterdam: Gordon and Breach, 1997.

———, and Khin-Maung-Gyi, Felix A. *Ethics of the Use of Human Subjects in Research*. New York: Garland Publishers, 2002.

Sidel, Victor W. "The Social Responsibilities of Health Professionals." *Journal of the American Medical Association* 276 (1996), 1679–81.

Slinger, Robert and Moher, David. "How To Assess New Treatments." *Western Journal of Medicine* 174 (2001), 182–86.

Smith, Trevor. *Ethics in Medical Research: A Handbook of Good Practice*. New York: Cambridge University Press, 1999.

Sonis, Jeffrey, et al. "Teaching of Human Rights in US Medical Schools." *Journal of the American Medical Association* 276 (1996), 1676–78.

Spece, Roy G.; Shimm, David S.; Spece, Shimm Buchanan; and Buchanan, Allen, eds. *Conflicts of Interest in Clinical Practice and Research*. New York: Oxford University Press, 1996.

Steinbook, Richard A. "Protecting Research Subjects—the Crisis at Johns Hopkins." *New England Journal of Medicine* 346 (2002), 716–20.

Sugarman, Jeremy, et al. "How Proxies Make Decisions about Research for Patients with Alzheimer's Disease." *Journal of the American Geriatrics Society* 49 (2001), 1110–19.

———; Mastroianni, Anna C. and Kahn, Jeffrey P., eds. *Research with Human Subjects: Selected Policies and Resources*. Frederick, MD: University Publishing Group, 1998.

Tangwa, Godfrey B. "Moral Agency, Moral Worth and the Question of Double Standards in Medical Research in Developing Countries." *Developing World Bioethics* 1 (2001), 156–62.

Temple, Robert and Ellenberg, Susan S. "Placebo-Controlled Trials and Active-Control Trials in the Evaluation of New Treatments. Part 1: Ethical and Scientific Issues." *Annals of Internal Medicine* 133 (2000), 455–63.

——— and Ellenberg, Susan S. "Placebo-Controlled Trials and Active-Control Trials in the Evaluation of New Treatments. Part 2: Practical Issues and Specific Cases." *Annals of Internal Medicine* 133 (2000), 464–70.

U. K., Health Department, Gene Therapy Advisory Committee. "Guidance on Making Proposals to Conduct Gene Therapy Research on Human Subjects." *Human Gene Therapy* 12 (2001), 711–20.

U. K., Medical Research Council. *Guidelines for Good Clinical Practice in Clinical Trials*. London, England: Medical Research Council, 1998.

U. S. Congress, General Accounting Office. *Biomedical Research: HHS Direction Needed to Address Financial Conflicts of Interest.* Washington, DC: U.S Government Printing Office, 2001.

U. S., Department of Health and Human Services. "Protection of Human Research Subjects." *Federal Register* 66 (2001), 56775–80.

U. S., National Bioethics Advisory Commission. *Ethical and Policy Issues in International Research: Clinical Trials in Developing Countries*. 2 vols. Washington, DC: U.S. Government Printing Office, 2001.

U. S., National Bioethics Advisory Commission. *Ethical and Policy Issues in Research Involving Human Participants.* 2 vols. Washington, DC: U.S. Government Printing Office, 2001.

U. S., National Bioethics Advisory Commission. *Research Involving Persons With Mental Disorders That May Affect Decision-making Capacity*. 2 vols. Washington, DC: U.S. Government Printing Office, 1999.

U. S., National Commission for the Protection of Research Subjects. *Institutional Review Boards: Report and Reccomendations and Appendix.* 2 vols. Washington, DC: U.S. Government Printing Office, 1978.

Vanderpool, Harold Y., ed. *The Ethics of Research Involving Human Subjects: Facing the 21st Century*. Frederick, MD: University Publishing Group, 1996.

Veatch, Robert M. *Case Studies in Medical Ethics*. Cambridge, MA: Harvard University Press, 1977, Chapter 11.

———. *The Patient as Partner: A Theory of Human Experimentation Ethics*. Bloomington, IN: Indiana University Press, 1987.

———. "Three Theories of Informed Consent." In U.S. National Commission for the Protection of Human Subjects. *The Belmont Report: Appendix:* Vol. II. Washington, DC: US Government Printing Office, 1978, 26–1 to 26–66.

Warnock, Mary. "The Control and Regulation of Scientific and Medical Research." *Clinical Medicine* 1 (July/August 2001), 261–63.

Weir, Robert F., and Horton, Jay R. "Genetic Research, Adolescents, and Informed Consent." *Theoretical Medicine* 16 (1995): 347–73.

Weijer, Charles. "The Ethical Analysis of Risk." *Journal of Law, Medicine and Ethics,* 28 (2000), 344–61.

———. "Protecting Communities in Research: Philosophical and Pragmatic Challenges." *Cambridge Quarterly of Healthcare Ethics* 8 (1999), 501–13.

Weijer, Charles, et al. "Clinical Equipoise and Not the Uncertainty Principle Is the Moral Underpinning of the Randomised Controlled Trial." *British Medical Journal* 321 (2000), 756–58.

———. "Protecting Communities in Research: Current Guidelines and Limits of Extrapolation." *Nature Genetics* 23 (1999), 275–80.

Weijer, Charles, and Anderson, James A. "The Ethics Wars: Disputes over International Research." *Hastings Center Report* 31 (May–June 2001), 18–20.

Weijer, Charles, and Emanuel, Ezekiel J. "Protecting Communities in Biomedical Research." *Science* 289 (2000), 1142–44.

Weisstub, David N., ed. *Research on Human Subjects: Ethics, Law and Social Policy*. Kidlington, UK: Pergamon, 1998.

Wendler, Dave and Prasad, Kiran. "Core Safeguards for Clinical Research With Adults Who Are Unable to Consent." *Annals of Internal Medicine* 135 (2001), 514–23.

Wiesner, Georgia L., Lewis, Susan, and Scott, Jennifer. "Human Subjects Research, Ethics, Family, and Pedigree Studies." In Thomas H. Murray and Maxwell J. Mehlman, eds. *Ethical, Legal, and Policy Issues in Biotechnology.* 2 vols. New York: John Wiley & Sons, 2000, 595–611.

PAST ABUSES OF HUMAN RESEARCH SUBJECTS

Advisory Committee on Human Radiation Experiments. *Final Report*. Washington, DC: U.S. Government Printing Office, October 1995.

Altman, Lawrence K. *Who Goes First?: The Story of Self-Experimentation in Medicine*. Berkeley, CA: University of California Press, 1998.

Aly, Gotz, Chroust, Peter, and Pross, Christian. *Cleansing the Fatherland: Nazi Medicine and Racial Hygiene.* Baltimore, MD: Johns Hopkins University Press, 1994.

Andrews, George. *MKULTRA: The CIA's Top Secret Program in Human Experimentation and Behavior Modification*. Winston-Salem, NC: Healthnet Press, 2001.

Annas, George J., and Grodin, Michael A., eds. *The Nazi Doctors and the Nuremberg Code: Human Rights in Human Experiments*. New York: Oxford University Press, 1992.

Barondess, Jeremiah A. "Care of the Medical Ethos, with Some Comments on Research: Reflections after the Holocaust." *Perspectives in Biology and Medicine* 43 (2000), 308–24.

Buchanan, Allen. "Judging the Past: The Case of the Human Radiation Experiments." *Hastings Center Report* 26 (May–June 1996), 25–30.

Gillmore, Don. *I Swear by Apollo: Dr. Ewen Cameron and CIA Brainwashing Experiments*. Montreal: Eden Press, 1987.

Grodin, Michael A. "The Japanese Analogue." *Hastings Center Report* 26 (September–October 1996), 37–8.

Faden, Ruth R. "The Advisory Committee on Human Radiation Experiments: Reflections on a Presidential Commission." *Hastings Center Report* 26 (September–October 1996), 5–10.

———, ed. *The Human Radiation Experiments: Final Report of the Advisory Committee*. New York: Oxford University Press, 1996.

———; Lederer, Susan E.; and Moreno, Jonathan D. "US Medical Researchers, the Nuremberg Doctors Trial, and the Nuremberg Code." *Journal of the American Medical Association* 276 (1996), 1667–71.

Freedman, Benjamin. "Research, Unethical." In Warren Thomas Reich, ed. *Encyclopedia of Bioethics*. Revised ed. New York: Simon and Schuster Macmillan, 1995, 2258–61.

Goodwin, Bridget. *Keen as Mustard: Britain's Horrific Chemical Warfare Experiments in Australia*. St. Lucia, Australia: University of Queensland Press, 1998.

Hanauske-Abel, Hartmut M. "Not a Slippery Slope or Sudden Subversion: German Medicine and National Socialism in 1933." *British Medical Journal* 313 (1996), 1453–63.

Harris, Sheldon H. *Factories of Death: Japanese Biological Warfare 1932–45 and the American Cover Up*. New York: Routledge, 1994.

Harkness, Jon M. "Nuremberg and the Issue of Wartime Experiments on US Prisoners: The Green Committee." *Journal of the American Medical Association* 276 (1996), 1672–75.

Hornblum. Allen M. *Acres of Skin: Human Experiments at Holmesburg Prison: A True Story of Abuse and Exploitation in the Name of Medical Science*. Baltimore, MD: Johns Hopkins University Press, 1998.

———. "They Were Cheap and Available: Prisoners as Research Subjects in Twentieth Century America." *British Medical Journal* 315 (1997): 1437–41.

King, Nancy M. P. and Stein, Jane, eds. *Beyond Regulations: Ethics in Human Subjects Research.* Chapel Hill, NC: University of North Carolina Press, 1999.

Lederer, Susan E. *Subjected to Science: Human Experimentation in America before the Second World War*. Baltimore, MD: Johns Hopkins University Press, 1995.

Lifton, Robert Jay. *The Nazi Doctors: Medical Killing and the Psychology of Genocide*. New York: Basic Books, 1986.

Jones, James H. *Bad Blood: The Tuskegee Syphilis Experiment*. New and expanded ed. New York: Free Press, 1993.

Katz, Jay, with the assistance of Alexander Morgan Capron and Elanor Swift Glass. *Experimentaiton with Human Beings*. New York: Russell Sage Foundation, 1972.

Mann, Jonathan M., et al., eds. *Health and Human Rights: A Reader*. New York : Routledge, 1999.

Moreno, Jonathan D. *Undue Risk: Secret State Experiments on Humans*. New York: Routledge, 2001.

Posner, Gerald. *Mengele: The Complete Story*. London: Futura, 1987.

Proctor, Robert N. "Nazi Science and Nazi Medical Ethics: Some Myths and Misconceptions." *Perspectives in Biology and Medicine* 43 (2000), 335–46.

———. *Racial Hygiene: Medicine under the Nazis*. Cambridge, MA: Harvard University Press, 1988.

Reverby, Susan M. "Everyday Evil." *Hastings Center Report* 26 (September–October 1996), 38–39.

———, ed. *Tuskegee's Truths: Rethinking the Tuskegee Syphilis Study*. Chapel Hill, NC: University of North Carolina Press, 2000.

Seidelman, William E. "Nuremberg Lamentation: For the Forgotten Victims of Medical Science." *British Medical Journal* 313 (1996), 1463–67.

Shevell, Michael I. "Neurology's Witness to History: The Combined Intelligence Operative Sub-Committee Reports of Leo Alexander." *Neurology* 47 (1996), 1096–1103.

Thomas, Stephen B, and Quinn, Sandra Crouse. "The Tuskegee Syphilis Study, 1932 to 1972: Implications for HIV Education and AIDS Risk Education Programs in the Black Community." *American Journal of Public Health* 81 (1991), 1498–1505.

Weindling, Paul. "Human Guinea Pigs and the Ethics of Experimentation: The *BMJ*'s Correspondent at the Nuremberg Medical Trial." *British Medical Journal* 313 (1996), 1467–70.

Welsome, Eileen. *The Plutonium Files: America's Secret Medical Experiments in the Cold War*. New York: Dial Press, 1999.

White, Robert M. "Unraveling the Tuskegee Study of Untreated Syphilis." *Archives of Internal Medicine* 160 (2000), 585–98.

Barnard, Neal D., Kaufman Stephen R. "Animal Research Is Wasteful and Misleading." *Scientific American* 276 (February 1997), 80–82.

Bateson, Patrick. "When to Experiment on Animals." *New Scientist* 109 (February 1986), 30–32.

Beauchamp, Tom L. "Problems in Justifying Research on Animals." In National Institutes of Health, *National Symposium on Imperatives in Research Use: Scientific Needs and Animal Welfare* (NIH Publication No. 85–2746, 1985), 79–87.

Bekoff, Marc, with Meaney, Carron A., eds. *Encyclopedia of Animal Rights and Animal Welfare.* Westport, CT: Greenwood Press, 1998.

Blum, Deborah. *The Monkey Wars.* New York: Oxford University Press, 1994.

Botting, Jack H., and Morrison, Andrian R. "Animal Research Is Vital to Medicine." *Scientific American* 276 (February 1997), 83–85.

Brody, Baruch A. *The Ethics of Biomedical Research : An International Perspective.* New York: Oxford University Press, 1998, Chapter 1.

Cavalieri, Paola, and Singer, Peter, eds. *The Great Ape Project: Equality Beyond Humanity.* New York: St. Martin's Press, 1994.

Cohen, Carl, and Regan, Tom. *The Animal Rights Debate.* Lanham, MD: Rowman and Littlefield, 2001.

Cohen, Carl. "The Case for the Use of Animals in Research." *New England Journal of Medicine* 315 (1986), 865–70.

———. "Do Animals Have Rights?" *Ethics and Behavior* 7 (1997), 91–102.

Cothran, Helen, ed. *Animal Experimentation: Opposing Viewpoints.* Chicago, IL: Greenhaven Press, 2002.

Day, Nancy. *Animal Experimentation: Cruelty or Science?* Hillside, NJ: Enslow Publishers, Inc., 2000.

De Deyn, Peter P., ed. *The Ethics of Animal and Human Experimentation.* London: John Libbey, 1994.

DeGrazia, David. *Taking Animal Seriously: Mental Life and Moral Status.* New York: Cambridge University Press, 1996.

Dolan, Kevin. *Ethics, Animals and Science.* Malden, MA: Blackwell Science, 1999.

Donovan, Josephine and Adams, Carol J., eds. *Beyond Animal Rights: A Feminist Caring Ethic for the Treatment of Animals.* New York: Continuum, 1996.

Finsen, Lawrence and Fensen, Susan. *The Animal Rights Movement in America: From Compassion to Respect.* New York: Twyane, 1994.

Fox, Michael Allen. *The Case for Animal Experimentation: An Evolutionary and Ethical Perspective.* Berkeley, CA: University of California Press, 1986.

Garner, Robert. *Political Animals: Animal Protection Politics in Britain and the United States.* New York: St. Martin's Press, 1998.

Gluck, John P.; DiPasquale, Tony; and Orlans, F. Barbara; eds. *Applied Ethics in Animal Research: Philosophy, Regulation and Laboratory Applications.* West Lafayette, IN: Purdue University Press, 2001.

Grayson, Lesley. *Animals In Research: For and Against.* London: British Library, 2000.

Greek, C. Ray and Greek, Jean Swingle. *Sacred Cows and Golden Geese: The Human Cost of Experiments on Animals.* New York: Continuum, 2000.

Groves, Julian McAllister. *Hearts and Minds: The Controversy over Laboratory Animals.* Philadelphia, PA: Temple University Press, 1997.

Hart, Lynette A., ed. *Responsible Conduct with Animals in Research.* Oxford: Oxford University Press, 1998.

Haugen, David. *Animal Experimentation.* Chicago: Greenhaven Press, 2000.

Hayhurst, Chris. *Animal Testing: The Animal Rights Debate.* New York: Rosen Publishing Group, 2000.

Jamieson, Dale, and Regan, Tom. "On the Ethics of the Use of Animals in Science." In Tom Regan and Donald VanDeVeer, eds. *And Justice for All.* Totowa, NJ: Rowman and Littlefield, 1982, 169–96.

Kahn, Jeffrey, and Dell, Ralph. "Animal Research: III. Law and Policy." In Warren Thomas Reich, ed. *Encyclopedia of Bioethics.* Revised ed. New York: Simon & Schuster Macmillan, 1995, 153–58.

Kleinig, John. "Research on Animals, Ethics, Principles Governing Research on Animals." In Thomas H. Murray and Maxwell J. Mehlman, eds. *Ethical, Legal, and Policy Issues in Biotechnology.* 2 vols. New York: John Wiley & Sons, 2000, 1014–20.

Krause, A. Lanny and Renquist, David, eds. *Bioethics and the Use of Laboratory Animals: Ethics in Theory and Practice.* Dubuque, IA: Gregory C. Beniot, 2000.

Kuhse, Helga. "Interests." *Journal of Medical Ethics* 11 (1985), 146–49.

LaFollette, Hugh. *Brute Science: Dilemmas of Animal Experimentation.* New York: Routledge, 1996.

Leader, Robert W., and Stark, Dennis. "The Importance of Animals in Biomedical Research." *Perspectives in Biology and Medicine* 30 (1987), 470–85.

McCloskey, H. J. "The Moral Case for Experimentation on Animals." *Monist* 70 (1987), 64–82.

Midgley, Mary. *Animals and Why They Matter.* 2nd ed. Athens: University of Georgia Press, 1984.

Monamy, Vaughn. *Animal Experimentation: A Guide for the Issues.* New York: Cambridge University Press, 2000.

Mukerjee, Madhusree. "Trends in Animal Research." *Scientific American* 276 (February 1997), 86–93.

National Research Council, Committee on Regulatory Issues in Animal Care, *Definition of Pain and Distress and Reporting Requirements for Laboratory Animals.* Washington, DC: National Academy Press, 2000.

"On Animal Experimentation: Seeking Common Ground." *Cambridge Quarterly of Healthcare Ethics* 8 (1999), 9–87.

Orlans, F. Barbara. *In the Name of Science: Issues in Responsible Animal Experimentation.* New York: Oxford University Press, 1993.

———; Beauchamp, Tom L., Dresser, Rebecca, and Gluck, John P., eds. *The Human Use of Animals: Case Studies in Ethical Choice.* New York: Oxford University Press, 1998.

Parascandola, Mark. "Animal Research." In Ruth, Chadwick, ed. *Encyclopedia of Applied Ethics.* San Diego, CA: Academic Press, 1998, I, 151–60.

Paul, Ellen Frankel and Paul, Jeffrey. *Why Animal Experimentation Matters: The Use of Animals in Medical Research.* New Brunswick, NJ: Transaction Publishers, 2001.

Pence, Gregory. *Classic Cases in Medical Ethics.* 3rd ed. New York: McGraw Hill Companies, Inc. 2000, Chapter 9.

Pluhar, Evelyn B. Beyond Prejudice: The Moral Significance of Human and Nonhuman Animals. Durham, NC: Duke University Press, 1995.

Regan, Tom. *The Case for Animal Rights*. Berkeley, CA: University of California Press, 1983.

———. *Defending Animal Rights*. Urbana, IL: University of Illinois Press, 2001.

Rollin, Bernard E. *The Unheeded Cry: Animal Consciousness, Animal Pain, and Science*. Ames, IA: Iowa State University Press, 1998.

Rowan, Andrew N. "The Benefits and Ethics of Animal Research." *Scientific American* 276 (February 1997), 79.

———. *Of Mice, Models, and Men: A Critical Evaluation of Animal Research*. Albany, NY: State University of New York Press, 1984.

———; and Loew, Franklin M.; with Weer, Joan C. *The Animal Research Controversy: Protest, Process, and Public Policy—An Analysis of Strategic Issues*. North Grafton, MA: Center for Animals and Public Policy, Tufts University School of Veterinary Medicine, 1995.

The Royal Society. *Statement of the Royal Society's Position on the Use of Animals in Research*. London: Royal Society, January 2002.

———. *The Use of Genetically Modified Animals*. London: Royal Society, 2001.

Rudacille, Deborah. *The Scalpel and the Butterfly: The War between Animal Research and Animal Protection*. New York: Farrar, Strauss and Giroux, 2000.

Russow, Lilly-Marlene. "Research on Animals, Ethics, and the Moral Status of Animals." In Thomas H. Murray and Maxwell J. Mehlman, eds. *Ethical, Legal, and Policy Issues in Biotechnology*. 2 vols. New York: John Wiley & Sons, 2000, 1003–1014.

Ryder, Richard. *Victims of Science*. Revised edition. London: National Anti-Vivisection Society, 1983.

Scruton, Roger. *Animal Rights and Wrongs*. London: Demos, 1998.

Sherry, Clifford J. *Animal Rights: A Reference Handbook*. Santa Barbara, CA: ABC-CLIO, 1994.

Singer, Peter, *Animal Liberation,* 2nd ed. New York: New York Review of Books, 1990.

———. "Animal Research: II. Philosophical Issues." In Warren Thomas Reich, ed. *Encyclopedia of Bioethics*. Revised ed. New York: Simon & Schuster Macmillan, 1995, 147–53.

Singleton, Rivers, Jr. "Transgenic Animals: An Overview." In Thomas H. Murray and Maxwell J. Mehlman, eds. *Ethical, Legal, and Policy Issues in Biotechnology*. 2 vols. New York: John Wiley & Sons, 2000, 1088–98.

Smith, Jane A. and Boyd, Kenneth M., eds. *Lives in the Balance: The Ethics of Using Animals in Biomedical Research*. New York: Oxford University Press, 1991.

Spicer, Carol Mason, ed. "Appendix: V. Ethical Directives Pertaining to the Welfare and Use of Animals." In Warren Thomas Reich, ed. *Encyclopedia of Bioethics*. Revised ed. New York: Simon and Schuster Macmillan, 1995, 2801–17.

Tannebaum, Jerry and Rowan, Andrew M. "Rethinking the Morality of Animal Research." *Hastings Center Report* 15 (October 1985), 32–43.

U. S. Congress, Office of Technology Assessment. *Alternatives to the Use of Animals in Research, Education, and Testing*. Washington, DC: OTA, 1984.

U. S. National Institutes of Health, *National Symposium on Imperatives in Research Animal Use: Scientific Needs and Animal Welfare*. Washington, DC: U.S. Government Printing Office, 1985.

U. S. National Institutes of Health, Office for Protection from Research Risks. *Public Health Service Policy on Human Care and Use of Laboratory Animals*. Bethesda, MD: Office for Protection from Research Risks, National Institutes of Health, 1986.

Van Zutphen, L. F. M., et al., eds. *Principles of Laboratory Animal Science : A Contribution to the Humane Use and Care of Animals and to the Quality of Experimental Results*. New York: Elsevier, 1993.

Whorton, James C. "Animal Experimentation: I. Historical Aspects." In Warren Thomas Reich, ed. *Encyclopedia of Bioethics*. Revised ed. New York: Simon and Schuster Macmillan, 1995, 143–47.

Wolfensohn, Sarah, et al. *Handbook of Laboratory Animal Management and Welfare*. New York: Oxford University Press, 1994.

BIBLIOGRAPHIES

Bishop, Laura Jane and Nolen, Anita Lonnes. "Animals in Research and Education: Ethical Issues." *Scope Note 40*. Washington, DC: National Reference Center for Bioethics Literature, Georgetown University, 2001.

Goldstein, Doris Mueller. *Bioethics: A Guide to Information Sources*. Detroit, MI: Gale Research Company, 1982. See under "Research Involving Human Subjects."

Kistler, John M. *Animal Rights: A Subject Guide, Bibliography, and Internet Companion*. Westport, CT: Greenwood Press, 2000.

Lineback, Richard H., ed. *Philosopher's Index*. Vols. 1–. Bowling Green, OH: Philosophy Documentation Center, Bowling Green State University. Issued quarterly. See under "Animal Experimentation," "Experimentation," and "Research."

Walters, LeRoy, and Kahn, Tamar Joy, eds. *Bibliography of Bioethics*. Vols. 1–. Washington, D.C.: Kennedy Institute of Ethics, Georgetown University. Issued annually. See under "Animal Experimentation," and "Human Experimentation."

WORLD WIDE WEB RESOURCES

Alternatives to Animal Testing on the Web: (http://altweb.jhsph.edu)

Johns Hopkins Center for Alternatives to Animal Testing: CAAT (http://caat.jhsph.edu)

National Library of Medicine: PubMed (http://www.ncbi.nlm.nih.gov/PubMed/)

National Library of Medicine: LocatorPlus (http://locatorplus.gov/)

University Microfilms: Periodical Abstracts (http://www.umi.com/proquest)

7.
Eugenics and Human Genetics

INTRODUCTION

The last decade of the twentieth century and the first decade of this new century have been exciting times for human genetics. The detailed sequencing of the human genome will be completed in 2003, exactly fifty years after the discovery of the double helix by James Watson and Francis Crick. Parallel genome projects have already provided the genetic sequences for the fruit fly, a roundworm called *C. elegans,* a mustardlike plant named *Arabidopsis,* and at least sixty types of bacteria.[1] Within a year or two the mouse genome will also be sequenced.

These dramatic achievements of multiple genome projects will provide new understandings of health and disease, information about human evolution and migration, and, more controversially, insight into genetic factors in, or influences on, human behavior. The readings in this chapter explore two medical applications of new genetic knowledge: genetic testing and screening on one hand and human gene transfer aimed at treating disease (sometimes called *human gene therapy*) on the other. In a more speculative vein, the final readings in the chapter consider the moral arguments for and against enhancing human capabilities by genetic means.

While new scientific findings offer grounds for optimism about the future, some past attempts to apply genetic knowledge suggest that caution and vigilance may also be warranted. The initial readings in this chapter recount government-sponsored attempts to improve society by intervening in the reproductive decisions, or modifying the reproductive capacities, of human beings. The first of these eugenic programs emerged in the United States during the first half of the twentieth century. A second program, modeled in part on the U.S. experience and the writings of American eugenicists, was enacted in Germany when that country was governed by Adolf Hitler and the National Socialists. The extreme conclusion, and in some ways the logical outcome, of the German program was the Holocaust.

EUGENICS PROGRAMS IN THE TWENTIETH CENTURY

The definition of *eugenics* is controversial. One simple definition is that eugenics means "the study of human improvement by genetic means."[2] If this definition is accepted, one can discover eugenic proposals in writings as old as Plato's *Republic,* where selective breeding was proposed as a means of improving society.[3] The actual word *eugenics* was coined in 1883 by an English scientist, Francis Galton, who was a cousin of Charles Darwin. In his first major book, *Hereditary Genius,* published in 1869, and in later works Galton advocated a system of arranged marriages between men and women of distinction, with the aim of producing a group of gifted children and ultimately an improved British population.

In the eugenic programs of the twentieth century, the element of coercion by the state was added to the notion of eugenics as a social goal. The first systematic attempts to develop mandatory eugenic programs occurred in several states of the United States. The central aim of these programs was to prevent reproduction by people who were judged to be feeble-minded. The method by which this aim was to be achieved was involuntary sterilization. Daniel Kevles's essay chronicles the history of eugenic sterilization in the United States.

While several state courts struck down mandatory sterilization statutes as unconstitutional, the U.S. Supreme Court found Virginia's involuntary sterilization law to be compatible with the guarantees of the U.S. Constitution. Oliver Wendell Holmes wrote for the Supreme Court's majority and argued that if Carrie Buck's mother, Carrie herself, and Carrie's daughter were all feeble-minded, the state of Virginia was justified in attempting to prevent any further reproduction by Carrie Buck through involuntary sterilization. In Holmes's chilling words, "Three generations of imbeciles are enough." The full text of the court's 1927 *Buck v. Bell* decision is reprinted in this chapter. In his essay "Carrie Buck's Daughter" paleontologist Stephen Jay Gould critically examines the factual premises on which the Supreme Court based its decision.

The eugenic programs undertaken in several states of the United States were closely monitored by academics and policymakers in other parts of the world, and especially in Germany. There the method of mandatory sterilization was found to be compatible both with the academic field called "racial hygiene" and with the political agenda of the National Socialists. Jonathan Glover discusses the theory and practice of the Nazi sterilization program during the 1930s, when approximately 350,000 persons deemed unfit to reproduce were sterilized. As is well known, this sterilization effort was but an initial step on the road that led eventually to the extermination of "unworthy" individuals and groups in Nazi killing centers and concentration camps.[4]

THE HUMAN GENOME PROJECT

There can be no doubt that we live in the golden age of genetics, especially human genetics. Even before the 1950s, Gregor Mendel's classic work on various modes of inheritance was available as a framework for understanding how certain traits, like the colors of flowers, are transmitted from one generation to the next. However, Watson and Crick's discovery of the molecular structure of DNA in 1953 and the rapid advances made feasible by recombinant DNA techniques from the 1970s to the present have opened up entirely new possibilities for genetic diagnosis and therapy.

The genetic structure of human cells is incredibly intricate and complex. Within the nuclei of each human cell there are forty-six chromosomes. These chromosomes, in turn, are comprised of 30,000–50,000 genes plus intervening sequences; the function of the intervening sequences is not yet well understood. The simplest units into which the genes and intervening sequences can be analyzed are individual nucleotides or bases, designated by the familiar letters A, C, G, and T; two corresponding nucleotides form a base pair. It is estimated that each human cell contains approximately 3 billion base pairs.

Through the early years of the twenty-first century, we will witness an intensive international effort to complete the sequencing of the human genome and to achieve a better understanding of human genetic variation. Francis Collins and Victor McKusick, two leaders of human genetics and the human genome project, analyze the impact that current research is likely to have on medical diagnosis and treatment. They note that new genetic information will facilitate the more timely and precise diagnosis of human disease, as well as suggesting new approaches to treatment, whether through gene transfer or better targeted drug therapy. Collins and McKusick warn, however, that the same personal genetic information that provides medical benefits may expose individuals to new kinds of social and financial hazards, especially if such information is employed to sort people into risk categories.

In an essay that combines history with ethical and political analysis, James Watson describes the sequence of events that led a reluctant community of U.S. biomedical scientists to accept the importance of mapping and sequencing the human genome. As Watson notes with satisfaction, he insisted that a fixed percentage of the human genome project budget—initially 3 percent, later 5 percent—be set aside to the study the ethical, legal, and social implications of the project. The ELSI program, as it came to be known, has allowed philosophers, theologians, lawyers, social scientists, and clinicians to perform normative research on issues like those discussed in the current chapter. At the conclusion of his essay Watson predicts that behavioral genetics and genetic enhancement will become important topics as genetic knowledge continues to accrue. He argues that the main lesson to be drawn from the eugenic excesses of the past is that governments must be prevented from telling citizens what to do, and what not to do, in the genetic sphere.

Philosophers Allen Buchanan, Dan Brock, Norman Daniels, and Daniel Wikler have written an important book entitled *From Chance to Choice: Genetics and Justice.*[5] In the excerpt from this book reprinted here the authors extrapolate from current developments in human genetics to create five future scenarios—case studies that illustrate the moral dilemmas that may be faced by our children and grandchildren. Buchanan and colleagues focus primary attention on what they term *direct genetic interventions,* such as human gene transfer, and on a single *indirect genetic intervention*—the use of carefully tailored drugs designed to alleviate diseases caused (at least in part) by genetic factors. However, they also consider issues arising at the interface of human reproduction and genetics: preimplantation diagnosis and embryo selection, prenatal diagnosis, and the genetic screening of newborns. Rejecting both the public health model and the personal services model, Buchanan and his colleagues seek to develop a third approach to the public policy issues raised by genetic research. The authors' constructive proposal draws heavily on John Rawls's theory of justice and on a robust notion of equal opportunity that is indebted both to Rawls and to the writings of Norman Daniels on just health care.

European scholar Svante Pääbo considers possible nonmedical implications of the human genome project. The findings of this research will help us as humans to reconstruct our ancient history—that is, our sites of origin and the patterns of migration and conquest that have led to the current configuration of human ethnic groups and nations. At the same time, however, the genome project will reveal to what extent the human genome contains genes that are closely related to corresponding genes in "simple" organisms like the fruit fly and roundworms. Further research will also delineate more clearly the similarities and differences between humans and our closest nonhuman relatives, the great apes. In Pääbo's view, the fact that humans and chimpanzees show 99 percent similarity in their DNA sequences may raise intriguing questions about traditional notions of human uniqueness.

GENETIC TESTING AND SCREENING

As noted by Collins and McKusick, the human genome project will make more precise genetic *testing* possible. This type of testing will be applicable to the diagnosis of disease, or even a higher-than-average predisposition to develop a certain kind of disease later in life. However, as the science develops, more sophisticated types of genetic testing may also make possible the discovery of at least approximate correlations between genes (or small constellations of genes) and complex behavioral traits—for example, exceptional memory or specific personality characteristics.[6] The techniques of genetic testing can be employed at any of several stages in the human life cycle: between the time of in vitro fertilization and the time of embryo transfer (preimplantation diagnosis); after implantation but before birth (prenatal diagnosis); immediately after birth (newborn genetic testing); during childhood or adolescence; and in adulthood (for example, when reproductive decisions are being made). It is not yet clear whether the genetic testing of sperm and egg cells can be performed in ways that are both highly accurate and nondestructive to the cells being tested. Genetic *screening* involves the use of genetic testing in large populations—for example, all newborn infants.

The three essays in this section consider multiple dimensions of genetic testing and screening. Patricia Roche and George Annas assert that genetic information about oneself is almost uniquely personal and constitutes a kind of coded "future diary." In their view, individual genetic information should be shared with others only after the individual in question has been thoroughly counseled and has given his or her explicit consent to the release of the information. Roche and Annas advocate uniform federal legislation to protect genetic privacy in the United States. Canadian scholar Michael Burgess questions the exclusive focus on disclosure and consent that often characterizes discussions of genetic testing and screening. Burgess argues that an open-minded and wide-ranging consideration of genetic testing's potential benefits and harms is a necessary complement to respect for individual autonomy. In the final essay of this section Lainie Friedman Ross and Margaret Moon consider the moral justifications for the genetic testing of children. Their subtle analysis distinguishes between tests that confirm a probable diagnosis and tests that, with a higher or lower probability, can predict a future disease state even in an asymptomatic child. Ross and Moon also discuss the conditions under which mass newborn screening programs are morally justified. Like Burgess, they argue for a thoughtful, nuanced evaluation of both medical and psychosocial benefits and harms.

HUMAN GENE TRANSFER RESEARCH

In the history of medicine, diagnosis is often the necessary prelude to a cure. It thus seems likely that the capacity to identify genetic diseases and susceptibilities will provide new impetus for already existing efforts to develop ways to correct, or at least to compensate for, genetic defects. The general name usually given to these therapeutic initiatives is *gene therapy*, or, more broadly, *genetic intervention*.

A central distinction in any discussion of genetic intervention is the distinction between reproductive and nonreproductive cells, which are often called germ-line and somatic cells, respectively. Somatic cells, like skin or muscle cells, contain the full complement of forty-six chromosomes and cannot transmit genetic information to succeeding generations. In other words, the genetic information contained in somatic cells stops with us and is not passed on to our descendants. In contrast, germ-line cells, the egg and sperm cells, contain only twenty-three chromosomes and are capable of transmitting genetic information to our progeny in the next generation, as well as to their children and grandchildren.

A second important distinction in discussions of human genetic intervention is that between the cure or prevention of disease on one hand and the enhancement of human capabilities on the other. A genetic approach to the treatment of cystic fibrosis clearly would be regarded as gene therapy. In contrast, the attempt to increase stature or to improve the efficiency of long-term memory—in a child whose height or memory fall within the normal range—would probably be regarded by most observers as an effort to enhance capabilities rather than to cure disease. The two distinctions discussed in this and the preceding paragraph can be arrayed in the following two-by-two matrix:

	Somatic	**Germ-line**
Cure or prevention of disease	1	2
Enhancement of capabilities	3	4

In the late 1980s and early 1990s, the name generally applied to somatic-cell gene transfer to treat disease was gene therapy. This phrase had originally been suggested by scientists in 1970 as a less frightening alternative to the then-prevalent phrase *genetic engineering.*[7] However, the term *therapy* was potentially misleading because it tended to obscure the experimental character of human gene transfer. By 1995 at the latest, it had also become clear that human gene transfer would not immediately produce the dramatic therapeutic results that both scientists and the public had anticipated. Thus, in the late 1990s, several commentators recommended that the word *therapy* be replaced by the more neutral term *transfer* and that the entire phrase describing this technique include the word *research.*[8] The phrase *human gene transfer research* is therefore employed in this introduction as a more neutral and more accurate descriptor than *human gene therapy.*

By the end of 2001, more than 500 formal gene transfer protocols had been submitted to the National Institutes of Health for formal public review. Of these, approximately 475 studies were oriented toward the alleviation of disease. Almost two-thirds of the disease-oriented studies were conducted in human subjects who were afflicted with various kinds of cancers. Another 10 percent of the studies involved subjects with genetic disorders—for example, cystic fibrosis, a progressive disease of the lungs. Still other studies enlisted people with HIV infection or AIDS.

During the year 2000 the first clear-cut success occurred in human gene transfer research. Alain Fischer and his colleagues at the Necker Hospital in Paris, France, demonstrated decisive improvement in several children born with a genetically caused condition called "severe combined immunodeficiency."[9] David, the so-called boy in the bubble, had suffered from the same disease in the 1970s and early 1980s.[10] Fischer and his colleagues succeeded in transferring the gene that produces a missing enzyme into enough of the children's bone marrow cells to produce a clinical benefit that has now persisted for up to two and one-half years.[11] Gene-transfer researchers hope that this improvement will be permanent and that the children's immune systems will function normally into adulthood.

The three essays on human gene transfer research discuss several facets of this promising, but still very young, field. Ninkunj Somia and Inder Verma review the difficulties that researchers have encountered in attempting to create *vectors* for transporting genes into target cells. The authors summarize the characteristics of an ideal vector but reluctantly concede that no such vector currently exists. In his essay Theodore Friedmann describes the requirements for ethically acceptable, publicly accountable human gene transfer research. He tacitly acknowledges that the public oversight system for this field of research was weakened in 1997 and urges that the monitoring of serious adverse events in gene-transfer studies be enhanced. In Friedmann's view, researchers, universities, and companies should scrupulously avoid even the appearance of financial conflicts of interest in conducting such studies. Australian scholar Julian Savulescu reviews the tragic death of an 18-year-old young man, Jesse Gelsinger, in a gene-transfer study conducted at the University of Pennsylvania. After documenting numerous deficiencies in the way the Penn study was conducted, Savulescu goes on to argue that gene-transfer research in infants afflicted with life-threatening disorders can be morally justifiable if certain conditions are fulfilled.

GENETIC ENHANCEMENT

The last three selections in this chapter consider the more speculative possibility that in the future genetic technology will be employed to enhance human capabilities. In an adventuresome essay Jonathan Glover expresses dissatisfaction with at least some aspects of human nature as we know it. He also attempts to demolish several of the standard ethical objections to genetic enhancement. In the end Glover adopts a "principle of caution" and advocates a mixed system of public oversight for genetic enhancement—one that allows substantial leeway to parents in making decisions about the characteristics of their children while at the same time providing for a social check on possible parental excesses.

Jon Gordon's essay provides a reality check to current philosophical debates about human genetic enhancement. He points to the technical difficulties that have attended laboratory research aimed at enhancing nonhuman mammals and plants. In addition, Gordon argues that fears or claims about "controlling human evolution" through genetic enhancement techniques are grossly inflated, given the large number of unenhanced children that would be simultaneously produced through more traditional means. According to Gordon, unfounded hyperbole about the potential for genetic enhancement could have the unfortunate consequence of prompting panicked lawmakers to ban important kinds of basic laboratory research.

Without unconditionally rejecting genetic enhancement, philosopher Erik Parens questions whether the goals that proponents of enhancement seek to achieve are, on balance, worthwhile. Parens argues that enhancement seeks to replace change with stability and to substitute control or predictability for chance. In addition, he suggests that proposals for genetic enhancement tend toward utopianism. For Parens change, chance, and struggle are important—perhaps even essential—elements of the good life.

L. W.

NOTES

1. Russell F. Doolittle, "Microbial Genomes Multiply," *Nature* 416, no. 6882 (18 April 2002), 697–700.

2. *Encyclopedia Britannica,* Micropaedia, "Eugenics," 1989, 593.

3. Plato, *Republic,* III (410), IV, 456–61.

4. For the history of Nazi policies on the "unfit" and the "unworthy," see the following works: Robert Jay Lifton, *The Nazi Doctors: Medical Killing and the Psychology of Genocide* (New York: Basic Books, 1986); Robert N. Proctor, *Racial Hygiene: Medicine under the Nazis* (Cambridge, MA: Harvard University Press, 1988); Michael Burleigh and Wolfgang Wipperman, *The Racial State: Germany 1933–1945* (Cambridge: Cambridge University Press, 1991); and Michael Burleigh, *Death and Deliverance: "Euthanasia" in Germany 1900–1945* (Cambridge: Cambridge University Press, 1994).

5. Allan Buchanan et al., *From Chance to Choice: Genetics and Justice* (New York: Cambridge University Press, 2000).

6. For a primer on behavioral genetics, see Robert Plomin et al., *Behavioral Genetics,* 3d ed. (New York: W. H. Freeman, 1997).

7. LeRoy Walters, "Gene Therapy: Overview," in Thomas H. Murray and Maxwell J. Mehlman, eds., *Encyclopedia of Ethical, Legal, and Policy Issues in Biotechnology,* 2 vols. (New York: John Wiley and Sons, 2000), 336–42.

8. Larry R. Churchill et al., "Genetic Research as Therapy: Implications of 'Gene Therapy' for Informed Consent," *Journal of Law, Medicine, and Ethics* 26, no. 1 (Spring 1998), 38–47.

9. Marina Cavazzana-Calvo et al., "Gene Therapy of Severe Combined Immunodeficiency (SCID)-X1 Disease," *Science* 288, no. 5466 (28 April 2000), 627–29.

10. See LeRoy Walters and Julie Gage Palmer, *The Ethics of Human Gene Therapy* (New York: Oxford University Press, 1997), xiii–xvi.

11. Salima Hacein-Bey-Abina et al., "Sustained Correction of X-Linked Severe Combined Immunodeficiency by *ex vivo* Gene Therapy," *New England Journal of Medicine* 346, no. 16 (18 April 2002), 1241–43.

Eugenics Programs in the Twentieth Century

DANIEL J. KEVLES

Eugenics and Human Rights

Daniel Kevles is the Stanley Woodward Professor of History at Yale University. He has published extensively about the history of science in America; the interplay of science and society past and present; and scientific fraud and misconduct. His publications include *In the Name of Eugenics: Genetics and the Uses of Human Heredity* (Harvard University Press) and *The Baltimore Case: A Trial of Politics, Science, and Character* (Norton).

During the Nazi era in Germany, eugenics prompted the sterilisation of several hundred thousand people, then helped lead to antisemitic programmes of euthanasia and ultimately, of course, to the death camps. The association of eugenics with the Nazis is so strong that many people were surprised at the news several years ago that Sweden had sterilised around 60,000 people (mostly women) between the 1930s and 1970s. The intention was to reduce the number of children born with genetic diseases and disorders. After the turn of the century, eugenics movements—including demands for sterilisation of people considered unfit—had, in fact, blossomed in the United States, Canada, Britain, and Scandinavia, not to mention elsewhere in Europe and in parts of Latin America and Asia. Eugenics was not therefore unique to the Nazis. It could, and did, happen everywhere.

ORIGINS OF EUGENICS

Modern eugenics was rooted in the social darwinism of the late 19th century, with all its metaphors of fitness, competition, and rationalisations of inequality. Indeed, Francis Galton, a cousin of Charles Darwin and an accomplished scientist in his own right, coined the word eugenics. Galton promoted the ideal of improving the human race by getting rid of the "undesirables" and multiplying the "desirables." Eugenics began to flourish after the rediscovery, in 1900, of Mendel's theory that the biological make up of organisms is determined by certain factors, later identified with genes. The application of mendelism to human beings reinforced the idea that we are determined almost entirely by our "germ plasm."

Eugenic doctrines were articulated by physicians, mental health professionals, and scientists—notably biologists who were pursuing the new discipline of genetics—and were widely popularised in books, lectures, and articles for the educated public of the day. Publications were bolstered by the research pouring out of institutes for the study of eugenics or "race biology." These had been established in several countries, including Denmark, Sweden, Britain, and the United States. The experts raised the spectre of social degeneration, insisting that "feebleminded" people (the term then commonly applied to people believed to be mentally retarded) were responsible for a wide range of social problems and were proliferating at a rate that threatened social resources and stability. Feebleminded women were held to be driven by a heedless sexuality, the product of biologically grounded flaws in their moral character that led them to prostitution and producing illegitimate children. "Hereditarian" biology attributed poverty and criminality to bad genes rather than to flaws in the social corpus.

A DRIVE FOR SOCIAL IMPROVEMENT

Much of eugenics belonged to the wave of progressive social reform that swept through western Europe and North America during the early decades of the

Reprinted from the *British Medical Journal* 1999;319:435–438, with permission from BMJ Publishing Group. Copyright © 1999, the British Medical Association.

century. For progressives, eugenics was a branch of the drive for social improvement or perfection that many reformers of the day thought might be achieved through the deployment of science to good social ends. Eugenics, of course, also drew appreciable support from social conservatives, concerned to prevent the proliferation of lower income groups and save on the cost of caring for them. The progressives and the conservatives found common ground in attributing phenomena such as crime, slums, prostitution, and alcoholism primarily to biology and in believing that biology might be used to eliminate these discordances of modern, urban, industrial society.

Race was a minor subtext in Scandinavian and British eugenics, but it played a major part in the American and Canadian versions of the creed. North American eugenicists were particularly disturbed by the immigrants from eastern and southern Europe who had been flooding into their countries since the late 19th century. They considered these people not only racially different from but inferior to the Anglo-Saxon majority, partly because their representation among the criminals, prostitutes, slum dwellers, and feebleminded in many cities was disproportionately high. Anglo-American eugenicists fastened on British data indicating that half of each generation was produced by no more than a quarter of married people in the preceding generation, and that the prolific quarter was disproportionately located among the "dregs" of society. Eugenic reasoning in the United States had it that if deficiencies in immigrants were hereditary and eastern European immigrants outreproduced natives of Anglo-Saxon stock, then inevitably the quality of the American population would decline.

POSITIVE AND NEGATIVE EUGENICS

Eugenicists on both sides of the Atlantic argued for a two pronged programme that would increase the frequency of "socially good" genes in the population and decrease that of "bad genes." One prong was positive eugenics, which meant manipulating human heredity or breeding, or both, to produce superior people; the other was negative eugenics, which meant improving the quality of the human race by eliminating or excluding biologically inferior people from the population.

In Britain between the wars, positive eugenic thinking led to proposals (unsuccessful ones) for family allowances that would be proportional to income. In the United States, it fostered "fitter family" competitions. These became a standard feature at a number of state fairs and were held in the "human stock" sections. At the 1924 Kansas Free Fair, winning families in the three categories—small, average, and large—were awarded a governor's fitter family trophy. "Grade A" individuals received a medal that portrayed two diaphanously garbed parents, their arms outstretched toward their (presumably) eugenically meritorious infant. It is hard to know exactly what made these families and individuals stand out as fit, but the fact that all entrants had to take an IQ test and the Wasserman test for syphilis says something about the organisers' views of necessary qualities.

Much more was urged for negative eugenics, notably the passage of eugenic sterilisation laws. By the late 1920s, sterilisation laws had been enacted in two dozen American states, largely in the middle Atlantic region, the Midwest, and California. By 1933, California had subjected more people to eugenic sterilisation than had all other states of the union combined. Similar measures were passed in Canada, in the provinces of British Columbia and Alberta. Almost everywhere they were passed, however, the laws reached only as far as the inmates of state institutions for the mentally handicapped or mentally ill. People in private care or in the care of their families escaped them. Thus, the laws tended to discriminate against poorer people and minority groups. In California, for example, the sterilisation rates of blacks and foreign immigrants were twice as high as would be expected from their representation in the general population.

SOCIETY BEFORE INDIVIDUAL RIGHTS

The sterilisation laws rode roughshod over private human rights, holding them subordinate to an allegedly greater public good. This reasoning figured explicitly in the US Supreme Court's eight to one decision, in 1927, in the case of Buck versus Bell, which upheld Virginia's eugenic sterilisation law. Justice Oliver Wendell Holmes, writing for the majority, averred: "We have seen more than once that the public welfare may call upon the best citizens for their lives. It would be strange if it could not call upon those who already sap the strength of the State for these lesser sacrifices, often not felt to be such by those concerned, in order to prevent our being swamped with incompetence. It is better for all the world, if instead of waiting to execute degenerate offspring for crime, or to let them starve for their imbecility, society can prevent those who are manifestly unfit from continuing their kind. The principle that sustains compulsory vaccination is broad enough to cover cutting the Fallopian tubes. . . . Three generations of imbeciles are enough."[1]

In Alberta, the premier called sterilisation far more effective than segregation and, perhaps taking a leaf from Holmes's book, insisted that "the argument of freedom or right of the individual can no longer hold good where the welfare of the state and society is concerned."[2,3]

Sterilisation rates climbed with the onset of the worldwide economic depression in 1929. In parts of Canada, in the deep south of the United States, and throughout Scandinavia, sterilisation acquired broad support. This was not primarily on eugenic grounds (though some hereditarian-minded mental health professionals continued to urge it for that purpose) but on economic ones. Sterilisation raised the prospect of reducing the cost of institutional care and of poor relief. Even geneticists who disparaged sterilisation as the remedy for degeneration held that sterilising mentally disabled people would yield a social benefit because it would prevent children being born to parents who could not care for them.

In Scandinavia, sterilisation was broadly endorsed by Social Democrats as part of the scientifically oriented planning of the new welfare state. Alva Myrdal spoke for her husband, Gunnar, and for numerous liberals like themselves when in 1941 she wrote, "In our day of highly accelerated social reforms the need for sterilization on social grounds gains new momentum. Generous social reforms may facilitate home-making and childbearing more than before among the groups of less desirable as well as more desirable parents. [Such a trend] demands some corresponding corrective."[4] On such foundations among others, sterilisation programmes continued in several American states, in Alberta, and in Scandinavia well into the 1970s.

EUGENICS UNDER FIRE

During the interwar years, however, eugenic doctrines were increasingly criticised on scientific grounds and for their class and racial bias. It was shown that many mental disabilities have nothing to do with genes; that those which do are not simple products of genetic make up; and that most human behaviours (including deviant ones) are shaped by environment at least as much as by biological heredity, if they are fashioned by genes at all. Science aside, eugenics became malodorous precisely because of its connection with Hitler's regime, especially after the second world war, when its complicity in the Nazi death camps was revealed.

All along, many people on both sides of the Atlantic had ethical reservations about sterilisation and were squeamish about forcibly subjecting people to the knife. Attempts to authorise eugenic sterilisation in Britain had reached their high water mark in the debates over the Mental Deficiency Act in 1913. They failed not least because of powerful objections from civil libertarians insistent on defending individual human rights. More than a third of the American states declined to pass sterilisation laws, and so did the eastern provinces of Canada. Most of the American states which passed the laws declined to enforce them, and British Columbia's law was enforced very little.

The opposition comprised coalitions that varied in composition. It came from mental health professionals who doubted the scientific underpinnings of eugenics and from civil libertarians, some of whom warned that compulsory sterilisation constituted "Hitlerisation." Sterilisation was also vigorously resisted by Roman Catholics—partly because it was contrary to church doctrine and partly because many recent immigrants to the United States were Catholics and thus disproportionately placed in jeopardy of the knife. For many people before the second world war, individual human rights mattered far more than those sanctioned by the science, law, and perceived social needs of the era.

The revelations of the holocaust strengthened the moral objections to eugenics and sterilisation, and so did the increasing worldwide discussion of human rights, a foundation for which was the Universal Declaration of Human Rights that the General Assembly of the United Nations adopted and proclaimed in 1948. Since then, the movement for women's rights and reproductive freedom has further transformed moral sensibilities about eugenics, so that we recoil at the majority's ruling in Buck versus Bell. History at the least has taught us that concern for individual rights belongs at the heart of whatever stratagems we may devise for deploying our rapidly growing knowledge of human and medical genetics.

NOTES

1. Buck v Bell [1927] 274 US 201–7.

2. Christian T. The mentally ill and human rights in Alberta: a study of the Alberta Sexual Sterilisation Act. Edmonton: Faculty of Law, University of Alberta, nd: 27.

3. McLaren A. Our own master race: eugenics in Canada, 1885–1945. Toronto: McClelland and Stewart, 1990.

4. Broberg G., Roll-Hansen N., eds. Eugenics and the welfare state: sterilization policy in Denmark, Sweden, Norway, and Finland. East Lansing: Michigan State University Press, 1996.

UNITED STATES SUPREME COURT

Buck v. Bell (1927)

Argued April 22, 1927. Decided May 2, 1927.

On Writ of Error to the Supreme Court of Appeals of the State of Virginia to review a judgment affirming a judgment of the Circuit Court for Amherst County directing the sterilization of an inmate of a Colony for Epileptics and Feeble Minded. Affirmed. . . .*

The facts are stated in the opinion.

Mr. I. P. Whitehead argued the cause and filed a brief for plaintiff in error:

The act of assembly of Virginia does not provide due process of law guaranteed by the 14th Amendment to the Constitution of the United States. . . .

The act of assembly of Virginia denies to the plaintiff and other inmates of the State Colony for Epileptics and Feebleminded the equal protection of the law guaranteed by the 14th Amendment to the Constitution of the United States. . . .

Mr. Aubrey E. Strode argued the cause and filed a brief for defendant in error:

The act affords due process of law. . . .

The act is a valid exercise of the police power.

The statute may be sustained as based upon a reasonable classification. . . .

MR. JUSTICE HOLMES delivered the opinion of the court:

This is a writ of error to review a judgment of the supreme court of appeals of the state of Virginia, affirming a judgment of the circuit court of Amherst county, by which the defendant in error, the superintendent of the State Colony for Epileptics and Feeble Minded, was ordered to perform the operation of salpingectomy upon Carrie Buck, the plaintiff in error, for the purpose of making her sterile. 143 Va. 310, 51 A.L.R. 855, 130 S. E. 516. The case comes here upon the contention that the statute authorizing the judgment is void under the 14th Amendment as denying to the plaintiff in error due process of law and the equal protection of the laws.

Carrie Buck is a feeble minded white woman who was committed to the State Colony above mentioned in due form. She is the daughter of a feeble minded mother in the same institution, and the mother of an illegitimate feeble minded child. She was eighteen years old at the time of the trial of her case in the circuit court, in the latter part of 1924. An Act of Virginia approved March 20, 1924, recites that the health of the patient and the welfare of society may be promoted in certain cases by the sterilization of mental defectives, under careful safeguard, etc.; that the sterilization may be effected in males by vasectomy and in females by salpingectomy, without serious pain or substantial danger to life; that the Commonwealth is supporting in various institutions many defective persons who if now discharged would become a menace but if incapable of procreating might be discharged with safety and become self-supporting with benefit to themselves and to society; and that experience has shown that heredity plays an important part in the transmission of insanity, imbecility, etc. The statute then enacts that whenever the superintendent of certain institutions including the above named State Colony shall be of opinion that it is for the best interests of the patients and of society that an inmate under his care should be sexually sterilized, he may have the operation performed upon any patient afflicted with hereditary forms of insanity, imbecility, etc., on complying with the very careful provisions by which the act protects the patients from possible abuse.

*Editor's note: Some references to other court decisions are omitted or abbreviated.

From *United States [Supreme Court] Reports* 274 (1927), 200–08.

The superintendent first presents a petition to the special board of directors of his hospital or colony, stating the facts and the grounds for his opinion, verified by affidavit. Notice of the petition and of the time and place of the hearing in the institution is to be served upon the inmate, and also upon his guardian, and if there is no guardian the superintendent is to apply to the circuit court of the county to appoint one. If the inmate is a minor notice also is to be given to his parents if any with a copy of the petition. The board is to see to it that the inmate may attend the hearings if desired by him or his guardian. The evidence is all to be reduced to writing, and after the board has made its order for or against the operation, the superintendent, or the inmate, or his guardian, may appeal to the circuit court of the county. The circuit court may consider the record of the board and the evidence before it and such other admissible evidence as may be offered, and may affirm, revise, or reverse the order of the board and enter such order as it deems just. Finally any party may apply to the supreme court of appeals, which, if it grants the appeal, is to hear the case upon the record of the trial in the circuit court and may enter such order as it thinks the circuit court should have entered. There can be no doubt that so far as procedure is concerned the rights of the patient are most carefully considered, and as every step in this case was taken in scrupulous compliance with the statute and after months of observation, there is no doubt that in that respect the plaintiff in error has had due process of law.

The attack is not upon the procedure but upon the substantive law. It seems to be contended that in no circumstances could such an order be justified. It certainly is contended that the order cannot be justified upon the existing grounds. The judgment finds the facts that have been recited and that Carrie Buck "is the probable potential parent of socially inadequate offspring, likewise afflicted, that she may be sexually sterilized without detriment to her general health and that her welfare and that of society will be promoted by her sterilization," and thereupon makes the order. In view of the general declarations of the legislature and the specific findings of the court obviously we cannot say as matter of law that the grounds do not exist, and if they exist they justify the result. We have seen more than once that the public welfare may call upon the best citizens for their lives. It would be strange if it could not call upon those who already sap the strength of the state for these lesser sacrifices, often not felt to be such by those concerned, in order to prevent our being swamped with incompetence. It is better for all the world, if instead of waiting to execute degenerate offspring for crime, or to let them starve for their imbecility, society can prevent those who are manifestly unfit from continuing their kind. The principle that sustains compulsory vaccination is broad enough to cover cutting the Fallopian tubes. Jacobson v. Massachusetts, 197 U.S. 11. Three generations of imbeciles are enough.

But, it is said, however it might be if this reasoning were applied generally, it fails when it is confined to the small number who are in the institutions named and is not applied to the multitudes outside. It is the usual last resort of constitutional arguments to point out shortcomings of this sort. But the answer is that the law does all that is needed when it does all that it can, indicates a policy, applies it to all within the lines, and seeks to bring within the lines all similarly situated so far and so fast as its means allow. Of course so far as the operations enable those who otherwise must be kept confined to be returned to the world, and thus open the asylum to others, the equality aimed at will be more nearly reached.

Judgment affirmed.

MR. JUSTICE BUTLER dissents.

STEPHEN JAY GOULD

Carrie Buck's Daughter

Stephen Jay Gould (d. 2002) was Professor of Geology and Zoology at Harvard University. His main interests lay in palaeontology and evolutionary biology. He was a frequent and popular speak on the sciences. His published work included *The Mismeasure of Man* (Norton), *The Panda's Thumb: More Reflections in Natural History* (Norton), and *The Flamingo's Smile* (Norton).

The Lord really put it on the line in his preface to that prototype of all prescriptions, the Ten Commandments:

> . . . for I, the Lord thy God, am a jealous God, visiting the iniquity of the fathers upon the children unto the third and fourth generation of them that hate me (Exod. 20:5).

The terror of this statement lies in its patent unfairness—its promise to punish guiltless offspring for the misdeeds of their distant forebears.

A different form of guilt by genealogical association attempts to remove this stigma of injustice by denying a cherished premise of Western thought—human free will. If offspring are tainted not simply by the deeds of their parents but by a material form of evil transferred directly by biological inheritance, then "the iniquity of the fathers" becomes a signal or warning for probable misbehavior of their sons. Thus Plato, while denying that children should suffer directly for the crimes of their parents, nonetheless defended the banishment of a personally guiltless man whose father, grandfather and great-grandfather had all been condemned to death.

It is, perhaps, merely coincidental that both Jehovah and Plato chose three generations as their criterion for establishing different forms of guilt by association. Yet we maintain a strong folk, or vernacular, tradition for viewing triple occurrences as minimal evidence of regularity. Bad things, we are told, come in threes. Two may represent an accidental association; three is a pattern. Perhaps, then, we should not wonder that our own century's most famous pronouncement of blood guilt employed the same criterion—Oliver Wendell Holmes's defense of compulsory sterilization in Virginia (Supreme Court decision of 1927 in *Buck v. Bell*): "three generations of imbeciles are enough."

Restrictions upon immigration, with national quotas set to discriminate against those deemed mentally unfit by early versions of IQ testing, marked the greatest triumph of the American eugenics movement—the flawed hereditarian doctrine, so popular earlier in our century and by no means extinct today . . . that attempted to "improve" our human stock by preventing the propagation of those deemed biologically unfit and encouraging procreation among the supposedly worthy. But the movement to enact and enforce laws for compulsory "eugenic" sterilization had an impact and success scarcely less pronounced. If we could debar the shiftless and the stupid from our shores, we might also prevent the propagation of those similarly afflicted but already here.

The movement for compulsory sterilization began in earnest during the 1890s, abetted by two major factors—the rise of eugenics as an influential political movement and the perfection of safe and simple operations (vasectomy for men and salpingectomy, the cutting and tying of Fallopian tubes, for women) to replace castration and other socially unacceptable forms of mutilation. Indiana passed the first sterilization act based on eugenic principles in 1907 (a few states had previously mandated castration as a puni-

Reprinted from *THE FLAMINGO'S SMILE: Reflections in Natural History,* by Stephen Jay Gould, by permission of W. W. Norton and Company, Inc. Copyright © 1985 by Stephen Jay Gould.

tive measure for certain sexual crimes, although such laws were rarely enforced and usually overturned by judicial review). Like so many others to follow, it provided for sterilization of afflicted people residing in the state's "care," either as inmates of mental hospitals and homes for the feeble-minded or as inhabitants of prisons. Sterilization could be imposed upon those judged insane, idiotic, imbecilic, or moronic, and upon convicted rapists or criminals when recommended by a board of experts.

By the 1930s, more than thirty states had passed similar laws, often with an expanded list of so-called hereditary defects, including alcoholism and drug addiction in some states, and even blindness and deafness in others. These laws were continually challenged and rarely enforced in most states; only California and Virginia applied them zealously. By January 1935, some 20,000 forced "eugenic" sterilizations had been performed in the United States, nearly half in California.

No organization crusaded more vociferously and successfully for these laws than the Eugenics Record Office, the semiofficial arm and repository of data for the eugenics movement in America. Harry Laughlin, superintendent of the Eugenics Record Office, dedicated most of his career to a tireless campaign of writing and lobbying for eugenic sterilization. He hoped, thereby, to eliminate in two generations the genes of what he called the "submerged tenth"—"the most worthless one-tenth of our present population." He proposed a "model sterilization law" in 1922, designed

> to prevent the procreation of persons socially inadequate from defective inheritance, by authorizing and providing for eugenical sterilization of certain potential parents carrying degenerate hereditary qualities.

This model bill became the prototype for most laws passed in America, although few states cast their net as widely as Laughlin advised. (Laughlin's categories encompassed "blind, including those with seriously impaired vision; deaf, including those with seriously impaired hearing; and dependent, including orphans, ne'er-do-wells, the homeless, tramps, and paupers.") Laughlin's suggestions were better heeded in Nazi Germany, where his model act inspired the infamous and stringently enforced *Erbgesundheitsrecht,* leading by the eve of World War II to the sterilization of some 375,000 people, most for "congenital feeble-mindedness," but including nearly 4,000 for blindness and deafness.

The campaign for forced eugenic sterilization in America reached its climax and height of respectability in 1927, when the Supreme Court, by an 8–1 vote, upheld the Virginia sterilization bill in *Buck v. Bell.* Oliver Wendell Holmes, then in his mid-eighties and the most celebrated jurist in America, wrote the majority opinion with his customary verve and power of style. It included the notorious paragraph, with its chilling tag line, cited ever since as the quintessential statement of eugenic principles. Remembering with pride his own distant experiences as an infantryman in the Civil War, Holmes wrote:

> We have seen more than once that the public welfare may call upon the best citizens for their lives. It would be strange if it could not call upon those who already sap the strength of the state for these lesser sacrifices. . . . It is better for all the world, if instead of waiting to execute degenerate offspring for crime, or to let them starve for their imbecility, society can prevent those who are manifestly unfit from continuing their kind. The principle that sustains compulsory vaccination is broad enough to cover cutting the Fallopian tubes. Three generations of imbeciles are enough.

Who, then, were the famous "three generations of imbeciles," and why should they still compel our interest?

When the state of Virginia passed its compulsory sterilization law in 1924, Carrie Buck, an eighteen-year-old white woman, lived as an involuntary resident at the State Colony for Epileptics and Feeble-Minded. As the first person selected for sterilization under the new act, Carrie Buck became the focus for a constitutional challenge launched, in part, by conservative Virginia Christians who held, according to eugenical "modernists," antiquated views about individual preferences and "benevolent" state power. (Simplistic political labels do not apply in this case, and rarely in general for that matter. We usually regard eugenics as a conservative movement and its most vocal critics as members of the left. This alignment has generally held in our own decade. But eugenics, touted in its day as the latest in scientific modernism, attracted many liberals and numbered among its most vociferous critics groups often labeled as reactionary and antiscientific. If any political lesson emerges from these shifting allegiances, we might consider the true inalienability of certain human rights.)

But why was Carrie Buck in the State Colony and why was she selected? Oliver Wendell Holmes upheld her choice as judicious in the opening lines of his 1927 opinion:

> Carrie Buck is a feeble-minded white woman who was committed to the State Colony. . . . She is the daughter of a feeble-minded mother in the same institution, and the mother of an illegitimate feeble-minded child.

In short, inheritance stood as the crucial issue (indeed as the driving force behind all eugenics). For if measured mental deficiency arose from malnourishment, either of body or mind, and not from tainted genes, then how could sterilization be justified? If decent food, upbringing, medical care, and education might make a worthy citizen of Carrie Buck's daughter, how could the State of Virginia justify the severing of Carrie's Fallopian tubes against her will? (Some forms of mental deficiency are passed by inheritance in family lines, but most are not—a scarcely surprising conclusion when we consider the thousand shocks that beset us all during our lives, from abnormalities in embryonic growth to traumas of birth, malnourishment, rejection, and poverty. In any case, no fair-minded person today would credit Laughlin's social criteria for the identification of hereditary deficiency—ne'er-do-wells, the homeless, tramps, and paupers—although we shall soon see that Carrie Buck was committed on these grounds.)

When Carrie Buck's case emerged as the crucial test of Virginia's law, the chief honchos of eugenics understood that the time had come to put up or shut up on the crucial issue of inheritance. Thus, the Eugenics Record Office sent Arthur H. Estabrook, their crack fieldworker, to Virginia for a "scientific" study of the case. Harry Laughlin himself provided a deposition, and his brief for inheritance was presented at the local trial that affirmed Virginia's law and later worked its way to the Supreme Court as *Buck v. Bell.*

Laughlin made two major points to the court. First, that Carrie Buck and her mother, Emma Buck, were feebleminded by the Stanford-Binet test of IQ then in its own infancy. Carrie scored a mental age of nine years, Emma of seven years and eleven months. (These figures ranked them technically as "imbeciles" by definitions of the day, hence Holmes's later choice of words—though his infamous line is often misquoted as "three generations of idiots." Imbeciles displayed a mental age of six to nine years; idiots performed worse, morons better, to round out the old nomenclature of mental deficiency.) Second, that most feeblemindedness resides ineluctably in the genes, and that Carrie Buck surely belonged with this majority. Laughlin reported:

> Generally feeble-mindedness is caused by the inheritance of degenerate qualities; but sometimes it might be caused by environmental factors which are not hereditary. In the case given, the evidence points strongly toward the feeble-mindedness and moral delinquency of Carrie Buck being due, primarily, to inheritance and not to environment.

Carrie Buck's daughter was then, and has always been, the pivotal figure of this painful case. I noted in beginning this essay that we tend (often at our peril) to regard two as potential accident and three as an established pattern. The supposed imbecility of Emma and Carrie might have been an unfortunate coincidence, but the diagnosis of similar deficiency for Vivian Buck (made by a social worker, as we shall see, when Vivian was but six months old) tipped the balance in Laughlin's favor and led Holmes to declare the Buck lineage inherently corrupt by deficient heredity. Vivian sealed the pattern—*three* generations of imbeciles are enough. Besides, had Carrie not given illegitimate birth to Vivian, the issue (in both senses) would never have emerged.

Oliver Wendell Holmes viewed his work with pride. The man so renowned for his principle of judicial restraint, who had proclaimed that freedom must not be curtailed without "clear and present danger"—without the equivalent of falsely yelling "fire" in a crowded theater—wrote of his judgment in *Buck v. Bell:* "I felt that I was getting near the first principle of real reform."

And so *Buck v. Bell* remained for fifty years, a footnote to a moment of American history perhaps best forgotten. Then, in 1980, it reemerged to prick our collective conscience, when Dr. K. Ray Nelson, then director of the Lynchburg Hospital where Carrie Buck had been sterilized, researched the records of his institution and discovered that more than 4,000 sterilizations had been performed, the last as late as 1972. He also found Carrie Buck, alive and well near Charlottesville, and her sister Doris, covertly sterilized under the same law (she was told that her operation was for appendicitis), and now, with fierce dignity, dejected and bitter because she had wanted a child more than anything else in her life and had finally, in her old age, learned why she had never conceived.

As scholars and reporters visited Carrie Buck and her sister, what a few experts had known all along became abundantly clear to everyone. Carrie Buck was a woman of obviously normal intelligence. For example, Paul A. Lombardo of the School of Law at the University of Virginia, and a leading scholar of *Buck v. Bell,* wrote in a letter to me:

> As for Carrie, when I met her she was reading newspapers daily and joining a more literate friend to assist at regular bouts with the crossword puzzles. She was not a sophisticated woman, and lacked social graces, but mental health professionals who examined her in later life confirmed my impressions that she was neither mentally ill nor retarded.

On what evidence, then, was Carrie Buck consigned to the State Colony for Epileptics and Feeble-Minded on January 23, 1924? I have seen the text of her commitment hearing; it is, to say the least, cursory and contradictory. Beyond the bald and undocumented say-so of her foster parents, and her own brief appearance before a commission of two doctors and a justice of the peace, no evidence was presented. Even the crude and early Stanford-Binet test, so fatally flawed as a measure of innate worth . . . but at least clothed with the aura of quantitative respectability, had not yet been applied.

When we understand why Carrie Buck was committed in January 1924, we can finally comprehend the hidden meaning of her case and its message for us today. The silent key, again as from the first, is her daughter Vivian, born on March 28, 1924, and then but an evident bump on her belly. Carrie Buck was one of several illegitimate children borne by her mother, Emma. She grew up with foster parents, J. T. and Alice Dobbs, and continued to live with them as an adult, helping out with chores around the house. She was raped by a relative of her foster parents, then blamed for the resulting pregnancy. Almost surely, she was (as they used to say) committed to hide her shame (and her rapist's identity), not because enlightened science had just discovered her true mental status. In short, she was sent away to have her baby. Her case never was about mental deficiency; Carrie Buck was persecuted for supposed sexual immorality and social deviance. The annals of her trial and hearing reek with the contempt of the well-off and well-bred for poor people of "loose morals." Who really cared whether Vivian was a baby of normal intelligence; she was the illegitimate child of an illegitimate woman. Two generations of bastards are enough. Harry Laughlin began his "family history" of the Bucks by writing: "These people belong to the shiftless, ignorant and worthless class of anti-social whites of the South."

We know little of Emma Buck and her life, but we have no more reason to suspect her than her daughter Carrie of true mental deficiency. Their supposed deviance was social and sexual; the charge of imbecility was a cover-up, Mr. Justice Holmes notwithstanding.

We come then to the crux of the case, Carrie's daughter, Vivian. What evidence was ever adduced for her mental deficiency? This and only this: At the original trial in late 1924, when Vivian Buck was seven months old, a Miss Wilhelm, social worker for the Red Cross, appeared before the court. She began by stating honestly the true reason for Carrie Buck's commitment:

> Mr. Dobbs, who had charge of the girl, had taken her when a small child, had reported to Miss Duke [the temporary secretary of Public Welfare for Albemarle County] that the girl was pregnant and that he wanted to have her committed somewhere—to have her sent to some institution.

Miss Wilhelm then rendered her judgment of Vivian Buck by comparing her with the normal granddaughter of Mrs. Dobbs, born just three days earlier:

> It is difficult to judge probabilities of a child as young as that, but it seems to me not quite a normal baby. In its appearance—I should say that perhaps my knowledge of the mother may prejudice me in that regard, but I saw the child at the same time as Mrs. Dobbs' daughter's baby, which is only three days older than this one, and there is a very decided difference in the development of the babies. That was about two weeks ago. There is a look about it that is not quite normal, but just what it is, I can't tell.

This short testimony, and nothing else, formed all the evidence for the crucial third generation of imbeciles. Cross-examination revealed that neither Vivian nor the Dobbs grandchild could walk or talk, and that "Mrs. Dobbs' daughter's baby is a very responsive baby. When you play with it or try to attract its attention—it is a baby that you can play with. The other baby is not. It seems very apathetic and not responsive." Miss Wilhelm then urged Carrie Buck's sterilization: "I think," she said, "it would at least prevent the propagation of her kind." Several years later, Miss Wilhelm denied that she had ever examined Vivian or deemed the child feebleminded.

Unfortunately, Vivian died at age eight of "enteric colitis" (as recorded on her death certificate), an ambiguous diagnosis that could mean many things but may well indicate that she fell victim to one of the preventable childhood diseases of poverty (a grim reminder of the real subject in *Buck v. Bell*). She is therefore mute as a witness in our reassessment of her famous case.

When *Buck v. Bell* resurfaced in 1980, it immediately struck me that Vivian's case was crucial and that evidence for the mental status of a child who died at age eight might best be found in report cards. I have therefore been trying to track down Vivian Buck's school records for the past four years and have finally succeeded. (They were supplied to me by Dr. Paul A. Lombardo, who also sent other documents, including Miss Wilhelm's testimony, and spent several hours answering my questions by mail and Lord knows how much time playing successful detective in re Vivian's school records. I have never met Dr. Lombardo; he did all this work for kindness, collegiality, and love of the game of knowledge, not for expected reward or even requested acknowledgment. In a profession—academics—so often marred by pettiness and silly squabbling over meaningless priorities, this generosity must be recorded and celebrated as a sign of how things can and should be.)

Vivian Buck was adopted by the Dobbs family, who had raised (but later sent away) her mother, Carrie. As Vivian Alice Elaine Dobbs, she attended the Venable Public Elementary School of Charlottesville for four terms, from September 1930 until May 1932, a month before her death. She was a perfectly normal, quite average student, neither particularly outstanding nor much troubled. In those days before grade inflation, when C meant "good, 81–87" (as defined on her report card) rather than barely scraping by, Vivian Dobbs received A's and B's for deportment and C's for all academic subjects but mathematics (which was always difficult for her, and where she scored D) during her first term in Grade 1A, from September 1930 to January 1931. She improved during her second term in 1B, meriting an A in deportment, C in mathematics, and B in all other academic subjects; she was placed on the honor roll in April 1931. Promoted to 2A, she had trouble during the fall term of 1931, failing mathematics and spelling but receiving A in deportment, B in reading, and C in writing and English. She was "retained in 2A" for the next term—or "left back" as we used to say, and scarcely a sign of imbecility as I remember all my buddies who suffered a similar fate. In any case, she again did well in her final term, with B in deportment, reading, and spelling, and C in writing, English, and mathematics during her last month in school. This daughter of "lewd and immoral" women excelled in deportment and performed adequately, although not brilliantly, in her academic subjects.

In short, we can only agree with the conclusion that Dr. Lombardo has reached in his research on *Buck v. Bell*—there were no imbeciles, not a one, among the three generations of Bucks. I don't know that such correction of cruel but forgotten errors of history counts for much, but I find it both symbolic and satisfying to learn that forced eugenic sterilization, a procedure of such dubious morality, earned its official justification (and won its most quoted line of rhetoric) on a patent falsehood.

Carrie Buck died last year. By a quirk of fate, and not by memory or design, she was buried just a few steps from her only daughter's grave. In the umpteenth and ultimate verse of a favorite old ballad, a rose and a brier—the sweet and the bitter—emerge from the tombs of Barbara Allen and her lover, twining about each other in the union of death. May Carrie and Vivian, victims in different ways and in the flower of youth, rest together in peace.

JONATHAN GLOVER

Eugenics: Some Lessons from the Nazi Experience

Joanthan Glover is Professor of Ethics at King's College, University of London, and the Director of the Centre for Medical Law and Ethics. For many years, Jonathan was Fellow of New College, Oxford. During his years at Oxford, Jonathan gained the reputation of being an outstanding lecturer and tutor. He is currently working on the philosophy of mental illness, in particular the nature of psychopathology.

In one way, the existence of bioethics is very cheering. It is a fine thing that in our time there is so much ethical discussion about what we should do with the remarkable new developments in biology and medicine. But it is also hard not to be struck by the feeling that much work in bioethics is un-philosophical, in the sense of being unreflective on its own methods.

In particular, much of bioethics seems uncritically Cartesian in approach, in a way which makes the whole subject too easy. People writing about certain practical issues, for instance in medical ethics, often start off with principles which are taken to be self-evident. Or else there is a perfunctory attempt to explain why these are the appropriate principles and then practical conclusions are simply derived from them. Often the result is the mechanical application of some form of utilitarianism to various bioethical problems. Or, alternatively, there is a list of several principles about autonomy, beneficence, and so on, which is again mechanically applied.

What worries me about this approach is that it does not reflect real ethical thinking, which is a two-way process. We do not just start off with a set of axioms and apply them to particular cases. We also try to learn from experience. There is something to be said for a more empirical approach to bioethics. This involves not only looking at principles and thinking about what they imply. It involves also looking at particular experiences which, collectively, we have had, and seeing what can be learnt from them. Perhaps from these experiences we can learn something about the sorts of approach it would be a good idea to adopt. Sometimes these historical experiences can teach us a different, but still useful, lesson about the kinds of approach it would be a good idea not to adopt. That is one of the reasons for looking at the Nazi experiment in eugenics.

Before talking about the Nazi episode, it is worth mentioning a quite different case which might also be described as, in one sense, a kind of eugenics. In thinking about the Nazis, it is important to bear in mind how very different their concerns were from the motives which sometimes make people these days want to be able to choose to have one kind of child rather than another.

A letter was published in an English newspaper, the *Guardian,* a few years ago. It was at a time when there was a move to try to lower the time limit for legal abortion. Part of the aim of this proposal was to restrict the possibility of so-called "therapeutic abortion," since many of the tests for medical disorders would not give results by the proposed new time limit. Behind the proposal was an opposition to abortion on the "eugenic" grounds of wanting a child without disability, as opposed to one who had a disability.

Two parents wrote to the *Guardian* in these terms:

> In December 1986 our newly born daughter was diagnosed to be suffering from a genetically caused disease

From John Harris and Søren Holm, eds., *The Future of Human Reproduction: Ethics, Choice, and Regulation* (Oxford: Clarendon Press, 1998). Reprinted with the permission of Oxford University Press.

called Dystrophic epidermolysis Bullosa (EB). This is a disease in which the skin of the sufferer is lacking in certain essential fibres. As a result, any contact with her skin caused large blisters to form, which subsequently burst leaving raw open skin that only healed slowly and left terrible scarring. As EB is a genetically caused disease it is incurable and the form that our daughter suffered from usually causes death within the first six months of life. In our daughter's case the condition extended to her digestive and respiratory tracts and as a result of such internal blistering and scarring, she died after a painful and short life at the age of only 12 weeks.

Following our daughter's death we were told that if we wanted any more children, there was a one-in-four probability that any child we conceived would be affected by the disease but that it was possible to detect the disease antenatally. In May 1987 we decided to restart our family only because we knew that such a test was available and that should we conceive an affected child the pregnancy could be terminated, such a decision is not taken lightly or easily . . .

We have had to watch our first child die slowly and painfully and we could not contemplate having another child if there was a risk that it too would have to die in the same way.

My reaction to this letter is one of complete sympathy with the parents' predicament and complete support for the decision that they took. Of course, this kind of decision raises very real questions. If you choose not to have a disabled child, there is a question about the impact on disabled people already alive, about what it does to the idea of equality of respect for the disabled. There is also an alarming slippery slope. How far should we go in choosing what kinds of people should be born? As soon as we start choosing at all, we enter a zone of great moral difficulty where there are important boundaries to be drawn.

But many people, when they think about this sort of issue, also have a feeling of horror and revulsion, linked in a vague way to the Nazi episode. Of course any morally serious person at our end of the twentieth century is bound to have reactions which are coloured by what the Nazis did. All the same, the Nazi episode is greatly misused in bioethics. People too readily reach for the argument that "the Nazis did this" and that therefore we should not. It is a poor case for eating meat that Hitler was a vegetarian. It is necessary to look and see precisely what the Nazis did, and to look a bit harder than people usually do at exactly what was wrong with what they did.

In the case of the decision not to have another child with EB, there are two issues. First, is choosing not to have a child with EB in itself a "eugenic" decision, in the objectionable way the Nazi policies were? Second, are we on a slippery slope, which may lead to objectionable Nazi-like policies?

It is worth making a brief mention of the parallel appeal to the Nazi example that is often made in the euthanasia debate. Here it is fairly obvious that the argument is used too crudely. The Nazi "euthanasia" programme (as the quotation marks indicate) was extraordinarily different from anything that other advocates of euthanasia support. The Nazi euthanasia programme was itself bound up with their ideas about eugenics. It was driven by a highly distinctive ideology. For them, it was not at all important to consider the interests of the individual person whose life was in question. Their project was one of tidying up the world, in the interest of what they called "racial hygiene."

The Nazi theorists were concerned with Darwinian natural selection. They were afraid that the "natural" selective pressures, which had functioned to ensure the survival of healthy and strong human beings, no longer functioned in modern society. Because of such things as medical care, and support for the disabled, people who in tougher times would have died were surviving to pass on their genes.

In the Nazi "euthanasia" programme, 70,723 mental patients were killed by carbon monoxide gas. The thinking behind this is not a matter of acting on the patients' wishes. Nor is it a matter of asking whether someone's life is such a nightmare for them that it is in their own interests that they should die. The thinking does not try to see things from the perspective of the individual person at all.

The bible of the Nazi "euthanasia" programme was a book by a lawyer, Karl Binding, and a psychiatrist, Alfred Hoche, called *Permission for the Destruction of Life Unworthy of Life*. In it, Karl Binding wrote: "The relatives would of course feel the loss badly, but mankind loses so many of its members through mistakes that one more or less hardly matters." That is very different from the agonized thought that goes into the decisions taken by doctors nowadays, when they wonder whether someone's life should be terminated. "One more or less hardly matters" is not the thinking behind the moral case for euthanasia.

The impersonal approach characteristic of the Nazi programme was expressed in 1939 in Berlin. Victor Brack chaired a meeting about who should be killed. The minutes report his remarks: "The number is arrived at through a calculation on the basis of a ratio of 1000 to 10 to 5 to 1. That means, out of 1000 people 10 require psychiatric treatment, of these 5 in residential form, and of these 1 patient will come out of the programme. If one applies this to the population of the Greater German Reich, then one must reckon with 65 to 75,000 cases. With this statement the question of who can be regarded as settled."[1]

This impersonal approach went all the way through the Nazi programme. A nurse described one of the first transports from the asylum of Jestetten in Württemberg: "The senior sister introduced the patients by name. But the transport leader replied that they did not operate on the basis of names but numbers. And in fact the patients who were to be transported then had numbers written in ink on their wrists, which had been previously dampened with a sponge. In other words the people were transported not as human beings but as cattle."[2]

We all know how the later murder of the Jews was preceded by transport in cattle trucks. Many of the people who ran the Nazis' so-called euthanasia programme moved to Poland to work in the extermination camps there. The ideology behind the murder of the Jews was a mixture of race hatred and the same racial hygiene outlook found in the euthanasia programme.

The ideology was one of racial purity. There was the idea that genetic mixing with other races lowered the quality of people. One of the great fathers of the Nazi eugenics movement was Dr. Eugen Fischer. Many years before, he had been to South Africa and in 1913 had published a study of people who he called "Rehoboth bastards." They were children of mixed unions between Boers and Hottentots. He reached the conclusion, on a supposedly scientific basis, that these children were, as he put it, "of lesser racial quality." He wrote that "We should provide them with the minimum amount of protection which they require, for survival as a race inferior to ourselves, and we should do this only as long as they are useful to us. After this, free competition should prevail and, in my opinion, this will lead to their decline and destruction."[3]

In 1933 Dr Fischer was made the new Rector of Berlin University. In his Rectoral Address he said: "The new leadership, having only just taken over the reins of power, is deliberately and forcefully intervening in the course of history and in the life of the nation, precisely when this intervention is most urgently, most decisively, and most immediately needed . . . This intervention can be characterized as a biological population policy, biological in this context signifying the safeguarding by the state of our hereditary endowment and our race." Fischer in 1939 extended this line of thinking specifically to the Jews. He said: "When a people wants to preserve its own nature it must reject alien racial elements. And when these have already insinuated themselves it must suppress them and eliminate them. This is self-defence."[4]

As well as belief in racial purity, there was the idea that in a given race only the "best people" should be encouraged to procreate. And the view was that those who are not "the best people" should be discouraged from having children, or even prevented from doing so. In 1934, one of the other fathers of the Nazi eugenics movement, Professor Fritz Lenz, said: "As things are now, it is only a minority of our fellow citizens who are so endowed that their unrestricted procreation is good for the race."[5] Fisher and Lenz, together with their colleagues, had perhaps more impact on the world than any other academics in the twentieth century. In 1923, Adolf Hitler, while confined in Landsberg prison, read their recently published textbook *Outline of Human Genetics and Racial Hygiene*. He incorporated some of its ideas in *Mein Kampf*.[6] These ideas influenced the Sterilization Law brought in when Hitler came to power in 1933. This made sterilization compulsory for people with conditions including schizophrenia, manic depression, and alcoholism.

This ideology is not one of the importance of the individual. There is a conception of the pure race and the biologically desirable human being. Reproductive freedom and individual lives are to be sacrificed to these abstractions. One medical model had great influence on the Nazis. It is an appalling medical model: the idea that in treating people who are "racially inferior," you are like the doctor who is dealing with a diseased organ in an otherwise healthy body. This analogy was put forward in a paper in 1940 by Konrad Lorenz, the very distinguished ethologist, now remembered for his work on aggression, and whose books on animals had an enormous charm. Lorenz wrote this:

> There is a certain similarity between the measures which need to be taken when we draw a broad biological analogy between bodies and malignant tumours, on the one hand, and a nation and individuals within it who have become asocial because of their defective constitution, on the other

hand . . . Fortunately, the elimination of such elements is easier for the public health position and less dangerous for the supra-individual organism, than such an operation by a surgeon would be for the individual organism.[7]

The influence in practice of this thinking can be seen very clearly in Robert Jay Lifton's book on the Nazi doctors. He quotes a doctor called Fritz Klein. Dr. Klein was asked how he would reconcile the appalling medical experiments he carried out in Auschwitz with his oath as a doctor. He replied: "Of course I am a doctor and I want to preserve life. And out of respect for human life, I would remove a gangrenous appendix from a diseased body. The Jew is the gangrenous appendix in the body of mankind."[8] This brings out the importance, not just of things people literally believe, but also of the imagery which colours their thinking. Dr Klein cannot literally have believed that Jews were a gangrenous appendix. It would be easier to think that the Nazis were all mad if they literally thought that.

The role of such imagery can be seen again in the way in which racism was given a biological justification. Appalling images likened Jews to vermin, or to dirt and disease. When all Jews were removed from an area, it was called "Judenrein"—clean of Jews. Hans Frank, talking about the decline of a typhus epidemic, said that the removal of what he called "the Jewish element" had contributed to better health in Europe. The Foreign Office Press Chief Schmidt said that the Jewish question was, as he put it, "a question of political hygiene."[9]

This kind of medical analogy was important in Nazi thinking. Hitler said, "The discovery of the Jewish virus is one of the greatest revolutions that have taken place in the world. The battle in which we are engaged today is of the same sort as the battle waged during the last century by Pasteur and Koch. How many diseases have their origin in the Jewish virus! . . . We shall regain our health only by eliminating the Jew."[10]

The medical analogies and the idea of racial hygiene were supplemented by the ideology of Social Darwinism. To study either Nazism or, further back, the origins of the First World War is to see how enormously more influential Social Darwinist ideas have been in our century than one would guess. Social Darwinist ideas were not confined to Germany. They originated in England. It would be unfair to blame Darwin, who was a very humane person, for these ideas. They were developed by people like Francis Galton and Karl Pearson. Before the First World War, Karl Pearson said that the nation should be kept up to a high pitch of external efficiency by contest, chiefly by way of war with inferior races. The influence of Social Darwinism in Germany was partly the result of the Englishman Houston Stewart Chamberlain, who became an adopted German nationalist, holding that the Germans were a superior race.

Social Darwinism fuelled the naval arms race between Germany and Britain, a contest which helped to cause the First World War. Admiral Tirpitz thought naval expansion was necessary because, if Germany did not join the biological struggle between races, it would go under. When the danger of the arms race was obvious, the British Foreign Secretary, Sir Edward Grey, proposed a naval moratorium on both sides. The German Chancellor, Bethmann-Hollweg, rejected Grey's proposal: "The old saying still holds good that the weak will be the prey of the strong. When a people will not or cannot continue to spend enough on its armaments to be able to make its way in the world, then it falls back into the second rank . . . There will always be another and a stronger there who is ready to take the place in the world which it has vacated."[11]

Nazism emerged against this background of belief in life as a ruthless struggle for survival. According to Social Darwinism, victory goes to the strong, the tough, and the hard rather than to those who are gentle and co-operative. The Nazis took this up. They extolled struggle and the survival of the fittest. This led them to abandon traditional moral restraints. One Nazi physician, Dr Arthur Guett, said: "The ill-conceived 'love of thy neighbour' has to disappear . . . It is the supreme duty of the . . . state to grant life and livelihood only to the healthy and hereditarily sound portion of the population in order to secure . . . a hereditarily sound and racially pure people for all eternity."[12]

The Nazis also extolled hardness, which they thought led to victory in the struggle for survival. Hitler was proud of his own hardness. He said, "I am perhaps the hardest man this nation has had for 200 years."[13] The belief in hardness came partly from Nietzsche. He was contemptuous of English biologists, and so was predictably cool about Darwin. Despite this, Nietzsche was in certain respects a Social Darwinist. He too thought compassion for the weak was sentimental nonsense, and advocated struggle and hardness.

Hitler, an admirer of the darker side of Nietzsche, was also a Social Darwinist. One day at lunch he said, "As in everything, nature is the best instructor, even as regards selection. One couldn't imagine a better activity on nature's part than that which consists in deciding the supremacy of one creature over another by means of a constant struggle." He went on to express disapproval of the way "our upper classes give way to a feeling of compassion regarding the fate of the Jews who we claim the right to expel."[14]

This outlook influenced the people who worked in the Nazi eugenic and "euthanasia" programmes. They felt guilty about feelings of compassion, which they were taught were a weakness to overcome. One Nazi doctor involved in killing psychiatric patients as part of the "euthanasia" programme expressed this in a letter to the director of the asylum where he worked, explaining his reluctance to take part in murdering the children there. He wrote,

> I am very grateful for you willingly insisting that I should take time to think things over. The new measures are so convincing that I had hoped to be able to discard all personal considerations. But it is one thing to approve state measures with conviction and another to carry them out yourself down to their last consequences. I am thinking of the difference between a judge and an executioner. For this reason, despite my intellectual understanding and good will, I cannot help stating that I am temperamentally not fitted for this. As eager as I often am to correct the natural course of events, it is just as repugnant to me to do so systematically, after cold blooded consideration, according to the objective principles of science, without being affected by a doctor's feeling for his patient . . . I feel emotionally tied to the children as their medical guardian, and I think this emotional contact is not necessarily a weakness from the point of view of a National Socialist doctor . . . I prefer to see clearly and to recognise that I am too gentle for this work than to disappoint you later.[15]

This apology for his concern for his patients, his emotional tie to these children, as "not necessarily a weakness in a National Socialist doctor," shows how deeply ingrained this ideology was.

What lessons can be drawn from this grim episode? Any conclusions from this more empirical approach to ethics have to be tentative. There is always the danger of the mistake attributed to generals and strategists, of preparing for the previous war. There will not be an exact rerun of the Nazi episode, so we have to be flexible in learning from it.

The Nazi episode is evil on such a grand scale that any conclusions drawn from it are likely to seem puny by comparison with the events themselves. But it is worth not being deterred by this, and, at the risk of banality, trying to focus on some of the things we should guard against.

One conclusion may be that it is a mistake to let any system of belief, including a system of ethics, become too abstract. There are dangers in getting too far away from ordinary human emotional responses to people. The worry behind "racial hygiene," the worry about the consequences of removing "natural" evolutionary selective pressures, was a thought you did not have to be a very evil person to have. We see it as a misguided thought, but it is still one a morally good person might have had. The danger is to get hooked on an idea, such as this one, and then to follow it ruthlessly, trampling on all the normal human feelings and responses to individual people in front of you. This is a general danger in ethics. Even a humane outlook such as utilitarianism can do great harm when applied with ruthless abstraction.

Another lesson, in our time fortunately a platitude, is that we should not be thinking in terms of racial purity and of lesser racial quality. It is not at all clear what these phrases mean. They are woolly and muddled ideas, which are manifestly incredibly dangerous. (I mention this platitude because sometimes what was once a platitude stops being one. Who, a few years ago, would have thought it worth stating that "ethnic cleansing" should be utterly rejected?)

There is need for more thought about the answer to the claim about the necessity of replacing evolutionary selective pressures. All of us shudder when we see where this kind of thought led, but few do the thinking to find out exactly what is wrong with the arguments.

It is worth mentioning one thought about this. The fact that we can deal with some disorders, so that people with them are able to survive and have children who then may inherit the disorder, is supposed to be the problem. But, in the case of a disorder where people find their lives worth living, it is not a disaster if they pass on their genes. In the Stone Age, people with poor sight may have lost out in the evolutionary competition. Glasses and contact lenses are among the reasons why they now survive to have children. Their lives are not a disaster, and there is no reason why it is a disaster if their children inherit shortsightedness. To the extent that modern medicine makes possible, not just survival, but a decent quality of life, the supposed problem to which eugenics seemed to be the answer is not a real one.

Another lesson is the dangers of the group approach. The Nazis thought mainly in terms of nations and races. In decisions about who is to be born, decisions for instance about access to fertility treatment or about genetic screening, it is important to look first and foremost at those immediately involved: at the person who may be born and at the family. In the case of the kind of reproductive intervention where we are choosing the creation of one person rather than another, our central thought ought to be about what one kind of life or another would be like from the point of view of the person living it.

The case is like that of euthanasia. If we are to justify euthanasia at all, it has to be justified by saying either that a particular person wants not to go on living, or, where the person is past expressing any view, that their life must seem to them so terrible that it would be a kindness to kill them. We have to look at things from inside in taking these decisions. (Of course this is very difficult, which is a reason for extreme caution.)

It is utterly repugnant that "euthanasia" should be defended for instance on grounds of general social utility, such as the cost of keeping certain people alive. Killing on those grounds is not euthanasia, despite the Nazi attempt to hijack the term for such policies. People now sometimes ignorantly misuse the Nazi policy as though it were a knock-down argument against genuine euthanasia. Those of us who study what the Nazis really did tend to dislike this propagandist move. As with the casual use of "fascist" to describe political opponents, it makes light of something truly terrible, and leaves us without a vocabulary for the real thing. But the one place where the argument from Nazism really does apply is where killing the old or the sick or the insane to benefit other people is advocated.

In the same sort of way, I find repugnant the idea that decisions about the kind of children to be born should be made on grounds of general social utility.

Finally, there are issues about Social Darwinism. Rather few people these days hold Hitler's maniac racist views. But Social Darwinism may be a continuing danger. A crude interpretation of some claims in sociobiology could lend support to a renewed Social Darwinism. In mentioning this, I am not lending support to one crude reaction against sociobiology, a reaction which takes the form of denying any genetic contribution to the explanation of human behaviour. That sort of absolute denial is going to lose out in the intellectual debate. No doubt sometimes the evidence will suggest the existence of a genetic component. But, if people propose social policies supposed to follow from this, we need to look very hard at the supporting arguments. Claims about simple links between biology and social policy are often backed by very dubious arguments. And it is not just that the thinking is poor. The Nazi experience suggests that the conclusions may also be dangerous. The victims of the Nazis were not killed just by gas but also by beliefs, which can be poisonous too.

NOTES

1. Quoted in J. Noakes and G. Pridham, *Nazism, 1919–1945,* iii: *Foreign Policy, War and Racial Extermination: A Documentary Reader* (Exeter, 1988), 1010.

2. Quoted ibid. 1023–4.

3. Quoted in Benno Muller-Hill, *Murderous Science: Elimination by Scientific Selection of Jews, Gypsies, and Others, Germany 1933–1945,* trans. George R. Fraser (Oxford, 1988), 7–8.

4. Quoted ibid. 10, 12.

5. Quoted ibid. 10.

6. Cf. Robert N. Proctor, *Racial Hygiene: Medicine under the Nazis* (Cambridge, Mass.: Harvard University Press, 1988).

7. Quoted in Muller-Hill, *Murderous Science,* 14.

8. Quoted in Robert Jay Lifton, *The Nazi Doctors: A Study in the Psychology of Evil* (London, 1986), 16.

9. Quoted in Raul Hilberg, *The Destruction of the European Jews,* student edn. (New York, 1985), 287.

10. *Hitler's Table Talk, 1941–44,* introd. Hugh Trevor-Roper (Oxford, 1988), 332.

11. Quoted in Michael Howard, 'The Edwardian Arms Race', in Michael Howard, *The Lessons of History* (Oxford, 1993).

12. Quoted in Lifton, *The Nazi Doctors.*

13. Hitler, 8 Nov. 1940, quoted in J. P. Stren, *Hitler: The Fuhrer and the People,* 62.

14. *Hitler's Table Talk,* 396–7.

15. Noakes and Pridham, *Nazism, 1919–1945,* iii. 1014–15.

The Human Genome Project

FRANCIS S. COLLINS AND
VICTOR A. MCKUSICK

Implications of the Human Genome Project for Medical Science

Francis S. Collin is the Director of the National Human Genome Research Institute and oversees the project aimed at mapping and sequencing all of the human DNA. In 1989 he helped to discover the CFTR gene, which is associated with cystic fibrosis.

Victor A. McKusick is Professor of Medical Genetics at the Johns Hopkins University. He has helped to introduce genetics into clinical medicine. His interests lie in the study and management of inherited diseases and predispositions.

Until recently, many physicians and other health care professionals considered medical genetics as the province of specialists in tertiary care medical centers, who spent their time evaluating unusual cases of mendelian disorders, birth defect syndromes, or chromosomal anomalies. Asked whether genetics was a part of their everyday practice, most primary care practitioners would say no. That is all about to change.

To be sure, there are numerous medical conditions found in children and adults that have a strong, indeed predominant, genetic basis. The continuously updated Online Mendelian Inheritance in Man (OMIM) lists many thousands of such conditions,[1] but offers a far too narrow view of the contribution of genetics to medicine. Except for some cases of trauma, it is fair to say that virtually every human illness has a hereditary component.[2] While common diseases, such as diabetes mellitus, heart disease, cancer, and the major mental illnesses, do not follow mendelian inheritance patterns, there is ample evidence from twin and pedigree studies over many decades showing that all of these disorders have important hereditary influences. In fact, for many common illnesses of developed countries, the strongest predictor of risk is family history.

Reprinted with permission from the *Journal of the American Medical Association* 285 (February 7, 2001), 540–44. Copyright © 2001 by the American Medical Association.

The role of heredity in most diseases is thus not in itself a new revelation. But in the past, it was considered unlikely that much could be done with this information other than to guide medical surveillance based on careful family history taking. A sea change is now underway, and it is likely that the molecular basis for these hereditary influences on common illnesses soon will be uncovered. Even though on average the quantitative contribution of heredity to the etiological characteristics of diseases like diabetes mellitus or hypertension may be modest, uncovering the pathways involved in disease pathogenesis will have broad consequences, pointing toward possible environmental triggers as well. The implications for diagnostics, preventive medicine, and therapeutics will be profound.

GENETICS IN THE 20TH CENTURY

In the spring of 1900, 3 different investigators rediscovered Mendel's laws.[3] With Garrod's recognition of their application to human inborn errors of metabolism, the science of human genetics acquired a foundation. But it remained for Watson and Crick half a century later to uncover the chemical basis of heredity, with their elucidation of the double helical structure of DNA.[4] The role of RNA as a messenger and the genetic code that allows RNA to be translated to protein emerged over the next 15 years. This was followed by the advent of recombinant DNA technology in the 1970s, offering the ability to obtain pure preparations of a particular DNA segment. However, sequencing of DNA was difficult until Sanger and Gilbert independently derived methods of sequencing DNA in 1977.[5,6] (It is remarkable indeed that the Sanger dideoxy method for DNA sequencing remains the basic technology on which the genetic revolution is being built, albeit with major advances in automation of the analysis that have come along in the last 15 years.)

The use of variable DNA markers for linkage analysis of human disorders was set forth in 1980.[7] Mapping of disorders by linkage previously had been severely limited by the relatively small number of usable protein markers, such as blood groups. The notion that any mendelian disorder could be mapped to a chromosomal region caught the imagination of geneticists. An early and stunning success of this approach, the mapping of the Huntington disease gene to chromosome 4 in 1983, gave a burst of confidence to this adventurous new approach.[8] But the difficulty of going from a linked marker to the actual disease locus proved profoundly difficult. Years of work were required to map a candidate region and search for potential candidate genes, and many investigators in the 1980s longed for a more systematic approach to the genome.

At the same time, potential advances in mapping and sequencing technology led certain scientific leaders, particularly in the US Department of Energy, to propose the possibility of an organized effort to sequence the entire human genome. In the late 1980s much controversy raged about such proposals, with many in the scientific community deeply concerned that this was technologically impossible and likely to consume vast amounts of funding that might be taken away from other more productive hypothesis-driven research. But with the strong support of a panel of the National Academy of Sciences,[9] and the enthusiasm of a few leaders in the US Congress, the Human Genome Project (HGP) was initiated in the United States by the National Institutes of Health and the Department of Energy in 1990.[10]

THE HUMAN GENOME PROJECT

From the outset, it was realized that a detailed set of plans and milestones would be necessary for a project of this magnitude. The technology for carrying out actual large-scale sequencing had not advanced to the point of being able to tackle the 3 billion base pairs of the human genome in 1990 nor were the necessary maps of the genome in hand to provide a scaffold for this effort.

Under the leadership of James Watson, it was decided to focus the first 5 years of the HGP on the development of genetic and physical maps of the human genome, which would themselves be of great value to scientists hunting for disease genes. The HGP also tackled mapping and sequencing of simpler model organisms, such as bacteria, yeast, the roundworm, and the fruit fly.[9–12] Considerable investments were made in improving technology. Perhaps the most unusual feature for a basic science enterprise, 3% to 5% of the budget was set aside from the outset for research on the ethical, legal, and social implications of this expected acceleration in obtaining genetic information about our species.[10] In the past, ethical, legal, and social analysis of the consequences of a scientific revolution often were relegated to other groups outside the scientific mainstream or lay dormant until a crisis developed. This time, the intention was to inspire a cohort of ethicists, social scientists, legal scholars, theologians, and others to address the coming dilemmas associated with increased knowledge about the genome, from social and legal discrimination on the basis of genetics to more philosophical issues such as genetic determinism.

The HGP has been international from the beginning. Although the United States made the largest investment, important contributions have been made by many countries, including Britain, France, Germany, Japan, China, and Canada. The original plan[9] called for completion of the sequence of the human genome by the year 2005, though there was limited confidence that this goal could be achieved. But one by one the intermediate milestones were accomplished. The HGP agreed at the outset to release all map and sequence data into the public domain. The availability of genetic and physical maps led to a considerable acceleration in the successful identification of genes involved in single gene disorders; while fewer than 10 such genes had been identified by positional cloning in 1990, that number grew to more than 100 by 1997.[13]

By 1996, the complete sequencing of several bacterial species and yeast led to the conclusion that it was time to attempt sequencing human DNA on a pilot scale. The introduction of capillary sequencing instruments and the formation of a company in the private sector promising to sequence the human genome for profitable purposes added further momentum to the effort. By 1999, confidence had gathered that acquiring the majority of the sequence of the 3 billion base pairs of the human genome could be attempted. In June 2000, both the private company and the international public sequencing consortium announced the completion of "working drafts" of the human genome sequence.

CURRENT RESEARCH FOCUS

Though the working draft of the human sequence represents a major milestone, a vast amount of additional work remains to be done to understand its function.

It is necessary to complete the sequence analysis by closing the gaps and resolving ambiguities. This finishing process already has been accomplished for chromosomes 21[14] and 22[15] and will be carried out for the remainder of the genome during the next 2 years.

The genomes of other organisms also will need to be sequenced. Probably the most powerful tool to identify the coding exons, as well as the regulatory regions, is a comparison of the sequence across different genomes. For that purpose, full-scale sequencing of the laboratory mouse genome already has been initiated, and the sequencing of the rat and zebrafish genomes will not be far behind. In both the public and private sectors, serious consideration is being given to the sequencing of other large vertebrate genomes, including the pig, dog, cow, and chimpanzee.

An intense effort is under way to develop a catalog of human variation. While human DNA sequences are 99.9% identical to each other, the 0.1% of variation is expected to provide many of the clues to the genetic risk for common illnesses.[16] A public-private partnership has formed to build this catalog of variants as quickly as possible and has identified more than 2 million of these single nucleotide polymorphisms. Of particular interest are those common variants that influence gene function.

Research Opportunities and Forecast: Genomics

Key research opportunities	Forecast
Define Complete List of All Human Genes and Proteins	Thousands of New Drug Targets for Heart Disease, Cancer, Diabetes, Asthma, etc
Define All Common Variants in the Genome, Determine Hereditary Factors in Virtually All Common Diseases, and Refine Technology for Low-Cost Genotyping	Individualized Preventive Medicine Based on Genetic Risk
	Pharmacogenomics to Improve Outcome of Drug Therapy
	Environmental Risk Factor Assessment Becomes Individual-Specific
Determine Regulatory Signals That Affect Expression of All Human Genes in Normal or Abnormal State	Therapies for Developmental Defects
	Precise Molecular Analysis of Malignancies, Guiding Choice of Therapy
Determine Structures of All Human Proteins, Using a Combination of Experimental and Computational Methods	"Designer Drugs" Based on Precise 3-Dimensional Information About Targets
Develop Safe and Effective Gene-Transfer Vectors for Many Different Tissues	Gene Therapy for Rare Single-Gene Disorders, and Some Common Ones
Vigorously Explore the Ethical, Legal, and Social Implications of Genome Research	Legal Safeguards Against Genetic Discrimination and Breaches of Privacy
	Effective Oversight of Clinical Application of Genetic Testing
	Mainstreaming of Genetics into the Practice of Medicine, With Achievement of "Genetic Literacy" Among Clinicians and Patients

A powerful set of technologies for studying gene expression is being developed and explored.[17] These methodologies, which allow analysis of the transcription of as many as 10000 genes in one experiment, make it possible to investigate the differences that occur between various tissue types and to explore the alterations in that expression pattern during disease. Such analyses have already been proved capable of identifying subtypes of certain malignancies that were identical by all other criteria.[18]

The same large-scale analysis strategies that have been applied so effectively to DNA and RNA also are being applied to proteins to characterize their structures, quantity, location in the cell, posttranslational modifications, and interaction partners.[19]

With the advent of these very large databases of information on sequence, variation, and expression, the field of computational biology is emerging as critically important to the future. Effective methods of sorting and analyzing the data will be required to glean biologically meaningful insights from the plethora of data.

The ethical, legal, and social implications research program has already fostered awareness of needs for intervention, particularly in the areas of privacy, genetic discrimination, guidelines for research, and education, and now focuses on the societal implications of increased information about human variation, in both medical and nonmedical situations.

THE 21ST CENTURY: CRITICAL ELEMENTS OF THE MEDICAL RESEARCH AGENDA

Obtaining the sequence of the human genome is the end of the beginning. As Knoppers has said, "As the radius of knowledge gets longer, the circumference of the unknown increases even more" (Bartha Knoppers, personal communication). For the full impact of advances in genetics to be felt in the practice of medicine, major challenges must be addressed.

Information about the human genome sequence and its variants must be applied to identify the particular genes that play a significant role in the hereditary contribution to common disease. This will be a daunting challenge. For a disease such as diabetes mellitus, 5 to 10 (or maybe more) genes are involved, each of which harbors a variant conferring a modest degree of increased risk. Those variants interact with each other and the environment in complex ways, rendering their identification orders of magnitude more difficult than for single gene defects. Nonetheless, with the combination of careful phenotyping (so that different disorders are not inadvertently lumped together) and sampling genetic variants at high density across the genome, it should be possible to identify disease gene associations for many common illnesses in the next 5 to 7 years.[2,16] One should not underestimate, however, the degree of sophistication in clinical investigation that will be necessary or the need for development of more efficient genotyping technology, such as the use of DNA chips or mass spectrometry, to make this kind of genome-wide survey a reality.

An understanding of the major pathways involved in normal homeostasis of the human organism must be developed along with how those pathways are deranged in illness. Identification of each gene that harbors a high-risk variant will point toward a critical pathway for that illness. Many of those will come as a surprise, since the current molecular understanding of most common diseases is rather limited.

Efficient, high-volume methods will need to be developed and applied to the design of small-molecule drugs to modulate disease-related pathways in the desired direction. The pharmaceutical industry has been gearing up for this opportunity, and most companies now expect that the majority of future drug development will come from the field of genomics. With the application of methods that systematically combine chemical components into drugs and of high-volume assays for efficacy, it is expected that compounds can be efficiently identified that block or stimulate a particular pathway. A gratifying recent example is the development of the drug STI-571, which was designed to block the kinase activity of the bcr-abl kinase.[20] This protein is produced as a consequence of the translocation between chromosomes 9 and 22, a chromosome rearrangement that is characteristic of and central to the etiology of chronic myelogenous leukemia. STI-571 blocks the ability of the bcr-abl kinase to phosphorylate its unknown substrate and shows dramatic results in early clinical trials on patients with far advanced chronic myelogenous leukemia.

Along with the design of new drugs, genomics also will provide opportunities to predict responsiveness to drug interventions, since variation in those responses is often attributable to the genetic endowment of the individual. Examples have been identified where common variants in genes involved in drug metabolism or drug action are associated with the likelihood of a good or bad response. The expectation is that such correlations will be found for many drugs over the next 10 years, including agents that are already on the market. This field of pharmacogenomics promises to individualize prescribing practices.[21]

The field of gene therapy, having sustained a series of disappointments over the past few years, especially with the death of a volunteer in a gene therapy trial in the fall of 1999, has gone back to wrestling with the basic science questions of finding optimal methods for gene delivery.[22] While the optimism of the early 1990s about providing quick solutions to a long list of medical problems was probably never fully justified, it is likely that the development of safer and more effective vectors will ensure a significant role for gene therapy in the treatment of some diseases. There already have been promising reports of the application of gene therapy for hemophilia B[23] and severe combined immunodeficiency.[24]

GENETICS IN THE MEDICAL MAINSTREAM

The power of the molecular genetic approach for answering questions in the research laboratory will catalyze a similar transformation of clinical medicine, although this will come gradually over the course of the next 25 years (Figure).

By the year 2010, it is expected that predictive genetic tests will be available for as many as a dozen common conditions, allowing individuals who wish to know this information to learn their individual susceptibilities and to take steps to reduce those risks for which interventions are or will be available. Such interventions could take the form of medical surveillance, lifestyle modifications, diet, or drug therapy. Identification of persons at highest risk for colon cancer, for example, could lead to targeted efforts to provide colonoscopic screening to those individuals, with the likelihood of preventing many premature deaths.

Predictive genetic tests will become applicable first in situations where individuals have a strong family history of a particular condition; indeed, such testing is already available for several conditions, such as breast and colon cancers. But with increasing genetic information about common illnesses, this kind of risk assessment will become more generally available, and many primary care clinicians will become practitioners of genomic medicine, having to explain complex statistical risk information to healthy individuals who are seeking to enhance their chances of staying well. This will require substantial advances in the understanding of genetics by a wide range of clinicians.[25] The National Coalition for Health Professional Education in Genetics, an umbrella group of physicians, nurses, and other clinicians, has organized to help prepare for this coming era.

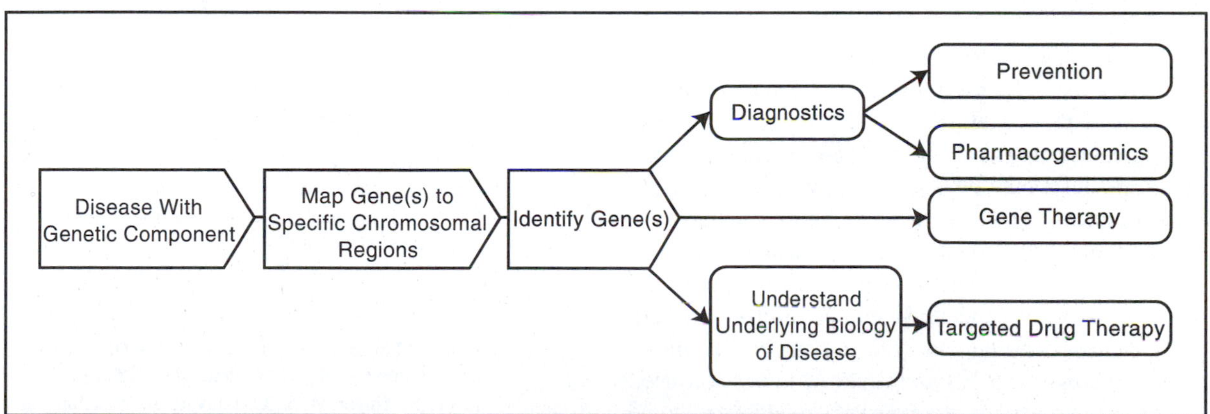

Figure. Steps Involved in a Genetic Approach to the Diagnosis and Treatment of Disease.
The rate of progress for applying a genetic approach to the diagnosis and treatment of each disease will be different depending on the research investment and the degree of biological complexity underlying the disease. First, the gene variants contributing increased disease risk must be identified by family studies and/or case-control studies. Diagnostic opportunities may then come along rather quickly, but will be of greatest clinical usefulness once prevention measures are developed that have proven benefit to those at high risk. Some gene variants will also show clinically useful associations with drug responsiveness (pharmacogenomics). In general, full-blown therapeutic benefits from identification of gene variants will take longer to reach mainstream medicine. In some instances, the gene itself will be the drug (gene therapy), while in others, a sophisticated knowledge of the underlying disease mechanism, built upon genetics, may allow the design of targeted and highly effective drug therapy.

Another crucial step is the passage of effective federal legislation to outlaw the use of predictive genetic information in the workplace and in obtaining health insurance.[26,27] Numerous surveys have indicated that the public is deeply concerned about the potential for discrimination, and some individuals have forgone acquiring genetic information about themselves, since assurances cannot be currently provided about discriminatory misuse of the information. Although more than 2 dozen states have taken some action in this regard, a patchwork of different levels of protection across the United States is not satisfactory and this vexing problem must be dealt with effectively at the federal level.

By 2020, the impact of genetics on medicine will be even more widespread. The pharmacogenomics approach for predicting drug responsiveness will be standard practice for quite a number of disorders and drugs. New gene-based "designer drugs" will be introduced to the market for diabetes mellitus, hypertension, mental illness, and many other conditions. Improved diagnosis and treatment of cancer will likely be the most advanced of the clinical consequences of genetics, since a vast amount of molecular information already has been collected about the genetic basis of malignancy. By 2020, it is likely that every tumor will have a precise molecular fingerprint determined, cataloging the genes that have gone awry, and therapy will be individually targeted to that fingerprint.

Despite these exciting projections, certain tensions also will exist. Access to health care, already a major problem in the United States, will complicate these new advances, unless our medical care systems change in significant ways. Anti-technology movements, already active in the United States and elsewhere, are likely to gather momentum as the focus of genetics turns even more intensely on ourselves. Though the benefits of genetic medicine will be profound, there will be those who consider this advancement unnatural and dangerous. Efforts at public education need to start now to explain the potential benefits and to be honest about the risks.

In conclusion, this is a time of dramatic change in medicine. As we cross the threshold of the new millennium, we simultaneously cross a threshold into an era where the human genome sequence is largely known. We must commit ourselves to exploring the application of these powerful tools to the alleviation of human suffering, a mandate that undergirds all of medicine. At the same time, we must be mindful of the great potential for misunderstanding in this quickly developing field and make sure that the advancement of the social agenda of genetics is equally as vigorous as the medical agenda.

REFERENCES

1. National Center for Biotechnology Information. Online Mendelian Inheritance in Man. Available at: http://www.ncbi.nlm.nih.gov/omim/. Accessed November 30, 2000.
2. Collins F. S. Shattuck Lecture: medical and societal consequences of the Human Genome Project. *N Engl J Med.* 1999;341:28–37.
3. Henig R. M. *The Monk in the Garden.* New York, NY: Houghton Mifflin; 2000.
4. Watson J. D., Crick F. H. C. Molecular structure of nucleic acids. *Nature.* 1953;171:737–738.
5. Sanger F., Nicklen S., Coulson A. R. DNA sequencing with chain-terminating inhibitors. *Proc Natl Acad Sci U S A.* 1977;74:5463–5467.
6. Maxam A. M., Gilbert W. A new method for sequencing DNA. *Proc Natl Acad Sci U S A.* 1977;74:560–564.
7. Botstein D., White R. L., Skolnick M., Davis R. W. Construction of a genetic linkage map in man using restriction fragment length polymorphisms. *Am J Hum Genet.* 1980;32:314–331.
8. Gusella J. F., Wexler N. S., Conneally P. M., et al. A polymorphic DNA marker genetically linked to Huntington's disease. *Nature.* 1983;306:234–238.
9. National Research Council, Committee on Mapping and Sequencing the Human Genome. *Mapping and Sequencing the Human Genome.* Washington, DC: National Academy Press; 2000.
10. US Department of Health and Human Services and Department of Energy. *Understanding Our Genetic Inheritance. The U.S. Human Genome Project: The First Five Years.* Washington, DC: US Dept of Health and Human Services; 1990.
11. Collins F. S., Galas D. A new five-year plan for the U.S. Human Genome Project. *Science.* 1993;262:43–46.
12. Collins F. S., Patrinos A., Jordan E., Chakravarti A., Gesteland R., Walters L. New goals for the U.S. Human Genome Project: 1998–2003. *Science.* 1998;282:682–689.
13. Collins F. S. Positional cloning moves from perditional to traditional. *Nat Genet.* 1995;9:347–350.
14. Hattori M., Fujiyama A., Taylor T. D., et al. The DNA sequence of human chromosome 21. *Nature.* 2000;405: 311–319.
15. Dunham I., Shimizu N., Roe B. A., et al. The DNA sequence of human chromosome 22. *Nature.* 1999;402:489–495.
16. Collins F. S., Guyer M. S., Chakravarti A. Variations on a theme: cataloging human DNA sequence variation. *Science.* 1997;278:1580–1581.
17. Lockhart D. J., Winzeler E. A. Genomics, gene expression and DNA arrays. *Nature.* 2000;405:827–836.
18. Bittner M., Meltzer P., Chen Y., et al. Molecular classification of cutaneous malignant melanoma by gene expression profiling. *Nature.* 2000;406:536–540.
19. Pandey A., Mann M. Proteomics to study genes and genomes. *Nature.* 2000;405:837–846.

20. Druker B. J., Lydon N. B. Lessons learned from the development of an abl tyrosine kinase inhibitor for chronic myelogenous leukemia. *J Clin Invest.* 2000;105:3–7.

21. Roses A. D. Pharmacogenetics and the practice of medicine. *Nature.* 2000;405:857–865.

22. Verma I. M. Gene therapy: beyond 2000. *Mol Ther.* 2000;1:493.

23. Kay M. A., Manno C. S., Ragni M. V., et al. Evidence for gene transfer and expression of factor IX in haemophilia B patients treated with an AAV vector. *Nat Genet.* 2000;24:257–261.

24. Cavazzana-Calvo M., Hacein-Bey S., de Saint Basile G., et al. Gene therapy of human severe combined immunodeficiency (SCID)-X1 disease. *Science.* 2000;288:669–672.

25. Collins F. S. Preparing health professionals for the genetic revolution. *JAMA.* 1997;278:1285–1286.

26. Hudson K. L., Rothenberg K. H., Andrews L. B., Kahn M. J. E., Collins F. S. Genetic discrimination and health insurance: an urgent need for reform. *Science.* 1995;270:391–393.

27. Rothenberg K., Fuller B., Rothstein M., et al. Genetic information and the workplace: legislative approaches and policy challenges. *Science.* 1997;275:1755–1757.

JAMES D. WATSON

Genes and Politics

James D. Watson is the President of the Cold Spring Harbor Laboratory and shared the Nobel Prize for the discovery of the structure of DNA. He has been a member of the Harvard faculty and was the first Director of the National Center for Human Genome Research at the National Institutes of Health, where he helped to launch the Human Genome Project.

• • •

GENUINE HUMAN GENETICS EMERGES FROM RECOMBINANT DNA METHODOLOGIES

Long holding back the development of human genetics as a major science was the lack of a genetic map allowing human genes to be located along the chromosomes on which they reside. As long as conventional breeding procedures remained the only route to gene mapping, the precise molecular changes underpinning most human genetic diseases seemed foreordained to remain long mysterious. The key breakthrough opening a path around this seemingly insuperable obstacle came in the late 1970s when it was discovered that the exact sequence (order of the genetic letters A, G, T, and C) of a given gene varies from one person to another. Between any two individuals, roughly 1 in 1000 bases are different, with such variations most frequently occurring within the noncoding DNA regions not involved in specifying specific amino acids. Initially most useful were base differences (polymorphisms) which affected DNA cutting by one of the many just discovered "restriction enzymes" that cut DNA molecules within very specific base sequences.

Soon after the existence of DNA polymorphisms became known, proposals were made that they could provide the genetic markers needed to put together human genetic maps. In a 1980 paper, David Botstein, Ron Davis, Mark Scolnick, and Ray White argued that human maps could be obtained through studying the pattern through which polymorphisms were inherited in the members of large multigenerational families. Those polymorphisms that stay together were likely to be located close to each other on a given chromosome. During the next 5 years, two groups, one led by Helen Donis-Keller in Massachusetts, the other led by Ray White in Utah, rose to this challenge, both using DNA from family blood samples stored at CEPH (Centre d'Étude de Polymorphisme Humain),

Reprinted with the permission of the author and the publisher from the *Journal of Molecular Medicine* 75 (September 1997), 632–36. Copyright © 1997 Springer-Verlag.

the mapping center established in Paris by Jean Dausset. By 1985, the mutant genes responsible for Huntington's disease and cystic fibrosis (CF) had been located on chromosomes 4 and 7, respectively.

By using a large number of additional polymorphic markers in the original chromosome 7 region implicated in CF, Francis Collins' group in Ann Arbor and L. C. Tsui's group in Toronto located the DNA segment containing the responsible gene. Its DNA sequence revealed that the CF gene coded for a large membrane protein involved in the transport of chloride ions. The first CF mutant they found contained three fewer bases than its normal equivalent and led to a protein product that was nonfunctional because of its lack of a phenylalanine residue.

THE HUMAN GENOME PROJECT: RESPONDING TO THE NEED FOR EFFICIENT DISEASE GENE MAPPING AND ISOLATION

Although the genes responsible for cystic fibrosis and Huntington's disease were soon accurately mapped using only a small number of DNA polymorphic markers, the genes behind many other important genetic diseases quickly proved to be much harder to map to a specific chromosome, much less assign to a DNA chromosomal segment short enough to generate hopes for its eventual cloning. All too obviously, the genes behind the large set of still very badly understood diseases like Alzheimer's disease, late-onset diabetes, or breast cancer would be mapped much, much sooner if several thousands more newly mapped DNA polymorphisms somehow became available. Likewise, the task of locating the chromosomal DNA segment(s) in which the desired disease genes reside would be greatly shortened if all human DNA were publicly available as sets of overlapping cloned DNA segments (contigs). And the scanning of such DNA segments to look for mutationally altered base sequences would go much faster if the complete sequence of all the human DNA were already known. However, to generate these importantly new resources for human genetics, major new sources of money would be needed. So, by early 1986, serious discussions began as to how to start, soon, the complete sequencing of the 3×10^9 [3 billion] base pairs that collectively make up the human genome (the Human Genome Project or HGP).

Initially, there were more scientific opponents than proponents for what necessarily would be biology's first megaproject. It would require thousands of scientists and the consumption of some $3 billion-like sums. Those disliking its prospects feared that, inevitably, it would be run by governmental bureaucrats not up to the job and would employ scientists too dull for assignment to this intellectually challenging research. Out of many protracted meetings held late in 1986 and through 1987, the argument prevailed that the potential rewards for medicine as well as for biological research itself would more than compensate for the monies the Human Genome Project would consume during the 15 years then thought needed to complete it. Moreover, completion of each of the two stages—the collection of many more mapped DNA markers and the subsequent ordering of cloned DNA segments into long overlapping sets (contigs)—would by themselves greatly speed up disease gene isolation.

Always equally important to point out, the 15 years projected to complete the Human Genome Project meant that its annual cost of $200 million at most would represent only 1–2% of the money spent yearly for fundamental biomedical research over the world. There was also the realization that some 100,000 human genes believed sited along their chromosomes would be much easier to find and functionally understand if genome sequences were first established for the much smaller, well-studied model organisms such as *Escherichia coli, Saccharomyces cerevisiae, Caenorhabditis elegans,* and *Drosophila melanogaster.* Thus, the biologists who worked with these organisms realized that their own research would be speeded up if the Human Genome Project went ahead.

The American public, as represented by their congressional members, proved initially to be much more enthusiastic about the objectives of the Human Genome Project than most supposedly knowledgeable biologists, with their parochial concerns for how federal monies for biology would be divided up. The first congressionally mandated monies for the Human Genome Project became available late in 1987, when many intelligent molecular geneticists still were sitting on the fence as to whether it made sense. In contrast, Congress, being told that big medical advances would virtually automatically flow out of genome knowledge, saw no reason not to move fast. In doing so, they temporarily set aside the question of what human life would be like when the bad genes behind so many of our major diseases were found. Correctly, to my mind, their overwhelming concern was the current horror of diseases like Alzheimer's, not seeing the need then to, perhaps prematurely, worry about the dilemmas arising when individuals are genetically shown at risk for specific diseases years before they show any symptoms.

GENOME ETHICS: PROGRAMS TO FIND WAYS TO AMELIORATE GENETIC INJUSTICE

The moment I began in October 1988 my almost 4-year period of helping lead the Human Genome Project, I stated that 3% of the NIH-funded component should support research and discussion on the Ethical, Legal, and Social Implications (ELSI) of the new resulting genetic knowledge. A lower percentage might be seen as tokenism, while I then could not see wise use of a larger sum. Under my 3% proposal, some $6 million (3% of $200 million) would eventually be so available, a much larger sum than ever before provided by our government for the ethical implications of biological research.

In putting ethics so soon into the Genome agenda, I was responding to my own personal fear that all too soon critics of the Genome Project would point out that I was a representative of the Cold Spring Harbor Laboratory that once housed the controversial Eugenics Record Office. My not forming a genome ethics program quickly might be falsely used as evidence that I was a closet eugenicist, having as my real long-term purpose the unambiguous identification of genes that lead to social and occupational stratification as well as to genes justifying racial discrimination. So I saw the need to be proactive in making ELSI's major purpose clear from its start—to devise better ways to combat the social injustice that has at its roots bad draws of the genetic dice. Its programs should not be turned into public forums for debating whether genetic inequalities exist. With imperfect gene copying always the evolutionary imperative, there necessarily will always be a constant generation of the new gene disease variants and consequential genetic injustice.

The issues soon considered for ELSI monies were far-ranging. For example, how can we ensure that the results of genetic diagnosis are not misused by prospective employers or insurers? How should we try to see that individuals know what they are committing themselves to when they allow their DNA to be used for genetic analyzing? What concrete steps should be taken to ensure the accuracy of genetic testing? And when a fetus is found to possess genes that will not allow it to develop into a functional human being, who, if anyone, should have the right to terminate the pregnancy?

From their beginnings, our ELSI programs had to reflect primarily the needs of individuals at risk of the oft tragic consequences of genetic disabilities. Only long-term harm would result in the perception of genetics as an honest science if ELSI-type decisions were perceived to be dominated either by the scientists who provided the genetic knowledge or by the government bodies that funded such research. And since women are even in the distant future likely to disproportionately share the burden of caring for the genetically disabled, they should lead the discussion of how more genetic knowledge is to come into our lives.

HUMAN HESITATIONS IN LEARNING THEIR OWN GENETIC FATE

With the initial distribution of American genome monies and the building and equipping the resulting genome centers taking 2 years, the Human Genome Project in its megaphase did not effectively start until the fall of 1990. Decisions to go ahead by funding bodies in the United States helped lead to the subsequent inspired creation of Genethon outside Paris by the French genetic disease charity, Association Française contre les Myopathies (AFM), as well as the building of the now immense Sanger Centre, just south of Cambridge, England, by the British medically oriented charity, the Wellcome Trust. Now effectively 7 years into its projected 15-year life, the Human Genome Project has more than lived up to its role in speeding up genetic disease mapping and subsequent gene cloning. It quickly made successful the search for the gene behind the fragile X syndrome that leads to severe mental retardation in boys preferentially affected by this sex-linked genetic affliction. The molecular defect found was an expansion of pre-existing three-base repetitive sequences that most excitingly increase in length from one generation to the next. The long mysterious phenomenon of anticipation, in which the severity of a disease grows through subsequent generations, was thus given a molecular explanation. Then at long last, in 1994, the gene for Huntington's disease was found. Its cause was likewise soon found to be the expansion of a repetitive gene sequence.

While the mapping to a chromosome per se of any disease gene remains an important achievement, the cloning of the disease gene itself is a bigger milestone. Thus, the 1990 finding by Mary Claire King that much hereditary breast cancer is due to a gene on chromosome 17 set off a big gene-cloning race. With that gene in hand, there was a chance that its DNA sequence would reveal the normal function of the protein it codes for. In any case, it gives its possessors the opportunity to examine directly the DNA from individuals known to be at risk for a disease to see whether they had the unwanted gene. Thus, when in 1993 the chromosome 17 breast cancer gene (BRCA1) was isolated by Myriad, the Utah disease gene-finding company, it could inform women so tested for BRCA1 whether or not they had the feared gene.

Initially, concerns were voiced that unbridled commercialization of this capability would all too easily give women knowledge they would not be psychologically prepared to handle. If so, the ethical way to prevent such emotional setbacks might be to regulate both how the tests were given and who should be allowed to be tested. I fear, however, that a major reason behind many such calls for regulation of genetic testing is the hidden agenda of wanting to effectively stop widespread genetic testing by making it so difficult to obtain. Now, however, calls for governmental regulation may fall on increasingly deaf ears. To Myriad's great disappointment, it appears that the great majority of women at 50% risk of being breast cancer gene carriers don't want to be tested. Rather than receive the wrong verdict, they seem to prefer living with uncertainty. Likewise, a very large majority of the individuals at risk for Huntington's disease are also psychologically predisposed against putting themselves at risk of possibly knowing of their genetic damnation.

Although we are certain to learn in the future of many individuals regretting that they subjected themselves to genetic tests and wishing they had been more forewarned of the potential perils of such knowledge, I do not see how the state can effectively enter into such decisions. Committees of well-intentioned outsiders will never have the intimate knowledge to assess a given individual's psychological need, or not, for a particular piece of scientific or medical knowledge. In the last analysis, we should accept the fact that if scientific knowledge exists, individual persons or families should have the right to decide whether it will lead to their betterment.

INARGUABLE EXISTENCE OF GENES PREDISPOSING HUMANS TO BEHAVIORAL DISORDERS

The extraordinarily negative connotation that the term eugenics now conveys is indelibly identified with its past practitioners' unjustified statements that behavioral differences, whether between individuals, families, or the so-called races, largely had their origins in gene differences. Given the primitive power of human genetics, there was no way for such broad-ranging assertions to have been legitimatized by the then methods of science. Even the eugenically minded psychiatrists' claims that defective genes were invariably at the root of their mental patients' symptoms were no more than hunches. Yet, it was by their imputed genetic imperfection that the mentally ill were first sterilized and then, being of no value to the wartime Third Reich, released from their lives by subsequent "mercy killings."

But past eugenic horrors in no way justify the "Not in Our Genes" politically correct outlook of many leftwing academics. They still spread the unwarranted message that only our bodies, not our minds, have genetic origins. Essentially protecting the ideology that all our troubles have capitalistic exploitative origins, they are particularly uncomfortable with the thought that genes have any influence on intellectual abilities or that unsocial criminal behavior might owe its origins to other than class or racially motivated oppression. Whether these scientists on the left actually believe, say, that the incidence of schizophrenia would seriously lessen if class struggles ended, however, is not worth finding out.

Instead, we should employ, as fast as we can, the powerful new techniques of human genetics to find soon the actual schizophrenia predisposing genes. The much higher concordance of schizophrenia in identical versus nonidentical twins unambiguously tells us that they are there to find. Such twin analysis, however, reveals that genetics cannot be the whole picture. Since the concordance rates for schizophrenia, as well as for manic-depressive disease, are more like 60%, not 100%, environmental predisposing factors must exist and, conceivably, viral infections that affect the brain are sometimes involved.

Unfortunately, still today, the newer statistical tricks for analyzing polymorphic inheritance patterns have not yet led to the unambiguous mapping of even one major schizophrenic gene to a defined chromosomal site. The only convincing data involve only the 1% of schizophrenics whose psychoses seemingly are caused by the small chromosome 22 deletions responsible also for the so-called St. George facial syndrome. Manic-depressive disease also has been more than hard to understand genetically. Only last year did solid evidence emerge for a major predisposing gene on the long arm of chromosome 18. This evidence looks convincing enough for real hopes that the actual gene involved will be isolated over the next several years.

Given that over half the human genes are thought to be involved in human brain development and functioning, we must expect that many other behavioral differences between individuals will also have genetic origins. Recently, there have been claims that both "reckless personalities" and "unipolar depressions" associate with specific polymorphic forms of genes coding for the membrane receptors involved in the transmission of signals between nerve cells. Neither claim now appears to be reproducible, but we should not be surprised to find some subsequent associations to hold water. Now anathematic to left-wing ideologues is the highly convincing report of a Dutch family, many of whose male members display particularly violent behavior. Most excitingly, all of the affected males possess a mutant gene coding for an inactive form of the enzyme monoamine oxidase. Conceivably having too little of this enzyme, which breaks down neurotransmitters, leads to the persistence of destructive thoughts and the consequential aggressive patterns. Subsequent attempts to detect in other violent individuals this same mutant gene have so far failed. We must expect someday, however, to find that other mutant genes that lead to altered brain chemistry also lead to asocial activities. Their existence, however, in no way should be taken to mean that gene variants are the major cause of violence. Nonetheless, continued denials by the scientific left that genes have no role in how people interact with each other will inevitably further diminish their already tainted credibility.

KEEPING GOVERNMENTS OUT OF GENETIC DECISIONS

No rational person should have doubts whether genetic knowledge properly used has the capacity to improve the human condition. Through discovering those genes whose bad variants make us unhealthy or in some other way unable to function effectively, we can fight back in several different ways. For example, knowing what is wrong at the molecular level should let us sometimes develop drugs that will effectively neutralize the harm generated by certain bad genes. Other genetic disabilities should effectively be neutralized by so-called gene therapy procedures restoring normal cell functioning by adding good copies of the missing normal genes. Although gene therapy enthusiasts have promised too much for the near future, it is difficult to imagine that they will not with time cure some genetic conditions.

For the time being, however, we should place most of our hopes for genetics on the use of antenatal diagnostic procedures, which increasingly will let us know whether a fetus is carrying a mutant gene that will seriously proscribe its eventual development into a functional human being. By terminating such pregnancies, the threat of horrific disease genes continuing to blight many families' prospects for future success can be erased. But even among individuals who firmly place themselves on the pro-choice side and do not want to limit women's rights for abortion, opinions frequently are voiced that decisions obviously good for individual persons or families may not be appropriate for the societies in which we live. For example, by not wanting to have a physically or mentally handicapped child or one who would have to fight all its life against possible death from cystic fibrosis, are we not reinforcing the second-rate status of such handicapped individuals? And what would be the consequences of isolating genes that give rise to the various forms of dyslexia, opening up the possibility that women will take antenatal tests to see if their prospective child is likely to have a bad reading disorder? Is it not conceivable that such tests would lead to our devoting less resources to the currently reading-handicapped children whom now we accept as an inevitable feature of human life?

That such conundrums may never be truly answerable, however, should not concern us too much. The truly relevant question for most families is whether an obvious good to them will come from having a child with a major handicap. Is it more likely for such children to fall behind in society or will they through such affliction develop the strengths of character and fortitude that lead, like Jeffrey Tate, the noted British conductor, to the head of their packs? Here I'm afraid that the word handicap cannot escape its true definition—being placed at a disadvantage. From this perspective, seeing the bright side of being handicapped is like praising the virtues of extreme poverty. To be sure, there are many individuals who rise out of its inherently degrading states. But we perhaps most realistically should see it as the major origin of asocial behavior that has among its many bad consequences the breeding of criminal violence.

Only harm, thus, I fear will come from any form of society-based restriction on individual genetic decisions. Decisions from committees of well-intentioned individuals will too often emerge as vehicles for seeming to do good as opposed to doing good. Moreover, we should necessarily worry that once we let governments tell their citizens what they cannot do genetically, we must fear they also have power to tell us what we must do. But for us as individuals to feel comfortable making decisions that affect the genetic makeups of our children, we correspondingly have to become genetically literate. In the future, we must necessarily question any government which does not see this as its responsibility. Will it so not act because it wants to keep such powers for itself?

THE MISUSE OF GENETICS BY HITLER SHOULD NOT DENY ITS USE TODAY

Those of us who venture forth into the public arena to explain what Genetics can or cannot do for society seemingly inevitably come up against individuals who feel that we are somehow the modern equivalents of Hitler. Here we must not fall into the absurd trap of being against everything Hitler was for. It was in no way evil for Hitler to regard mental disease as a scourge on society. Almost everyone then, as still true today, was made uncomfortable by psychotic individuals. It is how Hitler treated German mental patients that still outrages civilized societies and lets us call him immoral. Genetics per se can never be evil. It is only when we use or misuse it that morality comes in. That we want to find ways to lessen the impact of mental illness is inherently good. The killing by the Nazis of the German mental patients for reasons of supposed genetic inferiority, however, was barbarianism at its worst.

Because of Hitler's use of the term Master Race, we should not feel the need to say that we never want to use genetics to make humans more capable than they are today. The idea that genetics could or should be used to give humans power that they do not now possess, however, strongly upsets many individuals first exposed to the notion. I suspect such fears in some ways are similar to concerns now expressed about the genetically handicapped of today. If more intelligent human beings might someday be created, would we not think less well about ourselves as we exist today? Yet anyone who proclaims that we are now perfect as humans has to be a silly crank. If we could honestly promise young couples that we knew how to give them offspring with superior character, why should we assume they would decline? Those at the top of today's societies might not see the need. But if your life is going nowhere, shouldn't you seize the chance of jump-starting your children's future?

Common sense tells us that if scientists find ways to greatly improve human capabilities, there will be no stopping the public from happily seizing them.

ALLEN BUCHANAN, DAN W. BROCK, NORMAN DANIELS, AND DANIEL WIKLER

From Chance to Choice: Genetics and Justice

Allen Buchanan is Professor of Philosophy at Duke University. He publishes primarily in bioethics and political philosophy and currently serves as a member of the Advisory Council for the Human Genome Research Institute on goals and funding priorities for genomic research. Among his books are *Ethics, Efficiency, and the Market* (Rowman & Littlefield) and (with Dan Brock) *Deciding for Others: The Ethics of Surrogate Decision Making* (Cambridge University Press).

Dan W. Brock is Charles C. Tillinghast, Jr. University Professor, Professor of Philosophy and Biomedical Ethics, and Director of the Center for Biomedical Ethics at Brown University. He is a former staff philosopher on the President's Commission for the Study of Ethical Problems in Medicine. His books include *Life and Death: Philosophical Essays in Biomedical Ethics* (Cambridge), and (with Allen Buchanan) *Deciding for Others: The Ethics of Surrogate Decision Making* (Cambridge).

Norman Daniels is Goldthwaite Professor of Philosophy at Tufts University and Professor of Medical Ethics at Tufts Medical School. He has written widely in the philosophy of science, ethics, political and social philosophy, and medical ethics. Among his books are *Seeking Fair Treatment: From the AIDS Epidemic to National Health Care Reform* (Oxford) and (with Donald Light and Ronald Caplan) *Benchmarks of Fairness for Health Care Reform* (Oxford). He is currently working on *Just Health,* a substantial revision and expansion of his earlier book *Just Health Care.*

Daniel Wikler is a professor in the Program in Medical Ethics in the Department of the History of Medicine, and in the Department of Philosophy at the University of Wisconsin-Madison. His research focuses on ethical issues in health care and population health, including international health. He has served as President of the International Association of Bioethics, and staff philosopher to the President's Commission for the Study of Ethical Problems in Medicine. He has also served on study commissions and advisory boards for the Institute of Medicine, the Office of Technology Assessment, and other health policy agencies.

CHALLENGES OF THE GENETIC AGE

A powerful alliance of government, business, and science is propelling society into a new era in which human beings will possess a much greater understanding of the most basic functions of all forms of life. With this understanding will come unprecedented control over living things, including ourselves. Scientific knowledge of how genes work will empower human beings to cure and prevent diseases. It may also let us shape some of the most important biological characteristics of the human beings we choose to bring into existence.

Reprinted with permission of the authors and publisher from *From Chance to Choice: Genetics and Justice* by Allen Buchanan, Dan W. Brock, Norman Daniels, and Daniel Wilker. Cambridge University Press, 2000, pp. 1–21. Copyright © 2000 Cambridge University Press.

No one knows the limits of our future powers to shape human lives—or when these limits will be reached. Some expect that at most we will be able to reduce the incidence of serious genetic diseases and perhaps ensure that more people are at the higher end of the distribution of normal traits. More people may have long and healthy lives, and perhaps some will have better memory and other intellectual powers. Others foresee not only greater numbers of people functioning at high levels, but the attainment of levels previously unheard of: lives measured in centuries, people of superhuman intelligence, humans endowed with new traits presently undreamt of. One thing, however, is certain: Whatever the limits of our technical abilities turn out to be, coping with these new powers will tax our wisdom to the utmost.

PREVIEWS OF PERPLEXITIES

Consider a few of the perplexities with which the genetic revolution is likely to confront us in the future.

SCENARIO 1: GENETIC COMMUNITARIANISM

A disaffected member of what the media refer to as a religious cult announces that the group is attempting to implement its vision of the good society by "mass producing" human embryos cloned from the group's leaders. He claims that the group has its own genetics lab and hopes to adapt for use on humans techniques for cloning embryos commonly employed in the commercial production of animals. Several members of Congress express outrage and urge that the government take action against the religious group. A spokesperson for the American Civil Liberties Union says that if we value reproductive freedom and freedom of religion, we must respect the right of religious communities to attempt to transmit their beliefs and way of life to future generations, whether by the traditional methods of teaching and indoctrination or by the application of genetic technology.

SCENARIO 2: PERSONAL CHOICE OR PUBLIC HEALTH CONCERN?

A single, inexpensive blood test for prospective parents can detect high risk for virtually all serious genetic disorders as well as a broad range of genetic susceptibilities for illnesses. An initiative is a foot to provide mass genetic screening using this test. A government commission examining the feasibility of this proposal notes that the program's cost-effectiveness depends on whether a sufficient number of those tested "act on the knowledge of positive results—that is, whether they choose to avoid conception of affected fetuses." An advocate of the mass screening program says "this is a public health matter; people should not be free to inflict avoidable diseases on their children, especially if we are ever to have an affordable health care system that provides coverage for everyone." An opponent replies that "genetic services of any kind are strictly a matter of personal choice—respect for reproductive freedom requires this. People must be free to act on the test results as they see fit; any program that will result in pressures that limit reproductive freedom would be unacceptable."

SCENARIO 3: THE QUEST FOR THE PERFECT BABY

Excerpt from the introduction to a dissertation in a history of medicine written in 2040:

> In the 1990s, as in the preceding three decades, parents mainly practiced negative eugenics, using tests for major chromosomal defects such as Down syndrome and aborting "defective" fetuses. By 2020 the standards for acceptable babies had been raised: prospective parents routinely aborted fetuses that were otherwise healthy but that had genes that gave them a significantly higher than average risk of breast cancer, colorectal cancer, Alzheimer's dementia, or coronary artery disease. By 2030, the trend was toward even higher standards: Fetuses with any of a range of "undesirable" or "less than optimal" combinations of genes were routinely aborted, including those predicted not to be in the highest quintile with respect to intelligence or even height. Widespread use of these techniques by parents who could afford them began to raise the average level of health, physical strength and stature, and intellectual ability in the population, a trend encouraged by nationalist politicians. But the insistence of many parents that their child be in the upper quintile created a spiral in which no amount of genetic boost ever seemed enough.

SCENARIO 4: HEALTH CARE IN THE AGE OF GENETIC INTERVENTION

At a congressional hearing, Dr. Philip Jones testifies that the standard benefit package that all insurance companies are federally mandated to offer should be expanded to include what are popularly called "mood enhancer" drugs for all persons who have the "mild depression gene," even though these individuals do not usually meet existing criteria for having bipolar affective disorder. According to Jones, "What is important is whether clinical science can help people live better lives; the fact that a person's mood swings don't qualify as bipolar disorder isn't really important." A spokesperson for the National Association of Health Insurers protests, "Health care coverage stops where treatment for disease ends; there's a right to health care, but there's no right to be happy." Jones, shaking his head with a somewhat patronizing air, replies, "What we now know about the way genes affect the brain and hence the personality renders the distinction between psychiatric disorders and undesirable psychological conditions unimportant."

SCENARIO 5: THE GENETIC ENHANCEMENT CERTIFICATE

Katherine and Bill are applying for the same management position in a large firm. Included in Katherine's dossier is a genetic enhancement certificate from Opti-Gene, Inc. It certifies that the bearer has "benefited from cutting-edge genetic enhancement technology" and asserts that those who have had the package of services in question on average have fewer colds and other common respiratory infections, are less likely to suffer depression, and score higher on tests of memory skills. Bill, who cannot afford genetic enhancement, protests that "hiring on the basis of genetic enhancement is just as unfair as hiring on the basis of race or gender—it's a violation of equal opportunity and makes a travesty of the merit system." Katherine replies indignantly, "Merit means the position goes to the best candidate, and I am the best candidate, so what's the problem?"

THE NEED FOR SYSTEMATIC ETHICAL THINKING

Reflection on scenarios such as these prompts two sorts of self-doubt. We worry whether, like the sorcerer's apprentice, we will suffer the consequences of partial knowledge, overestimating our power to predict and control the causal chains we initiate through the application of our newfound knowledge. But we also worry about values. Even if we were more assured than we should be that our technical control will be complete, we would continue to wonder whether we will be able to distinguish between what we can do and what we ought to do. Do we have the ethical resources to use our genetic powers wisely and humanely? Or are we like hapless space-travelers embarking on an interstellar voyage equipped only with a pocket compass? Do existing ethical theories, concepts, and principles provide the materials for constructing more adequate instruments for moral navigation?

In the face of these doubts about whether our values will keep pace with our powers, there is an unfortunate tendency to rest content with inarticulate forebodings about the dangers of "playing God" when confronted with revelations of particular new genetic discoveries or technical breakthroughs. The admonition not to play God is useless, except as a general warning against hubris. It tells us nothing about how we should respond to any particular choice we may confront.

Something more is needed. A systematic vision of the moral character of the world we hope to be moving toward is required. The primary objective of this [essay], accordingly, is to make a contribution toward answering a single question: *What are the most basic moral principles that would guide public policy and individual choice concerning the use of genetic interventions in a just and humane society in which the powers of genetic intervention are much more developed than they are today?*

Accomplishing this will require responding to many other questions, among the most important of which are: What are the most important ethical problems to which greatly increased powers of genetic intervention will give rise? Are these new problems? How adequate are the resources of existing ethical theory to cope with them? And what sorts of ethical principles and distinctions are needed to help a society equipped with formidable powers of genetic intervention avoid the mistakes and evils of the eugenics movements of the late nineteenth and early to mid-twentieth centuries?

GENOMIC RESEARCH AND GENETIC INTERVENTION

THE HUMAN GENOME PROJECT AND RELATED GENETIC RESEARCH

Our knowledge of how genes function is growing at an almost imponderable rate. The Human Genome Project is ahead of schedule in achieving its goal of determining the sequence of the three million or so base pairs of nucleotides that make up the complete genetic material of a human being. Presumably the coming years will also bring a great expansion of our knowledge of how particular genes function. Almost daily, newspaper headlines proclaim startling and sometimes disquieting discoveries and feats of technological virtuosity, from the identification of a "fat gene" to the cloning of a sheep from an adult sheep's mammary cell. Eventually these advances will bear practical fruit: the ability to use knowledge of how genes function to intervene in significant ways in human life. The Human Genome Project, in part because of the impetus it has given to the rapid, worldwide sharing of information and technique, does much to guarantee that the stream of genetic knowledge will continue to increase in volume and speed.

Although it is the most highly publicized locus of research, the Human Genome Project does not stand alone. Many other projects for human genetic research are funded by the National Institutes of Health in the United States and by government agencies in other industrial countries. And private, commercial research efforts are increasingly capitalizing on the knowledge base provided by the Human Genome Project and other government-funded research and on the expertise of researchers in academic institutions, many of which are publicly funded. Although the research for this [essay] was funded by the program for Ethical, Legal, and Social Implications of the Human Genome Project of the National Institutes of Health, our concern is broader. We will speak generally of "human genomic research" or even more broadly of "advances in genetic knowledge," recognizing that the study of nonhuman organisms has contributed and will continue to contribute to an understanding of how genes function in human beings.

MODES OF GENETIC INTERVENTION

As a rough, initial categorization, modes of genetic intervention can first be divided into direct and indirect interventions. By "direct genetic interventions" we mean primarily two modes: gene therapy, in which normal or desirable genes are inserted into either somatic (body tissue) cells or germline cells (gametes—sperms or eggs—or embryos); and gene surgery, in which abnormal or undesirable genes are "switched off"—that is, deactivated so that they no longer produce their distinctive effects.

At present, gene therapy in human beings has been limited to somatic cells. For example, normal genes have been inserted into the bone marrow of patients who suffer from certain blood disorders due to the inability of their own genes to produce particular proteins. In the future, it is expected that gene therapy and gene surgery will be performed on human germline cells, with genes being inserted into or deactivated in gametes and embryos (fertilized eggs).

Gene therapy today involves the insertion of cloned normal genes—genes that occur naturally. Naturally occurring genes may come either from other human beings or from nonhuman animals. But it may eventually become possible to create new genes—that is, to synthesize new sequences of base pairs to produce effects that are not found in nature. Genes, after all, are just functionally significant sequences of base pairs.

From a technical standpoint, a fruitful combination of methods—at least for some conditions—would be to complement gene therapy on germline cells with gene surgery. The desirable gene would be introduced early enough in the gamete or embryo to replicate and keep reproducing throughout all the cells of the organism (rather than being inserted, decaying, and being reinserted into a particular tissue), and the undesirable gene would be "knocked out." Alternatively, recently isolated *totipotent* human embryo stem cells may eventually provide the ideal platform from which to develop a range of gene therapies. (A totipotent cell is one that can develop into any kind of tissue or organ, given the proper biochemical stimulation.)

In contrast to direct intervention, *indirect genetic intervention* means primarily genetic pharmacology and embryo selection. By *genetic pharmacology* we mean the use of knowledge about genes to design drugs that will either substitute for the chemical products that would be produced by a normal gene in an individual who has an abnormal one, augment the chemical products of normal genes or counteract the effects of an undesirable or abnormal gene (e.g., by disrupting the protein it produced; Lewontin 1997). Furthermore, someday novel sequences of base pairs—new genes synthesized in the laboratory—may produce drugs that will either ameliorate or prevent diseases, give individuals new desirable traits, or enhance desirable traits they already have or would have when they become fully developed. Embryo selection involves three main steps: "harvesting" embryos, subjecting them to DNA analysis, and implanting an embryo that possesses the preferred characteristics.

There is a third category of intervention that may be called genetic, though perhaps with some stretching of the term. It involves the application of knowledge about genes but without the use of either modifying genes, genetic pharmacology, or embryo selection. There are two subcategories: when genetic information is used in regard to reproductive decisions and when it is used to prevent or ameliorate genetically based diseases in an already existing individual. For convenience, we call the first group "reproductive genetic testing interventions" and the second "therapeutic genetic testing interventions."

Reproductive genetic testing interventions are done in response to information revealed by genetic testing, where the testing is performed either on persons who intend to have children or, after conception has occurred, on the fetus. In one sense, the difference between these modes of genetic testing and embryo selection is not great: In the latter, testing is done on embryos rather than on prospective parents or fetuses.

If such a test reveals a risk of genetic disease or of some other undesirable condition, any of several steps may be taken to reduce or eliminate the risk. If it is determined that a woman is carrying a fetus with a genetic defect such as the chromosomal anomaly known as Down syndrome, she may elect to abort the fetus. If a couple undergoes carrier testing (by a blood test) and learns that they both carry a gene for cystic fibrosis or Tay-Sachs disease, they may choose not to have children, to have children by sperm or by egg donation, or to adopt. At present we lack the capacity to use gene therapy, gene surgery, or genetic pharmacology in any of these cases. The only way to reduce the risk of having a child with an abnormal or undesired genetic condition is to avoid having that child.

The second subcategory, therapeutic genetic testing intervention, has been widely practiced in the United States in the case of the hereditary metabolic disorder phenylketonuria (PKU) for more than 30 years. A blood test is performed on infants at birth. If it is positive for PKU, a special diet is used to avoid the buildup of an enzyme that causes brain damage.

The gene for another potentially lethal genetic disorder, hereditary hemochromatosis, or inherited excessive iron storage disease, was identified by a private genetic technology company in 1996. A blood test for the two mutations that cause the disease has just become available. The treatment for hemochromatosis, like that for PKU, is remarkably "low-tech," consisting of regular phlebotomies (bloodlettings) to deplete stored iron. Because hereditary hemochromatosis is by far the most common serious genetic disease in the United States (approximately 4 persons per 1,000 of the Caucasian population are homozygous, i.e., have two copies of the mutation, and 1 in 10 is heterozygous, i.e., has one copy), and because treatment is inexpensive and effective, some argue that testing for hemochromatosis should become the next mass genetic screening program in this country.

In addition, knowledge of how genes work will lead to greater knowledge of how genes interact with different environments. Increasingly, we can expect to identify subgroups of the population who have genetic characteristics that may call for special environments if their physical or cognitive development is to be maximized. Here, unlike with PKU and hemochromatosis, tailoring an environment to the special developmental needs of a genotypic subgroup of the population may not be a matter of offering a therapy to treat a disease.

For example, we already know that some children benefit from special environments for learning to read or do mathematics. It may well turn out that there are genetic markers that will help pick out those with special learning needs or special needs for nutrition if their cognitive development is to be maximized. (It is already known that the Tohono O'Odham Indians of southern Arizona and Sonora, Mexico, experience extraordinarily high rates of diabetes on a "normal" white American diet but not when they eat their traditional foods.) Intervening to tailor environments to the needs of genotypic groups may not be genetic intervention as ordinarily understood, yet it is intervention based on knowledge of how genes work in various environments.

. . . [We will focus] mainly on direct genetic interventions and genetic pharmacology, with much of what we say having direct implications for embryo selection as well. The reason for this focus is twofold: First, some of the most fundamental ethical issues arise most clearly in the case of direct genetic interventions and genetic pharmacology. Second, there is already considerable literature on ethical issues in both genetic testing reproductive interventions and genetic testing therapeutic interventions (Cook-Deegan 1994; Andrews et al. 1994; Russo and Cove 1995).

Our reason for giving genetic pharmacology equal billing with direct genetic interventions perhaps warrants explanation. When ethical issues arising from the new genetics are discussed in the popular media—and even in the bioethics literature—the focus is often on "genetic engineering," a phrase that evokes images of scientists splicing genes together to create new kinds of organisms. Nonetheless, genetic pharmacology is likely to be one of the most potent applications of genetic science in the immediate future. (Venture capitalists, including some of the largest pharmaceutical companies, appear to agree with this prediction.) "Engineering" human embryos, if it occurs at all, will probably happen only in the relatively distant future. Dramatic advances in genetic pharmacology are a much nearer and surer prospect. Another alternative to the embryo engineering is embryo selection. Like genetic pharmacology, it seems to be more likely to see extensive use in the nearer future.

THE SHADOW OF EUGENICS

Even the brightest aspirations of the new genetics are from time to time dimmed by the shadow of eugenics. The very term has been in such bad odor since the era of Nazi "racial hygiene" (Proctor 1988) that few people today wish to be associated with eugenics. Indeed, controversies over the new genetics often proceed as if the rival parties assume that if it can be shown that someone's views are "eugenic," they are thereby discredited. Much energy is then spent in trying to attach the label to an opponent or avoid being labeled a eugenicist.

Such exercises tend to be long on rhetoric and short on cognitive content. Attitudes toward eugenics are much like the common view of Marx's *Das Capital*—people know it is wrong though they know little about it—or, more charitably, like the attitude toward Freud's theory of the unconscious: "He was on to something, but he went too far."

At present, neither those who assert that the new genetics is infected by the evils of the old eugenics nor those who indignantly defend the new genetics' moral purity have made a convincing case. Two things are needed for the satisfactory resolution of this controversy: an ethical autopsy on the old eugenics and an examination of the ethical presuppositions and implications of the new genetics. . . .

To evaluate the charge that the new genetics is infected by the evils of eugenics, it is necessary to unearth the ethical assumptions that provide the best justifications currently available for pursuing genetic knowledge and for attempting to use this knowledge to intervene in human lives. As with the attempt to articulate the underlying values of the eugenics movement, our task here requires considerable reconstruction, because those who endorse the expansion of our genetic knowledge and powers of intervention rarely make their ethical assumptions explicit, and they certainly offer nothing like a developed ethical theory. . . .

• • •

TWO MODELS FOR GENETIC INTERVENTION

THE PUBLIC HEALTH MODEL

[We have identified] two quite different perspectives from which genetic intervention may be viewed. The first is what we call the public health model; the second is the personal choice model.

The public health model stresses the production of benefits and the avoidance of harms for groups. It uncritically assumes that the appropriate mode of evaluating options is some form of cost-benefit (or cost-effectiveness) calculation. To the extent that the public health model even recognizes an ethical dimension to decisions about the application of scientific knowledge or technology, it tends to assume that sound ethical reasoning is exclusively consequentialist (or utilitarian) in nature. In other words, it assumes that whether a policy or an action is deemed to be right is thought to depend solely on whether it produces the greatest balance of good over bad outcomes.

More important, consequentialist ethical reasoning—like cost-benefit and cost-effectiveness calculations—assumes that it is not only possible but permissible and even mandatory to aggregate goods and bads (costs and benefits) across individuals. Harms to some can be offset by gains to others; what matters is the sum. Critics of such simple and unqualified consequentialist reasoning, including ourselves, are quick to point out its fundamental flaws: Such reasoning is distributionally insensitive because it fails to take seriously the separateness and inviolability of persons.

In other words, as simple and unqualified consequentialist reasoning looks only to the aggregate balance of good over bad, it does not recognize fairness in the distribution of burdens and benefits to be a fundamental value. As a result, it not only allows but in some circumstances requires that the most fundamental interests of individuals be sacrificed in order to produce the best overall outcome.

Consequentialist ethical theory is not unique in allowing or even requiring that the interests of individuals sometimes yield to the good of all. Any reasonable ethical theory must acknowledge this. But it is unique in maintaining that in principle such sacrifice is justified whenever it would produce any aggregate gain, no matter how small. Because simple and unqualified consequentialism has this implication, some conclude that it fails to appreciate sufficiently that each individual is an irreducibly distinct subject of moral concern.

The public health model, with its affinity for consequentialist ethical reasoning, took a particularly troubling form among some prominent eugenicists. Individuals who were thought to harbor "defective germ plasm" (what would now be called "bad genes") were likened to carriers of infectious disease. While persons infected with cholera were a menace to those with whom they came into contact, individuals with defective germ plasm were an even greater threat to society: They transmitted harm to an unlimited line of persons across many generations.

The only difference between the "horizontally transmitted" infectious diseases and "vertically transmitted" genetic diseases, according to this view, was that the potential harm caused by the latter was even greater. So if measures such as quarantine and restrictions on travel into disease areas that infringed individual freedom were appropriate responses to the former, then they were even more readily justified to avert the greater potential harm of the latter. This variant of the public health model may be called the *vertical epidemic model*. Once this point of view is adopted and combined with a simple and unqualified consequentialism, the risks of infringing liberty and of exclusion and discrimination increase dramatically.

THE PERSONAL SERVICE MODEL

Today eugenics is almost universally condemned. Partly in reaction to the tendency of the most extreme eugenicists to discount individual freedom and welfare for the supposed good of society, medical geneticists and genetic counselors since World War II have adopted an almost absolute commitment to "nondirectiveness" in their relations with those seeking genetic services. Recoiling from the public health model that dominated the eugenics movement, and especially from the vertical disease metaphor, they publicly endorse the view that genetic tests and interventions are simply services offered to individuals—goods for private consumption—to be accepted or refused as individuals see fit.

This way of conceiving of genetic interventions takes them out of the public domain, relegating them to the sphere of private choice. Advocates of the personal service model proclaim that the fundamental value on which it rests is individual autonomy. Whether a couple at risk for conceiving a child with a genetic disease takes a genetic test and how they use the knowledge thus obtained is their business, not society's, even if the decision to vaccinate a child for common childhood infectious diseases is a matter of public health and as such justifies restricting parental choice.

The personal service model serves as a formidable bulwark against the excesses of the crude consequentialist ethical reasoning that tainted the application of the public health model in the era of eugenics. But it does so at a prohibitive price: It ignores the obligation to prevent harm as well as some of the most basic requirements of justice. By elevating autonomy to the exclusion of all other values, the personal service model offers a myopic view of the moral landscape.

In fact, it is misleading to say that the personal service model expresses a commitment to autonomy. Instead, it honors only the autonomy of those who are in a position to exercise choice concerning genetic interventions, not all of those who may be affected by such choices. . . . [T]his approach wrongly subordinates the autonomy of children to that of their parents.

In addition, if genetic services are treated as goods for private consumption, the cumulative effects of many individual choices in the "genetic marketplace" may limit the autonomy of many people, and perhaps of all people. Economic pressures, including requirements for insurability and employment, as well as social stigma directed toward those who produce children with "defects" that could have been avoided, may narrow rather than expand meaningful choice. Finally, treating genetic interventions as personal services may exacerbate inequalities in opportunities if the prevention of genetic diseases or genetic enhancements are available only to the rich. It would be more accurate to say, then, that the personal service model gives free reign to some dimensions of the autonomy of some people, often at the expense of others.

A THIRD APPROACH

Much current thinking about the ethics of genetic intervention assumes that the personal service model is not an adequate moral guide. However, the common response to its deficiencies is not to resurrect the public health model associated with eugenics. Instead, there is a tendency to assume the appropriateness of the personal service model in general and then to erect ad hoc—and less than convincing—"moral firebreaks" to constrain the free choices of individuals in certain areas. For example, some ethicists have urged that the cloning of human beings be strictly prohibited, that there be a moratorium or permanent ban on human germline interventions, or that genetic enhancements (as opposed to treatments of diseases) be outlawed. In each case the proposed moral firebreak shows a distrust of the unalloyed personal service model but at the same time betrays the lack of a systematic, principled account of why and how the choices of individuals should be limited.

[We] aim to avoid both the lack of attention to the moral equality, separateness, and inviolability of persons that afflicted the eugenics movement's public health model of genetic intervention and the narrow concern with autonomous individual choice that characterizes the personal service model. We argue that although respect for individual autonomy requires an extensive sphere of protected reproductive freedoms and hence a broad range of personal discretion in decisions to use genetic interventions, both the need to prevent harm to offspring and the demands of justice, especially those regarding equal opportunity, place systematic limits on individuals' freedom to use or not use genetic interventions.

We try to develop a systematic, defensible moral framework for choices about the use of genetic intervention technologies. Our view steers a course between a public health model in which individuals count only so far as what they do or what is done to them affects the genetic health of "society" and a personal service model in which the choice to use genetic interventions is morally equivalent to the decision to buy goods for private consumption in an ordinary market. Because our account locates the ethics of genetic intervention within the larger enterprise of ethical theorizing, it avoids the arbitrariness and lack of system of the moral firebreaks approach.

ETHICAL ANALYSIS AND ETHICAL THEORY

Although we discuss ethical principles for individuals, our focus more often than not is primarily on ethical principles for institutions. In most cases we try to refine, and sometimes reinterpret or modify, institutional ethical principles that are quite familiar. Prominent examples include the principle that the basic institutions in a society should ensure equal opportunity and the principle of individual self-determination (or autonomy). We also evaluate certain distinctions, such as that between positive and negative genetic interventions or between treatments and enhancements, that some have tried to elevate to the status of institutional ethical principles.

PRINCIPLES FOR INSTITUTIONS

One of the main results of our analysis is that a proper respect for individual self-determination in the realm of reproductive choices must recognize an asymmetry between institutional ethical principles and those for private individuals who are prospective parents: In general, parents should have considerably more latitude to use genetic interventions to shape their children than governments should have to shape their citizens. So even though our emphasis is on institutional ethical principles, determining their proper scope and limits requires an exploration of principles for individuals.

A comprehensive ethical theory—which we do not pretend to provide here—would include an account of virtues as well as principles. Our concern is not to attempt to provide a theory of the connection between ethical virtues and choices concerning the uses of genetic interventions. Nevertheless, some of what we say has direct and important implications for the sorts of virtues persons will need to have, both in their capacities as private individuals and as citizens concerned with public policy, in a society of heightened genetic powers. In particular, we have a good deal to say about the attitudes toward genetically based disabilities and the commitments to "the morality of inclusion" that members of such a society must exhibit if our new powers are to be used justly and humanely.

By way of partial preview, this much can be said about the institutional ethical principles we believe are most essential for a just and humane society equipped with robust capabilities for genetic intervention. As a first approximation, we can say that among the most important principles are those of justice and the prevention of harm. This is hardly surprising or controversial. Things become more complex and interesting as we explore different concepts of what justice requires and different understandings of what constitutes harm, and as we attempt to ascertain the scope and limits of the obligation to prevent harm.

JUSTICE

Following Rawls (1971, p. 3), we focus on the justice of basic social institutions and only by implication on the justice of particular policies or actions. We identify two main headings under which considerations of justice arise in a society of developed powers of genetic intervention: equal opportunity and the morality of inclusion (the latter concept is introduced at the end of this section).

One important conception of equal opportunity requires protection against limitations on individuals' opportunities imposed by racial, ethnic, religious, or gender discrimination. This principle, we argue, is important but incomplete. We opt for a somewhat more inclusive concept of equal opportunity—a version of what John Roemer has called a level playing field conception, of which Rawls's notion of fair equality of opportunity is the most prominent exemplar. Level playing field conceptions require efforts to eliminate or ameliorate the influence of some or all other social factors that limit opportunity over and above discrimination.

The most direct and compelling implication of this conception of the principle of equal opportunity lies in the domain of just health care. Here we adopt the main lines of Norman Daniels's theory of just health care, as developed in several books and a number of articles over the past 15 years. The core idea is that a just health care system should strive to remove barriers to opportunity that are due to disease. ("Disease" here is understood as any "adverse departures from normal species functioning.")

Regardless of how the term "genetic disease" is defined, the etiologies of many diseases include a genetic component. If just health care puts a premium on eliminating barriers to opportunity posed by disease, the question is not whether or in what sense a disease is genetic, but whether there is an intervention (genetic or otherwise) that can cure or prevent it. Thus the level playing field conception has direct implications for genetic intervention: In general, genetic intervention will be an important means of achieving equal opportunity, at least through its use to cure or prevent disease.

We also argue that equal opportunity, as an important principle of justice, has another bearing on genetic intervention. This principle can impose conditions on access to genetic interventions that go beyond the prevention or cure of disease. If, for example, it should ever become possible to enhance some normal desirable characteristics, a consistent commitment to equal opportunity might rule out an unrestricted market for the dissemination of the relevant technology, for if valuable enhancements were available only to the better-off, existing inequalities in opportunity might be exacerbated. Under such conditions, equal opportunity might require either making the enhancements available to all, even those who cannot pay for them or preventing anyone from having them. How we respond to the fifth scenario sketched earlier—The Genetic Enhancement Certificate—will depend on whether justice requires constraints on unequal access to enhancement technologies.

A deeper and more perplexing question is whether equal opportunity may require or permit genetic interventions for the sake of preventing natural inequalities that do not constitute diseases. On the account we endorse, health care does not include everything of benefit that biomedical science can deliver. Health care, so far as it is a concern of justice, has to do only with the treatment and prevention of disease. However, we argue that some versions of the level playing field conception extend the requirements of equal opportunity, at least in principle, to interventions to counteract natural inequalities that do not constitute diseases.

The rationale for such an extension is straightforward: If one of the key intuitions underpinning a level playing field conception of equal opportunity is the conviction that people's opportunities should not be significantly limited due to factors that are wholly beyond their control, then it appears that equal opportunity may require the interventions to counteract the more serious opportunity-limiting effects of bad luck in the "natural lottery," regardless of whether the disadvantage conferred by a person's genes is a disease, strictly speaking, as in our fourth scenario (Health Care in the Age of Genetic Intervention).

Examples such as that of the person with the "mild depression gene" may pull one toward the conclusion that equal opportunity requires genetic interventions in such cases, even if the intervention is not treatment for a disease, for the same reason that equal opportunity requires efforts to counteract the effects of being born into a family of lower educational attainment. In both cases, it seems wrong that a person's opportunities should be limited by wholly undeserved and unchosen factors.

We will also see, however, that there are other interpretations of the level playing field conception that stop short of the conclusion that equal opportunity generally requires interventions to prevent natural disadvantages beyond the realm of disease. One such interpretation, which we believe to be Rawls's, does not hold that all undeserved disadvantages as such, including less desirable genetic endowments, require redress as a matter of justice. Instead, this understanding of equal opportunity only asserts that it is unjust to structure social institutions so as to base persons' entitlements to goods on their possession of natural advantages. According to this view, equal opportunity would not require intervention to prevent any and all instances in which an individual would have less desirable genetic endowments. Natural inequalities as such would not be problematic from the standpoint of justice. These alternative understandings of the level playing field conception of equal opportunity appear to have radically different implications for action: One seems to require what might be called genetic equality, the other does not. Thus, a satisfactory response to cases like our fourth scenario inevitably requires a sortie into the realm of ethical theorizing about the proper understanding and role of equality of opportunity in a theory of justice.

This divergence between different versions of the level playing field conception of equal opportunity provides the first illustration of one of the major aims of this [essay]: to explore how the prospects of genetic interventions with human beings challenge existing ethical theory. The challenge takes two distinct forms. First, the prospect of vastly increased powers of genetic intervention brings with it the inevitability of new choices, the contemplation of which stimulates us to articulate existing ethical theories in greater detail (in this case distinguishing different variants of level playing field theories of equal opportunity, which appear to have different practical implications). Second, by placing within human control features of our condition that we have heretofore regarded as given and unalterable (the fate assigned to us by the natural lottery), the prospect of genetic interventions forces us to rethink the boundary we have traditionally drawn between misfortune and injustice, and indeed between the natural and the social.

PREVENTING HARM

[W]e argue that the most straightforward and compelling case for developing and using genetic interventions is to fulfill one of the most basic moral obligations human beings have: the obligation to prevent harm. People have especially demanding obligations to prevent harm to their offspring, but through the agency of their political institutions, they also have obligations to prevent harm to others.

Taking seriously the potential of genetic interventions to prevent harm pushes the limits of ethical theory in two ways: first, by forcing us to ascertain more precisely the scope and limits of the obligation to prevent harm; and second, by putting pressure on our very understanding of how harm is to be understood in ethical theory. Meeting the first challenge requires us to determine how the sometimes conflicting values of reproductive freedom and the obligation to prevent harm limit each other. Meeting the second requires us to take a stand on a fundamental question of ethical theory: whether behavior is subject to ethical evaluation only if it worsens or betters the condition of particular, individual persons. Some genetic interventions—those that prevent a genetic impairment by preventing an individual who would have the impairment from coming into existence—cannot be described as preventing harm, if a harm is a worsening of the condition of a particular individual. If the individual does not exist, then the intervention cannot worsen his condition.

In addition, our exploration of the obligation to prevent harm through genetic interventions calls into question common dogmas concerning "nondirective" genetic counseling and the right to refuse medical treatment in cases of "maternal/fetal" conflict—where a woman who intends to carry a fetus to term refuses treatment that would prevent a disability in the future child. Thus, whether it is morally permissible to require or at least encourage individuals to avoid a high risk of transmitting a genetic disease (Scenario 2: Personal Choice or Public Health Concern?) will depend in part on how the obligation to prevent harm is understood.

LIMITS ON THE PURSUIT OF "GENETIC PERFECTION"

Parents, of course, are typically not just concerned with preventing harm to their children; they want what is best for them. As the capability for genetic intervention increases, however, ethical issues arise concerning the proper expression of this benevolent parental impulse. [W]e distinguish between permissible and obligatory genetic enhancements, examine the social implications of some of the enhancements that parents might consider undertaking for their children, and argue that what Joel Feinberg has called the child's right to an open future places significant limitations on what it is permissible for parents to do in this regard.

We also distinguish between the ethical implications of the pursuit of improvements by individual parents and those that might be pursued by collectivities in the name of some communitarian vision of human perfection. . . . [We will] provide some of the distinctions and principles needed for a sound ethical response to the issues raised in the Genetic Communitarianism and The Quest for a Perfect Baby scenarios.

THE MORALITY OF INCLUSION

The dawning of the age of genetic intervention also pushes the limits of theories of justice in another way—by calling into question the manner in which the fundamental problem of justice is characteristically framed.

Theories of justice generally begin with the assumption that the most fundamental problem is how to distribute fairly the burdens and benefits of a society—understood as a single, cooperative framework in which all members are active and effective participants. This way of formulating the issue of justice overlooks two vital points: first, that increasingly human beings can exert some control over the character of the basic cooperative framework within which the most fundamental questions of fair distribution arise; and second, that the character of the most basic cooperative framework in a society will determine who is and who is not "disabled." In other words, what the most basic institutions for production and exchange are like will determine the capacities an individual must have in order to be an effective participant in social cooperation (Wikler 1983; Buchanan 1993, 1996).

But if the choice of a framework of cooperation has profound implications for whether some people will be able to participate effectively, there is a prior question of justice: What is required for fairness in the choice of a society's most basic and comprehensive cooperative scheme? Attempting to answer this question stimulates us to gain a deeper understanding of the very nature of disability.

[W]e distinguish genetic impairments from disabilities that have a genetic component, noting that whether or to what extent a genetic impairment results in disability depends on the character of the dominant cooperative framework and the kinds of abilities required for effective participation in it. We then argue that there is an important but often ignored obligation to choose a dominant cooperative framework that is inclusive—that minimizes exclusion from participation on account of genetic impairments. If obligations of inclusion are to be taken seriously, they too impose significant restrictions on the personal choice model for the ethics of genetic intervention.

Justice in the choice of cooperative schemes turns out to be complex, however. The obligation of inclusion is not the sole morally relevant factor, so it cannot be a moral absolute. There is also the morally legitimate interest that persons have in having access to the most productive, enriching, and challenging cooperative scheme in which they are capable of being effective participants. Where there are significant differences in persons' natural assets, the obligation of inclusion and this legitimate interest can come into conflict.

However this conflict is resolved, we argue, a just society of considerable powers of genetic intervention may require changes in both directions: genetic interventions to enable individuals to be effective participants in social cooperation who would not otherwise be able to, and efforts to design the structure of cooperation in ways that make it possible for more people to be effective participants. Appreciation of the problem of justice in the choice of cooperative schemes leads us to the conclusion that regardless of whether we choose to use genetic interventions to promote inclusiveness or refuse to do so, we are in a very real sense choosing who will and who will not be disabled.

• • •

REFERENCES

Andrews, Lori B.; Fullerton, Jane E.; Holtzman, Neil A.; and Motulsky, Arno G., eds. *Assessing Genetic Risks: Implications for Health and Social Policy.* Washington, DC: National Academy Press, 1994.

Buchanan, Allen. "Genetic Manipulation and the Morality of Inclusion." *Social Philosophy and Policy* 13 (1996), 18–46.

Buchanan, Allen. "The Morality of Inclusion." *Social Philosophy and Policy* 10 (1993), 233–57.

Cook-Deegan, Robert. *The Gene Wars: Science, Politics, and the Human Genome.* New York: W. W. Norton and Co., 1994.

Lewontin, Richard C. "Science & 'The Demon-Haunted World': An Exchange." *New York Review of Books* (March 6, 1997), 51–2.

Proctor, Robert. *Racial Hygiene: Medicine Under the Nazis.* Cambridge, MA: Harvard University Press, 1988.

Rawls, John. *A Theory of Justice.* Cambridge, MA: Harvard University Press, 1971.

Russo, Enzo and Cove, David. *Genetic Engineering: Dreams and Nightmares.* Oxford, UK: W. H. Freeman/Spektrum, 1995.

Wikler, Daniel I. "Paternalism and the Mildly Retarded," in Rolf Sartorius, ed., *Paternalism.* Minneapolis: University of Minnesota Press, 1983, 83–94.

SVANTE PÄÄBO

The Human Genome and Our View of Ourselves

Svante Pääbo is one of the founding directors of the Max-Planck-Institute for Evolutionary Anthropology and Honorary Professor of Genetics and Evolutionary Biology at the University of Leipzig. He studies molecular evolution, with an emphasis on human history and origins. In particular, he works on the retrieval of DNA from archaeological and paleontological remains and comparative studies of genomes and gene expression in humans and the great apes.

Perhaps for the pragmatic biologist, the determination of the human genome sequence is a prosaic event—the delivery of a wonderfully powerful tool, but a tool nonetheless. For the general public, however, the human genome sequence is of enormous symbolic significance, and its publication [in] this issue[1] [of *Science*] and in this week's *Nature*[2] is likely to be greeted with the same awestruck feeling that accompanied the landing of the first human on the moon and the detonation of the first atomic bomb.

Why are certain achievements—the first lunar landing, atomic fission, the determination of the human genome sequence—imbued with such emblematic significance? The reason is, I believe, that they change how we think about ourselves. Landing a person on the moon gave us an extraterrestrial perspective on human life; atomic fission gave us the power to create enormous energy reserves and to extinguish all human life on Earth; and now the human genome sequence gives us a view of the internal genetic scaffold around which every human life is molded. This scaffold has been handed down to us from our ancestors, and through it we are connected to all other life on Earth.

How does the complete human genome sequence affect the way that we think about ourselves? Clearly, the availability of a reference human DNA sequence is a milestone toward understanding how humans have evolved, because it opens the door to large-scale comparative studies. The major impact of such studies will be to reveal just how similar humans are to each other and to other species.

The first comparisons will be between the human genome and distantly related genomes such as those of yeast, flies, worms, and mice. A glimpse of what this will show us comes from considering the fact that about 26,000 to 38,000 genes are found in the draft version of our own genome, a number that is only two to three times larger than the 13,600 genes in the fruit fly genome. Furthermore, some 10% of human genes are clearly related to particular genes in the fly and the worm. So, obviously, we share much of our genetic scaffold even with very distant relatives. The similarity between humans and other animals will become even more evident when genome sequences from organisms such as the mouse, with whom we share a more recent common ancestor, become available. For these species, both the number of genes and the general structure of the genome are likely to be very similar to ours. Although this has long been realized by insiders in the genetics community, the close similarity of our genome to those of other organisms will make the unity of life more obvious to everyone. No doubt the genomic view of our place in nature will be both a source of humility and a blow to the idea of human uniqueness.

However, the most obvious challenge to the notion of human uniqueness is likely to come from comparisons of genomes of closely related species. We already know that the overall DNA sequence similarity between humans and chimpanzees is about 99%.[3]

Reprinted with permission from *Science* 291 (16 February 2001), 1219–20. Copyright © 2001, American Association fot the Advancement of Science.

When the chimpanzee genome sequence becomes available, we are sure to find that its gene content and organization are very similar (if not identical) to our own. Perhaps it is our subconscious discomfort with this expectation that explains the slowness with which the genomics community has embraced the idea of a chimpanzee genome project. Be that as it may, with most of the human genome sequence now complete, it will be easy to determine the chimpanzee sequence using the human sequence as a guide to assembly. The result is sure to be an even more powerful challenge to the notion of human uniqueness than the comparison of the human genome to those of other mammals.

Yet the few differences between our genome and those of the great apes will be profoundly interesting because among them lie the genetic prerequisites that make us different from all other animals. In particular, these differences may reveal the genetic foundation for our rapid cultural evolution and geographic expansion, which started between 150,000 and 50,000 years ago[4] and led to our current overbearing domination of Earth. The realization that one or a few genetic accidents made human history possible will provide us with a whole new set of philosophical challenges to think about.

Large-scale comparisons of human genomes from many individuals are now possible with the emergence of high-throughput techniques for DNA sequence determination. The general picture already apparent from such studies is that the gene pool in Africa contains more variation than elsewhere, and that the genetic variation found outside of Africa represents only a subset of that found within the African continent.[5] From a genetic perspective, all humans are therefore Africans, either residing in Africa or in recent exile.

In view of the sad part that race and ethnicity still play in most societies, concerns that genetic analyses of different human populations could be abused are appropriate. Fortunately, from the few studies of nuclear DNA sequences, it is clear that what is called "race," although culturally important, reflects just a few continuous traits determined by a tiny fraction of our genes. This tiny fraction gives no indication of variations at other parts of our genome. Thus, from the perspective of nuclear genes, it is often the case that two persons from the same part of the world who look superficially alike are less related to each other than they are to persons from other parts of the world who may look very different (see the figure p. 498).[6] Although small segments of the genome—such as mitochondrial DNA and Y chromosomal DNA (which are inherited in an unusual way) or the few genes that encode visible traits (which may have been selected for)—show a pattern where the genes in a particular human population can be traced back to a single common ancestor, this is not the case for the vast majority of our genes. Indeed, one way in which we humans seem to differ from apes is that we have evolved with very little subdivision. This is surely because we are a young species (in evolutionary terms) and have a greater tendency for migration than many other mammals. I suspect, therefore, that genome-wide studies of genetic variation among human populations may not be so easy to abuse—in terms of using data as "scientific support" for racism or other forms of bigotry—as is currently feared. If anything, such studies will have the opposite effect because prejudice, oppression, and racism feed on ignorance. Knowledge of the genome should foster compassion, not only because our gene pool is extremely mixed, but also because a more comprehensive understanding of how our genotype relates to our phenotype will demonstrate that everyone carries at least some deleterious alleles. Consequently, stigmatizing any particular group of individuals on the basis of ethnicity or carrier status for certain alleles will be revealed as absurd.

From a medical standpoint, improved predictive capabilities provided by the identification of disease-associated alleles harbor great potential benefits but also problems. The benefits will come from using individualized risk assessment to modify the environmental and behavioral components of common diseases. Relatively minor measures implemented early in life may prove to be extremely effective in postponing or even preventing the onset of disease. But individualized risk assessment may come at the price of "genetic hypochondria," causing many to spend their lives waiting for a disease that may never arrive. Finally, increased medical predictive power obviously represents a societal challenge in terms of medical insurance, especially in countries that, unlike most Western European countries, are not blessed with health insurance systems that share risks in an equitable fashion among the whole population. Legislators in such countries would be wise to act now to counteract future temptations to "personalize" insurance risks. Later on, once powerful genetic diagnostic tests are in

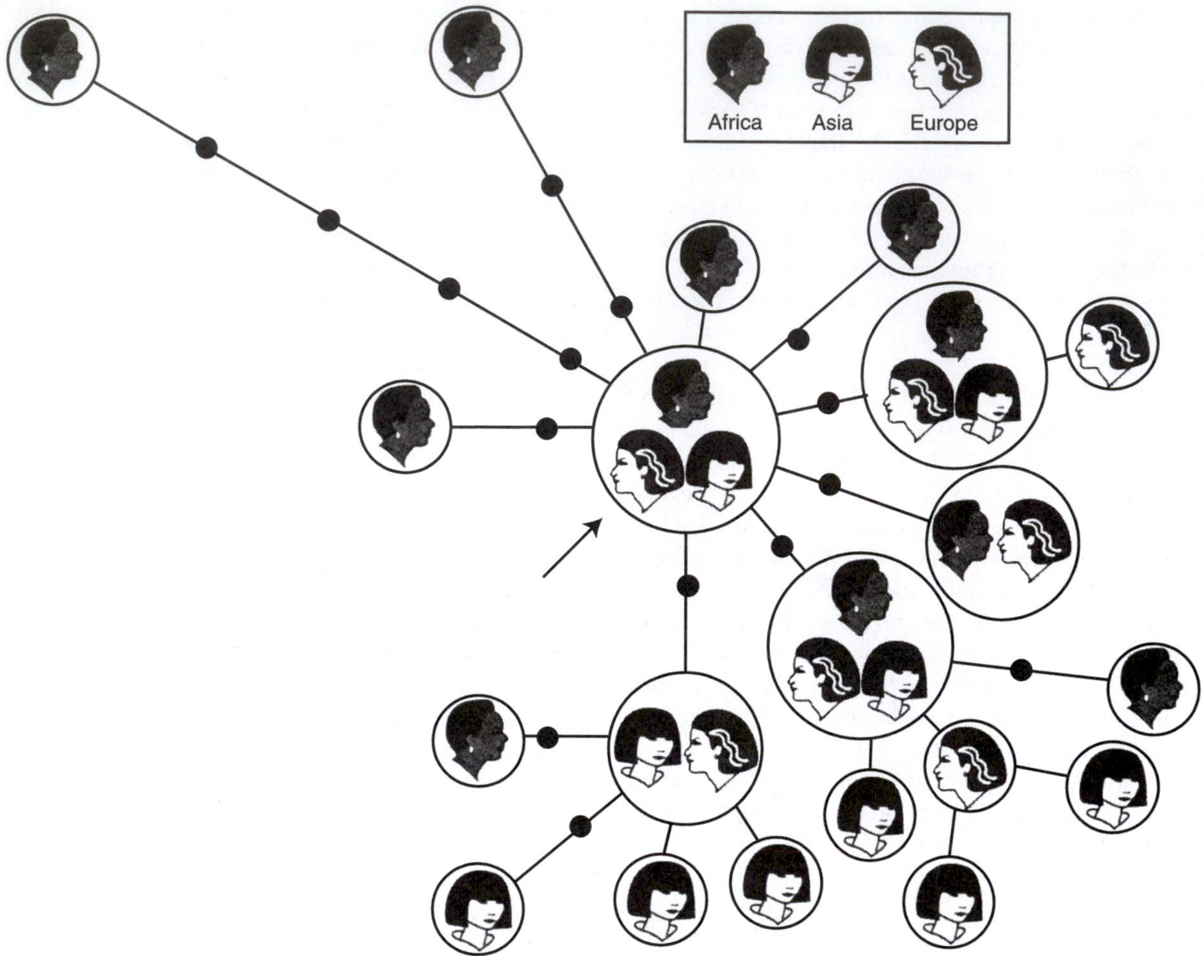

The global family. A network illustrating the relatedness of a series of DNA sequences within a 10,000-base pair segment of the human X chromosome sampled from 70 individuals worldwide. Identical DNA sequences found in people living on three different continents are illustrated by circles containing three faces; identical DNA sequences found in individuals from two continents are depicted as circles containing two faces; sequences that are found only among individuals inhabiting one continent are depicted as circles containing one face. A DNA sequence that is ancestral to all of the other sequences (arrow) is found in individuals from all continents. Black dots on the lines connecting the circles denote nucleotide substitutions in the DNA sequences. The network demonstrates that people from different continents often carry identical DNA sequences. Consequently, how a person looks gives little or no clue to what alleles he or she may carry at any particular locus. [Modified from (6)]

place, it will be hard to withstand pressure from the insurance lobby to prevent such legislation.

As we enter a genomic era in medicine and biology, perhaps the greatest danger I see stems from the enormous emphasis placed on the human genome by the media. The successes of medical genetics and genomics during the last decade have resulted in a sharp shift toward an almost completely genetic view of ourselves. I find it striking that 10 years ago, a geneticist had to defend the idea that not only the environment but also genes shape human development. Today, one feels compelled to stress that there is a large environmental component to common diseases, behavior, and personality traits! There is an insidious tendency to look to our genes for most aspects of our "humanness," and to forget that the genome is but an internal scaffold for our existence.

We need to leave behind the view that the genetic history of our species is *the* history par excellence. We must realize that our genes are but one aspect of our history, and that there are many other histories that are even more important. For example, many people in the Western world feel a connection to ancient Greece, from which arose fundamental features of Western architecture, science, technology, and political ideals (such as democracy). Yet, at best a tiny fraction of the gene pool of the Western industrialized world came from the ancient Greeks. Obviously, this fact in no way diminishes the importance of ancient Greece. So it is a delusion to think that genomics in isolation will ever tell us what it means to be human. To work toward that lofty goal, we need an approach that includes the cognitive sciences, primatology, the social sciences, and the humanities. But with the availability of the complete human genome sequence now at hand, genetics is in a prime position to play a prominent part in this endeavor.

REFERENCES

1. J. C. Venter *et. al.*, *Science* **291,** 1304 (2001).
2. International Human Genome Sequencing Consortium, *Nature* **409,** 860 (2001).
3. M.-C. King, A. C. Wilson, *Science* **188,** 107 (1975).
4. R. G. Klein, *The Human Career* (Univ. of Chicago Press, Chicago, IL, 1999).
5. L. B. Jorde, M. Bamshad, A. R. Rogers, *Bioessays* **20,** 126 (1998).
6. H. Kaessmann, F. Heissig, A. von Haeseler, S. Pääbo, *Nature Genet.* **22,** 78 (1999).

PATRICIA A. ROCHE AND
GEORGE J. ANNAS

Protecting Genetic Privacy

George Annas is Edward R. Utley Professor and Chair, Health Law Department, Boston University Schools of Medicine and Public Health. He is the author or editor of a dozen books on health law and ethics, including *The Rights of Patients* (Humana Press); *American Health Law* (Little, Brown); and *Some Choice: Law, Medicine and the Market* (Oxford University Press). He has held a variety of regulatory positions including Chair of the Massachusetts Health Facilities Appeals Board, Vice-Chair of the Massachusetts Board of Registration in Medicine, and Chair of the Massachusetts Organ Transplant Task Force.

Patricia Roche is Assistant Professor in Health Law, Boston University School of Public Health. She has lectured on issues raised by for-profit medicine and the privacy implications of new technologies, particularly developments in genetics. She has practiced law in Massachusetts since 1989, concentrating in family law.

The simultaneous publication of two versions of the human genome could be an important impetus to take more seriously the legal, ethical and social policy issues at stake in human genome research.[1,2] There are many such issues, and the one that has caused the most public concern is that of genetic privacy. As DNA sequences become understood as information, and as this information becomes easier to use in digitized form, public concerns about internet and e-commerce privacy (regarding the security with which an individual's private details are protected) will merge with concerns about medical record privacy and genetic privacy. In this paper, we outline the key public policy issues at stake in the genetic privacy debate by reviewing generally medical privacy, by asking whether genetic information is like other medical information, and by outlining the current controversies over privacy in genetic research. We conclude with some public policy recommendations.

Reprinted with permission from *Nature Reviews: Genetics* 2 (May 2001), 392–96. Copyright © 2001, Nature Publishing Group.

PRIVACY

Privacy is a complex concept that involves several different but overlapping personal interests. It encompasses informational privacy (having control over highly personal information about ourselves), relational privacy (determining with whom we have personal, intimate relationships), privacy in decision-making (freedom from the surveillance and influence of others when making personal decisions), and the right to exclude others from our personal things and places. In the United States, no single law protects all of these interests, and privacy law refers to the aggregate of privacy protections found in constitutions, statutes, regulations and common law.[3–9] Together, these laws reflect the value that US citizens place on individual privacy, sometimes referred to as "the right to be left alone" and the right to be free from outside intrusion, not as an end in itself, but as a means of enhancing individual freedom in various aspects of our lives. The centrality of individual freedom in Western societies is evident in the United States in state laws that establish a patient's right to make informed choices about treatment, that place an obligation on physicians to maintain patient confidentiality and that regulate the maintenance of medical records.

Privacy laws in the United States are fragmented because of the many sources of law, which includes the federal government and all 50 states. Legislative enactments are also often the result of negotiated agreements among segments of a diverse and often polarized society, rather than of a real consensus. This is perhaps most readily seen in the rules that govern highly sensitive and personal data in the United States. Unlike the approach of the European Data Protection Directive, which establishes similar rights and duties relative to different kinds of personal data (health and finance),[10] the United States has different rights and duties for personal information depending on the kind of information involved. Even for medical records, there are different rules that apply to the different types of information that they contain. For example, the United States has laws that govern generally medical record information,[11] as well as separate laws that govern specific types of medical information, such as HIV status,[12] substance-abuse treatment information[13] and mental health information.[14] New federal regulations apply the same privacy rules to all medical information except psychotherapy records.[9] Such exceptionalism has been criticized, and the primary argument against specific laws that are designed to protect genetic information is that such "genetic exceptionalism" would perpetuate the misconception that genetic information is uniquely private and sensitive.[15]

GENETIC PRIVACY

Is DNA-sequence information uniquely private or just like other sensitive information in an individual's medical record? If it is not unique, existing medical record confidentiality laws should be sufficient to protect genetic-sequence information, and no new laws would be needed. Those who support genetic exceptionalism (as we do) emphasize the distinguishing features of DNA-sequence information. The DNA molecule itself is a source of medical information and, like a personal medical record, it can be stored and accessed without the need to return to the person from whom the DNA was collected for permission. But DNA-sequence information contains information beyond an individual's medical history and current health status. DNA also contains information about an individual's future health risks, and in this sense is analogous to a coded "future diary."[16] As the code is broken, DNA reveals information about an individual's probable risks of suffering from specific conditions in the future. Our current obsession with genetic-sequence information means that it is likely to be taken more seriously than other information in a medical record that could also predict future risks, like high blood pressure or cholesterol levels. Information about the presence of proteins that specific genes might encode is also different from DNA-sequence information because the presence of certain proteins might change with time, and their levels, like cholesterol readings, can only be determined by retesting the patient personally. So, proteomics will not require new privacy rules, but rather the enforcement of existing privacy rules for medical records. DNA-sequence information might also contain information about behavioural traits that are unrelated to health status, although scepticism is called for in this area.[17]

Our use of the 'future diary' metaphor has been criticized as potentially perpetuating a mistaken view of genes as deterministic.[15] We understand this criticism, and also reject the idea that genes alone determine our future. Nevertheless, we continue to believe the future diary metaphor best conveys the private nature of genetic information itself. Our future medical status is not determined solely by genetics, any more than our past diaries are the only source for accurate information about our past (or even necessarily reflect it). DNA information, like a diary, however, is a uniquely private part of ourselves.

An individual's DNA can also reveal information about risks and traits that are shared with genetic relatives, and has been used to prove paternity and other relationships.[18] An individual's DNA has the paradoxical quality of being unique to that individual yet shared with others. Even if one believes that the DNA-sequence information extracted from an individual's DNA is no more sensitive than other medical information, this says nothing about the need to protect the DNA molecule itself. In this regard, we think it is useful to view the DNA molecule as a medical record in its own right. Having a DNA sample from an individual is like having medical information about the individual stored on a computer disk, except in this case the information is stored as blood or as other tissue samples. Like the computer disk, the DNA sequence can be "read" by the application of technology. So, regardless of the rules developed to control the use of genetic information when it is recorded in traditional paper and electronic medical records, separate rules are also needed to regulate the collection, analysis, storage and release of DNA samples themselves. This is because once a physician or researcher has a DNA sample, there is no practical need for further contact with the individual from whom the DNA was obtained, and DNA tests could be done on the stored sample (and thus on the individual) in their absence. Some of these tests might as yet be undeveloped but all will produce new genetic information about the individual.

DNA has also been culturally endowed with a power and significance exceeding that of other medical information.[19] Much of this significance is undoubtedly misplaced, but can be justified in so far as genetic information can radically change the way people view themselves and family members, as well as the way that others view them. The history of genetic testing, particularly in relation to rare monogenic diseases, such as Huntington disease, provides us with examples of this impact. Studies of individuals who have undergone testing in clinical settings show the changes in self-perception caused by positive, as well as negative, test results.[20,21] Individuals with a decreased risk of having a genetic disease have reported difficulty in setting expectations for their personal and professional lives in a more open-ended future. Adjustments seem to have been particularly difficult for those who have already made reproductive decisions based on the presumption that they were at high risk for developing a disease.[20] Consequently, it is good policy to provide genetic counselling before and after testing. And in the interests of protecting the privacy of children and adolescents, some institutions have also adopted a policy of refusing parental requests to test children for late-onset diseases when no medical intervention is available to prevent or alleviate the genetic condition.[22] Perhaps the principal reason why neither DNA-sequence information nor DNA samples themselves have been afforded special privacy protection is the strongly held view of many genetic researchers and biotechnology companies that privacy protections would interfere with their work. One court in the United States has addressed whether constitutional rights to privacy are implicated by genetic testing. In *Norman-Bloodsaw v. Lawrence Berkeley Laboratory,* employees of a research facility owned and operated by state and federal agencies alleged that non-consensual genetic testing by their employers violated their rights to privacy. Holding that the right to privacy protects against the collection of information by illicit means, as well as unauthorized disclosures to third parties, the court stated, "One can think of few subject areas more personal and more likely to implicate privacy interests than that of one's health or genetic make-up."[23]

DNA RESEARCH AND PRIVACY

Now that the human genome has been sequenced, attention is shifting to research on genetic variation that is designed to locate genes and gene sequences with disease-producing or disease-prevention properties.[24] Some researchers have already taken steps to form partnerships and create large DNA banks that will furnish the material for this research.[25,26] Others want to take advantage of the large number of stored tissue samples that already exist.[27] In the United States, for example, the DNA of about 20 million people is collected and stored each year in tissue collections ranging from fewer than 200 to more than 92 million samples.[28] Collections include Guthrie cards, on which blood from newborns has been collected for phenylketonuria screening since the 1960s, paraffin blocks used by pathologists to store specimens, blood-bank samples, forensic specimens and the US military's bank of samples for use in identifying bodily remains.[28]

Several factors have contributed to the proliferation of DNA banking: the relative ease with which DNA can be collected, its coincidental presence in bodily specimens collected for other reasons and its immutability. Regardless of the original purposes for storing specimens, however, as the ability to extract information from DNA increases and the focus of research shifts to genetic factors that contribute to human diseases and behaviours, repositories that contain the DNA of sizeable populations can be "gold mines" of genetic information. So, it is not surprising that there is considerable interest on the part of biomedical researchers, companies that market genomic data and the pharmaceutical industry, to stake claims on these informational resources[29] and to exploit them for their own purposes.

Commercial enterprises, as well as academic researchers, have equally strong interests in making it relatively easy to access DNA samples that can be linked to medical records for research purposes. Representatives of these constituencies have been vocal in arguing that requirements for informed consent and the right to withdraw data from ongoing research projects (two aspects of genetic privacy) would greatly hamper their research efforts.[30] When US federal rules apply to such research—as is the case with federally funded projects and any projects related to obtaining approval from the US Food and Drug Administration to market drugs or devices—the local Institutional Review Board (IRB) must approve the research protocol. These boards should not waive basic federal research requirements on informed consent (nor exempt researchers from them) except when the IRB determines that the research will be conducted in such a way that the subjects cannot be personally identified.[31] If existing research rules were consistently and diligently applied perhaps we could confidently state that the privacy of research subjects is adequately protected.[32] Today, however, such confidence would be misplaced.[32]

These privacy and consent issues are not limited to the United States (Box 1). The most internationally discussed DNA-based project has been deCODE Genetics in Iceland, a commercial project that has been opposed by the Iceland Medical Association, among others, for "ethical shortcuts," such as "opt-out" provisions that presume an individual's consent (see below).[33–35] The deCODE project, which has been endorsed by two acts of the Iceland parliament, involves the creation of two new databases: the first containing the medical records of all Iceland citizens, and the

second containing DNA samples from them (a third database, of genealogical records, already exists). deCODE intends to use these three databases in various combinations to identify genetic variations that could be of pharmaceutical interest. The chief ethical issues raised by this project are: first, the question of informed consent for inclusion of personal medical information in the database, which is at present included under the concept of presumed consent—this requires individuals to actively opt out of the research if they do not want their information in the database; second, informed consent for the inclusion of DNA in the DNA databank in an identifiable manner (whether encrypted or not, and no matter which entity holds the encryption key); and third, whether the right to withdraw from the research (including the right to withdraw both the DNA sample itself from the databank and all information generated about it) can be effectively exercised. Other issues include the security of the databases and community benefit from the research project itself.[35] Iceland is providing a type of ethical laboratory that will help identify the key issues involved in population-based genetic research, and might help to highlight why international privacy rules are desirable.

Box 1 Enterprises that raise challenging issues

- deCODE Genetics plans to computerize the patient records of the national health service of Iceland, and collect DNA samples from members of the population for genetic linkage analysis and association studies on common diseases. Results will be cross-referenced with information from publicly available genealogical information. Subscriptions to these databases are sold to researchers and information is entered into them on the basis of presumed consent.
- The UK Population Biomedical Collection, a joint initiative of the Medical Research Council and the Wellcome Trust, plans to focus on understanding the interactions between genes, environment and lifestyles in cancer and cardiovascular conditions. Their goal is to collect samples of up to 500,000 people and link these samples to an ongoing collection of the individuals' medical data. Investigators may be granted access to the results of genotyping, but not to the DNA samples.
- Ardais Corporation, a start-up biotechnology company that intends to enter into agreements with several major hospitals in the United States under which surgical patients will be asked for tissue that is left over from operations. These samples will be linked to records that detail the patient's medical history and family information. Tissue libraries and data will be licensed to researchers.
- Autogen Ltd, an Australian biotechnology firm that has secured exclusive rights to collect tissue samples and health data from the population of Tonga. The firm hopes to identify new disease-related genes and to aid the development of new drugs to prevent or treat common diseases, such as diabetes. It has pledged to abide by stringent ethical standards, to collect samples and data from individuals who voluntarily participate and to make the health database available to the Tongan people.

Although Icelanders themselves do not seem overly concerned with the adequacy of deCODE's plans to protect their personal privacy, other countries have not been as disposed to giving away the autonomy and privacy of their citizens so readily. Both Estonia and the United Kingdom, for example, have announced that their population-based DNA collections and research projects will contain strong consent and privacy-protection provisions.[36,37] The privacy problems inherent in large population-based projects could be avoided altogether by stripping DNA samples of their identifiers in a way that makes it impossible to link personal medical information with DNA samples (at least by using standard identifying methods). Of course, most researchers want to retain identifiers to do follow-up work or confirm diagnoses.[38] Such identification retention, however, puts individuals at risk of breach of confidentiality and invasion of privacy, and these risks are why both informed consent and strong privacy-protection protocols are ethically necessary for genetic research.[38] These considerations also apply to criminal DNA databases as even convicted felons have privacy rights.

Risks of disclosure of personal genetic information are so high that some prominent genetic researchers, including Francis Collins and Craig Venter, have suggested concentrating not on privacy rules, but rather on anti-discrimination legislation that is designed to protect individuals when their genetic information is disclosed, and when insurance companies, employers or others want to use that information against them.[39] We agree that anti-discrimination legislation is desirable, but it does not substitute for privacy rules that can prevent the genetic information from being generated in the first place without the individual's informed authorization.

This point is well illustrated by a law recently enacted in Massachusetts—a state with a population more than 20 times larger than the population of Iceland[40]—that has been mistakenly characterized in the US press as 'a sweeping set of genetic privacy protections.'[41] Under this new law, written informed consent is a prerequisite to predictive (but not diagnostic) genetic testing and to disclosing the results of such tests by entities and practitioners that provide health care. The law also limits the uses that insurers and employers can make of genetic information. However, it places no limitations on how researchers and biotechnology companies that engage in projects requiring the use of identifiable samples and identifiable genetic information conduct their activities. Apparently, those who drafted the statute believed that they need not be concerned about protecting research subjects because research with human subjects is regulated by the federal government, failing to recognize that many activities of genomic companies do not fall under the jurisdiction of the federal regulations.

POLICY RECOMMENDATIONS

We have argued in the past that a principal step to achieving genetic privacy would be the passage of a comprehensive federal genetic privacy law.[42,43] The primary purpose of such a law is to give individuals control over their identifiable DNA samples and the genetic-sequence information extracted from them. The model we suggest provides that individuals have a property interest in their own DNA—and that this property interest gives them control over it. Control could also, however, be obtained by requiring explicit authorization for the collection and use of DNA, including its research and commercial use. We believe that in the absence of authorization no one should know more about an individual's genetic make-up than that individual chooses to know themselves, and that an individual should also know who else knows (or will know) their private genetic information (see Box 2). Current US state laws at best offer some economic protections and a patchwork of genetic privacy protections. But existing state laws have significant gaps and inconsistently regulate those who engage in DNA banking and genetic research. Nevertheless, existing privacy laws provide models and a foundation that can be built on to protect genetic privacy and empower individuals in this genomic era. But until comprehensive federal legislation is passed in the United States, US citizens will have to rely on those who create and maintain DNA banks to design, implement and enforce self-imposed rules to protect individuals.

One proposal to deal with privacy issues and individual control over genetic information is to have DNA samples and medical records collected by a "third-party broker" of genetic information who would then, with the informed consent of the individual, make this information available to researchers in a coded form. A for-profit company, First Genetic Trust, has been formed in the United States to try out this model.[44] Individuals are solicited through the internet to participate in the Trust and all communication with those who participate, including consent to new studies, will take place over the internet. The purpose of

Box 2 Assessing genetic privacy

Laws or policies that purport to protect genetic privacy, at a minimum, should do the following:

- Recognize individual genetic rights particularly:
  - the right to determine if and when their identifiable DNA samples are collected, stored or analysed;
  - the right to determine who has access to their identifiable DNA samples;
  - the right to access to their own genetic information;
  - the right to determine who has access to their genetic information;
  - the right to all information necessary for informed decision-making about the collection, storage and analysis of their DNA samples and the disclosure of their private genetic information.
- Limit parental rights to authorize the collection, storage or analysis of a child's identifiable DNA sample so as preserve the child's future autonomy and genetic privacy.
- Prohibit unauthorized uses of individually identifiable DNA samples, except for some uses in solving crimes, determining paternity or identifying bodily remains.
- Prohibit disclosures of genetic information without the individual's explicit authorization.
- Strictly enforce laws and institutional policies.
- Provide accessible remedies for individuals whose rights are violated.
- Institute sufficient penalties to deter and punish violations.

the Trust is to assure individuals that no one would be able to use their DNA, or their personal medical information associated with it, without the individual's authorization. Some might criticize this approach as going too far in protecting participants, noting that consent is not generally necessary for IRB-approved research that does not involve identifiable data. Regardless of the fact that First Genetic Trust itself will not be engaged in research, as long as data held by the Trust can be linked to individuals, we think authorization should be required and that proposals such as this one are a step in the right direction.

Whether arrangements such as these will lead to significant public participation in genetic research remains to be seen. Despite the availability of tests for genes that predispose individuals to several diseases, including Huntington disease and some forms of breast and colon cancers, the number of people who choose to undergo clinical genetic testing has fallen far below the expectations of the companies that sell tests and of the physicians who believe their patients would benefit from them.[45] Why is the public, which is on the one hand fascinated with each advance in mapping the genome, the identification of particular genes and the possible association of a gene with particular human characteristics, simultaneously reticent to undergo genetic testing? Explanations that individuals give for avoiding genetic tests include fear of discrimination, concern over the impact on family members, lack of effective treatments and preference for uncertainty about the future.[46,47] Privacy protections have little, if any, impact on attitudes towards the future. Nevertheless, by regulating the creation, maintenance and disclosure of information, they can reduce privacy risks and provide some reassurance to those who might not otherwise participate in genetic research or clinical testing.

Once individual interests in privacy and in being treated fairly on the basis of genetic information have been addressed, only property issues remain. Individuals can be thought of as having a property right in their DNA, including, among other things, the right to restrict others from "trespassing" on their property without permission.[42] One US state, Oregon, incorporated an individual's right of ownership of DNA into its laws in 1995.[48] Objections that this law would inhibit research in that state echoed objections that researchers and industry have made elsewhere to explicit and strict privacy rules.[49,50] Acknowledging property interests in DNA need not impede research any more than respect for individual privacy would. Conversely, individuals are free to grant property rights in their DNA to researchers, and are much more likely to do so if their privacy can be guaranteed (as it can be if identifiers are not retained).

DNA can rightly be seen as containing uniquely

personal, powerful and sensitive information about individuals and their families. Some individuals want to know as much of this information about themselves as possible, and might be willing to share this information with their families and others. Others would rather remain ignorant about their own genetic makeup, and thus their risks for future illnesses, or at least to keep others ignorant of such information. We believe that individual choices are best served by policies that place primary control over an individual's DNA and genetic information in the hands of individuals. We also believe privacy protections will prove as necessary for the future of genetic research and clinical applications as they will be for the future of e-commerce. We believe that the sooner that reasonable genetic privacy protections are in place, the better it will be for all of us.

NOTES

1. International Human Genome Sequencing Consortium. Initial sequencing and analysis of the human genome. *Nature* **409,** 860–921 (2001).

2. Venter J. C. *et al.* The sequence of the human genome. *Science* **291,** 1304–1351 (2001).

3. Miller, A. R. Personal privacy in the computer age. *Mich. Law Rev.* **67,** 1091–1296 (1968).

4. *Griswald v. Connecticut,* 381 US 479 (1965).

5. *Meyer v. Nebraska,* 262 US 390 (1923).

6. Privacy Act of 1974 (Pub. L. 93–579, December 31, 1974, 88 Stat. 1896).

7. Family Educational Rights and Privacy Act of 1974 (FERPA) (Pub. L. 93–380, Title V, § 513, August 21, 1974, 88 Stat. 571).

8. Right to Financial Privacy Act of 1978 (RFPA) (Pub. L. 95–630, Title XI, November 10, 1978, 92 Stat. 3697).

9. Standards for Privacy of Individually Identifiable Health Information, 50 Fed. Reg. 250 (2000).

10. Swartz. J. P. M. in *Genetic Secrets* (ed. Rothstein, M.) 392–417 (Yale Univ. Press, New Haven, Connecticut, 1997).

11. California Health & Safety Code sec. 120980 (West 2000).

12. Connecticut Gen. Stat. sec. 19a–583 (West 1999).

13. 42 US Code sec. 290-dd (West 2000).

14. Florida State sec. 394. 4615 (West 2000).

15. Murray, T. H. in *Genetic Secrets* (ed. Rothstein, M.) 60–76 (Yale Univ. Press, New Haven, Connecticut, 1999).

16. Annas, G. J. Privacy rules for DNA databanks. *J. Am. Med. Assoc.* **270,** 2346–2350 (1993).

17. Billings, P. R., Beckwith, J. & Alper, J. S. The genetic analysis of human behavior: a new era? *Social Sci. Med.* **35,** 227–238 (1992).

18. Marshall, E. Which Jefferson was the father? *Science* **283,** 153–154 (1999).

19. Nelkin, D. & Lindee, M. S. *The DNA Mystique: The Gene as a Cultural Icon* (W. H. Freeman, New York, 1995).

20. Huggins, M. *et al.* Predictive testing for Huntington disease in Canada: adverse effects and unexpected results in those receiving a decreased risk. *Am. J. Med. Genet.* **42,** 504–515 (1992).

21. DudokdeWit, A. C. *et al.* Distress in individuals facing predictive DNA testing for autosomal dominant late-onset disorders: comparing questionnaire results with in-depth interviews. *Am. J. Med. Genet.* **75,** 62–74 (1998).

22. American Society of Human Genetics and American College of Medical Genetics. Ethical, legal and psychological implications of genetic testing in children and adolescents: points to consider. *Am. J. Hum. Genet.* **57,** 1233–1241 (1995).

23. *Norman-Bloodsaw v. Lawrence Berkeley Laboratory,* 135 F. 3d 1260 (1998). At 1269.

24. Kaiser, J. Environment institute lays plans for gene hunt. *Science* **278,** 569–570 (1997).

25. Pollack, A. Company seeking donors for a 'gene trust'. *NY Times* A1 (August 1, 2000).

26. Karet, G., Boguslavsky, J. & Studt, T. Unraveling human diversity. *Drug Discovery Dev.* November/December, S5–S14 (2000).

27. Grody, W. W. Molecular pathology, informed consent, and the paraffin block. *Diagn. Mol. Pathol.* **4,** 155–157 (1995).

28. National Bioethics Advisory Commission. *Report on the Use of Human Biological Material in Research: Ethical Issues and Policy Guidance* (Bethesda, Maryland, 1999).

29. Pezzella, M. DNA databases take shape at firms on two coasts. *Biotechnol. Watch* (September 18, 2000) at 2000 WL 7388705.

30. Korn, D. in *Genetic Testing and the Use of Information* (ed. Long, G.) 16–83 (American Enterprise, Washington DC, 1999).

31. 46 CFR sec. 46. 101(b)(4) (2000).

32. Office of Inspector General US Department of Health and Human Services. *Institutional Review Boards: A Time for Reform* (Washington DC, 2000).

33. Greely, H. T. Iceland's plan for genomics research: facts and implications. *Jurimetrics* **40,** 153–191 (2000).

34. Jonantansson, H. Iceland's Health Sector Database: a significant head start in the search for the biological holy grail or an irreversible error? *Am. J. Law Med.* **26,** 31–67 (2000).

35. Annas, G. J. Rules for research on human genetic variation—lessons from Iceland. *N. Engl. J. Med.* **342,** 1830–1833 (2000).

36. Frank, L. Storm brews over gene bank of Estonian population. *Science* **286,** 1262–1263 (1999).

37. McKie, R. The gene collection. *Br. Med. J.* **321,** 854 (2000).

38. Clayton, E. W. *et al.* Informed consent for genetic research on stored tissue samples. *J. Am. Med. Assoc.* **274,** 1786–1792 (1995).

39. CBS News: *This Morning* 6/27/00, Federal Document Clearing House transcript at 2000 WESTLAW 6654407.

40. 2000 Massachusetts Acts Chapter 254.

41. Misha, R. New law gives genetic privacy protection. *Boston Globe* B2 (August 23, 2000).

42. Annas, G. J., Glantz, L. H. & Roche, P. A. *The Genetic Privacy Act and Commentary* (available by request from the Health Law Department, Boston University School of Public Health, Boston Mass. and at http://www.busph.bu.edu/Depts/HealthLaw/) (1995).

43. Roche, P. A., Annas, G. J. & Glantz, L. H. The genetic privacy act: a proposal for national legislation. *Jurimetrics* **37,** 1–11 (1996).

44. Marshall, E. Company plans to bank human DNA profiles. *Science* **291,** 575 (2001).

45. Kolata, G. Public slow to embrace genetic testing. *NY Times* 16, 1 (March 27, 1998).

46. Gettig, B. Survey reveals attitudes towards genetic testing. *The Marker* **10,** 6–7 (1997).

47. Hall, M. A. & Rich. S. S. Genetic privacy laws and patients fear of discrimination by health insurers: the view of genetic counselors. *J. Law Med. Ethics* **28,** 245–257 (2000).

48. Oregon Revised Statutes § 659. 715 (1998).

49. O'Neill, P. Researchers fight to get a piece of you. *Portland Oregonian* (July 11, 1999) at 1999 WESTLAW 5358096.

50. Rosenberg, R. Biotechnology: a study in data collection, genomics companies go abroad to obtain samples citing obstacles in the United States. *Boston Globe* D4 (November 1, 2000).

MICHAEL M. BURGESS

Beyond Consent: Ethical and Social Issues in Genetic Testing

Michael Burgess holds the Chair in Biomedical Ethics at the Centre for Applied Ethics and in the Department of Medical Genetics at the University of British Columbia. His current research activities concern ethical issues raised by genetic knowledge and technology. He has served on committees with the Management Committee of the Canadian Genetic Assessment and Technology Program and the American Society of Human Genetics.

INFORMED CONSENT promotes patient participation and AUTONOMY in health-care decisions by requiring the provision of information and recognizing that patients must voluntarily authorize interventions. In the case of genetic testing, genetic counselling provides the means to achieve informed consent. Genetic counselling explains the nature, usefulness and risks associated with genetic tests, and assures that participation in genetic testing is autonomous, or based on participants' understanding of the relevant information. Because informed consent is highly dependent on comprehension of information and good communication, genetic counselling provides excellent support, although evaluation of counselling is not well established and some researchers express concern about the ability of counsellors to be non-directive.[1–3]

However, genetic testing raises issues that cannot be managed through informed consent. To begin with, there might be few, if any, clinical benefits from genetic testing. As far as genetic counselling is concerned, the STANDARD OF PRACTICE is primarily directed at imparting understanding of possible test results, because the net benefit of a genetic test is often highly dependent on how much the participant values the information and what they want to do with it (Box 1). Genetic counselling also involves careful

Box 1 Possible benefits from tests

Clinical

- Avoidance of onset of disease
- Curative treatment due to timely and accurate diagnosis
- Avoidance of harms from inappropriate treatment or monitoring
- Symptomatic treatment

Psychological or social

- Relief from uncertainty
- Personal planning
- Improved well-being
- Fulfilment of patient wishes to be tested

Public health

- Decrease population morbidity and/or mortality from genetic disease
- Decrease population frequency of treatment-related morbidity or mortality

Reprinted with permission from *Nature Reviews: Genetics* 2 (February 2001), 147–151. Copyright © 2001, Nature Publishing Group.

consideration of the social and psychological risks of genetic testing, but evolving social contexts, such as the workplace, the insurance industry and the family, shape whether and how these risks materialize. Genetic information produced by testing individuals also affects other family members, and those who share, or are perceived to share, a common genetic heritage.

Genetic testing therefore raises ethical issues that concern standard of practice, indeterminacy of risks and collective acceptability of risks and benefits. This article discusses each of these issues, indicating the extent to which informed consent addresses the ethical issues, and suggests fruitful avenues of research into the ethics of the social context of genetic practice.

GENETIC TESTING: A STANDARD OF PRACTICE

Because of the complexity of genetic information and its interpretation, genetic counselling has become a cornerstone of genetic research and clinical practice. Counsellors must explain the highly variable, and often changing, views about the relation between genetic test results and the associated conditions, as well as information about the conditions themselves and possible treatments or preventions.

One of the first and most influential studies of genetic testing for an adult onset disease was the predictive testing for Huntington disease. The concerns associated with predictive genetic testing[4,5] were managed in the Canadian multi-centre research protocol by requiring four pre-test and several post-test counselling sessions.[6] Although there were no definitive medical benefits in this instance, testing was felt to promote individual patient autonomy and emotional welfare. The conclusion of the Canadian study was that, with the provision of pre- and post-test counselling that included psychological assessments, genetic testing for Huntington disease did not pose unacceptable risks for consenting participants.[7] Clinical recommendations supporting genetic counselling of adults have been based on this research experience,[8] although in clinical practice and with other genetic tests, pre- and post-test counselling have become streamlined with little study of the effects of counselling itself or of modifications to clinical protocols.[9] The clinical availability of predictive testing for Huntington disease is based on the ethical assessment that the promotion of autonomy and the psychological and social benefits for people can justify the risks for those who want the test and undergo genetic counselling.

The case of Huntington disease illustrates the general trend for genetic testing to become the *de facto* standard of practice—available for those who wish to have the information once it is established that a genetic test can identify a genetic contribution to a disease. This is probably due to the low cost of the test, and the difficulty of justifying withholding the test on a clinical basis once it is established as accurate in the research context.[10,11] This emphasis on individual participant autonomy in the research setting might explain what some have referred to as "premature implementation" before establishing clinical benefit, particularly in the case of tests that are not predictive but that indicate an increase in disease susceptibility.[12]

There are, of course, genetic tests that direct clinical care. In the case of prenatal testing, the possibility of abortion as a clinical intervention does provide a clinical option with a clear outcome. A family history of colon cancer initiates invasive monitoring, and testing that eliminates a genetic contributor might reduce or eliminate the need for monitoring and the accompanying risks and discomforts. But, in many cases, the genetic information together with the choices that it provides to people are the primary benefits.

Providing access to a genetic test because it is accurate is different from evidence-based standards that are applied to other clinical interventions. These standards require that there is a measurable difference in clinical outcomes or population health measures for a test, screen or intervention to become the standard of practice. However, most genetic tests develop well in advance of effective interventions because of their usefulness in research. Many genetic tests are therefore available simply because they provide accurate information. This standard of practice does not protect patients from risks, but makes them responsible for evaluating whether the social and psychological risks are justified by the benefits. The historical association of genetics with eugenics has probably contributed to the vehemence with which patient autonomy and non-directive counselling have been asserted as the ethical standard for such assessments.[13]

Potential test participants cannot assume that there is benefit simply because genetic testing is offered as a clinical service. They have to evaluate for themselves whether the knowledge likely to result from the genetic test is beneficial. This poses an additional challenge to informed consent. It is not enough to provide information—patients must also be supported in evaluating their own responses and views of benefit. Policy decisions related to health-care insurance must also evaluate whether accurate genetic tests provide sufficient health benefits to justify coverage (and whether private and therefore unequal access constitutes a problem for justice in national health-care systems).[14] So it is not ethically sufficient to establish test accuracy and assure counselling and consent for test participants.

Participant evaluation of the benefits of testing engages a larger context than just the genetic counselling sessions. Media, marketing and some public enthusiasm for genetic testing and biotechnology in general will tend to raise participants' expectations of genetic testing.[15,16] Although the advent of preventive or ameliorating interventions will strengthen the benefits, the psychological and social risks will always be an important factor and make it difficult to consider genetic tests as being innocuous.

THE INDETERMINATE NATURE OF RISKS

Establishing the risks that are associated with genetic testing is also critical for both the standard of practice and for informed consent. In the absence of clear and dependable clinical benefits, the social and psychological risks might overwhelm the benefits. Even in cases for which there is clinical benefit from a particular test, the psychological and social risks should be disclosed in counselling, and there is a need for policies or regulation to minimize these risks. But evaluating the social and psychological risks (or benefits) that come from genetic testing and information is difficult. The same genetic information can pose harm or benefit owing to the highly variable nature of familial and social circumstances.

For example, a person told that they have not inherited the Huntington disease mutation might experience relief or increased responsibility for family members who are less fortunate. The experience of relief from being told that one is not at risk for a familial disease hardly needs explanation. But clinical reports, interviews and focus group discussions also describe the experiences of people receiving the same news whose relief is qualified by the misfortune of other family members, or who assume or are assigned caregiving responsibilities.[17] Whereas some people might experience caregiving roles as fulfilling and desirable, others find that their personal resources and social supports are inadequate, and describe their lives as still dominated by Huntington disease. Women receiving news that they have not inherited the mutation associated with breast cancer in their family certainly will experience relief, although they might also feel an obligation to educate family members and to encourage others at risk to seek genetic testing. For some, this responsibility might be grasped with enthusiasm, but for others, familial responses will be marginalizing. Although genetic counselling might include discussion of familial responses to genetic information as well as sharing of test results within the family, it is unrealistic to expect genetic counsellors or individual test participants to be able to anticipate the actual familial responses and personal experiences. The unpredictability of familial and personal responses makes it difficult to assess the net benefit of genetic testing for any individual.

Another context that will shape the social and psychological effects of genetic testing is the work place. On the positive side, the identification of a genetic contributor to an environmental sensitivity can motivate an intervention to reduce exposure to the specific environmental agent (if it is readily alterable).[18] But increased susceptibility identified by a genetic test might also lead employers to discriminate against some people to minimize employees' sick time. Liability, disability and life insurance create incentives for employers to increase scrutiny of those with genetic-based susceptibilities to minimize overhead costs or legal risks. It is not the genetic information itself that poses the risk, but individual and social system responses.[19,20]

Although confidentiality of health-care records could reduce some discriminatory uses of genetic testing information, it is controversial whether mere disclosure of the risks and the current privacy regulations for genetic information are adequate.[21,22] The privacy issue is particularly problematic for insurance policies, because insurance contracts are based on the sharing of medical information to assess risk and to establish proportionate or market-related premiums.[23–26] It is controversial whether broad social policy to restrict the insurance industry's access to genetic information is necessary to protect fair access to insurance,[27] despite strong international pressures either to restrict access or to require the provision of basic levels of insurance without scrutiny of medical records.[28–31] The various uses of genetic information in these social contexts emphasize the need to identify, evaluate and regulate for possible discrimination.

The occurrence of social and psychological effects,

and whether they are experienced as harms or benefits, is sensitive to many factors such as individual resources, family support, supportive social services, insurance company policies and social attitudes. Although informed consent must explain that these broader social contexts are relevant to assessing the effects of genetic testing, the actual effects remain unpredictable owing to the complexity and variability of social systems. Whenever genetic testing provides a definitive response to a pressing clinical problem, these more abstract concerns appropriately recede into the background. But when genetic tests provide primarily social or psychological benefits, these social contexts are critical for assessing whether the anticipated benefits will materialize, and whether the harms will be justified. Such an assessment is inevitably part of informed consent. But the genetic counselling must clearly articulate uncertainty about the harms and benefits of genetic testing.

Ethical evaluations of genetic tests must assess the social and psychological effects of testing and consider the actual and possible responses of social systems. Although informed consent and genetic counselling might disclose or discuss these ethical dimensions for the test candidate, they must not be construed as adequate to manage these risks. The social context is beyond the control of geneticists and participants; neither can be held responsible for deciding whether to expose the participant to effects that are essentially unstable and not universally experienced as good or bad. Ultimately, the acceptance of genetic testing in society must be accompanied by investment in social research that will identify social system responses, provide ethical and social analyses and alternatives for reform.

EFFECTS ON NON-CONSENTING PERSONS

Genetic testing produces information that is familial and not only individual. A participant's genetic test for an inherited mutation reveals whether they received the mutation from their parents, whether their siblings might have inherited the mutation, and whether their children could inherit it. The previous discussion of the subjectivity of non-clinical benefit established that the same test result could be beneficial or harmful, or some mix of the two, and that consent depended on the evaluation of the individual. But the model of consent presumes that harms and benefits can be isolated to consenting persons. Therefore, the combination of the familial effects of genetic testing and individual authorization of the acceptance of risks and benefits seems to entail the impractical requirement that every family member, for whom the test participant's information might have relevance, should provide consent before the participant is tested. The usual compromise is to suggest to a test candidate that he or she discuss the testing possibilities with family members, and, whenever possible, to first counsel and test potential carriers, such as parents. If the persons most likely to be affected by one family member's test are already tested, then the effects on the rest of the family will be minimized. But even if family members insist on their "right not to know," the presumption of the ethical sufficiency of informed consent for clinical services makes it difficult to justify refusing genetic testing to the consenting person.

The effects of genetic testing on groups larger than families are probably most familiar with inherited disease related to minorities or religious communities. Tay-Sachs disease, sickle cell anaemia and specific mutations associated with breast and ovarian cancers are the best-known examples. In these instances, historical reproductive and immigration patterns have preserved a degree of genetic homogeneity in ethnocultural communities, which makes the genetic contributions to some diseases easier to identify in these groups. Such communities are therefore attractive as research populations. It is important to recognize that the frequency of a condition in a specific population might not be higher than in the general population, but that the reduced heterogeneity makes it easier to search for meaningful genetic variations.[32] And it is this same association of heritage, race or social group with the identification of genetic risk that can lead to stigmatization of ethnic populations as genetically 'defective.'[33]

Informed consent of individual ethno-cultural COMMUNITY members is wholly inadequate for authorizing the acceptability of the risks of stigmatization for the entire group.[34,35] Even if there are collective benefits likely to accrue from the clinical testing of individuals or from research, consent from individual community members cannot authorize the acceptability of the effects to the community. Although researchers might sometimes seek authoritative acceptance by leaders, even this approach begs important ethical questions about the representativeness of leadership and heterogeneity of moral beliefs and judgments within communities.[36] The authority of leadership might, in some cases, require consent processes that encourage independence and strong confidentiality to leave room for people to refuse to participate.[37] Despite some views that if ethics gets in the way of science and benefits then the ethics should be examined,[38] there is considerable recognition that some kind of collective acceptability of research must be negotiated with identified populations.[39]

Untested and non-consenting members of disease-related charitable organizations and patient support groups can also experience the effects of genetic testing of persons within their group. For instance, a complex genetic disease might have several genetic components that interact with each other and with the environment in which the disease is manifested. Understanding these genetic components might differentiate between those who would benefit from one form of intervention rather than another, or show that environmental contributors can be controlled to avoid disease in some subset of the affected population. But characterization of the disease as genetic could lead to insurance discrimination for the entire population. Some persons with the disease who lack the social and financial resources so relevant to a sense of empowerment might assume fatalism with respect to the disease, avoiding possibly ameliorating measures. Affected persons might be stigmatized for not avoiding the environmental contributors. These are the effects on the population that result from a genetic understanding of disease and, as such, are the result of individuals' consent to genetic research on their own disease. Contrary to some attempts to extend informed consent to groups, the collective acceptability of research,[40] or its justifiability in the case of diverse opinion, requires detailed negotiation and specific ethical assessments.[41]

BEYOND CONSENT

Individualized ideas about autonomy and informed consent are a part of the CULTURE of bioethics in Western health-care practice and politics. Cultural studies indicate that the concept of culture should not be understood as a set of beliefs that explain the behaviour of others,[42] but instead as the nest of practices and assumptions that underlie everyday practice for all people, however diverse. Cultural dimensions shape what is considered desirable research for researchers, granting agencies, health-care systems and commercial enterprises, as well as for families, "ethnic groups" and groups organized around fund raising and research for particular diseases. In other words, the development of genetic testing as well as the trend towards genomic science are themselves cultural phenomena that can be understood as being made possible and supported by particular cultural views.[43]

The orientation towards accurate knowledge as a benefit independent of clinical relevance is a part of the culture of science and is promoted by a tradition that emphasizes individual autonomy. Resorting to the individual to assess net benefit in the face of ambiguity is a feature of liberal political philosophy. Contemporary bioethics tends to support the insulation of scientists, institutions and commercial producers from responsibility for social contexts in which scientific knowledge is used, without suggesting alternative responsible parties. Social research and explicit discussion of the culture of research, commercialization, and risk-orientated health education allow the wider public to participate in meaningful discussions about technology and health policy,[44–46] a critical but often neglected feature of democracy in this area.

Clinical research and health policy analysis must return to an evaluation of the clinical and non-clinical benefits related to the standard of practice. The current *ad hoc* addition of genetic tests to the standard of practice merely because they provide accurate genetic information is not justifiable. This is particularly true as social and psychological effects cannot be adequately described or predicted. Some of the most important research related to genetic testing has to do with the use of genetic information and ideas of inheritance in social institutions, ranging from the family to whole communities. Finally, as the social effects of genetic and inheritance information are better described, it will be vital to establish collaborative research with communities and other groups who have collective interests in the effects of research on themselves.

GLOSSARY

Autonomy The capacity to be rational and self-directing. Autonomy creates the possibility of moral responsibility, and is therefore accorded strong ethical protection in bioethics.

Community Communities usually share some element of value or practice that provides cohesiveness despite considerable heterogeneity. Aggregates might be identified as having a common feature, such as a disease, but lack any social cohesiveness. Disease-related groups might move from being an aggregate to a community as they organize activities around their common features.

Culture Culture is constituted by the practices and assumptions that underlie a group's everyday activities, and is typically heterogeneous and constantly evolving.

Informed consent A doctrine intended to assure patient participation in health-care decisions. It requires that the recommended and alternative interventions be explained, together with their harms and benefits. Authorization of treatment is based on comprehension of this information and voluntary agreement.
Standard of practice Historically rooted in clinical practice, the standard of practice is the service or intervention that is recognized by the relevant group of health professionals as appropriate care. The move to evidence-based standards of practice evaluates whether the benefits of a new intervention outweigh the possible harms.

NOTES

1. Rapp, R. Chromosomes and communication: the discourse of genetic counseling. *Med. Anthrop. Quart.* **2,** 143–157 (1988).

2. Lippman, A. in *The Future of Human Reproduction* (ed. Overall, C.) 182–194 (The Women's Press, Toronto, 1989).

3. Clarke, A. Is non-directive genetic counseling possible? *Lancet* **338,** 998–1001 (1991).

4. Farrer, L. A. Suicide and attempted suicide in Huntington disease: implications for preclinical testing of persons at risk. *Am. J. Med. Genet.* **24,** 305–3111 (1986).

5. Kessler, S. & Bloch, M. Social system responses to Huntington disease. *Family Processes* **28,** 59–68 (1989).

6. Fox, S., Bloch, M., Fahy, M. & Hayden, M. R. Predictive testing for Huntington disease: description of a pilot study in British Columbia. *Am. J. Med. Genet.* **32,** 211–216 (1988).

7. Benjamin, C. M. *et al.* and the Canadian collaborative groups for predictive testing for Huntington disease. Proceed with care: direct predictive testing for Huntington disease. *Am. J. Hum. Genet.* **55,** 606–617 (1994).

8. Quaid, K. A. Presymptomatic testing for Huntington disease: recommendations for counseling. *Am. J. Med. Genet.* **39,** 347–354 (1992).

9. Biesecker, B. B. & Marteau, T. M. The future of genetic counseling: an international perspective. *Nature Genet.* **22,** 133–137 (1999).

10. DeGrazia, D. The ethical justification for minimal paternalism in the use of the predictive test for Huntington's disease. *J. Clin. Ethics* **2,** 219–228 (1991).

11. Burgess, M. M. & Hayden, M. R. Patients' rights to laboratory data: trinucleotide repeat length in Huntington disease. *Am. J. Med. Genet.* **162,** 6–9 (1996).

12. Koenig, B. *et al.* Genetic testing for BRCA1 and BRCA2; recommendations of the Stanford program in genomics, ethics and society. *J. Women's Health* **7,** 531–545 (1998).

13. Kerr, A. & Cunningham-Burley, S. On ambivalence and risk: reflexive modernity and the new human genetics. *Sociology* **34,** 283–304 (2000).

14. Burgess, M. M. in *The Commercialization of Genetics Research: Ethical, Legal, and Policy Issues* (eds Caulfield, T. A. & Williams-Jones, B.) 181–194 (Kluwer Academic/Plenum Publishers, New York, 1999).

15. Nelkin, D. & Lindee, M. S., *The DNA Mystique: The Gene as a Cultural Icon* (New York: Freeman, 1995).

16. Harper, P. S. Direct marketing of cystic fibrosis carrier screening: commercial push or population need? *J. Med. Genet.* **32,** 249–250 (1995).

17. Huggins, M. *et al.* Predictive testing for Huntington disease in Canada: adverse effects and unexpected results in those receiving a decreased risk. *Am. J. Med. Genet.* **42,** 508 (1992).

18. Vineis, P. & Schulte, P. A. Scientific and ethical aspects of genetic screening of workers for cancer risk: the case of *N*-acetyltransferase phenotype. *J. Clin. Epidemiol.* **48,** 189–197 (1995).

19. MacDonald, C. & Williams-Jones, B. Ethics and genetics: susceptibility testing in the workplace. *J. Business Ethics* [35 (2002), 235–41.]

20. Lemmens, T. What about your genes? Ethical, legal and policy dimensions of genetics in the workplace. *Politics and the Life Sciences* **16,** 57–75 (1997).

21. Working Group on Ethical, Legal and Social Implications of Human Genome Research. *Genetic Information and Health Insurance. Report of the Task Force:* (National Institutes of Health, Bethesda, Maryland, 1993).

22. Abbott, A. Israel split on rights to genetic privacy. *Nature* **394,** 214 (1998).

23. McGleenan, T., Weising, U. & Ewald, F. (eds) *Genetics and Insurance* (Springer, New York, 1999).

24. NIH-DOE Working Group on Ethical, Legal, and Social Implications of Human Genome Research. *Genetic Information and Health Insurance* (Human Genome Project, Washington DC, 1993).

25. Lemmens, T. & Bahamin, P. in *Socio-Ethical Issues in Human Genetics* (ed. Knoppers, B. M.) 115–275 (Les Editions Yvons-Blais Inc., Cowansville, Quebec, 1998).

26. Greely, H. T. in *The Code of Codes: Scientific and Social Issues in the Human Genome Project* (eds Kelves, D. J. & Hood, L.) 274–280 (Harvard Univ. Press, Cambridge, Massachusetts, 1992).

27. McGleenan, T. & Wiesing, U. in *Genetics and Insurance* (eds McGleenan, T. *et al.*) 116–117 (Springer, New York, 1999).

28. Murray, T. Genetics and the moral mission of health insurance. *Hastings Center Report* **22,** 12–15 (1992).

29. Wilkie, T. Genetics and insurance in Britain: why more than just the Atlantic divides the English-speaking nations. *Nature Genet.* **20,** 119–121 (1998).

30. Dutch Health Council. *Genetics, Science & Society* (Dutch Health Council, The Hague, 1989).

31. Sandberg, P. Genetic information and life insurance: a proposal for an ethical European policy. *Social Sci. Med.* **40,** 1549–1559 (1995).

32. Collins, F. cited in Wadman, M. News: Jewish leaders meet NIH chiefs on genetic stigmatisation fears. *Nature* **392,** 851 (1998).

33. Editorial. Privacy matters. *Nature Genet.* **19,** 207–208 (1998).

34. Weijer, C., Goldsand, G. & Emanuel, E. J. Protecting communities in research: current guidelines and limits of extrapolation. *Nature Genet.* **23,** 275–280 (1999).

35. Weijer, C. Protecting communities in research: Philosophical and pragmatic challenges. *Cam. Q. Health Ethics* **8,** 501–513 (1999).

36. Burgess, M. M. & Brunger, F. in *The Governance of Health Research involving Human Subjects* (ed. McDonald, M.) 141–175 (Law Commission of Canada, Ottawa, 2000). Also see http://www.lcc.gc.ca/en/themes/gr/hrish/macdonald/macdonald.pdf

37. Foster, M. W., Berensten, D. & Carter, T. H., A model agreement for genetic research in socially identifiable populations. *Am. J. Hum. Genet.* **63,** 696–702 (1998).

38. Scheuermann, R. H. & Picker, L. J. Letter to the editor. *Nature* **392,** 14 (1998).

39. Council for International Organizations of Medical Sciences (CIOMS) *International Ethical Guidelines for Biomedical Research Involving Human Subjects* (CIOMS, Geneva, 1993).

40. Weijer, C., Goldsand, G. & Emanuel, E. J. Protecting communities in research: current guidelines and limits of extrapolation. *Nature Genet.* **23,** 275–280 (1999).

41. Burgess, M. M. & Brunger, F. in *The Governance of Health Research involving Human Subjects* (ed. McDonald, M.) 14–175 (Law Commission of Canada, 2000). Also see http://www.lcc.gc.ca/en/papers/macdonald/macdonald.pdf

42. Stephenson, P. in *A Cross-Cultural Dialogue on Health Care Ethics* (eds Coward, H. & Ratanakul, P.) 68–91. (Wilfrid Laurier Univ. Press, 1999).

43. Brunger, F. & Bassett, K. *Culture and Genetics in Socio-ethical Issues in Human Genetics* (ed. Knoppers, B. M.) 30–34 (Les Editions Yvon Blais Inc., Cowansville, Quebec, 1998).

44. Sclove, R. E. *Democracy and Technology* (The Guilford Press, New York, 1995).

45. Kerr, A:, Cunningham-Burley, S. & Amos, A. The new genetics and health: Mobilizing lay expertise. *Public Understanding of Science* **7,** 41–60 (1998).

46. Kerr, A., Cunningham-Burley, S. & Amos, A. Drawing the line: an analysis of lay people's discussions about the new genetics. *Public Understanding of Science* **7,** 113–133 (1998).

LAINIE FRIEDMAN ROSS AND MARGARET R. MOON

Ethical Issues in Genetic Testing of Children

Lainie Friedman Ross is Assistant Director at the MacLean Center for Clinical Medical Ethics at the University of Chicago. She has published widely on ethical issues in the field of pediatrics. Her most recent book is *Children, Families and Health Care Decision Making* (Clarendon Press).

Margaret R. Moon is the Senior Vice President and the Ethics and Medical Director of Doctors Community Healthcare Corporation. Her main interests lie in medical risk management and clinical ethics. In the past she held a dual appointment as Assistant Professor of Pediatrics and Medical Education and Director of the Clinical Ethics Service at the University of Illinois, Chicago.

Clinical genetics is an integral part of pediatrics. Genetic diseases are common in childhood: as many as 53 per 1000 children and young adults can be expected to have diseases with an important genetic component.[1] This rate increases to 79 per 1000 if congenital anomalies are included.[1] In addition, 12% to 40% of all pediatric hospitalizations are for genetic diseases and birth defects.[2–4] Despite its importance in primary care pediatrics, genetics has maintained its subspecialty status. Newborn screening for genetic diseases is the only aspect of genetics that has been incorporated as routine pediatric practice.[5]

Reprinted by permission of the authors and the publisher from the *Archives of Pediatrics and Adolescent Medicine* 154 (September 2000), 873–79. Copyright © 2000, American Medical Association.

The Human Genome Project is expanding knowledge of the genetic basis of disease at an incredible rate, and one by-product has been the development of new technology that makes widespread genetic testing feasible. Because there are not enough geneticists or genetic counselors to provide adequate counseling, primary care physicians will need to increase their knowledge about genetics and become the frontline providers of some of these services.[6] However, many primary care pediatricians are currently ill prepared to provide genetic counseling.[7–10] Even beyond the necessary medical knowledge, the development of new genetic technology raises ethical and social policy concerns that further challenge the primary care physician.[11,12]

The goal of this article is to help prepare pediatricians to respond to the ethical and policy challenges raised by the new genetics. Recent developments in genetics do not necessarily create new ethical concerns, but they highlight how social, political, and economic factors affect the implementation, use, and regulation of new biotechnologies. The ethical implications of these decisions need to be explored at the macro and micro levels. At the macro level, we examine the current policies and consensus statements regarding genetic testing of children, although our main focus is to provide pediatricians with a framework with which to interpret genetic testing in their own practice. Specifically, we examine the ethical issues raised in 3 clinical scenarios: (1) diagnostic genetic testing, (2) population-based genetic screening, and (3) carrier identification. The decision-making process is also described by 3 decision trees.

ETHICS OVERVIEW

To date, the Human Genome Project's greatest successes have been in gene discovery and the development of commercial genetic tests; gene therapy is still in an early experimental stage. Genetic testing of children can occur for a variety of reasons and in a variety of contexts, each of which raises a myriad of ethical questions, particularly with respect to consent and confidentiality.

Traditionally in pediatric medicine, parents are presumed to be best suited to make decisions for their children. Various arguments have been made to support parental control over medical decision making for minor children.[13–15] First, parents are presumed to have the child's best interests at heart, because they naturally care deeply for their children and because they are in a position to know the child best. Second, for parents to fulfill the responsibilities of child rearing, they need significant leeway in how they rear their children. This includes control over decisions about medical care, provided that the parents and their decisions are neither abusive nor neglectful. In part, this parental discretion is supported by the fact that many of the financial and emotional consequences of these decisions will be borne most heavily by the child and his or her parents. Third, society has an interest in supporting the family as the primary child-rearing institution. To do so requires that families be afforded a wide degree of privacy and freedom from governmental intrusion.

One constraint on parental control lies in our evolving understanding of children's autonomy and their role in the informed consent process. Historically, health care providers have downplayed the child's capacity for decision making, but the current attitude is to give greater weight to the child's developing decision-making capacity[16,17] and future autonomy.[18] We rely on parents to make decisions for their children while remaining open to the possibility that the child may have something important to add. However, parental autonomy is not and should not be absolute. The American Academy of Pediatrics argues that there are some situations in which parents should not be empowered to consent on their child's behalf and other situations in which the child's dissent ought to be binding.[16] Although the American Academy of Pediatrics does not make specific reference to genetic services, there are some genetics cases in which the parents' and child's interests may be in conflict. Evaluating parental requests requires finding the appropriate balance between the child's present and future needs and interests with the interests and needs of the families.[19–22]

Part of what makes genetics unique, however, is that knowledge about one family member might have great significance for other family members. To view decisions about genetic testing in the context of a single patient ignores the relationships and obligations that individuals have to those with whom they are genetically related because genetic information often applies to families as much as to individuals.[23,24] Confidentiality of genetic information requires clarification: confidentiality for whom and from whom? This is even more complex in pediatrics because of the role of the parents in the consent process.

In this article, we focus on the question of when genetic testing should be performed on children. Issues pertaining to the appropriate roles for parents and children in the consent process are addressed in another article.[25]

GENETIC SERVICES

TESTING HIGH-RISK CHILDREN

High-risk children are those who are symptomatic or are members of a family at high risk for a known genetic trait or disease.

Genetic testing is least controversial when an individual patient has some identifiable symptom or some specific risk factor that is best diagnosed via genetic testing. The use of genetic testing for confirming clinical diagnoses is indistinguishable from other therapeutic medical tests. The differential diagnosis of a child born with weak muscle tone and a large tongue includes the genetic condition of Down syndrome and the nongenetic condition of hypothyroidism; the former is tested by chromosomal analysis, the latter by endocrine function. The differential diagnosis of a child who has failure to thrive and chronic recurrent upper respiratory tract infections includes cystic fibrosis (CF), an autosomal recessive genetic condition, and acquired immunodeficiency syndrome, a nongenetic condition. In the symptomatic child, human immunodeficiency virus infection may be determined by Western blot or polymerase chain reaction testing (depending on the child's age and maternal antibody status), whereas CF can be diagnosed by measuring sweat chloride levels or by genetic mutational analysis. None of these tests are medically controversial in a symptomatic child provided that adequate consent is obtained.

If a patient has an extra chromosome 21 or 2 CF mutations, the clinician can conclude that the patient has Down syndrome or CF, respectively: the genetic test results confirm the clinical diagnoses. There is little controversy in these genetic tests when performed postnatally to provide appropriate clinical services for the affected child and family.

Contrast such tests with presymptomatic genetic testing used to identify disease in a currently healthy person known to be at risk. Testing for the genes for retinoblastoma or Huntington disease (HD) represent 2 such conditions. Both are autosomal dominant conditions, meaning that there is a 50% probability that an offspring of an affected adult (either symptomatic or presymptomatic) will inherit the gene. Both conditions are virtually 100% penetrant, which means that all individuals with the gene will become symptomatic. In hereditary retinoblastoma, most children present in the first year of life.[26] About 40% of retinoblastoma cases are familial, related to a mutation of a tumor suppressor gene on chromosome 13. Identification allows for targeted surveillance by frequent ophthalmologic examinations to minimize disease morbidity and mortality. The genetic test prevents unnecessary harm because it allows targeting of at-risk children in at-risk families. Children found to be positive for the gene are followed up with frequent ophthalmologic examinations (often under general anesthesia) to try to detect the disease early; children found to be negative for the gene are able to avoid frequent examinations. Without the test, all children in an at-risk family would have to undergo frequent ophthalmologic examinations. The genetic test optimizes treatment by enabling clinicians to focus on truly at-risk children and to avoid unnecessary medical surveillance of low-risk children from high-risk families.

In contrast, childhood onset of HD accounts for less than 5% of all affected individuals.[27] The value of testing children is to minimize uncertainty, to allow a person to incorporate positive or negative status as part of his or her self-concept, and to allow for better lifetime planning.[28,29] The risks to the child who has a positive test result are the potentially serious psychosocial sequelae that this information has on his or her relationships and interactions within the family, school, potential employers, and even with oneself.[28,29] The child who has a negative test result might also experience serious psychosocial sequelae ranging from survivor guilt to the possible social ostracization that occurs when one is perceived as different from siblings and parents.[28,29]

In retinoblastoma and HD, the tests are targeted to populations known to be at risk. The difference, however, is that there are preventive measures and treatments available for children with retinoblastoma, whereas there are neither preventive measures nor treatments that can minimize the morbidity of HD. Most genetic conditions are similar to HD in that they are currently untreatable, and diagnostic testing often offers no clear medical benefit to the patient. This does not mean that testing is necessarily harmful; rather, the calculation of benefit and risk will focus on psychosocial factors.

Retinoblastoma and HD are atypical genetic diseases in that they are almost 100% penetrant. Most genes and associated genetic tests, however, only identify an increased susceptibility, and their expression is widely variable, even within the same family. The probabilistic nature of genetic information adds further complexity to the ethical issues, in part because physicians and patients have a hard time understanding uncertainty and using such information in the decision-making process.[8–10,30] *BRCA1* testing for inheritable breast cancer exemplifies the point. A positive test result for the *BRCA1* gene identifies an increased risk of developing breast or ovarian cancer before age 65 years. In women of Ashkenazi Jewish ancestry with a positive family history, the probability can be as high as 85%.[31] Presymptomatic genetic diagnosis can offer some medical benefit for adult women, who can choose to undergo prophylactic mastectomy and oophorectomy, thereby reducing their chances of disease.[32] But there are currently no preventive measures appropriate for children or adolescents. Individuals who undergo testing for *BRCA1* and *BRCA2,* however, must understand that the gene is neither necessary nor sufficient for the development of breast cancer. *BRCA1* and *BRCA2* account for less than 10% of all breast cancers.[31] Even if a person has one of these inherited genetic predispositions, the fact is that the *BRCA1* mutation is only the first step in the development of breast or ovarian cancer. A "second hit," probably nongenetic, is required for a tumor to develop.[33–35] The nature of the second hit is not well specified, but a significant number of women with the *BRCA1* mutation avoid it.

Individuals who are not members of high-risk families can also test positive for *BRCA1* and *BRCA2*. Although they also have an increased risk of breast cancer compared with the general population, the risk is much lower than for members of high-risk families.[31,36] Parents might want to test their children for these genes because of family history, heightened awareness through an ill friend, or a community educational program. These parents need to know that presymptomatic genetic testing in low-risk families is often difficult to interpret. False-positive screening results might create a lasting burden of worry; alternatively, false-negative screening results might provide undue reassurance. As such, parents who request genetic testing of children for *BRCA1* need extensive counseling about what the test can and cannot do and how the results only provide information about increased or decreased disease susceptibility. A positive test result does not predict whether the disease will affect a particular individual, and it cannot predict at what age it might present, how aggressive the cancer might be, or whether it will be susceptible to standard chemotherapy.

For parents to interpret the risks and benefits of a particular genetic test, they need to understand the differences in (1) genetic testing in a child who is symptomatic, (2) genetic testing for the presence of a virtually 100% penetrant gene that has not yet expressed itself, and (3) genetic testing to determine increased susceptibility to a particular disease. The calculation of risks and benefits must take into account the technological quality of the test, its predictive value, its reliability, and its validity. Genetic technology is developing rapidly and is being introduced into the clinical setting early such that the actual quality of a test cannot be taken for granted and must be factored into decision making.[7,37,38]

The first step in helping parents calculate the risks and benefits is to delineate the possible medical benefits, if any, of genetic testing. Genetic testing that determines the cause of a child's symptoms has obvious medical benefits if treatments are available; and even if treatments are not available, the diagnosis can serve to prevent unnecessary additional workup. Genetic testing that diagnoses a presymptomatic child or a child with a genetic predisposition also has medical benefits when preventive or therapeutic measures are available at an early stage. But for most other genetic testing, there are no medical benefits. Even when genetic testing offers medical benefits, it is accompanied by and must be balanced with the possible medical risks created by false-negative and false-positive results.[7,39]

The next step is to consider the psychosocial benefits and risks. Empirical data on the emotional and psychosocial benefits and risks are inadequate and hard to come by. These issues are further complicated by the long time lag between genetic testing and diagnosis in childhood vs disease presentation in adulthood. The potential psychosocial benefits are (1) family uncertainty about the future can be reduced; (2) planning for the future can be more practical; and (3) parental expectations for the child's future can be more "realistic."[28,29] The potential psychosocial risks include (1) the possibility of stigmatization associated with genetic abnormality, even in the absence of phenotypic abnormality; (2) the potential for inhibiting parent-child bonding; (3) disruption of normal family relationships because of guilt on the part of parents or on behalf of the unaffected siblings (so-called survivor guilt); (4) the potential for a variation of the "vulnerable child syndrome"; and (5) modification of parental expectations (often subconsciously).[28,29] Little empirical data are available about how parents quantify the risks and benefits of presymptomatic and susceptibility testing in their children or how these children develop in contrast to their peers who were not diagnosed in childhood.

Other risks that must be incorporated into decisions about genetic testing include risks of discrimination related to genotypic abnormalities, even if the condition is not 100% penetrant, and concerns about the long-term privacy of genetic information. As a society, we are only in the early stages of understanding the relationship of genotype-phenotype correlation and the interaction of various genotypes with the environment. But this has not stopped different institutions from using this information in a discriminatory manner.[40–42]

Given that a risk-benefit analysis of most genetic tests will not yield an easy or obvious decision, pediatricians must learn to help their families navigate this decision-making process. Figure 1 summarizes a basic algorithm for decisions about genetic testing for children with known risk factors or symptoms. Genetic tests performed on children with symptoms or known risk factors that have immediate medical benefit to the child are ethically noncontroversial, despite the potential for psychosocial disruption. As medical benefits become less available, genetic testing becomes more controversial. The decision, however, whether to test a child will also take into account the psychosocial benefits and risks of testing for the child and the family. Although the values of the family are paramount, the pediatrician can help the family by ensuring that the whole range of possible scenarios is examined and that the family considers all of the possible implications and repercussions of testing.

The importance of the psychosocial analysis must not be underestimated. In many ways, the medical

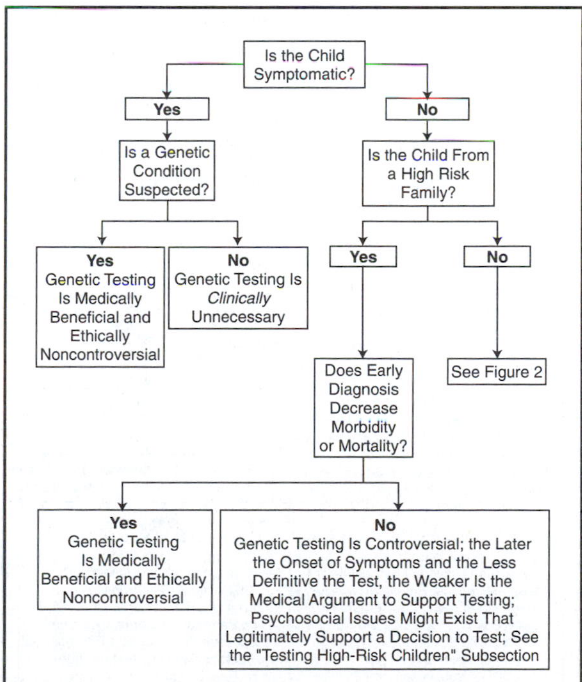

Figure 1. Genetic testing in high-risk children (i.e., children who have symptoms or are from a high-risk family).

benefit of genetic testing in pediatric patients is the simple question. More important and more difficult to know is the impact of testing, both immediate and long-term, on the child and family. Although some would argue that all requests for genetic tests that do not offer obvious and immediate medical benefit should be refused, we do not. It is conceivable that the psychosocial benefit of a test, even a test that has little or no medical benefit, might be decisive for a particular family. We believe that pediatricians need to work with families to ensure that they understand what the test does and does not offer and to ensure that the family has considered all the potential consequences and repercussions such information might have on the child during childhood and adulthood as well as on the family unit. Although we would tend to discourage parents from pursuing genetic information that offers no medical benefit, we realize that parents, not clinicians, must ultimately decide what is in the child's best interest. This includes weighing medical and nonmedical factors, many of which the pediatrician might not be cognizant of for this particular family in its particular circumstances.

GENETIC SCREENING

Genetic screening, in contrast to genetic testing, refers to testing whole populations for disease, usually without regard to particular risk factors. Population-based screening of children is most commonly done in the newborn period but can be done at other stages. Newborn screening is performed for a variety of medical conditions, both genetic and nongenetic. For example, thyroid disease, a nonmendelian condition, is included in all newborn state screens,[5] and the National Institutes of Health and the American Academy of Pediatrics recommend universal newborn screening for hearing loss in children that might or might not be genetic in origin.[43,44] Beyond the newborn period, it is also recommended that pediatricians screen targeted populations of children for lead[45,46] and tuberculosis.[47]

Newborn screening is an integral part of pediatrics. The list of genetic diseases varies by state, but screening for phenylketonuria, hemoglobinopathies, and galactosemia is nearly universal in the United States.[5] In 1994, the Institute of Medicine (IOM) recommended that population-based (newborn) screening programs fulfill 3 criteria: (1) there is a clear indication of benefit to the newborn, (2) a system is in place to confirm the diagnosis, and (3) treatment and follow-up are available for affected newborns. Additional criteria to justify screening whole populations include (1) that the condition is frequent and severe enough to be a public health concern; (2) that the condition causes a known spectrum of symptoms; and (3) that the screening test is simple and reliable, with low false-positive and false-negative rates.[11]

Medical data show that newborn screening for most conditions included in state screens is beneficial in reducing morbidity and mortality. In that regard, we support such testing, although we are against the current policy that mandates such testing without parental consent. We support parental consent because it gives authority to the parents, who are the appropriate surrogate decision-makers for their children.[39,48] Through the consent process, the parents would be informed about the conditions for which testing is offered, why follow-up might be necessary, and why follow-up should be done early. Currently, parental consent is sought in Maryland only, where fewer than 1 parent in 1000 refuses testing for their newborns.[49] Although this creates a possibility that an affected child will not be screened, the probability is much lower than the chance of missing an affected child because of a false-negative test result or because the specimen was inadequate or lost.[50]

An even more serious challenge for the future, however, is to evaluate carefully all new proposals for population-based screening programs, and not to institutionalize programs that do not meet, at minimum, the criteria enumerated by the IOM. Historically, newborn screens have not fulfilled these criteria at the time of implementation. For example, when newborn screening for sickle cell disease was first initiated, there was no known benefit to presymptomatic diagnosis.[11] Now that penicillin prophylaxis has been shown to reduce morbidity and mortality, newborn screening for sickle cell disease is a paradigm case of justifiable universal screening,[51] but that does not justify its earlier implementation. Even today, governments continue to test for conditions for which newborn testing has not been shown to benefit the newborn. For example, 2 states in the United States screen for CF despite the fact that data do not show that early initiation of therapy changes the course of disease.[52,53] In some countries, children are tested for Duchenne muscular dystrophy although there are no known early treatments.[54] The justification is to educate couples about their future reproductive risks. Early diagnosis can benefit the affected child because it will avoid unnecessary workup when symptoms develop. However, early diagnosis might place the child at risk because the parents might now view their healthy-appearing child as ill or even doomed and might bond poorly or otherwise neglect him or her. We believe that the expansion of universal newborn testing to these conditions is not warranted because the risks to the child, and possibly to the family, might outweigh the benefits.

On the other hand, there may be some genetic conditions that might not warrant universal screening because the cost of the test is too great or the cost-benefit analysis on a universal basis does not justify it. This does not mean, however, that genetic testing for this condition should never be offered. If there are identifiable groups who may be at increased risk for whom early diagnosis can decrease morbidity and mortality (eg, maple syrup urine disease in the Amish population or Gaucher disease in the Ashkenazi Jewish population), the medical benefits may support screening in these targeted populations. Even in low-risk communities, parental requests for specific genetic testing of their newborn may be justifiable. For example, we believe that parental anxiety alone may justify genetic testing, particularly when the condition is treatable. Parents who seek broad-spectrum testing of their newborn, however, need to be counseled that even the exclusion of a large number of genetic and nongenetic conditions does not promise a healthy child.

Our recommendations for universal screening are summarized in Figure 2, where we point out that,

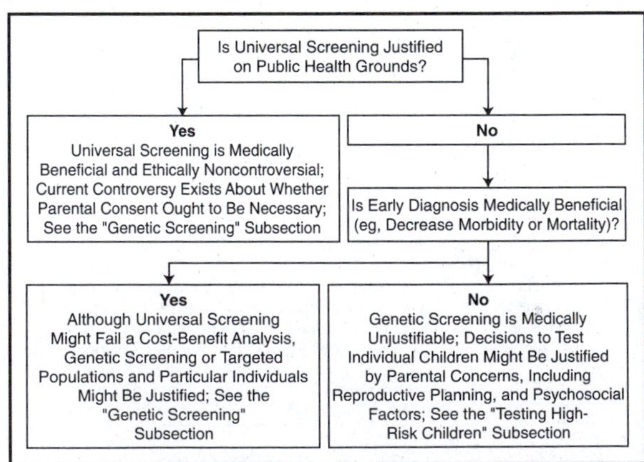

Figure 2. Genetic screening and testing in low-risk children (i.e., children who are asymptomatic and are from a low-risk family).

even when universal screening cannot be justified from a medical cost-benefit analysis, screening targeted populations or testing particular children may still be ethically permissible. Again, the final determination will depend on the psychosocial benefit-risk calculation made by the parents with appropriate counseling.

IDENTIFICATION OF CARRIER STATUS

All individuals carry several recessive genes that would prove lethal to a fetus if it received a double dose.[55] We all carry other recessive genes that are not lethal in the homozygous state but cause serious diseases. Carriers of recessive genes are often asymptomatic and unaware that they carry particular genes. For most recessive genetic traits, being a carrier confers no known medical morbidity. As such, tests to identify carrier status are not intended to provide a medical benefit to the patient, but they serve to provide information that may be important for reproductive decisions.

Carrier testing is most often done in the prenatal setting. Sometimes, however, carrier status is determined incidentally. For example, every child with a quantifiable amount of hemoglobin S on newborn screening in the United States is retested. Hemoglobin electrophoresis determines whether they are homozygous (sickle cell anemia) or heterozygous (sickle cell trait) for hemoglobin S. Currently, parents in the United States are told if their child is a carrier. This disclosure is not without controversy: the IOM recommends that parents not be told their child's trait status.[11] The IOM's justification is that the information has no clinical relevance but solely reproductive relevance, for which the child has a right to privacy and a right not to know.[11] We disagree with the IOM's recommendation insofar as it implies that the state has more right to information about a child than does his or her parents. Parents who receive such information need appropriate counseling to understand the distinction between clinical and reproductive relevance of this information so that they do not erroneously treat their child as "diseased" and can counsel their child effectively. Nevertheless, we also believe that there is a need for longitudinal research to determine the impact such knowledge has on children and adolescents and their families during the life cycle so that any policy changes can be based on empirical analysis of harms and benefits.

If informing parents of trait status when the information is determined incidentally is controversial, even more controversial is whether parents electively can request to test their children for carrier status. Often the interest is prompted by the diagnosis of a sibling or other relative with the disease.[56] We consider the possible scenarios and the framework with which to respond in Figure 3.

The arguments in favor of honoring the parents' requests are that being informed of carrier status in childhood might make it easier to accept that status and incorporate it into one's personal identity[57]; that it might be useful for other family members[58]; and that parents, not the state, are in a better position to decide if the benefits of knowledge outweigh the risks for a particular child.[25] The main arguments for refusing a parental request for carrier state testing are that it frustrates the child's right not to know as an

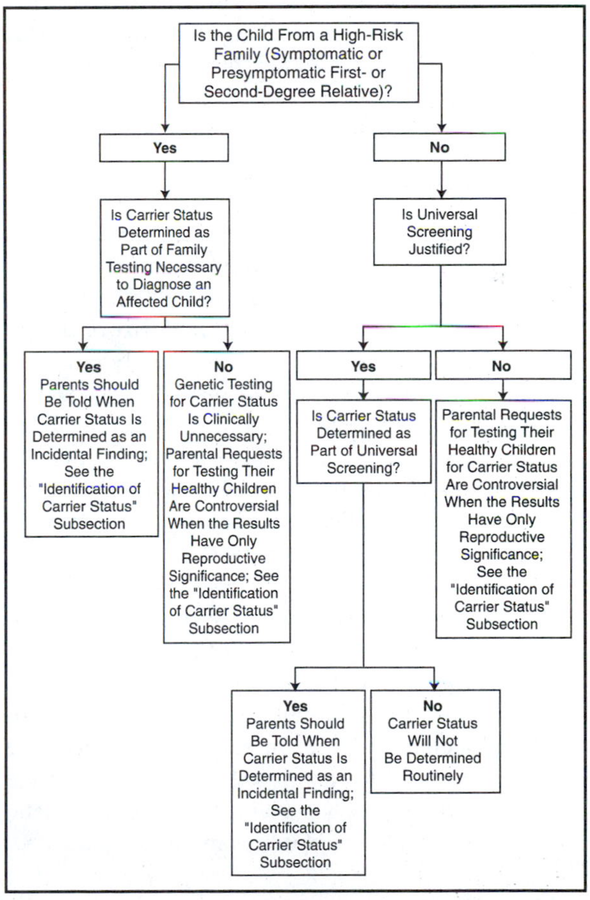

Figure 3. Genetic testing for carrier status (i.e., an autosomal recessive or sex-linked condition in which the carrier status confers no or minimal risk of morbidity or mortality but is important for reproductive decisions).

adult, it fails to respect the child's right to confidential reproductive knowledge, it may adversely impact the child's self-concept, and it may expose the child to unwarranted genetic discrimination. There is also concern that parental misunderstanding of test results will lead to treating the child who is a carrier as an ill or potentially ill child.[57]

Although we would neither encourage nor recommend carrier testing of children solely for informational purposes, we would not want to make a blanket prohibition of such testing in children. Rather, we are willing to respect parental requests, following appropriate counseling, on the grounds that they know what is best for the child and the family. Again, the importance of longitudinal research on the impact of such knowledge over the life cycle cannot be underestimated. Pediatricians need this information to help counsel families who request carrier testing of their children. In fact, we would be willing to reconsider our position if research found that knowledge of carrier status caused more harm than benefit for most children during the life cycle.

CONCLUSIONS

There are many different flavors of genetic testing: testing can be targeted or universalized in statewide screening programs; testing may uncover disease risk for which treatments may or may not exist or it may uncover information that has relevance only in the reproductive context; and testing may yield results of varying predictive value. Genetic testing is complicated because knowledge about one family member can have significant impact on other family members. This is further complicated in pediatrics because the decisions can have lifelong repercussions for the individual who did not consent himself or herself to this testing. Further research on the psychosocial and ethical implications of genetic information is needed to ensure that policies are designed that meet our needs as individuals and as members of families, communities, and society-at-large. In addition, primary care pediatricians need to familiarize themselves with the scientific and the psychosocial data regarding genetic services to better serve children and their families.

REFERENCES

1. Baird P. A., Anderson T. W., Newcombe H. B., Lowry R. B. Genetic disorders in children and young adults: a population study. *Am J Hum Genet*. 1988;42:677–93.
2. Hall J. G., Powers E. K., McIlvaine R. T., Ean V. H. The frequency and financial burden of genetic disease in a pediatric hospital. *Am J Med Genet*. 1978;1:417–436.
3. Scriver C. R., Neal J. L., Saginur R., Clow A. The frequency of genetic disease and congenital malformation among patients in a pediatric hospital. *CMAJ*. 1973;108:1111–1115.
4. Yoon P. W., Olney R. S., Khoury M. J., Sappenfield W. M., Chavez G. F., Taylor D. Contributions of birth defects and genetic diseases to pediatric hospitalizations: a population-based study. *Arch Pediatr Adolesc Med*. 1997;151:1096–1103.
5. American Academy of Pediatrics, Committee on Genetics. Newborn screening fact sheet. *Pediatrics*. 1996;98: 473–501.
6. Holtzman N. A. Primary care physicians as providers of frontline genetic services. *Fetal Diagn Ther*. 1993;8(suppl 1):213–219.
7. Holtzman N. A. *Proceed With Caution: Predicting Genetic Risks in the Recombinant DNA Era*. Baltimore, Md: The Johns Hopkins University Press; 1989.
8. Hofman K. J., Tambor E. S., Chase G. A., Geller G., Faden R. R., Holtzman N. A. Physicians' knowledge of genetics and genetic tests. *Acad Med*. 1993;68:625–632.
9. Giardiello F. M., Brensinger J. D., Petersen G. M., et al. The use and interpretation of commercial APC gene testing for familial adenomatous polyposis. *N Engl J Med*. 1997; 336:823–827.
10. Rowley P. T., Loader S., Levenkron J. C., Phelps C. E. Cystic fibrosis carrier screening: knowledge and attitudes of prenatal care providers. *Am J Prev Med*. 1993;9:261–266.
11. Andrews L., Fullarton J., Holtzman N., Motulsky A., eds. *Assessing Genetic Risks: Implications for Health and Social Policy*. Washington, DC: National Academy Press; 1994.
12. Marteau T., Richards M., eds. *The Troubled Helix: Social and Psychological Implications of the New Human Genetics*. New York, NY: Cambridge University Press; 1996.
13. Buchanan A., Brock D. *Deciding for Others: The Ethics of Surrogate Decision Making*. New York, NY: Cambridge University Press; 1990.
14. Blustein J. *Parents and Children: The Ethics of the Family*. New York, NY: Oxford University Press Inc; 1982.
15. Ross L. F. *Parents, Children, and Health Care Decision Making*. Oxford, England: Oxford University Press; 1998.
16. American Academy of Pediatrics, Committee on Bioethics. Informed consent, parental permission, and assent in pediatric practice. *Pediatrics*. 1995;95:314–317.
17. Alderson P., Montgomery J. *Health Care Choices: Making Decisions With Children*. London, England: Institute for Public Policy Research; 1996.
18. Feinberg J. The child's right to an open future. In: Aiken W., LaFollette H., eds. *Whose Child? Children's Rights, Parental Authority, and State Power*. Totowa, NJ: Littlefield, Adams & Co; 1980:124–153.
19. Sharpe N. F. Presymptomatic testing for Huntington disease: is there a duty to test those under the age of eighteen years? *Am J Med Genet*. 1993;46:250–253.
20. Patenaude A. F. The genetic testing of children for cancer susceptibility: ethical, legal and social issues. *Behav Sci Law*. 1996;14:393–410.
21. Cohen C. B. Wrestling with the future: should we test children for adult-onset genetic conditions? *Kennedy Inst Ethics J*. 1998;8:111–130.
22. Davis D. S. Genetic dilemmas and the child's right to an open future. *Rutgers Law J*. 1997;28:549–592.

23. American Society of Human Genetics Social Issues Subcommittee on Familial Disclosure. ASHG statement: professional disclosure of familial genetic information. *Am J Hum Genet.* 1998;62:474–483.

24. Deftos L. J. The evolving duty to disclose the presence of genetic disease to relatives. *Acad Med.* 1998;73:962–968.

25. Ross L. F. Genetic testing of children: who should consent? In: Burley J., Harris J., eds. *A Companion to Genethics: Ethics and the Genetic Revolution*. Oxford, England: Blackwell Publishers; 2000. Companions to Philosophy Series.

26. Birch J. M. Genes and cancer. *Arch Dis Child.* 1999;80:1–3.

27. Baraitser M. Huntington's chorea. In: Baraitser M., ed. *The Genetics of Neurological Disorders*. Oxford, England: Oxford Medical Publications; 1990:308–323.

28. American Society of Human Genetics Board of Directors and American College of Medical Genetics Board of Directors. ASHG/ACMG report: points to consider: ethical, legal and psychosocial implications of genetic testing in children and adolescents. *Am J Hum Genet.* 1995; 57:1233–1241.

29. Report of a Working Party of the Clinical Genetics Society (UK). The genetic testing of children. *J Med Genet.* 1994;31:785–797.

30. Davison C. Predictive genetics: the cultural implications of supplying probable futures. In: Marteau T., Richards M., eds. *The Troubled Helix: Social and Psychological Implications of the New Human Genetics*. Cambridge, England: Cambridge University Press; 1996:317–330.

31. Burke W., Daly M., Garber J., et al. Consensus statement: recommendations for follow-up care of individuals with an inherited predisposition to cancer, II: *BRCA1* and *BRCA2*. *JAMA.* 1997;277:997–1003.

32. Hartmann L. C., Schaid D. J., Woods J. E., et al. Efficacy of bilateral prophylactic mastectomy in women with a family history of breast cancer. *N Engl J Med.* 1999;340:77–84.

33. Armitage P., Doll R. A two-stage theory of carcinogenesis in relation to the age distribution of human cancer. *Br J Cancer.* 1957;11:161–169.

34. Ashley D. J. B. The two "hit" and multiple "hit" theories of carcinogenesis. *Br J Cancer.* 1969;23:313–328.

35. Knudson A. G. Hereditary cancer: two hits revisited. *J Cancer Res Clin Oncol.* 1996;122:135–140.

36. Malone K. E., Daling J. R., Thompson J. D., O'Brien C. A., Francisco L. V., Ostrander E. A. *BRCA1* mutations and breast cancer in the general population. *JAMA.* 1998;279:922–929.

37. Task Force on Genetic Testing. *Promoting Safe and Effective Genetic Testing in the United States: Final Report.* Baltimore, Md: The Johns Hopkins University Press; 1998.

38. Holtzman N. A., Murphy P. D., Watson M. S., Barr P. A. Predictive genetic testing: from basic research to clinical practice. *Science.* 1997;278:602–605.

39. Paul D. Contesting consent: the challenge to compulsory neonatal screening for PKU. *Perspect Biol Med.* 1999;42:207–219.

40. Billings P. R., Kohn M. A., de Cuevas J., Beckwith J., Alper J. S., Natowicz M. R. Discrimination as a consequence of genetic testing. *Am J Hum Genet.* 1992;50:476–482.

41. Duster T. *Backdoor to Eugenics*. New York, NY: Routledge; 1990.

42. Draper E. *Risky Business: Genetic Testing and Exclusionary Practices in the Hazardous Workplace*. New York, NY: Cambridge University Press; 1991.

43. NIH Consensus Statement. Early identification of hearing impairment in infants and young children. *NIH Consens Statement.* 1993;11:1–24.

44. American Academy of Pediatrics Joint Committee on Infant Hearing. Joint Committee on Infant Hearing 1994 position statement. *Pediatrics.* 1995;95:152–156.

45. American Academy of Pediatrics. Lead poisoning from screening to primary prevention. *Pediatrics.* 1993;92: 176–183.

46. Centers for Disease Control. *Preventing Lead Poisoning in Young Children*. Atlanta, Ga: US Dept of Health and Human Services; 1991.

47. American Academy of Pediatrics, Committee on Infectious Diseases. Update on tuberculosis skin testing of children. *Pediatrics.* 1996;97:282–284.

48. Annas G. J. Mandatory PKU screening: the other side of the looking glass. *Am J Public Health.* 1982;72:1401–1403.

49. Faden R., Chwalow J., Holtzman N. A., Horn S. D. A survey to evaluate parental consent as public policy for neonatal screening. *Am J Public Health.* 1982;72:1347–1352.

50. Holtzman N. A., Leonard C. O., Farfel M. R. Issues in antenatal and neonatal screening and surveillance for hereditary and congenital disorders. *Annu Rev Public Health.* 1981; 2:219–251.

51. Consensus Conference. Newborn screening for sickle cell disease and other hemoglobinopathies. *JAMA.* 1987; 258:1205–1209.

52. Genetic testing for cystic fibrosis. *NIH Consens US Statement.* 1997;15:1–37.

53. Wald N. J., Morris J. K. Neonatal screening for cystic fibrosis. *BMJ.* 1998;316:40–45.

54. Bradley D. M., Parsons E. P., Clarke A. J. Experience with screening newborns for Duchenne muscular dystrophy in Wales. *BMJ.* 1993;306:357–360.

55. Lee J. K., Lascoux M., Nordheim E. V. Number of lethal equivalents in human populations: how good are the previous estimates? *Heredity.* 1996;77:209–216.

56. Balfour-Lynn I., Madge S., Dinwiddie R. Testing carrier status in siblings of patients with cystic fibrosis. *Arch Dis Child.* 1995;72:167–168.

57. Fanos J. H. Developmental tasks of childhood and adolescence: implications for genetic testing. *Am J Med Genet.* 1997;71:22–28.

58. Bowman J. E. Genetics and African Americans. *Seton Hall Law Rev.* 1997;27:919–937.

Human Gene Transfer Research

THEODORE FRIEDMANN

Principles for Human Gene Therapy Studies

Theodore Friedmann is Professor of Pediatrics and Whitehill Professor of Biomedical Ethics at the University of California, San Diego (UCSD) and Director of the UCSD Program in Human Gene Therapy. He was one of the first to publish on the need for gene therapy for human disease. He is currently Chair of the NIH Recombinant DNA Advisory Committee.

The human gene therapy community finds itself struggling with technical and policy problems arising from several recently publicized adverse events in human gene therapy studies. The current discussion was catalyzed by the tragic death of Jesse Gelsinger, an 18-year-old patient with ornithine transcarbamylase (OTC) deficiency who died, apparently as a direct result of the experimental gene therapy studies being carried out by investigators at the University of Pennsylvania in Philadelphia and the National Children's Medical Center in Washington, DC.

Preliminary public review of the events leading to the tragedy in the Philadelphia OTC study was presented at a recent public meeting of the Recombinant DNA Advisory Committee (RAC) of the Office of Biotechnology Activities (OBA) of the National Institutes of Health. An ongoing Food and Drug Administration (FDA) investigation has already resulted in a compulsory hold of indefinite duration being placed on gene therapy studies at the Institute for Human Gene Therapy at the University of Pennsylvania and a voluntary hold on at least one other academic institution until possible deficiencies can be corrected. One commercially sponsored study was placed on temporary hold but now has been resumed. Additional inquiries by the involved universities, the Advisory Committee to the Director of the NIH, the United States Senate, and the executive branch are under way.

Reprinted with permission from *Science* 287 (March 24, 2000), 2163–65. Copyright © 2000, American Association for the Advancement of Science.

These events suggest that the gene therapy community has not fully succeeded in developing mechanisms to ensure the highest possible quality of clinical research. The intention of this discussion is to derive lessons from the preliminary information available and to reexamine the principles that constitute the foundation of clinical research in gene therapy.

HUMAN EXPERIMENTATION REQUIRES CAREFUL PATIENT SELECTION AND PROTECTION

Human disease and therapy are, eventually, best studied in human subjects. Codes of medical ethics recognize the importance of appropriate human studies, as long as they rest on strong basic and preclinical science and voluntary informed consent by patients. To be truly "informed," a patient's consent must be based on current and complete information of the procedures and their potential risks and benefits.

The patient population with potentially the most to gain in the Philadelphia OTC study, patients with the neonatal lethal form of the disease, were justifiably included in the initial study design. However, investigators were advised by their institutional review board (IRB) and medical ethics consultants that phase I experiments (in which dose and safety are being tested) would be ethically unacceptable in these infants because of the danger of implying a potential benefit to desperate parents. The next-best study population was used instead—less severely affected older patients from whom informed consent and meaningful data might be more readily obtained. There is debate in the medical ethics community whether this decision to exclude desperately ill newborns was appropriate. The quandary of patient selection in this case underscores this general dilemma in medical ethics and the unrealistic degree to which we have come to expect therapeutic results in phase I studies.

HUMAN EXPERIMENTATION INVOLVES RISKS

Human experimental studies, genetic or otherwise, are "experimental" precisely because the results are not known beforehand. Preclinical studies sometimes indicate adverse outcomes that can be readily avoided. In other instances, adverse results are found, only in retrospect, to have been foreshadowed by clues during early testing that investigators were neither alert nor wise enough to appreciate. In still other studies, adverse outcomes could not have been predicted in animals and limited human trials. Preclinical studies did not predict the discovery that the diet medication fen-phen is associated with potentially life-threatening cardiac valvular damage. Likewise, the recent withdrawal from the market by the FDA of a rotavirus vaccine came only after large-scale human experience with the vaccine.

ADVERSE RESULTS DO NOT INVALIDATE THE RATIONALE OF GENE THERAPY

Apparent "failures" in early phaseI/II or even phase III studies do not necessarily indicate a therapeutic wild-goose chase. Because gene therapy is highly experimental and many patients are desperately ill, serious adverse events and even deaths will occur. It is vital to understand the reasons for unexpected results or clinical failures to allow the development of corrected procedures and improved experimental methods. For example, problems with polio vaccines due to persistence of live disease-causing poliovirus in incompletely inactivated preparations and the presence of SV40 in the vaccine were identified early, corrected, and used to develop improved programs.

The development of gene therapy is similar to vaccine and drug development. Drug development is difficult and expensive, and gene therapy will not be simpler. The pharmaceutical industry, more mature and experienced than the gene therapy community, devotes enormous research and financial resources to studies of the biodistribution, pharmacological properties, stability, and metabolic properties of a potential new drug, as well as the physiological, immunological, and teratogenic effects on the host. Despite such care, because of the enormous complexity of human physiology and disease, and because even the most extensive animal data do not always faithfully predict responses in humans, adverse clinical responses have occurred and will again. The same understanding of pharmacokinetics and mechanisms has not been available for gene therapy trials. Some clinical applications have simply outstripped scientific understanding of the disease model or the properties of the vectors, resembling an army too far ahead of its supply lines. Despite clinical urgency, there is a need to develop a similar degree of rigor for gene transfer agents as for small molecule therapeutics or viral vaccines.

Despite the caveats regarding the need for better knowledge, the search for optimum methods should not paralyze attempts to use available tools to conduct clinical research studies. To make progress, one must accept the limitations of knowledge and simultaneously use available information to ease suffering and to continue research into improvements in technology.

INFORMED CONSENT IS CRUCIAL TO PATIENT PROTECTION

The single most important mechanism for ensuring patient protection from inherent risks of clinical experiments, unrealistic expectations, and potential conflicts of interest of the investigator is accurate and full disclosure of potential risks and benefits and a well-executed informed consent process. For gene therapy studies, the FDA and RAC review the adequacy of locally approved informed consent procedures during the protocol approval process. The FDA concluded that there were deficiencies in the informed consent process in the OTC study that resulted in incomplete disclosure of all potential risks to the subjects or their families. Additional troublesome public revelations of potential lapses in quality control and in patient protection have been made for other gene therapy studies.

Exaggerated expectations and potential conflicts of interest of investigators pose additional problems to the informed consent process. In 1995, an NIH advisory committee chaired by Stuart Orkin and Arno Motulsky criticized the gene therapy community for its overly optimistic public portrayal of gene therapy experiments and for unsubstantiated claims for efficacy.[1] There is still too ready a tendency by some in the gene therapy community to exaggerate potential benefits at the expense of full disclosure of potential risks. If that tendency is the result of optimism, it is at least unfortunate and should be guarded against. If it was determined that risks were intentionally omitted or misstated, appropriate sanctions by the gene therapy community and oversight bodies should be applied.

DEALING WITH FINANCIAL CONFLICT OF INTEREST

The issue of conflicts of interest is magnified by the very large role that biotechnology and pharmaceutical industries have come to play in gene therapy. In many cases, academic investigators have had to forge commercial collaborations to implement clinical studies because of the high costs (production and testing of a gene vector usually exceeds several hundred thousand dollars). Although commercial interactions have facilitated clinical studies, they have also introduced corporate financial interests and investigator economic conflicts. Therefore, at minimum, involved investigators should disclose direct commercial ties in the informed consent process. Those investigators with direct financial interest in the study outcome should recuse themselves from patient selection, the informed consent process, and study direction.

IMPROVEMENTS ARE NEEDED IN REVIEW AND REGULATION

During the early phase of clinical studies of human gene transfer, the RAC played a major role by providing an avenue for public evaluation of the scientific basis and patient protection aspects of a proposed study. The FDA shared responsibility for oversight of gene therapy studies through its traditional regulatory function of ensuring safety and efficacy. In 1997, in response to an advisory committee report to the NIH director, the FDA assumed the principal regulatory and oversight responsibility for gene therapy proposals, and the RAC was given the function of catalyzing public awareness and understanding of the issues of gene therapy. It also retained a secondary responsibility to determine whether studies submitted to the FDA utilized technological concepts and tools so novel that they required further public review.

An important difference between the RAC and FDA processes is that the RAC reviews of proposals and adverse-event reporting are public and open, whereas FDA is required by statute to carry out these functions privately and without provision for public disclosure. In a field as immature and filled with public interest and concern as gene therapy, more, rather than less, public review seems desirable. A cohesive mechanism must be developed in which primary regulatory control stays with the appropriate regulatory agency—the FDA—but which more effectively takes advantage of the advisory role of the RAC or a RAC-like body and also uses the RAC as a conduit for public discussion and disclosure before protocol approval. It is encouraging that discussions are under way between the RAC, FDA, and NIH through the Advisory Committee to the NIH director on potential mechanisms to provide this kind of process.

GENE THERAPY TRIALS REQUIRE IMPROVED MONITORING

For the field to progress, investigators must have more ready access to the clinical experience in other studies, and it is therefore particularly encouraging that the OBA has reaffirmed its intention to develop a gene therapy database that will make the occurrence and nature of adverse events available online to other gene therapy investigators.[2] Such a database can only succeed if investigators report their adverse events, and disclosure is useful only if mechanisms exist to collate, evaluate, and promulgate such information.

The existence of widely different reporting requirements has contributed to uncertainty and, quite probably, to deficiencies in reporting. The FDA requires that serious, unexpected, or related events be reported to the agency within 7 days if there is a patient death, or within 15 days for other serious adverse events. All other events are to be included in annual reports.[3] The words "serious," "unexpected," and "related" allow room for interpretation by investigators and study sponsors; the NIH requirements are less flexible. It is therefore possible, as the oversight agencies and several investigators have recently discovered, to be in compliance with the FDA requirements but not with the NIH guidelines. The NIH has recently proposed strengthening its reporting requirements through amendments of the NIH guidelines in which the definition of adverse events is clarified, and there is notification that such reports may not contain any confidential trade secrets or commercial and financial information.[4] The NIH has also notified all federally supported institutions to review their policies and procedures to ensure that they are in compliance with reporting requirements.[5] The FDA has stated that it will notify the RAC of the receipt of all adverse events in a gene therapy study.[6]

CONCLUSIONS

Scientific and policy problems in gene therapy studies, together with the explosive growth of clinical studies, challenge the academic gene therapy community, commercial biotechnology and pharmaceutical firms, regulatory agencies, and professional societies such as the American Society of Human Gene Therapy to work together to improve current practices and infrastructures. Announcements of new initiatives for FDA and NIH that would require earlier review of researcher's plans for monitoring safety and quarterly meetings to promote communication are encouraging developments. Further critical steps toward that goal would include RAC determination of the need for full public evaluation of protocols before investigational new drug (IND) assignment by FDA and IRB approval; the development of a single, uniform mechanism for reporting adverse events to the RAC, FDA, and other relevant agencies; establishment by OBA of its proposed public database of all adverse events; and nonparticipation of investigators with financial interests in study outcomes in patient selection, the informed consent process, and direct management of clinical studies. While there is need for improvements, there is also much to celebrate—major technical advances that promise imminent proof that the lives of patients can eventually be made better by gene therapy.

REFERENCES AND NOTES

1. S. Orkin and A. Motulsky, www.nih.gov/news/panelrep.html, 7 December 1995.
2. Testimony of A. Patterson, www4.od.nih.gov/oba/patterson2-00.pdf, 2 February 2000.
3. FDA Manual of Regulatory Standard Operating Procedures and Policies, www.fda.gov/cber/regsopp/91101.htm; www.fda.gov/cber/regsopp/91102.htm; and www.fda.gov/cber/ind/21cfr312.pdf.
4. Minutes of RAC meeting, 5 September 1999, www4.od.nih.gov/oba/9%2D99pro.htm.
5. Letter from A. Patterson to federally funded institutions, 22 November 1999.
6. Letter from K. Zoon to Investigational New Drug Sponsors and Principal Investigators, www.fda.gov/cber/ltr/gt110599.htm, 5 November 1999.

NIKUNJ SOMIA AND INDER M. VERMA

Gene Therapy: Trials and Tribulations

Ninkunj Somia was formerly a research associate at the Salk Institute working with Inder Verma. He is currently an Assistant Professor at the University of Minnesota. His research interests lie in gene therapy, and in particular, the targeting of retroviral vectors to specific cell types. More recently he has been developing novel uses for these vectors in the area of functional genomics.

Inder Verma is Professor and Co-Director of the Laboratory of Genetics at the Salk Institute, as well as Adjunct Professor of Biology at the University of California, San Diego. He has published extensively on the molecular basis for oncogenesis and on human gene therapy.

The basic concept of gene therapy is disarmingly simple—introduce the gene, and its product should cure or slow down the progression of a disease. Encompassed within this idea are a number of goals, including the treatment of both inherited and acquired disease. This approach requires a technology capable of gene transfer in a wide variety of cells, tissues and whole organs, but the delivery vehicles needed to ferry genetic material into a cell still represent the "Achilles heel" of gene therapy. An ideal vector should have the attributes outlined in Box 1. At present, not all of these attributes can be found in any one vector, although distinct classes of vector have different combinations of attributes.

The vectors available now fall into two broad categories—the non-viral and viral vectors. Non-viral vectors include naked DNA and LIPOSOMES.[1] Although non-viral vectors can be produced in relatively large amounts, and are likely to present fewer toxic or immunological problems, they suffer from inefficient gene transfer at present. Furthermore, expression of the foreign gene is transient. Given the need, in many diseases, for sustained and often high-level expression of the transgene, viral vectors are the most suitable vehicles for efficient gene delivery. . . .

Reprinted with permission from *Nature Reviews: Genetics* 1 (November 2000), 91–98. Copyright © 2000, Nature Publishing Group.

• • •

IMMUNE RESPONSE: THE BANE OF GENE THERAPY

The biggest challenge facing all viral vectors is the immune response of the host. The host defence mechanism functions at both the cellular level, by generating cytotoxic T cells, and at the humoral level, by generating antibodies to viral proteins. Cellular immunity eliminates the transduced cells, whereas humoral immunity precludes the repeat administration of the vector because the subsequent antibody response will be boosted by MEMORY CELLS.[5,6] The host immune system may also recognize the transgene product as foreign, and induce both cellular and humoral immunity.[7]

To minimize the cellular response, most vectors have been designed to prevent the synthesis of viral proteins following transduction. However, adenoviral vectors present a unique problem, because even the inactivated recombinant adenoviral vectors can elicit potent cytotoxic T-cell responses against viral proteins.[6] Therefore it is difficult to see how gutless vectors, which still require the full complement of viral structural proteins for efficient transduction, can bypass this host immune response. The humoral response is also most pertinent to adenoviral vectors because they do not integrate, and so suffer loss by cell

Box 1 Properties of the ideal gene therapy vector

Easy production
The vector should be easy to produce at high titre on a commercial scale. This consideration stems from the wide range of cell numbers that must be transduced—from a handful of stem cells capable of reconstituting the entire haematopoietic repertoire to 10^{11} or more cells to infect 5–10% of the liver. For widespread use, the vector should be amenable to commercial production and processing (such as concentration technology for delivery in small volumes), and should have a reasonable shelf-life for transport and distribution.

Sustained production
The vector, once delivered, should be able to express its genetic cargo over a sustained period or expression should be regulable in a precise way. Different disease states have different requirements (for example, regulated expression in diabetes and lifetime expression in haemophilia).

Immunologically inert
The vector components should not elicit an immune response after delivery. A humoral antibody response will make a second injection of the vector ineffective, whereas a cellular response will eliminate the transduced cells.

Tissue targeting
Delivery to only certain cell types is highly desirable, especially where the target cells are dispersed throughout the body (such as in the haematopoietic system), or if the cells are part of a heterogeneous population (such as in the brain). It is also important to avoid certain cells, such as dendritic cells, the "professional" antigen-presenting cells of the body, because of their role in mediating the immune response. Cell or tissue-targeted vectors present a great challenge, but also offer rich dividends for gene therapy approaches.

Size capacity
The vector should have no size limit to the genetic material it can deliver. The coding sequence of a therapeutic gene can vary from 350 base pairs for insulin, to over 12,000 base pairs for dystrophin. Furthermore, addition of appropriate regulatory sequences may be required for efficient transduction and expression of the foreign genetic material.

Replication, segregation or integration
The vector should allow for site-specific integration of the gene into the chromosome of the target cell, or should reside in the nucleus as an episome that will faithfully divide and segregate on cell division. Site-specific integration is a very desirable attribute because it eliminates the uncertainty of random integration into the host chromosome, and endogenous regulatory regions will control its expression under physiological conditions. The ability of the vector to be maintained as an episome could make the genetic elements independent of local chromatin environments, but faithful replication and segregation is needed if the vector is to be effective in systems such as stem cells.

Infection of dividing and non-dividing cells
As large numbers of cells (such as neurons, hepatocytes and myocytes) are postmitotic, vectors capable of efficiently transducing non-dividing cells are very desirable.

division and by DNA degradation, necessitating a repeat infection with the vector. The host raises neutralizing antibodies against viral proteins, thereby precluding any further infection. As there are scores of adenoviral SEROTYPES, one strategy to overcome this problem might be to use different serotypes.[3,7]

Retroviral, lentiviral and AAV [adeno-associated-viral] vectors do not seem to suffer from cytotoxic-T cell responses. It could be that the vectors are completely replication-defective, and that the incoming viral proteins do not elicit a cytotoxic T-cell response. Alternatively, the titres of at least the recombinant retro- or lentiviral vectors tested so far might not be sufficiently high to elicit an immune response. Antibody responses are also less of a concern, as retro- and lentiviral vectors integrate into the host genome and may not require subsequent transduction. Furthermore, for vectors engineered with the VSVG [vesicular stomatitis virus glycoprotein] protein, there are several strains of VSV that have different serotypes.[8] Antibodies to AAV-based vectors have been detected, which has prevented transduction by a second injection of the vector,[9] but this may also be overcome by using another serotype of AAV.[10]

Why some vectors are more immunogenic than others is a matter of considerable interest, and early hints indicate that antigen-presenting DENDRITIC CELLS may be important. In contrast to AAV-based vectors, it seems that adenoviral vectors efficiently transduce dendritic cells.[11] The route of administration also influences the immunological outcome,[12] and there is the question of pre-immunity in the host. Over 70% of the population may be carrying antibodies to adenovirus and AAV. What function might these pre-existing antibodies have in the efficiency of transduction or the toxicity of viral vectors? Are there sites in the body where the humoral response can be bypassed by the introduced vectors? Finally, the transgene itself may be highly immunogenic, particularly in hosts in which the transgene product was never made, due to either complete gene deletion or aberrant expression.[13] So, the gene therapy strategy in such hosts will also require the induction of TOLERANCE. Ultimately, individual patients may well require a therapeutic regimen tailored to their specific pathology, in the context of a genetic background that influences their immune response.

THE GELSINGER TRAGEDY

Jesse Gelsinger was barely 18 years old when he became the first patient to die in a Phase I gene therapy clinical trial. Although many patients have experienced severe adverse effects and even death during Phase I safety and toxicity studies, Jesse was the first patient in whom death could be directly attributed to the vector—an adenoviral vector.

Jesse suffered from deficiency of ornithine transcarbamylase (OTC), a metabolic enzyme required to break down ammonia. The total lack of this enzyme leads to death shortly after birth, owing to a build-up of ammonia. The partial presence of enzyme activity also leads to an accumulation of ammonia, but can be controlled by drugs and dietary intake. The aetiology of the disease, its associated morbidity, and the need for rapid production of the enzyme suggested that transient production of OTC by adenoviral vectors could extend the lifespan of OTC-deficient newborns, to allow implementation of a drug and dietary regime.[14]

The Phase I trial consisted of a study in which a cohort of patients with partial OTC activity were given escalating doses of second-generation (deleted for the *E1* and *E4* genes) adenoviral vectors. Jesse was in the last cohort, receiving up to 6×10^{13} recombinant adenoviruses particles containing the *OTC* gene. Within hours of intra-hepatic administration, he began to experience severe complications and died two days later. What went wrong? Was too much virus infused? Perhaps not, as another patient getting the same dose of the same vector did not suffer the same consequences. Were Jesse's adenoviral antibody titres higher? Again, there is no clear answer, as other patients with higher antibody titres did not have the same reaction. Perhaps there were other mitigating causes, like other viral infections or higher levels of ammonia before vector transduction. Are the animal models really reliable? Should we be screening patients for genetic variations, as immune responses are so heterogeneous? These are just some of the questions that have been raised, and several expert committees are now in the process of defining and refining new measures for gene therapy trials.

THE FIRST SUCCESSES

The field of gene therapy also has cause to celebrate. Alain Fischer and colleagues in Paris have successfully treated three young babies (1–11 months old), who suffer from a fatal form of severe combined immunodeficiency (SCID) syndrome.[15] SCID-X1 is an X-linked disorder characterized by an early block in T- and natural killer (NK) cell differentiation, due to mutations of the gene encoding the γC cytokine receptor subunit common to several interleukin receptors. A mutation in the γC subunit leads to disruption of signals required for growth, survival and differentiation of lymphoid progenitor cells.

Haematopoietic stem cells from the patients were transduced *ex vivo* with a recombinant mouse leukaemia viral vector containing the γC receptor gene and infused back into the young patients. After ten months, γC transgene expression in T- and NK cells was detected in the patients but, more importantly, T-, B- and NK-cell counts and function were comparable to those of age-matched controls. To all appearances, the recipients are clinically cured, and the fantastic promise of gene therapy is realized. Some concerns remain: only ten months of data are available, and expression of the transgene may be "shut-off." Also, very few patients have been treated so far. It remains to be seen if this approach will work for other diseases, because the success with SCID-X1 is probably owing to the strong selective advantage provided to the transduced lymphoid progenitors. Only those haematopoietic cells that express the γC receptor subunit can survive and differentiate. In earlier trials of SCID patients suffering from adenosine deaminase deficiency (ADA), PEG–ADA (a protein preparation with enzymatic activity) was administered to the patients in addition to the vector expressing the *ADA* gene. This may have prevented the selective advantage observed in the successful French trial.[16–18] The use of modified MLV [murine leukemia virus] vectors and the extensive manipulation of the stem cells (use of cytokines to stimulate cell proliferation) before transduction are a testimony to the continuous and incremental progress made in the field. We believe that with the availability of lentiviral vectors capable of transducing resting stem cells, the efficiency of transduction will improve even further.[19,20]

Haemophilia (A and B) is another excellent model system for gene therapy because the deficient protein does not have to be provided from its normal cellular source. Therefore, several vectors have been designed that transduce a range of cells to produce and secrete factor IX protein. Both the factor IX knockout mice and haemophilic dogs have turned out to be extremely beneficial pre-clinical model systems.[13,21,22] Further model systems will continue to be useful for preclinical studies, and promising results have recently been obtained in a mouse model of β-thalassaemia.[23] In another exciting human study, Kathryn High and colleagues at the University of Pennsylvania have treated several haemophilia B (factor IX-deficient) patients in a Phase I clinical trial with AAV vectors that contain the human *factor IX* gene.[2] The recombinant vector was injected intramuscularly, and preliminary results indicate that factor IX protein can be found in the serum of a patient. Although the levels of the factor IX protein expected to be produced by the low doses of injected AAV are not curative,[2] the treated patients did show some clinical benefits. No factor IX inhibitors were found, but neither could they be expected, because very low amounts of factor IX were being secreted. This is still a preliminary study, but nevertheless it bodes well for success in treating haemophilia.

THE NEXT PHASE

It was not long ago that the "battlecry" of the gene therapy community was "titres, titres, titres." Then it switched to "delivery, delivery, delivery," and now it is "expression, expression, expression." We have the appropriate titres of desirable vectors for delivering genes to patients. The emphasis now is on efficiency, safety and duration of expression. The issue of safety will always remain predominant, and the trend is to generate "minimal vectors" carrying the least amount of viral information needed for successful transduction.

Significant progress in vector development is occurring in the area of tissue- or cell-specific expression. . . .

• • •

PERSPECTIVES

The last two decades have witnessed the birth of the field of gene therapy, which has generated great hopes and great hypes. The promise of influencing the outcome of a vast array of diseases, ranging from birth defects to neurological disorders and from cancer to infectious diseases, although far-reaching, is not beyond reach. With the completion of the sequence of the human genome, over 50,000 genes will be available to the practitioners of gene therapy. The potential benefits for human health are vast, so how can the biomedical community move forward to realize this potential?

Geneticists will continue to identify the genetic contribution to disease. Virologists will generate safe and efficient viral vectors, and molecular biologists will help to design vectors capable of cell- and tissue-specific expression of the foreign genes carried by the transducing vectors. Immunologists will work out ways to prevent unwanted immunological consequences of the delivery vehicles and their cargo. Cell biologists will devise ways to facilitate gene transfer to various tissues and will take the lead in identifying stem cells. Clinicians will carry out clinical trials on humans with the best vectors that the scientists can supply. To achieve successful gene therapy, all branches of biology will have to contribute to this endeavour.

Society has an enormous stake in science, and scientists have an obligation not to promise more than they can deliver. Gene therapy is a young science that has undergone extreme scrutiny in the recent past. It is our responsibility to assure the public that the patient's health and welfare is of paramount concern. Adherence to accepted guidelines is incumbent on all investigators participating in clinical trials, and those wilfully violating the recommended practices will have to pay the consequences. The field of gene therapy has also been rocked by charges of conflict of interest, an area relatively new in biomedical science. Harmonized guidelines need to be put in place to allay the public's concern of real or perceived conflicts of interest. The science of gene therapy has many hurdles ahead, but they are surmountable.

GLOSSARY

Liposomes Artificial lipid vesicles. Liposomes fuse with the cell membrane to deliver their contents, such as DNA for gene therapy.
Episomes DNA molecules that are maintained in the nucleus without integrating into the chromosomal DNA.
Transduction The introduction of a gene into a target cell by a viral vector.
Haematopoiesis The programme of cellular differentiation leading to the formation of blood cells.
Memory cells Immune cells that are primed, after an initial exposure to an antigen, to make rapid response to subsequent exposure to the same antigen.
Serotypes Antigenically distinct forms that elicit different antibody responses by the immune system.
Dendritic cells These cells present antigen to T cells, and stimulate cell proliferation and the immune response.
Tolerance The lack of an immune response to a specific foreign protein.

NOTES

1. Li, S. & Huang, L. Nonviral gene therapy: promises and challenges. *Gene Ther.* **7,** 31–34 (2000).

2. Kay, M. A. *et al.* Evidence for gene transfer and expression of *factor IX* in haemophilia B patients treated with an AAV vector. *Nature Genet.* **24,** 257–261 (2000).

Gives the first hints of successful gene therapy in haemophilia B patients by using recombinant adeno-associated viral vectors. Expression of transduced *factor IX* could be detected in one patient.

3. Shenk, T. in *Fields Virology* (eds Fields B. N., Knipe D. M. & Howley P. M.) 2111–2148 (Lippincott-Raven, Philadelphia, 1996).

4. Morral, N. *et al.* Administration of helper-dependent adenoviral vectors and sequential delivery of different vector serotype for long-term liver-directed gene transfer in baboons. *Proc. Natl. Acad. Sci. USA* **96,** 12816–12821 (1999).

5. Dai, Y. *et al.* Cellular and humoral immune responses to adenoviral vectors containing *factor IX* gene: tolerization of *factor IX* and vector antigens allows for long-term expression. *Proc. Natl Acad. Sci. USA* **92,** 1401–1405 (1995).

6. Kafri, T. *et al.* Cellular immune response to adenoviral vector infected cells does not require *de novo* viral gene expression: implications for gene therapy. *Proc. Natl Acad. Sci. USA* **95,** 11377–11382 (1998).

Even physically inactivated adenoviral particles can generate a cytotoxic T-cell response, raising concerns about adenoviral vectors as suitable tools for long-term gene therapy.

7. Tripathy. S. K., Black, H. B., Goldwasser, E. & Leiden, J. M. Immune responses to transgene-encoded proteins limit the stability of gene expression after injection of replication-defective adenovirus vectors. *Nature Med.* **2,** 545–550 (1996).

8. Wagner, R. R., & Rose, J. K. in *Fields Virology* (eds Fields, B. N., Knipe D. M. & Howley, P. M.) 1121–1136 (Lippincott–Raven, Philadelphia, 1996).

9. Chirmule, N. *et al.* Humoral immunity to adeno-associated virus type 2 vectors following administration to murine and nonhuman primate muscle. *J. Virol.* **74,** 2420–2425 (2000).

10. Halbert, C. L., Rutledge, E. A., Allen, J. M., Russell, D. W. & Miller, A. D. Repeat transduction in the mouse lung by using adeno-associated virus vectors with different serotypes. *J. Virol.* **74,** 1524–1532 (2000).

11. Fields, P. A. *et al.* Role of vector in activation of T cell subsets in immune responses against the secreted transgene product *factor IX. Mol. Ther.* **1,** 225–235 (2000).

12. Xiao, W. *et al.* Route of administration determines induction of T-cell-independent humoral responses to adeno-associated virus vectors. *Mol. Ther.* **1,** 323–329 (2000).

13. Wang, L., Takabe, K., Bidlingmaier, S. M., III, C. R. & Verma, I. M. Sustained correction of bleeding disorder in hemophilia B mice by gene therapy. *Proc. Natl Acad. Sci. USA* **96,** 3906–3910 (1999).

14. Scriver, C. R. S., Beaudet, A. L., Sly, W. S. & Valle, D. V. (eds) *The Metabolic Basis of Inherited Disease* (McGraw–Hill, New York, 1989).

15. Cavazzana-Calvo, M. *et al.* Gene therapy of human severe combined immunodeficiency (SCID)-XI disease. *Science* **288,** 669–672 (2000).

The first definitive example of successful gene therapy, in three children suffering from SCID-XI. The haematopoietic stem cells from the patients were transduced by recombinant retroviruses expressing the γc-subunit, which is common to many interleukin receptors.

16. Kohn, D. B. *et al.* T lymphocytes with a normal *ADA* gene accumulate after transplantation of transduced autologous umbilical cord blood $CD34^+$ cells in ADA-deficient SCID neonates. *Nature Med.* **4,** 775–780 (1998).

17. Blaese, R. M. *et al.* T lymphocyte-directed gene therapy for ADA-SCID; initial trial results after 4 years. *Science* **270,** 475–480 (1995).

18. Bordignon, C. *et al.* Gene therapy in peripheral blood lymphocytes and bone marrow for ADA-immunodeficient patients. *Science* **270,** 470–475 (1995).

19. Miyoshi, H., Smith, K. A., Mosier, D. E., Verma, I. M. & Torbett, B. E. Transduction of human $CD34^+$ cells that mediate long-term engraftment of NOD/SCID mice by HIV vectors. *Science* **283,** 682–686 (1999).

20. Guenechea, G. *et al.* Transduction of human $CD34^+$ $CD38^-$ bone marrow and cord-derived SCID-repopulating cells with third-generation lentiviral vectors. *Mol. Ther.* **1,** 566–573 (2000).

References 19 and 20 show successful long-term transduction of human haematopoietic stem cells by lentiviral vectors, without the use of agents such as growth factors and cytokines.

21. Snyder, R. O. *et al.* Persistent and therapeutic concentrations of human factor IX in mice after hepatic gene transfer of recombinant AAV vectors. *Nature Genet.* **16,** 270–276 (1997).

22. Wang, L., Nichols, T. C., Read, M. S., Bellinger, D. A. & Verma, I. M. Sustained expression of therapeutic level of *factor IX* in hemophilia B dogs by AAV-mediated gene therapy in liver. *Mol. Ther.* **1,** 154–158 (2000).

23. May, C. *et al.* Therapeutic haemoglobin synthesis in thalassaemic mice expressing lentivirus-encoded human-globin. *Nature* **406,** 82–86 (2000).

JULIAN SAVULESCU

Harm, Ethics Committees and the Gene Therapy Death

Julian Savulescu is Director of the Ethics Program at the Murdoch Institute at the Royal Children's Hospital. He helped to establish the Oxford Institute for Ethics and Communication in Health Care Practice. Journals in which he has published include the *British Medical Journal, Bioethics,* and the *Journal of Medical Ethics.* His research interests encompass consent, advance directives, research ethics and resource allocation.

The recent tragic and widely publicised death of Jesse Gelsinger in a gene therapy trial has many important lessons for those engaged in the ethical review of research. One of the most important lessons is that ethics committees can give too much weight to ensuring informed consent and not enough attention to minimising the harm associated with participation in research. The first responsibility of ethics committees should be to ensure that the expected harm associated with participation is reasonable.

Jesse was an 18-year-old man with a mild form of ornithine transcarbamylase (OTC) deficiency, a disorder of nitrogen metabolism. His form of the disease could be controlled by diet and drug treatment. On September 13 1999 a team of researchers lead by James Wilson at the University of Pennsylvania's Institute for Human Gene Therapy (IHGT) injected 3.8×10^{13} adenovirus vector particles containing a gene to correct the genetic defect. He was the eighteenth and final patient in the trial. The virus particles were injected directly into the liver. He received the largest number of virus particles in a gene therapy trial.[1] Four days later he was dead from what was probably an immune reaction to the virus vector. This was the first death directly attributed to gene therapy. It resulted in worldwide publicity, an independent investigation, the Federal Drug Administration (FDA) suspending all trials at the IHGT, an FDA, and a senate subcommittee investigation.

Reprinted with permission from the *Journal of Medical Ethics* 27 (2001), 148–50. Copyright © 2001 by the BMJ Publishing Group.

At a special public meeting at the National Institutes of Health (NIH) in December 1999, James Wilson, also the director of the IHGT, said they still did not understand fully what had gone wrong.[2] Even though a massive dose had been used, only 1% of transferred genes reached the target cells. (None of the patients in the trial showed significant gene expression. Art Caplan, the University of Pennsylvania's outspoken bioethicist, is reported to have said: "if you cured anyone from a Phase 1 trial, it would be a miracle" and "there was never a chance that anyone would benefit from these experiments."[3]) Wilson claimed the death was the result of an anomalous response. Jesse's bone marrow had very low levels of red blood cell precursors, which probably predated the experiment. This may have reflected another genetic defect or a parvovirus infection. While most gene therapists at the meeting agreed that Jesse's response was unusual, some claimed it was foreseeable, given the ability of adenovirus to elicit an immune response and the high dose employed.[2]

The death also resulted in a wrongful death lawsuit which alleged[3]:

- that members of the IHGT team and others were careless, negligent and reckless in failing to adequately evaluate Jesse's condition and eligibility. Jesse had an ammonia level 30%-60% higher than the eligibility criterion stated in the protocol approved by the FDA;
- that the adenovirus vector was unreasonably dangerous;

- that storage of the vector for 25 months led researchers to underestimate its potency;
- that a conflict of interest existed. Researchers and members of the University of Pennsylvania held patents covering several aspects of the technology employed. Wilson and colleagues also hold equity holdings in Genovo, the private sector biotechnology collaborator in the project. These conflicts of interest were alleged to have not been disclosed to the participant;
- that researchers failed to notify the FDA of adverse events in prior patients and animals.

The lawsuit also named Art Caplan, director of the University of Pennsylvania's Bioethics Center. It was also suggested but not explicitly alleged that Caplan had a conflict of interest because his centre was funded by Wilson's department. The complaint also drew attention to Caplan's intervention to persuade Wilson and others to use older participants who could consent (but who had a mild form of the disease) rather than newborns who could not consent (but had an otherwise lethal form of the disease).[3]

Other concerns related to this trial have included[4]:

- Researchers continued to increase the dose despite signs of toxicity in other patients;
- Volunteers were recruited by direct appeal on a patient advocacy website which described "very low doses" and "promising results." Such appeals had been rejected by federal officials as being coercive.
- The original consent reviewed publicly by the NIH mentioned that monkeys had died from the treatment but the final version did not mention that.
- The NIH's Recombinant DNA Advisory Committee (RAC) discussed the potential for lethal liver inflammation related to this experiment in December 1995, after reviewing toxicity results in rhesus monkeys and the death of one monkey from an extremely high dose of a first-generation vector. They recommended administration through a peripheral vein rather than directly into the liver. Food and Drug Administration regulators were concerned about infection of reproductive cells (germ line modification) and made researchers go back to direct liver injection.[1]

In February 2000, at a separate hearing, Paul Geisinger, Jesse's father, asserted:

1. that his son had not been told important preclinical evidence of toxicity (including the deaths of monkeys);
2. that his son was led to believe that his participation would be clinically beneficial, despite this being a Phase 1 trial where no benefit was envisaged.[5]

James Wilson while acting as director of the IHGT, was also involved in several clinical trials and basic research. Judith Rodin, the University of Pennsylvania's president and William Danceforth, the lead author of an independent report into Jesse's death, said that Wilson was "overloaded."[6] The IHGT has been downsized and no longer conducts clinical trials. The Department of Health and Human Services has said it intends to introduce laws which will fine researchers up to $250,000 and instructions up to one million dollars for failing to meet new stricter standards.[6]

INTERSTING INSIGHTS

This experiment yields many interesting insights into the problems related to ethics review of research in general. But there is perhaps one lesson which is more important than all the others. Research ethics review is concerned primarily with two goals: ensuring that the expected harm involved in participation is reasonable and that participants give valid consent. The requirement to give valid consent has led many in the research ethics community to suggest that non-therapeutic research on incompetent patients is unethical. This trial illustrates *par excellence* the increasing and mistaken tendency of ethics committees to give too much weight to consent and to fail to give sufficient attention to protecting participants from harm.

One simple justification for conducting this trial in adults with the mild form of the disease rather than severely affected newborns goes like this. "There are serious risks including a risk of death associated with participation in this trial. Since the risks are significant, it is better that the trial be conducted on humans who consent to those risks rather than on those who cannot consent."

However, it is important to distinguish between the *chance* of a bad outcome occurring and *expected harm.* Expected harm is the probability of a harm occurring multiplied by the magnitude of that harm. Being harmed by an intervention is being made worse off than one would otherwise have been if that intervention had not been performed.

Consider an illustration using a quality adjusted life year (QALY) approach. Let's assume for simplicity's sake that the only harm in this experiment was death from the virus vector. Let's assign a value of 1 to perfect health and 0 to death. Jesse's existing quality of life was less than perfect, but still acceptable. Let's say it was 0.8. Assume that he would have lived another 50 years. Assume that the risk of the gene therapy killing him was small—1/10,000 (this is a conservative estimate: Jesse's death was the first death in nearly 400 gene therapy trials involving over 4000 patients).[7] That means that the expected harm of Jesse participating was $0.8 \times 50/10{,}000 = 40/10{,}000 = 0.004$ quality adjusted life year. This is a very small expected harm.

Now compare this to the expected harm that severely affected newborns would experience. Imagine that a newborn boy, who is already very likely to die of his disease, dies as a result of a similar gene therapy trial. Has he been harmed? He is not worse off than he would otherwise have been, since he would have died if the trial had not been conducted. He would have died of the severe form of the underlying disease. The magnitude of the expected harm to adult participants with milder forms of this disease was significantly greater than to newborns with the severe form of the disease.

Put simply, Jesse had something to lose while the seriously affected newborn did not. Even though the expected harm to Jesse prior to commencing the trial may have been small, why prefer a small expected harm to no harm? There is no good reason, regardless of whether someone is prepared to consent. It is irrational to prefer more harm to less harm.

The ethics committee which persuaded Wilson and colleagues to invite adults to participate either:

1. misunderstood the nature of expected harm and/or ethics committees' responsibilities in evaluating it, or
2. (more likely) gave greater weight to consent than to expected harm.

Attempting to draw lessons from Jesse's death, Friedmann, director of the Program in Human Gene Therapy at the University of California, stated: "The single most important mechanism for ensuring patient protection from inherent risks of clinical experiments, unrealistic expectations, and potential conflicts of interest of the investigator is accurate and full disclosure of potential risks and benefits and a well-executed informed consent process."[8]

Fine rhetoric but probably false. In Jesse's case, there were allegedly significant omissions in the consent process, allegedly involving failure to disclose relevant risks and conflicts of financial interest. But would these have made a difference? Jesse understood the trial would not cure him and there was a small chance it could hurt him. But, as his father said: "He wanted to help the babies. . . . My son had the purest intent." Indeed, strong intentions. He attempted to enrol when he was 17 but had to return when he turned 18 and was eligible.[7] Even if Jesse Gelsinger would not have participated if disclosure had been more frank, someone would have. (After all, one healthy person offered his own heart when Barney Clark received the first artificial heart!) The key to research review is not only consent, but a responsible objective evaluation of the reasonableness of harm in research.[9]

There are complex issues about whether this trial should have been conducted on human beings at all. But if it was justified, it would have been better to conduct it on newborns with the severe form of the disease. Sometimes it is better that an incompetent person participate in research than a competent person who can consent. Consent is important. But the fact that a human being is not able to consent should not paralyse ethics committees. It is a mistake to give more weight to consent than to expected harm. Ethics committees must make an evaluation of the expected harm and whether less harmful avenues should be pursued.

REFERENCES

1. Lehrman S. Virus treatment questioned after gene therapy death. *Lancet* 1999;**401**:517–8.
2. Marshall E. Gene therapy death prompts review of adenovirus vector. *Science* 1999; **286**: 2244–5.
3. Fox J. L. Gene-therapy death prompts broad civil lawsuit. *Nature Biotechnology* 2000;**18**: 1136.
4. Nelson D., Weiss R. Is Jesse's death a stain on the new science? *The Age* 1999 Dec 5: news section: 1.
5. Walters L. "Gene therapy: overview." In: Murray T., Mehlman MJ, eds. *Encyclopedia of ethical, legal and policy issues in biotechnology.* New York: Wiley, 2000: 341.
6. Smaglik P. Clinical trials end at gene therapy institute. *Nature* 2000; **405**: 497.
7. Verma I. M. A tumultuous year for gene therapy. *Molecular Therapy* 2000; **2**: 415–6.
8. Friedmann T. Principles for human gene therapy studies. *Science* 2000;**287**:2163–5.
9. Savulescu J. Safety of participants of non-therapeutic research must be ensured. *British Medical Journal* 1998;**16**:891–2.

JONATHAN GLOVER

Questions about Some Uses of Genetic Engineering

There is a widespread view that any project for the genetic improvement of the human race ought to be ruled out: that there are fundamental objections of principle. The aim of this discussion is to sort out some of the main objections. It will be argued that our resistance is based on a complex of different values and reasons, none of which is, when examined, adequate to rule out in principle this use of genetic engineering. The debate on human genetic engineering should become like the debate on nuclear power: one in which large possible benefits have to be weighed against big problems and the risk of great disasters. The discussion has not reached this point, partly because the techniques have not yet been developed. But it is also partly because of the blurred vision which fuses together many separate risks and doubts into a fuzzy-outlined opposition in principle.

1. AVOIDING THE DEBATE ABOUT GENES AND THE ENVIRONMENT

In discussing the question of genetic engineering, there is everything to be said for not muddling the issue up with the debate over the relative importance of genes and environment in the development of such characteristics as intelligence. One reason for avoiding that debate is that it arouses even stronger passions than genetic engineering, and so is filled with as much acrimony as argument. But, apart from this fastidiousness, there are other reasons.

The nature-nurture dispute is generally seen as an argument about the relative weight the two factors have in causing differences within the human species: "IQ is 80 per cent hereditary and 20 per cent environmental" versus "IQ is 80 per cent environmental and 20 per cent hereditary." No doubt there is some approximate truth of this type to be found if we consider variations within a given population at a particular time. But it is highly unlikely that there is any such statement which is simply true of human nature regardless of context. To take the extreme case, if we could iron out all environmental differences, any residual variations would be 100 per cent genetic. It is only if we make the highly artificial assumption that different groups at different times all have an identical spread of relevant environmental differences that we can expect to find statements of this kind applying to human nature in general. To say this is not to argue that studies on the question should not be conducted, or are bound to fail. It may well be possible, and useful, to find out the relative weights of the two kinds of factor for a given characteristic among a certain group at a particular time. The point is that any such conclusions lose relevance, not only when environmental differences are stretched out or compressed, but also when genetic differences are. And this last case is what we are considering.

We can avoid this dispute because of its irrelevance. Suppose the genetic engineering proposal were to try to make people less aggressive. On a superficial view, the proposal might be shown to be unrealistic if there were evidence to show that variation in aggressiveness is hardly genetic at all: that it is 95 per cent environmental. (Let us grant, most implausibly, that such a figure turned out to be true for the whole of humanity, regardless of social context.) But all this would show is that, within our species, the distribution of genes relevant to aggression is very uniform.

Reprinted with permission from *What Sort of People Should There Be?* (London: Penguin Books, 1984), pp. 25–33, 33–36, 41–43, 45–52. Copyright © 1984 Jonathan Glover. Reprinted with permission of Penguin Books Ltd.

It would show nothing about the likely effects on aggression if we use genetic engineering to give people a different set of genes from those they now have.

In other words, to take genetic engineering seriously, we need take no stand on the relative importance or unimportance of genetic factors in the explanation of the present range of individual differences found in people. We need only the minimal assumption that different genes could give us different characteristics. To deny *that* assumption you need to be the sort of person who thinks it is only living in kennels which make dogs different from cats.

2. METHODS OF CHANGING THE GENETIC COMPOSITION OF FUTURE GENERATIONS

There are essentially three ways of altering the genetic composition of future generations. The first is by environmental changes. Discoveries in medicine, the institution of a National Health Service, schemes for poverty relief, agricultural changes, or alterations in the tax position of large families, all alter the selective pressure on genes.[1] It is hard to think of any social change which does not make some difference to who survives or who is born.

The second method is to use eugenic policies aimed at altering breeding patterns or patterns of survival of people with different genes. Eugenic methods are "environmental" too: the difference is only that the genetic impact is intended. Possible strategies range from various kinds of compulsion (to have more children, fewer children, or no children, or even compulsion over the choice of sexual partner) to the completely voluntary (our present genetic counselling practice of giving prospective parents information about probabilities of their children having various abnormalities).

The third method is genetic engineering: using enzymes to add to or subtract from a stretch of DNA.

Most people are unworried by the fact that a side-effect of an environmental change is to alter the gene pool, at least where the alteration is not for the worse. And even in cases where environmental factors increase the proportion of undesirable genes in the pool, we often accept this. Few people oppose the National Health Service, although setting it up meant that some people with genetic defects, who would have died, have had treatment enabling them to survive and reproduce. On the whole, we accept without qualms that much of what we do has genetic impact. Controversy starts when we think of aiming deliberately at genetic changes, by eugenics or genetic engineering. I want to make some brief remarks about eugenic policies, before suggesting that policies of deliberate intervention are best considered in the context of genetic engineering.

Scepticism has been expressed about whether eugenic policies have any practical chance of success. Medawar has pointed out the importance of genetic polymorphism: the persistence of genetically different types in a population.[2] (Our different blood groups are a familiar example.) For many characteristics, people get a different gene from each parent. So children do not simply repeat parental characteristics. Any simple picture of producing an improved type of person, and then letting the improvement be passed on unchanged, collapses.

But, although polymorphism is a problem for this crudely utopian form of eugenics, it does not show that more modest schemes of improvement must fail. Suppose the best individuals for some quality (say, colour vision) are heterozygous, so that they inherit a gene A from one parent, and a gene B from the other. These ABs will have AAs and BBs among their children, who will be less good than they are. But AAs and BBs may still be better than ACs or ADs, and perhaps much better than CCs or CDs. If this were so, overall improvement could still be brought about by encouraging people whose genes included an A or B to have more children than those who had only Cs or Ds. The point of taking a quality like colour vision is that it may be genetically fairly simple. Qualities like kindness or intelligence are more likely to depend on the interaction of many genes, but a similar point can be made at a higher level of complexity.

Polymorphism raises a doubt about whether the offspring of the three "exceptionally intelligent women" fertilized by Dr. Shockley or other Nobel prize-winners will have the same IQ as the parents, even apart from environmental variation. But it does not show the inevitable failure of any large-scale attempts to alter human characteristics by varying the relative numbers of children different kinds of people have. Yet any attempt, say, to raise the level of intelligence, would be a very slow affair, taking many generations to make much of an impact. This is no reason for preferring to discuss genetic engineering. For the genetic engineering of human improvements, if it becomes possible, will have an immediate effect, so we will not be guessing which qualities will be desirable dozens of generations later.

There is the view that the genetic-engineering techniques requires will not become a practical possibility. Sir MacFarlane Burnet, writing in 1971 about using genetic engineering to cure disorders in people already born, dismissed the possibility of using a virus to carry a new gene to replace a faulty one in cells throughout the body: "I should be willing to state in any company that the chance of doing this will remain infinitely small to the last syllable of recorded time."[3] Unless engineering at the stage of sperm cell and egg is easier, this seems a confident dismissal of the topic to be discussed here. More recent work casts doubt on this confidence.[4] So, having mentioned this skepticism, I shall disregard it. We will assume that genetic engineering of people may become possible, and that it is worth discussing. (Sir MacFarlane Burnet's view has not yet been falsified as totally as Rutherford's view about atomic energy. But I hope that the last syllable of recorded time is still some way off.)

The main reason for casting the discussion in terms of genetic engineering rather than eugenics is not a practical one. Many eugenic policies are open to fairly straightforward moral objections, which hide the deeper theoretical issues. Such policies as compulsory sterilization, compulsory abortion, compelling people to pair off in certain ways, or compelling people to have more or fewer children than they would otherwise have, are all open to objection on grounds of overriding people's autonomy. Some are open to objection on grounds of damage to the institution of the family. And the use of discriminatory tax- and child-benefit policies is an intolerable step towards a society of different genetic castes.

Genetic engineering need not involve overriding anyone's autonomy. It need not be forced on parents against their wishes, and the future person being engineered has no views to be overridden. (The view that despite this, it is still objectionable to have one's genetic characteristics decided by others, will be considered later.) Genetic engineering will not damage the family in the obvious ways that compulsory eugenic policies would. Nor need it be encouraged by incentives which create inequalities. Because it avoids these highly visible moral objections, genetic engineering allows us to focus more clearly on other values that are involved.

(To avoid a possible misunderstanding, one point should be added before leaving the topic of eugenics. Saying that some eugenic policies are open to obvious moral objections does not commit me to disapproval of all eugenic policies. In particular, I do not want to be taken to be opposing two kinds of policy. One is genetic counselling: warning people of risks in having children, and perhaps advising them against having them. The other is the introduction of screening-programmes to detect foetal abnormalities, followed by giving the mother the option of abortion where serious defects emerge.)

Let us now turn to the question of what, if anything, we should do in the field of human genetic engineering.

3. THE POSITIVE-NEGATIVE DISTINCTION

We are not yet able to cure disorders by genetic engineering. But we do sometimes respond to disorders by adopting eugenic policies, at least in voluntary form. Genetic counselling is one instance, as applied to those thought likely to have such disorders as Huntington's chorea. This is a particularly appalling inherited disorder, involving brain degeneration, leading to mental decline and lack of control over movement. It does not normally come on until middle age, by which time many of its victims would in the normal course of things have had children. Huntington's chorea is caused by a dominant gene, so those who find that one of the parents has it have themselves a 50 per cent chance of developing it. If they do have it, each of their children will in turn have a 50 per cent chance of the disease. The risks are so high and the disorder so bad that the potential parents often decide not to have children, and are often given advice to this effect by doctors and others.

Another eugenic response to disorders is involved in screening-programmes for pregnant women. When tests pick up such defects as Down's syndrome (mongolism) or spina bifida, the mother is given the possibility of an abortion. The screening-programmes are eugenic because part of their point is to reduce the incidence of severe genetic abnormality in the population.

These two eugenic policies come in at different stages: before conception and during pregnancy. For this reason the screening-programme is more controversial, because it raises the issue of abortion. Those who are sympathetic to abortion, and who think it would be good to eliminate these disorders will be sympathetic to the programme. Those who think abortion is no different from killing a fully developed human are obviously likely to oppose the programme. But they are likely to feel that elimination of the disorders would be a good thing, even if not an adequate justification for killing. Unless they also disapprove of contraception, they are likely to support the genetic-counselling policy in the case of Huntington's chorea.

Few people object to the use of eugenic policies to eliminate disorders, unless those policies have additional features which are objectionable. Most of us are resistant to the use of compulsion, and those who oppose abortion will object to screening-programmes. But apart from these other moral objections, we do not object to the use of eugenic policies against disease. We do not object to advising those likely to have Huntington's chorea not to have children, as neither compulsion nor killing is involved. Those of us who take this view have no objection to altering the genetic composition of the next generation, where this alteration consists in reducing the incidence of defects.

If it were possible to use genetic engineering to correct defects, say at the foetal stage, it is hard to see how those of us who are prepared to use the eugenic measure just mentioned could object. In both cases, it would be pure gain. The couple, one of whom may develop Huntington's chorea, can have a child if they want, knowing that any abnormality will be eliminated. Those sympathetic to abortion will agree that cure is preferable. And those opposed to abortion prefer babies to be born without handicap. It is hard to think of any objection to using genetic engineering to eliminate defects, and there is a clear and strong case for its use.

But accepting the case for eliminating genetic mistakes does not entail accepting other uses of genetic engineering. The elimination of defects is often called "negative" genetic engineering. Going beyond this, to bring about improvements in normal people, is by contrast "positive" engineering. (The same distinction can be made for eugenics.)

The positive-negative distinction is not in all cases completely sharp. Some conditions are genetic disorders whose identification raises little problem. Huntington's chorea or spina bifida are genetic "mistakes" in a way that cannot seriously be disputed. But with other conditions, the boundary between a defective state and normality may be more blurred. If there is a genetic disposition towards depressive illness, this seems a defect, whose elimination would be part of negative genetic engineering. Suppose the genetic disposition to depression involves the production of lower levels of an enzyme than are produced in normal people. The negative programme is to correct the genetic fault so that the enzyme level is within the range found in normal people. But suppose that within "normal" people also, there are variations in the enzyme level, which correlate with ordinary differences in [the] tendency to be cheerful or depressed. Is there a sharp boundary between "clinical" depression and the depression sometimes felt by those diagnosed as "normal"? Is it clear that a sharp distinction can be drawn between raising someone's enzyme level so that it falls within the normal range and raising someone else's level from the bottom of the normal range to the top?

The positive-negative distinction is sometimes a blurred one, but often we can at least roughly see where it should be drawn. If there is a rough and ready distinction, the question is: how important is it? Should we go on from accepting negative engineering to accepting positive programmes, or should we say that the line between the two is the limit of what is morally acceptable?

There is no doubt that positive programmes arouse the strongest feelings on both sides. On the one hand, many respond to positive genetic engineering or positive eugenics with Professor Tinbergen's though: "I find it morally reprehensible and presumptuous for anybody to put himself forward as a judge of the qualities for which we should breed" [*Guardian,* 5 March, 1980].

But other people have held just as strongly that positive policies are the way to make the future of mankind better than the past. Many years ago H. J. Muller expressed this hope:

> And so we foresee the history of life divided into three main phases. In the long preparatory phase it was the helpless creature of its environment, and natural selection gradually ground it into human shape. In the second—our own short transitional phase—it reaches out at the immediate environment, shaking, shaping and grinding to suit the form, the requirements, the wishes, and the whims of man. And in the long third phase, it will reach down into the secret places of the great universe of its own nature, and by aid of its ever growing intelligence and cooperation, shape itself into an increasingly sublime creation—a being beside which the mythical divinities of the past will seem more and more ridiculous, and which setting its own marvellous inner powers against the brute Goliath of the suns and the planets, challenges them to contest.[5]

The case for positive engineering is not helped by adopting the tones of the mad scientist in a horror film. But behind the rhetoric is a serious point. If we decide on a positive programme to change our nature, this will be a central moment in our history, and the transformation might be beneficial to a degree we can now scarcely imagine. The question is: how are we to weigh this possibility against Tinbergen's objection, and against other objections and doubts?

For the rest of this discussion, I shall assume that, subject to adequate safeguards against things going wrong, negative genetic engineering is acceptable. The issue is positive engineering. I shall also assume that we can ignore problems about whether positive engineering will be technically possible. Suppose we have the power to choose people's genetic characteristics. Once we have eliminated genetic defects, what, if anything, should we do with this power? . . .

4. THE VIEW THAT OVERALL IMPROVEMENT IS UNLIKELY OR IMPOSSIBLE

There is one doubt about the workability of schemes of genetic improvement which is so widespread that it would be perverse to ignore it. This is the view that, in any genetic alteration, there are no gains without compensating losses. On this view, if we bring about a genetically based improvement, such as higher intelligence, we are bound to pay a price somewhere else: perhaps the more intelligent people will have less resistance to disease, or will be less physically agile. If correct, this might so undermine the practicability of applying eugenics or genetic engineering that it would be hardly worth discussing the values involved in such programmes.

This view perhaps depends on some idea that natural selection is so efficient that, in terms of gene survival, we must already be as efficient as it is possible to be. If it were possible to push up intelligence without weakening some other part of the system, natural selection would already have done so. But this is a naive version of evolutionary theory. In real evolutionary theory, far from the genetic status quo always being the best possible for a given environment, some mutations turn out to be advantageous, and this is the origin of evolutionary progress. If natural mutations can be beneficial without a compensating loss, why should artificially induced ones not be so too?

It should also be noticed that there are two different ideas of what counts as a gain or a loss. From the point of view of evolutionary progress, gains and losses are simply advantages and disadvantages from the point of view of gene survival. But we are not compelled to take this view. If we could engineer a genetic change in some people which would have the effect of making them musical prodigies but also sterile, this would be a hopeless gene in terms of survival, but this need not force us, or the musical prodigies themselves, to think of the changes as for the worse. It depends on how we rate musical ability as against having children, and evolutionary survival does not dictate priorities here.

The view that gains and losses are tied up with each other need not depend on the dogma that natural selection *must* have created the best of all possible sets of genes. A more cautiously empirical version of the claim says there is a tendency for gains to be accompanied by losses. John Maynard Smith, in his paper on "Eugenics and Utopia,"[6] takes this kind of "broad balance" view and runs it the other way, suggesting, as an argument in defence of medicine, that any loss of genetic resistance to disease is likely to be a good thing: "The reason for this is that in evolution, as in other fields, one seldom gets something for nothing. Genes which confer disease-resistance are likely to have harmful effects in other ways: this is certainly true of the gene for sickle-cell anaemia and may be a general rule. If so, absence of selection in favour of disease-resistance may be eugenic."

It is important that different characteristics may turn out to be genetically linked in ways we do not yet realize. In our present state of knowledge, engineering for some improvement might easily bring some unpredicted but genetically linked disadvantage. But we do not have to accept that there will in general be a broad balance, so that there is a presumption that any gain will be accompanied by a compensating loss (or Maynard Smith's version that we can expect a compensating gain for any loss). The reason is that what counts as a gain or loss varies in different contexts. Take Maynard Smith's example of sickle-cell anaemia. The reason why sickle-cell anaemia is widespread in Africa is that it is genetically linked with resistance to malaria. Those who are heterozygous (who inherit one sickle-cell gene and one normal gene) are resistant to malaria, while those who are homozygous (whose genes are both sickle-cell) get sickle-cell anaemia. If we use genetic engineering to knock out sickle-cell anaemia where malaria is common, we will pay the price of having more malaria. But when we eradicate malaria, the gain will not involve this loss. Because losses are relative to context, any generalization about the impossibility of overall improvements is dubious.

Unlike various compulsory eugenic policies, genetic engineering need not involve any interference with decision by couples to have children together, or with their decisions about how many children to have. And let us suppose that genetically engineered babies grow in the mother's womb in the normal way, so that her relationship to the child is not threatened in the way it might be if the laboratory or the hospital were substituted for the womb. The cruder threats to family relationships are eliminated.

It may be suggested that there is a more subtle threat. Parents like to identify with their children. We are often pleased to see some of our own characteristics in our children. Perhaps this is partly a kind of vanity, and no doubt sometimes we project on to our children similarities that are not really there. But, when the similarities do exist, they help the parents and children to understand and sympathize with each other. If genetic engineering resulted in children fairly different from their parents, this might make their relationship have problems.

There is something to this objection, but it is easy to exaggerate. Obviously, children who were like Midwich cuckoos, or comic-book Martians, would not be easy to identify with. But genetic engineering need not move in such sudden jerks. The changes would have to be detectable to be worth bringing about, but there seems no reason why large changes in appearance, or an unbridgeable psychological gulf, should be created in any one generation. We bring about environmental changes which make children different from their parents, as when the first generation of children in a remote place are given schooling and made literate. This may cause some problems in families, but it is not usually thought a decisive objection. It is not clear that genetically induced changes of similar magnitude are any more objectionable.

A related objection concerns our attitude to our remoter descendants. We like to think of our descendants stretching on for many generations. Perhaps this is in part an immortality substitute. We hope they will to some extent be like us, and that, if they think of us, they will do so with sympathy and approval. Perhaps these hopes about the future of mankind are relatively unimportant to us. But, even if we mind about them a lot, they are unrealistic in the very long term. Genetic engineering would make our descendants less like us, but this would only speed up the natural rate of change. Natural mutations and selective pressures make it unlikely that in a few million years our descendants will be physically or mentally much like us. So what genetic engineering threatens here is probably doomed anyway. . . .

[6.] RISKS AND MISTAKES

Although mixing different species and cloning are often prominent in people's thoughts about genetic engineering, they are relatively marginal issues. This is partly because there may be no strong reasons in favour of either. Our purposes might be realized more readily by improvements to a single species, whether another or our own, or by the creation of quite new types of organism, than by mixing different species. And it is not clear what advantage cloning batches of people might have, to outweigh the drawbacks. This is not to be dogmatic that species mixing and cloning could never be useful, but to say that the likelihood of other techniques being much more prominent makes it a pity to become fixated on the issues raised by these ones. And some of the most serious objections to positive genetic engineering have wider application than to these rather special cases. One of these wider objections is that serious risks may be involved.

Some of the risks are already part of the public debate because of current work on recombinant DNA. The danger is of producing harmful organisms that would escape from our control. The work obviously should take place, if at all, only with adequate safeguards against such a disaster. The problem is deciding what we should count as adequate safeguards. I have nothing to contribute to this problem here. If it can be dealt with satisfactorily, we will perhaps move on to genetic engineering of people. And this introduces another dimension of risk. We may produce unintended results, either because our techniques turn out to be less finely tuned than we thought, or because different characteristics are found to be genetically linked in unexpected ways.

If we produce a group of people who turn out worse than expected, we will have to live with them. Perhaps we would aim for producing people who were especially imaginative and creative, and only too late find we had produced people who were also very violent and aggressive. This kind of mistake might not only be disastrous, but also very hard to "correct" in subsequent generations. For when we suggested sterilization to the people we had produced, or else corrective genetic engineering for *their* offspring, we might find them hard to persuade. They might like the way they were, and reject, in characteristically violent fashion, our explanation that they were a mistake.

The possibility of an irreversible disaster is a strong deterrent. It is enough to make some people think we should rule out genetic engineering altogether, and to make others think that, while negative engineering is perhaps acceptable, we should rule out positive engineering. The thought behind this second position is that the benefits from negative engineering are clearer, and that, because its aims are more modest, disastrous mistakes are less likely.

The risk of disasters provides at least a reason for saying that, if we do adopt a policy of human genetic engineering, we ought to do so with extreme caution. We should alter genes only where we have strong reasons for thinking the risk of disaster is very small, and where the benefit is great enough to justify the risk. (The problems of deciding when this is so are familiar from the nuclear power debate.) This "principle of caution" is less strong than one ruling out all positive engineering, and allows room for the possibility that the dangers may turn out to be very remote, or that greater risks of a different kind are involved in *not* using positive engineering. These possibilities correspond to one view of the facts in the nuclear power debate. Unless with genetic engineering we think we can already rule out such possibilities, the argument from risk provides more justification for the principle of caution than for the stronger ban on all positive engineering. . . .

DECISIONS

Some of the strongest objections to positive engineering are not about specialized applications or about risks. They are about the decisions involved. The central line of thought is that we should not start playing God by redesigning the human race. The suggestion is that there is no group (such as scientists, doctors, public officials, or politicians) who can be entrusted with decisions about what sort of people there should be. And it is also doubted whether we could have any adequate grounds for basing such decisions on one set of values rather than another. . . .

1. NOT PLAYING GOD

Suppose we could use genetic engineering to raise the average IQ by fifteen points. (I mention, only to ignore, the boring objection that the average IQ is always by definition 100.) Should we do this? Objectors to positive engineering say we should not. This is not because the present average is preferable to a higher one. We do not think that, if it were naturally fifteen points higher, we ought to bring it down to the present level. The objection is to our playing God by deciding what the level should be.

On one view of the world, the objection is relatively straightforward. On this view, there really is a God, who has a plan for the world which will be disrupted if we stray outside the boundaries assigned to us. (It is *relatively* straightforward: there would still be the problem of knowing where the boundaries came. If genetic engineering disrupts the programme, how do we know that medicine and education do not?)

The objection to playing God has a much wider appeal than to those who literally believe in a divine plan. But, outside such a context, it is unclear what the objection comes to. If we have a Darwinian view, according to which features of our nature have been selected for their contribution to gene survival, it is not blasphemous, or obviously disastrous, to start to control the process in the light of our own values. We may value other qualities in people, in preference to those which have been most conducive to gene survival.

The prohibition on playing God is obscure. If it tells us not to interfere with natural selection at all, this rules out medicine, and most other environmental and social changes. If it only forbids interference with natural selection by the direct alteration of genes, this rules out negative as well as positive genetic engineering. If these interpretations are too restrictive, the ban on positive engineering seems to need some explanation. If we can make positive changes at the environmental level, and negative changes at the genetic level, why should we not make positive changes at the genetic level? What makes this policy, but not the others, objectionably God-like?

Perhaps the most plausible reply to these questions rests on a general objection to any group of people trying to plan too closely what human life should be like. Even if it is hard to distinguish in principle between the use of genetic and environmental means, genetic changes are likely to differ in degree from most environmental ones. Genetic alterations may be more drastic or less reversible, and so they can be seen as the extreme case of an objectionably God-like policy by which some people set out to plan the lives of others.

This objection can be reinforced by imagining the possible results of a programme of positive engineering, where the decisions about the desired improvements were taken by scientists. Judging by the literature written by scientists on this topic, great prominence would be given to intelligence. But can we be sure that enough weight would be given to other desirable qualities? And do things seem better if for scientists we substitute doctors, politicians or civil servants? Or some committee containing businessmen, trade unionists, academics, lawyers and a clergyman?

What seems worrying here is the circumscribing of potential human development. The present genetic lottery throws up a vast range of characteristics, good and bad, in all sorts of combinations. The group of people controlling a positive engineering policy would inevitably have limited horizons, and we are right to worry that the limitations of their outlook might become the boundaries of human variety. The drawbacks would be like those of town-planning or dog-breeding, but with more important consequences.

When the objection to playing God is separated from the idea that intervening in this aspect of the natural world is a kind of blasphemy, it is a protest against a particular group of people, necessarily fallible and limited, taking decisions so important to our future. This protest may be on grounds of the bad consequences, such as loss of variety of people, that would come from the imaginative limits of those taking the decisions. Or it may be an expression of opposition to such concentration of power, perhaps with the thought: 'What right have *they* to decide what kinds of people there should be?' Can these problems be side-stepped?

2. THE GENETIC SUPERMARKET

Robert Nozick is critical of the assumption that positive engineering has to involve any centralized decision about desirable qualities: "Many biologists tend to think the problem is one of *design,* of specifying the best types of persons so that biologists can proceed to produce them. Thus they worry over what sort(s) of person there is to be and who will control this process. They do not tend to think, perhaps because it diminishes the importance of their role, of a system in which they run a "genetic supermarket," meeting the individual specifications (within certain moral limits) of prospective parents. Nor do they think of seeing what limited number of types of persons people's choices would converge upon, if indeed there would be any such convergence. This supermarket system has the great virtue that it involves no centralized decision fixing the future human type(s)."[7]

This idea of letting parents choose their children's characteristics is in many ways an improvement on decisions being taken by some centralized body. It seems less likely to reduce human variety, and could even increase it, if genetic engineering makes new combinations of characteristics available. (But we should be cautious here. Parental choice is not a guarantee of genetic variety, as the influence of fashion or of shared values might make for a small number of types on which choices would converge.)

To those sympathetic to one kind of liberalism, Nozick's proposal will seem more attractive than centralized decisions. On this approach to politics, it is wrong for the authorities to institutionalize any religious or other outlook as the official one of the society. To a liberal of this kind, a good society is one which tolerates and encourages a wide diversity of ideals of the good life. Anyone with these sympathies will be suspicious of centralized decisions about what sort of people should form the next generation. But some parental decisions would be disturbing. If parents chose characteristics likely to make their children unhappy, or likely to reduce their abilities, we might feel that the children should be protected against this. (Imagine parents belonging to some extreme religious sect, who wanted their children to have a religious symbol as a physical mark on their face, and who wanted them to be unable to read, as a protection against their faith being corrupted.) Those of us who support restrictions protecting children from parental harm after birth (laws against cruelty, and compulsion on parents to allow their children to be educated and to have necessary medical treatment) are likely to support protecting children from being harmed by their parents' genetic choices.

No doubt the boundaries here will be difficult to draw. We already find it difficult to strike a satisfactory balance between protection of children and parental freedom to choose the kind of upbringing their children should have. But it is hard to accept that society should set no limits to the genetic choices parents can make for their children. Nozick recognizes this when he says the genetic supermarket should meet the specifications of parents "within certain moral limits." So, if the supermarket came into existence, some centralized policy, even if only the restrictive one of ruling out certain choices harmful to the children, should exist. It would be a political decision where the limits should be set.

There may also be a case for other centralized

restrictions on parental choice, as well as those aimed at preventing harm to the individual people being designed. The genetic supermarket might have more oblique bad effects. An imbalance in the ratio between the sexes could result. Or parents might think their children would be more successful if they were more thrusting, competitive and selfish. If enough parents acted on this thought, other parents with different values might feel forced into making similar choices to prevent their own children being too greatly disadvantaged. Unregulated individual decisions could lead to shifts of this kind, with outcomes unwanted by most of those who contribute to them. If a majority favour a roughly equal ratio between the sexes, or a population of relatively uncompetitive people, they may feel justified in supporting restrictions on what parents can choose. (This is an application to the case of genetic engineering of a point familiar in other contexts, that unrestricted individual choices can add up to a total outcome which most people think worse than what would result from some regulation.)

Nozick recognizes that there may be cases of this sort. He considers the case of avoiding a sexual imbalance and says that "a government could require that genetic manipulation be carried on so as to fit a certain ratio."[8] He clearly prefers to avoid governmental intervention of this kind, and, while admitting that the desired result would be harder to obtain in a purely libertarian system, suggests possible strategies for doing so. He says: "Either parents would subscribe to an information service monitoring the recent births and so know which sex was in shorter supply (and hence would be more in demand in later life), thus adjusting their activities, or interested individuals would contribute to a charity that offers bonuses to maintain the ratios, or the ratio would leave 1:1, with new family and social patterns developing." The proposals for avoiding the sexual imbalance without central regulation are not reassuring. Information about likely prospects for marriage or sexual partnership might not be decisive for parents' choices. And, since those most likely to be "interested individuals" would be in the age group being genetically engineered, it is not clear that the charity would be given donations adequate for its job.[9]

If the libertarian methods failed, we would have the choice between allowing a sexual imbalance or imposing some system of social regulation. Those who dislike central decisions favouring one sort of person over others might accept regulation here, on the grounds that neither sex is being given preference: the aim is rough equality of numbers.

But what about the other sort of case, where the working of the genetic supermarket leads to a general change unwelcome to those who contribute to it? Can we defend regulation to prevent a shift towards a more selfish and competitive population as merely being the preservation of a certain ratio between characteristics? Or have we crossed the boundary, and allowed a centralized decision favouring some characteristics over others? The location of the boundary is obscure. One view would be that the sex-ratio case is acceptable because the desired ratio is equality of numbers. On another view, the acceptability derives from the fact that the present ratio is to be preserved. (In this second view, preserving altruism would be acceptable, so long as no attempt was made to raise the proportion of altruistic people in the population. But is *this* boundary an easy one to defend?)

If positive genetic engineering does become a reality, we may be unable to avoid some of the decisions being taken at a social level. Or rather, we could avoid this, but only at what seems an unacceptable cost, either to the particular people being designed, or to their generation as a whole. And, even if the social decisions are only restrictive, it is implausible to claim that they are all quite free of any taint of preference for some characteristics over others. But, although this suggests that we should not be doctrinaire in our support of the liberal view, it does not show that the view has to be abandoned altogether. We may still think that social decisions in favour of one type of person rather than another should be few, even if the consequences of excluding them altogether are unacceptable. A genetic supermarket, modified by some central regulation, may still be better than a system of purely central decisions. The liberal value is not obliterated because it may sometimes be compromised for the sake of other things we care about.

3. A MIXED SYSTEM

The genetic supermarket provides a partial answer to the objection about the limited outlook of those who would take the decisions. The choices need not be concentrated in the hands of a small number of people. The genetic supermarket should not operate in a completely unregulated way, and so some centralized decisions would have to be taken about the restrictions that should be imposed. One system that would answer many of the anxieties about centralized decision-making would be to limit the power of the decision-makers to one of veto. They would then only check departures from the natural genetic lottery, and so the power to bring about changes would not be given to them, but spread through the whole population of potential parents. Let us call this combination of parental initiative and central veto a "mixed system." If positive genetic engineering does come about, we can imagine the argument between supporters of a mixed system and supporters of other decision-making systems being central to the political theory of the twenty-first century, parallel to the place occupied in the nineteenth and twentieth centuries by the debate over control of the economy.[10]

My own sympathies are with the view that, if positive genetic engineering is introduced, this mixed system is in general likely to be the best one for making decisions. I do not want to argue for an absolutely inviolable commitment to this, as it could be that some centralized decision for genetic change was the only way of securing a huge benefit or avoiding a great catastrophe. But, subject to this reservation, the dangers of concentrating the decision-making create a strong presumption in favour of a mixed system rather than one in which initiatives come from the centre. And, if a mixed system was introduced, there would have to be a great deal of political argument over what kinds of restrictions on the supermarket should be imposed. Twenty-first-century elections may be about issues rather deeper than economics.

If this mixed system eliminates the anxiety about genetic changes being introduced by a few powerful people with limited horizons, there is a more general unease which it does not remove. May not the limitations of one generation of parents also prove disastrous? And, underlying this, is the problem of what values parents should appeal to in making their choices. How can we be confident that it is better for one sort of person to be born than another?

4. VALUES

The dangers of such decisions, even spread through all prospective parents, seem to me very real. We are swayed by fashion. We do not know the limitations of our own outlook. There are human qualities whose value we may not appreciate. A generation of parents might opt heavily for their children having physical or intellectual abilities and skills. We might leave out a sense of humour. Or we might not notice how important to us is some other quality, such as emotional warmth. So we might not be disturbed in advance by the possible impact of the genetic changes on such a quality. And, without really wanting to do so, we might stumble into producing people with a deep coldness. This possibility seems one of the worst imaginable. It is just one of the many horrors that could be blundered into by our lack of foresight in operating the mixed system. Because such disasters are a real danger, there is a case against positive genetic engineering, even when the changes do not result from centralized decisions. But this case, resting as it does on the risk of disaster, supports a principle of caution rather than a total ban. We have to ask the question whether there are benefits sufficiently great and sufficiently probable to outweigh the risks.

But perhaps the deepest resistance, even to a mixed system, is not based on risks, but on a more general problem about values. Could the parents ever be justified in choosing, according to some set of values, to create one sort of person rather than another?

Is it sometimes better for us to create one sort of person rather than another? We say "yes" when it is a question of eliminating genetic defects. And we say "yes" if we think that encouraging some qualities rather than others should be an aim of the upbringing and education we give our children. Any inclination to say "no" in the context of positive genetic engineering must lay great stress on the two relevant boundaries. The positive-negative boundary is needed to mark off the supposedly unacceptable positive policies from the acceptable elimination of defects. And the genes-environment boundary is needed to mark off positive engineering from acceptable positive aims of educational policies. But it is not clear that confidence in the importance of these boundaries is justified. . . .

NOTES

1. Chris Graham has suggested to me that it is misleading to say this without emphasizing the painful slowness of this way of changing gene frequencies.

2. *The Future of Man* (The Reith Lectures, 1959), London, 1960, chapter 3; and in "The Genetic Improvement of Man," in *The Hope of Progress,* London, 1972.

3. *Genes, Dreams and Realities,* London, 1971, p. 81.

4. "Already they have pushed Cline's results further, obtaining transfer between rabbit and mouse, for example, and good expression of the foreign gene in its new host. Some, by transferring the genes into the developing eggs, have managed to get the new genes into every cell in the mouse, including the sex cells; those mice have fathered offspring who also contain the foreign gene." Jeremy Cherfas: *Man Made Life,* Oxford, 1982, pp. 229–30.

5. *Out of the Night,* New York, 1935. To find a distinguished geneticist talking like this after the Nazi period is not easy.

6. John Maynard Smith: *On Evolution,* Edinburgh, 1972; the article is reprinted from the issue on "Utopia" of *Daedalus, Journal of the American Academy of Arts and Sciences,* 1965.

7. *Anarchy, State and Utopia,* New York, 1974, p. 315.

8. Op. cit., p. 315.

9. This kind of unworldly innocence is part of the engaging charm of Nozick's dotty and brilliant book.

10. Decision-taking by a central committee (perhaps of a dozen elderly men) can be thought of as a "Russian" model. The genetic supermarket (perhaps with genotypes being sold by TV commercials) can be thought of as an "American" model. The mixed system may appeal to Western European social democrats.

JON W. GORDON

Genetic Enhancement in Humans

Jon W. Gordon is Professor of Obstetrics and Gynecology, Geriatrics and Human Genetics at the Mount Sinai School of Medicine. He has authored more than 100 articles and book chapters on the subjects of gene transfer and reproductive biology. He has also served on numerous government committees that consider the ethics of gene transfer, including the NIH Recombinant DNA Advisory Committee.

Dramatic advances in gene transfer technology since the early 1980s have prompted consideration of its use in humans to enhance phenotypic traits. The notion that genetic modification could confer special advantages on an individual has generated excitement. Controversial issues surround this prospect, however. A practical concern is determining how to ensure equal access to such advanced medical technologies. There has also been speculation that genetic enhancement might affect human evolution, and philosophical objections have been raised, based on the belief that to intervene in such fundamental biological processes is to "play God." Although such philosophical questions cannot be resolved through data analysis, we nevertheless have the tools in hand to objectively assess our state of progress. We can also assess the impact that promulgation of such technology might have on human evolution and formulate sensible guidelines for developing policies governing human genetic enhancements.

Reprinted with permission from *Science* 283 (26 March 1999), 2023–24. Copyright © 1999, American Association for the Advancement of Science.

DEFINING GENETIC ENHANCEMENT

Some experts have argued that "enhancement" can have different meanings depending on the circumstances. For example, when a disease is common, the risk for developing the disorder may be considered the norm, and genetic alleviation of that risk might be regarded as a form of enhancement.[1] This kind of semantic gamesmanship is misleading. The obvious public concern does not relate to improvement of traits for alleviation of deficiencies or reduction of disease risk, but to augmentation of functions that without intervention would be considered entirely normal. To raise the athletic capabilities of a schoolyard basketball player to those of a professional or to confer the talents of Chopin on a typical college music professor is the sort of genetic enhancement that many find troublesome. The experts in the gene transfer field should acknowledge the distinction in order to avoid causing public distrust and undermining the deliberative process.

Another important distinction is that between genetic changes that are heritable and those that cannot be genetically transmitted. At the present time, gene transfer approaches that involve the early embryo are far more effective than somatic cell gene therapy methodologies. Embryo gene transfer affords the opportunity to transform most or all cells of the organism and thus overcomes the inefficient transformation that plagues somatic cell gene transfer protocols. Moreover, the commonly used approaches to embryo gene insertion—pronuclear microinjection[2] and transfection of embryonic stem cells[3]—are associated with stable, high expression of donor DNA. Typically, however, genetic changes introduced into the embryo extend to the gametes and are heritable.

Scenarios can be constructed wherein introduced genes could be deleted from germ cells or early embryos derived from the treated individual. For example, transferred genes could reside on artificial chromosomes that could be deleted by activating a recombinase that induced recombination of the chromosome ends.[1] Such approaches, however, are currently only speculative. Germline gene transfer has already succeeded in several animal species. Because of this and the general belief that voluntary abstention from germline modification in humans is unlikely, a candid discussion of genetic enhancement must include the possibility that changes introduced will be transmitted to offspring.

THE STATE OF THE ART

Animal experiments thus far have attempted to improve what are intuitively regarded as "simple" traits such as growth rate or muscle mass. Efforts to genetically improve the growth of swine have involved insertion of transgenes encoding growth hormone.[4,5] Nevertheless, despite the fact that growth hormone transgenes are expressed well in swine, increased growth does not occur.[4,5] Although the transgenic animals fortuitously have less body fat,[5] these unexpected benefits cannot be extrapolated to human clinical protocols. Before a human embryo is treated with recombinant DNA, we must know exactly what we are doing.

Another spectacular failed attempt at enhancement resulted from efforts to increase muscle mass in cattle. When expressed in mice, the avian c-*ski* gene, the cellular counterpart of the retroviral *v-ski* oncogene, induced massive muscle hypertrophy.[6] This prompted efforts to produce cattle expressing a c-*ski* transgene. When gene transfer was accomplished, the transgenic calf initially exhibited muscle hypertrophy, but muscle degeneration and wasting soon followed. Unable to stand, the debilitated animal was killed.[7]

Why did these enhancement experiments fail? For clues, it is useful to compare modern-day gene transfer technology with the more traditional approach to genetic engineering: selective breeding. Selective breeding maximizes the reproductive efficiency of individuals that exhibit desired characteristics. The selection strategy is oblivious to the number of genes responsible for generating the phenotype. Swine selected for rapid growth may consume more food, produce more growth hormone, respond more briskly to endogenous growth hormone, divert proteins toward somatic growth, and possess skeletal anatomy that allows the animal to tolerate increased weight. Dozens or perhaps hundreds of genes may influence these traits, but in selective breeding, favorable alleles at all loci can simultaneously be selected. In contrast, gene transfer selects one relevant locus and attempts to improve it in isolation. It is little wonder that this approach, albeit potentially powerful and efficient, is more chancy, and has, despite more than 10 years of effort, failed to yield even one unequivocal success. Greater success has been achieved in genetic enhancement of plants, which are more easily manipulated genetically and reproductively; for example, see note 8.

Given the inherent limitations of the gene transfer approach to enhancement, discussion of extending such procedures to humans is scientifically unjustified. We clearly do not yet understand how to accomplish controlled genetic modification of even simple phenotypes. Where more complex traits such as intelligence are concerned, we have no idea what to do, and in fact we may never be able to use gene transfer for enhancement of such phenotypes. A useful way to appreciate the daunting task of manipulating intelligence through gene transfer is by considering the fact that a single cerebellar Purkinje cell may possess more synapses than the total number of genes in the human genome. There are tens of millions of Purkinje cells in the cerebellum, and these cells are involved in only one aspect of brain function: motor coordination. The genome only provides a blueprint for formation of the brain; the finer details of assembly and intellectual development are beyond direct genetic control and must perforce be subject to innumerable stochastic and environmental influences.

GENETIC ENGINEERING AND HUMAN EVOLUTION

Some have suggested that genetic enhancement and related reproductive technologies now give us the power to control human evolution. This solemn pronouncement is totally without scientific foundation. The evolution of the human species may be understood as a nonrandom change in allelic frequencies resulting from selective pressure. The change progresses over generations because individuals with specific patterns of alleles are favored reproductively. If new alleles were introduced by gene transfer, the impact on the species would be negligible. Every month worldwide approximately 11 million babies are born. The addition of one genetically modified individual could not significantly affect gene frequencies. Moreover, if the "enhanced" individual had his or her first child at the age of 20, then 2,640,000,000 unengineered children would be born during the interval between the birth and procreation of the gene recipient. Even if 1000 successful gene transfers were performed per year, a number not likely to be achieved in the foreseeable future, those newborns would constitute only 1/132,000 of all live births. Thus, any effort to enhance the human species experimentally would be swamped by the random attempts of Mother Nature.

Finally, there is no certainty that genetically enhanced individuals would have greater biological fitness, as measured by reproductive success. A genius or great athlete who has no children has no biological fitness as defined in evolutionary theory. For these reasons, neither gene transfer nor any of the other emerging reproductive technologies will ever have a significant impact on human evolution.

DEVELOPING POLICY

If we accept the notion that genetic enhancement is not practicable in the near future, what policies should we develop concerning the use of such technology? The decision to undertake any form of invasive medical intervention immediately renders the treatment subject a patient who has a right to informed consent as well as to protection from unjustifiably dangerous medical manipulation. Our inability to predict the consequences of an attempt at genetic enhancement makes informed consent impossible, and current knowledge from animal experiments tells us that embryo gene transfer is unsafe: The common approach of pronuclear microinjection is characterized by random integration of donor DNA, a lack of control of the number of gene copies inserted, significant rearrangements of host genetic material, and a 5 to 10% frequency of insertional mutagenesis.[9] Homologous recombination[10] in embryonic stem cells overcomes many of these shortcomings, but human embryonic stem cell transfection would necessarily be followed by nuclear transfer into enucleated oocytes. Because nuclear transfer in at least two animal models is associated with a low birth rate and a very high rate of late pregnancy loss or newborn death,[11] this procedure is also unsafe. The risks are so high and the documented efficacy is so low for gene transfer that it could not compare favorably to straightforward prenatal diagnosis even when a compelling need for therapy exists, as in cases of genetic disease. The use of gene transfer for elective purposes such as enhancement would stray far beyond the limits of acceptable medical intervention.

To attempt genetic enhancement with extant methods would clearly be medically unacceptable, but attempts to ban gene transfer legally could be a cumbersome approach to limiting its clinical use. Verification of compliance would be difficult. The diverse resources required for gene transfer necessitate that the procedure be carried out in facilities equipped for in vitro fertilization. Direct inspection would be required to uncover gene transfer procedures in such facilities. This would impose on the privacy of patients undergoing accepted assisted reproduction procedures such as sperm injection. Moreover, gene transfer can be easily concealed; in the case of pronuclear microinjection, only a few seconds are needed to complete the process. Legal restrictions can also be easily avoided by performing the procedure outside the area of jurisdiction.

Finally, and perhaps most important, broad legal restrictions incur the risk of limiting invaluable research. Exemplifying this problem is the current overly broad ban on federal funding for experiments with human embryos. The recent derivation of human embryonic stem cells from preimplantation embryos[12] has created important new research opportunities, accompanied by pressure to provide federal funds for the work. This pressure has led to the odd situation in which federal funds will likely be allowed for research with embryonic stem cells but not for manipulating human embryos to produce embryonic stem cell lines. If, as a society, we feel compelled to make a statement against genetic enhancement, we need not enact anticipatory legislation. Instead we can evaluate such manipulations as we would any other invasive clinical procedure. If we require that gene transfer be accompanied by informed consent, that it have a reasonable possibility of succeeding, that its cost not be excessive, that it have acceptable side effects and toxicities, that it not be accompanied by a burdensome requirement for long-term follow-up evaluation, and that it compare favorably with other treatment options, we will currently reject the procedure on all counts as medically unethical. Were entities such as the National Bioethics Advisory Commission or Congress to make such statements formally, no responsible physician would attempt genetic enhancement. Irresponsible use of technology can never be stopped, even by legislation.

Fear of genetic manipulation may encourage proposals to limit basic investigations that might ultimately lead to effective human gene transfer. History has shown that effort is far better spent in preparing society to cope with scientific advances than in attempting to restrict basic research. Gene transfer studies may never lead to successful genetic enhancement, but they are certain to provide new treatment and prevention strategies for a variety of devastating diseases. No less significant is the potential for this research to improve our understanding of the most complex and compelling phenomenon ever observed—the life process. We cannot be expected to deny ourselves this knowledge.

REFERENCES

1. G. Stock and J. Campbell, Eds., *Summary Report, Engineering the Human Germline Symposium* (University of California, Los Angeles, 1998).
2. J. W. Gordon *et al., Proc. Natl. Acad. Sci. U.S.A.* **77,** 7380 (1980); J. W. Gordon and F. H. Ruddle, *Science* **214,** 1244 (1981); F. Costantini and F. E. Lacy, *Nature* **294,** 92 (1981); R. L. Brinster *et al., Cell* **27,** 223 (1981).
3. M. J. Evans and M. H. Kaufman, *Nature* **292,** 154 (1981); G. R. Martin, *Proc. Natl. Acad. Sci. U.S.A.* **78,** 7634 (1981); S. L. Mansour, K. R. Thomas, M. R. Capecchi, *Nature* **336,** 348 (1988); S. Thompson *et al., Cell* **56,** 313 (1989).
4. V. G. Pursel *et al., Vet. Immunol. Immunopathol.* **17,** 303 (1987).
5. C. A. Pinkert, E. J. Galbreath, C. W. Yang, L. J. Striker, *Transgenic Res.* **3,** 401 (1994); M. B. *Solomon et al., J. Anim. Sci.* **72,** 1242 (1994).
6. P. Sutrave, A. M. Kelly, S. H. Hughes, *Genes Dev.* **4,** 1462 (1990).
7. R. A. Bowen *et al., Biol. Reprod.* **50,** 664 (1994).
8. K. J. Kramer and S. Muthukrishnan, *Insect. Biochem. Mol. Biol.* **27,** 887 (1997).
9. R. D. Palmiter and R. L. Brinster, *Annu. Rev. Genet.* **20,** 465 (1986); J. W. Gordon, *Int. Rev. Cytol.* **115,** 171 (1989).
10. O. Smithies, R. G. Grett, S. S. Boggs, M. A. Koralewski, R. S. Kucherlapati, *Nature* **317,** 230 (1981).
11. I. Wilmut *et al., ibid.* **385,** 810 (1997); T. Wakayama, A. C. F. Perry, M. Zucotti, K. R. Johnson, R. Yanagimachi, *ibid.* **394,** 369 (1998).
12. M. J. Shamblott *et al., Proc. Natl. Acad. Sci. U.S.A.* **95,** 13726 (1998); J. A. Thomson *et al., Science* **282,** 1145 (1998).

ERIK PARENS

The Goodness of Fragility: On the Prospect of Genetic Technologies Aimed at the Enhancement of Human Capacities

Erik Parens is the Associate for Philosophical Studies at the Hastings Center, a bioethics think tank in Garrison, New York. He has published extensively on the ethical and social questions raised by biotechnological advances; he is also editor of *Enhancing Human Traits: Ethical and Social Ramifications* (Georgetown University Press) and coeditor of *Prenatal Genetic Testing and the Disability Rights Critique* (Georgetown University Press).

Currently, genetic technology cannot be used to significantly enhance human capacities. Although, for instance, genetically engineered bovine somatotropin (BST) is now used to enhance the milk production of cows, no one suggests an analogous enhancement of humans. And while human growth hormone (hGH) has been administered to enhance the stature of children who are not hGH deficient, it is not clear whether the procedure has worked (White 1993).

Yet if it is true that humans cannot now significantly enhance their capacities with genetic technology, it is also true that they always have sought to enhance their capacities with whatever means have been available. For example, we enhance our intellectual capacities with education, our bodily capacities with exercise, and our capacity to attract sexual partners with a variety of cosmetic techniques. From this I infer two things: (1) that it would make no sense to argue that the enhancement of human capacities is, in itself, a bad thing; and (2) that when genetic technology gets to the point where enhancement is possible, there will be a powerful drive to employ it.

Indeed, there seems to be no reason why, in principle, the gene-therapy techniques used to replace defective genes with "healthy" ones could not be used to replace healthy genes with "enhanced" or "better" ones.[1] Nor is there any reason why, in principle, the genetic-engineering techniques used to make products that the body cannot make could not be used to make more of a product that the body already makes.

If today, a drug like fluoxetine (Prozac) can enhance the capacity of a significant minority of users to compete in a consumer society by raising the level of the neurotransmitter serotonin (Kramer 1993; Sherman 1994), then there is reason to think that genetic technology will be able to enhance human capacities in similarly significant ways.[2] Indeed, a recent issue of *Science* reports on researchers who generated mice that lacked the gene for one of the serotonin receptors (5-HT_{1B}) (Saudou et al. 1994). As one might predict from fluoxetine's ability to increase serotonin levels in humans by inhibiting the reuptake of serotonin, the researchers found that the aggressiveness of the mice was increased. While these researchers clearly did not have in mind the significant minority of fluoxetine users whose competitiveness is enhanced by increased levels of serotonin, they apparently did have in mind the possibility of using genetic technology to achieve the same therapeutic effect that drugs like fluoxetine have. Furthermore, although enhancing the aggressiveness of mice is a long way from enhancing the competitiveness of humans with genetic technology, such enhancements no longer seem the stuff of science fiction.

Given the apparently enduring desire of humans to enhance their capacities, and given the likelihood that

Reprinted by permission from *Kennedy Institute of Ethics Journal* 5 (June 1995), 141–53. Copyright © 1995 by the Johns Hopkins University Press.

new genetic technologies will at some point enable us to enhance our capacities in significant and perhaps unprecedented ways, now is the time for society to begin thinking about how far it ought to go in this regard.[3] While there are good and self-evident reasons to go in the direction of such enhancements, a chief aim of this essay is to reflect on some good and less evident reasons why our society ought to exercise extreme caution as it contemplates such a move.

Urging caution with respect to genetic enhancement is nothing new (see, e.g., President's Commission 1982; Davis and Englehardt 1983; Anderson, 1989; Walters 1991). But the problem does not admit of a neat solution. It is, rather, the sort of problem that requires ongoing engagement. My attempt to engage it will take the form of the following question: Will we, in some of our attempts to enhance humans, inadvertently improverish them by reducing what I will call their fragility.[4] Before beginning to answer this question, I want to make three preliminary points.

First, my use of the term "fragility" might seem strange. When I say that we are fragile creatures, I mean that we are creatures subject to change and to chance. In this essay I attempt to reflect upon what life would be like if we could significantly reduce the change and chance to which we—creatures whose forms are largely determined by the genetic hand dealt us by nature—have hitherto been subject.

Second, I am not trying to argue that genetic technology aimed at enhancement could rid life of fragility. Even if human beings were to become uniformly beautiful, marvelously tempered, hugely healthy, and massively smart, there still would be plenty of change and chance for everyone to be subject to. I am merely exploring that might be lost if, to an unprecedented extent, we could reduce our vulnerability to change and chance.

Finally, I am not making the unconditional or absolute claim that we ought never to use genetic technology to enhance human beings. Nor am I attempting to provide an algorithm that we could simply apply when faced with the prospect of a given technology. Rather, I am attempting to articulate a series of considerations that ought to be factored into any decision about whether to go ahead with a given technology aimed at enhancement. I undertake to articulate these considerations because, given the potential for prodigious benefits, we might overlook them. In the end, I will speculate about what besides benevolence inclines us to overlook such considerations as we contemplate the use of technologies aimed at the enhancement of human capacities.

THE DESIRE TO REDUCE CHANGE

One of the easiest ways to begin appreciating what is valuable about fragility is to think about the pleasure we take in our experience of some forms of the beautiful. Consider the ordinary experience of beholding other organisms—such as flowers. The intensity of one sort of pleasure we receive from beholding flowers depends decisively on their transience, on the fact that they undergo change. Crucial ingredients in our pleasure are our anticipation of the blossoming and our anxiety about, and memory of, its passing.

That the blossom comes into being and passes away may be a source of anxiety—but it is an anxiety that heightens our pleasure: this flower, in this form, is here but for a few, beautiful days. It may even be that this "little" anxiety in the face of the flower's coming into being and passing away is an occasion for our reflection upon the "great" anxiety we experience in the face of our own mortality. Though we often turn away from anxiety, both little and great, doing so is to turn away from an important part of being human and thus is to impoverish our experience.

The goodness of this sort of fragility receives one of its most beautiful expressions in the poetry of Wallace Stevens:

> Is there no change of death in paradise?
> Does ripe fruit never fall? Or do the boughs
> Hang always heavy in that perfect sky,
> Unchanging, yet so like our perishing earth,
> With rivers like our own that seek for seas
> They never find, the same receding shores
> That never touch with inarticulate pang? . . .
> Death is the mother of beauty. . . .[5]

If there is no change in paradise, then, according to Stevens, neither is there beauty of a fundamental sort.

If the attempt to reduce our subjection to change could affect for the worse our experience of some forms of the beautiful, it could do the same for our experience of caring and being cared for.[6] Suppose enhancement technology were aimed at removing the difficulties of aging, thereby altering our conception and experience of, for example, relationships between the generations. Given that figuring out how to care for a burgeoning elderly population is one of our most pressing social problems, it might, at first glance, seem quite wonderful if we could, say, enhance the capacities of ninety-five-year-olds so that they could act and feel like twenty-five-year-olds.

Furthermore, while we're thinking about trying to reduce the time spent on the elderly members of our society, we could also think about trying to reduce the time spent on the young. We could, I suppose, strive to discover an "acceleration hormone"—a hormone aimed at making children grow faster. Much money and energy would be saved if we could compress not only old age, but childhood too. I can well imagine the complaint that I have created a straw man. After all, children are sweet; no one would make such a proposal. But what about accelerating adolescence? No one ever claimed that adolescents are sweet; moreover, adolescence is a time of pain and danger to the people undergoing it, as well as to the rest of us. Compressing this difficult period could significantly reduce pain and the expenditure of valuable social resources.

I assume that one reason no one would assent to my modest proposal is that we think that we ought to caringly respond to the pain of adolescence rather than engineer a way around it. There is a point beyond which the reduction of our subjection to some sorts of change costs too much. Though it would be naive to forget just how burdensome the need for care can be to both the giver of care and the receiver, it would be equally naive to forget that the shared recognition and acceptance of human neediness can be profoundly valuable. That is, I take it to be valuable for us to recognize and accept our nature, and neediness is a constituent of that nature.

Further, as I will discuss more fully below, when we consider whether to proceed with a given technology aimed at enhancement, we ought to consider whether that technology threatens to reduce the great diversity of human forms. Given what appears to be a deep human tendency to fear and hate the different, we ought to be especially vigilant about promoting technologies that could—by engineering sameness—collude with that tendency. At the point where a given enhancement technology diminishes difference across the life span, where it promises to make us all look and act more alike, the good that is diversity across the life span is threatened.

In a word, before we attempt to enhance human beings by reducing their subjection to change—before attempting to reduce their fragility—we ought to consider how such attempts would affect the good that is our experience of some forms of the beautiful, the good that is relationships of care, and the good that is diversity across the life span.

THE DESIRE TO REDUCE CHANCE

Let me invite you now to think about the pleasure we take in our experience of some human excellences. Why is it, for example, that our knowledge of a runner's use of steroids diminishes our pleasure in his or her performance? Why is it that watching Ben Johnson run does not give track fans the same sort of pleasure as watching, say, Carl Lewis? Part of the reason is no doubt simply a sense of fairness: Johnson has an unfair, steroid-induced advantage. I want to suggest, however, that something subtler is at work as well. Part of our experience of the particular excellence of a winning runner resides in our intuition that this performance is the result of an extraordinary combination of human effort and chance. It could have been otherwise, and it almost always is, but this time a human being ran 100 meters in well under 10 seconds. To reduce the role of chance—to alter with steroids the hand that nature dealt the runner—is to diminish, if not ruin, our experience of this form of excellence.

Sport is neither the only, nor the most significant, area of human endeavor where chance plays a crucial role. When we speak of equal opportunity, for example, we mean that within the constraints of those gifts that come to people from the natural lottery, we give each an equal opportunity to compete. When there no longer is a natural lottery such as we have understood is heretofore, when what we are depends not upon the hand nature dealt us, but—even more than now—upon the hand our parents bought us, then concepts such as equal opportunity will have to undergo fundamental transformations.[7]

It is predictable, for example, that an even larger chasm will open between the rich who can afford enhancement treatment and the poor who cannot. This prediction rests on the assumption that enhancement treatment will be distributed unevenly, according to people's ability to pay. But let us change the assumption. What would happen if resources were not limited and enhancement treatment were available to all? At first glance, it might seem that nothing could be lost; it might seem that, finally, we had discovered how to make humankind happier. Reducing the chance to which humans are subject in the natural lottery might seem like a brilliant way to end the competitiveness and resentment that are the root of clashes in the kindergarten and on the battlefield. Imagine: Everyone could be porcelain-skinned, blond, blue-eyed, straight, tall, small-waisted, big-chested, smart, and nice. Nobody would have to have skin too dark anymore. Nobody would have to have hair too kinky anymore. Nobody would have to be gay. Nobody would be too short. Nobody would have too big a nose or too small a chest. Nobody would be too mean or too nice. Everybody would be just right (see Fielder 1985).

If society could in fact enhance away the "imperfections" resulting from chance, it could, once again, reduce one of its most pressing burdens: the burden of responding to the needs of those who are marginalized because they do not possess the specifications deemed valuable. And once again the questions arise: Would it be a good thing to reduce the diversity—to diminish the difference—that results from our subjection to chance? Would it be a good thing to reduce the need to respond to the vulnerability of others that results from our subjection to chance? For the reasons offered above in the context of attempting to reduce our subjection to change, my tentative answers to those questions are clear.

Just as I suggested that it is in exuberant moments—of imagining how much better life might be if we could rid it of change—that we forget about the goodness of change, so in exuberant moments we forget about the goodness of chance.[8] When we are carried away by our benevolent desires to reduce the suffering of vulnerable people and, less benevolently, their cost to society, we forget that the vulnerability of others not only burdens us (though it surely does so), but also elicits from us the awesome capacity to care for others. Although—and I cannot be too emphatic about this—it would be a profound mistake to romanticize the need to care for vulnerable others and the need of vulnerable others to be cared for, it would be equally mistaken to ignore the goodness that those relationships can possess.[9]

THE DESIRE FOR PARADISE

In my attempt to articulate the considerations that ought to be factored into any decision to implement a given technology aimed at enhancement, there operates an as-yet unarticulated premise involving a particular conception of the proper relationship between humans and the rest of the natural world. Indeed it seems that significantly different conceptions of the value and the meaning of human life—profoundly different conceptions of our proper relationship to ourselves and to the rest of the natural world—are at work in the argument between those who tend to favor enhancement technologies and those who tend to be critical of them. I would like now to suggest one way to begin thinking about that difference.

Those who tend to favor genetic enhancement proceed from a conception of the relationship between humans and the rest of the world much like that of Francis Bacon. Bacon's project to conquer and control nature is relentlessly commented upon, yet one element of the project is often forgotten. Bacon thinks that his project has a divine sanction; in *The New Organon* (I, cxxix), for instance, he writes that the human race has a "right over nature which belongs to it by divine bequest." Consistent with his Calvinism, Bacon believes, as one scholar succinctly puts it, that "the mission of science [is] to repair the damage done by the Fall of Man and to restore man to his original glory" (Finch 1963, p. xiii).[10]

It goes without saying that Bacon's project has benefited humankind enormously. It does not, however, go without saying that Bacon's project is embedded in a very particular conception of the proper relationship between humans and the rest of nature. In fact, we are so embedded in Bacon's conception that it does not seem particular to us at all. Medicine, for example, has been one of the greatest beneficiaries of that project's success. When Ronald Munson and Lawrence Davis (1992) argue in this journal that medicine ought to employ germ-line therapy for the treatment of disease, they speak as if the aim of medicine were self-evident. Like Bacon, they proceed as if the Western biomedical conception were ordained by God. Because the aim of medicine is self-evident for Munson and Davis, the only remaining problem is to find the means to achieve it. As they write, "The basic standard of evaluation [for medicine] must be practical or instrumental success with respect to its specific aim." What, in their view is the aim of medicine? It is to achieve "control over the factors affecting health. . . . [Knowledge] is important to medicine because it leads to control" (Munson and Davis 1992, p. 155). Given that control is the aim, and given that germ-line therapy "is the most effective form of control," they conclude that medicine has a prima facie duty to employ germ-line therapy.

Although the view that the proper relationship between humans and the rest of the world is one of control is so entrenched as to seem self-evident, there are alternative perspectives: certainly many feminists, environmentalists, and peoples from different cultures have articulated such views. But people in the bioethical conversation also have attempted to articulate an alternative vision; Hans Jonas is one such person.

Whereas Bacon proceeds from the assumption that the mission of science is to repair the damage done by the Fall of Man and to restore Man to his original glory, Jonas—to translate his thought into theological terms—proceeds from the assumption that leaving Paradise did not constitute a Fall at all, but rather marked the beginning of peculiarly difficult and good human life. Whereas Bacon thinks that creation needs restoration to a former state of perfection, Jonas thinks that creation is owed preservation in its altogether "imperfect" state. Whereas Bacon thinks that nature is ours to use in whatever ways conduce to our desires, Jonas thinks that because nature is in an important sense not ours—"being [is] strictly on loan" (1992, p. 36)—we ought not so to use it.[11]

The archenemy of the Baconian project—death—is of course the ultimate form of fragility. Whereas, according to Bacon, death is the enemy and life extension is medicine's "noblest goal" (Amundsen 1978, p. 27), according to Jonas, death is both a "bitter burden" and a "blessing." Following Heidegger, Jonas (1992, p. 36) writes of death: "only in confrontation with ever-possible not-being could being come to feel itself, affirm itself, make itself its own purpose." For Jonas, death is not an accidental part of life that we ought to try to overcome, but rather is an essential part of life, the goodness of which we need to try to understand.

Those who seek to understand the goodness of death—that ultimate form of fragility—hope that we are the sort of animals who can decide that, although technologies aimed at enhancement might gratify both pedestrian and noble desires, we won't go ahead with some of those technologies because to do so would be to lose too much that makes life good. As valuable as the human capacity for self-transformation and control of the world is, the human capacity to relinquish control and to resist the desire for transformation is equally valuable. We are the animals that can ask: When does that marvelous capacity to manipulate and control the world, when does that marvelous and peculiarly human capacity to change ourselves, go too far?

With respect to genetic technology, we can begin by saying that it goes too far when—in an attempt to establish paradise on earth—it threatens the good that is the pleasure we take in some forms of the beautiful and excellent, or when it threatens the good that is some relationships of care, or when it threatens the good that is the diversity of human forms. When we ask whether it makes a difference if we figure out when our capacity to manipulate and control the world and ourselves has gone too far, we might think about what that capacity has wrought, in the last forty years, on the diversity of life forms on this planet.

Since Watson and Crick discovered the double helix in 1953, the world's population has more than doubled and its economic activity has more than quadrupled (Kennedy 1993, p. 97). According to an appeal sent to Latin American presidents by Gabriel Garcia Marquez and others, "By the year 2000 three-quarters of America's tropical forests may have been felled and 50 percent of their species lost forever" (Kennedy 1993, p. 100). Thus, it is possible that in approximately the same time it will have taken us to garner the knowledge necessary to diminish the diversity of human forms by making ourselves more alike, we also will have reduced by one-half the diversity of other animal forms in some places.[12]

It seems to me that it would be profoundly tragic if the virtue that is our capacity for self-transformation became a vice. It would be profoundly tragic and paradoxical if what Nietzsche calls "the unfixed animal"—due to its capacity for change and its desire for perfection—were to "fix itself" (see Jonas 1974, p. 153).

Let me emphasize: It would be cruel, if not stupid, to suggest that we ought never to use genetic technology to heal the sick. It probably would be foolish to suggest that technology ought never to be used for the enhancement of human beings. So too would it be foolish to forget that without the desire to control and master the world there would be no desire to control and master ourselves.[13] My suggestion has not been that we should figure out a way to extirpate our desire to control and alter ourselves and the world; rather, it has been simply that we should think more deeply about how attempts at control and alteration that truly enhance life are different from those that impoverish it. It may be that thinking more deeply about that difference will entail rethinking some basic beliefs about our proper relationship to ourselves and the rest of nature.

To paraphrase the Czech novelist, Milan Kundera, whose native country has been subjected to relentless political violence in the name of establishing Paradise on earth, "Humankind's longing for Paradise is humankind's longing not to be human." No less than the nobility, we should remember the peril of that longing.

NOTES

1. I am keenly aware that, given the extent to which concepts such as health and enhancement are socially constructed, the distinction between treatment aimed at health and treatment aimed at enhancement is highly contestable. For an account of the reasonableness of the distinction, see Normal Daniels (1992).

2. Although Prozac's effectiveness is correlated with altered serotonin levels, research suggests that increased serotonin is a necessary, but not sufficient, cause for the effects now associated with Prozac. Nonetheless, my point remains: if we can enhance behavior with a drug like Prozac, it stands to reason that we can do the same with genetic technology.

3. It seems to me that we should respond to the prospect of genetic enhancement (somatic and germ-line) as Nelson Wivel and LeRoy Walters respond to the prospect of germ-line treatment aimed at the prevention of disease: "Because the readily identifiable technical problems necessarily consign germ-line gene modification to the relatively distant future, a discussion of the ethical issues might be viewed as an exercise in the abstract. . . . It [nonetheless] would, in our view, be a useful investment of time and energy to continue and in fact to intensify the public discussion . . . *even though the application of this new technology to humans is not likely to be proposed in the near future*" (Wivel and Walters 1993, p. 537, emphasis added).

4. Always in the background for me will be the words of Martha Nussbaum (1986, p. 2), "Human excellence is seen . . . in the Greek poetic tradition . . . as something whose very nature it is to be in need, a growing thing in the world that could not be made invulnerable and keep its own peculiar fineness."

5. My attention was first called to Stevens's "Sunday Morning" by Leon Kass's essay "Mortality and Morality: The Virtues of Finitude" (1985).

6. For the dangers of such "care talk," see Adrienne Asch (1993).

7. Concerning the implications of the genetic technologies for (1) our concept of equality of opportunity, (2) our conception of humans as responsible agents, and (3) our conception of normality, see Dan Brock (1992).

8. See Hans Jonas (1985, p. 500): "The random nature of the sexual process is both the irreplaceable blessing and the inescapable burden of our lot. . . ."

9. See Bruce Jennings, Daniel Callahan and Arthur Caplan (1988, p. 15): "The provision of care and social support for persons with chronic illness by temporarily well and able-bodied citizens reflects an acknowledgment of the links that join the sick and the well, the young and the old in a community of common humanness and vulnerability."

10. See also Charles Taylor's discussion of the Calvinist desire to "clean up the human mess" (Taylor, 1989, pp. 227–28).

11. Though here I am contrasting Jonas's world view with the Calvinist one, the respect in which Jonas's view is commensurate with much of Christian thought is clear.

12. This desire to McDonaldize the world—to reduce the diversity of animate and inanimate forms—is as deep as it is demanding of our attention. Benjamin R. Barber's (1992) "Jihad vs. McWorld" is pertinent. For a closely related argument, see James V. Neel (1993, p. 127): "The elucidation of the precise nature of our genetic material, four billion years in evolving, occurred only 40 years ago. Despite the incredible advances in molecular genetics, we still have a very limited knowledge of the anatomy of our DNA, but even less understanding of how it transacts its excruciatingly complex business. Right now the ecosystem is reeling under the impact of an intellectual arrogance which assumed unbridled license to perturb that system. We are a part of that ecosystem, the last frontier, so to speak. Is there any informed person who, surveying the current evidence of the profound consequences of precipitous human action, believes we are now ready for a serious consideration of how to mold ourselves genetically?"

13. Similarly, it would be foolish to suggest that Bacon and his contemporary followers are without awe or reverence for nature; there are, however, "reverences" or "awes" with different emphases. See Renée Fox's discussion of the difference between the awe Barbara McClintock brings to the study of molecular biology and the awe Albert Claude brings to it (Fox 1989, pp. 190–94).

REFERENCES

Amundsen, Darrel W. 1978. The Physician's Obligation to Prolong Life: A Medical Duty without Classical Roots. *Hastings Center Report* 8 (4): 23–30.

Anderson, W. French, 1989. Human Gene Therapy: Why Draw a Line? *Journal of Medicine and Philosophy* 14: 681–93.

Asch, Adrienne. 1993. Abused or Neglected Clients—Abusive or Neglectful Service Systems? In *Ethical Conflicts in the Management of Home Care,* ed. Rosalie A. Kane and Arthur L. Caplan, pp. 113–21. New York: Springer Publishing Co.

Barber, Benjamin R. 1992. Jihad vs. McWorld. *Atlantic Monthly* (March): 53–65.

Brock, Dan. 1992. The Human Genome Project and Human Identity. *Houston Law Review* 29 (1): 7–22.

Daniels, Norman. 1992. Growth Hormone Therapy for Short Stature: Can We Support the Treatment/Enhancement Distinction? *Growth: Genetics & Hormones* 8 (Supplement 1): 46–48.

Davis, Bernard D., and Engelhardt, H. Tristram, Jr. 1984. Genetic Engineering: Prospects and Recommendations. *Zygon* 19: 277–80.

Fielder, Leslie A. 1985. The Tyranny of the Normal. In *Which Babies Shall Live?,* ed. Thomas H. Murray and Arthur L. Caplan, pp. 151–60. Clifton, NJ: Humana Press.

Finch, Henry LeRoy, ed. 1963. *The Complete Essays of Francis Bacon.* New York: Washington Square Press.

Fox, Renée. 1989. *The Sociology of Medicine: A Participant Observer's View.* Englewood Cliffs, NJ: Prentice-Hall.

Jennings, Bruce; Callahan, Daniel; and Caplan, Arthur. 1988. Ethical Challenges of Chronic Illness. *Hastings Center Report* 18 (1, Special Supplement): 1–16.

Jonas, Hans. 1974. Biological Engineering—A Preview. In *Philosophical Essays: From Ancient Creed to Technological Man,* ed. Hans Jonas, pp. 141–67. Englewood Cliffs, NJ: Prentice-Hall.

——. 1985. Ethics and Biogenic Art. *Social Research* 52: 491–501.

——. 1992. The Burden and Blessing of Mortality. *Hastings Center Report* 22 (1): 34–40.

Kass, Leon. 1985. Mortality and Morality: The Virtues of Finitude. In *Toward a More Natural Science,* ed. Leon Kass, pp. 299–317. New York: The Free Press.

Kennedy, Paul. 1993. *Preparing for the Twenty-First Century*. New York: Random House.

Kramer, Peter D. 1993. *Listening to Prozac*. New York: Viking.

Munson, Ronald, and Davis, Lawrence H. 1992. Germ-Line Therapy and the Medical Imperative. *Kennedy Institute of Ethics Journal* 2: 137–58.

Neel, James V. 1993. Germ-Line Gene Therapy: Another View. *Human Gene Therapy* 4: 127–28.

Nussbaum, Martha. 1986. *The Fragility of Goodness*. New York: Cambridge University Press.

President's Commission for the Study of Ethical Problems in Medicine and Biomedical and Behavioral Research. 1982. *Splicing Life: The Social and Ethical Issues of Genetic Engineering with Human Beings*. Washington, DC: U.S. Government Printing Office.

Saudou, Frédéric; Amara, Djamel Aït; Dierich, Andrée; et al. 1994. Enhanced Aggressive Behavior in Mice Lacking 5-HT_{1B} Receptor. *Science* 265: 1875–78.

Sherman, Carl. 1994. Depression's Complex, Tangled Biologic Roots. *Clinical Psychiatry News* 22 (2): 3, 15.

Taylor, Charles. 1989. *Sources of the Self: The Making of the Modern Identity*. Cambridge: Harvard University Press.

Walters, LeRoy. 1991. Human Gene Therapy: Ethics and Public Policy. *Human Gene Therapy* 2: 115–22.

White, Gladys. 1993. Human Growth Hormone: The Dilemma of Expanded Use in Children. *Kennedy Institute of Ethics Journal* 3: 401–9.

Wivel, Nelson A., and Walters, LeRoy. 1993. Germ-Line Gene Modification and Disease Prevention: Some Medical and Ethical Perspectives. *Science* 262: 533–38.

SUGGESTED READINGS

GENERAL ISSUES

Andrews, Lori B., et al. "Genetics and the Law." *Emory Law Journal* 39 (1990), 619–853. Symposium.

Asch, Adrienne, and Geller, Gail. "Feminism, Bioethics, and Genetics." In Susan M. Wolf, ed., *Feminism and Bioethics: Beyond Reproduction*. New York: Oxford University Press, 1996, 318–50.

Annas, George J., and Elias, Sherman, eds. *Gene Mapping: Using Law and Ethics as Guides*. New York: Oxford University Press, 1992.

Bankowski, Zbigniew, and Capron, Alexander Morgan, eds. *Genetics, Ethics, and Human Values: Human Genome Mapping, Genetic Screening and Gene Therapy*. Geneva: Council for International Organizations of Medical Sciences, 1990.

Davis, Bernard D., ed. *The Genetic Revolution: Scientific Prospects and Public Perceptions*. Baltimore: Johns Hopkins University Press, 1991.

Evans, John H. *Playing God?: Human Genetic Engineering and the Rationalization of Public Bioethical Debate*. Chicago: University of Chicago Press, 2002.

Fletcher, Joseph. *The Ethics of Genetic Control: Ending Reproductive Roulette*. Garden City, NY: Anchor Books, 1974.

Frankel, Mark S., and Teich, Albert, eds. *The Genetic Frontier: Ethics Law, and Policy*. Washington, DC: American Association for the Advancement of Science, 1994.

Fukuyama, Francis. *Our Posthuman Future: Consequences of the Biotechnology Revolution*. New York: Farrar, Straus and Giroux, 2002.

Gert, Bernard, et al. *Morality and the New Genetics: A Guide for Students and Health Care Providers*. Boston: Jones and Bartlett, 1996.

Greely, Henry T. "Human Genome Diversity Project." In Thomas H. Murray and Maxwell J. Mehlman, eds., *Encyclopedia of Ethical, Legal, and Policy Issues in Biotechnology*. 2 vols. New York: John Wiley & Sons, 2000, 552–66.

Harris, John. *Clones, Genes, and Immortality: Ethics and the Genetic Revolution*. New York: Oxford University Press, 1998.

House of Commons, Select Committee on Science and Technology. *Human Genetics: The Science and Its Consequences* (Third Report). 4 vols. London: Her Majesty's Stationery Office, 1995. (HC41.)

Hubbard, Ruth, and Wald, Elijah. *Exploding the Gene Myth*. Boston: Beacon Press, 1993.

Kitcher, Philip. *The Lives to Come: The Genetic Revolution and Human Possibilities*. New York: Simon & Schuster, 1996.

Krimsky, Sheldon. *Biotechnics and Society: The Rise of Industrial Genetics*. Westport, CT: Praeger, 1991.

Kristol, William, and Cohen, Eric, eds. *The Future Is Now: America Confronts the New Genetics*. New York: Rowman & Littlefield, 2002.

Mahowald, Mary B., et al. "The New Genetics and Women." *Milbank Quarterly* 74 (1996), 239–83.

McGee, Glenn. *The Perfect Baby: A Pragmatic Approach to Genetics*. Lanham, MD: Rowman and Littlefield, 1997.

———. "Parenting in an Era of Genetics." *Hastings Center Report* 27 (March–April 1997), 16–22.

Nelkin, Dorothy, and Lindee, M. Susan. *The DNA Mystique: The Gene as a Cultural Icon*. New York: Freeman, 1995.

Ramsey, Paul. *Fabricated Man: The Ethics of Genetic Control*. New Haven: Yale University Press, 1970.

Rifkin, Jeremy. *The Biotech Century: Harnessing the Gene and Remaking the World*. New York: Penguin Putnam, 1998.

Suzuki, David, and Knudtson, Peter. *Genethics: The Clash between the New Genetics and Human Values*. Rev. updated ed. Cambridge, MA: Harvard University Press, 1990.

Tong, Rosemarie. "Feminist and Nonfeminist Perspectives on Genetic Screening, Diagnosis, Counseling, and Therapy." In Rosemarie Tong, ed., *Feminist Approaches to Bioethics: Theoretical Reflections and Practical Applications*. Boulder, CO: Westview Press: 213–42, 268–71.

U.S. Congress, Office of Technology Assessment. *New Developments in Biotechnology—Background Paper: Public Perceptions of Biotechnology*. Washington, DC: U.S. Government Printing Office, May 1987.

Wachbroit, Robert. "Genetic Determinism, Genetic Reductionism, and Genetic Essentialism." In Thomas H. Murray and Maxwell J. Mehlman, eds., *Encyclopedia of Ethical, Legal, and Policy Issues in Biotechnology*. 2 vols. New York: John Wiley & Sons, 2002, 352–56.

Walters, LeRoy. "Human Genetic Intervention and the Theologians: Cosmic Theology and Casuistic Analysis." In Lisa Sowle Cahill and James F. Childress, eds., *Christian Ethics: Problems and Prospects*. Cleveland: Pilgrim Press, 1996, 235–49.

Weir, Robert F., Lawrence, Susan C., and Fales, Evan, eds. *Genes and Human Self-Knowledge: Historical and Philosophical Reflections on Modern Genetics*. Iowa City, IA: Iowa University Press, 1994.

Wasserman, David T. "Behavioral Genetics, Human." In Thomas H. Murray and Maxwell J. Mehlman, eds., *Encyclopedia of Ethical, Legal, and Policy Issues in Biotechnology*. 2 vols. New York: John Wiley & Sons, 2000, 117–27.

Wolf, Susan M. "Beyond 'Genetic Discrimination'; Toward the Broader Harm of Geneticism." *Journal of Law, Medicine and Ethics* 23 (1995), 345–53.

Zweiger, Gary. *Transducing the Genome: Information, Anarchy, and Revolution in the Biomedical Sciences.* New York: McGraw-Hill, 2001.

EUGENICS PROGRAMS IN THE TWENTIETH CENTURY

Adams, Mark B., ed. *The Wellborn Science: Eugenics in Germany, France, Brazil, and Russia.* New York: Oxford University Press, 1990.

Allen, Garland E. "Is a New Eugenics Afoot?" *Science* 294 (2001), 59–61.

———. "The Social and Economic Origins of Genetic Determinism: A Case History of the American Eugenics Movement, 1900–1940, and Its Lessons for Today." *Genetica* 99 (1997), 77–88.

American Society of Human Genetics, Board of Directors. "Eugenics and the Misuse of Genetic Information to Restrict Reproductive Freedom." *American Journal of Human Genetics* 64 (1999), 335–38.

Barondess, Jeremiah A. "Medicine against Society: Lessons from the Third Reich." *Journal of the American Medical Association* 276 (1996), 1657–61.

Biesold, Horst. *Crying Hands: Eugenics and Deaf People in Nazi Germany.* Washington DC: Gallaudet University Press, 1999.

Burleigh, Michael, and Wippermann, Wolfgang. *The Racial State: Germany 1933–1945.* Cambridge: Cambridge University Press, 1991.

Carlson, Elof Axel. *The Unfit: A History of a Bad Idea.* Woodbury, NY: Cold Spring Harbor Laboratory Press, 2000.

China, People's Republic of. "Presidential Decree No. 33 of 27 October 1994 Promulgating the Law of the People's Republic of China on the Protection of Maternal and Child Health." *International Digest of Health Legislation* 46, no. 1 (1995), 39–42.

Dikötter, Frank. *Imperfect Conceptions: Medical Knowledge, Birth Defects, and Eugenics in China.* New York: Columbia University Press, 1998.

———. "Race Culture: Recent Perspectives on the History of Eugenics." *American Historical Review* 103 (1998), 467–78.

Dowbiggin, Ian Robert. *Keeping America Sane: Psychiatry and Eugenics in the United States and Canada, 1880–1940.* Ithaca, NY: Cornell University Press, 1997.

Dubow, Saul. *Scientific Racism in Modern South Africa.* New York: Cambridge University Press, 1995.

Duster, Troy. *Backdoor to Eugenics.* New York: Routledge, Chapman and Hall, 1990.

Field, Martha A., and Sanchez, Valerie A. *Equal Treatment for People with Mental Retardation: Having and Raising Children.* Cambridge, MA: Harvard University Press, 2001.

Gallagher, Nancy L. *Breeding Better Vermonters: The Eugenics Project in the Green Mountain State.* Hanover, NH: University Press of New England, 1999.

Galton, David J. and Galton, Clare J. "Francis Galton: and Eugenics Today." *Journal of Medical Ethics* 24 (1998), 99–105.

Gillham, Nicholas Wright. *A Life of Sir Frances Galton: From African Exploration to the Birth of Eugenics.* New York: Oxford University Press, 2001.

Haller, Mark H. *Eugenics: Hereditarian Attitudes in American Thought.* New Brunswick, NJ: Rutgers University Press, 1963.

Hesketh, Therese, and Zhu, Wei Xiang. "Maternal and Child Health in China." *British Medical Journal* 314 (1997), 1898–1900.

Kerr, Anne and Shakespeare, Tom. *Genetic Politics: From Eugenics to Genome.* Cheltenham, UK: New Clarion Press, 2002.

Kevles, Daniel J. "Eugenics: I. Historical Aspects." in Warren Thomas Reich, ed., *Encyclopedia of Bioethics.* Rev. ed. New York: Simon & Schuster Macmillan, 1995, 765–70.

———. *In the Name of Eugenics: Genetics and the Uses of Human Heredity.* Cambridge, MA: Harvard University Press, 1995.

King, David S. "Preimplantation Genetic Diagnostic and the 'New' Eugenics." *Journal of Medical Ethics* 25 (1999), 176–82.

Kline, Wendy. *Building of a Better Race: Gender, Sexuality, and Eugenics From the Turn of the Century to the Baby Boom.* Berkeley, CA: University of California Press, 2001.

Kühl, Stefan. *The Nazi Connection: Eugenics, American Racism, and German National Socialism.* New York: Oxford University Press, 2002.

Lappé, Marc. "Eugenics: II. Ethical Issues." In Warren Thomas Reich, ed., *Encyclopedia of Bioethics.* Rev. ed. New York: Simon & Schuster Macmillan, 1995, 770–77.

Larson, Edward J. *Sex, Race, and Science: Eugenics and the Deep South.* Baltimore, MD: Johns Hopkins University Press, 1996.

Lifton, Robert J. *The Nazi Doctors: Medical Killing and the Psychology of Genocide.* New York: Basic Books, 2000.

Ludmerer, Kenneth M. *Genetics and American Society: A Historical Appraisal.* Baltimore: Johns Hopkins University Press, 1972.

Lynn, Richard. *Eugenics: A Reassessment.* Westport, CT: Greenwood, 2001.

McGee, Glenn, and Magus, David. "Eugenics, Ethics." In Thomas H. Murray and Maxwell J. Mehlman, eds., *Encyclopedia of Ethical, Legal, and Policy Issues in Biotechnology.* 2 vols. New York: John Wiley & Sons, 2000, 199–204.

Micklos, David, and Carlson, Elof. "Engineering American Society: The Lesson of Eugenics." *Nature Reviews: Genetics* 1 (2000), 153–58.

Neri, Demetrio. "Eugenics." In *Encyclopedia of Applied Ethics.* vol. 2. San Diego, CA: Academic Press, 1998, 161–73.]

Neumann-Held, Eva M. "Can It Be a 'Sin' to Understand Disease? On 'Genes' and 'Eugenics' and an 'Unconnected Connection.' " *Medicine, Health Care and Philosophy* 4 (2001), 5–17.

Nies, Betsy Lee L. *Eugenic Fantasies: Racial Ideology in the Literature and Popular Culture of the 1920's.* New York: Routledge, 2001.

Paul, Diane B. *Controlling Human Heredity, 1865 to the Present.* Atlantic Highlands, NJ: Humanities Press International, 1995.

———. *The Politics of Heredity: Essays on Eugenics, Biomedicine, and the Nature-Nurture Debate.* Albany, NY: State University of New York Press, 1998.

Pearson, Veronica. "Population Policy and Eugenics in China." *British Journal of Psychiatry* 167 (1995), 1–4.

Pernick, Martin S. *The Black Stork: Eugenics and the Death of "Defective" Babies in American Medicine and Motion Pictures Since 1915.* New York: Oxford University Press, 1999.

———. "Eugenics and Public Health in American History." *American Journal of Public Health* 87 (1997), 1767–72.

Proctor, Robert N. "Genomics and Eugenics: How Fair Is the Comparison?" In George J. Annas and Sherman Elias, eds., *Gene Mapping: Using Law and Ethics as Guides.* New York: Oxford University Press, 1992, 75–93.

———. *Racial Hygiene: Medicine under the Nazis.* Cambridge, MA: Harvard University Press, 1988.

Rafter, Nicole Hahn. *Creating Born Criminals.* Urbana, IL: University of Illinois Press, 1998.

Reilly, Philip R. "Eugenic Sterilization in the United States." In Aubrey Milunsky and George J. Annas, eds., *Genetics and the Law III.* New York: Plenum Press, 1985, 227–241.

———. Eugenics, Ethics, Sterilization Laws." In Thomas H. Murray and Maxwell J. Mehlman, eds., *Encyclopedia of Ethical, Legal, and Policy Issues in Biotechnology.* 2 vols. New York: John Wiley & Sons, 2000, 204–14.

———. *The Surgical Solution: A History of Involuntary Sterilization in the United States.* Baltimore: Johns Hopkins University Press, 1991.

Roll-Hansen, Nils, and Broberg, Gunnar, eds. *Eugenics and the Welfare State: Sterilization Policy in Denmark, Sweden, Norway, and Finland.* East Lansing, MI: Michigan State University Press, 1996.

Romeo-Casabona, Carlos M. "Health and Eugenics Practices: Looking towards the Future." *European Journal of Health Law* 5 (1998), 241–60.

Selden, Steven. *Inheriting Shame: The Story of Eugenics and Racism in America,* New York: Teachers College Press, 1999.

Smith, J. David, and Nelson, K. Ray. *The Sterilization of Carrie Buck.* Far Hills, NJ: New Horizon Press, 1989.

Sofair, Andre N., and Kaldjian, Lauris C. "Eugenic Sterilization and a Qualified Nazi Analogy: The United States and Germany, 1930–1945." *Annals of Internal Medicine* 132 (2000), 312–19.

Stepan, Nancy Leys. *The Hour of Eugenics: Race, Gender, and Nation in Latin America.* Ithaca, NY: Cornell University Press, 1996.

Thomson, Mathew. *Problem of Mental Deficiency: Eugenics and Social Policy in Britain.* New York, Oxford University Press, 1998.

Wachbroit, Robert. "What Is Wrong with Eugenics?" In Edward Erwin, Sidney Gendin, and Lowell Kleiman, eds., *Ethical Issues in Scientific Research.* New York: Garland, 1994, 329–36.

Weindling, Paul. *Health, Race, and German Politics between National Unification and Nazism, 1870–1945.* Cambridge: Cambridge University Press, 1989.

Zenderland, Leila. *Measuring Minds: Henry Herbert Goddard and the Origins of American Intelligence Testing.* New York: Cambridge University Press, 1997.

THE HUMAN GENOME PROJECT

Andrews, Lori B., et al., Institute of Medicine, Committee on Assessing Risks. *Assessing Genetic Risks: Implications for Health and Social Policy.* Washington, DC. National Academy Press, 1994.

Balint Peter J., ed. *The Human Genome Project and Minority Communities: Ethical, Social, and Political Dilemmas.* Westport, CT: Greenwood, 2000.

Bishop, Jerry E., and Waldholz, Michael. *Genome: The Story of the Most Astonishing Scientific Adventure of Our Time—The Attempt to Map All the Genes in the Human Body.* New York: Simon & Schuster, 1990.

Bloom, Barry R., and Trach, Dang Duc. "Genetics and Developing Countries." *British Medical Journal* 322 (2001), 1006–1007.

Boyle, Philip J., et al. "Genetic Grammar: 'Health,' 'Illness,' and the Human Genome Project." *Hastings Center Report* 22 (July–August 1992; Supplement), S1–S20.

Brock, Dan W. "The Human Genome Project and Human Identity." In Robert F. Weir, Susan C. Lawrence, and Evan Fales, eds., *Genes and Human Self-Knowledge: Historical and Philosophical Reflections on Modern Genetics.* Iowa City: Iowa University Press, 1994: 18–33.

Buchanan, Allen, et al. *From Chance to Choice: Genetics and Justice.* New York: Cambridge University Press, 2000.

Cantor, Charles R. "How Will the Human Genome Project Improve Our Quality of Life?" *Nature Biotechnology* 16 (1998), 212–13.

Capron, Morgan Alexander. "Which Ills to Bear? Reevaluating the 'Threat' of Modern Genetics." *Emory Law Journal* 39 (1990), 665–96.

Clayton, Ellen W. "Through the Lens of the Sequence." *Genome Research* 11 (2001), 659–64.

Collins, Francis S. "Medical and Ethical Consequences of the Human Genome Project." *Journal of Clinical Ethics* 2 (1991), 260–67.

———. "Ahead of Schedule and under Budget: The Genome Project Passes Its Fifth Birthday." *Proceedings of the National Academy of Sciences* 92 (1995), 10821–23.

———. "Contemplating the End of the Beginning." *Genome Research* 11 (2001), 641–43.

———; Guyer, Mark S.; and Chakravarti, Aravinda. "Variations on a Theme: Cataloging Human DNA Sequence Variation." *Science* (1997), 1580–81.

Cook-Deegan, Robert M. *The Gene Wars: Science, Politics, and the Human Genome.* New York: W. W. Norton, 1993.

———. "Genome Mapping and Sequencing." in Warren Thomas Reich, ed., *Encyclopedia of Bioethics.* Rev. ed. New York: Simon & Schuster Macmillan, 1995, 1011–20.

Ganten, Detlev. "James D. Watson at the Congress of Molecular Medicine." *Journal of Molecular Medicine* 75 (1997), 615–17.

Glasner, Peter, et al., eds. *Genetic Imaginations: Ethical, Legal and Social Issues in Human Genome Research.* Aldershot, Hampshire, UK: Ashgate, 1998.

Green, Eric D., and Chakravarti, Aravinda. "The Human Genome Sequence Expedition: View from the 'Base Camp.' " *Genome Research* 11 (2001), 645–51.

Hanna, Kathi E. "The Ethical, Legal, and Social Implications Program of the National Center for Human Genome Research: A Missed Opportunity?" In Ruth Ellen Bulger, Elizabeth Meyer Bobby, and Harvey F. Fineberg, eds. Institute of Medicine, Committee on the Social and Ethical Impacts of Developments in Biomedicine. *Society's Choices: Social and Ethical Decision Making in Biomedicine.* Washington, DC: National Academy Press, 1995, 432–57.

Hedgecoe, Adam M. "Genome Analysis." In Ruth Chadwick, ed., *Encyclopedia of Applied Ethics.* San Diego, CA: Academic Press, 1998, 463–70.

Holtzman, Neil A. "Putting the Search for Genes in Perspective." *International Journal of Health Services* 31 (2001), 445–61.

Institute of Physics. "The Human Genome Project—What's the Public Got to Do with It?" *Public Understanding of Science* 8 (1999), 153–59.

Juengst, Eric T. "Respecting Human Subjects in Genome Research: A Preliminary Policy Agenda." In Harold Y. Vanderpool, ed., *The Ethics of Research Involving Human Subjects: Facing the Twenty-First Century.* Frederick, MD: University Publishing Group, 1996, 401–29.

———. "Self-Critical Federal Science? The Ethics Experiment within the U.S. Human Genome Project." *Social Philosophy and Policy* 13 (1996), 63–95.

Kaveny, M. Cathleen. "Jurisprudence and Genetics." *Health Progress* (March–April 2001), 43–47, 78.

Kevles, Daniel J., and Hood, Leroy, eds. *The Code of Codes: Scientific and Social Issues in the Human Genome Project*. Cambridge, MA: Harvard University Press, 1993.

Koonin, Steven E. "An Independent Perspective on the Human Genome Project." *Science* (1998), 36–37.

Lapham, E. Virginia, et al. "Genetic Discrimination: Perspectives of Consumers." *Science* 274 (1996), 621–24.

Lenoir, Noelle. "UNESCO, Genetics, and Human Rights." *Kennedy Institute of Ethics Journal* 7 (1997), 31–42.

Lewontin, Richard C. *It Ain't Necessarily So: The Dream of the Human Genome and Other Illusions*. New York: New York Review of Books, 2001.

McKusick, Victor A. "The Human Genome Project: Plans, Status, and Applications in Biology and Medicine." In George J. Annas and Sherman Elias, eds., *Genome Mapping: Using Law and Ethics as Guides*. New York: Oxford University Press, 1992, 18–42.

Mehlman, Maxwell J. and Botkin, Jeffrey R. *Access to the Genome: The Challenge of Equality*. Washington, DC: Georgetown University Press, 1998.

Meslin, Eric M., Thomson, Elizabeth J., and Boyer, Joy T. "The Ethical, Legal, and Social Implications Research Program at the National Human Genome Research Institute." *Kennedy Institute of Ethics Journal* 7 (1997), 291–98.

Murray, Thomas H., Rothstein, Mark A., and Murray, Robert F. Jr., eds. *The Human Genome Project and the Future of Health Care*. Bloomington and Indianapolis, IN: Indiana University Press, 1996.

National Research Council. *Mapping and Sequencing the Human Genome*. Washington, DC: National Academy Press, 1988.

Olson, Maynard V. "The Human Genome Project." *Proceedings of the National Academy of Sciences* 90 (1993), 4338–44.

Peters, Ted, ed. *Genetics: Issues of Social Justice*. Cleveland, OH: Pilgrim Press, 1998.

Ridley, Matt. *Genome: The Autobiography of a Species in 23 Chapters*. New York: HarperCollins, 2000.

Rosenberg, Alexander. "The Human Genome Project: Research Tactics and Economic Strategies." *Social Philosophy and Policy* 13 (1996), 1–17.

Rothman, Barbara Katz. *The Book of Life: A Personal and Ethical Guide to Race, Normality, and the Implications of the Human Genome Project*. Boston, MA: Beacon Press, 2001.

———. *Genetic Maps and Human Imaginations: The Limits of Science in Understanding Who We Are*. New York: W. W. Norton, 1998.

———. "Of Maps and Imaginations: Sociology Confronts the Genome." *Social Problems* 42 (1995), 1–10.

Rothstein, Mark A., ed. *Legal and Ethical Issues Raised by the Human Genome Project*. Houston, TX: University of Houston, Health Law and Policy Institute, 1991.

Rowen, Lee, Mahairas, Gregory, and Hood, Lee. "Sequencing the Human Genome." *Science* 278 (1997), 605–607.

Sloan, Philip R., ed. *Controlling Our Destinies: The Human Genome Project from Historical, Philosophical, Social, and Ethical Perspectives*. Notre Dame, IN: University of Notre Dame Press, 1997.

United Nations Educational, Scientific, and Cultural Organization. *Universal Declaration on the Human Genome and Human Rights*. Paris: UNESCO, 1997.

U.S. Congress, Office of Technology Assessment. *Mapping Our Genes—The Genome Projects: How Big, How Fast?* Washington, DC: U.S. Government Printing Office, April 1988.

Venter, J. Craig, et al. "Shotgun Sequencing of the Human Genome." *Science* 280 (1998), 1540–42.

Wade, Nicholas. *Life Script: How the Human Genome Discoveries Will Transform Medicine and Enhance Your Health*. New York: Simon & Schuster, 2001.

Watson, James D. *A Passion for DNA: Genes, Genomes, and Society*. Woodbury, NY: Cold Spring Harbor Laboratory Press, 2000.

———, et al. *The Human Genome*. New York: Palgrave Macmillan, 2001.

Weiss, Kenneth M. "In Search of Human Variation." *Genome Research* 8 (1998): 691–97.

World Health Organization, Advisory Committee on Health Research. *Genomics and World Health*. Geneva: World Health Organization, 2002.

GENETIC TESTING AND SCREENING, GENETIC INFORMATION

AAAS-ABA National Conference of Lawyers and Scientists and AAAS Committee on Scientific Freedom and Responsibility. *The Genome, Ethics, and the Law: Issues in Genetic Testing*. Washington, DC: American Association for the Advancement of Science, 1992.

Advisory Committee on Genetic Testing. *Code of Practice and Guidance on Human Genetic Testing Services Supplied to the Public*. London: Her Majesty's Stationery Office, 1997.

American Medical Association, Council on Ethical and Judicial Affairs, "Use of Genetic Testing by Employers." *Journal of the American Medical Association* 266 (1991), 1827–30.

Anderlik, Mary R., and Pentz, Rebecca D. "Genetic Information, Legal, Genetic Privacy Laws." In Thomas H. Murray and Maxwell J. Mehlman, eds., *Encyclopedia of Ethical, Legal, and Policy Issues in Biotechnology*. 2 vols. New York: John Wiley & Sons, 2000, 456–68.

Anderlik, Mary R. "Genetic Information, Legal, Genetics and the Americans with Disabilities Act." In Thomas H. Murray and Maxwell J. Mehlman, eds., *Encyclopedia of Ethical, Legal, and Policy Issues in Biotechnology*. 2 vols. New York: John Wiley & Sons, 2000, 468–78.

Andre, Judith, et al. "On Being Genetically 'Irresponsible.' " *Kennedy Institute of Ethics Journal* 10 (2000), 129–46.

Andrews, Lori B. *Future Perfect: Confronting Decisions about Genetics*. New York: Columbia University Press, 2001.

———, et al. Institute of Medicine, Committee on Assessing Genetic Risks. *Assessing Genetic Risks: Implications for Health and Social Policy*. Washington, DC: National Academy Press, 1994.

Annas, George J. "The Limits of State Laws to Protect Genetic Information." *New England Journal of Medicine* 345 (2001), 385–88.

Association of British Insurers. *Genetic Testing: ABI Code of Practice*. London: ABI, 1997.

Bartels, Dianne M., LeRoy, Bonnie S., and Caplan, Arthur L., eds. *Prescribing Our Future: Ethical Challenges in Genetic Counseling*. New York: Aldine De Gruyter, 1993.

Biesecker, Barbara Bowles. "Reproduction, Ethics, The Ethics of Reproductive Genetic Counseling: Nondirectiveness." In

Thomas H. Murray and Maxwell J. Mehlman, eds., *Encyclopedia of Ethical, Legal, and Policy Issues in Biotechnology.* 2 vols. New York: John Wiley & Sons, 2000, 977–983

Billings, Paul R., ed. *DNA on Trial: Genetic Identification and Criminal Justice*. Plainview, NY: Cold Spring Harbor Laboratory Press, 1992.

———, et al. "Discrimination as a Consequence of Genetic Testing." *American Journal of Human Genetics* 50 (1992), 476–82.

Bobinski, Mary Anne. "Genetic Information, Legal, ERISA Preemption, and HIPAA Protection." In Thomas H. Murray and Maxwell J. Mehlman, eds., *Encyclopedia of Ethical, Legal, and Policy Issues in Biotechnology.* 2 vols. New York: John Wiley & Sons, 2000, 427–40.

Botkin, Jeffrey R. "Reproduction, Law, Wrongful Birth, and Wrongful Life Actions." In Thomas H. Murray and Maxwell J. Mehlman, eds., *Encyclopedia of Ethical, Legal, and Policy Issues in Biotechnology.* 2 vols. New York: John Wiley & Sons, 2000, 996–1003.

Burke, Wylie, et al. "Recommendations for Follow-Up Care for Individuals with an Inherited Predisposition to Cancer. I. Hereditary Nonpolyposis Colon Cancer. Cancer Genetics Studies Consortium." *Journal of the American Medical Association* 277 (1997), 915–19.

Chadwick, Ruth, et al., eds. *The Ethics of Genetic Screening.* New York: Kluwer Academic Publishers, 1999.

———, et al. "Euroscreen 2: Towards Community Policy on Insurance, Commercialization and Public Awareness." *Journal of Medicine and Philosophy* 26 (2001), 263–72.

Clark, A. J. J., et al. *The Genetic Testing of Children.* Philadelphia, PA: Coronet Books, 1997.

Clayton, Ellen Wright. "Genetic Testing in Children." *Journal of Medicine and Philosophy* 22 (1997), 233–51.

———. "Genetic Testing Is Different." *Journal of Health Politics, Policy and Law* 26 (2001), 457–64.

Cunningham, George S. "Genetic Information, Legal, Regulating Genetic Services." In Thomas H. Murray and Maxwell J. Mehlman, eds., *Encyclopedia of Ethical, Legal, and Policy Issues in Biotechnology.* 2 vols. New York: John Wiley & Sons, 2000, 478–83.

DeGrazia, David. "The Ethical Justification for Minimal Paternalism in the Use of the Predictive Test for Huntington's Disease." *Journal of Clinical Ethics* 2 (1991), 219–28.

Doherty, Peter and Sutton, Agneta, eds. *Man-Made Man: Ethical and Legal Issues in Genetics.* Portland, OR: Four Courts Press, 1997.

Evans, James P., et al. "The Complexities of Predictive Genetic Testing." *British Medical Journal* 322 (2001), 1052–56.

Giannelli, Paul, Hoffman, Sharona, Wagner, Wendy. "Genetic Information, Law, Legal Issues in Law Enforcement DNA Databanks." In Thomas H. Murray and Maxwell J. Mehlman, eds., *Encyclopedia of Ethical, Legal, and Policy Issues in Biotechnology.* 2 vols. New York: Johns Wiley & Sons, 2000, 413–26.

Gostin, Larry. Genetic Discrimination: The Use of Genetically Based Diagnostic and Prognostic Tests by Employers and Insurers." *American Journal of Law and Medicine* 17 (1991), 109–44.

Grodin, Michael A., et al. "Susceptibility Genes and Neurological Disorders." *Archives of Neurology* 57 (2000), 1569–74.

Hoedemaekers, Rogeer, ten-Have, Henk, and Chadwick, Ruth. "Genetic Screening: A Comparative Analysis of Three Recent Reports." *Journal of Medical Ethics* 23 (1997), 135–41.

Holtzman, Neil A. *Proceed with Caution: Predicting Genetic Risks in the Recombinant DNA Era.* Baltimore: Johns Hopkins University Press, 1989.

———, and Watson, Michael S., eds. *Promoting Safe and Effective Genetic Testing in the United States: Final Report of the Task Force on Genetic Testing.* Baltimore, MD: Johns Hopkins University Press, 1998.

———, and Shapiro, David. "Genetic Testing and Public Policy." *British Medical Journal* 316 (1998), 852–56.

———, et al. "Predictive Genetic Testing: From Basic Research to Clinical Practice." *Science* 278 (1997), 602–605.

Huang, Anny. "Genetic Information, Legal, FDA Regulation of Genetic Testing." In Thomas H. Murray and Maxwell J. Mehlman, eds., *Encyclopedia of Ethical, Legal, and Policy Issues in Biotechnology.* 2 vols. New York: Johns Wiley & Sons, 2000, 441–55.

Hudson, Kathy L., et al. "Genetic Discrimination and Health Insurance: An Urgent Need for Reform." *Science* 270 (1995), 391–93.

Juengst, Eric T. "Genetic Information, Ethics, Family Issues." In Thomas H. Murray and Maxwell J. Mehlman, eds., *Encyclopedia of Ethical, Legal, and Policy Issues in Biotechnology.* 2 vols. New York: Johns Wiley & Sons, 2000, 390–96.

Kass, Nancy F. "The Implications of Genetic Testing for Health and Life Insurance." In Mark A. Rothstein, ed. *Genetic Secrets.* New Haven: Yale University Press, 1997, 299–316.

Koenig, Barbara A., et al. "Genetics Testing for BRCA1 and BRCA2: Recommendations of the Stanford Program in Genomics, Ethics, and Society." *Journal of Women's Health* 7 (1998), 531–45.

Knoppers, Bartha M. "Cancer Genetics: A Model for Multifactorial Conditions?" *Medicine and Law* 20 (2001), 177–82.

Laurie, Graeme. *Genetic Privacy: A Challenge to Medico-Legal Norms.* New York: Cambridge University Press, 2002.

Lerman, Caryn, et al. "BRCA1 Testing in Families with Hereditary Breast-Ovarian Cancer: A Prospective Study of Patient Decision Making and Outcomes." *Journal of the American Medical Association* 275 (1996), 1885–92.

Lippman, Abby. "Prenatal Genetic Testing and Screening: Constructing Needs and Reinforcing Inequities." *American Journal of Law and Medicine* 17 (1991), 15–50.

Long, Clarisa, ed. *Genetic Testing and Use of Information.* Washington, DC: The American Enterprise Institute for Public Policy Research, 1999.

Marshall, Eliot. "Fast Technology Drives New World of Newborn Screening." *Science* 294 (2001), 2272–74.

Marteau, Theresa M., and Crooyle, Robert T. "Psychological Responses to Genetic Testing." *British Medical Journal* 316 (1998), 693–96.

Matthews, Anne L. "Genetic Counseling." In Thomas H. Murray and Maxwell J. Mehlman, eds., *Encyclopedia of Ethical, Legal, and Policy Issues in Biotechnology.* 2 vols. New York: Johns Wiley & Sons, 2000, 342–52.

Naser, Curtis, and Alpert, Sheri. "Genetic Information, Ethics, Ethical Issues in Tissue Banking and Human Subject Research in Stored Tissues." In Thomas H. Murray and Maxwell J. Mehlman, eds., *Encyclopedia of Ethical, Legal, and Policy Issues in Biotechnology.* 2 vols. New York: Johns Wiley & Sons, 2000, 363–89.

National Academy of Sciences, Committee on DNA Technology in Forensic Science. *DNA Technology in Forensic Science*. Washington, DC: National Academy Press, 1992.

National Research Council, Committee for the Study of Inborn Errors of Metabolism. *Genetic Screening: Programs, Principles and Research*. Washington, DC: National Academy of Science, 1975.

Natowicz, Marvin R., Alper, Jane K., and Alper, Joseph S. "Genetic Discrimination and the Law." *American Journal of Human Genetics* 50 (1992), 465–75.

Neitzel, Heidemarie, et al., eds. *The New Genetics: From Research into Health Care: Social and Ethical Implications for Users and Providers*. New York: Springer-Verlag, 2001.

Nelkin, Dorothy, and Tancredi, Laurence. *Dangerous Diagnostics: The Social Power of Biological Information*. Chicago, IL: University of Chicago Press, 1994.

New York State Task Force on Life and the Law. *Genetic Testing and Screening in the Age of Genomic Medicine*. New York: The Task Force, November 2000.

Nuffield Council on Bioethics. *Genetic Screening: Ethical Issues*. London: The Council, 1993.

Organization for Economic Cooperation and Development (OECD) Staff. *Genetic Testing: Policy Issues For the New Millenium*. Organization for Economic Cooperation and Development, 2001.

Pagon, Roberta A., et al. "Genetic Testing." *Western Journal of Medicine* 174 (2001), 344–47.

Parens, Erik, Asch, Adrienne, and Powell, Cynthia. "Reproduction, Ethics, Prenatal Testing and the Disability Rights Critique." In Thomas H. Murray and Maxwell J. Mehlman, eds., *Encyclopedia of Ethical, Legal, and Policy Issues in Biotechnology*. 2 vols. New York: Johns Wiley & Sons, 2000, 957–69.

Peterson, James C. *Genetic Turning Points: The Ethics of Human Genetic Intervention*. Grand Rapids: William B. Eerdmans, 2001.

Powers, Madison. "Genetic Information, Ethics, Privacy and Confidentiality: Overview." In Thomas H. Murray and Maxwell J. Mehlman, eds., *Encyclopedia of Ethical, Legal, and Policy Issues in Biotechnology*. 2 vols. New York: John Wiley & Sons, 2000, 405–13.

———. "Privacy and the Control of Genetic Information." In Mark S. Frankel, and Albert Teich, eds., *The Genetic Frontier: Ethics, Law, and Policy*. Washington, DC: American Association for the Advancement of Science, 1994, 77–100.

Quaid, Kimberly A. "Genetic Information, Ethics, Informed Consent to Testing and Screening." In Thomas H. Murray and Maxwell J. Mehlman, eds., *Encyclopedia of Ethical, Legal, and Policy Issues in Biotechnology*. 2 vols. New York: Johns Wiley & Sons, 2000, 397–405.

Robertson, John A. "Ethical and Legal Issues in Preimplantation Genetic Screening." *Fertility and Sterility* 57 (1992), 1–11.

———. "Genetic Selection of Offspring Characteristics." *Boston University Law Review* 76 (1996), 421–82.

Rothman, Barbara Katz. *The Tentative Pregnancy: Prenatal Diagnosis and the Future of Motherhood*. New York: Viking Penguin, 1986.

Rothenberg, Karen H. "Genetic Information and Health Insurance: State Legislative Approaches." *Journal of Law, Medicine, and Ethics* 23 (1995), 312–19.

———, and Thomson, Elizabeth J., eds. *Women and Prenatal Testing. Facing the Challenges of Genetic Technology*. Columbus, OH: Ohio State University Press, 1994.

———, et al. "Genetic Information and the Workplace: Legislative Approaches and Policy Challenges." *Science* 275 (1997), 1755–57.

Rothstein, Mark A., ed. *Genetic Secrets: Protecting Privacy and Confidentiality in the Genetic Era*. New Haven: Yale University Press, 1997.

Shi, Michael M., and Bleavins, Michael R. "Pharmacogenetics." In Thomas H. Murray and Maxwell J. Mehlman, eds., *Encyclopedia of Ethical, Legal, and Policy Issues in Biotechnology*. 2 vols. New York: Johns Wiley & Sons, 2000, 880–88.

Smith, David H., et al. *Early Warning: Cases and Ethical Guidance for Presymptomatic Testing in Genetic Diseases*. Bloomington, IN: Indiana University Press, 1998.

Takala, Tuija. "Who Should Know about Our Genetic Makeup and Why? *Western Journal of Medicine* 175 (2001), 260–63.

Tauer, Carol A. "Genetic Testing and Discrimination." *Health Progress* (March–April 2001), 48–53, 71.

———. "Personal Privacy and the Common Good." *Health Progress* (March–April 2001), 36–42, 78.

Testart, Jacques. "The New Eugenics and Medicalized Reproduction." *Cambridge Quarterly of Healthcare Ethics* 4 (1995), 304–12.

Thomson, Elizabeth J., et al., eds. *Genetics and Public Health in the Twenty-First Century: Using Genetic Information to Improve Health and Prevent Disease*. New York: Oxford University Press, 2000.

U.S. Congress, Office of Technology Assessment. *Cystic Fibrosis and DNA Tests: Implications of Carrier Screening*. Washington, DC: U.S. Government Printing Office, August 1992.

———. *Genetic Monitoring and Screening in the Workplace*. Washington, DC: U.S. Government Printing Office, October 1990.

———. *Genetic Witness: Forensic Uses of DNA Tests*. Washington, DC: U.S. Government Printing Office, July 1990.

U.S. President's Commission for the Study of Ethical Problems in Medicine and Biomedical and Behavioral Research. *Screening and Counseling for Genetic Conditions*. Washington, DC: U.S. Government Printing Office, February 1983.

Welch, Charles A. "Sacred Secrets—The Privacy of Medical Records." *New England Journal of Medicine* 345 (2001), 371–72.

Wertz, Dorothy C., and Fletcher, John C., eds. *Ethics and Human Genetics: A Cross-Cultural Perspective*. Berlin and New York: Springer-Verlag, 1989.

Whitehouse, Peter J. and Post, Stephen G., eds. *Genetic Testing for Alzheimer Disease: Ethical and Clinical Issues*. Baltimore, MD: Johns Hopkins University Press, 1998.

Wolf, Susan M. "Beyond 'Genetic Discrimination': Toward the Broader Harm of Geneticism." *Journal of Law, Medicine and Ethics* 23 (1995), 345–53.

Xin, Mao, and Wertz, Dorothy C. "China's Genetics Services Providers' Attitudes towards Several Ethical Issues: A Cross-Cultural Survey." *Clinical Genetics* 52 (1997), 100–109.

Zallen, Doris Teichler. *Does It Run in the Family? A Consumers Guide to DNA Testing for Genetic Disorders*. Piscataway, NJ: Rutgers University Press, 1997.

HUMAN GENE TRANSFER RESEARCH AND GERM-LINE GENETIC INTERVENTION

Ackerman, Terrence F. and Nienhuis, Arthur W., eds. *Ethics of Cancer Genetics and Gene Therapy*. Totowa, NJ: Humana Press, 2001.

Agius, Emmanuel, et al., eds. *Germ-Line Intervention and Our Responsibilities to Future Generations, Vol. 55*. New York: Kluwer Academic Publishers, 1998.

Anderson, W. French. "Human Gene Therapy." *Science* 256 (1992), 808–13.

———. "Human Gene Therapy." *Nature* 392 Supplement (1998), 25–30.

———. "Excitement in Gene Therapy." *Human Gene Therapy* 12 (2001), 1483–84.

Billings, Paul R., et al. "Human Germline Gene Modification: A Dissent." *Lancet* 353 (1999), 1873–75.

Bonnicksen, Andrea A. "Gene Therapy, Ethics, and International Perspectives." In Thomas H. Murray and Maxwell J. Mehlman, eds., *Encyclopedia of Ethical, Legal, and Policy Issues in Biotechnology.* 2 vols. New York: Johns Wiley & Sons, 2000, 275–85.

Boylan, Michael, and Brown, Kevin E. *Genetic Engineering: Science and Ethics on the New Frontier.* Upper Saddle River, NJ: Pearson Education, 2001.

Clark, William R. *The New Healers.* New York: Oxford University Press, 1999.

Fletcher, John C., and Anderson, W. French. "Germ-Line Gene Therapy: A New Stage of Debate." *Law, Medicine and Health Care* 20 (1992), 26–39.

———, and Richter, Gerd. "Human Fetal Gene Therapy: Moral and Ethical Questions." *Human Gene Therapy* 7 (1996), 1605–14.

Fowler, Gregory, Juengst, Eric T., and Zimmerman, Burke K. "Germ-Line Gene Therapy and the Clinical Ethos of Medical Genetics." *Theoretical Medicine* 10 (1989), 151–65.

Frankel, Mark S., and "Facing Inheritable Genetic Modifications." *Science* 292 (2001), 1303.

———. *Human Inheritable Genetic Modifications: Assessing Scientific, Ethical, Religious, and Policy Issues.* Washington, DC: American Association for the Advancement of Science, 2000.

Friedmann, Theodore, ed. *The Development of Human Gene Therapy.* New York: Cold Spring Harbor Laboratory Press, 1999.

———. "The Evolution of Public Review and Oversight Mechanisms in Human Gene Transfer Research: Joint Roles of the FDA and NIH." *Current Opinion in Biotechnology* 12 (2001), 304–307.

———. *Gene Therapy: Fact and Fiction in Biology's New Approaches to Disease.* Woodbury, NY: Cold Spring Harbor Laboratory Press, 1994.

Gura, Trisha. "After a Setback, Gene Therapy Progresses . . . Gingerly." *Science* 291 (2001), 1692–97.

Hedgecoe, Adam M. "Gene Therapy." In Ruth Chadwick, ed. *Encyclopedia of Applied Ethics.* San Diego, CA: Academic Press, 1998, 383–90.

High, Katherine A. "Gene Therapy: A 2001 Perspective." *Haemophilia* 7 (2001), suppl. 1, 23–27.

Juengst, Eric T., ed. "Human Germ-Line Engineering." *Journal of Medicine and Philosophy* 16 (1991), 587–694. Thematic issue.

Kaji, Eugene H., and Leiden, Jeffrey M. "Gene and Stem Cell Therapies." *Journal of the American Medical Association* 285 (2001), 545–50.

Knight, Jonathan. "Biology's Last Taboo." *Nature* 413 (2001), 12–15.

Lyon, Jeff. *Altered Facts: Gene Therapy and the Retooling of Human Life.* New York: W. W. Norton, 1996.

McKenny, Gerald P. "Gene Therapy, Ethics, Religious Perspectives." In Thomas H. Murray and Maxwell J. Mehlman, eds., *Encyclopedia of Ethical, Legal, and Policy Issues in Biotechnology.* 2 vols. New York: Johns Wiley & Sons, 2000, 300–311.

Nelson, Robert. "Gene Therapy, Ethics, Germ Cell Gene Transfer." In Thomas H. Murray and Maxwell J. Mehlman, eds., *Encyclopedia of Ethical, Legal, and Policy Issues in Biotechnology.* 2 vols. New York: Johns Wiley & Sons, 2000, 292–300.

Nichols, Eve K., and Institute of Medicine, National Academy of Sciences. *Human Gene Therapy.* Cambridge, MA: Harvard University Press, 1988.

Pollack, Andrew. "Gene Therapy's Focus Shifts from Rare Illness." *New York Times,* August 4, 1998, p. F1.

Proctor, Robert N. "Genomics and Eugenics: How Fair Is the Comparison?" In George J. Annas and Sherman Elias, eds., *Gene Mapping: Using Law and Ethics as Guides.* New York: Oxford University Press, 1992, 75–93.

Resnik, David B. *Human Germ-Line Therapy: Scientific, Moral and Political Issues.* Georgetown, TX: Landes Bioscience, 1999.

Ross, Gail, et al. "Gene Therapy in the United States: A Five-Year Status Report." *Human Gene Therapy* 7 (1996), 1781–90.

Simon, Jurgen W., et al. *Interdisciplinary Approaches to Gene Therapy: Legal, Ethical, and Scientific Aspects.* New York: Springer, 1997.

Stock, Gregory, and Campbell, John eds. *Engineering the Human Germline: An Exploration of the Science and Ethics of Altering the Genes We Pass to Our Children.* New York: Oxford University Press, 2000.

Szebik, Imre, and Glass, Kathleen C. "Ethical Issues of Human Germ-Cell Therapy: A Preparation for Public Discussion." *Academic Medicine* 76 (2001), 32–38.

Tauer, Carol A. "Gene Therapy, Ethics, Gene Therapy for Fetuses and Embryos." In Thomas H. Murray and Maxwell J. Mehlman, eds., *Encyclopedia of Ethical, Legal, and Policy Issues in Biotechnology.* 2 vols. New York: Johns Wiley & Sons, 2000, 285–292.

Thompson, Larry. *Correcting the Code: Inventing the Genetic Cure for the Human Body.* New York: Simon & Schuster, 1994.

U.K. Department of Health, Gene Therapy Advisory Committee. "Guidance on Making Proposals to Conduct Gene Therapy Research on Human Subjects." *Human Gene Therapy* 12 (2001), 711–20.

U.S. President's Commission for the Study of Ethical Problems in Medicine and Biomedical and Behavioral Research. *Splicing Life: A Report on the Social and Ethical Issues of Genetic Engineering with Human Beings.* Washington, DC: U.S. Government Printing Office, November 1982.

Walters, LeRoy. "Ethical Issues in Human Gene Therapy." *Journal of Clinical Ethics* 2 (1991), 267–74.

———. "Human Gene Therapy: Ethics and Public Policy." *Human Gene Therapy* 2 (1991), 115–22.

Walters, LeRoy. "Gene Therapy: Overview." In Thomas H. Murray and Maxwell J. Mehlman, eds., *Encyclopedia of Ethical, Legal, and Policy Issues in Biotechnology.* 2 vols. New York: Johns Wiley & Sons, 2000, 336–42.

———, and Palmer, Julie G. "Germ-Line Gene Therapy." *The Ethics of Human Gene Therapy.* New York: Oxford University Press, 1997, 60–98.

———, and Palmer, Julie Gage. *The Ethics of Human Gene Therapy.* New York: Oxford University Press, 1997.

Willgoos, Christine. "FDA Regulation: An Answer to the Questions of Human Cloning and Germline Gene Therapy." *American Journal of Law & Medicine* 27 (2001), 101–24.

Wivel, Nelson A. "Gene Therapy, Ethics, Somatic Cell Gene Therapy." In Thomas H. Murray and Maxwell J. Mehlman, eds., *Encyclopedia of Ethical, Legal, and Policy Issues in Biotechnology.* 2 vols. New York: Johns Wiley & Sons, 2000, 310–21.

Wivel, Nelson A., and Walters, LeRoy. "Germ-Line Gene Modification and Disease Prevention: Some Medical and Ethical Perspectives." *Science* 262 (1993), 533–38.

GENETIC ENHANCEMENT

Cole-Turner, Ronald. "Do Means Matter? Evaluating Technologies of Human Enhancement." In Erik Parens, ed., *Enhancing Human Traits: Ethical and Social Implications.* Washington, DC: Georgetown University Press, 1998, 151–61.

Daniels, Norman. "Normal Functioning and the Treatment-Enhancement Distinction." *Cambridge Quarterly of Healthcare Ethics* 9 (2000), 309–22.

Engelhardt, Tristram H. "Germ-Line Genetics Engineering and Moral Diversity: Moral Controversies in a Post-Christian World." *Social Philosophy and Policy* 13 (1996), 47–62.

Gardner, William. "Can Human Genetic Enhancement Be Prohibited?" *Journal of Medicine and Philosophy* 20 (1995), 65–84.

Glover, Jonathan. *What Sort of People Should There Be?* New York: Penguin Books, 1984.

Juengst, Eric T. "Can Enhancement Be Distinguished from Prevention in Genetic Medicine?" *Journal of Medicine and Philosophy* 22 (1997), 125–42.

———. "Human Enhancement Uses of Biotechnology, Ethics, The Ethics of Enhancement." In Thomas H. Murray and Maxwell J. Mehlman, eds., *Encyclopedia of Ethical, Legal, and Policy Issues in Biotechnology.* 2 vols. New York: Johns Wiley & Sons, 2000, 503–07.

McKenny, Gerald. "Human Enhancement Uses of Biotechnology, Ethics, Therapy vs. Enhancement." In Thomas H. Murray and Maxwell J. Mehlman, eds., *Encyclopedia of Ethical, Legal, and Policy Issues in Biotechnology.* 2 vols. New York: Johns Wiley & Sons, 2000, 507–15.

Mehlman, Maxwell J. "Human Enhancement Uses of Biotechnology, Law, Genetic Enhancement, and the Regulation of Acquired Genetic Advantages. In Thomas H. Murray and Maxwell J. Mehlman, eds., *Encyclopedia of Ethical, Legal, and Policy Issues in Biotechnology.* 2 vols. New York: Johns Wiley & Sons, 2000, 515–27.

Muller, Hermann J. "The Guidance of Human Evolution." *Perspectives in Biology and Medicine* 3, (1959), 1–43.

Parens, Erik, ed. *Enhancing Human Traits: Ethical and Social Implications*. Washington, DC: Georgetown University Press, 1998.

Resnik, David B. "The Moral Significance of the Therapy-Enhancement Distinction in Human Genetics." *Cambridge Quarterly of Healthcare Ethics* 9 (2000), 365–77.

Scully, Jackie Leach, and Rehmann-Sutter, Christoph. "When Norms Normalize: The Case of Genetic 'Enhancement.' " *Human Gene Therapy* 12 (2001), 87–95.

Shapiro, Michael H. "Human Enhancement Uses of Biotechnology, Policy, Technological Enhancement, and Human Equality. In Thomas H. Murray and Maxwell J. Mehlman, eds., *Encyclopedia of Ethical, Legal, and Policy Issues in Biotechnology.* 2 vols. New York: Johns Wiley & Sons, 2000, 527–48.

Stock, Gregory. *Redesigning Humans: Our Inevitable Genetic Future.* Boston, MA: Houghton Mifflin, 2002.

Wachbroit, Robert. "Human Enhancement Uses of Biotechnology: Overview." In Thomas H. Murray and Maxwell J. Mehlman, eds., *Encyclopedia of Ethical, Legal, and Policy Issues in Biotechnology.* 2 vols. New York: Johns Wiley & Sons, 2000, 549–52.

Walters, LeRoy, and Palmer, Julie G. "Enhancement Genetic Engineering." *The Ethics of Human Gene Therapy*. New York: Oxford University Press, 1997, 99–142.

Whitehouse, Peter J., and Marling, Cynthia R. "Human Enhancement Uses of Biotechnology, Ethics, Cognitive Enhancement." In Thomas H. Murray and Maxwell J. Mehlman, eds., *Encyclopedia of Ethical, Legal, and Policy Issues in Biotechnology.* 2 vols. New York: Johns Wiley & Sons, 2000, 485–91.

GENE PATENTS

Brody, Baruch A. "Protecting Human Dignity and the Patenting of Human Genes." In Audrey R. Chapman, ed., *Perspectives on Genetic Patenting.* Washington, DC: American Association for the Advancement of Science, 1999, 111–26.

Chapman, Audrey R., ed. *Perspectives on Genetic Patenting.* Washington, DC: American Association for the Advancement of Science, 1999.

Cole-Turner, Ronald. "Patents and Licensing, Ethics, Organizations with Prominent Positions on Gene Patenting." In Thomas H. Murray and Maxwell J. Mehlman, eds., *Encyclopedia of Ethical, Legal, and Policy Issues in Biotechnology.* 2 vols. New York: Johns Wiley & Sons, 2000, 834–44.

Cook-Deegan, Robert M. and McCormack, Stephen J. "Patents, Secrecy, and DNA." *Science* 293 (2001), 217.

Doll, John J. "The Patenting of DNA." *Science* (1998), 689–90.

Gilbert, Penny X. and Walter, Claire. "Patents and the Human Genome Project—New Claims for Old?" *Trends in Biotechnology* 19 (2001), 49–52.

Grisham, Julie. "New Rules for Gene Patents." *Nature Biotechnology* 18 (2000), 921.

Guenin, Louis M. "Patents, Ethics, Human Life Forms." In Thomas H. Murray and Maxwell J. Mehlman, eds., *Encyclopedia of Ethical, Legal, and Policy Issues in Biotechnology.* 2 vols. New York: Johns Wiley & Sons, 2000, 866–80.

Heller, Michael A., and Eisenberg, Rebecca S. "Can Patents Deter Innovation? The Anticommons in Biomedical Research." *Science* (1998), 698–701.

Hermerén, Göran. "Patents and Licensing, Ethics, International Controversies." In Thomas H. Murray and Maxwell J. Mehlman, eds., *Encyclopedia of Ethical, Legal, and Policy Issues in Biotechnology.* 2 vols. New York: Johns Wiley & Sons, 2000, 817–25.

Hoedemaekers, Rogeer. "Commercialization, Patents and Moral Assessment of Biotechnology Products." *Journal of Medicine and Philosophy* 26 (2001), 273–84.

———. "Human Gene Patents: Core Issues in Multi-layered Debate." *Medicine, Health Care and Philosophy* 4 (2001), 211–21.

Jones, Philip B. C. "Patentability Requirements for Genes and Proteins: Perspectives from the Trilateral Patent Offices." *Journal of BioLaw and Business* 3 (2000), 5–15.

Katz, Dana, and Merz, Jon F. "Patents and Licensing, Policy, Patenting of Inventions Developed with Public Funds." In Thomas H. Murray and Maxwell J. Mehlman, eds., *Encyclopedia of Ethical, Legal, and Policy Issues in Biotechnology.* 2 vols. New York: Johns Wiley & Sons, 2000, 854–66.

Lui, Jacqueline. "Patenting Biotechnology Inventions in China." *Nature Biotechnology* 19 (2001), 83–84.

Poste, George. "The Case for Genomic Patenting." *Nature* 378 (1995), 534–36.

Resnik, David B. "DNA Patents and Human Dignity." *Journal of Law, Medicine and Ethics* 29 (2001), 152–65.

———. "The Morality of Human Gene Patents." *Kennedy Institute of Ethics Journal* 7 (1997), 43–61.

Svatos, Michele. "Patents and Licensing, Ethics, Ownership of Animal, and Plant Genes." In Thomas H. Murray and Maxwell J. Mehlman, eds., *Encyclopedia of Ethical, Legal, and Policy Issues in Biotechnology.* 2 vols. New York: Johns Wiley & Sons, 2000, 844–54.

Yanai, Itai. "Brave New Patents: The Law of DNA Worship." *Journal of BioLaw and Business* 4 (2001), 27–33.

BIBLIOGRAPHIES

Goldstein, Doris Mueller. *Bioethics: A Guide to Information Sources*. Detroit: Gale Research Company, 1982. See under "Genetic Intervention."

Lineback, Richard H., ed. *Philosopher's Index*. Vols. 1– . Bowling Green, OH: Philosophy Documentation Center, Bowling Green State University. Issued quarterly. See under "Genetic Engineering" and "Genetics."

Walters, LeRoy, and Kahn, Tamar Joy, eds. *Bibliography of Bioethics*. Vols. 1– . Washington, DC: Kennedy Institute of Ethics, Georgetown University. Issued annually. See under "Eugenics," "Gene Therapy," "Genetic Counseling," "Genetic Intervention," "Genetic Screening," and "Genome Mapping."

WORLD WIDE WEB RESOURCES

Kennedy Institute of Ethics Georgetown University: National Information Resource on Ethics and Human Genetics, *Scope Notes* (http://www.georgetown.edu/research/nrcbl/nirehg/scope.htm

National Library of Medicine: PubMed (http://www.ncbi.nlm.nih.gov/PubMed/)

National Library of Medicine: LocatorPlus (http:///locatorplus.gov/)

University Microfilms: Periodical Abstracts (http://www.umi.com/proquest)

8.
Reproductive Technologies and Human Embryonic Stem Cell Research

INTRODUCTION

This chapter first considers the moral quandaries faced by individuals or couples contemplating the conception, gestation, birth, and rearing of a child or multiple children. In the idealized traditional model, the members of a heterosexual couple make a rational decision about whether to have a child, or another child. If their decision is positive, they proceed to conceive a child by means of sexual intercourse. It is always understood, of course, that the process of rational decision making may occur after the unintended initiation of a pregnancy.

The idealized traditional model is not always realized in practice. In the latter decades of the twentieth century and the early years of the twenty-first century, health professionals and couples alike have made the general public increasingly aware of the problem of involuntary infertility. As a response to this problem, both older and newer technologies of assisted reproduction have been developed and increasingly employed. This chapter focuses first on a technique of assisted reproduction that has been widely employed in industrialized countries for almost twenty years—in vitro (test-tube) fertilization. In the second section of the chapter attention shifts to a reproductive technique that was first demonstrated in a mammal in early 1997, with the birth of "Dolly," a sheep produced by means of reproductive cloning.

In vitro fertilization and cloning can also be employed for nonreproductive purposes. In November 1998, researchers at the University of Wisconsin published a paper describing the successful derivation of human embryonic stem cells.[1] These stem cells have the capacity to develop into all of the approximately 260 cell types of the human body. Since the publication of the 1998 essay, there has been an international public debate about the ethical acceptability of removing cells from five-day-old human embryos to produce embryonic stem cells. This debate intensified in late 2001 and early 2002 when researchers at Advanced Cell Technology in Worcester, Massachusetts, announced that they had derived stem cells from human and monkey embryos that had been produced through cloning.[2]

THE PROBLEM OF INFERTILITY

The primary motivation for developing new reproductive technologies is, of course, involuntary infertility. The most comprehensive recent survey suggests that approximately 2.1 million (or 7.1 percent of) U.S. married couples were infertile in the mid-1990s.[3] (For this survey infertility was defined as not conceiving after at least twelve months of unprotected intercourse.) Similar surveys of cohabiting couples in Canada found that between 7 percent and 8.5 percent were infertile; the variation in rates depended on whether a one-year or two-year criterion was used for establishing infertility.[4] The causes of infertility vary from couple to couple but seem to include lower fertility rates among couples who defer having children until the spouses are in their thirties and the deleterious effects on fertility of sexually transmitted diseases like chlamydia.

But how should the problem of infertility be viewed, philosophically and ethically? Some critics of the new reproductive technologies have argued that infertility is not a disease and that medical intervention to alleviate infertility amounts to nothing more than doctoring the desires of patients.[5] However, other commentators have adopted a variety of alternative approaches. For example, the authors of the Warnock Committee report, published in 1984 in the United Kingdom, argued that even if infertility is not a disease in the strict sense, it is a bodily "malfunction" that health professionals can and should help to remedy.[6] Feminist author Barbara Katz Rothman has employed a different metaphor, suggesting that involuntary infertility should be regarded as a disability. While accepting the view that women should be totally free to choose whether or not to become parents, the author presents a nuanced approach to the problems faced by couples, and especially women, who are surprised to discover that they cannot easily bear children. With the aid of the disability metaphor, Katz Rothman notes that infertility can sometimes be prevented, sometimes cured. In other cases, the disabled person must simply find ways to compensate for the disability. Whatever path is chosen, the author argues, it is the person herself and not a successful reproductive outcome that should remain the central focus of attention.[7]

A 1998 decision of the U.S. Supreme Court paralleled Katz Rothman's analysis in the legal sphere. The question before the court was whether a woman's HIV infection placed a substantial limitation on her ability "to reproduce and to bear children" and, if so, whether reproduction is one of the "major life activities" covered by the Americans with Disabilities Act (ADA) of 1990. By a 5-4 margin, the Supreme Court agreed with Sidney Abbott that the limitations on her ability to reproduce *do* constitute a disability under the terms of the ADA.[8]

IN VITRO FERTILIZATION

The birth of Louise Brown in Lancashire, England, in 1978 inaugurated a new era in the history of the reproductive technologies. Louise had not been conceived inside her mother's body but in a Petri dish, where eggs removed from her mother had been mixed with sperm from her father, and where fertilization had taken place.

In vitro fertilization (literally, "fertilization in glass") is most often proposed as a technique for overcoming infertility in married couples. The simplest case involves the use of semen from the husband and eggs from the wife. No reproductive cells are donated to the couple, and no "surplus" embryos are produced. All embryos that result from in vitro fertilizations (IVF) contain the parents' genes, and all are transferred to the uterus of the wife in the hope that at least one pregnancy will be achieved. In addition, the simplest case involves no freezing and storage of early human embryos.

There are, of course, variations on this simplest case. Either the sperm cells or the egg cells or the early embryo may be derived from sources other than the husband and the wife (donors or vendors). Even if the sperm and egg cells are provided by the husband and wife, there are numerous options. The developing embryos may be tested for genetic or chromosomal abnormalities, frozen and stored, donated to other couples, provided for research, or allowed to die. Thus, multiple procedures that previously had been possible only with semen or prenatally (that is, after implantation) are now able to be performed after fertilization and before implantation.

IVF is no longer a radically new reproductive technology. In fact, it is estimated that approximately one million infants have been born worldwide with the assistance of IVF.[9] Nonetheless, as the essays in this chapter indicate, IVF raises a series of interesting metaphysical and ethical problems. John Robertson's essay provides an overview of ethical and public policy issues surrounding the practice of IVF, with special emphasis on the biological, moral, and legal status of preimplantation embryos. In the concluding sections of his essay Robertson also addresses what he calls "consumer protection issues" and the question of patient access to a relatively expensive reproductive technology. Susan Sherwin notes several topics treated by moral philosophers and theologians in their discussions of IVF, then proceeds to identify a series of feminist themes that have been neglected in traditional analyses. Among these themes are discriminatory criteria for selecting among candidates for IVF, unexamined assumptions about women's natural roles as mothers, and an undue emphasis on the importance of a genetic connection between parents and the children they rear.

Various countries have adopted widely divergent approaches to the public oversight of assisted reproductive technologies like IVF. In the United Kingdom, for example, the Human Fertilisation and Embryology Authority (HFEA) is a statutory body that regulates donor insemination, IVF, and research involving early human embryos.[10] The British agency publishes annual reports that detail the success rates of individual clinics with donor insemination and IVF. The HFEA also sets practice standards on matters as specific as the number of early embryos that can be transferred to the body of a woman in a given ovulatory cycle. Within the United States, the reproductive technologies have developed within an environment that can only be described as laissez-faire. A working group from the Institute for Science, Law, and Technology (ISLAT) in Chicago has proposed federal legislation that would set minimum standards for U.S. clinics that offer assistance in reproduction. According to the working group, these standards should cover such issues as approval of new techniques by a research review committee, more systematic data collection and reporting, and fuller disclosure to those who seek reproductive assistance. The group stops short of recommending a regulatory body like HFEA for the United States. The ISLAT working group's report is reprinted in this chapter.

CLONING

In the February 27, 1997, issue of *Nature,* Scottish researcher Ian Wilmut and his colleagues published an article modestly titled "Viable Offspring Derived from Fetal and Adult Mammalian Cells"[11] The one viable offspring derived from an adult mammalian cell was a sheep named "Dolly," who became an overnight celebrity. The research of Wilmut and his colleagues and subsequent success in the cloning of other mammals have stimulated a global debate on the question: Now or in the future, would it be morally justifiable to clone a human being?

Once again in this instance, conceptual clarification is necessary. *Cloning* can be defined quite technically as the transfer of the nucleus from a somatic (nonreproductive) cell into an egg cell from which the nucleus has been removed. The type of cloning that has provoked the most vigorous ethical discussion would transfer the nucleus of a cell taken from an already born individual into an enucleated egg cell. Someone who cloned a human being in this sense would be attempting to produce a genetically identical twin to a visible and recognizable individual—whether that individual were an infant, a college student, or a person nearing retirement age. Cloning, or *nuclear transfer,* for research rather than reproductive purposes will be discussed in the next section of this introduction.

In response to a request by then President Bill Clinton, the U.S. National Bioethics Advisory Commission (NBAC) completed an ethical evaluation of human cloning in just over three months. The commission's conclusion was that the cloning of a human being in 1997 or in the next few years would be unethical, both because many questions about the safety of the technique for offspring remained unresolved and because of broader social concerns about the technique that would require further deliberation. NBAC went on to recommend a legislative ban on human cloning in the United States—both in the public and private sectors—for a period of three to five years.

The remaining selections in this section summarize the major ethical arguments for and objections to human reproductive cloning. In an essay initially prepared for NBAC, Dan Brock analyzes the ethical arguments for and against cloning and concludes that they are quite evenly balanced. He advocates further public and professional debate and vigorous public oversight as preconditions for attempting to clone a human being. In a similar vein, British physician-philosopher Raanan Gillon focuses on the standard moral objections to human reproductive cloning and finds most of them to be unconvincing.

The opposition position to reproductive cloning is eloquently argued by physician-biochemist-philosopher Leon Kass, who currently serves as Chair of the President's Council on Bioethics appointed by President George W. Bush. Kass's "The Wisdom of Repugnance" was originally written and published in 1997, as the National Bioethics Advisory Committee deliberated on its policy recommendations to President Clinton. In the essay Kass argues that reproductive cloning differs from other assisted reproductive technologies like in vitro fertilization "in essential and important ways." His critique appeals to broad cultural themes such as the role of emotion in ethics and public policy, the importance of sexuality in human reproduction, and the American tendency to reduce profound problems affecting human nature to simple procedural questions. In Kass's view, the only safe course for industrialized societies to follow is a comprehensive legal ban on both reproductive cloning and the use of nuclear transfer in research. On the question of reproductive cloning, the panel appointed by the National Research Council agrees with Kass's proposal for a legislative ban. However, the panel's recommendations for at least a temporary ban on cloning are based primarily on the physical risks of the technique to pregnant women and their potential offspring rather than on broader social concerns.

HUMAN EMBRYONIC STEM CELL RESEARCH

As noted, the successful demonstration in 1998 that human embryonic stem cells can be produced opened new scientific possibilities but also raised new ethical questions. The final five selections in this chapter describe the techniques that can be employed to produce embryonic stem cells and argue the cases for and against such research.[12]

In humans, embryonic stem cells are derived from the inner cell mass of a five-day-old embryo called a *blastocyst*. At this stage of development a human embryo is comprised of between 100 and 200 cells, of which approximately 10 percent form the inner cell mass. The cells of the inner cell mass have already begun to differentiate into three types of cells, some of which will form the inner layer, the middle layer, and the outer layer of the later embryo if the embryo continues to develop. These cells are therefore said to be *pluripotent* or *multipotent* rather than *totipotent*. That is, the individual cells of the inner cell mass no longer have the potential to develop into human beings.

Several distinctions have been important in the international discussion of human embryonic stem research. The first distinction is between stem cells derived from embryos that have been produced through in vitro fertilization on one hand and stem cells derived from embryos that have been produced through nuclear transfer, or cloning, on the other. The second distinction is between (1) IVF embryos that are left over or unneeded in an infertility clinic after a couple has completed its reproductive plans, and (2) embryos created specifically for research purposes, whether by IVF or by nuclear transfer. A third distinction is much more subtle: It contrasts the *use* of embryonic stem cells that have already been produced from the *derivation* of stem cells. The derivation process results in the destruction or death of the embryo, whereas the act of using already derived stem cells does not, in itself, destroy embryos.

In the few years that have passed since the first successful production of human embryonic stem cells, philosophers, theologians, and public advisory bodies have employed these distinctions to formulate five positions on the ethics of this.

1. It is morally wrong both to derive human embryonic stem cells and to use stem cells that have been previously derived.
2. It is ethically acceptable to use already existing human embryonic stem cells but wrong to derive such cells.
3. It is ethically acceptable both to derive and to use human embryonic stem cells, but only if the embryos used for this purpose were originally created for reproductive purposes and are no longer needed for reproduction. However, it is morally wrong to create embryos for research purposes.
4. It is ethically acceptable both to derive and to use human embryonic stem cells that have been produced by means of in vitro fertilization, whether for reproductive or research purposes. However, it is morally wrong to create embryos by means of cloning, or nuclear transfer, and then to derive stem cells from them.
5. It is ethically acceptable both to derive and to use human embryonic stem cells without regard to the purpose for which the embryos were created or the technique by which the embryos were created.

In the United States the terms of the public debate about human embryonic stem cell research were set primarily by the National Bioethics Advisory Commission, which advocated the third option identified here, and the National Institutes of Health (and, at least tacitly, the Clinton administration), which espoused the second option. In August 2001 President George W. Bush also adopted a version of the second option when he decided what types of human embryonic stem cell research should be eligible for federal funding. Most other industrial democracies—for example, Canada, the Netherlands, Italy, Spain, Japan, and Australia—have settled on the third option. In contrast, countries as diverse as the United Kingdom, Sweden, Israel, and China have adopted versions of either the fourth or fifth option.

The commentaries reprinted in this chapter represent the full spectrum of ethical opinion. Gilbert Meilaender argues that all human embryonic stem cell research should be legally prohibited. His essay draws analogies from the practice of warfare to argue for an ethic focused on means rather than the medical benefits promised by advocates of embryonic stem cell research. The National Bioethics Advisory Commission (NBAC) argues for the ethical acceptability of an incremental approach that, for the present, derives embryonic stem cells only from left-over human embryos. Glenn McGee and Arthur Caplan, as well as two separate panels of the National Research Council, argue that the option of creating embryos through nuclear transfer and then deriving embryonic stem cells from them should be left open, in principle. In their view, research on such cells may be important for research on normal and abnormal cellular development in the short run and for the preparation of stem cells that are genetically matched to a particular patient and thus suitable for transplantation in the longer-term future. Both NBAC and the first National Research Council committee also accent the importance of transparent public oversight for all human embryonic stem cell research.

L.W.

NOTES

1. James A. Thomson, et al., "Embryonic Stem Cell Lines Derived from Human Blastocytes," *Science* 282 (1998), 1145–47.

2. Jose B. Cibelli, et al., "The First Human Cloned Embryo," *Scientific American* 286 (January 2002), 44–51; Jose B. Cibelli, et al., "Parthenogenetic Stem Cells in Nonhuman Primates," *Science* 295 (2002), 819.

3. Joyce C. Abma, et al., "Fertility, Family Planning, and Women's Health: New Data from the 1995 National Survey of Family Growth," *Vital and Health Statistics,* Series 23: Data from the *National Survey of Family Growth,* no. 19, May 1997, pp. 7 and 61.

4. New York State Task Force on Life and the Law, *Assisted Reproductive Technologies: Analysis and Recommendations for Public Policy* (New York: New York State Task Force, April 1998), 12–13.

5. See, for example, Leon R. Kass, "Making Babies: The New Biology and the 'Old' Morality," *Public Interest,* No. 26 (1972), 18–56.

6. U.K., Department of Health and Social Security, *Report of the Committee of Inquiry into Human Fertilisation and Embryology* (the Warnock Committee Report) (London: Her Majesty's Stationery Office, July 1984), pp. 8–10.

7. Barbara Katz Rothman, "Infertility as Disability" in *Recreating Motherhood: Ideology and Technology in a Patriarchal Society* (New York: W. W. Norton & Company, 1989), pp. 143–51.

8. U.S. Supreme Court, *Bragdon v. Abott, 524 U.S. [Supreme Court Reports],* 624 (1998).

9. These figures are based on the 1998 estimate of the ISLAT Working Group, which is reprinted in this chapter, and data from the American Society for Reproductive Medicine (ASRM), the Human Fertilisation and Embryology Authority (HFEA), and two infertility experts. According to ASRM, more than 175,000 live infants were delivered in the United States following IVF through 1999 (personal communication to the author by Eleanor Nicoll, ASRM, May 8, 2002). In the United Kingdom, the comparable figure is 52,402 infants born following IVF between 1983 and 1999 (personal communication to the author by Anne Furedi, HFEA, May 8, 2002). David Adamson, Clinical Assistant Professor of Obstetrics and Gynecology at Stanford University (personal communication to Eleanor Nicoll, ASRM, May 8, 2002) and Jean Cohen, Director of the Centre de Stérilité de l'Hôpital de Sèvres in Paris, have confirmed that one million is the approximate worldwide figure for 2002 (personal communication to the author, May 13, 2002).

10. The Web site for the Human Fertilisation and Embryology Authority is *www.hfea.gov.uk.*

11. Ian Wilmut, et al., "Viable Offspring Derived from Fetal and Adult Mammalian Cells," *Nature* 386 (1997), 810–13.

12. The questions surrounding the derivation and use of embryonic germ cells, which are derived from fetal tissue after induced abortion, are not discussed in detail in this chapter.

In Vitro Fertilization

JOHN A. ROBERTSON

IVF, Infertility, and the Status of Embryos

John A. Robertson holds the Vinson and Elkins Chair at the University of Texas School of Law at Austin. He has written and lectured widely on law and bioethical issues. He is the author of two books in bioethics—*The Rights of the Critically Ill* (Bantam Books) and *Children of Choice: Freedom and the New Reproductive Technologies* (Princeton University Press), and numerous articles on reproductive rights, genetics, organ transplantation, and human experimentation. He has served on or been a consultant to many national bioethics advisory bodies, and is currently Chair of the Ethics Committee of the American Society for Reproductive Medicine.

In vitro fertilization (IVF) emerged as a major treatment for infertility in the 1980s. Its reliance on extracorporeal fertilization of human eggs raises questions about the status, control, and disposition of embryos. As a high-tech reproductive procedure, it also presents issues of access, efficacy, and truthful disclosure that test the limits of procreative freedom. To explore these issues, this [essay] addresses the conflicts and controversies that arise when husband and wife provide egg and sperm for IVF.[1]

• • •

IN VITRO FERTILIZATION

IVF treats infertility problems by bypassing the natural place of fertilization in the fallopian tube. It operates by collecting eggs surgically after ovarian stimulation, fertilizing them in vitro in the laboratory, and, after 48–72 hours, placing the cleaving embryos into the uterus.

Originally developed to overcome tube blockage by bypassing the fallopian tubes altogether, IVF is increasingly used to treat infertility due to other conditions, such as endometriosis, cervical mucus problems, and the great number of cases of unexplained infertility. In addition, IVF can be used to treat oligospermia or low sperm count by putting sperm directly in contact with the egg in a dish, where there is a shorter distance to travel to conception. In severe cases, it would enable conception to occur by drilling of the egg's zona pellucida or by microinjection of [a] single sperm into the egg.

The first birth of a child from IVF occurred in 1978 in Great Britain, capping off a long period of research by Steptoe, Edwards, and others. Since then more than 30,000 children conceived in this way have been born worldwide. The United States has more than 180 programs offering IVF. Over 8,230 children have been born as a result of the procedure in the last four years alone.[2] However, IVF will not provide all patients with a baby. While the best programs have a success rate of 20 to 25 percent per egg retrieval cycle, many programs cannot approach this record.[3] At present women have to undergo on the average two IVF cycles to start a pregnancy, at a cost of $5,000 to $7,000 per cycle. Improvements in success rates will occur as research and experience with the technique grow.

To increase the chances of pregnancy, most IVF programs stimulate the ovaries to obtain multiple eggs, and place several fertilized eggs or embryos in the uterus in each IVF cycle (American programs place on average 3.5 embryos in the uterus per cycle). If too

From John A. Robertson, *Children of Choice: Freedom and the New Reproductive Technologies,* pp. 97–105, 107–11, 113–18. Copyright © 1994 by Princeton University Press. Reprinted by permission of Princeton University Press.

many fertilized eggs are placed in the uterus, there is a great risk of multiple pregnancy, and may create the need for selective reduction (abortion) of the pregnancy. Embryo freezing, now practiced in most clinics, permits extra embryos to be preserved and then thawed for use in later cycles. This will increase the overall efficacy of an egg retrieval cycle and reduce the costs or burdens of later cycles.

Increasingly, eggs are collected by means of ultrasound-guided transvaginal aspiration, which eliminates the need for laparoscopy and general anesthesia.[4] When tubes are patent, the embryos may also be placed directly into the fallopian tube, in a procedure known as ZIFT (zygote intrafallopian transfer). Egg and sperm may also be inserted directly into a patent tube before fertilization occurs (known as GIFT, or gamete intrafallopian transfer). Since the fallopian tube is the natural site of fertilization and early embryo development, these procedures may offer a better chance of success in certain cases.

SHOULD IVF BE DONE AT ALL?

Basic IVF raises many issues that force us to consider the scope and meaning of procreative liberty. At the most fundamental level, the question is whether IVF should occur at all. Engineering conception in the bright glare of the laboratory rather than the dark recesses of the fallopian tube strikes some people as wrong or undesirable. They would deny or severely limit access to this procedure.

Their objection has several strands. One is an antitechnology bias against medical interventions, especially reproductive interventions. A second strand is theological, exemplified by the Catholic position that any separation of the unitive (sexual) and procreative is improper. A third feminist strand sees any reproductive technology as exploiting the socially engrained view that infertile women are inadequate—that women must produce children for their husbands. IVF, which bombards a woman's body with powerful hormones and then invades the body to harvest eggs, is in their view a prime example of such an exploitive technology. It holds out the false promise of success when the chance of taking home a baby is actually quite low.[5] Finally, right-to-life groups would ban IVF because they think that it harms embryos.

Whatever the merits of these objections, they have not dampened demand or had a significant impact on public policy. Although a 1987 Vatican directive urged that civil law be enacted to ban procedures such as IVF, no state has done so and no groups appear to be lobbying for such a measure.[6] Indeed, the incidence of IVF in the United States (and throughout the world) continues to grow. In 1990, 19,079 stimulation cycles for IVF were reported, 16,405 of which went to egg retrieval, with an additional 3,750 retrieval cycles done for gamete intrafallopian transfer (GIFT), in which the egg and sperm are placed directly into the fallopian tube.[7]

If a law banning IVF or GIFT were passed, it would no doubt be found unconstitutional because it directly impeded the efforts of infertile married couples to have offspring, thus interfering with their fundamental right to procreate.[8] The moral objections to IVF made by the Catholic Church, feminists, and others do not constitute the compelling evidence of tangible harm necessary to justify interference with procreative liberty. Ancillary rules for the conduct of IVF, which are discussed below, should also have to satisfy the compelling-interest test when they substantially interfere with access to IVF.

EMBRYO STATUS ISSUES

IVF is unique because it externalizes the earliest stages of human life, and subjects it to observation and manipulation. Moral and legal controversies over basic IVF concern the control and disposition of embryos created in the process. What is the status of preimplantation embryos?[9] Who has dispositional control over them? What actions may be done with them?

These questions pit deeply felt views about respect for the earliest stages of human life against the needs of infertile couples to create embryos to serve their reproductive goals. Their resolution will have a great impact on the scope of procreative freedom and the use of IVF to treat infertility. The biological, moral, and legal status of the embryo is first discussed before issues of ownership and limitations on what may be done with embryos is addressed.

THE BIOLOGICAL STATUS OF EMBRYOS

Conception occurs when a single spermatozoa enters the egg and the chromosomes of each fuse into a single cell of forty-six chromosomes. Fertilization is not instantaneous, but occurs gradually over several hours after penetration of the egg by a single sperm.[10] At this stage a new and unique genome beginning a new generation exists within a single cell.[11]

During the next three days the one-celled zygote divides several times to become an undifferentiated aggregate of two, four, six, or eight cells. In IVF programs the embryo will be transferred to a uterus when it reaches the four-, six-, or eight-cell stage, some 48 to 72 hours after conception. In ZIFT, transfer directly into the fallopian tube occurs via laparoscopy at the one-cell or zygote stage. It is also at this stage that the embryo would be cryopreserved for later use.

Further growth produces the cell clusters of the morula and then blastocyst stage of development. At the blastocyst stage the simple cellular aggregate of the fertilized egg starts to show a central cavity surrounded by a peripheral cellular layer with some distinguishable inner cells.[12] The outer cells develop into a trophoblastic or feeding layer that becomes the placenta rather than the embryo proper. At this time only cells of the inner mass can give rise to an embryo.

The blastocyst stage marks the developing capability to interact with maternal cells of the uterine lining, which is essential for implantation and later development to occur. At six to nine days the developing cellular mass acquires the ability to implant or embed in the uterine wall as the placenta, jointly derived from embryonic and maternal cells, begins to form.[13] Implantation marks the beginning of pregnancy as a maternal state. At this stage the embryonic mass has a clearly distinguishable outer cellular layer which plays the major role in the implantation process. It is the as yet undeveloped inner cell mass, however, that is the source of the embryo proper. It is for this reason that preimplantation stages are more accurately called the "preembryo."

When the blastocyst is well established in the uterine wall (early in the second postfertilization week), the inner cell mass reorganizes into two layers that make up the embryonic disk. This first true rudiment of the embryo is the site of the formation of the embryonic axis, along which the major organs and structures of the body will be differentiated.[14] By the end of the fourth postconception week, the major organs are more fully formed and cardiovascular circulation has begun.[15] By the eighth week an anatomically recognizable human miniature exists, displaying very primitive neuromuscular function but still extremely immature by all structural and functional criteria.[16] The higher parts of the brain do not show any electrical activity or nerve cell connections until twelve weeks after conception.[17] If abortion does not occur, the birth of a newborn infant will complete the gestational process.

THE MORAL STATUS OF EMBRYOS

While scientists largely agree about these facts of zygote, preembryo, and embryo development, there is also a growing consensus about their moral significance. Three major ethical positions have been articulated in the debate of embryo status. At one extreme is the view of the embryo as a human subject after fertilization, which requires that it be accorded the rights of a person. This position entails an obligation to provide an opportunity for implantation to occur and tends to ban any action before transfer that might harm the embryo or that is not immediately therapeutic, such as freezing and embryo research. Its weakness is that it ignores the reality of biological development just described.

At the opposite extreme is the view that the embryo has a status no different from that of any other human tissue, and can be treated accordingly. Other than requiring the consent of those who have ownership or decision-making authority over embryos, no limits should be imposed on actions taken with them. The problem with this view is that it ignores the fact that a new genome has been formed and that actions with this tissue could affect whether a new child will be born.

The most widely held view of embryo status takes an intermediate position between the other two. It holds that the embryo deserves respect greater than that accorded to other human tissue, because of its potential to become a person and the symbolic meaning it carries for many people. Yet it should not be treated as a person, because it has not yet developed the features of personhood, is not yet established as developmentally individual, and may never realize its biologic potential.[18]

It is noteworthy that law, ethical commentary, and the reports of most official or professional advisory bodies share the view that the embryo has a special moral status less than that of a person. For example, the United States' Ethics Advisory Board unanimously agreed in 1979 that "the human preembryo is entitled to profound respect, but this respect does not necessarily encompass the full legal and moral rights attributed to persons."[19]

In 1984, the Warnock Committee in Great Britain took a similar position when it stated: "The human preembryo . . . is not under the present law of the United Kingdom accorded the same status as a living child or an adult, nor do we necessarily wish it to be accorded the same status. Nevertheless, we were agreed that the preembryo of the human species ought to have a special status."[20]

The Ontario Law Reform Commission (Canada), which completed an extensive review of the issue in 1985, also took this view, as have nearly all other professional and official advisory bodies that have reviewed the question of embryo status.[21] The most recent pronouncement to this effect came from the Tennessee Supreme Court in 1992 when it overturned a trial court finding that embryos were "children" but held that because of their special status they deserved "special respect."[22]

For the most part, only groups holding the view that "personhood" begins at conception have rejected this middle position. However, Father Richard McCormick, a noted Catholic bioethicist who believes that abortion is immoral, has looked carefully at the biologic facts about the embryo and concluded that because the embryo is not developmentally individual until implantation, it has not clearly been determined to be a person in Catholic theology.[23]

THE LEGAL STATUS OF EMBRYOS

Legal status—position or standing in law—will define what rights, if any, embryos have and what duties are owed to them, thus determining what might be done with these entities, and by whom.

Do Embryos Have Legal Rights? The advisory body conclusions parallel the traditional Anglo-American legal view of prenatal life. In that tradition, legal personhood does not exist until live birth and separation from the mother. Common law prohibitions on abortion protected fetuses only after quickening (roughly sixteen weeks of gestation). While many American states did pass restrictive abortion laws in the nineteenth and twentieth centuries, those laws applied only to termination of pregnancy, and thus did not address the status of preimplantation embryos outside the body. Wrongful death statutes did not compensate for the wrongful death of a fetus until the late 1940s, and then only if the fetus was viable at the time of the injury.

At the present time, then, the law does not regard embryos as rights-bearing entities, although it has recognized that prenatal actions could affect the postnatal well-being of persons. In most states the embryo is not a legal subject in its own right and is not protected by laws against homicide or wrongful death, nor is embryo discard prohibited. However, three states (Minnesota, Louisiana, and Illinois) have altered their homicide laws in such a way that they arguably ban the intentional destruction of extracorporeal embryos.[24] Aside from those states, the embryo generally has legal cognizance only if the interests of an actual person are at stake, such as when transfer occurs and offspring may be affected or when someone wrongfully interferes with another person's right to determine disposition of the embryo.

The biology of early human embryo development supports this legal status. Since the embryo does not have differentiated organs, much less the developed brain, nervous system, and capacity for sentience that legal subjects ordinarily have, it cannot easily be regarded as a legal subject. Indeed, the embryo is not yet individual, because twinning or mosaicism can still occur. It is not surprising that the law does not recognize the embryo itself as a legal subject.

This legal status of embryos is not dependent on the continued survival of *Roe v. Wade* and the right to abortion. Because abortion laws penalized termination of pregnancy, they never applied to the destruction of embryos before pregnancy occurred. Thus *Roe* has not been a direct barrier to states wishing to protect embryos in situations other than abortion. A reversal of *Roe v. Wade* is not necessary to have states protect extracorporeal embryos more extensively than they previously have. IVF programs are also free to set their own standards concerning the extent to which embryos will be protected.

Dispositional Control over Embryos. An important question of legal status concerns the locus and scope of decisional authority over embryos. "Who" has the right or authority to choose among available options for disposition of embryos is a question separate from "what" those dispositional options are.

The question of decisional authority is really the question of who "owns"—has a "property" interest in—the embryo. However, using terms such as "ownership" or "property" risks misunderstanding. Ownership does not signify that embryos may be treated in all respects like other property. Rather, the term merely designates who decides which legally available options will occur, such as creation, freezing, discard, donation, use in research, and placement in a uterus. Although the bundle of property rights attached to one's ownership of an embryo may be more circumscribed than for other things, it is an ownership or property interest nonetheless.

While the individuals who provided the gametes, the couple jointly, their transferees, the physicians or embryologists who directly create the embryos, or the IVF program or embryo storage bank that has actual possession are all possible candidates for decisional authority over embryos, the persons who provide the egg and sperm have the strongest claim to ownership of the embryo. The more interesting questions concern whether and how they have exercised that authority, and whether advance instructions for disposition will be binding if their preferences or circumstances change.

While legislation has not yet explicitly recognized the gamete providers' joint ownership of extracorporeal embryos, it is reasonable to assume that the courts would so hold when confronted with disputes raising this issue.[25] It is also likely that a right of survivorship in embryos would be recognized as well. The Uniform Anatomical Gift Act and other precedents concerning disposition of body parts support that view, even though they do not address it specifically.

Since most IVF programs and storage banks are likely to honor the couple's ownership, the issue would be directly joined only if a program or bank refused to follow the couple's dispositional instructions. The question would also arise if the program intentionally or negligently destroyed embryos.

• • •

Limits on the Scope of Authority over Embryos. Having seen that the gamete providers and their transferees have decisional authority over embryos, we now consider the limits that the state and IVF programs may impose on exercise of the authority. Is the couple's "ownership" of embryos absolute, or may the state qualify or limit it in certain ways? As noted previously, the answer to this question will depend on the reproductive interests implicated and the state's reasons for limiting the couple's ownership. While resolution of some issues will turn on views of embryo moral status, most will turn on the reproductive interests at stake and the degree to which procreative liberty is recognized. The main questions that arise here are limits on discard and freezing of embryos.

Discard or Nontransfer of Embryos. Because most IVF programs hyperstimulate the ovaries and retrieve multiple eggs, couples and programs must decide whether all fertilized eggs will be placed in the uterus, or whether surplus or unwanted embryos may be discarded or donated to others. If all fertilized eggs are to be placed in the uterus, the number fertilized may have to be limited, because of the very serious risks of multiple gestation.[26] Yet limiting the number fertilized might yield too few embryos to initiate a viable pregnancy. Freezing extra embryos may solve the problem in some cases, but not all frozen embryos will be placed in the woman producing them.

The procedure most likely to produce pregnancy is to fertilize all viable eggs, transfer only the three or four embryos that can safely be placed in the uterus at one time, and either freeze the remaining embryos, discard them, or donate them to others. A problem arises when people object to discard of embryos because they believe that embryos are persons with rights, or because they find the symbolic effects of such a practice distasteful and take action to implement their view.

Legally, IVF programs are free to determine their own policy about embryo discard, but must inform couples of their policies before embryos are created. Except in Minnesota, Louisiana, and possibly Illinois, destruction or discard of an embryo is not covered by homicide or other criminal laws.[27] While many programs will allow couples the option of discard, some will apply restrictive policies, either because of their own moral qualms or because of institutional constraints.[28]

An important public policy question is whether couples and programs should be free to decide these matters as they wish, or whether government should intervene to limit their choice. A limitation on embryo discard (by limiting the number of eggs that may be inseminated, banning discard, or requiring donation of unwanted embryos) would interfere with the procreative liberty of a couple that wished to employ this alternative.[29] Would such laws be constitutional? Are they desirable?

The constitutionality of laws that prevent the discard or destruction of IVF embryos is independent of the right to abortion established in *Roe v. Wade* and upheld in *Planned Parenthood v. Casey.*[30] *Roe* and *Casey* protect a woman's interest in not having embryos placed in her body and in terminating implantation (pregnancy) that has occurred. Under *Roe-Casey* the state would be free to treat external embryos as persons or give as much protection to their potential life as it chooses, as long as it did not trench on a woman's bodily integrity or other procreative rights.

Embryo protection laws, however, even if they do not infringe bodily integrity, do interfere with decisions about having biologic offspring and thus limit procreative choice. For example, laws that require donation of unwanted embryos in lieu of discard force people to have biologic offspring against their will, thus infringing the right not to procreate. Even if no child-rearing obligations follow, as would ordinarily be the case if the embryos are donated anonymously to others, the couple would still face the possibility that they had produced genetic offspring. One could argue that genetic reproduction *tout court* is such a significant personal event that it should be included in the fundamental right not to procreate. If this argument were accepted, a state's desire to signify the importance of human life by requiring donation of unwanted embryos would not constitute the compelling interest necessary to justify infringement of a fundamental right to avoid reproduction.

A counterargument to this position is that the Supreme Court is unlikely to recognize the right to avoid biologic offspring *tout court* as a fundamental right, and therefore the state's interest in protecting prenatal life provides a rational basis for embryo protection laws. *Griswold, Roe,* and *Casey* establish a right to avoid reproduction when reproduction is necessarily coupled with gestation or rearing burdens. Laws that mandate embryo donation impose only the psychological burden of having unknown biologic offspring. Such a purely psychosocial interest is not likely to be granted fundamental right status as part of the right to avoid reproduction. In that case a state concerned with protecting prenatal life would easily satisfy the rational basis test by which such a statute would be judged. The reaffirmation of *Roe v. Wade* in *Casey* does not lessen the state's power to protect extracorporeal embryos, because the right of women to end pregnancy is not at issue.

One could also argue that bans on embryo discard interfere with the right to procreate. By limiting the number of eggs that can be fertilized or requiring that extra embryos be donated, such policies will deter couples from using IVF to treat infertility, thus infringing their right to use noncoital means of procreation. The validity of this argument rests on the degree of deterrence that such policies entail. It is possible that this policy would not "unduly burden" efforts to treat infertility. After all, the couple may still undergo IVF. They just are limited in the number of eggs they can inseminate, or must accept anonymous donation of extras to others. If deemed unlikely to deter resort to IVF, embryo protection policies would not violate the freedom to procreate.

Resolving the question of embryo discard requires coming to terms with two very different value questions. One is the importance of the genetic tie *tout court*—an issue never previously faced in this way. The other is the detriment to values of respect for human life that flow from embryo discard. While the view of many people would be that embryos are too rudimentary to make embryo discard very costly in symbolic terms, some persons—and IVF programs—will hold different views. The values that people hold about these two aspects of reproduction will determine what policies ultimately control embryo discard.

Embryo Freezing. Cryopreservation or embryo freezing is a rapidly growing aspect of IVF practice. In 1990 there were 23,865 embryos frozen as a result of the IVF process, an increase of 14,657 over the number reported in 1988.[31] In addition, 3,290 frozen embryos were thawed and placed in a uterus, a 70 percent increase over 1988, resulting in 382 pregnancies and 291 live births. The frozen embryo cycles involved more than 129 clinics, with 19 clinics performing fifty or more transfer cycles.

Embryo freezing is growing in popularity for several reasons. It could increase the efficacy of IVF by making use of all retrieved eggs. By eliminating the need for additional stimulation and egg retrieval cycles, it reduces the physical and financial costs of later IVF cycles. It also reduces the chance that surplus embryos (those that cannot be safely implanted in the uterus) will be destroyed. Yet many aspects of embryo freezing are controversial and are likely to generate proposals to limit the practice.

Harm to Embryos. Persons opposed to embryo discard also object to embryo freezing on the ground that the freeze-thaw process harms or destroys embryos by damaging particular blastomeres or cells that render the embryo unable to divide further. It is true that frozen-thawed embryos divide and start pregnancies at a lesser rate than do fresh embryos, and that freezing does damage some blastomeres. It is not clear, however, whether the damaged embryos are viable, and thus would have successfully implanted if freezing had not occurred.

A ban on embryo freezing would actually reduce the number of embryos in existence. Rather than risk the possibility of multiple gestation (and the chance of selective reduction of the pregnancy), fewer embryos would be created, since all embryos would have to be placed in the uterus. This reduction might also lead to fewer IVF pregnancies, because one cannot always guarantee that fertilizing three or four eggs will yield three or four viable embryos (the optimal number of embryos to transfer).

Reasonable people, however, could find that embryo freezing is sufficiently respectful of prenatal human life that it should be permitted as an option for infertile couples trying to become pregnant through IVF. Fewer embryos are destroyed than by outright discard. Moreover, it leads to the creation of embryos that would never have existed if freezing were not available. Even if some embryos are harmed by the freezing process, the total number of embryos available for implantation has increased. Even if discard were prohibited, freezing seems more protective than destructive of embryos and should be permitted as part of procreative choice in the IVF process.

Length of Storage. For most infertile couples embryo storage will be temporary, with most frozen embryos thawed within six to eighteen months in efforts to start pregnancy. Technically, however, there may be no outer limit on the length of time that embryos could be frozen before they are thawed and implanted in a uterus. Inevitably, some embryos will end up being frozen for years, as plans change or other factors intervene. An important question for IVF programs and public policy is whether the length of storage should be limited.

Proposals for such limits vary, from set terms such as five to ten years to the reproductive life of the woman providing the egg. Time limits are thought to be easier to administer and more desirable, because it will prevent children from being born to women who are much older.[32] It will also prevent simultaneously conceived siblings from being born years apart.

As a matter of public policy, such considerations are not sufficient to justify time limits on embryo freezing. None of them pose such dangers to offspring—who might not otherwise be born—that the wishes of couples to freeze for longer periods should be infringed. IVF programs should assess more carefully the purposes of time limits on storage, and not impose them unless clearly necessary. If programs adopt such policies, they should clearly inform couples in advance and permit them to remove frozen embryos to other facilities when the period elapses.

Posthumous Implantation. Embryo freezing also makes possible the posthumous implantation and birth of children conceived before death occurs. While such cases will not be frequent, situations will arise in which the husband or wife dies before previously frozen embryos are thawed and implanted. A surviving wife may request that "her" embryos be implanted in her, so that she may reproduce the "child" that she and her now dead husband created. A surviving husband might wish [that] the thawed embryos be placed in a new partner or in a host uterus engaged for that purpose.

Respect for the procreative liberty of the surviving spouse should permit posthumous thawing and implantation to occur. The survivor has a real interest in procreating, which the frozen embryo serves well. The fear that the child will have only one parent is not sufficient to override the spouse's procreative liberty. Many children thrive with single parents, especially if they have the resources and support to parent, and births to women pregnant at the time of their husband's death occasionally occur. A law that prohibited posthumous implantation would infringe the survivor's procreative liberty, and is unnecessary. IVF programs should not set such a restriction.

The question is somewhat different if both husband and wife die while the embryos are frozen. If the couple has directed that any frozen embryos be donated for implantation, their wishes should be respected. On the other hand, if they directed or accepted the program's condition that remaining embryos would be discarded, that too may be honored. However, a state law that required all frozen embryos remaining at time of death of both to be implanted would probably not violate the procreative rights of the couple, since the prospect of posthumous donation is unlikely to influence their reproductive decision making.[33]

• • •

Resolving Disputes over Frozen Embryos. The practice of freezing embryos will also raise questions about embryo disposition when the couple divorces, dies, is unavailable, is unable to agree, or is in arrears in paying storage charges. As noted earlier, the best way to handle these questions is by dispositional agreements made at the time of creation or cryopreservation of embryos. Such agreements should be binding on the parties, and enforced even if their circumstances or desires change. IVF programs that have reasonable grounds for thinking that the agreements were freely and knowingly made should be free to rely on them, without more. This is the best policy to give all parties some control of the process, as well as reliable advance certainty about future outcomes. It also will reduce the administrative costs and difficulty of resolving any disputes that arise.

The advantage of relying on prior dispositional agreements to resolve disputes over frozen embryos is illustrated by the widely publicized 1989 Tennessee divorce case of *Davis v. Davis* concerning disposition of seven frozen embryos. The couple had made no prior agreement for embryo disposition in case of divorce or disagreement. At the time of divorce, the wife insisted that the embryos be available to her for thawing and placement in her uterus or donation to another couple. The husband objected to the idea of children from a marriage that had failed. The trial judge awarded "custody" of the embryos to the wife, on the ground that the embryos were "children" whose best interests required the chance to implant and come to term.

A Tennessee intermediate appellate court reversed the trial court decision, requiring that any disposition of the embryos be jointly agreed to by the husband and wife. The Tennessee Supreme Court affirmed this decision on somewhat different grounds.[34] It upheld advance agreements for disposition in the case of divorce or disagreement, but rejected the notion that the freezing of embryos alone constituted an agreement to later implantation. It also recognized that a right to "procreational autonomy" existed under both the United States and Tennessee constitutions that outweighed the state's "at best slight" interest in "the potential life embodied by these four- to eight-cell preembryos."[35]

In this case, however, the choice of the husband not to procreate conflicted with the wife's desire to use the embryos to procreate. To resolve that conflict, the Court compared the relative burdens and concluded that the burdens of unwanted reproduction to the husband, even if genetic only, outweighed the burden to the wife of not having the embryos donated to another couple, as she now desired. Even if she had wanted them for herself, her claim to have them would be strong only if she had no way to achieve parenthood by other reasonable means. If she could go through another IVF cycle without excessive burdens to her, her interest in procreating with the disputed embryos should not take precedence over the husband's wishes to avoid unwanted reproduction.

The Tennessee Supreme Court's decision is eminently sound and will be a major precedent for the conduct of IVF and the resolution of disputes about frozen embryos for years to come. It nicely illustrates the advantages of relying on a prior agreement in these cases, rather than having to balance the procreative interests anew in lengthy and expensive litigation.[36]

• • •

CONSUMER PROTECTION ISSUES

Questions about the control and disposition of embryos have attracted much attention, but questions of safety, efficacy, and access raise equally important policy issues. For most couples, the most important question concerning IVF is whether it will work. The ethical niceties of control over embryos may be much less important.

Unfortunately, IVF does not work nearly as often as people would like. In the very best programs, pregnancy and take-home baby rates are around 20 percent of IVF egg retrieval cycles, which means that fewer than one in ten IVF-created embryos implant and come to term. Only ten to twenty programs achieve this level of success. Many other programs have much weaker records, and many have very few pregnancies at all. One survey in 1987 found that over half of the then existing American IVF programs had never produced a live birth. Other programs have misstated their success rates to consumers and been the subject of Federal Trade Commission charges of misleading advertising.[37]

The reasons for this relatively poor track record are several. The whole process of IVF is extremely complicated with many unknowns. What eggs best fertilize, what culture medium to use for embryos, when to transfer, what instruments to use, and many other questions will determine the outcome of IVF. Also crucial is the skill and experience of the physicians involved, the reliability of their laboratories, and the age and condition of patients. It is no accident that the biggest and most experienced programs consistently have the highest success rates.

The efficacy situation raises three important policy issues for protecting consumers. One concerns the need to support and fund research to improve success rates. Because of pro-life opposition, the federal government funded no IVF research during the twelve years of the Reagan-Bush administrations. Under the Clinton administration, federal funding of IVF research will now occur, though the amount of funding will have to compete with the many other demands for the federal health research dollar.

A second policy issue is the need to make infertile couples more aware of the varying success rates of IVF programs, so that they can make informed choices about whether and where to seek IVF. Complaints from unhappy consumers about misleading claims by IVF clinics led Congressman Ron Wyden (D-Oregon) to conduct hearings and seek legislation that requires that IVF success rates be uniformly kept and accurately disclosed. Uniform reporting and disclosure will prevent infertile couples from being misled by claims of success rates overall vs. success of the particular clinic, or claims that successful fertilization and even clinical pregnancy is the equivalent of a liveborn child, the bottom line issue of interest to patients. Prodded by Congressman Wyden's interest, the American Fertility Society and the Society for Assisted Reproductive Technology began to collect and publish overall and clinic specific data about IVF, GIFT, and ZIFT success rates. The Fertility Clinic Success Rate and Certification Act of 1992 now requires that each IVF program report annually to the Centers for Disease Control their pregnancy success rates as defined in the act.[38]

A third policy issue is the need for oversight of the laboratory settings in which IVF programs handle human oocytes, sperm, and embryos. Laboratories vary widely in the quality and replicability of their procedures, and are thought to be an important factor in the wide variance in IVF success rates. The Fertility Clinic Success Rate and Certification Act of 1992 directs the Secretary of Health and Human Services to develop a model program for the certification of embryo laboratories. This program will be made available to states that wish to adopt it. The act also provides for states to have private accrediting bodies such as the College of American Pathology and the American Fertility Society, which have adopted a joint inspection program, conduct the certification. Greater attention to laboratory conditions and practices should improve the efficacy of IVF.

Questions of IVF efficacy and consumer awareness show that IVF, while a novel reproductive procedure, also presents policy problems typical of most new medical technologies. Medical zeal and interest in self-promotion may mislead patients about its efficacy, and induce women to undergo expensive, invasive procedures that may have less chance of helping them than they thought. A 1992 proposed public offering of stock in IVF America, a chain of IVF clinics that planned to expand across the country, revealed the importance of the profit motive in providing IVF services and the need for ongoing monitoring of the industry.[39] Laboratory certification and accurate disclosure of success rates relative to other clinics is an appropriate policy response to protect the procreative freedom of infertile couples. However, it is they who will have to decide whether the risks and benefits of the procedure are worth it.

FUNDING AND ACCESS ISSUES

Another important policy issue with IVF and other reproductive technologies is cost and access. IVF costs $5,000 to $7,000 per cycle and is often ineffective, with two or three cycles necessary to achieve pregnancy when it is successful. Insurance may pay none or only some of the costs, making IVF a procedure that only wealthier couples can afford. Indeed, the cost may be prohibitive for many middle-class couples.

The high cost of IVF raises questions of access and justice in allocation of health care resources. Given the high rate of infertility, its impact on couples, and insurance coverage of many kinds of infertility treatment, there is a reasonable case for including IVF in private or public health insurance plans. Ten states have laws that require insurance coverage of infertility services. Five of these states (Arkansas, Hawaii, Massachusetts, Maryland, and Texas) currently require health insurers to include IVF as an option.[40] Courts have also ruled that insurance plans that cover surgical repair of blocked fallopian tubes as treatment for an "existing physical or mental illness" must also cover IVF, though other courts have found that IVF is not a medically necessary treatment for illness.[41]

While insurance coverage will increase access to IVF, it also increases the cost of insurance for all policyholders. Depending on the size of the pool, however, this subsidy may not be unfair. Infertility may reasonably be viewed, because of its frequency, expense, and personal importance, as one of the health risks for which people should be insured. Spread over a large group, the cost of IVF coverage is relatively small. It should not be singled out for exclusion if other infertility services are covered.

On the other hand, a policy that covered no infertility services or which excluded IVF and other high-tech procedures might not be unreasonable. At a time of great strain in the health care system, limiting coverage for procedures based on judgments about their cost, efficacy, and benefits to patients is also reasonable. If choices have to be made, people might well prefer coverage for catastrophic or life-threatening illness and preventive services rather than for infertility.

Such a judgment would support exclusion of IVF (and other fertility treatments) from public insurance programs such as Medicaid as well. Despite stereotypes of unrestrained reproduction, the poor actually have higher rates of infertility due to poverty, nutrition, and more infectious disease than does the middle class. If infertility is considered an "illness" for which "medical treatment" is available, existing law would require that Medicaid cover IVF and other infertility treatments.

Yet many people would object to spending increasingly scarce Medicaid funds on IVF when life-threatening illnesses are not adequately covered. It is not surprising that the Oregon health care plan for rationing medical resources for Medicaid patients ranked infertility treatment near the bottom.[42] Such a ranking does deny the poor infertility services available to those who have the means to pay directly. Yet if differences between public and private funding of health care are to exist, one may reasonably conclude that infertility is one place to draw the line. Such a judgment illustrates the limitations of procreative liberty as a negative right that does not entitle people to government resources to fulfill their reproductive goals.

A final issue of access is the control that IVF programs exercise over who receives their services. Many IVF programs will not treat unmarried persons. Nearly all will test couples for HIV, and may refuse the procedure if one or both of the partners test positive.[43] Some may exclude couples whom they think are unstable or unfit parents. The exclusion is usually justified on the "ethical" ground of protecting offspring who would be born in disadvantageous circumstances. However, providing IVF services to these groups would not harm children who have no other way to be born, and thus may ethically be provided if a program is so inclined.[44] Because private IVF clinics have wide discretion in selecting patients for treatment, they may in most circumstances be legally free to set the criteria for selecting patients.

CONCLUSION

This account of IVF shows how different strands of procreative liberty and different views about the status of preimplantation embryos are entwined in the use of this technology. Restriction of IVF to protect embryos will, in most cases, interfere with an infertile couple's interest in procreating and may affect other reproductive interests.

Resolution of the ethical, legal, and policy conflicts that arise in IVF depends, for the most part, on determining the relative importance of these reproductive interests vs. the perceived threat to embryos and respect for prenatal life. The widely held view that the preimplantation embryo is not a person but deserves special respect would resolve most of these conflicts in favor of the infertile couple. However, a more protective view of embryo status would not necessarily exclude central aspects of IVF practice, including embryo freezing, even though it prevents embryo discard from occurring.[45]

A final point to note is how issues of efficacy and access turn out to be as important to IVF as issues of embryo status. The legal right to use IVF is embedded in a set of socioeconomic and structural circumstances that affect exercise of the right. Socially constructed attitudes about the need to overcome infertility will be a main determinant of use. Money also counts when one is seeking access to IVF. IVF shows that procreative liberty is not a fully meaningful concept unless one has the knowledge and means to obtain IVF from the best programs, or the will to resist its allure when its use seems excessive.

NOTES

1. The focus is on married couples because most women seeking IVF are married, and most IVF programs treat only married couples. Whether the state could prohibit single persons access to IVF is discussed later in the chapter.

2. Medical Research International, Society for Assisted Reproduction, the American Fertility Society, "In Vitro Fertilization-Embryo Transfer (IVF-ET) in the United States: 1990 Results from the IVF-ET Registry," *Fertility and Sterility* 57(1992):15. This study reports 2,345 deliveries from IVF in 1990. By extrapolation the number of births for the last four years is over eight thousand.

3. Success here is measured by take-home baby rate per stimulation or egg retrieval cycle, and not clinical pregnancy rate, which many programs use to improve their statistics.

4. Eventually egg retrieval will occur in the physician's office, which will reduce the costs of the procedure. Retrieving eggs during a natural cycle without stimulation will also reduce costs, though it may also reduce efficacy.

5. Elizabeth Bartholet vividly expresses concerns about infertile women feeling compelled by their own sense of inadequacy to try IVF and to keep trying because there "is often no logical stopping point." *Family Bonds: Adoption and the Politics of Parenting* (Boston: Houghton Mifflin, 1993), 202.

6. Catholic Church, Congregation for the Doctrine of the Faith, "Instruction on Respect for Human Life in Its Origin and on the Dignity of Procreation," *Origins* 16(1987):698–711.

7. 1990 Results from the IVF-ET Registry, note [2] supra at pp. 16–19.

8. See chapter 2 [not reprinted], where the argument for infertile married couples having the same right to reproduce that fertile married couples have is developed.

9. For the sake of convenience, the term "embryo" is used throughout this [essay] rather than the technically more accurate "preembryo." Embryo thus refers to all postfertilization, preimplantation stages of development.

10. Grobstein, "The Early Development of Human Embryos," *Journal of Medicine and Philosophy* 10(1985):213, 214. Much of the ensuing description is based on Grobstein's excellent survey of early human and mammalian development.

11. However, the fertilized egg is not yet individual, as only at implantation can a single new individual be identified. Also, recent studies suggest that a new genome is not expressed until the four- to eight-cell stage of development. See Braude, Bolton, and Moore, "Human Gene Expression First Occurs between the Four- and Eight-Cell Stages of Preimplantation Development," *Nature* 332(1988):459, 460.

12. Grobstein, "Early Development," 216–17.

13. Ibid., 219, 232.

14. Ibid., 219–20

15. Ibid., 223.

16. Ibid.

17. Ibid., 223–25.

18. This view parallels the view described in chapter 3 [not reprinted] of respecting fetuses because of their symbolic value. Although not persons or entities which themselves have rights, embryos are potent symbols of human life and deserve some degree of respect on that basis alone.

19. Department of Health and Human Services, the Ethical Advisory Board in the United States, U.S. Department of Health, Education and Welfare, Ethics Advisory Board, HEW Support of Research Involving Human In Vitro Fertilization and Embryo Transfer, 44 Fed.Reg. 35033 (1979).

20. The Warnock Committee Report in Great Britain, United Kingdom, Department of Health and Social Security, Report of the Committee of Inquiring into Human Fertilisation and Embryology (1984).

21. Ontario Law Reform Commission, Report on Human Artificial Reproduction and Related Matters (1985).

22. *Davis v. Davis,* 842 S.W.2d 588 (Tenn. 1992). In reaching that conclusion, the Court relied heavily on the American Fertility Society's report "Ethical Considerations of the New Reproductive Technologies," which articulated a view similar to that set forth in the text. *Fertility and Sterility* 46, (supp. 1) (1986):295–305.

23. "Who or What is a Preembryo?" *Kennedy Institute of Ethics Journal* 1(1991):1–15.

24. John A. Robertson, "In the Beginning: The Legal Status of Early Embryos," *Virginia Law Review* 76(1990):437, 452.

25. It follows then that an IVF program must have the consent of both partners before thawing, transferring, implanting, discarding, or donating embryos.

26. Elizabeth Rosenthal, "Cost of High-Tech Fertility: Too Many Tiny Babies," *New York Times,* 26 May 1992, discusses some of the problems of the higher rate of multigestational pregnancies that occurs when more than two embryos are placed in a woman's uterus. See also chapter 9 [not reprinted], where selective reduction of multifetal pregnancies is discussed.

27. See note 22.

28. Some programs will not permit discard of fresh embryos, but will allow embryos that have been frozen for a period of time to be discarded.

29. Although the issue raises questions of the couple's right to avoid genetic reproduction, the embryo discard policy might also influence their willingness to use IVF in the first place, thus implicating their right to reproduce as well.

30. *Roe v. Wade,* 410 U.S. 113 (1973); *Planned Parenthood v. Casey,* 112 S.Ct. 2791 (1992).

31. Medical Research International, 15, 21. [See note 2.]

32. Of course, it would not harm children to be born to older mothers, even if younger mothers are more desirable rearers of offspring, if the children in question had no alternative way of being born. See chapters 4 and 8 [not reprinted].

33. For further discussion of this issue, see J. Robertson, "Posthumous Reproduction," *Indiana Law Journal* (forthcoming, 1994).

34. 842 S.W.2d 588 (Tenn. 1992).

35. "When weighed against the interests of the individuals and the burdens inherent in parenthood, the state's interest in the potential life of these preembryos is not sufficient to justify any infringement upon the freedom of these individuals to make their own decisions as to whether to allow a process to continue that may result in such a dramatic change in their lives as becoming parents." *Davis v. Davis,* 842 S.W.2d 588, 602–03 (Tenn. 1992).

36. In cases where there is no prior agreement on disposition, the courts should, as the Tennessee court recommended, resolve such disputes according to whether the party wishing to preserve the embryos has a realistic possibility of achieving his or her reproductive goals by other means. If there are no alternative opportunities to reproduce, or if going through IVF again would be unduly burdensome, it may be fairer to award the embryos to the party for whom they represent the last chance to have offspring, as might occur if the wife has lost ovarian function since the embryos were preserved. In that case, the unconsenting party should also be relieved of child support obligations. In most cases, however, the party wishing the embryos to be destroyed should prevail. See Robertson, "Resolving Disputes over Frozen Embryos," *Hastings Center Report,* November/December 1989; Robertson, "In the Beginning," 473–83.

37. Robert Pear, "Fertility Clinics Face Crackdown, *New York Times,* 26 October 1992.

38. Public Law 102-493 (H.R.4773), 24 October 1992. The act calls for reporting of the live birth rate for IVF and other assisted reproductive techniques, defined as the ratio of live births divided (1) by the number of ovarian stimulation procedures attempted at each program, and (2) by the number of successful oocyte retrieval procedures performed by each program. Section 2(b)(2)(A) and (B). Virginia now also requires clinic-specific disclosure of success rates to patients before IVF treatments occur. Va. Code Ann. Sec. 54.1-2971.1 (Michie 1991).

39. Alison Leigh Cowan, "Can a Baby-Making Venture Deliver?" *New York Times,* 1 June 1992. However, the public offering was never made.

40. Ark. Code Ann. Sec. 23-85-137 (Michie 1992); Haw. Rev. Stat. Ann. Sec. 431:10A-116.5 (1992); Md. Ann. Code art. 48A, Sec. 354DD (1992); Tex. Ins. Code Ann. art. 3.51-6, Sec. 3A (West 1993).

41. *Egert v. Connecticut General Life Ins. Co.,* 900 F.2d 1032 (7th Cir.)(infertility an illness and IVF necessary to treat it); *Kinzie v. Physician's Liability Insur. Co.,* 750 P.2d 1140 (Okl. App. 1987)

(IVF not a medically necessary procedure under the insurance contract).

42. David C. Hadorn, "Setting Health Care Priorities in Oregon: Cost Effectiveness Meets the Rule of Rescue," *Journal of the American Medical Association* 265(1991):2218.

43. Such discrimination against persons with HIV may be a violation of the Americans with Disabilities Act, because HIV status qualifies as a disability within the meaning of that law and an infertility clinic may be considered a place of public accommodation. 42 U.S.C. 12182 (1990).

44. The patient groups in question may have a right against a state that denies them access to IVF or other reproductive services, but they would not have the same right to services from private actors unless civil rights or antidiscrimination laws apply. See chapters 2 and 4 [not reprinted].

45. Persons who view the fertilized egg and embryo as persons from the time of fertilization may differ over the extent to which IVF should be permitted at all. Some may permit it with no freezing, or with freezing but no embryo discard.

SUSAN SHERWIN

Feminist Ethics and In Vitro Fertilization[1]

Susan Sherwin is a Professor of Philosophy at Dalhousie University. Her interests lie in feminist theory, bioethics and ethics. She was the recipient of the Canadian Association of University Teachers' Sarah Shorten Award in 2000. Her publications include the books *No Longer Patient: Feminist Ethics and Health Care* (Temple University Press) and *The Politics of Women's Health Health: Exploring Agency and Autonomy* (Temple University Press).

New technology in human reproduction has provoked wide ranging arguments about the desirability and moral justifiability of many of these efforts. Authors of biomedical ethics have ventured into the field to offer the insight of moral theory to these complex moral problems of contemporary life. I believe, however, that the moral theories most widely endorsed today are problematic and that a new approach to ethics is necessary if we are to address the concerns and perspectives identified by feminist theorists in our considerations of such topics. Hence, I propose to look at one particular technique in the growing repertoire of new reproductive technologies, in vitro fertilization (IVF), in order to consider the insight which the mainstream approaches to moral theory have offered to this debate, and to see the difference made by a feminist approach to ethics.

I have argued elsewhere that the most widely accepted moral theories of our time are inadequate for addressing many of the moral issues we encounter in our lives, since they focus entirely on such abstract qualities of moral agents as autonomy or quantities of happiness, and they are addressed to agents who are conceived of as independent, non-tuistic individuals. In contrast, I claimed, we need a theory which places the locus of ethical concerns in a complex social network of interrelated persons who are involved in special sorts of relations with one another. Such a theory, as I envision it, would be influenced by the insights and concerns of feminist theory, and hence, I have called it feminist ethics.[2]

In this [essay], I propose to explore the differences between a feminist approach to ethics and other, more traditional approaches in examining the propriety of developing and implementing in vitro fertilization and related technologies. This is a complicated task, since each sort of ethical theory admits of a variety of interpretations and hence of a variety of conclusions on concrete ethical issues. Nonetheless, certain themes and trends can be seen to emerge. Feminist thinking is also ambivalent in application, for feminists are quite torn about their response to this sort of technology. It is my hope that a systematic theoretic evaluation of

From Marsha Hanen and Kai Nielsen, eds., *Science, Morality and Feminist Theory* (Calgary, Alberta: University of Calgary Press, 1987), pp. 265–84. Reprinted by permission of the author and the University of Calgary Press.

IVF from the point of view of a feminist ethical theory will help feminists like myself sort through our uncertainty on these matters.

Let me begin with a quick description of IVF for the uninitiated. In vitro fertilization is the technology responsible for what the media likes to call 'test tube babies.' It circumvents, rather than cures, a variety of barriers to conception, primarily those of blocked fallopian tubes and low sperm counts. In vitro fertilization involves removing ova from the woman's body, collecting sperm from the man's, combining them to achieve conception in the laboratory, and, a few days later, implanting some number of the newly fertilized eggs directly into the woman's womb with the hope that pregnancy will continue normally from this point on. This process requires that a variety of hormones be administered to the woman—which involve profound emotional and physical changes—that her blood and urine be monitored daily, and then at 3 hour intervals, [and] that ultrasound be used to determine when ovulation occurs. In some clinics, implantation requires that she remain immobile for 48 hours (including 24 hours in the head down position). IVF is successful in about 10–15% of the cases selected as suitable, and commonly involves multiple efforts at implantation.

Let us turn now to the responses that philosophers working within the traditional approaches to ethics have offered on this subject. A review of the literature in bioethics identifies a variety of concerns with this technology. Philosophers who adopt a theological perspective tend to object that such technology is wrong because it is not "natural" and undermines God's plan for the family. Paul Ramsey, for instance, is concerned about the artificiality of IVF and other sorts of reproductive technology with which it is potentially associated, e.g. embryo transfer, ova as well as sperm donation or sale, increased eugenic control, etc.:

> But there is as yet no discernible evidence that we are recovering a sense for man [sic] as a natural object . . . toward whom a . . . form of "natural piety" is appropriate . . . parenthood is certainly one of those "courses of action" natural to man, which cannot without violation be disassembled and put together again.[3]

Leon Kass argues a similar line in " 'Making Babies' Revisited."[4] He worries that our conception of humanness will not survive the technological permutations before us, and that we will treat these new artificially conceived embryos more as objects than as subjects; he also fears that we will be unable to track traditional human categories of parenthood and lineage, and that this loss would cause us to lose track of important aspects of our identity. The recent position paper of the Catholic Church on reproductive technology reflects related concerns:

> It is through the secure and recognized relationship to his [sic] own parents that the child can discover his own identity and achieve his own proper human development . . .
>
> Heterologous artificial fertilization violates the rights of the child; it deprives him of his filial relationship with his parental origins and can hinder the maturing of his personal identity.[5]

Philosophers partial to utilitarianism prefer a more scientific approach; they treat these sorts of concerns as sheer superstition. They carefully explain to their theological colleagues that there is no clear sense of "natural" and certainly no sense that demands special moral status. All medical activity, and perhaps all human activity, can be seen in some sense as being "interference with nature," but that is hardly grounds for avoiding such action. "Humanness," too, is a concept that admits of many interpretations; generally, it does not provide satisfactory grounds for moral distinctions. Further, it is no longer thought appropriate to focus too strictly on questions of lineage and strict biological parentage, and, they note, most theories of personal identity do not rely on such matters.

Where some theologians object that "fertilization achieved outside the bodies of the couple remains by this very fact deprived of the meanings of the values which are expressed in the language of the body and the union of human persons,"[6] utilitarians quickly dismiss the objection against reproduction without sexuality in a properly sanctified marriage. See, for instance, Michael Bayles in *Reproductive Ethics:* ". . . even if reproduction should occur only within a context of marital love, the point of that requirement is the nurturance of offspring. Such nurturance does not depend on the sexual act itself. The argument confuses the biological act with the familial context."[7]

Another area of disagreement between theological ethicists and their philosophical critics is the significance of the wedge argument to the debate about IVF. IVF is already a complex technology involving research on superovulation, "harvesting" of ova, fertilization, and embryo implants. It is readily adaptable to technology involving the transfer of ova and embryos, and hence their donation or sale, as well as to the "rental of womb space"; it also contributes to an increasing ability to foster fetal growth outside of the womb and, potentially, to the development of artificial wombs covering the whole period of gestation. It is already sometimes combined with artificial insemination and is frequently used to produce surplus fertilized eggs to be frozen for later use. Theological ethicists worry that such activity, and further reproductive developments we can anticipate (such as human cloning), violate God's plan for human reproduction. They worry about the cultural shift involved in viewing reproduction as a scientific enterprise, rather than the "miracle of love" which religious proponents prefer: "[He] cannot be desired or conceived as the product of an intervention of medical or biological techniques; that would be equivalent to reducing him to an object of scientific technology."[8] And, worse, they note, we cannot anticipate the ultimate outcome of this rapidly expanding technology.

The where-will-it-all-end hand-wringing that comes with this sort of religious futurology is rejected by most analytical philosophers; they urge us to realize that few slopes are as slippery as the pessimists would have us believe, that scientists are moral people and quite capable of evaluating each new form of technology on its own merits, and that IVF must be judged by its own consequences and not the possible result of some future technology with which it may be linked. Samuel Gorovitz is typical:

> It is not enough to show that disaster awaits if the process is not controlled. A man walking East in Omaha will drown in the Atlantic—if he does not stop. The argument must also rest on the evidence about the likelihood that judgment and control will be exercised responsibly . . . Collectively we have significant capacity to exercise judgment and control . . . our record has been rather good in regard to medical treatment and research.[9]

The question of the moral status of the fertilized eggs is more controversial. Since the superovulation involved in producing eggs for collection tends to produce several at once, and the process of collecting eggs is so difficult, and since the odds against conception on any given attempt are so slim, several eggs are usually collected and fertilized at once. A number of these fertilized eggs will be introduced to the womb with the hope that at least one will implant and gestation will begin, but there are frequently some "extras." Moral problems arise as to what should be done with these surplus eggs. They can be frozen for future use (since odds are against the first attempt "taking"), or they can be used as research material, or simply discarded. Canadian clinics get around the awkwardness of their ambivalence on the moral status of these cells by putting them all into the woman's womb. This poses the devastating threat of six or eight "successfully" implanting, and a woman being put into the position of carrying a litter; something, we might note, her body is not constructed to do.

Those who take a hard line against abortion and argue that the embryo is a person from the moment of conception object to all these procedures, and, hence, they argue, there is no morally acceptable means of conducting IVF. To this line, utilitarians offer the standard responses. Personhood involves moral, not biological categories. A being neither sentient nor conscious is not a person in any meaningful sense. For example, Gorovitz argues, "Surely the concept of person involves in some fundamental way the capacity for sentience, or an awareness of sensations at the very least."[10] Bayles says, "For fetuses to have moral status they must be capable of good or bad in their lives . . . What happens to them must make a difference to them. Consequently some form of awareness is necessary for moral status."[11] (Apparently, clinicians in the field have been trying to avoid this whole issue by coining a new term in the hopes of identifying a new ontological category, that of the "preembryo.")[12]

Many bioethicists have agreed here, as they have in the abortion debate, that the principal moral question of IVF is the moral status and rights of the embryo. Once they resolve that question, they can, like Engelhardt, conclude that since fetuses are not persons, and since reproductive processes occurring outside a human body pose no special moral problems, "there will be no sustainable moral arguments in principle . . . against in vitro fertilization."[13] He argues,

> in vitro fertilization and techniques that will allow us to study and control human reproduction are morally neutral instruments for the realization of profoundly important human goals, which are bound up with the realization of the good of others: children for infertile parents and greater health for the children that will be born.[14]

Moral theorists also express worries about the safety of the process, and by that they tend to mean the safety to fetuses that may result from this technique. Those fears have largely been put to rest in the years since the first IVF baby was born in 1978, for the couple of thousand infants reportedly produced by this technique to date seem no more prone to apparent birth defects than the population at large, and, in fact, there seems to be evidence that birth defects may be less common in this group—presumably because of better monitoring and pre and post natal care. (There is concern expressed, however, in some circles outside of the bioethical literature about the longterm effect of some of the hormones involved, in light of our belated discoveries of the effect of DES usage on offspring. This concern is aggravated by the chemical similarity of clomid, one of the hormones used in IVF, to DES.)[15]

Most of the literature tends to omit comment on the uncertainties associated with the effect of drugs inducing superovulation in the woman concerned, or with the dangers posed by the general anaesthetic required for the laparoscopy procedure; the emotional costs associated with this therapy are also overlooked, even though there is evidence that it is extremely stressful in the 85–90% of the attempts that fail, and that those who succeed have difficulty in dealing with common parental feelings of anger and frustration with a child they tried so hard to get. Nonetheless, utilitarian theory could readily accommodate such concerns, should the philosophers involved think to look for them. In principle, no new moral theory is yet called for, although a widening of perspective (to include the effects on the women involved) would certainly be appropriate.

The easiest solution to the IVF question seems to be available to ethicists of a deontological orientation who are keen on autonomy and rights and free of religious prejudice. For them, IVF is simply a private matter, to be decided by the couple concerned together with a medical specialist. The desire to have and raise children is a very common one and generally thought to be a paradigm case of a purely private matter. Couples seeking this technology face medical complications that require the assistance of a third party, and it is thought, "it would be unfair to make infertile couples pass up the joys of rearing infants or suffer the burdens of rearing handicapped children."[16] Certainly, meeting individuals' desires/needs is the most widely accepted argument in favour of the use of this technology.

What is left, then, in the more traditional ethical discussions, is usually some hand waving about costs. This is an extremely expensive procedure; estimates range from $1500 to $6000 per attempt. Gorovitz says, for instance, "there is the question of the distribution of costs, a question that has heightened impact if we consider the use of public funds to pay for medical treatment."[17] Debate tends to end here in the mystery of how to balance soaring medical costs of various sorts and a comment that no new ethical problems are posed.

Feminists share many of these concerns, but they find many other moral issues involved in the development and use of such technology and note the silence of the standard moral approaches in addressing these matters. Further, feminism does not identify the issues just cited as the primary areas of moral concern. Nonetheless, IVF is a difficult issue for feminists.

On the one hand, most feminists share the concern for autonomy held by most moral theorists, and they are interested in allowing women freedom of choice in reproductive matters. This freedom is most widely discussed in connection with access to safe and effective contraception and, when necessary, to abortion services. For women who are unable to conceive because of blocked fallopian tubes, or certain fertility problems of their partners, IVF provides the technology to permit pregnancy which is otherwise impossible. Certainly most of the women seeking IVF perceive it to be technology that increases their reproductive freedom of choice. So, it would seem that feminists should support this sort of technology as part of our general concern to foster the degree of reproductive control women may have over their own bodies. Some feminists have chosen this route. But feminists must also note that IVF as practiced does not altogether satisfy the motivation of fostering individual autonomy.

It is, after all, the sort of technology that requires medical intervention, and hence it is not really controlled by the women seeking it, but rather by the medical staff providing this "service." IVF is not available to every woman who is medically suitable, but only to those who are judged to be worthy by the medical specialists concerned. To be a candidate for this procedure, a woman must have a husband and an apparently stable marriage. She must satisfy those specialists that she and her husband have appropriate resources to support any children produced by this arrangement (in addition, of course, to the funds required to purchase the treatment in the first place), and that they generally 'deserve' this support. IVF is not available to single women, lesbian women, or women not securely placed in the middle class or beyond. Nor is it available to women whom the controlling medical practitioners judge to be deviant with respect to their norms of who makes a good mother. The supposed freedom of choice, then, is provided only to selected women who have been screened by the personal values of those administering the technology.

Further, even for these women, the record on their degree of choice is unclear. Consider, for instance, that this treatment has always been very experimental: it was introduced without the prior primate studies which are required for most new forms of medical technology, and it continues to be carried out under constantly shifting protocols, with little empirical testing, as clinics try to raise their very poor success rates. Moreover, consent forms are perceived by patients to be quite restrictive procedures and women seeking this technology are not in a particularly strong position to bargain to revise the terms; there is no alternate clinic down the street to choose if a women dislikes her treatment at some clinic, but there are usually many other women waiting for access to her place in the clinic should she choose to withdraw.

Some recent studies indicate that few of the women participating in current programs really know how low the success rates are.[18] And it is not apparent that participants are encouraged to ponder the medical unknowns associated with various aspects of the technique, such as the long term consequences of superovulation and the use of hormones chemically similar to DES. Nor is it the case that the consent procedure involves consultation on how to handle the disposal of "surplus" zygotes. It is doubtful that the women concerned have much real choice about which procedure is followed with the eggs they will not need. These policy decisions are usually made at the level of the clinic. It should be noted here that at least one feminist argues that neither the woman, nor the doctors have the right to choose to destroy these embryos: ". . . because no one, not even its parents, owns the embryo/fetus, no one has the *right* to destroy it, even at a very early development stage . . . to destroy an embryo is not an automatic entitlement held by anyone, including its genetic parents."[19]

Moreover, some participants reflect deep seated ambivalence on the part of many women about the procedure—they indicate that their marriage and status depends on a determination to do "whatever is possible" in pursuit of their "natural" childbearing function—and they are not helped to work through the seeming imponderables associated with their long term well-being. Thus, IVF as practiced involves significant limits on the degree of autonomy deontologists insist on in other medical contexts, though the non-feminist literature is insensitive to this anomaly.

From the perspective of consequentialism, feminists take a long view and try to see IVF in the context of the burgeoning range of techniques in the area of human reproductive technology. While some of this technology seems to hold the potential of benefitting women generally—by leading to better understanding of conception and contraception, for instance—there is a wary suspicion that this research will help foster new techniques and products such as human cloning and the development of artificial wombs which can, in principle, make the majority of women superfluous. (This is not a wholly paranoid fear in a woman-hating culture: we can anticipate that there will be great pressure for such techniques in subsequent generations, since one of the 'successes' of reproductive technology to date has been to allow parents to control the sex of their offspring; the "choice" now made possible clearly threatens to result in significant imbalances in the ratio of boy to girl infants. Thus, it appears, there will likely be significant shortages of women to bear children in the future, and we can anticipate pressures for further technological solutions to the "new" problem of reproduction that will follow.)

Many authors from all traditions consider it necessary to ask why it is that some couples seek this technology so desperately. Why is it so important to so many people to produce their "own" child? On this question, theorists in the analytic tradition seem to shift to previously rejected ground and suggest that this is a natural, or at least a proper, desire. Engelhardt, for example, says "The use of technology in the fashioning of children is integral to the goal of rendering the world congenial to persons."[20] Bayles more cautiously observes that "A desire to beget for its own sake . . . is probably irrational"; nonetheless, he immediately concludes, "these techniques for fulfilling that desire have been found ethically permissible."[21] R. G. Edwards and David Sharpe state the case most strongly: "the desire to have children must be among the most basic of human instincts, and denying it can lead to considerable psychological and social difficulties."[22] Interestingly, although the recent pronouncement of the Catholic Church assumes that "the desire for a child is natural,"[23] it denies that a couple has a right to a child: 'The child is not an object to which one has a right."[24]

Here, I believe, it becomes clear why we need a deeper sort of feminist analysis. We must look at the sort of social arrangements and cultural values that underlie the drive to assume such risks for the sake of biological parenthood. We find that the capitalism, racism, sexism, and elitism of our culture have combined to create a set of attitudes which views children as commodities whose value is derived from their possession of parental chromosomes. Children are valued as privatized commodities, reflecting the virility and heredity of their parents. They are also viewed as the responsibility of their parents and are not seen as the social treasure and burden that they are. Parents must tend their needs on pain of prosecution, and, in return, they get to keep complete control over them. Other adults are inhibited from having warm, stable interactions with the children of others—it is as suspect to try to hug and talk regularly with a child who is not one's own as it is to fondle and hang longingly about a car or a bicycle which belongs to someone else—so those who wish to know children well often find they must have their own.

Women are persuaded that their most important purpose in life is to bear and raise children; they are told repeatedly that their life is incomplete, that they are lacking in fulfillment if they do not have children. And, in fact, many women do face a barren existence without children. Few women have access to meaningful, satisfying jobs. Most do not find themselves in the centre of the romantic personal relationships which the culture pretends is the norm for heterosexual couples. And they have been socialized to be fearful of close friendships with others—they are taught to distrust other women, and to avoid the danger of friendship with men other than their husbands. Children remain the one hope for real intimacy and for the sense of accomplishment which comes from doing work one judges to be valuable.

To be sure, children can provide that sense of self worth, although for many women (and probably for all mothers at some times) motherhood is not the romanticized satisfaction they are led to expect. But there is something very wrong with a culture where childrearing is the only outlet available to most women in which to pursue fulfillment. Moreover, there is something wrong with the ownership theory of children that keeps other adults at a distance from children. There ought to be a variety of close relationships possible between children and adults so that we all recognize that we have a stake in the well-being of the young, and we all benefit from contact with their view of the world.

In such a world, it would not be necessary to spend the huge sums on designer children which IVF requires while millions of other children starve to death each year. Adults who enjoyed children could be involved in caring for them whether or not they produced them biologically. And, if the institution of marriage survives, women and men would marry because they wished to share their lives together, not because the men needed someone to produce heirs for them and women needed financial support for their children. That would be a world in which we might have reproductive freedom of choice. The world we now live in has so limited women's options and self-esteem, it is legitimate to question the freedom behind women's demand for this technology, for it may well be largely a reflection of constraining social perspectives.

Nonetheless, I must acknowledge that some couples today genuinely mourn their incapacity to produce children without IVF, and there are very significant and unique joys which can be found in producing and raising one's own children which are not accessible to persons in infertile relationships. We must sympathize with these people. None of us shall live to see the implementation of the ideal cultural values outlined above which would make the demand for IVF less severe. It is with real concern that some feminists suggest that the personal wishes of couples with fertility difficulties may not be compatible with the overall interests of women and children.

Feminist thought, then, helps us to focus on different dimensions of the problem than do other sorts of approaches. But, with this perspective, we still have difficulty in reaching a final conclusion on whether to encourage, tolerate, modify, or restrict this sort of reproductive technology. I suggest that we turn to the developing theories of feminist ethics for guidance in resolving this question.[25]

In my view, a feminist ethics is a moral theory that focuses on relations among persons as well as on individuals. It has as a model an inter-connected social fabric, rather than the familiar one of isolated, independent atoms; and it gives primacy to bonds among people rather than to rights to independence. It is a theory that focuses on concrete situations and persons and not on free-floating abstract actions.[26] Although many details have yet to be worked out, we can see some of its implications in particular problem areas such as this.

It is a theory that is explicitly conscious of the social, political, and economic relations that exist among persons; in particular, as a feminist theory, it attends to the implications of actions or policies on the status of women. Hence, it is necessary to ask questions from the perspective of feminist ethics in addition to those which are normally asked from the perspective of mainstream ethical theories. We must view issues such as this one in the context of the social and political realities in which they arise, and resist the attempt to evaluate actions or practices in isolation (as traditional responses in biomedical ethics often do). Thus, we cannot just address the question of IVF per se without asking how IVF contributes to general patterns of women's oppression. As Kathryn Payne Addleson has argued about abortion,[27] a feminist perspective raises questions that are inadmissible within the traditional ethical frameworks, and yet, for women in a patriarchal society, they are value questions of greater urgency. In particular, a feminist ethics, in contrast to other approaches in biomedical ethics, would take seriously the concerns just reviewed which are part of the debate in the feminist literature.

A feminist ethics would also include components of theories that have been developed as "feminine ethics," as sketched out by the empirical work of Carol Gilligan.[28] (The best example of such a theory is the work of Nel Noddings in her influential book *Caring*.[29]) In other words, it would be a theory that gives primacy to interpersonal relationships and woman-centered values such as nurturing, empathy, and cooperation. Hence, in the case of IVF, we must care for the women and men who are so despairing about their infertility as to want to spend the vast sums and risk the associated physical and emotional costs of the treatment, in pursuit of "their own children." That is, we should, in Noddings' terms, see their reality as our own and address their very real sense of loss. In so doing, however, we must also consider the implications of this sort of solution to their difficulty. While meeting the perceived desires of some women—desires which are problematic in themselves, since they are so compatible with the values of a culture deeply oppressive to women—this technology threatens to further entrench those values which are responsible for that oppression. A larger vision suggests that the technology offered may, in reality, reduce women's freedom and, if so, it should be avoided.

A feminist ethics will not support a wholly negative response, however, for that would not address our obligation to care for those suffering from infertility; it is the responsibility of those who oppose further implementation of this technology to work towards the changes in the social arrangements that will lead to a reduction of the sense of need for this sort of solution. On the medical front, research and treatment ought to be stepped up to reduce the rates of [puerperal] sepsis and gonorrhea which often result in tubal blockage, more attention should be directed at the causes and possible cures for male infertility, and we should pursue techniques that will permit safe reversible sterilization providing women with better alternatives to tubal ligation as a means of fertility control; these sorts of technology would increase the control of many women over their own fertility and would be compatible with feminist objectives. On the social front, we must continue the social pressure to change the status of women and children in our society from that of breeder and possession respectively; hence, we must develop a vision of society as community where all participants are valued members, regardless of age or gender. And we must challenge the notion that having one's wife produce a child with his own genes is sufficient cause for the wives of men with low sperm counts to be expected to undergo the physical and emotional assault such technology involves.

Further, a feminist ethics will attend to the nature of the relationships among those concerned. Annette Baier has eloquently argued for the importance of developing an ethics of trust,[30] and I believe a feminist ethics must address the question of the degree of trust appropriate to the relationships involved. Feminists have noted that women have little reason to trust the medical specialists who offer to respond to their reproductive desires, for commonly women's interests have not come first from the medical point of view.[31] In fact, it is accurate to perceive feminist attacks on reproductive technology as expressions of the lack of trust feminists have in those who control the technology. Few feminists object to reproductive technology per se; rather they express concern about who controls it and how it can be used to further exploit women. The problem with reproductive technology is that it concentrates power in reproductive matters in the hands of those who are not directly involved in the actual bearing and rearing of the child; i.e., in men who relate to their clients in a technical, professional, authoritarian manner. It is a further step in the medicalization of pregnancy and birth which, in North America, is marked by relationships between pregnant women and their doctors which are very different from the traditional relationships between pregnant women and midwives. The latter relationships fostered an atmosphere of mutual trust which is impossible to replicate in hospital deliveries today. In fact, current approaches to pregnancy, labour, and birth tend to view the mother as a threat to the fetus who must be coerced to comply with medical procedures designed to ensure delivery of healthy babies at whatever cost necessary to the mother. Frequently, the fetus-mother relationship is medically characterized as adversarial and the physicians choose to foster a sense of alienation and passivity in the role they permit the mother. However well IVF may serve the interests of the few women with access to it, it more clearly serves the interests (be they commercial, professional, scholarly, or purely patriarchal) of those who control it.

Questions such as these are a puzzle to those engaged in the traditional approaches to ethics, for they always urge us to separate the question of evaluating the morality of various forms of reproductive technology in themselves, from questions about particular uses of that technology. From the perspective of a feminist ethics, however, no such distinction can be meaningfully made. Reproductive technology is not an abstract activity; it is an activity done in particular contexts and it is those contexts which must be addressed.

Feminist concerns cited earlier made clear the difficulties we have with some of our traditional ethical concepts; hence, feminist ethics directs us to rethink our basic ethical notions. Autonomy, or freedom of choice, is not a matter to be determined in isolated instances, as is commonly assumed in many approaches to applied ethics. Rather it is a matter that involves reflection on one's whole life situation. The freedom of choice feminists appeal to in the abortion situation is freedom to define one's status as a childbearer, given the social, economic, and political significance of reproduction for women. A feminist perspective permits us to understand that reproductive freedom includes control of one's sexuality, protection against coerced sterilization (or iatrogenic sterilization, e.g. as caused by the Dalkon shield), and the existence of a social and economic network of support for the children we may choose to bear. It is the freedom to redefine our roles in society according to our concerns and needs as women.

In contrast, the consumer freedom to purchase technology, allowed only to a few couples of the privileged classes (in traditionally approved relationships), seems to entrench further the patriarchal notions of woman's role as childbearer and of heterosexual monogamy as the only acceptable intimate relationship. In other words, this sort of choice does not seem to foster autonomy for women on the broad scale. IVF is a practice which seems to reinforce sexist, classist, and often racist assumptions of our culture; therefore, on our revised understanding of freedom, the contribution of this technology to the general autonomy of women is largely negative.

We can now see the advantage of a feminist ethics over mainstream ethical theories, for a feminist analysis explicitly accepts the need for a political component to our understanding of ethical issues. In this, it differs from traditional ethical theories and it also differs from a simply feminine ethics approach, such as the one Noddings offers, for Noddings seems to rely on individual relations exclusively and is deeply suspicious of political alliances as potential threats to the pure relation of caring. Yet, a full understanding of both the threat of IVF, and the alternative action necessary should we decide to reject IVF, is possible only if it includes a political dimension reflecting on the role of women in society.

From the point of view of feminist ethics, the primary question to consider is whether this and other forms of reproductive technology threaten to reinforce the lack of autonomy which women now experience in our culture—even as they appear, in the short run, to be increasing freedom. We must recognize that the interconnections among the social forces oppressive to women underlie feminists' mistrust of this technology which advertises itself as increasing women's autonomy.[32] The political perspective which directs us to look at how this technology fits in with general patterns of treatment for women is not readily accessible to traditional moral theories, for it involves categories of concern not accounted for in those theories—e.g., the complexity of issues which makes it inappropriate to study them in isolation from one another, the role of oppression in shaping individual desires, and potential differences in moral status which are connected with differences in treatment.

It is the set of connections constituting women's continued oppression in our society which inspires feminists to resurrect the old slippery slope arguments to warn against IVF. We must recognize that women's existing lack of control in reproductive matters begins the debate on a pretty steep incline. Technology with the potential to further remove control of reproduction from women makes the slope very slippery indeed. This new technology, though offered under the guise of increasing reproductive freedom, threatens to result, in fact, in a significant decrease in freedom, especially since it is a technology that will always include the active involvement of designated specialists and will not ever be a private matter for the couple or women concerned.

Ethics ought not to direct us to evaluate individual cases without also looking at the implications of our decisions from a wide perspective. My argument is that a theory of feminist ethics provides that wider perspective, for its different sort of methodology is sensitive to both the personal and the social dimensions of issues. For that reason, I believe it is the only ethical perspective suitable for evaluating issues of this sort.

NOTES

1. I appreciate the helpful criticism I have received from colleagues in the Dalhousie Department of Philosophy, the Canadian Society for Women in Philosophy, and the Women's Studies program of the University of Alberta where earlier versions of this paper were read. I am particularly grateful for the careful criticism it has received from Linda Williams and Christine Overall.

2. Susan Sherwin, "A Feminist Approach to Ethics," *Dalhousie Review* 64, 4 (Winter 1984–85) 704–13.

3. Paul Ramsey, "Shall We Reproduce?" *Journal of the American Medical Association* 220 (June 12, 1972), 1484.

4. Leon Kass, '"Making Babies" Revisited,' *The Public Interest* 54 (Winter 1979), 32–60.

5. Joseph Cardinal Ratzinger and Alberto Bovone, "Instruction on Respect for Human Life in its Origin and on the Dignity of Procreation: Replies to Certain Questions of the Day" (Vatican City: Vatican Polyglot Press 1987), 23–24.

6. Ibid., 28.

7. Michael Bayles, *Reproductive Ethics* (Englewood Cliffs, NJ: Prentice-Hall 1984), 15.

8. Ratzinger and Bovone, 28.

9. Samuel Gorovitz, *Doctors' Dilemmas: Moral Conflict and Medical Care* (New York: Oxford University Press 1982), 168.

10. Ibid., 173.

11. Bayles, 66.

12. I owe this observation to Linda Williams.

13. H. Tristram Engelhardt, *The Foundations of Bioethics* (Oxford: Oxford University Press 1986), 237.

14. Ibid., 241.

15. Anita Direcks, "Has the Lesson Been Learned?" *DES Action Voice* 28 (Spring 1986), 1–4; and Nikita A. Crook, "Clomid," DES Action/Toronto Factsheet #442 (available from 60 Grosvenor St., Toronto, M5S 1B6).

16. Bayles, 32. Though Bayles is not a deontologist, he does concisely express a deontological concern here.

17. Gorovitz, 177.

18. Michael Soules, "The In Vitro Fertilization Pregnancy Rate: Let's Be Honest with One Another," *Fertility and Sterility* 43, 4 (1985) 511–13.

19. Christine Overall, *Ethics and Human Reproduction: A Feminist Analysis* (Allen and Unwin, forthcoming), 104 ms.

20. Engelhardt, 239.

21. Bayles, 31.

22. Robert G. Edwards and David J. Sharpe, "Social Values and Research in Human Embryology," *Nature* 231 (May 14, 1971), 87.

23. Ratzinger and Bovone, 33.

24. Ibid., 34.

25. Many authors are now working on an understanding of what feminist ethics entail. Among the Canadian papers I am familiar with are Kathryn Morgan's "Women and Moral Madness," Sheila Mullet's "Only Connect: The Place of Self-Knowledge in Ethics," [in Marsha Hanen and Kai Nielsen, eds., *Science, Monthly, and Feminist Theory* (Calgary, Alberta: University of Calgary Press, 1987)], and Leslie Wilson's "Is a Feminine Ethics Enough?" *Atlantis* (forthcoming).

26. Sherwin, "A Feminist Approach to Ethics."

27. Kathryn Payne Addelson, "Moral Revolution," in Marilyn Pearsall, ed., *Women and Values* (Belmont, CA: Wadsworth 1986). 291–309.

28. Carol Gilligan, *In a Different Voice* (Cambridge, MA: Harvard University Press 1982).

29. Nel Noddings, *Caring* (Berkeley: University of California Press 1984).

30. Annette Baier, "What Do Women Want in a Moral Theory?" *Nous* 19 (March 1985), 53–64, and "Trust and Antitrust," *Ethics* 96 (January 1986), 231–60.

31. Linda Williams presents this position particularly clearly in her invaluable work "But What Will They Mean for Women? Feminist Concerns About the New Reproductive Technologies," No. 6 in the *Feminist Perspectives* Series, CRIAW.

32. Marilyn Frye vividly describes the phenomenon of interrelatedness which supports sexist oppression by appeal to the metaphor of a bird cage composed of thin wires, each relatively harmless in itself, but, collectively, the wires constitute an overwhelming barrier to the inhabitant of the cage. Marilyn Frye, *The Politics of Reality: Essays in Feminist Theory* (Trumansburg, NY: The Crossing Press 1983), 4–7.

ISLAT WORKING GROUP*

ART into Science: Regulation of Fertility Techniques

Lori B. Andrews is Distinguished Professor of Law at Chicago-Kent Law School. She is also Director of the Institute for Science, Law and Technology at the Illinois Institute of Technology. Professor Andrews' most recent books are *The Body Bazaar: The Market for Human Tissue in the Biotechnology Age* (Crown Publishers), *Future Perfect: Confronting Decisions about Genetics* (Columbia University Press), and *The Clone Age: Adventures in the New World of Reproductive Technology.*

Nanette Elster is an Associate Professor at the Institute for Bioethics, Health Policy, and Law at the University of Louisville and in the Department of Obstetrics and Gynecology at the University of Louisville School of Medicine. She is the author or coauthor of numerous articles on genetic and reproductive health. Her area of particular interest is the impact of new biomedical technologies on women and children.

On 25 July 1998, Louise Brown, the first child born through in vitro fertilization, was 20 years old. Since her birth, 300,000 other children have been created worldwide by in vitro fertilization (IVF). Variations of the technology abound, including the use of donor gametes, transfer of the embryo into a surrogate, and preimplantation genetic screening of in vitro embryos. Potential parents now seemingly have greater control over how they bring children into the world. They can even, as did a California couple, choose an egg donor, sperm donor, and surrogate gestational mother, thus creating a child with five or more potential legal parents.[1]

The assisted reproductive technology (ART) industry, with an annual revenue of $2 billion,[2] is growing to serve an estimated one of six American couples who are infertile.[3] Annually, in the United States alone, approximately 60,000 births result from donor insemination,[4] 15,000 from IVF,[5] and at least 1000[6] from surrogacy arrangements. In contrast, only about 30,000 healthy infants are available for adoption.[7] What is striking about this comparison is that every state has an elaborate regulatory mechanism for adoption whereas only two states, Virginia and New Hampshire, have enacted legislation to comprehensively address ARTs.

Despite the fact that many families have been created with ART, the field has not been without problems. These include experimentation without appropriate review, use of embryos without consent, inadequate informed consent, conflicts regarding control over stored gametes and embryos, and failure to routinely screen donors for disease. Currently, the United States has taken a laissez-faire approach toward ART. In contrast, other countries combine outright prohibitions of certain procedures, such as sex selection for nonmedical purposes [for example, in Canada],[8] and licensing requirements to limit who may perform reproductive technologies [for example, in the United Kingdom].[9] Despite the existence of voluntary guidelines by the American Society [for] Reproductive Medicine abuses continue to occur.

*Working Group members: Lori Andrews and Nanette Elster, cochairs; Robert Gatter, Terri Finesmith Horwich, Ami Jaeger, Susan Klock, Eugene Pergament, Francis Pizzulli, Robyn Shapiro, Mark Siegler, Peggie Smith, and Shirley Zager. The Group is located at The Institute for Science, Law, and Technology (ISLAT), Illinois Institute of Technology, Chicago, IL 60661-3691, USA.

Reprinted with permission from *Science* 281 (July 31, 1998), 651–52. Copyright © 1998 by the American Association for the Advancement of Science.

Medical researchers in other fields risk losing federal funds or academic positions if they do not comply with human subjects' protections. Reproductive technologists, many of whom practice in private clinics, do not have such constraints.

REGULATION OF ART

In the United Kingdom a licensing authority was established under the Human Fertilization and Embryology Authority. When such an oversight group was suggested in the United States, reproductive technologists argued that they should not be singled out for regulations that do not apply to other areas of medicine. Yet enhanced regulation is justified in this area because the constraints usually in place in other fields of medicine are lacking here.

For several reasons, reproductive technology has been insulated from regulations that apply to other medical fields. For example, the political undertow from the abortion debate has led every administration from the late 1970s to the present to reject federal funding of embryo and fetal research. As a result, IVF clinics, which do not receive federal research funding, are not required to set up institutional review boards (IRBs) or to review innovative therapies under the human research subject regulations of the Department of Health and Human Services. In fact, IRB review is so rare in this field that it has been viewed as "remarkable."[10]

Unlike new drugs and new medical equipment, which are regulated by the Food and Drug Administration, no similar review of innovative ART medical procedures is required.[11] Consequently, if ART practitioners wanted to undertake an innovative and unproven technique like human cloning, there would be nothing to stop them (other than the legislative bans on human cloning in California and Michigan). In fact, one ART provider has suggested that even though the success rate of cloning is low (1 in 277 in the Dolly experiment), this may not be a barrier because all new reproductive technologies have high failure rates.[12]

ART also differs from other medical procedures because it is rarely covered by health insurance. For other types of health services, insurers, through managed care outcome studies and evaluation of services, have required proof of efficacy before medical services are reimbursed.

Additionally, medical malpractice litigation, which serves as a quality control mechanism in other areas of health care, does not work as well in the ART field because of the high failure rate (which means that patients do not know whether their lack of success was due to negligence or not). Risks to the children may not be discernible for many years, which may be past the period of time a statute of limitations on a legal suit has run. In "wrongful life" cases, courts have been reluctant to impose liability on medical providers and laboratories for children born with birth defects where the child would not have been born if the negligent act had been avoided.[13]

In 1992 a federal law was passed to require ART clinics to report success rates to the Centers for Disease Control.[14] Implementation was slow—the first report was published in December of 1997. In 1992 there was concern that the federal government did not have the constitutional authority to regulate ART clinics, because medicine is traditionally regulated at the state level. Since then, however, federal court cases have established Congress' ability to regulate medical clinics, whether or not they receive federal funds, if patients travel across state lines to use them, if supplies come from out of state, and if the doctors attend conferences in other states.[15] All of these factors are present in ARTs.

The consequences of the laissez-faire approach have been documented by the report of the New York State Task Force on Life and the Law.[16] They identified various major problems, such as clinics' lack of oversight, variability in success rates, failure to assess risks associated with ovarian hyperstimulation, failure to disclose multiple gestation risks, insufficient follow-up data collection efforts, and inconsistent reporting of risk data for egg donation.[16] Despite their criticisms, the New York Task Force would impose few new responsibilities on physicians to change practices or curb abuses. In contrast, we recommend a federal law to set a minimum standard requiring IRB approval of new ARTs, data collection, reporting, record keeping, and informed consent. Noncompliance would result in criminal or civil liability.

DATA COLLECTION, REPORTING, RECORDS

ART should be treated as a science. Currently, ART practitioners experiment on patients in the clinical setting without required peer review of research methods or protocol oversight. With ARTs, experimental techniques have been introduced rapidly in many of the more than 280 ART clinics in the United States without sufficient prior animal experimentation, randomized clinical trials, or the rigorous data collection that would occur in federally funded studies.[17,18]

Intracytoplasmic sperm injection (ICSI) has been used since 1993 as a therapy for male factor infertility. Only recently has it been observed that children born after this procedure are twice as likely to have major congenital abnormalities as children conceived naturally.[19] The newly discovered risks include an unbalanced chromosome complement and male infertility.[20] Children conceived through ICSI may experience mild or significant developmental delays during their first year more often than children conceived by natural conception or IVF.[21]

ART procedures may present risks to women as well. ARTs increase pregnancy-related risks to women—higher rates of preeclampsia, diabetes mellitus, bleeding, and anemia.[22] There is some indication that hormonal stimulation during ART may increase the risk of ovarian cancer.[23] Yet new techniques are used on women before being adequately researched in animals. IVF itself was applied to women years before it was applied to baboons, chimpanzees, or rhesus monkeys, leading some embryologists to observe that it seemed as if women have served as the model for the nonhuman primates.[24]

Our analysis of public health implications of ART indicates the need for more consistent record keeping and review. Sperm and egg donation account for more than 60,000 births annually, yet there is no uniform procedure for storing information regarding the donor, the resulting birth, and medical history information. The recent discovery that a California semen donor transmitted polycystic kidney disease to at least one child and possibly many other children,[25] and the case of Dr. Cecil Jacobson[26] who secretly inseminated over 70 of his patients with his own sperm, are striking examples.

Data should also be collected on long-term health risks of treating women with fertility drugs. Studies should be undertaken on ART children to assess the long-term medical and psychological effects of ART procedures, especially cryopreservation. All ART clinics should be required to obtain and maintain updated medical and family information about both donors and ART children, including any reported change in medical status of donors.

NUMBER OF EMBRYOS TRANSFERRED

Unlike England, where doctors are prohibited from implanting more than three or four embryos, the laws in the United States set no limits on how many embryos a physician may implant. The New York State Task Force deferred to the American Society for Reproductive Medicine's voluntary recommendation that generally only four embryos be transferred, but it is clear that the guidelines are not being followed. In fact, the recently published report by the Centers for Disease Control,[5] examining data collected from 281 ART programs in 1995, shows that in some programs seven or more embryos are being transferred during an IVF cycle. Out of ART births, 37% are multiples as compared with 2% in the general population. Multiple pregnancies present significant risks to the resulting children in terms of increased frequency of death within the first year and long-term disability.[27] We recommend that a federal law be adopted limiting the number of embryos transferred per cycle to women to four.

INFORMED CONSENT AND DISCLOSURE

Basic informed consent requires that the patient or patients be told the risks, benefits, and alternatives of a treatment. Clinics should, at minimum, be required by federal law to disclose pregnancy rates; how pregnancy is confirmed; the live birth rate for the clinic; and the risks, benefits, and specific procedures for the technique being considered. Clinics should also disclose the risks associated with fertility drugs. They should disclose the risks of multiple births, including potential medical and psychological problems for the offspring.

The clinic should be required to disclose all embryo disposition options: storage, donation for use by another couple (known or unknown), donation for research, or destruction. Moreover, the clinic should disclose which services it actually offers, including the costs, duration, and location of gamete and embryo storage, and which services it does not offer that other clinics do.

CONCLUSION

ART involves creating children and building families, a fundamental social value. These minimum scientific standards for the practice of ART were designed to protect the interests of all participants—couples, children, donors, and health care providers.

REFERENCES AND NOTES

1. *Buzzanca v. Buzzanca,* 72 Cal. Rptr. 280 (10 March 1998).
2. M. Beck *et al., Newsweek,* 17 January 1994, p. 54.

3. D. Kong, *The Boston Globe,* 4 August 1996, p. A35.

4. Personal communication with American Society [for] Reproductive Medicine, 2 April 1998. Information is based on anecdotal reports from 1994.

5. *1995 Assisted Reproductive Technology Success Rates, National Summary and Fertility Clinic Reports* [Centers for Disease Control (CDC), Atlanta, GA, 1997].

6. Personal communication with the Organization of Parents Through Surrogacy, 25 March 1997.

7. *Hotline Information Packet 1* (National Council for Adoption, Washington, DC, 1997).

8. *Government of Canada, New Reproductive and Genetic Technologies: Setting Boundaries, Enhancing Health* (Minister of Supply and Services Canada, Canada, 1996).

9. Human Fertilization and Embryology Act 1990, Ministry of Health, United Kingdom.

10. B. Harrison, *Atlanta Journal and Constitution,* 21 December 1997, p. D06, quoting Dr. Mark Sauer.

11. M. Siegler and L. Bergman, *Transplant. Proc.,* in press.

12. P. Kendall and W. Neikirk, *Chicago Tribune,* 25 February 1997, p. 1.

13. L. B. Andrews, *Hous. L. Rev.* 23, 149 (1992); M. Hibbert, proceedings from *Changing Conceptions: A Symposium on Reproductive Technologies,* Institute for Science, Law, and Technology, Chicago, IL, 1 to 26 December 1997 (Chicago: Chicago-Kent College of Law, 1997).

14. 42 U.S.C. 263a-1 through 263a-7 (Suppl. 1998).

15. *Abbott v. Bragdon,* 912 F. Supp. 580 (D. Me 1995) aff'd; 66 USLW 460 (U.S., 25 June 1998); *United States v. Wilson,* 73 F. 3d 675 (7th Circuit, 1995).

16. The New York State Task Force on Life and the Law, *Assisted Reproductive Technologies: Analysis and Recommendations for Public Policy* (1998).

17. K. Saunders, J. Spensley, J. Munro, G. Halasz, *Pediatrics* **97,** 688 (1996).

18. E. R. te Veld, A. L. van Baar, R. J. van Kooij, *Lancet* **351,** 1524 (1998).

19. J. Kurinczuk and C. Bower, *Br. Med. J.* **315,** 1260 (1997).

20. See, for example, P. A. In't Veld *et al., Lancet* **350,** 490 (1997).

21. J. R. Bowen, F. L. Gibson, G. I. Leslie, D. M. Saunders, *ibid.* **351,** 1529 (1998).

22. J. G. Schenken, *Fertil. Steril.* **61,** 411 (1994).

23. A. Venn *et al., Lancet* **346,** 995 (1995).

24. D. P. Wolf and M. M. Quigley, Eds., *Human in Vitro Fertilization and Embryo Transfer* (Plenum, New York, 1984), pp. 3–4.

25. See J. Marquis, *Los Angeles Times,* 9 August 1997, p. A1.

26. *U.S. v. Jacobson,* 785 F. Suppl. 563 (E. D. Va. 1992).

27. B. Guyer *et al., Pediatrics* **100,** 905 (1997).

DAN W. BROCK

Cloning Human Beings: An Assessment of the Ethical Issues Pro and Con

Dan W. Brock is Charles C. Tillinghast, Jr. University Professor, Professor of Philosophy and Biomedical Ethics, and Director of the Center for Biomedical Ethics at Brown University. He is a former staff philosopher for the President's Commission for the Study of Ethical Problems in Medicine. His books include *Life and Death: Philosophical Essays in Biomedical Ethics* (Cambridge University Press), and (with Allen Buchanan) *Deciding for Others: The Ethics of Surrogate Decision Making* (Cambridge University Press).

The world of science and the public at large were both shocked and fascinated by the announcement in the journal *Nature* by Ian Wilmut and his colleagues that they had successfully cloned a sheep from a single cell of an adult sheep (Wilmut, 1997). But many were troubled or apparently even horrified at the prospect that cloning of adult humans by the same process might be possible as well. The response of most scientific and political leaders to the prospect of human cloning, indeed of Dr. Wilmut as well, was of immediate and strong condemnation.

A few more cautious voices were heard both suggesting some possible benefits from the use of human cloning in limited circumstances and questioning its too quick prohibition, but they were a clear minority. A striking feature of these early responses was that their strength and intensity seemed far to outrun the arguments and reasons offered in support of them—they seemed often to be "gut level" emotional reactions rather than considered reflections on the issues. Such reactions should not be simply dismissed, both because they may point us to important considerations otherwise missed and not easily articulated, and because they often have a major impact on public policy. But the formation of public policy should not ignore the moral reasons and arguments that bear on the practice of human cloning—these must be articulated in order to understand and inform people's more immediate emotional responses. This essay is an effort to articulate, and to evaluate critically, the main moral considerations and arguments for and against human cloning. Though many people's religious beliefs inform their views on human cloning, and it is often difficult to separate religious from secular positions, I shall restrict myself to arguments and reasons that can be given a clear secular formulation.

On each side of the issue there are two distinct kinds of moral arguments brought forward. On the one hand, some opponents claim that human cloning would violate fundamental moral or human rights, while some proponents argue that its prohibition would violate such rights. While moral and even human rights need not be understood as absolute, they do place moral restrictions on permissible actions that an appeal to a mere balance of benefits over harms cannot justify overriding; for example, the rights of human subjects in research must be respected even if the result is that some potentially beneficial research is more difficult or cannot be done. On the other hand, both opponents and proponents also cite the likely harms and benefits, both to individuals and to society, of the practice. I shall begin with the arguments in support of permitting human cloning, although

From Martha C. Nussbaum and Cass R. Sunstein, eds., *Clones and Clones: Facts and Fantasies About Human Cloning* (New York: W. W. Norton & Company, 1998), 141–63. Reprinted by permission of W. W. Norton & Company.

with no implication that it is the stronger or weaker position.

MORAL ARGUMENTS IN SUPPORT OF HUMAN CLONING

IS THERE A MORAL RIGHT TO USE HUMAN CLONING?

What moral right might protect at least some access to the use of human cloning? A commitment to individual liberty, such as defended by J. S. Mill, requires that individuals be left free to use human cloning if they so choose and if their doing so does not cause significant harms to others, but liberty is too broad in scope to be an uncontroversial moral right (Mill, 1859; Rhodes, 1995). Human cloning is a means of reproduction (in the most literal sense) and so the most plausible moral right at stake in its use is a right to reproductive freedom or procreative liberty (Robertson, 1994a; Brock, 1994), understood to include both the choice not to reproduce, for example, by means of contraception or abortion, and also the right to reproduce.

The right to reproductive freedom is properly understood to include the right to use various assisted reproductive technologies (ARTs), such as in vitro fertilization (IVF), oocyte donation, and so forth. The reproductive right relevant to human cloning is a negative right, that is, a right to use ARTs without interference by the government or others when made available by a willing provider. The choice of an assisted means of reproduction should be protected by reproductive freedom even when it is not the only means for individuals to reproduce, just as the choice among different means of preventing conception is protected by reproductive freedom. However, the case for permitting the use of a particular means of reproduction is strongest when it is necessary for particular individuals to be able to procreate at all, or to do so without great burdens or harms to themselves or others. In some cases human cloning could be the only means for individuals to procreate while retaining a biological tie to their child, but in other cases different means of procreating might also be possible.

It could be argued that human cloning is not covered by the right to reproductive freedom because whereas current ARTs and practices covered by that right are remedies for inabilities to reproduce sexually, human cloning is an entirely new means of reproduction; indeed, its critics see it as more a means of manufacturing humans than of reproduction. Human cloning is a different means of reproduction than sexual reproduction, but it is a means that can serve individuals' interest in reproducing. If it is not protected by the moral right to reproductive freedom, I believe that must be not because it is a new means of reproducing, but instead because it has other objectionable or harmful features; I shall evaluate these other ethical objections to it later.

When individuals have alternative means of procreating, human cloning typically would be chosen because it replicates a particular individual's genome. The reproductive interest in question then is not simply reproduction itself, but a more specific interest in choosing what kind of children to have. The right to reproductive freedom is usually understood to cover at least some choice about the kind of children one will have. Some individuals choose reproductive partners in the hope of producing offspring with desirable traits. Genetic testing of fetuses or preimplantation embryos for genetic disease or abnormality is done to avoid having a child with those diseases or abnormalities. Respect for individual self-determination, which is one of the grounds of a moral right to reproductive freedom, includes respecting individuals' choices about whether to have a child with a condition that will place severe burdens on them, and cause severe burdens to the child itself.

The less a reproductive choice is primarily the determination of one's own life, but primarily the determination of the nature of another, as in the case of human cloning, the more moral weight the interests of that other person, that is the cloned child, should have in decisions that determine its nature (Annas, 1994). But even then parents are typically accorded substantial, but not unlimited, discretion in shaping the persons their children will become, for example, through education and other childrearing decisions. Even if not part of reproductive freedom, the right to raise one's children as one sees fit, within limits mostly determined by the interests of the children, is also a right to determine within limits what kinds of persons one's children will become. This right includes not just preventing certain diseases or harms to children, but selecting and shaping desirable features and traits in one's children. The use of human cloning is one way to exercise that right.

Public policy and the law now permit prospective parents to conceive, or to carry a conception to term, when there is a significant risk or even certainty that the child will suffer from a serious genetic disease.

Even when others think the risk or certainty of genetic disease makes it morally wrong to conceive, or to carry a fetus to term, the parents' right to reproductive freedom permits them to do so. Most possible harms to a cloned child are less serious than the genetic harms with which parents can now permit their offspring to be conceived or born.

I conclude that there is good reason to accept that a right to reproductive freedom presumptively includes both a right to select the means of reproduction, as well as a right to determine what kind of children to have, by use of human cloning. However, the specific reproductive interest of determining what kind of children to have is less weighty than are other reproductive interests and choices whose impact falls more directly and exclusively on the parents rather than the child. Even if a moral right to reproductive freedom protects the use of human cloning, that does not settle the moral issue about human cloning, since there may be other moral rights in conflict with this right, or serious enough harms from human cloning to override the right to use it; this right can be thought of as establishing a serious moral presumption supporting access to human cloning.

WHAT INDIVIDUAL OR SOCIAL BENEFITS MIGHT HUMAN CLONING PRODUCE?

LARGELY INDIVIDUAL BENEFITS

The literature on human cloning by nuclear transfer or by embryo splitting contains a few examples of circumstances in which individuals might have good reasons to want to use human cloning. However, human cloning seems not to be the unique answer to any great or pressing human need and its benefits appear to be limited at most. What are the principal possible benefits of human cloning that might give individuals good reasons to want to use it?

1. *Human cloning would be a new means to relieve the infertility some persons now experience.* Human cloning would allow women who have no ova or men who have no sperm to produce an offspring that is biologically related to them (Eisenberg, 1976; Robertson, 1994b, 1997; LaBar, 1984). Embryos might also be cloned, by either nuclear transfer or embryo splitting, in order to increase the number of embryos for implantation and improve the chances of successful conception (NABER, 1994). The benefits from human cloning to relieve infertility are greater the more persons there are who cannot overcome their infertility by any other means acceptable to them. I do not know of data on this point, but the numbers who would use cloning for this reason are probably not large.

The large number of children throughout the world possibly available for adoption represents an alternative solution to infertility only if we are prepared to discount as illegitimate the strong desire of many persons, fertile and infertile, for the experience of pregnancy and for having and raising a child biologically related to them. While not important to all infertile (or fertile) individuals, it is important to many and is respected and met through other forms of assisted reproduction that maintain a biological connection when that is possible; that desire does not become illegitimate simply because human cloning would be the best or only means of overcoming an individual's infertility.

2. *Human cloning would enable couples in which one party risks transmitting a serious hereditary disease to an offspring to reproduce without doing so* (Robertson, 1994b). By using donor sperm or egg donation, such hereditary risks can generally be avoided now without the use of human cloning. These procedures may be unacceptable to some couples, however, or at least considered less desirable than human cloning because they introduce a third party's genes into their reproduction instead of giving their offspring only the genes of one of them. Thus, in some cases human cloning could be a reasonable means of preventing genetically transmitted harms to offspring. Here too, we do not know how many persons would want to use human cloning instead of other means of avoiding the risk of genetic transmission of a disease or of accepting the risk of transmitting the disease, but the numbers again are probably not large.

3. *Human cloning to make a later twin would enable a person to obtain needed organs or tissues for transplantation* (Robertson, 1994b, 1997; Kahn, 1989; Harris, 1992). Human cloning would solve the problem of finding a transplant donor whose organ or tissue is an acceptable match and would eliminate, or drastically reduce, the risk of transplant rejection by the host. The availability of human cloning for this purpose would amount to a form of insurance to enable treatment of certain kinds of medical conditions. Of course, sometimes the medical need would be too urgent to permit waiting for the cloning, gestation, and development that is necessary before tissues or organs can be obtained for transplantation. In other

cases, taking an organ also needed by the later twin, such as a heart or a liver, would be impermissible because it would violate the later twin's rights.

Such a practice can be criticized on the ground that it treats the later twin not as a person valued and loved for his or her own sake, as an end in itself in Kantian terms, but simply as a means for benefiting another. This criticism assumes, however, that only this one motive defines the reproduction and the relation of the person to his or her later twin. The well-known case some years ago in California of the Ayalas, who conceived in the hopes of obtaining a source for a bone marrow transplant for their teenage daughter suffering from leukemia, illustrates the mistake in this assumption. They argued that whether or not the child they conceived turned out to be a possible donor for their daughter, they would value and love the child for itself, and treat it as they would treat any other member of their family. That one reason they wanted it, as a possible means to saving their daughter's life, did not preclude their also loving and valuing it for its own sake; in Kantian terms, it was treated as a possible means to saving their daughter, but not *solely as a means,* which is what the Kantian view proscribes.

Indeed, when people have children, whether by sexual means or with the aid of ARTs, their motives and reasons for doing so are typically many and complex, and include reasons less laudable than obtaining lifesaving medical treatment, such as having someone who needs them, enabling them to live on their own, qualifying for government benefit programs, and so forth. While these are not admirable motives for having children and may not bode well for the child's upbringing and future, public policy does not assess prospective parents' motives and reasons for procreating as a condition of their doing so.

4. Human cloning would enable individuals to clone someone who had special meaning to them, such as a child who had died (Robertson, 1994b). There is no denying that if human cloning were available, some individuals would want to use it for this purpose, but their desire usually would be based on a deep confusion. Cloning such a child would not replace the child the parents had loved and lost, but would only create a different child with the same genes. The child they loved and lost was a unique individual who had been shaped by his or her environment and choices, not just his or her genes, and more importantly who had experienced a particular relationship with them. Even if the later cloned child could not only have the same genes but also be subjected to the same environment, which of course is impossible, it would remain a different child than the one they had loved and lost because it would share a different history with them (Thomas, 1974). Cloning the lost child might help the parents accept and move on from their loss, but another already existing sibling or a new child that was not a clone might do this equally well; indeed, it might do so better since the appearance of the cloned later twin would be a constant reminder of the child they had lost. Nevertheless, if human cloning enabled some individuals to clone a person who had special meaning to them and doing so gave them deep satisfaction, that would be a benefit to them even if their reasons for wanting to do so, and the satisfaction they in turn received, were based on a confusion.

LARGELY SOCIAL BENEFITS

5. Human cloning would enable the duplication of individuals of great talent, genius, character, or other exemplary qualities. Unlike the first four reasons for human cloning which appeal to benefits to specific individuals, this reason looks to benefits to the broader society from being able to replicate extraordinary individuals—a Mozart, Einstein, Gandhi, or Schweitzer (Lederberg, 1966; McKinnell, 1979). Much of the appeal of this reason, like much support and opposition to human cloning, rests largely on a confused and false assumption of genetic determinism, that is, that one's genes fully determine what one will become, do, and accomplish. What made Mozart, Einstein, Gandhi, and Schweitzer the extraordinary individuals they were was the confluence of their particular genetic endowments with the environments in which they were raised and lived and the particular historical moments they in different ways seized. Cloning them would produce individuals with the same genetic inheritances (nuclear transfer does not even produce 100 percent genetic identity, although for the sake of exploring the moral issues I have followed the common assumption that it does), but it is not possible to replicate their environments or the historical contexts in which they lived and their greatness flourished. We do not know the degree or specific respects in which any individual's greatness depended on "nature" or "nurture," but we do know that it always depends on an interaction of them both. Cloning could not even replicate individuals' extraordinary capabilities, much less their accomplishments, because these too are the product of their inherited genes and their environments, not of their genes alone.

None of this is to deny that Mozart's and Einstein's extraordinary musical and intellectual capabilities, nor even Gandhi's and Schweitzer's extraordinary moral greatness, were produced in part by their unique genetic inheritances. Cloning them might well produce individuals with exceptional capacities, but we simply do not know how close their clones would be in capacities or accomplishments to the great individuals from whom they were cloned. Even so, the hope for exceptional, even if less and different, accomplishment from cloning such extraordinary individuals might be a reasonable ground for doing so.

Worries here about abuse, however, surface quickly. Whose standards of greatness would be used to select individuals to be cloned? Who would control use of human cloning technology for the benefit of society or mankind at large? Particular groups, segments of society, or governments might use the technology for their own benefit, under the cover of benefiting society or even mankind at large.

6. Human cloning and research on human cloning might make possible important advances in scientific knowledge, for example, about human development (Walters, 1982; Smith, 1983). While important potential advances in scientific or medical knowledge from human cloning or human cloning research have frequently been cited, there are at least three reasons for caution about such claims. First, there is always considerable uncertainty about the nature and importance of the new scientific or medical knowledge to which a dramatic new technology like human cloning will lead; the road to new knowledge is never mapped in advance and takes many unexpected turns. Second, we do not know what new knowledge from human cloning or human cloning research could also be gained by other means that do not have the problematic moral features to which its opponents object. Third, what human cloning research would be compatible with ethical and legal requirements for the use of human subjects in research is complex, controversial, and largely unexplored. Creating human clones solely for the purpose of research would be to use them solely for the benefit of others without their consent, and so unethical. But if and when human cloning was established to be safe and effective, then new scientific knowledge might be obtained from its use for legitimate, nonresearch reasons.

Although there is considerable uncertainty concerning most of human cloning's possible individual and social benefits that I have discussed, and although no doubt it could have other benefits or uses that we cannot yet envisage, I believe it is reasonable to conclude at this time that human cloning does not seem to promise great benefits or uniquely to meet great human needs. Nevertheless, despite these limited benefits, a moral case can be made that freedom to use human cloning is protected by the important moral right to reproductive freedom. I shall turn now to what moral rights might be violated, or harms produced, by research on or use of human cloning.

MORAL ARGUMENTS AGAINST HUMAN CLONING

WOULD THE USE OF HUMAN CLONING VIOLATE IMPORTANT MORAL RIGHTS?

Many of the immediate condemnations of any possible human cloning following Wilmut's cloning of Dolly claimed that it would violate moral or human rights, but it was usually not specified precisely, or often even at all, what rights would be violated (WHO, 1997). I shall consider two possible candidates for such a right: a right to have a unique identity and a right to ignorance about one's future or to an open future. Claims that cloning denies individuals a unique identity are common, but I shall argue that even if there is a right to a unique identity, it could not be violated by human cloning. The right to ignorance or to an open future has only been explicitly defended, to my knowledge, by two commentators, and in the context of human cloning, only by Hans Jonas; it supports a more promising, but in my view ultimately unsuccessful, argument that human cloning would violate an important moral or human right.

Is there a moral or human right to a unique identity, and if so would it be violated by human cloning? For human cloning to violate a right to a unique identity, the relevant sense of identity would have to be genetic identity, that is, a right to a unique unrepeated genome. This would be violated by human cloning, but is there any such right? It might be thought that cases of identical twins show there is no such right because no one claims that the moral or human rights of the twins have been violated. However, this consideration is not conclusive (Kass, 1985; NABER, 1994). Only human actions can violate others' rights; outcomes that would constitute a rights violation if deliberately caused by human action are not a rights violation if a result of natural causes. If Arthur deliberately strikes Barry on the head so hard as to cause his death, he violates Barry's right not to be killed; if lightning strikes Cheryl, causing her death, her right not to be killed has not been violated. Thus, the case of twins does not show that there could not be a right to a unique genetic identity.

What is the sense of identity that might plausibly be what each person has a right to have uniquely, that constitutes the special uniqueness of each individual (Macklin 1994; Chadwick 1982)? Even with the same genes, homozygous twins are numerically distinct and not identical, so what is intended must be the various properties and characteristics that make each individual qualitatively unique and different from others. Does having the same genome as another person undermine that unique qualitative identity? Only on the crudest genetic determinism, according to which an individual's genes completely and decisively determine everything else about the individual, all his or her other nongenetic features and properties, together with the entire history or biography that constitutes his or her life. But there is no reason whatever to believe that kind of genetic determinism. Even with the same genes, differences in genetically identical twins' psychological and personal characteristics develop over time together with differences in their life histories, personal relationships, and life choices; sharing an identical genome does not prevent twins from developing distinct and unique personal identities of their own.

We need not pursue whether there is a moral or human right to a unique identity—no such right is found among typical accounts and enumerations of moral or human rights—because even if there is such a right, sharing a genome with another individual as a result of human cloning would not violate it. The idea of the uniqueness, or unique identity, of each person historically predates the development of modern genetics. A unique genome thus could not be the ground of this long-standing belief in the unique human identity of each person.

I turn now to whether human cloning would violate what Hans Jonas called a right to ignorance, or what Joel Feinberg called a right to an open future (Jonas, 1974; Feinberg, 1980). Jonas argued that human cloning in which there is a substantial time gap between the beginning of the lives of the earlier and later twin is fundamentally different from the simultaneous beginning of the lives of homozygous twins that occur in nature. Although contemporaneous twins begin their lives with the same genetic inheritance, they do so at the same time, and so in ignorance of what the other who shares the same genome will by his or her choices make of his or her life.

A later twin created by human cloning, Jonas argues, knows, or at least believes she knows, too much about herself. For there is already in the world another person, her earlier twin, who from the same genetic starting point has made the life choices that are still in the later twin's future. It will seem that her life has already been lived and played out by another, that her fate is already determined; she will lose the sense of human possibility in freely and spontaneously creating her own future and authentic self. It is tyrannical, Jonas claims, for the earlier twin to try to determine another's fate in this way.

Jonas's objection can be interpreted so as not to assume either a false genetic determinism, or a belief in it. A later twin might grant that he is not determined to follow in his earlier twin's footsteps, but nevertheless the earlier twin's life might always haunt him, standing as an undue influence on his life, and shaping it in ways to which others' lives are not vulnerable. But the force of the objection still seems to rest on the false assumption that having the same genome as his earlier twin unduly restricts his freedom to create a different life and self than the earlier twin's. Moreover, a family environment also importantly shapes children's development, but there is no force to the claim of a younger sibling that the existence of an older sibling raised in that same family is an undue influence on the younger sibling's freedom to make his own life for himself in that environment. Indeed, the younger twin or sibling might gain the benefit of being able to learn from the older twin's or sibling's mistakes.

A closely related argument can be derived from what Joel Feinberg has called a child's right to an open future. This requires that others raising a child not so close off the future possibilities that the child would otherwise have as to eliminate a reasonable range of opportunities for the child autonomously to construct his or her own life. One way this right might be violated is to create a later twin who will believe her future has already been set for her by the choices made and the life lived by her earlier twin.

The central difficulty in these appeals to a right either to ignorance or to an open future is that the right is not violated merely because the later twin is likely to *believe* that his future is already determined, when that belief is clearly false and supported only by the crudest genetic determinism. If we know the later twin will falsely believe that his open future has been taken from him as a result of being cloned, even though in reality it has not, then we know that cloning will cause the twin psychological distress, but not that it will violate his right. Jonas's right to ignorance, and Feinberg's right of a child to an open future, are not not violated by human cloning, though they do point to psychological harms that a later twin may be likely to experience and that I will take up later.

Neither a moral or human right to a unique identity, nor one to ignorance and an open future, would be violated by human cloning. There may be other moral or human rights that human cloning would violate, but I do not know what they might be. I turn now to consideration of the harms that human cloning might produce.

WHAT INDIVIDUAL OR SOCIAL HARMS MIGHT HUMAN CLONING PRODUCE?

There are many possible individual or social harms that have been posited by one or another commentator and I shall only try to cover the more plausible and significant of them.

LARGELY INDIVIDUAL HARMS

1. Human cloning would produce psychological distress and harm in the later twin. No doubt knowing the path in life taken by one's earlier twin might often have several bad psychological effects (Callahan, 1993; LaBar, 1984; Macklin, 1994; McCormick, 1993; Studdard, 1978; Rainer, 1978; Verhey, 1994). The later twin might feel, even if mistakenly, that her fate has already been substantially laid out, and so have difficulty freely and spontaneously taking responsibility for and making her own fate and life. The later twin's experience or sense of autonomy and freedom might be substantially diminished, even if in actual fact they are diminished much less than it seems to her. She might have a diminished sense of her own uniqueness and individuality, even if once again these are in fact diminished little or not at all by having an earlier twin with the same genome. If the later twin is the clone of a particularly exemplary individual, perhaps with some special capabilities and accomplishments, she might experience excessive pressure to reach the very high standards of ability and accomplishment of the earlier twin (Rainer, 1978). These various psychological effects might take a heavy toll on the later twin and be serious burdens to her.

While psychological harms of these kinds from human cloning are certainly possible, and perhaps even likely in some cases, they remain at this point only speculative since we have no experience with human cloning and the creation of earlier and later twins. Nevertheless, if experience with human cloning confirmed that serious and unavoidable psychological harms typically occurred to the later twin, that would be a serious moral reason to avoid the practice. Intuitively at least, psychological burdens and harms seem more likely and more serious for a person who is only one of many identical later twins cloned from one original source, so that the clone might run into another identical twin around every street corner. This prospect could be a good reason to place sharp limits on the number of twins that could be cloned from any one source.

One argument has been used by several commentators to undermine the apparent significance of potential psychological harms to a later twin (Chadwick, 1982; Robertson, 1994b, 1997; Macklin, 1994). The point derives from a general problem, called the nonidentity problem, posed by the philosopher Derek Parfit, although not originally directed to human cloning (Parfit, 1984). Here is the argument. Even if all these psychological burdens from human cloning could not be avoided for any later twin, they are not harms to the twin, and so not reasons not to clone the twin. That is because the only way for the twin to avoid the harms is never to be cloned, and so never to exist at all. But these psychological burdens, hard though they might be, are not so bad as to make the twin's life, all things considered, not worth living. So the later twin is not harmed by being given a life even with these psychological burdens, since the alternative of never existing at all is arguably worse—he or she never has a worthwhile life—but certainly not better for the twin. And if the later twin is not harmed by having been created with these unavoidable burdens, then how could he or she be wronged by having been created with them? And if the later twin is not wronged, then why is any wrong being done by human cloning? This argument has considerable potential import, for if it is sound it will undermine the apparent moral importance of any bad consequence of human cloning to the later twin that is not so serious as to make the twin's life, all things considered, not worth living.

I defended elsewhere the position regarding the general case of genetically transmitted handicaps, that if one could have a *different* child without comparable burdens (for the case of cloning, by using a different method of reproduction which did not result in a later twin), there is as strong a moral reason to do so as there would be not to cause similar burdens to an already existing child (Brock, 1995). Choosing to create the later twin with serious psychological burdens instead of a different person who would be free of them, without weighty overriding reasons for choosing the former, would be morally irresponsible or wrong, even if doing so does not harm or wrong the later twin who could only exist with the burdens. These issues are too detailed and complex to pursue here and the nonidentity problem remains controversial and not fully resolved, but at the least, the argument for disregarding the psychological burdens to the later twin because he or she could not exist without them is controversial, and in my view mistaken. Such psychological harms, as I shall continue to call them, are speculative, but they should not be disregarded because of the nonidentity problem.

2. Human cloning procedures would carry unacceptable risks to the clone. There is no doubt that attempts to clone a human being at the present time would carry unacceptable risks to the clone. Further research on the procedure with animals, as well as research to establish its safety and effectiveness for humans, is clearly necessary before it would be ethical to use the procedure on humans. One risk to the clone is the failure to implant, grow, and develop successfully, but this would involve the embryo's death or destruction long before most people or the law consider it to be a person with moral or legal protections of its life.

Other risks to the clone are that the procedure in some way goes wrong, or unanticipated harms come to the clone; for example, Harold Varmus, director of the National Institutes of Health, raised the concern that a cell many years old from which a person is cloned could have accumulated genetic mutations during its years in another adult that could give the resulting clone a predisposition to cancer or other diseases of aging (Weiss, 1997). Risks to an ovum donor (if any), a nucleus donor, and a woman who receives the embryo for implantation would likely be ethically acceptable with the informed consent of the involved parties.

I believe it is too soon to say whether unavoidable risks to the clone would make human cloning forever unethical. At a minimum, further research is needed to better define the potential risks to humans. But we should not insist on a standard that requires risks to be lower than those we accept in sexual reproduction, or in other forms of ART.

LARGELY SOCIAL HARMS

3. Human cloning would lessen the worth of individuals and diminish respect for human life. Unelaborated claims to this effect were common in the media after the announcement of the cloning of Dolly. Ruth Macklin explored and criticized the claim that human cloning would diminish the value we place on, and our respect for, human life because it would lead to persons being viewed as replaceable (Macklin, 1994). As I have argued concerning a right to a unique identity, only on a confused and indefensible notion of human identity is a person's identity determined solely by his or her genes, and so no individual could be fully replaced by a later clone possessing the same genes. Ordinary people recognize this clearly. For example, parents of a child dying of a fatal disease would find it insensitive and ludicrous to be told they should not grieve for their coming loss because it is possible to replace him by cloning him; it is *their child who is dying* whom they love and value, and that child and his importance to them is not replaceable by a cloned later twin. Even if they would also come to love and value a later twin as much as they now love and value their child who is dying, that would be to love and value that *different child* for its own sake, not as a replacement for the child they lost. Our relations of love and friendship are with distinct, historically situated individuals with whom over time we have shared experience and our lives, and whose loss to us can never be replaced.

A different version of this worry is that human cloning would result in persons' worth or value seeming diminished because we would come to see persons as able to be manufactured or "handmade." This demystification of the creation of human life would reduce our appreciation and awe of human life and of its natural creation. It would be a mistake, however, to conclude that a person created by human cloning is of less value or is less worthy of respect than one created by sexual reproduction. At least outside of some religious contexts, it is the nature of a being, not how it is created, that is the source of its value and makes it worthy of respect. For many people, gaining a scientific understanding of the truly extraordinary complexity of human reproduction and development increases, instead of decreases, their awe of the process and its product.

A more subtle route by which the value we place on each individual human life might be diminished could come from the use of human cloning with the aim of creating a child with a particular genome, either the genome of another individual especially meaningful to those doing the cloning or an individual with exceptional talents, abilities, and accomplishments. The child then comes to be objectified, valued only as an object and for its genome, or at least for its genome's expected phenotypic expression, and no longer recognized as having the intrinsic equal moral value of all persons, simply as persons. For the moral value and respect due all persons to come to be seen as resting only on the instrumental value of individuals and of their particular qualities to others would be to fundamentally change the moral status properly accorded to persons. Individuals would lose their moral standing as full and equal members of the moral community, replaced by the different instrumental value each has to others.

Such a change in the equal moral value and worth accorded to persons should be avoided at all costs, but it is far from clear that such a change would result from permitting human cloning. Parents, for example, are quite capable of distinguishing their children's intrinsic value, just as individual persons, from their instrumental value based on their particular qualities or properties. The equal moral value and respect due all persons simply as persons is not incompatible with the different instrumental value of different individuals; Einstein and an untalented physics graduate student have vastly different value as scientists, but share and are entitled to equal moral value and respect as persons. It is a confused mistake to conflate these two kinds of value and respect. If making a large number of clones from one original person would be more likely to foster it, that would be a further reason to limit the number of clones that could be made from one individual.

4. Human cloning might be used by commercial interests for financial gain. Both opponents and proponents of human cloning agree that cloned embryos should not be able to be bought and sold. In a science fiction frame of mind, one can imagine commercial interests offering genetically certified and guaranteed embryos for sale, perhaps offering a catalogue of different embryos cloned from individuals with a variety of talents, capacities, and other desirable properties. This would be a fundamental violation of the equal moral respect and dignity owed to all persons, treating them instead as objects to be differentially valued, bought, and sold in the marketplace. Even if embryos are not yet persons at the time they would be purchased or sold, they would be being valued, bought, and sold for the persons they will become. The moral consensus against any commercial market in embryos, cloned or otherwise, should be enforced by law whatever the public policy ultimately is on human cloning.

5. Human cloning might be used by governments or other groups for immoral and exploitative purposes. In *Brave New World,* Aldous Huxley imagined cloning individuals who have been engineered with limited abilities and conditioned to do, and to be happy doing, the menial work that society needed done (Huxley, 1932). Selection and control in the creation of people was exercised not in the interests of the persons created, but in the interests of the society and at the expense of the persons created; nor did it serve individuals' interests in reproduction and parenting. Any use of human cloning for such purposes would exploit the clones solely as means for the benefit of others, and would violate the equal moral respect and dignity they are owed as full moral persons. If human cloning is permitted to go forward, it should be with regulations that would clearly prohibit such immoral exploitation.

Fiction contains even more disturbing or bizarre uses of human cloning, such as Mengele's creation of many clones of Hitler in Ira Levin's *The Boys from Brazil* (Levin, 1976), Woody Allen's science fiction cinematic spoof *Sleeper* in which a dictator's only remaining part, his nose, must be destroyed to keep it from being cloned, and the contemporary science fiction film *Blade Runner*. These nightmare scenarios may be quite improbable, but their impact should not be underestimated on public concern with technologies like human cloning. Regulation of human cloning must assure the public that even such far-fetched abuses will not take place.

CONCLUSION

Human cloning has until now received little serious and careful ethical attention because it was typically dismissed as science fiction, and it stirs deep, but difficult to articulate, uneasiness and even revulsion in many people. Any ethical assessment of human cloning at this point must be tentative and provisional. Fortunately, the science and technology of human cloning are not yet in hand, and so a public and professional debate is possible without the need for a hasty, precipitate policy response.

The ethical pros and cons of human cloning, as I see them at this time, are sufficiently balanced and uncertain that there is not an ethically decisive case either for or against permitting it or doing it. Access to human cloning can plausibly be brought within a moral right to reproductive freedom, but its potential legitimate uses appear few and do not promise substantial benefits. It is not a central component of the moral right to reproductive freedom and it does not uniquely serve any major or pressing individual or social needs. On the other hand, contrary to the pronouncements of many of its opponents, human cloning seems not to be a violation of moral or human rights. But it does risk some significant individual or social harms, although most are based on common public confusions about genetic determinism, human identity, and the effects of human cloning. Because most potential harms feared from human cloning remain speculative, they seem insufficient to warrant at this time a complete legal prohibition of either research on or later use of human cloning, if and when its safety and efficacy are established. Legitimate moral concerns about the use and effects of human cloning, however, underline the need for careful public oversight of research on its development, together with a wider public and professional debate and review before cloning is used on human beings.

REFERENCES

Annas, G. J. (1994). "Regulatory Models for Human Embryo Cloning: The Free Market, Professional Guidelines, and Government Restrictions." *Kennedy Institute of Ethics Journal* 4, 3:235–249.

Brock, D. W. (1994). "Reproductive Freedom: Its Nature, Bases and Limits," in *Health Care Ethics: Critical Issues for Health Professionals,* eds. D. Thomasma and J. Monagle. Gaithersburg, MD: Aspen Publishers.

Brock, D. W. (1995). "The Non-Identity Problem and Genetic Harm." *Bioethics* 9:269–275.

Callahan, D. (1993). "Perspective on Cloning: A Threat to Individual Uniqueness." *Los Angeles Times,* November 12, 1993:B7.

Chadwick, R. F. (1982). "Cloning." *Philosophy* 57:201–209.

Eisenberg, L. (1976). "The Outcome as Cause: Predestination and Human Cloning." *Journal of Medicine and Philosophy* 1:318–331.

Feinberg, J. (1980). "The Child's Right to an Open Future," in *Whose Child? Children's Rights, Parental Authority, and State Power,* eds. W. Aiken and H. LaFollette. Totowa, NJ: Rowman and Littlefield.

Harris, J. (1992). *Wonderwoman and Superman: The Ethics of Biotechnology.* Oxford: Oxford University Press.

Huxley, A. (1932). *Brave New World.* London: Chalto and Winders.

Jonas, H. (1974). *Philosophical Essays: From Ancient Creed to Technological Man.* Englewood Cliffs, NJ: Prentice-Hall.

Kahn, C. (1989). "Can We Achieve Immortality?" *Free Inquiry* 9:14–18.

Kass, L. (1985). *Toward a More Natural Science.* New York: The Free Press.

LaBar, M. (1984). "The Pros and Cons of Human Cloning." *Thought* 57:318–333.

Lederberg, J. (1966). "Experimental Genetics and Human Evolution." *American Naturalist* 100:519–531.

Levin, I. (1976). *The Boys from Brazil.* New York: Random House.

Macklin, R. (1994). "Splitting Embryos on the Slippery Slope: Ethics and Public Policy." *Kennedy Institute of Ethics Journal* 4:209–226.

McCormick, R. (1993). "Should We Clone Humans?" *Christian Century* 110:1148–1149.

McKinnell, R. (1979). *Cloning: A Biologist Reports.* Minneapolis, MN: University of Minnesota Press.

Mill, J. S. (1859). *On Liberty.* Indianapolis, IN: Bobbs-Merrill Publishing.

NABER (National Advisory Board on Ethics in Reproduction) (1994). "Report on Human Cloning Through Embryo Splitting: An Amber Light." *Kennedy Institute of Ethics Journal* 4:251–282.

Parfit, D. (1984). *Reasons and Persons.* Oxford: Oxford University Press.

Rainer, J. D. (1978). "Commentary." *Man and Medicine: The Journal of Values and Ethics in Health Care* 3:115–117.

Rhodes, R. (1995). "Clones, Harms, and Rights." *Cambridge Quarterly of Healthcare Ethics* 4:285–290.

Robertson, J. A. (1994a). *Children of Choice: Freedom and the New Reproductive Technologies.* Princeton, NJ: Princeton University Press.

Robertson, J. A. (1994b). "The Question of Human Cloning." *Hastings Center Report* 24:6–14.

Robertson, J. A. (1997). "A Ban on Cloning and Cloning Research is Unjustified." Testimony Presented to the National Bioethics Advisory Commission, March 1997.

Smith, G. P. (1983). "Intimations of Immortality: Clones, Cyrons and the Law." *University of New South Wales Law Journal* 6:119–132.

Studdard, A. (1978). "The Lone Clone." *Man and Medicine: The Journal of Values and Ethics in Health Care* 3:109–114.

Thomas, L. (1974). "Notes of a Biology Watcher: On Cloning a Human Being." *New England Journal of Medicine* 291:1296–1297.

Verhey, A. D. (1994). "Cloning: Revisiting an Old Debate." *Kennedy Institute of Ethics Journal* 4:227–234.

Walters, W. A. W. (1982). "Cloning, Ectogenesis, and Hybrids: Things to Come?" in *Test-Tube Babies,* eds. W. A. W. Walters and P. Singer. Melbourne: Oxford University Press.

Weiss, R. (1997). "Cloning Suddenly Has Government's Attention." *International Herald Tribune,* March 7, 1997.

WHO (World Health Organization Press Office). (March 11, 1997). "WHO Director General Condemns Human Cloning." World Health Organization, Geneva, Switzerland.

Wilmut, I., et al. (1997). "Viable Offspring Derived from Fetal and Adult Mammalian Cells." *Nature* 385:810–813.

LEON KASS

The Wisdom of Repugnance

Leon Kass is Addie Clark Harking Professor in the Committee on Social Thought and in the College of the University of Chicago. Kass has held academic positions in the field of medical ethics at the National Academy of Sciences, St. John's College, and the Kennedy Institute of Ethics at Georgetown University. Among his books are *Toward a More Natural Science: Biology and Human Affairs* (Free Press) and, with James Q. Wilson, *The Ethics of Human Cloning* (AEI Press). In August 2001, Professor Kass was named Chair of the new Council on Bioethics by President George W. Bush.

Our habit of delighting in news of scientific and technological breakthroughs has been sorely challenged by the birth announcement of a sheep named Dolly. Though Dolly shares with previous sheep the "softest clothing, woolly, bright," William Blake's question, "Little Lamb, who made thee?" has for her a radically different answer: Dolly was, quite literally, made. She is the work not of nature or nature's God but of man, an Englishman, Ian Wilmut, and his fellow scientists. What's more, Dolly came into being not only sexually—ironically, just like "He [who] calls Himself a Lamb"—but also as the genetically identical copy (and the perfect incarnation of the form or blueprint) of a mature ewe, of whom she is a clone. This long-awaited yet not quite expected success in cloning a mammal raised immediately the prospect—and the specter—of cloning human beings: "I a child and Thou a lamb," despite our differences, have always been equal candidates for creative making, only now, by means of cloning, we may both spring from the hand of man playing at being God.

After an initial flurry of expert comment and public consternation, with opinion polls showing overwhelming opposition to cloning human beings, President Clinton ordered a ban on all federal support for human cloning research (even though none was being supported) and charged the National Bioethics Advisory Commission to report in ninety days on the ethics of human cloning research. The commission (an eighteen-member panel, evenly balanced between scientists and nonscientists, appointed by the president and reporting to the National Science and Technology Council) invited testimony from scientists, religious thinkers and bioethicists, as well as from the general public. It is now deliberating about what it should recommend, both as a matter of ethics and as a matter of public policy.

Congress is awaiting the commission's report, and is poised to act. Bills to prohibit the use of federal funds for human cloning research have been introduced in the House of Representatives and the Senate; and another bill, in the House, would make it illegal "for any person to use a human somatic cell for the process of producing a human clone." A fateful decision is at hand. To clone or not to clone a human being is no longer an academic question.

TAKING CLONING SERIOUSLY, THEN AND NOW

Cloning first came to public attention roughly thirty years ago, following the successful asexual production, in England, of a clutch of tadpole clones by the technique of nuclear transplantation. The individual largely responsible for bringing the prospect and promise of human cloning to public notice was Joshua Lederberg, a Nobel Laureate geneticist and a man of large vision. In 1966, Lederberg wrote a remarkable article in *The American Naturalist* detailing the eugenic advantages of human cloning and other forms of genetic engineering, and the following year he

From the *New Republic* 216 (June 2, 1997), 17–26. Copyright 1997 the New Republic, Inc. Reprinted by permission of the author and publisher.

devoted a column in *The Washington Post,* where he wrote regularly on science and society, to the prospect of human cloning. He suggested that cloning could help us overcome the unpredictable variety that still rules human reproduction, and allow us to benefit from perpetuating superior genetic endowments. These writings sparked a small public debate in which I became a participant. At the time a young researcher in molecular biology at the National Institutes of Health (NIH), I wrote a reply to the *Post,* arguing against Lederberg's amoral treatment of this morally weighty subject and insisting on the urgency of confronting a series of questions and objections, culminating in the suggestion that "the programmed reproduction of man will, in fact, dehumanize him."

Much has happened in the intervening years. It has become harder, not easier, to discern the true meaning of human cloning. We have in some sense been softened up to the idea—through movies, cartoons, jokes and intermittent commentary in the mass media, some serious, most lighthearted. We have become accustomed to new practices in human reproduction: not just in vitro fertilization, but also embryo manipulation, embryo donation and surrogate pregnancy. Animal biotechnology has yielded transgenic animals and a burgeoning science of genetic engineering, easily and soon to be transferable to humans.

Even more important, changes in the broader culture make it now vastly more difficult to express a common and respectful understanding of sexuality, procreation, nascent life, family, and the meaning of motherhood, fatherhood and the links between the generations. Twenty-five years ago, abortion was still largely illegal and thought to be immoral, the sexual revolution (made possible by the extramarital use of the pill) was still in its infancy, and few had yet heard about the reproductive rights of single women, homosexual men and lesbians. (Never mind shameless memoirs about one's own incest!) Then one could argue, without embarrassment, that the new technologies of human reproduction—babies without sex—and their confounding of normal kin relations—who's the mother: the egg donor, the surrogate who carries and delivers, or the one who rears?—would "undermine the justification and support that biological parenthood gives to the monogamous marriage." Today, defenders of stable, monogamous marriage risk charges of giving offense to those adults who are living in "new family forms" or to those children who, even without the benefit of assisted reproduction, have acquired either three or four parents or one or none at all. Today, one must even apologize for voicing opinions that twenty-five years ago were nearly universally regarded as the core of our culture's wisdom on these matters. In a world whose once-given natural boundaries are blurred by technological change and whose moral boundaries are seemingly up for grabs, it is much more difficult to make persuasive the still compelling case against cloning human beings. As Raskolnikov put it, "man gets used to everything—the beast!"

Indeed, perhaps the most depressing feature of the discussions that immediately followed the news about Dolly was their ironical tone, their genial cynicism, their moral fatigue: "AN UDDER WAY OF MAKING LAMBS" (*Nature*), "WHO WILL CASH IN ON BREAKTHROUGH IN CLONING?" (*The Wall Street Journal*), "IS CLONING BAAAAAAAAD?" (*The Chicago Tribune*). Gone from the scene are the wise and courageous voices of Theodosius Dobzhansky (genetics), Hans Jonas (philosophy) and Paul Ramsey (theology) who, only twenty-five years ago, all made powerful moral arguments against ever cloning a human being. We are now too sophisticated for such argumentation; we wouldn't be caught in public with a strong moral stance, never mind an absolutist one. We are all, or almost all, postmodernists now.

Cloning turns out to be the perfect embodiment of the ruling opinions of our new age. Thanks to the sexual revolution, we are able to deny in practice, and increasingly in thought, the inherent procreative teleology of sexuality itself. But, if sex has no intrinsic connection to generating babies, babies need have no necessary connection to sex. Thanks to feminism and the gay rights movement, we are increasingly encouraged to treat the natural heterosexual difference and its preeminence as a matter of "cultural construction." But if male and female are not normatively complementary and generatively significant, babies need not come from male and female complementarity. Thanks to the prominence and the acceptability of divorce and out-of-wedlock births, stable, monogamous marriage as the ideal home for procreation is no longer the agreed-upon cultural norm. For this new dispensation, the clone is the ideal emblem: the ultimate "single-parent child."

Thanks to our belief that all children should be *wanted* children (the more high-minded principle we use to justify contraception and abortion), sooner or later only those children who fulfill our wants will be fully acceptable. Through cloning, we can work our wants and wills on the very identity of our children, exercising control as never before. Thanks to modern notions of individualism and the rate of cultural change, we see ourselves not as linked to ancestors and defined by traditions, but as projects for our own self-creation, not only as self-made men but also man-made selves; and self-cloning is simply an extension of such rootless and narcissistic self-re-creation.

Unwilling to acknowledge our debt to the past and unwilling to embrace the uncertainties and the limitations of the future, we have a false relation to both: cloning personifies our desire fully to control the future, while being subject to no controls ourselves. Enchanted and enslaved by the glamour of technology, we have lost our awe and wonder before the deep mysteries of nature and of life. We cheerfully take our own beginnings in our hands and, like the last man, we blink.

Part of the blame for our complacency lies, sadly, with the field of bioethics itself, and its claim to expertise in these moral matters. Bioethics was founded by people who understood that the new biology touched and threatened the deepest matters of our humanity: bodily integrity, identity and individuality, lineage and kinship, freedom and self-command, eros and aspiration, and the relations and strivings of body and soul. With its capture by analytic philosophy, however, and its inevitable routinization and professionalization, the field has by and large come to content itself with analyzing moral arguments, reacting to new technological developments and taking on emerging issues of public policy, all performed with a naïve faith that the evils we fear can all be avoided by compassion, regulation and a respect for autonomy. Bioethics has made some major contributions in the protection of human subjects and in other areas where personal freedom is threatened; but its practitioners, with few exceptions, have turned the big human questions into pretty thin gruel.

One reason for this is that the piecemeal formation of public policy tends to grind down large questions of morals into small questions of procedure. Many of the country's leading bioethicists have served on national commissions or state task forces and advisory boards, where understandably, they have found utilitarianism to be the only ethical vocabulary acceptable to all participants in discussing issues of law, regulation and public policy. As many of these commissions have been either officially under the aegis of NIH or the Health and Human Services Department, or otherwise dominated by powerful voices for scientific progress, the ethicists have for the most part been content, after some "values clarification" and wringing of hands, to pronounce their blessings upon the inevitable. Indeed, it is the bioethicists, not the scientists, who are now the most articulate defenders of human cloning: the two witnesses testifying before the National Bioethics Advisory Commission in favor of cloning human beings were bioethicists, eager to rebut what they regard as the irrational concerns of those of us in opposition. One wonders whether this commission, constituted like the previous commissions, can tear itself sufficiently free from the accommodationist pattern of rubber-stamping all technical innovation, in the mistaken belief that all other goods must bow down before the gods of better health and scientific advance.

If it is to do so, the commission must first persuade itself, as we all should persuade ourselves, not to be complacent about what is at issue here. Human cloning, though it is in some respects continuous with previous reproductive technologies, also represents something radically new, in itself and in its easily foreseeable consequences. The stakes are very high indeed. I exaggerate, but in the direction of the truth, when I insist that we are faced with having to decide nothing less than whether human procreation is going to remain human, whether children are going to be made rather than begotten, whether it is a good thing, humanly speaking, to say yes in principle to the road which leads (at best) to the dehumanized rationality of *Brave New World*. This is not business as usual, to be fretted about for a while but finally to be given our seal of approval. We must rise to the occasion and make our judgments as if the future of our humanity hangs in the balance. For so it does.

THE STATE OF THE ART

If we should not underestimate the significance of human cloning, neither should we exaggerate its imminence or misunderstand just what is involved. The procedure is conceptually simple. The nucleus of a mature but unfertilized egg is removed and replaced with a nucleus obtained from a specialized cell of an adult (or fetal) organism (in Dolly's case, the donor nucleus came from mammary gland epithelium). Since almost all the hereditary material of a cell is contained within its nucleus, the renucleated egg and the individual into which this egg develops are genetically identical to the organism that was the source of the transferred nucleus. An unlimited number of genetically identical individuals—clones—could be produced by nuclear transfer. In principle, any person, male or female, newborn or adult, could be cloned, and in any quantity. With laboratory cultivation and storage of tissues, cells outliving their sources make it possible even to clone the dead.

The technical stumbling block, overcome by Wilmut and his colleagues, was to find a means of reprogramming the state of the DNA in the donor cells, reversing its differentiated expression and restoring its full totipotency, so that it could again direct the entire process of producing a mature organism. Now that this problem has been solved, we should expect a rush to develop cloning for other animals, especially livestock, in order to propagate in perpetuity the champion meat or milk producers. Though exactly how soon someone will succeed in cloning a human being is anybody's guess, Wilmut's technique, almost certainly applicable to humans, makes *attempting* the feat an imminent possibility.

Yet some cautions are in order and some possible misconceptions need correcting. For a start, cloning is not Xeroxing. As has been reassuringly reiterated, the clone of Mel Gibson, though his genetic double, would enter the world hairless, toothless and peeing in his diapers, just like any other human infant. Moreover, the success rate, at least at first, will probably not be very high: the British transferred 277 adult nuclei into enucleated sheep eggs, and implanted twenty-nine clonal embryos, but they achieved the birth of only one live lamb clone. For this reason, among others, it is unlikely that, at least for now, the practice would be very popular, and there is no immediate worry of mass-scale production of multicopies. The need of repeated surgery to obtain eggs and, more crucially, of numerous borrowed wombs for implantation will surely limit use, as will the expense; besides, almost everyone who is able will doubtless prefer nature's sexier way of conceiving.

Still, for the tens of thousands of people already sustaining over 200 assisted reproduction clinics in the United States and already availing themselves of in vitro fertilization, intracytoplasmic sperm injection and other techniques of assisted reproduction, cloning would be an option with virtually no added fuss (especially when the success rate improves). Should commercial interests develop in "nucleus-banking," as they have in sperm-banking; should famous athletes or other celebrities decide to market their DNA the way they now market their autographs and just about everything else; should techniques of embryo and germline genetic testing and manipulation arrive as anticipated, increasing the use of laboratory assistance in order to obtain "better" babies—should all this come to pass, then cloning, if it is permitted, could become more than a marginal practice simply on the basis of free reproductive choice, even without any social encouragement to upgrade the gene pool or to replicate superior types. Moreover, if laboratory research on human cloning proceeds, even without any intention to produce cloned humans, the existence of cloned human embryos in the laboratory, created to begin with only for research purposes, would surely pave the way for later baby-making implantations.

In anticipation of human cloning, apologists and proponents have already made clear possible uses of the perfected technology, ranging from the sentimental and compassionate to the grandiose. They include: providing a child for an infertile couple; "replacing" a beloved spouse or child who is dying or has died; avoiding the risk of genetic disease; permitting reproduction for homosexual men and lesbians who want nothing sexual to do with the opposite sex; securing a genetically identical source of organs or tissues perfectly suitable for transplantation; getting a child with a genotype of one's own choosing, not excluding oneself; replicating individuals of great genius, talent or beauty—having a child who really could "be like Mike"; and creating large sets of genetically identical humans suitable for research on, for instance, the question of nature versus nurture, or for special missions in peace and war (not excluding espionage), in which using identical humans would be an advantage. Most people who envision the cloning of human beings, of course, want none of these scenarios. That they cannot say why is not surprising. What is surprising, and welcome, is that, in our cynical age, they are saying anything at all.

THE WISDOM OF REPUGNANCE

"Offensive." "Grotesque." "Revolting." "Repugnant." "Repulsive." These are the words most commonly heard regarding the prospect of human cloning. Such reactions come both from the man or woman in the street and from the intellectuals, from believers and atheists, from humanists and scientists. Even Dolly's creator has said he "would find it offensive" to clone a human being.

People are repelled by many aspects of human cloning. They recoil from the prospect of mass production of human beings, with large clones of look-alikes, compromised in their individuality; the idea of father-son or mother-daughter twins; the bizarre prospects of a woman giving birth to and rearing a genetic copy of herself, her spouse or even her deceased father or mother; the grotesqueness of conceiving a child as an exact replacement for another who has died; the utilitarian creation of embryonic genetic duplicates of oneself, to be frozen away or created when necessary, in case of need for homologous tissues or organs for transplantation; the narcissism of those who would clone themselves and the arrogance of others who think they know who deserves to be cloned or which genotype any child-to-be should be thrilled to receive; the Frankensteinian hubris to create human life and increasingly to control its destiny; man playing God. Almost no one finds any of the suggested reasons for human cloning compelling; almost everyone anticipates its possible misuses and abuses. Moreover, many people feel oppressed by the sense that there is probably nothing we can do to prevent it from happening. This makes the prospect all the more revolting.

Revulsion is not an argument; and some of yesterday's repugnances are today calmly accepted—though, one must add, not always for the better. In crucial cases, however, repugnance is the emotional expression of deep wisdom, beyond reason's power fully to articulate it. Can anyone really give an argument fully adequate to the horror which is father-daughter incest (even with consent), or having sex with animals, or mutilating a corpse, or eating human flesh, or even just (just!) raping or murdering another human being? Would anybody's failure to give full rational justification for his or her revulsion at these practices make that revulsion ethically suspect? Not at all. On the contrary, we are suspicious of those who think that they can rationalize away our horror, say, by trying to explain the enormity of incest with arguments only about the genetic risks of inbreeding.

The repugnance at human cloning belongs in this category. We are repelled by the prospect of cloning human beings not because of the strangeness or novelty of the undertaking, but because we intuit and feel, immediately and without argument, the violation of things that we rightfully hold dear. Repugnance, here as elsewhere, revolts against the excesses of human willfulness, warning us not to transgress what is unspeakably profound. Indeed, in this age in which everything is held to be permissible so long as it is freely done, in which our given human nature no longer commands respect, in which our bodies are regarded as mere instruments of our autonomous rational wills, repugnance may be the only voice left that speaks up to defend the central core of our humanity. Shallow are the souls that have forgotten how to shudder.

The goods protected by repugnance are generally overlooked by our customary ways of approaching all new biomedical technologies. The way we evaluate cloning ethically will in fact be shaped by how we characterize it descriptively, by the context into which we place it, and by the perspective from which we view it. The first task for ethics is proper description. And here is where our failure begins.

Typically, cloning is discussed in one or more of three familiar contexts, which one might call the technological, the liberal and the meliorist. Under the first, cloning will be seen as an extension of existing techniques for assisting reproduction and determining the genetic makeup of children. Like them, cloning is to be regarded as a neutral technique, with no inherent meaning or goodness, but subject to multiple uses, some good, some bad. The morality of cloning thus depends absolutely on the goodness or badness of the motives and intentions of the cloners: as one bioethicist defender of cloning puts it, "the ethics must be judged [only] by the way the parents nurture and rear their resulting child and whether they bestow the same love and affection on a child brought into existence by a technique of assisted reproduction as they would on a child born in the usual way."

The liberal (or libertarian or liberationist) perspective sets cloning in the context of rights, freedoms and personal empowerment. Cloning is just a new option for exercising an individual's right to reproduce or to have the kind of child that he or she wants. Alternatively, cloning enhances our liberation (especially women's liberation) from the confines of nature, the vagaries of chance, or the necessity for sexual mating. Indeed, it liberates women from the need for men altogether, for the process requires only eggs, nuclei and (for the time being) uteri—plus, of course, a healthy dose of our (allegedly "masculine") manipulative science that likes to do all these things to mother nature and nature's mothers. For those who hold this outlook, the only moral restraints on cloning are adequately informed consent and the avoidance of bodily harm. If no one is cloned without her consent, and if the clonant is not physically damaged, then the liberal conditions for licit, hence moral, conduct are met. Worries that go beyond violating the will or maiming the body are dismissed as "symbolic"—which is to say, unreal.

The meliorist perspective embraces valetudinarians and also eugenicists. The latter were formerly more vocal in these discussions, but they are now generally happy to see their goals advanced under the less threatening banners of freedom and technological growth. These people see in cloning a new prospect for improving human beings—minimally, by ensuring the perpetuation of healthy individuals by avoiding the risks of genetic disease inherent in the lottery of sex, and maximally, by producing "optimum babies," preserving outstanding genetic material, and (with the help of soon-to-come techniques for precise genetic engineering) enhancing inborn human capacities on many fronts. Here the morality of cloning as a means is justified solely by the excellence of the end, that is, by the outstanding traits or individuals cloned—beauty, or brawn, or brains.

These three approaches, all quintessentially American and all perfectly fine in their places, are sorely wanting as approaches to human procreation. It is, to say the least, grossly distorting to view the wondrous mysteries of birth, renewal and individuality, and the deep meaning of parent-child relations, largely through the lens of our reductive science and its potent technologies. Similarly, considering reproduction (and the intimate relations of family life!) primarily under the political-legal, adversarial and individualistic notion of rights can only undermine the private yet fundamentally social, cooperative and duty-laden character of child-bearing, child-rearing and their bond to the covenant of marriage. Seeking to escape entirely from nature (in order to satisfy a natural desire or a natural right to reproduce!) is self-contradictory in theory and self-alienating in practice. For we are erotic beings only because we are embodied beings, and not merely intellects and wills unfortunately imprisoned in our bodies. And, though health and fitness are clearly great goods, there is something deeply disquieting in looking on our prospective children as artful products perfectible by genetic engineering, increasingly held to our willfully imposed designs, specifications and margins of tolerable error.

The technical, liberal and meliorist approaches all ignore the deeper anthropological, social and, indeed, ontological meanings of bringing forth new life. To this more fitting and profound point of view, cloning shows itself to be a major alteration, indeed, a major violation, of our given nature as embodied, gendered and engendering beings—and of the social relations built on this natural ground. Once this perspective is recognized, the ethical judgment on cloning can no longer be reduced to a matter of motives and intentions, rights and freedoms, benefits and harms, or even means and ends. It must be regarded primarily as a matter of meaning: Is cloning a fulfillment of human begetting and belonging? Or is cloning rather, as I contend, their pollution and perversion? To pollution and perversion, the fitting response can only be horror and revulsion; and conversely, generalized horror and revulsion are prima facie evidence of foulness and violation. The burden of moral argument must fall entirely on those who want to declare the widespread repugnances of humankind to be mere timidity or superstition.

Yet repugnance need not stand naked before the bar of reason. The wisdom of our horror at human cloning can be partially articulated, even if this is finally one of those instances about which the heart has its reasons that reason cannot entirely know.

THE PROFUNDITY OF SEX

To see cloning in its proper context, we must begin not, as I did before, with laboratory technique, but with the anthropology—natural and social—of sexual reproduction.

Sexual reproduction—by which I mean the generation of new life from (exactly) two complementary elements, one female, one male, (usually) through coitus—is established (if that is the right term) not by human decision, culture or tradition, but by nature; it is the natural way of all mammalian reproduction. By nature, each child has two complementary biological progenitors. Each child thus stems from and unites exactly two lineages. In natural generation, moreover, the precise genetic constitution of the resulting offspring is determined by a combination of nature and chance, not by human design: each human child shares the common natural human species genotype, each child is genetically (equally) kin to each (both) parent(s), yet each child is also genetically unique.

These biological truths about our origins foretell deep truths about our identity and about our human condition altogether. Every one of us is at once equally human, equally enmeshed in a particular familial nexus of origin, and equally individuated in our trajectory from birth to death—and, if all goes well, equally capable (despite our morality) of participating, with a complementary other, in the very same renewal of such human possibility through procreation. Though less momentous than our common humanity, our genetic individuality is not humanly trivial. It shows itself forth in our distinctive appearance through which we are everywhere recognized; it is revealed in our "signature" marks of fingerprints and our self-recognizing immune system; it symbolizes and foreshadows exactly the unique, never-to-be-repeated character of each human life.

Human societies virtually everywhere have structured child-rearing responsibilities and systems of identity and relationship on the bases of these deep natural facts of begetting. The mysterious yet ubiquitous "love of one's own" is everywhere culturally exploited, to make sure that children are not just produced but well cared for and to create for everyone clear ties of meaning, belonging and obligation. But it is wrong to treat such naturally rooted social practices as mere cultural constructs (like left- or right-driving, or like burying or cremating the dead) that we can alter with little human cost. What would kinship be without its clear natural grounding? And what would identity be without kinship? We must resist those who have begun to refer to sexual reproduction as the "traditional method of reproduction," who would have us regard as merely traditional, and by implication arbitrary, what is in truth not only natural but most certainly profound.

Asexual reproduction, which produces "single-parent" offspring, is a radical departure from the natural human way, confounding all normal understandings of father, mother, sibling, grandparent, etc., and all moral relations tied thereto. It becomes even more of a radical departure when the resulting offspring is a clone derived not from an embryo, but from a mature adult to whom the clone would be an identical twin; and when the process occurs not by natural accident (as in natural twinning), but by deliberate human design and manipulation; and when the child's (or children's) genetic constitution is preselected by the parent(s) (or scientists). Accordingly, as we will see, cloning is vulnerable to three kinds of concerns and objections, related to these three points: cloning threatens confusion of identity and individuality, even in small-scale cloning; cloning represents a giant step (though not the first one) toward transforming procreation into manufacture, that is, toward the increasing depersonalization of the process of generation and, increasingly, toward the "production" of human children as artifacts, products of human will and design (what others have called the problem of "commodification" of new life); and cloning—like other forms of eugenic engineering of the next generation—represents a form of despotism of the cloners over the cloned, and thus (even in benevolent cases) represents a blatant violation of the inner meaning of parent-child relations, of what it means to have a child, of what it means to say "yes" to our own demise and "replacement."

Before turning to these specific ethical objections, let me test my claim of the profundity of the natural way by taking up a challenge recently posed by a friend. What if the given natural human way of reproduction were asexual, and we now had to deal with a new technological innovation—artificially induced sexual dimorphism and the fusing of complementary gametes—whose inventors argued that sexual reproduction promised all sorts of advantages, including hybrid vigor and the creation of greatly increased individuality? Would one then be forced to defend natural asexuality because it was natural? Could one claim that it carried deep human meaning?

The response to this challenge broaches the ontological meaning of sexual reproduction. For it is impossible, I submit, for there to have been human life—or even higher forms of animal life—in the absence of sexuality and sexual reproduction. We find asexual reproduction only in the lowest forms of life: bacteria, algae, fungi, some lower invertebrates. Sexuality brings with it a new and enriched relationship to the world. Only sexual animals can seek and find complementary others with whom to pursue a goal that transcends their own existence. For a sexual being, the world is no longer an indifferent and largely homogeneous *otherness,* in part edible, in part dangerous. It also contains some very special and related and complementary beings, of the same kind but of opposite sex, toward whom one reaches out with special interest and intensity. In higher birds and mammals, the outward gaze keeps a lookout not only for food and predators, but also for prospective mates; the beholding of the many splendored world is suffused with desire for union, the animal antecedent of human eros and the germ of sociality. Not by accident is the human animal both the sexiest animal—whose females do not go into heat but are receptive throughout the estrous cycle and whose males must therefore have greater sexual appetite and energy in order to reproduce successfully—and also the most aspiring, the most social, the most open and the most intelligent animal.

The soul-elevating power of sexuality is, at bottom, rooted in its strange connection to mortality, which it simultaneously accepts and tries to overcome. Asexual reproduction may be seen as a continuation of the activity of self-preservation. When one organism buds or divides to become two, the original being is (doubly) preserved, and nothing dies. Sexuality, by contrast, means perishability and serves replacement; the two that come together to generate one soon will die. Sexual desire, in human beings as in animals, thus serves an end that is partly hidden from, and finally at odds with, the self-serving individual. Whether we know it or not, when we are sexually active we are voting with our genitalia for our own demise. The salmon swimming upstream to spawn and die tell the universal story: sex is bound up with death, to which it holds a partial answer in procreation.

The salmon and the other animals evince this truth blindly. Only the human being can understand what it means. As we learn so powerfully from the story of the Garden of Eden, our humanization is coincident with sexual self-consciousness, with the recognition of our sexual nakedness and all that it implies: shame at our needy incompleteness, unruly self-division and finitude; awe before the eternal; hope in the self-transcending possibilities of children and a relationship to the divine. In the sexually self-conscious animal, sexual desire can become eros, lust can become love. Sexual desire humanly regarded is thus sublimated into erotic longing for wholeness, completion and immortality which drives us knowingly into the embrace and its generative fruit—as well as into all the higher human possibilities of deed, speech and song.

Through children, a good common to both husband and wife, male and female achieve some genuine unification (beyond the mere sexual "union," which fails to do so). The two become one through sharing generous (not needy) love for this third being as good. Flesh of their flesh, the child is the parents' own commingled being externalized, and given a separate and persisting existence. Unification is enhanced also by their commingled work of rearing. Providing an opening to the future beyond the grave, carrying not only our seed but also our names, our ways and our hopes that they will surpass us in goodness and happiness, children are a testament to the possibility of transcendence. Gender duality and sexual desire, which first draws our love upward and outside of ourselves, finally provide for the partial overcoming of the confinement and limitation of perishable embodiment altogether.

Human procreation, in sum, is not simply an activity of our rational wills. It is a more complete activity precisely because it engages us bodily, erotically and spiritually, as well as rationally. There is wisdom in the mystery of nature that has joined the pleasure of sex, the inarticulate longing for union, the communication of the loving embrace and the deep-seated and only partly articulate desire for children in the very activity by which we continue the chain of human existence and participate in the renewal of human possibility. Whether or not we know it, the severing of procreation from sex, love and intimacy is inherently dehumanizing, no matter how good the product.

We are now ready for the more specific objections to cloning.

THE PERVERSITIES OF CLONING

First, an important if formal objection: any attempt to clone a human being would constitute an unethical experiment upon the resulting child-to-be. As the animal experiments (frog and sheep) indicate, there are grave risk of mishaps and deformities. Moreover, because of what cloning means, one cannot presume a future cloned child's consent to be a clone, even a healthy one. Thus, ethically speaking, we cannot even get to know whether or not human cloning is feasible.

I understand, of course, the philosophical difficulty of trying to compare a life with defects against nonexistence. Several bioethicists, proud of their philosophical cleverness, use this conundrum to embarrass claims that one can injure a child in its conception, precisely because it is only thanks to that complained-of conception that the child is alive to complain. But common sense tells us that we have no reason to fear such philosophisms. For we surely know that people can harm and even maim children in the very act of conceiving them, say, by paternal transmission of the

AIDS virus, maternal transmission of heroin dependence or, arguably, even by bringing them into being as bastards or with no capacity or willingness to look after them properly. And we believe that to do this intentionally, or even negligently, is inexcusable and clearly unethical.

The objection about the impossibility of presuming consent may even go beyond the obvious and sufficient point that a clonant, were he subsequently to be asked, could rightly resent having been made a clone. At issue are not just benefits and harms, but doubts about the very independence needed to give proper (even retroactive) consent, that is, not just the capacity to choose but the disposition and ability to choose freely and well. It is not at all clear to what extent a clone will truly be a moral agent. For, as we shall see, in the very fact of cloning, and of rearing him as a clone, his makers subvert the cloned child's independence, beginning with that aspect that comes from knowing that one was an unbidden surprise, a gift, to the world, rather than the designed result of someone's artful project.

Cloning creates serious issues of identity and individuality. The cloned person may experience concerns about his distinctive identity not only because he will be in genotype and appearance identical to another human being, but, in this case, because he may also be twin to the person who is his "father" or "mother"—if one can still call them that. What would be the psychic burdens of being the "child" or "parent" of your twin? The cloned individual, moreover, will be saddled with a genotype that has already lived. He will not be fully a surprise to the world. People are likely always to compare his performances in life with that of his alter ego. True, his nurture and his circumstance in life will be different; genotype is not exactly destiny. Still, one must also expect parental and other efforts to shape this new life after the original—or at least to view the child with the original version always firmly in mind. Why else did they clone from the star basketball player, mathematician and beauty queen—or even dear old dad—in the first place?

Since the birth of Dolly, there has been a fair amount of doublespeak on this matter of genetic identity. Experts have rushed in to reassure the public that the clone would in no way be the same person, or have any confusions about his or her identity: as previously noted, they are pleased to point out that the clone of Mel Gibson would not be Mel Gibson. Fair enough. But one is shortchanging the truth by emphasizing the additional importance of the intrauterine environment, rearing and social setting: genotype obviously matters plenty. That, after all, is the only reason to clone, whether human beings or sheep. The odds that clones of Wilt Chamberlain will play in the NBA are, I submit, infinitely greater than they are for clones of Robert Reich.

Curiously, this conclusion is supported, inadvertently, by the one ethical sticking point insisted on by friends of cloning: no cloning without the donor's consent. Though an orthodox liberal objection, it is in fact quite puzzling when it comes from people (such as Ruth Macklin) who also insist that genotype is not identity or individuality, and who deny that a child could reasonably complain about being made a genetic copy. If the clone of Mel Gibson would not be Mel Gibson, why should Mel Gibson have grounds to object that someone had been made his clone? We already allow researchers to use blood and tissue samples for research purposes of no benefit to their sources: my falling hair, my expectorations, my urine and even my biopsied tissues are "not me" and not mine. Courts have held that the profit gained from uses to which scientists put my discarded tissues do not legally belong to me. Why, then, no cloning without consent—including, I assume, no cloning from the body of someone who just died? What harm is done the donor, if genotype is "not me"? Truth to tell, the only powerful justification for objecting is that genotype really does have something to do with identity, and everybody knows it. If not, on what basis could Michael Jordan object that someone cloned "him," say, from cells taken from a "lost" scraped-off piece of his skin? The insistence on donor consent unwittingly reveals the problem of identity in all cloning.

Genetic distinctiveness not only symbolizes the uniqueness of each human life and the independence of its parents that each human child rightfully attains. It can also be an important support for living a worthy and dignified life. Such arguments apply with great force to any large-scale replication of human individuals. But they are sufficient, in my view, to rebut even the first attempts to clone a human being. One must never forget that these are human beings upon whom our eugenic or merely playful fantasies are to be enacted.

Troubled psychic identity (distinctiveness), based on all-too-evident genetic identity (sameness), will be made much worse by the utter confusion of social identity and kinship ties. For, as already noted, cloning radically confounds lineage and social relations, for "offspring" as for "parents." As bioethicist James Nelson has pointed out, a female child cloned from her "mother" might develop a desire for a relationship to her "father," and might understandably seek out the father of her "mother," who is after all also her biological twin sister. Would "grandpa," who thought his paternal duties concluded, be pleased to discover that the clonant looked to him for paternal attention and support?

Social identity and social ties of relationship and responsibility are widely connected to, and supported by, biological kinship. Social taboos on incest (and adultery) everywhere serve to keep clear who is related to whom (and especially which child belongs to which parents), as well as to avoid confounding the social identity of parent-and-child (or brother-and-sister) with the social identity of lovers, spouses and co-parents. True, social identity is altered by adoption (but as a matter of the best interest of already living children: we do not deliberately produce children for adoption). True, artificial insemination and in vitro fertilization with donor sperm, or whole embryo donation, are in some way forms of "prenatal adoption"—a not altogether unproblematic practice. Even here, though, there is in each case (as in all sexual reproduction) a known male source of sperm and a known single female source of egg—a genetic father and a genetic mother—should anyone care to know (as adopted children often do) who is genetically related to whom.

In the case of cloning, however, there is but one "parent." The usually sad situation of the "single-parent child" is here deliberately planned, and with a vengeance. In the case of self-cloning, the "offspring" is, in addition, one's twin; and so the dreaded result of incest—to be parent to one's sibling—is here brought about deliberately, albeit without any act of coitus. Moreover, all other relationships will be confounded. What will father, grandfather, aunt, cousin, sister mean? Who will bear what ties and what burdens? What sort of social identity will someone have with one whole side—"father's" or "mother's"—necessarily excluded? It is no answer to say that our society, with its high incidence of divorce, remarriage, adoption, extramarital childbearing and the rest, already confounds lineage and confuses kinship and responsibility for children (and everyone else), unless one also wants to argue that this is, for children, a preferable state of affairs.

Human cloning would also represent a giant step toward turning begetting into making, procreation into manufacture (literally, something "handmade"), a process already begun with in vitro fertilization and genetic testing of embryos. With cloning, not only is the process in hand, but the total genetic blueprint of the cloned individual is selected and determined by the human artisans. To be sure, subsequent development will take place according to natural processes; and the resulting children will still be recognizably human. But we here would be taking a major step into making man himself simply another one of the man-made things. Human nature becomes merely the last part of nature to succumb to the technological project, which turns all of nature into raw material at human disposal, to be homogenized by our rationalized technique according to the subjective prejudices of the day.

How does begetting differ from making? In natural procreation, human beings come together, complementarily male and female, to give existence to another being who is formed, exactly as we were, *by what we are:* living, hence perishable, hence aspiringly erotic, human beings. In clonal reproduction, by contrast, and in the more advanced forms of manufacture to which it leads, we give existence to a being not by what we are but by what we intend and design. As with any product of our making, no matter how excellent, the artificer stands above it, not as an equal but as a superior, transcending it by his will and creative prowess. Scientists who clone animals make it perfectly clear that they are engaged in instrumental making; the animals are, from the start, designed as means to serve rational human purposes. In human cloning, scientists and prospective "parents" would be adopting the same technocratic mentality to human children: human children would be their artifacts.

Such an arrangement is profoundly dehumanizing, no matter how good the product. Mass-scale cloning of the same individual makes the point vividly; but the violation of human equality, freedom and dignity are present even in a single planned clone. And procreation dehumanized into manufacture is further degraded by commodification, a virtually inescapable result of allowing baby-making to proceed under the banner of commerce. Genetic and reproductive biotechnology companies are already growth industries, but they will go into commercial orbit once the

Human Genome Project nears completion. Supply will create enormous demand. Even before the capacity for human cloning arrives, established companies will have invested in the harvesting of eggs from ovaries obtained at autopsy or through ovarian surgery, practiced embryonic genetic alteration, and initiated the stockpiling of prospective donor tissues. Through the rental of surrogate-womb services, and through the buying and selling of tissues and embryos, priced according to the merit of the donor, the commodification of nascent human life will be unstoppable.

Finally, and perhaps most important, the practice of human cloning by nuclear transfer—like other anticipated forms of genetic engineering of the next generation—would enshrine and aggravate a profound and mischievous misunderstanding of the meaning of having children and of the parent-child relationship. When a couple now chooses to procreate, the partners are saying yes to the emergence of new life in its novelty, saying yes not only to having a child but also, tacitly, to having whatever child this child turns out to be. In accepting our finitude and opening ourselves to our replacement, we are tacitly confessing the limits of our control. In this ubiquitous way of nature, embracing the future by procreating means precisely that we are relinquishing our grip, in the very activity of taking up our own share in what we hope will be the immortality of human life and the human species. This means that our children are not *our* children: they are not our property, not our possessions. Neither are they supposed to live our lives for us, or anyone else's life but their own. To be sure, we seek to guide them on their way, imparting to them not just life but nurturing, love, and a way of life; to be sure, they bear our hopes that they will live fine and flourishing lives, enabling us in small measure to transcend our own limitations. Still, their genetic distinctiveness and independence are the natural foreshadowing of the deep truth that they have their own and never-before-enacted life to live. They are sprung from a past, but they take an uncharted course into the future.

Much harm is already done by parents who try to live vicariously through their children. Children are sometimes compelled to fulfill the broken dreams of unhappy parents; John Doe Jr. or the III is under the burden of having to live up to his forebear's name. Still, if most parents have hopes for their children, cloning parents will have expectations. In cloning, such overbearing parents take at the start a decisive step which contradicts the entire meaning of the open and forward-looking nature of parent-child relations. The child is given a genotype that has already lived, with full expectation that this blueprint of a past life ought to be controlling of the life that is to come. Cloning is inherently despotic, for it seeks to make one's children (or someone else's children) after one's own image (or an image of one's choosing) and their future according to one's will. In some cases, the despotism may be mild and benevolent. In other cases, it will be mischievous and downright tyrannical. But despotism—the control of another through one's will—it inevitably will be.

MEETING SOME OBJECTIONS

The defenders of cloning, of course, are not wittingly friends of despotism. Indeed, they regard themselves mainly as friends of freedom: the freedom of individuals to reproduce, the freedom of scientists and inventors to discover and devise and to foster "progress" in genetic knowledge and technique. They want large-scale cloning only for animals, but they wish to preserve cloning as a human option for exercising our "right to reproduce"—our right to have children, and children with "desirable genes." As law professor John Robertson points out, under our "right to reproduce" we already practice early forms of unnatural, artificial and extramarital reproduction, and we already practice early forms of eugenic choice. For this reason, he argues, cloning is no big deal.

We have here a perfect example of the logic of the slippery slope, and the slippery way in which it already works in this area. Only a few years ago, slippery slope arguments were used to oppose artificial insemination and in vitro fertilization using unrelated sperm donors. Principles used to justify these practices, it was said, will be used to justify more artificial and more eugenic practices, including cloning. Not so, the defenders retorted, since we can make the necessary distinctions. And now, without even a gesture at making the necessary distinctions, the continuity of practice is held by itself to be justificatory.

The principle of reproductive freedom as currently enunciated by the proponents of cloning logically embraces the ethical acceptability of sliding down the entire rest of the slope—to producing children ectogenetically from sperm to term (should it become feasible) and to producing children whose entire genetic makeup will be the product of parental eugenic planning and choice. If reproductive freedom means the right to have a child of one's own choosing, by whatever means, it knows and accepts no limits.

But, far from being legitimated by a "right to reproduce," the emergence of techniques of assisted reproduction and genetic engineering should compel us to reconsider the meaning and limits of such a putative right. In truth, a "right to reproduce" has always been a peculiar and problematic notion. Rights generally belong to individuals, but this is a right which (before cloning) no one can exercise alone. Does the right then inhere only in couples? Only in married couples? Is it a (woman's) right to carry or deliver or a right (of one or more parents) to nurture and rear? Is it a right to have your own biological child? Is it a right only to attempt reproduction, or a right also to succeed? Is it a right to acquire the baby of one's choice?

The assertion of a negative "right to reproduce" certainly makes sense when it claims protection against state interference with procreative liberty, say, through a program of compulsory sterilization. But surely it cannot be the basis of a tort claim against nature, to be made good by technology, should free efforts at natural procreation fail. Some insist that the right to reproduce embraces also the right against state interference with the free use of all technological means to obtain a child. Yet such a position cannot be sustained: for reasons having to do with the means employed, any community may rightfully prohibit surrogate pregnancy, or polygamy, or the sale of babies to infertile couples, without violating anyone's basic human "right to reproduce." When the exercise of a previously innocuous freedom now involves or impinges on troublesome practices that the original freedom never was intended to reach, the general presumption of liberty needs to be reconsidered.

We do indeed already practice negative eugenic selection, through genetic screening and prenatal diagnosis. Yet our practices are governed by a norm of health. We seek to prevent the birth of children who suffer from known (serious) genetic diseases. When and if gene therapy becomes possible, such diseases could then be treated, in utero or even before implantation—I have no ethical objection in principle to such a practice (though I have some practical worries), precisely because it serves the medical goal of healing existing individuals. But therapy, to be therapy, implies not only an existing "patient." It also implies a norm of health. In this respect, even germline gene "therapy," though practiced not on a human being but on egg and sperm, is less radical than cloning, which is in no way therapeutic. But once one blurs the distinction between health promotion and genetic enhancement, between so-called negative and positive eugenics, one opens the door to all future eugenic designs. "To make sure that a child will be healthy and have good chances in life": this is Robertson's principle, and owing to its latter clause it is an utterly elastic principle, with no boundaries. Being over eight feet tall will likely produce some very good chances in life, and so will having the looks of Marilyn Monroe, and so will a genius-level intelligence.

Proponents want us to believe that there are legitimate uses of cloning that can be distinguished from illegitimate uses, but by their own principles no such limits can be found. (Nor could any such limits be enforced in practice.) Reproductive freedom, as they understand it, is governed solely by the subjective wishes of the parents-to-be (plus the avoidance of bodily harm to the child). The sentimentally appealing case of the childless married couple is, on these grounds, indistinguishable from the case of an individual (married or not) who would like to clone someone famous or talented, living or dead. Further, the principle here endorsed justifies not only cloning but, indeed, all future artificial attempts to create (manufacture) "perfect" babies.

A concrete example will show how, in practice no less than in principle, the so-called innocent case will merge with, or even turn into, the more troubling ones. In practice, the eager parents-to-be will necessarily be subject to the tyranny of expertise. Consider an infertile married couple, she lacking eggs or he lacking sperm, that wants a child of their (genetic) own, and propose to clone either husband or wife. The scientist-physician (who is also coowner of the cloning company) points out the likely difficulties—a cloned child is not really their (genetic) child, but the child of only *one* of them; this imbalance may produce strains on the marriage; the child might suffer identity confusion; there is a risk of perpetuating the cause of sterility; and so on—and he also points out the advantages of choosing a donor nucleus. Far better than a child of their own would be a child of their own choosing. Touting his own expertise in selecting healthy and talented donors, the doctor presents the couple with his latest catalog containing the pictures, the health records and the accomplishments of his stable of cloning donors, samples of whose tissues are in his deep freeze. Why not, dearly beloved, a more perfect baby?

The "perfect baby," of course, is the project not of the infertility doctors, but of the eugenic scientists and their supporters. For them, the paramount right is not the so-called right to reproduce but what biologist Bentley Glass called, a quarter of a century ago, "the right of every child to be born with a sound physical and mental constitution, based on a sound genotype . . . the inalienable right to a sound heritage." But to secure this right, and to achieve the requisite quality control over new human life, human conception and gestation will need to be brought fully into the bright light of the laboratory, beneath which it can be fertilized, nourished, pruned, weeded, watched, inspected, prodded, pinched, cajoled, injected, tested, rated, graded, approved, stamped, wrapped, sealed and delivered. There is no other way to produce the perfect baby.

Yet we are urged by proponents of cloning to forget about the science fiction scenarios of laboratory manufacture and multiple-copied clones, and to focus only on the homely cases of infertile couples exercising their reproductive rights. But why, if the single cases are so innocent, should multiplying their performance be so off-putting? (Similarly, why do others object to people making money off this practice, if the practice itself is perfectly acceptable?) When we follow the sound ethical principle of universalizing our choice—"would it be right if everyone cloned a Wilt Chamberlain (with his consent, of course)? Would it be right if everyone decided to practice asexual reproduction?"—we discover what is wrong with these seemingly innocent cases. The so-called science fiction cases make vivid the meaning of what looks to us, mistakenly, to be benign.

Though I recognize certain continuities between cloning and, say, in vitro fertilization, I believe that cloning differs in essential and important ways. Yet those who disagree should be reminded that the "continuity" argument cuts both ways. Sometimes we establish bad precedents, and discover that they were bad only when we follow their inexorable logic to places we never meant to go. Can the defenders of cloning show us today how, on their principles, we will be able to see producing babies ("perfect babies") entirely in the laboratory or exercising full control over their genotypes (including so-called enhancement) as ethically different, in any essential way, from present forms of assisted reproduction? Or are they willing to admit, despite their attachment to the principle of continuity, that the complete obliteration of "mother" or "father," the complete depersonalization of procreation, the complete manufacture of human beings and the complete genetic control of one generation over the next would be ethically problematic and essentially different from current forms of assisted reproduction? If so, where and how will they draw the line, and why? I draw it at cloning, for all the reasons given.

BAN THE CLONING OF HUMANS

What, then, should we do? We should declare that human cloning is unethical in itself and dangerous in its likely consequences. In so doing, we shall have the backing of the overwhelming majority of our fellow Americans, and of the human race, and (I believe) of most practicing scientists. Next, we should do all that we can to prevent the cloning of human beings. We should do this by means of an international legal ban if possible, and by a unilateral national ban, at a minimum. Scientists may secretly undertake to violate such a law, but they will be deterred by not being able to stand up proudly to claim the credit for their technological bravado and success. Such a ban on clonal baby-making, moreover, will not harm the progress of basic genetic science and technology. On the contrary, it will reassure the public that scientists are happy to proceed without violating the deep ethical norms and intuitions of the human community.

This still leaves the vexed question about laboratory research using early embryonic human clones, specially created only for such research purposes, with no intention to implant them into a uterus. There is no question that such research holds great promise for gaining fundamental knowledge about normal (and abnormal) differentiation, and for developing tissue lines for transplantation that might be used, say, in treating leukemia or in repairing brain or spinal cord injuries—to mention just a few of the conceivable benefits. Still, unrestricted clonal embryo research will surely make the production of living human clones much more likely. Once the genies put the cloned embryos into the bottles, who can strictly control where they go (especially in the absence of legal prohibitions against implanting them to produce a child)?

I appreciate the potentially great gains in scientific knowledge and medical treatment available from embryo research, especially with cloned embryos. At the same time, I have serious reservations about creating human embryos for the sole purpose of experimentation. There is something deeply repugnant and fundamentally transgressive about such a utilitarian treatment of prospective human life. This total, shameless exploitation is worse, in my opinion, than the "mere" destruction of nascent life. But I see no added objections, as a matter of principle, to creating and using *cloned* early embryos for research purposes, beyond the objections that I might raise to doing so with embryos produced sexually.

And yet, as a matter of policy and prudence, any opponent of the manufacture of cloned humans must, I think, in the end oppose also the creating of cloned human embryos. Frozen embryonic clones (belonging to whom?) can be shuttled around without detection. Commercial ventures in human cloning will be developed without adequate oversight. In order to build a fence around the law, prudence dictates that one oppose—for this reason alone—all production of cloned human embryos, even for research purposes. We should allow for all cloning research on animals to go forward, but the only safe trench that we can dig across the slippery slope, I suspect, is to insist on the inviolable distinction between animal and human cloning.

Some readers, and certainly most scientists, will not accept such prudent restraints, since they desire the benefits of research. They will prefer, even in fear and trembling, to allow human embryo cloning research to go forward.

Very well. Let us test them. If the scientists want to be taken seriously on ethical grounds, they must at the very least agree that embryonic research may proceed if and only if it is preceded by an absolute and effective ban on all attempts to implant into a uterus a cloned human embryo (cloned from an adult) to produce a living child. Absolutely no permission for the former without the latter.

The National Bioethics Advisory Commission's recommendations regarding this matter should be watched with the greatest care. Yielding to the wishes of the scientists, the commission will almost surely recommend that cloning human embryos for research be permitted. To allay public concern, it will likely also call for a temporary moratorium—not a legislative ban—on implanting cloned embryos to make a child, at least until such time as cloning techniques will have been perfected and rendered "safe" (precisely through the permitted research with cloned embryos). But the call for a moratorium rather than a legal ban would be a moral and a practical failure. Morally, this ethics commission would (at best) be waffling on the main ethical question, by refusing to declare the production of human clones unethical (or ethical). Practically, a moratorium on implantation cannot provide even the minimum protection needed to prevent the production of cloned humans.

Opponents of cloning need therefore to be vigilant. Indeed, no one should be willing even to consider a recommendation to allow the embryo research to proceed unless it is accompanied by a call for *prohibiting* implantation and until steps are taken to make such a prohibition effective.

Technically, the National Bioethics Advisory Commission can advise the president only on federal policy, especially federal funding policy. But given the seriousness of the matter at hand, and the grave public concern that goes beyond federal funding, the commission should take a broader view. (If it doesn't, Congress surely will.) Given that most assisted reproduction occurs in the private sector, it would be cowardly and insufficient for the commission to say, simply, "no federal funding" for such practices. It would be disingenuous to argue that we should allow federal funding so that we would then be able to regulate the practice; the private sector will not be bound by such regulations. Far better, for virtually everyone concerned, would be to distinguish between research on embryos and baby-making, and to call for a complete national and international ban (effected by legislation and treaty) of the latter, while allowing the former to proceed (at least in private laboratories).

The proposal for such a legislative ban is without American precedent, at least in technological matters, though the British and others have banned cloning of human beings, and we ourselves ban incest, polygamy and other forms of "reproductive freedom." Needless to say, working out the details of such a ban, especially a global one, would be tricky, what with the need to develop appropriate sanctions for violators. Perhaps such a ban will prove ineffective; perhaps it will eventually be shown to have been a mistake. But it would at least place the burden of practical proof where it belongs: on the proponents of this horror, requiring them to show very clearly what great social or medical good can be had only by the cloning of human beings.

We Americans have lived by, and prospered under, a rosy optimism about scientific and technological progress. The technological imperative—if it can be done, it must be done—has probably served us well, though we should admit that there is no accurate method for weighing benefits and harms. Even when, as in the cases of environmental pollution, urban decay or the lingering deaths that are the unintended byproducts of medical success, we recognize the unwelcome outcomes of technological advance, we remain confident in our ability to fix all the "bad" consequences—usually by means of still newer and better technologies. How successful we can continue to be in such post hoc repairing is at least an open question. But there is very good reason for shifting the paradigm around, at least regarding those technological interventions into the human body and mind that will surely effect fundamental (and likely irreversible) changes in human nature, basic human relationships, and what it means to be a human being. Here we surely should not be willing to risk everything in the naïve hope that, should things go wrong, we can later set them right.

The president's call for a moratorium on human cloning has given us an important opportunity. In a truly unprecedented way, we can strike a blow for the human control of the technological project, for wisdom, prudence and human dignity. The prospect of human cloning, so repulsive to contemplate, is the occasion for deciding whether we shall be slaves of unregulated progress, and ultimately its artifacts, or whether we shall remain free human beings who guide our technique toward the enhancement of human dignity. If we are to seize the occasion, we must, as the late Paul Ramsey wrote,

> raise the ethical questions with a serious and not a frivolous conscience. A man of frivolous conscience announces that there are ethical quandaries ahead that we must urgently consider before the future catches up with us. By this he often means that we need to devise a new ethics that will provide the rationalization for doing in the future what men are bound to do because of new actions and interventions science will have made possible. In contrast a man of serious conscience means to say in raising urgent ethical questions that there may be some things that men should never do. The good things that men do can be made complete only by the things they refuse to do.

NATIONAL BIOETHICS ADVISORY COMMISSION

Cloning Human Beings

The idea that humans might someday be cloned—created from a single somatic cell without sexual reproduction—moved further away from science fiction and closer to a genuine scientific possibility on February 23, 1997. On that date, *The Observer* broke the news that Ian Wilmut, a Scottish scientist, and his colleagues at the Roslin Institute were about to announce the successful cloning of a sheep by a new technique which had never before been fully successful in mammals. The technique involved transplanting the genetic material of an adult sheep, apparently obtained from a differentiated somatic cell, into an egg from which the nucleus had been removed. The resulting birth of the sheep, named Dolly, on July 5, 1996, was different from prior attempts to create identical offspring since Dolly contained the genetic material of only one parent, and was, therefore, a "delayed" genetic twin of a single adult sheep.

This cloning technique is an extension of research that had been ongoing for over 40 years using nuclei derived from non-human embryonic and fetal cells. The demonstration that nuclei from cells derived from an adult animal could be "reprogrammed," or that the full genetic complement of such a cell could be reactivated well into the chronological life of the cell, is what sets the results of this experiment apart from prior work. In this report we refer to the technique, first described by Wilmut, of nuclear transplantation using nuclei derived from somatic cells other than those of an embryo or fetus as "somatic cell nuclear transfer."

Within days of the published report of Dolly, President Clinton instituted a ban on federal funding related to attempts to clone human beings in this manner. In addition, the President asked the recently appointed National Bioethics Advisory Commission (NBAC) to address within ninety days the ethical and legal issues that surround the subject of cloning human beings. This provided a welcome opportunity for initiating a thoughtful analysis of the many dimensions of the issue, including a careful consideration of the potential risks and benefits. It also presented an occasion to review the current legal status of cloning and the potential constitutional challenges that might be raised if new legislation were enacted to restrict the creation of a child through somatic cell nuclear transfer cloning.

The Commission began its discussions fully recognizing that any effort in humans to transfer a somatic cell nucleus into an enucleated egg involves the creation of an embryo, with the apparent potential to be implanted in utero and developed to term. Ethical concerns surrounding issues of embryo research have recently received extensive analysis and deliberation in our country. Indeed, federal funding for human embryo research is severely restricted, although there are few restrictions on human embryo research carried out in the private sector. Thus, under current law, the use of somatic cell nuclear transfer to create an embryo solely for research purposes is already restricted in cases involving federal funds. There are, however, no current federal regulations on the use of private funds for this purpose.

The unique prospect, vividly raised by Dolly, is the creation of a new individual genetically identical to an existing (or previously existing) person—a "delayed" genetic twin. This prospect has been the source of the overwhelming public concern about such cloning. While the creation of embryos for research purposes alone always raises serious ethical questions, the use of somatic cell nuclear transfer to create embryos

Reprinted from *Cloning Human Beings: Report and Recommendations of the National Bioethics Advisory Committee* (Rockville, MD: NBAC, June 1997), i–v.

raises no new issues in this respect. The unique and distinctive ethical issues raised by the use of somatic cell nuclear transfer to create children relate to, for example, serious safety concerns, individuality, family integrity, and treating children as objects. Consequently, the Commission focused its attention on the use of such techniques for the purpose of creating an embryo which would then be implanted in a woman's uterus and brought to term. It also expanded its analysis of this particular issue to encompass activities in both the public and private sector.

In its deliberations, NBAC reviewed the scientific developments which preceded the Roslin announcement, as well as those likely to follow in its path. It also considered the many moral concerns raised by the possibility that this technique could be used to clone human beings. Much of the initial reaction to this possibility was negative. Careful assessment of that response revealed fears about harms to the children who may be created in this manner, particularly psychological harms associated with a possibly diminished sense of individuality and personal autonomy. Others expressed concern about a degradation in the quality of parenting and family life.

In addition to concerns about specific harms to children, people have frequently expressed fears that the widespread practice of somatic cell nuclear transfer cloning would undermine important social values by opening the door to a form of eugenics or by tempting some to manipulate others as if they were objects instead of persons. Arrayed against these concerns are other important social values, such as protecting the widest possible sphere of personal choice, particularly in matters pertaining to procreation and child rearing, maintaining privacy and the freedom of scientific inquiry, and encouraging the possible development of new biomedical breakthroughs.

To arrive at its recommendations concerning the use of somatic cell nuclear transfer techniques to create children, NBAC also examined long-standing religious traditions that guide many citizens' responses to new technologies and found that religious positions on human cloning are pluralistic in their premises, modes of argument, and conclusions. Some religious thinkers argue that the use of somatic cell nuclear transfer cloning to create a child would be intrinsically immoral and thus could never be morally justified. Other religious thinkers contend that human cloning to create a child could be morally justified under some circumstances, but hold that it should be strictly regulated in order to prevent abuses.

The public policies recommended with respect to the creation of a child using somatic cell nuclear transfer reflect the Commission's best judgments about both the ethics of attempting such an experiment and our view of traditions regarding limitations on individual actions in the name of the common good. At present, the use of this technique to create a child would be a premature experiment that would expose the fetus and the developing child to unacceptable risks. This in itself might be sufficient to justify a prohibition on cloning human beings at this time, even if such efforts were to be characterized as the exercise of a fundamental right to attempt to procreate.

Beyond the issue of the safety of the procedure, however, NBAC found that concerns relating to the potential psychological harms to children and effects on the moral, religious, and cultural values of society merited further reflection and deliberation. Whether upon such further deliberation our nation will conclude that the use of cloning techniques to create children should be allowed or permanently banned is, for the moment, an open question. Time is an ally in this regard, allowing for the accrual of further data from animal experimentation, enabling an assessment of the prospective safety and efficacy of the procedure in humans, as well as granting a period of fuller national debate on ethical and social concerns. The Commission therefore concluded that there should be imposed a period of time in which no attempt is made to create a child using somatic cell nuclear transfer.[1]

Within this overall framework the Commission came to the following conclusions and recommendations:

I. The Commission concludes that at this time it is morally unacceptable for anyone in the public or private sector, whether in a research or clinical setting, to attempt to create a child using somatic cell nuclear transfer cloning. We have reached a consensus on this point because current scientific information indicates that this technique is not safe to use in humans at this time. Indeed, we believe it would violate important ethical obligations were clinicians or researchers to attempt to create a child using these particular technologies, which are likely to involve unacceptable risks to the fetus and/or potential child. Moreover, in addition to safety concerns, many other serious ethical concerns have been identified, which require much more widespread and careful public deliberation before this technology may be used.

The Commission, therefore, recommends the following for immediate action:

- A continuation of the current moratorium on the use of federal funding in support of any attempt to create a child by somatic cell nuclear transfer.
- An immediate request to all firms, clinicians, investigators, and professional societies in the private and non-federally funded sectors to comply voluntarily with the intent of the federal moratorium. Professional and scientific societies should make clear that any attempt to create a child by somatic cell nuclear transfer and implantation into a woman's body would at this time be an irresponsible, unethical, and unprofessional act.

II. The Commission further recommends that:

- Federal legislation should be enacted to prohibit anyone from attempting, whether in a research or clinical setting, to create a child through somatic cell nuclear transfer cloning. It is critical, however, that such legislation include a sunset clause to ensure that Congress will review the issue after a specified time period (three to five years) in order to decide whether the prohibition continues to be needed. If state legislation is enacted, it should also contain such a sunset provision. Any such legislation or associated regulation also ought to require that at some point prior to the expiration of the sunset period, an appropriate oversight body will evaluate and report on the current status of somatic cell nuclear transfer technology and on the ethical and social issues that its potential use to create human beings would raise in light of public understandings at that time.

III. The Commission also concludes that:

- Any regulatory or legislative actions undertaken to effect the foregoing prohibition on creating a child by somatic cell nuclear transfer should be carefully written so as not to interfere with other important areas of scientific research. In particular, no new regulations are required regarding the cloning of human DNA sequences and cell lines, since neither activity raises the scientific and ethical issues that arise from the attempt to create children through somatic cell nuclear transfer, and these fields of research have already provided important scientific and biomedical advances. Likewise, research on cloning animals by somatic cell nuclear transfer does not raise the issues implicated in attempting to use this technique for human cloning, and its continuation should only be subject to existing regulations regarding the humane use of animals and review by institution-based animal protection committees.
- If a legislative ban is not enacted, or if a legislative ban is ever lifted, clinical use of somatic cell nuclear transfer techniques to create a child should be preceded by research trials that are governed by the twin protections of independent review and informed consent, consistent with existing norms of human subjects protection.
- The United States Government should cooperate with other nations and international organizations to enforce any common aspects of their respective policies on the cloning of human beings.

IV. The Commission also concludes that different ethical and religious perspectives and traditions are divided on many of the important moral issues that surround any attempt to create a child using somatic cell nuclear transfer techniques. Therefore, we recommend that:

- The federal government, and all interested and concerned parties, encourage widespread and continuing deliberation on these issues in order to further our understanding of the ethical and social implications of this technology and to enable society to produce appropriate long-term policies regarding this technology should the time come when present concerns about safety have been addressed.

V. Finally, because scientific knowledge is essential for all citizens to participate in a full and informed fashion in the governance of our complex society, the Commission recommends that:

- Federal departments and agencies concerned with science should cooperate in seeking out and supporting opportunities to provide information and education to the public in the area of genetics, and on other developments in the biomedical sciences, especially where these affect important cultural practices, values, and beliefs.

NOTE

1. The Commission also observes that the use of any other technique to create a child genetically identical to an existing (or previously existing) individual would raise many, if not all, of the same non-safety-related ethical concerns raised by the creation of a child by somatic cell nuclear transfer.

RAANAN GILLON

Human Reproductive Cloning: A Look at the Arguments against It and a Rejection of Most of Them

Raanan Gillon is a Professor at Imperial College (London) in the Medical Ethics Unit. He has published widely in medical ethics in the *British Medical Journal* and was Senior Editor of, and a contributor to, *Principles of Health Care Ethics* (John Wiley & Sons). He is a member of British Medical Association's Ethics Committee and was for many years Editor of the *Journal of Medical Ethics*.

Human reproductive cloning—replication of genetically identical or near identical human beings—can hardly be said to have had a good press. Banned in one way or another by many countries including the United Kingdom,[1] execrated by the General Assembly of the World Health Organization as "ethically unacceptable and contrary to human integrity and morality,"[2] forbidden by the European Commission through its Biotechnology Patents Directive,[3] by the Council of Europe through its Bioethics Convention,[4] and by UNESCO through its Declaration on the Human Genome and Human Rights,[5] clearly human cloning arouses massive disapproval. What are the reasons, and especially the moral reasons, offered as justifications for this wholesale disapproval? In brief summary these seem to be: "yuk—the whole thing is revolting, repellent, unnatural and disgusting"; "it's playing God, hubris"; "it treats people as means and not as ends, undermines human dignity, human rights, personal autonomy, personality, individuality, and individual uniqueness; it turns people into carbon copies, photocopies, stencils, and fakes"; "it would be dangerous and harmful to those to whom it was done, as well as to their families; it would particularly harm the women who would be bearing the babies, and especially so if they were doing so on behalf of others as would probably be the case; it would harm societies in which it happened, changing and demeaning their values, encouraging vanity, narcissism, and avarice; and it would be harmful to future generations." "Altogether it would be the first massive step on a ghastly slippery slope toward"—here fill in the horror—'Hitler's Nazi Germany, Stalin's USSR, China's eugenic dictatorship; or, from the realms of literature, *Boys from Brazil,* mad dictators, and of course mad scientists in science fiction, Big Brother in *Nineteen Eighty-Four,* and the human hatcheries of *Brave New World*." "It would be unjust, contrary to human equality, and, as the European Parliament put it, it would lead to eugenics and racist selection of human beings, it would discriminate against women, it would undermine human rights, and it would be against distributive justice by diverting resources away from people who could derive proper and useful medical benefits from those resources." So, clearly, where it has not already been legally prohibited it should be banned as soon as possible.

Note that I have grouped these objections into five categories. The first constitute a highly emotionally charged group that includes yuk, horror, offence, disgust, unnaturalness, the playing of God, and hubris. Then come four clearly moral categories—those concerned with autonomy (in which for reasons given later I have included dignity); those concerned with harm; those concerned with benefit; and those concerned with justice of one sort or another, whether in the sense of simply treating people equally, of just allocation of inadequate resources, of just respect for

Reprinted with the permission of the author and the publisher from the *Journal of the Royal Society of Medicine* 92 (1999), 3–12.
Copyright © 1999 the Royal Society of Medicine.

people's rights, or in the sense of legal justice and the obeying of morally acceptable laws.

Two types of cloning have generated particular moral concern: the first involves taking a cell from a human embryo and growing it into a genetically identical embryo and beyond; the second, made famous by the creation of Dolly the sheep,[6] involves taking out the nucleus of one cell and putting into the resulting sac, or cell wall, the nucleus of another cell to be cloned. Strictly, the Dolly-type clone is not quite a clone because the cell wall also contributes a few genes, the mitochondrial genes, which are incorporated into the resulting organism, but the vast majority of the genes in a Dolly-type clone come from the nucleus, so that, for example, if a nucleus from one of my cells were implanted into a cell sac from someone else, and the resulting cell were grown into a human being, he would have a gene complement almost but not entirely identical to mine. On the other hand, clones that result from splitting off of cells from embryos and growing them have exactly the same gene content as the embryo from which they came. With either of these cloning techniques, the process can be carried to early stages of development for a variety of potentially useful purposes, without any intention or prospect of producing a developed human being (lumped together here as nonreproductive human cloning and referred to only in passing). The human cloning that produces the greatest concern, and is the main subject of this paper, is of course reproductive human cloning, which would aim to produce a human person with the same genes as some other human being.

HUBRIS, YUK, AND SO ON

First, then, the group of responses based on yuk, it's unnatural, it's against one's conscience, it's intuitively repellent, it's playing God, it's hubris—a group of responses that one hears very frequently. I have to admit that this sort of essentially emotional response tends to evoke a negative emotional response in me when it is used in moral argument, as it often is (by moral argument I mean, following David Raphael,[7] argument about what is good or bad, what is right or wrong, what ought or ought not to be done and about our values and norms). The trouble is that these gut responses *may* be morally admirable, but they may also be morally wrong, even morally atrocious, and on their own such gut responses do not enable us to distinguish the admirable from the atrocious. Think of the moral gut responses of your favorite bigots—for example, the ones who feel so passionately that homosexuality is evil, that black people are inferior, that women should be subservient to men, that Jews and Gypsies and the mentally retarded or mentally ill ought to be exterminated. People have existed—some still exist—who have these strong "gut beliefs" which they believe to be strong *moral* feelings, which indeed they believe to be their consciences at work; and my point here is that gut responses provide no way for us to distinguish those moral feelings that we know or strongly believe to be wrong, from the moral feelings that we ourselves have, which we know or strongly believe to be right. To discriminate between emotional or gut responses, or indeed between the promptings of deeply felt moral intuitions or of conscience, we must reflect, think, analyze in order to decide whether particular moral feelings are good or bad, whether they should lead to action or whether they should be suppressed (and yes, I think moral reflection shows that it is important to suppress, or even better reeducate so as to change, one's moral feelings when on analysis one finds they are wrong). Without such moral reflection the feeling itself, while it may be an important flag that warns us to look at the issues it concerns, is no more than that. With such reflection we may find that the flag is signaling an important moral perspective that we should follow; or we may find that the flag is signaling us to respond in a morally undesirable way.

An analogy which I like to use concerns medical practice. Doctors, especially surgeons, cut people up quite a lot; they (we) also stick their fingers in people's bottoms. Most of us, I imagine, would feel quite deeply that both of those activities are rather disgusting and not to be done; yet we know, through thought and reflection in our medical studies, that we had better overcome these deep feelings because in some circumstances it is right to cut people and in some circumstances it is right to put our fingers in people's bottoms. Both are extraordinary and counterintuitive things to do, but on analysis we find that they are sometimes the *right* thing to do. The same need for reflection, thought, and analysis applies to our deeply felt moral feelings in general. We need those deep moral feelings, those deep moral gut responses. Moral feelings are—here we may agree with Hume[8]—the mainsprings or drivers of our moral action. They lead us to action against social injustice and corruption, against the tyrant, the torturer, the sadist, the rapist, the sexual aggressor of children but—and now I part company with Hume—we need to reflect on and educate our moral feelings so as to select and develop the good ones, and deter and modify or preferably abolish the bad ones.

In the context of our deep feelings let's just remind ourselves about Huxley and his *Brave New World*.[9] It has become a trigger title, needing only utterance to provoke strong negative feelings, especially about the use of science and technology to control and predetermine people's feelings, attitudes, and behavior. From a rereading of *Brave New World* I was satisfied that Huxley's main target is not science and technology but rather their misapplication by the despotic state that systematically sets out to undermine the possibility of freedom—freedom in the sense of humanity's ability to make thought-out choices and live by them, autonomous freedom. But while Orwell, in his *Nineteen Eighty-Four,* imparted to us a horror of tyrannical social control, of "Big Brother is watching you," Huxley with *Brave New World* is more commonly perceived to have patterned our thoughts and feelings against "runaway science" and especially against genetics and the artificial reproduction of embryos, fetuses, and babies away from their mothers, so as to control every aspect of their development. Recall, as an example itself of conditioning (of Huxley's readers), the ghastly example early on in which babies are naturally attracted to books and to flowers, and then, to ensure that the particular class of worker that the babies are destined to become will detest flowers and books, are subjected to nasty noises, terrifying explosions, sirens, alarm bells, and finally, to make sure, electric shocks. Two hundred repetitions of the Pavlovian conditioning would cause them to grow up with what the psychologists used to call an *instinctive* hatred of books and flowers. "Reflexes unalterably conditioned. They'll be safe from books and botany all their lives," declared the director of hatcheries.

Later on infants are socially programmed while they sleep through "hypnopaedia," in which they are conditioned to have predetermined attitudes. Thus children predestined to be in the Beta class of citizen hear over and over again:

> "Alpha children wear grey. They work much harder than we do because they're so frightfully clever. I'm really awfully glad I'm a Beta, because I don't work so hard. And then we are much better than the Gammas and Deltas. Gammas are stupid. They all wear green, and Delta children wear khaki. Oh no, I *don't* want to play with Delta children. And Epsilons are still worse. They're too stupid."

So, the director concludes,

> "At last the child's mind is these suggestions, and the sum of the suggestions *is* the child's mind. . . . The adult's mind too—all his life long. . . . But all these suggestions are *our* suggestions." The Director almost shouted in his triumph. "Suggestions from the State," he banged the nearest table. . . . "Oh, Ford! . . . I've gone and woken the children."

We will return to *Brave New World,* but I do not think we need Huxley's warnings about childhood conditioning of our attitudes and beliefs and prejudices to know that, even in our ordinary lives, many of our strong attitudes and prejudices and beliefs have emerged as a result of childhood patterning. We have been programmed to some extent into our attitudes. The big difference, of course, is that as we grow up and are educated we are able to reflect on these attitudes and beliefs and to *decide* whether to own them or reject them. Nonetheless many of our deep moral attitudes and beliefs are firmly embedded from early childhood (as the book of *Proverbs* reminds us "Train up a child in the way he should go: and when he is old he will not depart from it") and, even if we decide that some of them are wrong, we have to work very hard if we want to change them. Huxley in *Brave New World* warns against despotic *misuse* of science and technology that, by painfully embedding attitudes and feelings in early infancy, and by later social prohibition or discouragement of reflection about those attitudes, makes the development of moral agency impossible or at least extremely difficult.

However, we have not been the recipients of such state conditioning and control in our own societies, and I find it difficult to understand the strength and depth and origins of the contemporary widespread hostility to the very idea of cloning human beings. Certainly the existence of contemporary nature's own human clones, identical twins, seems harmless enough *not* to account for such deep hostility to the idea of deliberate cloning, though in passing it may be relevant to note that, down the ages, twins have been mysteriously subject to ambivalent prejudices. Thus, apart from literary and dramatic jokes about them from the comedies of Plautus via Shakespeare to Stephen Sondheim, twins and their mothers have been persecuted in some societies, revered but also feared in others, for example as unnatural miscegenated offspring of gods. On the other hand, there may be quite strongly positive attitudes to twins. Wendy Doniger in a review in the *London Review of Books*[10] quotes from Lawrence Wright's work on twins on "the common fantasy that any one of us might have a clone, a Doppelganger; someone who is not only a human mirror, but also an ideal companion; someone who understands me perfectly, almost perfectly, because he is me, almost me."

We will return to the issue of identity, because the myth that genetic identity equals personal identity lies at the root of much misunderstanding about cloning. First, let us pursue in more detail the argument that cloning is *unnatural* and therefore wrong. What role does "unnatural" play in moral argument? Our first requirement is to disambiguate the term—what do we *mean* by unnatural in this context? Anything that occurs in nature could be said to be natural, but that sense of natural is not going to do much moral work for us, for we and what we do are natural, not unnatural, in this sense. In any case, right and wrong, good and bad, insofar as they occur in nature, also are equally natural in this sense, so that to say that something is natural will hardly help us distinguish between the two. Another sense of natural means unaffected by human intervention. But unless we wish to argue that all human interventions are bad and or wrong and all states of nature are good or right, then this sense of natural too is not much help for moral judgment. Think of all the truly horrible and morally undesirable things that occur in nature uninfluenced by humans; think too of all the human interventions in nature that are clearly morally desirable, but "unnatural" in this sense—including all medical interventions, and all the other activities by which we help each other, including the provision of food, housing, clothing, and heating.

But there are two more senses of unnatural that are of moral relevance. The first is that it is part of human nature to be a moral agent (with perhaps a few exceptions) and thus human people who behave immorally or even amorally are acting unnaturally in this sense of acting against their human nature. I personally find this theme of enormous moral importance and a way of linking theological natural law theory with secular morality. But it does not afford us any simple basis or method for moral assessment—instead it demands assessment of what the moral part of our human nature requires of us. So "natural" in this sense, important though it is as a moral concept, does not give us a way of deciding whether cloning and the other genetics activities are good or bad—it simply requires us to make such distinctions. Like the objections based on the 'yuk response', the deep moral intuition, the moral repugnance and the claim of conscience, the objection that cloning is unnatural, when used in this morally plausible sense, requires moral reflection and judgment, but does not itself provide that moral reflection and judgment. If—but only if—such reflection and judgment lead us to conclude that cloning is immoral, *then* we can say that cloning is unnatural in this morally relevant sense of going against our moral nature.

There is another sense of unnatural which I think is also of potential moral relevance. If we do something that weakens, undermines, destroys, or harms our human moral nature, then this is immoral and unnatural in the sense of antinatural or against nature; and that of course is of enormous moral significance not just in relation to cloning but for the whole of the new genetics enterprise. So, to show that any activity, such as cloning, is unnatural in a morally relevant sense we need to give *reasons* that demonstrate why it is contrary to our human moral nature, or why it will undermine that human moral nature. Until we can give such reasons let us be particularly careful to avoid pejorative claims about cloning being unnatural, not simply for the reasons I have just given, but also because it must be very hurtful for the world's identical twins to hear that they, by association, are considered to be "unnatural" and therefore that their existence is morally undesirable.

To continue with this range of somewhat mysterious objections to cloning and sometimes to the new genetics as a whole, we need to look now at hubris and playing God. *Hubris* is a pejorative term meaning a contemptuous arrogance, especially against God or the gods. *Playing at God* combines both an implicit accusation of hubris with an implicit accusation of immaturity and lack of skill—as when children play doctors, somewhat inefficiently. Suffice it to agree that contempt, arrogance, puerile immaturity, and lack of skill are all morally undesirable in one fulfilling a responsible task. But are these accusations justifiably made against the whole enterprise of human cloning, or indeed against the whole enterprise of the new genetics? One would require specific cases and examples rather than sweeping generalizations, which otherwise boil down to mere abuse. There clearly is an important moral issue here, especially in relation to the question of whether at present we can safely and sufficiently skillfully carry out reproductive cloning, even if we wish to do so, and I shall return to this. But, without specific evidence, it seems straightforwardly tendentious to brand the whole enterprise of human cloning, let alone the whole of the new genetics, as "hubris" and "playing God."

AUTONOMY AND PERSONAL IDENTITY

The next set of objections against cloning concerns personal identity and dignity, the undermining of autonomy, of individuality, of personality, of uniqueness, the production of carbon copies, photocopies, stencils, and fakes of human beings.

Even if reproductive cloning were to produce a person identical with the person from whom he or she was cloned, it is not clear to me why this should be immediately condemned as morally unacceptable, though the idea so greatly strains the imagination that one might argue that it would be irresponsible to try any such trick even if it were possible. But of course reproductive cloning would *not* produce two identical people—only two people with identical (or in the case of Dolly-type cloning near identical) sets of genes. Genetic identity neither means nor entails personal identity.

Once again the proof of this exists all around us, for genetically identical twins are obviously different people, even though their genes are identical or near identical (in a type-type sense of identity, such that billiard balls are type-type identical, even though each billiard ball is token identical only with itself). But this genetic type-type identity of people who are clones does not make them identical as people, in either sense.

Some commentators make a different criticism. It is not only personal identity that must not be replicated; nor must genetic identity, for that itself is morally important, indeed even a right, according to the European Parliament. They assert that every one of us has a right to his or her own genetic identity. Here there seems to be serious confusion or conflation between token identity, type-type identity, and uniqueness. On analysis the claim surely cannot be that we all have a right to our genetic identity in the sense of token identity (every thing being token identical with itself and with nothing else), for that is simply an analytic truth. We all, including identical twins, necessarily do have that sort of genetic token identity, and if it is not incoherent to describe this definitional truth as a right, it is certainly pointless. But if the claim is made in terms of type-type identity, whereby we are claimed to have a right to type-type genetic identity, then identical twins and any other human clones *do* have such genetic identity; that is precisely the sort of identity that they have (or near identity in the case of Dolly-type cloning). So presumably it is not genetic identity that the European Parliament can sensibly be claiming as a right. Perhaps instead it is genetic exclusivity or uniqueness. If I have such a right, then no one else is entitled to have the (type-type) identical genes that I have. It might be described as a claim right that one's genetic identity, in the sense of token identity, must be unique—in other words, a claim right *not* to have type-type genetic identity. But if that is the European Parliament's claim it is not merely bizarre; if taken seriously it is morally malignant, for it implies morally malignant consequences for identical twins, nature's existing examples of people who are clones. If we have this right to genetic uniqueness, then somebody must have the corresponding duty—the duty to destroy one of each pair of existing identical twins, both born and *in utero*. Fortunately such counterexamples, plus the general tendency of morally reflective people to be morally and legally unconcerned about the lack of genetic uniqueness of identical twins, indicate that genetic uniqueness is unlikely, *pace* the European Parliament, to be of moral importance, let alone a moral right, and still less a right that ought to be enshrined in law.

But maybe there is a difference between cloning that occurs naturally and cloning that occurs by intention? Perhaps it is deliberate cloning that is the problem, rather than the cloning that occurs naturally, in the sense of unmediated by human beings? And perhaps the problem is that such deliberate reproductive cloning somehow demeans human dignity? Certainly both the World Health Organization and the European Parliament have stated that such cloning would offend against human dignity. Well, once again we need to know what we mean by human dignity. We all know that human dignity is good and ought to be promoted and respected, but most of us, I suspect, would find it very difficult to say what we actually mean by human dignity and to explain why its violation is wrong.

The *Shorter Oxford English Dictionary* offers definitions such as "the quality of being worthy or honourable . . . worth, excellence . . . high estate, position or estimation . . . honour, rank"—definitions that indicate that to say that someone has dignity is to say that he or she is valued. But with this sort of understanding of "dignity," to say that cloning violates or offends against human dignity is simply to assert that it diminishes worth without in any way explaining *why* this should be so. Interestingly the *Encyclopedia of Philosophy,* the *Encyclopedia of Bioethics,* and the *Dictionary of Medical Ethics* all lack entries under "dignity." Those who wish to use infringement of human dignity as an argument against human reproductive cloning thus need to explain what they mean by the term. For me the most plausible account of human dignity is Immanuel Kant's. For him human dignity resides in our ability to be autonomous, to will or choose to act according to the moral law.[11] I suspect that many uses of the term "human dignity" are consistent with this Kantian notion that our human dignity is our ability to make autonomous choices for ourselves according to what we believe to be right. If so, when we commit ourselves to respecting human dignity, to treating others in ways that respect their human dignity, we mean roughly that we should treat them in ways that they themselves on reflection and deliberation would believe to be good or right ways; and that when we make decisions on behalf of people who cannot make their own decisions, we should try so far as we can to replicate the decisions they themselves would have autonomously chosen (or if they have not yet become autonomous, can be expected and desired to make were they autonomous).

If we accept some version of the Kantian meaning of human dignity and its basis in autonomous choice, then it is not at all clear to me why reproductive cloning should in any way undermine such dignity. Of course there might be ways of destroying or damaging that dignity by damaging the underlying genetic basis for such autonomous choice—and any such activity should be morally condemned precisely because of the damage to human dignity, a version of the reputable anti-human nature argument above. But no reason has been offered for accusing reproductive human cloning of damaging human dignity in this way.

Another objection to cloning that may also reside in the notion of human dignity is that we must never treat other people merely as means to an end, but always as ends in themselves—one of the versions of Kant's categorical imperative.[11] This claim is frequently misrepresented as a moral obligation never to use each other as means to an end, or as instruments or as tools or as objects. That misrepresentation is plainly wrong, for of course we morally can and morally do frequently use each other as means to an end, as tools, and it is highly desirable that we continue to do so. If I ask you to bend forward so that I can climb on your back in order to get over my garden wall to let myself in through the kitchen window because I have lost my key, I am using you as a means to my end, as an object, a sort of stepladder, an instrument or a tool. But I am not treating you *merely* as an object or a tool or an instrument. By asking and obtaining your permission I am treating you as an end in yourself as well as treating you as a means to my end. The issue is complicated with embryos because it is a matter of unresolved and passionate moral debate whether embryos and fetuses are within the scope of the Kantian requirement to treat each other as ends in themselves. Many of us believe that they are not, and thus would permit, for example, the cloning of human embryos for research purposes with disposal (i.e., destruction) of the experimented-on embryo at an early stage in its development. In the United Kingdom the law allows this sort of thing. On the other hand, many others would say that this is morally outrageous because the human embryo *does* fall within the scope of the Kantian categorical imperative, being itself a human person from the moment of its creation. I am not going to address that argument, but it is important to see how it complicates the issue of cloning, both sorts of cloning. For if in creating an embryo, by whatever method, we have created a person, then of course we must treat it as a person, and thus not use it merely as a means to an end. If, on the other hand, it is not yet a person then we may use it merely as a means to an end, as a research tool for example, and destroy it after such use. That is an unresolved philosophical or theological problem.

Suppose, however, we put aside that piece of the argument and revert to human reproductive cloning. Then the requirement always to treat people as ends in themselves, even when we also treat them as means, is entirely compatible with reproductive cloning. The issue surely turns, not on the method of reproduction, cloning or otherwise, that one may choose, but rather on how one actually treats and regards the child that results. Take the example of parents who seek to clone a child because they want to have another child with the same blood or marrow type, so that they can transplant some marrow from the new child into an existing child mortally ill with leukemia. Such a process would necessarily involve, it is often claimed, treating the new child merely as a means. Not at all, I would counterargue. The argument needs to be broken down into two parts. The first part concerns the question, why do and ought people decide to have children? In particular, is there any moral obligation to have a child only for the sake of the child-to-be? If so, then surely the vast majority of parents have behaved immorally, for while there must be many different reasons for having a child, I doubt that there exist very many parents who have decided to have a child because they decided there was now a need to have a new person in the world to whom duties were owed that he or she should exist. Much more commonly (and yes, this is mere supposition) people decide to have a child because they *want* a child for their own reasons or, perhaps more commonly, instincts. They feel like it, or they are ready to have children, or they want to fill a gap in their lives, or perhaps they want an heir, or someone to take over the business, or someone to look after them in their old age; all sorts of personal selfish reasons may operate, or none at all. My argument is that, until shown otherwise, we should accept that there is nothing wrong with making either a self-interested or an instrumental decision to have a child.

Having implemented such a decision, the second stage of the argument applies, for now, of course, mere self-interest can no longer be justified. Once there is another person created as a result of one's decision, then that person must be accorded the same moral respect as is due to all people and must not be treated merely as a means to an end, an object, a tool, an instrument. So while one may perfectly properly decide to have a child in order to provide a source of life-saving cord blood or marrow for one's existing child, one must of course then respect the new child as an end and never treat him or her merely as a means to an end. I can see no reason for the parents' instrumental motivation for having a child in any way necessitating their treatment of the new child merely as a means and not an end. If anything, I suspect that human psychological nature would tend to lead parents to treat such children even more lovingly and respectfully than usual.

I have given reasons for doubting that cloning would infringe the human dignity and autonomy of the cloned person. Let us now consider the dignity and autonomy of those who wish to engage in reproductive cloning. Such considerations favor noninterference on the grounds that in general people's autonomous choices for themselves should be respected, unless there are very strong moral reasons against doing so, and that this is particularly true in respect of those rather personal and private areas of choice, notably those concerning reproduction, sexuality, choice of partners, and decisions about babies. Intervention by the state, or anyone else, in these areas of private morality undermines the human dignity/autonomy of those people. Moreover, respect for people's dignity/autonomy in these areas is not only right in itself, but is also likely to lead to far greater overall good and far less harm than if we start erecting state apparatuses for intervention in these private areas.

I think this is Huxley's main message in *Brave New World*. Do not let government start to control our private decisions, our autonomy or our development. Do not let the apparatus for state control in these areas be developed. By leaving such choices decentralized not only will people's dignity/autonomy be respected—a good in itself—but human welfare generally will benefit. Similarly, beware state control of science and technology, for in the name of social order it will lead to the end of liberty. As Huxley later admits, this is an overstated case, and I am certainly not arguing for total libertarianism and absence of state controls either of citizens' behavior or of science and technology. But I am arguing against excessive state control, and in favor of a substantial zone of respect by the state for private autonomous choices where such respect does not entail harm to others. And so, I think, was Huxley.

HARMS AND BENEFITS

Which brings us to the next group of arguments, based on the harms and benefits of cloning. Let us briefly examine these in relation to the people cloned, their families, their societies and future generations. It is in the context of the social and personal harms of human reproductive cloning that *Brave New World* (and also the Ira Levin book of 1976, *Boys from Brazil,* in which clones of Hitler are bred in an attempt to rekindle the Nazi enterprise) has done so much to turn us against cloning, even succeeding in rendering the term pejorative. What was common to both of those books, but was especially evident in Huxley's novel, was that the cloning involved either selection of already impaired humanity for cloning (e.g., Levin and the cloning of

Hitlers) or the deliberate impairment of human embryos before they were cloned, as in Huxley's notion of "Bokanovsky's Process."

"Essentially," the director of hatcheries and conditioning explains, bokanovskification, or cloning, "consists of a series of arrests of development"—arrests by chilling the embryo, by X-raying it, by adding alcohol, and by oxygen starvation. When one of the students bravely asks what the benefit was of this process,

> the Director wheeled sharply round, "can't you see, can't you *see*?" He raised a hand; his expression solemn. "Bokanovsky's Process is one of the major instruments of social stability. . . . Ninety-six identical twins working ninety-six identical machines! . . . You really know where you are. For the first time in history." He quoted the planetary motto: "Community, Identity, Stability." Grand words. "If we could bokanovskify indefinitely, the whole problem would be solved" . . . standard Gammas, unvarying Deltas, uniform Epsilons . . . "But alas," the Director shook his head, "we *can't* bokanovskify indefinitely."

Note that Huxley has here combined and conflated three quite separate ideas. One is reproductive cloning; the second is a crude and simplistic genetic determinism (ascribed to the rulers of course and rejected by Huxley himself) whereby genetic identity equals personal identity; and the third is intervention in the cloning process to impair the normal development of the human embryo. But we have seen that cloning does not entail personal identity, and so far as we know cloning need not harm or impair the embryo.

But of course we do not yet know. Cloning by nuclear substitution has only just begun in mammals, with Dolly the sheep being one successful outcome out of 277 attempts to produce such a clone. Imagine that being done in human beings and the harms to the women producing the eggs and undergoing the unsuccessful implantations (as stated above, I am leaving unargued the issue of whether it is permissible to harm the human embryo itself for the purpose of such research).

Claims about the potential harms caused by human reproductive cloning are extensive. Animal experiments are reported to have produced many abnormal embryos and fetuses, many spontaneous abortions, and many abnormal births. Theoretical reasons are claimed to indicate that the offspring will be particularly prone to various diseases including those associated with premature aging. Psychological harms are predicted for individual children thus born, including resentment at having their genetic structure predetermined by their parents, resentment at having been conceived merely as means to benefit others (for example as blood or bone marrow sources), a sense of overwhelming burden if they have been cloned from someone with great achievements that they are supposed to emulate; confusion about their personal identity and relationships (if, for example, they are clones of one of their parents). Physical and emotional harms are also predicted for women bearing cloned embryos, including the high rate of failure and abnormality of the pregnancies; and if the women are also surrogates even more emotional harms can be anticipated (a point made by my colleague Donna Dickenson).

In addition to the general social disasters noted above, as envisaged in books such as *Brave New World* and *Boys from Brazil,* contemporary concerns include undermining of social values by opening the doors to racist eugenics, encouragement of "vanity, narcissism and avarice" as the U.S. Commission on Bioethics has reported,[12] and the creation of "a means of mass destruction" with "science out of control" as the Nobel Laureate scientist Joseph Rotblat is reported to have claimed.[13] Add to all this the concern of the European Parliament about "violation of the security of human genetic material," anticipated reduction in the genetic variability of the human race and the consequent threat to human evolution that the WHO is concerned about, and also worries about the geometric increase through germline inheritance of any mistakes that are created by cloning, and we see a wide range of anticipated harms that may result from cloning.

Once again we need to look at this range of harms rather more precisely. Let it be acknowledged immediately that *at present* the technique of human cloning is not well developed enough to be safely used in humans for reproduction, but this is not to acknowledge either that each of the preceding harm arguments is valid, or that the harm arguments that are currently valid are sufficiently strong to prevent further research into ways of reducing such harms—for example, by animal experimentation.

What, then, of the formidable lists of harms, mainly psychological harms, anticipated to affect children? In brief, I think we need to set against these purported and anticipated psychological harms of being a clone child the very important counterconsideration of what is the alternative for that particular child? This argument commonly irritates, sometimes enrages, but rarely convinces. Yet it seems valid, and I have not encountered plausible *counterarguments*. The alternative *for those children* is to not exist at all, so if we are genuinely looking at the interests of those children who are anticipated to have the various psychological problems of being clones, and the difficulties that undoubtedly we can anticipate those will raise, and if we are genuinely looking at those problems from the point of view of the child, then the proper question to ask is: What is preferable for that child? To exist but to have those problems, or not to exist at all? It is an argument that I learned from the so-called pro-life movement, though I suspect this is not a use that pro-lifers themselves would wish to make of it. I found that the argument radically changed the way I thought about anticipated harms. Of course, it in no way stops one from deciding, for example, not to have a baby, or to have an abortion, or not to pursue reproductive cloning. But it does force one, or should force one, to realize that one's reasons are unlikely to be the best interests of the child whom one is thinking of not having, but are instead one's own reasons and preferences, largely about the sort of world one wishes to participate in creating. And if that is the case, why should one's own reasons and preferences prevail over the reasons and preferences of those who do wish to carry out reproductive cloning? After all, they do not claim a right to prevent us from reproducing according to our preferences; why should we claim a right to prevent them from reproducing according to their preferences?

As for the arguments about the potential social harms of cloning, other than those based on safety of the techniques, it seems to me that they are either frankly implausible (the argument that cloning is a threat to further human evolution surely falls into this category, given the likely numbers of cloned versus more conventionally produced people), too weak to justify imposition on those who reject them (for instance the arguments that reproductive cloning encourages vanity, narcissism, and avarice), or powerful but misdirected. Thus it is not cloning, nor the techniques of the new genetics more broadly considered, that might lead to the social harms of racism, eugenics, mass destruction, or the violation of the security of genetic material, but rather social structures that permit dictatorships and other forms of immorally enforced control of people's behavior by their rulers. Those are the harms that we need to be concerned about; and the most important way of avoiding them—of avoiding oppression of all those who are oppressed by the strong, including the widespread oppression of women by men—is not to ban cloning or to become obsessed with the new genetics, but rather to reform those social structures that result in such harms and to maintain in good order those social structures that do largely avoid these harms.

What about the germ-line argument of dangers to future generations? Well certainly the genome resulting from reproductive cloning is germ-line transmissible, and any mistakes that occur can be passed on to future generations. But so too, of course, can any benefits. If, for example, a cloning technique results in the elimination of some genetic abnormality that would otherwise have been transmitted through the germ line, then the cascade effect is geometrically beneficial, just as, if a mistake results and is passed on through the germ line, that, too, is geometrically inheritable. Clearly, care is needed to minimize the chances of the latter and maximize the chances of the former. But in general, with ever increasing voluntary personal control over reproduction, it seems likely that even if genetic mistakes do occur, if they are severe people will be reluctant to pass them on to their offspring, thus reducing the risks of a cascade of negative genetic effects down the generations. On the other hand the precedent of deciding to prevent certain sorts of reproduction on the basis of the risk to future generations of deleterious genetic effects is itself one of the social harms—enforced eugenics—that opponents of the new genetics are usually very keen to avoid. The current orthodoxy that somatic genetic interventions that are beneficial can be accepted but that germ-line interventions, even if clearly beneficial, should be forbidden seems to be one of those undefended taboos that need to be rejected. If we develop a genetic intervention that helps one offspring we need very good reasons for denying it to that offspring's offspring.

In general, and in relation to possible harms of new techniques, we need to beware excessive concern with the "precautionary principle." Insofar as it tells us to avoid doing harm, it is an important moral concern to balance against our continuing search for new ways of doing good—of benefiting others. In other words, the principle of beneficence should always take into account the principle of non-maleficence, and the objective should be an acceptable probability of doing good with minimal and acceptable harm and risk of harm. But sometimes the precautionary principle is used as a sort of moral blunderbuss, like the use of *primum non nocere* when this is translated as "above all do no harm." That way lies a beneficence moratorium, with all applied medical research, indeed all new medical interventions, being banned, for whenever we seek to benefit we risk harming. The morally desirable use of the precautionary principle is to weigh anticipated benefits and their probabilities against anticipated harms and their probabilities, always aiming at a likely outcome of net benefit with minimal and acceptable harm and risk of harm.

So what about the benefits? I have been able to find less in the published work about the potential benefits of reproductive human cloning than about its potential harms. The same is not true about nonreproductive human cloning, for which a wide variety of impressive potential benefits has been claimed. These include production of useful pharmaceuticals from cloned transgenic animals; basic research into DNA and aspects of genetics, human reproduction and infertility, aging and *oncogenesis;* as well as the possible production of cloned human tissues and organs (for use, for example, in transplantation).[14] But even human reproductive cloning can be anticipated to provide certain benefits. For example, in rare cases Dolly-type cloning techniques could prevent inheritance of rare and disabling mitochondrial genetic disorders. The genetic abnormality being in the mitochondria, these cloning techniques make it possible to replace the cell membrane containing the defective mitochondria with an unaffected cell membrane and then to insert into that the unaffected genetic material in the cell nucleus. For the affected people such reproductive cloning could be of major benefit. A second potential benefit could arise where parents wish to have a further child, as already suggested, in order to provide, for example, compatible bone marrow or cord blood for an existing child who needs it to survive (I owe the cord blood example to Dr. Matjaz Zwitter). A third example of potential benefit might be where a car crash has led to the death of a husband and the fatal injury of the only child and where the surviving woman wishes to have a clone from the child as the only means of raising a child who is her husband's biological offspring. A further potential benefit of reproductive cloning might be to a couple who are carriers of a fatal recessive gene and prefer to clone a cell from one of them to avoid the genetic danger, rather than reproduce by means of other people's genetic material.

Given the limited potential benefits of reproductive human cloning, the benefit/harm analysis does not seem at present to create much moral pressure to undertake this activity (though in nonreproductive cloning there certainly seem to be a large number of potential benefits, with far fewer potential harms). Nonetheless, given that there are some benefits that may be anticipated from reproductive human cloning, given the counterarguments offered above to many of the claims that this would create major harms, and given the arguments from respect for reproductive and scientific autonomy, then at the very least we should thoroughly question contemporary absolutist proposals to ban human reproductive cloning for ever and a day—even if prudence and precaution indicate a temporary ban until the safety of such techniques can be researched and developed.

JUSTICE

But do the last set of moral arguments against human reproductive cloning—those based on justice—lead us to require a permanent ban on the technique? Justice arguments can usefully be considered from the point of view of rights-based justice; of straightforward egalitarian justice (according to the European Parliament, cloning is contrary to the principle of human equality because it leads to eugenics and racism), of legal justice (the requirements of morally acceptable laws); and finally, and perhaps in this context most important, of distributive justice—the fair or just distribution of scarce resources, including consideration of the opportunity costs of using such resources for one purpose rather than another.

The only rights-based arguments that I have found against reproductive human cloning are based on the right to have a genetic identity—a claim that I have examined above and found morally unacceptable in regard to identical twins. On the other hand, in favor of reproductive cloning are rights-based arguments claiming rights to reproductive autonomy and privacy and rights to carry out morally acceptable scientific research.

Egalitarian theories of justice are fine (everyone should be treated equally) provided they pass the Aristotelian test for theories of justice—notably, that it is equals who should be treated equally, while those who are not equal in a morally relevant sense ought *not* to be treated equally but treated unequally in proportion to the morally relevant inequality. Thus, cloning does not treat everyone as equal if it is not done for everyone, but that is not unjust; for not everyone *needs* cloning and not everyone *wants* cloning. However, the European Parliament has claimed that cloning is contrary to human equality because it leads to eugenics and racism. Suffice it to say that, while both racism and imposed eugenics are morally unacceptable (though not the sort of eugenics that stems from uncoerced reproductive choice, against which there are, I believe, no convincing moral arguments), there seem to be no reasons for believing that cloning is or entails either of these morally unacceptable phenomena. At best this is an empirical "slippery slope" type of argument; and there seems no reason to believe that the slipperiness of this slope is so uncontrollable that we should never start down it.

Legal justice arguments require us at least *prima facie* to obey morally acceptable laws. I will simply assert that by this is meant laws that have been created in a morally acceptable manner, rather than laws whose content one morally approves. From this point of view we should obey the many laws that have now been passed in morally acceptable ways which ban reproductive human cloning. That in no ways settles the question of whether their moral content *is* morally desirable, and the bulk of this paper has been arguing that permanent bans on such cloning are *not* morally desirable and should be reversed.

Distributive justice arguments seem to offer the most plausible case against development of human reproductive cloning, or at least against funding such development from community funds, simply because the anticipated benefit-harm ratio does not seem to justify the undoubted costs and especially the opportunity costs. But this argument does not rule out private funding of such research, nor does it result in a permanent ban on provision of state funding, should the anticipated benefits become substantially greater.

CONCLUSION

And so I conclude that all the arguments for a permanent ban on human reproductive cloning fail and that most of the arguments for even a temporary ban fail. However, four arguments in favor of a temporary ban do, I have indicated, currently succeed. The first is that at present the technique for human reproduction by cloning is simply not safe enough to be carried out in human beings. The second related argument is that, given these safety considerations, the benefits including respect for the autonomy of prospective parents and the scientists who would assist them are at present insufficient to outweigh the harms. The third is the argument from distributive justice, but this is only sufficient to prescribe a low priority for state funding for human reproductive cloning. And finally, respect for autonomy within a democratic society requires adequate social debate before decisions are democratically made about socially highly contentious issues so a moratorium is also needed to provide time for this full social debate and, with luck, for more informed, more deliberated, and less frantic decisions.

The issues that underlie, and in my view are far more morally important than the cloning debate and indeed much of the contemporary opposition to the new genetics are those that Huxley pointed to in *Brave New World*—notably that both science and government must be used as servants of the people and not as our masters. This is something that Huxley explicitly addresses in the foreword to his 1946 edition of *Brave New World,* where he points out that if he had written the book again he would not have had just two alternatives—essentially either the madness of state control or the madness of the savage's emotional and unreasoned lifestyle. He would also have included a middle way in which reason was used in pursuit of a reasonable life, in which science was applied for the benefit, for the *eudaemonia* or flourishing, of humankind.

The second issue that underlies the cloning debate, and indeed the overall debate about the new genetics, and is of deep moral importance, is the need to protect the genetic *underpinning of human autonomy and free will.* Some such basis, however complex, there must be; and in pursuing any sort of human genetic research and development, safeguarding and protecting that genetic kernel of what, to embroider on Aristotle, is humanity's specific attribute, notably our autonomous rationality—*that* must be the underlying moral challenge and moral imperative for the new genetics, along with its and our shared obligation to protect ourselves against the predations of the control freaks, whether they are the control freaks of state or religion or science or big business, or simply of crooked gangsters who seek to use us for their own ends. Those I think should be the central moral concerns in developing the new genetics, and that is the lesson that I have most vividly taken to heart from this excursus into the ethics of human reproductive cloning and from my rereading of Aldous Huxley's *Brave New World.* But let us also not forget the origin of Huxley's title—in Shakespeare's *Tempest.*

There the phrase does not have the negative connotations that Huxley has given it. Rather, Miranda is excited by the prospect of a new world of new people (and especially one wonderful new man), and a new life away from the tiny island on which she had been brought up and on which the only people she had ever seen till then were her father and Caliban. It is to the prospect of a new, more varied, and fuller world and life that she wonderingly refers when she exclaims "O brave new world, That has such people in't." Like her and like Huxley in his 1946 preface I think we should look more positively at our brave new world—the brave new world of genetics. We should learn Huxley's lessons, protect ourselves against the depredations of those who would unjustifiably control us, and realize that the potential problems lie less in cloning and genetics and more in politics and political philosophy—and of course in *their and our* underlying ethics.

REFERENCES

While the ideas and arguments in this are my own, many are similar to arguments put forward by others. In particular I would like to acknowledge the pioneering work in this area by Professor John Harris (See reference 13 for example), and the thorough analysis of the issues by the U.S. National Bioethics Advisory Commission (reference 12).

1. Human Genetics Advisory Commission (HGAC). *Cloning Issues in Reproduction, Science and Medicine.* London: HGAC, 1998.
2. World Health Organization. Resolution on cloning in human reproduction (50th World Health Assembly). Geneva: WHO, 1997.
3. European Parliament and Council. *Draft Directive on the Legal Protection of Biotechnical Inventions.* Brussels: European Parliament, 1997.
4. Council of Europe. *Protocol to the Convention on Human Rights and Biomedicine on the Prohibition of Cloning Human Beings.* Strasbourg: Council of Europe, 1997.
5. United Nations Economic and Social Council. *Universal Declaration on the Human Genome and Human Rights.* Paris: UNESCO, 1997.
6. Wilmut I., Schnieke A. E., McWhir J., Kind A. J., Campbell K. H. Viable offspring derived from fetal and adult mammalian cells. *Nature* 1997; 385:810–8.
7. Raphael D. D. *Moral Philosophy,* 2nd ed. Oxford: Oxford University Press, 1994:8.
8. MacIntyre A., ed. *Hume's Ethical Writings.* London: Collier-Macmillan, 1970.
9. Huxley A. *A Brave New World.* Harmondsworth: Penguin, 1955.
10. Doniger W. What did they name the dog? (Review of Wright L. Twins: Genes, *Environment and the Mystery of Identity.* London: Weidenfeld, 1997). *London Rev Books* March 19, 1998: 32.
11. Kant I., Groundwork of the metaphysic of morals. In: Paton H. J., ed. *The Moral Law.* London: Hutchinson, 1964.
12. National Bioethics Advisory Commission (USA). *Cloning Human Beings.* Rockville, Maryland: NBAC, 1997 [http://bioethics.gov/pubs.html].
13. Harris J. "Goodby Dolly?" The ethics of human cloning. *J Med Ethics* 1997; 23:353–60.
14. Winston R. *The Future of Genetic Manipulation.* London: Phoenix, 1997.

NATIONAL RESEARCH COUNCIL

Scientific and Medical Aspects of Human Reproductive Cloning

Human reproductive cloning is an assisted reproductive technology that would be carried out with the goal of creating a human being. It is currently the subject of much debate around the world, involving a variety of ethical, religious, societal, scientific, and medical issues. However, this report from the National Academies addresses only the scientific and medical aspects of human reproductive cloning. Consideration of the medical aspects has required the panel to examine issues of scientific conduct and human-subjects protection. But we have not attempted to address the issue of whether producing a new individual by reproductive cloning, if it were found to be scientifically safe, would or would not be acceptable to individuals or society. Instead, the panel defers to others on the fundamental ethical, religious, and societal questions, and presents this report on the scientific and medical aspects to inform the broader debate. Our report differs in this respect from the last major report on the topic in the United States, *Cloning Human Beings,* a 1997 report developed by the National Bioethics Advisory Commission.[1]

THE PANEL'S CONCLUSIONS AND RECOMMENDATIONS

The panel has examined and analyzed the scientific, medical, and legal literature on the issues and heard testimony at a workshop from experts in animal cloning, assisted reproductive technologies, and science, technology, and legal policy—including people who, on scientific and medical grounds, either oppose or defend human reproductive cloning. After carefully considering the issues raised, we conclude that the case has not been proved that human reproductive cloning would lead to fewer negative outcomes at this time than reproductive cloning of other mammals. We therefore make the following recommendations:

Human reproductive cloning should not now be practiced. It is dangerous and likely to fail. The panel therefore unanimously supports the proposal that there should be a legally enforceable ban on the practice of human reproductive cloning. For this purpose, we define human reproductive cloning as the placement in a uterus of a human blastocyst derived by the technique that we call nuclear transplantation. In reaching this conclusion, we considered the relevant scientific and medical issues, including the record from cloning of other species, and the standard issues that are associated with evaluating all research involving human participants.

The scientific and medical considerations related to this ban should be reviewed within 5 years. The ban should be reconsidered only if at least two conditions are met: (1) a new scientific and medical review indicates that the procedures are likely to be safe and effective and (2) a broad national dialogue on the societal, religious, and ethical issues suggests that a reconsideration of the ban is warranted.

Finally, the scientific and medical considerations that justify a ban on human reproductive cloning at this time are not applicable to nuclear transplantation to produce stem cells. Because of its considerable potential for developing new medical therapies for life-threatening diseases and advancing fundamental knowledge, the panel supports the conclusion of a recent National Academies report that recommended that biomedical research using nuclear transplantation to produce stem cells be permitted. A broad

Adapted with permission from Panel on Scientific and Medical Aspects of Human Cloning, *Scientific and Medical Aspects of Human Reproductive Cloning* (Washington, DC: National Academy Press, 2002), ES-1 to ES-5. Copyright © 2002 by the National Research Council. Courtesy of National Academy Press, Washington, DC.

national dialogue on the societal, religious, and ethical issues is encouraged on this matter.

THE FINDINGS THAT SUPPORT A BAN ON HUMAN REPRODUCTIVE CLONING

It is a serious event when any group that has potential authority over research intercedes to ban it, and the reasons must therefore be compelling. We are convinced that the scientific and medical data concerning the likely danger to the implanted fetus or the eventual newborn if reproductive cloning of humans is attempted in the near future are compelling.

The panel has based its support for the proposed ban on human reproductive cloning on the following findings:

Finding 1: The scientific and medical criteria used to evaluate the safety of reproductive cloning must be the potential morbidity and death of the woman carrying the clone as a fetus and of the newborn and the risk to women donating the eggs.

Finding 2: Data on the reproductive cloning of animals through the use of nuclear transplantation technology demonstrate that only a small percentage of attempts are successful; that many of the clones die during gestation, even in late stages; that newborn clones are often abnormal or die; and that the procedures may carry serious risks for the mother. In addition, because of the large number of eggs needed for such experiments, many more women would be exposed to the risks inherent in egg donation for a single cloning attempt than for the reproduction of a child by the presently used *in vitro* fertilization (IVF) techniques. These medical and scientific findings lead us to conclude that the procedures are now unsafe for humans.

Finding 3: At least three criteria would have to be fulfilled before the safety of human reproductive cloning could be established: (1) The procedures for animal reproductive cloning would have to be improved to such an extent that the levels of observed abnormalities in cloned animals, including nonhuman primates, were no more than that seen with existing human assisted reproductive technology (ART) procedures. If that could not be achieved, researchers would have to demonstrate that humans are different from other animals with regard to cloning-related defects. Reproducible data demonstrating that a successful reprogramming of the donor nucleus and proper imprinting can be achieved in animals would be essential, as would an understanding of the mechanisms responsible for such events. (2) New methods would have to be developed to demonstrate that the human preimplantation embryos produced through the use of nuclear transplantation technology are normal with respect to imprinting and reprogramming. That would best be done by first establishing the normal state of reprogramming and imprinting in nonhuman primates and then documenting that the processes in preimplantation human embryos are substantially similar. (3) Methods would have to be developed to monitor—effectively and comprehensively—preimplantation embryos and fetuses in the uterus for cloning-related defects, such as those outlined in Chapter 3; these include alterations in gene expression and imprinting.

Finding 4: The issues of responsible conduct of research raised by the prospect of cloning a person are those of medical ethics—in particular, the protection of the participants (the egg donor, the host mother, and the child produced through cloning) in any human cloning research. Participants in any human cloning research efforts require full protection as human research participants, although it should be noted that, as with fetal surgery, this protection cannot be extended fully to the cloned fetus. Human reproductive cloning has not been performed before, and its introduction, if it ever occurred, would require systematic research. That research would likely entail full review by institutional review boards and other human-subjects protections, including informed consent of donors and recipients of all biological materials.

Finding 5: If any attempts at human reproductive cloning were ever to occur, they would constitute research, not merely innovative therapy. Such research would then be subject to external technical and ethical review by review boards to ensure that the proposed experiments are both technically and ethically sound and that the rights and welfare of all research participants are protected. This institutional review process should be applied equally to both public- and private-sector research and be transparent to the public.

Finding 6: Because medical and scientific findings indicate that cloning procedures are currently not safe for humans, cloning of a human through the use of nuclear transplantation technology is not now appropriate. The panel believes that no responsible scientists or physicians are likely to undertake to clone a human. Nevertheless, no voluntary system that is established to restrict reproductive cloning is likely to be completely effective. Some organizations have already announced their intention to clone humans, and many of the reproductive technologies needed are widely accessible in private fertility clinics that are not subject to federal regulations. The panel therefore concludes that a legally enforceable ban that carries substantial penalties has a much greater potential than a voluntary system or moratorium to deter any attempt to clone a human using these techniques.

Finding 7: If no ban is imposed, it is possible that some organizations will attempt the reproductive cloning of humans. Although such attempts would most likely fail, there is a high probability they would be associated with serious risks to any possible fetus or newly born child and may harm the woman carrying the developing fetus.

Finding 8: There is concern that legislation or regulation that would ban reproductive human cloning would set a troubling precedent with respect to the restriction of innovative, experimental research and medical procedures. Modern scientific research proceeds rapidly, and its findings are unpredictable and often surprising. It is probable that at least every 5 years there will be significant new information regarding the issues of the safety and applicability of human cloning to medical practice. The above concern can be ameliorated by including in any legislation or regulation a requirement for an updated evaluation of the scientific, medical, and societal issues within 5 years. Such a requirement for periodic reviews would allow for extensive public debate regarding reproductive human cloning and the consideration of modifications to the legislation. Part of that evaluation would include a recommendation as to when the next such evaluation should be conducted.

Finding 9: Two activities will be particularly important for an updated evaluation of human reproductive cloning: a thorough scientific and medical review to evaluate whether the procedures are likely to be safe and effective and a broad national dialogue on the societal, religious, and ethical issues. As part of this process, any persons advocating the practice of human reproductive cloning would need to acknowledge the extent of the abnormalities seen in animal cloning experiments and to demonstrate that these problems—assuming that they persist—are unlikely to occur in humans.

Finding 10: Any future process designed to evaluate the scientific and medical evidence on cloning a person would likely need to involve scientists, physicians, ethicists, and the public. A public debate could be facilitated by a committee that issues regular updates on the state of the science surrounding animal cloning and reaches out to involved constituencies in a systematic manner. Such a body could derive its powers by executive order, by executive action within the Department of Health and Human Services under the Public Health Service Act, or by legislation. Among many other issues, the debate should be structured to inform the public that clones are not precise replicas, but persons with identical genetic material.

Finding 11: The science of cloning is an international one with research conducted throughout the world. Furthermore, the issue of human reproductive cloning is the subject of worldwide debate. A number of countries and international organizations have prepared reports and issued statements on the issue. Participation by the United States in such international debates about human reproductive cloning will be beneficial to any future process to evaluate the scientific and medical evidence on this issue.

Finding 12: The limited regulation and monitoring of experimental ART procedures in the United States means that important data needed for assessing novel ART procedures are in some cases lacking, in other cases incomplete and hard to find. Because the panel was not charged to investigate ART regulation and did not solicit expert testimony thereon, we make no recommendations regarding oversight of, registration of, or required data collection from ART clinics. But we do believe that a request from Congress or the Executive Branch for a panel of experts to study the matter and report its findings and recommendations publicly would probably be useful. Having such information is likely to be beneficial to any process of evaluating future scientific and medical evidence regarding both reproductive cloning and new ART procedures.

NATIONAL BIOETHICS ADVISORY COMMISSION

Ethical Issues in Human Stem Cell Research

INTRODUCTION

In November 1998, President Clinton charged the National Bioethics Advisory Commission with the task of conducting a thorough review of the issues associated with human stem cell research, balancing all ethical and medical considerations. The President's request was made in response to three separate reports that brought to the fore the exciting scientific and clinical prospects of stem cell research while also raising a series of ethical controversies regarding federal sponsorship of scientific inquiry in this area. Scientific reports of the successful isolation and culture of these specialized cells have offered hope of new cures for debilitating and even fatal illness and at the same time have renewed an important national debate about the ethics of research involving human embryos and cadaveric fetal material.

SCIENTIFIC AND MEDICAL CONSIDERATIONS

The stem cell is a unique and essential cell type found in animals. Many kinds of stem cells are found in the body, with some more differentiated, or committed, to a particular function than others. In other words, when stem cells divide, some of the progeny mature into cells of a specific type (e.g., heart, muscle, blood, or brain cells), while others remain stem cells, ready to repair some of the everyday wear and tear undergone by our bodies. These stem cells are capable of continually reproducing themselves and serve to renew tissue throughout an individual's life. For example, they constantly regenerate the lining of the gut, revitalize skin, and produce a whole range of blood cells.

From *Ethical Issues in Human Stem Cell Research: Executive Summary* (Rockville, MD: NBAC, September 1999).

Although the term *stem cell* commonly is used to refer to the cells within the adult organism that renew tissue (e.g., hematopoietic stem cells, a type of cell found in the blood), the most fundamental and extraordinary of the stem cells are found in the early stage embryo. These *embryonic stem (ES) cells,* unlike the more differentiated adult stem cells or other cell types, retain the special ability to develop into nearly any cell type. *Embryonic germ (EG) cells,* which originate from the primordial reproductive cells of the developing fetus, have properties similar to ES cells.

It is the potentially unique versatility of the ES and EG cells derived, respectively, from the early stage embryo and cadaveric fetal tissue that presents such unusual scientific and therapeutic promise. Indeed, scientists have long recognized the possibility of using such cells to generate more specialized cells or tissue, which could allow the generation of new cells to be used to treat injuries or diseases, such as Alzheimer's disease, Parkinson's disease, heart disease, and kidney failure. Likewise, scientists regard these cells as an important—perhaps essential—means for understanding the earliest stages of human development and as an important tool in the development of life-saving drugs and cell-replacement therapies to treat disorders caused by early cell death or impairment.

The techniques for deriving these cells have not been fully developed as standardized and readily available research tools, and the development of any therapeutic application remains some years away. Thus, ES and EG cells are still primarily a matter of intense research interest.

At this time, human stem cells can be derived from the following sources:

- human fetal tissue following elective abortion (EG cells),
- human embryos that are created by *in vitro* fertilization (IVF) and that are no longer needed by couples being treated for infertility (ES cells),
- human embryos that are created by IVF with gametes donated for the sole purpose of providing research material (ES cells), and
- potentially, human (or hybrid) embryos generated asexually by somatic cell nuclear transfer or similar cloning techniques in which the nucleus of an adult human cell is introduced into an enucleated human or animal ovum (ES cells).

In addition, although much promising research currently is being conducted with stem cells obtained from adult organisms, studies in animals suggest that this approach will be scientifically and technically limited, and in some cases the anatomic source of the cells might preclude easy or safe access. However, because there are no legal restrictions or new ethical considerations regarding research on adult stem cells (other than the usual concerns about consent and risks), important research can and should go forward in this area. Moreover, because important biological differences exist between embryonic and adult stem cells, this source of stem cells should not be considered an alternative to ES and EG cell research.

ETHICAL AND POLICY CONSIDERATIONS

The scientific reports of the successful isolation and culture of ES and EG cells have renewed a longstanding controversy about the ethics of research involving human embryos and cadaveric fetal material. This controversy arises from sharply differing moral views regarding elective abortion or the use of embryos for research. Indeed, an earnest national and international debate continues over the ethical, legal, and medical issues that arise in this arena. This debate represents both a challenge and an opportunity: a challenge because it concerns important and morally contested questions regarding the beginning of life, and an opportunity because it provides another occasion for serious public discussion about important ethical issues. We are hopeful that this dialogue will foster public understanding about the relationships between the opportunities that biomedical science offers to improve human welfare and the limits set by important ethical obligations.

Although we believe most would agree that human embryos deserve respect as a form of human life, disagreements arise regarding both what form such respect should take and what level of protection is required at different stages of embryonic development. Therefore, embryo research that is not therapeutic to the embryo is bound to raise serious concerns and to heighten the tensions between two important ethical commitments: to cure disease and to protect human life. For those who believe that the embryo has the moral status of a person from the moment of conception, research (or any other activity) that would destroy the embryo is considered wrong and should not take place. For those who believe otherwise, arriving at an ethically acceptable policy in this arena involves a complex balancing of a number of important ethical concerns. Although many of the issues remain contested on moral grounds, they co-exist within a broad area of consensus upon which public policy can, at least in part, be constructed.

For most observers, the resolution of these ethical and scientific issues depends to some degree on the source of the stem cells. The use of cadaveric fetal tissue to derive EG cell lines—like other uses of tissues or organs from dead bodies—is generally the most accepted, provided that the research complies with the system of public safeguards and oversight already in place for such scientific inquiry. With respect to embryos and the ES cells from which they can be derived, some draw an ethical distinction between two types of embryos. One is referred to as the *research embryo,* an embryo created through IVF with gametes provided solely for research purposes. Many people, including the President, have expressed the view that the federal government should not fund research that involves creating such embryos. The second type of embryo is that which was created for infertility treatment, but is now intended to be discarded because it is unsuitable or no longer needed for such treatment. The use of these embryos raises fewer ethical questions because it does not alter their final disposition. Finally, the recent demonstration of cloning techniques (somatic cell nuclear transfer) in nonhuman animals suggests that transfer of a human somatic cell nucleus into an oocyte might create an embryo that could be used as a source of ES cells. The creation of a human organism using this technique raises questions similar to those raised by the creation of research embryos through IVF, and at this time federal funds may not be used for such research. In addition, if the enucleated oocyte that was to be combined with a human somatic cell nucleus came from an animal other than a human being, other issues would arise about the nature of the embryo produced. Thus, each source of material raises ethical questions as well as scientific, medical, and legal ones.

Conscientious individuals have come to different conclusions regarding both public policy and private actions in the area of stem cell research. Their differing perspectives by their very nature cannot easily be bridged by any single public policy. But the development of public policy in a morally contested area is not a novel challenge for a pluralistic democracy such as that which exists in the United States. We are profoundly aware of the diverse and strongly held views on the subject of this report and have wrestled with the implications of these different views at each of our meetings devoted to this topic. Our aim throughout these deliberations has been to formulate a set of recommendations that fully reflects widely shared views and that, in our view, would serve the best interests of society.

Most states place no legal restrictions on any of the means of creating ES and EG cells that are described in this report. In addition, current Food and Drug Administration regulations do not apply to this type of early stage research. Therefore, because the public controversy surrounding such activities in the United States has revolved around whether it is appropriate for the federal government to sponsor such research, this report focuses on the question of whether the scientific merit and the substantial clinical promise of this research justify federal support, and, if so, with what restrictions and safeguards.

CONCLUSIONS AND RECOMMENDATIONS

This report presents the conclusions that the Commission has reached and the recommendations that the Commission has made in the following areas: the ethical acceptability of federal funding for research that either derives or uses ES or EG cells; the means of ensuring appropriate consent of women or couples who donate cadaveric fetal tissue or embryos remaining after infertility treatments; the need for restrictions on the sale of these materials and the designation of those who may benefit from their use; the need for ethical oversight and review of such research at the national and institutional level; and the appropriateness of voluntary compliance by the private sector with some of these recommendations.

THE ETHICAL ACCEPTABILITY OF FEDERAL FUNDING OF ES AND EG CELL RESEARCH BY THE SOURCE OF THE MATERIAL

A principal ethical justification for public sponsorship of research with human ES or EG cells is that this research has the potential to produce health benefits for individuals who are suffering from serious and often fatal diseases. We recognize that it is possible that the various sources of human ES or EG cells eventually could be important to research and clinical application because of, for example, their differing proliferation potential, differing availability and accessibility, and differing ability to be manipulated, as well as possibly significant differences in their cell biology. *At this time, therefore, the Commission believes that federal funding for the use and derivation of ES and EG cells should be limited to two sources of such material: cadaveric fetal tissue and embryos remaining after infertility treatments.* Specific recommendations and their justifications are provided below.

Recommendation 1: EG Cells from Fetal Tissue

Research involving the derivation and use of human EG cells from cadaveric fetal tissue should continue to be eligible for federal funding. Relevant statutes and regulations should be amended to make clear that the ethical safeguards that exist for fetal tissue transplantation also apply to the derivation and use of human EG cells for research purposes.

Considerable agreement exists, both in the United States and throughout the world, that the use of fetal tissue in therapy for people with serious disorders, such as Parkinson's disease, is acceptable. Research that uses tissue from aborted fetuses is analogous to the use of fetal tissue in transplantation. The rationales for conducting EG research are equally strong, and the arguments against it are not persuasive. The removal of fetal germ cells does not occasion the destruction of a live fetus, nor is fetal tissue intentionally or purposefully created for human stem cell research. Although abortion itself doubtless will remain a contentious issue in our society, the procedures that have been developed to prevent fetal tissue donation for therapeutic transplantation from influencing the abortion decision offer a model for creating such separation in research to derive human EG cells. Because the existing statutes are written in terms of tissue transplantation, which is not a current feature of EG cell research, changes are needed to make it explicit that the relevant safeguards will apply to research to derive EG cells from aborted fetuses. At present, no legal prohibitions exist that would inhibit the use of such tissue for EG cell research.

Recommendation 2: ES Cells from Embryos Remaining After Infertility Treatments

Research involving the derivation and use of human ES cells from embryos remaining after infertility treatments should be eligible for federal funding. An exception should be made to the present statutory ban on federal funding of embryo research to permit federal agencies to fund research involving the derivation of human ES cells from this source under appropriate regulations that include public oversight and review. (See Recommendations 5 through 9.)

The current ban on embryo research is in the form of a rider to the appropriations bill for the Department of Health and Human Services (DHHS), of which the National Institutes of Health (NIH) is a part. The rider prohibits use of the appropriated funds to support any research "in which a human embryo [is] destroyed, discarded, or knowingly subjected to risk of injury greater than that allowed for research on fetuses *in utero*" (Pub. L. No. 105-78, 513(a)). The term "human embryo" in the statute is defined as "any organism . . . that is derived by fertilization, parthenogenesis, cloning, or any other means from one or more human gametes or human diploid cells." The ban is revisited each year when the language of the NIH appropriations bill is considered.

The ban, which concerns only federally sponsored research, reflects a moral point of view either that embryos deserve the full protection of society because of their moral status as persons or that there is sufficient public controversy to preclude the use of federal funds for this type of research. At the same time, however, some effects of the embryo research ban raise serious moral and public policy concerns for those who hold differing views regarding the ethics of embryo research. In our view, the ban conflicts with several of the ethical goals of medicine and related health disciplines, especially healing, prevention, and research. These goals are rightly characterized by the principles of beneficence and nonmaleficence, which jointly encourage pursuing social benefits and avoiding or ameliorating potential harm.

Although some may view the derivation and use of ES cells as ethically distinct activities, we do not believe that these differences are significant from the point of view of eligibility for federal funding. That is, we believe that it is ethically acceptable for the federal government to finance research that both derives cell lines from embryos remaining after infertility treatments and that uses those cell lines. Although one might argue that some important research could proceed in the absence of federal funding for research that derives stem cells from embryos remaining after infertility treatments (i.e., federally funded scientists merely using cells derived with private funds), we believe that it is important that federal funding be made available for protocols that also derive such cells. Relying on cell lines that might be derived exclusively by a subset of privately funded researchers who are interested in this area could severely limit scientific and clinical progress.

Trying to separate research in which human ES cells are used from the process of deriving those cells presents an ethical problem, because doing so diminishes the scientific value of the activities receiving federal support. This separation—under which neither biomedical researchers at NIH nor scientists at universities and other research institutions that rely on federal support could participate in some aspects of this research—rests on the mistaken notion that the two areas of research are so distinct that participating in one need not mean participating in the other. We believe that this is a misrepresentation of the new field of human stem cell research, and this misrepresentation could adversely affect scientific progress for several reasons.

First, researchers using human ES cell lines will derive substantial scientific benefits from a detailed understanding of the process of ES cell derivation, because the properties of ES cells and the methods for sustaining the cell lines may differ depending on the conditions and methods that were used to derive them. Thus, scientists who conduct basic research and are interested in fundamental cellular processes are likely to make elemental discoveries about the nature of ES cells as they derive them in the laboratory. Second, significant basic research needs to be conducted regarding the process of ES cell derivation before cell-based therapies can be realized, and this work must be pursued in a wide variety of settings, including those exclusively devoted to basic academic research. Third, ES cells are not indefinitely stable in culture. As these cells are grown, irreversible changes occur in their genetic makeup. Thus, especially in the first few years of human ES cell research, it is important to be able to repeatedly derive ES cells in order to ensure that the properties of the cells that are being studied have not changed.

Thus, anyone who believes that federal support of this important new field of research should maximize its scientific and clinical value within a system of appropriate ethical oversight should be dissatisfied with a position that allows federal agencies to fund research using human ES cells but not research through which the cells are derived from embryos. Instead, recognizing the close connection in practical and ethical terms between derivation and use of the cells, it would be preferable to enact provisions applicable to funding by all federal agencies, provisions that would carve out a narrow exception for funding of research to use or to derive human ES cells from embryos that are being discarded by infertility treatment programs.

Recommendation 3: ES Cells from Embryos Made Solely for Research Purposes Using IVF

Federal agencies should not fund research involving the derivation or use of human ES cells from embryos made solely for research purposes using IVF.

ES cells can be obtained from human research embryos created from donor gametes through IVF for the sole purpose of deriving such cells for research. The primary objection to creating embryos specifically for research is that there is a morally relevant difference between generating an embryo for the sole purpose of creating a child and producing an embryo with no such goal. Those who object to creating embryos for research often appeal to arguments about respecting human dignity by avoiding instrumental use of human embryos (i.e., using embryos merely as a means to some other goal does not treat them with appropriate respect or concern as a form of human life).

In 1994, the NIH Human Embryo Research Panel argued in support of federal funding of the creation of embryos for research purposes in exceptional cases, such as the need to create banks of cell lines with different genetic make-ups that encoded various transplantation antigens—the better to respond, for example, to the transplant needs of groups with different genetic profiles. This would require the recruitment of embryos from genetically diverse donors.

In determining how to deal with this issue, a number of points are worth considering. First, it is possible that the creation of research embryos will provide the only way in which to conduct certain kinds of research, such as research into the process of human fertilization. Second, as IVF techniques improve, it is possible that the supply of embryos for research from this source will dwindle. Nevertheless, we have concluded that, either from a scientific or a clinical perspective, there is no compelling reason at this time to provide federal funds for the creation of embryos for research. At the current time, cadaveric fetal tissue and embryos remaining after infertility treatment provide an adequate supply of research resources for federal research projects.

Recommendation 4: ES Cells from Embryos Made Using Somatic Cell Nuclear Transfer into Oocytes

Federal agencies should not fund research involving the derivation or use of human ES cells from embryos made using somatic cell nuclear transfer into oocytes.

Somatic cell nuclear transfer of the nucleus of an adult somatic cell into an enucleated human egg likely has the potential of creating a human embryo. To date, although little is known about these embryos as potential sources of human ES cells, there is significant reason to believe that their use may have therapeutic potential. For example, the potential use of matched tissue for autologous cell replacement therapy from ES cells may require the use of somatic cell nuclear transfer. The use of this technique to create an embryo arguably is different from all the other cases we considered—due to the asexual origin of the source of the ES cells—although oocyte donation is necessarily involved. The Commission concludes that, at this time, federal funding should not be provided to derive ES cells from this source. Nevertheless, scientific progress and the medical utility of this line of research should be monitored closely.

REQUIREMENTS FOR THE DONATION OF CADAVERIC FETAL TISSUE AND EMBRYOS FOR RESEARCH

Potential donors of embryos for ES cell research must be able to make voluntary and informed choices about whether and how to dispose of their embryos. Because of concerns about coercion and exploitation of potential donors, as well as societal controversy about the moral status of embryos, it is important, whenever possible, to separate donors' decisions to dispose of their embryos from their decisions to donate them for research. Potential donors should be asked to provide embryos for research only if they have decided to have those embryos discarded instead of donating them to another couple or storing them. If the decision to discard the embryos precedes the decision to donate them for research purposes, then the research determines only how their destruction occurs, not whether it occurs.

Recommendation 5: Requirements for Donation to Stem Cell Research of Embryos That Would Otherwise Be Discarded After Infertility Treatment

Prospective donors of embryos remaining after infertility treatments should receive timely, relevant, and appropriate information to make informed and voluntary choices regarding disposition of the embryos. Prior to considering the potential research use of the embryos, a prospective donor should have been presented with the option of storing the embryos, donating them to another woman, or discarding them. If a prospective donor chooses to discard embryos remaining after infertility treatment, the option of donating to research may then be presented. (At any point, the prospective donors' questions—including inquiries about possible research use of any embryos remaining after infertility treatment—should be answered truthfully, with all information that is relevant to the questions presented.)

During the presentation about potential research use of embryos that would otherwise be discarded, the person seeking the donation should (a) disclose that the ES cell research is not intended to provide medical benefit to embryo donors; (b) make clear that consenting or refusing to donate embryos to research will not affect the quality of any future care provided to prospective donors; (c) describe the general area of the research to be carried out with the embryos and the specific research protocol, if known; (d) disclose the source of funding and expected commercial benefits of the research with the embryos, if known; (e) make clear that embryos used in research will not be transferred to any woman's uterus; and (f) make clear that the research will involve the destruction of the embryos.

To assure that inappropriate incentives do not enter into a woman's decision to have an abortion, we recommend that directed donation of cadaveric fetal tissue for EG cell derivation be prohibited. Although the ethical considerations supporting a prohibition of the directed donation of human fetal tissue are less acute for EG cell research than for transplantation, certain concerns remain. Potential donors of cadaveric fetal tissue for EG cell derivation would not receive a direct therapeutic incentive to create or abort tissue for research purposes in the same way that such personal interest might arise in a transplant context. However, we agree that the prohibition remains a prudent and appropriate way of assuring that inappropriate incentives, regardless of how remote they may be, are not introduced into a woman's decision to have an abortion. Any suggestion of personal benefit to the donor or to an individual known to the donor would be untenable and possibly coercive.

Recommendation 6: No Promises to Embryo Donors That Stem Cells Will Be Provided to Particular Patient-Subjects

In federally funded research involving embryos remaining after infertility treatments, researchers may not promise donors that ES cells derived from their embryos will be used to treat patient-subjects specified by the donors.

Existing rules prohibit the practice of designated donation, the provision of monetary inducements to women undergoing abortion, and the purchase or sale of fetal tissue. We concur in these restrictions and in the earlier recommendation of the 1988 Human Fetal Tissue Transplantation Research Panel that the sale of fetal tissue for research purposes should not be permitted under any circumstances. The potential for coercive pressure is greatest when financial incentives are present, and the treatment of the developing human embryo or fetus as an entity deserving of respect may be greatly undermined by the introduction of any commercial motive into the donation or solicitation of fetal or embryonic tissue for research purposes.

Recommendation 7: Commerce in Embryos and Cadaveric Fetal Tissue

Embryos and cadaveric fetal tissue should not be bought or sold.

If and when sufficient scientific evidence and societal agreement exist that the creation of embryos specifically for research or therapeutic purposes is justified (specifically through somatic cell nuclear transfer), prohibitions on directed donation should be revisited. For obvious reasons, the use of somatic cell nuclear transfer to develop ES cells for autologous transplantation might require that the recipient be specified.

THE NEED FOR NATIONAL OVERSIGHT AND REVIEW

The need for national as well as local oversight and review of human stem cell research is crucial. No such system currently exists in the United States. A national mechanism to review protocols for *deriving* human ES and EG cells and to monitor research using such cells would ensure strict adherence to guidelines and standards across the country. Thus, federal oversight can provide the public with the assurance that research involving stem cells is being undertaken appropriately. Given the ethical issues involved in human stem cell research—an area in which heightened sensitivity about the very research itself led the President to request that the Commission study the issue—the public and the Congress must be assured that oversight can be accomplished efficiently, constructively, and in a timely fashion, with sufficient attention to the relevant ethical considerations.

Recommendation 8: Creation and Duties of an Oversight and Review Panel

DHHS should establish a National Stem Cell Oversight and Review Panel to ensure that all federally funded research involving the derivation and/or use of human ES or EG cells is conducted in conformance with the ethical principles and recommendations contained in this report. The panel should have a broad, multidisciplinary membership, including members of the general public, and should (a) review protocols for the derivation of ES and EG cells and approve those that meet the requirements described in this report; (b) certify ES and EG cells lines that result from approved protocols; (c) maintain a public registry of approved protocols and certified ES and EG cell lines; (d) establish a database—linked to the public registry—consisting of information submitted by federal research sponsors (and, on a voluntary basis, by private sponsors, whose proprietary information shall be appropriately protected) that includes all protocols that derive or use ES or EG cells (including any available data on research outcomes, including published papers); (e) use the database and other appropriate sources to track the history and ultimate use of certified cell lines as an aid to policy assessment and formulation; (f) establish requirements for and provide guidance to sponsoring agencies on the social and ethical issues that should be considered in the review of research protocols that derive or use ES or EG cells; and (g) report at least annually to the DHHS Secretary with an assessment of the current state of the science for both the derivation and use of human ES and EG cells, a review of recent developments in the broad category of stem cell research, a summary of any emerging ethical or social concerns associated with this research, and an analysis of the adequacy and continued appropriateness of the recommendations contained in this report.

THE NEED FOR LOCAL REVIEW OF DERIVATION PROTOCOLS

For more than two decades, prospective review by an Institutional Review Board (IRB) has been the principal method for assuring that federally sponsored research involving human subjects will be conducted in compliance with guidelines, policies, and regulations designed to protect human beings from harm. This system of local review has been subject to criticism, and, indeed, in previous analyses we have identified a number of concerns regarding this system. In the course of preparing this report, we considered a number of proposals that would allow for the local review of research protocols involving human stem cell research, bearing in mind that a decision by the Commission to recommend a role for IRBs might be incorrectly interpreted as endorsing the view that human ES or EG cells or human embryos are human subjects and therefore would be under the purview of the Common Rule.

We adopted the principle, reflected in these recommendations, that for research to derive human ES and EG cells, a system of national oversight and review supplemented by local review would be necessary to ensure that important research could proceed—but only under specific conditions. We recognized that for research proposals involving the derivation of human ES or EG cells, many of the ethical issues associated with these protocols could be considered at the local level, that is, at the institutions at which the research would be taking place. For protocols using but not deriving ES cells (i.e., generating the cells elsewhere), a separate set of ethical deliberations would have occurred. In general, the IRB is an appropriate body to review protocols that aim to derive ES or EG cells. Although few review bodies (including IRBs) have extensive experience in reviewing protocols of this kind, they remain the most visible and expert entities available. It is for this reason, for example, that we make a number of recommendations (8, 9, 10, 11, and 12) that discuss the importance of developing additional guidance for the review of such protocols.

Recommendation 9: Institutional Review of Protocols to Derive Stem Cells

Protocols involving the derivation *of human ES and EG cells should be reviewed and approved by an IRB or by another appropriately constituted and convened institutional review body prior to consideration by the National Stem Cell Oversight and Review Panel. (See Recommendation 8.) This review should ensure compliance with any requirements established by the panel, including confirming that individuals or organizations (in the United States or abroad) that supply embryos or cadaveric fetal tissue have obtained them in accordance with the requirements established by the panel.*

RESPONSIBILITIES OF FEDERAL RESEARCH AGENCIES

Federal research agencies have in place a comprehensive system for the submission, review, and approval of research proposals. This system includes the use of a peer review group—sometimes called a study section or initial review group—that is established to assess the scientific merit of the proposals. In addition, in some agencies, such as NIH, staff members review protocols prior to their transmittal to a national advisory council for final approval. These levels of review provide an opportunity to consider ethical issues that arise in the proposals. When research proposals involve human subjects, federal agencies rely on local IRBs to review and approve the research in order to assure that it is ethically acceptable. (See Recommendation 9.) A grant application should not be funded until ethical issues that are associated with research involving human subjects have been resolved fully. Therefore, at every point in this continuum—from the first discussions that a prospective applicant may have with program staff within a particular institution to the final decision by the relevant national advisory council—ethical and scientific issues can be addressed by the sponsoring agency.

Recommendation 10: Sponsoring Agency Review of Research Use of Stem Cells

All federal agencies should ensure that their review processes for protocols using human ES or EG cells comply with any requirements established by the National Stem Cell Oversight and Review Panel (see Recommendation 8), paying particular attention to the adequacy of the justification for using such cell lines.

Research involving human ES and EG cells raises critical ethical issues, particularly when the proposals involve the derivation of ES cells from embryos remaining after infertility treatments. We recognize that these research proposals may not follow the paradigm usually associated with human subjects research. Nevertheless, research proposals being considered for funding by federal agencies must, in our view, meet the highest standards of scientific merit and ethical acceptability. To that end, the recommendations made in this report, including a proposed set of *Points to Consider in Evaluating Basic Research Involving Human ES Cells and EG Cells,* constitute a set of ethical and policy considerations that should be reflected in the respective policies of federal agencies conducting or sponsoring human ES or EG cell research.

ATTENTION TO ISSUES FOR THE PRIVATE SECTOR

Although this report primarily addresses the ethical issues associated with the use of federal funds for research to derive and use ES and EG cells, we recognize that considerable work in both of these areas will be conducted under private sponsorship. Thus, our recommendations may have implications for those working in the private sector. First, for cell lines to be eligible for use in federally funded research, they must be certified by the National Stem Cell Oversight and Review Panel described in Recommendation 8. Therefore, if a private company aims to make its cell lines available to publicly funded researchers, it must submit its derivation protocol(s) to the same oversight and review process recommended for the public sector, i.e., local review (see Recommendation 9) and for certification that the cells have been derived from embryos remaining after infertility treatments or from cadaveric fetal tissue.

Second, we hope that nonproprietary aspects of protocols developed under private sponsorship will be made available in the public registry, as described in Recommendation 8. The greater the participation of the private sector in providing information on stem cell research, the more comprehensive the development of the science and related public policies in this area.

Third, and perhaps most relevant, in an ethically sensitive area of emerging biomedical research it is important that all members of the research community, whether in the public or private sectors, conduct the research in a manner that is open to appropriate public scrutiny. The last two decades have witnessed an unprecedented level of cooperation between the public and private sectors in biomedical research, which has resulted in the international leadership position of the United States in this arena. Public bodies and other authorities, such as the Recombinant DNA Advisory Committee, have played a crucial role in enabling important medical advances in fields such as gene therapy by providing oversight of both publicly and privately funded research efforts. We believe that voluntary participation by the private sector in the review and certification procedures of the proposed national panel, as well as in its deliberations, can contribute equally to the socially responsible development of ES and EG cell technologies and accelerate their translation into biomedically important therapies that will benefit patients.

Recommendation 11: Voluntary Actions by Private Sponsors of Research That Would Be Eligible for Federal Funding

For privately funded research projects that involve ES or EG cells that would be eligible for federal funding, private sponsors and researchers are encouraged to adopt voluntarily the applicable recommendations of this report. This includes submitting protocols for the derivation of ES or EG cells to the National Stem Cell Oversight and Review Panel for review and cell line certification. (See Recommendations 8 and 9.)

In this report, we recommend that federally funded research to derive ES cells be limited to those efforts that use embryos remaining after infertility treatment. Some of the recommendations made in this context—such as the requirement for separating the decision by a woman to cease such treatment when embryos still remain and her decision to donate those embryos to research—simply do not apply to efforts to derive ES cells from embryos created (whether by IVF or somatic cell nuclear transfer) solely for research purposes, activities that might be pursued in the private sector. Nevertheless, other ethical standards and safeguards embodied in the recommendations, such as provisions to prevent the coercion of women and the commodification of human reproduction, remain vitally important, even when embryos are created solely for research purposes.

Recommendation 12: Voluntary Actions by Private Sponsors of Research That Would Not Be Eligible for Federal Funding

For privately funded research projects that involve deriving ES cells from embryos created solely for research purposes and that are therefore not eligible for federal funding (see Recommendations 3 and 4)

(a) professional societies and trade associations should develop and promulgate ethical safeguards and standards consistent with the principles underlying this report, and

(b) private sponsors and researchers involved in such research should voluntarily comply with these safeguards and standards.

Professional societies and trade associations dedicated to reproductive medicine and technology play a central role in establishing policy and standards for clinical care, research, and education. We believe that these organizations can and should play a salutary role in ensuring that all stem cell and embryo research conducted in the United States, including that which is privately funded, conforms to the ethical principles underlying this report. Many of these organizations already have developed policy statements, ethics guidelines, or other directives addressing issues in this report, and the Commission has benefited from a careful review of these materials. These organizations are encouraged to review their professional standards to ensure not only that they keep pace with the evolving science of human ES and EG cell research, but also that their members are knowledgeable about and in compliance with them. For those organizations that conduct research in this area but that lack statements or guidelines addressing the topics of this report, we recommend strongly that they develop such statements or guidelines. No single institution or organization, whether in the public or the private sector, can provide all the necessary protections and safeguards.

THE NEED FOR ONGOING REVIEW AND ASSESSMENT

No system of federal oversight and review of such a sensitive and important area of investigation should be established without simultaneously providing an evaluation of its effectiveness, value, and ongoing need. The pace of scientific development in human ES and EG cell research likely will increase. Although one cannot predict the direction of the science of human stem cell research, in order for the American public to realize the promise of this research and to be assured that it is being conducted responsibly, close attention to and monitoring of all the mechanisms established for oversight and review are required.

Recommendation 13: Sunset Provision for National Panel

The National Stem Cell Oversight and Review Panel described in Recommendation 8 should be chartered for a fixed period of time, not to exceed five years. Prior to the expiration of this period, DHHS should commission an independent evaluation of the panel's activities to determine whether it has adequately fulfilled its functions and whether it should be continued.

There are several reasons for allowing the national panel to function for a fixed period of time and for evaluating its activities before continuing. First, some of the hoped-for results will be available from research projects that are using the two sources we consider to be ethically acceptable for federal funding. Five years is a reasonable period of time to allow some of this information to amass, offering the panel, researchers, members of Congress, and the public sufficient time to determine whether any of the knowledge or potential health benefits are being realized. The growing body of information in the public registry and database described above (particularly if privately funded researchers and sponsors voluntarily participate) will aid these considerations.

Second, within this period the panel may be able to determine whether additional sources of ES cells are necessary in order for important research to continue. Two arguments are evident for supporting research using embryos created specifically for research purposes: one is the concern that not enough embryos remain for this purpose from infertility treatments, and the other is the recognition that some research requires embryos that are generated particularly for research and/or medical purposes. The panel should assess whether additional sources of ES cells that we have judged to be ineligible for federal funding at this time (i.e., embryos created solely for research purposes) are needed.

Third, an opportunity to assess the relationship between local review of protocols using human ES and EG cells and the panel's review of protocols for the derivation of ES cells will be offered. It will, of course, take time for this national oversight and review mechanism to develop experience with the processes of review, certification, and approval described in this report. Fourth, we hope that the panel will contribute to the national dialogue on the ethical issues regarding research involving human embryos. A recurring theme of our deliberations, and in the testimony we heard, was the importance of encouraging this ongoing national conversation.

The criteria for determining whether the panel has adequately fulfilled its functions should be set forth by an independent body established by DHHS. However, it would be reasonable to expect that the evaluation would rely generally on the seven functions described above in Recommendation 8 and that this evaluation would be conducted by a group with expertise in these areas. In addition, some of the following questions might be considered when conducting this evaluation: Is there reason to believe that the private sector is voluntarily submitting descriptions of protocols involving the derivation of human ES cells to the panel for review? Is the panel reviewing projects in a timely manner? Do researchers find that the review process is substantively helpful? Is the public being provided with the assurance that social and ethical issues are being considered?

SUMMARY

Recent developments in human stem cell research have raised hopes that new therapies will become available that will serve to relieve human suffering. These developments also have served to remind society of the deep moral concerns that are related to research involving human embryos and cadaveric fetal tissue. Serious ethical discussion will (and should) continue on these issues. However, in light of public testimony, expert advice, and published writings, we have found substantial agreement among individuals with diverse perspectives that although the human embryo and fetus deserve respect as forms of human life, the scientific and clinical benefits of stem cell research should not be foregone. We were persuaded that carrying out human stem cell research under federal sponsorship is important, but only if it is conducted in an ethically responsible manner. And after extensive deliberation, the Commission believes that acceptable public policy can be forged, in part, on widely shared views. Through this report, we not only offer recommendations regarding federal funding and oversight of stem cell research, but also hope to further stimulate the important public debate about the profound ethical issues regarding this potentially beneficial research.

GLENN McGEE AND ARTHUR L. CAPLAN

The Ethics and Politics of Small Sacrifices in Stem Cell Research

Glenn McGee is Associate Director and Assistant Professor at the University of Pennsylvania Center for Bioethics. The author of more than fifty articles on ethical issues in medicine, his books include *The Perfect Baby* (Rowman & Littlefield), *The Human Cloning Debate* (Berkeley Hills Books), and *Pragmatic Bioethics* (Vanderbilt University Press). He is an NBC News commentator, Director of www.bioethics.net, a 1998 Atlantic Fellow in Public Policy of the British Government and the Commonwealth Foundation, and a Commissioner on the National Molecular and Clinical Genetics Task Force of the FDA.

Arthur Caplan is the Director of the Center for Bioethics at the University of Pennsylvania. He has written widely in medical ethics, health policy, ethical issues in science and technology, and the history and philosophy of medicine and the life sciences. He has published articles in the *Annals of Internal Medicine* and the *Journal of the American Medical Association.* His books include *Due Consideration: Controversy in the Age of Medical Miracles* (John Wiley & Sons), *Moral Matters: Ethical Issues in Medicine and the Life Sciences* (John Wiley & Sons), and *If I Were a Rich Man Could I Buy a Pancreas?* (Indiana University Press).

• • •

MORAL SACRIFICE

. . . [T]he central moral issues in stem cell research have less to do with abortion than with the criteria for moral sacrifices of human life. Those who inveigh against the derivation and use of pluripotent stem cells make the assumption that an embryo has not only the moral status of human person, but also a sort of super status that outweighs the needs of others in the human community. It is wrong to abort or kill a human, they argue, and thus it is wrong to kill an embryo. But this argument, which is problematic when made about abortion more generally, is doubly so when made against the derivation of pluripotent stem cells from embryos.

Even if frozen human embryos are persons, symbolically or intrinsically, this in no way entails the right of a frozen embryo to gestation, or to a risk-free pathway into maturation. Adult and child human beings' right "to life" is, considered constitutionally and as a moral problem, at best a negative right against unwarranted violence by the state or individuals. There are, sadly, few positive rights involved. Americans cannot, for example, claim a right against the state to protect them against disease, disasters, adverse weather, and other acts of nature. If a frozen human embryo is a full human person, it still has no right to life *per se,* but rather a negative right against unwarranted violence and a weak positive right to a set of basic social services (police protection, fire protection, and the like). The question remains as to what constitutes unwarranted violence against an embryo, and for what reasons might an embryo ethically be destroyed—e.g., in the interest of saving the community. Adults and even children are sometimes forced to give life, but only in the defense or at least interest

From *Kennedy Institute of Ethics Journal* 9, (1999), 151–58.
Copyright © 1999 by The Johns Hopkins University Press.

of the community's highest ideals and most pressing interests. One would expect that the destruction of embryonic life, whatever its moral status, would also take place only under the most scrupulous conditions and for the best communal reasons. It bears noting that only those who consistently oppose all violence, destruction, or killing of any kind in the name of the state, the church, or the community can rationally oppose the destruction of an embryo solely by virtue of its status as a human person.

It remains to be shown what the common good is, and what sort of sacrifice an embryo should make in its interest. It is commonly held that no human being should be allowed to lie unaided in preventable pain and suffering. The desire to ameliorate the suffering of the ill motivated Hippocrates, St. Francis of Assisi, Cicero, and Florence Nightingale. It is a central tenet of contemporary medicine that disease is almost always to be attended to and treated because it brings such pain and suffering to its victims and to their family and communities. Trade-offs are made in the treatment of disease, against cost and other competing social demands. But both the Western ethic of rescue and the practical structure of contemporary health care and other social institutions make it clear that among the deepest moral habits of human life is that of compassion for the sick and vulnerable. One of the compelling tenets of the movement to prevent abortion is the argument that a pregnancy ought not be terminated for superficial reasons, but should be viewed as a responsibility to aid the developing human life and to prevent it from needless suffering.

It is the moral imperative of compassion that compels stem cell research. [The s]tem cell research consortium Patient's CURe [Coalition for Urgent Research] estimates that as many as 128 million Americans suffer from diseases that might respond to pluripotent stem cell therapies. Even if that is an optimistic number, many clinical researchers and cell biologists hold that stem cell therapies will be critical in treating cancer, heart disease, and degenerative diseases of aging such as Parkinson's disease. More than half of the world's population will suffer at some point in life with one of these three conditions, and more humans die every year from cancer than were killed in both the Kosovo and Vietnam conflicts. Stem cell research is a pursuit of known and important moral goods.

WHAT IS DESTROYED?

The sacrifice of frozen embryos is a curious matter. Set aside, again, the question of whether a frozen embryo is a human life or human person. Grant for a moment that a 100-cell human blastocyst, approximately the size of the tip of an eyelash and totally lacking in cellular differentiation, is a fully human person. What does such a person's identity mean, and in what ways can it be destroyed? What would it mean for such a person to die? When could such a death be justified? These questions require a new kind of analysis.

The human embryo from which stem cells are to be taken is an undifferentiated embryo. It contains mitochondria, cytoplasm, and the DNA of mother and father within an egg wall (which also contains some RNA). None of the identity of that embryo is wrapped up in its memory of its origins: it has no brain cells to think, no muscle cells to exercise, no habits. The 100-cell embryo has one interesting and redeeming feature, which as best anyone can tell is the only thing unique about it: its recombined DNA. The DNA of the embryo contains the instructions of germ cells from father and mother, and the earliest moments of its conception determined how the DNA of mother and father would be uniquely combined into a human person. The DNA of that person will, if the embryo survives implantation, gestation, and birth, continue to direct many facets of the growth and identity of our human person. At 100 cells, nuclear DNA is the only feature of the embryo that is not replaceable by donor components without compromising the critical features of the initial recombination of maternal and paternal genetic material after sex (or, in this case, *in vitro*).

Opponents of stem cell research make an anti-abortion argument, namely that the harvesting of pluripotent stem cells will require the destruction of the embryo. But while the cytoplasm, egg wall, and mitochondria of the embryo are destroyed, we just noted that none of these cellular components identifies the embryo at the 100-cell stage. The personifying feature of a 100-cell blastocyst is its DNA. Pluripotent stem cells from the harvested embryo are directed to form cell lines, each cell of which contains, in dormant form, the full component of embryonic DNA. The DNA in the cell lines has a much greater chance of continuing to exist through many years than does the DNA of a frozen embryo (which in most cases already will have been slated for destruction by the IVF clinic that facilitated the donation, and which would have no better than a 5 to 10 percent chance of successful implantation in any event). Although most

Americans are opposed to the "cloning" of adult human beings, it might be possible to harvest DNA from any of the stem-cell-based cell lines to make a new, nuclear-transfer-derived embryo, or in fact to make five or ten embryos, each of which would possess all of the DNA of the original embryo. In this sense, the critical, identifying features of the embryo would never have been destroyed in the first place, unless what one means by "destroying" an embryo is the loss of its first egg wall, cytoplasm, and mitochondria. The transfer of the nucleus from an embryo to an enucleated egg is a bit like a transplant, though here the donor and the donation are both the DNA. In the case of embryos already slated to be discarded after IVF, the use of stem cells may actually lend permanence to the embryo. Our point here is that the sacrifice of an early embryo, whether it involves a human person or not, is not the same as the sacrifice of an adult because the life of a 100-cell embryo is contained in its cells' nuclear material.

The task of balancing sacrifice in the community is one encountered by Solomon in the Judeo-Christian religious texts. Our institutions must enable us in the community to debate and identify the ideals that merit sacrifice, and the loss must be weighed with justice in mind. An embryo cannot reason and it cannot reject a sacrifice or get up and leave the community. For those who feel special responsibility to embryos, the vulnerability of the frozen embryo may suggest special consideration of the kind given to all moral actors in society who are for one reason or another without voice. The question remains, though: what need is so great that it rises to the level where every member of the human family, even the smallest of humans might sacrifice? Already it is clear that we believe that no need is more obvious or compelling than the suffering of half the world at the hand of miserable disease. Not even the most insidious dictator could dream up a chemical war campaign as horrific as the devastation wrought by Parkinson's disease, which destroys our grandparents, parents, and finally many of us.

If Parkinson's disease, or for that matter if a dictator could only be stopped through the destruction of an infant, most every human would blanch at the idea of such sacrifice. But that is not what is asked here. Even those who hold that an embryo is a person will not want to argue that the life of a 100-cell embryo is contained in its inessential components. Assuming that a developing embryo can be salvaged by transplanting its DNA, as we have described, it seems unreasonable to oppose the destruction of the embryo's external cellular material or to fear that the 100-cell embryo is killed in the transfer. The identity of the human embryo person, if it is a symbolic or intrinsic person, is tied at that stage to the DNA. That DNA is not lost or even injured by the harvesting of embryonic stem cells. This is not the sacrifice of the smallest and most vulnerable among us. We are debating the potential for temporary transplant of undifferentiated tissue and the DNA of such a "person," rather than the imminent destruction of an embryo discarded by a clinic. It is difficult to imagine those who favor just war opposing a war against such suffering given the meager loss of a few cellular components.

• • •

GILBERT MEILAENDER

The Point of a Ban: Or, How to Think about Stem Cell Research

Gilbert Meilaender is a Professor of Theology at Valparasio University. His published works fall generally into the area of religious ethics. He has a special interest in bioethics. He has served as an Associate Editor for the *Journal of Religious Ethics,* as an Associate Editor for *Religious Studies Review,* and as a member of the Editorial Board for the *Annual of the Society of Religious Ethics.* His most recent book is an edited volume titled *Working: Its Meaning and Its Limits* (University of Notre Dame Press).

In its report *Ethical Issues in Human Stem Cell Research,* the National Bioethics Advisory Commission says the following of the congressional ban on federally funded embryo research: "In our view, the ban conflicts with several of the ethical goals of medicine, especially healing, prevention, and research."[1] So inured have we become to such language that we fail to notice its oddity. Is it surprising that a ban should conflict with desirable goals? Or isn't that, in fact, why we sometimes need a ban—precisely to prohibit an unacceptable means to otherwise desirable ends? Taking note of this point—the oddity of NBAC's statement—should help us think about the issue of stem cell research. To explore the logic and make sense of a ban on stem cell research is my aim here. To be sure, such a ban may be persuasive chiefly for those who are concerned to affirm the dignity of the embryo, but the public debate need not be restricted to a seemingly endless argument about the embryo's status. Since many parties to the debate claim, at least, to agree that the embryo should be treated with "respect," it may be fruitful to explore other issues—in particular, the nature of moral reasoning and the background beliefs that underline such reasoning.

I propose to take a very long way round. Our understanding of what is at stake can be sharpened if we begin not with stem cell research but with a quite different moral question.

In the memoir of his service as a Marine in the Pacific theater of World War II, historian William Manchester writes at one point:

> Biak was a key battle, because Kuzumi had made the most murderous discovery of the war. Until then the Japs had defended each island at the beach. When the beach was lost, the island was lost; surviving Nips formed for a banzai charge, dying for the emperor at the muzzles of our guns while few, if any, Americans were lost. After Biak the enemy withdrew to deep caverns. Rooting them out became a bloody business which reached its ultimate horrors in the last months of the war. You think of the lives which would have been lost in an invasion of Japan's home islands—a staggering number of American lives but millions more of Japanese—and you thank God for the atomic bomb.[2]

Yet, one might argue—many have—that it would always be wrong to drop atomic bombs on cities, that doing so violates the rights of non-combatants. One might argue for a ban on that approach to waging war, even though in the instance cited by Manchester one can reasonably claim that such a ban would have conflicted with some of the ethical goals of statecraft: to minimize loss of life, and to seek peace and pursue it.

UTILITARIANISM OF EXTREMITY

How do we reason about such a ban in the ethics of warfare? There are, of course, different views about what is permitted in war, as there are different views

From the *Hastings Center Report* 31 (January-February 2001), 9–16. Reprinted by permission of the author and the Hastings Center.

on all important moral questions. But if we contemplate briefly the logic of one very widely read treatment—Michael Walzer's *Just and Unjust Wars*[3]—we will discover that it provides a helpful window into our consideration of banning federal support for stem cell research.

Following a well-trodden path, Walzer notes that there is a kind of dualism in just war theory. It requires two different sorts of moral judgments: about when it is permissible to go to war (what Walzer calls "the theory of aggression") and about what it is permissible to do in war (which he terms "the war convention"). These are two different sorts of judgments. If we are fortunate, they will cohere for us: that is, those who have just cause for going to war will be able to win without fighting in ways that are prohibited. Because, however, these really are two different moral judgments, there are moments when we face "dilemmas of war," when it may seem, for example, that those whose cause is just cannot win unless they violate the war convention.

Confronted by such a dilemma, we might reason in several different ways. We might adopt a simple utilitarian approach; indeed, as Walzer notes, "[i]t is not hard to understand why anyone convinced of the moral urgency of victory would be impatient" with the notion of a ban on certain means to that victory (p. 227). The more desirable the goals we pursue, the more tempting it will be to allow seemingly obvious utilitarian calculations to carry the day. If we take this route, the war convention provides us with rules of thumb at best. It offers some general guidelines about how to fight, which may be set aside whenever they conflict with the means required for those with just cause to win. To reason thus is in effect to conclude that the morality of war really involves only one kind of moral judgment: about when it is permissible to go to war. There is no genuine "dualism" in just war theory.

In an effort to preserve at least some sense that two different sorts of moral judgments are present, we might turn to what Walzer calls a "sliding scale." Roughly speaking, it means: Although there may be some rules that should never be violated, "the greater the injustice likely to result from my defeat, the more rules I can violate in order to avoid defeat" (p. 229). Some acts of war, even in a good cause, might still be wrong—if, for example, the destruction they bring is disproportionate to the good they seek to serve. But that "limit" is an essentially utilitarian one, and hence the sliding scale is simply a gradualist way of eroding the distinction between just war theory's two kinds of moral judgments. "The only kind of justice that matters is *jus ad bellum*" (p. 230). In short, the sliding scale is simply the timid person's avenue to utilitarian calculation.

The true alternative to such calculation seems to be a kind of moral absolutism: do justice even if the heavens fall. "To resist the slide, one must hold that the rules of war are a series of categorical and unqualified prohibitions, and that they can never rightly be violated even in order to defeat aggression" (p. 230). This is deontology with teeth. But it does, at least, acknowledge the force of each sort of moral judgment we make about war—what goals it would be desirable to realize, and what rights it is necessary to respect—and it permits the tension between these judgments to stand. It does not deny that winning in a just cause is often very important indeed; it simply refuses to reduce reasoning about how to fight to calculations of how best to win, and it does not gradually chip away at the rights recognized by the war convention by means of any sliding scale. In short, it acknowledges that a ban on fighting in certain ways will certainly make it more difficult to achieve the good ends sought in war, but it does not offer that fact as, in itself, an argument against such a ban. The morality of warfare involves both judgments about values to be realized and rights to be upheld. When important values cannot be realized without violating rights, it would be peculiar simply to note this fact as an argument in favor of violating rights—as if a ban on such violation were out of the question. It might be that we should do justice even if the heavens will fall, even if those values cannot then be realized or must be pursued in some slower, less certain, manner.

For such a position Walzer has considerable respect. Nevertheless, he himself adopts "an alternative doctrine that stops just short of absolutism. . . . It might be summed up in the maxim: do justice unless the heavens are (really) about to fall" (p. 231). This "utilitarianism of extremity" does not commit us to reasoning in terms of a sliding scale. Whether one's cause is relatively more or less just, the rules of the war convention apply with equal force, and we are not to chip away gradually at its limits. Ordinarily, a nation with just cause ought to accept defeat rather than try to win by fighting unjustly. Sometimes, however, in very special circumstances, a nation at war may face an enemy who simply "must" be defeated, whose possible victory constitutes "an ultimate threat to everything decent in our lives" (p. 253). The paradigmatic example of such an enemy, for Walzer, is the Nazi regime.

Confronting such an enemy, facing a defeat that threatens everything decent in human life, there might come a moment when we simply had to override the war convention and fight unjustly. This is no gradual erosion of moral limits such as the sliding scale permits. It is, rather, "a sudden breach of the convention, but only after holding out for a long time against the process of erosion" (p. 231). The deontological limits remain in place until the moment when we must reason in accord with a utilitarianism of extremity and override them.

How shall we recognize such a moment of supreme emergency—and, just as important, how not suppose that we face such a moment every time we are tempted to fight unjustly in a good cause? Walzer offers two criteria to help us delimit the moment, though of course criteria alone can never replace the discernment of wise men and women. It must be both strategically and morally necessary to override the war convention: no other strategy must be available to oppose the enemy, and the enemy must really constitute an ultimate threat to moral values. The moment is upon us only when we face an enemy who can be beaten in no other way, but who must be beaten. For Walzer, Britain's decision to bomb German cities—a decision made late in 1940—responded to such a moment of supreme emergency.[4] Civilians were targeted and the war convention overridden. Yet even in this moment of supreme emergency, Walzer argues, the war convention is "overridden," not "set aside." Logically puzzling though it may be, Walzer believes that political leaders who undertake such deeds bear a burden of criminality, even though they do what they must according to a utilitarianism of extremity.

The passage from William Manchester might be thought to make such an argument from supreme emergency. "You think of the lives which would have been lost in an invasion of Japan's home islands, . . . and you thank God for the atomic bomb." But Walzer believes the decision to drop the atomic bomb on Hiroshima was unjustified, and he argues that the American government did not face a moment of supreme emergency that necessitated a breach of the war convention. American policy sought from Japan an unconditional surrender, and Japanese policy was to make an invasion so costly that the Americans would prefer to negotiate a settlement. "[T]he continuation of the struggle was not something forced upon us. It had to do with our war aims. The military estimate of casualties was based not only on the belief that the Japanese would fight almost to the last man, but also on the assumption that the Americans would accept nothing less than unconditional surrender" (p. 267).

Since the Japanese government was not, in Walzer's view, "the moral equivalent of the Nazi regime," there was no imperative reason to demand unconditional surrender. It "should never have been asked" (p. 267). Of course, it would have been morally desirable—very desirable—to end the war quickly. And yes, it would have been morally desirable to end the war with a clear-cut victory. And of course it was morally desirable to minimize the loss of life. One can imagine those whose lives would have been lost had we refused to drop the bomb arguing that we might have saved them had we been less scrupulous. But for Walzer all that provided no persuasive reason to override the war convention. Hence the ban on bombing cities should never have been set aside here—good though the cause undeniably was. To say, "the ban on bombing civilians conflicts with several of the ethical goals of warfare and must therefore be set aside" would have been morally mistaken.

Two other features of Walzer's analysis need notice here before we turn to the issue of stem cell research. The first concerns his discussion of "The Dishonoring of Arthur Harris," and the second attends to the problem of nuclear deterrence. The very concept of supreme emergency assumes that, almost always, the deontological limits marked off by inviolable rights remain in place. Those limits are transgressed only in the most extreme instance of moral and strategic necessity. And they are never simply "set aside"; they are "overridden." Having been overridden, they must then be put back into place. Those who transgressed the ban and fought unjustly bear a burden of criminality. Walzer does not suppose that nation-states, especially victorious ones, could or should legally punish responsible leaders, but he does think that, after the fact, a way must be found to reinstate the overridden moral code. Thus Arthur Harris, chief of Britain's Bomber Command, who advocated bombing civilians and whose pilots carried out that terrorist policy, was the only one of Britain's top wartime commanders not rewarded after the war with a seat in the House of Lords. This "refusal to honor Harris," Walzer writes, "at least went some small distance toward re-establishing a commitment to the rules of war and the rights they protect." Supreme emergency must be a "moment." It must come to an end, and the moral law must be reacknowledged and reinstated.

To see that is to understand why one of the least successful features of Walzer's analysis of just war theory is his discussion of nuclear deterrence. The moral problem of deterrence—especially acute during the Cold War but still troubling today—is that one targets civilians, threatening almost unimaginable destruction, in order to avoid war altogether. For the many years of nuclear standoff between the United States and the Soviet Union, the posture of deterrence seemed to work (at least in the sense that nuclear weapons were used only to deter and not to fight). Walzer tries to make sense of this by suggesting that "[s]upreme emergency has become a permanent condition. Deterrence is a way of coping with that condition, and though it is a bad way, there may well be no other that is practical in a world of sovereign and suspicious states. We threaten evil in order not to do it, and the doing of it would be so terrible that the threat seems in comparison to be morally defensible" (p. 274). The benefits are so great that, horrifying as it is in principle, deterrence can become "easy to live with" (p. 271). The needed reinstatement of the moral code is deferred—indefinitely.

It is hard to find this persuasive. Having resisted any too easy transgressing of rights and limits, having confined utilitarian calculation to the moment of supreme emergency, Walzer simply settles for a permanent condition of supreme emergency. But, of course, when all moments are catastrophic, none is. In the dark of night all cats become gray, and we lose the ability to make needed and important moral distinctions.

STEM CELLS

In a recent article, Glenn McGee and Arthur Caplan argue for the moral justifiability—perhaps even obligatoriness—of stem cell research.[5] They suggest that NBAC and other scholars (in particular, John Robertson) have been too ready to accommodate research opponents who would ban any research that involves deliberate destruction of embryos. If advocates of research cede too much ground to these opponents, they never directly confront the objection, even though they argue for moving ahead (if with caution). By contrast, McGee and Caplan argue that even if one grants the humanity and personhood of the embryo, its destruction in stem cell research is justified because this research promises to relieve incalculable suffering. Therefore, "the moral imperative of compassion . . . compels stem cell research" (p. 153). The "central moral issues in stem cell research" have to do, McGee and Caplan say, "with the criteria for moral sacrifices of human life" (p. 152). (It is instructive to note that they tend to talk not about when life may be "taken," but about when it may be "sacrificed" or "allowed to die." Clearer language would make for a clearer argument.) Thus even if one grants the personhood of the embryo, they argue, the question whether the embryo's life may be taken is still unresolved, at least for most of us. Only those who oppose all killing of any kind "can rationally oppose the destruction of an embryo solely by virtue of its status as a human person" (p. 153). For most of us, who do not oppose all killing as unjustified, the question becomes: "what constitutes unwarranted violence against an embryo, and for what reasons might an embryo ethically be destroyed—e.g., in the interest of saving the community?" (p. 153).

When, if ever, is it permissible to sacrifice a human life in service of the common good? When is such killing warranted? For McGee and Caplan, "it is clear that . . . no need is more obvious or compelling than the suffering of half the world at the hand of miserable disease. Not even the most insidious dictator could dream up a chemical war campaign as horrific as the devastation wrought by Parkinson's disease" (pp. 155ff). Since it would be possible, they think, to salvage by transplantation the DNA of the embryo-to-be-destroyed, little would be lost other than easily replaceable cellular components (cytoplasm, mitochondria).[6] And they find it "difficult to imagine those who favor just war opposing a war against such suffering given the meager loss of a few cellular components" (p. 156).

Their argument might be summarized thus: "You think of the lives that will be lost because of serious diseases such as Parkinson's—a staggering number of lives—and you thank God for stem cell research." In the face of a structurally similar argument from William Manchester and others, Walzer suggested that the United States might have changed its war aims, and that unconditional surrender was an optional goal. McGee and Caplan never consider analogous possibilities. Only unconditional surrender of Parkinson's disease will do. Progress at relieving human suffering does not seem to be an optional goal. Nor apparently is slower progress, achieved by research techniques not involving the destruction of embryos, acceptable.

Perhaps McGee and Caplan suppose that we are in something like a moment of supreme emergency. If so, they have at best made a case for moral necessity—they have identified an enemy that must be defeated. They have not yet ventured to make a case for *strategic* necessity—to show that progress cannot be made, even if more slowly, by means that do not involve destruction of embryos. Further, the case for moral necessity commits us to accepting nothing less than the eradication of all horrible diseases. Conquer one, after all, and there will be another to be conquered. Supreme emergency becomes a permanent condition, and the "sacrifice" of human lives in service of the common good and the war against suffering never comes to an end. Indeed, knowing that our actions are compelled by "the moral imperative of compassion," we act with a good conscience, bear no burden of criminality, and feel no need to find ways to reinstate the moral code we have overridden. By comparison with Walzer's analysis of just war theory, this attempt to justify stem cell research seems all too casual.

Consider a different argument about yet another issue. In a brief piece about euthanasia, written in 1990 when Jack Kevorkian had suddenly garnered attention, William F. May adopted a position on euthanasia that is not unlike Walzer's lengthier argument on the morality of war.[7] Despite judging that the motivations behind the euthanasia movement were "understandable in an age when dying has become such an inhumanly endless business," May offered a number of reasons why acceptance of euthanasia would be bad policy. He argued that "our social policy should allow terminal patients to die but it should not regularize killing for mercy." Even the good end of relieving suffering brought on by "an inhumanly endless" process of dying did not lead May to set aside the ban on euthanasia. But he did recognize something like a moment when both moral and strategic necessity could come together in such a way as to persuade one to override that ban. "I can, to be sure, imagine rare circumstances in which I hope I would have the courage to kill for mercy—when the patient is utterly beyond human care, terminal, and in excruciating pain. . . . On the battlefield I would hope that I would have the courage to kill the sufferer with mercy." Even in such a "moment"—which can scarcely become anything like a "permanent condition"—May seems to think that the ban on killing is overridden rather than set aside and that a measure of guilt may remain. He writes that "we should not always expect the law to provide us with full protection and coverage for what, in rare circumstances, we may morally need to do. Sometimes the moral life calls us out into a no-man's-land where we cannot expect total security and protection under the law." This is the sort of argument one looks for if a ban is to be overridden.

Did NBAC do better than McGee and Caplan in offering such an argument? To some extent, it did, and although I find its approach defective, I have considerable respect for the seriousness with which it seems to have proceeded. For example, NBAC declines simply to weigh on some utilitarian balance possible relief of future suffering versus destruction of embryos. This becomes clear in its discussion of R. Alto Charo's proposal to bypass entirely the issue of the embryo's moral status. Charo suggests that we seek simply to balance deeply felt offense to some (who accept the full humanity of the embryo) over against potentially great health benefits for some future sufferers. "Thus, although it is clear that embryo research would offend some people deeply, she would argue that the potential health benefits for this and future generations outweigh the pain experienced by opponents of the research."[8]

This "Manchesterian" argument eliminates from the outset any possibility of a ban founded on a belief that certain wrongs ought never be done. NBAC rightly notes that, at least for anyone prepared to contemplate the possibility of a ban on embryo research, Charo's recommendation must seem to be sleight of hand. "It might be argued, for example, that placing the lives of embryos in this kind of utilitarian calculus will seem appropriate only to those who presuppose that embryos do not have the status of persons" (p. 51). NBAC does not simply say, "You think of the suffering that will go unrelieved and the lives that will be lost without this research—and you thank God for stem cell research." It at least recognizes the force of the sort of point raised over thirty years ago by Paul Ramsey:

> I may pause here to raise the question whether a scientist has not an entirely "frivolous conscience" who, faced with the awesome technical possibility that soon human life may be created in the laboratory and then be either terminated or preserved in existence as an experiment, or, who

> gets up at scientific meetings and gathers to himself newspaper headlines by urging his colleagues to prepare for that scientific accomplishment by giving attention to the "ethical" questions it raises—if he is not at the same time, and in advance, prepared to stop the whole procedure should the "ethical finding" concerning this fact-situation turn out to be, for any serious conscience, murder. It would perhaps be better not to raise the ethical issues, than not to raise them in earnest.[9]

NBAC's conscience is not that frivolous.

Nonetheless, it stops short of taking a ban fully seriously. Its alternative to simple utilitarian calculation seems to be a mode of reasoning analogous to Walzer's "sliding scale." Its stated aim is "to develop policies that demonstrate respect for all reasonable alternative points of view."[10] To that end, NBAC looks for ways to express "respect" for the embryo even if not the kind or degree of respect afforded the rest of us. Hence, for example, it offers the following as "a reasonable statement of the kind of agreement that could be possible on this issue": "Research that involves the destruction of embryos remaining after infertility treatments is permissible when there is good reason to believe that this destruction is necessary to develop cures for life-threatening or severely debilitating diseases" (p. 52). That is, the more urgent the cause, the more potential good to be gained from this research, the more respect for the embryo must give way to the research imperative.

That this is a kind of sliding scale becomes clear when we note one of the limits recommended by NBAC. Its report supports research on spare embryos to be discarded after IVF procedures but recommends against creating embryos solely as research subjects. But this is not a limit to be respected even if the heavens will fall—or even a limit to be overridden only if the heavens are about to fall. It is a limit to be chipped away at gradually, as the little words "at this time" in the following sentence indicate: "We do not, at this time, support the federal sponsorship of research involving the creation of embryos solely for research purposes. However, we recognize that in the future, scientific evidence and public support for this type of stem cell research may be sufficient in order to proceed" (p. 55).

This is a kind of "proceed with caution" view. One suspects that the chief "limit" to research discerned by NBAC involves not so much the status of the embryo as the status of "public support."[11] There is no sense here of a limit that could be overridden—if at all—only in a moment of supreme emergency, which overriding would involve a burden of criminality, and which limit would somehow have to be reinstated after the fact. Such an argument, if it could be made persuasively, would be a very strong expression of respect for embryos. NBAC does much less, however. From one perspective, in fact, perhaps NBAC's cautious sliding scale shows less respect for embryos than McGee and Caplan's "full speed ahead" approach, since one can read McGee and Caplan as justifying stem cell research with a kind of "supreme emergency as a permanent condition" argument. While I doubt that it really makes sense to posit such a permanent condition of supreme emergency, the attempt does at least acknowledge that nothing less than such extreme circumstances could even claim to justify embryo research. The more judicious, "at this time" approach of NBAC promises, by contrast, a kind of relentless "progress" in what is allowed. It is not really prepared ever to stop. It cannot contemplate or make sense of a ban.

ENDS AND MEANS

Perhaps we can understand, then, why some critics of stem cell research would not be persuaded by moral reasoning that uses simple utilitarian calculation, applies a "sliding scale," or appeals to "supreme emergency as a permanent condition." If we are among the unpersuaded, we are left to contemplate seriously a ban. To do that, however, may compel us to think also about the background beliefs—metaphysical and religious in character—that undergird all our moral reflection. In particular, we will be forced to ponder the degree to which relief of suffering has acquired the status of trump in our moral reasoning.

Why might one, even while granting the enormous benefits to be gained from stem cell research, be prepared to contemplate a ban on research that requires the destruction of embryos? How must one think for such a ban to make sense? Clearly, no ban can make sense if we say with McGee and Caplan that "no need is more obvious or compelling than the suffering of half the world at the hand of miserable disease." Nor could any ban make sense in the context of a search, such as NBAC's, for a public policy "consensus" that, while taking objections seriously, will always permit research to proceed. Indeed, despite NBAC's serious attempt to be fair-minded, its understanding of consensus ultimately excludes from consideration precisely those who might be willing to think in terms of a ban.

The very notion of a ban can make sense only if we consider that the fundamental moral question—for a community as for an individual—is *how* we live, not *how long*. If we act simply for the sake of future good, the day will come when those good effects reach an end—which is not a telos, but simply an end. We will have done evil in the present for a future good that does not come to pass.

In his meditations to himself, Marcus Aurelius writes: "Another [prays] thus: How shall I not lose my little son? Thou thus: How shall I not be afraid to lose him?"[12] That is, how shall I not be afraid if the alternative to losing him is doing wrong? In our tradition this emphasis on means over ends, on how rather than how long we live, has been grounded not only in such Stoic thought but also and primarily in Jewish and Christian belief.

It has provided the moral background that makes sense of doing justice even if the heavens are about to fall.

One who looks on life this way need not, of course, suppose that beneficence is unimportant or that relief of suffering is of little consequence. Weighty as such values are, however, they have no automatic moral trump. To appreciate this, we can consider passages from two twentieth century thinkers for whom it was clear that the most important moral question was how we live. In *The Screwtape Letters* C.S. Lewis created a series of letters from a senior devil to a junior tempter on the subject of how to tempt a mortal—with instructions that invert the moral world by inviting us to look at things from the perspective of Satan (for whom God must be "the Enemy"). So, for example, Screwtape advises Wormwood about the attitude toward time that he ought to cultivate in his patient:

> [N]early all vices are rooted in the Future. Gratitude looks to the Past and love to the Present; fear, avarice, lust, and ambition look ahead. . . . [The Enemy] does not want men to give the Future their hearts, to place their treasure in it. We do. . . . [W]e want a man hagridden by the Future—haunted by visions of an imminent heaven or hell upon earth—ready to break the Enemy's commands in the Present if by so doing we make him think he can attain the one or avert the other.[13]

Likewise, reflecting upon "the ethics of genetic control," Paul Ramsey noted the relatively greater importance of an "ethics of means" for religious thinkers:

> Anyone who intends the world as a Christian or as a Jew knows along his pulses that he is not bound to succeed in preventing genetic deterioration, any more than he would be bound to retard entropy, or prevent planets from colliding with this earth or the sun from cooling. He is not under the necessity of ensuring that those who come after us will be like us, any more than he is bound to ensure that there will be those like us to come after us. He knows no such absolute command of nature or of nature's God. This does not mean that he will do nothing. But it does mean that as he goes about the urgent business of doing his duty in regard to future generations, he will not begin with the desired end and deduce his obligation exclusively from this end. . . . And he will know in advance that any person, or any society or age, expecting ultimate success where ultimate success is not to be reached, is peculiarly apt to devise extreme and morally illegitimate means for getting there.[14]

My aim is not to inject religious beliefs into public discussion of stem cell research. On the contrary, my point is that such beliefs are already there. To see clearly the kind of background beliefs which might make a ban on stem cell research seem reasonable is also to realize that something like a religious vision of the human is at work in arguments *for* such research. Precisely insofar as a ban is not really an option, insofar as proponents of a ban cannot possibly be included in any proposed consensus, the argument for research is that we—human beings—bear ultimate responsibility for overcoming suffering and conquering disease. We know along our pulses that we are, in fact, obligated to succeed, compelled to ensure that future generations not endure suffering that we might have relieved. Possible future benefits so bind our consciences that we are carried along by an argument we might well reject in, say, the ethics of warfare. "You think of the suffering that will go unrelieved and the lives that will be lost without this research and you thank God for stem cell research."

It is quite true, of course, that a ban on stem cell research requiring destruction of embryos would mean that future sufferers could say to us: "You might have made more rapid progress. You might have helped me." To consider how we should respond to them is to contemplate the moral point of a ban: "Perhaps we could have helped you, but only by pretending that our responsibility to do good is godlike, that it knows no limit. Only by supposing, as modernity has taught us, that suffering has no point other than to be overcome by human will and technical mastery—that compassion means not a readiness to suffer with others but a determination always to oppose suffering as an affront to our humanity. We could have helped you only by destroying in the present the sort of world in which both we and you want to live—a world in which justice is done now, not permanently mortgaged in service of future good. Only, in short, by pretending to be something other than the human beings we are."

REFERENCES

1. National Bioethics Advisory Commission, *Ethical Issues in Human Stem Cell Research, Volume I: Report and Recommendations of the National Bioethics Advisory Commission* (Rockville, Md.: National Bioethics Advisory Commission, 1999), p. 69.

2. W. Manchester, *Goodbye Darkness: A Memoir of the Pacific War* (Boston and Toronto: Little, Brown and Company, 1980), p. 210.

3. M. Walzer, *Just and Unjust Wars: A Moral Argument with Historical Illustrations* (New York: Basic Books, 1977).

4. We should note the limits to Walzer's understanding of the supreme emergency faced by Britain: "For the truth is that the supreme emergency passed long before the British bombing reached its crescendo" (p. 261). Long after it was strategically necessary "the raids continued, culminating in the spring of 1945—when the war was virtually won—in a savage attack on the city of Dresden in which something like 100,000 people were killed" (p. 261).

5. G. McGee and A. Caplan, "The Ethics and Politics of Small Sacrifices in Stem Cell Research," *Kennedy Institute of Ethics Journal* 9, no. 2 (1999), pp. 151–58.

6. A puzzling feature of their argument, which I cannot unpack here, has to do with this claim that the trajectory of a human life, which clearly begins with the embryo, is of little importance. As long as certain elements (DNA) are salvaged and given a new trajectory, nothing has been lost. McGee and Caplan develop their claim too briefly for one really to know what its implications are for the matter of personal identity, but, surely, they need to say far more if they are to try to make this move persuasive.

7. W. F. May, "Rising to the Occasion of Our Death," *Christian Century* 107 (11–18 July 1990), pp. 662ff.

8. NBAC, *Ethical Issues in Human Stem Cell Research,* p. 51.

9. P. Ramsey, *Fabricated Man: The Ethics of Genetic Control* (New Haven, Conn.: Yale University Press, 1970), p. 13.

10. NBAC, *Ethical Issues in Human Stem Cell Research,* p. 51.

11. I do not wish to deny the obvious fact that a public commission such as NBAC must pay attention to and measure public support when it makes recommendations. Nevertheless, if one accepts a research ban as one choiceworthy moral option, then one must be open to the possibility that NBAC's responsibility might be to marshal public support for such a ban.

12. Marcus Aurelius, *Meditations,* tr. Long (South Bend, Ind.: Regnery-Gateway, 1956), VIII, 31, p. 100.

13. C. S. Lewis, *The Screwtape Letters* (New York: Macmillan, 1973), pp. 69–70.

14. See ref. 9, Ramsey, *Fabricated Man,* pp. 29–31.

NATIONAL RESEARCH COUNCIL AND INSTITUTE OF MEDICINE

Stem Cell Research and the Future of Regenerative Medicine

Stem cell research offers unprecedented opportunities for developing new treatments for debilitating diseases for which there are few or no cures. Stem cells also present a new way to explore fundamental questions of biology, such as determining the basic mechanisms of tissue development and specialization, which will be required for the development of therapies. However, our society holds diverse views about the morality of using early embryos for research, and we find ourselves searching for a consensus on how to proceed with this new avenue of research. Provocative and conflicting claims about the biology and biomedical potential of adult and embryonic stem cells have been made both inside and outside the scientific community. The committee considered those claims in light of the meaning and importance of the preliminary data from recent stem cell experiments. The following findings and recommendations constitute the final result of the committee's deliberations on these issues.

Adapted with permission from Committee on the Biological and Biomedical Applications of Stem Cell Research, *Stem Cell Research and the Future of Regenerative Medicine* (Washington, DC: National Academy Press, 2001), 36–39. Copyright © by the National Research Council and the Institute of Medicine. Courtesy of National Academy Press, Washington, D.C.

Finding 1: Experiments in mice and other animals are

necessary but not sufficient for medical advances in human regenerative medicine. There are substantial biological differences between animal and human development and between animal and human stem cells, although the full range of similarities and differences is not understood.

Recommendation: Studies with human stem cells are essential to make progress in the development of treatments for human disease, and this research should continue.

Finding 2: Current scientific data indicate that there are important biological differences between adult and embryonic stem cells and among adult stem cells found in different types of tissue. The therapeutic implications of these biological differences are not clear, and additional scientific data are needed on all stem cell types. Adult stem cells from bone marrow have so far provided most of the examples of successful therapies for replacement of diseased or destroyed cells. Their potential for fully differentiating into other cell types (such as brain, nerve, and pancreas cells) is still poorly understood and remains to be clarified. In contrast, embryonic stem cells studied in animals clearly are capable of developing into multiple tissue types and capable of long-term self-renewal in culture, features that have not yet been demonstrated with many adult stem cells. The application of stem cell research to therapy for human disease will require much more knowledge about the biological properties of all types of stem cells. The best available scientific and medical evidence indicates that research on both embryonic and adult human stem cells will be needed. Moreover, research on embryonic stem cells will be important to inform research on adult stem cells, and vice versa.

Recommendation: Although stem cell research is on the cutting edge of biological science today, it is still in its infancy. Studies of both embryonic and adult human stem cells will be required to most efficiently advance the scientific and therapeutic potential of regenerative medicine. Research on both adult and embryonic human stem cells should be pursued.

Finding 3: Over time, all cell lines in tissue culture change, typically accumulating harmful genetic mutations. There is no reason to expect stem cell lines to behave differently. In addition, most existing stem cell lines have been cultured in the presence of non-human cells or serum that could lead to potential human health risks. Consequently, vigilant monitoring of the integrity of existing cell lines is essential. In addition, the generation of new stem cell lines is likely to be important to replace those that become inviable and to increase understanding of the impact of long-term cell culture.

Recommendation: While there is much that can be learned using existing stem cell lines if they are made widely available for research, concerns about changing genetic and biological properties of these stem cell lines necessitate continued monitoring as well as the development of new stem cell lines in the future.

Finding 4: High quality, publicly funded research is the wellspring of medical breakthroughs. Although private, for-profit research plays a critical role in translating the fruits of basic research into medical advances that are broadly available to the public, the status of stem cell research is far from the point of providing therapeutic products. Without public funding of basic research on stem cells, progress toward medical therapies is likely to be hindered. In addition, public funding offers greater opportunities for regulatory oversight and public scrutiny of stem cell research.

Recommendation: Human stem cell research that is publicly funded and conducted under established standards of open scientific exchange, peer review, and public oversight offers the most efficient and responsible means to fulfill the promise of stem cells to meet the need for regenerative medical therapies.

Finding 5: Conflicting ethical perspectives surround the use of embryonic stem cells in medical research, particularly where the moral and legal status of human embryos is concerned. The differing perspectives are difficult to reconcile. Given the controversial nature of research with fetal and embryonic tissues, restrictions and guidelines for ethical conduct of such research have been developed.

Recommendation: If the federal government chooses to fund human stem cell research, proposals to work on human embryonic stem cells should be required to justify the decision on scientific grounds and should be strictly scrutinized for compliance with existing and future federally-mandated ethical guidelines.

Finding 6: The use of embryonic stem cells is not the first scientific advance to raise public concerns about ethical and social issues in biomedical research. Recombinant-DNA techniques likewise raised questions and were subject to intense debate and public scrutiny. In that case, a national advisory body, the Recombinant DNA Advisory Committee, was established at the National Institutes of Health to ensure that the research met with the highest scientific and ethical standards.

Recommendation: A national advisory group composed of outstanding researchers, ethicists, and other stakeholders should be established at NIH to oversee research on human embryonic stem cells. The group should include leading experts in the most current scientific knowledge relevant to stem cell research who can evaluate the technical merit of any proposed research on human embryonic stem cells. Other roles for the group could include evaluation of potential risks to research subjects and ensuring compliance with all legal requirements and ethical standards.

Finding 7: Regenerative medicine is likely to involve the implantation of new tissue in patients with damaged or diseased organs. A substantial obstacle to the success of transplantation of any cells, including stem cells and their derivatives, is the immune-mediated rejection of foreign tissue by the recipient's body. In current stem cell transplantation procedures with bone marrow and blood, success hinges on obtaining a close match between donor and recipient tissues and on the use of immunosuppressive drugs, which often have severe and potentially life-threatening side effects. To ensure that stem cell–based therapies can be broadly applicable for many conditions and people, new means of overcoming the problem of tissue rejection must be found. Although ethically controversial, the somatic cell nuclear transfer technique promises to have that advantage. Other options for this purpose include genetic manipulation of the stem cells and the development of a very large bank of ES cell lines.

Recommendation: In conjunction with research on stem cell biology and the development of potential stem cell therapies, research on approaches that prevent immune rejection of stem cells and stem cell-derived tissues should be actively pursued. These scientific efforts include the use of a number of techniques to manipulate the genetic makeup of stem cells, including somatic cell nuclear transfer.

NATIONAL RESEARCH COUNCIL

Using Nuclear Transplantation to Produce Embryonic Stem Cells

Stem cells are cells that have an extensive ability to self-renew and to differentiate (turn into specialized cells). Embryonic stem cells obtained from blastocysts (5-to-7-day-old preimplantation embryos of about 150 cells each) are particularly important because they can give rise to the widest variety of cells and are immortal. If embryonic stem cells are derived by nuclear transplantation using as—the somatic nucleus transferred into the egg—a nucleus from a patient, the resulting cells will be immunologically very similar to the patient's cells. However, the nuclear DNA donor and mitochondrial DNA donor will generally be different. Only if the egg donor is the mother of the patient or the patient herself, will the stem cells be genetically identical with the patient's cells—containing not only the same nuclear genome, but also the same mitochondrial DNA. As described in the recent report from the National Academies entitled *Stem Cells and the Future of Regenerative Medicine,* present research with such cells has the goal of producing cells and tissues for therapeutic transplantation with a reduced risk of rejection.[1] However, mitochondrial

Adapted with permission from Panel on *Scientific and Medical Aspects of Human Cloning, Scientific and Medical Aspects of Human Reproductive Cloning* (Washington, DC: National Academy Press, 2002), ES-11 to ES-12. Copyright © 2002 by the National Research Council. Courtesy of National Academy Press, Washington, D.C.

gene products that differ can elicit transplant rejection.

The panel recognizes that a blastocyst derived for scientific purposes by nuclear transplantation could be implanted in a human uterus in violation of a ban on reproductive cloning. But a legally enforceable ban that criminalizes the implantation step should be sufficient to prevent such proscribed activity. Moreover, because all nuclear transplantation experiments will require the participation of human subjects (the donor of the eggs and the donor of the somatic cell nuclei, who may be the same person or different persons), all this work would necessarily be regulated and controlled by the procedures and rules concerning human-subjects research—subjecting it to close scrutiny.

Stem cells derived directly from an adult's own tissues are an alternative to nuclear transplantation-derived embryonic stem cells as a source of cells for therapies. Two types of adult stem cells—bone marrow and skin stem cells—currently provide the only two stem cell therapies. But, as noted in the above mentioned report, many questions remain before the potential of other adult stem cells can be accurately assessed. Few studies on adult stem cells have sufficiently defined the stem cell by starting from a single isolated cell or defined the necessary cellular environment for correct differentiation or the factors controlling the efficiency with which the cells repopulate an organ. There is a need to show that the cells derived from introduced adult stem cells are contributing directly to tissue function and to improve the ability to maintain adult stem cells in culture without having the cells differentiate. Finally, most of the studies that have garnered so much attention have used mouse rather than human adult stem cells.

The previous report also notes that unlike adult stem cells, it is well established that embryonic stem cells can form multiple tissue types and be maintained in culture for long periods of time. However, embryonic stem cells are not without their own potential problems as a source of cells for transplantation. The growth of human embryonic stem cells in culture now requires a "feeder" layer of mouse cells that may contain viruses, and when allowed to differentiate the embryonic stem cells can form a mixture of cell types at once. Human embryonic stem cells can form benign tumors when introduced into mice, although this potential seems to disappear if the cells are allowed to differentiate before introduction into a recipient.

In addition to possible uses in therapeutic transplantation, embryonic stem cells and cell lines derived by nuclear transplantation could be valuable tools for both fundamental and applied medical and biological research.[1] This research would begin with the transfer of genetically defined donor nuclei from normal and diseased tissues. The resulting cell lines could be used to study how inherited and acquired alterations of genetic components might contribute to disease processes. The properties of the cell lines could be studied directly, or the embryonic stem cells could be studied as they differentiate into other cell types. For example, the way in which cells derived by nuclear transplantation from an Alzheimer's disease patient acted while differentiating into brain cells, compared with those derived from a normal patient, might yield new clues about Alzheimer's disease. Such cell lines could also be used to ensure that research covers a more genetically diverse human population than that represented in the blastocysts stored in IVF clinics, promoting studies of the causes and consequences of genetic diseases by allowing researchers to study how embryonic stem cells with different genetic endowments differ in the way that they form cell types and tissues. Finally, studies of genetic reprogramming and genetic imprinting will be substantially enhanced through the use of stem cells derived by nuclear transplantation, compared with studies with stem cells derived from other sources.

NOTE

1. Committee on Stem Cells and the Future of Regenerative Medicine, Board on Life Sciences and Board on Neuroscience and Behavioral Health. *Stem Cells and the Future of Regenerative Medicine. Report of the National Research Council and the Institute of Medicine.* 2001 Sep. [excerpt reprinted in this chapter.]

SUGGESTED READINGS

GENERAL ISSUES

Alpern, Kenneth D. *The Ethics of Reproductive Technology*. New York: Oxford University Press, 1992.

American Fertility Society, Ethics Committee. "Ethical Considerations of the New Reproductive Technologies." *Fertility and Sterility* 62, supplement 1 (1994), 1S–125S.

American Society for Reproductive Medicine. "Ethical Considerations of Assisted Reproductive Technologies." *Fertility and Sterility* 67, supplement 1 (1997), I–III.

Andrews, Lori B. *The Clone Age: Adventures in the New World of Reproductive Technology.* New York: Henry Holt, 1999.

———. "Control and Compensation: Laws Governing Extracorporeal Generative Materials." *Journal of Medicine and Philosophy* 14 (1989), 541–60.

Australia, National Health and Medical Research Council. *Long-Term Effects on Women from Assisted Conception*. Canberra: NH&MRC, 1996.

Bartels, Diane M., et al., eds. *Beyond Baby M: Ethical Issues in New Reproductive Techniques*. Clifton, NJ: Humana Press, 1990.

Blank, Robert H. *Regulating Reproduction*. New York: Columbia University Press, 1990.

Boling, Patricia Ann. *Expecting Trouble: Surrogacy, Fetal Abuse and New Reproductive Technologies*. Scranton, PA: Westview Press, 1995.

Cahill, Lisa Sowle. "Moral Traditions, Ethical Language, and Reproductive Technologies." *Journal of Medicine and Philosophy* 14 (1989), 497–522.

Canada, Law Reform Commission. *Medically Assisted Procreation*. Working Paper 65. Ottawa: Minister of Supply and Services, 1992.

Canada, Royal Commission on New Reproductive Technologies. *Proceed with Care: Final Report*. 2 vols. Ottawa: RCNRT, November 15, 1993.

Caplan, Arthur L. "And Baby Makes—Moral Muddles." In Arthur L. Caplan, *Am I My Brother's Keeper: The Ethical Frontiers of Biomedicine*. Bloomington and Indianapolis, IN: Indiana University Press, 1997, 3–21.

Cohen, Cynthia. "Reproductive Technologies: VII. Ethical Issues." In Warren Thomas Reich, ed., *Encyclopedia of Bioethics,* rev. ed. New York: Simon & Schuster Macmillan, 1995, 2233–41.

Corea, Gena. *Man-Made Women: How New Reproductive Technologies Affect Women*. Bloomington, IN: Indiana University Press, 1987.

———. *The Mother Machine: Reproductive Technologies from Artificial Insemination to Artificial Wombs*. New York: Harper & Row, 1985.

Edwards, Robert G., and Brody, Steven A. *Principles and Practice of Assisted Human Reproduction*. Edinburgh, UK: W. B. Saunders, 1995.

Franklin, Sarah. *Embodied Progress: A Cultural Account of Assisted Conception*. New York: Routledge, 1997.

Glover, Jonathan, et al. *Ethics of New Reproductive Technologies: The Glover Report to the European Commission*. DeKalb: Northern Illinois University Press, 1989.

Gosden, Roger G. *Designing Babies: The Brave New World of Reproductive Technologies*. New York: W. H. Freeman, 1999.

Harris, John. *Clones, Genes, and Immortality: Ethics and the Genetic Revolution*. Oxford: Oxford University Press, 1998. [Earlier edition entitled *Wonderwoman and Superman.*]

———, and Holm, Søren, eds. *The Future of Human Reproduction: Ethics, Choice and Regulation*. New York: Oxford University Press, 1998.

Holmes, Helen Bequaert. "Reproductive Technologies." In Lawrence C. Becker and Charlotte B. Becker, eds. *Encyclopedia of Ethics*. New York: Garland, 1992, 1083–89.

Hull, Richard T., ed. *Ethical Issues in the New Reproductive Technologies*. Belmont, CA: Wadsworth, 1990.

Humber, James M., and Almeder, Robert F., eds. *Biomedical Ethics Reviews, 1995: Reproduction, Technology, and Rights*. Totowa, NJ: Humana Press, 1996.

Institute of Medicine and National Research Council, Committee on the Basic Science Foundations of Medically Assisted Conception. *Medically Assisted Conception: An Agenda for Research*. Washington, DC: National Academy Press, 1989.

Kahn, Susan Martha. *Reproducing Jews: A Cultural Account of Assisted Conception in Israel*. Durham, NC: Duke University Press, 2000.

Kaplan, E. Ann, and Squier, Susan M., eds. *Playing Dolly: Technocultural Formations, Fantasies, and Fictions of Assisted Reproduction*. Piscataway, NJ: Rutgers University Press, 1999.

Kondratowicz, Diane M. "Approaches Responsive to Reproductive Technologies: A Need for Critical Assessment and Directions for Further Study." *Cambridge Quarterly of Healthcare Ethics* 6 (1997), 148–56.

Knoppers, Bartha M., and LeBris, Sonia. "Recent Advances in Medically Assisted Conception: Legal, Ethical and Social Issues." *American Journal of Law and Medicine* 17 (1991), 329–61.

Lauritzen, Paul. *Pursuing Parenthood: Ethical Issues in Assisted Reproduction*. Bloomington, IN: Indiana University Press, 1993.

LeRoy, Bonnie S., and Bartels, Dianne M. "Reproduction, Ethics, Sex Selection." In Thomas H. Murray and Maxwell J. Mehlman, eds. *Encyclopedia of Ethical, Legal, and Policy Issues in Biotechnology*. 2 vols. New York: John Wiley & Sons, 2000, 969–77.

Macklin, Ruth. *Surrogates and Other Mothers: The Debates over Assisted Reproduction*. Philadelphia: Temple University Press, 1994.

McCullough, Laurence B., and Chervenak, Frank A. *Ethics in Obstetrics and Gynecology*. New York: Oxford University Press, 1994.

Melo-Martin, Immaculada de. *Making Babies: Biomedical Technologies, Reproductive Ethics, and Public Policy*. Dordrecht and Boston: Kluwer Academic, 1998.

New York State Task Force on Life and the Law. *Assisted Reproductive Technologies: Analysis and Recommendations for Public Policy*. New York: TFLL, April 1998.

Overall, Christine. *Ethics and Human Reproduction: A Feminist Analysis*. Boston: Allen & Unwin, 1987.

———, ed. *The Future of Human Reproduction*. Toronto: The Women's Press, 1989.

Pellegrino, Edmund D.; Harvey, John Collins; and Langan, John P., eds. *Gift of Life: Catholic Scholars Respond to the Vatican Instruction*. Washington, DC: Georgetown University Press, 1990.

Roberts, Dorothy. *Killing the Black Body: Race, Reproduction, and the Meaning of Liberty*. Vancouver, WA: Vintage Books, 1998.

Robertson, John A. *Children of Choice: Freedom and the New Reproductive Technologies*. Princeton, NJ: Princeton University Press, 1994.

Rothman, Barbara Katz. *Recreating Motherhood: Ideology and Technology in a Patriarchal Society*. New York: W. W. Norton, 1989.

Rowland, Robyn. *Living Laboratories: Women and Reproductive Technology*. Bloomington, IN: Indiana University Press, 1992.

Ryan, Maura A. "The Argument for Unlimited Procreative Liberty: A Feminist Critique." *Hastings Center Report* 20 (July-August 1990), 6–12.

———. *Ethics and Economics of Assisted Reproduction: The Cost of Longing*. Washington, DC: Georgetown University Press, 2001.

Shenfield, F. and Surreau, Claude. *Ethical Dilemmas in Assisted Reproduction,* vol. 7. Boca Raton, FL: CRC Press, 1997.

Sherwin, Susan. "The Ethics of Babymaking" [book review essay]. *Hastings Center Report* 25 (March-April 1995), 34–37.

Singer, Peter and Wells, Deane. *Making Babies: The New Science and Ethics of Conception*. New York: Charles Scribner's Sons, 1985.

Steinberg, Deborah Lynn. *Bodies in Glass: Genetics, Eugenics, Embryo Ethics*. Manchester: Manchester University Press [distributed in the United States by St. Martin's Press], 1997.

Steinbock, Bonnie. *Life before Birth: The Moral and Legal Status of Embryos and Fetuses*. New York: Oxford University Press, 1992.

———. "Reproduction, Ethics, Moral Status of the Fetus." In Thomas H. Murray and Maxwell J. Mehlman, eds. *Encyclopedia of Ethical, Legal, and Policy Issues in Biotechnology.* 2 vols. New York: John Wiley & Sons, 2000, 947–56.

United Kingdom, Human Fertilisation and Embryology Authority. *Ninth Annual Report and Accounts*. London: HFEA, 2000. Available online at www.hfea.gov.uk

———. *The Patient's Guide to IVF [In Vitro Fertilization] Clinics.* London: HFEA, 2000.

U.S. Centers for Disease Control and Prevention; American Society for Reproductive Medicine and Society for Assisted Reproductive Technology; and RESOLVE. *1999 Assisted Reproductive Technology Success Rates.* 3 vols. Atlanta: CDC, December 2001.

U.S. Congress, Office of Technology Assessment. *Artificial Insemination: Practice in the United States—Summary of a 1987 Survey*. Background Paper. Washington, DC: U.S. Government Printing Office, August 1988.

———. *Infertility: Medical and Social Choices*. Washington, DC: U.S. Government Printing Office, May 1988.

Walters, LeRoy. "Ethics and New Reproductive Technologies: An International Review of Committee Statements." *Hastings Center Report* 17, supplement (June 1987), 3–9.

———. "Reproductive Technologies and Genetics." In Robert M. Veatch, ed. *Medical Ethics.* 2nd ed. Boston: Jones and Bartlett, 1997, 209–38.

Warnock, Mary, and United Kingdom Department of Health and Social Security, Committee of Inquiry into Human Fertilisation and Embryology. *A Question of Life: The Warnock Report on Human Fertilisation and Embryology*. New York: Basil Blackwell, 1985.

Worthington-White, Diana, et al. *Preimplantation Diagnosis of Genetic Diseases: A New Technique in Assisted Reproduction.* New York: John Wiley & Sons, 1993.

PARENTING AND THE FAMILY

Campbell, Courtney S., ed. *What Price Parenthood? Ethics and Assisted Reproduction.* Aldershot, Hampshire, UK: Ashgate, 1992.

Edwards, Jeanette, et al. *Technologies of Procreation: Kinship in the Age of Assisted Conception.* New York: Routledge, 1999.

Lauritzen, Paul. *Pursuing Parenthood: Ethical Issues in Assisted Reproduction.* Bloomington, IN: Indiana University Press, 1993.

Macklin, Ruth. "Artificial Means of Reproduction and Our Understanding of the Family." *Hastings Center Report* 21 (January–February 1991), 5–11.

Rothman, Barbara Katz. *The Tentative Pregnancy: How Amniocentesis Changes the Experience of Motherhood.* New York: W. W. Norton, 1993.

———. "Motherhood: Beyond Patriarchy." *Nova Law Review* 13 (1989), 481–86.

INFERTILITY

Abma, Joyce C., et al. "Fertility, Family Planning, and Women's Health: New Data from the 1995 National Survey of Family Growth." *Vital and Health Statistics,* Series 23. Data from the *National Survey of Family Growth,* no. 19, May 1997.

Chandra, Anjani, and Stephen, Elizabeth Hervey. "Impaired Fecundity in the United States: 1982–1995." *Family Planning Perspectives* 30 (January/February 1998), 34–42.

Fein, Esther B. "Calling Infertility a Disease, Couples Battle with Insurers." *New York Times,* February 22, 1998, p. 1.

New York State Task Force on Life and the Law. "The Prevalence of Infertility." *Assisted Reproductive Technologies: Analysis and Recommendations for Public Policy.* New York: TFLL, 1998, 10–16.

Rothman, Barbara Katz. "Infertility." In Barbara Katz Rothman, *Recreating Motherhood, Ideology and Technology in a Patriarchal Society.* New York: W. W. Norton, 1989.

Rothstein, Laura F. "Reproduction, Law, Is Infertility a Disability?" In Thomas H. Murray and Maxwell J. Mehlman, eds., *Encyclopedia of Ethical, Legal, and Policy Issues in Biotechnology.* 2 vols. New York: John Wiley & Sons, 2000: 983–988.

Shanner, Laura. "Bioethics through the Back Door: Phenomenology, Narratives, and Insights into Infertility." In L. Wayne Sumner and Joseph Boyle, eds., *Philosophical Perspectives on Bioethics*. Buffalo, NY: University of Toronto Press, 1996, 115–42.

United Kingdom Human Fertilisation and Embryology Authority. *The Patient's Guide to Infertility and IVF [In Vitro Fertilization].* London: HFEA, 2000. Available online at www.hfea.gov.uk

U.S. Congress, Office of Technology Assessment. *Infertility: Medical and Social Choices*. Washington, DC: U.S. Government Printing Office, May 1988.

U.S. Supreme Court. *Bragdon v. Abbott.* 524 *U.S. [Supreme Court]* Reports, 624, 1998.

Warnock, Mary, and United Kingdom Department of Health and Social Security, Committee of Inquiry into Human Fertilisation and Embryology. "Infertility." *Report on the Committee of Inquiry into Human Fertilisation and Embryology.* London: Her Majesty's Stationary Office, 1984, 8–10.

IN VITRO FERTILIZATION

Annas, George J. "Crazy Making: Embryos and Gestational Mothers." *Hastings Center Report* 21 (January-February 1991), 35–38.

Bonnicksen, Andrea L. *In Vitro Fertilization: Building Policy from Laboratories to Legislatures*. New York: Columbia University Press, 1991.

———. "Reproductive Technologies: IV. In Vitro Fertilization and Embryo Transfer." In Warren Thomas Reich, ed., *Encyclopedia of Bioethics,* rev. ed. New York: Simon & Schuster Macmillan, 1995: 2221–25.

Caplan, Arthur L. "The Ethics of In Vitro Fertilization." *Primary Care* 13 (1986), 241–53.

Capron, Alexander M. "Parenthood and Frozen Embryos: More Than Property and Privacy." *Hastings Center Report* 22 (September-October 1992), 32–33.

Cohen, Cynthia B., ed. *New Ways of Making Babies: The Case of Egg Donation*. Bloomington and Indianapolis, IN: Indiana University Press, 1996.

Dawson, Karen, and Singer, Peter. "Should Fertile People Have Access to In Vitro Fertilization?" *British Medical Journal* 300 (1990), 167–70.

Dyson, Anthony Oakley. *The Ethics of IVF.* Harrisburg, PA: Morehouse, 1995.

Fleischer, Eva. "Ready for Any Sacrifice? Women in IVF Programmes." *Issues in Reproductive and Genetic Engineering* 3 (1990), 1–11.

Hildt, Elisabeth, and Mieth, Dietmar. *In Vitro Fertilization in the 1990s: Towards Medical, Social, and Ethical Evaluation.* Aldershot, Hampshire, UK: Ashgate, 1998.

Jones, Howard W., Jr., and Cohen, Jean. "IFFS [International Federation of Fertility Societies] Surveillance '01," *Fertility and Sterility* 76 (5 Supplement 2; November 2001), S5–S36.

Klein, Renate D. "IVF Research: A Question of Feminist Ethics." *Issues in Reproductive and Genetic Engineering* 3 (1990), 243–51.

Lee, Ellie, ed. *Abortion Law and Politics Today.* New York: St. Martin's Press, 1998.

Rothman, Barbara Katz. "Not All That Glitters Is Gold." *Hastings Center Report* 22, supplement (July-August 1992), S11–S15.

Stephenson, Patricia, and Wagner, Marsden G., eds. *Tough Choices: In Vitro Fertilization and the Reproductive Technologies.* Philadelphia: Temple University Press, 1994.

Ten Have, Henk A. M. J., and Sass, Hans-Martin, eds. *Consensus Formation in Healthcare Ethics.* London: Kluwer Academic, 1998.

Tennessee Supreme Court. *Davis v. Davis. Southwestern Reporter,* SW.2d 842, 588–604 (1992).

Tong, Rosemarie. "Nonfeminist and Feminist Perspectives on Artificial Insemination and In-Vitro Fertilization." In Rosemary Tong, ed., *Feminist Approaches to Bioethics: Theoretical Reflections and Practical Applications.* Boulder, CO: Westview Press, 1997, 156–86, 261–65.

United Kingdom Human Fertilisation and Embryology Authority. *The Patients' Guide to IVF [In Vitro Fertilization] Clinics.* London: HFEA, 2000. Available online at www.hfea.gov.uk

U.S. Centers for Disease Control and Prevention; American Society for Reproductive Medicine and Society for Assisted Reproductive Technology; and RESOLVE. *1999 Assisted Reproductive Technology Success Rates.* 3 vols. Atlanta: CDC, December 2001.

Van der Wilt, Gert Jan. "Health Care and the Principle of Fair Equality of Opportunity: A Report from the Netherlands." *Bioethics* 8 (1994), 329–49.

SURROGATE PARENTING ARRANGEMENTS

Allen, Anita L. "Surrogacy, Slavery, and the Ownership of Life." *Harvard Journal of Law and Public Policy* 13 (1990), 139–49.

American College of Obstetricians and Gynecologists, Committee on Ethics. "Ethical Issues in Surrogate Motherhood." *Women's Health Issues* 1 (1991), 129–34. See also pp. 135–60.

Anderson, Elizabeth S. "Is Women's Labor a Commodity?" *Philosophy and Public Affairs* 19 (1990), 71–92.

Arneson, Richard J. "Commodification and Commercial Surrogacy." *Philosophy and Public Affairs* 21 (1992), 132–64.

Annas, George J. "Crazy Making: Embryos and Gestational Mothers." *Hastings Center Report* 21 (January-February 1991), 35–38.

Boling, Patricia Ann. *Expecting Trouble: Surrogacy, Fetal Abuse and New Reproductive Technologies.* Scranton, PA: Westview Press, 1995.

Capron, Alexander M. "Surrogate Motherhood: Legal Issues Raised by the New Reproductive Alternatives." In Mark I. Evans, et al., eds. *Fetal Diagnosis and Therapy: Science, Ethics, and the Law.* Philadelphia: J. B. Lippincott, 1989, 372–86.

———. "Whose Child Is This?" *Hastings Center Report* 21 (November-December 1991), 37–38.

———, and Radin, Margaret Jane. "Choosing Family Law over Contract Law as a Paradigm for Surrogate Motherhood." *Law Medicine, and Health Care* 16 (1988), 34–43.

Field, Martha A. *Surrogate Motherhood: The Legal and Human Issues,* expanded ed. Cambridge, MA: Harvard University Press, 1988.

Gostin, Larry, ed. *Surrogate Motherhood: Politics and Privacy.* Bloomington, IN: Indiana University Press, 1990.

Macklin, Ruth. *Surrogates and Other Mothers: The Debates over Assisted Reproduction.* Philadelphia: Temple University Press, 1994.

New Jersey Commission on Legal and Ethical Problems in the Delivery of Health Care. *After Baby M: The Legal, Ethical and Social Dimensions of Surrogacy.* Trenton, NJ: CLEPDHC, September 1992.

New Jersey Supreme Court. *In the Matter of Baby M. Atlantic Reporter* 537 A.2d 1227 (1988).

Posner, Richard A. "The Ethics and Economics of Enforcing Contracts of Surrogate Motherhood." *Journal of Contemporary Health Law and Policy* 5 (1989), 21–29.

Purdy, Laura M. "Surrogate Mothering: Exploitation or Empowerment?" *Bioethics* 3 (1989), 18–34.

Rae, Scott B. *The Ethics of Commercial Surrogate Motherhood: Brave New Families?* Westport, CT: Praeger, 1994.

Rothenberg, Karen H. "Gestational Surrogacy and the Health Care Provider: Put Part of the 'IVF Genie' Back in the Bottle." *Law, Medicine and Health Care* 18 (1990), 345–52.

Satz, Debra. "Markets in Women's Reproductive Labor." *Philosophy and Public Affairs* 21 (1992), 107–31.

Shapiro, Michael H. "How (Not) to Think about Surrogacy and Other Reproductive Innovations." *University of San Francisco Law Review* 28 (1994), 647–80.

Tong, Rosemarie. "Feminist and Nonfeminist Perspectives on Surrogacy." In Rosemary Tong, ed., *Feminist Approaches to Bioethics: Theoretical Reflections and Practical Applications.* Boulder, CO: Westview Press, 1997, 187–212, 266–68.

———. "Reproductive Technologies: V. Surrogacy." In Warren Thomas Reich, ed., *Encyclopedia of Bioethics,* rev. ed. New York: Simon & Schuster Macmillan, 1995, 2225–29.

Wadlington, Walter J. "Baby M: Catalyst for Family Law Reform?" *Journal of Contemporary Health Law and Policy* 5 (1989), 1–20.

Wertheimer, Alan. "Commercial Surrogacy." In Alan Wertheimer, ed., *Exploitation.* Princeton: Princeton University Press, 1996: 96–122.

REPRODUCTIVE CLONING

Andrews, Lori B. "Mom, Dad, Clone: Implications for Reproductive Privacy." *Cambridge Quarterly for Healthcare Ethics* 7 (1998), 176–86.

Boylan, Michael, and Brown, Kevin E. *Genetic Engineering: Science and Ethics on the New Frontier.* Upper Saddle River, NJ: Pearson Education, 2001.

Brannigan, Michael C. *Ethical Issues in Human Cloning.* New York: Seven Bridges Press, 2000.

Callahan, Daniel. "Cloning: Then and Now." *Cambridge Quarterly for Healthcare Ethics* 7 (1998), 141–44.

Chambers, Jean H. "May a Woman Clone Herself?" *Cambridge Quarterly of Healthcare Ethics* 10 (2001), 194–204.

Cohen, Cynthia B. "Ethical Issues in Embryonic Stem Cell

Research." *Journal of the American Medical Association* 285 (2001), 1439–40.

Cole-Turner, Ronald, ed. *Beyond Cloning: Religion and the Remaking of Humanity.* Harrisburg, PA: Trinity Press International, 2000.

———, ed. *Human Cloning: Religious Reponses.* Louisville: Westminster John Knox Press, 1997.

Dudley, William. *Ethics of Human Cloning.* Farmington Hills, MI: Gale Group, 2001.

Editors of *Scientific American. Understanding Cloning.* New York: Warner Books, 2002.

Eiseman, Elisa. "Cloning, Policy Issues." In Thomas H. Murray and Maxwell J. Mehlman, eds., *Encyclopedia of Ethical, Legal, and Policy Issues in Biotechnology.* 2 vols. New York: John Wiley & Sons, 2000, 157–72.

Fitzgerald, Kevin T. "Human Cloning: Analysis and Evaluation." *Cambridge Quarterly for Healthcare Ethics* 7 (1998), 218–22.

Hanna, Kathi E. "Cloning, Overview of Human Cloning." In Thomas H. Murray and Maxwell J. Mehlman, eds., *Encyclopedia of Ethical, Legal, and Policy Issues in Biotechnology.* 2 vols. New York: John Wiley & Sons, 2000, 148–57.

Harris, John. "Cloning and Human Dignity." *Cambridge Quarterly for Healthcare Ethics* 7 (1998), 163–67.

———. *Clones, Genes, and Immortality: Ethics and the Genetic Revolution.* Oxford: Oxford University Press, 1998.

Humber, James M., and Almeder, Robert F., eds. *Biomedical Ethics Reviews: Human Cloning.* Totowa, NJ: Humana Press, 1998.

Kaebnick, Gregory E. and Murray, Thomas H. "Cloning." In Ruth Chadwick, ed., *The Concise Encyclopedia of the Ethics of New Technologies.* San Diego: Academic Press, 2001, 51–64.

Kass, Leon R, and Wilson, James Q. *The Ethics of Human Cloning.* Washington, DC: American Enterprise Institute (AEI) Press, 1998.

Kimbrell, Andrew. *The Human Body Shop: The Engineering and Marketing of Life.* Washington, DC: Renery, 1998.

Klotzko, Arlene Judith, ed. *The Cloning Sourcebook.* New York: Oxford University Press, 2001.

Kolata, Gina. *Clone: The Road to Dolly, and the Path Ahead.* New York: William Morrow, 1998.

MacKinnon, Barbara, ed. *Human Cloning: Science, Ethics, and Public Policy.* Urbana, IL: University of Illinois Press, 2000.

McGee, Glenn. *The Perfect Baby: Parenthood in the New World of Cloning and Genetics.* 2d ed. Lanham, MD: Rowman and Littlefield, 2000.

———, ed. *The Human Cloning Debate.* 2d ed. Berkeley: Berkeley Hills Books, 2000.

National Research Council, *Scientific and Medical Aspects of Human Reproductive Cloning.* Washington, DC: National Academy Press, 2002.

Nussbaum, Martha C., and Sunstein, Cass R., eds. *Clones and Clones: Facts and Fantasies about Human Cloning.* New York: W. W. Norton, 1998.

Pence, Gregory E. *Who's Afraid of Human Cloning?* Lanham, MD: Rowman and Littlefield, 1998.

———, ed. *Flesh of My Flesh: The Ethics of Cloning Humans: A Reader.* Lanham, MD: Rowman and Littlefield, 1998.

Rantala, M. L., and Milgram, Arthur J., eds. *Cloning: For and Against.* Chicago: Carus, 1998.

Shostak, Stanley. *Becoming Immortal: Combining Cloning and Stem-Cell Therapy.* Albany, NY: State University of New York Press, 2001.

Silver, Lee M. "Cloning, Ethics, and Religion." *Cambridge Quarterly of Healthcare Ethics* 7 (1998), 168–72.

———. *Remaking Eden: How Genetic Engineering and Cloning Will Transform the American Family.* New York: Avon Books, 1998.

Stock, Gregory, and Campbell, John, eds. *Engineering the Human Germline: An Exploration of the Science and Ethics of Altering the Genes We Pass to Our Children.* New York: Oxford University Press, 2000.

Sunstein, Cass R., and Nussbaum, Martha, eds. *Clones and Clones: Facts and Fantasies about Human Cloning.* New York: W. W. Norton, 1998.

U.S. National Bioethics Advisory Commission. *Cloning Human Beings: Report and Recommendations of the National Bioethics Advisory Commission.* Rockville, MD: The Commission, June 1997.

Wakayama, T., et al. "Full-Term Development of Mice from Enucleated Oocytes Injected with Cumulus Cell Nuclei." *Nature* 394 (1998), 369–74.

Willgoos, Christine. "FDA Regulation: An Answer to the Questions of Human Cloning and Germline Gene Therapy." *American Journal of Law and Medicine* 27 (2001), 101–24.

Wilmut, Ian, et al. *The Second Creation: Dolly and the Age of Biological Control.* Cambridge, MA: Harvard University Press, 2001.

Wilmut, I., et al. "Viable Offspring Derived from Fetal and Adult Mammalian Cells." *Nature* 385 (1997), 810–13.

Winston, Robert. "The Promise of Cloning for Human Medicine." *British Medical Journal* 314 (1997), 913–14.

HUMAN EMBRYONIC STEM CELL RESEARCH

Capron, Alexander M. "Stem Cells: Ethics, Law and Politics." *Biotechnology Law Report* 20 (2001), 678–99.

Cohen, Cynthia B. "Ethical Issues in Embryonic Stem Cell Research." *Journal of the American Medical Association* 285 (2001), 1439–40.

Colman, Alan and Burley, Justine C. "A Legal and Ethical Tightrope." *EMBO Reports* 2 (2001), 2–5.

Green, Ronald M. *The Human Embryo Research Debates: Bioethics in the Vortex of Controversy.* New York: Oxford University Press, 2001.

———. "Human Subjects Research, Ethics, Research on Human Embryos." In Thomas H. Murray and Maxwell J. Mehlman, eds., *Encyclopedia of Ethical, Legal, and Policy Issues in Biotechnology.* 2 vols. New York: John Wiley & Sons, 2000, 630–41.

Holland, Suzanne, Lebacqz, Karen, and Zoloth, Laurie, eds. *The Human Embryonic Stem Cell Debate: Science, Ethics, and Public Policy.* Cambridge, MA: MIT Press, 2001.

Human Embryo Research. Farmington Hills, MI: Greenhaven Press, 2002.

National Research Council and the Institute of Medicine. *Stem Cells and the Future of Regenerative Medicine.* Washington, DC: National Academy Press, 2002.

Shostak, Stanley. *Becoming Immortal: Combining Cloning and Stem-Cell Therapy.* Albany, NY: State University of New York Press, 2001.

Singer, Peter, et al., eds. *Embryo Experimentation: Ethical, Legal and Social Issues.* New York: Cambridge University Press, 1990.

U.K., Department of Health, *Stem Cell Research: Medical Progress with Responsibility* (A Report from the Chief Medical Officer's

Expert Group Reviewing the Potential of Developments in Stem Cell Research and Cell Nuclear Replacement to Benefit Human Health). London: Department of Health, June 2000.

U.K., Parliament, House of Lords, Select Committee, Session 2001-02. *Stem Cell Research: Report from the Select Committee.* London: The Stationery Office, Limited, February 13, 2002. [HL Paper 83(i)].

REGULATING ASSISTED REPRODUCTION

Annas, George J. "The Shadowlands—Secrets, Lies, and Assisted Reproduction." *New England Journal of Medicine* 339 (1998), 935–39.

Charo, R. Alta. "Reproductive Technologies: VIII. Legal and Regulatory Issues." In Warren Thomas Reich, ed. *Encyclopedia of Bioethics,* rev. ed. New York: Simon & Schuster Macmillan, 1995, 2241–48.

Cohen, Cynthia B. "Unmanaged Care: The Need to Regulate New Reproductive Technologies in the United States." *Bioethics* 11 (1997), 348–65.

Gunning, Jennifer, and English, Veronica. *Human In Vitro Fertilization: A Case Study in the Regulation of Medical Innovation.* Aldershot, Hampshire, UK: Ashgate, 1993.

New York State Task Force on Life and the Law. *Assisted Reproductive Technologies: Analysis and Recommendations for Public Policy.* New York: TFLL, 1998.

Parsi, Kayhan P. "Reproduction, Law, Regulation of Reproductive Technologies." In Thomas H. Murray and Maxwell J. Mehlman, eds., *Encyclopedia of Ethical, Legal, and Policy Issues in Biotechnology.* 2 vols. New York: John Wiley and Sons, 2000, 988–96.

U.S. Centers for Disease Control and Prevention; American Society for Reproductive Medicine and Society for Assisted Reproductive Technology; and RESOLVE. *1999 Assisted Reproductive Technology Success Rates.* 3 vols. Atlanta: CDC, December 2001.

United Kingdom Human Fertilisation and Embryology Authority. *Code of Practice.* London: HFEA, 2001.

———. *Ninth Annual Report and Accounts.* London: HFEA, 2000.

———. *The Patients' Guide to IVF [In Vitro Fertilization] Clinics.* London: HFEA, 2000.

———. *The Patients' Guide to DI [Donor Insemination].* London: HFEA, 2000.

Warnock, Mary. "The Regulation of Technology." *Cambridge Quarterly for Healthcare Ethics* 7 (1998), 173–75.

BIBLIOGRAPHIES

Goldstein, Doris Mueller. *Bioethics: A Guide to Information Sources.* Detroit: Gale Research, 1982. See under "Reproductive Technologies."

Lineback, Richard H., ed. *Philosopher's Index.* Vols. 1– . Bowling Green, OH: Philosophy Documentation Center, Bowling Green State University. Issued quarterly. See under "Artificial Insemination," "Cloning," "In Vitro Fertilization," and "Surrogates."

Walters, LeRoy, and Kahn, Tamar Joy, eds. *Bibliography of Bioethics.* Vols. 1– . Washington, DC: Kennedy Institute of Ethics, Georgetown University. Issued annually. See under "Artificial Insemination," "Cloning," "In Vitro Fertilization," "Reproduction," "Reproductive Technologies," and "Surrogate Mothers."

WORLD WIDE WEB RESOURCES

National Library of Medicine: PubMed (http://www.ncbi.nlm.nih.gov/PubMed/)

National Library of Medicine: LocatorPlus (http://locatorplus.gov/)

University Microfilms: Periodical Abstracts (http://www.umi.com/proquest)

Part V
PUBLIC HEALTH

9.
The Global AIDS Epidemic and the Threat of Bioterrorism

INTRODUCTION

Public health deals with the well-being of populations rather than with one-on-one clinical relationships. In promoting the health of entire populations, the field of public health draws upon a variety of nonbiomedical techniques—the provision of clean water for human use, the sanitary disposal of human wastes, the draining of swamps to reduce the incidence of mosquito-borne infections, and the promotion of clean air standards to prevent respiratory disease. However, public health also employs biomedical tools—for example, childhood immunizations to prevent infectious diseases and newborn screening to detect and treat several rare genetic disorders.

The modern public health movement had its beginnings in Germany in the eighteenth century. In the nineteenth century, governments in Germany, France, Britain, and the United States undertook a variety of measures to promote the health of their populations. The close association of government with public health had the advantage of efficiency: Joint efforts by national and state health officials could reach entire populations and provide group benefits that individual initiatives by citizens and physicians could not easily provide. At the same time, however, the involvement of government in public health carried with it the ever-present possibility that the coercive power of the state would be employed to enforce the compliance even of unwilling citizens.

The current chapter explores two sample issues in the field of public health: the global AIDS epidemic and a more recent public concern, the threat of bioterrorism. As we shall see, the attempt to control and eventually to defeat the current epidemic of HIV infection and AIDS involves both governments and international public health agencies like the World Health Organization. At the same time, the decisions of individuals about their sexual behavior and their injection drug use will have a major impact on the long-term course of the epidemic. In the AIDS epidemic, the tension between individual liberty and state coercion has generally been resolved in favor of liberty, although the legal duty to warn unsuspecting sexual partners and the mandatory testing of newborn infants for HIV infection represent exceptions to this rule. The threat of bioterrorism, made much more vivid in the United States by the mailing of envelopes laced with anthrax spores, seems much less amenable to individual initiative. Governments, including their intelligence agencies, are in the forefront of the battle against what might be called "public health in reverse." The commentaries on appropriate responses to this threat reveal fundamental differences in the attempt to balance liberty and safety.

GENERAL ISSUES IN THE AIDS EPIDEMIC

No public health problem of the twenty-first century is as threatening to human welfare as the global epidemic of AIDS. From small beginnings in a few sites about 1980, this epidemic has spread to every continent on earth. By early 1992, almost 13 million people worldwide were infected with the human immunodeficiency virus (HIV), the virus that causes AIDS. Of these 13 million people, almost 3 million were estimated to have advanced to the end stage of HIV infection, the life-threatening clinical diagnosis of AIDS.[1] At the end of 1997, updated and more precise figures on the extent of the epidemic were collected by the Joint United Nations Programme on HIV/AIDS (UNAIDS) and the World Health Organization (WHO). These two public health agencies reported that 30.6 million people were living with HIV infection or AIDS in 1997. Of these, an estimated 21 million resided in sub-Saharan Africa.[2] By December 2001, these numbers had grown to an estimated 40 million people with HIV infection or AIDS, with more than 28 million of this total number living in sub-Saharan Africa.[3] An additional 25 million people have probably died in the epidemic.[4]

How is this virus transmitted, and why has the epidemic been so difficult to control? The simplest answer is that HIV infection is predominantly a sexually transmitted disease. Thus, it is associated with one of the strongest drives in human beings and with a sphere of behavior that is both intimate and private in most people's lives. There are, of course, other sexually transmitted diseases, but the ingenuity of twentieth-century medicine has provided effective treatments for bacterial diseases like syphilis and gonorrhea, if they are diagnosed early, and has helped people who contract genital herpes to cope with the discomfort of that chronic viral infection. Unlike these sexually transmitted diseases, however, HIV infection is at present incurable and uncontrollable. Its long-term effect, over the course of ten to twenty years, is to weaken the infected person's immune system until he or she becomes susceptible to a life-threatening secondary infection.

There are, to be sure, nonsexual modes of transmission for this potent virus. For example, in the early years of the epidemic, many hemophiliacs were infected through their use of clotting factor made from the blood products of HIV-infected people. Similarly, several thousand patients were infected through receiving HIV-infected blood transfusions. These modes of transmission have virtually ceased in industrialized countries because of reliable tests for antibody to the virus in blood and new methods of treating clotting factor that kill the virus. Still important as a mode of infection in some countries is the sharing of needles among injecting drug users. Because injecting drug use occurs despite being illegal in most of these countries, and because some injecting drug users are addicted to the drugs they inject, this mode of transmission is also quite difficult to control. A final important mode of transmission is from pregnant women to the fetuses they are carrying. In the United States the rate of maternal-fetal transmission is approximately 25 percent.

The essay by Anthony Fauci, Director of the U.S. National Institute of Allergy and Infectious Diseases, provides an overview of the AIDS epidemic near the turn of the century. According to Fauci, the best scientific evidence suggests that the most prevalent strain of the human immunodeficiency virus (HIV) "jumped" from a subspecies of chimpanzees to human beings—most probably in central-west Africa and perhaps fifty years ago.[5] Migrations, contact with multiple sexual partners, and international travel undoubtedly helped to spread HIV infection, which became visible in the United States only in 1981. Fauci notes that the AIDS epidemic is out of control and that no definitive path toward bringing the worldwide epidemic under control is currently on the horizon. Individual actions like safer sexual practices and public-health initiatives like needle-exchange programs have helped to slow the rate at which the infection is spreading in numerous settings, and combinations of antiretroviral drugs have prolonged survival and improved the quality of life for HIV-infected people who have access to such drugs. The most striking success of biomedical research in preventing HIV transmission has been the demonstration that antiretroviral drugs to pregnant women and to their newborn infants can reduce the incidence of HIV infection by two-thirds. In the long-term future the world awaits the development of a vaccine against HIV. However, as Fauci admits, the short-term prospects for an effective vaccine are virtually nil.

The selections provided by the UNAIDS program and Peter Lamptey present a picture of almost-unrelenting pessimism about the future of the epidemic, especially in the Third World. Lamptey asserts that the AIDS epidemic "is likely to surpass the Black Death as the worst pandemic ever." Yet the UNAIDS update sees signs of hope and highlights both international and national initiatives that may at least alleviate some of the consequences of the epidemic during the next decade.

With the essay by Lawrence Gostin and David Webber, the reader enters a rather different world—the U.S. setting in which the AIDS epidemic is increasingly concentrated among men who have sex with men, intravenous drug users, prisoners, and people living in urban poverty. Gostin and Webber illustrate the delicate balance that exists in the United States between civil liberties and the public good. They also note that people with HIV infection and AIDS have no guarantee of access to health care under existing U.S. law.

AIDS, JUSTICE, AND PUBLIC HEALTH

The three short essays in this section describe a yawning economic gap between the haves and the have-nots, which in many cases reflects a stark contrast between nations in the northern and southern hemispheres. Gavin Yamey and William Rankin express hope that a United Nations initiative on AIDS announced in 2001 will bear fruit. They argue that wealthy nations whose aggregate national income recently exceeded $21 trillion should be able to fund an initiative estimated to cost $7–10 billion per year. Yamey and Rankin are joined by Donald Berwick in their plea for reduced prices by pharmaceutical companies for the drugs needed to treat people with AIDS and to reduce the rate of perinatal transmission.

From their locations in London and Cape Town, Dorothy Logie and Solomon Benatar urge the wealthy nations to consider especially the plight of sub-Saharan Africa. This continent contains thirty-three of the world's fifty poorest countries. According to the authors, the AIDS epidemic should be seen in the context of international economic factors that make an effective medical and public-health response virtually impossible. These factors include accumulated debt to First World countries, economic adjustment policies required by the World Bank, falling foreign aid, a brain drain from Africa to wealthy nations, and the financial and human devastation caused by years of war on the continent. Despite all these challenges and problems, Logie and Benatar express "cautious Afro-optimism."

THE DUTY TO WARN AND THE DUTY NOT TO HARM

The duty to warn and the duty not to harm apply not just to health professionals, but to everyone. The authors of the three essays in the third part of this chapter examine the moral obligations of actual or potential sexual partners to each other. Charles Erin and John Harris argue the provocative thesis that anyone who knows that he or she is HIV positive, or has reason to think that he or she may be HIV positive, "has a moral duty to forewarn prospective partners of his [or her] HIV status and is responsible for their fate if he [or she] does not do so." The authors go on to argue that people who deliberately transmit HIV infection to sexual partners are guilty of committing a serious moral wrong and probably a crime, as well—the crime of reckless endangerment. Erin and Harris, however, argue on one hand against the criminalization of either offense, in part on grounds that enforcement of the law would be infeasible. On the other hand, to promote the full disclosure to potential sexual partners that they recommend, the authors argue for strong legal guarantees of protection against discrimination for people who fulfill their moral duty to disclose.

Writing seven years after the Erin-Harris essay was published, Rebecca Bennett, Heather Draper, and Lucy Frith disagree with the principal thesis of Erin and Harris. In their view, given the general social awareness that HIV infection can be sexually transmitted, even the HIV-positive person has no general duty to disclose his or her HIV status to possible sexual partners. Bennett, Draper, and Frith go on to develop a nuanced evaluation of different levels of risk and different levels of trust that can exist in sexual activities and relationships. They conclude by arguing that in extreme cases of reckless endangerment, where a victim has been both wronged and harmed by a sexual partner, criminal sanctions are appropriate.

The essay by Andrea Carlson Gielen and colleagues surveys the experiences of 257 HIV-infected women attending community and clinic sites in Baltimore, Maryland. More than 90 percent of the women surveyed were African-American, and fewer than half had completed a twelfth-grade education. According to the researchers, a substantial number of women had experienced negative social consequences because of their HIV-positive status: 24 percent reported the loss of friends, 23 percent had been insulted, and 21 percent had been rejected by their families. Ten of the women (or 4 percent) reported experiencing physical violence because of their infections. The authors conclude that policies on partner notification and the care of women at risk for domestic violence should be carefully tailored to individual situations.

TESTING AND SCREENING PROGRAMS

The essays in this section ask the questions: Under what circumstances should individuals be tested for HIV infection (through an antibody test), and should such testing be mandatory or voluntary? Debate about these questions has been a central feature of the AIDS policy discussion since a reasonably accurate antibody test became available in mid-1985. Note that the answers to the questions depend in part on the facts about how HIV infection is transmitted. That is, if HIV infection were transmitted through the air like the common cold or influenza, the risk of horizontal transmission to bystanders and casual acquaintances would be considerably higher and the argument for widespread testing and screening correspondingly stronger. In addition, the facts about whether an effective treatment—or, in the case of vertical transmission from pregnant woman to fetus, a preventive intervention—exists may also influence one's judgments about the moral justification for testing and screening programs.

The first two essays in this part focus on proposals to screen pregnant women for HIV infection. As the excerpt from the Institute of Medicine (IOM) committee report indicates, the shape of the ethical questions surrounding prenatal HIV testing was radically changed by the decisive results of a randomized, placebo-controlled clinical trial. In November 1994, AIDS researchers reported that treatment of pregnant women and newborn infants with AZT (also called Zidovudine) reduced the rate of HIV infection in the infants by two-thirds—from 25.5 percent to 8.3 percent.[6] This clinical result was the most dramatic success story in the AIDS epidemic until that time. The question therefore arose: Should all pregnant women be required to be tested for HIV infection? In 1999, the members of the IOM committee appointed to study this topic recommended that all pregnant women be tested for HIV infection, "with patient notification, as a routine component of prenatal care." This policy can be justified on the basis of justice (the equal treatment of all pregnant women) and beneficence (the probable discovery of HIV-infected pregnant women who would not otherwise have known that they are infected). However, the relationship of the proposed IOM committee policy to the ethical principle of respect for the autonomy of persons is more problematic.

Bernard Lo, Leslie Wolf, and Sohini Sengupta subject the IOM recommendations to a searching ethical review. The authors begin by pointing out that in most clinical settings patients "opt in" when they decide to undergo a test, rather than having to "opt out" of a test that will be done unless one clearly and explicitly refuses the test in advance. Lo and colleagues go on to identify several unanswered questions about the proposed new policy. For example, what are the actual preferences of pregnant women about prenatal HIV testing? Do pregnant women understand that they may refuse the test? And would an HIV-positive pregnant women be coerced to accept drug therapy for the sake of the fetus she is carrying? At the end of their essay, the authors tentatively accept the proposed policy, subject to the proviso that its consequences in practice should be further studied. They also argue that the unique circumstances of HIV transmission from pregnant woman to fetus are not parallel in any other clinical setting and that the extraordinary policies recommended for this setting should not be extended to other settings.

The essay by Stephen Morin adopts a more descriptive approach, surveying trends in HIV testing during the late 1990s. On the issues of confidentiality, name-based reporting, mandatory partner notification, the criminalization of an HIV-positive person's "willful exposure" of others to harm, the public health rationale has increasingly taken precedence over concerns about the protection of individual privacy and autonomy. Like Lo and colleagues, Erin recommends that the actual effect of these increasingly coercive policies be carefully evaluated.

AIDS VACCINE TRIALS

The two essays in this short section seek to anticipate ethical questions that, for the most part, lie in the future. As noted by Anthony Fauci, the task of developing a vaccine against AIDS is a major scientific and medical challenge, in part because the virus mutates rapidly and in part because it attacks a critical part of the human immune system. By early 2002, only a few large-scale (Phase III) AIDS trials had been conducted, and none had been unambiguously successful.

The essay by Dale Guenter, Jose Esparza, and Ruth Macklin summarizes the outcome of a multi-year consultative process sponsored by the Joint United Nations Programme on HIV/AIDS (UNAIDS). Reiterating themes introduced earlier in this chapter by Logie and Benatar, the three authors reject the language of "developed" and "developing" countries in favor of identifying social and economic factors that "influence the degree of vulnerability of the prospective subject population to exploitation or harm." The authors of this document clearly want to avoid any selection of subjects that is based simply on the convenience of wealthy countries or of companies seeking to gain approval for the vaccines that they have produced. However, settings in which the prevalence of HIV is high—on the order of 20–30 percent among young adults—have the most to gain from the development of an effective vaccine. All participants in the consultation process were agreed that HIV-negative participants in vaccine trials must be counseled about how to reduce their risk of acquiring HIV infection, even though the risk-reducing measures may extend the trials and reduce the differences in outcome between or among treatment groups. Particularly contentious issues were the availability of expensive therapies to subjects who become infected during the course of vaccine trials and the moral and legal obligations of trial sponsors to provide the vaccine to host countries at reasonable cost after the conclusion of a trial.

From their vantage point in South Africa, Malegapuru William Makgoba and his colleagues express the hope that an effective vaccine against AIDS will be available within seven to ten years. The authors urge the establishment of private-public partnerships in the effort to speed vaccine development. At the same time, however, they clearly want to set limits on the ability of commercial firms to profit from their success. When a successful vaccine is developed, the authors argue, there will still be questions of access to the vaccine and its potential utility against multiple subtypes of HIV. Makgoba and colleagues express the hope that one day HIV infection will be overcome as smallpox and polio have been conquered by biomedical technology.

THE THREAT OF BIOTERRORISM

The final section of this chapter would not have been included had this sixth edition been prepared a year earlier. In the fall of 2001, citizens and public officials in the United States found themselves confronted by a problem that until then had seemed distant and theoretical. An unknown person, presumably either a terrorist or a sociopath, sought to infect members of the news media and members of the U.S. Congress through mailing lethal anthrax spores to their offices. This unprecedented attack, at least for the United States, has focused national attention on the threat that public health in reverse—either through bioterrorism or biological warfare—could pose to the citizens of any targeted nation.

The first two essays in this section describe the biological agents that are most likely to be used by bioterrorists. Even before the autumn of 2001, U.S. public health expert Donald Henderson had been warning that smallpox and anthrax posed the most important threats to civilian populations. In their essay, British researchers Robert Spencer and Nigel Lightfoot provide a comparison of the number of civilian lives likely to be lost in case of attacks with nuclear, chemical, and biological weapons. The authors recommend a combination of responses to the bioterrorism threat—international agreements, disarmament programs, improved detection systems, and vaccines and/or antidotes for the protection of civilian populations.

The final three essays explore how public health law have been affected by, and may be applied in response to, biological terrorism or biological warfare. Joseph Barbera and colleagues discuss the circumstances under which large-scale quarantine would be justified in the case of a major attack with biological weapons. The authors review historical examples of quarantine and propose guidelines that, in their view, would be both effective and nondiscriminatory. In the final two essays of this book, lawyers Lawrence Gostin and George Annas provide contrasting assessments of a Model State Emergency Health Powers Act developed by Gostin and his colleagues in 2001. Both authors agree on the importance of strengthening a public-health infrastructure that has been neglected and underfunded by the U.S. federal government for many years. In other respects, however, the views of Gostin and Annas are diametrically opposed, with Gostin giving precedence to the prevention of harm while Annas accents the primacy of individual liberty in a constitutional society.

L.W.

NOTES

1. For further details on these estimates, see Jonathan Mann, Daniel J. M. Tarantola, and Thomas W. Netter, eds., *AIDS in the World* (Cambridge, MA: Harvard University Press, 1992).

2. United Nations Joint Programme on HIV/AIDS and World Health Organization, *Report on the Global HIV/AIDS Epidemic, June 1998* (Geneva: UNAIDS/WHO, 1998), 6.

3. Joint United Nations Programme on HIV/AIDS and World Health Organization, *AIDS Epidemic Update: 2001* (Geneva: UNAIDS and WHO, December 2001), 3.

4. Peter R. Lamptey, "Reducing Heterosexual Transmission of AIDS in Poor Countries," *British Medical Journal* 324 (January 26, 2002), 207–11 [reprinted in this chapter].

5. See also Feng Gao et al., "Origin of HIV-1 in the Chimpanzee *Pan troglodytes troglodytes*," *Nature* 397 (February 4, 1999), 436–41.

6. Edward M. Connor et al., "Reduction of Maternal-Infant Transmission of Human Immunodeficiency Virus Type 1 with Zidovudine Treatment: Pediatric AIDS Clinical Trials Group Protocol 076 Study Group," *New England Journal of Medicine* 331 (November 3, 1994), 1173–80.

General Issues in the AIDS Epidemic

ANTHONY S. FAUCI

The AIDS Epidemic: Considerations for the 21st Century

Anthony S. Fauci is Director of the National Institute of Allergy and Infectious Diseases at the National Institutes of Health. He has made many contributions to basic and clinical research into immune-mediated disease. His main research interests lie in understanding the mechanisms of HIV infection and the body's response to AIDS. He is a member of the National Academy of Sciences, the American Philosophical Society, and the Institute of Medicine of the National Academy of Sciences.

Humankind has been besieged throughout its evolution by microorganisms that pose a continual challenge to the survival of the species.[1] Although such ancient killers as tuberculosis and malaria persistently take a toll of millions of lives per year, occasionally the emergence or reemergence of a microbe results in an unexpected, catastrophic pandemic with global public health consequences. As we prepare to leave the 20th century, it is worth reflecting on the fact that within the framework of an enormous but constant burden of a variety of infectious diseases, as well as a number of mini-epidemics, this century has witnessed two such unexpected cataclysmic events.

One, the influenza A pandemic of 1918, was due to an old, but reemerging microbe. Influenza had been a problem for centuries, but in that one winter of 1918–1919, it was responsible for the deaths of approximately 25 million people worldwide and 550,000 people in the United States.[2]

The other pandemic, the acquired immunodeficiency syndrome (AIDS), is due to a newly recognized microbe, the human immunodeficiency virus (HIV).[3] The world first became aware of this new disease in the summer of 1981, and it has exploded in successive waves in various regions of the world. Still, as we enter the 21st century, the catastrophic

Reprinted with permission from the *New England Journal of Medicine,* 341 (September 30, 1999), 1046–50. Copyright © 1999 by the Massachusetts Medical Society.

potential of the pandemic may still not have been fully realized. As we prepare to enter the new millennium, it is appropriate to reflect on the origins of this epidemic, what has occurred over the past 18 years, what has been accomplished from a scientific and public health perspective, and what the prospects are for the future.

THE ORIGINS OF HIV

Recent molecular epidemiologic data have clearly indicated that HIV type 1 (HIV-1) evolved with the *Pan troglodytes troglodytes* subspecies of chimpanzee and was present in that subspecies for centuries.[4] The virus apparently does not readily cause disease in the chimpanzee. As is the case with many viruses, HIV at a particular point (or points) in time "jumped" species to infect human beings; hence, it almost certainly originated as a zoonotic infection. HIV type 2, the less prevalent and less virulent species of HIV, is remarkably similar genetically to the simian immunodeficiency virus that is endemic among sooty mangabeys.[5]

The most likely mechanism of transmission of HIV-1 from chimpanzees to humans was by contamination of a person's open wound with the infected blood of a chimpanzee, probably when the chimpanzee was being butchered for the purposes of consumption.[6] Chimpanzees have traditionally served as a source of nutrition for humans in certain parts of sub-Saharan Africa. Any of a number of mutations in the viral genome that would have allowed successful transmission of the virus from chimpanzees to humans probably took place intermittently over the centuries.[4] Indeed, it is likely that sporadic cases of transmission to humans were continually occurring unnoticed over the course of decades, and perhaps centuries.

As with other microbes, transmission may not result in an epidemic unless certain conditions are present.[1] An intermittent HIV infection in a rural village in Africa might have been passed on to an infected person's sexual partner and would probably have resulted in the deaths of the infected persons without further spread, thus representing a dead end for the virus. Only when demographic and social conditions allowed rapid spread of the virus among people did an epidemic actually begin to emerge. These conditions included massive migration from rural areas to urban areas; the breakup of family units due to the migratory nature of employment opportunities, with its attendant sexual promiscuity and extensive frequenting of commercial sex workers; and contamination of the blood supply.[7]

Such were the seeds of the epidemic in Africa. The introduction of the epidemic to developed countries, such as the United States, followed relatively soon after the "gay revolution" that had its origins in the riot at the Stonewall Inn, a bar frequented by homosexual men, in New York City in 1969.[8] The demographic setting of the high-risk homosexual practices that were concentrated in cities such as New York, San Francisco, and Los Angeles in the 1970s and early 1980s unfortunately made this population of predominantly young adults a perfect target for an epidemic of sexually transmitted disease. Similar patterns soon followed in other developed countries, such as Canada, Australia, and those of western Europe.

SCOPE OF THE EPIDEMIC

AIDS continues to exact an enormous toll throughout the world, in both human and economic terms. In the United States, an estimated 650,000 to 900,000 people are infected with HIV,[9] of whom more than 200,000 are unaware of their infection.[10] Through 1998, 688,200 cumulative cases of AIDS and 410,800 AIDS-related deaths had been reported to the Centers for Disease Control and Prevention (CDC).[11]

The demographic characteristics of those affected by the epidemic have changed dramatically since the first cases were reported in 1981. Unlike the early days of the HIV and AIDS epidemic in the United States, when the affected population consisted overwhelmingly of homosexual men, leading some to assume incorrectly that the epidemic would remain contained within the gay population, today new cases of HIV infection result predominantly from injection-drug use and heterosexual contact, with a disproportionate representation among minority populations.[11] The numbers of cases of AIDS (per 100,000 population) reported in 1998 in the United States were 66.4 for non-Hispanic blacks, 28.1 for Hispanics, 8.2 for non-Hispanic whites, 7.4 for American Indians and Alaska Natives, and 3.8 for Asians and Pacific Islanders. Women are increasingly affected; the proportion of U.S. cases reported among women and adolescent girls more than tripled between 1985 and 1998, from 7 percent to 23 percent.[11]

It is often said that the HIV and AIDS epidemic in the United States and other developed countries has reached a plateau, since the number of new infections per year is no longer on an accelerating trajectory but has leveled off. However, in the United States it is estimated that this plateau has reached an unacceptable level of 40,000 new infections per year, a rate that is believed to have remained relatively constant throughout the 1990s.[12] Of these newly infected people, the CDC estimates that half are younger than 25 years of age and were infected sexually.[13] As the number of new cases per year among homosexual men has decreased dramatically, the number of new infections among heterosexuals, particularly among women, has accelerated greatly, producing a deceptive plateau. In the United States we are in fact seeing new waves of the epidemic among different demographic groups.

The same phenomenon of successive waves is reflected dramatically in the global pattern of the epidemic, with sub-Saharan Africa currently bearing the greatest burden of the epidemic worldwide.[14] In addition, the number of HIV infections in the countries of the former Soviet Union has escalated sharply over the past few years.[14] However, the trajectory of the infection rate in the Indian subcontinent and Southeast Asia indicates that without dramatically successful preventive measures, these regions will bear the greatest burden of the epidemic as we enter the 21st century.[14] The estimated number of infections in China is still relatively low; however, there is potential for an explosive spread of HIV in that nation of more than 1 billion people.

The magnitude of the epidemic is huge. As of the end of 1998, there were more than 33 million people worldwide with HIV infection or AIDS, 43 percent of them female, according to estimates by the Joint United Nations Programme on HIV/AIDS (UNAIDS).[14] An estimated 5.8 million new HIV infections occurred worldwide during 1998—approximately 16,000 each day. More than 95 percent of these new infections occurred in developing countries. In 1998, HIV infection or AIDS was the fourth leading cause of death worldwide, resulting in an estimated 2.3 million deaths.[15] If the current trend in the incidence of HIV infection continues, more than 40 million people will be infected with HIV as we enter the new millennium.

In addition to the enormous human tragedy associated with HIV and AIDS, the economic costs of the epidemic are staggering, posing a serious impediment to the growth and economic stability of many developing countries. It is estimated that the annual economic burden of HIV infection is $14 billion for costs associated with prevention and treatment alone.[16] In many countries, the epidemic is depleting a limited pool of skilled workers and managers and will neutralize previously realized gains in development by slashing life expectancy. According to the United Nations Population Division, by 2010 to 2015 life expectancy in the nine countries in Africa with the highest prevalence of HIV infection will fall on average by 16 years.[17] It is also clear that this epidemic will produce political instability in some nations and in communities within these nations.

THE SUCCESSES AND LIMITATIONS OF ANTIRETROVIRAL THERAPY

In the United States and other developed countries, the numbers of new AIDS diagnoses and deaths have fallen substantially during the past three years. The age-adjusted death rate from AIDS declined 48 percent from 1996 to 1997[18]; similar decreases have been noted in western Europe and Australia.[19,20] These trends are due to several factors, including improved prophylaxis against opportunistic infections and improved treatment, the growing experience among health professionals in caring for HIV-infected patients, improved access to health care, and the decrease in the number of new HIV infections due to prevention efforts and to the fact that a substantial proportion of persons with high-risk behavior are already infected.

However, the most influential factor has clearly been the increased use of potent anti-HIV drugs, generally administered in combinations of three or more agents and usually including a protease inhibitor.[19,21–23] Such combinations are known as highly active antiretroviral therapy. The development of therapies for HIV infection has been remarkably successful, reflecting an effective synergy among government, industry, and academia. Sixteen anti-HIV drugs are now licensed by the Food and Drug Administration. These drugs have had dramatic effects in reversing the extent of illness in many patients with advanced disease, as well as in preventing the progression of disease in those who are relatively healthy.

Consensus guidelines have been developed for the use of highly active antiretroviral therapy in adults and adolescents, as well as in children and in HIV-infected pregnant women.[24–26] These guidelines, when appropriately applied, have greatly improved the prognosis for HIV-infected people and have markedly reduced the risk of HIV transmission from mother to baby.

Despite the enormous beneficial effects of highly active antiretroviral therapy, many HIV-infected people have unfortunately not had adequate responses to the regimens, cannot tolerate the toxic effects, or have difficulty complying with treatment that involves large numbers of pills, myriad interactions with other drugs, and complicated dosing schedules in which intake of food and liquids must be taken into account.[24] Even in patients who are successfully treated with highly active antiretroviral therapy and have extremely low levels of HIV-1 RNA in plasma, the virus persists in sanctuaries where the drugs cannot reach it or in a latent form on which drugs have no effect.[27–30] In addition, the emergence of strains of HIV that are resistant to currently available drugs is a widespread and growing problem.[31]

Although there is evidence of improvement in immune-system function in most patients who receive combination antiretroviral therapy, complete normalization of the immune system and complete eradication of the virus from the body appear unlikely with currently available therapies. The persistence of latent HIV despite therapy that successfully suppresses detectable levels of HIV-1 RNA in plasma is particularly problematic and suggests that lifelong treatment may be necessary with drugs that are currently expensive and difficult to tolerate for prolonged periods.[32–36] In patients in whom plasma HIV-1 RNA had been suppressed by highly active antiretroviral therapy to below detectable levels for a median of 390 days, levels invariably rebounded within 3 weeks after the cessation of therapy.[37]

Therefore, the development of a new generation of therapies remains a major priority. Currently, all licensed antiretroviral medications are directed at one of two viral enzymes, reverse transcriptase or protease. Many new treatment strategies are being developed and tested, including the use of drugs that prevent the virus from entering a cell and those that prevent the integration of the provirus into nuclear DNA. In addition, approaches to purging the virus from its latent reservoirs in certain cells and tissues are being vigorously pursued, as are methods to boost HIV-specific immune responses.[38]

PREVENTION OF HIV INFECTION

In developing countries in which the per capita allocation for health care spending may be only a few dollars a year, anti-HIV therapies are invariably beyond the reach of all but the privileged few. This situation underscores the need for effective, low-cost tools for HIV prevention that can be used in these settings as well as in the United States and other developed countries. Even if such therapies were feasible on a global scale, it is clear that treatment is not the solution to the global HIV problem. Unlike microbial scourges, such as malaria and tuberculosis (among many others), for which there is very little that people can do to prevent infection, HIV infection in adults is entirely preventable by behavior modification. Researchers have shown that several approaches to prevention, when properly executed, can be effective. These approaches include education and behavior modification, the promotion and provision of condoms, the treatment of other sexually transmitted diseases, drug-abuse treatment (for example, methadone maintenance for injection-drug users), access to clean needles and syringes for injection-drug users, and the use of antiretroviral drugs to interrupt the transmission of the virus from mother to infant.[39]

The use of antiretroviral drugs in pregnant women with HIV infection and their infants is an extraordinarily successful prevention strategy.[40] The rate of mother-to-child transmission of HIV in the United States has been cut to negligible levels among women and infants treated with an extended regimen of zidovudine therapy. Recent studies by the CDC, the National Institutes of Health (NIH), and others have shown that substantially shorter regimens of antiretroviral drugs, which would be more feasible in poorer countries, can also reduce perinatal HIV transmission dramatically.[41,42] A brief and affordable regimen of therapy administered to the mother around the time of delivery could potentially prevent HIV infection in hundreds of thousands of babies per year. An interim analysis of a study in Uganda indicates that two doses of nevirapine—one given to the mother at the onset of labor and one given to the infant within 72 hours after birth—can markedly reduce the incidence of perinatal transmission of HIV.[43]

Other methods of preventing HIV transmission may also help slow the epidemic of HIV and AIDS. For example, researchers are developing and testing topical microbicides, substances that a woman could use in her vagina before sexual intercourse to prevent the transmission of HIV and other sexually transmitted diseases.[44] UNAIDS and other organizations have also facilitated the widespread use of the female condom in Africa. These interventions may help empower women to protect themselves in situations in which they are unable to avoid sexual relations with HIV-infected partners or cannot persuade their partners to use a condom. This latter issue reflects the relation between the prevention of HIV transmission and human rights that was eloquently articulated by the late Jonathan Mann.[45]

DEVELOPMENT OF AN HIV VACCINE

Historically, vaccines have provided a safe, cost-effective, and efficient means of preventing illness, disability, and death from infectious diseases.[46] The solution to the HIV pandemic is the development and availability of a safe and effective vaccine against the infection. Indeed, such a goal remains the highest priority of AIDS research. A major scientific obstacle to the accomplishment of this goal has been the difficulty in establishing the precise correlates of protective immunity against HIV infection. To speed the pace of discovery, many public and private agencies have dramatically increased the resources devoted to research on HIV vaccines. For example, at the NIH, funding for HIV-vaccine research rose from $100.5 million in fiscal year 1995 to an estimated $194.1 million in fiscal year 1999. To date, more than 3000 uninfected volunteers have enrolled in more than 50 HIV-vaccine studies sponsored by the NIH (including two phase 2 intermediate-sized trials), involving 27 vaccines.

As part of a broad portfolio of research, recent NIH-supported studies have assessed so-called vectored vaccines: harmless viruses (e.g., canarypox) that are genetically altered to make HIV proteins. These vaccines have been administered to volunteers in combination with a separate vaccine made of a purified HIV envelope protein. Results have been encouraging. In phase 1 and phase 2 studies, the combination approach has appeared safe and has evoked both cellular and humoral immune responses that may have a role in providing protection from HIV infection.[47] Three vectors, as well as other HIV proteins, are currently being compared to determine which combination produces the most vigorous immune response.

Meanwhile, a large-scale study of a vaccine based on the surface proteins of two strains of HIV was recently undertaken in the United States by a private company, with an additional phase 3 study to be conducted in Thailand.[48] Finally, a phase 1 trial of canarypox-vectored vaccine for HIV infection has been initiated in Uganda in a growing effort to involve scientists from developing countries in the research effort.

CONCLUSIONS

The HIV pandemic has posed a formidable challenge to the biomedical-research and public health communities of the world. What began as a handful of recognized cases among homosexual men in the United States has become a global pandemic of such proportions that it clearly ranks as one of the most destructive microbial scourges in history. We are at a pivotal point in the evolution of this historic event as we enter the new millennium. Biomedical research has provided the tools for the development of treatments as well as a still elusive vaccine. It has become apparent over the past few years that minimizing the destructive impact of this epidemic will require partnerships between the public and private sectors as well as a stronger political will among the nations of the world. Unless methods of prevention, with or without a vaccine, are successful, the worst of the global pandemic will occur in the 21st century.

REFERENCES

1. Krause R. M. Introduction to infectious diseases: stemming the tide. In: Krause R. M., ed. Emerging infections. New York: Academic Press, 1998: 1–22.

2. History of influenza. In: Kilbourne E. D. Influenza. New York: Plenum Medical Book, 1987:3–22.

3. Fauci A. S. The human immunodeficiency virus: infectivity and mechanisms of pathogenesis. Science 1988;239:617–22.

4. Gao F., Bailes E., Robertson D. L., et al. Origin of HIV-1 in the chimpanzee *Pan troglodytes troglodytes.* Nature 1999;397:436–41.

5. Hirsch V. M., Olmsted R. A., Murphey-Corb M., Purcell R. H., Johnson P. R. An African primate lentivirus (SIVsm) closely related to HIV-2. Nature 1989;339:389–92.

6. Weiss R. A., Wrangham R. W. From Pan to pandemic. Nature 1999;397:385–6.

7. Quinn T. C., Fauci A. S. The AIDS epidemic: demographic aspects, population biology, and virus evolution. In: Krause R. M., ed. Emerging infections. New York: Academic Press, 1998:327–63.

8. Kramer L. Reports from the holocaust: the story of an AIDS activist. London: Cassell, 1994.

9. Karon J. M., Rosenberg P. S., McQuillan G., Khare M., Gwinn M., Petersen L. R. Prevalence of HIV infection in the United States, 1984 to 1992. JAMA 1996;276:126–31.

10. Sweeney P. A., Fleming P. L., Karon J. M., Ward J. W. Minimum estimate of the number of living HIV infected persons confidentially tested in the United States. In: Program and abstracts of the Interscience Conference on Antimicrobial Agents and Chemotherapy, Toronto, September 28–October 1, 1997. Washington, D.C.: American Society for Microbiology, 1997:245. abstract.

11. HIV/AIDS surveillance report. Vol. 10. No. 2. Atlanta: Centers for Disease Control and Prevention, 1998:1–43.

12. Rosenberg P. S. Scope of the AIDS epidemic in the United States. Science 1995;270:1372–5.

13. Rosenberg P. S., Biggar R. J., Goedert J. J. Declining age

at HIV infection in the United States. N Engl J Med 1994; 330:789–90.

14. AIDS epidemic update: December, 1998. Geneva: Joint United Nations Programme on HIV/AIDS (UNAIDS), World Health Organization, 1998.

15. The world health report 1999: making a difference. Geneva: World Health Organization, 1999.

16. Removing obstacles to healthy development. Geneva: World Health Organization, 1999.

17. Department of Economic and Social Affairs of the United Nations Secretariat. The demographic impact of HIV/AIDS. New York: United Nations, 1999.

18. Hoyert D. L., Kochanek K. D., Murphy S. L. Deaths: final data for 1997. Natl Vital Stat Rep 1999;47(19):1–104.

19. Mocroft A., Vella S., Benfield T. L., et al. Changing patterns of mortality across Europe in patients infected with HIV-1. Lancet 1998;352:1725–30.

20. Dore G. J., Brown T., Tarantola D., Kaldor J. M. HIV and AIDS in the Asia-Pacific region: an epidemiological overview. AIDS 1998;12:Suppl B: S1–S10.

21. Palella F. J. Jr, Delaney K. M., Moorman A. C., et al. Declining morbidity and mortality among patients with advanced human immunodeficiency virus infection. N Engl J Med 1998; 338:853–60.

22. Vittinghoff E., Scheer S., O'Malley P., Colfax G., Holmberg S. D., Buchbinder S. P. Combination antiretroviral therapy and recent declines in AIDS incidence and mortality. J Infect Dis 1999; 179:717–20.

23. Detels R., Munoz A., McFarlane G., et al. Effectiveness of potent antiretroviral therapy on time to AIDS and death in men with known HIV infection duration. JAMA 1998;280:1497–503.

24. Guidelines for the use of antiretroviral agents in HIV-infected adults and adolescents. MMWR Morb Mortal Wkly Rep 1998;47(RR-5):43–82. (See updates at http://www.hivatis.org.)

25. Guidelines for the use of antiretroviral agents in pediatric HIV infection. MMWR Morb Mortal Wkly Rep 1998;47(RR-4): 1-43. (See updates at http://www.hivatis.org.)

26. Public Health Service Task Force recommendations for the use of antiretroviral drugs in pregnant women infected with HIV-1 for maternal health and for reducing perinatal HIV-1 transmission in the United States. MMWR Morb Mortal Wkly Rep 1998;47(RR-2):1–30. (See updates at http://www.hivatis.org.)

27. Chun T. W., Engel D., Berrey M. M., Shea T., Corey L., Fauci A. S. Early establishment of a pool of latently infected, resting CD4(+) T cells during primary HIV-1 infection. Proc Natl Acad Sci U S A 1998;95:8869–73.

28. Chun T. W., Stuyver L., Mizell S. B., et al. Presence of an inducible HIV-1 latent reservoir during highly active antiretroviral therapy. Proc Natl Acad Sci U S A 1997;94:13193–7.

29. Finzi D., Hermankova M., Pierson T., et al. Identification of a reservoir of HIV-1 in patients on highly active antiretroviral therapy. Science 1997;278:1295–300.

30. Wong J. K., Hezareh M., Gunthard H. F., et al. Recovery of replication-competent HIV despite prolonged suppression of plasma viremia. Science 1997;278:1291–5.

31. Durant J., Clevenbergh P., Halfon P., et al. Drug-resistance genotyping in HIV-1 therapy: the VIRADAPT randomised controlled trial. Lancet 1999;353:2195–9.

32. Furtado M. R., Callaway D. S., Phair J. P., et al. Persistence of HIV-1 transcription in peripheral-blood mononuclear cells in patients receiving potent antiretroviral therapy. N Engl J Med 1999;340:1614–22.

33. Zhang L., Ramratnam B., Tenner-Racz K., et al. Quantifying residual HIV-1 replication in patients receiving combination antiretroviral therapy. N Engl J Med 1999;340:1605–13.

34. Pomerantz R. J. Residual HIV-1 disease in the era of highly active antiretroviral therapy. N Engl J Med 1999;340:1672–4.

35. Finzi D., Blankson J., Siliciano J. D., et al. Latent infection of CD4+ T cells provides a mechanism for lifelong persistence of HIV-1, even in patients on effective combination therapy. Nat Med 1999;5:512–7.

36. Chun T. W., Engel D., Mizell S. B., et al. Effect of interleukin-2 on the pool of latently infected, resting CD4+ T cells in HIV-1-infected patients receiving highly active anti-retroviral therapy. Nat Med 1999;5:651–5.

37. Harrigan P. R., Whaley M., Montaner J. S. Rate of HIV-1 RNA rebound upon stopping antiretroviral therapy. AIDS 1999;13: F59–F62.

38. Cooper D. A., Emery S. Latent reservoirs of HIV infection: flushing with IL-2? Nat Med 1999;5:611–2.

39. Coates T. J., Collins C. Preventing HIV infection. Sci Am 1998;279:96–7.

40. Connor E. M., Sperling R. S., Gelber R., et al. Reduction of maternal–infant transmission of human immunodeficiency virus type 1 with zidovudine treatment. N Engl J Med 1994;331:1173–80.

41. Mofenson L. M. Short-course zidovudine for prevention of perinatal infection. Lancet 1999;353:766–7.

42. Saba J. The results of the PETRA intervention trial to prevent perinatal transmission in sub-Saharan Africa. Chicago: Foundation for Retrovirology and Human Health, 1999. (See http://www.retroconference.org/99/lect_symposia/sym_session8.htm.) (See NAPS document no. 05531 for 19 pages, c/o Microfiche Publications, 248 Hempstead Tpke., West Hempstead, NY 11552.)

43. Guay L. A., Musoke P., Fleming T., et al. Intrapartum and neonatal single-dose nevirapine compared with zidovudine for prevention of mother-to-child transmission of HIV-1 in Kampala, Uganda: HIVNET 012 randomised trial. Lancet 1999;354;795–802.

44. Elias C., Coggins C. Female-controlled methods to prevent sexual transmission of HIV. AIDS 1996;10:Suppl 3:S43–S51.

45. Mann J. M. Medicine and public health, ethics and human rights. Hastings Cent Rep 1997;27(3):6–13.

46. Folkers G. K., Fauci A. S. The role of US government agencies in vaccine research and development. Nat Med 1998;4: Suppl:491–4.

47. Evans T. G., Keefer M. C., Weinhold K. J., et al. A canarypox vaccine expressing multiple human immunodeficiency virus type 1 genes given alone or with rgp 120 elicits broad and durable CD8+ cytotoxic T lymphocyte responses in seronegative volunteers. J Infect Dis 1999;180:290–8.

48. Francis D. P., Gregory T., McElrath M. J., et al. Advancing AIDSVAX to phase 3: safety, immunogenicity, and plans for phase 3. AIDS Res Hum Retroviruses 1998;14:Suppl 3:S325–S331.

JOINT UNITED NATIONS PROGRAMME ON HIV/AIDS AND WORLD HEALTH ORGANIZATION

AIDS Epidemic Update

GLOBAL OVERVIEW

Twenty years after the first clinical evidence of acquired immunodeficiency syndrome was reported, AIDS has become the most devastating disease humankind has ever faced. Since the epidemic began, more than 60 million people have been infected with the virus. HIV/AIDS is now the leading cause of death in sub-Saharan Africa. Worldwide, it is the fourth-biggest killer.

At the end of 2001, an estimated 40 million people globally were living with HIV. In many parts of the developing world, the majority of new infections occur in young adults, with young women especially vulnerable. About one-third of those currently living with HIV/AIDS are aged 15–24. Most of them do not know they carry the virus. Many millions more know nothing or too little about HIV to protect themselves against it.

EASTERN EUROPE AND CENTRAL ASIA—STILL THE FASTEST-GROWING EPIDEMIC

Eastern Europe—especially the Russian Federation—continues to experience the fastest-growing epidemic in the world, with the number of new HIV infections rising steeply. In 2001, there were an estimated 250 000 new infections in this region, bringing to 1 million the number of people living with HIV. Given the high levels of other sexually transmitted infections, and the high rates of injecting drug use among young people, the epidemic looks set to grow considerably.

Reprinted with the permission of the Joint United Nations Programme on HIV/AIDS and the World Health Organization from *AIDS Epidemic Update: December 2001* (Geneva: UNAIDS (WHO, 2001), pp. 1–4, 7–9, and 16–18. Copyright © 2001 by UNAIDS/WHO.

ASIA AND THE PACIFIC—NARROWING WINDOWS OF OPPORTUNITY

In Asia and the Pacific, an estimated 7.1 million people are now living with HIV/AIDS. The epidemic claimed the lives of 435 000 people in the region in 2001. The apparently low national prevalence rates in many countries in this region are dangerously deceptive. They hide localized epidemics in different areas, including some of the world's most populous countries. There is a serious threat of major, generalized epidemics. But, as Cambodia and Thailand have shown, prompt, large-scale prevention programmes can hold the epidemic at bay. In Cambodia, concerted efforts, driven by strong political leadership and public commitment, lowered HIV prevalence among pregnant women to 2.3% at the end of 2000—down by almost a third from 1997.

SUB-SAHARAN AFRICA—THE CRISIS GROWS

AIDS killed 2.3 million African people in 2001. The estimated 3.4 million new HIV infections in sub-Saharan Africa in the past year mean that 28.1 million Africans now live with the virus. Without adequate treatment and care, most of them will not survive the next decade. Recent antenatal clinic data show that several parts of southern Africa have now joined Botswana with prevalence rates among pregnant women exceeding 30%. In West Africa, at least five countries are experiencing serious epidemics, with adult HIV prevalence exceeding 5%. However, HIV prevalence among adults continues to fall in Uganda, while there is evidence that prevalence among young

Table 1 Global Summary of the HIV/AIDS Epidemic, December 2001

Number of people living with HIV/AIDS	Total	40 million
	Adults	37.2 million
	Women	*17.6 million*
	Children under 15 years	2.7 million
People newly infected with HIV in 2001	Total	5 million
	Adults	4.3 million
	Women	*1.8 million*
	Children under 15 years	800 000
AIDS deaths in 2001	Total	3 million
	Adults	2.4 million
	Women	*1.1 million*
	Children under 15 years	580 000

people (especially women) is dropping in some parts of the continent.

THE MIDDLE EAST AND NORTH AFRICA—SLOW BUT MARKED SPREAD

In the Middle East and North Africa, the number of people living with HIV now totals 440 000. The epidemic's advance is most marked in countries (such as Djibouti, Somalia and the Sudan) that are already experiencing complex emergencies. While HIV prevalence continues to be low in most countries in the region, increasing numbers of HIV infections are being detected in several countries, including the Islamic Republic of Iran, the Libyan Arab Jamahiriya and Pakistan.

HIGH-INCOME COUNTRIES—RESURGENT EPIDEMIC THREATENS

A larger epidemic also threatens to develop in the high-income countries, where over 75 000 people acquired HIV in 2001, bringing to 1.5 million the total number of people living with HIV/AIDS. Recent advances in treatment and care in these countries are not being consistently matched with enough progress on the prevention front. New evidence of rising HIV infection rates in North America, parts of Europe and Australia is emerging. Unsafe sex, reflected in outbreaks of sexually transmitted infections, and widespread injecting drug use are propelling these epidemics, which, at the same time, are shifting more towards deprived communities.

LATIN AMERICA AND THE CARIBBEAN—DIVERSE EPIDEMICS

An estimated 1.8 million adults and children are living with HIV in Latin America and the Caribbean—a region that is experiencing diverse epidemics. With an average adult HIV prevalence of approximately 2%, the Caribbean is the second-most affected region in the world. But relatively low national HIV prevalence rates in most South and Central American countries mask the fact that the epidemic is already firmly lodged among specific population groups. These countries can avert more extensive epidemics by stepping up their responses now.

STRONGER COMMITMENT

Greater and more effective prevention, treatment and care efforts need to be brought to bear. During the year 2001, the resolve to do so became stronger than ever.

History was made when the United Nations General Assembly Special Session on HIV/AIDS in June 2001 set in place a framework for national and international accountability in the struggle against the epidemic. Each government pledged to pursue a series of many benchmark targets relating to prevention, care, support and treatment, impact alleviation, and children orphaned and made vulnerable by HIV/AIDS, as part of a comprehensive AIDS response. These targets include the following:

- To reduce HIV infection among 15–24-year-olds

Table 2 Regional HIV/AIDS Statistics and Features, End of 2001

Region	Epidemic started	Adults and children living with HIV/AIDS	Adults and children newly infected with HIV	Adult prevalence rate (*)	% of HIV-positive adults who are women	Main mode(s) of transmission (#) for adults living with HIV/AIDS
Sub-Saharan Africa	late '70s early '80s	28.1 million	3.4 million	8.4%	55%	Hetero
North Africa & Middle East	late '80s	440 000	80 000	0.2%	40%	Hetero, IDU
South & South-East Asia	late '80s	6.1 million	800 000	0.6%	35%	Hetero, IDU
East Asia & Pacific	late '80s	1 million	270 000	0.1%	20%	IDU, hetero, MSM
Latin America	late '70s early '80s	1.4 million	130 000	0.5%	30%	MSM, IDU, hetero
Caribbean	late '70s early '80s	420 000	60 000	2.2%	50%	Hetero, MSM
Eastern Europe & Central Asia	early '90s	1 million	250 000	0.5%	20%	IDU
Western Europe	late '70s early '80s	560 000	30 000	0.3%	25%	MSM, IDU
North America	late '70s early '80s	940 000	45 000	0.6%	20%	MSM, IDU, hetero
Australia & New Zealand	late '70s early '80s	15 000	500	0.1%	10%	MSM
TOTAL		40 million	5 million	1.2%	48%	

*The proportion of adults (15 to 49 years of age) living with HIV/AIDS in 2001, using 2001 population numbers.

Hetero (heterosexual transmission), IDU (transmission through injecting drug use), MSM (sexual transmission among men who have sex with men).

by 25% in the most affected countries by 2005 and, globally, by 2010;

- By 2005, to reduce the proportion of infants infected with HIV by 20%, and by 50% by 2010;
- By 2003, to develop national strategies to strengthen health-care systems and address factors affecting the provision of HIV-related drugs, including affordability and pricing. Also, to urgently make every effort to provide the highest attainable standard of treatment for HIV/AIDS, including antiretroviral therapy in a careful and monitored manner to reduce the risk of developing resistance;
- By 2003, to develop and, by 2005, implement national strategies to provide a supportive environment for orphans and children infected and affected by HIV/AIDS;
- By 2003, to have in place strategies that begin to address the factors that make individuals particularly vulnerable to HIV infection, including underdevelopment, economic insecurity, poverty, lack of empowerment of women, lack of education, social exclusion, illiteracy, discrimination, lack of information and/or commodities for self-protection, and all types of sexual exploitation of women, girls and boys;
- By 2003, to develop multisectoral strategies to address the impact of the HIV/AIDS epidemic at the individual, family, community and national levels.

Increasingly, other stakeholders, including nongovernmental organizations and private companies worldwide, are making clear their determination to boost those efforts.

New resources are being marshalled to lift spending to the necessary levels, which UNAIDS estimates at US$7–10 billion per year in low- and middle-income countries. The global fund called for by United Nations Secretary-General Kofi Annan has attracted about US$1.5 billion in pledges. In addition, the World Bank plans major new loans in 2002 and 2003 for HIV/AIDS, with a grant equivalency of over US$400 million per year. All the while, more countries are boosting their national budget allocations towards AIDS responses. Several 'least developed countries' have received, or are in line for, debt relief that could help them increase their spending on HIV/AIDS.

More private companies are also stepping up their efforts. Guiding some of their interventions is a new international code of conduct on AIDS and the workplace, which was ratified earlier this year by members of the International Labour Organization (the new, eighth cosponsoring organization of UNAIDS).

The challenge now is to build on the newfound commitment and convert it into sustained action—both in the countries and regions already hard hit, and in those where the epidemic began later but is gathering steam.

• • •

RECLAIMING THE FUTURE

The impact of the AIDS epidemic is being increasingly felt in many countries across the world. Southern Africa continues to be the worst affected area, with adult prevalence rates still rising in several countries. But elsewhere, also, in countries often already burdened by huge socioeconomic challenges, AIDS threatens human welfare, developmental progress and social stability on an unprecedented scale.

The AIDS epidemic has a profound impact on growth, income and poverty. It is estimated that the annual per capita growth in half the countries of sub-Saharan Africa is falling by 0.5–1.2% as a direct result of AIDS. By 2010, per capita GDP in some of the hardest hit countries may drop by 8% and per capita consumption may fall even farther. Calculations show that heavily affected countries could lose more than 20% of GDP by 2020. Companies of all types face higher costs in training, insurance, benefits, absenteeism and illness. A survey of 15 firms in Ethiopia has shown that, over a five-year period, 53% of all illnesses among staff were AIDS-related.

DEVASTATING CYCLES

An index of existing social and economic injustices, the epidemic is driving a ruthless cycle of impoverishment. People at all income levels are vulnerable to the economic impact of HIV/AIDS, but the poor suffer most acutely. One quarter of households in Botswana, where adult HIV prevalence is over 35%, can expect to lose an income earner within the next 10 years. A rapid increase in the number of very poor and destitute families is anticipated. Per capita household income for the poorest quarter of households is expected to fall by 13%, while every income earner in this category can expect to take on four more dependents as a result of HIV/AIDS.

In sub-Saharan Africa, the economic hardships of the past two decades have left three-quarters of the continent's people surviving on less than US$2 a day. The epidemic is deepening their plight. Typically, this impoverished majority has limited access to social and health services, especially in countries where public services have been cut back and where privatized services are unaffordable.

In hard-hit areas, households cope by cutting their food consumption and other basic expenditures, and tend to sell assets in order to cover the costs of health care and funerals.

Studies in Rwanda have shown that households with a HIV/AIDS patient spend, on average, 20 times more on health care annually than households without an AIDS patient. Only a third of those households can manage to meet these extra costs.

According to a new United Nations Food and Agricultural Organization (FAO) report, seven million farm workers have died from AIDS-related causes since 1985 and 16 million more are expected to die in the next 20 years. Agricultural output—especially of staple products—cannot be sustained in such circumstances. The prospect of widespread food shortages and hunger is real. Some 20% of rural families in Burkina Faso are estimated to have reduced their agricultural work or even abandoned their farms because of AIDS. Rural households in Thailand are seeing their agricultural output shrink by half. In 15% of these instances, children are removed from school to take care of ill family members and to regain lost income. Almost everywhere, the extra burdens of care and work are deflected onto women—especially the young and the elderly.

Families often remove girls from school to care for sick relatives or assume other family responsibilities, jeopardizing the girls' education and future prospects. In Swaziland, school enrolment is reported to have fallen by 36% due to AIDS, with girls most affected. Enabling young people—especially girls—to attend school and, hopefully, complete their education, is essential. South Africa's and Malawi's universal free primary education systems point the way. Schemes to provide girls with second-chance schooling are another option.

DEVELOPMENT AND STABILITY THREATENED

Meanwhile, the epidemic is claiming huge numbers of teachers, doctors, extension workers and other human resources. In some countries, health-care systems are losing up to a quarter of their personnel to the epidemic. In Malawi and Zambia, for example, five-to-six-fold increases in health worker illness and death rates have reduced personnel, increasing stress levels and workload for the remaining employees.

Teachers and students are dying or leaving school, reducing both the quality and efficiency of educational systems. In 1999 alone, an estimated 860 000 children lost their teachers to AIDS in sub-Saharan Africa. In the Central African Republic, AIDS was the cause of 85% of the 300 teacher deaths that occurred in 2000. Already, by the late 1990s, the toll had forced the closure of more than 100 educational establishments in that country. In Guatemala, studies have shown that more than a third of children orphaned by HIV/AIDS drop out of school. In Zambia, teacher deaths caused by AIDS are equivalent to about half the total number of new teachers the country manages to train annually.

Replacing skilled professionals is a top priority, especially in low-income countries where governments depend heavily on a small number of policy-makers and managers for public management and core social services. In heavily affected countries, losing such personnel reduces capacity, while raising the costs of recruitment, training, benefits and replacements. A successful response to AIDS requires that essential public services, such as education, health, security, justice and institutions of democratic governance, be maintained. Each sector has to take account of HIV/AIDS in its own development plans and introduce measures to sustain public sector functions. Such actions might include fast-track training, as well as the recruitment of key civil servants and the reallocation of budgets towards the most essential services.

Countries that explore innovative ways of maintaining and rebuilding capacity in government will be better equipped to contain the epidemic. Equally valuable are labour and social legislation changes that boost people's rights, more effective and equitable ways of delivering social services, and more extensive programmes that benefit those worst hit by the epidemic (especially women and orphans).

COPING WITH CRISIS

In the worst-affected countries, steep drops in life expectancies are beginning to occur, most drastically in sub-Saharan Africa, where four countries (Botswana, Malawi, Mozambique and Swaziland) now have a life expectancy of less than 40 years. Were it not for HIV/AIDS, average life expectancy in sub-Saharan Africa would be approximately 62 years; instead, it is about 47 years. In South Africa, it is estimated that average life expectancy is only 47 years, instead of 66, if AIDS were not a factor (see Figure [1]). And, in Haiti, it has dropped to 53 years (as opposed to 59). The number of African children who had lost their mother or both parents to the epidemic by the end of 2000—12.1 million—is forecast to more than double over the next decade. These orphans are especially vulnerable to the epidemic, and the impoverishment and precariousness it brings.

As more infants are born HIV-positive in badly affected countries, child mortality rates are also rising. In the Bahamas, it is estimated that some 60% of deaths among children under the age of five are due to AIDS, while, in Zimbabwe, the figure is 70%.

Unequal access to affordable treatment and adequate health services is one of the main factors accounting for drastically different survival rates among those living with HIV/AIDS in rich and poor countries and communities. Public pressure and UN-sponsored engagements with pharmaceutical corporations (through the Accelerating Access Initiative), along with competition from generic drug manufacturers, has helped drive antiretroviral drug prices down. But prices remain too high for public-sector budgets in low-income countries where, in addition, health infrastructures are too frail to bring life-prolonging treatments to the millions who need it.

Backed by a strong social movement, Brazil's government has shown that those barriers are not

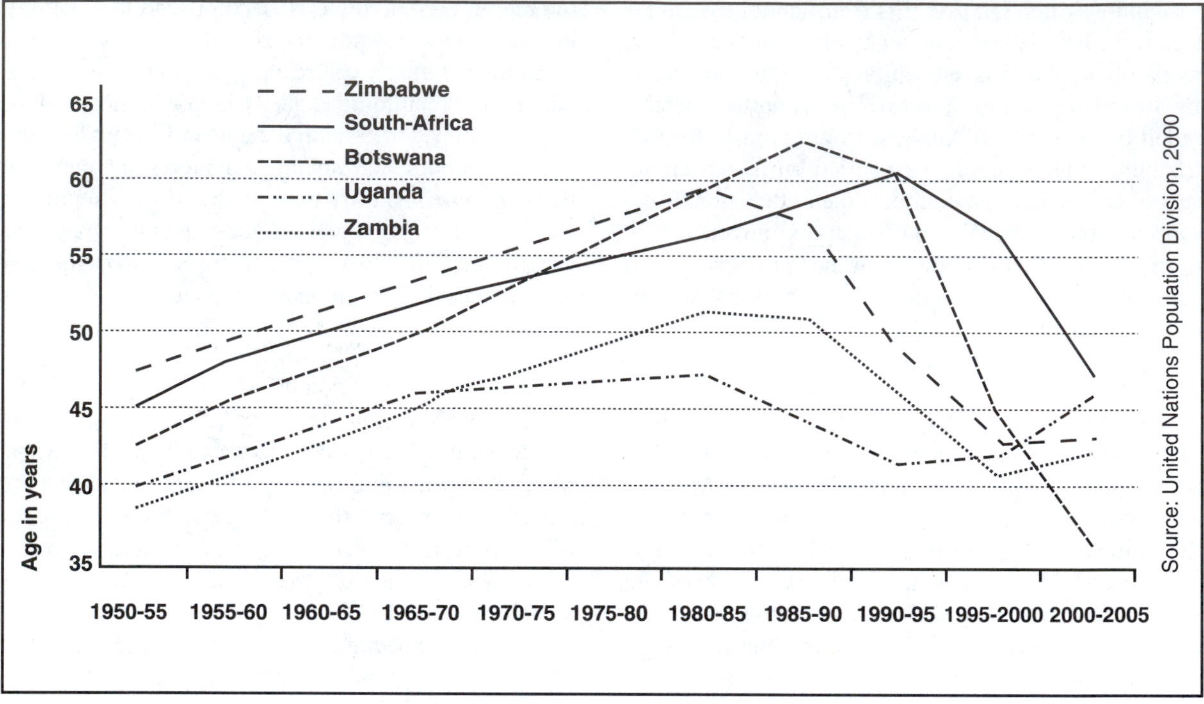

Figure [1]. Changes in life expectancy in selected African countries with high HIV prevalence, 1950–2005

impregnable and that the use of cheaper drugs can be an important element of a successful response. Along with Brazil, countries such as Argentina and Uruguay also guarantee HIV/AIDS patients free antiretroviral drugs. In Africa, several governments are launching programmes to provide similar drugs through their public health systems, albeit on a limited scale, at first.

In all such cases, though, clearing the hurdle of high prices is essential but not enough. Also indispensable are functioning and affordable health systems. Massive international support is needed to help countries meet that challenge.

• • •

SUB-SAHARAN AFRICA

Sub-Saharan Africa remains the region most severely affected by HIV/AIDS. Approximately 3.4 million new infections occurred in 2001, bringing to 28.1 million the total number of people living with HIV/AIDS in this region.

The region is experiencing diverse epidemics in terms of scale and maturity. HIV prevalence rates have risen to alarming levels in parts of southern Africa, where the most recent antenatal clinic data reveal levels of more than 30% in several areas. In Swaziland, HIV prevalence among pregnant women attending antenatal clinics in 2000 ranged from 32.2% in urban areas to 34.5% in rural areas; in Botswana, the corresponding figures were 43.9% and 35.5%. In South Africa's KwaZulu-Natal Province, the figure stood at 36.2% in 2000.

At least 10% of those aged 15–49 are infected in 16 African countries, including several in southern Africa, where at least 20% are infected. Countries across the region are expanding and upgrading their responses. But the high prevalence rates mean that even exceptional success on the prevention front will now only gradually reduce the human toll. It is estimated that 2.3 million Africans died of AIDS in 2001.

This notwithstanding, in some of the most heavily affected countries there is growing evidence that prevention efforts are bearing fruit. One new study in

Zambia shows urban men and women reporting less sexual activity, fewer multiple partners and more consistent use of condoms. This is in line with earlier indications that HIV prevalence is declining among urban residents in Zambia, especially among young women aged 15–24.

According to the South African Ministry of Health, HIV prevalence among pregnant women attending antenatal clinics reached 24.5% in 2000. About one-in-nine South Africans (or 4.7 million people) are living with HIV/AIDS. Yet, there are possibly heartening signs that positive trends might be increasingly taking hold among adolescents, for whom prevalence rates have dropped slightly since 1998. Large-scale information campaigns and condom distribution programmes appear to be bearing fruit. In South Africa, for instance, free male condom distribution rose from 6 million in 1994 to 198 million five years later. In recent surveys, approximately 55% of sexually active teenage girls reported that they always use a condom during sex. But these developments are accompanied by a troubling rise in prevalence among South Africans aged 20–34, highlighting the need for greater prevention efforts targeted at older age groups, and tailored to their realities and concerns.

Progress is also being made on the treatment and care front. In the southern African region, relatively prosperous Botswana has become the first country to begin providing antiretroviral drugs through its public health system, thanks to a bigger health budget and drug price reductions negotiated with pharmaceutical companies.

Within the context of a public/private partnership between five research-and-development pharmaceutical companies and five United Nations agencies, there is increasing access to antiretroviral therapy in Africa. As of the end of 2001, more than 10 African countries were providing antiretroviral therapy to people living with HIV/AIDS.

In five West African countries—Burkina Faso, Cameroon, Côte d'Ivoire, Nigeria and Togo—national adult prevalence rates already passed the 5% mark in 2000. Countries such as Nigeria are boosting their spending on HIV/AIDS and extending their responses nationwide. This year, Nigeria launched a US$240-million HIV/AIDS Emergency Action Plan. Determined prevention efforts in Senegal continue to bear fruit, thanks to the prompt political support for its programmes.

On the eastern side of the continent, the downward arc in prevalence rates continues in Uganda—the first African country to have subdued a major HIV/AIDS epidemic. HIV prevalence in pregnant women in urban areas has fallen for eight years in a row, from a high of 29.5% in 1992 to 11.25% in 2000. Focusing heavily on information, education and communication, and decentralized programmes that reach down to village level, Uganda's efforts have also boosted condom use across the country. In the Masindi and Pallisa districts, for instance, condom use with casual partners in 1997–2000 rose from 42% and 31%, respectively, to 51% and 53%. In the capital, Kampala, almost 98% of sex workers surveyed in 2000 said they had used a condom the last time they had sex.

But despite such success, huge challenges remain. New infections continue to occur at a high rate. Most people with HIV do not have access to antiretroviral therapy. Already, by the end of 1999, 1.7 million children had lost a mother or both parents to the disease. Providing them with food, housing and education will test the resources and resolve of the country for many years to come.

Uganda's experience underlines the fact that even a rampant HIV/AIDS epidemic can be brought under control. The axis of any effective response is a prevention strategy that draws on the explicit and strong commitment of leaders at all levels, that is built on community mobilization, and that extends into every area of the country.

Although they are exceptionally vulnerable to the epidemic, millions of young African women are dangerously ignorant about HIV/AIDS. According to UNICEF, more than 70% of adolescent girls (aged 15–19) in Somalia and more than 40% in Guinea Bissau and Sierra Leone, for instance, have never heard of AIDS. In countries such as Kenya and the United Republic of Tanzania, more than 40% of adolescent girls harbour serious misconceptions about how the virus is transmitted. One of the targets fixed at the UN General Assembly Special Session on HIV/AIDS in June 2001 was to ensure that at least 90% of young men and women should, by 2005, have the information, education and services they need to defend themselves against HIV infection. As in other regions of the world, most countries in sub-Saharan Africa are a considerable way from fulfilling that pledge.

The vast majority of Africans living with HIV do not know they have acquired the virus. One study has found that 50% of adult Tanzanian women know where they could be tested for HIV, yet only 6% have been tested. In Zimbabwe, only 11% of adult women have been tested for the virus. Moreover, many people who agree to be tested prefer not to return and discover the outcome of those tests. However, other obstacles remain. A study in Abidjan, Côte d'Ivoire, shows that 80% of pregnant women who agree to undergo a HIV test return to collect their results. But of those who discover they are living with the virus, fewer than 50% return to receive drug treatment for the prevention of mother-to-child transmission of the virus.

More than half of the women who know they have acquired HIV, and who were surveyed by Kenya's Population Council this year, said they had not disclosed their HIV status to their partners because they feared it would expose them to violence or abandonment. Not only are voluntary counselling and testing services in short supply across the region, but stigma and discrimination continue to discourage people from discovering their HIV status.

Accumulating over the past year have been many encouraging developments. Thirty-one countries in the region have now completed a national HIV/AIDS strategic plan and another 12 are developing such a plan. Several regional initiatives to roll back the epidemic are under way. Some, such as those grouping countries in the Great Lakes region, the Lake Chad Basin and West Africa, are concentrating their efforts on reducing the vulnerability of refugee and other mobile populations. The political commitment to turn the tide of AIDS appears stronger than ever. Gatherings such as the 2000 African Development Forum meeting last December, and the Organization of African Unity Summit on HIV/AIDS, Tuberculosis and Other Related Infectious Diseases in April 2001, appear to be cementing that resolve. At the latter meeting, Heads of State agreed to devote at least 15% of their countries' annual budgets to improving health sectors. Fewer than five countries had reached that level in 2000.

AIDS has become the biggest threat to the continent's development and its quest to bring about an African Renaissance. Most governments in sub-Saharan Africa depend on a small number of highly skilled personnel in important areas of public management and core social services. Badly affected countries are losing many of these valuable civil servants to AIDS. Essential services are being depleted at the same time as state institutions and resources come under greater strain and traditional safety nets disintegrate. In some countries, health-care systems are losing up to a quarter of their personnel to the epidemic. People at all income levels are vulnerable to these repercussions, but those living in poverty are hit hardest. Meanwhile, the ability of the state to ensure law and order is being compromised, as the epidemic disrupts institutions such as the courts and the police. The risks of social unrest and even socio-political instability should not be underestimated.

PETER R. LAMPTEY

Reducing Heterosexual Transmission of HIV in Poor Countries

Peter R. Lamptey is President of the AIDS Institute of Family Health International (FHI), where he serves as Director of the U.S.-Agency-for-International-Development-funded Implementing AIDS Prevention and Care (IMPACT) Project. He also directed FHI's AIDS Control and Prevention Project, the largest international HIV/AIDS prevention program undertaken, with more than 750 projects in 45 countries in Africa, Asia, Latin America, and the Caribbean. Dr. Lamptey's career has included worldwide consulting on HIV, AIDS, nutrition, and family planning, and lecturing appointments at the University of Ghana Medical School and the University of North Carolina School of Public Health.

The HIV/AIDS pandemic has devastated many countries, reversing national development, widening the gap between rich and poor people, and pushing already stigmatised groups closer to the margins of society.[1] It has killed millions of people, decimated families and communities, and adversely affected the lives of hundreds of millions. AIDS stands to kill more than half the young adults in the most severely affected countries.[1]

By the end of 2001 an estimated 65 million people worldwide had been infected with HIV—25 million had died and 40 million were living with HIV or AIDS, most of whom have no access to the lifesaving drugs available in industrialised countries.[1] Countries in sub-Saharan Africa and South and South East Asia are the worst affected (fig 1).

The pandemic continues its relentless spread—about 14 000 people are infected each day. This article describes the impact on health and the economic and social impact of the HIV/AIDS pandemic in poor countries, discusses the many factors that promote the heterosexual transmission of HIV, highlights successes around the world in preventing infection, and outlines some of the challenges for the future.

Reprinted with permission from the *British Medical Journal* 324 (January 26, 2002), 207–211. Copyright © 2002 by the British Medical Association.

METHODS

I performed searches of Medline, AIDS databases, global HIV and AIDS libraries (with particular emphasis on the UNAIDS website and its publications), the US Bureau of Census, and publications of the United Nations Development Programme. I also relied on personal experience through my work with Family Health International and the implementation of HIV/AIDS prevention and care programmes in more than 60 of the world's poorest countries.

THE IMPACT OF HIV/AIDS ON POPULATIONS

The HIV and AIDS pandemic is having a devastating demographic impact. Gains in life expectancy over the past half century have been reversed (fig 2). Infant mortality and adult mortality have increased by more than 50% in some countries.[1] Figure 3 shows the projected population structure of Botswana with and without the AIDS epidemic for the year 2020. The change from a normal population pyramid to a chimney shape reflects the disproportionate death rate among the young, sexually active, and productive segments of the population. As a result large numbers of young children and older adults will have to be supported by a shrinking proportion of productive adults.

The pandemic threatens to reverse the progress that has been made by the already fragile economies of poor countries. But the most severe economic impact is at the level of households, and affected

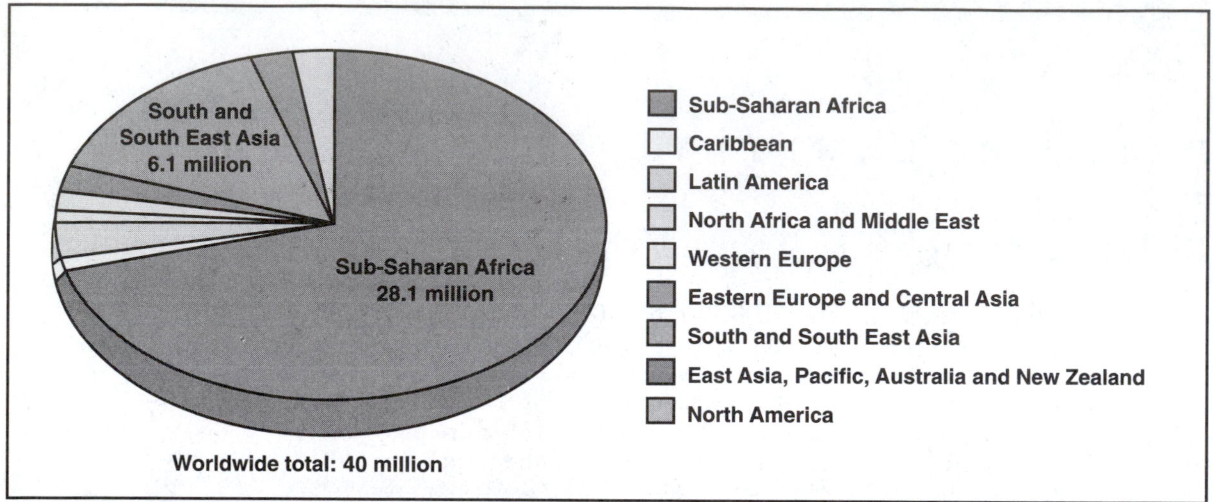

Figure 1 Global distribution of adults and children living with HIV or AIDS at end of 2001

families often become impoverished. In Ethiopia and Tanzania the average costs of basic treatment of the symptoms of AIDS and of funeral and mourning expenses amount to several times the average annual household income.[2] A study in Thailand showed that agricultural output was halved in a third of rural families affected by AIDS, which also threatens their food security.[1]

HETEROSEXUAL TRANSMISSION OF HIV

Heterosexual intercourse is the most common mode of transmission of HIV in poor countries. In Africa slightly more than 80% of infections are acquired heterosexually, while mother to child transmission (5–15%) and transfusion of contaminated blood account for the remaining infections.[3] In Latin America most infections are acquired through men having sex

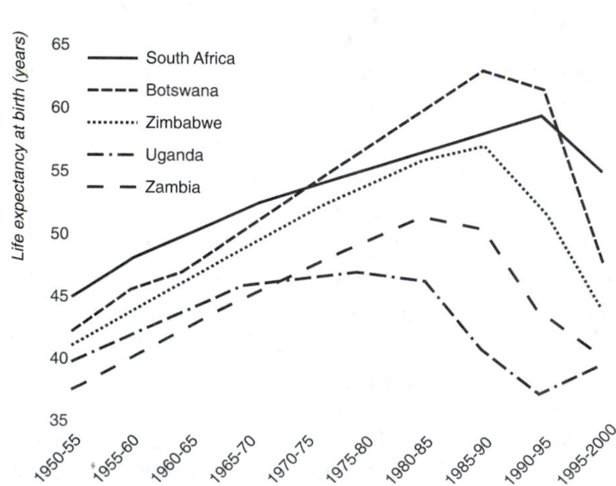

Figure 2 Life expectancy in some countries in sub-Saharan Africa with a high prevalence of HIV

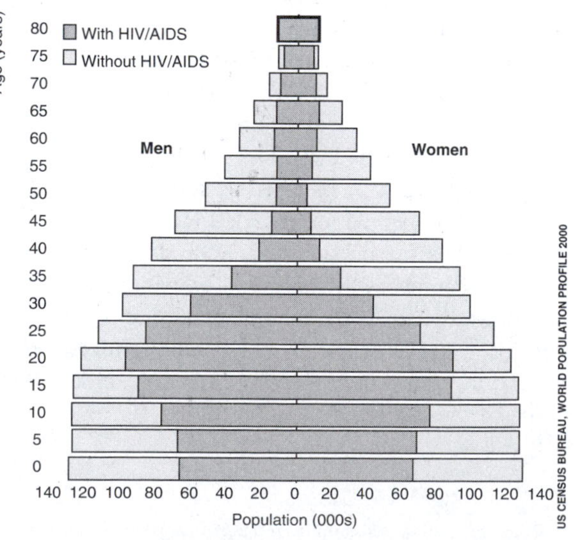

Figure 3 Projected population structure of Botswana in 2020 with and without HIV/AIDS

Impact of HIV and AIDS

- Gains in life expectancy have been reversed in many countries
- Infant mortality and adult mortality have increased by more than 50% in severely affected countries
- More than 13 million children, mostly in Africa, have lost one or both parents to AIDS
- Loss of income, cost of treatment, and burial expenses severely deplete income of affected households

with men and through misuse of injected drugs, but heterosexual transmission is rising. Heterosexual contact and injection of drugs are the main modes of HIV transmission in South and South East Asia.[1]

The rapid spread of HIV in poor countries has been attributed to several factors (box).[1] Besides these risk factors pertaining to individuals, societal factors beyond the control of individuals are important in the transmission of HIV and other sexually transmitted infections.

Despite the explosive spread of HIV and AIDS, there have been several successful interventions to reduce the heterosexual spread of HIV. The mainstays of these programmes are interventions to change behaviour, improved access to condoms to reduce the risk of infection and decrease vulnerability to HIV, and the effective management of sexually transmitted infections.[4–7]

DECREASING THE RISK OF INFECTION SLOWS THE EPIDEMIC

Interventions to reduce risky behaviours are aimed at high risk sexual behaviours such as frequent change of sexual partners, unprotected sexual intercourse, sex at a young age among adolescents, and poor behaviour in seeking treatment for sexually transmitted infections. Such interventions also aim to change situations where there is a greater risk of being infected with HIV, such as circumstances that lead to coercive sex. To change their behaviour people need to have some basic knowledge of HIV and be aware of their risk for HIV infection.[7] They must be taught a set of protective skills and offered access to appropriate services and products, such as condoms. They must also perceive their environment to be supportive of changing or maintaining safe behaviours.

Key factors in the heterosexual transmission of HIV

- Frequent change of sexual partners
- Unprotected sexual intercourse
- Presence of sexually transmitted infections and poor access to treatment
- Lack of male circumcision
- Social vulnerability of women and young people
- Economic and political instability of the community

Ways to reduce heterosexual transmission of HIV

- Better recognition of the symptoms of sexually transmitted infections and improved behaviour in seeking treatment
- Better management of sexually transmitted infections
- Sexual abstinence or delayed onset of sex, especially in adolescents
- Fewer sexual partners
- Safer sex practices, including consistent, correct use of condoms
- Supportive social environment to sustain behavioural change
- Reduced stigma and discrimination against people with HIV
- Promotion of male circumcision

Interventions to change behaviour can be targeted at the general population or at high risk groups (the people who are at most risk of acquiring and transmitting HIV). Programmes for the general population are designed to improve awareness, knowledge, and attitudes, to change social norms, and to create a supportive environment. The groups at the highest risk of acquiring HIV are typically sex workers and their clients, people who are highly mobile, such as long distance truck drivers and migrant workers, and the military and police.

Among the most successful interventions are those targeted at sex workers and their clients.[7] In Nairobi, Kenya, behaviour change programmes among these groups increased the percentage of sex workers who reported always using a condom from less than 5% in 1985 to more than 85% in the mid-1990s and reduced the annual incidence of HIV from 47% to about 1% over the same period.[8] In Thailand and Cambodia, programmes promoting 100% use of condoms in brothels have successfully reduced HIV transmission in sex workers and their clients, as well as in the general population.[1,6,9] . . .

DECREASING VULNERABILITY DECREASES RISK OF INFECTION

Vulnerability refers to individual and societal factors that increase the risk of HIV infection. Societal factors include poverty, unemployment, illiteracy, gender inequities, cultural practices, lack of information and services, and human rights abuses.[10] These factors greatly increase the vulnerability of women, young people, and other marginalised groups. For example, illiterate women with limited skills, few job opportunities, and limited access to health information and services are more likely than other women and the population as a whole to engage in unprotected sex for money, thereby increasing their vulnerability and risk of HIV infection.[11,12] Child prostitution in South East Asia and financial enticement of young girls by adult men in many countries increase vulnerability of girls to HIV.[1] Interventions to address vulnerability seek to change adverse policies, social norms, and harmful cultural practices as well as to create income generation schemes and programmes for orphans and other vulnerable children. The most vulnerable population groups in many countries include adolescent girls, women, sex workers, illegal immigrants, orphans, and displaced people.

Behaviour change interventions address two factors: what places people and communities at risk, and why they are at risk.[1] Reducing the risk of HIV infection slows the epidemic. By decreasing vulnerability we can decrease the risk of infection and the impact of the epidemic. By decreasing the impact of the epidemic we can likewise reduce vulnerability to HIV and AIDS.

TREATING SEXUALLY TRANSMITTED INFECTIONS REDUCES HIV TRANSMISSION

There are more than 300 million new cases of curable sexually transmitted infections throughout the world each year, with a global distribution that closely mirrors that of HIV. Each new infection not only increases the risk of HIV transmission but also carries the potential of other serious complications—miscarriage, stillbirths, infertility, ectopic pregnancy, and severe congenital infections.

Epidemiological studies have shown that people with a sexually transmitted infection are more susceptible to acquiring HIV infection and that the presence of a sexually transmitted infection increases the risk of spreading HIV to an uninfected person.[13] The behavioural risk factors for HIV are similar to those for sexually transmitted diseases, and HIV alters the epidemiology of some sexually transmitted infections.[14–16]

Treating sexually transmitted infections reduces HIV transmission

- Worldwide more than 300 million new cases of sexually transmitted infections occur each year, mostly in poor countries
- The global distributions of sexually transmitted infections and HIV are similar
- Sexually transmitted infections are an important cause of ill health, especially in women and children
- The presence of sexually transmitted infections increases the transmission of HIV
- Effective management of sexually transmitted infections can reduce the risk of HIV infection

In a study in Malawi, the successful treatment of men with both HIV and other sexually transmitted infections led to a threefold reduction in the concentration of HIV in semen two weeks after treatment.[17] Effective management of sexually transmitted infections can reduce the risk of HIV transmission and acquisition as well as reduce the serious health, social, and economic consequences of sexually transmitted infections. In Thailand a reduction of the incidence of curable sexually transmitted infections by more than 80% in five years, through improved treatment and promotion of condom use, led to a decline in the prevalence of HIV in sex workers, their clients, and the military.[9] In rural Mwanza, Tanzania, improving the case management of sexually transmitted infections through "syndromic" management (a diagnosis is made by matching a syndrome or group of easily recognised symptoms to well defined aetiologies, avoiding the need for sophisticated laboratory tests) in clinics reduced the incidence of HIV infection by 40%.[14–16] While the same intervention in Rakai, Uganda, had no effect on HIV transmission, it did show that in an area with a mature HIV epidemic, such as Rakai, services to manage sexually transmitted diseases need to be long term and that an important target group is adolescents. From the Rakai and Mwanza interventions we have learnt that prevention and treatment or control of sexually transmitted diseases can be very effective at reducing the incidence of HIV in areas where prevalence of these diseases is high and prevalence of HIV is low.[14–16]

HIV TREATMENT PROMOTES PREVENTION

An effective HIV prevention programme is one that is comprehensive and that addresses a community's prevention, care, and treatment needs. Essential components of a comprehensive programme include HIV testing and voluntary counselling, prevention of mother to child transmission, clinical care, and antiretroviral treatment (fig 4). Testing combined with voluntary counselling is an effective, pivotal strategy in HIV prevention and care for people with the virus, providing many benefits for people who test positive as well as for those who remain HIV negative.[18] A randomised controlled trial in Kenya, Tanzania, and Trinidad showed that voluntary counselling and testing significantly reduced high risk sexual behaviour among individuals and couples.[18]

Providing care and treatment enhances the efficacy of prevention programmes in several ways. Access to care and treatment helps to reduce the stigma associated with HIV infection, allows testing of more people, and may promote change in behaviour. But studies in industrialised countries have shown that there is a tendency for high risk sexual behaviour to increase when effective treatment becomes available.[19] Prevention services must therefore provide ongoing counselling for people on antiretroviral drugs about the need to continue to practise safe sex.

The use of antiretroviral drugs to prevent mother

Key challenges for the future

- Increasing resources for prevention and care
- Reducing stigma and discrimination
- Building the capacity in poor countries for an expanded and comprehensive response to the pandemic
- Scaling up interventions
- Improving access to care and treatment
- Improving programmes aimed at orphans and other vulnerable children
- Improving technologies, such as vaccines and microbicides

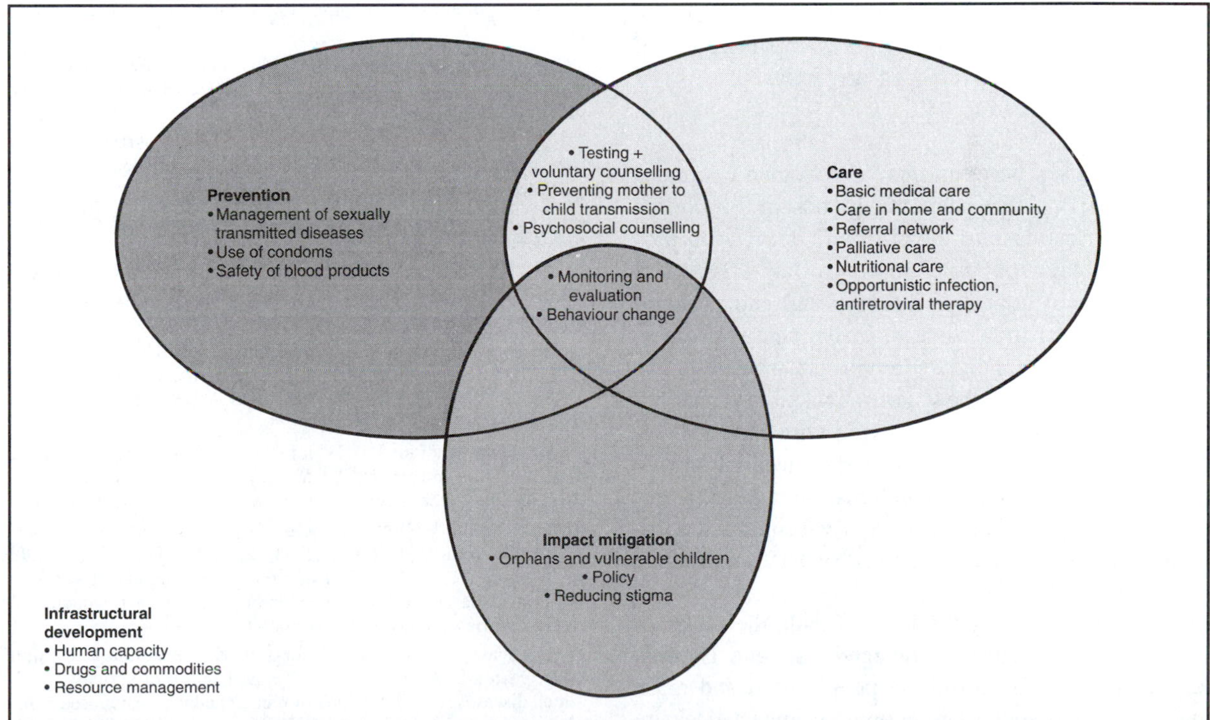

Figure 4 Components of a comprehensive HIV/AIDS programme

HIV treatment enhances prevention

- Prevention programmes are more effective in the context of comprehensive HIV/AIDS services
- Effective antiretroviral treatment reduces the risk of sexual transmission of HIV
- However, access to antiretroviral drugs may lead to an increase in high risk behaviour

to child transmission of HIV exemplifies the power of biological prevention strategies.[19] Recent work in Uganda has shown that the concentration of HIV in the blood—and, by extension, in genital secretions—determines the efficiency of the sexual transmission of HIV within serodiscordant couples.[19] These observations, together with extensive work with macaques, indicate that antiretroviral drugs can reduce the transmission of HIV. This has important implications: the extensive use of antiretroviral drugs in a population may reduce the sexual transmission of HIV from infected individuals to their uninfected partners, and antiretroviral drugs given (before or after exposure) at the community level can prevent the acquisition of HIV. However, no studies of antiretroviral prophylaxis in humans have yet been done, largely because of the difficulty in developing research strategies capable of proving the benefit of prophylaxis.[19]

CONCLUSIONS

Unprotected sex between men and women continues to fuel the HIV/AIDS pandemic in most of the world's poor countries, despite the efforts of prevention programmes. Major obstacles to controlling HIV/AIDS are the lack of adequate international and national commitment to the problem, inadequate resources, the lack of an expanded and comprehensive response to the pandemic, and the stigma attached to—and discrimination against—people living with HIV.

The cost and limitations of current technologies—such as male and female condoms, microbicides, antiretroviral drugs, diagnostics and vaccines—also inhibit efforts to contain the spread of HIV and reduce the impact of AIDS.

In the 14th century the Black Death, the most severe pandemic in history, ravaged Asia and Europe, leaving more than 40 million people dead and making a profound social and economic impact. Despite the impressive advances in medicine since then, HIV/AIDS is likely to surpass the Black Death as the worst pandemic ever. We urgently need an effective and safe vaccine, an affordable cure, and intensified prevention, care, and support programmes.

NOTES

1. UNAIDS. *AIDS epidemic update—December 2001.* www.unaids.org/epidemic_update/report_dec01/index.html (accessed 8 Jan 2002).

2. Delay P., Stanecki K., G. Ernberg. Introduction. In: Lamptey P., Gayle H., eds. *HIV/AIDS prevention and care in resource-constrained settings: a handbook for the design and management of programs.* Arlington, VA: Family Health International, 2002.

3. Mhalu F. S., Lyamuya E. Human immunodeficiency virus infection and AIDS in east Africa: challenges and possibilities for prevention and control. *East Afr Med J* 1996;73:13–9.

4. Flanagan D., Mahler H., Makinwa B. Case study #13: creating and applying a tool for upgrading behavior change skills on-the-job. In Makinwa B., O'Grady M., eds. *FHI/UNAIDS best practices in HIV/AIDS prevention collection.* Arlington, VA: UNAIDS and Family Health International, 2001.

5. Lamptey P. Prevention does work! [Plenary presentation.] 13th international AIDS conference, Durban, South Africa, 9–14 July 2000.

6. Cambodian Ministry of Health, Cambodia Sentinel Surveillance in collaboration with National Center for HIV/AIDS, Dermatology and STD (NCHADS) and Family Health International. 2000 HSS Survey. (Unpublished data.)

7. Larivee C., Lamptey P., Zeitz P., eds. Module 2: technical strategies. In: *Strategies for an expanded and comprehensive response (ECR): a handbook for designing and implementing HIV/AIDS programs.* Arlington, VA: Family Health International, 2001.

8. Universities of Nairobi and Manitoba. *The STD project, sex workers intervention programs. CIDA funded.* Nairobi: University of Nairobi, 2001.

9. UNAIDS. Best practice digest: STI/HIV—100% condom use programme for sex workers. www.unaids.org/bestpractice/digest/files/condoms.html (accessed 8 Jan 2002).

10. UNAIDS. *Reducing women's vulnerability to HIV infection.* Geneva: UNAIDS, 1996.

11. UNICEF Innocenti Research Centre. *Domestic violence against women and girls.* Florence, Italy: Innocenti Research Centre, 2000. (*Innocenti Digest* No 6, June 2000.)

12. AIDS Consortium. Vulnerability of the girl child to HIV/AIDS. Report of seminar organised by the working group on children and HIV/AIDS of the UK NGO AIDS Consortium, London, November 1999.

13. Over M., Piot P. HIV infection and sexually transmitted diseases. In: Jamison D. T., Mosley W. H., Measham A. R., Babadilla J. L., eds. *Disease control priorities in developing countries.* New York: Oxford University Press, 1993:445–529.

14. Grosskurth H., Mosha F., Todd J., Mwijarubi E., Klokke A., Senkoro K., et al. Impact of improved treatment of sexually transmitted diseases on HIV infection in rural Tanzania: randomised controlled trial. *Lancet* 1995;346:530–6.

15. Wawer M. J., Sewankambo N. K., Serwadda D., Quinn T. C., Paxton L. A., Kiwanuka N., et al. Control of sexually transmitted diseases for AIDS prevention in Uganda: a randomised community trial. Rakai Project Study Group. *Lancet* 1999;353:525–35.

16. Grosskurth H., Gray R., Hayes R., Mabey D., Wawer M.

Control of sexually transmitted diseases for HIV-1 prevention: understanding the implications of the Mwanza and Rakai trials. *Lancet* 2000;355:WA8–14.

17. Cohen M. S., Hoffman I. F., Royce R. A., Kazembe P., Dyer J. R., Daly C. C., et al. Reduction of concentration of HIV-1 in semen after treatment of urethritis: implications for prevention of sexual transmission of HIV-1. AIDSCAP Malawi Research Group. *Lancet* 1997;349:1868–73.

18. Efficacy of voluntary HIV-1 counseling and testing in individuals and couples in Kenya, Tanzania, and Trinidad: a randomised trial. The voluntary HIV-1 counseling and testing efficacy study group. *Lancet* 2000;356:103–12.

19. Colebunders R., Perriens J., VanPraag E. Management of HIV disease and its complications, in resource-constrained settings. In: Lamptey P., Gayle H., eds. *HIV/AIDS prevention and care in resource-constrained settings: a handbook for the design and management of programs*. Arlington, VA: Family Health International, 2002.

LAWRENCE O. GOSTIN AND DAVID W. WEBBER

HIV Infection and AIDS in the Public Health and Health Care Systems: The Role of Law and Litigation

Lawrence Gostin is Professor of Law at Georgetown University and Professor of Public Health at the Johns Hopkins University. He is also Director of the Center for Law and the Public's Health and Editor of the Health Law and Ethics section of the *Journal of the American Medical Association*. His latest book is *Public Health Law: Power, Duty, Restraint* (University of California Press and the Milbank Memorial Fund).

David W. Webber is a lawyer who specializes in legal issues related to HIV/AIDS and other infectious diseases. He founded the AIDS Law Project of Pennsylvania, a nonprofit public interest law firm. He has written extensively on HIV legal issues. Recently he edited and contributed to the third edition of *AIDS and the Law* (John Wiley & Sons). He is also the editor-in-chief of the *AIDS and Public Policy Journal*.

The epidemic of human immunodeficiency virus (HIV) infection and the acquired immunodeficiency syndrome (AIDS) has had powerful personal, social, and economic effects throughout America—in employment, housing, insurance, education, prisons, and many other aspects of life.[1] Yet, perhaps the most profound effects of the epidemic have been in the public health and health care systems.[2] Public health and medicine have responsibilities to monitor, prevent, and treat HIV infection. At the same time, the nation has struggled with the task of reconciling patients' rights to privacy and nondiscrimination with collective rights to public health protection.

Given the high degree of ongoing social conflict caused by the epidemic, it is not surprising that, unlike past infectious disease outbreaks, attempts to resolve contentious issues consistently involve the courts and legislatures at all levels. Furthermore, because of the high level of patient activism and advocacy, as well as immediate public access to new developments in scientific and medical information, including that available via the Internet, law and policymaking have not been the exclusive preserve of medical experts or other professional specialists. The resulting

Reprinted with permission from the *Journal of the American Medical Association* 279 (April 8, 1998), 1108–13. Copyright © 1998 by the American Medical Association.

democratization of policymaking processes has heightened the impact that legislatures and courts have had on the public health and health care systems.

Deeply divisive questions have emerged relating to informed consent for HIV testing, named HIV reporting, confidentiality vs the duty to warn, and an HIV-infected physician's right to practice. These and many other questions have come to be decided by legislatures and courts. The results are by no means uniform or consistent. Court decisions in similar cases sometimes conflict, and legislatures in different jurisdictions at times take markedly different approaches. Nevertheless, legislation and litigation provide a window through which the HIV epidemic's troubling questions, arising in relation to the delivery of health care services and the formulation of complex public health policy, can be examined.

This article is part of the AIDS Litigation Project,[3,4] which has reviewed nearly 600 cases reported in the federal and state courts in the United States between 1991 and 1997. The methods involved a federal and 50-state computer and library search of all reported cases involving HIV infection or AIDS. This article discusses an important subset of litigation relating to HIV/AIDS in the public health and health care systems. (The complete AIDS Litigation Project report can be found in the Library section of the HIV/AIDS Information Center at http://www.ama-assn.org.)

IDENTIFYING CASES OF HIV INFECTION: TESTING AND REPORTING

Issues of law and public policy take on new urgency as the HIV/AIDS epidemic experiences a paradigm shift. Combination antiviral therapies and clinical prophylaxes provide for the first time an opportunity for a longer, higher quality of life for persons living with HIV.[5] Combination therapies have markedly reduced the incidence of AIDS,[6] have lowered rates of perinatal transmission,[7,8] and potentially may diminish infectiousness by decreasing viral load. With these new treatment opportunities, it becomes critically important to identify persons at the earliest stages of HIV infection and to ensure full and fair access to the health care system.

Testing, since the approval of an HIV antibody test in early 1985,[9] has been considered essential for HIV prevention. With more recent advances in antiviral and prophylactic treatments, testing has also become important as an entrée into the health care system. Public health and medical authorities recommend that all persons at risk should know their serologic status, and many want to see the "routinization" of HIV testing. A broad range of testing services are desirable, such as testing by primary care clinicians and hospitals, public clinics, "alternative" (anonymous) test sites, and home testing. The technological development of "rapid" tests and analyses of saliva and urine will make testing easier for the public.

Despite the manifest clinical and public health benefits, testing may result in loss of privacy, increased social stigma, and discrimination. As a result, many state legislatures have enacted special requirements for HIV testing. State legislation requires informed consent, often in writing, as well as pretest and posttest counseling. While counseling and consent are thought to be important to enhance patient autonomy, ironically, they do make it more burdensome for health care professionals to "routinize" HIV testing and bring it into the mainstream of medicine.

Voluntary testing is almost universally recommended, and most states have abided by an ethic of voluntarism. Compulsory, nonconsensual testing has been undertaken only in limited circumstances and principally for nonmedical purposes. Thus, mandatory tests are imposed, for example, on US military[10] and foreign service personnel,[11] immigrants,[12] and certain sex offenders.[13,14] In the health care setting, however, compulsory testing violates statutory and common law requirements for informed consent and may violate nondiscrimination statutes[15] or constitutional prohibitions against unreasonable searches and seizures.[16] Although a Pennsylvania court held that HIV testing without patient consent or knowledge did not violate state common law doctrines of informed consent or invasion of privacy,[17] that ruling was subsequently overturned by statute.[18]

Some states permit nonconsensual HIV testing of patients in limited circumstances. An Alabama statute, for example, allows testing without consent if (1) the patient is at "high risk" of infection; (2) knowledge of the patient's serologic status is necessary for medical care; or (3) knowledge of HIV status is needed for the protection of health care personnel. A federal district court found the high-risk classification to be unconstitutional because a patient could be arbitrarily classified, but upheld the other 2 classifications.[19] Many states allow compulsory testing to determine the HIV status of a patient in the event of an injury to a health care worker, emergency response employee, or corrections officer that poses a risk of HIV transmission.

Scientific evidence that anti-HIV therapy could significantly reduce perinatal transmission, together with new treatment opportunities for newborns, has led legislatures to consider mandatory testing of pregnant women and newborn infants. Under federal law, states must at a minimum follow Centers for Disease Control and Prevention (CDC) guidelines recommending counseling and voluntary testing for all pregnant women. If federally set targets for reduction of perinatal HIV transmission are not met, mandatory measures ensue.[20] At the state level, several legislatures have enacted laws that mandate counseling and make voluntary testing available. These federal and state statutes may set a standard of care in tort, so that failure to counsel and offer testing to pregnant women may result in physician liability for wrongful life or wrongful birth in the event that the infant is born with HIV infection.[21] New York has enacted a law requiring mandatory testing of newborns, even though a positive antibody test reveals the serologic status of the mother. New York's law also requires disclosure to the mother and protects confidentiality.[22] That law is currently under court challenge on constitutional grounds.[23]

Since the earliest moments of the epidemic, all states have required named reporting of CDC-defined AIDS. By contrast, 28 states require HIV reporting,[24] and 3 additional states conduct HIV surveillance for pediatric cases only.[25] All HIV reporting states except Maryland and Texas are name based.[26] The CDC recently recommended that all states move to a system of HIV surveillance.[6] The CDC also recommends that states (unless otherwise required by state law) provide alternative test sites where names of persons with HIV infection are not reportable. Ten states proscribe nonreportable, anonymous testing.[27] North Carolina's closure of publicly funded anonymous HIV test sites was upheld as a valid exercise of the state's public health powers.[28]

The predominantly voluntary approach to HIV testing and the absence of a national HIV surveillance system has resulted in concerns that HIV/AIDS has acquired a special or "exceptional" status.[29] In New York State, prominent medical organizations sued to compel the health commissioner to include HIV in the official list of sexually transmitted diseases (STDs). By failing to classify HIV as an STD, the commissioner declined to trigger his powers for compulsory testing, reporting, and contact tracing. New York's highest court held that the classification of diseases was within the commissioner's discretion and affirmed the reasonableness of his belief that the exercise of mandatory powers would not serve an important public health purpose.[30]

PRIVACY, DUTY TO WARN, AND THE RIGHT TO KNOW

Privacy of HIV data has been thought to be necessary for both patient autonomy and public health.[31] Privacy safeguards against social stigma and discrimination and allows each person to make decisions for herself concerning disclosure. Privacy also supports trusting clinical relationships and participation in public health services such as testing, counseling, and partner notification. Most states have HIV-specific statutes requiring confidentiality of HIV data.[32] Litigation claiming wrongful disclosure of HIV-related information has been commenced against numerous individual and institutional providers during the course of the epidemic, including hospitals,[33] physicians,[34] and health departments.[35]

Guided by the mandates of the provider-patient privilege and state HIV confidentiality laws, health care professionals are generally prohibited from revealing a patient's HIV-related information.[36] In fact, some state privacy statutes specifically protect HIV information within the health care or social service setting.[37] Intentional disclosure is only 1 way to breach confidentiality. A health care facility's negligent failure to protect a medical record from disclosure may also violate privacy.[38] However, not all disclosures result in liability. If the health care provider can present a compelling reason for disclosure, a court may allow it. The courts balance the need for the disclosure against the harm done to both the individual's privacy and the public interest and often have little difficulty finding against the individual's privacy right. Using such a test, a Pennsylvania court authorized a hospital to disclose a physician's HIV status to 280 patients who had received invasive procedures.[39] In another case, a court held that a public health agency's disclosure of confidential HIV information to aid in a criminal prosecution was permissible; the criminal activity was deemed a waiver of confidentiality.[40] In contrast, another court prohibited law enforcement access to public health records.[41]

A major tension exists between confidentiality and the "right to know." Health care workers and others who perceive themselves to be at risk for HIV infection in the workplace claim the right to know the HIV status of patients or others. Generally, because infection control precautions in the health care setting are both the standard of practice and highly effective, right-to-know claims are difficult to maintain. For example, a surgeon's lawsuit alleging emotional distress caused by learning, after the fact, that his surgical patient was HIV positive was rejected.[42] Similarly, if morticians and emergency response employees use universal infection control precautions, the risk of HIV transmission is negligible. Nevertheless, federal law authorizes, under certain circumstances, disclosure of HIV information to morticians and emergency response workers upon their request.[43] But whether right-to-know claims will be successful in generating damage awards seems questionable. In a West Virginia case, a mortician filed a tort action against a hospital for failing to inform him that a corpse he had handled was contaminated with HIV. The court found no liability in the absence of actual exposure.[44]

FEAR OF HIV EXPOSURE IN THE HEALTH CARE SETTING

Many cases have been filed by patients claiming that individual or institutional health care providers are liable for exposing them to the risk of HIV transmission without their knowledge. Patients argue that health care professionals negligently caused them emotional distress by failing to warn or failing to prevent some contact that is perceived to pose a risk of transmission. These plaintiffs seek compensation for their mental distress and anguish. Recognizing the litigious nature of American society, many courts limit fear of HIV claims by requiring proof that the plaintiff's mental distress is a result of circumstances posing an actual risk of HIV transmission. Plaintiffs who fear an objectively nonexistent or unprovable risk generally will not be compensated.[45,46] Furthermore, many courts limit compensation to distress occurring during the "window of anxiety," the period between learning of possible exposure and obtaining a reliable HIV-negative test result.[47] In 1 case, a surgical patient provided her own blood for transfusion, but the surgeon transfused another donor's blood. This negligence caused emotional distress that, in light of plaintiff's precautions, was in the court's view both reasonable and foreseeable.[48]

HIV-INFECTED HEALTH CARE PROFESSIONAL'S DUTY TO DISCLOSE

Several courts have held that health care professionals have a duty to disclose their HIV status to patients or health authorities, assuming that their professional activities pose a risk of transmission to patients. The Maryland Court of Appeals ruled that a surgeon has a duty to inform his patients of his infection; even if the patient has not actually been exposed and tests HIV negative, the contact with the surgeon may subsequently give rise to a claim for the infliction of mental distress due to fear of transmission.[49] Courts justify orders to disclose based on a duty to protect patients and on the doctrine of informed consent.[39] Requiring disclosure to patients, of course, can severely jeopardize a health care professional's career. To avoid this result, some states allow the professional to continue practicing, with appropriate restrictions and supervision, but without disclosing his or her HIV status.

THE DUTY TO WARN THIRD PARTIES AT RISK

Many state laws permit, but do not require, disclosure by physicians to third parties known to be at significant future risk of HIV transmission from patients known to be infected.[50] Thus, if a physician reasonably believes that a patient will share drug injection equipment or have unprotected sex without informing a partner of the risk, the physician has discretion to inform the partner. Under some disclosure laws, the physician is required to first counsel the patient to refrain from the risk behavior, and, in providing the third-party warning, the physician is prohibited from disclosing the patient's identity. In the absence of state laws permitting such disclosure, physicians may be held liable for breach of confidentiality for disclosing patient information to sex partners.[51]

The "duty to warn" may extend to nonpatient third parties in other contexts, based on the provider's primary duty to the patient. Thus, health care professionals have a duty to inform patients that they have been transfused with HIV-contaminated blood, and this duty may extend to third parties. A physician in 1 case failed to inform a teenager or her parents that she had been transfused with HIV-contaminated blood. When the young woman's sexual partner tested positive for HIV, the court upheld his claim against the physician based on the physician's failure to inform the patient.[52] Similarly, courts have held that a health care professional's duty to inform a patient of his or her HIV infection may extend to those the patient foreseeably puts at risk such as a spouse[53] or family member caregiver.[54] On the other hand, courts have ruled that disclosure is wrongful in cases in which the third party, such as a family member, is not at actual risk of infection, or the physician has no knowledge that the patient has failed to disclose to the partner.[55]

PREVENTION AND TREATMENT: PHYSICIAN STANDARDS OF CARE

NEGLIGENT DIAGNOSIS OF HIV/AIDS

Patients who have been erroneously informed that they are HIV-infected, when in fact they are not, have filed suit against their health care providers for negligent infliction of emotional distress. Some of these plaintiffs have argued that an HIV-positive diagnosis is a "death sentence" that inflicts extreme psychological harm. To limit recovery to only those cases involving a significant claim for compensation, some courts have refused to award damages unless the mental distress arose from or led to physical injury. For example, courts have held that increased blood pressure is not an adequate injury, but that adverse effects of AIDS treatments or a patient's attempt at suicide would suffice to justify liability.[56] Other courts have not imposed a physical injury requirement.[57]

Providers may also be liable for negligently failing to diagnose HIV infection. In 1 case, a jury awarded more than $1 million in a case in which an earlier diagnosis would have delayed by 1 year the onset of symptoms, disability, and death.[58] A physician may also be liable for unnecessary delay in notifying a patient of exposure to HIV[59] and may be liable to the patient's sexual partner who is subsequently infected.[52] However, providers have not been held liable for failure to diagnose and effectively treat HIV unless the plaintiff has shown a causal connection between their failure and the injury suffered.[60] In the early years of the epidemic, failure to diagnose HIV infection did not expose the provider to significant liability, since treatment options and likelihood of success in treatment were limited. But as treatments for HIV illness develop to higher levels of efficacy, failure to render a prompt diagnosis or failure to initiate prompt and appropriate treatment may expose providers to increasing liability.

DISTRIBUTION OF DRUG INJECTION EQUIPMENT

Public health[61] and medical[62] authorities recommend that physicians counsel drug users to use a new syringe and needle for every injection. Syringe exchanges have been established at the state and local levels to prevent transmission of HIV and other blood-borne pathogens.[63] Nevertheless, a web of state statutes create criminal offenses for the sale, distribution, or possession of syringes and needles.[64,65] These laws pose the threat of prosecution to public health officials and community activists who distribute sterile needles and syringes, and, in some cases, prosecutions have resulted. The Washington Supreme Court, however, upheld syringe exchange as a valid public health measure. The court reasoned that the health department had acted in pursuance of an AIDS statute that granted the department the general power to implement prevention strategies.[66] Federal law prohibits use of federal funds for syringe exchange until the secretary of health and human services certifies that exchanges are effective in preventing HIV infection and do not encourage drug use.[67]

DISCRIMINATION AND ACCESS TO CARE

The HIV epidemic has been characterized by a high level of social opprobrium against those infected or suspected of being infected. As a result, individuals with HIV infection routinely encounter discrimination in many aspects of their lives. Discrimination in the health care setting, however, is especially pernicious, depriving patients of necessary services and undermining their trust in the system's commitment to provide them with the care they need. If individuals fear discrimination in health care, they may forgo testing or fail to discuss their health and risk behaviors. Furthermore, because health care professionals are viewed by the general public as being well informed, their actions set a poor example for others attempting to respond to the epidemic in a nondiscriminatory fashion.

Institutional health care providers and other employers have a duty to provide a reasonably safe workplace. The use of barrier techniques on a universal basis has been the officially sanctioned approach to workplace safety. As a result, discrimination against patients is rarely, if ever, justified by a provider's fear of transmission. The Occupational Safety and Health Administration's (OSHA's) blood-borne pathogen safety standard[68] has been challenged as overly broad,[69] but remains the primary safety standard. Although employer noncompliance with infection control standards may give rise to a justifiable refusal to work, the underlying fear must have an objective basis.[70] Employee claims of occupational transmission (or fear of occupational transmission) are generally covered by worker compensation statutes,[71] which provide exclusive remedies for work-related claims against employers.[72]

DEFINITION OF "DISABILITY" UNDER THE ADA: THE SUPREME COURT'S FIRST AIDS CASE

An array of laws at the federal, state, and local levels prohibit discrimination on the basis of a person's disability or health status.[1] The primary federal nondiscrimination statute is the Americans With Disabilities Act (ADA) of 1990,[73,74] although the laws of many states and localities also specifically prohibit discrimination against individuals living with HIV/AIDS.

The ADA provides that no individual "shall be discriminated against on the basis of disability in the full and equal enjoyment of the goods, services, facilities, privileges, advantages, or accommodations of any place of public accommodation."[75] The ADA's definition of "public accommodation" specifically includes hospitals and professional offices of health care providers.[76] Similarly, New York's highest court ruled that the offices of private dentists are considered places of public accommodation under New York law.[77]

A critically important issue under the ADA is whether persons with asymptomatic HIV infection have a "disability" and thus are protected under the ADA.[78] Disability is defined as a physical or mental impairment that substantially limits 1 or more of the major life activities of the individual, a record of such impairment, or being regarded as having such an impairment.[79] In the past, many courts have ruled or assumed as undisputed that HIV infection, as the underlying cause of a life-threatening illness, is a disability. However, several recent court decisions have held that HIV does not automatically qualify as a disability, and in each case there must be an individualized determination as to whether the infection actually limits, in a substantial way, a major life activity. Given the advent of new combination therapies that significantly delay the onset of disabling symptoms, this judicial view could markedly undermine legal protection against discrimination for persons with asymptomatic or mildly symptomatic HIV infection. The ADA's legislative history, however, indicates that Congress intended to include HIV infection within the definition of disability, and the Equal Employment Opportunity Commission's regulations embody that view.[80] In its first AIDS case ever, the Supreme Court will decide whether and to what extent persons with HIV infection are protected under the ADA.

In *Abbott v Bragdon,*[81] a dentist refused to fill a dental cavity of an HIV-infected patient. The patient then brought suit alleging that the refusal violated the ADA. The dentist conceded that his professional office was covered by the ADA, but argued that providing services to the infected patient, because of the risk of HIV transmission, would pose a direct threat to his health. Additionally, he argued that the plaintiff, who did not have symptoms of HIV illness, was not an individual with a disability under the ADA. The lower courts rejected the dentist's defenses, concluding that the dentist was unable to show that in 1994, when the case arose, there was evidence that treating an infected patient posed a significant risk. The plaintiff's infection, which she testified resulted in her decision against becoming pregnant, was viewed as substantially limiting the major life activity of reproduction. The Supreme Court has agreed to consider 3 questions presented by the case: (1) whether reproduction is a major life activity; (2) whether asymptomatic HIV infection is a per se disability under the ADA; and (3) whether the courts should defer to a health care provider's reasonable professional judgment.

The ADA's coverage also extends to individuals merely regarded as having a disability. Thus, it is unlawful to discriminate against an individual based on the misperception that the person is infected with HIV under the ADA as well as under the laws of many states.[82] Persons discriminated against because of their association with a person with HIV infection are also protected,[83] as are persons retaliated against because of their opposition to discrimination.[84]

THE HEALTH CARE PROFESSIONAL'S DUTY TO TREAT

Courts have consistently held that health care professionals have a legal duty to treat patients living with HIV/AIDS.[85] Health care professionals must, of course, exercise appropriate clinical judgment. If a professional lacks the skill appropriate to render competent care, she may legally refuse to treat the person and may lawfully refer him elsewhere.[86] A clinician cannot, however, simply reject or refer an HIV-infected patient solely because of his or her HIV status.

The courts have had to decide the difficult question whether and to what degree a health care professional can treat HIV-infected persons differently from other patients. Although CDC and OSHA standards require use of "universal" precautions applicable to all patients without regard to infection status, imposition of special precautions for HIV-infected patients has been upheld.[87] One court, finding that special precautions may be necessary for certain procedures, ruled that a dentist may lawfully refuse to treat a patient who refuses to reveal HIV-related information.[88] But another court ruled that the use of special precautions, which resulted in delay of services, beyond those recommended by the CDC constituted unlawful discrimination.[89]

NONDISCRIMINATION IN HEALTH INSURANCE

Access to health care is often contingent on the ability to pay or the availability of insurance coverage. Federal and state law provides little or no protection from adverse coverage decisions provided the insurance company uses sound actuarial data. However, an employer's decision to place severe limits on coverage for HIV/AIDS, but not on comparable diseases, may be unlawful under the ADA.[90,91] A central question in determining the extent of health insurance coverage is whether certain services are "medically necessary." In an important case, the Eleventh Circuit Court of Appeals held that skilled nursing care was "medically necessary" and should be reimbursed under an employer's self-funded health benefits plan.[92]

HIV-INFECTED HEALTH CARE PROFESSIONALS

Federal law[93] requires states to comply with CDC guidance[94] that recommends an individualized determination of whether HIV-infected physicians engaging in "exposure-prone" procedures can safely practice. At present the CDC and the American Medical Association are reevaluating their policies in light of epidemiologic evidence showing that the risk to patients, even from invasive procedures, is negligible. The judiciary has had to decide whether HIV-infected health care professionals pose a significant risk to their patients, and thus are not qualified to continue to practice. Several courts have upheld decisions to prohibit HIV-infected health care professionals who perform invasive procedures.[95,96] These courts have reasoned that the severity of harm if HIV infection were transmitted justifies practice restrictions. However, the Ninth Circuit Court of Appeals held that a physician's practice could not be restricted if he did not primarily perform invasive procedures. The physician, a general internist, was employed by the Federal Bureau of Investigation (FBI). The agency refused to refer patients to the physician after suspecting that he was HIV positive. The court ruled that the FBI had failed to make adequate inquiries about the physician's infection control procedures: "The record shows that Dr. Doe and the hospital were entirely forthcoming about these procedures, but that their explanations fell on deaf ears."[97]

PRISONER HEALTH CARE

Access to adequate health care for prison inmates living with HIV/AIDS has been a long-term problem.[98] Gross inadequacies in state prison health care systems may rise to a constitutional violation.[99] In New York, inmates living with HIV/AIDS challenged the state's delivery of medical, mental health, educational, and prevention services. The court ordered the state to release records enumerating the inmates, both living and deceased, who had been diagnosed as having AIDS or AIDS-related illnesses, in order to aid in the court's determination as to whether the prison authorities deliberately neglected the inmates' health care needs.[100] Inadequate medical care and lack of HIV education services resulted in a court-imposed remedial plan in another case.[101] But when a showing of deliberate indifference is lacking, federal constitutional claims against prison officials will fail.[102]

CONCLUSION

Considerable progress has been made—socially and legally—during the first 2 decades of the HIV/AIDS epidemic. Reductions in social stigma and new statutes to protect privacy and proscribe discrimination have emerged. The serious consequences of the epidemic, however, are not over. While instances of gross abuse are less frequent, intolerance and animus stubbornly persist. Even legal advances have been eroded with some courts denying antidiscrimination protection for persons with asymptomatic HIV infection, and upholding discrimination against HIV-infected health care professionals despite the extremely low risks.

Systematic efforts to confront the HIV/AIDS epidemic are needed: (1) expanded and nondiscriminatory access to health care; (2) expansion of counseling, testing, and other prevention services; (3) educational campaigns to promote tolerance and reduce social stigma; and (4) better laws to protect privacy and prohibit discrimination. The health care and public health systems need these and other kinds of new strategies to reduce the deep personal and social burdens of HIV disease in the United States.

REFERENCES

1. Webber D. W., ed. *AIDS and the Law*. 3rd ed. New York, NY: John Wiley & Sons Inc; 1997.

2. Gostin L. O., ed. *AIDS and the Health Care System*. New Haven, Conn: Yale University Press; 1990.

3. Gostin L. O. The AIDS Litigation Project: a national review of court and Human Rights Commission decisions, I: the social impact of AIDS. *JAMA*. 1990;263:1961–1970.

4. Gostin L. O. The AIDS Litigation Project: a national review of court and Human Rights Commission decisions, II: discrimination in education, employment, housing, insurance, and health care. *JAMA*. 1990;263:2086–2093.

5. Carpenter C. C. J., Fischl M. A., Hammer S. M., et al. Antiretroviral therapy for HIV infection in 1997. *JAMA*. 1997;277:1962–1969.

6. Centers for Disease Control and Prevention. Update: trends in AIDS incidence—United States, 1996. *MMWR Morb Mortal Wkly Rep.* 1997;46:861–867.

7. Peckham C., Gibb D. Mother-to-child transmission of the human immunodeficiency virus. *N Engl J Med.* 1995;333:298–302.

8. Fiscus S. A., Adimora A. A., Schoenbach V. J., et al. Perinatal HIV infection and the effect of zidovudine therapy on transmission in rural and urban counties. *JAMA*. 1996;275:1483–1494.

9. Centers for Disease Control. Provisional Public Health Service interagency recommendations for screening donated blood and plasma for antibody to the virus causing acquired immunodeficiency syndrome. *MMWR Morb Mortal Wkly Rep.* 1985;34:1–5.

10. 32 CFR §§58.1–58.6 (1997).

11. *American Fed'n of Gov't Employees, Local 1812 v US Dep't of State,* 662 F Supp 50 (DDC 1987).

12. Gostin L. O., Cleary P. D., Mayer K., Brandt A., Chittenden E. Screening and exclusion of international travelers and immigrants for public health purposes: an evaluation of United States policy. *N Engl J Med.* 1990;322:1743–1746.

13. *US v Ward,* 131 F3d 335 (3d Cir 1997).

14. Gostin L. O., Lazzarini Z., Alexander D. D., et al. HIV testing, counseling, and prophylaxis after sexual assault. *JAMA*. 1994;271:1436–1444.

15. *T.E.P. v Leavitt,* 840 F Supp 110 (D Utah 1993).

16. *Glover v Eastern Neb Community Office of Retardation,* 686 F Supp 243 (D Neb 1988), *aff'd,* 867 F2d 461 (8th Cir), *cert denied,* 493 US 932 (1989).

17. *Doe v Dyer-Goode,* 566 A2d 889 (Pa Super Ct 1989).

18. Pa Stat Ann tit 35, §7607.

19. *Hill v Evans,* No. 91-A-626-N, 1993 WL 595676 (MD Ala Oct 7, 1993).

20. 42 USC §300ff-34.

21. *Anastosopoulos v Perakis,* 644 A2d 480 (Me 1994).

22. New York Department of Health, Maternal-Pediatric HIV Prevention and Care Program. *HIV Counseling and Testing of Newborns as Part of the Comprehensive Newborn Testing Program.* Albany: New York Dept of Health Maternal-Pediatric HIV Prevention and Care Program; 1997. Memorandum 97-2.

23. *R.Z. v Pataki,* Index No. 97-112960 (Sup Ct NY County, complaint filed July 18, 1997).

24. Alabama, Arizona, Arkansas, Colorado, Florida, Idaho, Indiana, Louisiana, Michigan, Minnesota, Mississippi, Missouri, Nebraska, Nevada, New Jersey, New Mexico, North Carolina, North Dakota, Ohio, Oklahoma, South Carolina, South Dakota, Tennessee, Utah, Virginia, West Virginia, Wisconsin, Wyoming.

25. Connecticut, Texas, and Oregon.

26. Gostin L. O., Ward J. W., Baker A. C. National HIV case reporting for the United States. *N Engl J Med.* 1997;337:1162–1167.

27. Alabama, Idaho, Michigan, Nevada, North Carolina, Ohio, South Carolina, South Dakota, Tennessee, and Wyoming.

28. *ACT-UP Triangle v Comm'n for Health Servs,* 483 SE2d 388 (NC 1997), *rev'g* 472 SE2d 605 (NC Ct App 1996).

29. Bayer R. Public health policy and the AIDS epidemic: an end to HIV exceptionalism. *N Engl J Med.* 1991;324:1500–03.

30. *New York State Soc'y of Surgeons v Axelrod,* 572 NE2d 605 (NY 1991).

31. *Report of the Presidential Commission on the Human Immunodeficiency Virus Epidemic.* Washington, DC: US Government Printing Office; 1988.

32. Gostin L. O., Lazzarini Z., Neslund V. S., et al. The public health information infrastructure: a national review of the law on health information privacy. *JAMA*. 1996;275:1921–1927.

33. *Doe v Methodist Hosp,* 639 NE2d 683 (Ind Ct App 1994).

34. *Doe v Marselle,* 675 A2d 835 (Conn 1996), *rev'g* 660 A2d 871 (Conn App Ct 1995).

35. *Estate of Benson v Minnesota Bd of Medical Practice,* 526 NW2d 634 (Minn Ct App 1995).

36. *Doe v Roe,* 588 NYS2d 236 (Sup Ct Onondaga County 1992), *rev'd in part,* 599 NYS2d 350 (App Div 1993), *subsequent opinion,* 620 NYS2d 666 (App Div 1994).

37. NY Pub Health Law §2782.

38. *Estate of Behringer v Medical Ctr,* 592 A2d 1251 (NJ Super Ct Law Div 1991).

39. *In re* Milton S. Hershey Medical Ctr, 634 A2d 159 (Pa 1993), *aff'g* 595 A2d 1290 (Pa Super Ct 1991).

40. *State v Stark,* 832 P2d 109 (Wash Ct App 1992).

41. *State v J. E.,* 606 A2d 1160 (NJ Super Ct Law Div 1992).

42. *Ordway v County of Suffolk,* 583 NYS2d 1014 (Sup Ct Suffolk County 1992).

43. 42 USC §300ff-76(4).

44. *Funeral Servs by Gregory, Inc v Bluefield Community Hosp,* 413 SE2d 79 (WVa 1991), *overruled in part by Courtney v Courtney,* 437 SE2d 436 (WVa 1993).

45. *Kaufman v Physical Measurements, Inc,* 615 NYS2d 508 (App Div 1994).

46. *Barrett v Danbury Hosp,* 654 A2d 748 (Conn 1995).

47. *Madrid v Lincoln County Medical Ctr,* 923 P2d 1154 (NM 1996), *aff'g* 909 P2d 14 (NM Ct App 1995).

48. *Hoffman v Brandywine Hosp,* 661 A2d 397 (Pa Super Ct 1995).

49. *Faya v Almaraz,* 620 A2d 327 (Md 1993).

50. Gostin L. O., Hodge J. Piercing the veil of secrecy in HIV/AIDS and other sexually transmitted diseases: theories of privacy and disclosure in partner notification: contact tracing, the "right to know," and the "duty to warn." *Duke J Gender Law & Policy*. In press.

51. *N. O. L. v District of Columbia,* 674 A2d 498 (DC 1996).

52. *Reisner v Regents of Univ of Cal,* 37 Cal Rptr 2d 518 (Ct App 1995).

53. *Garcia v Santa Rosa Health Care Corp,* No. 13-94-482-CV, 1996 Tex App LEXIS 824 (Tex App 13 Dist 1996), *substituted opinion upon reh'g,* 1996 Tex App LEXIS 2513 (Tex App 13 Dist June 20, 1996).

54. *J. B. v Sacred Heart Hosp,* 635 So2d 945 (Fla 1994), *certified question at* 996 F2d 276 (11th Cir 1993).

55. *Diaz Reyes v US,* 770 F Supp 58 (DPR 1991), *aff'd without opinion,* 971 F2d 744 (1st Cir), *cert denied,* 504 US 957 (1992).

56. *R. J. v Humana of Fla, Inc,* 652 So2d 360 (Fla 1995).

57. *Bramer v Dotson,* 437 SE2d 773 (WVa 1993).

58. *Doe v McNulty,* 630 So2d 825 (La Ct App 1993), *cert denied,* 631 So2d 1167 (La 1994).

59. *Mixon v Cason,* 622 So2d 825 (Ala 1993).

60. *Baker v English,* 894 P2d 505 (Ore Ct App 1995), *aff'd in part & rev'd in part,* 932 P2d 57 (Ore 1997).

61. Centers for Disease Control and Prevention. *HIV Prevention Bulletin: Medical Advice for Persons Who Inject Illicit Drugs.* Atlanta, Ga: Centers for Disease Control and Prevention; May 9, 1997.

62. Normand J., Vlahov D., Moses L. E., eds. *Preventing HIV Transmission: The Role of Sterile Needles and Bleach.* Washington, DC: National Academy Press; 1995.

63. Burris S., Finucane D., Gallagher H., Grace J. The legal strategies used in operating syringe exchange programs in the United States. *Am J Public Health.* 1996;86:1161–1166.

64. Gostin L. O., Lazzarini Z., Jones T. S., et al. Prevention of HIV/AIDS and other blood-borne diseases among injection drug users: a national survey on the regulation of syringes and needles. *JAMA.* 1997;277:53–62.

65. Gostin L. O., Lazzarini Z. Prevention of HIV/AIDS among injection drug users: the theory and science of public health and criminal justice approaches to disease prevention. *Emory Law J.* 1997;46:587–696.

66. *Spokane County Health Dist v Brockett,* 839 P2d 324 (Wash 1992).

67. Pub L No. 105-78, Title V, §§505–506, 1997 USCCAN (111 Stat) 1467, 1515.

68. Occupational Safety and Health Administration. Blood borne pathogens. 29 CFR §1910.1030 (1997).

69. *American Dental Ass'n v Martin,* 984 F2d 823 (7th Cir 1993).

70. *Armstrong v Flowers Hosp,* 33 F3d 1308 (11th Cir 1994), *aff'g* 812 F Supp 1183 (MD Ala 1993).

71. Miller P., Tereskerz D., Jagger J. Occupationally acquired HIV. *Am J Public Health.* 1997;87:1558–1562.

72. *Elliott v Dugger,* 579 So2d 827 (Fla Dist Ct App 1991), *prior opinion,* 542 So2d 392 (Fla Dist Ct App 1989).

73. 42 USC §§12101 *et seq.*

74. Gostin L., Beyer H., eds. *The Americans With Disabilities Act: What It Means for All Americans.* Baltimore, Md: Brookes Publishing Co; 1993.

75. 42 USC §12182(a).

76. 42 USC §12181(7).

77. *Cahill v Rosa,* 674 NE2d 274 (NY 1996), *rev'g* 632 NYS2d 614 (App Div 1995).

78. Parmet W. E., Jackson D. H. No longer disabled: the legal impact of the new social construction of HIV. *Am J Law Med.* 1997;23:7–44.

79. 42 USC §12102(2).

80. 29 CFR §1630, appendix at 339 (1996).

81. *Abbott v Bragdon,* 107 F3d 934 (1st Cir 1997), *aff'g* 912 F Supp 580 (D Me 1995), *cert granted,* 118 SCt 554 (1997).

82. *Sanchez v Lagoudakis,* 486 NW2d 657 (Mich 1992), *subsequent opinion,* 552 NW2d 472 (Mich Ct App 1996).

83. *Finley v Giacobbe,* 827 F Supp 215 (SD NY 1993).

84. *Sherer v Foodmaker, Inc,* 921 F Supp 651 (ED Mo 1996).

85. *Howe v Hull,* 873 F Supp 72 (ND Ohio 1994).

86. *Schulman v State Div of Human Rights,* 641 NYS2d 134 (App Div 1996), *rev'd,* 677 NE2d 284 (NY 1997), *on remand,* 658 NYS2d 70 (App Div 1997).

87. *North Shore Univ Hosp v Rosa,* 657 NE2d 483 (NY 1995), *aff'g* 600 NYS2d 90 (App Div 1993).

88. *Doe v Kahala Dental Group,* 808 P2d 1276 (Haw), *reconsideration denied,* 841 P2d 1074 (Haw 1991).

89. *Sharrow v Bailey,* 910 F Supp 187 (MD Pa 1995).

90. *EEOC Interim Guidance on Application of the ADA to Health Insurance.* Washington, DC: Equal Employment Opportunities Commission; June 8, 1993.

91. *Carparts Distrib Ctr, Inc v Automotive Wholesalers Ass'n,* 37 F3d 12 (1st Cir 1994), *rev'g* 826 F Supp 583 (D NH 1993).

92. *Florence Nightingale Nursing Serv v Blue Cross & Blue Shield,* 832 F Supp 1456 (ND Ala 1993), *aff'd,* 41 F3d 1476 (11th Cir), *cert denied,* 115 S Ct 2002 (1995).

93. Pub L No. 102–141, Title VI, §633, 1991 USCCAN (105 Stat) 834, 876–77, *reprinted in note to* 42 USC §300ee-2.

94. Centers for Disease Control and Prevention. Recommendations for preventing transmission of human immunodeficiency virus and hepatitis B virus to patients during exposure-prone invasive procedures. *MMWR Morb Mortal Wkly Rep.* 1991;40(RR-8):1–9.

95. *Bradley v Univ of Tex M. D. Anderson Cancer Ctr,* 3 F3d 922 (5th Cir 1993) (per curiam), *cert denied,* 114 SCt 1071 (1994).

96. *Mauro v Borgess Medical Ctr,* 886 F Supp 1349 (WD Mich 1995).

97. *Doe by Lavery v Attorney Gen'l,* 44 F3d 715 (9th Cir 1995), *superseded without opinion,* 62 F3d 1424 (9th Cir), *vacated and remanded sub nom Reno v Doe by Lavery,* 116 SCt 2543 (1996).

98. Burris S. Prisons, law and public health: the case for a coordinated response to epidemic diseases behind bars. *Univ Miami Law Rev.* 1992;47:291–329.

99. *Hetzel v Swartz,* 917 F Supp 344 (MD Pa 1996).

100. *Inmates of NY State With HIV v Cuomo,* No. 90-CV-252, 1991 US Dist LEXIS 1488 (ND NY Feb 7, 1991).

101. *Madrid v Gomez,* 889 F Supp 1146 (ND Cal 1995).

102. State *ex rel Peeples v Anderson,* 653 NE2d 371 (Ohio 1995).

GAVIN YAMEY AND WILLIAM W. RANKIN

AIDS and Global Justice

Gavin Yamey received his B.A. degree (Physiological Sciences) from Oxford University. He later graduated from University College London Medical School. Before joining the *British Medical Journal (BMJ),* he worked in general medicine at a variety of London hospitals, and was a registrar in neurological rehabilitation at the Homerton Hospital Regional Neurological Rehabilitation Unit. He has been the deputy editor of *Western Journal of Medicine* and an assistant editor at the *BMJ.*

William W. Rankin is President of the Global AIDS Interfaith Alliance (GAIA), a nongovernmental organization for preventing HIV transmission in developing countries. He is a Fellow of the College of Preachers at Washington's National Cathedral, a member of the International Advisory Board of the Graduate School of International Relations and Pacific Studies at the University of California, San Diego, and a member of the board of the San Francisco Holocaust Memorial and Education Fund. He has authored three books, more than forty articles in refereed journals, and several book chapters.

"The bottom line is, the people who are dying from AIDS don't matter in this world."[1]

. . . In his *Theory of Justice,* John Rawls, perhaps the most important moral philosopher of the 20th century, argued that justice is required when there is a struggle for scarce resources and when life is brief.[2] Both of these conditions are met in those countries devastated by HIV. [Therefore, we should] demand actions that are based on justice: the distribution of antiretroviral drugs to the world's poorest people; the empowerment of women; the urgent search for an HIV vaccine; and the care and education of children orphaned by AIDS.

Wealthy countries must take the lead in acting justly. Their colonisation of the regions now struggling with rising HIV rates, like India and Africa, left behind a legacy of exploitation and oppression and an ongoing power imbalance between rich and poor countries.[3,4] Part of this imbalance is economic. The aggregate national income of wealthy countries recently surpassed $21 trillion annually. These countries quickly came up with astounding sums of money for an antiterrorism campaign, so they could surely find the $7–10 billion needed annually to fight HIV.[5]

The creation of the new global fund to fight AIDS, tuberculosis, and malaria sent a message that the world does care about HIV/AIDS. But ever since its proposal by Kofi Annan last year, there has been intense speculation about whether the fund will be able to meet its aims,[6] which are "to attract, manage and disburse additional resources through a new public-private partnership."[7] It was supposed to be operational by the end of last year. How is it performing?

On its first aim, the answer is poorly. The total pledges to the fund ($1.7bn,[8] or about $700m for this fiscal year) are hugely disproportionate to what is needed. As for management and disbursal, these remain a mystery. There were three meetings last year of a transitional working group and a 14 member board will meet for the first time on 28 January, after

Reprinted with permission from the *British Medical Journal* 324 (January 26, 2002), 181–82. Copyright © 2002 by the British Medical Association.

which resources will be disbursed. Yet there is still almost no public knowledge about exactly what the fund will pay for (perhaps treatments, health systems support, or both), and how it will make its funding decisions. This is worrying. We need reassurance that the fund will avoid the major pitfalls—lack of governance and poor accountability—that have plagued other public-private health initiatives.[9]

In thinking about justice and the global fund, Rawls might ask a simple question. Will the fund change the life of, say, a pregnant woman with HIV living in Malawi, whose husband has died of AIDS and who is caring for three children? This depends on four things, which, echoing Rawls, we could call the "conditions of justice."

Firstly, it must pay to treat those already infected. Treatment must include antiretroviral drugs. Yet in its statement of underlying principles, the fund's transitional working group says it will pursue "an integrated and balanced approach."[10] Is this coded language for saying that treatment will not be a priority? Médecins Sans Frontières thinks so. In a letter to the group, Bernard Pecoul, director of Médecins Sans Frontières' access to essential medicines campaign, expressed concern that, "because donors and some in the international health community traditionally favour prevention at the expense of treatment, patients already infected will be written off as not sufficiently cost effective to treat."[11] . . . Emily Bass, a Ugandan woman, calls on the world "to acknowledge that you cannot talk about prevention without treatment."[12]

Secondly, the fund must respond to the local needs of the poorest countries themselves, and not to donors' priorities. The ideal scenario is arguably one in which the fund supports a poor country that has put forward a technically feasible proposal. It is promising that the fund's board will have an equal number of members from donor and recipient countries—hopefully this will translate into an equal power relationship.

Thirdly, the fund must purchase drugs at the lowest cost possible, which in some cases might be generic versions. The fund's board, however, includes a representative from the pharmaceutical industry, in a voting seat. The fund must not end up underwriting the drug patent monopolies currently enjoyed by industry.

Fourthly—and this is the most important condition of justice—the fund must show measurable success. It must do something new and different in fighting HIV/AIDS, where previous global initiatives have failed. Donor money is not flowing into the fund because donors currently see no guarantee from their investment. For the fund to thrive, it has to address this lack of confidence. It has to show that it can cut deaths due to AIDS, prevent new HIV infections, and support care of orphans.

When the philosopher Thucydides was asked when justice would come to Rome, he famously replied that it would come when those who are not injured are as indignant as those who are. So let us all feel indignant about the worsening HIV pandemic—as if "we all have AIDS"[13]—and let us make sure that the global fund turns this anger into action.

NOTES

1. Sherry J. Quoted in Gellman, B. The belated global response to AIDS in Africa. *Washington Post* 2000;5 Jul:A01.

2. Rawls J. *Theory of justice.* Revised ed. Cambridge, MA: Harvard University Press, 1999.

3. Heath E. Colonial Rule. In: Appiah K. A., Gates H. L. Jr, eds. *Africana: the Encyclopedia of the African and African American experience*. New York: Basic Books, 1999:485–9.

4. Hochschild A. *King Leopold's ghost*. New York: Houghton Mifflin, 1998.

5. Attaran A., Sachs J. Defining and refining international donor support for combating the AIDS pandemic. *Lancet* 2001; 357:57–61.

6. Brugha R., Walt G. A global health fund: a leap of faith? *BMJ* 2001;323:152–4.

7. www.globalfundATM.org/overview.html [accessed 15 January 2002]

8. www.un.org/News/ossg/aids.htm [accessed 15 January 2002]

9. Yamey G. Global campaign to eradicate malaria. *BMJ* 2001;322:1191–2.

10. www.globalfundatm.org/principles.html [accessed 15 January 2002]

11. Pecoul B. Open letter to members of the transitional working group and technical support secretariat of the Global Fund to Fight AIDS, Tuberculosis and Malaria. http://lists.essential.org/pipermail/ip-health/2001-November/002386.html [accessed 14 January 2002]

12. Akiki F. S. The Focus on Women Kampala declaration: Ugandan women call for action on HIV/AIDS. *BMJ* 2002;324:247.

13. Berwick D. "We All Have AIDS": the case for reducing the cost of HIV medicines to zero. *BMJ* 2002;324:214–8.

DONALD M. BERWICK

We All Have AIDS

Donald M. Berwick is President and Chief Executive Officer of the Institute for Healthcare Improvement. He is also a Clinical Professor of Pediatrics and Health Care Policy at the Harvard Medical School. He has published widely in health care policy, decision analysis and health care quality management. He also chaired groups such as the Agency for Health Care Policy and Research and the National Advisory Council of the Agency for Healthcare Research and Quality.

In many occupied nations during World War II, the Nazis ordered Jews to wear a yellow star, as prelude to their destruction. But not in Denmark. According to legend, the Danish king, Christian X, threatened that, if Danish Jews were to wear the star, he would, too. The story is almost certainly a myth, but its meaning is not. Despite the Nazi occupation, Denmark rescued the overwhelming majority of its Jews. "If some Danes are under siege," the story means to say, "then all Danes are under siege. So, for now, we are all Jews."

Now we all have AIDS. No other construction is any longer reasonable. The earth has AIDS; 36.1 million people at the end of the year 2000. In Botswana, 36 percent of adults are infected with HIV; in South Africa 20 percent. Three million humans died of AIDS in the year 2000, 2.4 million of them in sub-Saharan Africa. That is a Holocaust every two years; the entire population of Oregon, Iowa, Connecticut or Ireland dead last year, and next year, and next. More deaths since the AIDS epidemic began than in the Black Death of the Middle Ages. It is the most lethal epidemic in recorded history. Prevention will be the most important way to attack AIDS everywhere, but treatment matters, too. We can treat AIDS effectively. We cannot cure its victims, but we can extend their healthy lives by years—with luck, by decades. We can reduce its transmission from infected mother to unborn child by two-thirds or more. We are seeing the effects of advancing science plus enlightened public health policies in the United States, where the toll of AIDS began to fall in 1997.

Successful, life-prolonging management of HIV infection is not simple. Important dimensions include education, social support and life-style interventions that are extremely difficult to achieve in the developed nations, and many times more so in impoverished nations. But it is a mistake to ignore the role of medications. In New York, San Francisco or Nairobi, no matter how different the cultural challenges, the correct mainstay of lifesaving care for the unborn child or the infected adult is medicine, given in a timely, scientifically accurate and reliable way. Most people on earth with HIV and AIDS do not get those medicines. The barriers are partly social and logistical, but the overwhelming barrier is cost. At current prices, one year of triple drug therapy for an HIV-positive person costs $15,000. Recent, welcome changes by a few progressive pharmaceutical companies, like Merck & Co., promise to reduce that cost by thousands of dollars per year.

But keep in mind that no legend claims King Christian talked of putting on only half a yellow star.

Here is what the world needs: free anti-AIDS medicines. The devastated nations of the world need AIDS medicines at no cost at all, or, at a bare minimum, medicines available at exactly their marginal costs of manufacture, not loaded at all with indirect costs or amortized costs of development. No hand-waving or

Berwick, Donald M. "We All Have AIDS." *Washington Post,* June 26, 2001, A17. Reprinted with the permission of the author.
Copyright © 2001 by Donald M. Berwick.

accounting maneuvers—for all practical purposes, free. Here is how it could happen: the board chairs and executives of the world's leading drug companies decide to do it, period. To the anxious corporate lawyers, the incredulous stockholders, the cynical regulators and the suspicious public, they say, together, the same thing:

"The earth has AIDS, and therefore we all, for now, have AIDS. Therefore, we are taking one simple action that will save millions and millions of lives. We choose to do it, together, and we will use the intelligence of our own forces to figure out how to make it possible, while preserving the futures of our companies."

No one could stop them; none would dare try. For the small profit they would lose, they would gain the trust and gratitude of the entire world. They would have created a story to be told for a millennium, and those who depend on the prudence of these leaders—on their "fiduciary responsibility"—might chose then not to blame them but to join them in celebration, as fiduciaries of humankind.

The names of the people who can say this, together, include these: Raymond Gilmartin, (chairman and CEO of Merck & Co.); Sir Richard Sykes and Jean-Pierre Garnier (respectively chairman and CEO of GlaxoSmithKline); Charles A. Heimbold, Jr, and Peter Dolan (respectively chairman/CEO and president of Bristol-Myers Squibb); Dr. Franz B. Humer (chairman and CEO of Roche). There are others; they know who they are. These few souls, with this act, would ultimately save the lives of more human beings than died in the Holocaust—perhaps two or three times over.

If a Nobel Prize followed, it would be redundant. The memory of the deed would likely outlive even the story of the Danish king who joined his people in their need.

DOROTHY E. LOGIE AND
SOLOMON R. BENATAR

Africa in the 21st Century: Can Despair Be Turned to Hope?

Dorothy Logie is the Referral Advisor for General Practice at Glasgow University. Her interests lie in international health policy, health care in sub-Saharan Africa, HIV/AIDS and promoting international primary health care. The countries she focuses on the most are in Western and Southern Africa.

Solomon Benatar is Professor of Medicine and Director of the University of Cape Town Bioethics Centre; Visiting Professor in Public Health Sciences and Medicine at the University of Toronto's Joint Centre for Bioethics; and Chairperson of South Africa's Ministerial Committee on Health Research Ethics.

The free flow of trade and money around the world has brought economic growth for the fortunate in the largest and strongest economies but has also created widening gaps in wealth and health between, and within, countries. These polarising forces have intensified in the past decade, creating a hundred million poor within the rich "core" in addition to the 1.3 billion people in the "periphery" who exist on $1 a day or less.[1]

AFRO-PESSIMISM

Sub-Saharan Africa is the most dramatic loser. Here poverty is at its most stark and marginalisation from the global economy most pronounced. The continent contains 33 of the world's 50 poorest countries. Improvements in health, education, and living standards have reversed in the past two decades, and standards continue to fall. By the end of the decade, two thirds of Africans will live in "absolute poverty."[2] More than half still lack safe water and 70% are without proper sanitation; 40 million children are not in primary school. Infant mortality is 55% higher than in the rest of the world's low income, developing countries, and average life expectancy, at 51 years, is 11 years less.[3] Malaria and tuberculosis are increasing, and in parts of central, southern, and eastern Africa 30–40% of pregnant women are now HIV positive.[2]

Poverty causes ill health, but ill health also imposes immense economic costs on individuals, their families, and society. African productivity could increase by 15% if illness and disability were attacked more strenuously.[4] The economic cost of malaria is estimated at 1% of gross national product, while AIDS strikes adults in their most productive years (figure). In families with AIDS, the children are forced to leave school early to work, weakening their long term financial prospects. New ways of coping with the cost of illness (selling cattle or land) cause further long term economic hardship (J. Tumwine, personal communication).

WHERE DOES BLAME LIE?

Many of Africa's setbacks have been associated with global economic policies over the past two decades which, in a complex way, reinforce the legacies of colonialism and imperialism and exacerbate Africa's internal problems. These external forces include:

- A crippling debt of $300 billion which soaks up one fifth of Africa's savings and drains the continent of more than it receives in aid or loans.[6] More money is spent on debt servicing than on health and education. In Uganda, which has one

Reprinted with permission from the *British Medical Journal* 315 (November 29, 1997). Copyright © 1997 by the British Medical Association.

of the highest maternal and infant mortality rates and an AIDS epidemic, the government spends $2.50 (£1.69) per head of the population annually on health—and $15 per head on debt servicing.[7] In Zambia, where for every $1 spent on health care $4 is spent on debt servicing, infant mortality is rising in the face of collapsing provision of health care, clean water, and sanitation[6]

- The World Bank's economic adjustment policies, which have restricted social spending and encouraged export manufacture at the expense of food production. User fees have excluded poor people from health and education and have especially affected women, contributing to their lack of empowerment to restrict the number of children they bear,[8] while the population of the continent grows at 3% a year[3]
- Trade protectionism, which has played a large part in the region's stagnation. Low commodity prices have lost Africa $45–55 billion between 1980 and 1992[9]
- Falling foreign aid. Aid from rich countries has fallen to a trickle, well short of the UN target of 0.7%, and the trend is downward. Foreign aid has failed to bear economic fruit, entangled as it is with promoting trade and arms sales and sustaining the opulent lives of despots. Donors' experience of investing in health is also disappointing where there are low levels of health financing: inappropriately targeted aid can fragment a fragile health service; projects collapse after investment ceases because of inadequate empowerment of local personnel; donors demand quick and measurable results to satisfy their funding sources[10]

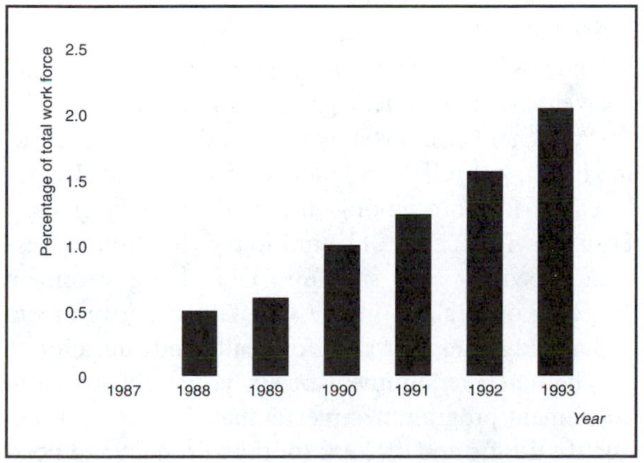

Mortality in 20 Zambian companies. Reprinted with permission.[5]

- The brain drain; encouraged by active recruitment by some northern countries, this is causing an exodus of Africa's ablest professionals, engineers, scientists, physicians, and technical workers
- War—in the 1980s an almost invisible war, waged by South Africa and the United States, destabilised much of southern Africa. History will record the terrible scars: "A million and a half or more dead, millions displaced from their homes, with economies in ruins, millions facing starvation and disease."[11]

But Africa too must bear responsibility for its current state. Poor governance, tribalism, pervasive corruption, and a lack of democracy have caused social and political tensions resulting, in extreme cases, in collapse of states, with devastating humanitarian consequences. Weakness of political commitment to fund better health and social services, accompanied by a disinclination to develop preventive and primary health, has meant that few people (mainly those in cities) have benefited from health expenditure.[4] Failure to value women's contribution to society and the denial of women's rights has had a huge negative impact on the health of African women and their families.[8]

CAN AFRICA'S RELENTLESS SLIDE BE HALTED?

However, these generalisations are only part of Africa's reality and it is neither fair nor objective to overlook the resilience of the African people or their achievements. For example, after independence, Zimbabwe's primary education increased from 36% of school age children enrolled in 1960 to 79% in 1980, and child mortality halved.[12] More recently, peace has returned to Angola, Ethiopia, Eritrea, and Mozambique. In South Africa, apartheid and its evil legacy has been dismantled without civil war, which brings hope that fundamental shifts can occur through thinking and acting in the best interest of future generations.

CAUTIOUS AFRO-OPTIMISM

In the past year, three international events have given rise to cautious optimism that Africa's health, and economy, can be improved. Firstly, the World Bank's new president, James Wolfensohn, has staked his reputation on alleviating poverty.[13] Secondly, the United Nations has embarked on a joint venture (the special initiative for Africa), pooling the expertise of all its agencies and those of the World Bank.[14] Thirdly, there has been an important movement on debt relief (the highly indebted poor countries initiative).[15]

THE UN SPECIAL INITIATIVE FOR AFRICA

In March 1996, the UN agencies launched a 10 year, $25 billion initiative for Africa to reduce poverty and to coordinate follow up from the global conferences of the 1990s (box). Eighty five per cent of this money (controlled by Africans themselves) will go to expanding basic education and health. Social development cannot take place without peace, so transparent governance and conflict prevention are high on the agenda. The health plans (box) emphasise cost effective packages of basic health care and more equitable use of public funds, but many are disappointed that charges imposed at the point of delivery of care are still promoted, with their detrimental effect on health seeking behaviour and their potential for weakening preventive health.[16]

What makes this programme different from other high profile efforts to help Africa? Firstly, it has not been imposed from the outside but is based on home grown themes reflecting Africa's own development priorities. Secondly, there is a commitment to listen not just to governments but to ordinary people, including non-governmental organisations. And thirdly, there are none of the conditions (meaning that "if you don't adopt our priorities you don't get the money") which have so dominated Africa's development over the past decade. Even so, African organisations are concerned that the annual allocation of $2.5 billion will not be "new" but redirected money. "The people of Africa," says President Rawlings of Ghana, "will know it [the special initiative] is successful when we see schools where there were no schools, when we have health services where those services were inadequate before, when households have access to safe water."[17]

Key goals of the UN special initiative for Africa

1. Primary education for all children within 10 years, with emphasis on girls
2. Basic health for all, with improved quality of and access to primary health care
3. Improved security of food and water
4. Safe water for drinking and cooking
5. Improved irrigation, drought management, soil nutrition
6. Improved sanitation
7. Transparent, responsible government by improving an independent judiciary and the electoral process and making public administration more accountable
8. Improved public information, particularly radio broadcasting
9. Support for women in food production (African women produce 80% of the continent's food supply)

UNSIA's health plan

- Targeting the commonest preventable diseases
- Promoting the essential drugs programme
- Increasing and strengthening Africa's existing 40 000 primary care centres
- Decentralising health planning and administration
- Integrating the delivery of reproductive health care
- Giving women a say in decisions on health
- Improving health promotion

HIGHLY INDEBTED POOR COUNTRIES INITIATIVE

1996 brought an unprecedented opportunity to diminish the debt crisis of the poorest countries (box). The World Bank and International Monetary Fund accepted that some debts cannot be repaid and that the flow of money from poor to rich countries must be stopped. Although there are problems in the design (slow implementation, thresholds of debt sustainability too high, and debt relief not adequately set into a broader programme of human development), the initiative provides new thinking.

But already the initiative has received a setback. Uganda, with an excellent economic track record and six years of adjustment programmes, was to be the first to benefit (followed by the Ivory Coast and Burkina Faso), but relief was blocked for one year by political in-fighting among donors. This delay means Uganda will receive £119 million ($193 million) less than hoped for (and six times Ugandan government spending on health)—money the Uganda government had already planned to use for health and education.[18]

The harsh requirement of six years' adherence to adjustment programmes means that Ethiopia will not qualify till the end of 2000 (despite drought and post-war reconstruction); Mozambique, Tanzania, Niger, and Zambia will not qualify till 2002 or later; and Rwanda may not qualify at all despite its desperate post-genocide reconstruction.

There is an increasing groundswell of demand for a one-off debt cancellation of the poorest countries to mark the start of the new millennium.[19] This "once only" gesture would not set a precedent for repeated cancellation—the "moral hazard" so feared by the international financial institutions—but would accept that both creditors (like the Swiss banks accepting the illegal booty of dictators) and debtors have made mistakes. Starting the new millennium by such a gesture, and structuring new loans with greater accountability, could remove a great barrier to progress and justice.

AFRO-PRAGMATISM: ON A KNIFE EDGE?

South Africa represents the continent's problems in microcosm. The apartheid regime borrowed to oppress and kill people; now, those who suffered are being asked to repay the debt. Like the rest of Africa, South Africa has a fast growing population (swollen by illegal immigration) which puts pressure on overstretched housing, education, and health and swells unemployment—which, in turn, unleashes violence and crime. Like the rest of Africa, the country faces a balancing act between achieving economic growth by participating in globalised free markets (with their potential to enrich some people at the expense of others) and redistributing resources through paradigm shifts in approaches to health, education, housing, and other socioeconomic inequalities.[20]

A mixture of hope and fear underlies the call for a "new push for Africa": hope that internal reconstruction, with greater focus on democracy and new visions of external support, can create sustainable development; fear because Africa has been marginalised and eliminated from the foreign policy agenda of most wealthy nations, and the window of opportunity to achieve these goals will not remain open indefinitely. As has been recognised in South Africa, policies which exclude peoples, nations, or continents have only limited potential and must eventually be replaced by longer term visions.

But no more should be expected of Africa than can be delivered by wealthy nations, who in turn must set an example through reform of their consumption patterns and energy expenditure. It is vital that industrialised countries acknowledge the adverse role they play in Africa. Pessimism, based on economic considerations, should be countered by an understanding that the cost of eradicating poverty is less than people imagine, about 1% of global income.[1] Effective debt relief for the 20 poorest countries is even cheaper, with a price tag of $5.5 billion—the cost of building Euro-Disney.[21]

Highly indebted poor countries initiative: principles

- All creditors (bilateral and multilateral) will work together for comprehensive debt reduction
- Debt will be approached from a completely different angle—namely, the ability of the debtor to pay, as opposed to meeting the creditor's claims
- In judging the economic performance of countries, note will be taken of their performance in social indicators such as health, education, and sanitation
- The International Monetary Fund, in a major policy shift, has agreed, in some cases, to provide grants for the payment of debt service as opposed to loans

NOTES

1. United Nations Development Programme. *Human development report.* New York, Oxford: Oxford University Press, 1997:9, 116.
2. Bergstrom S., Mocumbi P. Health for all by the year 2000? *BMJ* 1996;313:316.
3. United Nations. *Implementation strategy for the health sector. United Nations Special Initiative for Africa.* New York: United Nations, 1996.
4. World Bank. *Better health in Africa: experience and lessons learned.* Washington, DC: World Bank, 1994:24.
5. AIDS and the work place. *South African Economist* 1997 April 15:7.
6. Oxfam. *The Oxfam poverty report.* Oxford: Oxfam, 1996.
7. Oxfam. *Poor country debt relief: false dawn or new hope for poverty reduction?* Oxford: Oxfam, 1997. (International position paper.)
8. Harrison K. The importance of the educated healthy woman in Africa. *Lancet* 1997;349:644–7.
9. Flanders S. New ways for Africa. *Financial Times* 1997 April 14:13.
10. LaFond A. Sustaining primary health care. London: Earthscan, 1996.
11. Gervasi S., Wong S. The Regan doctrine and destabilisation of Southern Africa. In: George A, ed. *Western state terrorism.* Cambridge: Quality Press, 212–52.
12. Cornia G. A., ed. *Africa's recovery in the 1990s.* Florence: Unicef, 1992:19.
13. The World Bank, listening and learning [editorial]. *Lancet* 1996;347:411.
14. *The UN System-wide Special Initiative for Africa.* UN. New York: United Nations, 1996.
15. Pettifor A. World Bank/IMF proposals for comprehensive debt relief for the Poorest Countries. London: Debt Crisis Network, 1996. (Available from PO Box 100, London SE1 7RT.)

16. Woodward D. User charges for health services in developing countries: an approach to analysing the effects on utilisation and health outcomes. Discussion paper prepared for the Department for International Development, May 1997. (Available on the internet: http://cichich.ucl.ac.uk)

17. Novicki M. A new impetus for African development. *Africa Recovery* 1996 May:12.

18. Oxfam. *Debt relief and poverty reduction: new hope for Uganda.* Oxford: Oxfam, 1996.

19. Jubilee 2000. *A debt cutter's handbook.* London: Jubilee 2000, 1996.

20. Benatar S. Towards social justice in the new South Africa. *Medicine, Conflict and Global Survival* 1997;13:229–39.

21. Brittain V., Elliott L. Dollar-a-day losers in the global economy. *Guardian* 1997 June 12:12.

The Duty to Warn and the Duty Not to Harm

CHARLES A. ERIN AND JOHN HARRIS

Is There an Ethics of Heterosexual AIDS?[1]

Charles A. Erin is a Professor at the Manchester School of Law. He has published on diverse issues in bioethics, and his current research interests include self ownership, the commodification of the human body, freedom of movement, and the relationship between human values and rational arguments.

John Harris is the Sir David Alliance Professor of Bioethics at the Manchester School of Law. He is a member of the United Kingdom Human Genetics Advisory Commission and of the Ethics Committee of the British Medical Association. He is the author or editor of fourteen books and over one hundred and fifty papers.

THE THREAT OF AIDS IS GENDER NEUTRAL

It seems that in the West the once widely accepted view that AIDS is predominantly a disease affecting homosexuals may be returning reinforced with the conviction that AIDS is a syndrome affecting only those heterosexuals who indulge in 'deviant practices'—promiscuity, intravenous drug use, or association with prostitutes. Various scientific reports lend support to this view, and this in turn makes it a point of discussion for ethicists and jurists. Consider, for example, the following passage from Orr (1990):

> It is often claimed that prostitutes and intravenous drug-users are the means through which AIDS will be heterosexually transmitted to the general public. Recent studies suggest that it is, in fact, intravenous drug use which poses the vastly greater risk.[95]

And Orr's note 95 (Orr (1990)):

> According to the Centers for Disease Control, heterosexual transmission of the virus in the United States is mostly from intravenous drug-users (75 per cent)—A.R. Moss, 'AIDS and intravenous drug use: the real heterosexual epidemic' *BMJ* 294 (1987) 389.

The complacency of the general population appears to be sustained by any reports which tend to marginalize those believed to be at risk of infection, and the perceived insulation that results from the view that HIV/AIDS is a problem for *others* is, manifestly, dangerous. Such an attitude can lead heterosexuals who do not believe themselves to be promiscuous, do not

Reprinted from *AIDS and the Heterosexual Population,* edited by Lorraine Sherr, pp. 241–52. Copyright © 1993 by Gordon and Breach Publishing Group.

use intravenous drugs or associate with prostitutes to feel a false sense of security, perhaps even to believe that they are immune to the threat of infection by HIV. Whilst it may be true that certain groups within society—homosexuals, intravenous drug users—are *more* at risk of infection, the fact remains that the entire world population *is* at risk to this pandemic, irrespective of sexual orientation. Whilst lifestyle may affect the *level* of risk, the *absolute* risk of HIV infection is independent of such considerations.

Two issues have, however, emerged as special problems for AIDS as it affects the heterosexual population although, as indicated, they are by no means confined to that population. The first is consequent upon the probability that it is a widely, though quietly, accepted (but not scientifically confirmed), rule of thumb that the risk to a woman of becoming infected with HIV through unprotected sexual intercourse ('unsafe sex') with an infected man is greater than that to a man of contracting HIV through unprotected sexual intercourse with an infected woman. This may be thought of as an important feminist dimension of heterosexual AIDS.

The second problem is one that has been highlighted in a number of press reports and scare stories (e.g. Graves, 1992; Hunt, 1992; Mullin, 1992; Seaton, 1992). It is the problem of apparently (or, in any event, allegedly) deliberate attempts to infect others via sexual intercourse or, possibly, by other reckless or deliberate means. Both these issues will be examined in turn.

FEMINISM AND HETEROSEXUAL AIDS

Almond (1990) points out:

> . . . following the phase in which AIDS has been seen as a discrimination issue and, in particular, a homosexual or gay rights issue, it should now be regarded as a feminist issue. For the next stage of the virus is one in which the pattern is increasingly one of men infecting women.

Even if the 'rule of thumb' was accepted as an established scientific fact, considering AIDS as a feminist issue in this way is still to ignore the fact that AIDS affects us all. Relative infectivity may vary according to such features as gender or sexual orientation, but the vulnerability to transmission does not, and it is this fact which is of overriding importance.

The moral principles germane to a discussion of the ethics of AIDS are universal principles of justice and individual responsibility which are not altered by application to one particular group within society.

Almond continues in the same passage:

> This will be a transitory phase, however, for in the end AIDS is *everyone's* issue. Even complacent mature heterosexuals looking back on twenty or more years of settled marriage will find that the virus affects *their* lives too, in the threat that it poses to their sons and daughters.

This is true, but "complacent mature heterosexuals" in "settled" relationships are themselves exposed to the *threat* posed by HIV/AIDS even if they do not 'stray'. They may, perhaps, require a blood transfusion at some time and the recent French experience (e.g. Webster 1992; Witcher & Petre 1992) is evidence that it is not just their children who are at *risk* to AIDS. But this is not our point: those who do not consider themselves to be at risk—those who may choose to abstain from sexual intercourse, intravenous drug use, are not haemophiliacs, and never need a blood transfusion—remain under *threat* from HIV/AIDS. Indeed those who understand the transmission of HIV, will regard this threat as a reason for not 'straying'.

The *ethics* of AIDS are then the same for heterosexuals and homosexuals alike. The mode of transmission—heterosexual relations, homosexual relations, transfusion of infected blood, intravenous drug use—do not alter the ethics. Justice is of its very nature universal and morality cannot be simply relative to particular groups. It is worth digressing for a moment to say why this must be so.

THE IMPOSSIBILITY OF MORAL RELATIVITY

While it is true that there are many different moral outlooks and perspectives, and perhaps equally many and various moral theories, all presuppose the possibility of moral argument. This is because if something is right or wrong, good or bad, there must be some reason why this is so. And once reasons enter into the discussion, moral argument has begun. Reasons can always be scrutinised for their adequacy. There are better or worse reasons, reasons supported by better or worse arguments, reasons underpinned by more or less established or plausible evidence. Of course, arguments may not always be resolved. Sometimes the evidence relevant to a solution is unclear or unevenly balanced or the particular arguments deployed on either side are inconclusive. But moral arguments, if they are genuine, are always in principle resolvable. It is not coherent, for example, to believe that murder is wrong, but think that it is only wrong here and now, but not in another time or place, or for another culture or group; wrong only for people of this society and time, or for people with those beliefs (Harris, 1985).

Neither can citing God as a source of moral conviction or of particular moral imperatives help us to avoid the inevitability of moral argument. As Russell (1957) borrowing an argument originally used by Socrates,[2] so eloquently demonstrated:

> The point I am concerned with is that, if you are quite sure there is a difference between right and wrong, you are then in this situation: is that difference due to God's fiat or is it not? If it is due to God's fiat, then for God Himself there is no difference between right and wrong, and it is no longer a significant statement to say that God is good. If you are going to say, as theologians do, that God is good, you must then say that right or wrong have some meaning that is independent of God's fiat, because God's fiats are good and not bad independently of the mere fact that he made them.

This leaves the inevitable task of trying to formulate the ethical principles that should guide society's response to heterosexual HIV/AIDS.

JUSTICE AND INDIVIDUAL RESPONSIBILITY

The two most apposite moral considerations seem to be, on the one hand, the moral responsibilities of the individual towards others and, secondly, justice, which is here relevant to the way a community treats its individual members (Erin & Harris, [1993]). To summarize, they are as follows:

i. Central to any conception of justice is the ethical principle of equality which demands that each person within a community should be shown the same respect, concern, and protection as is accorded to any other;
ii. Consequently, no individual or group within the community should be unfairly discriminated against;
iii. Irrespective of premeditation or intent, the individual is responsible for what he/she *knowingly or recklessly* causes, either through his/her action or inaction.

JUSTICE, INDIVIDUAL RESPONSIBILITY AND DELIBERATE OR RECKLESS HIV TRANSMISSION

So what are the implications of the principle of justice and the moral imperative of individual responsibility for HIV/AIDS? One can consider here the case of deliberate or reckless transmission of HIV. It should be emphasized that what is said here bears application to both heterosexually and homosexually transmitted HIV.

RESPONSIBILITY AND THE INDIVIDUAL

Individual responsibility has two aspects in this context. There are the responsibilities both of potential transmitters of HIV and of potential receivers to be accounted for. Consider potential transmitters first. This group may be sub-divided into those who *know* they are HIV seropositive and those who do not. However, among the members of this latter sub-group are those who *have reason to believe* that they may be HIV seropositive. There is no morally relevant difference between the obligations of this group and of those who have had their HIV seropositive status confirmed. Members of both groups know that they may constitute a mortal danger to others in certain circumstances.

It is this feature of AIDS that makes it almost unique among diseases and which imposes strict obligations on the individual.

Quite simply, the individual who knows that he[3] is HIV seropositive or who has reason to believe that he may be, has a moral duty to forewarn prospective partners of his HIV status and is responsible for their fate if he does not. It is important to be clear about just why this is so.

ANALOGIES WITH LAW AND HEALTH CARE PRACTICE

It is tempting to draw analogies with law and with health care practice here, although it will be argued that ultimately such analogies fail.

In common law, any 'laying on of hands' or for that matter of other bodily parts is battery (and the threat of it is assault) unless the recipient has freely and full-heartedly consented. In current health care practice it is now almost universally accepted that for such consent to be valid it must be fully informed. At the very least this must mean that the subject of the touching must know all relevant facts including the likely consequences of such touching (Harris, 1985). Clearly, the fact that illness and almost certain death are a significant risk of the touching in question must be a relevant fact upon which any valid consent would have to be based. Whether the common law regarding assault and battery coincides with what would be regarded as acceptable current health care practice is a moot point. The law relating to consent to sexual intercourse where there is a danger of sexually transmitted disease, for example, is based on a number of Victorian cases and on the sexually transmitted diseases envisaged in those cases which were not fatal. These cases are a poor guide to what the courts would decide today although, in one, a man called Bennet was convicted of indecent assault for having sex with a thirteen year old girl while infected with a sexually transmitted disease. The court held that although the girl was below the 'age of consent', such consent as there was had been obtained by fraud and was therefore invalid (Arnheim, 1992). Arguably, no consent to intercourse could be valid if it was made in ignorance of the HIV seropositive status of one of the partners or in ignorance of the known probability of such status, whether or not the law would today regard lack of information or the withholding of information about HIV seropositive status as vitiating consent to intercourse. However, there is perhaps a better legal precedent for thinking about the responsibilities of the potential transmitter of HIV.

Another approach might be to regard the law and ethics of battery and its relationship to consent as irrelevant because of the specially serious risks associated with AIDS. It may be that a better guide would be the law regarding either grievous bodily harm or the administration of a 'noxious' thing. Both of these perspectives are covered in English law by the *Offences Against The Person Act 1861*. Under this act, the most serious of the assault genus of offences is that where the intent is to cause grievous bodily harm. Hence the consent of the 'victim' is probably irrelevant to the commission of the offence. The 1861 Act also deals with the administration of "any Poison or other destructive or noxious Thing" (*Offences Against The Person Act 1861*, s. 23). Clearly, if a person poisons another's coffee, he needs neither to assault nor batter her. Moreover, his act is not the less culpable because she consents to drink the coffee in ignorance of its possibly lethal contents.[4] This seems a better analogy for the knowing or reckless exposure by one person of another to HIV/AIDS. However, again, it is perhaps not quite close enough.

It might well be claimed that the HIV seropositive individual or the person who has reason to believe that she might be such an individual, lacks or may lack, the intent to harm that is requisite for the commission of the offences against the person under consideration. The moral, as opposed to the legal question is as to whether lack of the requisite intent is relevant.

THE MORAL CULPABILITY OF HIV TRANSMISSION

People are responsible for what they knowingly bring about (Harris, 1980). The individual who knows he is HIV seropositive and has sexual intercourse with another person without forewarning that person of his status has disregarded his moral obligation to disclose HIV status, and has thus undermined the autonomy of his sexual partner and put that partner at risk of HIV infection. Such an individual is responsible for the wrong done to the person he or she places at risk. He is responsible for the death of that person if, as a result of contracting HIV through sexual contact with him, she dies of AIDS. Even if they do not consequently contract HIV there is still responsibility for knowingly exposing another person to considerable risk.

That this is a separate and considerable wrong whether or not the risk materialises can be seen by considering the case of other hazards. Suppose someone were to allow a possibly lethal chemical effluent to run off into a public street. They would be culpable whether or not anyone actually succumbed to its effects.

The potential transmitter has neglected her moral obligation to forewarn and is to blame for any detriment to her sexual partner directly consequent upon her lack of disclosure. The individual who has reason to believe she may be HIV seropositive and neglects to forewarn her sexual partner of her at-risk status is equally at fault and equally culpable for any detrimental consequences to her sexual partner resulting directly from her lack of disclosure.

It might be thought that the current less than complete understanding of infectivity, particularly the apparent variation in infectivity during the various stages after infection with HIV, undermines this claim; that the fact that it is not certain that sexual intercourse with an HIV seropositive person *will* result in transmission of HIV nullifies the obligation to forewarn and thus provides extenuation of the infector's responsibility and culpability. But this is analogous to saying that an individual who, without warning, fires a machine gun indiscriminately into a crowd mortally wounding someone is not responsible for that person's injury and not guilty of murder (or at the very least manslaughter) when she dies of her wounds because he could not know for sure when firing that anyone would actually be hit.[5]

RESPONSIBILITY AND THE POTENTIAL RECEIVER

What of the responsibilities of the potential receiver? To begin, it is perhaps worth noting that not all those who might be considered potential receivers of deliberate HIV infection are 'victims' of deliberate infection.[6] There will be, it seems fair to assume, those who will have been infected previously by whatever transmission mode, but who have not previously had their HIV status confirmed one way or the other. All those who have suffered a lack of forewarning are, however, victims to an assault on their autonomy, but, to simplify matters, consider the case of a person whose HIV seronegative status has been confirmed.

CONTRIBUTORY NEGLIGENCE: A DUTY OF SELF-PROTECTION?

In the United Kingdom, as elsewhere, government AIDS education campaigns have focused on convincing the individual citizen of the wisdom of practising 'safe sex'. There is no such thing as *safe* sex, of course, merely *safer* sex, and while one cannot provide oneself with total protection against HIV transmission through sexual intercourse, one can considerably reduce the chances of transmission by that mode by, for example, the use of condoms. Practising protected intercourse may be thought of as the 'common sense' approach. It is far from clear, however, that the individual has a *duty* to do so. If this was the case, it might be claimed that the individual's duty of self-protection relieves the potential transmitter of the duty to forewarn. Such a claim is fundamentally flawed, as has been discussed elsewhere (Erin & Harris, [1993]):

> It is sometimes claimed that every individual has the obligation to protect herself and that there is consequently no duty to warn. This principle has two major flaws. The first is that it assumes that people will actually protect themselves in obedience to the principle. The second is that it assumes that the protective steps that they might take will be adequate.
>
> We will just look a little more closely at both these flaws. It may be the case, for example, that all workers at a nuclear plant should wear protective clothing at all times. It does not follow from the soundness of such a rule that worker A, seeing that worker B is without her protective clothing on this particular occasion, has no obligation not to turn on a machine that emits dangerous radiation or to warn worker B before turning on the machinery. Or, even if all *are* wearing protective clothing, that there is no obligation not to increase the dangerous radiation above the levels to which the workers have consented to be exposed and are expecting to receive.
>
> The second flaw is equally important. Since there is no such thing as '*safe* sex', merely less hazardous sex, it is important that each individual makes his/her own informed judgment about the level of risk they are prepared to run in each particular case. One might, for example, think that the risk that one's partner has AIDS is low and that this combined with the further lowering of the risk by practising protected intercourse was an aggregate risk worth running. One's assessment might be different if one knew that the first of the two risks was not small but, rather, 100%. This is why health care professionals often want to know (and rightly) the HIV status of patients for particular procedures even though they take routine precautions against infection during those procedures. Equally, and for the same reasons, patients have a legitimate interest in knowing the HIV status of health care professionals.

If this were not true, it would follow that, for example, a woman who walks alone at night has no cause for complaint if she is assaulted. It was, so it might analogously be claimed, her duty to protect herself by avoiding such conduct and she has only herself to blame.

DISCHARGING ONE'S RESPONSIBILITIES

Whilst individuals clearly have an interest in self-protection, it should not be afforded the same moral stature as the duty to forewarn others of the risks they are, or may be taking on by agreeing to sexual relations. Such disclosure is necessary for an individual to make an informed, autonomous judgement as to whether she is prepared to run those risks in the particular instance. Uninfected individuals are justified in being interested. That is, they have a right to demand that their sexual partners are open and honest with them regarding HIV status and risk category. It is only on this basis that their autonomy is safeguarded. And it is only on this basis that 'common sense' comes into play: whilst it is sensible, and advisable, that all persons educate themselves in the epidemiology of HIV/AIDS, particularly in the known HIV transmission modes, the decision of whether or not to indulge in sexual intercourse with a partner, and whether or not to practice 'saf*er* sex', depends on frank disclosure from one's partner.[7]

VOLENTI NON FIT INJURIA

If an HIV seropositive individual *does* inform any sexual partner of his HIV status, and the partner nevertheless indulges in sexual intercourse, whether protected or unprotected, he is a volunteer to the respective risks. This latter individual has made an informed consent and must bear responsibility for any consequences detrimental to himself. The HIV seropositive person who discloses his HIV status has discharged his responsibilities to his partner.

DELIBERATE TRANSMISSION AND THE CRIMINAL LAW

Should the deliberate or reckless transmission of HIV be considered a criminal offence in law; if so, what type of criminal offence? It is necessary to be explicit as to what is meant by *deliberate* transmission: it refers to the case of a person who knows she is HIV seropositive and, despite this knowledge, knowingly or recklessly does something where there is a possibility of passing on the virus, by whatever transmission mode, to another person (whom she does not know to be HIV seropositive) and does not shoulder her moral responsibility to disclose her HIV status to that person *prior* to that act. It is clear that where ignoring a moral responsibility can jeopardize the very lives of others and can lead to their deaths, this is a sufficiently serious matter, other things being equal, to justify criminalization. But are other things equal?

Firstly, assuming the moral symmetry of acts and omissions (Harris, 1980 *passim*), we are forced to accept that it does not make a moral difference whether non-disclosure was a result of misrepresentation (denying HIV seropositive status when asked) or as a result of non-representation (not offering the information in the absence of solicitation). Non-disclosure thus most nearly constitutes fraud in law.

There are three potential ways of considering the criminalization of deliberate HIV transmission. The first hinges on the issue of fraudulent representation. There is precedent (although by no means a conclusive precedent) for considering fraudulent representation as the basis of the charge of rape where sexual intercourse is the mode of transmission. Thus, if a woman consents to sexual intercourse with a man who has represented himself as single when he is actually married, and she would not have consented if she had been made aware of his married status, there is a case for saying she has been raped. Equally, if a person consents to sexual intercourse with an HIV seropositive individual who has not disclosed his HIV status, and that person would not have consented if she had been apprised of this information, there is a case for charging rape. Note that this approach encompasses the rape of both females and males. And note also that this approach would deem a crime to have been committed whether or not the victim of that crime contracted HIV as a result of intercourse with the perpetrator and whether or not the victim eventually died of AIDS.

The second alternative is to consider deliberate transmission as either attempted manslaughter or murder, or actual manslaughter or murder. If ('attempted') transmission is done recklessly, then the appropriate charge would likely be (attempted) manslaughter; if ('attempted') transmission is done knowingly, the appropriate charge would likely be (attempted) murder. It should be noted here that the *attempted* charge can, in principle, be brought where transmission has not occurred. Where sexual intercourse does result in transmission of HIV from a non-disclosing HIV seropositive individual to a seronegative individual, it is a moot point whether the crime committed could be considered in law as manslaughter (if done recklessly) or murder (if done knowingly), the point being that the manslaughter/murder victim is likely to be a living person for some considerable time after the putative crime is committed. However, taking into consideration the current state of the art of HIV/AIDS epidemiology which indicates strongly that the person who contracts HIV *will* eventually die of AIDS leads us to believe that, if the manslaughter/murder option is to be taken up, this is how the crime in this scenario should be viewed. The victim of the crime has, after all, been given a 'death sentence'.

The third option is to borrow a concept from American law, and create a new offence specifically to fit the circumstances of this new disease and perhaps call it 'reckless endangerment'.

THE POINT OF CRIMINALIZATION

It is likely that, whichever of the above approaches was to be chosen, the chances of a successful conviction would be slim. Firstly, it would need to be shown that the alleged victim of the crime was not HIV seropositive prior to the crime being committed. Secondly, it would probably need to be shown that the crime's perpetrator knew that he was HIV seropositive. Finally, there are various problems thrown up by the fact that transmission usually occurs during acts which are private and usually intimate. However, just as the charge of rape within marriage may be a difficult charge to prove one way or the other, the point of criminalizing such an act is to send out the emphatic message that rape within marriage is *morally wrong,* that it is a crime, whether or not it is likely to be successfully prosecuted in any particular case.

The key question is not "whether what has occurred is a criminal offence but whether it should be made a crime" (Brazier, 1992). In this paper it has been argued that the deliberate or reckless transmission of HIV, or 'attempts' at such transmission are not only a most serious moral wrong but also, in all probability, a crime. Whether it should be made, or where it already is, remain a criminal offence in law is a further and separate question and one it seems on balance should be answered in the negative.[8]

KNOWING HIV TRANSMISSION SHOULD NOT BE A CRIMINAL OFFENCE

There would be immense practical, social and even moral difficulties in the way of making the knowing transmission of HIV into a criminal offence. In the first place it is probably undesirable and dysfunctional to take any steps which would have the effect of further stigmatizing those with HIV/AIDS by treating them all as potential rapists or murderers.[9] Just as part of the point of criminalizing an activity is to send out clear and emphatic messages about what is tolerable behaviour in a society, so part of the point of not criminalizing an activity is to secure an analogous outcome: in this case, to try to minimize such wrongful and unjustified stigmatization as already exists. This is particularly appropriate where criminalization, while understandable and perhaps even defensible, is in fact unlikely to do any good in the sense of reducing the prevalence of such 'crimes' or in compensating victims (e.g. Orr, 1990).

There are a number of reasons to suppose criminalization would be ineffective. If intent were made the essence of the crime it would be difficult to prove. If recklessness were sufficient there would be so many mitigating circumstances alleged in every case as to render any deterrent effect problematic.

It would be difficult to improve upon Brazier's account of the scenario for any alleged victim in such a trial (Brazier, 1992): "The defence would say it was not *their* client who infected Ms X but one of several other men who they would show she slept with".

This said, two firm and inescapable conclusions follow, and these are the conclusions of this paper also. The first is that, while knowing transmission of HIV is a crime both in morality and probably also in law, it should not become, or, where it already is, remain a criminal offence. It should be recognised on all sides that those who are HIV seropositive or who believe that they may be should accept their responsibility not to endanger the lives of others. It may seem harsh to emphasize this point where those on whom the burden of disclosure falls are already themselves sufferers of a terrible disease and likely also to be victims of unfair and indefensible discrimination insofar as their HIV status is known. It is essential that society recognises that it has special and powerful obligations to those who are HIV seropositive. Such people should receive substantial protections against discrimination in employment, housing, health care and in all other respects be treated as equals in any society. These protections have been outlined in detail elsewhere (Erin & Harris, [1993]; Harris, 1992) and for this reason will not be rehearsed here.

The second is that *anyone* and *everyone* has the most powerful of motives to protect innocent third parties from becoming the objects of knowing or reckless transmission. This will include those such as doctors and other health care workers who come by their knowledge of someone's HIV seropositive status in a confidential or quasi-confidential role. The duty of confidentiality is not absolute and where it conflicts with the obligation to protect people at risk of their very lives it surely must give way to such an overwhelming moral priority (Harris, 1985).

As Brazier (1992) has suggested in the context of the Birmingham case in which a man who, contrary to medical and other advice, allegedly continued to have unprotected sex with several women without warning them of his condition:

> To protect such women, doctors might have to publish his name in the press and perhaps include a photograph.

However, it should be reaffirmed that the most effective means of preventing the spread of HIV and of protecting people from contracting it is to encourage those who are HIV seropositive "to come forward and seek diagnosis of their condition and advice on how to care for themselves and others" (Brazier, 1992). And, more importantly, we must ensure that, when they do, they are protected against discrimination and ensure also that they are able to provide for themselves and their families, and this we must do at public expense if necessary (Erin & Harris, [1993] *passim*).

NOTES

1. This paper was written as part of the development of the project for the Commission of the European Communities entitled "AIDS: Ethics, Justice and European Policy". The authors gratefully acknowledge the stimulus and support provided by the Commission.

2. Plato (1954) *The Euthyphro,* in *The Last Days of Socrates,* transl. H. Tredennick (Harmondsworth: Penguin) 10B–11B.

3. We have switched the gender of the personal pronouns throughout for the sake of equality and elegance.

4. Here, as elsewhere, we are grateful to our colleague Margaret Brazier for her stimulating legal advice.

5. Steinbock comes to similar conclusions for slightly different reasons (Steinbock (1989) pp 27ff.). Steinbock locates the obligation to disclose in a duty of concern for welfare rather than, as do we, in an obligation not to harm.

6. Or of infection on the occasion in question.

7. The assumption here is that it is autonomous individuals which are under consideration, that is, individuals capable of authentic action. Insofar as they are not, it is, of course, pointless to make any recommendations as to what they should do. However, it is often too readily assumed that those under various sorts of pressure lose their autonomy.

8. Despite the fact that in the United States, for example, there is precedent for the (attempted) knowing transmission of HIV being considered in law as attempted manslaughter and attempted murder (Hermann, 1991, pp 296–297) and 20 states have already passed laws making knowing transmission of HIV a criminal offence (Bayer, 1991, p 46).

9. In the hysterical way that some feminists have sought to stigmatize all men as potential rapists.

REFERENCES

Almond, B. (1990) "Introduction: War of the world" in Brenda Almond (ed.) *AIDS: A Moral Issue—The Ethical, Legal And Social Aspects* (London: MacMillan) p 1–21.

Arnheim, M. (1992) *The Guardian,* 24 June.

Bayer, R. (1991) "AIDS, public health, and civil liberties" in F. G. Reamer (Ed.) *AIDS & Ethics* (New York: Columbia University Press) p 26–49.

Brazier, M. (1992) *The Guardian,* 24 June.

Erin, C. A., Harris, J. (1993) "AIDS: Ethics, Justice, and Social Policy", *Journal of Applied Philosophy,* **10,** 165–173.

Grayes, D. (1992) "Dilemma over Aids man who infected four women", *The Daily Telegraph,* 23 June, p. 1, cols. 1–7.

Harris, J. (1980) *Violence & Responsibility* (London: Routledge & Kegan Paul).

Harris, J. (1985) *The Value of Life: An Introduction to Medical Ethics* (London: Routledge).

Harris, J. (1992) *Wonderwoman & Superman: The Ethics of Human Biotechnology* (Oxford: Oxford University Press).

Hermann, D. H. J. (1991) "AIDS and the law" in F. G. Reamer (Ed.) *AIDS & Ethics* (New York: Columbia University Press) p 277–309.

Hunt, L. (1992) "HIV victim on "revenge" sex spree may be detained", *The Independent,* 23 June, p. 1, cols. 2–4.

Mullin, J. (1992) "Man "set out to spread HIV" ", *The Guardian,* 23 June, p. 1, cols. 4–6.

Orr, A. (1990) "The legal implications of AIDS and HIV infection in Britain and the United States" in Almond (1990) p 112–139.

Russell, B. (1957) "Why I am not a Christian" in Paul Edwards (Ed.), *Why I am not a Christian* (London: George Allen and Unwin).

Seaton, C. (1992) "Woman dies as HIV man ignores advice and spreads Aids", *The Times* [London], 23 June, p. 3, cols. 1–3.

Steinbock, B. (1989) "Harming, wronging and AIDS", in James M. Humber & Robert F. Almeder (Eds.) *AIDS and Ethics, Biomedical Ethics Reviews 1988,* (Clifton, New Jersey: Humana Press).

Webster, P. (1992) "French doctors go on trial in case of Aids-infected blood", *The Independent,* 23 June, p. 7, cols. 5–7.

Witcher, T., Petre, J. (1992) "Doctors on trial over HIV-infected transfusions", *The Daily Telegraph,* 23 June, p. 10, col. 8.

REBECCA BENNETT, HEATHER DRAPER, AND LUCY FRITH

Ignorance Is Bliss? HIV and Moral Duties and Legal Duties to Forewarn

Rebecca Bennett is a Lecturer in Bioethics at the Manchester School of Law and a fellow of the Institute of Medicine, Law and Bioethics. She has published widely on diverse issues in bioethics. Her recent publications are *Dementia* (2nd ed., Chapman and Hall) and *HIV and AIDS Testing, Screening and Confidentiality* (Oxford University Press).

Heather Draper is a lecturer in Biomedical Ethics at the Medical School, University of Birmingham. She is also an honorary lecturer in the Department of General Practice at the University of Liverpool. Her interests are in the fields of medical ethics and law.

Lucy Frith is a lecturer in Health Care Ethics at the University of Liverpool and a Fellow of the Institute of Medicine, Law and Bioethics. Her research interests include reproductive technologies, resource allocation in health care, and patient consent and confidentiality. Her publications have appeared in *Bioethics, Nursing Law and Ethics* and *Human Reproduction*.

[INTRODUCTION]

In 1997, a court in Cyprus jailed Pavlos Georgiou for fifteen months for knowingly infecting a British woman, Janet Pink, with HIV-1 through unprotected sexual intercourse. Pink met Georgiou in January 1994 whilst on holiday. She discovered that she had contracted the virus from him in October 1994 but continued the relationship until July 1996 when she developed AIDS. She returned to the UK for treatment and reported Georgiou to the Cypriot authorities.[1]

There have been a number of legal cases involving deliberate transmission of HIV, but most have involved forced exposure to infected bodily fluids for example, rape or biting, and have been dealt with using the existing legislation for rape or assault. While it is often difficult to prove responsibility for transmission in cases of forced exposure to HIV, it is even more contentious in cases like those of Janet Pink where an individual has consented to sex but claims that he/she was not forewarned of his/her partner's HIV-positive status. At present there is no specific criminal offence of having unprotected sexual intercourse without disclosing one's HIV-positive status but a prosecution could possibly be brought under any one of a number of existing offences.[2] *Perhaps a change of policy needs to be considered. The Home Office has issued a consultation document which outlines a proposal that will allow the criminalisation of intentional transmission of diseases, like HIV, that are likely to cause serious harm. This revised legislation would cover all other potentially fatal diseases (including salmonella and legionnaire's disease, for instance) but seems primarily to be targeted at HIV transmission. Should transmission of HIV through consensual sex, without the HIV-positive status of the individual being disclosed, be an offence? This question, and that of*

Reprinted with permission from the *Journal of Medical Ethics* 26, (2000), 9–15. Copyright © 2000 by the BMJ Publishing Group.

whether there is a moral obligation to disclose a positive HIV status prior to having a sexual relationship is the subject of this paper.

CRIMINALISATION AND MORAL OBLIGATIONS

It has been argued that "the generally acknowledged threat of a steady and inexorable growth in the incidence of HIV infection represents a sufficient threat to require all reasonable methods of containment to be seriously examined including use of the criminal law."[2] In jurisdictions such as the USA the criminal law has been used to punish those who have deliberately or recklessly transmitted HIV. Smith suggests that the criminal law in the UK should be used to punish deliberate transmission of HIV.[3] First, he argues that the harms caused through HIV transmission in the form of physical and emotional trauma are considerable. Second, although the detection/deterrence rate would be low, he believes that specific criminalisation would underscore the social rejection of what are highly dangerous practices.

The criminalisation of such behaviour is fraught with practical problems, not least that of enforcement. It would be exceedingly difficult to establish in court that the offence had been committed because it would be difficult to prove whether a sexual partner had or had not been adequately forewarned of a partner's HIV positivity. However, that prosecution for intentional HIV transmission would probably be relatively rare and difficult to prove, does not provide an argument against prosecution itself. Prosecution for rape within marriage is also relatively rare and difficult to prove, however, by putting into place legislation criminalising such an act, not only can justice be seen to be done in at least a few cases but also an important message about the absolute wrongness of rape within marriage is established. Criminalising the non-consensual transmission of HIV could be justified along the same lines. If those who knowingly put sexual partners at risk of HIV infection without forewarning of this known risk are behaving in a morally abhorrent way, it may be that the status of this behaviour as unacceptable should be signalled in the law.

Thus, when considering the possibility of a legal duty of HIV-positive individuals to forewarn sexual partners of their positive status, it is important to determine whether it is reasonable to suppose that individuals have a moral duty to forewarn sexual partners of their HIV positivity. A convincing argument establishing the likelihood of a moral duty to forewarn in these circumstances will drive any policy debate towards considering criminalisation of HIV transmission. Determining the extent of any moral duty to forewarn may also inform other areas of policy, for instance, contact tracing, or even forewarning by health care professionals when those with HIV refuse to forewarn. If it can be established that strong moral obligations can be attributed to an HIV-positive individual then it may be that these moral obligations should be transformed into legal obligations.

HIV AND MORAL OBLIGATIONS

It seems uncontentious to assert that individuals have a general moral obligation to avoid harming or wronging others whenever possible. This is a general obligation and not one restricted to the transmission of HIV. What needs to be examined is the question of whether this general obligation not to harm or wrong others implies specific obligations with regard to possible HIV transmission. What is not clear in the case of HIV transmission is whether the obligation to prevent transmission falls solely (or even largely) on the shoulders of those who are already infected, or whether it is down to everyone to do their best to protect themselves against transmission.

MORAL OBLIGATIONS OF HIV-NEGATIVE INDIVIDUALS

In a liberal society it is difficult to formulate an uncontentious argument in support of a moral obligation on the part of HIV-negative individuals to protect themselves from HIV infection. Granted the common liberal structure of societies with the emphasis on liberty and autonomy, then a "self-protection obligation" would seem irretrievably incompatible. Promoting individual autonomy and freedom seems necessarily to entail promoting the legitimacy of risky choices. The decision to run the risk of HIV infection seems on a par with engaging in dangerous sports or careers, or heavy drinking and smoking. Protecting oneself from HIV infection is clearly the prudent thing to do, but there may be no moral obligation to do so.

The relationship between self-protection and the protection of others Alternatively, it may be that a duty of self-protection arises from a duty to protect others. Those on whom others rely for financial or other support may well have a duty to protect themselves from HIV in order to maintain this support. It may also be the case that individuals have a duty to protect themselves from HIV infection in order not to make avoidable calls on health care resources. But, an obligation to protect oneself in order to protect others from financial or other hardship or distress, if it exists, is not specific to HIV. If such a duty exists, it exists generally, and all individuals would be obliged to do everything possible to ensure their good health, not only by avoiding communicable diseases but also by modifying lifestyle choices from motor racing to eating junk food. Even granted that a general obligation of self-protection exists, it is something that should be heeded in wider policy considerations regarding individuals' responsibility for health, or should not be considered at all. To consider such an obligation only within the framework underlying policy on HIV is an act of discrimination against those with HIV.

Self-inflicted harm? Evidence of a self-preservation duty relating specifically to HIV infection would weaken the case for specific obligations on the part of HIV-positive individuals to warn others and would provided a strong argument against policies which diminish the freedom of those infected with HIV. However, evidence for a specific self-preservation duty relating to HIV is not forthcoming. For a self-preservation obligation to seem plausible it would have to be more generally applicable and exist in a society which upheld vastly different values and expectations than a society based on a general commitment to liberalism.

But even granted we accept this conclusion, if it can be shown that HIV infection via consensual sexual contact is an instance of self-inflicted harm this will impact on analysis of the responsibilities of HIV-positive individuals, and in turn on recommendations for policy. If the responsibility for infection lies with those who become infected then criminalisation of HIV again seems inappropriate.

For HIV transmission via consensual sexual contact to be categorised as an instance of self-inflicted harm, it would have to be shown that an individual consented to the risk of infection. In cases where an individual was unaware of the specific risk involved, a categorisation of self-harm could not be confidently applied. Thus, the question that needs to be addressed is now one of how much information must be available for consent to risk of HIV infection to be valid, and whether valid consent would indeed render any resulting harm self-inflicted?

Informed consent Charles Erin and John Harris claim that one has an absolute duty to forewarn sexual partners of one's HIV-positive status. Their claim is based on their high regard for autonomy and informed consent.[4] They argue that forewarning allows those considering a sexual relationship to make an informed, autonomous choice about whether or not to run the risk of infection. Erin and Harris argue that, once forewarned of the risk of HIV infection, the individual is free to take an autonomous decision and is accordingly responsible for his or her actions. Individuals who become infected as a result of fully forewarned consensual sex are responsible for this harm, the harm is self-inflicted. Accordingly, HIV-infected individuals can be said to have fulfilled their moral obligations towards sexual partners, regarding HIV, as long as they fully forewarn of their infection.

However, even if this is accepted, it is not clear that an individual is necessarily being deceived when a sexual partner does not disclose his or her HIV positivity because a failure to disclose need not preclude an autonomous choice. With sex education in schools and extensive educational campaigns and media coverage it is reasonable to suppose that most adults are aware of the existence of HIV and have some elementary knowledge of its transmission routes. It is arguable then, that it can be assumed that any consent given to, say, "high-risk" sexual activity includes consent to the background risk of HIV infection without specific information about the particular sexual partner in question.

Erin and Harris reject this line of thought.[5] They argue that consent to sexual contact is invalidated if any information which may cause a potential partner to refuse consent to sexual activity is withheld. But this view does not translate readily to other circumstances. For instance, it would be difficult for a woman who becomes pregnant to blame her partner for this on the grounds that he did not warn her of this possibility. It is not unreasonable for men to suppose that women who are competent to consent to sex are also aware of the risk of pregnancy and it is not, therefore, morally irresponsible of them to fail to make a specific warning about this risk.

The basis of Erin and Harris's claim is that the risk assessment individuals may make when they believe that the risk of their sexual partner being HIV-positive is low, is very different from the risk assessment after their partner has told them that he or she is HIV-positive. For Erin and Harris, consent to sexual contact is invalidated if any information which may cause a sexual partner to refuse consent to sexual activity is withheld. It would, however, seem difficult to establish that an individual's failure to disclose his or her HIV-positive status would legally be considered to negate the validity of the consent to sexual contact. In the case of Hegarty v Shine, for instance, a claim in battery brought by a woman who contracted syphilis from her lover failed.[6] The court held that she had consented to sexual intercourse and that the disease did not affect the validity of her consent. It is perhaps necessary to draw a distinction here between consent to sex and consent to the risk of infection. It is difficult to argue that failure to disclose infection with a potentially fatal sexually transmitted disease (STD) renders an otherwise consensual sexual act as rape or battery. However, it may be that while the consent to the sexual contact is valid in such cases, the consent to risk of infection is invalid. Consent to the possibility that a partner is infected may well be significantly different from consent where the partner is in fact infected, especially where the sexual partner is in fact infected, especially where the sexual partner is aware of his or her HIV positivity.

OBLIGATIONS OF HIV-POSITIVE INDIVIDUALS

So far, we have looked at a general obligation to forewarn and have rejected this. We will now turn to the question of whether there might be a duty to forewarn in specific circumstances.

Levels of risk One specific circumstance which might have a bearing on the obligation to forewarn is the level of risk to which someone is being exposed. Erin and Harris tend to lump together all kinds of sexual relationships and then describe all as carrying an absolute risk because HIV disease will ultimately result in premature death. Equally, because not everyone who suspects that they may be HIV-positive takes an HIV test, there are good reasons to claim that those who have "reason to believe"[7] that they may have contracted the virus be treated on a par with those who know that they have. Taken together, this means that the scope for a general obligation to forewarn is very wide indeed.

As a recent, high profile trial in the USA has illustrated, the term "sexual relationship" can mean many different things. To restrict the term "sexual partner" to those who engage in coital[8] relations is far too conservative. Those who engage in very intimate physical activity for pleasure which does not involve penetration are surely more than good friends! This said, there is a legal tradition of sexual partners in terms of coital relations. According to Black's *Law Dictionary,* oral sex, for instance, is not technically adultery.[9] It was, of course, this issue of whether oral sex constituted "sexual relations" that formed the basis of President Clinton's legal defence in the Monica Lewinsky scandal. Yet any definition of a sexual partner based on coital relations, while being easy to apply, would seem woefully inadequate. On this definition, for instance, there could be no such thing as lesbian sexual partners.

All sexual activity is not equally risky. Many sexual liaisons only involve a very low risk of infection, for example, kissing, mutual masturbation or oral sex using an appropriate barrier to infection ie condoms or dental dam. In sexual liaisons where risks are extremely low it is possible to act in a responsible and morally justifiable way without forewarning partners of one's HIV infection. The duty to forewarn, cannot, therefore apply equally to all sexual partners.

To accept that those who have reason to believe that they are HIV-positive have a moral obligation to disclose this fact where there is any risk to others would entail widespread forewarning, even where the risks are low. An HIV-infected individual's duty to forewarn would cover not only both high and low risk sexual activity, but also any other kind of activity involving close contact no matter how low the actual risk of transmission actually was. For Erin and Harris it is not just potential sexual partners to whom we owe a duty of disclosure, but whomsoever we risk infecting, however slight this risk is—or indeed however unjust or beyond our control their own activities may be. For instance, one becomes obliged to forewarn one's flatmates of one's status just in case one of them, or one of their guests, decides to use one's toothbrush or razor without permission. Effectively, Erin and Harris seem committed to the view that if one suspects one is HIV-positive, this information must be made public.

Such a conclusion is incompatible with a liberal society. The level of risk of transmission must be allowed to influence the strength of any moral obligation to forewarn others of HIV infection. Whilst one may be justified in withholding information about one's HIV status from one's flatmates as long as one minimises the risk of infection by disposing carefully of any spilled blood etc, it is much less acceptable that one withholds information about one's

HIV-positive status from an individual with whom one intends to have unprotected penetrative sex. Perhaps there is a moral duty to forewarn where there is a significant risk of infection.

Levels of trust There are other problems raised by the Erin and Harris's stance on absolute disclosure. The duty to forewarn, according to this view, in addition to not being influenced by the very different levels of risk involved, does not take into account the significance of different levels of trust and expectation that may exist in a sexual relationship. According to Erin and Harris, irrespective of how casual the partner, the kind of activity being undertaken and however small the risk, those who believe themselves to be HIV-positive must forewarn. Even in the context of other views Erin and Harris hold about social justice, this insistence on an absolute duty to disclose seems unnecessarily stringent, and, if the aim is to reduce the spread of infection, seems likely to fail because even if it is observed (which seems unlikely) it will result in some kind of bland, universal disclaimer prior to sexual activity which, very quickly, no one will take seriously.

But the strength of their view lies in the intuition that there are at least *some* circumstances where disclosure *is* morally required, such as between long term partners or those contemplating unsafe sex—perhaps in order to have children. So, whilst there might be good grounds for dismissing an absolute duty to disclose, it is undesirable to move from this to a position to one where there is *never* an obligation to disclose HIV positivity.

The key point is that our obligations to our sexual partners may change over time and depending upon the circumstances. This means that our moral obligations shift from one of self-protection—which in effect requires us to assume that everyone is HIV-positive until proven negative—to an obligation to disclose when, within a relationship, there is a false assumption of negativity. Once partners—for whatever reason—come to assume that each is HIV-negative, then there is an obligation on a partner who believes or knows herself to be HIV-positive to disclose this, particularly if some change in risk-taking is about to occur—such as, for instance, a change from the use of condoms to unprotected intercourse. This understanding of the moral obligation to disclose addresses several of the problems inherent in the Erin and Harris argument.

First, it permits couples to arrive at an assumption of negativity by a variety of routes which reflect the different ways in which sexual relationships are formed in contemporary society, and the different ways in which couples develop longer term relationships. For instance, some individuals may take positive steps to ascertain their HIV status and insist that partners do the same. Others practise unsafe sex without apparent adverse effects and come to assume that each is negative. For still others, the decision to have unsafe sex is a statement about what they are prepared to risk to achieve closeness with the other, or is a statement of trust in the other, or of the emotional investment in the relationship. Attaching a moral value to the assumption of negativity provides a flexible point at which trust in relationships can be said to have developed. It is a point which is not based either on duration of the relationship, type of sexual activity or particular risks taken. But it is the point at which it might be argued that a relationship has moved from the casual to one of mutual moral obligation. False assumption of negativity also requires disclosure in established relationships, like those formed before HIV was considered to be a risk. Because the criteria of assumption of negativity is flexible and enables individuals to distinguish between different kinds of relationships, it does not place unrealistic demands on comparative strangers. There is a duty to disclose HIV positivity to sexual partners only when there has been an assumption of negativity, and one knows this assumption to be false. There remains, however, a general duty upon everyone not to make rash assumptions of negativity. To make a rash assumption would be to fail in one's obligation to protect one's self.

Second, there are good moral reasons to distinguish between different kinds of relationships. In arguing that there is an absolute moral obligation to disclose even a suspicion of HIV positivity, in effect, one is arguing that most cases of HIV transmission are not just cases of harm to others but wrongs or serious injustices to others. Clearly, HIV infection is always a harm, but not so obviously a wrong, especially as there is such a range of risk, and risks (like that in the example of the toothbrush or razor) which might be taken without the consent of the infected person. Under this view of obligations, HIV transmission would only be a wrong as well as a harm if it occurred as a result of a failure to correct a false assumption of negativity. This correction of a false assumption need not necessarily take the form of a disclosure of HIV positivity. In the context of casual relationships, a more appropriate correction might be to remind one's partner that such assumptions should not be made about *anyone*. Likewise, modification of behaviour might also be a response to a false assumption.

IS THERE AN OVERRIDING MORAL OBLIGATION NOT TO HARM?

Erin and Harris argue that: "If an HIV seropositive individual does inform any sexual partner of his HIV status, and the partner nevertheless indulges in sexual intercourse, whether protected or unprotected, he is a volunteer to the respective risks. This latter individual had made an informed consent and must bear responsibility for any consequences detrimental to himself. The HIV seropositive person who discloses his HIV status has discharged his responsibilities to his partner."[10]

The claim here is that while deliberate or reckless transmission of HIV or attempts at such transmission are "not only a serious moral wrong but also, in all probability, a crime"[11] they cease to be morally wrong if consent to risk of infection is obtained. However, if knowing transmission of HIV is viewed as morally wrong then it would seem to follow that it is wrong whether the uninfected person is forewarned of the risk or not.

Assuming an individual has a general obligation to do no harm where s/he has the option of doing no harm, can this obligation to do no harm be nullified by another's consent to be harmed? Can it ever be morally justifiable to harm someone?

Clearly, there are cases where consent to harm makes the infliction of the harm morally justifiable. For instance, if a woman can save her sister by donating one of her kidneys, there would seem to be good reasons to suppose that while the removal of her kidney would be a harm, if she consents, the infliction of the harm would be morally justifiable as the consequences of not donating it may be a much greater harm. In cases where the possible harm involved is temporary and not debilitating then it may be that the benefits to the individuals involved are such that the risk of harm is worth taking.

Consent to the risk of HIV infection may be given for many reasons, all of which may be very significant in, say, the context of a long term relationship. It may be that the uninfected partner wants to prove how much he/she cares about his/her partner, or to increase the quality of their sex lives or even to have a child together. However, HIV disease is still ultimately fatal. It is arguable that there are few benefits that could outweigh the harm of a fatal disease. One of the strongest moral obligations must be an obligation not to kill others. This obligation is clearly not absolute but where killing is deemed morally permissible it is usually as the lesser of two evils, for instance in war or instances of euthanasia. However, it is difficult to imagine a circumstance which absolves one of one's obligation not to kill other people by infecting them with a fatal condition like HIV, and it is not clear that gaining their consent to this harm makes a significant moral difference.

Acknowledging that concern for consent seems to miss the point here suggests that if an HIV-infected individual consistently avoids "high risk" activities in an attempt to protect his sexual partners from infection, then he has discharged at least some of his moral responsibility towards his partners. So, could it be that instead of having a moral obligation to forewarn others who may be at risk of an HIV infection before they consent to any sexual contact, the infected individual actually has an obligation to protect others from infection. If an HIV-positive individual does have a moral obligation to refrain from activities that expose others to a high risk of infection, then the argument for forewarning appears redundant.

On the wrongs of knowing transmission, we offer one further and final observation. At some point in the widespread debate about HIV transmission, we must explore the relative worth which is to be attached to sexual expression and sexual gratification. This relative worth needs to be assessed both in terms of different relationships, and in terms of the value to the individual versus his/her moral obligation to avoid avoidable harms. Without such an analysis, we are unable to pass judgment either on the behaviour of those who engage in risky activity following a failed attempt to rectify a false assumption of negativity, or on the behaviour of those who continue to have risky sex despite knowing the danger to themselves of HIV transmission. If sexual expression and gratification are extremely valuable, then some known or unknown risk-taking may be justified with reference to the good that such sex bestows on the individuals concerned. If sexual expression and gratification can be afforded only very conditional value, then it may indeed be wrong knowingly to take risks with HIV transmission to achieve even substantial sexual expression and gratification. Likewise, it may also be wrong to place one's concerns to protect one's highly valued sex life above one's concerns to protect one's partner against transmission.

Between committed couples, the question about the value of sexual expression might be even more difficult to determine, but it is certainly something that couples themselves need to—and certainly do—address. But, until this question of value is resolved, it is difficult to argue that the decisive issue is that of disclosure.

HIV, MORAL OBLIGATIONS AND LEGAL SANCTIONS

Although Erin and Harris suggest that HIV-positive individuals have a strong moral duty to disclose their status to their intended sexual partners they reject the use of the criminal law as a means by which such disclosure could be encouraged. Their concern is that such legislation would discourage those who believe they may be infected from coming forward to be tested. Since Erin and Harris assert a general obligation to disclose, is it reasonable for them to shy away from translating this obligation into a legal one?

There are good reasons to suppose that if criminal sanctions were applicable to all cases of HIV transmission, whatever the circumstances, this would not only be morally unacceptable but also unjustifiable in terms of public health efficacy. As this paper has demonstrated, the ascription of moral responsibility in many cases of HIV transmission are complex, especially those where forewarning has taken place, or "high risk" activities have been avoided, or the "at risk" individual has an obligation to attempt to protect him/herself. In such cases it will be very difficult, if not impossible to establish a compelling case that the partner who is aware of his/her HIV positivity is solely responsible for the HIV transmission. In many cases of HIV transmission, at least via consensual acts, it seems probable that the responsibility for any resulting harm is, in some sense, held jointly by both partners. In such cases it is unhelpful to prosecute one or both of the parties involved. We suggest that the criminalisation of HIV transmission is justifiable only where there is a good case for placing the responsibility for the resulting harm with one partner, that is, where the "plaintiff" is both harmed by HIV infection and wronged by not being forewarned of her partner's known HIV-positive status. If criminalisation of deliberate or reckless HIV transmission is restricted to those cases where there is clear and unequivocal evidence of both harming and wronging, it is hoped that such legislation would allow the punishment of a serious moral crime, while avoiding any unhelpful consequences in terms of public health.

PROBLEMS WITH CRIMINALISATION OF HIV TRANSMISSION

While it seems there may be a good case for criminalising some extreme cases of reckless or deliberate HIV transmission, the criminalisation of transmission of HIV alone is unjustifiable. If criminal sanctions are used then they should be available where there has been the deliberate or reckless transmission of any communicable disease which leads to death or serious injury. This is in line with the recommendations of the Law Commission which suggests that the deliberate or reckless transmission of disease should be potentially subject to criminal prosecution.[11]

CRIMINAL LIABILITY IF THE 'VICTIM' KNOWS THE HIV STATUS OF THE 'OFFENDER'

We have suggested that if criminalisation of HIV transmission is to be seriously considered, its applicability should be restricted to cases where reckless or deliberate transmission has occurred. Criminalising cases where forewarning occurs is not advocated. While we may disagree with Erin and Harris's assertion that by forewarning an HIV-positive individual has fulfilled his/her moral obligations regarding HIV to his/her partner, the complexity of the moral obligations involved mean that criminalising his/her behaviour will not always be appropriate and thus should be avoided. However, this needs to be clarified with regard to existing legislation. It is as important for unhelpful legislation to be repealed as it is for appropriate legislation to be introduced. At present even if disclosure takes place before the parties have penetrative sex, if the partner of an HIV-positive person becomes infected as a result, a criminal offence may have been committed. English law does not allow a person to consent to the infliction on him/herself of any harm, however grave.[12] The Law Commission in recent recommendations supports this approach. It recommends that a person should not be able to consent to the infliction of a "seriously disabling injury" and that both perpetrator and victim of such an injury would be guilty of a criminal offence.[13]

It can be argued that there is a public policy interest in avoiding such harm which may arise through deliberate consensual action which leads to the transmission of HIV. Indeed, ultimately society as a whole has to bear the financial burden of counselling and medical care required in the future. But on the other hand, to criminalise sexual conduct, even where the infliction of harm is involved, in a situation in which both parties are competent, consenting adults, is intrusion upon an individual's right of privacy, a right recognised in article 8 of the *European Convention on Human Rights*.

CONCLUSION

There is a real danger that the criminalisation of HIV transmission may produce consequences that are not only morally unjustifiable but also unhelpful in terms of public health aims. To avoid these undesirable consequences, criminalisation of HIV should be restricted to the small minority of cases of HIV transmission that constitute serious moral wrongs. It is our assertion that criminal punishment of HIV transmission should only be applicable where there is clear evidence that an individual was not only harmed but also wronged when s/he became infected with HIV. That is, where an individual was infected with HIV by a person who was aware of his infection but failed to warn his partner of this fact and also failed to attempt to protect against transmission or where it was reasonable for the partner to assume negativity. Likewise, where transmission was a deliberate attempt to kill the subject. If and only if legislation could be developed that would restrict criminalisation to such cases should it be enacted. In addition, if criminal sanctions are to be available in these cases of HIV transmission, then they should also be available in comparable cases, that is, where there has been deliberate or reckless transmission of any communicable disease that leads to death or serious injury.

REFERENCES

1. Mitchell P. Cypriot sentences for infecting woman with HIV-1. *Lancet* 1997;**422:**350.

2. Smith K. J. M. Dangerous sexual behaviour and the law. In: Morgan D., Lee R., eds. *Deathrites*. London: RKP, 1994: 270.

3. Smith K. J. M. Dangerous sexual behaviour and the law. In: Morgan D., Lee R., eds. *Deathrites*. London: RKP, 1994.

4. Erin C. A., Harris J. Is there an ethics of heterosexual AIDS?. In: Sherr L., ed. *AIDS and the heterosexual population*. London: Harwood, 1993. Erin C. A., Harris J. AIDS: ethics, justice, and social policy. *Journal of Applied Philosophy* 1993; **10:**165–73.

5. See reference 4: Sherr L., ed: 245.

6. See reference 4: Sherr L., ed.

7. See reference 4: Sherr L., ed: 244.

8. "Coitus" is defined in *Webster's American heritage dictionary of the English language* [3rd ed], Houghton Mufflin, 1992, electronic format, as: "sexual union between a male and a female involving the insertion of the penis into the vagina".

9. Black H. C. *Black's law dictionary: definitions of the terms and phrases of America* [6th ed]. St Paul, Minnesota: West Publishing Company, 1990.

10. See reference 4: Sherr L., ed: 248.

11. The Law Commission no 128 at para 15.17 and the Criminal Law Bill clauses 2–5.

12. R v Brown [1993] 2 ALL ER 75.

13. The Law Commission no 139 para 4.51 and 6.84.

ANDREA CARLSON GIELEN, LINDA FOGARTY, PATRICIA O'CAMPO, JEAN ANDERSON, JEAN KELLER, AND RUTH FADEN

Women Living with HIV: Disclosure, Violence, and Social Support

Andrea Carlson Gielen is a Professor and Deputy Director of the Center for Injury Research and Policy at the Johns Hopkins Bloomberg School of Public Health. Her research interests are in the development and evaluation of community and clinic-based programs that address health behavior problems affecting women and children, primarily among low-income families in urban areas. She has contributed chapters to *Integrating Behavioral and Social Sciences with Public Health* (American Psychological Association) and to the *Health Promotion Handbook* (Mosby).

Linda Fogarty is an Assistant Research Professor in the faculty of Social and Behavioral Sciences at Johns Hopkins Bloomberg School of Public Health. Her research interests include the quality of clinical care, HIV prevention, and clinician-patient communication and its influences on informed consent, treatment decision making and treatment outcomes. She has published in the *Journal of Health Psychology* and the *Journal of Community Health.*

Patricia O'Campo is an Associate Professor in the Department of Population and Family Health Sciences at the Johns Hopkins Bloomberg School of Public Health. She has a doctorate in epidemiology. Her research interests lie in applying epidemiologic methods to a wide range of women's and maternal and child health issues like contraceptive practices, HIV infection among women, and violence toward women.

Jean Anderson is an Associate Professor of Gynecology and Obstetrics at the Johns Hopkins School of Medicine. Her research interests lie in obstetrical and gynecological issues related to HIV and genital tract infections. She is an expert in treating women with HIV.

Jean Keller is a Research Associate and a Physician's Assistant in the Department of Gynecology and Obstetrics at the Johns Hopkins School of Medicine. Her interests lie in the fields of gynecologic care and family planning.

Ruth Faden is Philip Franklin Wagley Professor of Biomedical Ethics and Executive Director of the Bioethics Institute at the Johns Hopkins University. She is also a Senior Research Scholar at the Kennedy Institute of Ethics, Georgetown University, and former chair of the President's Advisory Committee on Human Radiation Experiments. Among her books are *AIDS, Women and the Next Generation* (Oxford), edited with Gail Geller and Madison Powers, *A History and Theory of Informed Consent* (Oxford), written with Tom L. Beauchamp, and *HIV, AIDS, and Childbearing* (Oxford), edited with Nancy Kass.

INTRODUCTION

People with HIV generally are encouraged to inform appropriate others of their infection status, including, for example, sexual partners who may be at risk, as well as friends and family who might provide assistance with medical and complicated medication regimens. Yet, disclosure has been identified as an important psychological stressor for HIV-positive women.[1] Fear of abandonment and rejection, public ignorance and stigma, loss of children and housing, and potential violence have all been reported as barriers to disclosure.[2–4] Nevertheless, it appears that most women eventually do disclose their status to others. Three prior studies[3–5] of HIV-positive women have reported disclosure rates in the range 72%–98%. A study of 20 HIV-positive women who were tested during pregnancy found that 65% had not disclosed to any friends, and 25% had not disclosed to family members, but this somewhat discrepant finding may be due to the very small sample size or the short time between when women learned they were positive and the interview (6–36 months).[2]

Others may learn of a woman's HIV status either through her specific disclosure or through word of mouth when her status becomes known to friends and family.[4] Very little is known about the impact on women of both intended and unintended disclosure to others. Lester et al.[2] compared 20 HIV-positive and 20 HIV-negative postpartum women and found that HIV-positive women were more depressed and anxious and reported more discrimination by health care providers and more social isolation. Gillman and Newman[3] found that disclosure was associated positively with receiving more emotional and personal support, although 8% of women who disclosed to more than 10 people reported receiving no support, and 8% reported receiving support from only 1 person. Our own previous study[4] found that just over one-quarter of a sample of 50 HIV-positive women experienced negative consequences when others learned of their status; the consequences included rejection or abandonment (22%) and verbal or physical assault (4%). Rothenberg et al.[6] reported that, among 136 HIV/AIDS health care providers, 24% had at least 1 female patient who experienced violence as a result of HIV disclosure. Vlahov and colleagues[7] recently reported that in a cross-sectional survey of HIV-positive women, the rate of physical or sexual attack as an adult did not differ by disclosure of test results to sexual partners, although these results are somewhat difficult to interpret because the question about violence was a cumulative measure of abuse during adulthood by any perpetrator. Nevertheless, in this sample, rates of violence during adulthood were quite high: 66% reported having been abused physically, and 46% reported having been abused sexually or raped.[7] Thus, whether violence is a substantial risk of disclosure remains an open question. Understanding the risks to women and their experiences when others learn of their HIV status is critical to formulating sound partner notification policies, as well as to developing appropriate interventions for women living with the disease.

In 1991, the Centers for Disease Control and Prevention began a multisite demonstration project of behavioral interventions to promote reproductive health in women at risk and HIV-positive women. At our site, baseline interviews were conducted with a sample of HIV-positive women at the time they enrolled in the intervention trial. The purposes of this paper are to (1) describe the frequency of women's disclosure of their HIV status and (2) examine the extent to which they experience adverse social and physical consequences as a result of being HIV positive. To understand better the context of women's lives in which these events occur, we also describe women's social support network, their history of interpersonal violence, and the relationship between these experiences and negative consequences of being HIV positive. We hypothesized that women who disclosed to more people, had less social support, and had a history of interpersonal violence would be more likely to experience negative social and physical consequences of being HIV positive.

METHODS

SAMPLE RECRUITMENT

A total of 322 HIV-positive women were recruited between April 7, 1993, and June 21, 1995, from both clinic and community sites in Baltimore, Maryland. The majority of subjects were recruited from two hospital-based clinical settings—one adult outpatient HIV clinic (n = 213, 66%) and one pediatric outpatient clinic serving children of HIV-positive women (n = 59, 18%). The remaining women were referred from a community-based outpatient HIV treatment clinic

Reprinted with permission from the *Journal of Urban Health* 77 (September 2000), 480–90. Copyright © 2000 The New York Academy of Medicine.

(n = 11, 3%) or were referred informally by other project participants or by outreach workers employed by the project (n = 39, 12%). The HIV status of all participants was confirmed either by medical records or, if records were unavailable, by an HIV test.

Women were eligible for the study if they were between 18 and 44 years old, not currently pregnant, and mentally and physically healthy enough to participate (as judged by the attending physician, charge nurse, or the recruiter). A study interviewer screened all potential participants for study criteria, described the study, and obtained signed informed consent. The study was approved by the hospital's institutional review board.

To protect patients' confidentiality, names of women who declined to participate were not retained in study records. These women, particularly those identified in the clinics, therefore were likely to be approached more than once over the course of the 2-year recruitment period. Because the names of the women who were approached and declined and the number of times they were approached are not recoverable information, a true refusal rate could not be calculated. To assess the degree to which our sample was representative of the clinic population, we compared the sample distribution with that of the primary recruiting clinic for the same time period by examining 95% confidence intervals (CIs) around the point estimates for each variable in each distribution. Overlapping CIs indicated that our sample was no different from the clinic population as a whole on age and intravenous drug use history. Nonoverlapping CIs indicated that the sample included proportionally more African-American women and women with less than a 9th grade education and proportionally fewer women with more than a 12th grade education.

MEASURES

Women were paid $10 for completing the baseline interview and $5 for transportation. Interviews were conducted in a private office, and child care was available. Interviews lasted 40 to 90 minutes and included numerous topics, such as information related to HIV and reproductive health, HIV risk behaviors and beliefs, disclosure, violence, and social support. The subset of items relevant to the specific research questions of this paper are presented here.

Demographic and clinical characteristics Age, education, ethnicity, and number of children living with the woman were collected for all participants. HIV-related clinical information obtained from the women included the length of time they reported knowing they were HIV positive, history of intravenous drug use, and partner's HIV status.

Disclosure Women were asked how many people, besides doctors and nurses, they had told that they were HIV positive. Answer options were categorized as no one, 1 person, 2–5 people, or more than 5 people.

Social support We selected three domains of social support that we believed would be most relevant to women in our samples. *Social network* was measured by asking women how many relatives and how many friends they felt close to and summing the responses. *Confidant* was measured by asking women if there was anyone in particular they could confide in or talk to about themselves or their problems. *Instrumental support* was measured by summing affirmative responses to two questions that asked women if they had someone they could count on to (1) lend or give them money and (2) take them in if they needed a place to stay.

History of physical and sexual violence Women were asked whether, as an adult, they had ever been (1) pushed, grabbed, or slapped; (2) kicked, bit, or hit; (3) beat up; (4) threatened with a knife or gun or had a knife or gun used against them; and (5) sexually abused or raped. Items 1–4 were adapted from the Conflict Tactics Scale, in which Items 2–4 are considered severe physical violence,[8] and Item 5 measures sexual violence. The number of affirmative responses to the severe violence items (2–5) were summed to construct the history of violence scale score, which ranged from 0 to 4.

Negative consequences Two measures were used to construct the negative consequences variable. First, if a woman responded that she had experienced any of the five violent events described above, she was asked if she thought it happened because she was HIV positive. If she answered yes, it was counted as HIV-related violence and was included in the dependent variable as a negative consequence, but excluded from the history of violence independent variable (described above) to avoid double counting the same event and to disentangle background violence from that related to others learning that the woman was HIV positive. Second, all women were asked the following: "I'd like to ask you about some bad consequences that some women have experienced because they are HIV positive. Have any of the following things happened to you that you think were caused by your being HIV positive?" Have you been insulted or sworn at; had trouble getting or keeping a job; lost some of your friends; been turned out of your home; had your boyfriend/husband reject you; had other family members reject you. A summary score was calculated across all questions to reflect the total number of negative consequences women reported having experienced because of their HIV status.

ANALYSES

We first describe the sample characteristics and women's experiences of disclosure, social support, violence, and negative consequences. Bivariate comparisons relevant to the study aims are presented using Pearson *r*, *t* test, and Fisher exact tests. Logistic regression analysis was used to examine the extent to which demographic and clinical characteristics, disclosure, social support, and a history of violence are related to whether women experience negative social and physical consequences of being HIV positive.

RESULTS

SAMPLE

Of the 322 women recruited, the first 65 (20%) were not asked questions about the negative consequences and therefore were excluded from this analysis. When the demographic and clinical characteristics of the remaining 257 women were compared to the 65 women not included, no statistically significant differences were found.

DEMOGRAPHIC AND CLINICAL CHARACTERISTICS

The average age of participants was 32.7 years. Most women were African-American (92%), and more than one-half (54%) had less than a 12th grade education (Table I). A majority were never married (62%) and living with at least one child (60%). Over one-half of the women had used intravenous drugs, and 19% were currently with an HIV-positive male partner, although 45% did not have a main partner at the time of the interview. Of the women, 30% reported knowing they were HIV positive for 5 years or more.

DISCLOSURE

Only 8 women (3%) had not told anyone of their HIV status at the time of the interview (Table I); 6 of these women had known they were positive for 12 months or less. A majority of the sample (64%) reported having disclosed their HIV status to five or more people. The correlation between the length of time (in months) a woman knew she was positive and the reported number of people told was Pearson $r = 0.142$, $P = .023$.

SOCIAL SUPPORT

Most women reported having a confidant (89%) and numerous people who they felt close to in their social networks (mean = 8.1) (Table I). There were 68% who reported having someone they could count on for money and a place to stay, although 16% reported having no one they could count on for either. We compared the women with no instrumental support to the remainder of the sample on demographic and clinical characteristics and on their disclosure history. The absence of instrumental support was associated only with the average number of months women knew they were positive; women with no instrumental support had known they were positive for an average of 29 months, compared to 44 months for the remainder of the sample ($t = 3.1$, $P = .002$).

HISTORY OF VIOLENCE

A history of physical and sexual violence was widespread in this sample (Table I), including 26% who had been threatened with a knife or gun or had one used against them, and 27% who had been raped. In total, 62% reported having experienced at least one event; 28% experienced one type; and 34% reported two or more types of violent events.

NEGATIVE CONSEQUENCES

When asked specifically about negative consequences of being HIV positive, women most frequently reported the loss of friends (24%), followed closely by reports of being insulted (23%) and being rejected by family (21%) (Table II). In total, 56% reported experiencing no negative consequences, 16% reported one, 11% reported two, and 17% reported experiencing three or more.

There were 10 women (4%) who reported experiencing violence that they thought was attributable directly to their HIV status. The violence reported by

Table I Sample Characteristics, 257 Women Living with HIV, Baltimore, Maryland, 1993–1995

Study variables	Percentage*	Study variables	Percentage*
Demographics		Social support	
Age		Social network (# of people)	
<30	30	0	3
30–34	32	1–5	50
≥35	39	>5	47
Ethnicity		Confidant	
African-American	92	No	11
Other	8	Yes	89
Education (years)		Instrumental support score	
<12	54	0	16
12, GED	32	1	16
≥13	14	2	68
Marital status		Violence history	
Never married	62	Kicked, bit, or hit	
Married	8	No	65
Divorced/separated	24	Yes	35
Widowed	6	Beaten up	
Main partner status		No	66
HIV+	19	Yes	34
HIV−	25	Threatened with or used a knife or gun	
HIV unknown	10		
No main partner	45	No	74
Years HIV positive		Yes	26
<3	43	Sexually abused or raped	
3–4	27	No	73
≥5	30	Yes	27
Ever used IV drugs		Total violence scale score (# of types)	
No	44		
Yes	56	0	38
Disclosure		1	28
Number of people told status		≥2	34
0	3		
1–4	33		
≥5	64		

*May not add to 100% due to rounding.

these women included being pushed, grabbed, or slapped (N = 4); kicked, bit, or hit (N = 1); beaten up (N = 1); threatened with knife or gun or had one used against them (N = 3); and raped (N = 1). We compared these 10 women with the remainder of the sample on all study variables, and the two groups appeared similar on all measures with the following exceptions. Women who experienced HIV-related violence appeared more likely to have less than 12 years of education (90% versus 52%, $P = .022$) and to report experiencing more other negative consequences, including having trouble getting or keeping a job (40% versus 9%, $P = .013$); losing their home (50% versus 10%, $P = .002$); and being rejected by their families (70% versus 19%, $P = .001$).

RELATIONSHIP BETWEEN NEGATIVE CONSEQUENCES, DISCLOSURE, VIOLENCE, AND SOCIAL SUPPORT

Logistic regression was used to examine the probability of experiencing any negative consequences as a function of all of the study variables. Instrumental social support was dichotomized to compare women who had both types of support versus all others. All study variables were entered first into the model, and those that were significant at $P \leq .10$ were retained and entered into the final model (Table III).

TABLE II Negative Consequences of Living with HIV Among 257 Women, Baltimore, Maryland, 1993–1995

Type of negative consequence	Percentage
Physical violence or rape	4
Insulted or sworn at	23
Trouble getting or keeping a job	10
Lost friends	24
Turned out of home	11
Rejected by boyfriend/husband	9
Rejected by other family members	21

A history of physical or sexual violence was associated positively with experiencing negative consequences attributable to being HIV positive (OR = 1.4, 95% CI 1.11–1.74). There was a marginally statistically significant relationship between experiencing negative consequences and both having disclosed one's HIV status to more people and being younger.

DISCUSSION

In this sample of women, the majority of whom knew they were HIV positive for less than 5 years, almost all (97%) had disclosed their status to others, which is consistent with our previous qualitative study[4] and higher than other reports from smaller samples of HIV-positive women[1–3] and from another large sample recently reported.[7] Disclosure was not related to reported levels of social support, which were generally quite high in this sample. However, 16% reported having no one they could count on for money or a place to stay if they needed it.

Violence during adulthood was widespread in this sample, with 62% having experienced some form of severe physical or sexual violence, including sexual abuse or rape (27%), being beaten up (34%), and experiencing weapon-related violence (26%). These rates generally are consistent with two existing studies of HIV-positive women. In a study of 90 HIV-positive pregnant women, 53% reported ever having experienced domestic violence.[9] Zierler et al.[10] found that 35% of 74 HIV positive women reported having been raped as an adult. These rates among HIV-positive women appear higher than other studies of violence against women living in low-income urban areas, which have reported rates of physical violence of 25% to 34% and rates of 20% for sexual abuse by a partner.[11–13]

In a study comparing rates between HIV-positive and sociodemographically similar HIV-negative women, Vlahov et al.[7] found that rates of adult violence did not differ between 764 HIV-positive women and 367 HIV-negative women (66% vs. 69%, respectively). HIV-positive women experienced significantly lower rates of recent physical or sexual violence in the 6 months preceding the interview (5% vs. 8%, respectively).[7] Given the differences in sampling methods, time frames, questions, and perpetrators in this small body of literature, further research seems warranted.

Particular attention needs to be paid to measures of violence. A limitation in our study, as in others, is that simply counting violence as present or absent does not represent frequency and severity of the violence or its potential harm adequately. We tried to address this limitation by counting the number of different types of violence women experienced rather than simply using a dichotomous variable. Because of the substantial rates of violence in these women's lives, it may be that women experience the same violence after seroconversion as before, but after seroconversion, they attribute it to their HIV status. A longitudinal design comparing HIV-positive and HIV-negative women's violence experience over time would help address this limitation.

Regardless of the actual comparative risk, it is also relevant and important to describe the experiences and needs of women living with HIV. In that regard, we found substantial evidence that HIV-positive women experience social harms when others learn they are positive. Negative consequences associated with being HIV positive were widespread, with 44% of the sample reporting at least one problem, and almost one-quarter of the sample reporting that they lost friends, were rejected by their family, or had been insulted by others because they were HIV positive.

TABLE III Odds Ratios of Experiencing Any Negative Consequence of Living with HIV Among 257 Women, Baltimore, Maryland, 1993–1995: Multiple Logistic Regression Results

Variables Included in Final Model	Odds Ratio	95% Confidence Interval
History of violence	1.39	1.11, 1.74
Number of people told	1.66	1.01, 2.72
Age	0.95	0.91, 0.99
Instrumental support (both vs. other)	0.58	0.33, 1.02

Although the adverse consequences related to HIV reported here represent the women's perceptions, this should not undermine the validity of the findings. Rather, these results can be interpreted as indicating that there remains substantial stigma associated with being a woman infected with HIV.

Logistic regression analysis indicated that women who had experienced a history of severe physical or sexual violence were at increased risk for negative consequences, adjusting for age and the number of people the women had disclosed to, both of which were marginally significant. Interestingly, other sociodemographic characteristics, length of time since diagnosis, partner characteristics, and social support variables did not contribute significantly to experiencing negative consequences. This suggests that there is no simple profile of women at greatest risk for negative consequences, such as women with a history of intravenous drug use or with HIV-negative partners. Future studies should reexamine the influence of social support because, due to time constraints on the interview, we were restricted in the number of items we could choose.

Fortunately, very few women in our sample (4%) reported experiencing violence that they thought was attributable directly to others learning they were HIV positive. It is troubling, however, that this last group of women also reported disproportionately more other negative consequences of being HIV positive, such as losing their jobs and their homes and being rejected by their family. These data suggest that there may be a core group of HIV-positive women who are particularly badly affected by others learning of their status. This group also had a smaller proportion of women who graduated from high school, which may leave them with limited opportunities and resources to overcome such negative experiences.

Because our sample closely mirrored the recruiting clinic's population of HIV-positive women, results should be generalizable to other HIV-infected women receiving care in inner-city teaching hospitals. Nonetheless, it is important to note that these women may not be representative of HIV-infected women who are not receiving care.

As symptoms of HIV disease become manifest, women eventually will come into contact with the medical care system. Thus, health care providers can use the results of this study in several ways. First, partner notification policies must acknowledge and be responsive to the potential negative consequences associated with others learning that a woman is HIV infected. Young women, those who disclose to more people, and those with a history of physical or sexual violence appear to be at increased risk for negative social consequences such as losing friends, jobs, and housing and being rejected by family. Screening women for these risk factors may help individualize recommendations about disclosure. Second, support services and programs should be available to ameliorate the negative consequences that appear to be widespread among HIV-infected women. Finally, the high rates of historical violence in the lives of these women underscore the need for routine screening and intervention for domestic violence in all settings that provide health care to women living with HIV.

REFERENCES

1. Semple S. J., Patterson T. L., Temoshok L. R., et al. Identification of psychobiological stressors among HIV-positive women. *Women Health.* 1993;20(4):15–36.

2. Lester P., Partridge J. C., Chesney M. A., Cooke M. The consequences of a positive prenatal HIV antibody test for women. *J Acquir Immune Defic Syndr Hum Retrovirol.* 1995;10:341–349.

3. Gillman R. R., Newman B. S. Psychosocial concerns and strengths of women with HIV infection: an empirical study. *Fam Soc J Contemp Hum Serv* 1996;131–141.

4. Gielen A. C., O'Campo P., Faden R. R., Eke A. Women's disclosure of HIV status. Experiences of mistreatment and violence in an urban setting. *Women Health.* 1997;25(3):19–31.

5. Carter R. Disclosure of HIV serostatus to male sexual partners. Paper presented at: *HIV and Women Conference;* February 23, 1995; Washington, DC. Abstract TP481.

6. Rothenberg K. H., Paskey S. J., Reuland M. M., Zimmerman S. I., North R. L. Domestic violence and partner notification: implications for treatment and counseling of women with HIV. *J Am Med Womens Assoc.* 1995;50(3&4):87–93.

7. Vlahov D., Wientge D., Moore J., et al. Violence among women with or at risk for HIV infection. *AIDS Behav.* 1998;2(1):53–60.

8. Straus M. A., Hamby S. L., Boney-McCoy S., Sugarman D. B. The revised conflict tactics scales (CTS2): development and preliminary psychometric data. *J Family Issues.* 1996;17(3):283–316.

9. Shannon M. T., Dahrough B. M., Pantell R. H., Landers D. V. Domestic violence in HIV-infected pregnant women. Paper presented at: *HIV and Women Conference;* February 23, 1995; Washington, DC. Abstract TD 2–123.

10. Zierler S., Witbeck B., Mayer K. Sexual violence against women living with or at risk for HIV infection. *Am J Prev Med.* 1996;12(5):304–310.

11. Gin N. E., Rucker L., Frayne S., Cygan R., Hubbell F. A. Prevalence of domestic violence among patients in three ambulatory care internal medicine clinics. *J Gen Intern Med.* 1991;6:317–322.

12. Brown V. B., Melchior L. A., Reback C. J., Huba G. J. Mandatory partner notification of HIV test results: psychological and social issues for women. *AIDS Public Policy J.* Summer 1994;86–92.

13. Gielen A. C., O'Campo P., Faden R. R., Kass N. E., Xue X. Interpersonal conflict and physical violence during the childbearing year. *Soc Sci Med.* 1994;39(6):781–787.

INSTITUTE OF MEDICINE AND NATIONAL RESEARCH COUNCIL

Reducing the Odds: Preventing Perinatal Transmission of HIV in the United States

NATURAL HISTORY, DETECTION, AND TREATMENT OF HIV INFECTION IN PREGNANT WOMEN AND NEWBORNS

Perinatal transmission can occur antepartum (during pregnancy), intrapartum (during labor and delivery), and postpartum (after birth), but most mother-to-infant transmission appears to occur intrapartum. The ACTG 076 protocol showed that antiretroviral therapy could reduce perinatal transmission to 8% in some populations (Connor et al., 1994), and subsequent studies have suggested that rates of 5% or lower are possible.

To maximize prevention efforts, women must be identified as HIV-infected as early as possible during pregnancy. Early diagnosis of HIV infection allows the mother to institute effective antiretroviral therapy for her own health. This treatment is also capable of significantly reducing perinatal transmission. HIV-infected pregnant women can also be referred to appropriate psychological, social, legal, and substance abuse services. Babies born to HIV-positive mothers can be started on ZDV within hours of birth, as in the ACTG 076 regimen. Mothers who know they are HIV-positive can be counseled not to breast-feed their infants.

In terms of preventing perinatal transmission, newborn HIV testing has fewer benefits than maternal testing. When maternal serostatus is unknown, however, newborn HIV testing permits early identification and evaluation of exposed infants, allows for initiation of *Pneumocystis carinii* pneumonia (PCP) prophylaxis in the first months of life to prevent life-threatening bouts of PCP infection, may prevent transmission through breast-feeding or in future pregnancies, and could lead to mothers being treated for their own infection.

THE CONTEXT OF SERVICES FOR WOMEN AND CHILDREN AFFECTED BY HIV/AIDS

Women and children in the United States, including those at risk for or with HIV/AIDS, receive their health care from a variety of sources. Their care is financed by a mixture of public and/or private insurance and public funds. Its content and quality are influenced by public and professional organizations. Its oversight and regulation are achieved through a combination of national, state, and local authorities. Major modifications in Medicaid and welfare programs, the increasing number of uninsured, and the growing presence of managed care in both the public and the private sectors, are having a significant impact on the health care system, affecting not only the availability of quality services, but access to those services as well.

The federal government, with support from state and sometimes local governments, as well as foundations, charitable agencies, and other groups, has established special programs to provide HIV- and AIDS-related care to women and children. All states and territories have an AIDS program funded by the Centers for Disease Control and Prevention (CDC) and Health Resources and Services Administration

Adapted with permission from Committee on Perinatal Transmission of HIV, *Reducing the Odds: Preventing Perinatal Transmission of HIV in the United States* (Washington, DC: National Academy Press, 1999), 4–7, 135–36. Copyright © 1999 by the National Research Council and the Institute of Medicine. Courtesy of National Academy Press.

(HRSA). Moreover, an array of federal, state, and local laws, regulations, policies, institutions, and financing mechanisms shapes the services in any given locality and determines who has access to those services.

The complex patterns of medical care, financing mechanisms, program authority, and organizations that influence care make it difficult to institute uniform policies for reducing perinatal HIV transmission. In addition, the multiple lines of funding responsibility and accountability have made it extremely difficult to educate providers and convince them of the necessity of testing all pregnant women, as called for in the PHS counseling and testing guidelines (CDC, 1995b).

The resulting structure of the health care system presents a number of barriers to the treatment of HIV-positive women, which include—using the prevention chain as a framework—

- financial and access barriers that may discourage women from seeking prenatal care,
- time constraints that may discourage physicians from counseling pregnant patients about the importance of testing,
- prenatal care sites that may not have the staff to overcome the language and cultural barriers that may cause women to refuse testing, and
- financial and logistical problems that may make testing and treatment difficult.

IMPLEMENTATION AND IMPACT OF THE PUBLIC HEALTH SERVICE COUNSELING AND TESTING GUIDELINES

Since the publication of the ACTG 076 findings in 1994, there has been a concerted national effort to bring the benefits of HIV testing and appropriate treatment to as many women and children as possible. Reviewing the results of these efforts, the committee must make a qualified response to its congressional charge to assess "the extent to which state efforts have been effective in reducing the perinatal transmission of HIV." The committee interprets this charge to include the efforts of national as well as state and local health agencies, and professional organizations at both levels. The data reviewed indicate that, on the whole,

1. there have been substantial public and private efforts to implement the PHS recommendations,
2. prenatal care providers are more likely now than in the past to counsel their patients about HIV and the benefits of ZDV and to offer and recommend HIV tests,
3. women are more likely to accept HIV testing and ZDV if indicated, and
4. there has been a large reduction in perinatally transmitted cases of AIDS.

The number of children born with HIV, however, continues to be far above what is potentially achievable, so much more remains to be done. There is substantial variability from state to state in the way that the PHS guidelines have been implemented, but no evidence to suggest that any particular approach is more successful than others in preventing perinatal HIV.

[RECOMMENDATION]

UNIVERSAL HIV TESTING, WITH PATIENT NOTIFICATION, AS A ROUTINE COMPONENT OF PRENATAL CARE

To meet the goal that all pregnant women be tested for HIV as early in pregnancy as possible, and those who are positive remain in care so that they can receive optimal treatment for themselves and their children, *the committee's central recommendation is for the adoption of a national policy of universal HIV testing, with patient notification, as a routine component of prenatal care.*

There are two key elements to the committee's recommendation. The first is that HIV screening should be *routine with notification.* This means that the test for HIV would be integrated into the standard battery of prenatal tests and women would be informed that the HIV test is being conducted and of their right to refuse it. This element addresses the doctor–patient relationship, and can reduce barriers to patient acceptance of HIV testing. Most importantly, this approach preserves the right of the woman to refuse the test. If it is followed, women would not have to deal with the burden of disclosing personal risks or potential stereotyping; the test would simply be a part of prenatal care that is the same for everyone. Routine testing will also reduce burdens on providers such as the need for costly extensive pretest counseling and having discussions about personal risks that many providers think are embarrassing. A policy of routine testing might also help to reduce physicians' risk of liability to women and children, where providers incorrectly guess that a woman is not at risk for HIV infection.

The second key element to the recommendation is that screening should be *universal,* meaning that it applies to all pregnant women, regardless of their risk factors and of prevalence rates where they live. The benefit of universal screening is that it ameliorates the stigma associated with being "singled out" for testing, and it overcomes the problem that many HIV-infected women are missed when a risk-based or prevalence-based testing strategy is employed (Barbacci et al., 1991).

Making prenatal HIV testing universal also has broad social implications. First, if incorporated into standard prenatal testing procedures, the costs of universal HIV screening are low, and the benefits are high. Assuming that the marginal cost of adding an ELISA test to the current prenatal panel is $3 per woman and the prevalence of HIV in pregnant women is 2 per 10,000, the committee's calculations . . . show that the cost of routine prenatal testing is $15,600 per HIV-positive woman found. Even if the cost of the test is $5 and the prevalence 1 per 10,000, the cost per case found is $51,100. Taken in the context of the cost of caring for an HIV-infected child, even though not all women found to be HIV-positive will benefit, these figures indicate the clear benefits of routine prenatal HIV testing.

Second, universal screening is the only way to deal with possible geographic shifts in the epidemiology of perinatal transmission. Although perinatal AIDS cases are currently concentrated in eastern states, particularly New York, New Jersey, and Florida, there have been shifts in the prevalence of HIV in pregnant women, including an increase in the South in the early 1990s. Changes in the regional demographics of drug use can also lead to changes in the distribution of HIV infection in pregnant women. Given the uncertainty of these trends, the committee considered universal testing the most prudent method to reduce perinatal transmission despite possible regional fluctuations.

Third, it would help to reduce stigmatization of groups by calling attention to a communicable disease that does not have inherent geographic barriers or a genetic predisposition. Focusing on the communicable disease aspect may allow national education programs that would otherwise be difficult, discouraging infected individuals from hiding themselves and thus not benefiting from care, and discouraging a "blame the victim" mentality.

• • •

REFERENCES

Barbacci M. B., Repke J. T., Chaisson R. E. Routine prenatal screening for HIV infection. *Lancet* 337:709–11, 1991.

CDC. U.S. Public Health Service recommendations for human immunodeficiency virus counseling and voluntary testing for pregnant women. *MMWR* 44(RR-7), 1995b.

Connor E. M., Sperling R. S., Gelber R., Kiselev P., Scott G., O'Sullivan M. J., VanDyke R., Bey M., Shearer W., Jacobson R. L., Jimenez E., O'Neill E., Bazin B., Delfraissy J. F., Culnane M., Coombs R., Elkins M., Moye J., Stratton P., Balsley J. Reduction of maternal–infant transmission of human immunodeficiency virus type 1 with zidovudine treatment. Pediatric AIDS Clinical Trials Group Protocol 076 Study Group. *N Engl J Med* 331(18):1173–1180, 1994.

BERNARD LO, LESLIE WOLF, AND SOHINI SENGUPTA

Ethical Issues in Early Detection of HIV Infection to Reduce Vertical Transmission

Bernard Lo is Director of the Center for AIDS Prevention Studies Ethics Core, a Professor of Medicine and Director of the Program in Medical Ethics at the University of California, San Francisco. He is a member of the Board of Health Sciences Policy, the Institute of Medicine, and the Board of Directors of the American Society of Law, Medicine, and Ethics. He was formerly a member of the National Bioethics Advisory Commission. His publications include (with A. Alpers) "Physician-Assisted Suicide in Oregon: A Bold Experiment," in *Resolving Ethical Dilemmas: A Guide for Clinicians* (Williams & Wilkins).

Leslie E. Wolf is an Assistant Professor of Medicine at the University of California, San Francisco. She also works in the Medical Ethics Program and the Center for AIDS Prevention Studies. Her publications are found in journals like the *Western Journal of Medicine* and *IRB*.

Sohini Sengupta is a former postdoctoral fellow at the Center for AIDS Prevention Studies at the University of California, San Francisco. His publications are found in journals like *AIDS Care* and *Health Education Research.*

Early detection of HIV infection offers the hope that transmission of HIV may be reduced through effective preventive measures. A dramatic example of the benefits of early detection is the prevention of vertical transmission of HIV. Vertical transmission of HIV can be substantially reduced if antiretroviral therapy is administered to HIV-infected pregnant women during pregnancy, labor, and delivery, and to the infant in the neonatal period.[1] Early prenatal testing for HIV is the crucial first step in reducing transmission in this setting. A 1998 Institute of Medicine (IOM) report has recommended substantial changes in HIV testing policies in the prenatal setting, so that prenatal HIV testing would be a routine and universal part of pregnancy care.[2] The American College of Obstetrics and Gynecology and the American Academy of Pediatrics have supported these recommendations.[3] However, early detection of HIV through more widespread prenatal HIV testing also raises difficult ethical and policy issues. This article analyzes issues that must be worked out if routine, universal prenatal HIV testing is to be adopted and if such early detection is to be translated into more effective prevention of maternal-child transmission. We also discuss whether these proposed policy changes have merit in other clinical settings.

Vertical transmission of HIV has been a priority area for earlier detection because the source of exposure is easily identifiable and because infants cannot take steps to protect themselves. In addition, there is compelling evidence that transmission is significantly reduced if pregnant women identified as seropositive receive antiretroviral therapy. AIDS Clinical Trials Group Study 076 showed that zidovudine reduced

Reprinted with permission from the *Journal of Acquired Immune Deficiency Syndrome* 25 (2000), S136–S143. Copyright © (2000), Lippincott Williams & Wilkins, Inc., Philadelphia.

transmission from 25% to 8%.[1] Subsequent randomized controlled trials have demonstrated that shorter courses of antiretroviral therapy also reduce vertical transmission.[4–7] Since the publication of ACTG 076 and Centers for Disease Control recommendations that prenatal HIV testing be offered to all pregnant women, the rates of perinatal transmission and the number of reported cases of perinatally transmitted AIDS in the U.S. have decreased by almost 50%.[8,9] More aggressive treatment with combination antiretroviral therapy may reduce perinatal transmission even further.[10]

The public health goal should be to identify all HIV-infected pregnant women before delivery, so that they can be offered prenatal and intrapartum antiretroviral therapy. However, approximately 15% of HIV-infected women in the U.S. receive no prenatal care. Most of these women are black, live in urban areas, and use injection drugs.[2] Furthermore, the percentage of women in prenatal care who are offered HIV testing by their provider varies from state to state, ranging from 50%–75%.[2] This finding is disconcerting because most women accept prenatal HIV testing, particularly when providers strongly recommend it.[2] Thus, lack of prenatal testing is an important barrier to preventing vertical transmission of HIV.

PROPOSED POLICIES FOR ROUTINE UNIVERSAL PRENATAL HIV TESTING

HIV testing early in pregnancy is the essential first step in further reducing vertical transmission of HIV. The 1998 IOM panel charged with evaluating the effectiveness of efforts to reduce perinatal transmission concluded that requirements for pretest counseling and written informed consent were significant barriers to prenatal HIV testing. In light of the proven effectiveness of antiretroviral therapy for preventing vertical transmission, the panel called for significant changes in HIV testing policies for pregnant women in the U.S. The panel recommended that universal HIV testing with patient notification be a routine part of prenatal care.[2]

DEVELOPMENT OF HIV TESTING POLICIES

Early in the epidemic, HIV testing was recognized to have serious social and psychological risks of stigma and discrimination.[11] People identified as HIV-positive may be rejected by their families or suffer discrimination in employment, access to health care, and housing if the confidentiality of their test results is breached. Domestic violence against HIV-infected women was identified as a particular risk.[12] The benefits of early diagnosis to individual patients were uncertain because there was no proven treatment at that time. Because HIV testing was regarded as different from other blood tests, states required pretest counseling and specific written informed consent.[13] Special protections for confidentiality of HIV test results also were enacted in an era when draconian measures like quarantine were suggested for individuals known to be seropositive.[14–17] Anonymous test sites were established. Many states required specific written permission from the patient to disclose HIV test results to third parties.

The IOM panel determined that the clear evidence that antiretroviral therapy reduces vertical transmission justified changing prenatal HIV testing policies. These recommendations make prenatal HIV testing policies similar to policies of routine prenatal testing for syphilis, rubella immunity, and Rh incompatibility. However, objections have been raised against routine prenatal HIV testing. Critics fear that pregnant women may not be explicitly told that the test will be done and thus may have no real option to refuse. Hence, the process may seem mandatory rather than voluntary to pregnant women. Furthermore, opponents argue that routine testing discriminates against pregnant women by eliminating the protections of specific written consent and pretest counseling required for HIV testing in other settings.

In the U.S. system, the states have the authority to regulate HIV testing. If the IOM recommendations are to be implemented, most states will have to revise their laws regarding HIV testing. Thus the IOM recommendations regarding prenatal testing will be debated in the states. Research can contribute to this debate. Ethical analysis can identify and clarify pertinent issues and suggest how to resolve them. Analysis of current state laws on HIV testing can indicate what laws need to be changed if routine prenatal testing is to be adopted. Even without changes in state laws, the IOM recommendations, together with the support of the American Academy of Pediatrics and the American College of Obstetricians and Gynecologists, are likely to change the standard of practice. If a mother who was not tested for HIV infection during pregnancy has an infected child, she would have a plausible malpractice suit if the obstetrician had not recommended prenatal HIV testing. However, it must be noted that most women who give birth to

HIV-infected children are poor and not well educated and therefore unlikely to bring a lawsuit.

The ethical rationale for routine universal prenatal HIV testing is to protect the public health and to prevent the transmission of a fatal illness to third parties who cannot protect themselves. Although such HIV testing also benefits the pregnant woman, the benefit to the patient being tested would not in itself justify the recommended policy. In clinical care, the standard practice is to obtain informed consent from patients for medical interventions.[18] This clinical policy is justified by the ethical principle of respect for persons. The default position is that interventions are not carried out unless the patient gives consent. Stated another way, the patient must "opt in" in order to receive the intervention. In many clinical situations, specific consent is not obtained for tests such as a blood count or cholesterol level. These tests have no medical or psychosocial risks. A doctor may simply ask the patient to have "routine" tests done, without specifying which tests will be done. Very few patients decline such tests. Presumably, most patients, if offered a discussion of the risks and benefits of such tests, would agree to testing. In contrast, many public health interventions, such as tuberculosis screening, are carried out on an "opt out" basis. That is, the intervention is done unless the individual objects. This reverses the presumption in clinical practice that consent is needed. This compromise of patient autonomy is accepted by society because the public health intervention offers clear benefits in preventing serious harm to third parties, the risks to the person being tested are minimized, and the infringement of autonomy seems appropriate in light of the benefits.

Making prenatal HIV testing universal is justified by the ethical principles of justice and beneficence. Targeting HIV testing tends to stigmatize groups that are identified as being at high risk. Making testing universal will reduce stigma and discrimination because individuals will not be singled out for testing based on assessments of risk. Furthermore, universal testing should identify more seropositive pregnant women, because both physicians and patients are uncomfortable discussing high-risk behaviors. Patients may not know whether they are at risk because they do not know their partners' level of risk. Also, physicians who are uncomfortable with risk assessment often do not offer HIV testing.

DEFINITION OF ROUTINE PRENATAL HIV TESTING

The word *routine* can be used in different ways, and it is important to define clearly what routine prenatal testing means. *Routine* is derived from the same Latin stem as the words *route, rote,* and *rut.*[19] Thus, *routine* refers to a regular course or procedure, a habitual or mechanical performance, or something found in the ordinary course of events.[19] With regard to prenatal testing, the danger is that routine prenatal HIV testing will become so habitual or mechanical that pregnant women may not realize that they have the option to decline testing. Thus, the decision to be tested may not really be an autonomous choice. Another danger is that caregivers and patients may forget that HIV testing has much greater psychosocial risks than other blood tests and that prenatal HIV testing differs from HIV testing in other settings. In addition, what seems routine to health care workers may be a daunting experience to patients.

Several ethical issues regarding routine prenatal HIV testing need to be addressed in order to ensure that pregnant women's autonomous choices are respected. These include the notification that HIV testing will be done unless that patient objects and an offer to discuss the risks and benefits of testing in more detail.

NOTIFICATION OF PATIENTS ABOUT ROUTINE PRENATAL HIV TESTING

The IOM recommends that physicians inform pregnant women explicitly that the test will be done unless they object. This provision helps ensure that prenatal testing is a voluntary choice by the pregnant woman. However, this requirement may not be observed in state law or in practice. Currently Texas and Arkansas allow prenatal HIV testing without specific consent. In Texas, clinicians must inform women that the test will be done unless they object.[20] In Arkansas, however, there is no statutory requirement that pregnant women be notified that they have the right to refuse.[21] Furthermore, even if laws require health care workers to notify pregnant women that they may refuse, such notification may not occur in clinical practice. In their desire to increase prenatal HIV testing, physicians and nurses may gloss over this point when discussing HIV tests with pregnant patients. If notification does not occur, the risks of prenatal HIV testing may not be minimized. For example, a woman may be concerned about domestic violence or rejection by her partner. If such concerns are identified, caregivers can discuss how test results may be disclosed to her privately and what steps she can take to decrease the risks of domestic violence.

DISCUSSION OF THE RISKS AND BENEFITS OF HIV TESTING

The IOM recommendations would abolish pretest counseling for prenatal HIV testing. This is a dramatic policy change because almost all states currently require such pretest counseling. Some states even specify information that must be discussed with patients before HIV testing. For example, New York requires that patients be told that confidentiality may be breached and discrimination may occur.[22] Proponents of routine prenatal HIV testing argue that it is counterproductive for health care providers to describe the risks of testing in detail because these risks are far outweighed by the benefits of preventing vertical transmission. Furthermore, proponents contend that it is misleading to suggest that women who deliver infants in New York state can avoid having their HIV status known. In New York, neonates must be tested if the mother's HIV status is unknown, even without the consent of the mother.[22] Such neonatal testing, of course, also indicates whether the mother is infected. In these circumstances, the woman has little choice as to whether her HIV status is determined; her only choice is whether that information is available at a time when the most effective preventive measures can be instituted.

If pretest counseling is abolished for prenatal HIV testing, what should health care workers say to pregnant patients about the risks and benefits of HIV testing? To say nothing may be misleading, suggesting that the risks of HIV testing are no greater than the risks of a test for syphilis, Rh titers, rubella antibodies, or blood sugar, which are all routine prenatal tests. Perhaps an acceptable middle ground would be for health care workers to offer to discuss the benefits and risks of prenatal HIV testing in more detail with each pregnant woman. Without an explicit offer of a more detailed discussion, patients may be hesitant to ask questions.

UNANSWERED QUESTIONS REGARDING ROUTINE PRENATAL HIV TESTING

The IOM recommendations to abolish pretest counseling in the prenatal situation leave many questions unanswered. Empirical research can help address those questions.

IS ROUTINE PRENATAL HIV TESTING ACCEPTABLE TO PREGNANT WOMEN?

A policy of routine prenatal HIV testing will be feasible only if it is acceptable to pregnant women. The long-term cooperation of seropositive pregnant patients is essential in preventing vertical transmission. To minimize the risk of vertical transmission, HIV-infected women must take antiretroviral therapy and must administer it to the child after birth. Although prenatal regimens may be simpler than combination regimens of highly active antiretroviral therapy, they still must be taken several times a day, optimally over many weeks. In addition, HIV-infected mothers should use bottle-feeding because HIV can be transmitted to the infant through breastfeeding.[23,24] To gain the cooperation of seropositive women with recommended care, we must avoid policies that ignore their perspectives or that may lead to mistrust or confrontation.

It is crucial to understand the perspectives of pregnant women regarding routine prenatal HIV testing, particularly the views of women at increased risk for HIV. A number of empirical questions need to be studied. First, do pregnant women understand the policy of routine prenatal HIV testing? In particular, do they appreciate the difference between routine testing and mandatory testing? Do they understand the rationale for the policy and the benefits of prenatal HIV testing? Does making testing universal—having all pregnant women be tested, regardless of their apparent risk for HIV—relieve concerns that routine testing is discriminatory? Does their understanding of routine testing affect their willingness to agree to testing?

A second question is what are the concerns of pregnant women regarding routine prenatal HIV testing? Do pregnant women have concerns that refusal to take an HIV test, or positive HIV test results, will be used against them in their medical care or in child abuse or child custody hearings? Do they fear that domestic violence may occur as a result of a positive HIV test result or even as a result of taking an HIV test? Do women feel that prenatal HIV testing devalues them as people, that the policy stems from a concern for preventing harm only to the infant who will be born? Unless the concerns of pregnant women are understood, steps cannot be taken to address them and thereby reduce the barriers to prenatal HIV testing.

Third, how can routine prenatal HIV testing be presented so that it is most acceptable to pregnant women? Social marketing, which segments the population of pregnant women into subgroups, may be particularly helpful in addressing the following questions. How can the policy of routine prenatal HIV testing best be described? How can misunderstandings be corrected or avoided? How can patient concerns be most effectively addressed?

ARE SAFEGUARDS FOR PREGNANT WOMEN ADEQUATE?

To the extent that pregnant women have realistic concerns that HIV test results may be used against them, those concerns need to be addressed.

Women may fear that refusal of prenatal HIV testing may result in charges of child neglect or abuse. However, refusal of prenatal testing per se should not be considered neglect or abuse. First, in the majority of cases, refusal of testing will not result in an avoidable case of mother-to-child transmission of HIV. In most cases, the child will be seronegative, either because the woman is seronegative or because transmission occurs in only a minority of HIV-infected pregnant women. Second, even if it is known that a pregnant woman is seropositive, forcibly administering antiretroviral therapy over her objections is both impractical and difficult to justify ethically. Third, many other actions by pregnant women are not considered child neglect or abuse, even though they put the fetus at risk. Examples are alcohol and substance abuse during pregnancy. Although such behaviors are ill-advised and morally reprehensible, they are not legally punishable. The autonomy of pregnant women is given particular respect because interventions directed at the fetus are necessarily interventions on the pregnant woman. Pregnant women are granted more discretion to do what they consider best than parents are granted after children are born.

Legal safeguards can protect pregnant women against discrimination on the basis of their choice about prenatal HIV testing. In Maryland, pregnant women cannot be denied prenatal care if they refuse an HIV test, and the results of prenatal HIV testing are not discoverable or admissible in criminal, civil, or administrative procedures[25]. Thus, refusal of prenatal HIV testing cannot be used in proceedings about child custody or child neglect or abuse. Similar protections that address pregnant women's concerns should be adopted in other states.

WHAT IS THE IMPACT OF ROUTINE PRENATAL HIV TESTING?

The policy of routine prenatal HIV testing has been recommended in order to achieve specific public health goals. If routine prenatal HIV testing is adopted, it would be important to evaluate whether those goals in fact are achieved. Does routine prenatal HIV testing increase the number of pregnant women who receive HIV testing before the third trimester? Does the policy increase the number of pregnant women who start antiretroviral therapy? Does the policy reduce the number of HIV-infected infants? Are there any adverse consequences of the policy? Specifically, is there any evidence that the policy is leading pregnant women to forego or delay prenatal care? If new HIV testing policies deter pregnant women from prenatal care, infants may be harmed by increased prematurity or birth defects.

IS ROUTINE PRENATAL HIV TESTING COST-EFFECTIVE?

Because resources for HIV prevention and care are limited, the cost-effectiveness of routine prenatal HIV testing cannot be ignored. Resources devoted to routine prenatal HIV testing cannot be spent on other HIV prevention programs or other worthwhile social programs. Hence the marginal cost effectiveness of routine prenatal testing must be compared to that of other preventive programs, such as increased outreach to injection drug users, which may identify more seropositive persons and therefore more opportunities to prevent transmission. However, prevention of vertical transmission may be given higher priority than its cost-effectiveness per se warrants. Public opinion gives special importance to preventing cases where HIV transmission can be traced to specific individuals and where exposed individuals cannot protect themselves.[26–28] Other situations in which society is willing to spend considerable resources on preventing a few cases of HIV include transmission from blood transfusions and from health care worker to patients.[26–28] However, the public may be less willing to support more cost-effective prevention programs if cases of transmission can not be readily identified as failures of the program.[29]

ADDITIONAL PREVENTION ISSUES AFTER HIV TESTING

Prenatal HIV testing is only the first of a series of steps that must occur for optimal prevention of vertical transmission. Other steps in the series also raise ethical dilemmas.

A policy of routine prenatal HIV testing will fail to prevent vertical HIV transmission in cases where the pregnant woman receives no prenatal care. As previously noted, approximately 15% of HIV-infected pregnant women in the U.S. present for obstetrical care for the first time while in labor.[2] Even at this late stage of pregnancy, vertical transmission may still be prevented if HIV infection can be quickly identified. Recent randomized trials in developing countries show that antiretroviral therapy initiated during labor and delivery also reduces perinatal transmission of HIV significantly.[5,7] Thus, if HIV-infected women could be identified among those women who first present for care during labor, there would still be an opportunity to institute effective measures to prevent vertical transmission.

Rapid HIV testing offers a means to identify HIV-infected pregnant women who first present for care during labor.[30] Rapid HIV tests can be performed in about 10 minutes. Thus, if a woman presents in labor without previous prenatal care or prenatal HIV testing, it can be quickly determined whether she is seropositive. Because the negative predictive value of a single rapid test is high, a woman who tests negative can be considered HIV-negative if the rapid test is unreactive. If the rapid test is reactive, the Centers for Disease Control suggests that it is appropriate to make clinical decisions without a confirmatory test when time is limited.[31] The positive predictive value of the rapid test can be increased if it is combined with another rapid test. However, currently only one rapid HIV test is approved by the Food and Drug Administration for use in the United States.

Several specific clinical and ethical issues must be addressed regarding rapid prenatal HIV testing during labor and delivery.

First, is it appropriate for physicians to initiate antiretroviral therapy on the basis of a rapid HIV test, which may be a false positive test?[31] The benefits of acting upon a potentially false-positive test must be weighed against the risks. The benefit is the opportunity to reduce perinatal transmission substantially. In the intrapartum period, the primary risks are the stigma and anxiety of a false-positive diagnosis of HIV in the mother and the adverse consequences if confidentiality is broken, such as rejection by the woman's partner or family.

The second issue is whether a physician may initiate antiretroviral treatment during labor after obtaining the woman's assent to routine emergency therapy, rather than full informed consent. By assent, we mean the patient's affirmative acceptance of treatment based upon a clinician's recommendation of the therapy. In contrast, informed consent requires physicians to discuss with the patient the diagnosis, prognosis, risks, and benefits of treatment, and alternatives.

The third issue concerns HIV-infected women who lack the capacity to make medical decisions during labor and delivery (for example, because they are intoxicated). May the medical team begin antiretroviral therapy under a doctrine of implied consent to emergency treatment? In an emergency, if treatment must be instituted immediately to prevent serious harm, it is presumed that patients would want treatment started without their explicit consent.[32] The situation may be more complicated than in usual cases of emergency treatment for patients who lack decision-making capacity. For example, after an automobile accident, physicians often turn to next of kin for authorization to treat an injured patient who cannot give consent. In the case of HIV infection, asking the woman's partner or other family to authorize treatment may be inappropriate because it may breach confidentiality and result in social harms, including rejection or even domestic violence.

REFUSAL OF MEASURES TO PREVENT VERTICAL TRANSMISSION

After a pregnant woman is identified as HIV-infected, the next step in the chain of preventing prenatal HIV infection is the administration of antiretroviral therapy. However, some pregnant women do not want antiretroviral therapy. This may be an informed decision made after careful consideration of the benefits and risks of treatment. Consider a pregnant woman with two seronegative children. She fears that her partner will learn that she is taking antiretroviral therapy and infer that she is HIV-positive. If this occurs, she believes that he will force her and her children out of his home. She concludes that the risk of homelessness outweighs the benefits of reducing the risk of vertical transmission. The woman is an autonomous moral agent, who must be allowed to weigh the benefits and burdens of antiretroviral therapy for herself. The ethical principle of respect for the autonomy of patients and the legal doctrine of informed consent allow competent pregnant patients to refuse treatment, even highly beneficial therapies. As a practical matter, it would be extremely difficult to force pregnant women to take medications over a period of many weeks over their objections. In such a situation, however, physicians should offer the woman intrapartum antiretroviral therapy, which she may be willing to accept. Steps can be taken to reduce the likelihood that the partner will discover her infection, such as avoiding labeling intravenous solutions with the name of the antiretroviral agent. Of course, the woman may still refuse intrapartum therapy.

Still other ethical dilemmas may arise after childbirth. An HIV-infected woman who assented to intrapartum therapy may, upon more reflection, decline antiretroviral therapy to the infant after birth and insist on breastfeeding. After childbirth, interventions can be administered to the child without violating the bodily integrity of the mother, unlike the prenatal situation. Moreover, there are precedents for overriding the refusal of parents to provide highly effective therapies to children.[33,34] By analogy, is it ethically warranted for physicians to seek to administer antiretroviral therapy to the infant over the objections of the seropositive mother or to keep her from breastfeeding? In this situation, respect for the autonomy of parents to make medical decisions for their children must be balanced against the best interests of the infant.

IMPLICATIONS FOR EARLY DETECTION AND PREVENTION IN OTHER CLINICAL SETTINGS

In the prenatal setting, several changes in public policy have been suggested to enhance the use of measures known to prevent vertical HIV transmission. These policy changes include routine testing without pretest counseling or written consent and rapid HIV testing during labor. Are similar policy changes advisable in other situations of HIV prevention? Some arguments that support changes in prenatal HIV testing policy also support similar changes in other clinical settings. Written informed consent to HIV testing and pretest counseling may be seen as reasons for low rates of HIV testing in high-prevalence populations. Changes in HIV testing policies are justified as a public health measure if they will lead to reduced HIV transmission, without significant adverse consequences for the individuals tested.

There are important differences between perinatal HIV transmission and HIV transmission in other settings. First, and most important, pregnancy differs from other clinical situations of HIV transmission in ethically significant ways. In pregnancy, the entity at risk for acquiring HIV infection is readily identified. The fetus who is exposed to HIV in utero is in no position to take steps to reduce potential harms. Arguably, no other being at risk for HIV is so vulnerable and dependent. This vulnerability has been the justification for other public policies that establish "routine" prenatal testing of women for other conditions.[35] which generally evoke little opposition from pregnant women. There are few other clinical situations where routine testing is mandated by state laws, even for conditions that may be stigmatizing. The discrepancy between written consent for prenatal HIV testing and "routine" prenatal testing for syphilis, Rh incompatibility, and other conditions has been criticized for implying that HIV testing is less beneficial or more dangerous than these other tests. The situation is significantly different when HIV is transmitted through sexual intercourse or sharing of injection drug paraphernalia. Those at risk for transmission in these contexts may not be readily identifiable and, unlike a fetus, may be able to take steps to prevent infection, e.g., by refraining from high-risk behaviors.

Second, the evidence that early detection reduces HIV transmission is stronger in the prenatal setting. The evidence is compelling that antiretroviral therapy to the woman before and during delivery, coupled with antiretroviral therapy to the child after birth, significantly reduces mother-to-child HIV transmission. To be sure, there are no clinical trials demonstrating that routine, universal prenatal HIV testing increases the number of pregnant women identified as seropositive or reduces the number of HIV-infected infants. However, unless routine, universal prenatal HIV testing has undesirable consequences such as deterring pregnant women from prenatal care, it is unlikely to have adverse consequences on perinatal transmission. In other clinical contexts, the evidence supporting changes in HIV testing policies are weaker. As detailed elsewhere in the symposium, there is growing evidence that HIV testing and counseling are effective in reducing HIV transmission. However, studies demonstrating the effectiveness of counseling and testing have all been carried out with full informed consent for HIV testing and pretest counseling. It is not clear whether patients will adopt behavioral changes if HIV testing is carried out routinely without full informed consent.

Third, when a pregnant woman presents in labor without previous antiretroviral therapy, there is a small window of opportunity to administer antiretroviral therapy before delivery. Thus the arguments to justify rapid HIV testing for women who present in labor without HIV testing may be stronger than arguments to justify rapid testing in other clinical contexts where there are opportunities for the patient to return for further discussion of therapeutic alternatives.

These clinical and ethical differences between vertical HIV transmission and other situations of HIV transmission must be kept clearly in mind when analogous policies to enhance early HIV detection are considered in other contexts. In our view, making HIV testing routine in other clinical settings is not justified. The acceptance of routine prenatal testing for other conditions, as a matter of both public policy and clinical practice, makes the requirement for written consent for HIV testing anomalous. The issue of pretest counseling regarding HIV infection in other settings is less clear. Arguably, public knowledge about HIV transmission is now sufficiently accurate that the benefits of pretest counseling are much less than when HIV testing policies were first formulated. Communicating information about HIV may no longer be as a high a priority as increasing the use of HIV testing in persons at risk. To the extent that pretest counseling is shown to be a significant barrier to physicians recommending HIV testing, pretest counseling may need to be reconsidered. Posttest counseling targeted to the patient's HIV status may be an effective alternative to pretest counseling. If patient failure to return for HIV test results is a problem, it might be addressed through the use of two rapid HIV tests, so that the results can be given to the patient the same day.

In conclusion, early detection of HIV infection during pregnancy offers the opportunity to institute antiretroviral therapy that prevents vertical transmission and also provides benefit to the pregnant woman. However, policies to encourage earlier detection also raise ethical issues regarding the definition and implementation of routine universal prenatal testing, the connection between prenatal HIV testing and the right of women to refuse antiretroviral therapy, and the care of pregnant women who present in labor without prenatal HIV testing. These ethical and policy issues must be clarified and resolved in order for HIV prevention programs to be acceptable to the public and effective in achieving their goals.

REFERENCES

1. Connor E., Sperling R., Gelber R., et al. Reduction of maternal-infant transmission of human immunodeficiency virus type 1 with zidovudine treatment. *N Engl J Med* 1994;331:1173–80.

2. Institute of Medicine Committee on Perinatal Transmission of HIV. *Reducing the odds: preventing perinatal transmission of HIV in the United States*. Washington DC: National Academy Press, 1998.

3. American Academy of Pediatrics and American College of Obstetricians and Gynecologists. Human immunodeficiency virus screening. *Pediatrics* 1999;104:128.

4. Altman L. Spare AIDS regime is found to reduce risk to newborns. *New York Times* February 2, 1999, 1999:1A.

5. Department of Health and Human Services. Researchers identify a simple, affordable drug regimen that is highly effective in preventing HIV infection in infants of mothers with the disease [press release]. Available at: http://www.niaid.nih.gov. Accessed October 28, 2000.

6. Blanche S., Rouzioux C., Mandelbrot L., Delfraissy J. F., Mayaux M. J. Zidovudine-lamivudine for prevention of mother to child HIV-1 transmission [abstract 267]. Paper presented at 6th Conference on Retroviruses and Opportunistic Infections. January 31–February 4, 1999; Chicago, IL.

7. Saba J. Interim analysis of early efficacy of three short ZDV/3TC combination regimens to prevent mother-to-child transmission of HIV-1: the PETRA trial [abstract S7]. Paper presented at 6th Conference on Retroviruses and Opportunistic Infections. 1999; Chicago, IL.

8. National Center for HIV STD & TB Prevention. *Perinatal HIV prevention update*. National Center for HIV STD & TB Prevention; 1997.

9. Centers for Disease Control. Update: perinatally acquired HIV/AIDS—United States, 1997. *MMWR* 1997;46:1086–92.

10. Centers for Disease Control. Public Health Service Task Force recommendations for the use of antiretroviral drugs in pregnant women infected with HIV-1 for maternal health and for reducing perinatal HIV-1 transmission in the United States. *MMWR* 1998;47:1–30.

11. Lo B., Steinbrook R. L., Coates T., Cooke M., Walters E., Hulley S. B. Voluntary HIV screening: weighing the benefits and harms. *Ann Intern Med* 1989;110:727–33.

12. North R. L., Rothenberg K. H. Partner notification and the threat of domestic violence against women with HIV infection. *N Engl J Med* 1993;329:1194–6.

13. Gostin L. O., Webber D. W. HIV infection and AIDS in the public health and health care systems. *JAMA* 1998;279:1108–13.

14. Bayer R. Public health policy and the AIDS epidemic: an end to HIV exceptionalism? *N Engl J Med* 1991;324:1500–4.

15. Gostin L. O. Public health strategies for confronting AIDS: legislative and regulatory policy in the United States. *JAMA* 1989;261:1621–9.

16. Gostin L., Curran W. J. AIDS screening, confidentiality, and the duty to warn. *Am J Public Health* 1987;77:361–5.

17. Gostin L., Curran W. J. Legal control measures for AIDS: reporting requirements, surveillance, quarantine, and regulation of public meeting places. *Am J Public Health* 1987;77:214–8.

18. Lo B. *Resolving ethical dilemmas: a guide for clinicians*, 2nd ed. Philadelphia: Lippincott Williams & Wilkins. 2000:19–29.

19. Hypertext Webster Gateway. *Webster's revised unabridged dictionary* (1913). http://work.ucsd.edu:5141/egi-bin/http_webster?routine&method=exact. Accessed October 28, 2000.

20. Tex. Health & Safety Code, §81.090 (1997).

21. Ark. Stat. Ann., §20-15-905 (1994).

22. New York CLS Pub Health, §2781(3) (1999).

23. Van de Perre P. Postnatal transmission of the human immunodeficiency virus type 1 and the breastfeeding dilemma. *Am J Obstet Gynecol* 1995;173:483–7.

24. Dunn D., Newell M., Ades A., Peckham C. Risk of human immunodeficiency virus type 1 transmission through breastfeeding. *Lancet* 1992;340:585–8.

25. Maryland Health-General Code Ann., §18-338.2 (1997).

26. AuBuchon J. P., Birkmeyer J. D., Busch M. P. Safety of the blood supply in the United States: opportunities and controversies. *Ann Intern Med* 1997;127:904–9.

27. Daniels N. HIV-infected professionals, patient rights, and the "switching dilemma." *JAMA* 1992;267:1368–71.

28. Lo B., Steinbrook R. Health care workers infected with the human immunodeficiency virus: the next steps. *JAMA* 1992;267:1000–5.

29. Calabresi G., Bobbitt P. *Tragic choices*. New York: Norton, 1978.

30. Minkoff H., O'Sullivan M. The case for rapid HIV testing during labor. *JAMA* 1998;279:1743–4.

31. Centers for Disease Control. Update: HIV counseling and testing using rapid tests—United States, 1995. *MMWR* 1998;47: 211–5.

32. Appelbaum P., Lidz C., Meisel A. *Informed consent: legal theory and clinical practice*. New York: Oxford University Press. 1987.

33. American Academy of Pediatrics Committee on Bioethics. Informed consent, parental permission, and assent in pediatric practice. *Pediatrics* 1995;95:314–7.

34. Wadlington W. Medical decision making for and by children: tensions between parent, state, and child. *University of Illinois Law Review* 1994;1994:311–36.

35. Acuff K. I. Prenatal and newborn screening: state legislative approaches and current practice standards. In: Faden R. R., Geller G., Powers M., eds. *AIDS, women and the next generation*. New York: Oxford University Press, 1991:121–65.

STEPHEN F. MORIN

Early Detection of HIV: Assessing the Legislative Context

Stephen F. Morin is Associate Adjunct Professor of Medicine and Director of the Policy Center within the University of California, San Francisco AIDS Research Institute. He has served as part of the associate staff to the House Appropriations Committee. He has played a part in almost every AIDS-related battle at the federal level. His current work is on ways to improve HIV counseling and testing programs and on setting priorities for international HIV prevention research.

Throughout its history, the AIDS epidemic has sparked intense political debate about the role the government should play in addressing public health challenges.[1] Lawmakers at every level have found it difficult to strike a balance between invoking the extensive powers given to health officials to protect the public health and protecting the privacy and dignity of people living with HIV and AIDS. Legislative controversies have often involved policies regarding HIV testing: who should be tested, when people should be tested, where testing should be made available, and who should have access to test results. Today, however, medical advances have altered the landscape and vastly increased the potential importance of early HIV detection, returning the focus with new intensity to HIV testing policies.

Reprinted with permission from the *Journal of Acquired Immune Deficiency Syndrome* 25 (2000), S144–S150. Copyright © 2000 Lippincott Williams & Wilkins, Inc., Philadelphia.

This paper describes the legislative environment that has emerged over the last several years in the United States, particularly in state legislatures. Research presented here identified a significant trend toward more mandatory testing for broader classes of people and away from protecting the confidentiality of HIV test results. New laws make it apparent that in many instances legislators may not have considered that their actions may discourage early detection of HIV infection. Thus, recent legislative trends may raise new barriers to the generally acknowledged goal of getting more HIV-infected Americans identified and into treatment as early as possible.

In the United States, state and local health departments have historically handled local implementation of public health policies, whereas the federal government has provided resources, technical assistance, program guidance, and information on national trends. In assessing the current legislative environment, this analysis focuses primarily on legislative action by states. The National Conference of State Legislatures maintains a web-based summary of state legislation specifically addressing HIV testing from 1997 through 1999. In this article, only legislation that was passed by state legislatures and signed into law is considered. The general themes and purpose of HIV testing legislation are reviewed and analyzed.

The analysis identifies several major themes: limiting confidentiality of HIV test results, mandating name-based HIV reporting, partner notification and the testing of newborns, and criminalizing nondisclosure in sexual and needle-sharing situations. Proposals currently before the United States Congress reflect many of these same themes. This article assesses these public policies within the context of new HIV treatment options and the emerging public health priority of promoting early HIV detection.

BACKGROUND

State and federal governments promote the public health in a number of ways. One approach targets individuals and is designed to shape behaviors for the benefit of public health. Examples include laws prohibiting drunk driving and outlawing the sale of cigarettes to minors, as well as speed limit and seat belt laws designed to reduce automobile-related injuries. Regarding HIV, all 50 states have laws against its intentional transmission.

Another approach entails government-funded programs that directly promote public health. Examples include social marketing campaigns to reduce drunk driving or to reduce demand for tobacco products. Similar marketing campaigns may be used to promote knowing one's HIV status, to reduce HIV-related stigma, and to promote abstinence or condom use. Other government programs may promote public health by increasing availability of safety devices such as child safety seats to prevent injury. Programs to make condoms or clean needles available are HIV-related examples. These approaches attempt to use the resources of government to change the behavior of groups or communities, with the goal of advancing public health.

Public health policies may also directly affect the physical environment in which these behaviors occur. For example, water is fluoridated to improve dental health. The automobile industry is regulated to require certain safety standards, e.g., air bags and seat belts. Similar health and safety regulations are imposed on the airline industry, e.g., carry-on luggage requirements and nonsmoking policies. In addition, there are many examples of workplace health and safety standards, many of which, such as ergonomic standards, are the subject of controversy and public debate. Screening the blood supply for HIV and other blood-borne pathogens is an HIV-related example of an environmental intervention that has proven to be highly effective. In short, legislatures routinely debate how best to promote the public health, and employ several different methods of intervention.

Substantial investment in AIDS research over two decades has brought about expanded HIV treatment options that not only have brought new hope to people living with HIV but also have required new government policies and altered the impact of old laws and policies. Pessimism, which for many years characterized scientific discussions on HIV disease, has now given way to restrained optimism about controlling viral replication.

Under new guidelines for the treatment of HIV-infected individuals,[2,3] decisions such as when to begin therapy or to change drug combinations are made based on monitoring viral load, T-cell counts, and physical symptoms. In general, these recommendations argue for earlier and more aggressive treatment. The long-term benefit of treatment for healthier individuals with T-cell counts >500 has yet to be documented. Thus, decisions about early intervention for these asymptomatic individuals must balance a number of factors that influence risk and benefit. But for asymptomatic individuals with T-cells count <500, or anyone with a high viral load, the guidelines recommend treatment be offered. Therefore, where symptoms appear before HIV testing takes place, an opportunity to consider the full range of treatment options has been missed. In light of such HIV treatment advances, policy makers must reassess how best to promote the public health goal of early HIV detection. Social marketing campaigns and other educational approaches are needed,[4] as well as laws and policies that enhance the potential personal benefits of being tested.

The new optimism over early intervention with combination therapies has placed an increased emphasis on the role of testing in both treatment and prevention. Often, HIV testing serves as the necessary gateway to treatment. However, most of the legislation regarding HIV testing dates to the middle to late 1980s, when the HIV antibody test was new and effective medical treatments had not yet been developed. At that time antibody testing was similar to genetic testing in that the results could be psychologically distressing but it was not clear what useful medical options might be available. Thus, early laws placed emphasis on pretest counseling and informed consent.

Publicly supported testing and counseling programs began at the time the HIV antibody test was licensed in 1985, primarily to divert people from donating blood as a means of finding out their HIV status. This practice was dangerous because of the so-called window period between infection and the development of measurable antibodies.[5] Later, testing, in combination with counseling, became a vital part of the public health strategy to prevent new infections. Even in the absence of effective medical treatments, health departments believed that knowledge of serostatus could bolster resolve to practice safe behaviors, encourage HIV-positive individuals to protect their loved ones, and encourage HIV-negative individuals to stay uninfected. Research studies have confirmed the importance of counseling and testing as a prevention intervention.[6]

The Centers for Disease Control and Prevention (CDC) estimates that 650,000 Americans are HIV-infected and know their status and are therefore able to seek treatment.[7] One study in the United States found that 36% of individuals diagnosed with AIDS were first tested for HIV within 2 months of their AIDS diagnosis, and 51% within a year of AIDS diagnosis.[8] Although these data were gathered from 1990–1992, it remains true that many individuals lose the documented benefits of early intervention because they are tested so late in the course of their infection.

New treatment options are also changing the content and importance of test-related counseling. For those who test positive, greater emphasis needs to be placed on scheduling additional testing to determine the length of time the individual has been infected, the damage done to the immune system, and the amount of virus in the blood. Thus, in addition to preventing further transmission, counseling services now seek to reduce the time between HIV testing and initiating primary care for HIV disease.

Increasingly, scientists, public health officials, and advocates have come to consensus about the importance of early HIV detection for both access to treatment and prevention.[9] However, these same players, as well as legislators, must understand concerns about HIV-related stigma and the confidentiality of HIV test results before they can effectively promote HIV testing to at-risk populations.

CONFIDENTIALITY

State legislatures are clearly moving toward limiting rather than expanding HIV-related confidentiality statutes. This trend may work at cross-purposes to the goal of promoting early HIV detection. Confidentiality protections for HIV test results are an important public policy for establishing "risk-free" environments in which individuals will be more inclined to learn their HIV status and seek medical care.

After the HIV antibody test was first licensed, state legislatures and the CDC developed an alternative system of publicly funded testing sites where individuals could be tested either anonymously or with strict confidentiality protections. Strong protections for more traditional sites also were adopted in most instances. To further promote confidence among potentially infected individuals that HIV testing would remain voluntary and would not result in harmful legal or personal consequences, state laws were adopted that required specific informed consent for HIV testing[10] and provided penalties for wrongful disclosure of HIV status. These public policies were established to preempt potential negative consequences to testing that might discourage it.

An analysis of recent state legislation addressing HIV confidentiality is presented in Figure 1. A clear trend exists in bills signed into law from 1997 through 1999 toward amending confidentiality statutes to permit exceptions, rather than expanding confidentiality protections, e.g., increasing the penalty for unlawful disclosure (Information obtained from the StateServ web site: address: http://stateserv.hpts.org/public/pubhome.nsf). Most of these limitations involve laws designed to protect so-called Good Samaritans, such as police, corrections officers, and emergency medical technicians (14 of 28), or to test criminal offenders or those accused of criminal offenses (9 of 28). The remaining laws are on newborn testing (2 of 28) and name-based HIV reporting (3 of 28), both of which will be discussed later.

"Good Samaritan" laws are primarily a response to the concerns of emergency medical personnel and law enforcement officers who are distressed by the potential for HIV infection from exposure to blood or other bodily fluids. In general, these laws allow testing so that the exposed person can know the HIV status of the person who is the source of the exposure, even

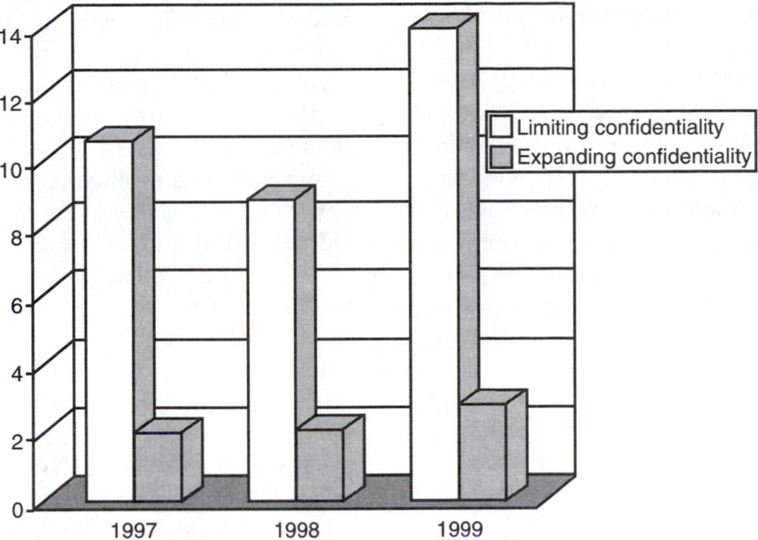

Figure. 1. Recent state legislation on HIV confidentiality

without his or her consent. These laws differ from CDC guidelines for postexposure prophylaxis in occupational settings,[11] which do not require involuntary testing of the individual who is the source of the exposure. Instead, guidance is given to assist the clinician in assessing the severity of the potential risk and in offering or recommending postexposure treatment.

Testing of criminal offenders involves mandatory testing of prison inmates or, in some cases, laws permitting testing of individuals accused of specific acts of sexual assault and disclosure of serostatus to victims. Legislative debates on the emotional issue of sexual assault involve many of the same arguments as with emergency medical personnel. At present, the CDC has not developed specific guidelines for postexposure treatment after sexual assault, and developing such guidance is complicated by the criminal justice context of these cases.

NAME-BASED REPORTING

Another legislative and administrative trend is toward name-based HIV case reporting, a policy that has the potential to discourage early HIV testing. Although AIDS cases have always been required to be reported, cases of HIV infection have been considered differently because patients are not yet seriously ill. Proponents of HIV name-based reporting argue that HIV should be treated like any other sexually transmitted disease (STD) for which names are reported. They also argue that having the name assists with referral to medical care, risk reduction counseling, and partner notification. Opponents argue that the public health benefit of name-based reporting is outweighed by the deterrent effect it has on HIV testing and early identification. They also contend that name-based reporting is not necessary to achieve referral to medical care, risk reduction counseling, and/or partner notification. Whether the benefits to individual and public health outweigh the risks is still the subject of heated debate.[12]

The name-based reporting issue has re-emerged largely because the new treatments have changed AIDS surveillance. With the development of more effective therapies, which significantly delay the onset of AIDS for many people, experts believe the number of AIDS cases and deaths are no longer reliable measures for monitoring the epidemic.[13] Recently, the CDC recommended that all states implement HIV case surveillance as an extension of AIDS case surveillance, which is a name-based reporting system.[7] Recognizing that name-based reporting is not acceptable in some states, the CDC is providing technical assistance to those states implementing unique coded systems.[14] By the end of 1999, 37 states had adopted or were implementing name-based HIV case surveillance, 6 states had adopted or were implementing unique coded systems and the issue remained unresolved in the remaining 7 states.[15]

As the controversial issues surrounding surveillance are debated in legislatures, policy makers would be wise to consider the implications of such policies for early HIV detection. Although proponents argue that names assist with referral to medical care, a recent study found that in name-based reporting states follow-up contacts were not associated with moving people into care earlier.[16] The question becomes, then, is name-based reporting the deterrent to HIV testing that its opponents argue it to be?

The answer to this question appears to depend on the target groups that may be priorities for promoting early identification. A study of six states that adopted name-based HIV reporting looked at the 12 months before and after implementation of the new policy and found the overall level of testing went up in three states, was level in two states, and declined in one state.[17] However, several studies have found that the potential deterrent effect of name-based reporting is the greatest in groups at highest risk of HIV infection. Though knowledge of state policies was low among all individuals never before tested, the deterrent effect was minimal on heterosexuals at STD clinics, moderate among injection drug users, and highest among men who have sex with men.[18] A number of other studies have found a potential deterrent effect among men who have sex with men[19–23] and for Latinos and African Americans.[24]

A recent San Francisco study found that HIV name-based reporting might have a particular deterrent effect on those at very high risk.[25] The study examined gay men who were repeat anonymous testers and also reported at least one episode of unprotected anal sex with a partner who was HIV-infected or of unknown serostatus in the last year. It found that 68% would not be tested if names were to be reported. Even after explaining the public health benefits of name reporting, only 58% said they would be tested. This suggests that among those at greatest risk a change in attitude toward testing, and toward the public health system as a whole, must precede the change to a name-based reporting system. Otherwise, behavior may undermine the benefits of testing and HIV surveillance. As critics have noted, moving to a system of name-based HIV surveillance may drive the epidemic underground.[10]

PARTNER NOTIFICATION

Another trend identified in state legislation is a move toward mandating health department-mediated partner notification. Currently, all states receiving CDC funding for HIV prevention activities are required to establish procedures for the confidential, voluntary notification of sexual and needle-sharing partners.[26] These partner notification services, which are perhaps better termed "partner counseling" services, are considered part of primary prevention efforts.[27]

The new treatment opportunities have been used by some to argue for a return to a narrow "find-and-treat" STD model for responding to the HIV epidemic. Some members of Congress, who argue that AIDS should be treated like other STDs, are advocating legislation that would require states to adopt name-based reporting policies and shift prevention resources to contact tracing and health department-mediated partner notification programs. Other members of Congress believe that, although they are an important part of HIV prevention, partner-counseling services must be assessed in terms of their relative priority. The CDC has established a process for HIV prevention community planning where these kinds of decisions about resource allocation for maximum prevention effectiveness are made.

Two states have recently moved to mandate name-based HIV reporting and couple it with health department-mediated partner notification. Advocates for this policy argue that having the name of the infected person allows the health department to notify sexual and needle-sharing partners and urge these people to get tested themselves. However, recent research[16] found that individuals who had been tested anonymously reported notifying as many sexual and needle-sharing partners as those whose names had been reported to health departments. Mandatory approaches to contacting partners and connecting them to HIV services are potentially problematic because voluntary cooperation is needed for these services to be effective. Partner notification can be done only as a voluntary activity. These laws may be viewed as barriers to early detection if they are perceived as "mandatory" by people living with HIV; they may be accepted as a valued service if perceived as voluntary, with a goal of assisting people in preventing further transmission.[28]

CRIMINALIZATION OF NONDISCLOSURE

As of 1999, 31 states had enacted legislation making nondisclosure of HIV status in certain situations a criminal offense.[29] An analysis of state legislation enacted between 1996 and 1999 reveals a distinct trend toward more (from 26 to 31 states) and tougher "willful exposure" laws. The interest in criminal statutes has been fueled by highly publicized cases of multiple HIV transmission by a single person in Missouri and in New York State.[30,31] These laws differ from state to state; some are broad in scope, whereas others are narrowly focused on specific sexual acts. Some states wrote laws with specific provisions regarding donating blood or organs, sharing needles, practicing prostitution, soliciting prostitutes, and potentially transmitting HIV to corrections or emergency health workers by persons with knowledge of an HIV/AIDS diagnosis. An analysis of these state statutes indicates that the specific sexual behaviors prohibited without disclosure are often poorly defined.[32,33]

Research has not yet gauged the extent of knowledge of these statutes among those HIV-infected, nor has it tried to assess the statutes' deterrent impact. One state, which has maintained confidential HIV surveillance records for many years, recently enacted a law that requires public health officials to reveal previous HIV testing information about people charged with a sexual offense when requested by the criminal justice system. Under this law, an individual convicted of a sexual offense can be sentenced to three times the maximum penalty for that offense if public health records show the individual had been notified of his or her HIV infection prior to the crime.[34] Because the legislation applies regardless of when the previous HIV test took place, it contradicts the informed consent for the initial HIV testing, which was intended for public health purposes only. While the legislature is acting to punish particularly deplorable criminal conduct, the unintended consequences also need to be assessed.

This trend toward criminalization of nondisclosure or "willful exposure" has not been studied in terms of its effect on early detection of HIV. However, it seems logical to argue that increasing an individual's risk of enhanced criminal penalty could deter HIV testing and early detection. In addition, retroactively invalidating the conditions of informed consent for testing has the potential to undermine trust in the public health system.

NEWBORN TESTING AND REDUCING PERINATAL TRANSMISSION

Three states now require the HIV-testing of newborns, hoping this practice will allow for early access to treatment for infected infants and provide an opportunity to caution mothers about potential transmission to uninfected infants through breast feeding. Testing of newborns is actually testing the antibody status of the mothers. Thus, opponents note that requiring antibody testing of newborns is actually mandatory testing of the mothers. They argue for voluntary approaches they believe are more likely to encourage the cooperation of pregnant women. These newborn testing laws have been controversial. Congress has also adopted targeted goals for reduction of perinatal transmission, which if not achieved would trigger mandatory testing of newborns as a condition of receiving HIV-related federal funding (Ryan White CARE Act Reauthorization, 42 USC Sec. 300ff–34).

Advances in treatments have also resulted in medical options to reduce the risk of transmission from an infected mother to her newborn through administering antiretroviral treatment to the mother.[35] Since these advances, the number of perinatal cases of AIDS has dropped by 75%, from a high of between 1,000 and 2,000 in the early 1990s, to between 250 and 500 in 1998[36]. This progress has led to discussion of the possibility of eliminating perinatal cases of HIV in the United States. These advances have also led to legislation in several states.

A recent Institute of Medicine Committee on Perinatal Transmission of HIV report[35] also addressed the possibilities for reducing perinatal HIV transmission. The committee recommended a national policy of "universal" HIV testing for pregnant women as a "routine" procedure, including posttest notification for women who test positive. These recommendations have several implications for state legislation. In order to implement such guidelines fully, many states would need to amend HIV testing statutes to remove a pretest and posttest counseling requirement. The implications for informed consent are even more important.

Currently, 33 states require specific informed consent for HIV testing, often in writing. The implication of routine testing is that it has raised the debate about moving from "informed consent" to "informed right of refusal." A study found that most people would accept HIV testing if they need to "opt out" of the test while fewer would be tested if they needed to "opt in" to taking a test by request.[37] The goal of moving people who are infected into early care is in part motivating the policy discussions toward removing the barriers to testing. Thus, pretest counseling and specific informed consent are now viewed by some as barriers to HIV testing.

The Institute of Medicine panel's conclusion that specific informed consent may be viewed as a harmful barrier to testing is a source of concern to those who have advocated specific informed consent and civil penalties for wrongful disclosure as deterrents to rogue testing.[38] At this point it is not clear how these issues will play out in a legislative context over the next several years. And, it is not clear how these policy trends will effect voluntary early HIV identification.

IMPLICATIONS AND CONCLUSION

It is now widely recognized that new treatment opportunities offer hope to those who are infected with HIV. That hope can only be realized if systems are in place that encourage individuals at risk to seek HIV testing, as well as to make maximum use of health care services as early as possible in the course of the infection. This article outlines some of the legislative trends that have emerged in the last several years in state legislatures, and suggests that some recently passed laws could be barriers to, rather than facilitators of, early HIV testing. If these laws discourage testing, the question becomes what price does public and personal health pay for the stricter legal environment.

In order to consent fully to HIV testing, individuals must understand the benefits that may result from medical treatment and the potential to prevent further HIV transmission. Potential risks of HIV testing include possible psychological distress associated with a positive test result, as well as potential limitations in employment and insurance coverage. State legislatures have added to these risks the requirements that one's name be reported to the health department, and that one may be required to disclose the names of sexual or needle-sharing partners. In addition, once an individual is aware of infection, the potential exists for criminal penalties for nondisclosure of HIV status in certain situations. These added risks and requirements create an atmosphere in which at-risk individuals and communities often draw the conclusion—rightly or wrongly—that HIV testing is not in their best interest.

Much of the state legislation on HIV testing from 1997 through 1999 expresses the goal of helping HIV-infected people obtain care. The effect of many of these policies, however, is not well known or evaluated. At the federal level, states are often referred to as laboratories for new ideas and policies. Thus, it seems important to direct greater attention to the careful evaluation of these state-level policy interventions. Scientists and public health officials must help determine whether legislated policies increase or decrease early identification of HIV as an important outcome measure in assessing such initiatives.

Developing effective policies to promote early identification of HIV will require consultation, discussion, and compromise by public health officials at all levels of government and by affected individuals, communities, and other stakeholders. Legislative policy makers also need to be part of the collective discussions on ways to promote early HIV detection.

REFERENCES

1. Shilts R. *And the band played on: politics, people and the AIDS epidemic*. New York: Penguin Books, 1988:640.

2. National Institutes of Health. *Report of the NIH panel to define the principles of therapy of HIV infection.* Bethesda, MD: NIH; 1997.

3. Department of Health and Human Services. *Guidelines for the use of antiretroviral agents in HIV-infected adults and adolescents*. Washington, DC: Dept. of Health and Human Services; 2000.

4. Valdiserri R. O. HIV counseling and testing: its evolving role in HIV prevention. *AIDS Educ Prev* 1997, 9(3 suppl):2–13.

5. Valdiserri R. O., Holtgrave D. R., West G. R. Promoting early HIV diagnosis and entry into care. *AIDS* 1999, 13:2317–30.

6. Kamb M. L., Fishbein M., Douglas J. M., et al. Efficacy of risk-reduction counseling to prevent human immunodeficiency virus and sexually transmitted diseases: a randomized controlled trial. Project RESPECT Study Group. *JAMA* 1998, 280:1161–7.

7. Centers for Disease Control. Guidelines for national human immunodeficiency virus case surveillance, including monitoring for human immunodeficiency virus infection and acquired immunodeficiency syndrome. *MMWR* 1999, 48:1–28.

8. Wortley P. M., Chu S. Y., Diaz T., et al. HIV testing patterns: where, why, and when were persons with AIDS tested for HIV? *AIDS* 1995, 9:487–92.

9. Kaiser Family Foundation. *Understanding the impact of new treatments on HIV testing.* Palo Alto, CA: Kaiser Family Foundation; 1998.

10. Burris S. Driving the epidemic underground? a new look at the law and the social risk of HIV testing. *AIDS Public Policy* 1997, 12:67–87.

11. Centers for Disease Control. Public Health Service guidelines for the management of health-care worker exposures to HIV and recommendations for postexposure prophylaxis. Centers for Disease Control and Prevention. *MMWR* 1998, 47:1–33.

12. Colfax G. N., Bindman A. B. Health benefits and risks of reporting HIV-infected individuals by name. *Am J Public Health* 1998, 88:876–9.

13. Gostin L. O., Ward J. W., Baker A. C. National HIV case reporting for the United States: a defining moment in the history of the epidemic. *N Engl J Med* 1997, 337:1162–7.

14. Centers for Disease Control. *Guidelines for national human immunodeficiency virus case surveillance, including monitoring for human immunodeficiency virus infection and acquired immunodeficiency syndrome.* Atlanta, GA: Centers for Disease Control and Prevention; 1999.

15. AIDS Policy & Law, HIV case surveillance: CDC advocates names, but doesn't rule out use of coded identifiers. *AIDS Policy & Law* 1999; 14.

16. Osmond D. H., Bindman A. B., Vranizan K., et al. Name-based surveillance and public health interventions for persons with HIV infection. *Ann Intern Med* 1999, 131:775–79.

17. Nakashima A. K., Horsley R., Frey R. L., Sweeney P. A., Weber J. T., Fleming P. L. Effect of HIV reporting by name on use of HIV testing in publicly funded counseling and testing programs. *JAMA* 1998, 280:1421–6.

18. Hecht F. M. HIV testing among populations at risk for HIV infection: nine states, November 1995–December 1996. *MMWR* 1998, 47:1086–91.

19. Johnson W. D. The impact of mandatory reporting on HIV seropositive persons in South Carolina. Paper presented at the Fourth International Conference on AIDS, June 12–16, 1998; Stockholm, Sweden.

20. Kegeles S. M., Catania J. A., Coates T. J., Pollack L. M., et al. Many people who seek anonymous HIV-antibody testing would avoid it under other circumstances. *AIDS* 1990, 4:585–8.

21. Kegeles S. M., Coates T. J., Lo B., Catania J. A. Mandatory reporting of HIV testing would deter men from being tested. *JAMA* 1989, 261:1275–6.

22. Hirano D. Anonymous HIV testing: the impact of availability on demand in Arizona. *Am J Public Health* 1994, 84:2008.

23. Reed, G. The impact of mandatory name reporting on HIV testing and treatment. Paper presented at the Poster Presentation for the XI International Conference on AIDS, July 7–12, 1996; Vancouver, Canada.

24. Fordyce E. J., Sambula S., Stoneburner R. Mandatory reporting of human immunodeficiency virus testing would deter blacks and Hispanics from being tested. *JAMA* 1989, 262:349.

25. Dilley J. W., McFarland W., Sullivan P., Discepola M. Psychosocial correlates of unprotected anal sex in a cohort of gay men attending an HIV-negative support group. *Aids Educ Prev* 1998, 10:317–26.

26. Centers for Disease Control. *HIV partner counseling and referral services.* Atlanta, GA: Centers for Disease Control and Prevention: 1998.

27. West G. R., Stark K. A. Partner notification for HIV prevention: a critical reexamination. *AIDS Educ Prev* 1997, 9(3 suppl):68–78.

28. Shriver M. D., Everett C., Morin S. F. Structural interventions to encourage primary HIV prevention among people living with HIV. *AIDS* 2000, 14(1 suppl):51–6.

29. National Conference of State Legislatures. *Criminal transmission and exposure to HIV.* Washington, D.C.: National Conference of State Legislatures; 1999.

30. Barron, J. Officials link man to at least 10 girls infected with HIV. *New York Times,* October 28, 1997: A1.

31. Sauerwein K., Bryan B. "Boss man" sex partners now grow to over 100. *St. Louis Post-Dispatch,* April 24, 1997: A1.

32. Russell S. Lawmakers pass bill to criminalize intentional transmission of HIV. *The San Francisco Chronicle.* August 22, 1998: A15.

33. Sanchez L., Wilson S. *Criminalization of HIV transmission and exposure.* Issue Brief: Health Policy Tracking Service 1998. Available at: http://stateserv.hpts.org. Accessed October 25, 2000.

34. Sanko J. Bill gets tough on rapists with HIV. *Denver Rocky Mountain News,* February 24, 1999: 12A.

35. Stoto M. A., Almaria D. A., McCormick M. C. *Reducing the odds: preventing perinatal transmission of HIV in the United States.* Washington, D.C.: Institute of Medicine; 1999.

36. Centers for Disease Control. *Status of perinatal HIV prevention: U.S. declines continue.* Atlanta, GA: Centers for Disease Control and Prevention; 1999.

37. Irwin K. L., Valdiserri R. O., Holmberg S. D. The acceptability of voluntary HIV antibody testing in the United States: a decade of lessons learned. *AIDS* 1996, 10:1707–17.

38. Burris S. HIV surveillance: ethical and policy issues. Paper presented at the Early Detection of HIV: Emerging Issues in HIV Prevention and Care, July 29, 1999; Washington, D.C.

AIDS Vaccine Trials

DALE GUENTER, JOSE ESPARZA, AND RUTH MACKLIN

Ethical Considerations in International HIV Vaccine Trials: Summary of a Consultative Process Conducted by the Joint United Nations Programme on HIV/AIDS

Dale Guenter is Assistant Professor of Family Medicine at McMaster University. His areas of interest include social determinants of health, HIV primary care and prevention, applying population health approaches in primary care, primary care in developing countries, and research ethics. His international interests have taken him to developing countries to conduct workshops on ethical issues in HIV vaccine trials for the United Nations Joint Program on HIV/AIDS.

Jose Esparza is Senior Adviser for Vaccine and Clinical Trials to the World Health Organization/Joint United Nations Programme on HIV/AIDS Vaccine Initiative. His expertise lies in HIV vaccines and trials and cohort studies.

Ruth Macklin is a Professor of Bioethics in the Department of Epidemiology and Social Medicine at the Albert Einstein College of Medicine. She serves as Vice President of the Council of International Organizations of Medical Sciences. Her recent publications include *Against Relativism: Cultural Diversity and the Search for Ethical Universals in Medicine* (Oxford University Press) and *Surrogates and Other Mothers: The Debates over Assisted Reproduction* (Temple University Press).

INTRODUCTION

As we approach the beginning of the third decade of the HIV epidemic, it is clear that developing an effective HIV vaccine presents a formidable challenge. As of the end of 1999, while therapeutic pharmaceutical research has made major advances, only two phase III efficacy trials of closely related candidate HIV vaccines have been initiated, in the US and Thailand. Many candidate HIV vaccines have proceeded to the point of testing for safety and immunogenicity in human subjects (phase I and II clinical trials), but multiple factors have slowed progression to the final step of randomised, controlled, large-scale, phase III efficacy trials. The challenges have been scientific, logistical, political and economic.

Planning the appropriate design and location for HIV vaccine trials gives rise to ethical issues that require special attention. The HIV epidemic is characterized by distinctive biological and social factors that must be considered in the harm/benefit analysis for individuals participating in HIV vaccine research. First, the global prevalence of disease and death related to HIV is increasing at a rate unmatched by any other agent. Although AIDS was unknown in 1980, HIV is today the most important infectious disease in the world. AIDS is now the major cause of death in Africa, and fourth worldwide. The burden of disease has been greatest in the poorest countries; more than 95% of all HIV infections occur in developing countries, and Africa is home to two out of every three

Reprinted with permission from the *Journal of Medical Ethics* 26 (2000), 37–43. Copyright © 2000 by the BMJ Publishing Group.

people living with HIV or AIDS. Despite intense national and international efforts to control the HIV pandemic, more than 16,000 HIV infections occur every day. Treatments currently available are inadequate since they do not lead to cure, but at best slow the progression of disease. The most effective treatment—antiretroviral medication—is complicated to administer, requires close medical monitoring, can cause significant adverse effects and is extremely costly. These logistical and economic barriers render treatment inaccessible for many populations, creating a sense of urgency to develop a safe, effective and globally accessible HIV preventive vaccine to complement other strategies.

HIV is also unique in that development of an effective vaccine will likely require that clinical trials be conducted among numerous different populations, including some with a relatively low level of social and economic development. This is true for several reasons. First, the large majority of HIV infections occur in developing countries, and phase III efficacy trials will need to be conducted in populations with a high incidence of new HIV infections in order to produce valid and timely results. High incidence populations in industrialised countries are already participating in current trials, but the incidence in many developing countries is much higher and affects larger populations. Second, the genetic and antigenic variability of HIV may require that candidate vaccines be tested in different areas of the world where different HIV strains are prevalent. It is possible, though not yet known, that a vaccine preventing infection with one HIV subtype may not prevent infection with another HIV subtype. Finally, it may be necessary to evaluate the efficacy of candidate vaccines in a variety of populations where the predominant route of transmission of the virus differs, and where different cofactors could influence vaccine protection.

The unique social consequences of HIV infection must also be considered in the ethical analysis of vaccine trials. People infected with HIV have experienced stigma, marginalisation, and discrimination in many forms. Volunteers participating in HIV vaccine trials may be falsely identified as HIV-positive simply through their association with a trial, or by developing falsely positive HIV antibody tests as a result of receiving candidate vaccines. Thus, the risk of social and psychological harm for human subjects participating in vaccine research is substantial.

While previous ethical statements have articulated the principles of ethical research,[1–4] and some have provided guidance on the application of these principles to international research settings,[2,3] several of the issues emerging from HIV vaccine trials have illuminated important gaps. The Joint United Nations Programme on HIV/AIDS (UNAIDS) has identified these areas of ethical uncertainty as a priority for accelerated discussion and formulation of relevant guidance.

THE CONSULTATION PROCESS

The process began with a consultation in Geneva in September 1997. Representatives from developed and developing countries began to identify the major ethical challenges that needed to be confronted in relation to international HIV vaccine research. The result of this meeting was a plan to organise regional workshops in order to seek views from communities and interested parties around the world. Three countries representing different geographical regions were invited to host these workshops in April and May, 1998. Brazil, Thailand and Uganda were chosen because of their previous involvement in HIV vaccine trials, their familarity with the relevant scientific and social issues, and their imminent need to develop greater familiarity with the ethical implications of vaccine research. Biomedical and social scientists, community members, non-government organisations, activists, persons living with HIV/AIDS, ethicists, lawyers and government representatives participated in the workshops. An average of thirty participants representing the host country and other countries in the region attended each of the three workshops, which lasted three days.

SEVERAL OBJECTIVES

The workshops had several objectives. The first was to familiarise participants with important scientific details related to HIV vaccines and the design of clinical trials. The second was to discuss relevant social, political and economic conditions, and economic conditions in the local context that would have ethical implications for proposed vaccine research. Finally, the intent was to establish a continuing discourse on HIV vaccine ethics both locally and in the international community.

A hypothetical case-scenario was used to facilitate workshop discussions. This case was framed as an HIV preventive vaccine trial proposal that involved a sponsor company or agency from a developed country, and a proposed study population and researchers from a developing country. In each region, the case was translated from English in written or oral form into one or more languages, depending on the preference of the local organisers.

An introductory session outlined the important scientific aspects of HIV preventive vaccines, and the basic principles of biomedical research ethics. However, no ethical guidance documents or statements were referred to during the course of the workshops, unless they were introduced by the participants. A set of open-ended questions was used to facilitate discussion on specific topics (for example, informed consent), with the same questions being used in all three regions. The case was discussed in depth in small groups, and then further with all participants at the table. Important ethical issues were identified by the group, and on many of these issues a consensus was reached. For those issues on which consensus could not be reached, the points of controversy were defined and articulated. Final statements were written and agreed upon separately for each of the three workshops. An additional workshop was organised in Washington, DC, USA in May, 1998 to discuss specific issues related to bilateral collaboration.

The outcomes of the workshops were presented at a meeting in Geneva in June, 1998, along with a draft document that condensed these outcomes into a set of proposed ethical guidance statements. About 70 individuals participated in this discussion, including representatives from each of the regional workshops, the World Health Organisation, the Council of International Organisations of Medical Sciences (CIOMS), UNAIDS, research funding agencies in developed countries, public health organisations, activist groups, biomedical and social scientists, ethicists, and the media.

OUTCOMES OF THE CONSULTATION PROCESS

Each of the three regional workshops discussed the same general topics. The results of these discussions are summarised in the following sections.

"DEVELOPING COUNTRY" AND "DEVELOPED COUNTRY" TERMINOLOGY

Participants from all of the regions expressed their concern about the inadequacy of terminology used to categorise countries of advantage and disadvantage. Previous ethical documents have drawn a distinction between "developed" and "developing" countries or communities.[2] "Developing" countries have generally been perceived as deserving of additional protection to prevent harm or exploitation as a result of biomedical research. However, the usefulness of the developing/developed terminology for assessing risk of harm and exploitation was seen to be limited. It refers primarily to economic considerations, while many other factors are relevant in HIV vaccine research. It also separates nations into two categories, whereas in reality they are distributed along a spectrum.

In place of the developing/developed terminology, each region described the factors that are likely to influence the degree of vulnerability of the prospective subject population to exploitation or harm. These include the following:

1. Limited economic development;
2. Inadequate protection of human rights in general, and more specifically, discrimination on the basis of HIV antibody status;
3. Inadequate community/cultural experience with, or understanding of, scientific research;
4. Limited political awareness of the importance and process of vaccine research;
5. Limited availability of health care and treatment options;
6. Limited ability of individuals in the community to provide informed consent, often based on class, gender, etc;
7. Insufficient formal experience with, or capability to conduct, ethical or scientific review of proposed research, and
8. Insufficient infrastructure and technical capacity to conduct the proposed research.

Most countries and communities are characterised to varying degrees by some or all of these conditions. However, as the number or severity of these characteristics increases, the potential for harm or exploitation also increases. These factors contribute to a disparity in real or perceived power between sponsor(s) and host countries, make it difficult for residents of a host country to make informed, reasoned and independent choices, and increase the potential for social harm to occur.

URGENCY FOR VACCINE DEVELOPMENT VERSUS PROTECTION OF HUMAN SUBJECTS

One major source of ethical tension appeared to be relevant to many of the specific topics discussed during the consultation process. The experience of the HIV epidemic was clearly desperate for many of the developing countries participating in the workshops. The moral charge to expedite development of an effective vaccine appeared at times to conflict with the ethical imperative to safeguard the rights and welfare of communities and individuals participating in vaccine trials, especially when such safeguards would require time to put into place. Workshop participants struggled to resolve this tension. The degree to which resolution was reached is reflected in the sections that follow.

SELF-DETERMINATION VERSUS PROTECTIONISM

Many of the developing countries represented at the workshops endeavoured to define their own level of readiness to take responsibility for determining whether to participate in vaccine trials. Current ethical guidelines that address research in developing countries lean in the direction of protectionism. For example, the conduct of phase I and II trials in developing countries has been discouraged.[2] The rationale is that there is a greater risk inherent with early trials, and that the potential for exploitation or harm in these settings cannot be justified. Participants from all the regions concluded, however, that, with certain safeguards in place, it would be appropriate for developing countries to participate in phase I and II clinical trials when there was a valid scientific rationale. This might expedite the progression to phase III efficacy trials, and may be the only way to determine safety and immunogenicity for the specific subtype of virus being targeted in the host country. In addition, phase I and II trials would provide host countries with important capacity-building experience in reviewing and conducting research, and building public and political support prior to the much larger and more complex phase III trials.

Conditions that would need to be fulfilled prior to conducting HIV vaccine trials in developing countries might include the following:

1. The vaccine is expected to be effective against a strain of HIV virus that is a relevant public health problem in the host country;
2. The host country has, or with assistance can develop, adequate scientific capability and administrative infrastructure for the successful conduct of the proposed research;
3. The host country has, or with assistance can develop, the capability to conduct scientific and ethical review, and
4. Community members, policy makers, ethicists and researchers in the host country have determined that their residents will be adequately protected from harm or exploitation, and that the vaccine development programme is responsive to the health needs and priorities in their country.

ACHIEVING RESEARCH OBJECTIVES VERSUS PREVENTING HIV INFECTION

Efficacy trials of HIV vaccines are successful only if new infections are occurring among trial participants. It is necessary to demonstrate a difference in incidence between the control group and the vaccinated group if efficacy is to be proven. However, it is also true that HIV can be prevented with reductions in risk behaviour. Although most risk behaviour modification strategies have proven insufficient to reduce HIV incidence to zero, the most rigorous approaches have been proven significantly to decrease the rate of new infections. This introduces what might be perceived as a conflict of interest between researchers, who hope to prove that the vaccine is effective, and trial participants, whose interest it is to defend themselves from infection by any methods possible.

Throughout the consultation process, contributors agreed that "high quality" HIV prevention counselling must be provided for all trial participants. Exactly what information should be conveyed through what specific methods was not agreed upon. The degree to which items such as condoms and sterile syringes should be made available remained a point of controversy, although some degree of access to these was broadly supported. In addition, some suggested that those responsible for providing prevention strategies should be independent, or at least at arm's length, from those whose main interest was the research.

TREATMENT AND CARE FOR PARTICIPANTS CONTRACTING HIV

The most contentious issue arising from the consultation process was whether there is an ethical imperative for participants in an HIV vaccine trial to be provided with treatment, should they become infected during the course of the trial. Infection would likely occur as a result of ongoing risk behaviour in some who are assigned to a control arm, and also in some assigned to the arm receiving the candidate vaccine if it failed to be protective. Workshop participants within each region reached a consensus on the question of treatment, but the consensus reached was different for each region. Positions ranged from providing the "best proven" treatment, to providing the level of treatment that is readily available within the host country. This debate has continued to the present. Several specific questions have arisen. Is there an ethical obligation for trial sponsors and investigators to provide treatment when the intervention being tested is a vaccine rather than a therapy? Is the cost of providing treatment likely to be prohibitive for conducting vaccine trials in developing countries? Is providing treatment likely to constitute an unreasonable inducement to participate in a trial when there is minimal treatment available to the general population? Once treatment is started, is there an ethical obligation to provide this beyond the duration of the trial, and, if there is an ethical justification for providing treatment, what components should be included in the treatment package?

The justification for providing treatment has been made from several perspectives. It might be hypothesised (although it has not been proven) that participation in an HIV preventive vaccine trial could lead to increased risk behaviour among the participants. Those who participate in vaccine trials will be informed that they should not consider themselves to be protected from infection, since neither the placebo nor the candidate vaccine are known to be effective. They will also be informed of the behaviours that will put them at risk of infection, and how to avoid exposure to HIV. However, it is possible that even with this information, research subjects will believe that they are protected to some degree by their participation in the trial, and will increase their risk behaviour, making HIV infection more likely. Under this hypothesis, it is not the vaccine itself that causes an increase in HIV risk, but rather people's beliefs and perceptions about the significance of receiving an experimental vaccine.

GLOBAL SOCIAL JUSTICE

Another perspective arises from the framework of global social justice. This argument points to the disparity in economic resources that exists between countries. HIV preventive vaccine trials will likely be funded by sponsors from countries with greater wealth and better health care than the host country populations in which they are eventually tested. In many of the potential host countries, there is no treatment available to the general population. In addition, sponsor companies are likely to profit from the eventual sale of preventive HIV vaccines. Providing treatment to those infected with HIV during vaccine trials in developing countries would be a step towards addressing an ethical obligation for international researchers to contribute towards equality of resources.

Those who agree on providing treatment must eventually identify the components that would be included in an ethical treatment package. The focus on combination antiretroviral medication is a relatively recent phenomenon. Although this is clearly the most effective therapy that has been available since the epidemic was recognised, it continues to be extremely expensive, non-curative, complex to administer and monitor, and accompanied by numerous adverse effects. Treatment and prevention of opportunistic infections, palliative care, nutrition, spiritual support, psychological support and rehabilitation, among others, are also important components of care for those infected with HIV.

Some have proposed that appropriate treatment is "the best proven therapy" anywhere in the world. This reference to the Declaration of Helsinki implies that all proven treatment modalities relevant to HIV and its complications should be made available for the lifetime of the individual.[5] There are several barriers to providing "best proven therapy". First, it is often difficult for experts to reach consensus on what the best proven treatment is. Then, if consensus is reached, economic cost and technical feasibility play a role in locations where infrastructure in services such as health care, laboratory and transportation are not secured. Without adequate infrastructure for monitoring individuals taking complex medical regimens, there could be a significant risk of harmful effects as a result of treatment. Finally, if expensive and sophisticated treatment is provided in a context where no treatment is generally available, this may constitute undue inducement to participate in a trial.

An alternative proposal arising from the consultations was to provide access to a level of treatment that approaches as closely as possible the best proven treatment, that is, "the highest attainable". Sponsors could consider ways in which their activities might build up not only research capacity in a host country, but also capacity to deliver health services. Efforts could be made to build this capacity in ways that are likely to be integrated into the infrastructure of the host country, and are not likely to disappear when the research is completed. As an example, this could happen through the reinforcement of laboratories, health centres and non-government organisations in the host country.

During the process of consultation there was general agreement that where no treatment is available to the general population, sponsors and investigators are obligated to ensure that some form of treatment is made available to study participants. However, whether an international ethical standard should uphold the provision of the best proven treatment, the highest attainable treatment, or a procedure for decision making where controversy persists, is still a point of vigorous discussion in the global community.

ACCESS AND AVAILABILITY OF A PROVEN HIV VACCINE

Participants in all regions expressed disapproval of the historic practice of testing pharmaceutical products in developing countries without ensuring access for residents of the host country to successful products resulting from the research. Agreement was not reached on how accessibility could be ensured, nor on how broadly a new product should be made available. Workshop participants acknowledged the complexity of designing economic and political mechanisms capable of ensuring availability even before a product has been tested. There was consensus that volunteers who receive a placebo in a vaccine trial should be offered the final vaccine product once it is approved and licensed. Others who were considered to be candidates for such a vaccine were those at risk of infection in the general population of the host country, and similar populations in other developing countries. However, whether access and availability should be extended to this degree remains a point of debate.

Effective incentives for fostering development of HIV vaccines, and for ensuring the ultimate availability of vaccines to the populations that need them most, were identified as an area of priority for future work. Suggested strategies included financial rewards through the market place and public subsidies, technology transfer, and negotiation of intellectual property.

COMMENT

This process of international consultation has resulted in several notable outcomes. Most importantly, individuals in countries that are relatively unfamiliar with biomedical research and research ethics have become part of an ongoing, informal discussion on the ethical dilemmas encountered in HIV vaccine trials. This global discussion is critical. It constitutes one step toward equalising what is likely to be an inherently unequal balance of power between collaborating countries. Through enhanced capacity to participate in ethical debate—to analyse and articulate the ethical issues most relevant in the local context—countries and communities anticipating involvement in research will be better equipped to ensure that the rights and welfare of human subjects are safeguarded. To this end, UNAIDS has proceeded to initiate a series of training workshops on ethics for members of ethical review committees and community representatives in developing countries.

It was anticipated that the consultation process would lead to the development of an ethical guidance document that could provide direction to those involved in planning and reviewing international HIV vaccine research. Since the final meeting in Geneva in June, 1998, a draft document has been prepared and distributed for comment. It was clear from the June, 1998 meeting and from the responses to the draft that a consensus had been reached on a substantive ethical standard for many of the identified issues. However, consensus could not be reached on a substantive solution to the question of treatment for those infected with HIV during the course of a trial. Although some have suggested that international guidelines ought to uphold a standard for a decision making procedure for such areas of ethical controversy, many have expressed concern with an approach that does not offer a substantive standard to be applied globally. UNAIDS plans to publish its own position statement and guidance in the near future.

Because these consultations were carried out in regions of the world far removed from one another culturally as well as geographically, it might be thought that lack of agreement on some issues stemmed from cultural differences. There is no denying that different cultures and subgroups within societies exhibit a variety of moral beliefs and practices. These empirical facts yield the descriptive thesis known as "cultural relativity". It is certainly true that southeast Asian nations, countries in South America and the Caribbean, and the region of east Africa have many cultural variations in beliefs and practices. But as striking as these variations may be, they did not play a role in those instances where participants in the consultations reached different conclusions about what was ethically required. Nor was cultural relativity a factor in failure to arrive at consensus in the final meeting in Geneva, at which several additional countries and regions were represented.

Where one might have expected some disagreement stemming from cultural diversity, for example, in the requirements for individual informed consent to participate in vaccine trials, there was striking uniformity of agreement among the three regional consultations. Although procedural steps in obtaining consent may vary from one country or region to another, participants in all three regional consultations unanimously concurred that in no circumstances, such as cultures in which women are normally not accorded decision-making authority, may the requirement for individuals to provide voluntary, informed consent on their own behalf be abandoned or weakened.

ECONOMIC DISPARITY

The lack of consensus that did emerge on several points had little to do with different norms or values in different countries and everything to do with the economic disparity between industrialised and resource-poor countries, and with countries along the spectrum of economic development. Resulting from these economic disparities is a different level of medical care in wealthier countries and poorer nations. The chief point of controversy, as noted above, was whether there is an ethical obligation to provide treatment for HIV and its associated complications for participants in an HIV vaccine trial. Disagreements about whether such an obligation exists, and if so, who bears that responsibility, arise from different views about what justice requires and what wealthy sponsors owe to resource-poor countries in which the research is carried out.

A remaining unanswered question is whether an ethical double standard exists if participants in vaccine trials who become infected in some countries are assured access to the best proven therapy, while those in other countries will never be provided with treatment. One side in this debate points to the provision in the Declaration of Helsinki that requires assurance of access to the best proven therapy,[5] and argues that to depart from that principle is to adopt a double standard. This side contends that ethical principles may not be "relativised" to different economic circumstances. In contrast, as one commentator observed regarding an analogous controversy: "The real double standard lies not in the way the trials are being conducted, but in the inequity in access to medicines in different countries."[6] On the latter view, ethical obligations may be relativised to different economic circumstances and disparities in the health infrastructure in different countries. However that debate is to be resolved, it is not a case of ethical relativism stemming from cultural variation.

DISCLAIMERS

This article does not represent the official position of UNAIDS. A guidance document on ethical considerations in international HIV vaccine trials is to be released which will describe the UNAIDS policy.

REFERENCES

1. World Medical Association. *Declaration of Helsinki.* Somerset West, Republic of South Africa: 48th General Assembly, World Medical Association, 1996.

2. Council for International Organisations of Medical Sciences. *International ethical guidelines for biomedical research involving human subjects.* Geneva: Council for International Organisations of Medical Sciences (CIOMS) in collaboration with the World Health Organisation (WHO), 1993.

3. International Conference on Harmonisation of Technical Requirements for Registration of Pharmaceuticals for Human Use (European Union, Japan, USA). *Guideline for good clinical practice (ICH harmonised tripartite guideline),* 1997.

4. World Health Organisation. *Guidelines for good clinical practice (GCP) for trials on pharmaceutical products.* Geneva: WHO technical report series, no 850, 1995.

5. See reference 1:article II. 3.

6. Piot P. Ethics of placebo-controlled trials of zidovudine to prevent the perinatal transmission of HIV in the Third World. [letter]. *New England Journal of Medicine* 1998;**338:**839.

MALEGAPURU WILLIAM MAKGOBA, NANDIPHA SOLOMON, AND TIMOTHY JOHAN PAUL TUCKER

The Search for an HIV Vaccine

Malegapuru William Makgoba is President of the Medical Research Council of South Africa and leader of the South African AIDS Vaccine Initiative. His task has been to develop a strategy for dealing with South Africa's AIDS epidemic. Among the awards he has received are the United Kingdom Department of Health's National Health Service Distinction and Meritorious Award and Dr. G. E. Malherbe Award for outstanding contribution to Education, Science and Industry. He has published widely in the field of immunology.

Nandipha Solomon is the Executive Manager for Corporate Communications and Marketing for the Medical Research Council of South Africa.

Timothy Johan Paul Tucker is the Director of the South African AIDS Vaccine Initiative, an Honorary Consultant Virologist at Groote Schuur Hospital, and a Fellow of the College of Pathologists of South Africa. His research interests have included HIV and hepatitis viruses. He has published nationally and internationally, has presented at international conferences, and is on the editorial board and review board of international journals.

HIV infections and deaths from AIDS continue to ravage many countries around the world, with most infected people living in the poorest nations.[1] In terms of morbidity and mortality, the HIV/AIDS pandemic is worse than the Black Death of the 14th century. The search for an HIV vaccine was seen as the logical solution to the burgeoning epidemic soon after the discovery of HIV, but early enthusiasm became muted as the realities of the challenge became evident.[2–4]

Nevertheless, there are scientific reasons why there is hope that an HIV vaccine will ultimately be developed. Firstly, studies of non-human primates that were given candidate vaccines based on HIV or SIV (simian immunodeficiency virus) have shown either complete or partial protection against infection with the wild type virus.[5,6] Secondly, successful vaccines have been developed against other retroviruses.[7] Thirdly, almost all humans develop some form of immune response to HIV infection, with some exposed people remaining uninfected or developing immune responses that are protective or that are able to control the viral infection over long periods.[8] Some people have remained free of disease for up to 20 years, often with undetectable viral loads.[9,10] A group of sex workers from Nairobi and South Africa has remained HIV negative despite continuing high risk exposure; resistance to HIV infection in these people is thought to be due to their ability to mount protective immune responses to HIV, rather than to any innate host genetic factors.[11,12] This group has provided insights into strategies for developing a vaccine.

Reprinted with permission from the *British Medical Journal* 324 (January 26, 2002), 211–13. Copyright © 2002 by the British Medical Association.

Potential developments

An effective, affordable, and accessible HIV vaccine is within reach

Equitable public-private partnerships between researchers, manufacturers, and distributors and partnerships between rich and poor countries are the best strategy for the development of the vaccine

Successful vaccine development entails adequate investment in the countries that carry the burden of the HIV/AIDS pandemic

If we fail to provide the world with an effective HIV vaccine, future generations will judge us harshly, because this failure will be due not to lack of ability or resources but to politics

WILL AN APPROPRIATE HIV VACCINE EVER BE DEVELOPED?

The answer to this depends on a complex interplay of politics, science, institutions and their organisation, and public-private partnerships.

POLITICS

Many political realities will need to be accepted if the global health community is to develop an HIV vaccine:

- Vaccines are a public good and should be supported worldwide
- Rich countries have the expertise and experience to develop and test HIV vaccines but do not have sufficient numbers of patients to conduct clinical trials of efficacy
- Most poor countries have poor infrastructure and inadequate resources to conduct major trials of an HIV vaccine but are fertile ground for such trials. Thus, rich and poor nations are obliged to cooperate in the successful development of an HIV vaccine
- Any trial of an HIV vaccine must take into account the history of exploitation and abuse of vulnerable people in clinical trials. All research has the potential to introduce unequal power relations between the researchers and the trial participants, particularly when the researchers are from a rich nation and the participants are from a poor nation
- Rich countries want to do research in poor countries. Poor countries often have weak research infrastructure and regulatory institutions, allowing rich countries to exert more control over the research and over intellectual property rights
- Most countries lack the political will and commitment—reflected in inadequate investment—to develop an HIV vaccine.

SCIENCE

The current impressive knowledge of the genotypic, phenotypic, pathological, and clinical aspects of HIV/AIDS reflects the substantial scientific discourse that has occurred around the world over the past two decades. However, the current knowledge base remains inadequate, in that it has failed to elucidate the most critical item on the HIV vaccinologist's wish list: the correlates of protection against HIV. Until these are defined with accuracy, as has been the case with other infectious agents, such as hepatitis B, the required "height of the high jump bar" will remain speculative.

Another problem is that animal models for investigating candidate vaccines are inadequate. Results from studies of candidate vaccines in small animal models are invaluable, but their applicability to the development of an HIV vaccine in humans may be tenuous. Products that have an acceptable safety record in animal studies should be used as rapidly as possible in human studies, because human studies will give critical insights into the potential success or failure of a vaccine that far outweigh those from any animal data.

INSTITUTIONS

Science has traditionally moved relatively slowly and cautiously in the transition from laboratory development of new agents to commercialisation. Yet in the case of HIV vaccines the scientific community is, for humanitarian reasons, under pressure to move with urgency. The scientific and corporate communities are being asked to "think out of the box" and to break down traditional modes of operations, while still maintaining the highest values of science and ethics, in developing an HIV vaccine.

For almost a decade after the discovery of HIV a concerted and coordinated international effort to produce a vaccine was slow to develop. But a number of initiatives have helped to create a scientific framework for rapidly testing hypotheses and products. The International AIDS Vaccine Initiative (IAVI), whose mission is the development of and worldwide access to an HIV vaccine, has helped to keep the need for a vaccine high on the agendas of many governments. Following from IAVI's advocacy, changes in the scientific priorities of traditional institutions, such as the National Institutes of Health, the WHO, and the European Union's HIV vaccine platform, have also helped, as has the establishment of regional vaccine development programmes in poor countries, such as the South African AIDS Vaccine Initiative.

This new framework gives the public and private sectors the chance to become partners in getting important academic, financial, and logistic support. Effective coordination, maintenance, and expansion of these structures are essential. Equally important is the need for cooperation among these international bodies, to ensure that the efforts are not inhibited by organisational pride, traditions, or the desire to be first.

Levels of political will to support global initiatives to develop an HIV vaccine will largely determine the rate of their progress and success. Such political support will need to come from the highest levels of government and from global bodies such as the United Nations. Vaccines are but a part of the message of prevention that all governments should be endorsing, along with progressive policies on sex education, condom distribution, needle exchange programmes, and appropriate treatment. State and private sector funding of national and international vaccine programmes should be given the highest priority.

Political support for these programmes needs to be independent of other international crises. For example, our response to the events of 11 September should not deflect attention from the urgent need to develop a vaccine against the greatest threat ever to humanity from an infectious disease. Yet compare the rapid and committed response by the US government to the threat of anthrax with many governments' lack of support for development of an HIV vaccine over the past two decades.

PUBLIC-PRIVATE PARTNERSHIPS

Political processes should seek to maximise the synergies between government and the private sector through public-private partnerships. Over decades the private sector has been the mainstay of vaccine production and distribution, and thus the private sector's expertise needs to be harnessed to produce and distribute an appropriate HIV vaccine.

Vaccines have never been as commercially successful as other medical treatments, and so entering the field of HIV vaccine development is a risk for companies. Most of the initial uptake of an effective vaccine will have to be in countries with a high prevalence; and as these countries are heavily indebted, they will not have the resources to buy and distribute the vaccine. Governments of the rich countries will have to work with IAVI, the World Bank, the United Nations, the WHO, and the private sector to ensure that commercial guarantees are in place to give the private sector an incentive to move into this field. These commercial agreements will have to give attention to:

- Setting limits on exploitation of intellectual property
- "Guaranteed" markets
- Price controls in poor countries
- Limiting liability in the event of a small number of adverse events (such as with polio), and
- Ways to increase global manufacturing capacity.

Equally important will be the need for all countries, irrespective of wealth, to develop strategies to incorporate HIV vaccines into national vaccination programmes.

WHAT WILL WE DO WITH AN HIV VACCINE?

TARGET POPULATIONS

Even when we do develop an HIV vaccine, there is no guarantee that it will be used appropriately. This is why we should determine the rules for access to and distribution of the vaccine before making it widely available. The rules for distribution of an HIV vaccine must break with the present rules for access to new drugs and vaccines whereby priority is given to wealthy nations and people, who do not bear the burden of this disease. We see this problem in the current unequal access to antiretroviral drugs. HIV vaccines must be given firstly to the poorest and most vulnerable people in our global society. This will be a difficult challenge, as our current experience with polio vaccines in poor countries has shown, where warfare and social dislocation have often prevented the distribution of vaccines.

High risk populations in rich countries will also need to be targeted. Commercial sex workers, high risk gay men, haemophiliac people, injecting drug users, and children born to HIV positive mothers will need to be protected (or partially protected) by these vaccines.

To ensure adequate manufacture and distribution

of the vaccine, we will need accurate measures of the numbers of people in different regions that will require vaccination. This will be a difficult task that will need to involve governments and society.

How the vaccine will be used initially will be determined by the rates of full and partial protection given by the early generation of vaccines. If the early vaccines offer only marginal protection, there may be reason to use these only in high risk groups and then wait for more successful vaccines to be developed for use in lower risk groups. The same principle applies to any major side effects: these will be tolerated by and be acceptable to low risk populations only in the setting of very high predicted levels of protection.

Timing of administration of HIV vaccines will be complex and will need to take local factors into consideration. Decisions will need to be made whether to include HIV vaccines from birth in an expanded immunisation programme or whether to wait until preadolescence (or whether to immunise at both ages). Data on protection in these two settings of vertical and sexual transmission will help in these decisions.

SUBTYPES OF HIV

The number of described HIV subtypes increases constantly, and their relevance to protective immunity remains unresolved. The possibility of immune responses to specific subtypes will continue to haunt HIV vaccinologists until adequate data confirm or deny that cross protection can occur between subtypes. This matter will be difficult to deal with once a successful vaccine is identified in one or more geographical areas. For example, if a vaccine developed from the subtype B virus was found to be successful in an efficacy trial in the US, will this product then be seen as a compulsory alternative to a placebo arm in another study in a region in which subtype C is predominant? Because of their regional distribution, HIV subtypes have assumed a political and national importance, which could interfere with important international trials of efficacy.

CONCLUSION

It is generally agreed that the development of an affordable, appropriate, and effective HIV vaccine is within reach—within 7–10 years. Vaccines are the only hope for the control and possible elimination of HIV infection, as was the case with smallpox and polio, which have been fully or partially eliminated by global vaccination programmes. How we distribute the vaccine will be a test of our international ethics and humanitarian objectives, and our generation will be judged by its success or failure in making a vaccine and ensuring equitable access to it.

NOTES

1. UNAIDS. *Aids epidemic update: December 2001.* www.unaids.org/epidemic_update/report_dec01/index.html (accessed 9 Jan 2002).

2. Cohen J. Shooting blanks. "Science" writer Jon Cohen speaks of how the search for an HIV vaccine has strayed. Interview by Bob Roehr. *IAPAC Mon* 2001;7:268–70.

3. Hulskotte E. G., Geretti A. M., Osterhaus A. D. Towards an HIV-1 vaccine: lessons from studies in macaque models. *Vaccine* 1998;16:904–15.

4. Joy A. K., Dale C. J., Kent S. J. Can HIV infection be prevented with a vaccine? *Drugs R D* 1999;1:431–40.

5. Amara R. R., Villinger F., Altman J. D., Lydy S. L., O'Neil S. P., Staprans S. I., et al. Control of a mucosal challenge and prevention of AIDS by a multiprotein DNA/MVA vaccine. *Science* 2001;292:69–74.

6. Barouch D. H., Fu T., Montefiori D. C., Lewis M. G., Shiver J. W., Letvin N. L. Vaccine-elicited immune responses prevent clinical AIDS in SHIV(89.6P)-infected rhesus monkeys. *Immunol Lett* 2001;79:57–61.

7. Pu R., Tellier M. C., Yamamoto J. K. Mechanism(s) of FIV vaccine protection. *Leukemia* 1997;11(suppl 3):98–101S.

8. Rowland-Jones S. L., McMichael A. Immune responses in HIV-exposed seronegatives: have they repelled the virus? *Curr Opin Immunol* 1995;7:448–55.

9. Cao Y., Qin L., Zhang L., Safrit J., Ho D. D. Virologic and immunologic characterization of long-term survivors of human immunodeficiency virus type 1 infection. *N Engl J Med* 1995;332:201–8.

10. Pantaleo G., Menzo S., Veccarezza M., Graziosi C., Cohen O. J., Demarest J. F., et al. Studies in subjects with long-term nonprogressive human immunodeficiency virus infection. *N Engl J Med* 1995;332:209–16.

11. Rowland-Jones S. L., Dong T., Fowke K. R., Kimani J., Krausa P., Newell H., et al. Cytotoxic T cell responses to multiple conserved HIV epitopes in HIV-resistant prostitutes in Nairobi. *J Clin Invest* 1998;102:1758–65.

12. Kaul R., Plummer F. A., Kimani J., Dong T., Kiama P., Rostron T., et al. HIV-1-specific mucosal CD8+ lymphocyte responses in the cervix of HIV-1-resistant prostitutes in Nairobi. *J Immunol* 2000;164:1602–11.

DONALD A. HENDERSON

The Looming Threat of Bioterrorism

Donald A. Henderson is Director of the Office of Public Health Preparedness for the U.S. Department of Health and Human Services. He is the founding director of the Johns Hopkins Center for Civilian Biodefense Studies. He also directed the World Health Organization's global smallpox eradication campaign. He has received the National Medal of Science, National Academy of Sciences Public Welfare Medal, and the Edward Jenner Medal from the Royal Society of Medicine.

The past 4 years have been marked by escalating concerns in the United States about the threat of biological weapons. At first, discussions about the implications of this threat and its possible scenarios were confined primarily to those in the military, diplomatic, law enforcement, and intelligence communities and to those concerned with arms reduction issues. Only recently have the civilian medical and public health communities begun to be engaged in examining the practical challenges posed by this threat. Professional societies for the first time have begun to incorporate discussions of bioterrorism in national meetings. On the international scene, in 1998 the World Health Organization (WHO) decided to establish an expert group to review and revise its 1970 landmark document, *Health Aspects of Chemical and Biological Weapons*.[1]

Clearly, there is growing public awareness of the threat of bioterrorism, and there is nascent concern among medical and public health professionals as well. This is important because if real progress is to be made in addressing this difficult problem, a substantially greater input of good science, medicine, and public health will be needed.

Reprinted with the permission of the authors and the publisher from *Science* 283 (February 26, 1999), 1279–82. Copyright © 1999, American Association for the Advancement of Science.

BEGINNINGS OF A NATIONAL RESPONSE

The threat of bioterrorism has not been ignored. Substantial national preparedness measures were taken in June 1995 with Presidential Decision Directive 39 (PDD-39), which was further elaborated in May 1998 by PDD-62 and PDD-63, all classified documents. PDD-39 defined the broad responsibilities and coordination relationships among the federal agencies involved.[2] PDD-62 and PDD-63 sought to define a better organizational structure. The Federal Bureau of Investigation (FBI) was assigned lead responsibility for crisis management, in implementing measures to resolve the immediate emergency and to investigate the scene with the goal of gathering evidence to support criminal prosecution of a perpetrator. The federal lead role in coordinating subsequent assistance, termed consequence management, was delegated to the Federal Emergency Management Agency. The Public Health Service's Office of Emergency Preparedness (OEP) was asked to coordinate all health and medical assistance. However, OEP was given few funds with which to do this, and the Department of Health and Human Services (HHS), in which OEP is housed, was itself provided with virtually no new resources. The dominant role and most of the funds were assigned to the Department of Defense (DOD) under the 1997 Defense Against Weapons of Mass Destruction Act. The act directed DOD to develop and implement a domestic preparedness program to improve the ability of local, state, and federal agencies to cope with chemical, biological, and nuclear threats and to conduct exercises and preparedness tests.

Metropolitan Medical Response Teams, funded by OEP, are now being trained in a program that will eventually reach 120 major cities.[3] These teams are to be composed of first responders (fire fighting, law enforcement, and emergency medical personnel) that are already employed by their municipal governments. Limited funds are available for training and for the cities to lease equipment but not for operating costs. Meanwhile, 10 National Guard units of 22 full-time people each, called Rapid Assessment and Initial Detection Teams, are being trained. One unit is planned for each federal region. Under consideration is the possibility of providing one or more such units for each state. The units will be on a standby basis, able to be mobilized quickly should a chemical or biological substance be released. Two other specialized units, each consisting of several hundred people, have been established—the Marine Corps' Chemical and Biological Incident Response Force and the Army's Technical Escort Unit. Additional resources have also been provided to the FBI to permit additional agents to be hired, intelligence efforts are being augmented, and DOD and the Department of Energy have mounted greatly expanded research programs. Research areas include the development of environmental detection devices for chemical agents and some for biological agents, plus the development of equipment such as masks and suits for working in chemically contaminated areas.

THE CHALLENGE OF BIOLOGICAL AGENTS

Of the weapons of mass destruction (nuclear, chemical, and biological), the biological ones are the most greatly feared,[4] but the country is least well prepared to deal with them. Virtually all federal efforts in strategic planning and training have so far been directed toward crisis management after a chemical release or an explosion. Should such an event occur, fire, police, and emergency rescue workers would proceed to the scene and, with the FBI assuming lead responsibility, stabilize the situation, deal with casualties, decontaminate, and collect evidence for identification of a perpetrator. This exercise is not unfamiliar. Spills of hazardous materials, explosions, fires, and other civil emergencies are not uncommon events.

The expected scenario after release of an aerosol cloud of a biological agent is entirely different (Table 1). The release could be silent and would almost certainly be undetected. The cloud would be invisible, odorless, and tasteless. It would behave much like a gas in penetrating interior areas. No one would know until days or weeks later that anyone had been infected (depending on the microbe). Then patients would begin appearing in emergency rooms and physicians' offices with symptoms of a strange disease that few physicians had ever seen. Special measures would be needed for patient care and hospitalization, obtaining laboratory confirmation regarding the identity of microbes unknown to most laboratories, providing vaccine or antibiotics to large portions of the population, and identifying and possibly quarantining patients. Trained epidemiologists would be needed to identify where and when infection had occurred, so as to identify how and by whom it may have been spread. Public health administrators would be challenged to undertake emergency management of a problem alien to their experience and in a public environment where pestilential disease, let alone in epidemic form, has been unknown.

The implicit assumption has frequently been that chemical and biological threats and the responses to them are so generically similar that they can be readily handled by a single "chembio" expert, usually a chemist. This is a serious misapprehension (Table 1).

First responders to a biological weapons incident (in contrast to an explosion or chemical release) would be emergency room physicians and nurses, family physicians, infectious disease specialists, infection control practitioners, epidemiologists, hospital and public health administrators, and laboratory experts. Surprisingly, to date there has been little involvement of any of these groups in planning for appropriate responses or in training. One recent measure to address this deficit is the convening, by the Hopkins Center, of a national Working Group on Civilian Biodefense, which is composed of government and nongovernment experts. The principal goal of this group has been to identify which biological agents require priority attention and what should be the most appropriate response to each.

EMERGENCE OF THE BIOWEAPONS THREAT

Bioweapons programs began to receive substantial attention during World War II. An infamous Japanese program ceased with the end of the war, but programs in the United States, Canada, the Soviet Union, and the United Kingdom expanded steadily until 1972.[5]

Table 1. Important Distinctions between Chemical and Biological Terrorism

Chemical terrorism	Biological terrorism
Speed at which attack results in illness	
Rapid—usually minutes to hours after attack	Delayed—usually days to weeks after attack
Distribution of affected patients	
Downwind area near point of release	Widely spread through city or region; major international epidemic in worst-case scenario
First responders	
Paramedics, firefighters, police, emergency rescue workers, and law enforcement	Emergency department physicians and nurses, infectious disease physicians, infection control practitioners, epidemiologists, public health officials, hospital administrators, and laboratory experts
Release site of weapon	
Quickly discovered; possible and useful to cordon off area of attack	Difficult to identify; probably not possible or useful to cordon off area of attack
Decontamination of patients and environment	
Critically important in most cases	Not necessary in most cases
Medical interventions	
Chemical antidotes	Vaccines and/or antibiotics
Patient isolation/quarantine	
After decontamination there is no need	Crucial if easily communicable disease is involved (such as smallpox); advance hospital planning for isolating large numbers of patients is critical

At that time, the Biological and Toxin Weapons Convention (BWC) was opened for signature and was eventually ratified by 140 nations, including the Soviet Union and Iraq.[6] It called for the termination of all research on offensive bioweapons and the destruction of existing stocks of agents. The Western countries complied but, as time passed, other countries took an interest in developing their own capacities. There was no mechanism for verification of this. In the United States during the 1970s and 1980s, there was a mood of complacency about bioterrorism; funds for defensive activities all but evaporated, and a highly regarded research program and team were partially dismantled.

That complacency has been shattered in recent years by events in Iraq and Japan, by revelations from Soviet defectors that documented the extent of the program in Russia, and by the disclosure that at least 10 nations now have a biological weapons capacity.[7] Discoveries during and after the 1990 Gulf War brought new concerns about bioweapons.[8] Iraq used chemical weapons in the Iran-Iraq war; it was known to be developing a nuclear capability; and there were signs that it had been engaged in developing anthrax as a weapon. Concerns about anthrax arose too late, however, for enough vaccine to be produced to vaccinate more than a small proportion of the allied forces. After the war, it was learned that Iraq's bioweapons program was substantially larger and more advanced than had been appreciated. In 1995, with the defection of the President's son-in-law Hussein Karnel Hassan, Iraqi documents were obtained that portrayed an operation of previously unknown scope and sophistication. The acknowledged production included 20,000 liters of botulinum toxin and 8000 liters of anthrax spore suspension. SCUD missiles with a range of 300 to 600 km and carrying 400-lb bombs had been outfitted with botulinum toxin and anthrax warheads, and drone aircraft had been equipped with aerosol dispersal systems. Iraq's bioweapons capability remains intact.

In 1995, the sarin gas attack on metropolitan Tokyo by the Japanese religious cult Aum Shinrikyo came as an unexpected surprise. This little known cult foresaw the coming of an apocalyptic war from which its followers would emerge to assume control first of Japan and then the world.[9] To speed this process, they sought to use weapons of mass destruction to kill hundreds of thousands, if not millions, and to spread panic. Only in 1998 was it learned that the cult had actually sought to aerosolize anthrax and botulinum toxin throughout metropolitan Tokyo on eight occasions between 1990 and 1995. Although its leader has been imprisoned, the cult remains intact and legal today; it operates electronic, computer, and other stores with a net revenue of $30 million annually. It is said to have about 5000 adherents in Japan and to have branches in Russia, Ukraine, Belarus, and Kazakhstan.[10]

Perhaps of greatest concern is the status of Russia's bioweapons establishment. The scope of the Soviet program and details of its operation have become increasingly available during the 1990s as a result of defections by senior officials of its bioweapons program. The signing of the BWC in 1972 is reported to have been seen by the Soviet Union as an opportunity to gain an advantage over its Cold War adversaries. Accordingly, a massive expansion of its bioweapons program was begun.[11] The eradication of smallpox and the cessation of vaccination in 1980 were considered another opportunity to be exploited. A program was begun to produce smallpox virus on a very large scale and to weaponize it. By 1989, this had been achieved with a production capacity of dozens of tons of smallpox virus annually. Ken Alibek, a former first deputy chief of research and production for the Russian biological weapons program, has reported that smallpox virus had been mounted in intercontinental ballistic missiles and in bombs for strategic use.

The biological weapons R&D programs in the former Soviet Union were funded and managed by at least two different entities: the first, called Biopreparat, was in the Ministry of Medical and Microbiological Industry; the second was in the Ministry of Defense. Still operative is a significant proportion of a multilaboratory complex (the vestiges of Biopreparat) extending across at least eight different cities, which once employed 60,000 workers. One of these laboratories, the Russia State Research Center of Virology and Biotechnology, is located in Koltsovo, Novosibirsk Region.[12] It houses one of the two WHO-sanctioned repositories of smallpox virus [the other being the U.S. Centers for Disease Control (CDC)]. It has extensive biosafety level 4 containment facilities, permitting it to work with the most virulent pathogens, and is currently utilizing smallpox, Marburg, and hemorrhagic fever viruses in recombinant research studies. Like other laboratories in Russia, it is experiencing financial difficulties; substantial numbers of scientists have departed and security is more lax. Where the scientists have gone is unknown, but Libya, Iran, Syria, Iraq, and North Korea have actively been recruiting such expertise.[13] Relative to Biopreparat, far less is known about the activities of the biological weapons programs centered in the Ministry of Defense.[14]

A mixture of rogue states and well-financed religious cults with scientists desperately seeking funds creates a volatile situation with potentially serious consequences.

PROBABLE AGENTS

Any one of thousands of biological agents that are capable of causing human infection could be considered a potential biological weapon. Realistically, only a few pose serious problems. The NATO handbook dealing with potential biological warfare agents lists 31 infectious agents.[15] Only a very small number of these, however, can be cultivated and dispersed effectively so as to cause cases and deaths in numbers that would threaten the functioning of a large community. Other factors also determine which microbes are of priority concern: specifically, the possibility of further human-to-human spread, the environmental stability of the organism, the size of the infectious dose, and the availability of prophylactic or therapeutic measures.

A Russian panel of bioweapons experts reviewed the microbial agents and concluded that there were 11 that were "very likely to be used." The top four were smallpox, plague, anthrax, and botulism.[16] Lower on their list were tularemia, glanders, typhus, Q fever, Venezuelan equine encephalitis, and Marburg and influenza viruses. Each of the four top-rated agents is associated with high case fatality rates when dispersed as an aerosol. The rates range upward from 30% for smallpox to more than 80% for anthrax. Smallpox and anthrax have other advantages in that they can be grown reasonably easily and in large quantities and are sturdy organisms that are resistant to destruction. They are thus especially suited to aerosol dissemination to reach large areas and numbers of people.

Plague and botulinum toxin are less likely prospects. From experience in the now defunct U.S. bioweapons development program, producing and dispensing substantial quantities of plague organisms or botulinum toxin[17] pose virtually insurmountable problems. Thus, smallpox and anthrax are effectively alone at the top of the list among potential agents.

LIKELY PERPETRATORS

Some argue that almost anyone with intent can produce and dispense a biological weapon. It is unlikely, however, that more than a few would be successful in obtaining any of the top-rated agents in a form suitable to be dispensed as an aerosol. Naturally occurring cases of plague, anthrax, and botulism do occur on almost every continent and so provide a potential source for strains. However, there is considerable variation in the virulence of different strains, and a high level of expertise, which is much less obtainable than the agents themselves, is needed to identify an especially pathogenic one. Moreover, producing these particular organisms in large quantity and in the ultra-small particle form needed for aerosolization is beyond the average laboratory.

Soviet laboratories had the sophistication and capacity to produce all of the most pathogenic organisms in large quantities. It is assumed that a number of other countries now also possess this capacity because the costs of equipping and staffing a bioweapons laboratory are modest when compared to those required for a nuclear or chemical facility. Any group with sufficient resources could purchase prepared supplies of aerosolizable organisms and could transport them easily, because only small quantities are needed to inflict casualties over a very wide area. No mechanisms currently exist for screening to intercept such materials at state or national borders.

Discrete outbreaks of less virulent organisms could certainly be propagated by dissident groups with less access to resources and sophisticated laboratories. One such outbreak occurred in 1984, when members of the Rajneeshi religious sect introduced *Salmonella typhimurium* into salad bars in Dallas, Oregon.[18] In all, some 750 people became ill; none died or were hospitalized. Other episodes of this type could occur but would be unlikely to panic or cripple a city as would an outbreak of smallpox or anthrax.

GREATEST THREATS: SMALLPOX AND ANTHRAX

Of the potential biological weapons, smallpox and anthrax pose by far the greatest threats, albeit because of different clinical and epidemiological properties. So far there have been no examples of the potential devastation of biological weapons like those provided

by nuclear weapons during World War II. Epidemics of smallpox in Yugoslavia (1972)[19] and of anthrax in the Soviet Union (1979)[20] after an accidental release from the Sverdlosk bioweapons production facility provide some sense of the magnitude and nature of the problems posed.[23]

Comprehensive reviews of these two diseases and consensus views as to appropriate medical and public health responses have already been completed by the working group convened by the Hopkins Center.[21]

Smallpox poses an unusually serious threat; in part, because virtually everyone is now susceptible, vaccination having stopped worldwide 20 or more years ago as a result of the eradication of the disease. Because of waning immunity, it is probable that no more than 20% of the population is protected. Among the unprotected, case fatality rates after infection with smallpox are 30%. There is no treatment. Virus, in aerosol form, can survive for 24 hours or more and is highly infectious even at low dosages.[22]

An outbreak in which as few as 100 people were infected would quickly tax the resources of any community. There would be both actual cases and people with a fever and rash for whom the diagnosis was uncertain. In all, 200 or more patients would probably have to be treated in the first wave of cases. Most of the patients would be extremely ill with severe aching pains and high fever and would normally be hospitalized. Hospitalization poses problems, however. Because of the risk of widespread transmission of the virus, patients would have to be confined to rooms under negative pressure that were equipped with special filters to prevent the escape of the virus. Hospitals have few rooms so ventilated; there would, for example, probably be less than 100 in the Washington, D.C., metropolitan area.

A vaccination program would have to be undertaken rapidly to protect as many as possible of those who had been in contact with the patients. Vaccination given within 3 to 4 days after exposure can protect most people against a fatal outcome and may prevent the disease entirely. It is unlikely, however, that smallpox would be diagnosed early enough and vaccination programs launched rapidly enough to prevent infection of many of the people exposed during the first wave. Few physicians have ever seen smallpox and few, if any, have ever received training in its diagnosis. Moreover, mounting a vaccination campaign requires time unless there has been advance planning, and no city has yet done such planning. The human immunodeficiency virus epidemic and the more general issue of vaccine complications among immunosuppressed populations introduce added complexity to decision-making regarding smallpox vaccination administration.

A second wave of cases would be almost inevitable. From experiences with smallpox imported into Europe over the past 40 years, it is estimated that there would be at least 10 secondary cases for every case in the first wave,[23] or 1000 cases in all, appearing some 14 days after the first wave. Vaccination would initially be needed for health workers, essential service personnel, and contacts of patients at home and at work. With mounting numbers of cases, contacts, and involved areas, mass vaccination would soon be the only practical approach. That would not be possible, however, because present vaccine supplies are too limited, there being approximately 5 to 7 million doses currently available. To put this number in perspective, in New York City in 1947, 6 million people were vaccinated over approximately 1 week in response to a total of eight cases of smallpox. Moreover, there are no longer any manufacturers of smallpox vaccine. Best estimates indicate that substantial additional supplies could not be ensured sooner than 36 months from the initial outbreak.

A scenario for an inhalation anthrax epidemic is of no less concern. Like smallpox, the aerosol would almost certainly be unobtrusively released and would drift throughout a building or even a city without being noticed. After 2 to 3 days, infected individuals would appear in emergency rooms and doctors' offices with a variety of nonspecific symptoms such as fever, cough, and headache. Within a day or two, patients would become critically ill and then die within 24 to 72 hours. It is doubtful that antibiotic therapy given after symptoms develop would be of benefit. The case fatality rate is 80% or greater.

Although anthrax does not spread from person to person, it has another dangerous attribute. Individuals who are exposed to an aerosol may abruptly develop illness up to 8 weeks after the initial exposure. Cases can be prevented by the administration of antibiotics, but such treatment would have to be continued daily for at least 60 days. This period might be shortened by the prompt administration of vaccine. Experimental studies suggest that two doses of vaccine given 15 days apart may provide protection beginning 30 days after the initial inoculation. At this time, however, there is no vaccine available for civilian use; building of stockpiles of antibiotics is still in the planning stage, and no city at present has a plan for distributing antibiotics so as to ensure that drugs are given over a 60-day period.

A LOOK AT THE FUTURE

Biologists, especially those in medicine and public health, are as critical to confronting the problems posed by biological weapons as are physicists in dealing with nuclear threats and chemists with chemical weapons. During 1998, steps were taken to facilitate such involvement. Nonetheless, the need to discuss bioterrorism in national forums remains. One first step was the National Symposium on Medical and Public Health Response to Bioterrorism convened by the HHS, the Hopkins Center, and 12 other sponsoring organizations on 16 and 17 February 1998.

In May, Assistant Secretary Margaret Hamburg was assigned responsibility for developing a strategic plan for HHS. Formerly New York City Commissioner of Health, she guided the nation's most advanced counter-terrorist planning effort from the perspective of public health and medical consequence management. At the request of the president and with bipartisan support from Congress, $133 million was appropriated to HHS for fiscal 1999 for countering biological and chemical threats, $51 million of which is for an emergency stockpile of antibiotics and vaccines. Most of the funds are allocated to the CDC, primarily for the strengthening of the infectious disease surveillance network and for enhancing the capacity of federal and state laboratories. This is not a large sum of money, considering the needs of a fragile public health infrastructure extending over 50 states and at least 120 major cities, but it is a beginning.

The provision of funds to HHS is consonant with the general belief that the most effective step now is to strengthen the public health and infectious disease infrastructure. An augmented full-time cadre of professionals at the state and local level would represent, for biological weapons, a counterpart to the National Guard Rapid Assessment and Initial Detection Teams for chemical weapons. Rather than being on a standby basis, however, the biological cadre would also serve to strengthen efforts directed toward dealing with new and emerging infections and food-borne diseases.

Developing these experts, however, requires a considerable training effort, given the variety of specialists that are needed for preparation and response. First, there is a need to train primary care doctors in early recognition of the most important disease threats and to intensify the training of emergency room physicians and nurses. Infectious disease specialists and hospital epidemiologists must also become versed in case recognition and in steps to take if a suspicious case is detected. There is a need to train laboratory directors and key staff in laboratories with designated responsibilities for lab diagnosis. Moreover, state and local health officers and epidemiologists require training in, among other things, detection, surveillance, and management of epidemic disease.

National Institutes of Health- and CDC-administered research agendas are needed to attract both university and private sector talents to address a host of constraints and problems. Among the most critical needs now are improved vaccines, available in large supply, for both smallpox and anthrax. Areas for vaccine improvement include increasing overall efficacy; in the case of smallpox, reducing complications and in the case of anthrax, reducing the number of inoculations. Feasibility studies suggest that substantially improved second-generation vaccines can be developed quickly.

Finally, there is a need both now and in the longer term to pursue measures that will prevent acts of terrorism. Whatever can be done to strengthen the provisions of the BWC deserves all possible support. The strengthening of our intelligence capabilities so as to anticipate and perhaps interdict terrorists is of the highest priority. The fostering of international cooperative research programs to encourage openness and dialogue as is now being done with Russian laboratories is also important.

Once the medical community rallied to support Lown and Chazov[24] in educating peoples and policymakers everywhere about the dread realities of a nuclear winter. Perhaps the same should now be done with respect to the realities of biological weapons, which are now considered to be a more serious threat than the nuclear ones.

REFERENCES

1. WHO Group of Consultants, *Health Aspects of Chemical and Biological Weapons* (WHO, Geneva, 1970).

2. J. B. Tucker, *J. Am. Med. Assoc.* **278,** 369 (1997).

3. House Government Reform and Oversight Committee; National Security, International Affairs and Criminal Justice Subcommittee; U.S. House of Representatives, *Department of Defense Role in the Federal Response to Domestic Terrorism* (Washington, DC, 1998).

4. R. Danzig and P. B. Berkowsky, *J. Am. Med. Assoc.* **278,** 431 (1997).

5. G. W. Christopher *et al., ibid.,* p. 412.

6. R. P. Kadlec *et al., ibid.,* p. 351.

7. M. Leitenberg, *Asian Perspect.* **21,** 7 (1997).

8. R. A. Zilinskas, *J. Am. Med. Assoc.* **278,** 418 (1997).

9. S. WuDunn *et al.,* "How Japan germ terror alerted world," *New York Times,* 26 May 1998, p. A1.

10. J. Miller, "Some in Japan fear authors of subway attack are regaining ground," *New York Times,* 11 October 1998, p. A12.

11. K. Alibek, "Terrorist and intelligence operations: Potential impact on the U.S. economy" (testimony provided before the Joint Economic Committee, 20 May 1998).

12. R. Preston, *The New Yorker* **74** (no. 3), 52 (1998).

13. J. Miller and W. J. Broad, "Iranians, bioweapons in mind, lure needy ex-Soviet scientists," *New York Times,* 8 December 1998, p. A1.

14. M. Leitenberg, *Biologicals* **21,** 187 (1993).

15. Departments of the Army, Navy, and Air Force, *NATO Handbook on the Medical Aspects of NBC Defensive Operations* (Washington, DC, February 1996).

16. A. A. Vorobjev *et al., "Criterion Rating" as a Measure of Probable Use of Bioagents as Biological Weapons* (presented to the Working Group on Biological Weapons Control of the Committee on International Security and Arms Control, National Academy of Sciences, Washington, DC, 1994).

17. W. C. Patrick, "Analysis of botulinum toxin, type A, as a biological warfare threat" (unpublished paper, 1998).

18. T. J. Totok *et al., J. Am. Med. Assoc.* **278,** 389 (1997).

19. F. Fenner *et al., Smallpox and Its Eradication* (WHO, Geneva, 1988).

20. M. Meselsohn *et al., Science* **266,** 1202 (1994).

21. Working Group on Civilian Biodefense, in preparation.

22. P. F. Wehrle *et al., Bull. WHO* **43,** 669 (1970).

23. D. A. Henderson, *Emerging Infect. Dis.* **4,** 488 (1999).

24. S. H. Miller, "Nobel Peace Prize recipients warn of nuclear war dangers," *Boston Globe,* 12 December 1985, p. 62.

ROBERT C. SPENCER AND
NIGEL F. LIGHTFOOT

Preparedness and Response to Bioterrorism

Robert C. Spencer works with the Public Health Laboratory at the Bristol Royal Infirmary. He is chairman of the Hospital Infection Society. He is also an Assistant Editor for the *Journal of Hospital Infection*.

Nigel F. Lightfoot is the Group Director of Public Health Laboratory Service North, in Newcastle-upon-Tyne. The laboratory service seeks to protect the population of England from infection through detection, diagnosis, surveillance, prevention and control of infections and communicable diseases.

INTRODUCTION

Recently, former U.S. President Bill Clinton stated that biological warfare (BW) and bioterrorism pose two of the greatest threats to the military and civilian population of the U.S.A.[1,2] In the military scenario the most likely mode of delivery of BW agent(s) would be by aerosol, the particle size of which would be in the 0.3–5 μm diameter range.[3,4] Such particles could be delivered by missiles, bomblets with aerosol nozzles, aircraft with underbelly tanks and spray nozzles (so called "line source lay-down") or by aerosol generators on small boats, trucks or cars or, alternatively in concealed ground positions 1–50 km upwind of the target population.

Against this background, the "What If" programme broadcast on Radio 4 on 1 April 1999, examined the political, strategic and medical consequences of a BW attack on Washington D.C. The scenario envisaged a substantial line source attack with *Bacillus anthracis* under ideal weather conditions—at night with a light wind (Table I). The results, as one would have predicted, was that medical resources would be rapidly overwhelmed within hours, once symptoms began to develop, by the sick, the "worried well" and a population demanding vaccination and antibiotics (Table II).[5] There would be a total breakdown of law and order, with up to a third of the population attempting to flee the city. It has been estimated by mathematical modelling that the economic impact of such a bioterrorist attack with anthrax would be $26.2 billion per 100 000 persons exposed.[6] In a "Table Top" exercise conducted in the U.S.A in 1998, where the scenario was a BW attack across the U.S.–Mexican border with a smallpox–Marburg chimera, the predicted outcomes were similar. The exercise also revealed the immense difficulties for local and state officials in coping with a major terrorist strike and highlighted a disturbing lack of interagency coordination among federal officials. These two large-scale scenarios show that even sophisticated healthcare delivery systems would not be able to cope with the large numbers of casualties expected in such an attack. Even if faced with a much smaller bioterrorist attack, say, in the business class section of a Boeing 747, how many microbiologists could recognize pneumonic plague or identify *B. anthracis* on a culture plate. Few physicians have ever seen a case of smallpox. Therefore diagnosis is certain to be delayed. Commonly prescribed antibiotics for community acquired pneumonia would be ineffective. Deliberate release of potential bioweapons may not be promptly detected by the medical authorities. This has been shown by the activities of the Rajneeshee cult in the U.S.A., who deliberately contaminated restaurant salad bars with salmonella in an attempt to influence local politics,[7] and

From *Journal of Infection* 43 (2001), 104–10. Copyright © 2001 The British Infection Society.

Table I Optimal Dissemination of Biological Warfare Agent under Ideal Conditions

- Infectious dose is <100 particles/organisms
- Viability and virulence do not dissociate
- Concentration of agent is 10^{10}/ml
- Weather conditions optimal*
  –moderate inversion
  –relative humidity appropriate*
  –wind direction steady @ 20 km/h
- Extended line laydown at midnight at a height of 100 m
- Agent disseminated for 50 km at 5 l/km
- At least 10% of material appears in resulting aerosol and particles <5 μm diameter

*1 inch of rainfall would remove 99% of 5 μm particles but only 10% of 3 μm particles.

the activities of the Aum Shinrikyo sect in Japan prior to the Tokyo sarin nerve gas attack in 1995.[8]

So why now? Why is bioterrorism back on the political, military and medical agenda, overt vs. covert.[9–13] This small review will attempt to answer some of these questions by giving some background information on history, international protocols, the agents, impact of new technologies, detection, protection and deterrence and what the future may hold.

HISTORY

There is strong circumstantial historical evidence that BW agents have been used in warfare.[14] The Tartars are said to have broken the siege of Kaffa (Feodossia) during the 14th century by catapulting the plague-infected corpses of their soldiers over the city walls.[15]

Table II Effects of Attacks by Nuclear, Chemical and Biological Weapons

System	Fatalities
1. 1 megaton nuclear bomb	500 000–2 million
2. 1000 kg sarin nerve gas (line source with agent drifting on wind)	
(a) Clear day	300–700
(b) Overcast	400–800
(c) Clear night	3000–8000
3. 100 kg anthrax spores (line source with agent drifting on wind)	
(a) Clear day	130 000–460 000
(b) Overcast	420 000–1.4 million
(c) Clear night	1–3 million

The subsequent epidemic of bubonic plague forced the city's surrender and the Venetian defenders fled, allegedly initiating the major plague outbreak—The Black Death—that swept through Europe between 1348 and 1350 and in which 30% of Europe's population died. Blankets and clothing from victims of smallpox were allegedly given to the local Indian population in North America, resulting in epidemics that decimated their population.[16] During the First World War, Germany attempted to interrupt food supplies and infect draft animals with anthrax and glanders.[17] The Japanese allegedly dropped plague infected fleas on Chinese cities during the Sino–Japanese War in the 1930s and experimented on live prisoners of war with many agents at the notorious Unit 731 based in Manchuria.[18] Dr Paul Fildes headed the British effort at Porton Down in the 1940s and by November 1940 had determined that the most effective way to use a BW agent would be to disseminate an aerosol of lung-retention size particles from a liquid suspension of bacteria in a bursting munition, such as a bomb, so that effective concentrations would be inhaled by anyone in the target size.[19,20] The British BW offensive effort concentrated on anthrax and between 1942 and 1943 anthrax bombs were tested on the island of Gruinard, off the north-west coast of Scotland. The so-called N-bomb contained 106 special bomblets charged with anthrax spores. Another effort was the production of over 5 million anthrax-infected cattle cakes, which would have been dropped over Germany in an attempt to decrease meat stocks by some 30%. Events overtook plans to put these into operation. The Russians were not idle, and at its peak in the 1970s and 1980s the system known as Biopreparat employed over 50 000 people in BW research, mainly at Kirov (plague), Zagorsk (smallpox) and Sverdlovsk (anthrax).[21] In 1979, a sudden outbreak of pulmonary anthrax occurred in Sverdlovsk down wind of a military complex, compound 19, because of the failure to activate air filters. Between 66 and 105 people died.[22] The defection of two scientists, Vladimir Pasechnik (multiresistant plague) and Kamatjan Alibekov (anthrax talc) gave Western governments an insight into the USSR effort. The United States invested heavily in BW research after the Second World War with dispersal experiments over San Francisco (*Serratia marcescens*) and the New York subway (*Bacilus globigii*).[23] By 1969 they had weaponized seven anti-human BW agents and three anti-crop agents, but

President Nixon then announced that the U.S. was unilaterally abandoning its biological and toxin weapons. It has been argued that Nixon renounced BW agents because they were militarily insignificant when compared with American's nuclear arsenal. The British expert Gradon Carter strongly opposes such a suggestion, arguing that the abandonment of BW arose for purely political considerations.[20]

INTERNATIONAL MEASURES

The basic international law prohibiting the use of BW is contained in the 1925 Geneva Protocol. The protocol was, in effect, a "no-first-use" agreement between countries, as it did not prevent BW being researched or preparations made for its use, in defence. In 1969 the United Nations General Assembly passed resolution 2603A which made recommendations on the interpretation of the Geneva Protocol. Following President Nixon's decision to halt BW research and deployment, the world moved to the Biological and Toxin Weapons Convention (BTWC) which was signed on 10 April 1972 and entered into force on 26 March 1975, with four review conferences in 1980, 1986, 1991 and 1996. This Convention bans the development, production, other acquisition and stockpiling of biological agents and toxins except for peaceful purposes. It also bans the transfer of such agents and toxins to assist a BW programme in a foreign country. The provisions of the Convention are implemented in the U.K. through the 1974 Biological Weapons Act.

A shortcoming of the BTWC is that there are no effective verification provisions and a very limited requirement for States Parties to provide transparency of certain legitimate activities. Greater transparency is badly needed because of the undoubted "dual-use" potential of any modern biotechnology or pharmaceutical pilot plant or full scale manufacturing facility. Without casting any aspersions on the *bona fides* of these research and development (R&D) and industrial sectors, the technical reality is that many such sites would have the skills and equipment to change production to BW with a fair expectation of success and only a minimum risk of accidents. The BTWC States Parties have accordingly been working in Geneva since 1975 in drafting a Protocol that will add mandatory provisions for declarations, for visits to declared facilities, and for investigations of facilities and in the "field" to address any future accusations of noncompliance. It is hoped that most of the States Parties to the Convention will see the benefit of the Protocol in deterring BW, and will want to sign up to it. The Protocol will also need to address the pressure from developing countries for an increased focus on the requirements of Article X of the Convention, which requires States Parties to facilitate the exchange of technology. These negotiations are coming to a critical point. Support from academia and industry is needed more than ever. Industry groups in the U.S. and in a number of other Western countries support the overall objective to strengthen the Convention, but are critical of the concept of random transparency visits. These critics maintain that such visits may compromise a facility's legitimate, competitive trade secrets. What seems to be ignored is that the Chemical Weapons Convention which came into force in 1977 has been successfully operating rather more intrusive routine inspections, using "managed access" to protect industrial confidentiality.

Another international activity intended to increase confidence over BW compliance was the confidential interaction between the U.S., U.K. and Russia based on their 1992 Trilateral Joint Statement. This followed a statement by President Yeltsin about activities of the former Soviet Union with respect to the BTWC.

In parallel with transparency of national activities, export controls on certain high risk items are seen as an important mechanism to prevent the acquisition and development of weapons anywhere in the world, including acquisition by non-state actors. Diversion through countries lacking effective export control machinery is a real risk. In the U.K., EU-agreed controls on "dual-use" items are operated through the Dual-Use and Related Goods (Export Controls) Regulations 1996. This legislation includes lists of human pathogens (including zoonoses) and toxins, animal pathogens, plant pathogens, and key items of production and downstream processing equipment. BW-related items are also covered by the "military lists" of the Export of Goods (Control) Order 1994.

The Chemical Weapons Convention (CWC) which came into force in 1997 outlaws chemical weapons, which would include weapons based on toxins. The CWC requires declarations of specified facilities and has a professional inspectorate capable of mounting inspections in response to a challenge from a State Party. The U.K.'s obligations under the CWC are implemented by the Department of Trade and Industry through the Chemical Weapons Act 1996.

THE AGENTS

BW agents are defined as "living organisms, whatever their nature, or infected material derived from them, which are used for hostile purposes and intended to cause disease or death in man, animals or plants, and which depend for their efforts on their ability to multiply in the person, animal or plant attacked."[3] To be an effective BW agent the micro-organism should meet specific criteria as shown in Table III.[3] Of the approximately 160 known disease-causing species that directly or indirectly affect man, about 30 have been discussed in the open literature as having BW potential (Table IV).[3] When factors such as ease of production, infectivity, toxicity and ability to be spread by aerosol dissemination [are considered], there are two agents that lead the pack—anthrax and smallpox. Pulmonary anthrax has at least an 90% case-fatality rate, though non-contagious from person to person.[24,25] Although the standard treatment has been penicillin, treatment with ciprofloxacin is now recommended if given prior to pulmonary symptoms developing. Smallpox is highly contagious, with a case-fatality rate in excess of 30%. Many experts believe that stocks of smallpox virus exist outside the two World Health Organization (WHO) designated high security laboratories of Center for Disease Control (CDC) Atlanta and Biotechnology Koltsovo, Novosibirsk. It is possible that smallpox virus exists in the arsenals of nations or terrorist groups. Worldwide the supply of smallpox vaccine is <50 million doses. In the U.S.A. it is estimated that there are 5–7 million doses for a population of 260 million. No one knows if these vaccines are still efficacious, as production stopped 20 years ago. Even a crash programme to develop a modern cell-cultured vaccine would take 3 years at a cost of $120 million. On 22nd April 1999, President Clinton sought to delay the planned destruction of U.S. smallpox stocks, whilst awaiting the development of a modern anti-smallpox vaccine.

Table III Desired Properties of Biological Warfare Agent

- Consistently produce a known effect: death or disease
- Highly contagious and effective in low doses
- A short and predictable incubation time
- Target population should have little or no immunity
- Little or no treatment available
- Aggressor should have means to protect own forces and civilians
- Suitable for mass production, robust and stable during production, storage, transportation and in munitions
- Stable during dissemination
- Low persistence after delivery to allow prompt occupation by invading forces

Table IV List of Potential Biological Warfare Agents

- Bacteria, Rickettsia, Chlamydia, Fungi, Viruses
- Microbial toxins
- Animal toxins
- Plant and seaweed toxins
- Snake and spider toxins
- Neuropeptides

1960s	20/31 were bacteria or fungi
1990s	19/21 are viruses

BIOLOGICAL WARFARE DELIVERY SYSTEMS

Many possible types of delivery mechanisms have been described from the very crude—back of a truck as used by Aum Shinrikyo—to the highly sophisticated MIRV (Multiple Independent Re-entry Vehicle) with its own cooling system mounted on an intercontinental ballistic missile. Cruise missiles have been described as the ideal BW delivery system because of their ability to lay down a toxic cloud close to the ground (at an altitude of about 100 m). Their subsonic speeds would avoid problems of the agent overheating when ejected into a wind stream. Such a system would rival nuclear fallout in terms of area covered and expected fatalities (Table II).[26]

WARNING AND DETECTION OF A BIOLOGICAL WARFARE ATTACK

BW aerosols are usually invisible, odourless and taste free. The first evidence of a BW attack may be the large number of casualties appearing within hours or days following attack. But at what point does the military commander, or the public health doctor in the civilian sector, begin to ask the obvious—is this a natural or intentional disease outbreak? How would we know that it was intentional; are there features which allow us to differentiate correctly between natural and deliberate outbreak scenarios? The answers to these questions will depend on a medical threat assessment using various differentiating criteria. Algorithms have been developed which summarize positive and negative data relevant to the prediction that a given epidemic is either man-made or due to natural causes.[27,28]

Because all this would take time, governments have invested hugely in developing physical protection (especially with regard to the armed forces) and particularly so called "real-time detection."[29,30] These are intended to provide a warning if not in minutes, then in hours. The LIDAR (Light Detection and Ranging) System has been used experimentally to detect natural and artificially induced aerosol clouds. Once detected, concentrated samples of cloud are analysed by BIDS (Biointegrated Detection System). This provides a plot of particle size (using an aerodynamic particle sizer); it detects and classifies bacterial cells and measures DNA content (by flow cytometry), measures ATP content (by bioluminescence) and identifies the specific agent (by immunoassays). It is reported that the first three tests are completed in 4 min and the immunoassay in 20 min. Thermocyclers for use with polymerase chain reaction (PCR) technology were deployed during Operation Desert Storm/Granby to augment conventional detection methods. Recently the Advanced Nucleic Acid Analyser (ANAA) has been described, able to detect 500 cfu of *Erwinia herbicola,* (as a surrogate for *Yersinia pestis*), in 15 min. Other technologies include BRACIS (Biological, Radiological and Chemical Information System)—a portable computer that predicts the path of a contaminant and the area in which it will form dangerous concentrations. In the U.K., interest has been shown in an integrated three tier system to detect, collect and identify agents in the field—IBDS (Integrated Biological Detection System). It permits detection by light scattering, down to 10 000 particles in 1–10 μ range; collection by determining presence of microbial material by ATP capture and identification by antibody reaction. The time required to produce a result is said to be less than 5 min. Canadian workers have examined a number of analytical techniques to provide real-time detection—mass spectrometry, liquid chromatography, flow cytometry, infrared and supercritical fluid extraction. CIBADS (Canadian Integrated Biological/Chemical Agent Detection System) is due to enter service soon. This system will also incorporate FLAPS (Fluorescence Aerodynamics Particle Sizer) which will be able to distinguish biological aerosol particles from inanimate material such as sand. The ideal real-time detector should weigh no more than 2 kg, identify as few as two particles of 20 potential BW agents in a sample of air, should not give false-positive readings and ideally, cost less than $5000. One interesting research proposal involves electronic chips containing live nerve cells incorporated in mice. The chip will "chatter" until something kills it; BW agents having a characteristic signature (the BW equivalent of the coal miners' canary!).

Whatever detection system is adopted it must be sited on the battlefield, whereas an identification system may be sited off the battlefield. Armed forces are easier to protect than the civilian population: immunization programmes can be used (some vaccines are not available for the civilian population), prophylactic antibiotics may be effective (U.S. Army alone had 30 million doses of ciprofloxacin available for Desert Storm, and the U.K. intended to use ciprofloxacin as first line treatment with doxycycline as an alternative), and personal particulate respirators can be provided (current research is aimed at producing a light weight version that can be worn without discomfort, for prolonged periods of time).

TODAY, TOMORROW

Terrorism has been defined as an act or threat of violence against non-combatants with the object of exacting revenge, intimidating or otherwise influencing an outcome.[9] So why bioterrorism and why now?[31] Traditionally, political terror groups were trying to get a seat at the conference table and to establish the legitimacy of their cause with a few deaths and much publicity. Today, fundamentalists are less interested in establishing legitimacy, so numerous deaths, and wide notoriety are the aims. Examples are the Oklahoma (1996) and World Trade Center New York (1993 and 2001) attacks, the activities of the Aum Shinrikyo, (which had attempted at least four separate bioterrorist strikes, before the Tokyo Sarin attack in 1995) and the Rajneeshee religious cult (which infected 751 people via 10 restaurants, with *Salmonella typhimurium* in an attempt to influence local politics[7] in Wasco County, Oregon). As potential adversaries know they are unable to win a conventional challenge to the U.S. or NATO, they are more likely to try to use so called "asymmetric methods" such as BW.[32]

Any modern pharmaceutical facility can produce BW agents and this dual-use problem also makes it easier for countries to conceal BW programmes. Genetic engineering can be done in a small building with a few PhD researchers, using tabletop equipment, available cheaply worldwide. Kathleen Bailey, former assistant director of U.S. Arms Control and Disarmament Agency is "absolutely convinced" that a major biological arsenal could be built in a room 15 feet square with only $10 000 worth of equipment. In 1995, Larry Harris demonstrated the ease with which BW agents could be obtained when he almost succeeded in receiving cultures of the plague bacillus by Federal Express with no more than a credit card and a false letterhead. Even then the U.S. Authorities could only prosecute him for mail fraud. . . .

To counter BW threats there must be a coordinated response between diplomacy, a military response (whether it be a flexible or an escalatory deterrent), and a defensive approach which would convince political enemies that a credible defensive deterrence against BW exists.[33–35] Such a system would include research and development of adequate real-time detection systems, warning devices, individual and collective protection for military and civilian use (masks, protective clothing and shelters) and medical countermeasures (improved diagnosis, antibiotics and vaccines). An effective system for delivering these measures must also be in place.

Undoubtedly there is a current, and future, need to pursue measures that will prevent acts of terrorism by a combination of integrated efforts. Whatever can be done to strengthen the BTWC deserves all possible support. Increased intelligence capabilities so as to anticipate and interrupt terrorist activity is of the highest priority. International cooperative research programmes to encourage openness and dialogue, as is being done with Russian scientists, are also important, as proposed in Section X of BTWC. Future specific technologies, especially those of genetic engineering, that will impact on BW agent preparation are shown in Table V.[26] Current offensive bioweapons are probably extremely primitive compared to what may be possible 25–50 years from now. There will inevitably be developments in recombinant DNA/genetic engineering, computer-aided orthomolecular drug design, fermentation, mammalian cell culture, peptide synthesis and understanding of the biophysics of cell membranes. Of particular concern is the development of recombinant DNA organisms to target specific races or ethnic groups. . . .

Table V Novel Agents That Could Be Produced by Genetic Engineering

- Benign micro-organisms, genetically altered to produce a toxin, venom or bioregulator
- Micro-organisms resistant to antibiotics, standard vaccines and therapeutics
- Micro-organisms with enhanced aerosol and environmental stability
- Immunologically altered micro-organisms able to defeat standard identification, detection and diagnostic methods
- Combinations of the above four types with improved delivery systems
- Ethnic or racially targeted agents.

Coordinated national contingency arrangements must be made . . . for dealing with a possible attack. At the same time, every effort must be made to achieve a successful conclusion to the negotiations over the protocol to strengthen the verification of the Biological Weapons Convention. This, we believe, offers the best route to achieving a reduction in the possibility that biological weapons will ever be used in warfare or terrorist attacks.

In the meantime we will leave the final word with William S. Cohen, Defence Secretary U.S.A., who in 1997 said, "there is no single defence against this (BW) threat. Instead we must treat it as if it were a chronic disease, being constantly alert to the early symptoms and ready to employ, rapidly, a combination of treatments."

REFERENCES

1. Presidential Decision Directive 39. *Responsibilities to detect, defeat, prevent and manage the consequence of WMD terrorism,* 1997.

2. Presidential Decision Directive 62. *Combating Terrorism Directive,* 1998.

3. Spencer R. C., Wilcox M. H. Agents of biological warfare. *Rev Med Microbiol* 1993; **4:** 138–143.

4. Dando M. R. *Biological warfare in the 21st Century: biotechnology and the proliferation of biological weapons.* London: Brassey's, 1994.

5. World Health Organization. *Health aspects of chemical and biological weapons.* Geneva: WHO, 1970.

6. Kaufmann A. F., Meltzler M. I., Schmid G. P. The economic impact of a bioterrorist attack. *Emerging Infect Dis* 1997; **3:** 83–94.

7. Torok T. J., Tauxe R. V., Wise R. P. *et al.* A large community outbreak of salmonellosis caused by intentional contamination of restaurant salad bars. *JAMA* 1997; **287:** 384–395.

8. Okumara T., Suzuki K., Fukuda A. *et al.* The Tokyo subway sarin attack: disaster management, parts 1–3, community, hospital, national and international responses. *Acad Emerg Med* 1998; **5:** 613–628.

9. Stern J. *The Ultimate Terrorist.* Cambridge, Mass: Harvard, 1999.

10. Rosen P. Coping with bioterrorism. *Br Med J* 2000; **320:** 71–72.

11. Henderson D. A. The looming threat of bioterrorism. *Science* 1999; **283:** 1279–1282.

12. Wise R. Bioterrorism: thinking the unthinkable. *Lancet* 1998; **351:** 1378.

13. Barnham M., Lightfoot N. F. Coping with the bioterrorism threat. *ACP News* 2000; 12–14.

14. Geissler E., van Courtland Moon J. E. (eds.) *Biological and Toxin Weapons: research, development and use from the Middle Ages to 1945*. Oxford: Oxford University Press, 1999.

15. Poupard J. A., Miller L. A. History of biological warfare: catapults to capsomers. *Annals NY Acad Sci* 1992; **666:** 9–20.

16. Wheelis M. Biological warfare before 1914. In: Geissler E., van Courtland Moon J. E. (eds.) *Biological and Toxin Weapons: research, development and use from the Middle Ages to 1945*. Oxford: Oxford University Press 1999, pp 8–34.

17. Wheelis M. Biological sabotage in World War 1. In: Geissler E., van Courtland Moon J. E. (eds.) *Biological and Toxin Weapons: research, development and use from the Middle Ages to 1945*. Oxford: Oxford University Press, pp 35–62.

18. Harris S. Japanese biological warfare research on humans: a case study of microbiology and ethics. *Annals NY Acad Sci* 1992; **666:** 21–52.

19. Carter G. B. *Chemical and Biological Defence at Porton Down: 1916–2000*. London, HMSO, 2000.

20. Carter G. B. Biological warfare and biological defence in the United Kingdom: 1940–1979. *RUSI J* 1992; **137:** 67–74.

21. Alibeck K. *Biohazard*. London: Hutchinson, 1999.

22. Guillemin J. *Anthrax: the Investigation of a Deadly Outbreak*. Berkley, Cal: University of California Press, 1999.

23. Cole L. A. *The Eleventh Plague: Politics of Biological and Chemical Warfare*. New York: WH Freeman, 1997.

24. Pile J. C., Malone J. D., Eitzen E. M., Freidlander A. M. Anthrax as a potential biological warfare agent. *Arch Intern Med* 1998; **158:** 429–434.

25. Dixon T. C., Meselson M., Guillemin J., Hauna P. C. Anthrax—review article. *New Eng J Med* 1999; **341:** 815–825.

26. British Medical Association. *Biotechnology Weapons and Humanity*. Amsterdam: Harwood Academic, 1999.

27. Franz D. R., Jahrling P. B., Friedlander A. M. *et al.* Clinical recognition and management of patients exposed to biological warfare agents. *JAMA* 1997; **278:** 399–403.

28. Noah D. L., Ostroff S. M., Sobel A. L., Kildew J. A. Biological warfare training: infectious disease outbreak differentiation criteria. *Mil Med* 1998; **163:** 198–201.

29. Boiarski A. A., Bowen G. W., Durnford J., Kenny D.V., Shaw M. J. *State-of-the-art report on biological warfare agent detection technologies*. (Rep No: SPO900-94-D-0002). Ft. Belvoir, VA: Chemical and biological defense information analysis center, 1995.

30. Boyle R. E., Laughlin L. L. *History and Technical Evaluation of the U.S. Bio/Toxin Detection Program*. Arlington VA: Battelle Memorial Institute, 1995.

31. Siegrist D. W., Graham J. M. *Countering biological terrorism in the US: an understanding of issues and status*. New York: Oceana Publications, 1999.

32. Newman N. J. *Asymmetric Threats to British Military Intervention Operations*. London: *RUSI*, 2000.

33. Wiener S. L. Strategies of biowarfare defense. *Mil Med* 1987; **152:** 25–32.

34. Lebeda F. J. Deterence of biological and chemical warfare, a review of policy options. *Mil Med* 1997; **162:** 156–161.

35. Office of Technology Assessment. *Proliferation of Weapons of Mass Destruction: assessing the risks*. OTA-ISC-559. United States Congress, 1993.

JOSEPH BARBERA, ANTHONY MACINTYRE, LARRY GOSTIN, TOM INGLESBY, TARA O'TOOLE, CRAIG DeATLEY, KEVIN TONAT, AND MARCI LAYTON

Large-Scale Quarantine Following Biological Terrorism in the United States: Scientific Examination, Logistic and Legal Limits, and Possible Consequences

Joseph Barbera is Professor of Engineering Management and Systems Engineering and Co-Director of the Institute for Crisis, Disaster, and Risk Management at the George Washington University. He was formerly Director of the Disaster Medicine Program at the Ronald Reagan Institute of Emergency Medicine.

Anthony Macintyre is an Assistant Professor of Emergency Medicine at the George Washington University. His interests include disaster medicine, emergency medical services and international emergency medicine. He has published in the *Journal of the American Medical Association.*

Tom Inglesby is the Deputy Director of the Johns Hopkins Center for Civilian Biodefense Studies, and a faculty member of the Division of Infectious Diseases at the Johns Hopkins University School of Medicine. He was a principal designer, author and controller of the *Dark Winter* exercise of June 2001. He has published numerous articles in the *Journal of the American Medical Association* and is a special editor of the section "Confronting Biological Weapons" for the journal *Clinical Infectious Diseases.* He has served in advisory and consultative capacities to federal and state agencies on issues related to bioterrorism preparedness.

Tara O'Toole is the Director of the Johns Hopkins University Center for Civilian Biodefense Strategies and a member of the faculty of the School of Hygiene and Public Health. She has served as Assistant Secretary of Energy for Environment Safety and Health and has been a Senior Analyst at the Congressional Office of Technology Assessment (OTA) directing and participating in studies of health impacts on workers and the public due to environmental pollution resulting from nuclear weapons production, among other projects.

Craig DeAtley is a Physician's Assistant and Associate Professor of Emergency Medicine and Health Care Sciences at the George Washington University Medical Center.

Marcelle Layton is the Assistant Commissioner for Communicable Diseases at the New York City Department of Health.

Reprinted with permission from the *Journal of the American Medical Association* 286 (December 5, 2001), 2711–17. Copyright © 2001 by the American Medical Association.

During the past few years, the US government has grown increasingly concerned about the threat that biological terrorism poses to the civilian population.[1–3] A number of events have occurred that have raised awareness about the potential threat of bioterrorism. These include the suspected attempt to disseminate anthrax by Aum Shinrikyo in Japan,[4] widespread occurrence of bioterrorist hoaxes,[5] and revelations about the bioweapons programs in the former Soviet Union[6] and Iraq.[7] Most recently, the anthrax-related deaths, illnesses, and exposures in Florida and the New York City and Washington, DC, areas have generated even more concern.[8,9] It is now generally acknowledged that a large-scale bioterrorist attack is plausible and could conceivably generate large numbers of seriously ill exposed individuals, potentially overwhelming local or regional health care systems.[10–12] In the event of a large bioterrorist attack with a communicable disease, the potential for person-to-person transmission of the disease would create serious health care and emergency management problems at the local and federal levels.

Throughout history, medical and public health personnel have contended with epidemics and, in the process, evolved procedures to lessen morbidity and mortality. Historically, quarantine was a recognized public health tool used to manage some infectious disease outbreaks, from the plague epidemic in the 13th century to the influenza epidemics of the 20th century. During the past century in the United States, professional medical and public health familiarity with the practice of quarantine has faded. A review of the medical literature found no large-scale human quarantine implemented within US borders during the past 8 decades.[13] Despite this lack of modern operational experience, local, state, and federal incident managers commonly propose or have called for quarantine in the early or advanced stages of bioterrorism exercises.[14] Management of some incidents that later proved to be hoaxes included the quarantine of large numbers of people for periods of hours while the purported biological weapon was analyzed.[4,15] A striking example of the inclination to resort to quarantine was demonstrated during a recent federally sponsored national terrorism exercise, TOPOFF 2000.[16,17] During the biological terrorism component of this drill, a national, large-scale geographic quarantine was imposed in response to a growing pneumonic plague epidemic caused by the intentional release of aerosolized *Yersinia pestis,* the bacteria that causes plague. An array of significant political, practical, and ethical problems became apparent when quarantine was imposed.

Given the rising concerns about the threat of bioterrorism and the concomitant renewed consideration of quarantine as a possible public health response to epidemics, it is important that the implications of quarantine in the modern context be carefully analyzed.

QUARANTINE VS. ISOLATION

One of the first challenges to address is the lack of a precise definition of *quarantine*. In the historical context, quarantine was defined as detention and enforced segregation of persons suspected to be carrying a contagious disease. Travelers or voyagers were sometimes subjected to quarantine before they were permitted to enter a country or town and mix with inhabitants. The term *quarantine* is derived from the Italian *quarante,* which refers to the 40-day sequestration imposed on arriving merchant ships during plague outbreaks of the 13th century.[18]

In the modern era, the meaning of the term *quarantine* has become less clear. The *Oxford English Dictionary* defines *quarantine* as "a period of isolation imposed on a person, animal or thing that might otherwise spread a contagious disease."[19] Unfortunately, during modern bioterrorism response exercises, this term has been used broadly and confusingly to include a variety of public health disease containment measures, including travel limitations, restrictions on public gatherings, and isolation of sick individuals to prevent disease spread. The authors believe it is most appropriate to use *quarantine* to refer to compulsory physical separation, including restriction of movement, of populations or groups of healthy people who have been potentially exposed to a contagious disease, or to efforts to segregate these persons within specified geographic areas. For clarity in this article, this action is termed *large-scale quarantine* to differentiate it from incidents of exposure by only a few persons. To avoid confusion, we do not use the terms *quarantine* and *isolation* interchangeably. We use the term *isolation* to denote the separation and confinement of individuals known or suspected (via signs, symptoms, or laboratory criteria) to be infected with a contagious disease to prevent them from transmitting disease to others.[20,21] It is operationally important that medical and public health emergency managers use accurate terminology.

LEGISLATIVE FRAMEWORK FOR DISEASE CONTAINMENT

The moral authority for human quarantine is historically based on the concept of the public health contract.[22] Under the public health contract, individuals agree to forgo certain rights and liberties, if necessary, to prevent a significant risk to other persons. Civil rights and liberties are subject to limitation because each person gains the benefits of living in a healthier and safer society.[23]

The statutory authority for the imposition of quarantine in the United States originated at a local level during the colonial period. Massachusetts established state quarantine powers in the first comprehensive state public health statute in 1797.[24(pp238–239),25] At approximately the same time (1796), a federal statute authorized the president to assist in state quarantines.[26] The act was later replaced by a federal inspection system for maritime quarantines.[27] Thereafter, the federal government became more active in regulating the practice of quarantine, and a 19th-century conflict between federal and state quarantine powers resulted. In the ensuing federalism debate, the states maintained that they had authority pursuant to police power.[28–30] The federal government maintained that its preeminent authority was derived from regulatory powers over interstate commerce. Today, states are primarily responsible for the exercise of public health powers. However, if the exercise of quarantine clearly would affect interstate commerce, the federal government may claim that its authority is supreme.[31,32] Following is a brief summary of which institutions or levels of government have statutory authority to apply quarantine in distinct contexts.

LOCAL OUTBREAKS IN THE UNITED STATES

When an infectious disease is confined to a specific locale, the authority for quarantine usually rests with local or state public health officials. The authority is generally relinquished to the state when the event affects more than a single community or has the potential to spread across jurisdictional boundaries within the state. The individuality of each state authority has led to a widely divergent group of regulations providing for the use of quarantine.[33] Few local and state jurisdictions, however, have established specific policies and procedures to assist officials in deciding whether an individual event merits imposition of quarantine.[34]

INTERSTATE AND NATIONAL OUTBREAKS

The federal government has the authority to enact quarantine when presented with the risk of transmission of infectious disease across state lines.[35] Legislation stipulates that this is an executive decision to be made by the president. Once the decision has been made, the Centers for Disease Control and Prevention (CDC) is the federal agency authorized to manage federal quarantine actions.[36] The implementation apparatus for such an order could involve federal assets from other agencies, such as the Department of Defense or the Federal Emergency Management Agency, deploying in support of federal, state, or local authorities.[37] The federal government may also assert supremacy in managing specific intrastate incidents if so requested by that state's authorities or if it is believed that local efforts are inadequate.[35,38] Other legal venues for federal action may exist but have not been well delineated.[39]

FOREIGN OUTBREAKS AND US BORDER CONTROL

For travelers seeking to enter the United States, the CDC has the authority to enact quarantine. At the turn of the 20th century, the Marine Hospital Service (forerunner to the modern US Public Health Service) established this federal power.[40] The authority was later delegated to the CDC's Division of Global Migration and Quarantine, currently consisting of 43 employees in the field and 30 at department headquarters in Atlanta, Ga.[41] In areas where Division of Global Migration and Quarantine personnel are not stationed, Immigration and Naturalization Service and US Customs Service personnel are trained to recognize travelers with potential illness of public health significance. While rarely used, detention of arriving individuals, including US citizens, is authorized to prevent the entry of specified communicable diseases into the United States. Using definitions delineated in this article, the detention of arriving passengers with visible signs of illness would be termed *isolation*.[42]

Currently, federal law authorizes cooperative efforts between the federal government and the states related to planning, training, and prevention of disease epidemics and other health emergencies.[43] Despite this, lines of authority between federal and state/local jurisdictions have not been sufficiently tested to ensure that all essential parties have clear understanding of the boundaries and interface between these potentially conflicting authorities. In a large-scale or rapidly evolving natural or deliberate biological incident, confusion and conflict in this public health authority may result. This issue was demonstrated in the TOPOFF exercise.[16,17]

Extensive reviews of the legal basis for quarantine actions have been published elsewhere and will not be reviewed in detail here.[21,44,45] Perhaps the most important understanding that can be extracted from these reviews is that though legal powers exist to quarantine in many contexts, the imposition of quarantine would likely be challenged in the courts using modern interpretations of civil liberties provided by the US Constitution. Additionally, courts have suggested that, in the event of a quarantine, detainees would have to be provided with reasonable amenities to reduce harm (eg, adequate shelter and medical care). Ultimately, extensive quarantines would likely cause the judicial system to become a slow and deliberate arbitrator between the conflicting ideals of public health and individual civil liberties. The CDC and many states are currently in the process of reexamining the legal authority for public health actions, including quarantine.[46,47]

HISTORICAL ILLUSTRATIONS OF ADVERSE CONSEQUENCES OF QUARANTINE

United States history has demonstrated that quarantine actions themselves may cause harm. Large-scale quarantine today can be expected to create similar problems, perhaps to a greater degree. Three historical events in the United States provide examples of the unintended consequences of quarantine implementation.

INCREASED RISK OF DISEASE TRANSMISSION IN THE QUARANTINED POPULATION

One of the most controversial US quarantines was imposed by the New York City Port Authority in 1892 on ships traveling from Europe, where a cholera outbreak had occurred.[48] Cholera had been detected among immigrants, and the subsequent public health response included quarantining passengers aboard arriving vessels. Passengers of lower socioeconomic standing were clearly subjected to separate, more severe conditions than wealthy passengers. Authorities sequestered these impoverished immigrants below deck without sanitary provisions during the confinement. Cholera spread disproportionately among the poor on board the vessels and resulted in at least 58 deaths on one ship alone.[48]

MISTRUST IN GOVERNMENT RECOMMENDATIONS LED TO VIOLENCE

The municipality of Muncie, Indiana, was confronted with an outbreak of smallpox in 1893.[49] Public health officials had great difficulty convincing citizens that intrusive public health actions were necessary, in part because the diagnosis of smallpox was repeatedly challenged. Many infected citizens were isolated under home detention and their presumably uninfected family members were quarantined with them. Entire neighborhoods were quarantined by patrolling armed guards; violators were incarcerated. Mandatory vaccination was instituted. Violence broke out as some civilians resisted the public health impositions, and several public officials were shot. Public health officials ultimately concluded that their quarantine actions had been "an utter failure" as the public had repeatedly defied their quarantine efforts.[49]

ETHNIC BIAS ADVERSELY ALTERED PUBLIC HEALTH DECISION MAKING

A quarantine was instituted in the Chinese neighborhood of San Francisco, California, in 1900, after plague was diagnosed in several inhabitants.[50] The boundaries for the quarantine were arbitrarily established such that only Chinese households and businesses were included. This resulted in severe economic damage to the once-thriving Chinese business community. A federal court found the quarantine unconstitutional on grounds that it was unfair—health authorities acted with an "evil eye and an unequal hand."[51]

KEY CONSIDERATIONS IN QUARANTINE DECISIONS

In most infectious disease outbreak scenarios, there are alternatives to large-scale quarantine that may be more medically defensible, more likely to effectively contain the spread of disease, less challenging to implement, and less likely to generate unintended adverse consequences. Decisions to invoke quarantine, therefore, should be made only after careful consideration of 3 major questions examined within the specific context of a particular outbreak: (1) Do public health and medical analyses warrant the imposition of large-scale quarantine? (2) Are the implementation and maintenance of large-scale quarantine feasible? and (3) Do the potential benefits of large-scale quarantine outweigh the possible adverse consequences?

1. DO PUBLIC HEALTH AND MEDICAL ANALYSES WARRANT THE IMPOSITION OF LARGE-SCALE QUARANTINE?

Decision makers must consider whether large-scale quarantine implementation at the time of discovery of disease outbreak has a reasonable scientific chance of substantially diminishing the spread of disease. There is no valid public health or scientific justification for any type of quarantine in the setting of disease outbreaks with low or no person-to-person transmission, such as anthrax. Despite this, quarantine has been invoked in anthrax bioterrorism hoaxes in recent years.[4,15] Among the many diseases that are termed contagious (ie, capable of being spread by contact with sick persons), only a limited number could pose a serious risk of widespread person-to-person transmission. Of these contagious diseases with potential for widespread person-to-person transmission, only a limited number confer sufficient risk of serious illness or death to justify consideration of the sequestration of large groups or geographic areas. In addition to the agent characteristics, available treatment and prophylaxis options also create the context for the decision process. Public health responses must be accurately tailored to meet the specific risks and resource needs imposed by individual agents.

There are imaginable contexts in which a large-scale smallpox outbreak would generate reasonable considerations for quarantine. But even in the setting of a bioterrorist attack with smallpox, the long incubation period (10–17 days) almost ensures that some persons who were infected in the attack will have traveled great distances from the site of exposure before the disease is recognized or quarantine could be implemented. Subsequent issues with quarantine will remain problematic.

2. ARE THE IMPLEMENTATION AND MAINTENANCE OF LARGE-SCALE QUARANTINE FEASIBLE?

If medical and public health principles lead to a judgment that quarantine is an effective and necessary action to stop the spread of a dangerous disease outbreak, the next set of issues that should be considered involves the logistics of actually establishing the large-scale quarantine. These issues are applicable to local, state, and federal decision makers.

Is There a Plausible Way to Determine Who Should Be Quarantined? Are there practically available criteria for defining and identifying a group or a geographic area that is at higher risk of transmitting a dangerous disease? As noted, depending on the disease-specific incubation period and due to the mobility of modern society, it is probable that a population exposed to a biological weapon will have dispersed well beyond any easily definable geographic boundaries before the infection becomes manifest and any disease containment measures can be initiated. Even within a specific locale, it will be initially impossible to clearly define persons who have been exposed and, therefore, at risk of spreading the disease. A quarantine of a neighborhood would potentially miss exposed individuals, but a large-scale quarantine of a municipality could include many with no significant risk of disease. Currently proposed or functional health surveillance systems have not yet demonstrated adequate proficiency in rapid disease distribution analysis.[52,53]

Are Resources Available to Enforce the Confinement? The human and material resources that would be required to enforce the confinement of large groups of persons, perhaps against their will, would likely be substantial, even in a modest-sized quarantine action. The behavioral reaction of law enforcement or military personnel charged with enforcing quarantine should also be considered. It is possible that fear of personal exposure or public reaction to enforcement actions may compromise police willingness to enforce compliance.

Can the Quarantined Group Be Confined for the Duration During Which They Could Transmit the Disease? Quarantine will not be over quickly. The period during which confined persons could develop disease might be days or weeks, depending on the specific infectious agent. Development of illness among detainees could prolong the confinement of those remaining healthy. Resources and political resolve must be sufficient to sustain a quarantine of at least days, and probably weeks. Furthermore, the multiple needs of detainees must be addressed in a systematic and competent fashion. During previous events, the courts have required that those quarantined be detained in safe and hygienic locations.[44] Adequate food and other necessities must be provided. Competent medical care for those detained is an ethical and possibly constitutional requirement.[21] Transferring supplies across quarantine lines can be difficult, as can recruiting qualified medical personnel to enter quarantined areas. The shortage of trained medical persons to adequately care for quarantine detainees should be anticipated and was clearly demonstrated during the influenza epidemic of 1918.[13,54]

Given the presumption that biological terrorism would impose multiple competing demands for human and material resources within the affected region, decision makers must weigh the costs and benefits of devoting available assets to the maintenance of quarantine.

3. DO THE POTENTIAL BENEFITS OF LARGE-SCALE QUARANTINE OUTWEIGH THE POSSIBLE ADVERSE CONSEQUENCES?

If valid public health and medical principles lead to a judgment that quarantine is an effective and necessary action to stop the spread of a dangerous disease outbreak, and it is established that a quarantine could logistically be put into place, the possible unintended adverse consequences of a quarantine action must then be carefully considered.

What Are the Health Risks to Those Quarantined? As noted herein, there are US historical examples in which persons with clear evidence of infection with a contagious disease have been quarantined together with persons with no evidence of infection.[48,49] It is now beyond dispute that such measures would be unethical today, but a recent event illustrates that this ethical principle might still be disregarded or misunderstood.[55] A passenger returning to the United States was noted to be ill and vomiting on an airline flight, and the passenger's consequent subconjunctival hemorrhages were initially mistaken to be a sign of a coagulopathic infection. On arrival at a major US airport, the plane was diverted and quarantined by airport authorities with all passengers on board, including the potential index case. They were released after an hour-long period of investigation, when public health authorities arrived and concluded that there was no dangerous contagion. Had this been an actual contagious disease, quarantined passengers may have been subjected to an increased risk by continued confinement on the parked aircraft with the ill person. At a minimum, passengers should have been allowed to disembark and remain in an area separate from the index case while this person was being evaluated.

What Are the Consequences if the Public Declines to Obey Quarantine Orders? It is not clear how those quarantined would react to being subjected to compulsory confinement. Civilian noncompliance with these public health efforts could compromise the action and even become violent. Historical quarantine incidents have generated organized civil disobedience and wholesale disregard for authority. Such conditions led to riots in Montreal, Quebec, during a smallpox epidemic in 1885.[24(pp285–286)] Some might lose confidence in government authorities and stop complying with other advised public health actions (eg, vaccination, antibiotic treatment) as well. The possibility also exists for development of civilian vigilantism to enforce quarantine, as occurred in New York City in 1892.[48] The rules of engagement that police are expected to follow in enforcing quarantine must be explicitly determined and communicated in advance. Protection of police personnel and their families against infection would be essential to police cooperation.

What Are the Consequences of Restricting Commerce and Transportation to and from the Quarantine Area? Halting commercial transactions and the movement of goods to and from quarantined areas will have significant economic effects that may be profound and long-term and reach well beyond the quarantined area. Much modern business practice relies on just-in-time supply chains. Shortages of food, fuel, medicines and medical supplies, essential personnel, and social services (sanitation) should be anticipated and provisions must be in place to deal with such issues. Postquarantine stigmatization of the geographic location and of the population quarantined should be anticipated.

CONCLUSIONS AND RECOMMENDATIONS

PUBLIC HEALTH DISEASE CONTAINMENT MEASURES MUST BE BASED ON SCIENTIFIC, DISEASE-SPECIFIC ANALYSIS

The essential first step in developing any disease containment strategy is to determine if the disease at issue is communicable. If not, then no consideration of quarantine should be pursued. If the disease of concern is contagious, then the specific mechanism of disease transmission must drive the disease containment strategy (eg, spread by cough at close distances or possibly over longer range, as has occurred in smallpox outbreaks; infrequent spread by cough at close distance, as in some plague outbreaks; or spread through person-to-person contact, as in Ebola outbreaks). Some progress in delineating disease containment strategies for bioterrorism-induced outbreaks has already occurred in the form of consensus public health and medical recommendations,[56–58] though more diseases must be addressed and public health actions examined. Political leaders in particular need to understand that a single strategy for limiting the spread of all contagious diseases is not appropriate and will not work. The political consequences of public health actions such as large-scale quarantine must also be carefully examined and understood. Modern US disaster response has consistently focused on assistance to those directly affected; in the case of bioterrorism, response will focus on both those potentially infected and those actually infected. With implementation of quarantine, the perception may be that those potentially and actually infected have instead been secondarily harmed by response actions.

In an outbreak of a contagious disease, disease containment may be more effectively achieved using methods that do not attempt to contain large groups of people. As noted, persons with clinical or laboratory evidence demonstrating infection with a contagious disease should be isolated, separate from those who do not have clinical or laboratory evidence of that contagious disease. Depending on the illness, this isolation may be primarily respiratory, body fluid, or skin contact isolation rather than full physical separation from all healthy people.

Additional, population-based public health intervention strategies should also be considered. Depending on the context, rapid vaccination or treatment programs, widespread use of disposable masks (with instructions), short-term voluntary home curfew, restrictions on assembly of groups (eg, schools, entertainment sites), or closure of mass public transportation (buses, airliners, trains, and subway systems) are disease containment steps that may have more scientific credibility and may be more likely to result in diminished disease spread, more practically achievable, and associated with less adverse consequences. For clarity, these alternative disease control measures should not be termed *quarantine* or *quarantine actions*.

INVEST IN NEW INFORMATION TOOLS AND EMERGENCY MANAGEMENT SYSTEMS THAT WOULD IMPROVE SITUATIONAL AWARENESS DURING DISEASE OUTBREAKS

During large-scale contagious disease outbreaks, decision makers would be critically dependent on the availability of timely, accurate information about what is happening and what interventions are desirable and feasible. Emergency management and public health officials will need real-time case data and the analytic capacity to determine the epidemiological parameters of the outbreak to make the most appropriate disease containment decisions. Clinicians will seek information about the natural history and clinical management of the illness and ongoing analyses of the efficacy of treatment strategies. Rapid communication between the medical and public health communities may be especially important and in most locales is currently not conveyed by electronic means or through routine, well-exercised channels.

PROVIDE INCENTIVES TO FOSTER SPECIFIC PUBLIC ACTIONS

Positive incentives may help to persuade the public to take actions that promote disease containment. The ready provision of adequate medical expertise, appropriate vaccines or antibiotics, or distribution of disposable face masks to the public in specific circumstances are examples of incentives that may positively influence population behavior to promote disease containment. Allowing family members to voluntarily place themselves at some defined, calculated risk of infection to care for their sick loved ones might encourage participation in a community's overall disease containment strategy. Assisting family members in these efforts by offering them some forms of protection against the disease could be a valuable aspect of an integrated disease containment strategy. For example, distribution of barrier personal protective equipment and education aimed at discouraging potentially dangerous burial rituals were successful interventions in controlling viral hemorrhagic fever in Africa.[59]

DEVOTE RESOURCES TO DEVELOPING ROBUST PUBLIC COMMUNICATION STRATEGY COMMENSURATE WITH THE CRITICAL IMPORTANCE OF THIS ACTION

The development of strategies for communicating with the public throughout a disease outbreak is of paramount importance. Objectives of this strategy would include informing the public through multiple appropriate channels of the nature of the infectious disease and the scope of the outbreak, providing behavioral guidelines to help minimize spread of illness, and conveying details about how to get prompt access to effective treatment. Ideally, such messages would be conveyed by informed, widely recognized health experts such as the state health commissioner or US surgeon general. In a bioterrorist attack, the media's appetite for information will be limitless and health authorities must be prepared to provide accurate and useful information on a nearly continuous basis.[60] Advanced planning and preparation for such a media storm is essential. Once public credibility is lost, it will be difficult or impossible to recover. A well-informed public that perceives health officials as knowledgeable and reliable is more likely to voluntarily comply with actions recommended to diminish the spread of the disease. Effective information dissemination would work to suppress rumors and anxiety and enlist community support.

It is clear that public health strategies for the control of potential epidemics need to be carefully reevaluated. This process should ensure that civil rights and liberties are kept at the forefront of all discussions, as recently proposed by the congressionally created Gilmore Commission.[3] Further delineation of the authority to impose quarantine is required, and the political and psychological implications must be addressed. Given the complex multidisciplinary nature of this problem, further analysis of possible disease containment strategies would ideally include experts from the fields of medicine, public health, mental health, emergency management, law, ethics, and public communication. The process should specifically examine the various alternatives to quarantine that may be more effective and more feasible in addressing the containment of an infectious outbreak. Strict definition of terms such as *quarantine* must be maintained. With modern, in-depth understanding of specific diseases, more specific and medically valid response is appropriate than that used in the era of poor scientific understanding that established the practice of quarantine. The resulting work from this effort could provide a more comprehensive systems approach to disease containment in general.

Disclaimer: The opinions and findings in this article are those of the authors and should not be construed as official policies or positions of the US Public Health Service or the New York City Department of Health.

REFERENCES

1. *Improving Local and State Agency Response to Terrorist Incidents Involving Biological Weapons: Interim Planning Guide.* Aberdeen, Md: US Army Soldier and Biological Chemical Command, Domestic Preparedness Office; August 1, 2000.

2. *Road Map for National Security: Imperative for Change: The Phase III Report of the United States Commission on National Security/21st Century.* Washington, DC: United States Commission on National Security/21st Century; January 31, 2001.

3. *Toward a National Strategy for Combating Terrorism. Second Annual Report to Congress of the Advisory Panel to Assess Domestic Response Capabilities for Terrorism Involving Weapons of Mass Destruction.* December 15, 2000. Available at: http://www.rand.org/nsrd/terrpanel/terror2.pdf. Accessed October 30, 2001.

4. Senate Government Affairs Permanent Subcommittee on Investigations. Global proliferation of weapons of mass destruction: a case study on the Aum Shinrikyo. October 31, 1995. Available at: http://www.fas.org/irp/congress/1995_rpt/aum/part05.htm. Accessed May 25, 2001.

5. Bioterrorism alleging use of anthrax and interim guidelines for management—United States, 1998. *MMWR Morb Mortal Wkly Rep.* 1999;48:69–74.

6. US General Accounting Office. *Biological Weapons: Effort to Reduce Former Soviet Threat Offers Benefits, Poses New Risks.* Washington, DC: US General Accounting Office; April 2000. GAO/NSIAD-00-138.

7. Zilinskas RA. Iraq's biological weapons: the past as future? *JAMA.* 1997;278:418–24.

8. Notice to readers: ongoing investigation of anthrax—Florida, October 2001. *MMWR Morb Mortal Wkly Rep.* 2001; 50:877.

9. Centers for Disease Control and Prevention. CDC summary of confirmed cases of anthrax and background information. October 23, 2001. Available at: http://www.bt.cdc.gov/DocumentsApp/Anthrax/10232001pm/10232001pm.asp. Accessed October 24, 2001.

10. Carter A., Deutsch J., Zelicow P. Catastrophic terrorism. *Foreign Affairs.* 1998;77:80–95.

11. Office of Technology Assessment. *Proliferation of Weapons of Mass Destruction.* Washington, DC: Government Printing Office; 1993. OTA-ISC-559, 53–55.

12. Cilluffo F., Cardash S., Lederman G. *Combating Chemical, Biological, Radiological and Nuclear Terrorism: A Comprehensive Strategy.* Washington, DC: Center for Strategic and International Studies Homeland Defense Project; May 2001.

13. Gemhart G. A forgotten enemy: PHS's fight against the 1918 influenza pandemic. *Public Health Rep.* 1999;114:559–561.

14. Mayor's Office of Emergency Management, New York City. *Draft After Action Report for Operation RED-Ex Recognition, Evaluation, and Decision Making Exercise.* New York, NY: Mayor's Office of Emergency Management; May 2001.

15. Horowitz S. B'nai B'rith package contained common bacteria. *Washington Post.* April 29, 1997:B2.

16. *Top Officials (TOPOFF) 2000 Exercise Observation Report Volume 2: State of Colorado and Denver Metropolitan Area.* Washington, DC: Office for State and Local Domestic Preparedness Support, Office of Justice Programs, Dept of Justice, and Readiness Division, Preparedness Training, and Exercises Directorate, Federal Emergency Management Agency; December 2000.

17. Inglesby T. Lessons from TOPOFF. Presented at: Second National Symposium on Medical and Public Health Response to Bioterrorism; November 28, 2000; Washington, DC.

18. Cumming H. The United States quarantine system during the past 50 years. In: Ravenel M, ed. *A Half Century of Public Health.* New York, NY: American Public Health Association; 1921:118–32.

19. *Oxford English Dictionary*. 2nd ed. Oxford, England: Oxford University Press; 1989:983.

20. Jackson M., Lynch P. Isolation practices: a historical perspective. *Am J Infect Control*. 1985;13:21–31.

21. Gostin L. *Public Health Law: Power, Duty, Restraint*. New York, NY, and Berkeley, Calif: Milbank Memorial Fund and University of California Press; 2000.

22. Merritt D. The constitutional balance between health and liberty. *Hastings Cent Rep*. December 1986: 2–10.

23. Gostin L. Public health, ethics, and human rights: a tribute to the late Jonathan Mann. *J Law Med Ethics*. 2001;29:121–130.

24. Hopkins D. *Princes and Peasants: Smallpox in History*. Chicago, Ill: University of Chicago Press; 1983.

25. Chapin C. State and municipal control of disease. In: Ravenel M, ed. *A Half Century of Public Health*. New York, NY: American Public Health Association; 1921:133–160.

26. Act of May 27, 1796, ch 31, 1 Stat 474 (repealed 1799).

27. Act of February 25, 1799, ch 12, 1 Stat 619.

28. Freund E. *The Police Power: Public Policy and Constitutional Rights*. New York, NY: Amo Press; 1904:124–130.

29. Lee B. H. Limitations imposed by the federal constitution on the right of the states to enact quarantine laws. *Harvard Law Rev*. 1889;2:267, 270–82.

30. *Hennington v Georgia,* 163 US 299, 309 (1896).

31. *Gibbons v Ogden,* 22 US 1, 205–06 (1824).

32. *Compagnie Française de Navigation á Vapeur v Louisiana State Bd of Health,* 186 US 380, 388 (1902).

33. Gostin L. Controlling the resurgent tuberculosis epidemic: a 50-state survey of TB statutes and proposals for reform. *JAMA*. 1993;269:255–61.

34. Conright K. TOPOFF 2000: lessons learned from the Denver venue. Presented at: National Disaster Medical System Conference on Lifesaving Interventions; April 28, 2001; Dallas, Tex.

35. 42 USC §264a (2001).

36. 65 *Federal Register* 49906 (2000) (in reference to 21 CFR §1240).

37. United States Government Interagency Domestic Terrorism Concept of Operations Plan. January 2001. Available at: http://www.fas.org/irp/threat/conplan.html. Accessed May 4, 2001.

38. 65 *Federal Register* 49906 (2000) (amendment in reference to: Measures in the event of inadequate control, 42 USC §70.2).

39. Gostin L. Public health law in a new century, II: public health powers and limits. *JAMA*. 2000;283:2979–84.

40. Knight W. The history of the US Public Health Service. 1999. Available at: http://www.usphs.gov/html/history.html. Accessed November 4, 2001.

41. Centers for Disease Control and Prevention, Division of Global Migration and Quarantine. History of quarantine. Available at: http://www.cdc.gov/ncidod/dq/history.htm. Accessed April 28, 2001.

42. Centers for Disease Control and Prevention. *Public Health Screening at US Ports of Entry: A Guide for Federal Inspectors*. Atlanta, Ga: National Center for Infectious Disease; March 2000. Available at: http://www.cdc.gov/ncidod/dq/operations.htm. Accessed November 4, 2001.

43. 42 USC §243a (2001).

44. Gostin L. The future of public health law. *Am J Law Med.* 1990;16:1–32.

45. Parmet W. AIDS and quarantine: the revival of an archaic doctrine. *Hofstra Law Rev*. 1985;14:53–90.

46. Gostin L. Public health law reform. *Am J Public Health.* 2001;91:1365–68.

47. Cole T. When a bioweapon strikes, who will be in charge? *JAMA*. 2000;284:944–48.

48. Markel H. "Knocking out the cholera": cholera, class, and quarantines in New York City, 1892. *Bull Hist Med.* 1995; 69:420–57.

49. Eidson W. Confusion, controversy, and quarantine: the Muncie smallpox epidemic of 1893. *Indiana Magazine of History*. 1990;LXXXVI:374–98.

50. Risse G. "A long pull, a strong pull, and all together": San Francisco and Bubonic Plague, 1907–1908. *Bull Hist Med.* 1992;66:260–86.

51. *Jew Ho v Williamson,* 103 F1024 (CCD Cal 1900).

52. Defense Advanced Research Projects Agency epidemiology software used during presidential inauguration [press release]. March 9, 2001. Available at: http://www.darpa.mil/body/newsitems/encompass_release.doc. Accessed November 4, 2001.

53. Centers for Disease Control and Prevention. Supporting public health surveillance through the National Electronic Disease Surveillance System (NEDSS). Available at: http://www.cdc.gov/nchs/otheract/phdsc/presenters/nedss.pdf. Accessed April 14, 2001.

54. Ross I. The influenza epidemic of 1918. *American History Illustrated*. 1968;3:12–17.

55. Szanislo M. Plane quarantined due to passenger's illness. *Boston Herald*. October 25, 2000:2.

56. Inglesby T. V., Henderson D. A., Bartlett J. G., et al, for the Working Group on Civilian Biodefense. Anthrax as a biological weapon: medical and public health management. *JAMA*. 1999;281:1735–1745.

57. Henderson D. A., Inglesby T. V., Bartlett J. G., et al, for the Working Group on Civilian Biodefense. Smallpox as a biological weapon: medical and public health management. *JAMA*. 1999;281:2127–37.

58. Inglesby T. V., Dennis D. T., Henderson D. A., et al, for the Working Group on Civilian Biodefense. Plague as a biological weapon: medical and public health management. *JAMA*. 2000; 283:2281–90.

59. Outbreak of Ebola hemorrhagic fever—Uganda, August 2000–January 2001. *MMWR Morb Mortal Wkly Rep*. 2001; 50:73–77.

60. Ball-Rokeach S., Loges W. Ally or adversary? using media systems for public health. *Prehosp Dis Med*. 2000;15:62–69.

LAWRENCE O. GOSTIN

Law and Ethics in a Public Health Emergency

Lawrence Gostin is professor of law at Georgetown University and professor of public health at the Johns Hopkins University. He is also director of the Center for Law and the Public's Health and editor of the Health Law and Ethics section of the *Journal of the American Medical Association.* His latest book is *Public Health Law: Power, Duty, Restraint* (University of California Press, 2000).

In 1974, the Surgeon General informed Congress that it was time to "close the book on infectious diseases." So sure was the United States that modern biomedicine would solve the problem of infectious diseases that government was already cutting funding from state and local public health agencies and beginning a massive build-up of biotechnology research and development. Having declared victory over infectious diseases, the new war would be waged against diseases of modern western civilization, principally cardiovascular disease and neoplasms.

The United States was also unconcerned about bioterrorism. To be sure, America has experienced bioterrorism in 1984 when the Rajneeshee cult contaminated salad bars in rural Oregon, causing over 750 cases of Salmonella poisoning. But the government and citizenry felt that America's geographic isolation meant it would be relatively immune from upheavals abroad.

Of course, the perception of safety and security evaporated on 11 September 2001. And then on 4 October, authorities confirmed the first cases of inhalational anthrax in Florida, beginning a period in which five people died, hundreds were tested, and thousands treated. Although the method of delivery through the postal service was inefficient, the anthrax outbreak exposed the nation's vulnerability.

A sustained debate ensued about the public health system's preparedness to detect and respond quickly and effectively to bioterrorism and naturally occurring infectious diseases. Do public health agencies have sufficient laboratory capacity, information systems, and work force? Are there sufficient stockpiles of safe and effective vaccines and treatments? Do health and safety agencies efficiently share information and coordinate activities? Is communication to the public clear and authoritative? Unfortunately, the answer to these questions, and many others, is that the United States is ill prepared.[1]

CRUMBLING FOUNDATIONS

The lack of preparedness for bioterrorism and naturally occurring infectious diseases is due primarily to insufficient financing. Before the recent influx of funding for homeland security,[2] traditional population-based public health services received approximately 1 percent of all health dollars, with the rest going to health care and biotechnology.[3] At the federal level, over 95 percent of the health budget went to nondiscretionary spending, principally Medicaid and Medicare. Congress allocated half of the remaining 5 percent to the National Institutes of Health, whose budget has been approximately doubling in each of the last several years. The Public Health Service agencies together shared the remainder.[4] Even in the president's new bioterrorism budget for homeland security, biotechnology and health care take the lion's share leaving relatively little for prevention.[5]

What is wrong with this picture? Expenditures on biotechnology and health care are not improper, but they are now out of proportion to the benefit derived.

From the *Hastings Center Report* 32 (March–April 2002), 9–11. Reprinted with permission of the author and the Hastings Center.

Biotechnology and health care contribute to only a small percentage of the population's health (estimated at less than 5 percent), but receive an inordinately high percentage of health funding (more than 95 percent). On the other hand, population-based services (such as sanitation, pure food and water, safe products and roads) contribute much more to health and longevity, but have been starved of resources.[6]

Individual health care services dominate federal and state budgets because of the values dominant in America. Both ends of the political spectrum celebrate personal freedom and choice—the political left emphasizes civil liberties while the political right focuses on markets and free enterprise. In this political climate, the public sees government as inefficient and burdensome. People would rather see ever-increasing advances in clinical medicine and freedom of choice in health care than stable and well-funded agencies regulating for the public welfare. The nation has lost the tradition of classical republicanism that valued the collective benefits of health, safety, and security.[7]

PUBLIC HEALTH LAW REFORM

Another important reason for the lack of preparedness is that public health laws are antiquated. Many of these laws date back to the early twentieth century and predate modern science, medicine, and constitutional law.[8] Consequently, these laws do not provide a clear mission, essential services, or powers necessary for public health agencies to be effective.[9] These antiquated laws are often unconstitutional since they lack clear standards and procedural safeguards. Vague public health care laws may be challenged in a crisis, adding to indecision and delay; more fundamentally, existing laws do not provide a hedge against arbitrary action and unfairness in the exercise of public health powers.

To rectify the problems of antiquity, inadequacy, and unfairness, the Robert Wood Johnson "Turning Point" program funded the development of a model public health law in collaboration with a consortium of states. The "Public Health Statute Modernization" Project, which began in 2001, had a three-year time horizon, with little public and political impetus for speedy reform. Following the events of 11 September and 4 October, however, the need for law reform captured the attention of political leaders. On 6 October, I received a call from Gene Matthews, general counsel of the Centers for Disease Control and Prevention (CDC), asking the Center for Law and the Public's Health to draft a Model State Emergency Health Powers Act (MSEHPA). Because the CDC feared the governors would introduce their own legislation in the absence of a model, Matthews asked for a draft within three to four weeks.

That began an intensive drafting process in collaboration with members of the National Governors Association, the National Conference of State Legislatures, the National Association of Attorneys General, the Association of State and Territorial Health Officials, and the National Conference of State and National Association of County and City Health Officials. The model law, or a version of it, has been introduced in nearly half of the states, with many more expected to consider it.

MSEHPA has been developed using an open and deliberative process. Federal agencies such as the CDC and Department of Justice provided intellectual support during its development, as did high-level staff of state governors, legislators, attorney generals, and health commissioners. The Center for Law and the Public's Health received thousands of comments about the model law from national organizations, academic institutions, practitioners, corporations, and the general public, and it has been widely discussed in the media.[10] Despite this rigorous and inclusive process, it has provoked criticism from a civil liberties and property rights perspective. As one governor's chief of staff said in a private meeting commenting on the model law: "The far left has met the far right, leaving the vast majority of Americans in the middle unprotected."

THE MODEL LAW

MSEHPA (available at www.publichealthlaw.net) is intended to support the vital functions of public health agencies while safeguarding personal and proprietary interests: planning, surveillance, management of property, and protection of persons. The planning and surveillance functions would be implemented immediately, but the measures affecting property and persons would be triggered only after a state's governor declares a public health emergency.

Declaration of a Public Health Emergency. A public health emergency is narrowly defined in the model law as involving an imminent threat caused by bioterrorism or a new or re-emerging infectious agent or biological toxin that poses a high probability of a large number of deaths or serious disabilities. Civil libertarians objected to a previous draft of the definition on two grounds: that it would permit compulsory powers against persons living with HIV/AIDS, and that state governors would have too much discretion. In response, the definition of a public health emergency was modified to exclude endemic diseases such as HIV/AIDS and to place checks on the governor. The legislature may, by majority vote, discontinue the state of emergency at any time. Similarly, the judiciary may overturn an emergency declaration if the governor has not complied with the standards and procedures in the model law. This reflects a preference for constitutional checks and balances, providing a role for each branch of government.

Emergency Planning. The governor must appoint a Public Health Emergency Planning Commission to design a plan for coordination of services; procurement of necessary materials and supplies; housing, feeding, and caring for affected populations; and vaccination and treatment. The planning requirement is important because most states do not have a systematic design for handling a public health emergency. Planning raises significant ethical issues, notably the proper criteria allocating vaccines, medicines, and health care services. On what basis should scarce resources be allocated: need, benefit, age, or utility? The model law does not resolve the numerous ethical or policy issues but insists that a rational plan be devised through a deliberative process.

Surveillance. MSEHPA addresses measures necessary to detect and monitor infectious disease outbreaks. It requires prompt disease reporting, interviewing, and contact tracing. Existing law often does not facilitate, and may even hinder, surveillance. For example, most states do not require reporting of many of the critical agents of bioterrorism.[11] Consequently, if a case of smallpox or hemorrhagic fever is known or suspected, there is no assurance that public health authorities will be promptly notified. MSEHPA also facilitates exchange of health information if necessary to prevent, identify, or investigate a public health emergency. Existing state laws, due to privacy concerns, often prohibit the sharing of health information between public health agencies and health care organizations, and among public health agencies in different states. While individuals have the right to expect a certain amount of privacy to prevent harms and embarrassment, a balance needs to be struck to ensure public health and safety. Consider the potential impact of a case of bioterrorism in New York City, if a health officer could not exchange data with the public safety officer, monitor hospitals and pharmacies for unusual clusters of symptoms, or obtain health records from New Jersey or Connecticut.

Management of Property. MSEHPA authorizes the public health authority to close, decontaminate, or procure facilities and materials to respond to a public health emergency; dispose of infectious waste safely; perform appropriate burials; and obtain and deploy health care supplies. These powers are necessary to ensure sufficient availability of vaccines, medicines, and hospital beds, and sufficient power to regulate, close, or destroy dangerous facilities. The political right has engaged in a sustained attack on these provisions, claiming that they interfere with the freedom to own and control personal property. Indeed, the drafters have been lobbied by virtually every major corporate sector, including the food, transportation, hospital, and pharmaceutical industries, some of which have hired large law firms to help press their case.

Although the right to possess and enjoy private property is important, owners have always been subject to the restriction that property not be used in a way that poses a health hazard.[12] MSEHPA provides a right of compensation to owners only if the government "takes" private property for public purposes—if, for example, it confiscates private stocks of drugs to treat patients or takes over a private hospital to quarantine persons exposed to infection. No compensation would be provided for a "nuisance abatement"—closing a facility that poses a public health threat or destroying property contaminated with smallpox or anthrax. Although entrepreneurs may complain that such private losses are unfair, MSEHPA fully comports with modern constitutional law and enlightened public policy.[13] If government were forced to compensate for all nuisance abatements, it would significantly chill public health regulation.

Protection of Persons. MSEHPA permits public health authorities to physically examine, test, vaccinate, or treat individuals to prevent or ameliorate an infectious condition, and to isolate or quarantine individuals to prevent or limit the transmission of an infectious disease. Civil libertarians have argued that individuals should be neither confined nor compelled to receive vaccines or treatment. But this view has never been accepted even in the most liberal societies. It is generally accepted that persons who pose a significant risk to the public may be subject to restraint. MSEHPA's powers of vaccination, treatment, and civil confinement are not new, but have been part of public health law since the founding of the republic. The exercise of these powers has also been upheld by the courts on grounds of community health and security: "There are manifold restraints to which every person is necessarily subject for the common good. On any other basis organized society could not exist with safety to its members."[14]

To ensure an appropriate sphere of liberty and justice, MSEHPA contains many safeguards that do not exist in most statutes: vaccines and treatments cannot be imposed on persons who would suffer harm; cultural and religious beliefs must be respected; and the needs of persons isolated or quarantined must be met, including food, clothing, shelter, and health care. Orders for isolation or quarantine are subject to judicial review, with full procedural due process.

THE FUTURE OF PUBLIC HEALTH

In many ways, America has the public health system it deserves—under-funded, ill prepared, and dispirited. The government has starved public health agencies of resources, allowing the public health infrastructure to deteriorate. The public has valued high-glamour genetics and high-technology biomedicine over basic prevention and population-based services. And the legislature has neglected the legal foundations of public health. The law lacks a coherent vision of an appropriate mission, essential services, powers, and safeguards for public health agencies.

The *Institute of Medicine Report on Public Health Preparedness,* due to be published this year, will set out the intellectual critique of the public health system. The events of 11 September and 4 October will provide the impetus for change. Now it is time to change the nation's values, priorities, and funding to recognize the overwhelming importance of assuring the conditions in which the people can be healthy, safe, and secure.

NOTES

1. Institute of Medicine, *The Future of Public Health* (Washington, D.C.: National Academy Press, 1988); Centers for Disease Control and Prevention, *Pubilc Health's Infrastructure: A Status Report,* submitted to the Appropriations Committee of the United States Senate in 2001.

2. Protecting the Homeland: The President's Budget for 2003 (4 February 2002), available at http://www.whitehouse.gov/omb/budget/fy2003/pdf/bud05.pdf, at p. 5.

3. K.W. Eilbert et al., *Measuring Expenditures for Essential Public Health Services* 17 (Washington, D.C.: Public Health Foundation, 1996). See also Centers for Disease Control, "Estimated National Spending on Prevention: United States, 1988," *Morbidity & Mortality Weekly Report* 41 (1992): 529, 531.

4. See J.I. Boufford and P.R. Lee, *Health Policies for the 21st Century: Challenges and Recommendations for the U.S. Department of Health and Human Services* (New York: Milbank Memorial Fund, 2001).

5. S. Gorman, "Shortchanging Prevention?" *National Journal,* 9 February 2002, 391.

6. L.O. Gostin, J.P. Koplan, and F. Grad, "The Law and the Public's Health: The Foundations," in *Law in Public Health Practice,* ed. R.A. Goodman, et al. (New York: Oxford University Press, forthcoming).

7. D.E. Beauchamp, "Community: The Neglected Tradition of Public Health," *Hastings Center Report* 15 (1985): 28–36.

8. L.O. Gostin, S. Burris, and Z. Lazzarini, "The Law and the Public's Health: A Study of Infectious Disease Law in the United States," *Columbia Law Review* 99 (1999): 59–128.

9. L.O. Gostin, "Public Health Law Reform," *American Journal of Public Health* 91 (2001): 1365–68.

10. J. Gillis, "States Weighing Laws to Fight Bioterrorism." *The Washington Post,* 19 November 2001.

11. H. Horton et al., "Disease Reporting as a Tool for Bioterrorism Preparedness," *Journal of Law, Medicine and Ethics,* forthcoming.

12. Commonwealth v. Alger, 7 Cush. 53, 84–85 (1851).

13. Lucas v. South Carolina Coastal Council, 505 U.S. 1992 (1992).

14. Jacobson v. Massachusetts, 197 U.S. 11, 26 (1905).

GEORGE J. ANNAS

Bioterrorism, Public Health, and Civil Liberties

George Annas is Edward R. Utley Professor and Chair, Health Law Department, Boston University Schools of Medicine and Public Health. He is the author or editor of a dozen books on health law and ethics, including *The Rights of Patients: The Basic ACLU Guide to Patient Rights* (Humana Press), *Some Choice: Law, Medicine, and the Market* (Oxford University Press), and *Standard of Care: Law of American Bioethics* (Oxford University Press). He has held a variety of regulatory positions including Chair of the Massachusetts Health Facilities Appeals Board, Vice-Chair of the Massachusetts Board of Registration in Medicine, and Chair of the Massachusetts Organ Transplant Task Force.

The prospect of having to deal with bioterrorist attack, especially one involving smallpox, has local, state, and federal officials rightly concerned.[1,2] Before September 11, most procedures for dealing with a bioterrorist attack against the United States were based on fiction. Former President Bill Clinton became engaged in the bioterrorism issue in 1997, after reading Richard Preston's novel *The Cobra Event.*[3] In Tom Clancy's 1996 *Executive Orders,*[4] the United States is attacked by terrorist using a strain of Ebola virus that is transmissible through the air. To contain the epidemic, the President declares a state of emergency, orders that all nonessential businesses and places of public assembly be closed, and suspends all interstate travel by airplane, train, bus, and automobile. In defending the order, the fictional President makes a statement that is now often used to justify major changes in our criminal laws: "The Constitution is not a suicide pact."[4]

The anthrax attacks through the U.S. mail demonstrated that the federal government must provide better planning, coordination, and communication with the public, as well as better drugs and vaccines.[5,6] What remains more controversial is whether we must give up any civil liberties to deal with this "different kind of war." What steps should the government take to prepare for a bioterrorist attack involving the use of smallpox or another contagious agent, and which level of government, state or federal, should take the lead?

Reprinted with permission from the *New England Journal of Medicine* 346 (April 25, 2002), 1337–42. Copyright © 2002 by the Massachusetts Medical Society.

BIOTERRORISM AND PUBLIC HEALTH

The prospect of a bioterrorist attack and the actual attacks in Florida, the District of Columbia, New York, New Jersey, and Connecticut have changed public health in the United States. Since the founding of the country, public health has been considered primarily the business of the states. The reason is that when the former colonies delegated powers to the federal government in the U.S. Constitution, they retained the authority to protect the public's health and safety, usually referred to as the state's "police powers."[7,8] The federal government may, nonetheless, affect public health and safety through its constitutional authority to spend money, regulate interstate and foreign commerce, and provide for national defense. The Congress established the Public Health Service and the Centers for Disease Control and Prevention (CDC) with federal money and used its authority under the commerce clause of the Constitution to establish the Food and Drug Administration (FDA). The creation of these federal agencies, however, did not alter the states' responsibility for public health; the anthrax attacks did.

Bioterrorism—the deliberate release of a harmful biologic agent to intimidate civilians and their government—constitutes a threat to public health that differs from any other public health threat that our country has faced. An act of bioterrorism is both a state and a federal crime, and it can also be an act of war.[9] Because of our highly developed transportation system, communicable diseases can be spread widely in a short period of time. All these factors make it reasonable to view bioterrorism as an inherently federal matter under both the national-defense and commerce clauses of the Constitution. Thus, the Federal Bureau of Investigation (FBI) and the CDC took the lead in investigating all the anthrax mail attacks. Moreover, had the attacks originated outside the country, the U.S. military and the Central Intelligence Agency would have been called on to respond.

BUILDING A MODERN PUBLIC HEALTH SYSTEM

In the immediate aftermath of the September 11 attacks and the subsequent anthrax attacks through the U.S. mail, hospitals, cities, states, and federal officials began developing or revisiting protocols to deal with possible biologic attacks in the future. The federal response has so far emphasized the stockpiling of drugs and vaccines that could be used to respond to an attack, especially one involving smallpox.[10] Other proposals have included improving the public health infrastructure of the country (especially the ability to monitor diagnoses made in emergency departments and pharmacy sales of relevant drugs) and training emergency medical personnel to recognize and treat the diseases most likely to be caused by a bioterrorist attack (such as anthrax, smallpox, and plague).[11] Major efforts are also under way to improve coordination and communication among local, state, and federal officials who are responsible for responding to emergencies and to delineate more clearly the lines of authority involving "homeland security." All these measures are reasonable and responsible steps our government should take.

Properly worried that many state public health laws are outdated and perhaps inadequate to permit state officials to contain an epidemic caused by a bioterrorist attack, the CDC has advised all states to review the adequacy of their laws, with special attention to provisions for quarantining people in the event of a smallpox attack.[12] In addition, the CDC released a proposed model act for the states, the Model State Emergency Health Powers Act, on October 23, 2001.[12,13] The act was constructed by the Center for Law and the Public's Health at Georgetown University and Johns Hopkins University and was pieced together from a variety of existing state laws.

THE ORIGINAL MODEL STATE EMERGENCY HEALTH POWERS ACT

The original model act permits the governor to declare a "state of public health emergency," and this declaration, in turn, gives state public health officials the authority to take over all health care facilities in the state, order physicians to act in certain ways, and order citizens to submit to examinations and treatment, with those who refuse to do so subject to quarantine or criminal punishment. The model act specifies that public health officials and those working under their authority are immune from liability for their actions, including actions that cause permanent injury or death; the only exceptions are in cases of gross negligence and willful misconduct. A public health emergency (the condition that requires the governor to declare a state of public health emergency) is defined as "an occurrence or imminent threat or an illness or health condition, caused by bioterrorism, epidemic or pandemic disease, or [a] novel and highly fatal infectious agent or biological toxin, that poses a substantial risk of a significant number of human fatalities or incidents of permanent or long-term disability.[13]

The declaration of a state of public health emergency permits the governor to suspend state regulations, change the functions of state agencies, and mobilize the militia. Under the model act, all public health personnel will be issued special identification badges, to be worn "in plain view," that "shall indicate the authority of the bearer to exercise public health functions and emergency powers. . . .[13] Public health personnel may "compel a health care facility to provide services or the use of its facility if such services or use are reasonable and necessary for emergency response . . . [including] transferring the management and supervision of the health care facility to the public health authority."

According to the act's provisions, public health personnel have exceptionally broad powers, and failure of physicians and citizens to follow their orders is a crime. Section 502 of the act, which covers mandatory medical examinations and testing, states:

> Any person refusing to submit to the medical examination and/or testing is liable for a misdemeanor. If the

public health authority is uncertain whether a person who refuses to undergo medical examination and/or testing may have been exposed to an infectious disease or otherwise poses a danger to public health, the public health authority may subject the individual to isolation or quarantine. . . . Any [health care provider] refusing to perform a medical examination or test as authorized herein shall be liable for a misdemeanor. . . . An order of the public health authority given to effectuate the purposes of this subsection shall be immediately enforceable by any peace officer.[13]

Section 504, on vaccination and treatment, states, "Individuals refusing to be vaccinated or treated shall be liable for a misdemeanor. If, by reason of refusal of vaccination or treatment, the person poses a danger to the public health, he or she may be subject to isolation or quarantine. . . . An order of the public health authority given to effectuate the purposes of this Section shall be immediately enforceable by any peace officer."[13]

THE NEED FOR NEW STATE LAWS ON BIOTERRORISM

Of course, state public health, police, fire, and emergency planners should be clear about their authority, and to the extent that it encourages states to review their emergency laws, the model act is constructive. On the other hand, many of the provisions of this act, especially those giving public health officials authority over physicians and hospitals, as well as authority to enforce a quarantine in the absence of meaningful standards, seem to be based on the assumption that neither physicians nor citizens are likely to cooperate with public health officials in the event of a bioterrorist attack. This assumption, in turn, seems to be based on the results of theoretical planning exercises involving simulated bioterrorist attacks, including the Top Officials 2000 (Top Off) and Dark Winter exercises.[12] Top Off was an exercise that simulated a bioterrorist attack on Denver that involved the use of aerosolized *Yersinia pestis,* the bacteria that causes plague.[14] Dark Winter simulated a smallpox attack on Oklahoma City.[15] Using these simulated cases as a basis for legislation is unreasonable, given the extremely high level of voluntary cooperation on the part of the public, physicians, and hospitals after both the September 11 terrorist attacks and the subsequent anthrax attacks.

In my opinion, the model act poses several problems. First, proposed laws should respond to real problems. It is not at all clear what problem the model act is intended to solve, and this makes it extremely difficult to evaluate.

Second, the authority to respond to a bioterrorist attack or a new epidemic that the model act provides is much too broad, since it applies not just to real emergencies such as a smallpox attack but also to nonemergency conditions as diverse as annual influenza epidemics and the AIDS epidemic.[16,17]

Third, although it may make sense to put public health officials in charge of responding to a smallpox attack, it may not make sense to put them in charge of responding to every type of bioterrorist event. In the event of a bioterrorist attack, the state public health department has a major role in limiting the public's exposure to the agent. However, the tasks of identifying affected persons, reporting them, treating them, and taking preventive actions will be performed by physicians, nurses, emergency medical personnel, and hospitals. The primary role of public health authorities will usually be, as it was in the wake of the anthrax attacks, to provide guidance to the public and other government officials in identifying and dealing with the disease and to provide laboratory facilities where exposure can be evaluated and diagnoses definitively established.[5,6,18]

Fourth, there is no evidence from either the September 11 attacks or the anthrax attacks that physicians, nurses, or members of the public are reluctant to cooperate in the response to a bioterrorist attack or are reluctant to take drugs or vaccines recommended by public health or medical officials. In fact, medical personnel in the affected areas volunteer their time and expertise to help victims of the September 11 attacks, and the public lined up to be tested for anthrax and stockpiled ciprofloxacin.[19] The public demand for testing and treatment was so great that the CDC had to issue recommendations against both.

Of course, anthrax, unlike smallpox, is not spread from person to person. The situation might have been different if smallpox had been used as a biologic weapon or if thousands or tens of thousands of people had been infected with anthrax. Nonetheless, there is no empirical evidence that draconian provisions for quarantine, such as those outlined in the model act, are necessary or desirable. Persons with smallpox, for example, are most infectious only after fever and a rash have developed,[12] and then they are usually so sick that they are likely to accept whatever care is available. Moreover, according to Barbera et al., the "long incubation period (10–17 days) almost ensures that some persons who are infected in the [smallpox] attack will have traveled great distances from the site of the exposure before the disease is recognized or quarantine could be implemented."[14] The key to an effective public health response is identifying and helping those who have been exposed. Even with a sufficient supply of smallpox vaccine, a quarantine enforced by the police would probably not be effective in controlling an outbreak of smallpox.[12,14,20] This is a major reason for the current recommendation that smallpox vaccine be made available to the public on a voluntary basis.[21]

Finally, even if it is concluded that a quarantine law may be useful to respond to a bioterrorist attack (e.g., as a means of ensuring that the few unwilling Americans, if any, would be treated, vaccinated, or quarantined), it should be a federal law, not a state law. The reason is that bioterrorism is a matter of national security, not just of state police powers. The existing federal quarantine law is based on the commerce clause of the Constitution (with special provisions for cholera, plague, smallpox, typhus, and yellow fever), and Congress could examine and update it to deal with bioterrorism.[22,23] The governors of the states involved in the anthrax attacks all realized that bioterrorism is fundamentally a federal issue and quickly called for action from both the FBI and the CDC to deal with the attacks.

CIVIL LIBERTIES AND PUBLIC HEALTH EMERGENCIES

The model act is based on the belief that in public health emergencies, there must be a trade-off between the protection of civil rights and effective public health interventions. There is, of course, precedent for this belief, and the preamble to the model act cites the 1905 case of *Jacobson v. Massachusetts* in stating the proposition that "the whole people covenants with each citizen, and each citizen with the whole people, that all shall be governed by certain laws for the 'common good.' "[8,13] *Jacobson v. Massachusetts* involved a state statute that permitted local boards of health to require vaccination when they deemed it "necessary for the public health or safety." There were no provisions for quarantine in the statute, and refusal to be vaccinated was punishable by a $5 fine. Refusal was anticipated in the early 1900s because vaccination itself was controversial, there were no antibiotics, physicians were not widely trusted, science and medicine were in their infancy, and hospitals were primarily "pesthouses."[24] Trade-offs between civil liberties (the right to refuse treatment) and public health interventions (mandatory vaccination) seemed necessary in such circumstances.[25]

In *Jacobson v. Massachusetts,* the Supreme Court cited the military draft as the precedent for upholding the Massachusetts law. The point is not that the Constitution does not give the government wide latitude to respond in times of war and public health emergencies—it does. The point is that trade-offs between civil rights and public health measures are not always required and can be counterproductive. Just as we have been able to abolish the draft and rely on all-volunteer armed forces, so it seems reasonable to think that we can rely on Americans to follow the reasonable instructions of government officials for their own protection.

Today, almost 100 years after *Jacobson,* both medicine and constitutional law are radically different.[7] We now take constitutional rights much more seriously, including the right of a competent adult to refuse any medical treatment, even life-saving treatment.[26] Of course, we would still permit public health officials to quarantine persons with a serious communicable disease, such as infectious tuberculosis, but only if they could not or would not accept treatment and thus put others at risk for exposure.[27] Even then, however, we would require public officials to use the "least restrictive alternative" and resort to quarantine only after other interventions, such as directly observed therapy, had failed.[27] Provisions for quarantine are also accompanied by due-process rights, including the right to legal representation and the right to a hearing.[27]

The model act seems to have been drafted for a different age; it is more appropriate for the United States of the 19th century than for the United States of the 21st century. Today, all adults have the constitutional right to refuse examination and treatment, and such a refusal should not result in involuntary confinement simply on the whim of a public health official. At the very least, persons suspected of having a contagious disease should have the option of being examined by physicians of their own choice and, if isolation is necessary, of being isolated in their own homes.[27] The requirement that physicians treat patients against their will and against the physicians' medical judgement under penalty of criminal law has no precedent and makes no sense. Moreover, state governors already have broad emergency powers; there is no compelling reason to expand them.

Just as important as the constitutional questions posed by the model act is the pragmatic question of whether it is likely to undermine the public's trust in public health—trust that is absolutely essential for containing panic in a bioterrorist-induced epidemic. Unlike the situation at the turn of the last century, for example, we have televised news 24 hours a day, cell phones, and automobiles, making a large-scale quarantine impossible unless the public believes that it is absolutely necessary to prevent the spread of fatal disease and is fairly and safely administered. Enactment of a law that made it a crime to disobey a public health officer would rightly engender distrust, because it would suggest that public officials could not provide valid reasons for their actions.

The necessity of maintaining the public's trust also means that the argument that, in a public health emergency, there must be a trade-off between effective public health measures and civil rights is simply wrong. As the AIDS epidemic has demonstrated, the promotion of human rights can be essential for dealing effectively with an epidemic.[28] Early in the course of the AIDS epidemic, public health officials recognized that mandatory screening for human immunodeficiency virus would simply help drive the epidemic underground, where it would spread faster and wider. Likewise, draconian quarantine measures would probably have the unintended effect of encouraging people to avoid public health officials and physicians rather than to seek them out. In this regard, the protection of civil liberties is a core ingredient in a successful response to a bioterrorist attack. Provisions that treat citizens as the enemy, with the use of the police for enforcement, are much more likely to cost lives than to save them. This is one reason why there has not been a large-scale quarantine in the United States for more than 80 years and why experts on bioterrorism doubt that such a quarantine wold be effective.[14,20]

THE REVISED MODEL ACT

On December 21, 2001, in response to criticisms of the model act, including those I have summarized, a revised version was released.[29] No one any longer considers the act a "model." Instead, it is now labeled a "draft for discussion." The new version does "not represent the official policy, endorsement, or views" of anyone, including the authors themselves and the CDC.[29]

Although the revised act can be viewed as a modest improvement, all the fundamental problems remain. Failure to comply with the orders of public health officials for examination or treatment is no longer a crime but results in isolation or quarantine. Criminal penalties continue to apply to failure to follow isolation or quarantine "rules" that will be written at a future time. Physicians and other health care providers can still be required "to assist" public health officials, but cooperation is now coerced as "a condition of licensure" instead of a legal requirement with criminal penalties for noncompliance. The quarantine provisions have been improved, with a new requirement that quarantine or isolation be imposed by "the least restrictive means necessary" and stronger due-process protection, including hearings and legal representation for those actually quarantined.[29] Nonetheless, on the basis of a written directive by a public health official, a person can still be quarantined for 15 days before a hearing must be held, and the hearing itself can be for groups of quarantined persons rather than individuals.[29]

Some of the revised quarantine provisions seem even more arbitrary. A major criticism of the original version of the act was the extreme vagueness of its standard for quarantine, which invited the arbitrary use of force. According to the original version, quarantine can be ordered if a public health official is "uncertain whether a person who refused to undergo medical examination or testing may have been exposed to an infectious disease or otherwise poses a danger to public health." In the revised version, the standard is even vaguer. Quarantine can be ordered when the person's refusal to be examined or tested "results in uncertainty regarding whether he or she has been exposed to or is infected with a contagious or possibly contagious disease or otherwise poses a danger to public health."[29] This is no standard at all; it simply permits public health authorities to quarantine anyone who refuses to be examined or treated, for whatever reason, since all refusals will result in uncertainty. If one were already certain, one would not order the test. At the hearing, if requested, the standard for a continued quarantine appears to be the finding that the person would "significantly jeopardize the public health authority's ability to prevent or limit the transmission of a contagious or possibly contagious disease to others." This standard also makes no sense because the public health focus, I think, should be on the person's condition and on the determination of whether it poses a danger to others, not on the public health authority's ability to function.

These vague standards are especially troublesome because the act's incredible immunity provision remains unchanged. Thus, all state public health officials and all private companies and persons operating under their authority are granted immunity from liability for their actions (except for gross negligence or willful misconduct), even in the case of death or permanent injury. Out-of-state emergency health care providers have even greater protection; they are given immunity from liability for everything but manslaughter. In my opinion, such immunity is something public health authorities should not want (even though it may have superficial appeal), because it means that they are not accountable for their actions, no matter how arbitrary. The immunity provision thus serves only to undermine the public's trust in public health authorities. Citizens should never be treated against their will by their government, but if they ever are, they should be fully compensated for injuries suffered as a result.

CONCLUSIONS

All sorts of proposals were floated in the wake of the September 11 attacks—some potentially useful, such as irradiation of mail at the facilities that had been targeted, and some potentially dangerous, such as the use of secret military tribunals and measures that would erode lawyer–client confidentiality, undermine our constitutional values, and make us less able to criticize authoritarian countries for similar behavior. I think the Model State Emergency Health Powers Act is one of the dangerous proposals.

Bioterrorism is primarily a federal, not a state, issue, and actions undertaken to prevent and respond to bioterrorism should be a federal priority.[30] Laws that provide funding for training in the recognition and treatment of diseases caused by pathogens that could be used as biologic weapons deserve support, as do laws that improve communication and coordination in response to such an attack. The Biological and Toxin Weapons Convention also deserves our support.[31] In my opinion, laws that treat Americans and their physicians as the enemy and grant broad, arbitrary powers to public health officials without making them accountable do not deserve support and distract us from important work that needs to be done. The fear and frenzy that prompted state legislatures to consider new antiterrorist laws after September 11 seem to have abated, and reason may yet prevail over panic.[32] Of course the Constitution is not a suicide pact, but we do not have to sacrifice civil liberties for an effective public health response to a bioterrorist attack.

REFERENCES

1. Tucker J. B. Scourge: the once and future threat of smallpox. New York: Atlantic Monthly Press, 2001.
2. Gillis J., Connolly C. U.S. details response to smallpox: cities could be quarantined and public events banned. Washington Post. November 27, 2001:A1.
3. Preston R. The cobra event. New York: Random house, 1997.
4. Clancy T. Executive orders. New York: G.P. Putnam, 1996.
5. Lipton E., Johnson K. Tracking bioterror's tangled course. New York Times. December 26, 2001:A1.
6. Altman L. K., Kolata G. Anthrax missteps offer guide to fight next bioterror battle. New York Times. January 6, 2002 (Section 1):1.
7. Wing K. R. The law and the public's health. 5th ed. Chicago: Health Administration Press, 1999.
8. Jacobson v. Massachusetts, 197 U.S. 11 (1905).
9. Fidler D. P. The malevolent use of microbes and the rule of law: legal challenges presented by bioterrorism. Clin Infect Dis 2001;33:686–9.
10. Stolberg S. G. Health secretary testifies about germ warfare defenses. New York Times. October 4, 2001:B7.
11. Miller J., Engelberg S., Broad W. Germs: biological weapons and America's secret war. New York: Simon & Schuster, 2001.
12. Interim smallpox response plan and guidelines, for distribution to state and local public health bioterrorism response planners, November 21, 2001 draft. Guide C: isolation and quarantine guidelines. Atlanta: Centers for Disease Control and Prevention, 2001.
13. The Model State Emergency Health Powers Act: as of October 23, 2001. Atlanta: Centers for Disease Control and Prevention, 2001. (Accessed April 5, 2002, at http://www.publichealthlaw.net/MSEHPA/MSEHPA.pdf.)
14. Barbera J., Macintyre A., Gostin L., et al. Large-scale quarantine following biological terrorism in the United States: scientific examination, logistic and legal limits, and possible consequences. JAMA 2001;286:2711–7. [Reprinted in this chapter.]
15. Marlands L. Bioterror: all the rules change. Christian Science Monitor. December 17, 2001:1.
16. Marlands L. Bioterror act: the wrong response. National Law Journal. December 17, 2001:18.
17. Parmet W. E., Mariner W. K. A health act that jeopardizes public health. Boston Globe. December 1, 2001:A15.
18. Stolberg S. G., Miller J. Bioterror role an uneasy fit for the C.D.C. New York Times. November 11, 2001;A1.
19. Martinez B., Harris G. Anxious patients plead with doctors for antibiotics. Wall Street Journal. October 15, 2001:B1.
20. Osterholm M. T., Schwartz J. Living terrors: what American needs to know to survive the coming bio-terrorist catastrophe. New York: Delacorte Press, 2000.
21. Bicknell W. J. The case for voluntary smallpox vaccination. N Engl J Med 2002:346:1323–5.
22. Public Health Service Act, as amended, 42 U.S.C. 264 (1983).

23. Quarantine, inspection, licensing: interstate quarantine, 42 C.F.R. 70.1-8 (2000).

24. Rosenberg C. E. The care of strangers: the rise of America's hospital system. New York: Basic Books, 1987.

25. Albert M. R., Ostheimer K. G., Breman J. G. The last smallpox epidemic in Boston and the vaccination controversy, 1901–1903. N Engl J Med 2001;344:375–9.

26. Annas G. J. The bell tolls for a constitutional right to physician-assisted suicide. N Engl J Med 1997;337:1098–103.

27. *Idem.* Control of tuberculosis: the law and the public's health. N Engl J Med 1993;328:585–8.

28. Mann J. M., Gostin L., Gruskin S., Breman T., Lazzarini Z., Fineberg H. V. Health and human rights. Health Hum Rights 1994;1:6–23.

29. The Model State Emergency Health Powers Act: as of December 21, 2001. Atlanta: Centers for Disease Control and Prevention, 2001. (Accessed April 5, 2002, at http://www.publichealthlaw.net/MSEHPA/MSEHPA2.pdf.)

30. Kellman B. Biological terrorism: legal measures for preventing a catastrophe. Harv J Law Public Policy 2001;24:417–85.

31. Scharf M. P. Clear and present danger: enforcing the international ban on biological and chemical weapons through sanctions, use of force, and criminalization. Mich J Int Law 1999;20:477–521.

32. Gavin R. Frenzy to adopt terrorism laws starts to recede. Wall Street Journal. March 27, 2002:B1.

SUGGESTED READINGS

ETHICS AND PUBLIC HEALTH

Adler, Nancy and Newman, Katherine. "Socioeconomic Disparities in Health: Pathways and Policies. Inequality in Education, Income, and Occupation Exacerbates the Gaps between the Health 'Haves' and 'Have-Nots.' " *Health Affairs* 21 (March–April 2002), 60–76.

Albert, Michael R.; Ostheimer, Kristen G.; and Breman, Joel G. "The Last Smallpox Epidemic in Boston and the Vaccination Controversy, 1901–1903." *New England Journal of Medicine* 344 (2001), 375–79.

Beauchamp, Dan E., and Steinbock, Bonnie, eds. *New Ethics for the Public's Health*. New York: Oxford University Press, 1999.

Bhutta, Zulfiqar. "Ethics in International Health Research: A Perspective from the Developing World." *Bulletin of the World Health Organization* 80 (2002), 114–20.

Bradley, Peter, and Burls, Amanda, eds. *Ethics in Public and Community Health*. New York: Routledge, 2000.

Callahan, Daniel, and Jennings, Bruce. "Ethics and Public Health: Forging a Strong Relationship." *American Journal of Public Health* 92 (2002), 169–76.

Coughlin, Steven S.; Goodman, Kenneth W.; and Soskolne, Colin L., eds. *Case Studies in Public Health Ethics*. Washington, DC: American Public Health Association Publications, 1997.

Evans, Timothy; Diderichsen, Finn; Bhuiya, Abbas; Wirth, Meg; and Whitehead, Margaret, eds. *Challenging Inequities in Health: From Ethics to Action*. New York: Oxford University Press, 2001.

Gostin, Lawrence O. *Public Health Law: Power, Duty, Restraint.* Berkeley, CA: University of California Press, 2000.

———. *Public Health Law and Ethics: A Reader*. Berkeley, CA: University of California Press, 2002.

Hodges, Frederick M.; Svoboda, J. Steven; and Van Howe, Robert S. "Prophylactic Interventions on Children: Balancing Human Rights with Public Health." *Journal of Medical Ethics* 28 (2002), 10–16.

Levin, Betty Wolder, and Fleischman, Alan R. "Public Health and Bioethics: the Benefits of Collaboration." *American Journal of Public Health* 92 (2002), 165–67.

McGinnis, J. Michael; Williams-Russo, Pamela; and Knickman, James R. "The Case for More Active Policy Attention to Health Promotion. To Succeed, We Need Leadership That Informs and Motivates, Economic Incentives That Encourage Change, and Science That Moves the Frontiers." *Health Affairs* 21 (March–April 2002), 78–93.

Mechanic, David. "Disadvantage, Inequality, and Social Policy. Major Initiatives Intended to Improve Population Health May Also Increase Health Disparities." *Health Affairs* 21 (March–April 2002), 48–59.

Roberts, Marc, and Reich, Michael R. "Ethical Analysis in Public Health." *Lancet* 359 (2002), 1055–59.

Schuklenk, Udo, and Ashcroft, Richard E. "Affordable Access to Essential Medication in Developing Countries: Conflicts between Ethical and Economic Imperatives." *Journal of Medicine and Philosophy* 27 (2002), 179–95.

Tauber, Alfred I. "Medicine, Public Health, and the Ethics of Rationing." *Perspectives in Biology and Medicine* 45 (2002), 16–30.

Upshur, Ross. "Principles for the Justification of Public Health Intervention." *Canadian Journal of Public Health* 93 (2002), 101–103.

AIDS: GENERAL ISSUES

Allen, James R., et al. "AIDS: The Responsibilities of Health Professionals." *Hastings Center Report* 18, special supplement (April-May 1988), S1–S32.

Almond, Brenda, ed. *AIDS: A Moral Issue—The Ethical, Legal and Social Aspects*. New York: St. Martin's Press, 1990.

Battin, Margaret P. "Going Early, Going Late: The Rationality of Decisions about Suicide in AIDS." *Journal of Medicine and Philosophy* 19 (1994), 571–94.

Bayer, Ronald. "Science, Politics, and AIDS Prevention Policy." *Journal of Acquired Immune Deficiency Syndromes and Human Retrovirology* 14, supplement 2 (1997), S22–S29.

———. "AIDS: I. Public-Health Issues." In Warren Thomas Reich, ed., *Encyclopedia of Bioethics*. Rev. ed. New York: Simon & Schuster Macmillan, 1995: 108–13.

———. "AIDS and Ethics." In Robert M. Veatch, ed. *Medical Ethics*. 2d ed. Sudbury, MA: Jones and Bartlett, 1997: 395–413.

———, and Stryker, Jeff. "Ethical Challenges Posed by Clinical Progress in AIDS." *American Journal of Public Health* 87 (1997), 1599–1602.

———. *Private Acts, Social Consequences: AIDS and the Politics of Public Health*. New York: Free Press, 1989.

———. "Science, Politics, and AIDS Prevention Policy." *Journal of Acquired Immunodeficiency Syndromes and Human Retrovirology.* 14 (suppl. 2; 1997), 522–29.

Benatar, Solomon. "AIDS in the 21st Century." *New England Journal of Medicine* 342 (2000), 515–17.

———. "The HIV/AIDS Pandemic: A Sign of Instability in a Complex Global System." *Journal of Medicine and Philosophy* 27 (2002), 163–77.

Berridge, Virginia. *AIDS in the UK: The Making of a Policy, 1981–1994.* New York: Oxford University Press, 1996.

Blendon, Robert J.; Donelan, Karen; and Knox, Richard A. "Public Opinion and AIDS: Lessons for the Second Decade." *Journal of the American Medical Association* 267 (1992), 981–86.

Brandt, Allan M. "The Syphilis Epidemic and Its Relationship to AIDS." *Science* 239 (1988), 375–80.

Brennan, Troyen A. "The Challenge of AIDS." In Troyen A. Brennan, *Just Doctoring: Medical Ethics in the Liberal State*. Berkeley, CA: University of California Press, 1991, 147–74, 264–68.

Cameron, Miriam E. *Living with AIDS: Experiencing Ethical Problems*. Newbury Park, CA: Sage, 1993.

Cook, Molly, et al. "Informal Caregivers and the Intention to Hasten AIDS-Related Death." *Archives of Internal Medicine* 158 (1998), 69–75.

Daniels, Norman. "Insurability and the HIV Epidemic: Ethical Issues in Underwriting." *Milbank Quarterly* 68 (1990), 497–525.

Dickens, Bernard M. "Legal Rights and Duties in the AIDS Epidemic." *Science* 239 (188), 580–87.

Epstein, Steven. *Impure Science: AIDS, Activism, and the Politics of Knowledge*. Berkeley, CA: University of California Press, 1996.

Erin, Charles A., and Harris, John. "AIDS: Ethics, Justice, and Social Policy." *Journal of Applied Philosophy* 10 (1993), 167–73.

Faden, Ruth R., and Kass, Nancy E., eds. *HIV, AIDS, and Childbearing: Public Policy, Private Lives.* New York: Oxford University Press, 1996.

———. "Women as Vessels and Vectors: Lessons from the HIV Epidemic." In Susan M. Wolf, ed., *Feminism and Bioethics: Beyond Reproduction*. New York: Oxford University Press, 1996, 252–81.

Foley, Kathleen M. "Competent Care for the Dying Instead of Physician-Assisted Suicide" [Editorial]. *New England Journal of Medicine* 336 (1997), 54–58.

Gostin, Lawrence O. "The AIDS Litigation Project: A National Review of Court and Human Rights Commission Decisions" [Two Parts]. *Journal of the American Medical Association* 263 (1990), 1961–70, 2086–93.

———, ed. *AIDS and the Health Care System.* New Haven: Yale University Press, 1990.

———, and Lazzarini, Zita. *Human Rights and Public Health in the AIDS Pandemic*. New York: Oxford University Press, 1997.

———, et al. "Prevention of HIV/AIDS and Other Blood-Borne Diseases among Injection Drug Users: A National Survey on the Regulation of Syringes and Needles." *Journal of the American Medical Association* 277 (1997), 53–62.

———, and Webber, David W. "HIV Infection and AIDS in the Public Health and Health Care Systems: The Role of Law and Litigation." *Journal of the American Medical Association* 279 (1998), 1108–13.

Graubard, Stephen R., ed. *Living with AIDS*. Cambridge, MA: MIT Press, 1990.

Hastings Center. *AIDS: An Epidemic of Ethical Puzzles*. Brookfield, VT: Dartmouth, 1991.

Humber, James M., and Almeder, Robert F. *Biomedical Ethics Reviews, 1988: AIDS and Ethics*. Clifton, NJ: Humana Press, 1989.

Institute of Medicine, Committee for the Oversight of AIDS Activities. *Confronting AIDS: Update 1988*. Washington, DC: National Academy Press, 1988.

Juengst, Eric T., and Koenig, Barbara A., eds. *The Meaning of AIDS: Implications for Medical Science, Clinical Practice, and Public Health Policy*. New York: Praeger, 1989.

Kahn, James. "Success and Sadness." *Journal of the American Medical Association* 280 (1998), 89.

Kass, Nancy E., et al. "Homosexual and Bisexual Men's Perceptions of Discrimination in Health Services." *American Journal of Public Health* 82 (1992), 1277–79.

Kondro, Wayne. "Canadian AIDS Doctor Convicted of Physician-Assisted Suicide." *Lancet* 351 (1998), 121.

Kopelman, Loretta M., and van Niekerk, Anton A. "AIDS and Africa." *Journal of Medicine and Philosophy* 27 (2002), 139–42.

Lo, Bernard. "Ethical Dilemmas in HIV Infection: What Have We Learned?" *Law, Medicine and Health Care* 20 (1992), 92–103.

———. "AIDS: II. Health-Care and Research Issues." In Warren Thomas Reich, ed., *Encyclopedia of Bioethics*. Rev. ed. New York: Simon & Schuster Macmillan, 1995, 113–20.

Loewy, Erich H., ed. "Ethical and Communal Issues in AIDS." Thematic issue. *Theoretical Medicine* 11 (1990), 173–226.

Mann, Jonathan, and Tarantola, Daniel, eds. *AIDS in the World II: Global Dimensions, Social Roots, and Responses*. New York: Oxford University Press, 1996.

———, and Netter, Thomas W., eds. *AIDS in the World: A Global Report*. Cambridge, MA: Harvard University Press, 1992.

McKenzie, Nancy F., ed. *The AIDS Reader: Social, Political, Ethical Issues*. New York: Meridian, 1991.

Miller, Heather G.; Turner, Charles F.; and Moses, Lincoln E., eds. *AIDS: The Second Decade*. Washington, DC: National Academy Press, 1990.

Minkoff, Howard, & Santoro, Nanette. "Ethical Considerations in the Treatment of Infertility in Women with Human Immunodeficiency Virus Infection." *New England Journal of Medicine* 342 (2000), 1748–50.

Mohr, Richard D. *Gays/Justice: A Study of Ethics, Society, and Law*. New York: Columbia University Press, 1988.

Murphy, Timothy F. "No Time for an AIDS Backlash." *Hastings Center Report* 21 (March-April 1991), 7–11.

———. "AIDS." In Ruth Chadwick, ed., *Encyclopedia of Applied Ethics*. San Diego, CA: Academic Press, 1998, 111–22.

National Research Council, Commission on Behavioral and Social Sciences and Education, Committee on AIDS Research and the Behavioral, Social, and Statistical Sciences. *AIDS: Sexual Behavior and Intravenous Drug Use*. Edited by Charles F. Turner, Heather G. Miller, and Lincoln E. Moses. Washington, DC: National Academy Press, 1989.

———, Panel on Monitoring the Social Impact of the AIDS Epidemic. *The Social Impact of AIDS in the United States.* Washington, DC: National Academy Press, 1993.

Nelkin, Dorothy; Willis, David P.; and Parris, Scott V., eds. *A Disease of Society: Cultural and Institutional Responses to AIDS*. New York: Cambridge University Press, 1991.

Nichols, Eve K., Institute of Medicine, National Academy of Sciences. *Mobilizing against AIDS*. Newly rev. and enlarged ed. Cambridge, MA: Harvard University Press, 1989.

Parmet, Wendy E., and Jackson, Daniel J. "No Longer Disabled: The Legal Impact of the New Social Construction of HIV." *American Journal of Law and Medicine* 23 (1997), 7–43.

Onwuteaka-Philipsen, Bregje D., and van der Wal, Gerrit. "Cases of Euthanasia and Physician Assisted Suicide among AIDS Patients Reported to the Public Prosecutor in North Holland." *Public Health* 112 (1998), 53–56.

Pierce, Christine, and VanDeVeer, Donald, eds. *AIDS: Ethics and Public Policy*. Belmont, CA: Wadsworth, 1990.

Reamer, Frederic G., ed. *AIDS and Ethics*. New York: Columbia University Press, 1991.

Rosenbrock, Rolf; Dubois-Arber, Francoise; Moers, Martin; Pinell, Patrice; Schaeffer, Doris; and Setbon, Michel. "The Normalization of AIDS in Western European Countries." *Social Science & Medicine* 50 (2000), 1607–29.

Ross, Lainie Friedman. "Genetic Exceptionalism vs. Paradigm Shift: Lessons from HIV." *Journal of Law, Medicine and Ethics* 29 (2001), 141–48.

Rubenstein, William B.; Eisenberg, Ruth; and Gostin, Lawrence O. *The Rights of People Who Are HIV Positive: The Authoritative ACLU Guide to the Rights of People Living with HIV Disease and AIDS*. Carbondale, IL: Southern Illinois University Press, 1996.

Schuklenk, Udo; Chokevivat, Vichai; Del Rio, Carolos; Gbadegesin, Segun; and Magis, Carlos. "AIDS in the Developing World." In Ruth Chadwick, ed., *Encyclopedia of Applied Ethics*. San Diego, CA: Academic Press, 1998, 123–27.

———, ed. *AIDS: Society, Ethics and Law*. Hampshire, UK: Ashgate, 2001.

Shilts, Randy. *And the Band Played On*. New York: Penguin, 1988.

Slome, Lee R., et al. "Physician-Assisted Suicide and Patients with Human Immunodeficiency Virus Disease." *New England Journal of Medicine* 336 (1997), 417–21.

United Nations Joint United Nations Programme on HIV/AIDS (UNAIDS) and World Health Organization. *AIDS Epidemic Update*. Geneva: UNAIDS/WHO, 2001.

U.S. Congress. "Americans with Disabilities Act of 1990" (Public Law No. 101-336). *[United States] Statutes at Large* 104, pp. 327 ff.

U.S. National Commission on AIDS. *AIDS: An Expanding Tragedy—The Final Report of the National Commission on AIDS*. Washington, DC: U.S. Government Printing Office, 1993.

Walters, LeRoy. "Ethical Issues in the Prevention and Treatment of HIV Infection and AIDS." *Science* 239 (1988), 597–603.

Wang, Yan Guang. "AIDS and Bioethics: Ethical Dilemmas Facing China in HIV Prevention: A Report from China." *Bioethics* 11 (1997), 323–27.

Weinberg, Peter D.; Hounshell, Jennie; Sherman, Laurence A.; Godwin, John; Ali, Shirin; Tomori, Cecilia; et al. "Legal, Financial, and Public Health Consequences of HIV Contamination of Blood and Blood Products in the 1980s and 1990s." *Annals of Internal Medicine* 136 (2002), 312–19.

Wolffers, Ivan. "Biomedical and Development Paradigms in AIDS Prevention." *Bulletin of the World Health Organization* 78 (2000), 267–73.

Zhu, T. "An African HIV-1 Sequence from 1959 and Implications for the Origin of the Epidemic." *Nature* 391 (February 5, 1998), 594–97.

THE DUTY TO WARN AND THE DUTY NOT TO HARM

Altman, Lawrence L. "Sex, Privacy and Tracking H.I.V. Infections." *New York Times,* November 4, 1997, Al.

Bayer, Ronald. "AIDS Prevention—Sexual Ethics and Responsibility." *New England Journal of Medicine* 334 (1996), 1540–42.

———. "Discrimination, Informed Consent, and the HIV Infected Clinician." *British Medical Journal* 314 (1997), 915–16.

Bird, Sheila M., and Leigh Brown, Andrew J. "Criminalisation of HIV Transmission: Implications for Public Health in Scotland." *British Medical Journal* 323 (2001) 1174–77.

Blatchford, Oliver; O'Brien, Sarah J.; Blatchford, Mary; and Taylor, Avril. "Infectious Health Care Workers: Should Patients Be Told?" *Journal of Medical Ethics* 26 (2000), 27–33.

Brennan, Troyen A. "Transmission of the Human Immunodeficiency Virus in the Health Care Setting—Time for Action." *New England Journal of Medicine* 324 (1991), 1504–09.

Christie, Timothy. "Recalcitrant HIV-Positive Persons: The Problem of People Who Are Unwilling or Unable to Prevent the Transmission of Communicable Diseases." *Health Law in Canada* 20 (2000), 53–57.

Cochran, Susan D., and Mays, Vickie M. "Sex, Lies, and HIV." *New England Journal of Medicine* 322 (1990), 774–75.

Daniels, Norman. "HIV-Infected Professionals, Patient Rights, and the 'Switching Dilemma.'" *Journal of the American Medical Association* 267 (1992), 1368–71.

Dickens, Bernard M. "Confidentiality and the Duty to Warn." In Lawrence O. Gostin, ed., *AIDS and the Health Care System*. New Haven: Yale University Press, 1990, 98–112, 259–61.

Erridge, Peter. "The Rights of HIV Infected Healthcare Workers: Ignoring Them May Put the Public at Risk" [Editorial]. *British Medical Journal* 312 (1996), 1625–26.

Fein, Esther B. "Medical Professionals with H.I.V. Keep Silent, Fearing Reprisals." *New York Times,* December 21, 1997, 41, 45.

Fleck, Leonard, and Angell, Marcia. "Please Don't Tell!" [Case Study]. *Hastings Center Report* 21 (November-December 1991), 39–40.

Freedman, Benjamin. "Violating Confidentiality to Warn of a Risk of HIV Infection: Ethical Work in Progress." *Theoretical Medicine* 12 (1991), 309–23.

Gostin, Larry. "The HIV-Infected Health Professional: Public Policy, Discrimination, and Patient Safety. *Law, Medicine and Health Care* 18 (1990), 303–10.

Harris, John, and Holm, Søren. "Is There a Moral Obligation Not to Infect Others?" *British Medical Journal* 311 (1995), 1215–17.

Lo, Bernard, and Steinbrook, Robert. "Health Care Workers Infected with the Human Immunodeficiency Virus: The Next Steps." *Journal of the American Medical Association* 267 (1992), 1100–05.

Macklin, Ruth. "HIV-Infected Psychiatric Patients: Beyond Confidentiality." *Ethics and Behavior* 1 (1991), 3–20.

Murphy, Timothy F. "Health Care Workers with HIV and a Patient's Right to Know." *Journal of Medicine and Philosophy* 19 (1994), 553–69.

Rose, Joseph W. "To Tell or Not To Tell: Legislative Imposition of Partner Notification Duties For HIV Patients." *Journal of Legal Medicine* 22 (2001), 107–23.

Rothenberg, Karen H., and North, Richard L. "Partner Notification and the Threat of Domestic Violence against Women with HIV Infection." *New England Journal of Medicine* 329 (1993), 1194–96.

———, and Paskey, Stephen J. "The Risk of Domestic Violence and Women with HIV Infection: Implications for Partner Notification, Public Policy, and the Law." *American Journal of Public Health* 85 (1995), 1569–76.

———, et al. "Domestic Violence and Partner Notification: Implications for Treatment and Counseling of Women with HIV." *Journal of the American Medical Women's Association* 50 (1995), 87–93.

Schoeman, Ferdinand. "AIDS and Privacy." In Frederic G. Reamer, ed., *AIDS and Ethics*. New York: Columbia University Press, 1991: 240–76.

Schorr, Andrew F. "Health Care Workers, Patients, and HIV: An Analysis of the Policy and Ethical Debate." *Pharos* 58 (1995), 7–13.

Simon, Stephanie; Hartz, Jay N.; and Micco, Guy. "A Family's

Right to Know?" [Case Study and Commentaries]. *Cambridge Quarterly of Healthcare Ethics* 6 (1997), 93–99.

Simone, Simone J., and Fulero, Solomon M. "Psychologists' Perceptions of Their Duty to Protect Uninformed Sex Partners of HIV-Positive Clients." *Behavioral Sciences and the Law* 19 (2001), 423–36.

Smolkin, Doran. "HIV Infection, Risk Taking, and the Duty to Treat." *Journal of Medicine and Philosophy* 22 (1997), 55–74.

Stein, Michael D. "Sexual Ethics: Disclosure of HIV-Positive Status to Partners." *Archives of Internal Medicine* 158 (1998), 253–57.

U.S. Supreme Court. *Bragdon v. Abbott*. June 25, 1998. United States [Supreme Court] Reports No. 97–156.

TESTING, SCREENING, AND REPORTING PROGRAMS

Akiki, Faith Spicer. "The Focus on Women Kampala Declaration: Ugandan Women Call for Action on HIV/AIDS." *British Medical Journal* 324 (2002), 247.

American College of Obstetricians and Gynecologists. "Human Immunodeficiency Virus: Ethical Guidelines for Obstetricians and Gynecologists." *ACOG Committee Opinion* 255 (2001).

Ammann, Arthur J. "Unrestricted Routine Prenatal HIV Testing: The Standard of Care." *Journal of the American Medical Women's Association* 50 (1995), 83–84.

Angell, Marcia. "A Dual Approach to the AIDS Epidemic" [Editorial]. *New England Journal of Medicine* 324 (1991), 1498–1500.

Asch, David A., and Patton, James P. "Conflicts over Post-Exposure Testing for Human Immunodeficiency Virus: Can Negotiated Settlements Help?" *Journal of Medicine and Philosophy* 19 (1994), 41–59.

Bassett, Mary Travis. "Ensuring a Public Health Impact of Programs to Reduce HIV Transmission from Mothers to Infants: The Place of Voluntary Counseling and Testing." *American Journal of Public Health* 92 (2002), 347–51.

Bayer, Ronald, and Fairchild, Amy L. "Women's Rights, Babies' Interests: Politics, and Science in the Debate of Newborn HIV Screening." In Howard L. Minkoff.; Jack A. DeHovitz; and Ann Duerr, eds. *HIV Infection in Women*. New York: Raven Press, 1995, 293–307.

———. "Rethinking the Testing of Babies and Pregnant Women for HIV Infection." *Journal of Clinical Ethics* (1996), 85–89.

———. "Surveillance and Privacy." *Science* 290 (2000), 1898–99.

Bennett, Rebecca, and Erin, Charles A., eds. *HIV and AIDS: Testing, Screening and Confidentiality*. New York: Oxford Unversity Press, 2001.

Berger, Jeffrey T.; Rosner, Fred; and Farnsworth, Peter. "The Ethics of Mandatory HIV Testing in Newborns." *Journal of Clinical Ethics* 7 (1997), 77–84.

Brandt, Allan M.; Cleary, Paul D.; and Gostin, Lawrence O. "Routine Hospital Testing for HIV: Health Policy Considerations." In Lawrence O. Gostin, ed., *AIDS and the Health Care System*. New Haven: Yale University Press, 1990, 125–39, 264–67.

Britton, Carolyn Barley. "An Argument for Universal HIV Counseling and Voluntary Testing of Women." *Journal of the American Medical Women's Association* 50 (1995), 85–86.

Centers for Disease Control and Prevention. "U.S. Public Health Service Recommendations for Human Immunodeficiency Virus Counseling and Voluntary Testing for Pregnant Women." *Morbidity and Mortality Weekly Report* 44 (1995), 1–15.

———. "Revised Guidelines for HIV Counseling, Testing, and Referral." *Morbidity and Mortality Weekly Report* 50 (2001), 1–57.

———. "Revised Recommendations for HIV Screening of Pregnant Women." *Morbidity and Mortality Weekly Report* 50 (2001), 63–85.

Childress, James F. "Mandatory HIV Screening and Testing." *Practical Reasoning in Bioethics*. Bloomington: Indiana University Press, 1997, 95–118, 339–43.

Christie, Timothy. "HIV Serostatus Disclosure: Legal, Scientific and Ethical Considerations." *Health Law in Canada* 22 (2002), 70–76.

Cooper, Elizabeth B. "HIV Disease in Pregnancy: Ethics, Law, and Policy." *Obstetrics and Gynecology Clinics of North America* 24 (1997), 899–910.

Crawford, Colin. "Protecting the Weakest Link: A Proposal for Universal, Unblinded Pediatric HIV Testing, Counseling and Treatment." *Journal of Community Health* 20 (1995), 125–41.

D'Amelio, Raffaele; Tuerlings, Emmanuelle; Perito, Olga; Biselli, Roberto; Natalicchio, Sergio; and Kingma, Stuart. "A Global Review of Legislation on HIV/AIDS: The Issue of HIV Testing." *Journal of Acquired Immune Deficiency Syndromes* 28 (2001), 173–79.

Danziger, Renée, and Gil, Noel. "HIV Testing and HIV Prevention in Sweden" [Article and Commentary]. *British Medical Journal* 316 (1998), 293–96.

David, Dena S. "Mandatory HIV Testing in Newborns: Not Yet, Maybe." *Journal of Clinical Ethics* 7 (1996), 191–92.

De Cock, Kevin M., and Johnson, Anne M. "From Exceptionalism to Normalisation: A Reappraisal of Attitudes and Practices around HIV Testing." *British Medical Journal* 316 (1998), 290–93.

Dresser, Rebecca. "Should Consent Be Required for an HIV Test?" In Adam Zeman, and Linda L. Emanuel, eds., *Ethical Dilemmas in Neurology*. London: W.B. Saunders, 2000, 13–21.

Dumois, Ana O. "The Case Against Mandatory Newborn Screening for HIV Antibodies." *Journal of Community Health* 20 (1995), 143–59.

Faden, Ruth; Geller, Gail; and Powers, Madison, eds. *AIDS, Women and the Next Generation*. New York: Oxford University Press, 1991.

Gorsky, Robin D., et al. "Preventing Perinatal Transmission of HIV—Costs and Effectiveness of a Recommended Intervention." *Public Health Reports* 111 (1996), 335–41.

Gostin, Lawrence O.; Ward, John W.; and Baker, A. Cornelius. "National HIV Case Reporting for the United States: A Defining Moment in the History of the Epidemic." *New England Journal of Medicine* 337 (1997), 1162–67.

Gunderson, Martin; Mayo, David J.; and Rhame, Frank S. *AIDS: Testing and Privacy*. Salt Lake City: University of Utah Press, 1989.

———. "Routine HIV Testing of Hospital Patients and Pregnant Women: Informed Consent in the Real World." *Kennedy Institute of Ethics Journal* 6 (1996), 161–82.

Hardy, Leslie M., ed. Institute of Medicine, Committee on Prenatal and Newborn Screening for HIV Infection. *HIV Screening of Pregnant Women and Newborns*. Washington, DC: National Academy Press, 1991.

Hecht, Frederick M.; Chesney, Margaret A.; Lehman, J. Stan; Osmond, Dennis; Vranizan, Karen; Colman, Shoshana; et al. "Does HIV Reporting by Name Deter Testing?" *AIDS* 14 (2000), 1801–08.

Hernandez, Raymond. "Law Requires Giving Results of H.I.V. Tests of Newborns." *New York Times,* June 27, 1996, B4.

Institute of Medicine and National Research Council, Committee on Perinatal Transmission of HIV. *Reducing the Odds: Preventing Perinatal Transmission of HIV in the United States.* Washington, DC: National Academy Press, 1998.

Katz, Anne. "HIV Screening in Pregnancy: What Women Think." *Journal of Obstetric, Gynecologic, and Neonatal Nursing,* 30 (2001), 184–91.

Kopelman, Loretta M. "Informed Consent and Anonymous Tissue Samples: The Case of HIV Seroprevalence Studies." *Journal of Medicine and Philosophy* 19 (1994), 525–52.

Landers Daniel, V., and Sweet, Richard L. "Reducing Mother-Infant Transmission of HIV—The Door Remains Open" [Editorial]. *New England Journal of Medicine* 334 (1996), 1664–65.

Leary, Warren E. "Medical Panel Urges H.I.V. Tests for All Pregnant Women." *New York Times,* October 15, 1998, A24.

Lovvorn, Amy E.; Quinn, Sandra Crouse; and Jolly, David H. "HIV Testing of Pregnant Women: A Policy Analysis." *Journal of Public Health Policy* 18 (1997), 401–32.

Madison, Mellinda. "Tragic Life or Tragic Death: Mandatory Testing of Newborns for HIV—Mothers' Rights versus Children's Health." *Journal of Legal Medicine* 18 (1997), 361–86.

McIntyre, James and Gray, Glenda. "What Can We Do to Reduce Mother to Child Transmission of HIV?" *British Medical Journal* 324 (2002), 218–21.

Minkoff, Howard, and Willoughby, Anne. "Pediatric HIV Disease, Zidovudine in Pregnancy, and Unblinding Heelstick Surveys: Reframing the Debate on Prenatal HIV Testing." *Journal of the American Medical Association* 274 (1995), 1165–68.

———. "The Future of Prenatal HIV Testing." *Acta Paediatrica, Supplement* 421 (1997), 72–77.

———, and O'Sullivan, Mary Jo. "The Case for Rapid HIV Testing during Labor." *Journal of the American Medical Association* 279 (1998), 1743–44.

"Name Brands: The Effects of Intrusive HIV Legislation on High-Risk Demographic Groups." *Harvard Law Review* 113 (2000), 2098–2115.

O'Brien, Maura. "Mandatory HIV Antibody Testing Policies: An Ethical Analysis." *Bioethics* 3 (1989) 273–300.

Ploughman, Penelope. "Public Policy versus Private Rights: The Medical, Social, Ethical, and Legal Implications of the Testing of Newborns for HIV." *AIDS and Public Policy Journal* 10 (1995/1996), 182–204.

Potts, Malcolm. "Thinking about Vaginal Microbicide Testing." *American Journal of Public Health* 90 (2000), 188–90.

Samson, Lindy, and King, Susan. "Evidence-Based Guidelines for Universal Counseling and Offering of HIV Testing in Pregnancy in Canada." *Canadian Medical Association Journal* 158 (1998), 1149–57.

Schneider, Carl E. "Testing Testing." *Hastings Center Report* 27 (July-August 1997), 22–23.

Sherr, Lorraine, ed. *AIDS and the Heterosexual Population.* Chur, Switzerland: Harwood Academic Publishers, 1993.

Sternlight, Jean R. "Mandatory Non-Anonymous Testing of Newborns for HIV: Should It Ever Be Allowed?" *John Marshall Law Review* 29 (1994), 373–91.

Rogers, David E., and Osborn, June E. "Another Approach to the AIDS Epidemic." *New England Journal of Medicine* 325 (1991), 806–08.

U.S. Congress, House Committee on Commerce, Subcommittee on Health and the Environment. *HIV Testing of Women and Infants.* 104th Congress, 1st Session, May 11, 1995. Washington, DC: U.S. Government Printing Office, 1995.

Wilfert, Catherine M. "Mandatory Screening of Pregnant Women for the Human Immunodeficiency Virus." *Clinical Infectious Diseases* 19 (1996), 664–66.

Working Group on HIV Testing of Pregnant Women and Newborns. "HIV Infection, Pregnant Women and Newborns: A Policy for Information and Testing." *Journal of the American Medical Association* 264 (1990) 2416–20.

CLINICAL RESEARCH ON HIV/AIDS

"Administration of Zidovudine During Late Pregnancy and Delivery to Prevent Perinatal HIV Transmission—Thailand, 1996–1998." *Morbidity and Mortality Weekly Report* 47 (1998), 151–54.

Altman, Lawrence K. "F.D.A. Authorizes First Full Testing for H.I.V. Vaccine." *New York Times,* June 4, 1998, A1.

Angell, Marcia. "The Ethics of Clinical Research in the Third World." *New England Journal of Medicine* 337 (1997), 847–49.

———. "Tuskegee Revisited." *Wall Street Journal,* October 28, 1997, A22.

Annas, George J., and Grodin, Michael A. "Human Rights and Maternal-Fetal HIV Transmission Prevention Trials in Africa." *American Journal of Public Health* 88 (1998), 560–63.

Bagenda, Danstan, and Musoke-Mudido, Philippa. "We're Trying to Help Our Sickest People, Not Exploit Them." *Washington Post,* September 28, 1997, C3.

Bayer, Ronald. "Ethical Challenges Posed by Zidovudine Treatment to Reduce Vertical Transmission of HIV." *New England Journal of Medicine* 331 (1994), 1123–25.

———. "The Debate over Maternal-Fetal HIV Transmission Prevention Trials in Africa, Asia, and the Caribbean: Racist Exploitation or Exploitation of Racism?" *American Journal of Public Health* 88 (1998), 567–70.

———. "Ethical Challenges of HIV Vaccine Trials in Less Developed Nations: Conflict and Consensus in the International Arena." *AIDS* 14 (2000), 1051–57.

Benatar, Solomon R. "Distributive Justice and Clinical Trials In the Third World." *Theoretical Medicine* 22 (2001), 169–76.

Bloom, Barry R. "The Highest Attainable Standard: Ethical Issues in AIDS Vaccines." *Science* 279 (1998), 186–88.

Centers for Disease Control and Prevention. "Recommendations of the U.S. Public Health Service Task Force on the Use of Zidovudine to Reduce Perinatal Transmission of Human Immunodeficiency Virus." *Morbidity and Mortality Weekly Report* 43 (1994), 1–20.

Cohen, Jon. "Ethics of AZT Studies in Poorer Countries Attacked." *Science* 276 (1997), 1022.

Connor, Edward M., et al. "Reduction of Maternal-Infant Transmission of Human Immunodeficiency Virus Type 1 with Zidovudine Treatment." *New England Journal of Medicine* 331 (1994), 1173–80.

Cooley, D. R. "Distributive Justice and Clinical Trials in the Third World." *Theoretical Medicine* 22 (2001), 151–67.

de Zoysa, Isabelle; Elias, Christopher J.; and Bentley, Margaret E. "Ethical Challenges in Efficacy Trials of Vaginal Microbicides for HIV Prevention." *American Journal of Public Health* 88 (1998), 571–75.

De Zulueta, Paquita. "Randomised Placebo-Controlled Trials and HIV-Infected Pregnant Women In Developing Countries. Ethical Imperialism or Unethical Exploitation?" *Bioethics* 15 (2001), 289–311.

Grady, Christine. "HIV Preventive Vaccine Research: Selected Ethical Issues." *Journal of Medicine and Philosophy* (1994), 595–612.

———. *The Search for an AIDS Vaccine: Ethical Issues in the Development and Testing of a Preventive HIV Vaccine.* Bloomington, IN: Indiana University Press, 1995.

Gray, Joni N.; Lyons, Phillip M.; and Melton, Gary B. *Ethical and Legal Issues in AIDS Research.* Baltimore: Johns Hopkins University Press, 1995.

Halsey, Neal A., et al. "Ethics and International Research" [Editorial]. *British Medical Journal* 315 (1997), 965–66.

Karim, Salim S. A. "Placebo Controls in HIV Perinatal Transmission Trials: A South African's Viewpoint." *American Journal of Public Health* 88 (1998), 564–66.

Karlawish, Jason H. T., and Lantos, John. "Community Equipoise and the Architecture of Clinical Research." *Cambridge Quarterly of Healthcare Ethics* 6 (1997), 385–96.

Kerns, Thomas A. *Ethical Issues in HIV Vaccine Trials in Developing Nations.* New York: St. Martin's Press, 1997.

Kuhn, Louise, and Stein, Zena. "Infant Survival, HIV Infection, and Feeding Alternatives." *American Journal of Public Health* 87 (1997), 926–31.

Lackey, Douglas P. "Clinical Trials in Developing Countries: A Review of the Moral Issues." *Mount Sinai Journal of Medicine* 68 (2001), 4–12.

Leider, Philip A. "Domestic AIDS Vaccine Trials: Addressing the Potential for Social Harm To the Subjects of Human Experiments." *California Law Review* 88 (2000), 1185–32.

Lurie, Peter, and Wolfe, Sidney M. "Unethical Trials of Interventions to Reduce Perinatal Transmission of the Human Immunodeficiency Virus in Developing Countries." *New England Journal of Medicine* 337 (1997), 853–56.

Marshall, Eliot. "Controversial Trial Offers Hopeful Result." *Science* 279 (1998), 1299.

Marwick, Charles. "Bioethics Group Considers Transnational Research." *Journal of the American Medical Association* 279 (1998), 1425.

Mbidde, Edward. "Bioethics and Local Circumstances" [Editorial]. *Science* 279 (1998), 155.

Merson, Michael H., et al. "Ethics of Placebo-Controlled Trials of Zidovudine to Prevent the Perinatal Transmission of HIV in the Third World" [Letters]. *New England Journal of Medicine* 338 (1998), 836–41.

Mugerwa, Roy D.; Kaleebu, Pontiano; Mugyenyi, Peter; Katongole-Mbidde, Edward; Hom, David L.; Byaruhanga, Rose; et al. "First Trial of the HIV-1 Vaccine in Africa: Ugandan Experience." *British Medical Journal* 324 (2002), 226–29.

Phanuphak, Praphan. "Ethical Issues in Studies in Thailand of the Vertical Transmission of HIV." *New England Journal of Medicine* 338 (1998), 834–35.

Robb, Merlin L.; Khambaroong, Chirasak; and Nelson, Kenrad E. "Studies in Thailand of the Vertical Transmission of HIV" [Letter]. *New England Journal of Medicine* 338 (1998), 843–44.

Schuklenk, Udo, and Hogan, Carlton. "Patient Access to Experimental Drugs and AIDS Clinical Trial Designs: Ethical Issues." *Cambridge Quarterly of Healthcare Ethics* 5 (1996), 400–09.

Stolberg, Sheryl Gay. "Placebo Use Is Suspended in Overseas AIDS Trials." *New York Times* February 19, 1998, A16.

Thomas, Kerns. *Ethical Issues in HIV Vaccine Trials in Developing Nations.* New York: St. Martin's Press, 1996.

Varmus, Harold, and Satcher, David. "Ethical Complexities of Conducting Research in Developing Countries." *New England Journal of Medicine* 337 (1997), 1003–05.

Wadman, Meredith. "Controversy Flares over AIDS Prevention Trials in Third World." *Nature* 389 (1997), 894.

Zion, Deborah. "Ethical Considerations of Clinical Trials to Prevent Vertical Transmission of HIV in Developing Countries." *Nature Medicine* 4 (1998), 11–12.

THE THREAT OF BIOTERRORISM AND BIOLOGICAL WARFARE

Alibek, Ken W. and Handelman, Stephen. *Biohazard: The Chilling True Story of the Largest Covert Biological Weapons Program in the World Told from Inside by the Man Who Ran It.* New York: Dell, 2000.

Balmer, Brian. *Britain and Biological Warfare: Expert Advice and Science Policy, 1930–65.* New York: Palgrave Macmillan, 2001.

Beeching, Nicholas J., et al. "Biological Warfare and Bioterrorism." *British Medical Journal* 324 (2002), 336–39.

"Biological and Chemical Terrorism: Strategic Plan for Preparedness and Response. Recommendations of the CDC Strategic Planning Workgroup." *Morbidity and Mortality Weekly Report* 49 (2000), 1–14.

British Medical Association. *Biotechnology, Weapons and Humanity.* New York: Taylor & Francis, 1999.

Gani, Raymond, and Leach, Steve. "Transmission Potential of Smallpox in Contemporary Populations." *Nature* 414 (2001), 748–51, 1056.

Geissler, Erhard; Ellis Van Courtland Moon, John; and Ellis Moon, John, eds. *Biological and Toxin Weapons: Research, Development and Use from the Middle Ages to 1945.* New York: Oxford University Press, 1999.

Hammond, Peter M., and Carter, Gradon. *From Biological Warfare to Healthcare: Porton Down 1940–2000.* New York: Palgrave Macmillan, 2002.

Henderson, Donald A., and Ingelsby, Thomas. *Bioterrorism: Guidelines for Medical and Public Health Management.* Chicago: American Medical Association, 2002.

———, et al. "Smallpox as a Biological Weapon." *Journal of the American Medical Association* 281 (1999), 2127–37.

Henretig, Fred. "Biological and Chemical Terrorism Defense: A View from the 'Front Lines' of Public Health." *American Journal of Public Health* 91 (2001), 718–20.

Inglesby, Thomas V., et al. "Anthrax as a Biological Weapon." *Journal of the American Medical Association* 281 (1999), 1735–45.

———, et al. "Plague as a Biological Weapon." *Journal of the American Medical Association* 283 (2000), 2281–90.

———, et al. "Preventing the Use of Biological Weapons: Improving Response Should Prevention Fail." *Clinical Infectious Diseases* 30 (2000), 926–29.

Institute of Medicine. *Chemical and Biological Terrorism: Research and Development to Improve Civilian Medical Response.* Washington, DC: National Academy Press, 1999.

Khan, Ali S.; Morse, Stephen; and Lillibridge, Scott. "Public-Health Preparedness for Biological Terrorism in the USA." *Lancet* 356 (2000), 1179–82.

———, and Ashford, David A. "Ready or Not—Preparedness for Bioterrorism." *New England Journal of Medicine* 345 (2001), 287–89.

Lane, H. Clifford, and Fauci, Anthony S. "Bioterrorism on the Home Front." *Journal of the American Medical Association* 286 (2001), 2595–97.

Lederberg, Joshua, ed. *Biological Weapons: Limiting the Threat.* Cambridge, MA: MIT Press, 1999.

Linkie, Matthew. "The Defense Threat Reduction Agency: A Note on the United States' Approach to the Threat of Chemical and Biological Warfare." *Journal of Contemporary Health Law and Policy* 16 (2000), 531–63.

Miller, Judith; Broad, William J.; and Engelberg, Stephen. *Germs: Biological Weapons and America's Secret War.* New York: Simon & Schuster, 2001.

Morbidity and Mortality Weekly Report. "Update: Investigation of Bioterrorism-Related Anthrax and Interim Guidelines for Exposure Management and Antimicrobial Therapy, October 2001." *Journal of the American Medical Association* 286 (2001), 2226–32.

National Research Council, Committee on R&D Needs for Improving Civilian Medical Response to Chemical and Biological Terrorism Incidents. *Chemical and Biological Terrorism.* Washington, DC: National Academy Press, 1999.

O' Hanlon, Michael; Orszag, Peter; Daalder, Ivo; Destler, Mac; Gunter, David; Litan, Robert; et al. *Protecting the American Homeland.* Washington, DC: Brookings Press, 2002.

O'Toole, Tara, and Inglesby, Thomas V. "Facing the Biological Threat." *Lancet* 356 (2000), 1128–29.

Pesik, Nicki, et al. "Terrorism and the Ethics of Emergency Medical Care." *Annals of Emergency Medicine* 37 (2001), 642–46.

Rosen, Peter. "Coping With Bioterrorism." *British Medical Journal* 320 (2000), 71–72.

Royal Society. *Measures for Controlling the Threat from Biological Weapons.* London: The Society, 2000.

Stone, Richard. "WHO Puts Off Destruction of U.S., Russian Caches." *Science* 295 (2002), 598–99.

Tucker, Jonathan B. *Toxic Terror: Assessing Terrorist Use of Chemical and Biological Weapons.* Cambridge, MA: MIT Press, 2000.

Voelker, Rebecca. "Bioweapons Preparedness Chief Discusses Priorities in World of 21st-Century Biology." *Journal of the American Medical Association* 287 (2002), 573–75.

———. "Will Focus on Terrorism Overshadow the Fight against AIDS?" *Journal of the American Medical Association* 286 (2001), 2081–83.

Zilinskas, Raymond A., ed. Biological Warfare: Modern Offense and Defense. London: Lynne Rienner, 2000.

———. "Iraq's Biological Weapons: The Past as Future?" *Journal of the American Medical Association* 278 (1997), 418–24.

BIBLIOGRAPHIES

Lineback, Richard H., ed. *Philosopher's Index.* Vols. 1– . Bowling Green, OH: Philosophy Documentation Center, Bowling Green State University. Issued quarterly. See under "AIDS," "HIV," "biological warfare," and "terrorism."

Walters, LeRoy, and Kahn, Tamar Joy, eds. *Bibliography of Bioethics.* Vols. 1– . Washington, DC: Kennedy Institute of Ethics, Georgetown University. Issued annually. See under "AIDS and "war."

WORLD WIDE WEB RESOURCES

Bartlett, John G.; O' Toole, Tara; and Mair, Michael, eds. *Bioterrorism and Public Health: An Internet Resource Guide.* Montvale, NJ: Medical Economics Company, 2002.

National Library of Medicine: PubMed (http://www.ncbi.nlm.nih.gov/PubMed)

National Library of Medicine: LocatorPlus (http://locatorplus.gov)

University Microfilms: Periodical Abstracts (http://www.umi.com/proquest)